D0907003

DICTIONARY
of VIRGINIA
BIOGRAPHY

VOLUME 3
Caperton–Daniels

DICTIONARY
of VIRGINIA
BIOGRAPHY

VOLUME 3

Caperton–Daniels

SENIOR EDITOR

Sara B. Bearss

EDITORS

John G. Deal, Donald W. Gunter, Marianne E. Julienne,
John T. Kneebone, Brent Tarter, and Sandra Gioia Treadway

ASSISTANT EDITORS

Katharine E. Harbury, Jennifer R. Loux,
G. W. Poindexter, and William Bland Whitley

THE LIBRARY OF VIRGINIA

RICHMOND • 2006

Library of Congress Cataloging-in-Publication Data will be found on the last printed page of this book.

Standard Book Number: ISBN 0-88490-206-4

Library of Virginia, Richmond, Virginia.
© 2006 by the Library of Virginia.
All rights reserved.
Printed in the United States of America.

This book is printed on acid-free paper meeting the requirements of the American Standard for Permanence of Paper for Printed Library Materials.

A Preservation and Access Reference Materials Grant from the National Endowment for the Humanities supported the completion of this volume. Any views, findings, conclusions, or recommendations expressed in this publication do not necessarily reflect those of the National Endowment for the Humanities.

Jacket design: Sara Daniels Bowersox, *Graphic Designer*, Library of Virginia.

INTRODUCTION

The *Dictionary of Virginia Biography* is the first scholarly, comprehensive biographical reference work on Virginia. Many of the entries offer the first reliable biography ever printed about their subjects. The 471 biographies in the third volume range chronologically from Sir Thomas Dale (d. 1619), who twice served as acting governor of Virginia, to Richard Bernard Caspari (1942–2000), a pioneering arthroscopic surgeon. In between, readers will find biographies of participants in and chroniclers of Bacon's Rebellion; two colonial planters whose wealth and imperious bearing won them the sobriquet "king"; a surgeon general of the United States Public Health Service; the greatest third baseman never to play major-league baseball; a Continental army soldier sent undercover to attempt the capture of Benedict Arnold; twentieth-century chiefs of the Mattaponi and Pamunkey Indians; a Broadway producer and a Hollywood star; two Civil War generals, father and son, who fought on opposite sides; a Danville ichthyologist; two convicted murderers; the Mother of Country Music; founders of Liberia and of the Christian Children's Fund; and a documents expert who gave critical testimony in the Charles Lindbergh Jr. kidnapping trial.[1] Other biographies feature the Sleeping Prophet, the Heller of the Hollow, and the Angel of Happy Hollow.[2] Together, the biographies in volume 3 paint a vibrant portrait of Virginia's past.

Thorough research in underused primary sources has corrected errors and uncovered new information about even the most well-known subjects. Previous biographies of John Snyder Carlile (1817–1878), a passionate proponent of the Union who was instrumental in the creation of West Virginia as a separate state, have not named his parents. Carlile's biography in this volume is the first to do so and to lay out the volatile, peripatetic nature of his formative years. The biography of the Baptist missionary Lott Cary (ca. 1780–1828) uncovers for the first time his appearance in a 1797 estate inventory, identifies his second wife by name, and establishes a previously unknown fourth marriage. Also discovered through careful examination of archival and election records were two long-forgotten African American members of the House of Delegates (George William Cole, of Essex County, and Johnson Collins, of Brunswick County) whose names appear in no reference book of nineteenth-century black officeholders.

The *DVB* highlights many women, African Americans, Indians, and others whose lives have never before been studied. By broadening the definition of who, and what, is important, the compiled biographies have begun to reshape the narrative of Virginia's history. Emerging from the margins to expand and enrich the commonwealth's story are such groups as nineteenth-century African American political leaders, reform-minded twentieth-century clubwomen, and a cavalcade of artists, musicians, and writers. Contributors' research is raising intriguing questions about more-familiar topics, including the business affairs of colonial planters, partisan alignments in post–Civil War politics, and the multilayered influence of twentieth-century civic leaders. Similar insights await in almost every biography. Researchers can use the bricks and mortar of the *DVB* biographies as the raw materials to construct new histories of Virginia and to provide a deeper, more thorough understanding of the lives of all Virginians.

SELECTION CRITERIA

The *DVB* provides biographical information about Virginians who, regardless of place of birth or death, made significant contributions to the history or culture of their locality, state, or nation. From late in the sixteenth through the eighteenth centuries, the term *Virginia* was applied to territory extending much farther north, south, and west on the North American continent than the state's modern-day borders. For the purposes of the *DVB*, Virginia is defined by the state's current geographic boundaries, plus Kentucky before its separate statehood in 1792 and West Virginia before its statehood in 1863. This definition excludes from consideration in the *DVB* the District of West Augusta, a disputed area claimed by both the colonies of Virginia and Pennsylvania, but includes Alexandria County during the years it was ceded to the District of Columbia as part of the nation's capital.

With few exceptions, no person is included who did not live a significant portion of his or her life in Virginia. Although born in Virginia, the writer Willa Cather, the explorer William Clark, the statesman Henry Clay, and the emancipator Edward Coles left the state, and their careers became inextricably linked with other places. Biographies of such figures have not been included in volume 3. Other persons of national or international importance—such as the naturalist Mark Catesby, the singer Cass Elliot (born Ellen Naomi Cohen), and the painter Conrad Wise Chapman—spent only brief time in Virginia. Their limited contributions to Virginia's history and culture do not justify including entries on them in the *Dictionary of Virginia Biography*.

A biographical reference work such as the *DVB* cannot possibly include every interesting or successful person who lived in the past, but it should encompass all those who had an important influence on their communities or who achieved extraordinary recognition from their contemporaries or from posterity. The definition of significance necessarily varies from century to century, from one geographic region to another, and from one field of endeavor to another. Race and gender are also often important factors. A more thorough explication of the selection criteria appears at the beginning of volume 1.

Certain categories of people, most of whom were involved in public life, are included automatically because their participation in events of great consequence has made them frequent subjects of requests for biographical information. The categories of automatic inclusion are Virginia-born presidents of the United States; governors and lieutenant governors of Virginia (including absentee royal governors); members of the governor's Council during the colonial period and of the Council of State between 1776 and its abolition in 1851; Speakers of the House of Burgesses, the House of Delegates, and the Senate of Virginia; African American and female members of the General Assembly elected before 2000; Virginia members of the Continental Congress, the Confederation Congress, the United States Congress, and the Confederate States Congress; cabinet officers of the United States and the Confederate States governments resident in Virginia when appointed; justices of the Supreme Court of the United States and judges of the United States appellate and district courts resident in Virginia when appointed; judges of the highest appellate court in Virginia; attorneys general of Virginia; members of all Virginia constitutional conventions from 1776 through 1902; Virginia's delegates to the federal constitutional convention of 1787; members of the Virginia ratification convention of 1788 and of the secession convention of 1861; judges of the Virginia State Corporation Commission; general officers from Virginia in the American Revolution, the War of 1812, and the Civil War; recipients of major national or international awards, such as the Pulitzer and Nobel Prizes; presidents of important national or international organizations; and presidents of the major institutions of higher education in Virginia.

Most of the people in the *Dictionary of Virginia Biography* do not fall into one of these categories of automatic inclusion. Rather, they are Virginians whose lives and careers made them exceptional in their communities or professions. Some are associated with unusually important or notorious events; others are included because they became legendary figures and require a reliable biographical entry that separates fact from fiction. As a historical reference work, the *Dictionary of Virginia Biography* does not include persons living at the time of publication. No one who died after 31 December 2000 appears in volume 3.

Classified indexes to the first three volumes are posted on the Library of Virginia's Web site. At the conclusion of the project a comprehensive index to the *DVB* will be published as the final volume.

EDITORIAL STAFF

Since the appearance of the second volume of the *Dictionary of Virginia Biography*, the project staff has said farewell to one editor and welcomed several new colleagues. John T. Kneebone, one of the original project editors, left the Library of Virginia in October 2002 and is now an associate professor of history at Virginia Commonwealth University. The *DVB*'s loss is an immeasurable gain for students of southern and public history. This volume continued to benefit from his enthusiasm, dedication, expertise, and critical eye as he honed prose, caught gaffes, and raised insightful questions on a volunteer basis.

A generous grant from the National Endowment for the Humanities made it possible for the *Dictionary* to add three assistant editors to the staff. Katharine E. Harbury, G. W. Poindexter, and William Bland Whitley joined the editorial team in the summer of 2004. Their wide-ranging knowledge, skill, and dedication has improved every page. A fourth assistant editor, Jennifer R. Loux, began work during the summer of 2005. Her energy, tenacity, and understanding of southern history have likewise proved invaluable.

ACKNOWLEDGMENTS

Any project of this scope would have been impossible without contributions from numerous sources. The editors of the *Dictionary of Virginia Biography* are deeply grateful to all those associated with the Library of Virginia who have brought the third volume to successful completion. They are especially grateful to the Librarian of Virginia, Nolan T. Yelich, and to the members of the Library Board for their continuing support and encouragement.

The talented and dedicated historians, editors, archivists, librarians, and other specialists on the Library of Virginia's staff have provided valuable assistance to the project at every stage. Many deserve special mention. Edward D. C. Campbell, Jr., and Ann N. Harris have provided key support for the *Dictionary* project at critical times. One could not ask for finer or more congenial colleagues. The Library's crack team of archivists, particularly Roger E. Christman, Laura Drake Davis, Gerald P. Gaidmore II, Trenton E. Hizer, Alexander H. Lorch III, Jennifer Davis McDaid, Craig S. Moore, Ryan K. Smith, Patricia Ferguson Watkinson, and Minor T. Weisiger, generously alerted the *DVB* staff to new, unprocessed, or little-known collections that resolved many research quandaries. Mary Clark was unfailingly helpful in guiding the project staff through the mysteries of government documents. Tom Camden and the other Special Collections librarians patiently and cheerfully served the rare treasures and fragile, unwieldy tomes under their care, even when the *DVB* editors needed only to verify the punctuation on a title page or a single quotation. The staff of the Virginia Newspaper Project, directed by Errol Somay, provided many valuable research leads. The unflappable Ted Polk and David Grabarek often went above and beyond the call of duty to secure requested materials on interlibrary loan. Their creativity and perseverance are much appreciated. The technical expertise and good humor of Greta Bollinger were critical in managing the project database, which tracks almost 20,000 candidates for inclusion and the work done on each. Rose Schooff again proved indispensable by designing the classified indexes on the Library's Web site. Our excellent colleagues in Financial Services, particularly Bill Guyton, deserve special commendation for promptly filling many complicated and out-of-the-ordinary requests for foreign currency and for money orders (the latter required after the project staff discovered that the District of Columbia's Vital Records Division would not accept checks from the Commonwealth of Virginia but would accept money orders from 7-Eleven).

The *DVB* has benefited immeasurably from the eagle-eyed attention to detail of copy editors Emily J. Salmon and Ann E. Henderson. The latter also secured the illustrations and permissions for the dust jacket. Sara Daniels Bowersox provided the stately design of both the volume and the dust jacket. Other Library staff members who have offered indispensable advice, conducted specialized research, run down sources, checked facts, visited cemeteries, read proof, and done whatever else has been necessary to move the project forward are Barbara C. Batson, Gregg D. Kimball, Maria Kimberly, Patricia A. Kloke, and Amy Winegardner. The *DVB* editors also gratefully acknowledge the contributions of the project's enthusiastic, dedicated interns and volunteers, particularly Stephen Alexander, Dianna L. Bisbee, Elizabeth T. Broadbent, Cheryl Collins, Philip J. Dean, Elizabeth Hill, Kevin T. Lett, Susan Y. Miller, Amanda Morrell, Virginia Nawrocki, Sarah Jane Perkins, Terry L. Stoops, and Ann Drury Wellford. Deserving of special mention are Lucy Southall Colebaugh and Stephen A. Maguire, who generously gave their time to the project and whose handiwork may be seen on each and every page of the third volume.

The editors and contributors have visited the major research libraries containing materials relating to Virginia history as well as many other specialized repositories, museums, historical societies, and research centers across Virginia and the nation. Without exception, the staffs of these institutions have offered gracious assistance to the *Dictionary of Virginia Biography* project, for which the Library of Virginia is deeply grateful. Interlibrary loan departments, local reference librarians, college and university registrars and alumni offices, archives of professional organizations, and the keepers of vital statistics on both sides of the Atlantic have proved unfailingly prompt and helpful in answering queries and tracking down elusive details. It is impossible to thank them all individually or to express gratitude to each of the hundreds of researchers who have generously shared their knowledge, enthusiasm, and insights. The editors particularly thank the following people who provided assistance of an extraordinary nature for this volume: Richard L. Baker, U.S. Army Military History Institute; Brooks Miles Barnes, Eastern Shore Public Library; Jeanette Bergeron, Crumley Lutheran Archives, Columbia, South Carolina; Paul Blewitt, Canterbury Cathedral Archives; Steven Brown, Hargrett Library, University of Georgia; Jackie Cohan, Alexandria Archives and Records Center; David Comegys, AuSable, New York; Jolene Diven, International Conference of Funeral Service Examining Boards, Inc.; Lucious Edwards, Virginia State University; David Evans, Sara Hightower Regional Library, Rome, Georgia; Harold M. Forbes, West Virginia and Regional

History Collection, West Virginia University; David A. Franz, Ogdensburg Public Library, Ogdensburg, New York; Stephen Freeth, Keeper of Manuscripts, Guildhall Library, London; William M. Gardner, National Association of Secretaries of State; Rosemary Graham and Susie Stepanek, Pikes Peak Library District, Colorado Springs, Colorado; Tom Harkness, West Lothian Family History Society, West Lothian, Scotland; the staff of the Historical Society of Seabrook, New Hampshire; David W. Jackson, Jackson County Historical Society Archives, Independence, Missouri; Diane B. Jacob, Preston Library, Virginia Military Institute; Joan Echtenkamp Klein, Claude Moore Health Sciences Library, University of Virginia; Jodi L. Koste, Tompkins-McCaw Library, Virginia Commonwealth University; Dennis K. Kruse, American Society of Naval Engineers; Patricia M. LaPointe, Memphis–Shelby County Public Library, Tennessee; Devon Lee, University of North Carolina Library; Beverly Marks, Gilmer County clerk, Glenville, West Virginia; Lashe Mullins, White Hall State Historic Site, Richmond, Kentucky; Margaret Nolan, AuSable, New York; John Parascandola, U.S. Public Health Service; Tyler Paul, Saint Catherine's School, Richmond; Hilary Kanupp Perez, North Carolina State Archives; Sheila B. Phipps, Jonnie B. Deel Memorial Library, Clintwood; Frances S. Pollard, Virginia Historical Society; Jeanne Powers, Bristol Public Library; AnnMarie F. Price, Virginia Historical Society; the staff of the Sargeant Memorial Room, Norfolk Public Library; Kevin Shupe, Gunston Hall Plantation; Ray Smith, U.S. Army Heritage and Education Center; Wendie L. Summers, Lynchburg City School Board; Robert Teagle, Historic Christ Church, Irvington; Lisa Thompson, Kentucky Department for Libraries and Archives, Frankfort; Joel Thoreson, Evangelical Lutheran Church in America, Chicago, Illinois; Robert J. Vejnar, II, Emory and Henry College; Kathleen Walczak, National Funeral Directors Association; Edie White, Bel Air Branch, Harford County Public Library, Maryland; Linda Whitaker, Richmond; Gina Woodward, Earl Gregg Swem Library, College of William and Mary; and Virginia Yeager, Robert F. Kidd Library, Glenville State College, Glenville, West Virginia.

A final word of thanks and recognition goes to Helen C. Agüera and most especially to Joseph B. Herring, both at the National Endowment for the Humanities, for their encouragement and guidance in preparing the *Dictionary*'s first grant application in 2003. Thanks in part to their assistance, an NEH Preservation and Access Reference Materials Grant, awarded for 2004–2006, supported the completion of this volume. Any views, findings, conclusions, or recommendations expressed in this publication do not necessarily reflect those of the National Endowment for the Humanities.

The 294 contributors who researched and wrote the 471 biographies in this volume deserve a special place in Paradise. For the love of Virginia history, they carved time from their full professional and personal lives in order to accept the challenge of time-consuming and often difficult research. Not satisfied with relying on inexact, incomplete, or incorrect secondary accounts, they tracked their subjects using the most authentic surviving primary sources. Having found mounds of new, interesting evidence, they then faced the daunting task of constructing tight, concise biographies in six hundred words or fewer. Nothing deterred them. Several contributors finished their biographies while facing serious health issues or recovering from accidents, one completed his assigned entry while traveling through the Panama Canal, and another proofed his galleys while serving at the United States Naval Station at Guantanamo Bay. Their collective talents and energy shine through every biography.

[1] William Carver, Edmund Cheesman, and James Crewes (participants in Bacon's Rebellion) and Jane Dennison Carson, Ann Cotton, and John Cotton (chroniclers of the rebellion); planters Robert Carter (ca. 1664–1732) and John Custis (ca. 1629–1696); surgeon general Hugh Smith Cumming; third baseman Raymond Emmett

Dandridge; Continental army soldier John Champe; Chiefs George Major "Wahunsacook" Cook, George F. "Thunder Cloud" Custalow, and Otha Thomas "Blue Wing" Custalow; producer Richmond Dillard Crinkley and actor Joseph Cheshire Cotten; Generals Philip St. George Cooke and John Rogers Cooke (1833–1891); ichthyologist Russell Jordan Coles; criminals Thomas Judson Cluverius and George Crawford; musician Maybelle Addington Carter; Lott Cary (a founder of Liberia) and Joseph Calvitt Clarke (founder of the Christian Children's Fund); and document examiner Harry Evans Cassidy.

[2] Edgar Cayce, Robert Walter Childress, and Mary Elizabeth "Toddy" Collins, respectively.

Abbreviations and Short Titles

Acts of Assembly	*Acts of the General Assembly of Virginia, Passed at the Session of . . .* (1730–). Title varies over time.
Adm	Admiralty Papers, PRO.
Adventurers of Purse and Person	John Frederick Dorman, ed., *Adventurers of Purse and Person, Virginia, 1607–1624/5,* 4th ed. (2004–).
AHR	*American Historical Review.*
Annals of Congress	*Debates and Proceedings in the Congress of the United States* (1st–18th Congresses, 1789–1824, published 1834–1856), also known as *Annals of the Congress of the United States.*
AO	Exchequer and Audit Department Papers, PRO.
Atkinson and Gibbens, *Prominent Men*	George W. Atkinson and Alvaro F. Gibbens, *Prominent Men of West Virginia* (1890).
bap.	Baptized.
Billings, *Effingham Papers*	Warren M. Billings, ed., *The Papers of Francis Howard, Baron Howard of Effingham, 1643–1695* (1989).
Branch Papers	*The John P. Branch Historical Papers of Randolph-Macon College* (1901–1918); new ser. (1951–1956).
Brown, *Cabells*	Alexander Brown, *The Cabells and Their Kin: A Memorial Volume of History, Biography, and Genealogy,* 2d ed., rev. (1939).
Bruce, *Rhetoric of Conservatism*	Dickson D. Bruce Jr., *The Rhetoric of Conservatism: The Virginia Convention of 1829–30 and the Conservative Tradition in the South* (1982).
Bruce, *University of Virginia*	Philip Alexander Bruce, *History of the University of Virginia, 1819–1919: The Lengthened Shadow of One Man* (1920–1922).
Bruce, Tyler, and Morton, *History of Virginia*	Philip Alexander Bruce, Lyon Gardiner Tyler, and Richard L. Morton, *History of Virginia* (1924).
BT	Board of Trade Papers, PRO.

BVS	Bureau of Vital Statistics, Commonwealth of Virginia.
BW	Bounty Warrants (1779–1860), Office of the Governor, RG 3, LVA.
Byrd Correspondence	Marion Tinling, ed., *The Correspondence of the Three William Byrds of Westover, Virginia, 1684–1776* (1977).
C	Chancery Papers, PRO.
Caldwell, *History of the American Negro*	Arthur B. Caldwell, ed., *History of the American Negro*, vol. 5: *Virginia Edition* (1921).
Calendar of Virginia State Papers	William P. Palmer et al., eds., *Calendar of Virginia State Papers and Other Manuscripts, 1652–1869* (1875–1893).
Catlin, *Convention of 1829–30*	George Catlin, *The Convention of 1829–30*, VHS; painting reproduced with key in Hall, *Portraits*, 271–274.
Cavaliers and Pioneers	Nell Marion Nugent, *Cavaliers and Pioneers: Abstracts of Virginia Land Patents and Grants, 1623–1800* (1934–1999).
Census	United States Census Schedules, Records of the Bureau of the Census, RG 29, NARA. References are to Lists of Inhabitants unless otherwise indicated.
Circuit Court Ended Cases	United States Circuit Court, Virginia District, Ended Cases, LVA.
Clay Papers	James F. Hopkins et al., eds., *The Papers of Henry Clay* (1959–1992).
CO	Colonial Office Papers, PRO.
Compiled Service Records	Compiled Service Records of Confederate Soldiers (1861–1865), War Department Collection of Confederate Records, RG 109, NARA. Records of soldiers who served in units raised by Virginia, records of general and staff officers and nonregimental enlisted men, and records of soldiers in units raised directly by the Confederate government are the groupings cited most frequently, roughly in that order. The exact subsection used is given only when it is not easily conjectured from the subject's service history.
Convention of 1901–1902 Photographs	Virginia Convention of 1901–1902, [*Photographs of Members*], unpublished bound photograph album of convention members [1902], copies at LVA, UVA, and VHS.

Cunningham, *Circular Letters of Congressmen*	Noble E. Cunningham Jr., ed., *Circular Letters of Congressmen to Their Constituents, 1789–1829* (1978).
CW	John D. Rockefeller Jr. Library, Colonial Williamsburg Foundation, Williamsburg.
Debates and Proceedings of 1850–1851 Convention	*Register of the Debates and Proceedings of the Va. Reform Convention* (1851).
Debates and Proceedings of 1867–1868 Convention	*Debates and Proceedings of the Constitutional Convention of the State of Virginia* (1868).
Documents of 1867–1868 Convention	*Documents of the Constitutional Convention of the State of Virginia* [1868].
Dorman, *Claiborne of Virginia*	John Frederick Dorman, comp., *Claiborne of Virginia: Descendants of Colonel William Claiborne, the First Eight Generations* (1995).
Draper MSS	Lyman C. Draper Papers, Wisconsin Historical Society, Madison, Wis.
Duke	Duke University, Durham, N.C.
DVB Files	*Dictionary of Virginia Biography* Editorial Files, LVA.
E	Exchequer Papers, PRO.
Evans, *Confederate Military History*	Clement A. Evans, ed., *Confederate Military History Extended Edition* (1899; repr. 1987–1989).
Executive Journals of Council	Henry R. McIlwaine, Wilmer L. Hall, and Benjamin J. Hillman, eds., *Executive Journals of the Council of Colonial Virginia* (1925–1966).
Foote, *Sketches of Virginia*	William Henry Foote, *Sketches of Virginia, Historical and Biographical* (1850–1856).
Freedmen's Bank Records	Registers of Signatures of Depositors, Freedmen's Savings and Trust Company (1865–1874), Records of the Office of the Comptroller of the Currency, RG 101, NARA.
Freedmen's Bureau Records	Records of the Assistant Commissioner for the State of Virginia (1865–1869), Bureau of Refugees, Freedmen, and Abandoned Lands, RG 105, NARA.
French Biographies	S. Bassett French MS Biographical Sketches, Personal Papers Collection, LVA.

Glass and Glass, *Virginia Democracy*	Robert C. Glass and Carter Glass Jr., *Virginia Democracy* (1937).
Hall, *Portraits*	Virginius Cornick Hall Jr., *Portraits in the Collection of the Virginia Historical Society: A Catalogue* (1981).
Hampton	Hampton University, Hampton.
Harrison, *Virginia Carys*	Fairfax Harrison, *The Virginia Carys: An Essay in Genealogy* (1919).
Hayden, *Virginia Genealogies*	Horace Edwin Hayden, *Virginia Genealogies: A Genealogy of the Glassell Family* . . . (1891).
HCA	High Court of Admiralty Papers, PRO.
Hening, *Statutes*	William Waller Hening, ed., *The Statutes at Large: Being a Collection of All the Laws of Virginia, from the First Session of the Legislature, in the Year 1619* . . . (1809–1823).
Henry and Spofford, *Eminent Men*	William Wirt Henry and Ainsworth R. Spofford, *Eminent and Representative Men of Virginia and the District of Columbia of the Nineteenth Century* (1893).
Hume, "Membership of Convention of 1867–1868"	Richard L. Hume, "The Membership of the Virginia Constitutional Convention of 1867–1868: A Study of the Beginnings of Congressional Reconstruction in the Upper South," *VMHB* 86 (1978): 461–484.
Hummel and Smith, *Portraits and Statuary*	Ray O. Hummel Jr. and Katherine M. Smith, *Portraits and Statuary of Virginians Owned by The Virginia State Library, The Medical College of Virginia, The Virginia Museum of Fine Arts, and Other State Agencies: An Illustrated Catalog* (1977).
Huntington	Huntington Library, Art Collections, and Botanical Gardens, San Marino, Calif.
Jackson, *Free Negro Labor*	Luther Porter Jackson, *Free Negro Labor and Property Holding in Virginia, 1830–1860* (1942).
Jackson, *Negro Office-Holders*	Luther Porter Jackson, *Negro Office-Holders in Virginia, 1865–1895* (1945).
JAH	*Journal of American History.*
Jamerson, *Speakers and Clerks, 1776–1996*	Bruce F. Jamerson, ed., *Speakers and Clerks of the Virginia House of Delegates, 1776–1996* (1996).

Jefferson Papers	Julian P. Boyd et al., eds., *The Papers of Thomas Jefferson* (1950–).
Jefferson Papers: Retirement Series	J. Jefferson Looney et al., eds., *The Papers of Thomas Jefferson: Retirement Series* (2004–).
JHB	Henry R. McIlwaine and John Pendleton Kennedy, eds., *Journals of the House of Burgesses of Virginia, 1619–1776* (1905–1915).
JHD	Virginia General Assembly, House of Delegates, *Journal of the House of Delegates of the Commonwealth of Virginia* (1776–).
Journal of 1829–1830 Convention	*Journal, Acts, and Proceedings of a General Convention of the Commonwealth of Virginia* [1830].
Journal of 1850–1851 Convention	*Journal, Acts, and Proceedings of a General Convention of the State of Virginia* [1851].
Journal of 1867–1868 Convention	*Journal of the Constitutional Convention of the State of Virginia* [1868].
Journal of 1901–1902 Convention	*Journal of the Constitutional Convention of Virginia* [1902].
Journal of Confederate Congress	*Journal of the Congress of the Confederate States of America, 1861–1865*, 58th Cong., 2d sess., 1904–1905, Senate Doc. 234, serials 4610–4616.
Journal of Second Wheeling Convention	*Journal of the Convention Assembled at Wheeling, on the 11th of June, 1861* (1861).
Journals of Council of State	Henry R. McIlwaine et al., eds., *Journals of the Council of the State of Virginia, 1776–1791* (1931–1982).
JSH	*Journal of Southern History*.
JSV	Virginia General Assembly, Senate, *Journal of the Senate of Virginia* (1776–).
Kaminski, *Ratification*	John P. Kaminski et al., eds., *The Documentary History of the Ratification of the Constitution: Ratification of the Constitution by the States*, vols. 8–10: *Virginia* (1988–1993).
Kingsbury, *Virginia Company*	Susan Myra Kingsbury, ed., *The Records of the Virginia Company of London* (1906–1935).

Kukla, *Speakers and Clerks, 1643–1776*	Jon Kukla, *Speakers and Clerks of the Virginia House of Burgesses, 1643–1776* (1981).
LC	Library of Congress, Washington, D.C.
Legislative Journals of Council	Henry R. McIlwaine, ed., *Legislative Journals of the Council of Colonial Virginia* (1918–1919; 2d ed., 1979).
LOMC	Land Office Military Certificates (1782–1876), Virginia Land Office, RG 4, LVA.
Lowe, "Virginia's Reconstruction Convention"	Richard G. Lowe, "Virginia's Reconstruction Convention: General Schofield Rates the Delegates," *VMHB* 80 (1972): 341–360.
LVA	The Library of Virginia, Richmond.
Lynch, *Custis Chronicles: Migration*	James B. Lynch, Jr., *The Custis Chronicles: The Years of Migration* (1992).
Lynch, *Custis Chronicles: Virginia Generations*	James B. Lynch, Jr., *The Custis Chronicles: The Virginia Generations* (1997).
Madison: Congressional Series	William T. Hutchinson et al., eds., *The Papers of James Madison* (1962–1991).
Madison: Presidential Series	Robert A. Rutland et al., eds., *The Papers of James Madison: Presidential Series* (1984–).
Madison: Secretary of State Series	Robert J. Brugger et al., eds., *The Papers of James Madison: Secretary of State Series* (1986–).
Manarin, *Senate Officers*	Louis H. Manarin, *Officers of the Senate of Virginia, 1776–1996* (1997).
Marshall Papers	Herbert A. Johnson et al., eds., *The Papers of John Marshall* (1974–2006).
Meade, *Old Churches*	William Meade, *Old Churches, Ministers, and Families of Virginia* (1857).
Military Service Records	Military Service Records, World War I History Commission Records, RG 66, LVA.
Minutes of Council and General Court	Henry R. McIlwaine, ed., *Minutes of the Council and General Court of Colonial Virginia*, 2d ed. (1979).
MOC	Museum of the Confederacy, Richmond.

Morton, *Virginia Lives*	Richard Lee Morton, comp., *Virginia Lives: The Old Dominion Who's Who* (1964).
MVHR	*Mississippi Valley Historical Review.*
NARA	National Archives and Records Administration, Washington, D.C.
NCAB	*National Cyclopædia of American Biography* (1891–1984).
n.d.	No date.
n.p.	No page number.
OR	United States War Department, *The War of the Rebellion: A Compilation of the Official Records of the Union and Confederate Armies* (1880–1901).
ORN	United States Department of the Navy, *Official Records of the Union and Confederate Navies in the War of the Rebellion* (1894–1927).
Pecquet du Bellet, *Virginia Families*	Louise Pecquet du Bellet, *Some Prominent Virginia Families* (1907; repr. 1976).
Pollard Questionnaires	John Garland Pollard, comp., data for biographical sketches of members of the Virginia Convention of 1901–1902, compiled 1901, VHS.
por., pors.	Portrait or portraits, identifying location of an original or a source reproducing a photograph, painting, engraving, drawing, or sculpture of the subject.
Pratt, *General Assembly, 1852*	William A. Pratt, *Virginia General Assembly* (March–April 1852), VHS; composite daguerreotype by the Virginian Daguerrean Gallery reproduced in the Chrysler Museum exhibition brochure *Mirror of an Era: The Daguerreotype in Virginia* (1989).
Prerogative Court of Canterbury	Prerogative Court of Canterbury Registered Wills, Principal Probate Registry, London, Eng.
Presidential Pardons	Virginia Case Files for United States Pardons (1865–1867), United States Office of the Adjutant General, RG 94, NARA.
PRO	Public Record Office, London, Eng.

Proceedings and Debates of 1829–1830 Convention	*Proceedings and Debates of the Virginia State Convention of 1829–1830* (1830).
Proceedings and Debates of 1901–1902 Convention	*Report of the Proceedings and Debates of the Constitutional Convention, State of Virginia* (1906).
Quarles, *Worthy Lives*	Garland R. Quarles, *Some Worthy Lives: Mini-Biographies, Winchester and Frederick County* (1988).
Reese, *Journals and Papers of 1861 Convention*	George H. Reese, ed., *Journals and Papers of the Virginia State Convention of 1861* (1966).
Reese and Gaines, *Proceedings of 1861 Convention*	George H. Reese and William H. Gaines Jr., eds., *Proceedings of the Virginia State Convention of 1861* (1965).
Resolutions of 1901–1902 Convention	[*Resolutions of the Constitutional Convention of 1901–1902*] [1901–1902].
Revolutionary Virginia	William J. Van Schreeven, Robert L. Scribner, and Brent Tarter, eds., *Revolutionary Virginia, the Road to Independence: A Documentary Record* (1973–1983).
RG	Record Group.
Sainsbury, *Calendar of State Papers, Colonial Series*	W. Noël Sainsbury et al., eds., *Calendar of State Papers, Colonial Series* (1860–1963).
SCC Charter Book	State Corporation Commission Charter Book, RG 112, LVA.
ser.	Series.
SHSP	*Southern Historical Society Papers* (1876–1959).
Slemp and Preston, *Addresses*	C. Bascom Slemp and Thomas W. Preston, eds., *Addresses of Famous Southwest Virginians* [1939].
Smith, *Complete Works*	Philip L. Barbour, ed., *The Complete Works of Captain John Smith (1580–1631)* (1986).
Smith, *Letters of Delegates*	Paul H. Smith et al., eds., *Letters of Delegates to Congress, 1774–1789* (1976–2000).
Southern Claims Commission	Records of the Commissioners of Claims (Southern Claims Commission), 1871–1880, Department of the Treasury, RG 56, NARA.
SP	State Paper Office, PRO.

Sprague, *American Pulpit*	William B. Sprague, *Annals of the American Pulpit; or Commemorative Notices of Distinguished American Clergymen of Various Denominations* (1866–1877).
Stephenson and McKee, *Virginia in Maps*	Richard W. Stephenson and Marianne M. McKee, eds., *Virginia in Maps: Four Centuries of Settlement, Growth, and Development* (2000).
Stoner, *Seed-Bed*	Robert Douthat Stoner, *A Seed-Bed of the Republic: A Study of the Pioneers in the Upper (Southern) Valley of Virginia* (1962).
Supplement, 1850–1851 Convention Debates	Numbered and dated supplements issued with *Richmond Enquirer, Richmond Examiner, Richmond Times, Richmond Republican, Richmond Republican Advocate,* and *Richmond Whig* (1850–1851).
T	Treasury Office Papers, PRO.
Tompkins-McCaw	Special Collections and Archives, Tompkins-McCaw Library, Virginia Commonwealth University, Richmond.
Tyler, *Encyclopedia*	Lyon Gardiner Tyler, ed., *Encyclopedia of Virginia Biography* (1915).
Tyler, *Men of Mark*	Lyon Gardiner Tyler, ed., *Men of Mark in Virginia* (1906–1909); 2d ser. (1936; anonymously edited). References are to original series unless otherwise indicated.
Tyler's Quarterly	*Tyler's Quarterly Historical and Genealogical Magazine.*
UNC	University of North Carolina at Chapel Hill, N.C.
United States Reports	*Cases Argued and Decided in the Supreme Court of the United States* (title varies; first ninety volumes originally issued in seven distinct editions of separately numbered volumes with *United States Reports* volume numbers retroactively assigned; original volume numbers here given parenthetically; citations are to original pagination).
UTS	Union Theological Seminary and Presbyterian School of Christian Education, Richmond.
UVA	University of Virginia, Charlottesville.
VBHS	Virginia Baptist Historical Society, University of Richmond, Richmond.

VCU	Virginia Commonwealth University, Richmond.
VHS	Virginia Historical Society, Richmond.
Virginia Reports	*Cases Decided in the Supreme Court of Appeals of Virginia* (title varies; issued consecutively for the highest appellate court of Virginia under its variant names of Court of Appeals of Virginia [to 1830], Supreme Court of Appeals of Virginia [1830–1971], and the Supreme Court of Virginia [since 1971]; first seventy-four volumes originally issued in ten distinct editions of separately numbered volumes with *Virginia Reports* volume numbers retroactively assigned; original volume numbers here given parenthetically; citations are to original pagination).
Virginia State Bar Association Proceedings	*Proceedings of the Annual Meeting of the Virginia State Bar Association*; variant titles include *Report of the Annual Meeting.*
VMHB	*Virginia Magazine of History and Biography.*
VMI	Virginia Military Institute, Lexington.
VPI	Virginia Polytechnic Institute and State University, Blacksburg.
VRHC	Valentine Richmond History Center, Richmond.
W&L	Washington and Lee University, Lexington.
W&M	College of William and Mary, Williamsburg.
Washington: Colonial Series	W. W. Abbot et al., eds., *The Papers of George Washington: Colonial Series* (1983–1995).
Washington: Confederation Series	W. W. Abbot, Dorothy Twohig, et al., eds., *The Papers of George Washington: Confederation Series* (1992–1997).
Washington: Presidential Series	Dorothy Twohig, W. W. Abbot, et al., eds., *The Papers of George Washington: Presidential Series* (1987–).
Washington: Retirement Series	W. W. Abbot, Dorothy Twohig, et al., eds., *The Papers of George Washington: Retirement Series* (1998–1999).
Washington: Revolutionary War Series	Philander D. Chase, W. W. Abbot, et al., eds., *The Papers of George Washington: Revolutionary War Series* (1985–).

Washington Diaries	Donald Jackson and Dorothy Twohig, eds., *The Diaries of George Washington* (1976–1979).
Wells and Dalton, *Virginia Architects*	John E. Wells and Robert E. Dalton, *The Virginia Architects, 1835–1955: A Biographical Dictionary* (1997).
Willard and Livermore, *Woman of the Century*	Frances E. Willard and Mary A. Livermore, eds., *A Woman of the Century: Fourteen Hundred-Seventy Biographical Sketches Accompanied by Portraits of Leading American Women in All Walks of Life* (1893).
Winfree, *Laws of Virginia*	Waverly K. Winfree, comp., *The Laws of Virginia: Being a Supplement to Hening's The Statutes at Large, 1700–1750* (1971).
WMQ	*William and Mary Quarterly.*
WPA Biographies	Biographical Files, Virginia Writers' Project, Work Projects Administration Papers, LVA.
WVSA	West Virginia State Archives, Charleston, W.Va.
WVU	West Virginia University, Morgantown, W.Va.

DICTIONARY
of VIRGINIA
BIOGRAPHY

VOLUME 3
Caperton–Daniels

CAPERTON, Allen Taylor (21 November 1810–26 July 1876), member of the Convention of 1850–1851, the Convention of 1861, and the Confederate States Senate, was born at Elmwood, the Monroe County residence of his parents, Hugh Caperton, who won election to a single term in the House of Representatives in 1813, and his first wife, Jane Erskine Caperton. Although Monroe County was far from the frontier by the time Caperton was born, his family had close connections to the pioneers. His paternal grandfather, Adam Caperton, took part in Dunmore's War and in 1782 was killed in a battle with Native Americans in the Kentucky District. His maternal grandmother, Margaret Handley Paulee Erskine, was a captive of other Indians at about the same time, and it is possible that Caperton was the one who preserved her story in a memorandum published in 1912 as the *Old Record of the Captivity of Margaret Erskine, 1779.*

Caperton attended an academy in Huntsville, Alabama, returned to Virginia to attend another in Lewisburg, and in 1828 matriculated at the University of Virginia. After one year he entered Yale University, from which he received an A.B. in 1832. Caperton studied law in Staunton with Briscoe Gerard Baldwin (later a judge of the Virginia Supreme Court of Appeals) and then returned to Monroe County, where he qualified as an attorney in May 1834. On 19 September 1833 he married Harriet Echols. They had six daughters and one son and lived at Elmwood after his father's death in 1847. By 1850 Caperton owned more than a dozen tracts of land totaling more than 1,000 acres. He held ten slaves in 1850 and forty-three in 1860, along with thirteen more who belonged to his wife.

Elected to the House of Delegates in 1841, Caperton served on the Committee for Courts of Justice and on the minor Committee on the Public Library. From 1843 until 1845 he was a private, stockholding director of the James River and Kanawha Company. Throughout his life a strong advocate of government support for canals, railroads, and other internal improvements, he was a Whig and in 1844 was a candidate for presidential elector for Henry Clay. That same year Caperton won election to a four-year term in the Senate of Virginia from the district comprising the counties of Floyd, Giles, Greenbrier, Mercer, Monroe, Montgomery, and Pulaski. He sat on the Committees of Internal Improvement and of General Laws.

In 1850 Caperton entered a four-candidate field and in August of that year won one of three seats representing Giles, Mercer, Monroe, and Tazewell Counties in a convention called to revise the state constitution. He was a member of the Committee on the Basis and Apportionment of Representation named at the beginning of the deliberations and of the eight-member special committee appointed on 12 May 1851 to prepare the final text of the compromise article on apportionment of the General Assembly. Caperton stood with other representatives from the western counties in advocating representation based on the number of white residents without taking property and slaves into account, but he was absent when the final votes on the compromise were taken in the committee of the whole and on the floor of the convention. He supported taxing slaves according to their market value and not per capita, a calculation he believed had placed a disproportionate tax burden on western farmers. He did not vote on final passage of the constitution on 31 July 1851.

Caperton won election to the House of Delegates in 1857 and 1859 for two consecutive terms. He was a member of the Committee on Finance and the Joint Committee on the Library during his first term, and during his second he served on the Committee of Schools and Colleges and was ranking member of the Committee on Finance. On 4 February 1861 he and his brother-in-law John Echols were elected to represent Monroe County in the state convention called in response to the secession crisis. Caperton was named to the Committee on Privileges and Elections. On 4 April 1861 he voted against secession, but two weeks later, proclaiming that "war is upon us, and we are compelled to make the best of it," he asked for unity between the eastern and western regions of Virginia and on 17 April voted in favor of secession. Although Caperton agreed with other westerners that slaves should be taxed on their market value, a proposition that eastern slaveholders resisted until the spring of 1861, he opposed taking up that issue at that time for fear of widening divisions within the state.

In the autumn of 1861 Caperton was a presidential elector for Jefferson Davis and the following year was provost marshal for the Confederate government in Monroe County. On 17 January 1863 the General Assembly elected Caperton to succeed the recently deceased William Ballard Preston, a Whig from Montgomery County, in the Confederate States Senate. The legislators had argued for two days about whether it was politic to select another westerner or another Whig to serve with Robert Mercer Taliaferro Hunter, an easterner and a Democrat, and if so, who the westerner or Whig should be. Although Caperton received scattered votes from the beginning of the balloting, he did not emerge as a strong candidate until midway through the voting and finally won election on the twentieth ballot. He took his seat nine days later and began serving on the Committees on the Judiciary and on Engrossment and Enrollment, the Special Committee on Hospitals, and a select committee to investigate charges of violence United States forces committed against Confederate civilians and their property. Caperton lost his seat on the judiciary committee in 1864 but gained seats on the Committees on Foreign Relations and on Indian Affairs and became chair of the Committee on Accounts. In December 1864 he temporarily joined the Committee on Post-Offices and Post-Roads. He remained in Richmond through the adjournment of the second, and final, session of the Second Confederate Congress on 18 March 1865.

After the Civil War, Caperton became a Democrat and continued to practice law in Monroe County, where he worked to bring the undeveloped coal and timber resources of West Virginia to the attention of northern investors. In 1875 the West Virginia legislature elected him to the United States Senate. Caperton took office on 5 March 1875 and was appointed to the Committees on Claims, on Railroads, and on the Revision of the Laws. Consistent with his antebellum support of Henry Clay and with his postwar involvement in the economic development of West Virginia, Caperton continued to argue while in the Senate that the national government had a constructive and constitutional role to play in fostering national economic growth. Allen Taylor Caperton died suddenly, probably of heart disease, in Washington, D.C., on 26 July 1876 and was buried in Green Hill Cemetery, in Union, West Virginia.

Biographies in Benjamin Perley Poore, comp., *The Political Register and Congressional Directory, . . . 1776–1878* (1878), 319, Atkinson and Gibbens, *Prominent Men*, 268–269, Oren F. Morton, *A History of Monroe County, West Virginia* (1916), 322–324, and George W. Atkinson, ed., *Bench and Bar of West Virginia* (1919), 32; Bernard M. Caperton, *The Caperton Family* (1973), 77–82; Caperton family Bible records (1781–1877), at LVA and VHS, with birth, marriage, and death dates and Caperton's record of births among the family's slaves, and Caperton family Bible records (1781–1929), LVA, recording Caperton's children; Caperton letters in Caperton Family Miscellaneous Papers and Guthrie-Caperton Family Papers, Filson Historical Society, Louisville, Ky., and Caperton Family Papers, VHS; *Richmond Enquirer*, 30 Aug., 3 Sept. 1850; *Journal of 1850–1851 Convention*, 58, 216; *Supplement, 1850–1851 Convention Debates*, no. 37; Reese and Gaines, *Proceedings of 1861 Convention*, 1:39, 2:19–23, 3:163, 4:100–102 (quotation on 102), 144–145; *JHD*, Jan. 1863 sess., 26–38; *Daily Richmond Enquirer*, 14, 16, 17, 19 Jan. 1863; *Journal of Confederate Congress*, 3:20, 31, 74, 414, 4:10, 11; *Congressional Record*, 44th Cong., 1st sess., 8, 1029–1031, 4663–4665; *Centennial Exposition: Speech of Allen T. Caperton, of West Virginia, in the Senate of the United States, February 11, 1876* (1876); obituaries in *Washington Evening Star* and *Wheeling Daily Register*, both 27 July 1876, and *Union [W.Va.] Border Watchman*, 28 July, 4 Aug. 1876; *Memorial Addresses on the Life and Character of Allen T. Caperton* (1877), including frontispiece por.

CONNIE PARK RICE

CAPERTON, Hugh (17 April 1781–9 February 1847), member of the House of Representatives, was born in Greenbrier County and was the son of Elizabeth Miller Caperton and her first husband, Adam Caperton, who was killed on 22 March 1782 in an Indian skirmish in the Kentucky District. Little is known of Caperton's childhood or education. He established his home, Elmwood, near Union in the part of Greenbrier County that in 1799 became Monroe County. Early in his political career, he was at times called Hugh Caperton Jr. to distinguish him from an uncle of the same name. On 11 February 1806 Caperton married Jane Erskine. Among their four daughters and six sons was Allen Taylor Caperton, a member of the constitutional convention of 1850–1851, the secession convention of 1861, and the Confederate States Senate. After the death of his first wife on 20 May 1831, Hugh Caperton married the widow Delilah B. Alexander Beirne on 16 January 1834. There were no children from the second marriage, and Delilah Caperton died on 8 August 1845.

While representing Monroe County in the House of Delegates from 1810 to 1813, Caperton served on the Committee for Courts of Justice during his first two terms and on the Committee of Claims during his third. In 1813 he was elected to the United States House of Representatives from the Seventh Congressional District comprising Cabell, Greenbrier, Kanawha, Mason, Monroe, Randolph, and Wood Counties. Caperton, a Federalist, rarely spoke but tended to vote on issues and bills in Congress with the younger members of his party who embraced partisan politics and adapted the Jeffersonian party apparatus for their own use. He did not serve on any standing committees but was a member of the Joint Committee for Enrolled Bills. After his term expired Caperton chose not to run for reelection.

From 1826 to 1830 Caperton once again represented Monroe County in the House of Delegates. He served on the Committee of Privileges and Elections during each of his four terms. During the 1827–1828 session he sat on the Committee of Roads and Internal Navigation, and during the 1828–1829 session he was appointed to the Joint Committee to Examine the Expenditures of the Treasury and to the Committee to Examine the Expenditures of the Second Auditor.

When not serving in the House of Delegates or in Congress, Caperton returned to Monroe County to oversee Elmwood and his business interests. He was involved in at least four mercantile enterprises, held stock in the White and Sulphur Springs Turnpike and in the James River and Kanawha Company, and in 1835 was elected a director of the latter company. By the time of his death, Caperton owned more than one hundred slaves and numerous properties, including at least five plantations; a house, tavern, and storehouse in Union; and another house in Lewisburg. He left to his heirs more than $35,000 in cash, bonds, and slaves, as well as land, furni-

ture, stocks, and other property. Hugh Caperton died on 9 February 1847 in Monroe County and was buried in Green Hill Cemetery, in Union.

Biography in David Hackett Fischer, *The Revolution of American Conservatism: The Federalist Party in the Era of Jeffersonian Democracy* (1965), 383–384; birth, marriage, and death dates in Caperton family Bible records (1781–1877), at LVA and VHS; Caperton correspondence in Caperton Family Papers, Hugh Blair Grigsby Papers, and Preston Family Papers, VHS; *Richmond Enquirer*, 11, 18 May 1813, 26 Apr. 1815; *Journal of the House of Representatives*, 13th Cong., 3d sess., 582; will (with birth date) and estate inventory in Monroe Co. Will Book, 4:242–248, 361–362, printed in John Hays Caperton and William Alexander Gordon, *The Killing of Adam Caperton by Indians . . .* (1918), 33–42 (por. between 6 and 7).

TRENTON E. HIZER

CAPPON, Lester Jesse (18 September 1900–24 August 1981), archivist and historian, was born in Milwaukee, Wisconsin, and was the son of Jesse Cappon, a carpenter, and Mary Elizabeth Geisinger Cappon. A gifted pianist and passionate lover of music, he earned a diploma at the Wisconsin Conservatory of Music in 1920. After receiving a B.A. in history from the University of Wisconsin, in Madison, in 1922 and an M.A. the following year, he taught English at an all-male high school in Milwaukee for the 1923–1924 academic term. Cappon received a second master's degree from Harvard University in 1925 and a Ph.D. in 1928. Arthur Meier Schlesinger (1888–1965) directed his dissertation on the southern iron industry through 1865. On 25 June 1932 Cappon married Dorothy Elizabeth Bernet, a teacher in La Crosse, Wisconsin. They had one son and one daughter.

While completing his doctoral studies Cappon was a research associate at the University of Virginia's Institute for Research in the Social Sciences during the 1926–1927 academic year. He returned to that position for two years beginning in 1928. In 1930 Cappon accepted appointments as both assistant professor of history at the University of Virginia and the first archivist of the university library. In the latter post, which he held until 1940, he won praise for initiating and sustaining the movement to identify, locate, collect, preserve, and publish guides to the records of Virginia's past. Cappon compiled and published such detailed reference works as *Bibliography of*

Virginia History since 1865 (1930), *Virginia Newspapers, 1821–1935: A Bibliography with Historical Introduction and Notes* (1936), and "Bibliography of Original Baptist Church Records in the Virginia Baptist Historical Society, University of Richmond," in the University of Virginia Library's *Annual Report of the Archivist* (1937).

Cappon's familiarity with Virginia manuscript resources led to his service as director of the Virginia Historical Records Survey from 1936 to 1937. Asked to prepare guidelines for recording the history of the Second World War, he published *A Plan for the Collection and Preservation of World War II Records* (1942) and *War Records Projects in the States, 1941–43* (1944), and from 1944 to 1945 he was director of the Virginia World War II History Commission. Cappon edited two periodicals, *Papers of the Albemarle County Historical Society* from 1940 to 1945 and the monthly *War Records Collector* in 1944 and 1945. His vision and experience allowed him to move easily and often across the artificial barriers erected by specialists in academic history, archival science, and genealogy.

Shortly after being promoted to associate professor in 1945, Cappon left Charlottesville to become the first editor of publications for the Institute of Early American History and Culture, a new institution founded by the College of William and Mary and Colonial Williamsburg, Incorporated (later the Colonial Williamsburg Foundation). Once settled in a restored eighteenth-century house on Duke of Gloucester Street in Williamsburg, he became a vital part of the life of the college and town. For ten years as editor of publications, Cappon labored in the institute's offices over the stores on Duke of Gloucester Street along with the brilliant editor of the *William and Mary Quarterly*, Douglass Greybill Adair, and the distinguished directors of the institute, Carl Bridenbaugh and Lyman Henry Butterfield, to make the fledgling institute a center of early American studies. During these years he completed, with Stella Frances Duff (later Neiman), the massive and indispensable *Virginia Gazette Index, 1736–1780* (1950) and in 1949 served as president of the Southern Historical Association. From 1945 to 1952 he also was archivist of Colonial Williamsburg and then became an archival consultant for its research collection.

After the departure of Butterfield early in 1955, Cappon became acting director of the institute, and later that year the governing council made the appointment permanent. Heartened by this decision and buoyed by learning that his steadily encroaching deafness could be arrested, the new director moved quickly and decisively. He brought to Williamsburg two extraordinarily able and dynamic young historians who proved to be perfect fits for the institute. Lawrence William Towner cemented the *Quarterly*'s status as the most admired American scholarly journal of history, and James Morton Smith soon had the institute sending forth an uninterrupted flow of well-received books on early America. As early American history moved to the center of American historiography, the institute during the 1950s and 1960s created a flowering of colonial American studies. Cappon organized conferences for historians of early America to come together and explore the frontiers of their various areas of study, and he brought to Williamsburg for two years of postdoctoral work a succession of the most promising young historians. The resulting books by these research fellows, all published by the institute, were uniformly distinguished and in several instances seminal.

Cappon initiated and raised funds for a project to collect and publish a documentary edition of the papers of John Marshall, an undertaking organized in 1966. While making the institute the world center for its field of study, Cappon twice served as interim editor of the *William and Mary Quarterly*, from 1955 to 1956 and again in 1963. He maintained a prolific output of articles in such journals as the *American Archivist*, the *Journal of Southern History*, and the *William and Mary Quarterly* on bibliography; historical editing; changing standards of professional training of archivists, documentary editors, and historians; and the expanded horizons possible when archivists, genealogists, and historians cooperated. Cappon served as president of the Society of American Archivists for the 1956–1957 term and in 1959 published his classic *Adams-Jefferson Letters: The Complete Correspondence between Thomas Jefferson and Abigail and John Adams*. He was a founding director of the University Press of Virginia.

Cappon retired as director of the institute on 1 July 1969. His wife had died on 11 August 1965, and although he maintained a residence in Williamsburg, he spent most of his time in retirement in Chicago at the Newberry Library. By the arrangement of Towner, who had headed the Newberry since leaving the *William and Mary Quarterly* in 1961, Cappon became a senior fellow at the library and assembled a staff there to aid him in preparing the magnificent *Atlas of Early American History: The Revolutionary Era, 1760–1790* (1976), which in 1977 received from the Reference and User Services Association the Dartmouth Medal for an Outstanding Reference Work. His incomparable career as an archivist and editor won him election in 1980 as the second president of the Association for Documentary Editing. To mark his eightieth birthday in 1980 the Newberry Library mounted a retrospective exhibition of his writings, "Lester J. Cappon: The First Eighty Years."

Lester Jesse Cappon suffered a heart attack while striding down the sidewalk near the Newberry Library and died on 24 August 1981. He was buried in the cemetery of Emmanuel Episcopal Church in Greenwood, Albemarle County. The Newberry Library established a documentary editing fellowship in his honor.

Morton, *Virginia Lives*, 158; Harry Clemons, "Lester J. Cappon: An Appreciation," in *General Index to First Fifteen Annual Reports on Historical Collections, University of Virginia Library, 1931–1945* (1947), 3–8, including partial bibliography of Cappon's writings; retirement tribute by Wilcomb E. Washburn in *WMQ*, 3d ser., 26 (1969): 323–326 (por. by David Silvette on 322); oral history interview, conducted by Stephen M. Rowe on 12 May 1976, in "The Reminiscences of Lester Jesse Cappon" (typescript, 1976), W&M; Richard J. Cox, ed., *Lester J. Cappon and the Relationship of History, Archives, and Scholarship in the Golden Age of Archival Theory* (2004); Lester J. Cappon Papers, including diaries, research notes, and MS drafts, W&M; other Cappon materials in Lester Jesse Cappon Papers, UVA, and Lawrence W. Towner Papers, Newberry Library, Chicago, Ill.; Wisconsin BVS Marriage Certificate, Milwaukee; presidential addresses published as "The Provincial South," *JSH* 16 (1950): 5–24, and "Tardy Scholars Among the Archivists," *American Archivist* 21 (Jan. 1958): 3–16; obituaries in *Charlottesville Daily Progress*, *Richmond News Leader*, and *Richmond Times-Dispatch*, all 26 Aug. 1981, *New York Times*, 27 Aug. 1981, *Chicago Tribune*, 29 Aug., 16 Sept. 1981, and *Williamsburg Virginia Gazette*, 2 Sept. 1981; memorials in *Newsletter of the Association for Documentary Editing* 3 (Dec. 1981): 11, by James Morton Smith in *American Archivist* 45 (winter 1982): 105–108 (por. on 106), in *JSH* 48 (1982): 153–154, and by Lawrence W. Towner in *WMQ*, 3d ser., 39 (1982): 397–398.

W. W. ABBOT

CAPPS, Washington Lee (31 January 1864–31 May 1935), naval officer, was born in Portsmouth and was the son of Washington Tazewell Capps and Frances Bernard Capps. At age sixteen he was appointed to the United States Naval Academy, from which he graduated third in a class of forty-six in June 1884. After spending two years at sea as a naval cadet, Capps was promoted to ensign on 1 July 1886 and sent to Scotland to study naval architecture at the University of Glasgow. Following his graduation from the university, he was appointed an assistant naval constructor on 6 June 1888 and remained in Glasgow for another year. From his return to the United States in May 1889 until January 1896 Capps served at the Department of the Navy in Washington, D.C., at a commercial shipyard in Philadelphia, at the navy yard in New York, and at the Bureau of Construction and Repair in Washington.

Appointed a naval constructor on 28 January 1895, Capps became superintendent of naval construction in San Francisco in February 1896. During the Spanish-American War he served on the staff of Commodore George Dewey and arrived in the Philippines in July 1898, more than two months after the American navy defeated the Spanish fleet in Manila Bay. Capps supervised the raising of several Spanish vessels from the bay and their repair in Hong Kong. On 5 August 1899 he was promoted to commander. Returning to Washington, D.C., Capps served on the Board of Inspection and Survey from October 1899 to March 1901 and as head of the construction department at the Brooklyn Navy Yard from March 1901 through October 1903.

On 1 November 1903 Capps was appointed chief constructor of the navy and chief of the Bureau of Construction and Repair. He was reappointed for a second four-year term in 1907. Naval construction nearly doubled while Capps was chief of the bureau. The navy enlarged and modernized the fleet and designed and built its first four dreadnoughts. Capps oversaw important developments in battleship design, including the skeleton mast and the centerline turret arrangement for heavy guns. A series of accidents on the newest battleships between 1903 and 1906 disclosed design defects, notably in the ammunition hoists inside the gun turrets. Critics of the board demanded that line officers receive more control over ship design, but Capps argued that the accidents were the result of bad decisions made by line officers already serving on the board, not of mistakes by naval architects. He disagreed with a proposal to reorganize the navy department that would have transferred powers held by staff officers to line officers. Capps resigned as chief of the bureau on 1 October 1910, at which time he received a permanent commission as chief constructor with the rank of rear admiral.

From October 1913 to February 1914 Capps represented the United States in London at the International Conference on the Safety of Life at Sea and chaired the conference's Committee on the Safety of Construction. The conference endorsed his proposal that ships be subdivided with watertight side and crosswise compartments to reduce the danger of sinking. Capps became president of the navy's Board on Hull Changes, Atlantic Coast, in September 1912, a member of the Navy Yard Commission in 1916, and president of the Naval War Claims Board in 1917.

In 1917 Capps became senior member of the Navy Compensation Board with responsibility for supervising naval shipbuilding expenditures. On 24 July of that year the president appointed him general manager of the Emergency Fleet Corporation charged with directing the merchant shipbuilding program. The following November much of Capps's authority was transferred to the president of the corporation, who was also chair of the shipping board. Citing health reasons but also perhaps because he disapproved of the changes, Capps resigned as general manager effective 3 December 1917. He received the Navy Distinguished Service Medal for his service on the Compensation Board, the General Munitions Board, and the Emergency Fleet Corporation during World War I.

Capps continued to sit on the Board on Hull Changes, the Naval War Claims Board, and the Navy Commission until his death, although he was officially transferred to the retired list on 31 January 1928. A founding member of the Society of Naval Architects and Marine Engineers, he was its secretary from 1893 to 1895 and again from 1901 to 1903 and president from 1919 to 1921. On 28 December 1911 Capps married Edna Ward, an admiral's daughter, in Roslyn, New York. They had no children. Washington Lee Capps died at his home in Washington, D.C., on 31 May 1935 and was buried in Arlington National Cemetery. In his honor the troop transport USS *Admiral W. L. Capps* was commissioned in September 1944.

Biographies in *NCAB*, 100:54–55 (por.), Bruce, Tyler, and Morton, *History of Virginia*, 4:444–445, and William B. Cogar, ed., *Dictionary of Admirals of the U.S. Navy* (1991), 2:41; birth and death dates in *Register of the Commissioned and Warrant Officers of the United States Navy and Marine Corps, January 1, 1912* (1912), 98–99, and *July 1, 1935* (1935), 508, respectively; some Capps documents, including student notebook and exercise book, in Bernard Family Papers, and unidentified clippings in scrapbook in Couper Family Papers, both VHS; Capps correspondence in Arthur S. Link et al., eds., *The Papers of Woodrow Wilson* (1966–1994), 43:260, 270, 271, 45:103, 117; works include *Statements of Rear-Admiral Charles W. Rae, Chief of Bureau of Steam Engineering, and Rear-Admiral Washington Lee Capps, Chief of Bureau of Construction and Repair, . . . Mar. 1, 1906*, 59th Cong., 1st sess., 1906, House Committee on Naval Affairs, serial 113, *Report Concerning Certain Alleged Defects in Vessels of Navy*, 60th Cong., 1st sess., 1908, Senate Committee on Naval Affairs Doc. 297, serial 5265, and *Statement of Washington Lee Capps, Chief Constructor and Rear-Admiral . . .* , 60th Cong., 2d sess., 1909, House Committee on Naval Affairs, serial 8; *New York Times*, 12 July 1910, 29 Dec. 1911, 20 Jan. 1914, 25 July 1917; obituaries in *New York Times*, *Norfolk Ledger-Dispatch*, *Portsmouth Star*, and *Washington Post*, all 1 June 1935, and Society of Naval Architects and Marine Engineers *Transactions* 43 (1935): 308–311.

GERALD P. GAIDMORE II

CAPPS, William (fl. 1609–1630), member of the first General Assembly, was born in England, probably between 1580 and 1585, but nothing regarding his parentage or early years has been confirmed. In the employment of the Virginia Company of London in May 1609, he departed England in one of the company's ships bound for Virginia and most likely reached the colony in August 1609. Over the next few years the company granted Capps patents to several tracts of land at Kecoughtan, at the southeastern end of the Peninsula, and he later acquired land in the area that became Princess Anne County. He directed the shipment of supplies to the colony and often transported colonists, including a group of one hundred people early in 1622. He also planted tobacco and raised livestock.

Capps represented Kecoughtan in the first Virginia assembly, which met in Jamestown from 30 July to 4 August 1619. He was the fifth of eight men the Speaker named to a committee to review parts of the company's 1618 charter, known as the Great Charter, and to recommend modifications beneficial to the colony. The assembly also petitioned the company's London council to give Kecoughtan an English name, and the following year it named the site Elizabeth City in honor of the daughter of King James I.

During the 1620s Capps made several trips between Virginia and England. He advised the company officials on affairs in the colony but thought it prudent before returning to Virginia in 1622 to obtain an authenticated certificate that the company's officers held him in high esteem. By then Capps had made some enemies. He criticized various company officials early in the 1620s and in April 1621 filed a petition charging that Governor Sir George Yeardley had appropriated his land on the pretense that it was company property. The company compensated Capps by allowing him headrights to patent more land, but he nourished a grudge against the governor and privately accused him of being a "right worthie Statesman, for his owne profit." In March 1623 Capps complained to John Ferrar, deputy treasurer of the company, about the company's administration and charged that another of its officers had seized all of his swine, which during seven years of Capps's management had increased to a valuable herd. He was a cantankerous man. In 1628 the governor's Council forced him to apologize for calling a man a "rogue & theefe" and in the spring of the following year found him guilty of not regularly attending church according to law.

Capps was in England at the time of the Powhatan Uprising of 1622. When he returned to Virginia afterward and found that a large por-

tion of the colonists had died, he declared that the event had "burst the heart of all the rest." Whether the Catharine Capps who was reported as recently deceased in Elizabeth City about that time was his wife is not certain. He had a namesake son who was born in the mid-1610s, but the son is not listed among the victims or the survivors, and his whereabouts immediately after the uprising are not known.

In the autumn of 1622 Capps joined William Claiborne and several other veteran Virginia planters in petitioning the Crown "on the behalf of themselves and the rest of your poore distressed Subjects of that Plantation." They complained of the company's mismanagement and asked the king to take the colony and the tobacco trade under his protection. Capps's grievances and others like them from respectable and experienced colonists influenced the king's decision in 1624 to revoke the company's charter and to make Virginia a royal colony.

Capps made a successful transition from responsible company employee in the 1610s to responsible planter and royal agent in the 1620s. He never again held public office, but the king employed him to deliver official instructions to the governor and Council. Capps shared his sovereign's skepticism of building the colony's economy solely on tobacco cultivation, and he experimented with other sources of income. In 1621 he and some other men contracted to ship 100,000 pounds of sassafras to England, and two years later Capps asked that brickmakers, carpenters, and sawyers be sent to Virginia along with enough provisions to support them for a year while promising to take responsibility for building guesthouses at Elizabeth City and Jamestown. Later, in 1628, the Council ordered him to find a place on the Eastern Shore to experiment with making salt by solar evaporation of seawater.

Returning by February 1628 from one of his trips to England, Capps carried orders from the king that the colonists search for mines, plant grapevines, and establish new industries in Virginia. The king's accompanying authorization to the governor to call the assembly into session was the Crown's first official recognition of the assembly's right to participate in the government of the colony. In February 1629 Capps petitioned the governor and Council for leave to return to England again on his business, which "consisteth cheifly on the kings affaires." The governor and Council denied him permission to depart, but evidently believing that the king's business was more important than the governor's permission, Capps left the colony anyway later that year. He returned to Virginia again sometime in 1630 with another set of instructions from the king.

That is the last time that Capps's name appears in surviving records relating to the colony. A William Capps resided in Lower Norfolk County in the 1640s and 1650s, but his age indicates that he was the colonist's son. The date and place of William Capps's death are not known. The will of a mariner of that name, of Wapping, Middlesex County, England, written on 16 March 1625 and proved in the Prerogative Court of Canterbury on 7 May 1633, mentions a wife Edy, or Editha, Capps and a son Benjamin Capps. Another William Capps died overseas on an unrecorded date before his widow, Mary Capps, received letters of administration from the same court on 10 January 1637. It is not certain that either was the Virginia merchant and burgess.

Family information in Frances G. Howell, *William Capps of Jamestowne, Va., and His Johnston Co., N.C., Descendants* (1998), 3–20 (including an erroneous marriage), and Couper Family Papers, VHS, with family chart printed in *VMHB* 59 (1951): chart 5, following 127; Kingsbury, *Virginia Company*, 1:460–461, 471, 579, 585, 609, 615, 2:43, 105, 3:580–581, 4:37–39, 76–79, 159, 558; William J. Van Schreeven and George H. Reese, eds., *Proceedings of the General Assembly of Virginia, July 30–August 4, 1619* (1969), 12–13, 26–27; *Minutes of Council and General Court*, 134–135, 169 (second quotation), 174, 194; petition to king, ca. 1622, PRO CO 1/2, fol. 110 (fourth quotation); Capps to John Ferrar, 31 Mar. 1623, PRO 30/15/2, no. 322; Capps to Doctor Wynston, ca. 1623, PRO 30/15/2, no. 323 (first and third quotations); king to governor and Council, ca. 1627, PRO CO 1/4, fol. 84; Capps to governor and Council, 20 Feb. 1628, PRO CO 1/5, fol. 9 (fifth quotation); witness examinations concerning Capps, Nov. 1629, PRO CO 1/5, fol. 85; final references to Capps in Virginia in Sir John Harvey to Sir Dudley Carleton, viscount Dorchester, 29 May 1630, PRO CO 1/5, fol. 195–197, and to Sir Robert Heath, 31 May 1630, Colonial Papers, RG 1, LVA; assertion that Capps was appointed to the governor's Council in 1627 (*WMQ*, 1st ser., 6 [1898]: 194–195) not documented and probably erroneous; Prerogative Court of Canterbury, Russell

43; Marc Fitch, ed., *Index to Administrations in the Prerogative Court of Canterbury . . . , 1631–1648* (1986), 6:72.

DAPHNE GENTRY

CARAVATI, Charles Martin (31 May 1899–21 April 1991), medical educator, was born in Richmond and was the son of Henry L. Caravati, a native of Italy, and Lena M. Mahoney Caravati. His father died when Caravati was still a child, and he grew up with his two brothers in a Richmond household composed of his mother, his Irish maternal grandmother, and his uncle. After completing high school at a Catholic academy in Baltimore, Caravati attended Richmond College (later the University of Richmond) during the 1916–1918 academic years. He entered the Medical College of Virginia in 1918, was a private in the Student Army Training Corps during World War I, and in 1922 received an M.D. Caravati served his internship and residency at Providence Hospital, in Washington, D.C., from 1922 to 1924 and then returned to Richmond, where he opened a private practice and began a long career as a member of the faculty at the Medical College of Virginia (later the Virginia Commonwealth University Medical Center). On 15 November 1929 he married Mary Virginia Dore, a Staunton nurse, who died on 30 January 1950. They had one son, named for Caravati, who became a Richmond dermatologist and was president of the Medical Society of Virginia for the 1985–1986 term. On 19 October 1956 Caravati married Virginia Tabb Mason Love, a Hampton widow. They had no children, and she died on 20 September 1985.

Caravati maintained a general practice from 1924 to 1932, when he began to concentrate on internal medicine, especially gastroenterology. In 1941 he completed postgraduate study at the Johns Hopkins Hospital and Clinic in Baltimore and later became a diplomate of the American Board of Internal Medicine. During World War II, Caravati served in the United States Army Medical Corps and rose from major to colonel. He was posted to Walter Reed General Hospital, in Washington, D.C., from July to October 1942, was chief of gastrointestinal services and then chief of medical services at Percy Jones General Hospital, in Battle Creek, Michigan, from October 1942 to November 1944, and was chief of medical services at Woodrow Wilson General Hospital, near Staunton, from late in 1944 until January 1946, when he retired from the service. During the war his family accompanied him to each station.

Caravati resumed his Richmond practice and professorship at the Medical College of Virginia in 1947. He was assistant dean and director of continuing education from 1966 until his retirement in June 1969. Named emeritus professor of medicine at MCV in July 1969, he continued to teach until 1972. Caravati also served as a senior medical consultant at McGuire Veterans Hospital, in Richmond, and as a consultant to other Richmond-area hospitals. During his long career he published more than thirty articles in such professional medical journals as the *American Journal of Digestive Disease*, *Annals of Internal Medicine*, *Gastroenterology*, and the *Journal of the American Medical Association*, as well as the *Southern Medical Journal* and *Virginia Medical Monthly*. Caravati was a fellow, governor, regent, and master of the American College of Physicians and chaired the gastroenterology sections of both the Southern and American Medical Associations. He received the first annual Louise Obici Memorial Hospital award in 1965 for outstanding contributions to medicine, the Golden Apple Award for teaching from MCV's class of 1971, a distinguished service award from the Southern Medical Association in 1972, and a special citation from its gastroenterology section five years later. He was elected in 1970 an alumnus member of Alpha Omega Alpha Honor Medical Society.

In October 1949 Caravati was surprised to read in a newspaper that Pope Pius XII had named him a Knight Commander of the Order of Saint Sylvester for his wartime service to his country, outstanding medical service to Richmond-area priests and nuns, and tireless efforts toward establishing a Catholic hospital in Richmond. In 1976 Caravati received the Brotherhood award of the Richmond chapter of the National Conference of Christians and Jews (later the National Conference for Community and Justice). He sat on the boards of the Dooley School, Elk Hill Farm, the Little Sisters of the Poor, the Medical College of Virginia Foundation, Saint Joseph's Villa, and Sheltering Arms Hospital.

A charming man of genial personality and wit, Caravati was deeply attached to his hometown. His hobbies included fishing and managing the Goochland County farm that he bought about 1950, an interest he shared with his daughter-in-law. A member for many years of the Deep Run Hunt Club, Caravati was injured in a fall in October 1935. His ear was severely lacerated, and for the rest of his life he wore a prosthetic ear. After his retirement Caravati turned his research talents to history. He wrote *Medicine in Richmond, 1900–1975* (1975) for the Richmond Academy of Medicine and *Major Dooley* (1978), a biography of the Richmond attorney and railroad executive James Henry Dooley, for the Maymont Foundation. Charles Martin Caravati died in Richmond on 21 April 1991 and was buried in the city's Mount Calvary Cemetery.

Birth date in Military Service Records; BVS Marriage Register, Richmond City (1929); information provided by son, Charles Martin Caravati (2003); Caravati interview, 15 Jan. 1987, in MCV Oral History Collection, Caravati alumnus file in Records of MCV Alumni Association, Caravati Faculty File in Emeriti Faculty, Records of the Vice President for Health Sciences 86/Apr/4, all at Tompkins-McCaw; *Richmond Catholic Virginian*, 28 Oct., 4 Nov. (por.), 16 Dec. 1949; *Richmond Times-Dispatch*, 20 Oct. 1956, 14 Mar. 1965, 17 Oct. 1976; Virginius Dabney, *Virginia Commonwealth University: A Sesquicentennial History* (1987), 364–365; obituaries and editorial tributes in *Richmond News Leader* and *Richmond Times-Dispatch*, both 22 (pors.), 23 Apr. 1991; memorial in *Virginia Medical Quarterly* 119 (1992): 115–116.

GAIL V. TATUM

CARDWELL, Richard Henry (1 August 1846–19 March 1931), Speaker of the House of Delegates and judge of the Virginia Supreme Court of Appeals, was born in Madison, Rockingham County, North Carolina, and was the son of Richard Perrin Cardwell and Elizabeth Martin Dalton Cardwell. His father died while Cardwell was still an infant, and his mother raised him and his two brothers, both of whom died fighting for the Confederacy. Cardwell attended public and private schools in North Carolina and in 1863 enlisted in the Junior Reserves of North Carolina. In May 1864 he became a private in Company F of the 1st Confederate Engineer

Troops but soon required extended furloughs because of poor health. He retired from active duty and worked in the enrolling department of North Carolina until the end of the Civil War.

On 9 February 1865 Cardwell married Kate Howard, a Virginia native, in Rockingham County, North Carolina. They had four daughters and three sons, one of whom, William Duval Cardwell, also became Speaker of the House of Delegates. By 1870 Cardwell had moved to Hanover County, Virginia, where he farmed and studied law. Licensed to practice in 1874, he opened an office in Richmond while maintaining his home in Hanover County. Elected to the House of Delegates from Hanover County as a Democrat in 1881, Cardwell won reelection six times and served from 7 December 1881 until 2 March 1894. He was a member of the Committees for Courts of Justice, on Counties, Cities, and Towns, and on Immigration in his first term. In his second term he exchanged seats on the two last-named committees for a seat on the Committee on Federal Relations and Resolutions and the chair of the Committee on Propositions and Grievances. In his third term he retained the chairmanship and also served on the Committees on Officers and Offices at the Capitol, on Public Property, and on Roads and Internal Navigation.

Cardwell strongly campaigned for Democrats in the 1883 state legislative elections in which the party regained control of the General Assembly, and in 1884 he was a Democratic presidential elector. In November 1884 the General Assembly unanimously elected him a county court judge for Hanover, but he declined to serve. A widely respected public speaker and debater as well as a skilled parliamentarian, Cardwell frequently presided over his party's state conventions. In 1887 his tireless work for the Democratic Party was rewarded with his election as Speaker of the House of Delegates. He won reelection three times without opposition or with only token opposition.

From 1890 to 1892 Cardwell served on a commission charged to resolve with the state's creditors the issue of Virginia's antebellum public debt, and in 1892 he chaired a joint legislative committee formed to settle boundary disputes between Virginia and Maryland related to fishing and oyster-culling rights on the Pocomoke and Potomac Rivers. On 6 January 1894 the assembly elected him and four other Democrats to the Supreme Court of Appeals to replace the five judges that the Readjusters had elected when they controlled the legislature. Cardwell resigned as Speaker on 2 March 1894 and took his seat on the court along with the other new judges on 5 January 1895.

Membership on the court was remarkably stable and without dissension during the almost twenty-two years Cardwell sat on the bench. Three of the other four judges served for twenty of those years. The court's docket consisted largely of civil and procedural cases and a few appeals in criminal cases. Most of the court's workload concerned private, not public, law and arose from legal questions involving such matters as contracts, wills, and personal injuries. Dissents were infrequent, and Cardwell dissented in only a few cases either in brief opinions or sometimes with no published reason. His opinions for the court, like those of his fellow judges, were largely devoid of dicta or discursive commentary, relied heavily on judicial precedents, and were deferential to the state legislature. Among his more important decisions, Cardwell wrote the opinion of the court in *New York, Philadelphia, and Norfolk Railroad Company* v. *Board of Supervisors of Northampton County* (1896), holding that a county school tax on the property of a railroad company was an unconstitutional usurpation of state legislative authority. In the combined cases of *Commonwealth* v. *Henry* and *Commonwealth* v. *Shannon* (1909), Cardwell wrote the opinion of the court that upheld the constitutionality of the previous year's so-called Byrd Liquor Law. He also joined the other judges in *Taylor* v. *Commonwealth* (1903), which affirmed the validity of the Constitution of 1902 even though it had been proclaimed in effect rather than been submitted to the voters for ratification through referendum. Cardwell was president of the Supreme Court of Appeals for five months before retiring on 16 November 1916 because of serious eye trouble.

For a decade beginning in 1920 Cardwell served on the board of the Virginia Manual Labor

School for Colored Boys at Hanover (later the Virginia Industrial School Board for Colored Children). His wife died on 21 January 1909, and Richard Henry Cardwell died at his home, Prospect Hill, on 19 March 1931. He was buried in Woodland Cemetery, near Ashland in Hanover County.

Biographies in R. A. Brock, *Virginia and Virginians* (1888), 2:773–774, *NCAB*, 29:188–189, Glass and Glass, *Virginia Democracy*, 2:37–40, and Jamerson, *Speakers and Clerks, 1776–1996*, 105 (por. on 104); birth and death dates from BVS Death Certificate, Hanover Co.; Rockingham Co., N.C., Marriage Bonds (bond dated 7 Feb. 1865); *Richmond Dispatch*, 28 Sept. 1892; *Richmond Times-Dispatch*, 25 Oct. 1916; *Richmond News Leader*, 6 Jan. 1932; Thomas R. Morris, *The Virginia Supreme Court: An Institutional and Political Analysis* (1975), 22–23, 36, Appendices B, C, and E; *New York, Philadelphia, and Norfolk Railroad Company* v. *Board of Supervisors of Northampton County* (1896), *Virginia Reports*, 92:661–669; *Taylor* v. *Commonwealth* (1903), *Virginia Reports*, 101:829–832; *Commonwealth* v. *Henry* and *Commonwealth* v. *Shannon* (1909), *Virginia Reports*, 110:879–896; *Virginia Law Register*, new ser., 2 (1916): 619–620; obituaries and editorial tributes in *Richmond News Leader* and *Richmond Times-Dispatch*, both 20 Mar. 1931; obituary and account of funeral in *Ashland Herald-Progress*, 26 Mar. 1931; memorial in *Virginia State Bar Association Proceedings* (1931), 135–139.

THOMAS R. MORRIS

CARDWELL, William Duval (12 April 1868–27 June 1954), Speaker of the House of Delegates, was born in Madison, Rockingham County, North Carolina, and grew up in Hanover County, Virginia, to which his parents, Richard Henry Cardwell and Kate Howard Cardwell, moved about a year after his birth. Cardwell's father was a farmer and lawyer who represented the county in the House of Delegates from 1881 to 1894 and was Speaker of the House from 1887 until he was elected to the Virginia Supreme Court of Appeals in 1894. Cardwell attended Randolph-Macon College for two years before entering the law school of the University of Virginia, from which he graduated in 1889. He then became a partner in his father's Richmond law firm but continued to reside on a farm in Hanover County until 1919, when he moved to Ashland. About 1936 he moved to Richmond. Cardwell engaged in oystering on rented land in Northampton County and purchased two small islands on the Atlantic Ocean–side of the Eastern Shore.

Beginning about 1896 he was for many years an examiner of records for the judicial district that for most of his service comprised the counties of Caroline, Hanover, King George, Spotsylvania, and Stafford and the city of Fredericksburg.

In 1899 Cardwell was elected to a two-year term in the House of Delegates from Hanover County and was subsequently reelected three times without serious opposition. He was not an active legislator, but he offered a few bills pertaining to his constituents and supported legislation favorable to railroad interests. Cardwell served on the Committees on the Chesapeake and its Tributaries (which he chaired in 1904), for Courts of Justice, and on Immigration (which he chaired during the 1901–1902 session). Between 1900 and 1903 he also chaired a joint committee to examine the practices of oyster inspectors and other issues related to the oyster industry. In 1901 he was appointed to the Committee on Rules and became more involved in the procedural matters of the House.

Cardwell was elected Speaker of the House on 10 January 1906 after two other aspirants withdrew before the House Democratic caucus. The caucus probably selected him because of his loyalty to the political machine of Thomas Staples Martin, a former railroad lawyer and then United States senator, and his longtime friendship with the new governor, Claude Augustus Swanson. The Cardwells are the only father and son to hold the office of Speaker other than Sir John Randolph and Peyton Randolph (d. 1775), who presided over the House of Burgesses in the eighteenth century. Known as an excellent parliamentarian, Cardwell presided over the first session of the House in its new chamber in the enlarged State Capitol. In appointing committee members and assigning chairmanships, he rewarded his and Swanson's associates. Cardwell shuffled leadership positions and gave the new governor considerable influence with the House.

Hinting at new business opportunities in the Norfolk area, Cardwell unexpectedly announced on 22 April 1907 that he would not seek another term in the General Assembly. The following year the Norfolk and Western Railway Company retained his services and in 1925 named him associate counsel. He also served as counsel for the Virginia Railway Association. Having been active in a Hanover County cavalry troop before entering politics, Cardwell obtained a lieutenant's commission in the naval reserve in April 1917, even though he was almost fifty years old when the United States entered World War I. He commanded seven local boats that patrolled the coastline for German submarines.

Cardwell never abandoned his political interests. He remained friendly with Swanson, supported him in subsequent elections for the United States Senate, and represented his interests to other politicians behind the scenes. For many years Cardwell chaired both the Hanover Democratic Committee and the Third Congressional District committee, which secured him a position on the state central committee.

On 10 April 1890 Cardwell married Jane Price Gregory. They had three sons and three daughters. After her death on 18 December 1937, he married a Richmond widow, Frances Omohundro Sullivan, on 8 September 1943. Cardwell retired from law practice in 1949 and moved to Altamonte Springs, Florida. In 1952 he completed a fifteen-page memoir entitled *Random Recollections*. William Duval Cardwell died at his home in Maitland, Florida, on 27 June 1954 and was buried in Richmond's Hollywood Cemetery two days later.

Cardwell, *Random Recollections* (1952), copy at VHS; biographies in Bruce, Tyler, and Morton, *History of Virginia*, 4:191, Glass and Glass, *Virginia Democracy*, 2:249–250, and Jamerson, *Speakers and Clerks, 1776–1996*, 117 (por. on 116); BVS Marriage Register, Hanover Co. (1890); *Richmond Times-Dispatch*, 9, 10, 11, 17 Jan. 1906, 23 Apr. 1907; *Richmond News Leader*, 16 June 1936, 13 Apr. 1953; Henry C. Ferrell Jr., *Claude A. Swanson of Virginia: A Political Biography* (1985), 73, 132–133, 136, 137; William G. Thomas, *Lawyering for the Railroad: Business, Law, and Power in the New South* (1999), 140; obituaries in *Richmond News Leader* and *Richmond Times-Dispatch*, both 28 June 1954.

RONALD L. HEINEMANN

CARLILE, John Snyder (16 December 1817–24 October 1878), member of the Convention of 1850–1851, of the House of Representatives, of the Convention of 1861, of the First and Second Wheeling Conventions of 1861, and of the United States Senate, was born in Winchester and was the only child of Jonathan Carlile, a lawyer, and Elizabeth Snyder Carlile. Contrary to an accepted family tradition that Carlile's father died when he was young, Jonathan Carlile was an abusive alcoholic who squandered his wife's inheritance and whose conduct forced the family to move frequently. After he deserted his family in Bedford County, Pennsylvania, Elizabeth Carlile returned to Hampshire County, where she operated a school. On 17 December 1833 she petitioned the Virginia General Assembly for divorce, and after that request was rejected she obtained a judgment of divorce in Bedford County, Pennsylvania, on 22 August 1836. At age fourteen Carlile left his mother's school to begin working as a store clerk. Seven years later he became an independent merchant, but his business failed, leaving him to pay off his creditors. He then studied law and about 1840 gained admittance to the Virginia bar. Carlile practiced in Harrison and Taylor Counties and in Beverly, in Randolph County, and in Philippi, in Barbour County, during the 1840s. He married Mary Ellen Gittings in Harrison County on 5 March 1846. They had three sons and three daughters, one of whom died in childhood.

A Democrat, Carlile won election in April 1847 to a four-year term in the Senate of Virginia from the district comprising Barbour, Marion, Monongalia, Preston, Randolph, and Taylor Counties. During his first assembly session he was appointed to the Committees of Courts of Justice and on the Militia and to a joint committee to examine the bonds of public officers. In the 1848 session he was a member of the Committees on the Militia and of General Laws. During the 1849 and 1850 sessions he sat on the Committees of General Laws and of Internal Improvements and also chaired the important Committee of Privileges and Elections.

On 22 August 1850 Carlile was one of four delegates elected to represent the counties of Barbour, Braxton, Gilmer, Jackson, Lewis, Randolph, and Wirt in the convention that met in Richmond from 14 October 1850 to 1 August 1851 to revise Virginia's constitution. He was named to the Committee of Elections and the Committee on the Executive Department and Ministerial Officers. One of the convention's most frequent and active debaters, Carlile out-spokenly supported democratic reforms, including the popular election of most public officers and judges of the Virginia Supreme Court of Appeals and a proposal to allow governors to seek reelection. He called for a state census in 1855 and every tenth year thereafter so that the General Assembly could frequently redraw legislative districts based on the white population. On 16 May 1851 Carlile voted with the convention majority in favor of a compromise on the basis of legislative apportionment that established a western majority in the House of Delegates but retained an eastern majority in the Senate. On 31 July he also voted for the new constitution that the convention successfully submitted to popular referendum later that year.

Carlile moved to Clarksburg, in Harrison County, early in the 1850s and joined the new American (Know Nothing) Party. In the spring of 1855 he was the only nominee of that party to win election to the House of Representatives from Virginia. He defeated the incumbent Democrat, Charles Swearinger Lewis, by a narrow margin in the sixteen-county Eleventh Congressional District. In the Thirty-fourth Congress, Carlile received the lowest-ranking seat on the relatively insignificant House Committee on Accounts. In an extended speech, delivered on 21 June 1856, he denounced the Democratic Party's adoption of the principle of squatter sovereignty. Carlile feared that slave owners might lose their property if they moved into a western territory and opponents of slavery there voted to make the territory free. He published the speech in pamphlet form, in part to rebut charges circulated in Virginia by critics of the American Party that the Know Nothings were in league with abolitionists. Carlile made no major speeches during the remainder of his term and in the spring of 1857 lost his reelection bid to a Democrat, Albert Gallatin Jenkins.

In February 1861 Harrison County voters elected Carlile one of two delegates to represent them in the convention called to frame Virginia's response to the secession crisis. A few days after the convention opened, an observer writing for the *Wheeling Daily Intelligencer* characterized him as a "man of fine talents—a ready, keen,

solid, and impressive man." Carlile was "somewhat singular looking, being very sallow and angular in his face, flat on his head, compact and well knit in his framework. He has a rich deep voice, fine power of expression, impertur[b]able coolness and a great deal of tact."

Throughout the convention, Carlile spoke passionately in favor of the Union and against secession, which he denounced as the product of a Southern conspiracy, as "self murder," and as "an insult to all reasonable living humanity, and a crime against God." Emphasizing that he was a slave owner by purchase and not by mere inheritance (at that time he may have owned only one slave) and consequently was not to be confused with Republicans or abolitionists, he argued that slavery was more secure with Virginia in the Union than if the state seceded. One of the acknowledged leaders of the western Virginia Unionists, Carlile was the target of secessionist criticism. He was once assaulted and on another occasion observed a crowd outside his boardinghouse brandishing a rope and threatening to hang him. He voted against secession when the motion failed on 4 April 1861 and again when it passed on 17 April. Carlile quickly left Richmond and returned to Clarksburg to continue his campaign against secession. Because of his continued support for the Union, on 29 June 1861 by a vote of 83 to 1 the convention expelled him.

Soon after returning to Clarksburg, Carlile and other Unionists there issued an address to the people of western Virginia calling on Unionists to convene in Wheeling in May to develop a response to the rebellion in Richmond. He urged the resulting convention to draft a proclamation for a new state government. The convention voted to await the results of the referendum on secession but appointed Carlile to a committee that later summoned the Second Wheeling Convention after a majority of voters in eastern Virginia approved the state's secession from the Union. At the June session he chaired both the Committee on Rules and the influential Committee on Business and took the lead in drafting "A Declaration of the People of Virginia," which the delegates adopted on 17 June 1861. It stated the rationale of the convention's decision to declare the state offices of Virginia vacant, after which the convention elected a new governor and other officers and created the reorganized state government that President Abraham Lincoln recognized as the legitimate authority in Virginia. At the convention session in August of that year Carlile called for organizing northwestern Virginia counties as a new state. In a dramatic speech on 8 August, he enjoined, "Cut the knot now! Cut it now! Apply the knife!" In spite of his enthusiasm, the convention refused to separate from Virginia at that time, but it appointed Carlile to a six-member committee to consider establishing a new state. Carlile's committee reported a dismemberment ordinance, adopted by the convention on 20 August, that proposed creating the state of Kanawha from thirty-nine Virginia counties, with the possibility of later adding seven more.

In the meantime, on 23 May 1861, in spite of a prohibition that the Richmond convention had issued, voters in many western Virginia counties elected members of the United States House of Representatives, and Carlile regained his former seat with little opposition. A few days after being sworn in, he resigned to take his seat in the United States Senate, to which some western members of the General Assembly, meeting irregularly in Wheeling, elected him unanimously on 9 July 1861. Carlile served in the Senate until his term expired on 3 March 1865 and sat on the Committee on Public Lands and the Committee on Territories. He persisted in his Unionism but was often at odds with Republicans in Congress and with the administration. Carlile opposed allowing the army to free or arm escaped slaves, and until the end of the Civil War he continued to affirm the constitutionality and propriety of slavery. He voted against the bill passed on 3 April 1862 to abolish the institution in the District of Columbia but was not present to record his vote in the Senate on 8 April 1864 when that body proposed the Thirteenth Amendment to the Constitution abolishing slavery throughout the nation. Increasingly censorious of Lincoln's conduct of the war, Carlile sharply criticized the administration, Congress, and the Republican Party in speeches in Indianapolis in July 1862 and in New York in April 1863. On 15 June 1864 Lincoln ordered Carlile's arrest on suspicion of treason.

On 23 June 1862 the Senate Committee on Territories submitted a bill for the admission to the Union of West Virginia as a new state. The bill included several Shenandoah Valley counties where support for the Confederacy remained strong and that had not been represented in the constitutional convention or named in its application for statehood. Carlile was credited with adding those counties to the statehood bill in committee, but he disapproved of including them in the new state without first holding a referendum or recalling the convention to obtain the consent of the inhabitants of those counties. The Senate declined to include the eastern counties in the bill (although Berkeley and Jefferson Counties voted on 28 May 1863 to join West Virginia and Congress later approved their inclusion). After the Senate voted to require the new state to adopt a plan of gradual emancipation, Carlile attacked the bill on the grounds that Congress could not dictate the terms of a new state constitution. He spoke and voted against the statehood bill, which passed the Senate on 14 July 1862. Carlile's opposition to the bill led the Restored Virginia assembly to call for his resignation, but he ignored the resolution.

Carlile's contemporaries had difficulty identifying a consistent set of principles underlying his conduct, and many of his longtime friends consequently vilified him. His political turns in the 1860s seemed to confirm his son's assessment that "he would espouse what he considered to be a principle or the proper cause and he would throw the whole force of his intellect and zeal into the advocacy of it—uncaring for personal consequences." Carlile's political career effectively ended with the expiration of his term in March 1865. He moved to Frederick, Maryland, but, unable to rejuvenate his political fortunes there, he returned to Clarksburg in the summer of 1868. Carlile endorsed the Republican presidential candidate, Ulysses Simpson Grant, that year and the following year asked in return to be appointed minister to Brazil. Instead, Grant named him minister to Sweden, but Republican senators, reinforced by sharp objections from many West Virginians, blocked confirmation of the nomination. In 1869 Carlile unsuccessfully campaigned for a seat representing Harrison County in the West Virginia House of Delegates.

John Snyder Carlile lived his last years on his farm near Clarksburg, West Virginia, and died in that town on 24 October 1878. He was buried in the local Odd Fellows Cemetery.

Birth date on gravestone and in Charles Lanman, *Dictionary of the United States Congress, Containing Biographical Sketches of Its Members . . .* (1859), 93–94; parents identified in *Sherrard et als. v. Carlisle* (1855), in John M. Patton Jr. and Roscoe B. Heath, eds., *Reports of Cases Decided in the Special Court of Appeals of Virginia* (1856), 1:12–33; biographies in Atkinson and Gibbens, *Prominent Men*, 207–208, *Appletons' Cyclopædia of American Biography* (1887), 1:526, by son William D. Carlile in William P. Willey, *An Inside View of the Formation of the State of West Virginia* (1901), 207–210 (fourth quotation on 208), George W. Atkinson, *Bench and Bar of West Virginia* (1919), 14–15, and Dorothy Davis, *History of Harrison County, West Virginia* (1970), 171–199, 204–205, 832–833 (por. on 155); Harrison Co. Marriage Records (1784–1851), 3:210; Carlile letters in various collections at LC, LVA, Pierpont Morgan Library, University of Rochester, UVA, and WVU; major public addresses published as *The Cincinnati Platform* (1856), *Letter of John S. Carlile to the People of the Eleventh Congressional District of Virginia* (1857), *Speech of John S. Carlile, of Harrison, in the Virginia State Convention, Delivered Thursday, March 7, 1861* (1861), in *Wheeling Daily Intelligencer*, 10 Aug. 1861 (third quotation), *Speech of Hon. John S. Carlile, of Virginia, On the Bill to Confiscate the Property and Free the Slaves of Rebels; Delivered in the Senate of the United States, March 11, 1862* (1862), *Remarks of John S. Carlile, of Virginia, at the Mass Convention, at Indianapolis, on the 30th Day of July, 1862* (1862), in *Richmond Examiner*, 22 Apr. 1863 (abstracted in *New York Times*, 8 Apr. 1863), and in *New York Times*, 20 Aug. 1868; *Journal of 1850–1851 Convention*, esp. 25, 59, 419, and Appendix, 22; *Debates and Proceedings of 1850–1851 Convention*, esp. 75, 373–376; *Supplement, 1850–1851 Convention Debates*, esp. nos. 16, 42, 69–70; *Wheeling Daily Intelligencer*, 21 Feb. 1861 (first quotation); *Clarksburg Register*, 22 Mar. 1861 (with middle name); Reese and Gaines, *Proceedings of 1861 Convention*, esp. 1:156–160, 348–350, 448–482 (second quotation on 477), 2:146–150, 154–159, 311–322, 3:163, 253–254, 276–279, 323–326, 411–415, 562–565, 718–720, 4:144; *Journal of Second Wheeling Convention*; Granville Davisson Hall, *The Rending of Virginia: A History* (1902), including por. on 237; Virgil A. Lewis, ed., *How West Virginia Was Made* (1909); John Y. Simon et al., eds., *The Papers of Ulysses S. Grant* (1967–), 19:314; *Senate Executive Journal*, 41st Cong., special sess., 122, 245, 247–248; obituaries in *New York Times* and *Wheeling Daily Register*, both 25 Oct. 1878, *Wheeling Daily Intelligencer*, 26 Oct. 1878, and *Clarksburg Telegram*, 2 Nov. 1878.

JONATHAN M. BERKEY

CARLIN, Charles Creighton (8 April 1866–14 October 1938), member of the House of Representatives, was born in Alexandria and was the son of William H. Carlin and Frances Eskridge

Carlin. His father died in 1870, and Carlin sold newspapers and worked as an errand boy in a china shop and later as a night operator at the telephone exchange to help support his mother and sisters. He attended the public schools and for a short time enrolled at the Alexandria Academy before taking a job with a telephone company in Rome, Georgia. About 1885 C. C. Carlin, as he usually gave his name, returned to Alexandria and began studying law at the National University (later the National Law Center at the George Washington University) in Washington, D.C., while at the same time serving as Alexandria's deputy treasurer and as commissioner of accounts for the corporation court. After graduating in 1891 he was admitted to the bar and set up a practice in Alexandria, where for a time he earned extra income as the city correspondent for the *Washington Post*. On 28 October 1891 Carlin married Lillian E. Broders, daughter of a prominent businessman. They had two sons.

In July 1893 Carlin was elected to a four-year term on the Alexandria board of aldermen but resigned the following April after being appointed the city's postmaster, a position he held until March 1898. According to a story widespread at the time, Carlin had led a delegation that met with President Grover Cleveland to discuss the group's candidate for postmaster. Believing the original candidate incompetent, the president decided to select a member of the delegation instead, and Carlin's compelling speech so impressed the group that they chose him for the position with the president's approval. For much of his life Carlin was a Virginia delegate to the Democratic National Conventions, although in 1932 and 1936 he was a member of the District of Columbia's delegation. At the 1896 convention he backed the pro-silver candidate, William Jennings Bryan, over the fiscally conservative Cleveland, who supported the gold standard. In 1904 Carlin was a presidential elector from the Eighth Congressional District for the Democratic ticket led by Alton B. Parker, of New York.

Following the death of Democrat John Franklin Rixey in February 1907, Carlin joined the field of candidates competing for the nomination for the vacant Eighth District seat in the

United States House of Representatives. In the primary he exhibited a candor and wit that attracted a large following, although rivals charged that he attempted to buy votes with money and liquor. On 5 November 1907 Carlin trounced his Republican opponent to win election representing the city of Alexandria and the counties of Alexandria, Culpeper, Fairfax, Fauquier, King George, Loudoun, Louisa, Orange, Prince William, and Stafford. Reelected to the House six times, he served without interruption until 1919. During his first term he sat on the third Committee on Elections and the Committee on Coinage, Weights, and Measures. Carlin served on these committees again during his second term and also was placed on the Committee on the Judiciary. During his third term he served again on the Committee on Elections and was appointed to the Committee on Accounts. He continued on the Committee on the Judiciary for the remainder of his congressional career and in 1913 became ranking member.

During his first term Carlin sought to restore Jefferson Davis's name to the abutment of the Cabin John Bridge (later the American Legion Memorial Bridge), in Montgomery County, Maryland, from which it had been removed during the Civil War, and he spoke against Theodore Roosevelt's order to strike "In God We Trust" from United States coins. Recognizing the possible military applications of Wilbur Wright and Orville Wright's historic flight, he unsuccessfully pushed for an appropriation from the House Committee on Military Affairs to fund aviation advances. Carlin introduced legislation that resulted in construction of the Francis Scott Key Bridge and the Memorial Bridge over the Potomac River and of the Mount Vernon Memorial Highway linking the nation's capital with George Washington's home. Recognizing his contributions to transportation, his Alexandria constituents proposed naming a new road Carlin Avenue in December 1915, but he declined the honor.

During his fourth term Carlin introduced a bill to establish a national university in Washington, D.C., and legislation designed to create an interstate highway system. He supported antitrust legislation and in 1914 helped engineer the passage of the Clayton Anti-Trust Act. That same year he was also instrumental in passing the Federal Trade Commission Act. During the First World War, he helped bring the Virginia Shipbuilding Corporation to Alexandria, thus creating thousands of jobs.

Carlin won reelection in November 1918 but on 5 March of the following year, citing health concerns, a desire to resume practicing law, and the Democrats' loss of control of the House, announced that he would not serve in the Sixty-sixth Congress. He entered a partnership with his son Keith Charles Carlin in the Washington firm of Carlin, Carlin, and Hall and for many years enjoyed a prominent practice. In 1919 Carlin purchased the *Alexandria Gazette*. His namesake son later served as publisher and editor of the paper.

In February 1920 Carlin reversed his earlier position and urged the Virginia General Assembly to ratify the Nineteenth Amendment granting woman suffrage. Remaining politically active, he was a floor manager for Franklin Delano Roosevelt at the 1932 Democratic National Convention. In 1936 he moved to Washington, D.C., and in November of that year National University recognized his public service with an honorary law degree. Following a long illness Charles Creighton Carlin died on 14 October 1938 at his Washington residence. City offices in Alexandria closed during the funeral procession that carried his body to the city's Ivy Hill Cemetery for burial.

Feature article in *Fairfax Herald,* 1 Mar. 1907 (por.); Alexandria City Marriage Register; Alexandria City Board of Aldermen Minutes, 22:134, 171; *Fairfax Herald,* 15 Feb., 22, 29 Mar., 21 June, 1, 8 Nov. 1907, 24 Apr., 3 July 1908, 12 Apr., 28 June 1918, 7 Mar., 19 July 1919; *Washington Post,* 24 Feb. 1907, 19, 31 Dec. 1915, 16 Nov. 1916, 6 Mar. 1919, 4 Feb. 1920; Election Records, no. 183, RG 13, LVA; *Congressional Record,* 60th Cong., 1st sess., 3384–3385, 63d Cong., 2d sess., 9268–9270, 64th Cong., 1st sess., 2905, 2911–2914; obituaries in *Alexandria Gazette* (por. and editorial tribute), *Richmond Times-Dispatch,* and *Washington Post,* all 15 Oct. 1938; memorial in *Virginia State Bar Association Proceedings* (1939), 162–165.

BRUCE M. JONES

CARLYLE, John (6 February 1720–by 17 October 1780), merchant, was the son of William Carlyle, an apothecary-physician, and Rachel

Murray Carlyle. He may have been born in the city of Carlisle, where his parents lived and from which the family took its name, in Cumberland County, England, or a few miles away at his mother's family estate, Murraythwaite, in Dumfriesshire, Scotland. Eight of his nine brothers and sisters died in early childhood. Carlyle apprenticed at the mercantile house of William Hicks in the coastal town of Whitehaven and may have made his first voyage to Virginia in 1739. On 24 September of that year a John Carlyle witnessed two deeds in Prince William County. Carlyle moved to Virginia about two years later and joined other relatives who had already settled in the Chesapeake Bay region. Registering his power of attorney as a factor, or agent, for Hicks at the Prince William County courthouse on 27 July 1741, he intended to make his fortune working for Hicks in the Maryland and Virginia markets and then return home.

Sometime early in the 1750s, Carlyle and Hicks amicably separated. During the next two decades Carlyle formed several partnerships to conduct business with the British Isles, in the Caribbean, and with western Europe. He imported coal, convicts, rum, slaves, and sugar, and he exported flour, grain, iron from his own foundry, lumber, and tobacco. For his amusement as well as for profit, he imported, bred, and raised racehorses. Carlyle resided in Truro Parish, in Fairfax County, before moving to what became Alexandria. He engaged in business in the upper counties of the Northern Neck and as far inland as the boundary drawn in 1757 that separated the new county of Loudoun from Fairfax County. He steadily acquired tracts of land, servants, and slaves, and he developed contacts and made friends with other successful men of commerce and members of the area's elite families, most notably the wealthy Fairfaxes.

On 31 December 1747 Carlyle married Sarah Fairfax, daughter of William Fairfax, a member of the governor's Council. They had five daughters and two sons, but only two of the daughters lived beyond childhood. Sarah Carlyle died on 22 January 1761 following the birth of her seventh child. On 22 October of that year Carlyle married Sybil West, daughter of Hugh West, one of the early developers of Alexandria. Of their three

sons, two died in infancy. Sybil Carlyle died on 17 March 1769 as a consequence of her fourth pregnancy, which terminated in a miscarriage.

Together with the Fairfaxes and their relations, Augustine Washington and Lawrence Washington, Carlyle joined the Ohio Company in hopes of winning a royal grant of land in the Ohio River valley. Selling or leasing the land to new settlers promised to repay their investment as well as create lucrative commercial opportunities for residents in the Potomac River valley. To bring their plans to fruition they needed a seaport, and they petitioned the General Assembly to establish a new town to be built on land of the Alexander and West families at the mouth of Great Hunting Creek in Fairfax County. In 1749 the assembly complied and designated Carlyle one of the eleven trustees of the new town, which was named Alexandria in honor of one of the founding families. In March of that same year Carlyle became a justice of the peace in Fairfax County, and by the end of 1755 he was a colonel in the militia.

Early in the 1750s Carlyle built his family a grand stone Georgian mansion in Alexandria and saw to the details of its construction himself. It was by far the most splendid structure in the new town. He resided there for more than twenty-five years. As a trustee he administered to the town's needs in education, public health and sanitation, streets, safety, and the town market, and as a justice of the peace and leading citizen he oversaw the construction of the courthouse, bridges, churches, docks, roads, a school, and warehouses. Although a Presbyterian, he may have also attended services of the Church of England, and he was a Freemason.

During the early years of the French and Indian War, Carlyle served in 1754 as commissary to the Virginia militia's Ohio River expedition and the following year as Alexandria commissary to the British expeditionary forces. He employed his commercial experience and contacts to obtain, transport, and store fodder for the horses and powder, shot, shoes, tools, uniforms, victuals, and weapons for the troops, but his skill could not solve all the supply problems that the colonial and British forces faced. Carlyle's important role in preparing for the

British campaign in the West, together with his elegant residence at the seaport closest to the frontier, made his house the natural headquarters for Major General Edward Braddock in the spring of 1755. In Carlyle's house the general met with governors of five colonies and planned his ultimately disastrous campaign.

Carlyle supported the colony's protests against British policies during the decade after the war and in 1774 was a member of the Alexandria Town and Fairfax County Committees. He most likely took part in procuring small arms, fieldpieces, and ammunition for the local volunteer companies. During the Revolutionary War his only living son, George William Carlyle, served in the legion commanded by Lieutenant Colonel Henry "Light-Horse Harry" Lee (1756–1818) and on 8 September 1781, at age fifteen, was killed in the engagement at Eutaw Springs, South Carolina.

Carlyle was one of the most prominent and respectable merchants and community leaders in northern Virginia. His magnificent house in Alexandria testified to his success and eminence. He owned several town lots and two plantations in Fairfax County, and his more than sixty slaves raised the value of his personal estate there to more than £2,800. He also owned land in Berkeley and Culpeper Counties. When Carlyle composed his will in the spring of 1780, he provided for the education of his one surviving son and a grandson and set aside £500 from which Alexandria's Presbyterian church was to draw the annual earnings to care for the congregation's poor. John Carlyle died, probably in his Alexandria home, sometime not long before 17 October 1780, when his will was proved in the Fairfax County Court. He was buried, as he had specified in his will, with the bodies of his first wife and their children in the cemetery of the Alexandria Presbyterian Church.

James D. Munson, *Colo. John Carlyle, Gent.: A True and Just Account of the Man and His House* (1986), with cover por. by John Hesselius; John Carlyle Papers and John Carlyle family Bible (including marriage dates and birth date derived from age at first marriage), Carlyle House Historic Park, Alexandria, Northern Virginia Regional Park Authority; Carlyle letters and other documents in Carlyle Family Papers, VHS, in Fairfax of Cameron MSS, Virginia Colonial Records Project microfilm (location of originals no longer known), and in George Washington Papers, LC; W. W. Abbot, ed., "General Edward Braddock in Alexandria: John Carlyle to George Carlyle, 15 August 1755," *VMHB* 97 (1989): 205–214; Prince William Co. Deed Book, D:224–227 (possible first appearance in Virginia), E:348–349 (power of attorney); *Revolutionary Virginia*, 1:133, 2:88, 203, 209, 4:402, 403, 456, 5:90, 7:131, 729; J. Everette Fauber, *Restoration of the John Carlyle House, Alexandria, Virginia* (1980); will and estate inventory in Fairfax Co. Will Book, D-1:203–207, 368–393.

JAMES D. MUNSON

CARNE, Richard Libby (5 October 1826–18 February 1911), educator, was born in Alexandria and was the son of Richard Levi Carne, a merchant, and Cecelia Latruite Shakes Carne. Educated at home by his mother until age nine because of his delicate constitution, Carne in 1835 entered Saint John's Academy, a Jesuit school recently established by the priests of Saint Mary's Catholic Church, his home parish in Alexandria. There he studied French, Greek, and Latin for five years before beginning to work in his father's hardware store. In 1847 the parish priest invited Carne to reopen Saint John's, which had closed in 1841, and to return as a teacher. In spite of having no formal training beyond his early study at the academy, Carne reorganized the school and was its principal teacher and administrator for the next forty-five years. He opened the revived Saint John's with one assistant and seven pupils. With occasional help from his younger brother, William Francis Carne, and his mother, the academy prospered, and by 1850 the school enrolled seventy-two students. It operated even during the Civil War and educated the sons of soldiers in both armies. In 1868 Georgetown College (later Georgetown University) awarded Carne an honorary A.M. in recognition of his accomplishments as an educator.

While continuing his duties at Saint John's Academy, Carne embraced a new role in 1870, when he became the first superintendent of the public schools of the city and county of Alexandria (later Arlington County). Virginia's first superintendent of public instruction, William Henry Ruffner, named experienced educators and respected local administrators such as Carne when establishing the new system of free public schools required by the Constitution of 1869. As a Catholic promoting public schools in a religiously mixed community, Carne was perhaps particularly sensitive to the challenge of finding the appropriate role of religion in the new system and sought to exclude Scriptures from the classroom. Ruffner essentially deferred to community desires about Bible reading and religious content in the local schools. Ironically, Carne's success in creating a respected public school system in Alexandria contributed to a steady loss of pupils at Saint John's Academy, which closed in 1895. Carne served as superintendent of the county's schools until 1880, when the management of the county system was given to a separate administrator, but he remained city superintendent until 1882. In that year, following the Readjuster Party's victory in the statewide and assembly elections, Carne's brother William F. Carne became city superintendent. After the Democratic Party regained the majority in the assembly and control of the executive branch, Richard L. Carne was reappointed superintendent of the city schools in 1886.

In 1892 Carne turned his life in a new direction. At age sixty-six, he left Saint John's Academy and public education and entered the priesthood, fulfilling a lifelong calling for which he had intermittently studied since age fifteen. The bishop of the Diocese of Richmond ordained him at Saint Mary's Catholic Church in Alexandria on 1 November 1892. Carne was assistant pastor at the Sacred Heart Catholic Church in Richmond from 1893 to 1895 and then chaplain at the Old Point Comfort College in Fort Monroe in 1903 and 1904. Returning to Alexandria about 1907 to live with his sister and brother-in-law, Carne served as a chaplain to the Catholic community there and for Saint Mary's Academy. After more than a week in a coma Richard Libby Carne died in Alexandria on 18 February 1911 and was buried in the cemetery of Saint Mary's Catholic Church.

Biographies in *Virginia School Journal* 1 (1892): 215 (por.), and *St. Mary's: 200 Years for Christ, 1795–1995* (1995), 181–182 (por.); some Carne correspondence, including autobiographical letter to Charles Macksey, 12 Jan. 1906, in Georgetown University Archives, Washington, D.C.; works include Carne, *A Brief Sketch of the History of St. Mary's Church, Alexandria, Va.* (1874), and farewell address to Saint John's Academy, in *Academy Journal* 23 (Aug. 1892): n.p.; Saint John's Academy Records, Alexandria Public Library; pastoral assignments provided by Office of Archives, Catholic Diocese of Richmond (2003); obituaries in *Washington Post* and *Washington Sunday Star*, both 19 Feb. 1911, the latter reprinted in part in *Georgetown College Journal* (Mar. 1911), 325–326; obituary and account of funeral in *Alexandria Gazette*, 20, 22 Feb. 1911.

CATHERINE A. JONES

CARNE, William Francis (17 August 1832–20 December 1909), journalist and writer, was born in Alexandria and was the son of Richard Levi Carne, a merchant, and Cecelia Latruite Shakes Carne. He worked as a clerk in his father's hardware store and early in the 1850s assisted his elder brother, Richard Libby Carne, in reviving Saint John's Academy, a Jesuit boys' school in Alexandria associated with Saint Mary's Parish. Carne also studied law, received a license to practice in 1857, and joined a local firm. Despite his employment as an attorney and teacher, journalism and writing were his passions. In his diary on 9 September 1853, he cheerfully recorded an auspicious event, his first receipt of financial compensation for his writing.

Carne worked in a variety of capacities on several local journals, for newspapers published in Baltimore and Washington (among them the *Washington Evening Star* and the *Washington National Republican*), and for a brief time in New York. His Alexandria residence positioned him well to cover the national government as a Washington correspondent for the *Baltimore Sun* for more than a quarter of a century beginning in 1871. Although Carne expended the greater part of his journalistic energies reporting on the nation's capital, he also researched and wrote about the history on the south side of the Potomac River.

Carne's most frequent subject was the colonial and Revolutionary history of northern Virginia, with particular interest in the life of George Washington, whom he regarded as a model and a hero. He wrote regularly about Washington for a variety of audiences. Among his publications were "Washington as a Burgher" for *Harper's New Monthly Magazine* and "A New Leaf From Washington's Boy Life" for *St. Nicholas*, a children's magazine. Carne also used Washington's life as a measure by which to assess and defend an important and controversial public figure of his own lifetime, Robert

Edward Lee, in an essay entitled "Washington's Example" for the *Fairfax Herald* of 26 October 1900.

Beginning in 1860 and continuing through the 1870s, Carne wrote an extended series of articles entitled "Annals of Alexandria" for the *Alexandria Gazette*. The first installment appeared at a time when sectional tensions were intense and the nation took renewed interest in its Revolutionary origins. In the "Annals" and elsewhere, as in "Washington's Catholic Aide-de-Camp," published in *Catholic World,* Carne was particularly attentive to the role of Catholics in the early history of the region. The "Annals of Alexandria" articles served as the source for several short historical essays that he wrote on the history of the city and that were published in 1983 in a collected edition. As both an attorney and a local historian, Carne was the logical choice of the Alexandria town council to compile a revised edition of the town's code, which was enacted in December 1873 and published the following year with a brief history of Alexandria local government; and on 9 March 1880 he delivered the oration at the centennial celebration of the incorporation of the town. In addition to his historical writing, Carne produced several other publications, including a brief romantic tale of colonial days, *Narrative of John Trust* (1883), sometimes called *Story of the Female Stranger*, which he reprinted in a short *History of Alexandria* in 1896. He also published the *Alexandria Business Book* (1897), a promotional work that included a directory of local businesses, a history of the city, and an account of the city's contemporary economic life.

For most of his life Carne was a Democrat, but during the 1880s he supported the Readjusters, perhaps because of that party's concern for the state's public school system, which had been created in 1870. That political affiliation led to his appointment in 1882 as superintendent of the Alexandria city schools. He replaced his brother Richard L. Carne, who had been superintendent since 1870 and remained loyal to the Democratic Party. After the Democrats regained control of the state government, they replaced the Readjuster superintendents with Democrats. In 1886 Carne relinquished the office to his brother, who

resumed his former work on behalf of public education, to which they were both committed.

On 21 May 1861 Carne married Emma Virginia Markell. They had one son and two daughters, one of whom died in infancy, before his wife's death on 4 March 1874. He married Cornelia A. Stoutenburgh on 10 August 1875. They had one son and one daughter. William Francis Carne died at his home in Alexandria on 20 December 1909 and was buried in the graveyard at Saint Mary's Catholic Church.

Biography in T. Michael Miller, ed., *Alexandria's Forgotten Legacy: The Annals of Wm. F. Carne* (1983), iii–viii; birth date in baptismal record, Saint Mary's Catholic Church, Alexandria, printed in *St. Mary's: 200 Years for Christ, 1795–1995* (1995), 236; BVS Marriage Register, Arlington Co. (formerly Alexandria Co.), 1861, Alexandria City, 1875; William F. Carne Diary (1853–1854), Alexandria Public Library; publications include Carne, *The Charter and Laws, of the City of Alexandria, Va., and an Historical Sketch of Its Government* (1874), "Centennial Oration," in *Celebration of the First Centennial of the Municipal Government of the City of Alexandria, Virginia* (1880), 24–46, "Washington as a Burgher," *Harper's New Monthly Magazine* 60 (1880): 353–365, "A New Leaf From Washington's Boy Life," *St. Nicholas* 14 (1887): 373–375, and "Washington's Catholic Aide-de-Camp," *Catholic World* 50 (1890) 437–445; Alexander J. Wedderburn, *Souvenir Virginia Ter Centennial of Historic Alexandria, Va., Past and Present* (1907), por. on unnumbered page 76; obituaries in *Alexandria Gazette*, 21 Dec. 1909 (with editorial tribute), *Baltimore Sun*, 22 Dec. 1909, and *Fairfax Herald*, 24 Dec. 1909.

CATHERINE A. JONES

CARNEAL, William Leigh (24 October 1881–23 February 1958), architect, was born in Richmond and was the son of William Luther Carneal and Laura Epps Carneal. He was educated in Richmond public schools and at a private preparatory school in the city, graduated from the Virginia Military Institute in 1903, and then worked as a clerk in his father's Richmond hardware store for three years. In 1906 Carneal joined the firm of the Richmond architect Claude K. Howell. The following year he established his own independent architectural practice and designed several houses along the city's Grove Avenue. In 1908 Carneal and the engineer James Markham Ambler Johnston formed the partnership Carneal and Johnston Architects and Engineers.

World War I interrupted Carneal's architectural career. He served in the United States Army

Ordnance Department in Washington, D.C., with the rank of captain. In Philadelphia on 12 September 1919 he married Edna Lea. They had no children, separated in 1925, and obtained an uncontested divorce on 14 June 1928. On 21 August 1932 Carneal married Estelle Robinson Sullivan, daughter of a railroad executive in Atlanta, Georgia. They had no children. Having completed at least five years of professional work and met other requirements, Carneal petitioned the Virginia Military Institute for an alumnus professional degree in civil engineering, granted in 1924.

For eighty years the firm of Carneal and Johnston (known from 1928 to 1945, when Oscar Pendleton Wright was a partner, as Carneal, Johnston, and Wright) shaped the appearance of Richmond and central Virginia. It had designed more than 1,300 public and commercial structures by the time Carneal retired in 1950. He and his partners won praise for their literacy in historical styles applied to thoroughly modern buildings. Their designs ranged from the utilitarian, such as a simple stable building for the City of Richmond in 1912, to large commissions for some of Virginia's most important and monumental structures. Among the most prominent of these Richmond commissions were the State Office Building (later the Washington Building) in Capitol Square (1922–1923), the Virginia War Memorial Carillon in Byrd Park (1932) in association with the Boston firm of Cram and Ferguson, the State Highway Commission Building (1937), and, in cooperation with Baskervill and Son, the Virginia State Library and Supreme Court of Appeals Building (1939–1940).

Carneal and Johnston also designed two apartment buildings and several houses for Richmond's premier residential street, Monument Avenue. Among the grandest was the residence for Henry S. Wallerstein (1915), which featured the popular Collegiate Gothic style, as did the First Virginia Regiment Armory (1913) on Marshall Street and buildings for the University of Richmond campus. One of the most whimsical of its designs is the Richmond Dairy Company Building (1913) on Marshall Street, its corner milk-bottle towers unmistakably signaling the purpose of the structure. More stolid in appearance but well known locally are many of the Richmond banking and retail stores erected during the decades after the First World War.

Carneal and Johnston was one of the most influential architectural firms in Richmond for much of the twentieth century, but during Carneal's tenure the company did not limit its work to the capital. It designed more than twenty buildings for the Virginia Agricultural and Mechanical College and Polytechnic Institute (later Virginia Polytechnic Institute and State University) and helped determine the overall design of the Blacksburg campus. Carneal and Johnston designed more than a dozen buildings for the Virginia Military Institute, in Lexington, over the course of three decades and another thirteen for Saint Joseph's Academy and Orphan Asylum (later Saint Joseph's Villa), in Henrico County.

Elected the first president of the Virginia Society of Architects in 1939, Carneal was at various times president of the University Club and a member of the boards of the Richmond Chamber of Commerce and the Commonwealth Club. He was a vice president of the Gresham Court Apartment House Corporation, whose Richmond structure Carneal and Johnston designed in 1909. Carneal's principal interest outside the realm of architecture and commerce was a long-term relationship with the Richmond Male Orphan Society (later the Richmond Home for Boys and since July 2004 the Virginia Home for Boys and Girls). Besides designing its main building (ca. 1923–1924), he served on its board from 1924 to 1949, from 1930 to 1933 as vice president and after 1933 as president.

William Leigh Carneal died in Richmond on 23 February 1958 and was buried in Hollywood Cemetery. He was survived by his second wife and by the architectural firm of Carneal and Johnston.

Biographies in *NCAB*, 46:339, and Wells and Dalton, *Virginia Architects*, 67–75; autobiographical information, including birth date, provided on 27 Apr. 1939, WPA Biographies; BVS Birth Register, Richmond City (recording birth of unnamed son on 24 Oct. 1881); dates of first marriage and divorce confirmed by BVS; some firm architectural drawings at LVA and VPI; *Richmond Times-Dispatch*, 3 Nov. 1927, 8 Sept. 1939, 29 Jan. 1949; *Richmond News Leader*, 18 Dec. 1928, 31 July 1942; *Commonwealth* 6 (Oct. 1939): 41, 47–48; Charles E. Brownell et al., *The Making of*

Virginia Architecture (1992), 88, 102, 176, 191, 348–349; obituaries in *Richmond News Leader* and *Richmond Times-Dispatch*, both 24 Feb. 1958 (both with pors. and both with birth date of 4 Oct. 1881 repeated in later publications).

SELDEN RICHARDSON

CARPENTER, Caius Hunter (23 June 1883–24 February 1953), football player, was born in Louisa County and was the son of James Clivie Carpenter and Sallie Lewis Herring Carpenter. About 1891 the family moved to Clifton Forge, where the father was a railroad contractor and president of the First National Bank. Hunter Carpenter, as he was known, received private tutoring and attended a local school before entering the Virginia Agricultural and Mechanical College and Polytechnic Institute (later Virginia Polytechnic Institute and State University) in 1898. Although he had never played football and his father had instructed him to focus on his studies and avoid sports, Carpenter tried out for the school team.

Turn-of-the-century college football fielded eleven men playing both offense and defense. There was no passing game, and players wore little protective gear or padding for the popular but violent sport that produced many injuries and occasionally even deaths. At 128 pounds the fifteen-year-old Carpenter was too slight for such combat, but he made the team at 150 pounds during his sophomore year and was used sparingly at fullback. In his third year he shifted to the halfback position in which he displayed the gifts that made him a legendary player. During part of that season he played under the false name Walter Brown to avoid provoking his father, who later relented on learning of his son's exploits.

Weighing about 200 pounds in 1901, Carpenter combined football savvy with breakaway speed and aggressive running to overpower or evade tacklers. A talented field-goal kicker, he also called the plays. The Polytechnics won six of seven games, and Carpenter was named team captain for 1902 and selected to the first All-Southern team. Newspapers showered him with superlatives. The *Roanoke Times* observed, "Any one who knows what a football is, knows of Carpenter, the best runner, one of the best punters, the hardest tackler, and the hardest man to get off his feet in the south." A member of the Class

of 1902, Carpenter graduated in June 1903 with a B.S. in civil engineering and returned to VPI that autumn as a graduate student. During the 1903 season his team won five of six games, including an 11–0 upset of a United States Naval Academy team in which he scored all of the points.

Carpenter attended law classes at the University of North Carolina during the 1904–1905 school year. He continued to play football in hopes of besting the University of Virginia, a feat no VPI team had yet accomplished, but again he was denied victory. Carpenter's Tarheel teammates elected him captain for the 1905 season, but he chose instead to return to Blacksburg for further postgraduate study and another crack at the University of Virginia on the gridiron. Managers of the University of Virginia's athletic association unsuccessfully attempted to disqualify Carpenter and several other VPI players from the 1905 game between the archrival schools on the grounds that they were professionals. Carpenter shone in the 11–0 win in Charlottesville on 4 November of that year, even though officials nullified two touchdowns he scored. He left the field before the game ended after knocking out one of the Virginia players (the brother of the umpire) who had hit him repeatedly during the contest. After public name-calling erupted in the Charlottesville press, Carpenter's father threatened legal action. As a result of their strained relations, Virginia and VPI suspended athletic competition and did not meet again on the football field until 1923. Carpenter's team won nine of ten games in the 1905 season and defeated a powerful United States Military Academy team by a score of 16–6. The *Washington Post* hailed VPI as the southern football champion of 1905.

Compared by some to Jim Thorpe, Carpenter was one of the first players to attract widespread attention to football in Virginia, but his name never appeared on the All-American team. According to some accounts, Walter Camp, who helped invent American football and who made the All-American selections, acknowledged that Carpenter was the country's finest halfback but could not place him on the team because he had never seen him play. An all-around athlete, Carpenter also played baseball for at least three years at VPI and was team captain in 1902, twice won best-athlete accolades at VPI's annual Field Day events, and excelled at tennis.

After leaving VPI, Carpenter constructed railway lines in West Virginia under his father's direction and later worked for a Tennessee railroad. On 5 June 1907 he married Kathryn Anne Reilly in Huntington, West Virginia. They moved to New York State and had two sons. Carpenter operated a contracting business and helped build an aqueduct to supply water to New York City. Before World War I he constructed a section of subway in Brooklyn, but excavation cave-ins and rising labor and material costs plunged him into debt. Early in the 1920s he worked in Richmond. After several years he returned to New York, where he prospered in construction and real estate. Arrested in December 1925 for running rum from Canada into New York City and held on $20,000 bond, Carpenter was among thirty-three defendants indicted in November 1926 for conspiracy to violate the Prohibition liquor and tariff laws. Though accused of managing the rum ring's subheadquarters at Hempstead, on Long Island, he won acquittal on 20 January 1927. The next year Carpenter's wife received a judgment of divorce against him in Reno, Nevada. She retained custody of their sons and lived in Salem, Ohio, while Carpenter resided in Gardiner, Ulster County, New York, where he operated an apple orchard. On 11 April 1933 he married Beatrice Elizabeth Moore Tiffany, also of Gardiner, who had one son from a previous marriage that had ended in divorce earlier that year. Carpenter lost most of his financial assets in the Great Depression. During World War II he worked on several government construction projects.

After suffering a stroke in the autumn of 1952, Caius Hunter Carpenter died of cerebral thrombosis in a hospital in Middletown, New York, on 24 February 1953. His family scattered his cremated remains near Gardiner. Four years after his death he became the first Virginia Polytechnic Institute player to be inducted into the College Football Hall of Fame, and in 1973 the Virginia Sports Hall of Fame inducted him.

Biography in *A History of the Class of 1902 of Virginia Polytechnic Institute, Blacksburg, Virginia* (1955), 22–24; feature articles by nephew Deverton Carpenter in *Roanoke World-News*, 10–12, 14–16 Nov. 1938; newspaper clippings, photographs, scrapbooks, and nomination form to the National Football Hall of Fame (17 May 1956), including letters of support, all in C. Hunter Carpenter Papers, VPI; BVS Birth Register, Louisa Co.; Cabell Co., W.Va., Marriage Register (1907); State of New York Department of Health, Ulster Co. Marriage License (including year and circumstances of divorce) and Marriage Certificate (1933); *Roanoke Times*, 24 Oct. 1902 (quotation); *Norfolk Virginian-Pilot*, 28 Nov. 1902; *Washington Post*, 18 Feb. 1906, 19 Nov. 1926, 21 Jan. 1927; *New York Times*, 4 Dec. 1925, 19 Nov. 1926, 19, 21 Jan. 1927; Abe Goldblatt and Robert W. Wentz Jr., *The Great and the Near Great: A Century of Sports in Virginia* (1976), 139 (por.); Harry Downing Temple, *The Bugle's Echo: A Chronology of Cadet Life at the Military College at Blacksburg, Virginia, The Virginia Agricultural and Mechanical College and The Virginia Polytechnic Institute* (1996–1998), esp. 2:1029 (por.); death notice in *New York Times*, 25 Feb. 1953; obituaries in *Richmond News Leader, Richmond Times-Dispatch, Roanoke Times* (por.), *Roanoke World-News*, and *Winchester Evening Star*, all 25 Feb. 1953, and *Clifton Forge Daily Review* and *New Paltz [N.Y.] Independent*, both 26 Feb. 1953; editorial tribute in *Richmond Times-Dispatch*, 26 Feb. 1953.

STEVE CLARK

CARPENTER, Miles Burkholder (12 May 1889–7 May 1985), sculptor, was born in Lancaster County, Pennsylvania, and was the son of Wayne M. Carpenter, a farmer, and Elizabeth R. Burkholder Carpenter. He attended a one-room school and with his ten siblings worked on the Mennonite family's farm. In the spring of 1902 the family moved to Virginia, where his father acquired a 340-acre farm near Waverly, in Sussex County, and also constructed a sawmill. On 19 May 1915 Carpenter married Mary Elizabeth Stahl, of Carbon County, Pennsylvania. They had one son.

With financial assistance from his father Carpenter purchased a vacant factory in Waverly about 1912 and soon began operating a lumber mill that produced finished wood for local builders. He added his own sawmill to his enterprise and also began making and selling ice. For several years beginning about 1915 Carpenter joined a partner in operating an open-air theater showing silent movies. Occasionally tinkering with wood scraps, he made a violin and incised trinket boxes. During a slow period in his successful lumber business in 1941 he began whittling to pass the time. His first carving, a primitive polar bear, delighted his wife, who encouraged him to create more animals. The building boom following World War II left Carpenter little opportunity for further woodcarving until several accidents suffered while operating machinery caused him to close his lumber mill in the mid-1950s.

Carpenter's affinity for woodcarving probably derived from the rich Pennsylvania German folk art culture, a functional and ornamental tradition that inspired other members of his family to build furniture and clocks. His subjects included animals, especially birds, dogs, monkeys, pigs, and snakes, and human figures often expressing the artist's quirky reflections on biblical subjects or on such current events as the war in Vietnam, the Watergate scandal, or the 1973 protest at Wounded Knee, South Dakota. He also carved celebrity portraits of such notables as Charlie Chaplin and Elvis Presley, usually with an eye to their commercial value. His favored tools included chisels, files, hatchets, pocketknives, and saws.

Carpenter created sculptures in a naive style using both whittling and assemblage. After sanding, polishing, and preparing each piece, he painted it, usually with enamel house paint. He dressed many of his human figures in handmade clothes. Some works included moving parts or sound effects, such as one multipiece sculpture of a female pig feeding a litter of piglets in a pen that he equipped with a noisemaker that squealed when squeezed. His early sculptures were representational, often small and carefully detailed. Later in his career driftwood, twisting tree limbs and roots, and other found pieces of wood inspired him to create larger, more interpretational works such as the nightmarish *Root Monster* and *Sea Monster Catching a Fish*. Of these fantastical, often deeply symbolic pieces Carpenter observed, "I see the hidden objects there and bring them almost to life." He produced the majority of his carvings after his wife's death on 5 November 1966.

Carpenter displayed his colorful sculptures at the roadside stand where he sold ice, drinks, and produce. To attract customers he carved a 200-pound watermelon, a piece eventually acquired by the Abby Aldrich Rockefeller Folk Art Museum at Colonial Williamsburg. By the 1970s his work had drawn the attention of collectors, including Herbert Waide Hemphill Jr. One of the preeminent folk art enthusiasts of the twentieth century and a founder of what became the American Folk Art Museum in New York, Hemphill helped win critical acclaim for Carpenter's work. The sculptor received one-man shows at Virginia Commonwealth University in 1974 and 1985 and at the Yorktown Visitor Center in 1980. The Hand Workshop Art Center, in Richmond, and Radford University mounted centennial retrospectives in 1989 and 1990, respectively. Carpenter's imaginative carvings have been included in numerous group exhibitions across the country and featured in publications on American folk art. Few other twentieth-century Virginia folk artists elicited such national enthusiasm. In 1981 the president invited Carpenter to the White House, and the next year the sculptor received a Visual Artist Fellowship from the National Endowment for the Arts. In 1982 he published his autobiography, *Cutting the Mustard*.

Miles Burkholder Carpenter died in a Petersburg hospital on 7 May 1985 and was buried in Waverly Cemetery. The following year the Miles B. Carpenter Museum opened at his Waverly home to display his work and to provide an arts facility for area residents.

Carpenter, *Cutting the Mustard* (1982), with birth and marriage dates, quotation on 70, and several pors.; *Miles Carpenter: The Wood Carver from Waverly* (1985), exhibition catalog including Mar. 1985 interview of Carpenter; Chris Gregson, "Miles Carpenter: The Man and His Art," *Folk Art Messenger* 2 (spring 1989): 1, 3; solo and group exhibitions listed in *Miles Carpenter: A Second Century* (1990); Carpenter materials in Jeff and Jane Camp Papers, Archives of American Art, Smithsonian Institution, Washington, D.C.; Robert Bishop, *American Folk Sculpture* (1974), 10–11, 178, 202, 321; Herbert W. Hemphill Jr. and Julia Weissman, *Twentieth-Century American Folk Art and Artists* (1974), 218–219; Jay Johnson and William C. Ketchum Jr., *American Folk Art of the Twentieth Century* (1983), 38–39; *Richmond Times-Dispatch*, 6 Oct. 1974, 3 Aug. 1975, 10 May 1982, 2 June 1985, 6, 21 May 1989; *Richmond News Leader*, 16 Aug. 1976, 18 Sept. 1980; *New York Times*, 12 Sept. 1976; obituaries in *Richmond News Leader*, 7 May 1985, *Richmond Times-Dispatch*, 8 May 1985, *Washington Post*, 10 May 1985, and *Wakefield Sussex-Surry Dispatch*, 15 May 1985.

Tom H. Ray

CARR, Dabney (27 April 1773–8 January 1837), judge of the Virginia Court of Appeals, was born at Spring Forest, the Goochland County plantation of his parents, Dabney Carr (1743–1773), a lawyer, and Martha Jefferson Carr. His elder brother Peter Carr later served several terms in the House of Delegates and received posthumous notoriety when accused of fathering six of Sally Hemings's children. When Dabney Carr was three weeks old, his father died. His mother raised him with help from her brother, Thomas Jefferson, who supervised his education. While Jefferson was in France in diplomatic service, James Madison (1751–1836) kept him informed of Carr's academic progress. For several years Carr attended Hampden-Sydney College, where he showed diligence and promise, but in 1789 his mother removed him and early the next year enrolled him in Matthew Maury's school in Albemarle County, where he studied French and Greek.

Carr read law, was admitted to the bar on 5 September 1796, and practiced in Albemarle and adjoining counties. He was commonwealth's attorney of Albemarle County from 6 April 1801 through the end of March 1811. While living in Charlottesville, Carr formed lasting friendships with Francis Walker Gilmer and William Wirt, and together they nourished their interests in literature by making use of the extensive Gilmer and Jefferson libraries. Carr went on to write literary pieces for newspapers and contributed one article under the pseudonym Obadiah Squaretoes to Wirt's series of newspaper essays that were collected and published in 1814 under the title *The Old Bachelor.* Carr's entry pretended to ridicule the idea that women should be educated and not subordinate to their fathers and husbands. In June 1802 Carr married a cousin, Elizabeth Carr. They had two sons, both of whom died young, and two daughters. Giving the lie to his Squaretoes essay, Carr personally supervised his daughters' excellent education and taught them French.

On 26 March 1811 the governor gave Carr an interim appointment to the seat on the General Court that Carr's friend William H. Cabell had vacated when named to the Court of Appeals, but at its next session the General Assembly passed over Carr and elected another man. At that same time, however, the assembly created a new district court of chancery to meet at Winchester and on 29 January 1812 elected Carr the judge, or chancellor, of that court. He moved to Winchester and presided over the court until the assembly elevated him to the Court of Appeals on 24 February 1824. Carr then moved to Richmond, where he lived until his death. He had a reputation for being hard working, honest, and fair. Carr took careful notes of the arguments presented to the court and thoroughly researched the questions of law. Deferential to the opinions of others, he did not interrupt the lawyers before him when he asked questions of them and never appeared prejudiced toward them. His judicial opinions were thorough and clearly written in a straightforward and unpretentious style, entirely unlike his private and literary writings. Believing himself unqualified to teach, he declined Jefferson's offer of the law chair at the new University of Virginia in April 1825.

Well-respected and kind, Carr was known for his liberal hospitality. When he lived in Winchester, his physician advised him to begin taking long daily walks to prevent the gravel, a term that then referred to gallstones or kidney stones. When the weather was bad he walked indoors at the market house. Carr's exercise regimen included flinging his arms in the air as he walked, action that gave rise to rumors he was eccentric. When Carr moved to Richmond, he purposely did not live near the Capitol and continued his long daily walks to and from work. In both exercise and attending court, he was diligent and regularly sat on the bench until the last month of his life. Dabney Carr died at his residence on the outskirts of Richmond on 8 January 1837 and was buried in the city's Shockoe Cemetery.

Biography in *Southern Literary Messenger* 4 (1838): 65–70, with erroneous May 1772 birth date; birth and baptism dates in W. Mac[farlane] Jones, ed., *The Douglas Register . . .* (1928), 168; marriage date in William Wirt to Carr, June 1802, William Wirt Papers, Maryland Historical Society, and Wirt to Carr, 23 Mar. 1803, William Wirt Letters to Dabney Carr, LVA; family history in W. G. Stanard, "Library of Dabney Carr, 1773, with a Notice of the Carr Family," *VMHB* 2 (1895): 223–224; Carr correspondence and documents in Thomas Jefferson Papers, LC, William Wirt Letters to Dabney Carr, LVA, William Wirt Papers, Maryland Historical

Society, William Wirt Letters, UNC, Carr-Cary Papers, Francis Walker Gilmer Papers, Thomas Jefferson Papers, and other collections, all UVA, and various collections, VHS; Obadiah Squaretoes essay in William Wirt, *The Old Bachelor*, 2d ed. (1814), 48–54; Court of Appeals opinions in *Virginia Reports*, vols. 23–34 (vol. 2 of Randolph's *Reports* through vol. 7 of Leigh's *Reports*); *Virginia Cavalcade* 16 (spring 1967): 39 (por.); Anya Jabour, "Male Friendship and Masculinity in the Early National South: William Wirt and His Friends," *Journal of the Early Republic* 20 (2000): 83–111; copy of will, Acc. 28458, LVA; death notice in *Richmond Whig and Public Advertiser*, 10 Jan. 1837 (variant death date of 9 Jan. 1837); obituary, death date, and memorial resolutions of Richmond bar copied from lost issue of *Richmond Enquirer* in *Washington Daily National Intelligencer*, 13 Jan. 1837.

F. THORNTON MILLER

CARR, David Green (24 May 1809–7 April 1883), member of the Convention of 1867–1868, was born in Laurens, Otsego County, New York. The son of George Carr and Mary Greene Carr, he was said to be descended from Rhode Island's colonial governor Caleb Carr. His early life is undocumented, but by 1833 he had married Hannah Burnside. They had three sons and three daughters. Carr moved his family to Virginia, where in April 1853 he purchased 380 acres of farmland near the village of San Marino in Dinwiddie County. Sometime after Hannah Carr died of cancer in January 1856, Carr returned to New York, where by 1858 he had married Susan Marlette Walker, a physician's widow. By 1860 the couple was living on the farm in Dinwiddie. They had at least one daughter.

Carr became active in the Republican Party and was one of five men chosen to represent Dinwiddie County at the party's first state convention, held in Richmond on 17 and 18 April 1867. He served on the Committee on Permanent Organization. On 22 October 1867 Carr was one of two men elected to represent Dinwiddie and Prince George Counties in a convention called to rewrite the state constitution. In both counties he received a scattering of white votes and overwhelming support from African Americans. In the convention he chaired the Committee on the Pardoning Powers and was ranking member of the Committee on Currency, Banking, and Insurance Companies. He seldom spoke or proposed business, but on 4 January 1868 he introduced a resolution calling for the Virginia

Military Institute to be "obliterated" and stipulating that the value of the property fund public schools. Aligned with the Radical Republicans, Carr sided with the majority in the key roll-call votes including provisions for disfranchisement and test-oath clauses designed to keep some former Confederate officers and officials from voting or holding public office. On 17 April 1868 he voted in favor of the new constitution, which included such reforms as universal manhood suffrage, the establishment of a public school system, and popular election in a greater number of local offices. In July 1869 Virginians approved the constitution but rejected the controversial disabling clauses.

In June 1869 military authorities announced Carr's appointment to the Dinwiddie County board of election registrars. Carr again ran for office and easily outdistanced his opponent to represent Dinwiddie, Greensville, and Sussex Counties in the Senate of Virginia from October 1869 to March 1871. The *Petersburg Index* reported with displeasure the election of "Previous Question" Carr, maintained that his victory derived from his "most slavish and absolute control" of the black community, and unfairly grouped him with carpetbaggers who came to the state after the Civil War. Carr served on the Committees on Federal Relations, on Finance, on Public Institutions, and on Roads and Internal Navigation.

In 1869 President Ulysses S. Grant nominated Carr to be collector of customs at the United States Custom House in Petersburg, an appointment confirmed by Congress on 21 April 1870. In January 1872 Carr relinquished his farm to a son and moved to Petersburg. He was no longer customs collector by 1874 but returned to that position after Rutherford B. Hayes became president in 1877. He remained in office until shortly before his death. David Green Carr died of chronic gastric inflammation at his Petersburg home on 7 April 1883. Despite Carr's record as a Radical Republican, the editor of the *Petersburg Daily Index-Appeal* remembered him as a highly respected, courteous man with many sterling qualities. Carr was buried in Blandford Cemetery alongside his second wife, who had died on 22 July 1882, and one of his daughters.

Birth date on gravestone; David W. Carr, "Descendants of Governor Caleb Carr of Rhode Island" (1994 typescript), 24, 44, New York State Historical Association, Cooperstown, N.Y.; Census, Otsego Co., N.Y., 1840, 1850, Dinwiddie Co., 1860; Election Records, no. 427, RG 13, LVA; *Debates and Proceedings of 1867–1868 Convention*, 60, 210 (first quotation), 645, 703, 704; Hume, "Membership of Convention of 1867–1868," 481; Lowe, "Virginia's Reconstruction Convention," 356; *Petersburg Index*, 24 Oct. 1867, 2 June, 9 July 1869 (second and third quotations); *General Orders and Circulars, Headquarters First Military District, 1869* (1870), "Returns of Election of July 6, 1869," 11; Dinwiddie Co. Will Book, 10:379–380; full name in BVS Death Register, Petersburg; death notice and memorial in *Petersburg Daily Index-Appeal*, 9 Apr. 1883.

DONALD W. GUNTER

CARR, Peter (2 January 1770–17 February 1815), principal in a cause célèbre, was born in Saint James Northam Parish, Goochland County, most likely at the Spring Forest plantation of his parents, Dabney Carr (1743–1773), a lawyer, and Martha Jefferson Carr, sister of Thomas Jefferson. Dabney Carr and Jefferson formed so close a friendship that after Carr's death, Jefferson took full responsibility for the education of Peter Carr and the younger of his two brothers, Dabney Carr (1773–1837), later a judge of the Virginia Court of Appeals. During diplomatic service in France, Jefferson had to content himself with writing Peter Carr some much-quoted letters on education while entrusting his informal guardianship to James Madison (1751–1836). Carr attended Walker Maury's academies in Orange and Williamsburg and studied from 1786 until about 1789 at the College of William and Mary and as a private student of George Wythe. About 1790 Carr began to study law at Spring Forest and Monticello under Jefferson's direction. He was admitted to the bar in the summer of 1793 but practiced only briefly.

Late in 1794 Carr inherited some slaves and about 500 acres of land in Louisa County. He lived at Monticello until August 1796, when construction projects there caused him to move into Charlottesville. On 6 June 1797 Carr married Esther "Hetty" Smith Stevenson, a widow with one son and the sister of Robert Smith, who later served in Jefferson's cabinet, and Samuel Smith, a Maryland congressman. Of the Carrs' four sons and four daughters, two sons and one daughter died in infancy. After 1798 Carr lived with his

family at Carrsbrook, a 900-acre estate about five miles north of Charlottesville that the Carrs initially borrowed and then purchased from Wilson Cary Nicholas, Hetty Carr's brother-in-law and later governor of Virginia. By the time of his death Carr also possessed 199 acres of adjoining land, at least fourteen slaves, and ten horses.

Carr was a passionate political supporter of Jefferson and the Republican Party, but his first effort to advance their interests failed. Under the pseudonym John Langhorne, he addressed a letter to George Washington on 25 September 1797 commiserating with him on alleged calumnies directed at the former president in his retirement. After Washington dispatched a predictably cautious reply, a local Federalist informed him of the subterfuge and charged that Carr had hoped to elicit an indiscreet response. The incident dealt a final blow to Washington's already deteriorating relationship with Jefferson but otherwise achieved nothing.

Carr's subsequent political career was more straightforward. After a failed attempt to win election to the House of Delegates in 1799, he supported Jefferson during the 1800 presidential campaign, Carr became a justice of the peace for Albemarle County on 18 April 1801, and about the same time he was elected to represent the county in the House of Delegates. He served three consecutive one-year terms, from 1801 to 1804, and won the same seat a final time for the 1807–1808 session. In all but his third term Carr sat on the Committee for Courts of Justice, and he also served on the Committee of Propositions and Grievances in his first term. He chaired the Committee of Privileges and Elections and served on two minor committees during the 1803–1804 session. Carr lost his bid for reelection in 1808 and was defeated again a year later when he ran for the state senate. A supporter in the latter campaign urged Carr to display less pride and more familiarity with the voters, attitudes that may help explain these failures.

Carr collaborated in the great project of Jefferson's retirement, the promotion of education. An accomplished student of English literature with an exceptionally melodious speaking voice, Carr in 1811 opened a successful but short-lived academy at Carrsbrook. In 1803 he had been named a founding trustee of the Albemarle Academy, an institution that existed only on paper until 25 March 1814, when he joined four other trustees in an attempt at its revival that included adding Jefferson to the governing board. On 5 April, Carr was named president, in which capacity Jefferson wrote him a long and frequently cited letter on 7 September 1814 outlining his educational philosophy and urging the board to raise its sights and found a college. The Albemarle Academy Carr helped reinvigorate evolved into Central College and later into the University of Virginia.

Despite his widely acknowledged gifts, Carr failed to realize Jefferson's hopes for a distinguished legal or political career, at least in part because of the self-indulgence, corpulence, and "extreme indolence" of which he stood accused in an otherwise affectionate memoir by a much-younger cousin. Carr's notoriety came long after his death with the assertion that between 1795 and 1808 he had fathered at least three sons and three daughters of Thomas Jefferson's slave Sally Hemings. In 1802 James Thomson Callender, a waspish Richmond journalist, publicly accused Jefferson of fathering the children. Circumstantial evidence seemed to corroborate the charge. Jefferson was at Monticello when each Hemings child was conceived, and there were no documented Hemings pregnancies during his long absences. Jefferson allowed two of her surviving children to escape from slavery and freed the other two in his will, even though he emancipated very few other slaves. Sally Hemings's son Madison Hemings in the 1870 Ohio census and an 1873 newspaper article maintained that Jefferson was his father, an assertion supported by Israel Jefferson, another former Jefferson slave.

Descendants of Jefferson's white daughters, many of his admirers, and some historians sought to refute the allegation. In an 1862 memoir Jefferson's former overseer Edmund Bacon denied Jefferson was the father of the Hemings children but failed to name another man. Secondhand accounts of two conversations, written in 1858 and 1868, reported that Jefferson's grandson Thomas Jefferson Randolph had fixed the blame on Peter Carr and his younger brother Samuel Carr. One version explicitly named Peter Carr as the father of Sally Hemings's children, identified his brother as the father of offspring by another Jefferson slave, and described the Carrs shedding tears of remorse about the public furor over Jefferson's supposed responsibility. In the other, the Carr brothers allegedly found their uncle's predicament amusing, and in relating the story Randolph's sister concluded that Samuel Carr was responsible. From the initial publication of the first of these accusations in 1951, most Jefferson scholars, despite the absence of any contemporary evidence naming the Carrs or placing them at Monticello at the critical times, accepted these later, obviously contradictory stories as exculpatory of Jefferson and speculated on whether Peter Carr or Samuel Carr, both of whom lived reasonably close to Monticello, was the father. Samuel Carr probably did form other interracial sexual liaisons, but he had been raised by relatives in Maryland and seems to have been much farther removed from Jefferson and the Monticello social circle as an adult. Peter Carr was therefore often accepted as the likely father of the Hemings children until the publication in 1997 of Annette Gordon-Reed's monograph *Thomas Jefferson and Sally Hemings: An American Controversy*, which made a strong case for Jefferson's paternity. The following year a DNA analysis conclusively ruled out both Carrs, established Jefferson or a male-line relative as the father, and, in conjunction with the other evidence, suggested Jefferson himself was the most credible candidate.

After a British army burned Washington in August 1814, Carr joined the contingent of militia guarding the approaches to Richmond. The British moved instead against Baltimore, and he returned home, but the rigors of service in a hastily constructed encampment undermined his already delicate health. Two weeks after complaining to Jefferson of rheumatism, ague, and fever, Peter Carr died at Carrsbrook on 17 February 1815. As he had requested in his will, he probably was buried near his parents and children in the family cemetery at Monticello, but no gravestone survives.

Elizabeth Dabney Coleman, "Peter Carr of Carr's-Brook (1770–1815)," *Papers of the Albemarle County Historical Society* 4 (1943/1944): 5–23; birth and baptism dates in W. Mac[farlane] Jones, ed., *The Douglas Register . . .* (1928),

168, confirmed in Carr to Thomas Jefferson, 29 May 1789, in *Jefferson Papers*, 15:157; Carr letters in Thomas Jefferson Papers, Massachusetts Historical Society, Boston, and in Carr-Cary Papers (including marriage date and list of children in notes later subjoined to Martha Jefferson Minor to Virginia Cary, 28 Nov. 1831, and two undergraduate orations), Alexander Garrett Papers, and Thomas Jefferson Papers, all UVA; Albemarle Co. Deed Book, 20:409–411; N. Carolyn McCollum, "Carrsbrook" (unpublished report, Architecture in Virginia series, UVA School of Architecture, 1998); Langhorne incident documented in *Washington: Retirement Series*, esp. 1:373–375, 409, 475–477, 509–511; Bruce, *University of Virginia*, 1:116–134; Ellen Randolph Coolidge to Henry Randall, 10 July 1853, Coolidge Letter Book (1856–1858), 31, Ellen Wayles Randolph Coolidge Correspondence, UVA (quotation); the most elaborate speculation on Carr as father of the Hemings children is Douglass Adair, "The Jefferson Scandals," in his *Fame and the Founding Fathers*, ed. Trevor Colbourn (1974), 160–191; Annette Gordon-Reed, *Thomas Jefferson and Sally Hemings: An American Controversy* (1997), with Randolph's charges against the Carrs reprinted on 254–260; Helen F. M. Leary, "Sally Hemings's Children: A Genealogical Analysis of the Evidence," *National Genealogical Society Quarterly* 89 (2001): 165–207; Ellen G. Miles, *Saint-Mémin and the Neoclassical Profile Portrait in America* (1994), 263–264 (por.); will in Thomas Jefferson Papers, UVA, and Albemarle Co. Will Book, 6:129–130; death notice in *Richmond Enquirer*, 1 Mar. 1815; unsigned tribute by William Wirt in *Richmond Enquirer*, 4 Mar. 1815.

J. JEFFERSON LOONEY

CARRELL, James Peery (13 February 1787–28 October 1854), composer, was the son of Agnes Peery Gibson Carrell and her second husband, Charles Carrell, and was born probably in Washington County. Soon after his birth his parents moved to Russell County, where he later attended school for a few months but otherwise educated himself through extensive reading. Carrell lived in Lebanon, in November 1804 became deputy clerk of court, in November 1810 was appointed master commissioner in chancery, and beginning in October 1819 was one of the county's school commissioners. Elected clerk of the Russell County Court on 2 August 1825 (confirming an interim appointment on 7 July of that year), Carrell served in that position until his death. He was also a farmer who owned about 640 acres of land in Russell County. On 30 November 1809 Carrell married Martha George Peery, of Tazewell County. They had two sons, one of whom died late in his teens.

About 1837 Carrell became a local preacher in the Methodist Church. He was elected to deacon's orders in 1841, ordained a deacon on 9 October 1843, and made an elder in 1847. In 1843 Carrell invited "an aged and experienced minister" of his acquaintance to preach in Lebanon in order to quiet "Radicals" who "proposed a discussion of the impropriety of *our* church gover[n]ment, and the superior excellency of *theirs* over ours." He was a generous contributor to and trustee of the Lebanon Methodist Church. On 3 January 1846 Carrell was the featured speaker at the dedication of its first building, and on 27 December 1852 he deeded the congregation the land on which the church stood.

Through money and land donations Carrell also supported the female academy in Lebanon, and in 1836 he served on a nine-member committee (later enlarged to thirteen) that the Holston Methodist Conference appointed to draft a constitution for Emory and Henry College. Carrell's $500 pledge was among the largest gifts to the new college's inaugural subscription. He provided at least one student with a scholarship, and he regularly served on the board of visitors. In March 1852 he was one of the original incorporators of the Lebanon Savings Bank.

The avocation for which Carrell is best known is music. He composed tunes for hymns in the emerging shape-note tradition. Developed about 1800, this simplified system of musical notation used four distinctive shapes to denote the interval from the pitch. Taught in singing schools, the system enabled people otherwise lacking formal training to learn quickly how to read music. In 1821 Carrell's *Songs of Zion, being a small collection of tunes, principally original, with appropriate lines, adapted to Divine Worship* was published in Harrisonburg. Now lost, this work was the most likely source for a number of Carrell's tunes that other compilers subsequently published. William Walker's influential shape-note book, *The Southern Harmony, and Musical Companion* (1835), contained two of Carrell's songs, "The Mouldering Vine" and "Messiah," and the latter is still found in the most frequently used modern version (1991) of *The Sacred Harp*, first published in 1844 by Benjamin Franklin White and the book that has given its name to Sacred Harp singing.

David L. Clayton, a Frederick County farmer and vocal music teacher, collaborated with Carrell on *The Virginia Harmony: A New and Choice Selection of Psalm and Hymn Tunes, Anthems and Set Pieces*, published in Winchester in 1831. The volume omitted "Messiah" and "The Mouldering Vine" but contained twenty-two other tunes that Carrell wrote, with such names as "Anticipation," "The Dying Penitent," "Lexington," "The Pilgrim's Song," "Sharon," and "Staunton." A second edition released five years later retained both names on the title page but credited Clayton with the work of revision and enlargement, which added one more of Carrell's tunes but dropped eight others.

Clayton and Carrell's 1831 edition of *Virginia Harmony* was long credited as the first to publish the tune now always used with John Newton's classic hymn "Amazing Grace." Clayton and Carrell entitled the tune "Harmony Grove" and assigned other words to it. Early in the 1990s, however, the tune was discovered under two other names in Benjamin Shaw and Charles H. Spilman's *Columbian Harmony* (1829). Under yet another title, "New Britain," the tune was first linked to the words of "Amazing Grace" in 1835 in Walker's *Southern Harmony.*

James Peery Carrell died on 28 October 1854 and was buried in the Old Lebanon Cemetery. He bequeathed $1,000 apiece to a Methodist publishing house in Nashville and to the missionary society of the Methodist Episcopal Church South. Carrell's assets included more than $7,000 in debts due him and successfully collected for his estate. He also owned five slaves, having manumitted a woman in December 1816. In his will he urged his son to treat them with forbearance but instructed "if any of them should become unmanageable, that they be sold to some master they may select, provided he will pay a fair price."

Biographies in George Pullen Jackson, *White Spirituals in the Southern Uplands: The Story of the Fasola Folk, Their Songs, Singings, and "Buckwheat Notes"* (1933), 34–38 (including por. facing 36 and birth date from gravestone, no longer legible), and *The Heritage of Russell County, Virginia, 1786–1988* (1985–1989), 2:46–47; middle name in Russell Co. Deed Book, 5:475; Tazewell Co. Marriage Register, 1:18; several Carrell letters to David Campbell and undated obituary clipping from the *Abingdon Virginian* (noting variant birth year of 1786 and death "in the 68th year of his age") in Campbell Family Papers, Duke; other published works include Carrell, *Jehovah invited to his Temple: Discourse, delivered at the Dedication of the Methodist E. Church, at Lebanon, Russell Co., Va., January 3, 1846* (1846); Russell Co. Deed Book, 13:99–100; Russell Co. Law Order Book, 8:57–58; Land Tax Returns, Russell Co., 1854, RG 48, LVA; annual session minutes and recommendation orders, Holston Methodist Conference, and quarterly conference minutes, Lebanon Circuit, Holston Conference Archives, Emory and Henry College; subscription book, Emory and Henry College, and Carrell to George Eakin, 1 June 1843 (first quotation), Eakin Papers, Emory and Henry College Archives; Harry Lee Eskew, "Shape-Note Hymnody in the Shenandoah Valley, 1816–1860" (Ph.D. diss., Tulane University, 1966), 100–114; Steve Turner, *Amazing Grace: The Story of America's Most Beloved Song* (2002), 116–126; will, estate inventory and bill of sale, and estate settlement in Russell Co. Will Book, 6:534–535 (second quotation), 7:15–18, 56–58; Russell Co. Death Register.

J. JEFFERSON LOONEY

CARRINGTON, Alexander Berkeley (27 January 1862–26 January 1936), tobacco company executive, was the son of Alexander Broadnax Carrington, a Presbyterian minister, and his first wife, Fannie Isabella Venable Carrington. Berkeley Carrington, as he was known, was born in Prince Edward County and spent his first three years at his mother's family home there while his father served as a chaplain in the Army of Northern Virginia. He passed the remainder of his childhood and early adolescence in Charlotte County. At age sixteen he moved to Danville to work in the tobacco business of his uncle, Paul C. Venable, and later with the tobacco company Pace and Talbott. On 11 November 1891 Carrington married Mary Miller Taylor, of Danville. They had three sons and one daughter. In 1898 Carrington purchased Venable's well-known Italianate brick residence on Holbrook Avenue, where he lived for the rest of his life.

In 1891 Carrington became a partner in Dibrell Brothers, which purchased leaf tobacco from growers and processed, stored, and shipped it to and for manufacturers of tobacco products. He left the company in 1902 to work for the American Tobacco Company in Durham, North Carolina, but about 1904 he returned to Danville and with Richard Louis Dibrell and Herbert Lee Boatwright formed the triumvirate that created the modern Dibrell Brothers, Inc., with Carrington as vice president from July 1905. After

Dibrell's death in 1920, Carrington became president of the corporation. During the next decade the company expanded its operations in Europe and opened offices in Africa and the Far East. The company's tobacco sales increased by 43 percent and its net equity by 200 percent. Dibrell Brothers became one of the largest leaf tobacco firms in the South and one of the best known in the world. The company had fourteen domestic subsidiaries as well as branch offices in Antwerp, London, Manila, and Shanghai. To no one's surprise, in 1925 Carrington was elected president of the Tobacco Association of the United States, a position he held until 1934, when poor health forced him into semiretirement. In 1942 Carrington's namesake son, who succeeded him as president of Dibrell Brothers, also was elected president of the Tobacco Association of the United States.

Carrington acquired the courtesy title of colonel as an honorary member of the staff of Governor Andrew Jackson Montague from 1902 to 1906 and for the remainder of his life was referred to as Colonel Carrington. Active in Danville's civic life, he was a Shriner and a Freemason, and as president of the Masonic Building Corporation in 1920, he was partly responsible for the construction of the city's tallest building, the Masonic Temple. In local politics Carrington was a member of the board of aldermen from 1911 to 1919, for part of that time as chairman. From 1920 to 1923 he sat on Danville's common council, and he also chaired the city's school board. He was president of the Mutual Building and Loan Association and of the Westbrook Elevator Manufacturing Company, which had a nationwide market. Among other business concerns, Carrington was vice president of the Atlantic and Danville Railway and chairman of the board of Danville's First National Bank. He was a trustee of Hampden-Sydney College, president of the local Young Men's Christian Association and of the Danville Chamber of Commerce, a director of the Virginia State Chamber of Commerce, and chair of the First Presbyterian Church board of deacons and of the boards of Memorial Hospital of Danville and the Hughes Memorial Home for orphans. In Danville dur-

ing the first third of the twentieth century, a reference to "the colonel" meant Carrington.

Alexander Berkeley Carrington died of myocarditis in a Danville hospital on 26 January 1936, one day before his seventy-fourth birthday. He was buried in the family plot at Green Hill Cemetery in Danville. On the day of his funeral, Dibrell Brothers as a mark of respect closed its corporate headquarters in Danville and suspended business in all its foreign offices.

Biographies in *NCAB*, 38:144, Brown, *Cabells*, 623, and George Washington Dame, *Historical Sketch of Roman Eagle Lodge*, 2d ed. rev. (1939), 239–243; BVS Marriage Register, Danville; Alexander Berkeley Carrington, "History of Dibrell Brothers" (typescript, 12 Jan. 1933), and Jack I. Hayes Jr., "A History of Dibrell Brothers: 1873–1990," 1–15, in unpublished guide to the archives of Dibrell Brothers, Inc., both Dibrell Brothers Papers, Archives, Dimon, Inc., Danville; *Commonwealth* 2 (Sept. 1935): 19; Danville Tobacco Association, Inc., *100 Years of Progress, 1869–1969* (1969), 41–42; *Dibrell Brothers, Incorporated, 1873–1973* (1973); Mary Cahill and Gary Grant, *Victorian Danville: Fifty-Two Landmarks: Their Architecture and History* (1977), 40; BVS Death Certificate, Danville; obituaries and editorial tributes in *Danville Bee*, 27 Jan. 1936 (por.), and *Danville Register*, 28 Jan. 1936.

JACK IRBY HAYES JR.

CARRINGTON, Edward (11 February 1749–28 October 1810), Continental army officer and member of the Confederation Congress, was born on his family plantation in the part of Goochland County that became Cumberland County later that year. He was the son of George Carrington (1711–1785), who emigrated from Barbados and became a major landowner, and Anne Mayo Carrington, and was also a younger brother of Paul Carrington (1733–1818), a member of the Conventions of 1776 and 1788 and a judge of the Virginia Court of Appeals. During the summer of 1771 Carrington traveled to Barbados to make arrangements to collect his father's part of an inheritance. He returned to Virginia in the autumn of 1772, studied law, and was licensed to practice in Cumberland County in June 1773.

In March 1775 Carrington accompanied his brother Paul Carrington to the second of the Revolutionary Conventions, which met in Richmond, and stood outside the Henrico Parish Church to hear Patrick Henry make his "liberty or death" speech. According to a tradition set down more than a century later, Carrington was so impressed that he stated then that he wished to be buried on the spot where he stood. In 1775 and 1776 he was a member of, and sometime secretary for, the Cumberland County Committee, which in the summer of 1775 sent him to Philadelphia to purchase gunpowder for the county militia. In the autumn of that year Carrington became captain of a company of minutemen that he recruited in Cumberland County, and in February 1776 the Virginia Committee of Safety commissioned him a second lieutenant in one of its new artillery companies.

On 30 November 1776 the Continental Congress named Carrington lieutenant colonel of the 1st Regiment of Virginia Artillery, his commission to date from the creation of the regiment on 26 November. Described by Thomas Jefferson as being "industrious but not always as discreet as well meaning," Carrington clashed with Governor Patrick Henry the following summer over the appointment of officers, for which he apologized after Congress threatened to dismiss him. Carrington had a distinguished and successful military career and became deputy quartermaster general in January 1781. As chief of artillery under Nathanael Greene later in the year, he commanded artillery at the Battles of Guilford Court House and Hobkirk's Hill, as well as at the siege of Yorktown. On 26 April 1782 Congress rejected Carrington's application to become commander of a Pennsylvania artillery regiment because that state reserved the right to make the appointment.

In the spring of 1783 when Carrington's service in the army concluded, he returned to Cumberland County and the following year was elected to the first of two consecutive one-year terms in the House of Delegates. He was a member of the Committees for Courts of Justice and of Propositions and Grievances in the May 1784 session and in the session of October 1785 added to those two assignments a seat on the Committee of Privileges and Elections. In June 1784 the General Assembly designated Carrington to present to the Confederation Congress the state's claim for compensation for wartime expenditures in the Northwest. The next November he fell one vote short of being elected to the Council of State.

On 15 November 1785 the assembly chose Carrington as one of Virginia's five delegates to Congress. Reelected in November 1786 and October 1787, he attended from 3 March to 4 December 1786, from 26 March to 10 November 1787, and from early in May to 10 October 1788. Service in Congress reinforced the nationalist outlook that Carrington and many other Continental army officers had developed during the war. He joined attempts to reform the nation's militia and to strengthen its finances. Although he had a few reservations about the proposed constitution submitted to the states for ratification late in 1787, Carrington supported the document and in the spring of 1788 sought election to the Virginia ratification convention from Powhatan County, but Patrick Henry's numerous local allies who opposed the Constitution defeated him.

That defeat was the result of Carrington's advocacy of the Constitution, not of personal unpopularity. A few weeks later Powhatan County voters elected him to the House of Delegates. By then Carrington had returned to New York, where Congress was meeting, and therefore he missed the summer session of the assembly that year, but he kept Virginia's supporters of the Constitution posted on the progress of ratification in the northern states. On 24 October 1788, shortly after Carrington took his seat in the assembly and was appointed to the Committees of Commerce, for Courts of Justice, of Privileges and Elections, and of Propositions and Grievances, Patrick Henry engineered a vote depriving him of his seat in the House of Delegates, based on a law forbidding any person to be simultaneously a member of the General Assembly and of Congress. Carrington was immediately reelected and named to the Committees of Claims, of Privileges and Elections, and of Propositions and Grievances. During the final weeks of the session he opposed calls for a second constitutional convention. In 1789 he won election for a second term as a delegate from Powhatan County and was again assigned to the Committees for Courts of Justice and of Privileges and Elections. He had made an unsuccessful campaign for presidential elector earlier that year but lost to an opponent of the Constitution. Carrington might have run for a seat in the House of Representatives in 1789 had he believed that an advocate of the Constitution could have been elected.

An occasional visitor at Mount Vernon, Carrington advised George Washington on appointments and Virginia politics. On 26 September 1789 the president appointed him United States marshal for the District of Virginia. In that capacity Carrington administered the 1790 federal census in the state. He received the more lucrative office of supervisor of federal excise revenue for Virginia in the spring of 1791, and his old army friend Alexander Hamilton, then secretary of the treasury, later seriously considered him for appointment as comptroller of the Treasury Department. Although Carrington shared the reservations of his good friend James Madison about federal assumption of the state debts, he supported Hamilton's financial program, including federal chartering of a national bank. Along with John Marshall, he organized a public meeting in Richmond on 17 August 1793 to condemn the French minister, Edmond-Charles-Édouard Genet, who had encouraged anti-Federalist opposition to Washington's administration, and to defend Washington's proclamation of neutrality during the conflict between France and Great Britain. In 1795 Carrington declined presidential invitations to serve as a commissioner supervising construction of public buildings in the District of Columbia and as secretary of war. Three years later when possible war with France threatened, Washington suggested that Carrington be appointed quartermaster general of the United States Army.

On 8 December 1792 Carrington married a childless Richmond widow, Elizabeth Jaquelin Ambler Brent, daughter of Jaquelin Ambler, then treasurer of Virginia. She helped found the Female Humane Association of the City of Richmond. They had no children. Carrington had moved to Richmond by then, and he became one of the city's leading citizens. He was a charter member and officer of the Society of the Cincinnati, joined the Henrico Parish vestry in 1797, was a founding trustee in 1803 of the Richmond Academy, and was an original member of the board of the Bank of Virginia, chartered in 1804.

In June 1808 he joined other Richmond citizens in forming a committee to promote manufacturing. Carrington served as mayor of Richmond for one-year terms beginning in April 1807 and April 1809, and he was the foreman of the trial jury that on 1 September 1807 acquitted Aaron Burr of treason.

Edward Carrington died at his home in Richmond on 28 October 1810. The city council held a massive funeral, featuring a procession of state, city, and church officials. Carrington was buried outside the east entrance of the Henrico Parish (later Saint John's Episcopal) Church, near where he had stood listening to Patrick Henry in March 1775.

Garland Evans Hopkins, "The Life of Edward Carrington, A Brief Sketch," *Americana* 34 (1940): 458–474; Charles Konigsberg, "Edward Carrington, 1748–1810, 'Child of the Revolution': A Study of the Public Man in Young America" (Ph.D. diss., Princeton University, 1966), with bibliography of manuscripts; birth date and extensive biographical notes in Carrington family Bible records, Peyton Rodes Carrington Collection, Acc. 22517, LVA; Carrington correspondence and documents in several collections at LC, LVA, UVA, VHS, and Papers of Continental Congress, RG 360, NARA; James C. Brandow, "A Young Virginian's Visit to Barbados, 1771–1772," *Journal of the Barbados Museum and Historical Society* 35 (1976): 73–86; William Wirt Henry, *Patrick Henry: Life, Correspondence and Speeches* (1891), 1:270; *Revolutionary Virginia*; Richard K. Showman et al., eds., *The Papers of General Nathanael Greene* (1976–); Harold C. Syrett et al., eds., *The Papers of Alexander Hamilton* (1961–1987); *Jefferson Papers* (quotation on 10:225); Kaminski, *Ratification*; *Madison Papers: Congressional Series*; *Marshall Papers*; Smith, *Letters of Delegates*, vols. 23–25; *Washington Papers: Confederation Series, Presidential Series,* and *Retirement Series*; Henrico Co. Marriage Bonds; *Richmond Virginia Gazette, and General Advertiser*, 12 Dec. 1792; *Virginia Cavalcade* 36 (1987): 103 (por.); obituaries and accounts of funeral in *Richmond Enquirer* and *Richmond Virginia Patriot*, both 30 Oct., 2 Nov. 1810, and *Richmond Virginia Argus*, 30 Oct. 1810.

STUART LEIBIGER

CARRINGTON, Elizabeth Jaquelin Ambler Brent

CARRINGTON, Elizabeth Jaquelin Ambler Brent (11 March 1765–15 February 1842), a founder of the Female Humane Association of the City of Richmond, was born in Yorktown and was the daughter of Jaquelin Ambler, a prosperous merchant, and Rebecca Burwell Ambler. During the American Revolution the family moved to Richmond, where her father served on the Council of State and became state treasurer in 1782. On 31 March 1785 she married William

Brent, of Stafford County, who died suddenly on 15 June of that year. She married Edward Carrington, a former member of the Confederation Congress, in Richmond on 8 December 1792. She had no children from either marriage and was widowed a second time on 28 October 1810. Her family connections and two marriages tied her closely to many of Virginia's other leading families. Two of her sisters, for instance, married the Richmond attorneys Daniel Call and John Marshall.

Carrington's life epitomized the changes in the lives of elite women in Virginia from the colonial period into the antebellum era. There were no academies for young women in the colony, so her father educated her at home, and she read widely. During the Revolutionary War the family fled Yorktown before the advancing British forces. The separation from her native town was the beginning of a revealing correspondence with her friend Mildred Smith (later Mildred Smith Dudley). Their initial topic was a French officer's seduction and abandonment of their orphaned acquaintance, Rachel Warrington, and the subsequent birth of an illegitimate son. Recognizing the importance of a proper education to help young women distinguish false appearances from true, particularly with respect to men, Ambler and Smith articulated a predominant theme in contemporary novels, the rising literary genre of their generation, that reverberated throughout their adult lives. Years later Carrington began a novel based on Warrington's experience. The introduction and first chapter embodied the author's sympathetic attitude toward the mother and emphasized the necessity for women to be prepared to detect dangers to themselves. Carrington never completed or published the book, to which she gave the title *Variety or the vicissitudes of Long life*.

A committed Episcopalian, Carrington faithfully sought to keep afloat the Henrico Parish (later Saint John's Episcopal) Church in Richmond during a long period of Anglican decline following the Revolution. Her father and second husband were both parish vestrymen, and she contributed money to the church and attended the occasional services held there during its bleakest years. Carrington abhorred the deism

of the postrevolutionary age and in her letters particularly scorned Thomas Paine, author of *The Age of Reason*.

Carrington's belief in female education together with her religious sensibilities and memory of Rachel Warrington undoubtedly led her about 1805 to help found the Female Humane Association of Richmond for the relief of female orphans, probably the first such organization in Virginia. Carrington joined Mary Spear Nicholas, wife of the state's attorney general, Philip Norborne Nicholas, and Jean Moncure Wood, wife of former governor James Wood, in drawing up a constitution and bylaws early in 1808, and in December 1810 they and twenty-seven other association members petitioned the General Assembly for an act of incorporation, passed in January 1811. The statute incorporating the Female Humane Association of the City of Richmond omitted naming any male trustees and therefore granted the association's officers a host of legal rights, including the ability to buy and sell property, enter into contracts, and bring suits in court, that were denied them individually as married women.

Carrington was secretary when the association was incorporated and held the office as late as 1833, when a list of members and officers was printed. After initial success and the erection of an asylum, or orphanage, in 1813, the association suffered hard financial times and during the 1820s was forced to retrench, reduce the number of orphans it cared for, and narrow its objective to the care and education of destitute white girls. In 1828 the association instituted an annual fund-raising fair. Even during its lean years the association saved many orphans from lives of poverty and prostitution and literally provided them with asylum in a world where it was dangerous to lack male protectors. Modest as it was in the beginning, the association represented the entrance of women into a public sphere that had been the exclusive province of men and met an important social need that government had ignored. The association's work has survived through several transmutations. Its modern successor, the Memorial Foundation for Children, dispersed more than $905,000 in 2002 in support of educational and cultural programs.

Early in 1834 Carrington supported the successful efforts of her driver William Caswell, a former slave, to obtain permission to remain in Virginia. Carrington's petition to the General Assembly in his behalf specifically mentioned Caswell's contribution to her work for the association. Elizabeth Jaquelin Ambler Brent Carrington died in Richmond on 15 February 1842 and probably was buried beside her second husband in the churchyard of the city's Saint John's Episcopal Church. A simple announcement of her funeral was all the family issued or expected to appear in print, but the *Richmond Enquirer* published an unusual and perceptive obituary. Stating that family connections conferred "no small distinction on this lady," the editor went beyond that conventional characterization and recognized Carrington's pivotal leadership in the city: "Her intelligent and cultivated mind; her generous heart; her active and diffusive charity, of which the Female Humane Association of Richmond furnishes one enduring memorial"; and her "practical piety" made her one of Virginia's most "distinguished women."

Biographical information in Carrington letters (birth date in Carrington to Ann Ambler Fisher, 10 Oct. 1796, and first marriage date of 31 Mar. 1785 and death date of William Brent in letter to Mildred Smith, 10 July 1785), and draft novel, n.d., in Elizabeth Jaquelin Ambler Brent Carrington Papers, CW (photocopies and typescript copies in Elizabeth Jaquelin Ambler Brent Carrington Papers at LC and VHS, respectively); some letters excerpted in "An Old Virginia Correspondence," *Atlantic Monthly* 84 (1899): 535–549; Henrico Co. Marriage Bonds, 26 Mar. 1785, 8 Dec. 1792; variant first marriage date of 26 Mar. 1785 in *Richmond Virginia Gazette or the American Advertiser*, 9 Apr. 1785; *Richmond Virginia Gazette, and General Advertiser*, 12 Dec. 1792; Memorial Foundation for Children Records, LVA; Legislative Petitions, Richmond City, n.d. [13 Dec. 1810, 31 Jan. 1834], RG 78, LVA; *Acts of Assembly*, 1810–1811 sess., 86–87; Catherine Kerrison, "By the Book: Eliza Ambler Brent Carrington and Conduct Literature in Late Eighteenth-Century Virginia," *VMHB* 105 (1997): 27–52; death notices in *Daily Richmond Whig*, 16, 17 Feb. 1842; obituary in *Richmond Enquirer*, 17 Feb. 1842 (quotations).

CATHERINE KERRISON

CARRINGTON, George (1 July 1711–7 February 1785), surveyor, member of the House of Burgesses, and founder of the Carrington family in Virginia, was born in Saint Phillips Parish, Barbados, and was the son of Paul Carrington, a physician, and his second wife, Henningham Codrington Carrington. About 1723 he and his kinsmen, the merchant Joseph Mayo and the surveyor William Mayo, immigrated to Virginia. He worked as an assistant storekeeper with Joseph Mayo, but a family tradition that he accompanied William Mayo on the 1728 expedition to survey the boundary between Virginia and North Carolina is not corroborated by the records of the survey. Surveying, however, led Carrington to become a large landowner. Like William Mayo and William Cabell (1700–1774), with whom he was occasionally associated, Carrington eventually patented several thousand acres of land in the area that became Albemarle, Buckingham, Cumberland, and Goochland Counties. On 26 June 1732 he married William Mayo's daughter, Anne Mayo. They had three daughters and eight sons, including Edward Carrington, a member of the Confederation Congress, and Paul Carrington (1733–1818), a member of the Conventions of 1776 and 1788 and judge of the Virginia Court of Appeals.

Carrington served as a justice of the peace and sheriff of Goochland County, churchwarden and vestryman for Southam Parish, and member of the House of Burgesses beginning in the February 1746 session, when he replaced the recently deceased William Randolph. Completing that term, Carrington represented the county again during the 1748–1749 sessions, at which he was a member of the Committee for Courts of Justice.

Carrington's Boston Hill estate was in the southern part of Goochland County that in 1749 became Cumberland County. Carrington was the first surveyor of the new county and a justice of the peace for more than three decades. In 1752 he was named a colonel in the militia and presiding judge of the court. Carrington represented Cumberland County in the House of Burgesses from 1752 to 1765 and was appointed to the Committees for Courts of Justice, Claims, and Trade. During the October 1764 session he accepted the position of county sheriff and was succeeded in the House by Thomas Prosser. During the 1765 session, however, Carrington returned to replace Prosser, whom the burgesses had expelled. Carrington became county lieutenant in September 1775 and was an organizer and chair of the Cumberland County Committee in 1775 and 1776.

Carrington represented Cumberland County in the House of Delegates during the 1778–1781 and 1783 terms. A well-respected, senior member of the assembly, he served on the major standing committees including Courts of Justice, Propositions and Grievances, and Trade. Several times he also was appointed ranking member of the Committee of Public Claims and the Committee of Privileges and Elections or chair of the Committee for Religion. On 4 November 1783 a fellow delegate nominated Carrington to substitute for the absent Speaker of the House, but he declined.

George Carrington died at Boston Hill on 7 February 1785. His wife died eight days later, and they were buried together there in the same grave. Carrington died without completing his will. His estate, by one estimate, consisted of about 32,000 acres of land and personal property, including eighteen slaves, worth more than £1,300. His children tried to divide the estate equitably, according to his stated intentions.

James C. Brandow, "The Origin of the Carrington Family of Virginia," *National Genealogical Society Quarterly* 70 (1982): 246–270; birth, marriage, and death dates and other family history in Carrington family Bible records, Peyton Rodes Carrington Collection, Acc. 22517, LVA; Carrington Family Papers, VHS; Brown, *Cabells*, 54–55, 171–173, 182–183; numerous references in *Executive Journals of Council*, vols. 4–6, *JHB*, *JHD*, and *Revolutionary Virginia*, vols. 2–7; incorrect assertion that Carrington was a member of the Conventions of 1774–1776 and 1788 (Carrington family Bible records) repeated in Alice Read, *The Reads and Their Relatives* (1930), 123–126, Garland Evans Hopkins, *Colonel Carrington of Cumberland* (1942), 75–76, and Cumberland County Historical Society, Inc., *Cumberland County Virginia and Its People* (1983), 87–88; estate records in Cumberland Co. Will Book, 2:348–356, 399–404, and Cumberland Co. Order Book (1784–1786), 200; obituary in *Richmond Virginia Gazette or the American Advertiser*, 5 Mar. 1785.

JOHN G. DEAL

CARRINGTON, George (21 June 1758–27 May 1809), member of the Convention of 1788, was the son of Paul Carrington (1733–1818) and his first wife, Margaret Read Carrington, and was born probably at his father's plantation, Mulberry Hill, in the portion of Lunenburg County

that in 1764 became Charlotte County. His father served in public office for nearly half a century and was a judge of the Virginia Court of Appeals and a member of the Conventions of 1776 and 1788, and his younger brother Paul Carrington (1764–1816) served briefly as Speaker of the Senate of Virginia before becoming a judge of the General Court. Like others in his family, Carrington may have attended the College of William and Mary, but incomplete student records do not include his name. In August 1776, at age eighteen, he succeeded his father, probably on his father's recommendation, as clerk of Halifax County. Carrington held the office for twenty-one years, but while he was absent serving in the army from 1780 to 1783, hired deputies officiated in his name.

According to family tradition, Carrington left home in August 1780, without the knowledge of his family, and joined the cavalry regiment commanded by Henry "Light-Horse Harry" Lee (1756–1818). As quartermaster with the rank of cornet, Carrington served under his uncle, Lieutenant Colonel Edward Carrington (later a member of the Confederation Congress), and in July 1781 saw combat at Quinby's Bridge, north of Charleston, South Carolina. British cavalry captured Carrington in April 1782 while he was reconnoitering in the vicinity of nearby Dorchester. He was a prisoner of war until sometime the following year and after his exchange remained attached to Lee's command until discharged with the rank of lieutenant in October 1783.

As a result of his service in the army, Carrington became an original member of the Virginia chapter of the Society of the Cincinnati and also received a warrant for $2,666^2/_3$ acres of western land. He obtained grants for the land in Ohio in 1796 and 1805 and also owned an interest in nearly 4,000 acres in Kentucky. Carrington was a member of the vestry of Antrim Parish and served as its treasurer. He married Sarah Coles Tucker on 1 April 1784. They had eight sons and two daughters, all of whom survived to adulthood.

On 24 March 1788 Carrington and his wife's uncle, Isaac Coles, were elected to represent Halifax County in the convention called to consider the proposed constitution of the United States.

His father represented Charlotte County, making them one of two father-son pairs in the convention. Reportedly an eloquent speaker and very popular with his neighbors, Carrington was identified before the convention as a likely opponent of ratification. He attended all twenty-six days of the convention but took no recorded part in its debates. On 25 June 1788 Carrington voted in favor of requiring amendment of the Constitution before ratification. After that motion was defeated, he voted against ratification. Two days later he supported efforts to limit the federal government's powers of taxation. Carrington's opposition to the Constitution is interesting in light of his father's vote for ratification and the strong influence in favor of the Constitution that George Washington is thought to have had on former officers of the Continental army.

In May 1787 Carrington was commissioned a colonel in the county militia, and in September 1793 he was appointed lieutenant colonel and commander of the 69th Regiment in the reorganized state militia. Following a revision of the militia command structure in December 1795, Carrington became brigadier general of the 11th Brigade. He was often referred to thereafter as General George Carrington to distinguish him from his namesake son and other relatives of the same name. He retired at the end of December 1798.

Carrington was elected to a four-year term in the Senate of Virginia in 1798 to represent the counties of Charlotte, Halifax, and Prince Edward. He was a member of the Committee of Privileges and Elections and on 24 December 1798 voted for resolutions opposing the Alien and Sedition Acts. After serving one term in the Senate, Carrington was elected to the House of Delegates from Halifax County for a one-year term in 1802, during which he sat on the Committees of Privileges and Elections and for Courts of Justice. He had been a presidential elector in 1792 and was appointed a commissioner to supervise the presidential election of 1800 in the county.

Carrington lived at Oak Hill, his estate on the south bank of the Dan River near the original site of South Boston, which was founded on his property in 1796. He owned more than 2,850 acres of land in Halifax County and at the time of his death had more than fifty slaves. In 1803 he built a dam and a water gristmill on the Hyco River in southern Halifax County. George Carrington died suddenly of a ruptured blood vessel at his home on 27 May 1809 and was buried probably on his estate.

Birth date in Carrington family Bible records, Peyton Rodes Carrington Collection, Acc. 22517, LVA, in Paul Carrington family Bible as recorded in Agnes Gamble Carrington Marshall, comp., genealogical notes on the Carrington family (1861), VHS, in Herbert A. Claiborne notes (1883) compiled by Nathaniel Francis Cabell and undated typescript genealogical notes in Carrington Family Papers, both VHS, and in Hugh Blair Grigsby, *History of the Virginia Federal Convention of 1788* (1890–1891), 2:375 (with incorrect name of father); William B. Coles, *The Coles Family of Virginia: Its Numerous Connections, from the Emigration to America to the Year 1915* (1931), 85, with incorrect birth date of 21 Nov. 1756; Carrington Family Papers, LVA and VHS; BW; LOMC; Halifax Co. Marriage Bond Register, 1:6; Henry Lee, *Memoirs of the War in the Southern Department of the United States* (1812), 2:152–155; Richard K. Showman et al., eds., *The Papers of General Nathanael Greene* (1976–), 9:150–152, 11:64, 74–75; F. Claiborne Johnston, Jr., "Federalist, Doubtful, and Antifederalist: A Note on the Virginia Convention of 1788," *VMHB* 96 (1988): 341; Kaminski, *Ratification*, 10:1539, 1541, 1557, 1565; Halifax Co. Deed Book, 10:105, 17:353, 42:480–482; Samuel Shepherd, ed., *The Statutes at Large of Virginia* (1835), 2:48; will and estate inventory in Halifax Co. Will Book, 8:99–101, 167–173; obituary in *Richmond Enquirer*, 6 June 1809.

F. CLAIBORNE JOHNSTON, JR.

CARRINGTON, Isaac Howell (7 March 1827–30 January 1887), provost marshal of Richmond during the Civil War, was born in that city at the residence of his great-grandfather, Robert Gamble. He was the son of Paul Sydenham Carrington, a Charlotte County planter, and Emma Catherine Cabell Carrington. Well connected to the influential families of Virginia, he was a grandson of William H. Cabell, a former governor and then judge of the Virginia Court of Appeals, and of Paul Carrington (1764–1816), a Speaker of the Senate of Virginia and judge of the General Court. Carrington was raised in Charlotte County and studied in local schools before attending the University of North Carolina from 1842 to 1844 and the University of Virginia, where he studied law, from 1845 to 1846. He read law with James Murray Whittle in Pittsylvania County and practiced with him until the Civil War began. On 19 April 1853 Carrington married a cousin, Mary Claiborne Coles. They had two daughters and two sons. One of Carrington's sons was stillborn, the other drowned as a child, and his wife died of liver disease on 8 March 1860.

On 12 June 1861 Carrington was commissioned a major in the 38th Regiment Virginia Infantry and was mustered into Confederate service on the same day. The regiment arrived too late to participate in the First Battle of Manassas (Bull Run) and saw little action before going into winter quarters. Carrington was ill and absent from 13 January to the end of February 1862, but he was present in April when the regiment was posted to the Middle Peninsula. At the election of officers on 12 May 1862, Carrington was not reelected. He served as chief of staff to Brigadier General John Buchanan Floyd for several months and then late in May 1863 applied for a position as a judge of the courts-martial established under a recent act of the Confederate Congress. On 16 June 1863 Carrington was appointed assistant quartermaster with the rank of captain to date from 29 May, but soon thereafter he declined the position.

On 14 July 1863 the Confederate secretary of war appointed Carrington a commissioner of prisoners in Richmond and instructed him to report as well on persons suspected of disloyalty to the Confederacy. The health of the prisoners of war provoked censure from Carrington's counterparts in the United States Army and from the United States Sanitary Commission. Carrington reported in November 1863 that the prisoners were being properly provided with food and shelter, but throughout the war prisoners died, and criticism continued. The condition of the prisoners remained a subject of intense debate long after the war ended.

In March 1864 the secretary of war appointed Carrington provost marshal for the city of Richmond with responsibility for issuing passports to all persons leaving the city. He signed such a pass on 15 June 1864 for President Jefferson Davis. Carrington also tried to monitor the actions of suspected deserters, spies, stragglers, and other people who might threaten local security. In mid-February 1865 his commanding officer, Lieutenant General Richard Stoddert Ewell,

ordered him to make plans to destroy the cotton, tobacco, and military and naval stores that might be in danger of capture. On 2 April 1865 Carrington was also appointed superintendent for recruiting African American soldiers for the Confederate States Army, but on that same day the Confederate government abandoned Richmond, leaving the city undefended.

Carrington prepared to burn the warehouses and posted guards to prevent interference. He notified the city fire chief and requested that firefighters and equipment be ready to prevent the flames from spreading. Unfortunately, the wind began to blow soon after the first warehouses were set ablaze. Aided by disorderly residents and soldiers, who were drinking the capital's alcohol supply as city officials tried to destroy it and who even chopped up the fire hoses, the flames spread unchecked during the night. Much of the business district of Richmond was destroyed in the fire and accompanying riot.

Carrington left the city soon after dawn on 3 April, surrendered in Danville, and was paroled as a prisoner of war on 4 May 1865. He escaped blame for the Richmond fire, which fell on Ewell, but he was accused of complicity in the improper use of thousands of dollars in United States funds and gold that Union prisoners of war in Richmond had turned over after their capture. The army arrested Carrington on 12 May after his return to Richmond and investigated the fate of the money sent for relief of the prisoners. Exonerated, he was released on 29 June and took the oath of allegiance on the following day. Carrington then applied for a pardon and enclosed documents indicating that he had been cleared of suspicion in the misappropriation of the prisoner funds. On 20 September 1865 he received a presidential pardon.

On 7 November 1865 Carrington married Anne Seddon Smith at Glen Roy in Gloucester County. They had three sons and four daughters, but death struck his second family as it had his first. Only two sons and two daughters lived to adulthood. Carrington resumed the practice of law in partnership with the Richmond attorney Robert Ould, the former Confederate agent for prisoner exchange, who also had been arrested during the investigation of the prisoner fund.

They earned a high reputation in the emerging field of corporate law. After Ould's death in 1882, Carrington practiced law with Edward Henry Fitzhugh for several years. A member of the board of visitors of the University of Virginia from 1873 until 1875, Carrington became president of the Richmond Bar Association in February 1886 and was holding that office at his death.

In August 1886 Isaac Howell Carrington suffered an attack of Bright's disease and died in Richmond on 30 January 1887. He was buried in the city's Hollywood Cemetery.

George L. Christian, "Reminiscences of Some of the Dead of the Bench and Bar of Richmond: Major Isaac H. Carrington," *Virginia Law Register* (1909): 16; Brown, *Cabells*, 619–621; Alice Read, *The Reads and Their Relatives* (1930), 256–258; William B. Coles, *The Coles Family of Virginia: Its Numerous Connections, from the Emigration to America to the Year 1915* (1931), 240, 285–286; Pittsylvania Co. Marriage Bonds (1853); BVS Marriage Register, Gloucester Co. (1865); Compiled Service Records; G. Howard Gregory, *38th Virginia Infantry*, 1st ed. (1988), 1–2, 85; *OR*, 1st ser., vol. 46, pt. 1, 1293, 2d ser., 6:116, 530–531, 544–546, 8:512, 529, 572, 635, 671–672, 4th ser., 3:1194; Presidential Pardons; John O. Peters, *Tale of the Century: A History of the Bar Association of the City of Richmond, 1885–1985* (1985), 2, 4 (por.), 21, 109; BVS Death Register, Richmond City; obituaries in *Richmond Daily Times* and *Richmond Dispatch*, both 1 Feb. 1887; memorial resolutions in *Southern Churchman*, 3 Feb. 1887.

EMILY J. SALMON

CARRINGTON, Paul (5 March 1733–22 June 1818), member of the Convention of 1776 and of the Convention of 1788 and judge of the Virginia Court of Appeals, was the son of George Carrington (1711–1785) and Anne Mayo Carrington and was born in the southern portion of Goochland County that in 1749 became Cumberland County. His father, an emigrant from Barbados, was a surveyor and member of the House of Burgesses, and one of his younger brothers, Edward Carrington, was a member of the Confederation Congress. Details of Carrington's early education are unclear, but in 1750 he went to Lunenburg County to read law under Clement Read, then the county clerk and a member of the House of Burgesses. In May 1755 Carrington received a license to practice law, and on 1 October of that year he married Read's daughter, Margaret Read. They lived at Mulberry Hill on the Staunton River in the part of Lunenburg that in 1764 became Charlotte County. Before she died on 1 May 1766, they had two daughters and three sons, including George Carrington (1758–1809), who was a member of the Convention of 1788, and Paul Carrington (1764–1816), who briefly served as Speaker of the Senate of Virginia and was a judge of the General Court.

Soon after he began practicing law, Carrington was appointed king's attorney for Bedford County on 3 May 1756, and during the next twenty years he also served as king's attorney for several other counties, including Charlotte, Lunenburg, and Mecklenburg. He became a major in the Lunenburg County militia in 1761 and was a colonel in the Charlotte County militia in 1764. On 11 April 1772 the governor appointed him county lieutenant, or commander, of the Charlotte County militia. Carrington represented Charlotte County in the House of Burgesses from 1765 to 1776. He was a member of the Committees of Propositions and Grievances, of Privileges and Elections, of Religion, and to Examine the State of the Treasury. From 17 November 1772 until August 1776 Carrington was clerk of Halifax County. He was a founding trustee of Hampden-Sydney College and served on its board for forty-three years, from 1775 until his death in 1818.

Carrington consistently supported the colony's protests against British taxes on and regulation of American commerce during the 1770s, and in January 1775 he organized and was elected chair of the Charlotte County Committee formed to enforce the nonimportation resolutions that the Virginia Convention and the First Continental Congress had adopted and to prepare for the defense of the colony. Carrington represented Charlotte County at all five of the Revolutionary Conventions held between August 1774 and July 1776. On 17 August 1775 the Third Convention appointed him to the Virginia Committee of Safety that in effect governed the colony between September 1775 and July 1776. At the Fifth Convention, which met between 6 May and 5 July 1776, Carrington served on the Committee of Privileges and Elections and the committee charged with preparing a Virginia declaration of rights and the first Virginia constitution. Present for forty-seven days of the fifty-two-day convention, Carrington voted for independence, approval of the Declaration of Rights, and adoption of the Constitution of 1776.

Carrington represented Charlotte, Halifax, and Prince Edward Counties in the new Senate of Virginia during the 1776 and 1777–1778 assemblies. He chaired the Committee of Privileges and Elections during his first year and was ranking member during the second year. As one of the wealthiest and most respected men in Charlotte County, he was a natural choice to represent the county in the convention called in 1788 to consider the proposed constitution of the United States. He and his son George Carrington made one of two father-son pairs in the convention. Carrington attended every day from 2 June through 27 June 1788 and served on the Committee of Privileges and Elections and the committee to recommend amendments to the Constitution. He did not speak often during the proceedings, but on the first day he nominated his close friend Edmund Pendleton for president. Carrington voted against requiring amendment of the Constitution before ratification but supported restrictions on congressional taxing authority. Although he reportedly had reservations about the Constitution, he voted for ratification on 25 June 1788.

When the commonwealth established its first judicial system, the General Assembly elected Carrington on 23 January 1778 one of the original judges of the new General Court. As a member of the court, he was ex officio a judge of the Court of Appeals (consisting of members of the General Court, the High Court of Chancery, and the Court of Admiralty) after its creation in May 1779. Carrington was chief judge of the General Court from 1780 until 1788. When the state's judiciary was reorganized on 22 December 1788, he was one of the first five judges appointed to the new Court of Appeals. After forty-two years of public service and twenty-nine years as a judge, Carrington retired on 1 January 1807. He did not want to remain too long as some of his colleagues had done, holding on until their deaths.

Carrington was a quiet, unassuming jurist who rarely took the lead but preferred instead to cede that role to such strong-willed judges as Edmund Pendleton and Spencer Roane. Known for his impartiality, Carrington wrote opinions that were concise and direct, based more on practical judgment than on complicated legal learning. His integrity was so well respected that family members and biographers often recounted the story of how he settled the estate of his father. George Carrington died in 1785 without completing his will, leaving Paul Carrington heir to all of his father's estate, which included thousands of acres of land and more than £1,300 in personal property. Rather than keep the whole himself, Carrington tried to divide it among his siblings as his father had wished.

On 6 March 1792 Carrington married fifteen-year-old Priscilla Sims in Halifax County. Before she died on 15 September 1803, they had at least two sons, and their only daughter married Walter Coles, a five-term member of the House of Representatives. Following his retirement in 1807, Carrington returned to Mulberry Hill in Charlotte County. One of his last public acts was to serve as a presidential elector in 1808. Paul Carrington died at his estate on 22 June 1818 and was buried there between his two wives.

Birth date in Carrington family Bible records, Peyton Rodes Carrington Collection, Acc. 22517, LVA; birth and death dates from Paul Carrington family Bible as recorded in Agnes Gamble Carrington Marshall, comp., genealogical notes on the Carrington family (1861), VHS; birth date incorrectly adjusted for calendar change in Brown, *Cabells*, 223–226, and repeated in several other accounts; biographies in (4 Call) *Virginia Reports*, 8:xviii, Hugh Blair Grigsby, *The Virginia Convention of 1776* (1855), 97–105, and Henry C. Riely, "Paul Carrington," *Virginia State Bar Association Proceedings* (1927), 450–464; Alice Read, *The Reads and Their Relatives* (1930), 119–122; confusion with namesake son in Grigsby, *The History of the Virginia Federal Convention of 1788* (1890–1891), 2:369–370, repeated in several other accounts; Carrington Family Papers, LVA and VHS; Lunenburg Co. Index to Marriage Bonds (1755); Halifax Co. Marriage Bonds Register, 1:25 (1792); *Richmond Virginia Gazette, and General Advertiser*, 4 Apr. 1792; Alfred J. Morrison, *The College of Hampden-Sydney: Calendar of Board Minutes, 1776–1876* (1912), 171; Herbert Clarence Bradshaw, *History of Hampden-Sydney College*, vol. 1: *From the Beginnings to the Year 1856* (1976), por. plate xiv; Timothy S. Ailsworth et al., *Charlotte County, Rich Indeed: A History from Prehistoric Times through the Civil War* (1979), 279–281; numerous references in *Revolutionary Virginia*, vols. 1–7, and Kaminski, *Ratification*; David John Mays, *Edmund Pendleton, 1721–1803: A Biography* (1952), 2:191, 228, 270, 274, 298–299, 348; Charlotte Co. Will Book, 4:195–196; obituary in *Richmond Enquirer*, 7 July 1818 (with variant death date of 23 June 1818).

JOHN G. DEAL

CARRINGTON, Paul (20 September 1764–8 January 1816), Speaker of the Senate of Virginia and judge of the General Court, was born at Mulberry Hill, the Charlotte County estate of his parents, Paul Carrington (1733–1818) and his first wife, Margaret Read Carrington. His father was a delegate to the Conventions of 1776 and 1788 and a judge of the General Court and of the Virginia Court of Appeals. His uncle Edward Carrington served in the Confederation Congress, and his elder brother George Carrington (1758–1809) was a delegate to the Convention of 1788. Carrington probably entered Hampden-Sydney College in 1776, but according to family tradition he left while still a teenager in order to fight in the Revolutionary War. He saw action at the battles of Guilford Court House in March 1781 and of Green Spring, in James City County, in July of that year. After the war he studied at the College of William and Mary, from which he graduated in 1783. In Halifax County on 24 August 1786 Carrington married Mildred Howell Coles, whose uncle Isaac Coles was a member of the Convention of 1788 and of the House of Representatives. They had five sons and two daughters.

Carrington represented Charlotte County in the House of Delegates during the 1786–1787 and 1787–1788 assemblies. He served on the Committees of Propositions and Grievances and of Courts of Justice. He was elected to represent Charlotte, Halifax, and Prince Edward Counties in the Senate of Virginia for the four-year term beginning in 1791. Carrington chaired a committee to revise the rules and orders of the Senate in 1791 and the following year was ranking member of a committee to examine enrolled bills. During the 1793 session he served on the Committee of Privileges and Elections and a committee to examine the treasurer's accounts. On 13 November 1794 Carrington was elected Speaker of the Senate. He resigned on 18 December of that year in order to accept an appointment to the General Court. Carrington's was the shortest tenure of any Speaker of the Senate of Virginia.

As a judge of the General Court, Carrington presided at trials in Charlotte and surrounding counties and heard appeals from county courts. He also met from time to time in Richmond with other members of the court to hear appeals in criminal cases, the General Court being then the only court with appellate jurisdiction in such instances. In February 1808 the General Assembly established twelve Superior Courts of Law to relieve the congestion of the General Court in the adjudication of common-law actions. Each court was presided over by a judge of the General Court who held sessions twice a year in each county of the district. These courts were often referred to as circuit courts. Carrington was probably assigned to the Third District comprising the counties of Bedford, Campbell, Charlotte, Franklin, Halifax, Henry, Patrick, and Pittsylvania. In 1809 the legislature added another district consisting of Charlotte, Franklin, Halifax, Henry, Mecklenburg, Patrick, and Pittsylvania Counties. Carrington was reassigned to this Sixth District, which first met in April 1809. He served as judge for both the Superior Court and General Court until his death.

Like his father, Carrington was a trustee of Hampden-Sydney College and served on its board from 1803 until at least 1814 and probably until his death. He owned nearly 1,500 acres of land and at the time he died possessed more than seventy slaves and a library of 327 volumes. After a month-long illness Paul Carrington died at his Sylvan Hill estate in Charlotte County on 8 January 1816. His widow died on 24 April 1840. Both are buried at Berry Hill, in Halifax County.

Birth date from Paul Carrington family Bible as recorded in Agnes Gamble Carrington Marshall, comp., genealogical notes on the Carrington family (1861), VHS, and on gravestone; Manarin, *Senate Officers*, 24–25 (por.); Alice Read, *The Reads and Their Relatives* (1930), 240–242; incorrect identification as member of the Convention of 1788 in Hugh Blair Grigsby, *The History of the Virginia Federal Convention of 1788* (1890–1891), 2:369–370, repeated in many later accounts of Carrington and of the convention; Carrington Family Papers, LVA and VHS; Halifax Co. Marriage Bonds Register, 1:10; Alfred J. Morrison, *The College of*

Hampden-Sidney: Calendar of Board Minutes, 1776–1876 (1912), 175; Herbert Clarence Bradshaw, *History of Hampden-Sydney College*, vol. 1: *From the Beginnings to the Year 1856* (1976), 105; Timothy S. Ailsworth et al., *Charlotte County, Rich Indeed: A History from Prehistoric Times through the Civil War* (1979), 281–284, 422, 453; will and estate inventory in Charlotte Co. Will Book, 4:52, 62–65; obituary in *Richmond Enquirer*, 23 Jan. 1816.

JOHN G. DEAL

CARROLL, Daniel Lynn (10 May 1797–23 November 1851), president of Hampden-Sydney College, was born in Fayette County, Pennsylvania, and was the son of William Carroll and Mary Lynn Carroll, both natives of Ireland. He grew up on his father's farm and received a sporadic education that stimulated his intellectual curiosity. His father had been raised a Catholic and his mother a Presbyterian; and when Carroll was about twenty years old, he joined the Presbyterian Church. From an early age he contemplated a career in the ministry. His advanced education delayed by the need to assist his family in economic hard times, Carroll worked on a farm and in an iron factory and taught school to help support his parents and siblings. He enrolled in the preparatory department at Jefferson College (later Washington and Jefferson College), was admitted to the freshman class after eight months, and graduated in 1823, having completed two years of study simultaneously.

In the spring of 1824 D. L. Carroll, as he was usually known as an adult, entered the Princeton Theological Seminary, where he remained three and a half years. He married Anna Turk Halstead, of New York, on 25 September 1827. They had three daughters and three sons. As he was nearing the completion of his studies that same year, he followed the recommendation of his mentor, Archibald Alexander, and accepted a position as minister of a church in Newburyport, Massachusetts. Carroll found the climate so intolerable that he resigned after preaching only two services. He was then called to serve in a Congregational church in Litchfield, Connecticut, where he was ordained and installed as minister in October 1827. Finding the climate there also difficult to bear, he was forced to flee New England during the winters and eventually resigned on 4 March 1829. Carroll then accepted the pulpit of the First Presbyterian Church in Brooklyn, New York, where he remained until the summer of 1835, when an illness of the throat forced him to resign. While in New York, Carroll received a doctorate of divinity from New York University.

A former Connecticut colleague, Benjamin Franklin Stanton, who was a member of the Hampden-Sydney College board of trustees and pastor of the College Church, proposed in June 1835 that Carroll be appointed to the vacant presidency of the college. After seeking advice from Alexander, himself a former president of Hampden-Sydney, Carroll accepted the office. He was inaugurated at the autumn commencement on 25 September 1835. Carroll's address on that occasion was an eloquent exposition of his views on education, particularly as they applied to Hampden-Sydney. He was a powerfully emotive speaker whose careful preparation and substantive lectures were popular and effective. The board had Carroll's inaugural address printed as a pamphlet, which received favorable notice in the December 1835 issue of the *Southern Literary Messenger*. While he resided in Virginia two other of his public orations also appeared in print, his sermon on the role of clergymen, delivered at an 1835 ordination ceremony, and his 1838 lecture on literature to the Franklin Literary Society of Randolph-Macon College.

Carroll was an effective administrator and popular instructor. His fashionable appearance, elegant taste, urbane manner, and good humor helped him maintain his popularity with the students even as he dealt with an outbreak of gambling, but a revival took place on the campus during his presidency, too. Among the students on whom he made a lasting positive impression was Robert Lewis Dabney, who became one of the most prominent southern Presbyterians of the nineteenth century. Hampden-Sydney was still a small college when Carroll was president, and its financial condition was precarious. An appeal that he and the board made to the General Assembly for public assistance failed to produce an appropriation. During Carroll's administration the college in 1837 established a medical school in Richmond that in 1854 separated from Hampden-Sydney and became the Medical College of Virginia.

In 1837 a group of strict Calvinists who defended the Westminster Confession of Faith produced a rupture in the Presbyterian Church. Led by George Addison Baxter, president of the neighboring Union Theological Seminary and acting president of Hampden-Sydney for one term before Carroll's arrival, they expelled adherents of the so-called New School theology of modified Calvinism taught by Nathaniel William Taylor, of New Haven, Connecticut. Many leading Virginia Presbyterians and members of the Hampden-Sydney board were Old School Presbyterians, but Carroll supported the New School theology. Consequently, late in September 1838 Carroll resigned effective at the end of the academic session. His departure was evidently amicable.

Carroll moved back to Pennsylvania and was pastor of the First Presbyterian Church of the Northern Liberties in Philadelphia from 1838 until February 1844, when for health reasons he resigned. From then until his retirement in November 1845 he was corresponding secretary for the New York State Colonization Society. Carroll resided for the remainder of his life in Philadelphia and Newark, Delaware, and spent his winters in the milder clime of Savannah, Georgia. He published two volumes of his sermons, one in 1846 and the other in 1847, both mistakenly issued under the name David L. Carroll. One of his lectures on the slave trade from the first volume received favorable comment from the *African Repository, and Colonial Journal*, which reprinted it in November 1846.

On 23 November 1851 Daniel Lynn Carroll died at his home in Philadelphia. Following funeral services there and in his former church in Brooklyn, he was buried in Brooklyn's Green-Wood Cemetery.

Biography, including birth and marriage dates from information family and friends provided, in Sprague, *American Pulpit*, 4:697–705; Alfred Nevin, *Encyclopædia of the Presbyterian Church in the United States of America . . .* (1884), 127; Alfred J. Morrison, *The College of Hampden-Sidney: Calendar of Board Minutes, 1776–1876* (1912), 108–119; Herbert Clarence Bradshaw, *History of Hampden-Sydney College*, vol. 1: *From the Beginnings to the Year 1856* (1976), 210–229, 368–369 (por. plate v); John Luster Brinkley, *On This Hill: A Narrative History of Hampden-Sydney College, 1774–1994* (1994), 143–163; publications include *Inaugural Address of the Rev. D. L. Carroll, D.D., President of Hampden Sydney College, Delivered on His Induction into That Office* (1835), *The Ministerial Office: A Sermon, Delivered before the West Hanover Presbytery, October 25, 1835, at the Ordination of the Rev. B. M. Smith* (1836), *An Address Delivered before the Franklin Literary Society of Randolph Macon College, Virginia, June 19th, 1838* (1838), and reports and letters in *African Repository, and Colonial Journal* 20 (1844): 225–232, ibid. 21 (1845): 84–85, 242–246; his *Sermons and Addresses on Various Subjects* (1846), and a second series, *Sermons and Addresses on Various Subjects* (1847), both appeared under the name David L. Carroll.

CHRISTIAN HIGGINS

CARROLL, John Wesley (3 March 1832–9 February 1898), tobacco manufacturer, was born in Staunton. His parents, Jacob S. Carroll and Isabella Layman Carroll, died before he was seven years old, and he was raised by relatives in Augusta County. Late in the 1840s he moved to Lynchburg and received training as a cabinet-maker in the shop of Folkes and Winston. In 1850 Carroll became the business partner of the Lynchburg tobacco manufacturer William Crumpton and that same year, on 29 October, married Crumpton's daughter, Sarah Elizabeth Crumpton. They had three sons and four daughters before her death on 5 June 1877. On 31 July 1878 Carroll married Sarah Frances Adams, with whom he had two sons and one daughter.

In 1859 Carroll opened his own factory for the manufacture of smoking tobacco and in his first year of operation produced a modest amount of products worth $36,500. He soon became known for his Lone Jack tobacco brand, a name purportedly derived from his victory in a card game with a single jack in his hand but that was more likely based on his childhood nickname and the fact that he was orphaned. Carroll continued production during the Civil War, and his was among the best-quality smoking tobacco manufactured in the immediate postwar years. In 1867 Carroll purchased the former Crumpton factory and nearly doubled his output. After his factory burned the following year, he rebuilt on a larger scale. He distributed his products across much of the United States and exported them to Africa, Asia, Europe, and South America. Carroll's success during this period may have partially resulted from collusion with federal revenue agents, who possibly allowed him to pay taxes on his tobacco after it was sold rather than when it was manufactured or else to avoid the tax entirely. He remained in the tobacco business until his death, although the popularity of his smoking tobacco declined after the 1870s. In 1879 Carroll began to experiment with producing cigarettes, but his focus remained on loose smoking tobacco. In 1883 some Lynchburg tobacconists created the short-lived Lone Jack Cigarette Company, of which Carroll was a principal stockholder. Lone Jack was one of the earliest cigarette manufacturers to employ James Albert Bonsack's innovative cigarette-rolling machine, but the company did not survive more than a few years.

In addition to his tobacco interests, Carroll participated in a variety of other Lynchburg business and commercial real estate ventures. In February 1887 he invested $10,000 as a special partner in Aunspaugh and Cobbs, a dry goods emporium, and from 1893 until his death he was president of and the largest stockholder in the Hotel Carroll, on Main Street. His extensive commercial real estate holdings in Lynchburg alone were valued at $180,000 at the time of his death, and his expansive estate required his administrators to post a then-record $1 million bond after he died intestate. By 1875 Carroll was serving on the board of managers for the Mutual Building Fund Association of Lynchburg, during the 1870s and 1880s he was a director of the Lynchburg National Bank, and in 1890 he was a founding director of the Lynchburg Trust Company (later the Lynchburg Trust and Savings Bank). In 1882 he was a founding director of the Lynchburg Foundry and Machine Company, which later became the Glamorgan Company, a manufacturer of Bonsack's cigarette-rolling machine. He was the founding vice president of the Lynchburg Ice and Refrigerator Company in 1885. Carroll also served on the board of directors for the Lynchburg Female Orphan Asylum (sometimes designated the Miller Female Orphan Asylum) from May 1875 until his death.

Active in civic affairs, Carroll was elected in April 1864 to the Lynchburg city council. Chosen council president on 1 July 1871 by a margin of only one vote, he served continuously in that office until his retirement on 1 July 1895 and reportedly missed only two meetings. During his long tenure Lynchburg greatly expanded its city services by constructing public schools, creating a street railway system, improving the public water system, and providing electricity for streetlights to meet the demands of the city's growing population, which nearly tripled from 6,853 inhabitants in 1860 to 19,709 in 1890.

John Wesley Carroll suffered a stroke about 1895, and his health declined steadily until his death in Lynchburg on 9 February 1898. He was buried in Presbyterian Cemetery in that city. Three months later the city council appropriated funds to commission a portrait of its longtime president.

NCAB, 10:483–484 (por.); biographies in Rosa Faulkner Yancey, *Lynchburg and Its Neighbors* (1935), 282–283, and Samuel H. Williams, *A Brief History of Miller Home, Lynchburg Female Orphan Asylum, Lynchburg, Virginia* (1964), 64; Lynchburg Marriage Register (1850, 1878); Nannie May Tilley, *The Bright-Tobacco Industry: 1860–1929* (1948), 306, 509, 526–527, 538, 542, 606, 634; Philip Lightfoot Scruggs, *Lynchburg, Virginia: " . . . Its Industry, Enterprise and Correct Course"* (1972), 140–141, 170; *Sketchbook of Lynchburg: A Story as Told in 1887* (1987), 46, 125–128; Lynchburg City Council Minutes, 1864–1895, 1898; por. by Flavius Fisher, Lynchburg Museum System; estate settlement in *Lynchburg News*, 18 Feb. 1898; obituary and editorial tribute in *Lynchburg News*, 10 Feb. 1898.

MARIANNE E. JULIENNE

CARSON, James Marsh (22 March 1910–1 June 1987), president of Richard Bland College, was the son of William Dukes Carson and Harriett Eleanor DeVeaux Carson. Born on the family farm outside Sumter, South Carolina, he graduated from high school in nearby Summerton, in Clarendon County, in 1928, and from the Citadel, with a major in chemistry, in 1932. Carson supervised public schools in Oswego, Sumter County, and in Pamplico, Florence County, South Carolina, from 1932 to 1935 and taught science at a Sumter high school from 1937 to 1939. In the two-year interim he directed educational programs at Civilian Conservation Corps camps in Georgia and South Carolina and in 1939 rejoined the CCC as an administrator.

Carson married a teacher, Susan Elizabeth Thomas, on 23 June 1936. They had one son and one daughter. Carson enrolled in the Medical College of the State of South Carolina (later the Medical University of South Carolina) for the

1940–1941 academic year, but he was at the same time a lieutenant in the army reserves and was called to active duty in January 1941 and deployed to Schofield Barracks in Hawaii. During the Japanese attack on Pearl Harbor, he commanded an antiaircraft battery. Carson served in staff positions and in the field in the Pacific theater until July 1943, when he returned to the United States. He was an instructor and executive officer during the remaining years of World War II and rose to the rank of major. Taken into the regular army in 1947, he studied psychology and guidance at the University of South Carolina that same year and graduated with a master's degree in education. For almost a decade after the war ended Carson attended and also taught at the School of Military Government for Far Eastern Civil Affairs at the University of Virginia, the Command and General Staff College, the Strategic Intelligence School, and the Anti-Aircraft Artillery School. He was serving at Douglas MacArthur's general headquarters in Tokyo at the outbreak of the Korean War and received the Bronze Star for his work as an intelligence officer during that conflict. From January 1952 to August 1953 Carson commanded the mobile 507th Antiaircraft Artillery Automatic Weapons Battalion.

Carson then returned to the United States and became chief of the Human Research Division, Continental Army Command, at Fort Monroe in Virginia. From 1955 to 1959 he taught military science and tactics at the College of William and Mary, during which time enrollment in the Reserve Officers' Training Corps, under his command, almost doubled. From July 1959 through August 1960 he served in Korea with the United Nations Command and was promoted to colonel on 1 December 1959. In 1960 Carson was an adviser to the Virginia Army National Guard. He retired from the army on 31 May 1961.

That same year, Alvin Duke Chandler, chancellor of the College of William and Mary, persuaded Carson to become the director of Richard Bland College, a new junior college affiliated with William and Mary and located at the site of the old Petersburg Training School and Hospital. Carson personally hired the campus staff and the first faculty members, and he interviewed and accepted the first students. A firm believer

in higher education and a capable administrator after his years in the army, he was an effective advocate for the college and often addressed civic, educational, or social groups to engage regional support for the junior college and ensure its success. During its first twelve years the college's faculty more than tripled, enrollment grew from 265 day and evening students to more than 900, and about 5,000 students graduated from its classes.

Richard Bland College's curriculum offered classes in many fields, including adult education courses. The college also hosted a cultural center for the community. Carson had an open-door policy and personally advised many student organizations. He worked with legislators to secure funding for construction of new educational buildings and a student center and for renovation of the buildings in which the first college classes had been held. Carson's title became president on 1 July 1969, and with the support of the board of William and Mary, he moved toward his goal of establishing a technical education program and expanding the college into a four-year institution by 1973. The opening of nearby John Tyler Community College, which satisfied some of the local demand for technical education, and an adverse court decision in 1971 halted the proposed expansion. Deeply disappointed, Carson retired on 31 August 1973.

Carson spent his retirement in Williamsburg, where he was an active member of retired officers' associations, Bruton Parish Church, the Rotary Club, and the Hospice. He also served as president of the local Meals on Wheels and as a director of the Colonial Capital Branch of the Association for the Preservation of Virginia Antiquities. James Marsh Carson died of congestive heart failure in a Williamsburg hospital on 1 June 1987 and was buried in Arlington National Cemetery.

Carson family Bible records (with birth and marriage dates) and personal and professional records provided by son, James Marsh Carson Jr. (2003); *The Flat Hat*, 19 May 1959; *Richmond News Leader*, 1 June 1961, 17 Oct. 1972; *Petersburg Southside Virginia News*, 8 June, 16 Nov. 1961; *Petersburg Progress-Index*, 21 Mar. 1965, 7 Feb. 1966, 7 Nov. 1969, 19 Feb. 1970, 20 Sept. 1972; *Hopewell News*, 21 Oct. 1969, 21 Sept. 1972; *Richmond Times-Dispatch*, 21 Sept. 1972; interview with Donald J. Herrman, 16 Aug. 1976, Oral History

Collection, W&M; bound volume of college clippings and publicity, Richard Bland College Library; other information about early Richard Bland College career provided by James B. McNeer (2003); Susan H. Godson et al., *The College of William and Mary: A History* (1993), 2:798, 817–818, 852; obituaries in *Hopewell News*, *Petersburg Progress-Index* (por.), *Richmond News Leader*, *Richmond Times-Dispatch* (por.), *Williamsburg Virginia Gazette*, all 3 June 1987, and *William and Mary News*, 17 June 1987.

VIRGINIA ROSE CHERRY

CARSON, Jane Dennison (29 August 1909–9 November 1984), historian, was born in Marion into a staunchly Presbyterian family that highly valued education. Her parents, Sanford James Carson, a druggist, and Juliett Estelle Guy Carson, named her for her paternal grandmother. Carson's father moved several times while she was a child. The family was living in Farmville when her mother died of tuberculosis on 29 November 1920. A year later her father married Margaret E. Erwin in Charlottesville. Where the Carsons lived after 1921 is unknown, but her father had either died or left Virginia by the time the 1930 census was taken.

Because of the frequent moves, it is not certain where Carson attended elementary or high school, but in 1930 she received a B.A. from Flora MacDonald College, in Red Springs, North Carolina, a Presbyterian school for women that was later absorbed into Saint Andrews Presbyterian College, in Laurinburg. After graduating, she taught for several years in rural Virginia public schools, beginning in the autumn of 1931 at a two-room school in Charlotte County, where she taught fourth, fifth, and sixth grades. Carson later shared stories of her experiences as a country schoolteacher with her friend and colleague Burke Davis, who used her as the model for the character Cassie Carson in his 1965 novel *The Summer Land*.

In the mid-1930s Carson enrolled in graduate school at the University of Virginia and received a master's degree in history in 1937 after completing a thesis on William Beverley, a member of the colonial governor's Council. Carson continued her graduate work at the university with Thomas Perkins Abernethy, a prominent historian of the American South. While writing her dissertation, the first in-depth scholarly study of Virginia's most important seven-

teenth-century governor, Sir William Berkeley, Carson served as a history instructor at Mitchell College (later Mitchell Community College) in Statesville, North Carolina, and from 1947 to 1950 at H. Sophie Newcomb Memorial College in New Orleans. She also worked for a short time as a manuscripts assistant at the University of Virginia's Alderman Library. On completing her doctorate in 1951, Carson became a fully credentialed historian at a time when the profession was predominantly a male preserve and few women secured permanent academic appointments.

In 1952 Carson began working as an assistant to Lyman Henry Butterfield, director of the Institute of Early American History and Culture at the College of William and Mary. A collaborative endeavor between the college and Colonial Williamsburg, Incorporated (later the Colonial Williamsburg Foundation), the institute had been founded in 1943 to foster research and publication on the history of colonial America. Abernethy was one of its founders and may have recommended Carson for the position. She served as the director's assistant and as a lecturer in history at William and Mary until the end of 1954, when Butterfield left the institute. In February 1955 Carson joined the Research Department of Colonial Williamsburg, which was then expanding its staff and the scope of its research activities. Until the mid-1950s its research program supported the physical restoration of the colonial capital, but the foundation then widened its interests to embrace the cultural, economic, political, social, and religious history of eighteenth-century Virginia in order to provide context for its interpretive programming. Carson remained at Colonial Williamsburg engaged in research and writing for the remainder of her career.

In addition to her continuing interest in colonial politics, Carson immersed herself in such topics of social and cultural history as family life, foodways, colonial visitors' travel accounts and observations, housekeeping, reading habits, games, amusements, music, and dance. The detailed, carefully researched reports that she and her colleagues generated filled gaps in historians' understanding of the eighteenth-century South and anticipated by nearly two decades serious scholarly interest in early Virginia and the Chesapeake region. Desiring to share these research findings with a wider audience, Colonial Williamsburg in the mid-1960s published several of the reports as softcover books, including four of Carson's titles in 1965: *Colonial Virginians at Play*, *James Innes and His Brothers of the F.H.C.*, *Travelers in Tidewater Virginia, 1700–1800: A Bibliography*, and *We Were There: Descriptions of Williamsburg, 1699–1859*. Her *Colonial Virginia Cookery* appeared in 1968. Both it and the popular *Colonial Virginians at Play* were reprinted in the 1980s. Carson also contributed an essay on Innes to *The Old Dominion: Essays for Thomas Perkins Abernethy*, a 1964 festschrift. Long before southern women's history emerged as a field of study, Carson conducted research on such Virginia women as Frances Culpeper Stephens Berkeley, Ann Cary "Nancy" Randolph Morris, and Clementina Rind. Her biographies of Berkeley and Rind appeared in 1971 in the pathbreaking *Notable American Women* series.

Carson became the ultimate authority on historical authenticity to whom everyone at Colonial Williamsburg turned. She also shared her expertise on the colonial period in conversation and correspondence with other scholars and the public, who regularly wrote her seeking information and advice. In 1963 Carson resumed teaching in William and Mary's history department and was a lecturer through the 1974–1975 academic year. She retired from Colonial Williamsburg on 1 September 1974. Thereafter, Carson served as a resident consultant to Colonial Williamsburg and worked on a screenplay about eighteenth-century science, which the foundation released as the film *A Glorious System of Things* (1983). She published in 1976 what one reviewer called a "gem of a book" on Bacon's Rebellion for the Jamestown Foundation and in 1979 a study of Patrick Henry for the Virginia Independence Bicentennial Commission. A few months before her death Carson consulted with the founding editors of the *Dictionary of Virginia Biography* about Virginia women's history.

Diminutive in stature, with sparkling blue eyes, a playful sense of humor, a sharp wit, and a probing intellect, Carson had many close friends in the historical profession and in Williamsburg. Like many other professional women of her generation, she never married. Jane Dennison Carson died in a Richmond hospital on 9 November 1984. A memorial service took place at Williamsburg Presbyterian Church five days later. Her remains were cremated.

Birth date in Social Security application, Social Security Administration, Office of Earnings Operations, Baltimore, Md.; variant birth date of 28 Aug. 1909 on BVS Death Certificate, Richmond City, confirmed by BVS; Carson correspondence in Rockefeller Library, CW, in Williams Family Papers, VHS, and in *DVB* Files; information provided by Thad W. Tate (2004); *Colonial Williamsburg News*, Mar. 1955, July 1962, 18 Sept. 1974; *WMQ*, 3d ser., 35 (1978): 417 (quotation); obituaries in *Richmond News Leader*, 12 Nov. 1984, *Newport News Daily Press*, 13 Nov. 1984, and *Williamsburg Virginia Gazette* (with editorial tribute and por.) and *Norfolk Virginian-Pilot*, both 14 Nov. 1984; memorial in *Colonial Williamsburg* 7 (winter 1985): 15 (por.).

SANDRA GIOIA TREADWAY

CARSON, William (ca. 1774–by 21 January 1856), member of the Council of State, was the son of Jane Carson (maiden name unknown) and Simon Carson, a farmer who had begun by leasing and then purchasing land late in the 1750s in that part of Frederick County that in 1772 became Dunmore County and during the American Revolution changed its name to Shenandoah County. He was born probably on his father's farm near the Shenandoah River. Nothing is known of his education. Carson was a small-scale farmer with modest property holdings and only brief service from 1809 to 1811 on the county court.

In 1811 Carson won election to the House of Delegates. He served on the Committee of Claims and was reelected in 1812 and each of the next two years. During his second term he sat on the Committee to Examine the Executive Expenditures and in his second and third terms on the Committee of Propositions and Grievances. In the special session in the spring of 1813 he was appointed to a select committee to revise "An Act Providing for the Defence of the State Against Invasion or Insurrection." In 1814 Carson won a coveted seat on the Committee of Privileges and Elections, and on 14 November of that year the General Assembly elected him to the Council of State.

Often regarded as a steppingstone for promising young legislators, the Council met regularly in Richmond to advise the governor. Carson did not take his seat until 21 June 1815, thus missing the remaining meetings during the War of 1812. At first he attended regularly, though occasionally taking time off to return home, but after the summer of 1816 his attendance became sporadic and his absences longer, and he often neglected when present even to sign the daily record of the Council's proceedings. On 1 January 1818 Carson asked the General Assembly to replace him when it held its scheduled meeting later that day to remove two members of the Council as required by the state constitution. The assembly agreed, and he attended his last meeting on 8 January of that year.

A dislike for Council service, or perhaps for the prolonged stays it required in Richmond, did not mean that Carson lost interest in politics. He returned to the House of Delegates for the assemblies of 1827–1828, 1828–1829, and 1831–1832, and after his portion of Shenandoah County became Warren County in 1836, he represented it and Clarke County in the 1836–1837 assembly and again in 1839. Either because he had lost status or often arrived too late to be appointed to a choice committee, Carson usually served on one or two relatively inconsequential committees and received significant assignments only in the 1827–1828 and 1828–1829 sessions, when he was a member of the Committee of Propositions and Grievances, and in the 1836–1837 session, when he was a member of the Committee on Agriculture and Manufactures. Carson concluded his legislative career in the Senate of Virginia from the district composed of Hardy, Page, Shenandoah, and Warren Counties for the four-year term beginning in December 1839. An elderly senator with no recognized special legislative interest, he served during the 1839–1840 and 1842–1843 sessions on the Committee of Privileges and Elections, for three years on a joint committee appointed to examine the public armory, and for two years on a joint committee appointed to examine the condition of the state penitentiary.

Carson's private life is not well documented. It is likely that his loss of interest in the Council

resulted from a temporary enlargement of personal responsibilities. The 1820 census records that an adult woman over age forty-five and nine children then resided in his household. In the absence of any record of a marriage or other indication that he had children, it is probable that during the 1810s he had taken in a widowed sister or a relative's widow and children and had discharged his duties to them before he returned to active political life in 1827. Carson was living alone with two slaves when the census enumerator visited him in 1830, and he continued to live on his farm with a few slaves until his death. In 1852 he wrote a short will naming no wife or direct descendants, designating two nephews as his heirs, and emancipating one male slave. William Carson died on an unrecorded date before 21 January 1856, when his will was proved in the Warren County Court. His personal estate, which then included six slaves, was valued at a little more than $5,700.

Parents identified in Shenandoah Co. Will Book, D:461–462, and Shenandoah Co. Deed Book, C:513–514, DD:282–283; Census, Shenandoah Co., 1810, 1820, 1830; Census, Warren Co., 1840, 1850 (giving age as seventy-six on 29 June 1850); Personal Property Tax Returns, Shenandoah Co. (1810–1825), RG 48, LVA; election to and removal from Council in *JHD*, 1814–1815 sess., 68, and *JHD*, 1817–1818 sess., 77, 78; Council service documented in Council of State Journal, 1815–1818, RG 75, LVA; will, estate inventory, and estate sale in Warren Co. Will Book, C:1, 12–15.

BRENT TARTER

CARSON, William Edward (8 October 1870–25 March 1942), chair of the State Commission on Conservation and Development, was born in Enniskillen, Ireland (later Northern Ireland), and was the son of Samuel Carson and Anne Lougheed Carson. By 1870 his father had purchased land in Warren County, where he later founded a lime-manufacturing business that was chartered in 1891 as Carson Lime Company. In October 1885 young Carson and two of his brothers joined their father and older siblings in Virginia at Riverton, near Front Royal. Ten years later he became general manager of a successor manufacturing operation, incorporated in 1904 as the Riverton Lime Company.

Carson lived with his father and stepmother, Sarah H. Carson, until 1905, when he built an elaborate Queen Anne–style house that he called Killahevlin (listed in 1993 on the Virginia Landmarks Register and the National Register of Historic Places) in anticipation of his marriage to Agnes Holladay McCarthy, of Richmond. They were married in the Seventh Street Christian Church in Richmond on 9 May 1906. Two of Carson's attendants reveal how effectively he had established connections with the upper echelons of Virginia's political leadership. His best man was the Winchester attorney Richard Evelyn Byrd (1860–1925), who two years later became Speaker of the House of Delegates, and one of the groomsmen was Byrd's brother-in-law, Congressman Henry DeLaWarr Flood. The Carsons lived in Riverton and had one son and two daughters.

From 1908 to 1919 Carson was chairman of the board of directors of the National Lime Manufacturers Association (after its merger late in 1918 with the Hydrated Lime Bureau renamed the National Lime Association) and in 1919 was elected to one term as the association's president. From 1923 to 1926 he served on the Hampton Roads Port Commission. Active also in politics, Carson chaired the Seventh District Democratic Committee from 1910 until 1940. In 1925 he managed the successful gubernatorial campaign of Harry Flood Byrd (1887–1966). The following year Byrd named Carson chair of the State Commission on Conservation and Development, which was established in March 1926 and which consolidated the state Water Power and Development Commission and the commonwealth's geological and forestry offices. The commission oversaw the state's promotion of natural resources for economic growth and had broad powers to condemn private land to create public parks. Continuing to live in Riverton, Carson directed the work of the commission's component parts from home.

He and Byrd believed that historic and natural resources were keys to developing a flourishing tourism industry in Virginia. One of Carson's innovative and enduring programs was the placement of markers at historic sites along the state's highways, perhaps the first such program in the country. The centerpiece of his vision was to acquire land at minimum state cost for the proposed Shenandoah National Park. He and his brother, Adam Clarke "Kit" Carson, drafted the bill that the General Assembly enacted in 1928 to permit the commission to condemn private property for the park. Late in the following year Carson purchased the fishing rights to more than 10,000 acres along the Rapidan River in Madison County, within the proposed park boundary, and then convinced Herbert Hoover to use the site as a presidential fishing retreat. Two years later Carson persuaded the president and Congress to appropriate money to begin construction of Skyline Drive, fully five years before the dedication of Shenandoah National Park.

Carson took leading roles in the creation of the Colonial National Monument (after June 1936 Colonial National Historical Park), linking the historic sites of Jamestown, Williamsburg, and Yorktown, and in the transfer to the National Park Service of Richmond Battlefield Park (after 1934 Richmond National Battlefield Park). He arranged in 1938 for the Civilian Conservation Corps to develop the Front Royal Recreation Park (later the Front Royal Country Club) on land Carson and his wife donated in memory of his namesake son who had died early in 1925. While Carson was chair, the commission created Virginia's state park system, which initially comprised six parks: Douthat, in Alleghany and Bath Counties; Fairy Stone, in Patrick County; Hungry Mother, in Smyth County; Seashore (later First Landing), in Princess Anne County; Staunton River, in Halifax County; and Westmoreland, in the county of that name. The Civilian Conservation Corps did most of the work, and the federal government paid most of the bills. From 1935 until 1940 Carson was a vice president of the National Conference on State Parks.

In 1932 Governor John Garland Pollard proclaimed Carson the outstanding public servant in the state, and the New York Southern Society awarded him its Parchment of Distinction, an honor he shared that year with Douglas Southall Freeman and John D. Rockefeller Jr. The American Scenic and Historic Preservation Society of New York presented Carson the Honorable Cornelius Amory Pugsley Silver Medal in 1935 for his work establishing parks and commemorating historic sites. In 1941 his achievements in Virginia earned Carson his own historic marker, placed in Front Royal, and in 1948 a peak in Shenandoah National Park was named for him.

Carson's authoritative management style alienated some state Democratic Party leaders. In 1934, after the General Assembly converted the commission chair from a part-time advisory role to a fulltime professional position, Carson announced that his personal business interests as president of Riverton Lime Company (after 1935 Riverton Lime and Stone) required him to relinquish the chairmanship. In 1936 the British Scientific and Industrial Research Society elected him a fellow in recognition of his contributions to lime and mortar technology. William Edward Carson died at Killahevlin in Riverton on 25 March 1942 and was buried in the Carson family plot in Prospect Hill Cemetery in Front Royal.

Biographies in Winfield Scott Downs, ed., *Encyclopedia of American Biography*, new ser. (1943), 202–205, and National Conference on State Parks, *25th Anniversary Yearbook: Park and Recreation Progress* (1946), 24–25 (por.); BVS Marriage Register, Richmond City; *Richmond Times-Dispatch*, 10 May 1906, 10 Dec. 1932, 4 Jan. 1934, 22 Sept. 1941; *Richmond News Leader*, 4 Oct. 1932, 13 Mar. 1935; William E. Carson Scrapbooks, Acc. 30463, LVA; Carson letters in Herbert Hoover Presidential Library–Museum, West Branch, Iowa, in Henry D. Flood Papers, LC, in E. Griffith Dodson Papers, Acc. 25244, State Commission on Conservation and Development Records, RG 18, and Harry Flood Byrd, John Garland Pollard, and George Campbell Peery Executive Papers, all RG 3, LVA, in Civilian Conservation Corps Collection and Ferdinand L. Zerkel Collection, both Shenandoah National Park Archives, Luray, and in Harry Flood Byrd (1887–1966) Papers, UVA; works include Carson, *Conserving and Developing Virginia* (1935); Dennis Elwood Simmons, "The Creation of Shenandoah National Park and the Skyline Drive, 1924–1936" (Ph.D. diss., UVA, 1978); John F. Horan Jr., "Will Carson and the Virginia Conservation Commission, 1926–1934," *VMHB* 92 (1984): 391–415; Darwin Lambert, *The Undying Past of Shenandoah National Park* (1989), 209–226, 237, 254; obituaries in *New York Times, Richmond News Leader, Richmond Times-Dispatch*, and *Winchester Evening Star*, all 26 Mar. 1942, *Front Royal Warren Sentinel*, 2 Apr. 1942 (por.), and *Planning and Civic Comment* 8 (Apr. 1942): 51; editorial tributes in *Richmond News Leader*, 26 Mar. 1942, and *Richmond Times-Dispatch*, 27 Mar. 1942.

REED L. ENGLE

CARTER, Alvin Pleasant Delaney (15 December 1891–7 November 1960), song collector and musician, was born in a log cabin near Maces

Spring, in Scott County. The eldest of the eight children of Robert C. Carter, a farmer, and Mollie Arvella Bays Carter, he was a dreamer who found himself out of step with life in the Southwest Virginia mountains. A. P. Carter was a restless man who seldom stayed focused on tasks long enough to see them through to completion. Family members described him as nervous, a condition that manifested itself in trembling hands and a quavering voice. His formal education was meager. Lacking the instincts and passions of a farmer, Carter worked as a carpenter and as a traveling fruit-tree salesman. In 1911 he went to Richmond, Indiana, where he was briefly a carpenter for a railroad company. Later he spent six months in Detroit, Michigan, seeking work in the building industry. At various times Carter operated his own sawmill and gristmill and ran a grocery store.

Although Carter had little interest in farming and failed to achieve prosperity in his other career endeavors, music captured his attention and brought him success, not in terms of financial wealth, but in the form of enduring fame and immutable respect. Both of Carter's parents came from musical families. His father was a fiddler and his mother a singer of hymns and ballads that had been handed down through her family. As a youth Carter learned to play the jew's harp, guitar, and fiddle, despite his mother's aversion to the last instrument, to which she objected on religious grounds. Although his achievements as an instrumentalist were unremarkable, Carter's bass voice earned him early credibility as a musician. In singing schools held from time to time in the community he learned the seven-shape-note singing method that evolved in western Virginia after the Civil War, rather than the traditional four-note system found in popular prewar songbooks such as *Sacred Harp*, and had lessons in composition, harmony, voice, sight-reading, and rhythm. Carter also attended the singing schools of his uncle Flanders Bays, a well-known singing-school teacher who traveled a wide circuit in southwestern Virginia. An astute pupil who soon mastered the basics of music, Carter, when time allowed, assisted his uncle in conducting the singing schools in churches, schools, and other gathering places.

While on one of his tree-selling excursions in 1914 Carter heard Sara Elizabeth Dougherty playing an autoharp and singing the disaster ballad "Engine 143." They married in Scott County on 18 June 1915, set up housekeeping in a two-room cabin that Carter built with the help of his family and neighbors, and by 1919 had moved to Maces Spring. They had two daughters and one son. From the beginning the new Carter household was filled with music, as the husband and wife sang together to the accompaniment of his fiddle and guitar and her autoharp. Sara Carter joined the church choir of which her husband had long been a member, and occasionally the two of them performed together before audiences. In 1926, out of respect for his mother's religious convictions regarding fiddle playing, Carter rejected an offer from the Brunswick-Balke-Collender Company, which wanted to record the Carters' square dance tunes and bill the act as "Fiddlin' Doc."

In March 1926 Carter's brother, Ezra J. "Eck" Carter, married Maybelle Addington, who was Sara Dougherty Carter's first cousin. Maybelle Carter began playing guitar and singing tenor harmony with her cousin and brother-in-law, with Sara Carter singing lead and playing the autoharp and A. P. Carter singing bass. The group attracted considerable local attention and soon was in demand for performances at various community socials.

Undaunted by bad roads and a flat-tire-prone automobile, the three Carters made their way to Bristol, on the Virginia-Tennessee border, in July 1927 to audition for the Victor Talking Machine Company and on 1 August impressed the scout, Ralph Sylvester Peer, with their performances. The Carters recorded "Bury Me under the Weeping Willow," "Little Log Cabin by the Sea," "Poor Orphan Child," and "The Storms Are on the Ocean" in Peer's makeshift studio and returned the next morning to record two additional songs, "Single Girl, Married Girl" and "The Wandering Boy." These Bristol recording sessions proved to be a watershed event in the history of country music and launched the career of the Carter Family, one of the most important acts in that genre of American popular music.

For the next sixteen years, Carter devoted his energies to the music of the Carter Family. He collected, composed, arranged, and rehearsed songs for the group's recording sessions. He negotiated contracts with record companies and sought to keep the Carter Family music before the public through radio and personal appearances. Carter was an indefatigable song hunter, and the original Carter Family recorded almost 300 releases on a variety of labels for the Victor Talking Machine Company (later RCA Victor Records), American Record Corporation, and Decca Records. The repertoire, arranged to fit the Carter Family style, included hymns, spirituals, blues, ballads of British origin, nineteenth-century popular songs, occupational songs, and an occasional novelty tune. Carter assiduously canvassed ephemeral publications, old-timers living in neighboring hills and valleys, shape-note hymnals, black musicians such as the blues player Lesley Riddle, and sheet music in his search for material for the Carter Family and supplemented the songs obtained from external sources with his own original compositions. Among the Carter Family's memorable songs are "Can the Circle Be Unbroken," "I'm Thinking Tonight of My Blue Eyes," "Keep on the Sunny Side," "Wabash Cannonball," and "Wildwood Flower."

Carter's frequent absences collecting songs put strains on his marriage, and by 1932 Sara Carter had begun an affair with his first cousin, Coy W. Bays (later Bayes). Early in 1933 Carter and his wife separated, and on 15 October 1936 they divorced. Their three children remained with A. P. Carter. Despite this family schism, Carter and his former wife continued to perform together, even after her remarriage in 1939, and the group later expanded to include one of Carter's children and Maybelle Carter's three daughters. The Carter Family, through their phonograph records, became well-known among country music aficionados in the United States. Their music began to reach a much wider audience by the winter of 1937–1938, when the group started broadcasting regularly over several powerful Mexican border stations. Not bound by the 50,000-watt power restriction imposed by the government on radio stations in the United States, such border stations as XEG and XERA reached much of North America with a signal that often exceeded 500,000 watts. The Carter Family received other significant radio exposure over WBT in Charlotte, North Carolina, where they were heard from the autumn of 1942 to the spring of 1943. When the contract with WBT expired in March 1943, the original Carter Family disbanded. They had made their last recordings on 14 October 1941 in RCA Victor's New York studio.

Carter spent the last years of his life in Maces Spring, where he operated a country store (after his death the museum of the Carter Family Memorial Music Center, Incorporated). Between 1952 and 1956 he, his former wife, and their children Janette Carter and Joe Carter recorded occasionally as the Carter Family or the A. P. Carter Family for Acme Records, a minor independent recording company headquartered in Tennessee. He received a citation of achievement from the performing-rights organization BMI in 1959 for his arrangement of the Victorian parlor song "Jimmie Brown, the Newsboy," recorded by Lester Flatt, Earl Scruggs, and the Foggy Mountain Boys. Alvin Pleasant Delaney Carter died in Kingsport, Tennessee, on 7 November 1960 and was buried in Mount Vernon United Methodist Church Cemetery in Maces Spring. In 1970 the original Carter Family was the first musical group inducted into the Country Music Hall of Fame in Nashville, and that same year A. P. Carter was inducted into the Nashville Songwriters Hall of Fame. The National Academy of Recording Arts and Sciences recognized the Carter Family's 1935 Banner label recording of "Can the Circle Be Unbroken (Bye and Bye)" and 1928 RCA Victor recording of "Wildwood Flower" as enduring works of historical significance with Grammy Hall of Fame Awards in 1998 and 1999, respectively. The recordings that the group made in 1927 were still being reissued in the twenty-first century, and professional entertainers acknowledging a debt to the influence of Carter Family music have become legion.

Scott Co. Birth Register (name recorded as Pleasant Alvin Carter); BVS Marriage Register, Scott Co. (variant marriage date of 20 June 1915); divorce confirmed by BVS (marriage date of 18 June 1915 on judgment of divorce); Archie Green, "The Carter Family's 'Coal Miner's Blues,'" *Southern Folklore Quarterly* 25 (1961): 226–237; John Atkins et al., eds., *The Carter Family*, Old Time Music Booklet 1 (1973); Atkins, "The Carter Family," in Bill C. Malone and Judith McCulloh, eds., *Stars of Country Music: Uncle Dave Macon to Johnny Rodriguez* (1975), 95–120; June Carter Cash, *Among My Klediments* (1979); Mark Dawidziak, "It All Began in Bristol," *Commonwealth* 48 (Feb. 1981): 17–23; Irwin Stambler and Grelun Landon, *The Encyclopedia of Folk, Country and Western Music*, 2d ed. (1983), 94–97; Janette Carter, *Living with Memories* (1983); Ed Kahn, "The Carter Family on Border Radio," *American Music* 14 (1996): 205–217; Wayne W. Daniel, "The Legacy of A. P. Carter: A Famous Singer, Arranger, and Song Preserver Who Might Have Been a Famous Fiddler," *The Devil's Box* 31 (summer 1997): 24–28; John Rice Irwin, *A People and Their Music: The Story Behind the Story of Country Music* (2000), 20–59; Charles Wolfe, "Jake and Doc and May: The Carter Family Goes to the End of the World," *Bluegrass Unlimited* 34 (Feb. 2000): 22–27; Mark Zwonitzer with Charles Hirshberg, *Will You Miss Me When I'm Gone? The Carter Family and Their Legacy in American Music* (2002), pors.; Katie Doman, "Something Old, Something New: The Carter Family's Bristol Session Recordings," and Gladys Carter Millard, "I Remember Daddy," in Charles K. Wolfe and Ted Olson, eds., *The Bristol Sessions: Writing about the Big Bang of Country Music* (2005), 66–86, 172–182; original Carter Family discography in Kip Lornell, *Virginia's Blues, Country, and Gospel Records, 1902–1943: An Annotated Discography* (1989), 35–58; *The Carter Family on Border Radio*, John Edwards Memorial Foundation 101 (n.d.), recording with brochure notes by Archie Green, William H. Koon, and Norm Cohen; *The Carter Family: In the Shadow of Clinch Mountain*, Bear Family Records 15865 (2000), including discography by Tony Russell and Richard Weize and companion book by Charles K. Wolfe (pors.); obituaries in *Gate City Herald*, 11 Nov. 1960, and *Billboard*, 14 Nov. 1960.

WAYNE W. DANIEL

CARTER, Beirne Blair (24 January 1924–11 January 1989), businessman and philanthropist, was born in Richmond and was the son of Robert Hill Carter and Alice Small Blair Carter. Educated locally at Saint Christopher's School, he matriculated at the Virginia Military Institute in 1942 but after six months left to enter the army. Carter served as an infantry sergeant in Europe during World War II and was wounded at the Battle of the Bulge. He resumed his education after the war and in 1948 received a B.S. in commerce from the University of Virginia. The following year Carter went to work for the Virginia Tractor Company, in Richmond. On 25 April 1953 he married Elisabeth Ross Reed, of Richmond. They had one daughter and divorced on 13 January 1975.

The Virginia Tractor Company, which his father headed, held the statewide franchise of

Caterpillar Incorporated and sold heavy construction equipment. In 1952 the Virginia district was divided, and Carter moved to Salem and became president of the new firm, Carter Machinery Company, with forty employees and the exclusive right to sell Caterpillar equipment in western Virginia. By the 1970s Carter had built his company into one of the most successful Caterpillar franchises in the world. The company sold tractors and other heavy equipment to contractors during the heyday of coal hauling and the beginning of interstate highway construction. He later purchased the franchise for eastern Virginia held by his brother, and by 1988 Carter Machinery employed 850 people in Virginia and West Virginia.

After Carter's health began to fail as a consequence of cancer, he tried to transfer the state franchise to his daughter or to a publicly held corporation, but Caterpillar refused. Early in 1988 the General Assembly passed a bill imposing restrictions on a manufacturer's ability to dictate franchise changes, an act designed to enable Carter to dispose of his company as he pleased. Caterpillar took Carter Machinery to court, but after the assembly hastily amended the bill to make it retroactive, the company settled the dispute and bought Carter Machinery for approximately $125 million.

Although not a well-known public figure, Carter played important roles in the region's and state's economic life. He served as president of the Roanoke Valley United Way and as a director of the American Frontier Culture Foundation, the Atlantic Rural Exposition, Inc. (which staged the annual State Fair of Virginia), Bank of Virginia, First Federal Savings and Loan Association in Roanoke, Virginia Commonwealth Bankshares, the Roanoke Valley Chamber of Commerce, and the Roanoke Symphony Society. During the 1970s Carter sat on a state advisory board on industrial development as well as two advisory boards at the University of Virginia. He was a vestryman of Saint John's Episcopal Church, in Roanoke, and led in establishing Big Brothers and Big Sisters organizations in that city.

In 1986 Carter created the Beirne Carter Foundation, an independent charitable organization emphasizing grants in health, education, local history, nature, ecology, and youth programs. By 2003 the foundation had distributed about $15 million to approximately 400 Virginia organizations, with the largest grants to programs in social and community services, education, arts and humanities, and historic preservation. In 1988, while being treated for cancer, Carter gave more than $3 million to establish the Beirne B. Carter Center for Immunology Research at the University of Virginia, where scientists work to develop new ways to diagnose and treat human diseases. He also donated $4 million for the Carter Athletic Center at the private North Cross School, in Roanoke, of which he was a trustee for twenty-five years. He gave $1 million, the largest individual gift in its history, to Saint Christopher's School, in Richmond, and he was a major benefactor of the historic Christ Episcopal Church, in Irvington, Lancaster County.

Soon after selling Carter Machinery he moved to Richmond. Beirne Blair Carter died of sinus cancer in a hospital in that city on 11 January 1989 and was buried in a family plot at Christ Episcopal Church Glendower, in Albemarle County.

Feature article in *Roanoke Times and World-News*, 22 June 1988 (por.); information from family records provided by daughter, Mary Ross Carter Hutcheson, and by Elisabeth Ross Reed Carter; other information provided by Talfourd Kemper (2003) and by Lucille A. Lindamood, grant administrator, Beirne Carter Foundation (2003); *Richmond News Leader*, 25 Apr. 1953, 12 Oct. 1988; *Richmond Times-Dispatch*, 26 Apr. 1953, 17 July, 13, 16 Oct. 1988; *Virginia Business* 3 (Sept. 1988): 7; *Inside UVA*, 1 Nov. 1988; obituaries in *Richmond News Leader*, *Richmond Times-Dispatch*, and *Roanoke Times and World-News*, all 12 Jan. 1989.

GEORGE A. KEGLEY

CARTER, Charles (ca. 1707–26 April 1764), planter and member of the House of Burgesses, was the son of Robert "King" Carter (ca. 1664–1732), a land baron and member of the governor's Council, and Elizabeth Landon Willis Carter. It was the second marriage of both his parents. His elder half brother John Carter (d. 1742) became secretary of the colony and also a councillor, and his younger brother, Landon Carter, served with him in the House of Burgesses. Carter and his brothers were educated in England. After his return to Virginia early in 1724 he moved to one of his father's estates near Urbanna, in Middlesex County. The governor appointed Carter naval officer, or customs official, for the Rappahannock District on 1 November 1729 and on the following 29 April named him a justice of the peace for Middlesex County.

After the death of his father Carter moved to King George County to the Stanstead plantation, which he inherited. Later he purchased nearby Cleve, where he resided for the rest of his life. He was often referred to as Charles Carter of Cleve to distinguish him from several relatives of the same name. About 1728 Carter married Mary Walker, of Yorktown. They had three daughters and two sons before her death early in 1742. Their eldest daughter, Mary Walker Carter, married Carter's nephew Charles Carter (1732–1806), who served with him in the House of Burgesses, and their only surviving son, Charles Carter (1732–1796), also served with him in the House of Burgesses and later sat on the Council of State. On 25 December 1742 Carter married Anne Byrd, the seventeen-year-old daughter of William Byrd (1674–1744), of whose estate he was an executor. They had six daughters and two sons before she died on 11 September 1757. Carter courted at least two women, including the widow Martha Dandridge Custis, before he married sixteen- or seventeen-year-old Lucy Taliaferro about 9 June 1763. They had one daughter who was born a few weeks before his death.

Carter was a trustee for the establishment of the towns of Falmouth, in King George County (after 1776 Stafford County), Leedstown, in King George County (later Westmoreland County), and Port Royal, in Caroline County, and he was a commissioner in the 1730s and again in the 1740s to determine the boundaries of the Northern Neck. Carter served as a justice of the peace in King George County beginning in 1734 and became county lieutenant, or commanding officer of the militia. In September 1734 he stood for election to the House of Burgesses, lost, and unsuccessfully challenged the result. Two years later Carter won election to the House of Burgesses from King George County but had his victory contested on the ground that he had

offered life leases to one or more men to make them qualified to vote for him. The challenger failed to gather evidence properly, and the Committee of Privileges and Elections recommended that the challenge be dismissed. Carter served in every session of the assembly from 1736 until his death and quickly became one of the most influential burgesses. On his first day as a member he seconded the nomination of John Robinson (1705–1766) for Speaker, and during that session he took the lead in attempting to tighten enforcement of the duty on the importation of slaves, served on a committee that examined the treasurer's accounts, and also sat on a committee appointed to draft a bill to secure titles to land grants issued by the proprietors of the Northern Neck.

Lieutenant Governor William Gooch recommended Carter for the governor's Council late in 1742, but another man received the appointment. Throughout his career in the assembly Carter usually served on committees appointed to frame petitions to the Crown or to draft bills and major state papers on such topics as finance. In the October 1748 assembly session Carter succeeded Edwin Conway, who had temporarily retired from the House, as Robinson's right-hand man. Carter chaired the Committee of Propositions and Grievances and routinely presided during debate in the committee of the whole, which allowed Robinson to exercise his power effectively without fear of adverse rulings from the chair. Until his death, Carter remained, next to the Speaker, the most influential member of the House of Burgesses, even as the next generation of legislators, such as Richard Bland and Peyton Randolph (d. 1775), emerged early in the 1760s. Along with Robinson, Randolph, his kinsman Carter Burwell, and his brother Landon Carter, he was appointed in 1756 as one of the directors to oversee the colony's financing of troops to protect the Virginia frontier during the Seven Years' War.

While his father was an agent for the Fairfax family, Carter received grants for large amounts of land in the Piedmont counties of the Northern Neck Proprietary, and he subsequently inherited large tracts from his father. Carter spent much of his life improving his huge landholdings and seeking to diversify the productions of his plantations. He constructed flour mills that served a wide community and grew a variety of crops for market. Carter and his brothers developed a copper mine, he owned equipment for a large distillery and for processing nut oils, and he built a bakery that produced ship biscuits for the maritime market. About 1746 he began construction of the great, seven-bay house at Cleve.

Carter was equally committed to the diversification of the colony's economy and the development of the Piedmont and the backcountry. He worked in the 1750s with other colonial gentlemen to obtain grants to large tracts of land in the West, and in 1754 he persuaded George Washington to survey the Potomac River above the falls in pursuit of their mutual interest in opening the upper regions of that river to navigation.

In 1759 Carter sponsored a bill to create a committee to encourage economic diversification in Virginia and award "bounties or premiums for the more speedy and effectual bringing to perfection any art or manufacture of service to the public." As committee chair, he initiated an extended correspondence with the Royal Society for the Encouragement of Arts, Manufactures and Commerce, in London. Carter shared the results of his experiments and the trials other planters made with a variety of raw goods and manufactures, ranging from hemp and salted fish to naval stores and viniculture. The society awarded him a medal in 1763 for his attempt to produce wine in Virginia. Carter hoped to improve the colony's economy and the profitability of its plantations by fostering new exports to replace tobacco, which he feared would saturate the European market. Carter was one of the pioneers in transforming the plantation economy of northern Virginia from tobacco production to grains and other commodities.

When Carter wrote his will in 1762 he sought to extend his vision of economic improvement under the direction of a secure class of planter families. He instructed his executors to implement his full plan of agricultural reform at Cleve, and he granted a favored slave, Benjamin Boyd, a continued role in the maintenance of the estate's manufactures, as well as an annual income. Carter made substantial provision for all of his

children, daughters as well as sons, and younger sons as well as his firstborn, and he ordered that his younger sons study law in London in order to prepare themselves for their varied business affairs in the colony. Carter used his will as an attempt to instill in his family a code of behavior that shunned material ostentation and emphasized genteel manners. Charles Carter died at his home in King George County on 26 April 1764 of "a dropsey" that may have been induced by the use of narcotics to relieve pain or reduce fever. He was buried probably on his estate at Cleve.

Family relationships, with conjectural birth date, in Katharine L. Brown, *Robert "King" Carter, Builder of Christ Church* (2001), 84, 88–89; Carter business papers and letters in *Byrd Correspondence*, vol. 2, in *The Carter Family Papers, 1659–1797, in the Sabine Hall Collection* (1967 microfilm), in *Washington: Colonial Series*, 1:128–129, 196–197, 3:36–37, 64–65, 4:280–281, in various collections at LVA (esp. Carter Family Papers [1718–1833], Acc. 25840), UVA, and VHS, in earl of Romney's Deposit and Wyatt Family Papers, vol. 2, both British Library, and in Guard Books, Royal Society for the Encouragement of Arts, Manufactures and Commerce, London; second marriage date, probably from Byrd family records, in *VMHB* 35 (1927): 376; third marriage date in King George Co. Deed Book, 4:539–542; numerous references in *JHB*, with election challenges in *JHB, 1727–1740*, 195, 208–209, 251, 256, 263–264; Hening, *Statutes*, 7:288–290 (first quotation on 289); Robert Leroy Hilldrup, "A Campaign to Promote the Prosperity of Colonial Virginia," *VMHB* 67 (1959): 410–428; numerous entries in Jack P. Greene, ed., *The Diary of Colonel Landon Carter of Sabine Hall, 1752–1778* (1965; repr. 1987), with death date and possible cause on 1:266 (second quotation), 2:898; will in King George Co. Will Book, 1:169–210, printed with family history notes in Fairfax Harrison, ed., "The Will of Charles Carter of Cleve," *VMHB* 31 (1923): 39–69 (por. facing 39).

BRUCE A. RAGSDALE

CARTER, Charles (1732–28 June 1806), planter and member-elect of the Council of State, was the son of John Carter (d. 1742) and Elizabeth Hill Carter and grandson of Robert "King" Carter (ca. 1664–1732). He was born probably at Shirley, the Charles City County plantation where his parents lived while his father was secretary of the colony and a member of the governor's Council. Carter's father died in July 1742, and several years later his mother married Bowler Cocke, who moved from Henrico County to Shirley plantation. Carter was educated at the Gloucester County grammar school of William

Yates, a clergyman who later briefly served as president of the College of William and Mary, and at the college. He then assumed management of Corotoman, the Lancaster County plantation that he had inherited from his father. Carter resided there for two decades and supervised that and his other properties on the Northern Neck and elsewhere. He purchased Nanzatico, a 2,200-acre King George County plantation, from his financially strapped cousin Charles Carter (1732–1796). Following the deaths of his mother and Bowler Cocke in 1771, Carter made extensive repairs and renovations to the main house at Shirley and moved there permanently about 1775.

Carter's success as a planter and entrepreneur made him one of the wealthiest men in Virginia. At the time of his death in 1806, his will enumerated more than 13,000 acres in thirteen Virginia counties and at least 710 slaves. In addition to his extensive landholdings Carter operated a large mill near Corotoman, lent substantial sums of money to other planters, and provided in his will for investing some assets in bank stocks or similar securities. He was also a sometime administrator and trustee of the complicated estate left by his brother-in-law, the councillor William Byrd (1728–1777). Although Carter's uncle, Landon Carter, characterized him as an inefficient plantation manager, the uncle's pessimistic frame of mind and negative assessments of nearly everyone suggest that the criticism was overstated.

Carter became a justice of the peace in Lancaster County on 17 July 1761 and served until he moved to Charles City County. He was a vestryman of Christ Church Parish for several years before leaving Lancaster County, and on the eve of the Revolution he was a member of the board of visitors of the College of William and Mary. Carter served in the House of Burgesses representing Lancaster County continuously from 1758 until the Revolution. He gradually emerged late in the 1760s as a reasonably responsible member who was routinely appointed to the Committees on Privileges and Elections, on Propositions and Grievances, and for Religion. Throughout the imperial crises of the 1760s and early 1770s Carter supported Virginia protests of parliamentary measures. Lancaster freeholders elected him to the county committee in February 1775 and to the Revolutionary Conventions that met in August 1774 and in March, July, and December 1775. In September 1775 he angered Landon Carter by endorsing nonimportation of British goods but opposing the termination of exportation to Great Britain and its Caribbean colonies. He argued that exports were needed to provide money for the war and to enable Virginians to pay their debts. Although Carter was not elected in April 1776 to the fifth and final Revolutionary Convention, probably because by then he had moved to Shirley, on 29 June 1776 that convention elected him to the Council of State. He declined the appointment and never took the oath of office.

Sometime in the mid-1750s Carter married his first cousin Mary Walker Carter, daughter of Charles Carter (ca. 1707–1764), who represented King George County in the House of Burgesses for many years. They had two daughters and six sons (including one set of twins) before her death on 30 January 1770. Late in November of that year he married Ann Butler Moore. Of their eight daughters and seven sons, four children died in infancy, and one was stillborn. As had been the case in his generation and the generations of his parents and grandparents, nearly all of the Carter children who lived to adulthood married into respected Virginia families. The best-known example was the marriage in 1793 of his and Ann Butler Moore Carter's eldest daughter, Ann Hill Carter, to Henry "Light-Horse Harry" Lee (1756–1818).

Carter remained active in the affairs of the church and attended annual Episcopal Church conferences in Virginia from 1789 to 1793 as a lay delegate from Westover Parish. Charles Carter died at Shirley on 28 June 1806. His will directed that he be buried near the bodies of his parents (probably at Shirley or in the graveyard of the Westover Parish church) "without any funeral pomp and nothing but the burial service [to] be read over my grave by the parson of the parish (should we be so fortunate as to have one among us)."

Carter family Bible records (1732–1913), Acc. 24430, LVA, with birth and death dates and birth dates of children; a few Carter documents at CW and VHS; Hening, *Statutes*,

8:464–468; *Williamsburg Virginia Gazette* (Rind), 22 Feb. 1770; ibid. (Purdie and Dixon), 29 Nov. 1770; numerous references in Jack P. Greene, ed., *The Diary of Colonel Landon Carter of Sabine Hall, 1752–1778* (1965; repr. 1987); Catherine M. Lynn, "Shirley Plantation: A History" (M.A. thesis, University of Delaware, 1967), 69–88; *Revolutionary Virginia*, esp. 7:655, 692–693; Joanne Young, *Shirley Plantation: A Personal Adventure for Ten Generations* (1981), 27–39; Thomas Allen Glenn, *Some Colonial Mansions and Those Who Lived in Them* (1899), por. on 249; will and estate inventory in Charles City Co. Will Book (1789–1808), 653–663 (quotation on 653), 666–667, 709–725; obituary in *Richmond Enquirer*, 22 July 1806.

ALBERT H. TILLSON JR.

CARTER, Charles (15 October 1732–29 April 1796), member of the Council of State, was most likely born in Christ Church Parish in Middlesex County, where he was christened on 15 November 1732. The son of Charles Carter (ca. 1707–1764), a wealthy planter and later a member of the House of Burgesses, and his first wife, Mary Walker Carter, and also a grandson of the land baron Robert "King" Carter (ca. 1664–1732), he was closely related to many of the colony's leading families. Among his influential uncles were John Carter (d. 1742), secretary of the colony and a member of the governor's Council, and Landon Carter, a noted planter, writer, and member of the House of Burgesses. On 22 November 1753 Carter married Elizabeth Chiswell, daughter of the land speculator and mine operator John Chiswell, of Hanover County. They had five sons and two daughters.

As a young man Carter became notorious for an extravagant lifestyle. That and his bright red face earned him the nickname Blaze. His reckless behavior so alienated his father that in 1762 the father settled the primary family estate, Cleve, in King George County, on Carter's younger half brother and forced him to acknowledge that he had received ample provision from his father in land and slaves and that his father had paid some of Carter's large debts. After his father's death two years later, Carter contested the will and prevailed on the General Assembly to break the entail on several family properties. He then sold some of the land and borrowed money from his wife's brother-in-law Speaker John Robinson (1705–1766) in order to purchase Nanzatico, a 2,200-acre plantation in King George County, but he was unable to pay the full price of £6,600.

Carter probably hired William Buckland to build a spacious new house there. According to a persistent local tradition, Carter first erected the house on one spot and had scarcely moved into it before he took it down and erected it on another. After the extent of his indebtedness became known as a consequence of a scandal involving Robinson's estate, Carter lost a court judgment and sold his interest in Nanzatico to his cousin Charles Carter (1732–1806) and moved his family to Ludlow, a nearby family plantation in Stafford County. He was sometimes referred to thereafter as Charles Carter of Ludlow to distinguish him from other relatives sharing his name.

A lesser light in one of the greatest planting families of eighteenth-century Virginia, Carter exemplified the traditional gentry pattern of public service in spite of his financial perils. His indebtedness and loss of land did not prevent him from serving as a justice of the peace in both of the counties in which he lived and becoming a colonel in the militia. In 1756 Carter was elected to the House of Burgesses from King George County. Regularly reelected, he served for fifteen years. He usually held a seat on the Committee of Propositions and Grievances, which his father chaired, and took a responsible part in the assembly's work. Carter may have stood for the House from Stafford County in 1771 after relocating there, but if so, he was not elected. He may have won an interim election two years later, but he did not take his House seat again until the short session of May 1774. Carter served on the Committees on Privileges and Elections and of Propositions and Grievances in the final meeting of the House of Burgesses in June 1775.

Carter supported the colony's protests against British policies on the eve of the American Revolution and served in the first four conventions that met between the summer of 1774 and January 1776. He left the fourth convention to begin directing the production of saltpeter at several northern Virginia manufactories. Although he was not elected to the fifth and climactic Revolutionary Convention, he served in the House of Delegates from October 1776 until October 1779, when he gave up his seat to become sheriff of

Stafford County. During most sessions Carter was named to the Committees of Privileges and Elections (which he chaired during the two 1778 sessions), of Propositions and Grievances, and of Religion. He returned to the House of Delegates again in 1782 and 1783, resumed his seats on the three major standing committees, and in the October 1782 and October 1783 assembly sessions chaired the Committee of Propositions and Grievances.

Carter favored adoption of the Constitution in 1788 and was an unsuccessful candidate for the Virginia ratification convention. By letting a private letter from George Washington endorsing the proposed constitution become public, Carter perhaps aided the cause more than he would have had he been elected. In 1789 Carter won election to a four-year term in the Senate of Virginia representing the counties of King George, Stafford, and Westmoreland. On 28 November of that year, less than six weeks into the first session, the General Assembly elected Carter to the Council of State, for which service he earned a welcomed salary. He took his seat on 2 December 1789 and served faithfully, though uneventfully, for fourteen months. On 12 November 1790, in compliance with the state constitution, the assembly removed two members, Carter and his kinsman Carter Braxton. Carter attended his last meeting on 8 February 1791.

Despite his financial reversals, Carter retained considerable property, including a large number of slaves, and he tried to produce profitable crops. Creditors continued to hound him, and he eventually lost almost all of his remaining real property, including Ludlow, which he offered for sale in the spring of 1788. He moved to Fredericksburg, where his wife was reduced to advertising for boarders attending a nearby academy. Once a great planter, Carter repeatedly appealed to Washington during the 1790s for assistance for his sons, one of whom he had bound to a Philadelphia coachmaker and two others to planters. A fourth son studied medicine in Philadelphia. Through the generosity of his cousin Charles Carter (1732–1806), who allowed Carter's wife to retain the earnings of several slaves whom Carter had been forced to sell him, the Carters kept just out of poverty during their

final years. Charles Carter died in Fredericksburg on 29 April 1796 and was buried in the Willis family cemetery in that town.

Birth and christening dates in *The Parish Register of Christ Church, Middlesex County, Va., from 1653 to 1812* (1897), 135; marriage date and variant birth date of 22 Nov. 1732 in Carter family Bible records (1737–1809), VHS; father's will in King George Co. Will Book, 1:169–210, printed with family history notes in Fairfax Harrison, ed., "The Will of Charles Carter of Cleve," *VMHB* 31 (1923): 39–69; several Carter letters in George Washington Papers, LC, printed in part in *Washington: Confederation Series*, vols. 4–6, *Washington: Presidential Series*, vols. 6, 7, 10; numerous references in Jack P. Greene, ed., *The Diary of Colonel Landon Carter of Sabine Hall, 1752–1778* (1965; repr. 1987); Hening, *Statutes*, 8:218–222; King George Co. Deed Book, 5:756–757; *Virginia Herald, and Fredericksburg Advertiser*, 27 Mar. 1788; Kaminski, *Ratification*, 8:276–281, 479, 9:601, 613; *JHD*, Oct. 1789 sess., 77, and Oct. 1790 sess., 53–54; *Journals of Council of State*, 5:137, 256; George Green Shackelford, "Nanzatico, King George County, Virginia," *VMHB* 73 (1965): 393–402; undated posthumous credit reports by William Waller Hening in PRO T 79/73, fols. 19–20, 23–24, and T 79/91, 133–135; wills of Carter and widow in Fredericksburg District and Superior Court Bonds, Wills, and Inventories, A-3:229–230; death notice in *Virginia Herald, and Fredericksburg and Falmouth Advertiser*, 3 May 1796.

JAMES P. WHITTENBURG

CARTER, Charles Samuel (20 December 1878–14 May 1968), banker and Democratic Party leader, was born in the Rye Cove community in Scott County and was the son of Cowan Whitefield Carter and Mary Emily Gillenwater Carter, whose families had lived in southwestern Virginia for generations. His father, a farmer, served one term as county sheriff and several terms on the county board of supervisors. Carter was educated in the county's public schools and graduated in 1900 from Shoemaker College, a preparatory school in Gate City. He also attended Bristol Business College in Bristol, on the Virginia-Tennessee border.

C. S. Carter, as he was referred to professionally, or Sam Carter, as he was familiarly known, began his long, successful business career clerking in a store in Keystone, West Virginia. He moved to Big Stone Gap, in Wise County, and clerked in another store before opening a haberdashery in 1905. He served on the Wise County school board from 1905 to 1920 and joined the Freemasons and the Shriners. Carter championed economic development of the region. He sat on Wise County's board of trade, was first president of the county's industrial investment corporation, and during World War I chaired the county's war bond drive. On 11 July 1906 Carter married Ida Mae Specht, of Roanoke. They had three sons.

Carter began a sixty-year banking career late in 1907 when he helped reorganize the financially troubled Interstate Finance and Trust Company and was named to its board of directors. He was president of the bank from 1916 until 1920, when he moved to Bristol. He lived there for the remainder of his life and became president of Dominion National Bank in that city. Influential among Virginia bankers, he was acknowledged as the dean of banking in southwestern Virginia and the neighboring region of eastern Tennessee. Carter was president of the Virginia Bankers Association for the 1929–1930 term, and in his presidential address less than a year after the stock market crash he recommended that the state's banks cooperate for their mutual advantage and charge fees for all the services they provided their depositors and customers. Small-town banks, he argued, especially needed such financial resources. Carter chaired Group One of the Tennessee Bankers Association and served on several committees of the American Bankers Association.

Carter also invested in coal mines and real estate in southwestern Virginia and continued his civic involvement while living in Bristol, where he served on the local school board, as president of the chamber of commerce, and as a steward in the Methodist Episcopal Church. He regularly attended state and national Democratic Party conventions and was a presidential elector in 1924. Carter became an important political leader in the region and for more than thirty years was a key adviser to Harry Flood Byrd (1887–1966), leader of the business-oriented faction of the Democratic Party that dominated state politics for decades. Carter worked closely with Byrd and Everett Randolph Combs, of Russell County, to break the Republican Party's hold on local and congressional offices in the Ninth Congressional District, which included all the counties in southwestern Vir-

ginia. Beginning with a Democratic victory in the 1922 congressional campaign and the defeat of a proposal to finance road construction with bonds, southwestern Democrats helped Byrd seize and hold control of the party apparatus.

After Byrd became governor in 1926 and Combs moved to Richmond, Carter grew increasingly influential and in 1934 became chair of the Ninth District Democratic Committee. He was also a longtime member of the state central committee. One of a small circle of elected officials and businessmen on whom Byrd relied for political advice and monetary muscle necessary to maintain control of Virginia politics, Carter operated quietly and behind the scenes to ensure that the conservative economic and racial policies of Byrd's party organization remained dominant in the state until the 1960s. In a district known for its fierce partisanship and extralegal political practices, Carter used his influence to combat a Republican revival, but he was less successful in overcoming Democrats who opposed Byrd's hostility to the New Deal. The Ninth District regularly elected to Congress a supporter of New Deal policies, John William Flannagan.

In 1935 Carter won appointment to the State Commission on Conservation and Development (later the Virginia Conservation Commission and at the time of his retirement the Board of Conservation and Economic Development) and served until June 1962, except for the years 1938–1942 when a Byrd opponent was governor. Carter chaired that influential commission from 1948 until 1958. The commission's creation of the state park system was its principal achievement, but it also promoted economic development, exploitation and management of natural resources, and tourism at state historic sites. Carter was mentioned in 1946 as a compromise candidate for the United States Senate, but he never ran for statewide office.

Carter sat on the board of Emory and Henry College from 1925 to 1946, after 1930 as chair. During that time and in spite of the Great Depression, the college pulled through a decade of financial struggle, placed its finances on a solid footing, and dramatically increased its enrollment. Believing that education was a sound investment in society, Carter in 1966 gave the college stock valued at more than $100,000 with which to establish a student loan fund. He also served on the board of Arlington Hall Junior College for women, in Arlington County, from 1932 until 1942.

Following a long illness, Charles Samuel Carter died in Bristol on 14 May 1968 and was buried in Mountain View Cemetery in that city. The author of one obituary accurately characterized him as the "dean of Virginia's non-office holding statesmen."

Biographies with birth date in Bruce, Tyler, and Morton, *History of Virginia*, 6:423–424 (por. facing 423), and Glass and Glass, *Virginia Democracy*, 3:165–166; some Carter letters in George Campbell Peery, Colgate Whitehead Darden Jr., and James Lindsay Almond Jr. Executive Papers, all RG 3, LVA, and Harry Flood Byrd (1887–1966) Papers and Everett Randolph Combs Papers, both UVA; *Big Stone Gap Post*, 10, 17 Aug. 1905, 12 July 1906, 12, 19 Apr., 2 Aug. 1916, 31 Jan. 1917, 9 Jan. 1918, 25 Aug. 1920; *Roanoke Times*, 14 July 1906; *Richmond Times-Dispatch*, 11 Aug. 1946; *Bristol Herald Courier*, 25, 26 May 1956; presidential address printed in Virginia Bankers Association *Proceedings* (1930), 26–29; *Commonwealth* 23 (July 1956): 52–53, 77; obituaries in *Bristol Herald Courier* (por. and quotation), *Bristol Virginia-Tennessean*, and *Roanoke World-News*, all 15 May 1968.

MINOR T. WEISIGER

CARTER, Dale (14 October 1802–30 December 1878), member of the Convention of 1850–1851, was born in the part of Russell County that was carved off in 1814 to form part of Scott County. He was the son of John Carter, a farmer, and his first wife, Sarah Margaret Frazier Carter. Little information exists about Carter's childhood or education. He probably studied law with a local attorney or judge, and on 4 September 1827 he qualified as an attorney in Russell County. On 15 December 1829 Carter married Elizabeth Campbell Smith. She inherited from her father a farm about five miles west of Lebanon, on which the Carters built their home. They had four sons and four daughters. A grandson, Henry Carter Stuart, served as governor of Virginia from 1914 until 1918.

Carter's early legal career, although active, appears to have been unremarkable. Of more consequence was his concentration on farming and land speculation. In the decades before the Civil War he purchased or obtained through grants large tracts of land—perhaps as much as 65,000 acres—in southwestern Virginia, Kentucky, and Tennessee. In Russell County alone Carter acquired more than 9,750 acres, about one-third of which he resold or otherwise disposed of. Carter's county real estate holdings, valued at $25,000 in 1850 and $81,000 in 1860, placed him among the area's wealthiest citizens. He owned four slaves in 1830, ten in 1840, seventeen in 1850, and twenty-six in 1860.

In August 1850 Carter, a Democrat, finished third in an eight-candidate field and won election to fill one of three seats representing the district of Lee, Russell, and Scott Counties in a convention summoned to revise the state constitution. He served on the preliminary Committee of Elections and the standing Committee on the Right of Suffrage and Qualifications of Persons to be Elected. Although Carter was present for most of the votes while the convention sat from 14 October 1850 until 1 August 1851, he did not often participate in the debates that preceded them. As the convention neared its conclusion, however, he spoke simply but eloquently on 5 April 1851 in behalf of his southwestern constituents and called for unrestricted voting rights for all adult white males. On 16 May 1851 Carter voted in favor of a key compromise on apportionment of representation in the General Assembly but on 31 July voted against the final passage of the constitution.

Carter represented Russell County in the House of Delegates in the assembly that met from 7 December 1857 until 8 April 1858. He served on the prestigious Committee of Finance. During the Civil War, Carter was sympathetic to the Southern cause, but age and caution led him to sit out the conflict quietly cultivating his farm and responding when necessary to Confederate requisitions of supplies and labor. In September 1863 the county court sent Carter to Richmond as its agent to explain to the governor why drought and the proximity of the competing armies prevented Russell County from responding to the governor's requisition of able-bodied male slaves to work on fortifications around the capital. At the close of the war Carter's great wealth required him to seek a presidential pardon, which he received on 26 October 1865.

Carter returned to Richmond to represent Buchanan, Russell, and Tazewell Counties in the Senate of Virginia from 4 December 1865 through 29 April 1867. During the first session he sat on the Committees on Finance and on Public Institutions and also chaired the Committee on Enrolled Bills. During the second session he was a member of the Committees on Finance and on Federal Relations, and during the extra session in March and April 1867 he served on the Committees on Finance, on Federal Relations, and on General Laws. Named to a joint committee after two Senate colleagues declined appointment, Carter proceeded to Washington, D.C., with seven other Virginia legislators and on 10 February 1866 presented President Andrew Johnson with five resolutions passed by the General Assembly supporting presidential reconstruction and affirming that involuntary servitude, except as punishment for crime, had been abolished.

Dale Carter spent his final years farming in Russell County, where he died on 30 December 1878. He was buried on his farm.

Biographies in Joseph Lyon Miller, *The Descendants of Capt. Thomas Carter of "Barford," Lancaster County, Virginia* ... (1912), 246–247 (por. facing 236), and D. C. Pratt, *Russell County: Virginia's Bluegrass Empire* (1968), 108, 110; Russell Co. Common Law Order Book, 2:96, 14:492; *Richmond Enquirer*, 3, 10 Sept. 1850; *Journal of 1850–1851 Convention*, 419, and Appendix, 22; *Supplement, 1850–1851 Convention Debates,* no. 51; Presidential Pardons; *JSV*, 1865–1866 sess., 194, 207, and appended *Report of the Joint Committee of the General Assembly of Virginia Appointed to Convey Certain Resolutions to the President of the United States*, 12 Feb. 1866, Doc. 5; David Yancy Lyttle, 7 Dec. 1898 interview recorded in John Jay Dickey Diary, Pearl Day Bach Papers, Morehead State University, Morehead, Ky.; Alice E. Meade, "Dale Carter Home" (1937 typescript), in Works Progress Administration, Virginia Historical Inventory, LVA; estate accounts in Russell Co. Will Book, 9:501–508, 10:34–36, 213–224; death notice in *Richmond Daily Dispatch,* 3 Jan. 1879; obituary in *Marion Patriot and Herald,* 9 Jan. 1879 (with variant age at death of seventy-eight).

ANN DRURY WELLFORD

CARTER, Edward (d. by 13 November 1682), member of the Council, was born most likely in England, but the date and place of his birth and the names of his parents are not known. He married a woman named Anne (surname unrecorded), had a daughter of the same name, and lived for part of his young adulthood in London. Carter settled in Virginia sometime in the 1640s or early in the 1650s. He may have been related to several of the Carters who had lived south of the James River since the early years of the colony, and he may have been engaged in commerce before moving from England to Virginia. Loss of early local records and the presence of other men of the same name during his residence in Virginia complicate and obscure family and business relationships. His kinship to John Carter (ca. 1613–1670), who resided in Lancaster County and served with him on the governor's Council, was probably close but is unclear.

Carter acquired three plantations in Nansemond (then still sometimes called Upper Norfolk) County and was appointed a lieutenant colonel in the militia before being elected early in 1658 to represent the county in the House of Burgesses. He attended the assembly session that met for three weeks beginning in March 1658 and the session that met for one week in March 1659. Soon afterward Carter moved to Lancaster County and purchased one plantation and patented land for another. He also acquired property in Maryland.

Within a year after the March 1659 assembly, Carter became a member of the governor's Council. Few records of the Council survive to document his service or indicate when it began and when it ceased. He was present in March 1660 when the Council and House of Burgesses elected Sir William Berkeley governor pending receipt of a royal commission from Charles II, and he attended the Council's meeting as the Quarter Court on 17 October of that year. In 1663 Carter and other Council members joined the governor in signing a remonstrance to the Crown protesting the grant of the Northern Neck to the king's favorites. Carter and several of his fellow councillors complained to the king during the summer of 1667 that the proprietor of Maryland had blocked an agreement to reduce tobacco production and thus to increase the crop's price, and about that same time Carter also signed a letter that the governor and Council sent to the king concerning the colony's defense during the Second Anglo-Dutch War (1665–1667). The last meeting of the Council that Carter is known to have attended took place on 28 September 1667.

About 1668 Carter returned to England, terminating his membership on the Council. He resided at Edmonton, in Middlesex County, just outside London. Shipping records and other documents indicate that he engaged in trade between London and Virginia until the mid-1670s or later. He exported woolens and other goods to the colony and imported tobacco and furs. Carter also owned land in the parish of Chalfont Saint Peter in Buckinghamshire, England. He was one of five men who received from the estate of his fellow Virginia Council member Daniel Parke (d. 1679) money to purchase a mourning ring.

Carter married a second time, but whether before or after returning to England is unknown. His second wife's given name was Elizabeth, and she was probably the mother of the two daughters and possibly of his namesake son whom he mentioned when he signed his will on 18 October 1682. Carter appointed his wife executrix of his estate and empowered her to sell his colonial property if necessary to support the family. Edward Carter died probably at Edmonton and was buried on 13 November 1682, presumably in the middle aisle of the Church of Saint Dunstan in the East, in London, as his will specified. In 1685 his widow named John Purvis, a noted London sea captain and publisher of one of the earliest volumes of Virginia laws, as her attorney in fact to dispose of some of the Virginia and Maryland properties. He sold one of the Lancaster County plantations in 1686. Four years later, in her capacity of executrix, Elizabeth Carter patented 764 acres of land in Nansemond County.

Noel Currer-Briggs, *The Carters of Virginia: Their English Ancestry* (1979), 31, 33; *Cavaliers and Pioneers*, 1:387, 445, 480, 2:196, 238, 294, 337, 342; numerous references in Lancaster Co. records beginning in 1660; attendance as burgess and councillor recorded in Hening, *Statutes*, 1:430, 506, 526, in Egerton MSS 2395, fols. 360–362, British Library, in PRO CO 1/21, fols. 109–112, 118–121, and in *Minutes of Council and General Court*, 491; will in Prerogative Court of Canterbury, Cottle 128; power of attorney and sale of plantation in Lancaster Co. Deeds, Etc., 6: fols. 87–91; burial recorded in R. H. D'Elboux, ed., *The Registers of St. Dunstan in the East, London, 1653–1691*, part 2 (1955), 106.

LISA L. HEUVEL

CARTER, George Lafayette (10 January 1857–30 December 1936), industrialist, was born in Carroll County and was the son of Walter Crockett Carter and Lucy Ann Jennings Carter. As a youth Carter helped his father on the family farm and attended a country school during the winter. At age sixteen he secured employment as a clerk in a Hillsville store. Sometime after 1880 Carter became a buyer for the Wythe Lead and Zinc Mine Company, in Wythe County, and later rose to manager and bookkeeper. During the 1880s the railroad contractor George T. Mills hired him as vice president and general manager of the Dora Iron Furnace that Mills was building in Pulaski. After Mills died, Carter became president of the company and completed construction of the ironworks. On 9 April 1895, in Carroll County, Carter married Mayetta Wilkinson, daughter and sister of business associates. Their only child was a son born the following year.

Building on his investments, Carter persuaded two charcoal iron producers to merge their extensive properties with the Dora Iron Furnace. He purchased several small mines in Wise County and constructed about 700 coke ovens, which he organized as Tom's Creek Coal and Coke Company. Carter acquired the Crozier Furnace, in Roanoke, and in October 1897 incorporated all these properties as the Carter Coal and Iron Company, which he later sold at a handsome profit.

In 1899 Carter established the Virginia Iron, Coal, and Coke Company with himself as president and director. The business, capitalized at $10 million, consolidated the leading iron, coal, and coke properties in southwestern Virginia and eastern Tennessee. It controlled sixteen modern blast furnaces that had a production capacity of 900,000 tons of pig iron per year, 150,000 acres of coal lands including five active coal mines, and 60,000 acres of iron ore lands and mines. Originally the company maintained its principal office in Pulaski, but by early in 1901 Carter had moved its headquarters to Bristol. The discovery of rich iron ore deposits outside the region intensified competition, and after the company defaulted on loan payments in 1901, the courts placed it in receivership. When it was sold, Carter recouped several hundred thousand dollars.

Undaunted by the failure of Virginia Iron, Coal, and Coke, Carter pursued his goal of securing an outlet for the southwestern Virginia coalfields. In 1902 he established the Clinchfield Coal Company and began to amass hundreds of thousands of acres in the mineral-rich region and to acquire small railroads. One of these he renamed the South and Western Railway and extended its route. The greatest expansion took place between 1905 and 1908, and in March of the latter year Carter received a charter for the redesignated Carolina, Clinchfield, and Ohio Railway to link his vast coalfield holdings with the Great Lakes and Ohio Valley manufacturing region and the southern Piedmont textile mills. Slicing through the Appalachian Mountains, the railroad ran 211 miles from Dante, in Russell County, to Bostic, in Rutherford County, North Carolina, and included thirty-five tunnels, six major bridges, and an exceptionally low grade for easier transportation of heavy coal cars. One of the most ambitious rail undertakings in the East and reputed to be one of the most expensive railroads in America, it cost between $125,000 and $195,000 per mile and required backing from investors in several states, including the New York financier Thomas Fortune Ryan, a native Virginian. By 1915 the completed railroad extended almost 300 miles from Elkhorn City, in Pike County, Kentucky, through Virginia, Tennessee, and North Carolina to its terminus at Spartanburg, South Carolina.

In 1903 Carter launched the *Bristol Herald* and four years later oversaw its merger with the *Bristol Courier* to form the *Herald Courier*. The establishment of the *Herald* was an unusual venture for a man who disliked publicity as much as Carter did. Indeed, to conceal his identity as owner he bankrolled three newspapermen as a cover and prohibited the editors from printing his name for any reason. He sold the newspaper in 1919.

About 1907 Carter moved his family and business offices to Johnson City, Tennessee, where he lived for approximately ten years. About 1913 Carter stepped down as president and sold his stock in the Carolina, Clinchfield, and Ohio Railway. He also divested himself of land in Kingsport, Tennessee, and banks and other businesses in Tennessee and Virginia. His new venture, the $10 million Carter Coal Company, became one of the largest coal producers in the country with land in Virginia, West Virginia, and Kentucky. By 1920 Carter had moved to Coalwood, a remote mining town he built in McDowell County, West Virginia, to focus on developing his coal-mining operations there. In 1922 he sold Carter Coal to Consolidation Coal Company for $12 million. The subsequent decline in the coal industry caused Consolidation to default on its payments, and in March 1933 control of Carter Coal and its holdings reverted to Carter. That same year Carter, then living in Washington, D.C., where Carter Coal was headquartered, went into semiretirement and became vice president. He installed his son, James Walter Carter, as company president.

In that capacity the younger Carter challenged the constitutionality of the Bituminous Coal Conservation Act of 1935 in the Supreme Court of the United States. Also known as the Guffey Coal Act, it allowed the federal government to regulate coal prices as well as wages, hours, and working conditions of miners throughout the country. In *Carter* v. *Carter Coal Co. et al.* (1936), the Court ruled in James Carter's favor.

Described by contemporaries as an empire builder, Carter attracted an estimated $100 million of new capital to eastern Tennessee and southwestern Virginia. He owned hundreds of thousands of acres of land as well as banks, mills, and other business enterprises in southwestern Virginia and nearby areas of eastern Kentucky, Tennessee, and West Virginia. His Carolina, Clinchfield, and Ohio Railway spurred the development of many industrial towns and cities along its route, most notably Kingsport and Johnson City, both in Tennessee. Among other contributions, Carter organized support and donated money and land for the establishment of East Tennessee State Normal School (later East Tennessee State University) in Johnson City. The Carter Coal Company Store in Coalwood is listed on the National Register of Historic Places. George Lafayette Carter died of pneumonia on 30 December 1936 in a Washington, D.C., hospital. He was buried in a private cemetery in Hillsville.

Tyler, *Men of Mark*, 2:64–67; biography in *Bristol Herald Courier*, 1 July 1956; O. K. Morgan, "George L. Carter, Empire Builder," in Luther F. Addington, ed., *History of Wise County (Virginia)* (1975), 222–227 (variant birth year of 1858); Willie Nelms, "George Lafayette Carter: Empire Builder," *Virginia Cavalcade* 30 (1980): 12–21 (pors.); birth date in Carter family Bible records (1772–1888), LVA; BVS Marriage Register, Carroll Co. (giving age on 9 Apr. 1895 as twenty-eight years, two months, and twenty-nine days and implying birth on 11 Jan. 1867); SCC Charter Book; Carolina, Clinchfield, and Ohio Railway Records and Virginia Iron, Coal, and Coke Company Records, both East Tennessee State University; *Moody's Manual of Corporation Securities* (1901), 940–941; J. O. Lewis, "The Costliest Railroad in America," *Scientific American Supplement*, no. 1752, 31 July 1909; *Manufacturers Record* 63 (9 Jan. 1913): 61; *Moody's Manual of Investments, American and Foreign, Industrial Securities* (1934), 1116; *Carter v. Carter Coal Co. et al.* (1936), *United States Reports*, 298:238–341; obituaries in *Bristol Herald Courier*, *New York Times*, *Richmond Times-Dispatch*, and *Washington Post* (por.), all 31 Dec. 1936.

VINCENT BROOKS

CARTER, Harry Gilmore (8 November 1886–10 April 1926), physician, was born probably in Northumberland County and was the son of Elias J. Carter, a farmer, and Arabella Betts Carter. He received his education at a private school in Kilmarnock, in Lancaster County, and attended the College of William and Mary, where he played tennis and competed on the football and baseball teams. He graduated with a B.A. in 1908 and returned to Northumberland County as the principal of Heathsville's high school. In 1910 Carter matriculated at the Medical College of Virginia, in Richmond, and during his studies there supported himself by teaching at a local private school and at night in the public schools. After receiving an M.D. in 1914, he completed an internship at an Abingdon hospital before entering private practice with a partner in Emporia in 1915. On 28 June 1916 Carter married Mabel E. Holland, of Baltimore. They had one son and one daughter.

When the United States entered World War I in 1917, Carter considered military service but was diagnosed with tuberculosis after a physical examination and sent to the Catawba sanatorium, near Roanoke. He remained there several months until he had recovered enough to be appointed a part-time medical assistant at Salem's Mount Regis Sanatorium, and in November of that year he became an assistant physician at Gaylord Farm Sanatorium, in Connecticut.

On 22 March 1918 Carter was appointed the superintendent and medical director of the newly constructed Piedmont Sanatorium, the first large-scale public facility in the United States for treating African American tuberculosis patients. The Virginia State Board of Health opened Piedmont at the urging of the Negro Organization Society and Agnes Dillon Randolph, a department director at the State Board of Health and executive secretary of the Virginia Tuberculosis Association, which raised $5,000 toward the sanatorium's construction. Tuberculosis was a significant problem among the black population, and early in the twentieth century African Americans in Virginia died from the disease at a rate more than twice that of whites. Little research had been done on its treatment in African Americans, and few beds were available for black patients in sanatoria throughout the country, especially in the South. Piedmont, located in Burkeville, in Nottoway County, received its first patients on 22 April 1918, and by September the original building had been filled and a second constructed to accept a total of seventy patients.

Carter, like many other white physicians, feared the spread of tuberculosis in the white population as a result of its close contact with African Americans, particularly domestic servants. He hoped, however, to demonstrate that it was possible to cure tuberculosis as well as to disseminate information about personal hygiene and clean living conditions so that the disease would become less of a scourge. He sought early diagnosis so that treatment would be most effective and believed that educating African American community leaders about the importance of early treatment was essential in the fight to lower tuberculosis rates. In January 1920 Carter began offering courses at Piedmont to instruct black physicians in the early detection of the disease. Piedmont also provided a two-year training school for African American nurses specializing in the care of tuberculosis patients.

During his eight years at Piedmont Sanatorium, Carter expanded the facility to a capacity of almost 150 and treated more than 1,700 patients, half of whom were discharged in improved health if not fully cured. He shared his research in lectures before such groups as the

National Tuberculosis Association, the North Atlantic Tuberculosis Association, the Old Dominion Medical Society, and the Virginia Medical Society, as well as through the publication of his lectures and annual reports to the State Board of Health. In 1920 Carter was a member of the advisory board for a committee established by the General Assembly to study tuberculosis in Virginia, and two years later William and Mary awarded him a Phi Beta Kappa key for his work.

Harry Gilmore Carter died of pulmonary tuberculosis at Piedmont Sanatorium on 10 April 1926. He was buried in Loudon Park Cemetery in his wife's hometown of Baltimore, Maryland. Piedmont Sanatorium continued operating until 1967, when it was transferred to the state's Department of Mental Hygiene and Hospitals, and in 1977 became Piedmont Geriatric Hospital, the only state-operated psychiatric hospital for the elderly in Virginia.

Arthur W. Hafner, ed., *Directory of Deceased American Physicians, 1804–1929* (1993), 255; birth date of Nov. 1886 in Census, Northumberland Co., 1900; Northumberland Co. likely birthplace from parents' enumeration there by the 1880 and 1900 censuses and from registered birth of elder sister there in 1883; BVS Death Certificate, Nottoway Co., gives variant birthplace of "Kilmarnock, Northumberland Co.," and variant birth date of 8 Nov. 1884 but records age at death as thirty-nine years and six months; College of William and Mary *Colonial Echo* (1908), 21 (por.); marriage license reported in *Baltimore Sun*, 29 June 1916 (age given as twenty-nine); Carter's writings compiled in *Papers of Dr. H. G. Carter (Deceased)* . . . (1929); *Annual Report of the State Board of Health and the State Health Commissioner*, 1918–1926; Marion M. Torchia, "Tuberculosis among American Negroes: Medical Research on a Racial Disease, 1830–1950," *Journal of the History of Medicine and the Allied Sciences* 32 (1977): 252–279; obituaries in *Baltimore Sun* and *Richmond Times-Dispatch*, both 12 Apr. 1926, *Blackstone Courier*, 16 Apr. 1926, and *Virginia Medical Monthly* 53 (1926): 138–139 (birthplace of Northumberland Co.); memorials in *American Review of Tuberculosis* 14 (1926): 344–345 (variant birthplace of Lancaster Co.), and *Sunbeams* 10 (June 1926): 14–16 (variant birthplace of Kilmarnock, Lancaster Co.).

MARIANNE E. JULIENNE

CARTER, Henry Rose (25 August 1852–14 September 1925), epidemiologist, was the son of Henry Rose Carter, a successful farmer, and Emma Caroline Coleman Carter. His elder brother Hill Carter served in the Convention of 1901–1902. Born at Clifton plantation, in Caroline County, Carter moved with his family in 1855 to North River plantation, in Hanover County, where he received much of his early education. He attended a Louisa County academy and graduated from the University of Virginia in 1873 as a civil engineer. Carter remained at the college for the 1874–1875 academic year as an assistant instructor in applied mathematics while also taking classes in modern languages. A broken leg and possible permanent disability turned his interest to medicine, and in 1879 he graduated from the University of Maryland School of Medicine. On 29 September 1880 Carter married Laura Eugenia Hook, of Cairo, Illinois. They had two sons and one daughter.

On 5 May 1879 Carter entered the Marine-Hospital Service (later the United States Public Health Service) as assistant surgeon. During the next decade he served at hospital stations in Boston; Cairo, Illinois; Memphis; New Orleans; and San Francisco. From January 1888 until 1892 he was quarantine officer at Ship Island, in the Gulf of Mexico off Biloxi, Mississippi, and at the Chandeleur Islands, off the coast of Louisiana. During this posting Carter prepared standardized regulations governing disinfection of ships and quarantine of ships' companies that became the basis for the United States maritime quarantine system.

Yellow fever became a major part of Carter's research while at Ship Island. Throughout the 1890s the hospital service posted him to areas suffering yellow fever epidemics, and in November 1897 he contracted the disease. His suppression of the epidemic in McHenry, Stone County, Mississippi, in 1898 was the first time the disease had been controlled in warm weather. Because yellow fever epidemics in Cuba were considered a threat to the United States, in January 1899 Carter was ordered to the island as an inspector and on 2 June of that year was detailed as a quarantine officer there. From September 1899 until February 1900 he served temporary assignments in Florida, New Orleans, and Washington, D.C., before returning to Cuba and being promoted to chief quarantine officer on 21 June 1900. On the island Carter implemented his maritime quarantine and disinfection procedures.

Carter's work during the Mississippi epidemic of 1898, which he described in an article for the *New Orleans Medical and Surgical Journal* in 1900, confirmed his hypothesis about the extrinsic incubation of yellow fever in an intermediate host. Carter's observation led to Walter Reed's identification of the mosquito as the conveyer of the disease. For this achievement Carter was nominated to share the 1906 Nobel Prize in medicine.

In 1904 Carter became chief quarantine officer of the Isthmian Canal Commission and from 1905 until 1909 was director of hospitals in Panama. He was second in command to Colonel William Crawford Gorgas in overseeing public health during the construction of the Panama Canal. That great engineering feat could not have been achieved without the work of Carter, Gorgas, and Reed. Because of Carter's outstanding work in combating yellow fever, he received an honorary LL.D. in 1910 from the University of Maryland, and his service in Panama led to his commission as assistant surgeon general on 6 March 1915, to date from 4 March.

From 1913 until his retirement in 1920, Carter studied malaria and used mosquito control to suppress the disease. For nearly two years after being placed on waiting orders he served as sanitary adviser in Peru. He published numerous articles on yellow fever and malaria, and during World War I he directed efforts to control malaria in army camps. Because Henry Rose Carter was one of the nation's leading epidemiologists, the International Health Board of the Rockefeller Foundation asked him to write a history of yellow fever. Following Carter's death in Washington, D.C., on 14 September 1925 and his burial in Woodland Cemetery in Hanover County, Virginia, his daughter and assistant, Laura Armistead Carter, helped complete his manuscript, which was published in 1931 as *Yellow Fever: An Epidemiological and Historical Study of Its Place of Origin*.

Southern Medical Journal 8 (1915): 544–547; Jane Stafford, "Henry Rose Carter," *Hygeia* 4 (1926): 201–202 (por.); Howard A. Kelly and Walter L. Burrage, eds., *Dictionary of American Medical Biography* (1928), 203–204; T. H. D. Griffitts, "Henry Rose Carter: The Scientist and the Man," *Southern Medical Journal* 32 (1939): 841–848; Elihu D. Richter, "Henry R. Carter—An Overlooked Skeptical Epidemiologist," *New England Journal of Medicine* 277 (1967): 734–738 (por.); Henry Rose Carter Papers (including 1912 autobiographical sketch, bibliography of Carter's works compiled by his daughter, certificates and degrees, and letter from John W. Ross to the members of the Medical Nobel Committee, 9 Jan. 1906) and Philip S. Hench Walter Reed Yellow Fever Collection, both Claude Moore Health Sciences Library, UVA; Henry Rose Carter Papers, National Library of Medicine, Bethesda, Md.; major publications include Carter, "A Note on the Interval between Infecting and Secondary Cases of Yellow Fever from the Records of the Yellow Fever at Orwood and Taylor, Miss., in 1898," *New Orleans Medical and Surgical Journal* 52 (1900): 617–636, "The Period of Incubation of Yellow Fever: A Study from Unpublished Observations," *Medical Record* 59 (1901): 361–367, and *Yellow Fever*, ed. Laura Armistead Carter and Wade Hampton Frost (1931), including bibliography of Carter's writings on 275; personnel records, U.S. Public Health Service, RG 90, NARA; obituaries in *Richmond News Leader* (editorial tribute on 15 Sept. 1925), 14 Sept. 1925, *New York Times*, *Richmond Times-Dispatch* (editorial tribute on 16 Sept. 1925), and *Washington Post*, all 15 Sept. 1925, *Journal of the American Medical Association*, 26 Sept. 1925, and *Virginia Medical Monthly* 53 (1925): 474; memorials in *Boston Evening Globe*, 24 Nov. 1925, and *American Journal of Tropical Medicine* 5 (1925): 385–388.

ELIZABETH NEWSOME WEAKLEY

CARTER, Hill (12 April 1846–15 January 1918), member of the Convention of 1901–1902, was born at Clifton, the Caroline County plantation of his parents, Henry Rose Carter, a well-to-do farmer, and Emma Caroline Coleman Carter. His younger brother Henry Rose Carter (1852–1925) became a distinguished epidemiologist whose research was critical in controlling yellow fever. In 1855 his father settled the family at North River, a plantation in the Beaverdam area of northern Hanover County, where Carter attended a local school. Not quite eighteen years old when he enlisted in Confederate service on 1 April 1864, he served as a private in the Amelia Light Dragoons, Company G of the 1st Virginia Cavalry. Carter was wounded at the Battle of Spotsylvania Court House in May and later saw action in Jubal Anderson Early's Shenandoah Valley campaign. Captured on 12 March 1865 at Fredericks Hall in Louisa County, he remained in a Union prison at Point Lookout, Saint Mary's County, Maryland, until his release on 24 June 1865 after taking the oath of allegiance.

Carter studied law at Washington College (later Washington and Lee University) under

John White Brockenbrough during the academic year 1868–1869 and received a bachelor's degree at the close of the term. He was admitted to the Hanover County bar late in 1870 and during the next decade served as commonwealth's attorney for the county. A resident of Ashland, Carter joined the Richmond lawyers Alexander Hamilton Sands and William Josiah Leake to establish the firm Sands, Leake and Carter (later Leake and Carter) in the Virginia capital. On 23 December 1873 he married Emily H. Redd, of Caroline County. They had six sons and another child who did not live to adulthood.

Carter became a leader of the Hanover County and state bars. Enjoying a reputation as a well-rounded lawyer, he handled both criminal and civil cases. Carter appeared in numerous civil actions before the Virginia Supreme Court of Appeals and in 1899 argued *Richmond v. Southern Bell Telephone and Telegraph Company* before the Supreme Court of the United States. Noted for the thoroughness of his preparation and the strength of his presentation, he eloquently but unsuccessfully defended the accused murderers in the sensational trials of Samuel Hardy in Nansemond County in 1908 and of Henry Clay Beattie Jr. in Chesterfield County in 1911.

A lifelong Democrat, Carter served as a presidential elector for Winfield Scott Hancock in 1880. Campaigning on a neutral platform and without opposition, Carter won election on 23 May 1901 to represent Hanover County in the state constitutional convention that met from 12 June 1901 until 26 June 1902. He was appointed to the temporary Committee of Privilege and Election and to the standing Committees on the Preamble and Bill of Rights and on the Legislative Department. Carter addressed the convention several times on varying subjects including shortening the preamble to the Bill of Rights and the method of adopting the constitution. He argued against an eminent domain provision, the popular election of judges, and a liquor license amendment. In the Committee on the Legislative Department he was coauthor of two minority reports upholding the ban on public funding for private institutions and against broadening the scope of compensation for damaged private

property. In June 1901 Carter introduced a resolution limiting the suffrage to men age twenty-one or older who owned property worth at least $100 and who had paid both property and poll taxes. On 4 April 1902 he voted with the majority in favor of restrictive voter registration requirements designed to reduce the number of black and poor white voters, and on 29 May he again sided with the majority to proclaim the new constitution in effect rather than submit it to the electorate for ratification. On 6 June, Carter voted for adoption of the constitution.

After the convention adjourned, Carter resumed practicing law. Hill Carter died at his home in Ashland on 15 January 1918 of blood poisoning caused by a gangrenous left foot and complicated by diabetes. He was buried two days later in Woodland Cemetery in Hanover County.

Birth date in Pollard Questionnaires; Compiled Service Records; BVS Marriage Register, Hanover Co.; *Richmond v. Southern Bell Telephone and Telegraph Company* (1899), *United States Reports*, 174:761–778; *Hardy* v. *Commonwealth* (1910), *Virginia Reports*, 110:910–934; J. Bunyan Jones, *History of the Case of the Commonwealth of Virginia vs. Samuel Hardy . . .* (1910); *A Full and Complete History of the Great Beattie Case . . .* (1911), 76; Election Records, nos. 47, 102, RG 13, LVA; *Richmond Dispatch*, 24 May 1901; *Richmond Times*, 12 June 1901; *Journal of 1901–1902 Convention*, 486–487, 504, 535, and appended "Minority Report of the Committee on the Legislative Department" and "Second Minority Report of the Committee on the Legislative Department"; *Proceedings and Debates of 1901–1902 Convention*, 1:164–173, 707–711, 1376–1380, 2:2114–2116, 3188–3197; *Resolutions of 1901–1902 Convention*, no. 97; *Convention of 1901–1902 Photographs* (por.); BVS Death Certificate, Hanover Co.; obituaries in *Richmond News Leader*, 16 Jan. 1918 (por.), and *Richmond Times-Dispatch*, 17 Jan. 1918; memorial in *Virginia State Bar Association Proceedings* (1918), 95–98.

CATHERINE T. MISHLER

CARTER, James B. (ca. 1816–11 January 1870), member of the Convention of 1867–1868, was born into slavery, probably in Chesterfield County and probably of mixed-race ancestry. The names of his parents are undocumented, and nothing is known about his life during slavery. After the Civil War he was described as a boot-and shoemaker, so it is possible that he received some training as a cobbler. Although the list of convention delegates compiled by Virginia's military commander, Brigadier General John

McAllister Schofield, states that Carter was illiterate, he managed to acquire enough education, either while a slave or after emancipation, to be able to sign his name, and comments he made on the floor of the Underwood Convention suggest that he could read as well.

Possibly Carter escaped to the North during the Civil War, but he was living in Chesterfield County in February 1866, when he was taxed 28 cents as a male Negro over age twenty-one. He next appears in the public record in December of that year when he purchased two lots in the community of Swansboro, near Manchester, from William H. Brander, a wealthy farmer who may have been Carter's former owner. Carter probably practiced his trade as a shoemaker until 1868 or 1869, when he and a partner opened a grocery under the name of Smith and Carter. The store stood on a lot in Manchester that Carter bought in April 1868 for $425, most likely with the money he earned as a delegate to the state constitutional convention.

Carter had entered politics by April 1867, when he represented Chesterfield County at a convention of black and white Republicans who met in Richmond to prepare for the upcoming constitutional convention. The First Reconstruction Act, passed by Congress in March, mandated new constitutions for the former Confederate states in addition to placing the South under military rule and granting freedmen the right to vote. Chesterfield County Radical Republicans convened in Manchester to select candidates for the convention, and on 3 October 1867 a meeting of African American Republicans recommended Carter. A respected member of his community, Carter was nominated unanimously at the county's Radical convention held four days later. Charles Howell Porter, son-in-law of former United States senator Lemuel Jackson Bowden and a future member of the House of Representatives, and Samuel F. Maddox, a Pennsylvania native who later served in the General Assembly, overcame opposition to join Carter on the Radical ticket. African Americans in the district consisting of Chesterfield and Powhatan Counties turned out in large numbers on 22 October 1867 in their first opportunity to vote in a Virginia election. They overwhelmingly supported holding a convention and easily elected the Radical candidates, who also received votes from at least ten whites.

The convention opened on 3 December 1867, and nine days later Carter was appointed to the Committee on County and Corporation Courts and County Organizations. He remained silent during the first two months of the convention but spoke on 17 January 1868 in favor of continuing night sessions in order to complete the convention's business more quickly. Carter commented that too many delegates were wasting too much time with long speeches on irrelevant topics, whereas he had come to listen to the debates and "conceive whatever I believe to be right in the formation of this Constitution." On 28 January he again spoke out in favor of limiting speeches to half an hour. He also introduced several resolutions on the convention floor, including one that the General Assembly pass a law requiring students to attend public schools at least three months of every year. Carter voted with the Radicals on nearly all issues that came up during the convention, although he did side with the Conservatives against requiring racial integration in public schools. On 17 April 1868 he joined the majority in approving the new constitution, which mandated universal manhood suffrage, created a new system of publicly funded schools, and transformed the organization of county government.

The day after the convention closed, Carter attended a Radical meeting at the State Capitol to discuss appointments to state offices and nominations for Congress. Carter does not appear to have taken part in any further political activities, however, and he did not seek office in the elections held in July 1869. Carter had married a woman named Alice, surname unknown, by 7 January 1869, when he sold his two lots in Swansboro and mortgaged his lot in Manchester for $115. It is not known whether Carter and his wife had been married before or after emancipation or whether they had any children, because no marriage or births were ever recorded under their names in Chesterfield County. James B. Carter died at his home in Manchester early in the morning of 11 January 1870 and was buried from the African Baptist church (later First Baptist Church, South Richmond) in that town.

Jackson, *Negro Office-Holders*, 7; Chesterfield Co. Deed Book, 49:74, 51:97–98, 175–177, 53:624–625; Land Tax Returns, Chesterfield Co. (1869–1872), RG 48, LVA; Personal Property Tax Returns, Chesterfield Co. (1866–1869), RG 48, LVA; *Daily Richmond Enquirer*, 18 Apr. 1867; *Richmond Daily Dispatch*, 5, 8, 24, 25 Oct. 1867; *Richmond Daily Enquirer and Examiner*, 5, 8, 9 (Carter referred to as "Brander's Jim" and as "self-appointed ambassador North during the war"), 12 Oct. 1867; *Richmond Whig*, 24 Oct., 2 Nov. 1867; *Daily Richmond Whig*, 20 Apr. 1868; *Debates and Proceedings of 1867–1868 Convention*, 491–492 (quotation), 603, 640, 702; Hume, "Membership of Convention of 1867–1868," 481; Lowe, "Virginia's Reconstruction Convention," 354; death notice (indicating death "in the fifty-fifth year of his age") in *Richmond Daily Dispatch*, 12 Jan. 1870.

MARIANNE E. JULIENNE

CARTER, James Thomas (13 February 1874–19 November 1959), attorney and business leader, was born in Richmond and was the son of Elsie Russell Carter and William Henry Carter, a shoemaker and watchman. He attended Richmond public schools but quit during his teens to help support his family. At age sixteen Carter went to work as driver, personal attendant, office assistant, and porter for George Llewellyn Christian, a prominent Richmond attorney and retired judge who had lost his left foot and part of his right heel in Confederate military service. Impressed with the importance of education to an urban-dwelling African American, Carter in the mid-1890s received private instruction in bookkeeping, shorthand, and typing from white teachers at the Smithdeal Business College, in Richmond. After Carter completed the course, Christian promoted him to full-time bookkeeper, stenographer, and typist for his law firm. Carter was then the only African American holding such a responsible position in a leading firm of white Richmond lawyers. Carter worked for Christian for about twenty years.

On 29 November 1900 Carter married Mary Elizabeth Harper. Later an influential civic leader, especially in the causes of social work and domestic training, she was education and industrial secretary of the Phyllis Wheatley Branch of the Young Women's Christian Association from 1928 until her death on 3 November 1931. She earned a B.A. in education at Virginia Union University in June 1927 and at the time of her death taught industrial relations at the university's Francis J. Torrance School of Race Relations. The Carters' only child, a son, died in August 1927, shortly before he was to enter the law school of the University of Michigan.

Following his marriage, Carter began reading in Christian's law library during his free time. He honed his legal knowledge by taking a correspondence course administered by instructors at the University of Richmond and the University of Virginia. In 1916 Carter passed the state bar examination and was one of only a few who passed in all subject areas on his first attempt. His law practice attained similar success. Many black-owned corporations in central Virginia, including the Commercial Bank and Trust Company, employed him as attorney, and in 1918 he became general counsel of the Southern Aid Society of Virginia, the oldest African American insurance company in the United States. In April 1921, following the sudden death of the company's president, the board elected Carter the society's fourth president. His reputation in the black business community soared, and the following year the stockholders of the Commercial Bank and Trust Company elected Carter president of the bank. In 1931, after Commercial merged with and became Consolidated Bank and Trust Company, he served as vice president, and later he sat on the board of directors.

For fifteen years before 1929 Carter had held office, including grand treasurer, in the Improved Benevolent and Protective Order of Elks of the World. In that year he formed a renegade Virginia branch with the same name. The original order, maintaining that it held rights to the name, successfully sued Carter and three associates, and Carter's Virginia chapter lost its charter. Nevertheless, Carter remained active in benevolent and social organizations as well as in the legal and business communities. His appointment in June 1935 as vice supreme master of the National Ideal Benefit Society made front-page news in the *Richmond Planet*. At various times he was a Freemason and member of the National Association for the Advancement of Colored People, the Urban League, and several other fraternal and service organizations; he was also chairman of the board of Richmond Community Hospital, a director of Bankers' Fire Insurance Company, of Durham, North Carolina, and superintendent of the Sunday school at Second Baptist Church, of which he was a member for more than sixty years. During World War II, Carter served as an adviser for the Selective Service Questionnaire Board and as a commissioner in chancery of the court of law and equity in Richmond. In 1941 Virginia Union University awarded him an honorary law degree.

James Thomas Carter was still president and general counsel of the Southern Aid Society when he died in Richmond on 19 November 1959. He was buried in the city's Evergreen Cemetery.

Biographies in Joseph J. Boris, ed., *Who's Who in Colored America*, 2d ed. (1928/1929), 72, and M. S. Stuart, *An Economic Detour: A History of Insurance in the Lives of American Negroes* (1940), 233–234 (por. facing 230); BVS Birth Register, Richmond City; variant birth date of 13 Feb. 1875 in index to Richmond City Department of Public Health Birth Records; BVS Marriage Register, Richmond City; one Carter letter, 14 Nov. 1931, in Lucy Randolph Mason Papers, *Operation Dixie: The C.I.O. Organizing Committee Papers, 1946–1953* (1980 microfilm); Southern Aid Society of Virginia Records, Acc. 36805, LVA; *Richmond Planet*, 30 Apr. 1921, 18 Feb. 1922, 13 Aug. 1927, 15 June 1935; *Richmond News Leader*, 4 Nov. 1931; obituary of wife by Lucy Randolph Mason in *Richmond Times-Dispatch*, 5 Nov. 1931; Charles H. Wesley, *History of the Improved Benevolent and Protective Order of Elks of the World, 1898–1954* (1955), 227–229; John A. Cutchins, *Memories of Old Richmond (1881–1944)* (1973), 120; obituaries in *Richmond News Leader* and *Richmond Times-Dispatch*, both 20 Nov. 1959; obituary and account of funeral in *Richmond Afro American*, 28 Nov. 1959.

ALEXANDER H. LORCH III

CARTER, John (ca. 1613–10 January 1670), member of the Council, was born into an English family with commercial and kinship connections to members of the Virginia Company of London. He was probably the son of John Carter, a London vintner, and his second wife, Bridget Benion Carter. Historians once described Carter as an unhappy royalist who fled England after the execution of Charles I in 1649, but he had traveled to Virginia as early as 1635, when he gave his age as twenty-two on boarding the *Safety* on 10 August. He may have been the John Carter, of London, age about twenty-three, who sailed to Virginia in 1637 but whose ship was captured by the Spanish. Literate in English and proba-

bly in Latin, Carter was better prepared to succeed than some of his contemporaries. Like many other young men with commercial connections, he may have made multiple crossings of the Atlantic while learning the tobacco trade. Carter's familial relationship to Edward Carter (d. 1682), who served with him in the House of Burgesses and on the governor's Council, was probably close but is unknown.

Carter almost certainly decided to settle permanently in Virginia sometime before he was elected a burgess from Upper Norfolk County (later Nansemond County) for the assembly that met in January and June 1642. He also sat in the assembly that met on 2 March 1643, when for the first time the burgesses convened as a separate house. He represented Nansemond County again in the 1649 assembly. In 1642 Carter obtained the first of several grants of land on the north bank of the Rappahannock River in what became Lancaster County nine years later. There he established Corotoman, which became the family seat, and during the next quarter century amassed several thousand acres by patents and purchases. He received his largest single grant, for 4,000 acres, in 1665 for transporting to Virginia eighty people, including twenty-one of African origin or descent.

By 1652 Carter was a major in the county militia and soon thereafter became a colonel. Representing Lancaster County in the assemblies of 1654–1655 and 1658, Carter in the spring session of 1658 chaired committees that presented proposed revisions of the colony's laws to Governor Samuel Mathews (d. 1660) and that defended the burgesses' rights when the House got into a dispute with the governor and Council. On 13 March 1658 the burgesses elected Carter to the governor's Council, a selection the House confirmed on 3 April of that year, but on 15 March 1659 the assembly postponed a decision whether to reelect him. Carter served in the House of Burgesses again in the spring of 1659 and was present in Jamestown when news arrived of the death of Oliver Cromwell and the succession of his son, Richard Cromwell, as lord protector. A royalist, Carter objected so sternly that on 8 April 1659 the governor issued a warrant for his arrest. How long Carter remained in custody and the result of the arrest are not known. He returned to Jamestown again as a burgess for the March 1660 assembly, which elected Sir William Berkeley governor pending receipt of a commission from the restored king, Charles II.

After Berkeley's reelection, Carter won reappointment to the Council. Records of the governor's Council are scarce, a consequence of the destruction of most of the official documents, and the date of his appointment is not known. Carter joined other Council members and Berkeley in March 1663 in complaints after the king granted the Northern Neck to several court favorites, and that same spring he took part in negotiating an agreement that the Virginia and Maryland Councils concluded to reduce tobacco production in hopes of raising the crop's price. Carter was busy with his own affairs and could not attend all the recorded Council meetings in Jamestown, but he was present in June 1667 when the governor and Council wrote the king concerning the colony's defense during the Second Anglo-Dutch War (1665–1667) and remained a member until his death.

Carter exemplified the success that young men of urban backgrounds could attain in the middle third of the seventeenth century by entering the tobacco trade and becoming Virginia landowners and planters. The inventory of his estate, taken in July 1670, listed more than thirty indentured servants, with the amount of time left in each of their terms of service, and more than forty persons of African origin or descent, none of whom had a stated limit on future service. The distinction suggests that Carter, like other leading planters of his time, was shifting to a greater reliance on black laborers held in lifetime service.

Carter's success in business and in acquiring land, together with his political prominence, made him an increasingly attractive marriage partner in a society in which women were still in short supply. He founded one of the greatest of the colonial Virginia families. Carter married Jane Glyn, perhaps before settling in Virginia. The date and place of their marriage and the time of her death are not known. They had a daughter, who married a member of the Maryland governor's Council, and two sons. One of them died

young, and the other, John Carter (d. 1690), served in the assembly during the summer of 1676. Carter married Eleanor Eltonhead Brocas, the recent widow of the Council member William Brocas, in 1655. They are not known to have had any children before her death not long thereafter. On a trip to England in 1656 Carter married Anne Carter, who soon died, also without having any recorded children. By early in the 1660s Carter had married Sarah Ludlow. They had one daughter, who died in infancy, and one son, Robert Carter (ca. 1664–1732), before her death. On 24 October 1668 Carter executed a marriage agreement and then or very soon afterward married Elizabeth Sherley. Their son died probably early in the 1690s.

John Carter died, probably at Corotoman, on 10 January 1670 and was buried at the first Christ Church in Lancaster County, a parish and a church he had helped build. His fifth wife, one daughter, and three sons survived him, among them Robert Carter, who eclipsed him and who, because of his vast accumulation of wealth, other Virginians called King Carter.

Noel Currer-Briggs, *The Carters of Virginia: Their English Ancestry* (1979), 14–24, 59–60, 102–104; age twenty-two on 10 Aug. 1635 (PRO E 157/20, fol. 56); public records pertaining to Carter abstracted in Christine Jones, *John Carter I of "Corotoman," Lancaster County, Virginia* (1977); legislative career and first election to Council documented in *JHB, 1619–1659*, 108, 110–113, and Hening, *Statutes*, vols. 1–2; 1659 arrest records in Lancaster Co. Deeds Etc., 2:185–186; Egerton MSS 2395, fols. 360–362, British Library; PRO CO 1/17, fol. 68, CO 1/21, fols. 109–112; fifth marriage settlement in Lancaster Co. Deeds Etc., 4:63; original signed will in Lancaster Co. Wills and Administrations (1652–1800), LVA; will recorded on 9 Jan. 1722 in Lancaster Co. Wills Etc., 10:416–419; estate inventory, 29 July 1670, in Lancaster Co. Fiduciary Records (1651–1773), LVA; names of first four wives and Carter's death date (10 Jan. 1669 Old Style) on gravestone.

MARTIN H. QUITT

CARTER, John (1695 or 1696–31 July 1742), secretary of the colony and member of the Council, was born probably at Corotoman, the Lancaster County plantation of his parents, Robert "King" Carter (ca. 1664–1732) and his first wife, Judith Armistead Carter. His younger half brothers included Charles Carter (ca. 1707–1764), who represented King George County in the

House of Burgesses, and Landon Carter, who represented Richmond County in the assembly. Carter's father, an extraordinarily successful merchant and planter and rising political figure, had high ambitions for him and sent him to England to be educated. Carter attended Mile End School, in London, entered the Middle Temple to study law in April 1713, and at age eighteen matriculated at Trinity College, University of Cambridge, on 12 January 1714. He became part of a small and frequently changing community of Virginians in London, most of whom were there on business or for their education. Carter lived very well in England and occasionally exceeded the £200 per year his father allowed him. A £50 bill from a tailor aggravated Robert Carter, who consoled himself that at least Carter had maintained a good character. "To have spent so much money upon a dunce or a blockhead," his father admitted, would have been "most intolerable." Like many other young gentlemen, Carter did not graduate from the university, but unlike many others, he completed his legal education and was called to the bar on 27 May 1720.

Carter represented his father's business interests in London and briefly acted as the colony's solicitor under an appointment from the lieutenant governor and Council. Carter's father, who had become a leading member of the Council, purchased for him the patent for the office of secretary of the colony. Carter received his appointment on 21 June 1722 and that winter returned to Virginia. The secretary's office, which he held for life, was both lucrative and politically powerful. The secretary was the colony's record keeper. He appointed all of the clerks of the county courts and received from each a portion of the fees that the clerks were allowed in lieu of a salary. The secretary also earned fees from more than sixty different services, such as issuing writs for the election of burgesses and making out and recording land patents. By the time of Carter's death, his annual income as secretary was estimated at £1,800. When a vacancy on the Council occurred in 1723, Robert Carter pressed to have John Carter named to that office, too, and on 23 January 1724 King George I made the appointment. Father and son served on the Council together until the father's death almost nine years later.

Although Carter was efficient and responsible in both offices, some men, including Lieutenant Governor Hugh Drysdale, were concerned about the extent of the power of the secretary and perhaps worried about a potential for corruption if he retained the authority to appoint all of the county clerks. Drysdale mentioned his concerns to the Board of Trade, prompting Carter in 1727, not long after Drysdale's death, to defend his conduct and the perquisites of the office. He asserted that he had not sold clerkships or illegally profited from his position. Secretaries of the colony retained the right to appoint county clerks and receive a portion of their incomes until the Revolution. Carter remained ambitious, and later in 1727 he attempted to obtain appointment as deputy auditor of the royal revenue in Virginia, another influential and lucrative office, but that effort was unsuccessful. He held his seat on the Council and the position of secretary until his death.

Carter married Elizabeth Hill, of Charles City County, on 3 October 1723. They had one daughter, later the first wife of William Byrd (1728–1777), and three sons, one of whom, Charles Carter (1732–1806), represented Lancaster County in the House of Burgesses. The marriage gave Carter and his wife ownership of Shirley plantation, which she inherited following the death of her father. Carter lived at Shirley until the death of his own father in 1732 and thereafter divided his time among Shirley, Corotoman, and a town house that he owned in Williamsburg. He was a busy man, especially after he and his half brothers undertook to administer their father's enormous estate. Carter did most of the work, which occupied him until his death. His own estate demanded his close attention as well. By that time it consisted of about 52,000 acres of land, on which he raised tobacco and grain and where hundreds of tenants and slaves lived and labored. Carter also continued to operate his father's mercantile concern in Lancaster County, and like his father he was a substantial trader in slaves.

Carter's life epitomized the eighteenth-century Virginia elite. He held powerful and profitable public offices; he was related to many of the colony's other leading families, among them

Braxton, Burwell, Byrd, Harrison, Hill, Page, and Randolph; and he raced blooded horses, attended cockfights, and socialized with friends and neighbors. He also erected an imposing mansion at Shirley, an elegant plantation house that remains the property's most famous landmark. Completed about 1738, it symbolized Carter's status as one of the colony's wealthiest gentlemen. Not long afterward, while Carter was still in his early forties, his health began to decline. He attended the Council for the last time on 3 November 1741 and was reported during that winter to be "very ill of the Dropsy in the Belly." John Carter signed his will on the following 1 July and died, probably at Shirley or in Williamsburg, on 31 July 1742. Most likely he was buried at Shirley or in the graveyard of the Westover Parish church.

Biographies in George Selden Wallace, *The Carters of Blenheim: A Genealogy of Edward and Sarah Champe Carter of "Blenheim," Albemarle County, Virginia* (1955), 1–2, 11 (por.), 16, and Catherine M. Lynn, "Shirley Plantation: A History" (M.A. thesis, University of Delaware, 1967), 34–65; age recorded as eighteen on 12 Jan. 1714 in John Venn and J. A. Venn, comps., *Alumni Cantabrigienses* (1922), 1:300; Sir Henry F. MacGeagh and H. A. C. Sturgess, comps., *Register of Admissions to the Honourable Society of the Middle Temple* (1949), 1:272; John Carter correspondence in Carter Family Letter Book (1732–1782), UVA; marriage date in Robert Carter to Micajah Perry, 17 Oct. 1723, Robert Carter Letter Book (1723–1724), UVA; appointment as secretary in British Library, Add. MSS 36125; appointment to Council in PRO CO 5/1319, fol. 161; John Carter to secretary of state, 22 Jan. 1727 with enclosure, PRO CO 5/1337, fols. 97–104; Louis B. Wright, ed., *Letters of Robert Carter, 1720–1727: The Commercial Interests of a Virginia Gentleman* (1940), 4 (first quotation); Junius Rodes Fishburne Jr., "The Office of Secretary of State in Colonial Virginia" (Ph.D. diss., Tulane University, 1971), 346–363; Theodore R. Reinhart, ed., *The Archaeology of Shirley Plantation* (1984); William Beverley to Chr. Smyth, 10 Mar. 1742, William Beverley Letter Book, New York Public Library, printed in *WMQ*, 1st ser., 3 (1895): 229 (second quotation); date of lost will in Hening, *Statutes*, 8:465; Caroline Co. estate accounts and inventory in Carter Family Papers (1728–1892), VHS; death date in William Gooch to secretary of state, 28 July 1742, with postscript of 1 Aug. 1742, PRO CO 5/1337, fols. 265–266.

EMORY G. EVANS

CARTER, John Armistead (15 November 1808–12 January 1895), member of the Convention of 1850–1851 and of the Convention of 1861, was born probably at his father's ancestral seat, Sabine Hall, in Richmond County. He was the son of Landon Carter (1757–1820) and his second wife, Mary Burwell Armistead Carter. Following his father's death, Carter's legal guardians directed the completion of his education. He attended Phillips Academy, in Andover, Massachusetts, and entered the University of Virginia in February 1826, but in May of that year he and several other students were expelled for violating the school rules. Carter attended the Winchester law school of Henry St. George Tucker (1780–1848) from 1827 to 1829 and then settled in Loudoun County (where his family had long owned property) and practiced law in Leesburg. He married Richardetta L. DeButts on 12 February 1834. They had at least one son before she died in Baltimore on 10 May 1847.

Though trained as a lawyer, Carter prospered as a planter and was listed in the 1850 census as a farmer who owned thirty-two slaves and real estate worth $32,000. Ten years later he owned twenty-six slaves and valued his land at $37,000 and his personal property at more than $26,000. A Whig, Carter won election to represent Loudoun County in the House of Delegates for two one-year terms beginning in 1842, but he did not run for reelection in 1844. During both assembly sessions he sat on the Committee of Roads and Internal Navigation, and during the second session he was a member of the Committee of Propositions and Grievances.

On 22 August 1850 Carter received the most votes of seven candidates vying for three seats representing Loudoun County in a convention called to revise the state constitution. He served on the Committee on the Legislative Department of the Government. As a slaveholder, Carter might have been expected to side with the other eastern delegates on questions of apportioning seats in the General Assembly, but he spoke forcefully in March 1851 in favor of basing legislative representation solely on the white male population and of universal white manhood suffrage. He voted on 16 May of that year for a compromise plan that ceded the western counties a majority of seats in the House of Delegates and left the eastern counties with a majority in the state senate. On 31 July 1851 Carter voted to approve the constitution that the convention submitted to a successful referendum later that year.

Loudoun County voters elected Carter to the Senate of Virginia in 1859. Serving through the term's completion in the spring of 1861, he was named to the Committee on Agriculture and Commerce, the Committee on Finance and Claims, and a joint committee to examine the first auditor's office. Carter's moment of greatest prominence came during the secession crisis. Few in Loudoun County advocated secession during the winter of 1860–1861, and local men adopted resolutions urging compromise and negotiation to bring the crisis to a peaceful conclusion. On 4 February 1861 Carter narrowly defeated the third-place candidate to win one of two Loudoun County seats in the convention called to consider Virginia's response to the secession of the Deep South states. He spoke infrequently during the convention and tended to address procedural matters or points of clarification, as he had during the earlier convention. He voted against sending peace commissioners to Washington, D.C., but later supported their efforts, and he voted against secession on 4 April 1861. Trying to preserve peace and the status quo as long as negotiations continued, Carter in his one extended speech, on 9 April 1861, asked that the United States not attempt to hold federal installations in seceded states and that seceded states not attempt to seize federal installations. On 17 April, in the wake of the firing on Fort Sumter and Abraham Lincoln's call for troops, the convention voted in favor of secession, but Carter again opposed the motion and explained that he was following his conscience rather than orders from his constituents.

Unlike many other Unionists who left Richmond following the second vote on secession, Carter remained and took part in the final days of the convention's first session as it created an army and voted to join the Confederacy. Like many other Virginians and his Loudoun constituents, who endorsed secession in the May 1861 referendum, he abandoned his Unionism once the war began, and he signed the Ordinance of Secession. Carter returned to Richmond for the short second session of the convention in June and for the third session in November. He

took no other part in the Civil War, but his son served in the Confederate cavalry. On 28 August 1865 Carter swore the oath of allegiance and applied for a presidential pardon necessitated by his participation in the secession convention and the continued high value of his property, even though his barns, stables, and other outbuildings had been destroyed during local fighting.

After the war Carter shared his Loudoun County farmhouse with his son's family. In 1873 he won election to the first of two consecutive terms in the House of Delegates. In the 1874–1875 assembly session he served on the Committee on Finance, and during the following session he sat on the Committee on the Chesapeake and Its Tributaries. For both terms he chaired the Committee on Immigration. As Carter grew older his eyesight failed, and he became an invalid. John Armistead Carter died at his Loudoun County residence on 12 January 1895.

Birth date in French Biographies; guardian accounts and letters in Carter Papers (1667–1862), W&M; Loudoun Co. Marriage Records (1794–1850), 85; Alexandria Gazette, 31 Mar. 1843; Richmond Enquirer, 27, 30 Aug. 1850; Journal of 1850–1851 Convention, 419, and Appendix, 22; Supplement 1850–1851 Convention Debates, no. 38; Reese and Gaines, Proceedings of 1861 Convention, 3:163, 368, 437–438, 440–442, 4:119, 144; Charles P. Poland Jr., "Loudoun County during the Civil War: A Study of a Border County in a Border State" (M.A. thesis, American University, 1962), 13–23; Presidential Pardons; obituary in Leesburg Mirror, 24 Jan. 1895.

ANNE SARAH RUBIN

CARTER, Landon (18 August 1710–22 December 1778), writer and member of the House of Burgesses, was the son of Robert "King" Carter (ca. 1664–1732) and his second wife, Elizabeth Landon Willis Carter, who was a wealthy widow at the time of their marriage. Landon Carter was born probably at Corotoman, the family's seat in Lancaster County. His father was one of the most prominent public figures of his generation and was probably the wealthiest man in Virginia at the time of his death. Carter's elder half brother John Carter (d. 1742) became secretary of the colony and a member of the governor's Council, and his elder brother Charles Carter (ca. 1707–1764) represented King George County in the House of Burgesses for many years. When he was nine years old, Landon

Carter accompanied two of his elder brothers to London, where at the private school of Solomon Low he received the classical education of a young English gentleman. He demonstrated a strong inclination for learning and was allowed to stay for four years after his brothers returned to Virginia in 1723 and 1724. When Carter returned in May 1727, his father found him well qualified for any business and at first thought of apprenticing him to a London counting house for a career as a Virginia merchant but instead taught him plantation management. After a brief stay at the College of William and Mary, Carter returned to Corotoman and managed some of his father's land in Northumberland County.

In 1732 Carter married Elizabeth Wormeley, a member of a Virginia family almost as wealthy and as well connected as his own. They had three sons and one daughter before her death in January 1740. Carter's father died in 1732 and left him a very large estate, much of it in Richmond County. Carter settled there during the winter of 1733–1734 and spent the remainder of his life as a successful plantation owner, improving his estate and establishing himself as one of the county's leading men. On 22 September 1742 he married Maria Byrd, the fifteen-year-old daughter of the councillor and writer William Byrd (1674–1744). They had one daughter. Carter's second wife died in November 1745. Early in 1747 he married a neighbor, Elizabeth Beale. They had five daughters, two of whom survived childhood, before she died late in the 1750s. Each marriage increased Carter's landholdings. Sometime late in the 1730s or early in the 1740s he built Sabine Hall, a Georgian dwelling overlooking six gardened terraces and the Rappahannock River. It is listed on the Virginia Historic Landmarks Register and the National Register of Historic Places.

Like his father and brothers, Carter early assumed an important role in public life. In September 1734 he became a justice of the peace and member of the quorum of the county court. From this position he helped to dispense justice and administer the county until his death forty-four years later. Sometime in the 1740s the vestry of Lunenburg Parish elected him a member, which he remained for the rest of his life. About

the same time Carter became county lieutenant in command of the militia. He continued as head of the militia until new regulations that decreased his control over the troops caused him to resign early in 1776. Carter was less immediately successful in securing elective office. Richmond County voters rejected him three times between 1735 and 1748 before finally electing him in 1752 to represent them in the House of Burgesses.

Carter was one of the most prominent members of the House. At his first session he was appointed to two powerful standing committees, on Privileges and Elections and on Propositions and Grievances, and from 1757 until 1761 he chaired the Committee for Courts of Justice. An inexhaustible writer, he prepared numerous formal addresses and became a public defender of the House by publishing pamphlets and newspaper essays upholding its stand during its controversy with Lieutenant Governor Robert Dinwiddie over the pistole fee and also by defending the assembly's issue of paper currency and its passage of the Two Penny Act. Carter's legislative career lasted until 1768, when he lost an election, a defeat he attributed in part to his constituents' perception that "I did not familiarize myself among the People."

Along with his brother Charles Carter, Landon Carter was named in 1756 as one of the directors to oversee the colony's financing of troops to protect the Virginia frontier from French and Indian incursions. A strong advocate of vigorous measures during the Seven Years' War, Carter also consistently opposed British encroachments on American rights after 1763. He claimed the distinction of first raising the alarm against the Stamp Act in Virginia by inspiring the House to protest it in the autumn of 1764, six months before Patrick Henry's famous resolutions of May 1765. During the following decade Carter poured forth a steady stream of essays supporting the American cause. From December 1774 through the middle of 1776 he chaired the Richmond County Committee. Though he disagreed with Thomas Paine's *Common Sense*, preferring to be compelled to independence rather than to seek it actively, he gave wholehearted support to the Revolutionary War until his death.

Carter

Carter was probably the most prolific published author of his generation in Virginia. He produced at least four major political pamphlets: *A Letter from a Gentleman in Virginia to the Merchants of Great Britain Trading to that Colony* (1754), *A Letter to a Gentleman in London, from Virginia* (1759), *A Letter to the Right Reverend Father in God, the Lord B——p of L——n* (1760), and *The Rector Detected, Being a Just Defense of the twopenny Act, Against the Artful Misrepresentations of the Reverend John Camm* (1764). Carter also wrote nearly fifty essays for the *Virginia Gazette*s, the *Maryland Gazette*, and other newspapers in both England and America. A dedicated improver, he acquired a large library and composed scientific papers that won him election to the American Philosophical Society in 1769 and to the Virginian Society for the Promotion of Usefull Knowledge in 1774.

From 1752 to 1778 Carter kept a diary, one of the most revealing personal documents for mid-eighteenth-century Virginia. When he wrote his will in 1770, he made ample provisions for his children, giving large dowries to his four surviving daughters and large estates to his three sons. Including property transferred to his sons before his death, his estate consisted of nearly 50,000 acres of land, as many as 500 slaves, and a large capital investment in buildings, livestock, and personal possessions—a fortune few other Virginians of his generation could match. Landon Carter died at Sabine Hall on 22 December 1778 and was buried there.

Jack P. Greene, ed., *The Diary of Colonel Landon Carter of Sabine Hall, 1752–1778* (1965; repr. 1987), esp. 1:468 (recording Carter reached age sixty on 18 Aug. 1770), 2:736 (death of first wife), 1008 (quotation), and frontispiece por.; Greene, *Landon Carter: An Inquiry into the Personal Values and Social Imperatives of the Eighteenth-Century Virginia Gentry* (1967); Greene, ed., " 'Not to be Governed or Taxed, but by . . . our Representatives': Four Essays in Opposition to the Stamp Act by Landon Carter," *VMHB* 76 (1968): 259–300; Rhys Isaac, *Landon Carter's Uneasy Kingdom: Revolution and Rebellion on a Virginia Plantation* (2004); second marriage in William Byrd (1674–1744) to Daniel Parke Custis, 23 Sept. 1742, in *Byrd Correspondence,* 2:595; death notice of second wife in *Williamsburg Virginia Gazette*, 5–12 Dec. 1745; marriage agreement between Carter and Elizabeth Beale, dated 9 Feb. 1747 and recorded 1 June 1747, in Richmond Co. Deed Book, 10:410–412; Carter letters in Sabine Hall Papers, UVA, and Carter Family Papers, including estate inventory, W&M; Walter Ray Wineman, *The Landon Carter Papers in the University of Virginia Library: A Calendar and Biographical Sketch* (1962); scientific papers include "Observations concerning the Fly-Weevil, that destroys the wheat . . . " (1768), in *Transactions, of the American Philosophical Society* 1 (1771): 205–217; *Revolutionary Virginia*; Thomas Dabney Wellford, "Sabine Hall," in Elizabeth Lowell Ryland, ed., *Richmond County, Virginia: A Review Commemorating the Bicentennial, 1776–1976* (1976), 130–141, quoting family Bible record for death date; Richmond Co. Will Book, 7:336–344.

JACK P. GREENE

CARTER, Leslie Dillon (24 October 1895–23 March 1992), army officer, was born in Salem and was the son of Edward R. Carter, a businessman, and Anne Katherine Dillon Carter. He graduated from Salem High School and enrolled in Roanoke College, but in July 1917, three months after the United States entered World War I and a year short of graduation, he left college and enlisted as a corporal in the army's Signal Corps. In February 1918 Carter received a commission as a second lieutenant in the infantry reserve and was posted to Hawaii. Commissioned a first lieutenant in the regular army and assigned to the cavalry on 1 July 1920, he attended the cavalry school at Fort Riley, Kansas, and later the signal school in New Jersey. On 6 December 1924 while stationed with the 6th Cavalry Regiment at Fort Oglethorpe, in Georgia, Carter married Elizabeth Fleming, daughter of an army colonel. They had two sons, both of whom became army officers.

Carter served in the Philippines from 1928 to 1930 and was recorder for the cavalry board at Fort Riley from 1930 to 1935. Promoted to captain on 21 June 1931, he graduated from the Command and General Staff School in 1936 and served three years in command of a cavalry troop at Fort Myer, Virginia. Carter was promoted to major on 1 August 1939 and in December of that year was appointed intelligence officer at the Panama Canal. He became a lieutenant colonel on 18 April 1941.

On 1 February 1942, less than two months after the United States entered World War II, Carter was promoted to colonel. He spent the spring in Washington, D.C., as part of a military intelligence group and served from July 1942 until March 1943 as executive officer of the army's American Intelligence Command at Miami Beach, Florida. Carter then took command of the 44th Armored Regiment at Camp Campbell, near Hopkinsville, Kentucky. Joining American preparations for operations in Western Europe, he arrived in England in January 1944 and was assigned to the First Army Group as an intelligence officer before being transferred in June to VII Corps headquarters. After D-Day the corps spearheaded an advance across northern France and Belgium before joining with Russian forces near Berlin in April 1945. During this time Carter helped direct intelligence operations under rapidly changing combat conditions. He supervised the collection, analysis, and dissemination of intelligence; correlated prisoner-of-war interrogations, photographic reconnaissance, and intercepted communications; and compiled intelligence summaries for commanders. Before Germany's surrender on 8 May he left for his new assignment in the Philippines, where he participated in planning for the invasion of Japan.

In October 1945 Carter returned to the Canal Zone as chief of staff for the Antilles Department and later served in that capacity in Puerto Rico. He became chief of staff of the Ground General School at Fort Riley in August 1948 and assistant commandant in December. Promoted to brigadier general on 13 February 1951, he served from the following June until February 1953 as chief of staff of the Second Army headquartered at Fort Meade, near Laurel, Maryland. Carter was promoted to major general on 6 March and from May until October 1953 was acting commanding general of the Second Army.

In October 1953 Carter went to Japan as chief of staff for the army's Far East Command. Appointed commanding general of the 25th Infantry Division, in Korea, in May 1954, he was a member of the United Nations Military Armistice Commission during the winter of 1954–1955 and regularly took part in tedious and largely fruitless negotiations with representatives of North Korea. Returning to Washington in May 1955, Carter served on the Army Review Board in the Office of the Secretary of the Army. In June 1956 he was appointed special assistant to the Second Army commander

for reserve affairs and stationed in Richmond. He retired from active duty on 31 December 1956 and moved to a house he had purchased in Chesterfield County.

Carter's army decorations included three Legions of Merit and two Bronze Stars. The French government recognized him with the Legion of Honor and the Croix de Guerre with Palm, and Belgium also awarded him its Croix de Guerre. From South Korea he received a Distinguished Service Medal. Roanoke College awarded Carter a bachelor's degree in June 1955, even though he had never returned to complete the classes he missed after leaving school in 1917, and at the same commencement the college awarded him an honorary doctorate in science. When he died in 1992, Carter was designated a distinguished alumnus of Roanoke College.

Carter was active in several community organizations in the Richmond vicinity during his retirement years, including the Red Cross, and he also took part in Republican Party politics. He was director of the Valentine Museum (later the Valentine Richmond History Center) from 1961 through August 1966, and his wife during part of that time was president of the board of Retreat for the Sick Hospital in Richmond. Leslie Dillon Carter died at his home in Chesterfield County on 23 March 1992 and was buried in Arlington National Cemetery.

Official army biography, Mar. 1955, U.S. Army Military History Institute, Department of the Army, Carlisle, Pa.; biographical file, June 1956 (with birth date of 24 Oct. 1895), U.S. Army Center of Military History, Fort McNair, Washington, D.C.; BVS Birth Register, Roanoke Co. (variant birth date of 24 Nov. 1895); information provided by son Leslie Dillon Carter Jr., who confirmed birth date of 24 Oct. 1895 (2003); *Roanoke Times*, 7 Dec. 1924, 6 Jan. 1957 (por.); *New York Times*, 25 Aug., 7 Sept. 1953, 5 Nov. 1954, 10 Feb., 23 Mar., 6 Apr. 1955; *Richmond Times-Dispatch*, 12 Aug. 1956, 9 Sept. 1966; *Richmond News Leader*, 19 Dec. 1956, 25 June 1957, 5 Nov. 1964, 12 Aug. 1966; *Salem Times Register*, 10 Jan. 1957; obituary in *Richmond News Leader*, 25 Mar. 1992.

FRANK D. ENGLISH JR.

CARTER, Maybelle Addington (10 May 1909–23 October 1978), musician, was born in the Copper Creek community near Nickelsville, in Scott County. One of ten children of Hugh Jack Addington and Margaret Elizabeth Kilgore Addington, she learned a variety of traditional

Appalachian songs and tunes from her banjo-playing mother as well as from siblings, relatives, and neighbors. Performing as a child at social gatherings with her family's informal band, Addington sang and played the banjo and autoharp, although by her teenage years she had adopted the guitar as her primary instrument. Her style of playing, modeled loosely on old-time banjo techniques, required plucking the melody on the bass strings while strumming the rhythm on the high strings and became so influential among later guitar players that it was dubbed the "Carter lick."

One of the people with whom Addington performed regularly when young was her older first cousin Sara Elizabeth Dougherty, who lived with Addington's aunt after her own mother died and who in June 1915 married Alvin Pleasant Delaney "A. P." Carter. On 12 March 1926 Addington eloped to Bristol, on the Virginia-Tennessee state line, with A. P. Carter's younger brother Ezra J. "Eck" Carter, whom she had known only about four months. The couple settled in Maces Spring, a rural community in Poor Valley. There Carter began performing regularly with Sara Carter, who sang the lead vocal melody and accompanied on the autoharp, and A. P. Carter, who sang bass, collected and arranged songs, and managed the family singing group.

Late in July 1927 the trio traveled by automobile over rough roads to a makeshift studio in Bristol, where the producer Ralph Sylvester Peer was recording performances by various Appalachian musicians for commercial release on the Victor Talking Machine Company label. On 1 and 2 August the Carters recorded six tracks, including "Bury Me under the Weeping Willow," "Single Girl, Married Girl," "The Storms Are on the Ocean," and "The Wandering Boy," released on three double-sided 78 rpm records issued under the name the Carter Family. Strong sales led to more recording sessions for the trio, beginning with one in Camden, New Jersey, on 9 May 1928. Through commercial records, radio, and concerts, the Carter Family quickly developed a national reputation as one of the most influential acts in the emergent popular music genre then called hillbilly music and eventually known as country music.

Carter played the guitar and occasionally the autoharp on the trio's early recordings and during the 1930s began to sing tenor harmony behind Sara Carter's lead vocals. Her fame continued to be based on her guitar style, and her guitar arrangements on the Carter Family's recordings of such songs as "The Cannon-Ball," "Keep on the Sunny Side," and "Wildwood Flower" remain among the most-imitated instrumental parts in country music history. A number of Carter's guitar accompaniments on the group's 1930s recordings reveal the significant influence on her playing style of the African American blues musician Lesley Riddle, a family acquaintance who accompanied A. P. Carter on song-collecting expeditions.

Despite Sara Carter and A. P. Carter's marital difficulties, separation, and 1936 divorce, the original members of the Carter Family continued to perform together into the 1940s. Between 1938 and 1942 the Carter Family spent winters in Texas, where they performed over several Mexican border radio stations whose powerful ultrahigh-frequency signals blanketed all of North America and occasionally reached Asia, Europe, and South America. Appearing with the trio on these radio shows were Carter's three daughters, Anita Carter, Helen Carter, and Valerie June Carter, as well as A. P. Carter and Sara Carter's daughter Janette Carter.

The original Carter Family had its final recording session as a trio on 14 October 1941 in RCA Victor's New York studio. Their nearly 300 recordings, made over a fourteen-year period and released on the American Record Corporation, Decca, and RCA Victor labels, encompassed most types of songs popular in early twentieth-century southwestern Virginia homes, ranging from ballads, sentimental nineteenth-century parlor songs, and hymns to blues. Many of the songs the Carter Family recorded were familiar to record buyers throughout the southeastern United States, yet such songs were transformed in A. P. Carter's striking arrangements.

After performing regularly on radio station WBT in Charlotte, North Carolina, from the autumn of 1942 to the spring of 1943, the trio disbanded in March 1943. Teaming up with her daughters as Mother Maybelle and the Carter

Sisters, Carter traveled the South for several years performing over various radio stations, including WRVA in Richmond on the *Old Dominion Barn Dance*, WNOX in Knoxville, Tennessee, and KWTO in Springfield, Missouri. By 1950 Carter had moved to Nashville and joined the Grand Ole Opry. She occasionally wrote and composed songs for her group's repertoire, including "I've Got a Home in Glory," "A Jilted Love," "The Kneeling Drunkard's Plea," "Lonesome Homesick Blues," and "Walk a Little Closer." In 1961 the country music star Johnny Cash invited Carter and her daughters to tour with him. Exposure to a wider audience led to renewed recording opportunities, including, at Cash's urging, a 1966 reunion album with Sara Carter and other releases on the Columbia Records and Kapp labels.

After leaving the Grand Ole Opry in 1967, Carter continued to appear at leading venues of the 1960s folk music revival, including the 1967 Newport Folk Festival, often playing the autoharp rather than the guitar. Between 1969 and 1971 she performed regularly on the ABC television variety show of Johnny Cash, who in March 1968 had married Carter's twice-divorced daughter June Carter. Maybelle Carter won favor among a younger generation of fans, who gave her the moniker the Mother of Country Music. In 1970 the Carter Family was the first group voted into the Country Music Hall of Fame. Carter's participation in the recording of the Nitty Gritty Dirt Band's landmark all-star album *Will the Circle Be Unbroken* (1972) secured her reputation as one of the most distinctive and revered musicians in country music history. The Carter Family's 1935 Banner label recording of "Can the Circle Be Unbroken (Bye and Bye)" and 1928 RCA Victor recording of "Wildwood Flower" received Grammy Hall of Fame Awards from the National Academy of Recording Arts and Sciences in 1998 and 1999, respectively, as enduring works of historical significance.

Ezra Carter, who worked as a mail clerk for a railroad company during the Great Depression and later served as manager of Mother Maybelle and the Carter Sisters, died on 22 January 1975. Maybelle Addington Carter, having endured both arthritis and Parkinson's disease in her last years,

died suddenly of a respiratory ailment in a Nashville hospital on 23 October 1978 and was buried in Woodlawn Memorial Park East (later Hendersonville Memory Gardens) in Hendersonville, Tennessee. Her Maces Spring home is on both the Virginia Landmarks Register and the National Register of Historic Places.

Archie Green, "The Carter Family's 'Coal Miner's Blues,'" *Southern Folklore Quarterly* 25 (1961): 226–237; John Atkins et al., eds., *The Carter Family*, Old Time Music Booklet 1 (1973); Atkins, "The Carter Family," in Bill C. Malone and Judith McCulloh, eds., *Stars of Country Music: Uncle Dave Macon to Johnny Rodriguez* (1975), 95–120; June Carter Cash, *Among My Klediments* (1979); Mark Dawidziak, "It All Began in Bristol," *Commonwealth* 48 (Feb. 1981): 17–23; Janette Carter, *Living with Memories* (1983); Irwin Stambler and Grelun Landon, *The Encyclopedia of Folk, Country and Western Music*, 2d ed. (1983), 94–98; Mary A. Bufwack and Robert K. Oermann, *Finding Her Voice: The Saga of Women in Country Music* (1993), esp. 50–59, 149–151, 303; Ed Kahn, "The Carter Family on Border Radio," *American Music* 14 (1996): 205–217; Charles Wolfe, "Jake and Doc and May: The Carter Family Goes to the End of the World," *Bluegrass Unlimited* 34 (Feb. 2000): 22–27; Mark Zwonitzer with Charles Hirshberg, *Will You Miss Me When I'm Gone? The Carter Family and Their Legacy in American Music* (2002), pors. and variant marriage date of 13 Mar. 1926, derived from Carter interview, on 66; Katie Doman, "Something Old, Something New: The Carter Family's Bristol Session Recordings," in Charles K. Wolfe and Ted Olson, eds., *The Bristol Sessions: Writing about the Big Bang of Country Music* (2005), 66–86; original Carter Family discography in Kip Lornell, *Virginia's Blues, Country, and Gospel Records, 1902–1943: An Annotated Discography* (1989), 35–58; *The Carter Family on Border Radio*, John Edwards Memorial Foundation 101 (n.d.), recording with brochure notes by Archie Green, William H. Koon, and Norm Cohen; *The Carter Family: In the Shadow of Clinch Mountain*, Bear Family Records 15865 (2000), including several 1963 and 1973 Carter interviews, discography by Tony Russell and Richard Weize, and companion book by Charles K. Wolfe (pors.); Sullivan Co., Tenn., Marriage Ledger; obituaries in *Richmond News Leader* and *Richmond Times-Dispatch*, both 24 Oct. 1978, *Bristol Herald Courier*, 24, 25 Oct. 1978, *Nashville Tennessean*, 24, 25, 26 Oct. 1978, and *New York Times*, 6 Nov. 1978.

TED OLSON

CARTER, Peter Jacob (29 May 1845–19 July 1886), member of the House of Delegates, was born into slavery in the town of Eastville, in Northampton County. His parents were named Jacob and Peggie. According to family tradition, his father, whose surname was probably Carter, was the son of Pierre De Carte, a free native of West Africa, and an enslaved Virginia woman.

Carter, a younger brother and sister, and their mother belonged to Calvin H. Read, a schoolteacher who may have taught Carter to read. By 1858 Read had moved to Baltimore. To repay $1,000 he had borrowed from his wife's separate estate, he deeded to her on 5 December 1860 Carter, two of his siblings, and their mother, all enumerated in the deed as residing in Northampton County.

In November 1861 Union troops occupied the Eastern Shore and held the area for the remainder of the Civil War. Carter escaped from slavery, and on 30 October 1863 in Eastville he enlisted in Company B of the 10th Regiment United States Colored Infantry. Arrested for mutiny early in February 1864 and imprisoned at Camp Hamilton, he was released on 22 May after the charges were withdrawn and then returned to duty with his regiment at Bermuda Hundred. Carter served with the quartermaster department from September through December 1865 and then on detached duty with the Bureau of Refugees, Freedmen, and Abandoned Lands from January through April 1866. He mustered out on 17 May 1866 at Galveston, Texas.

Carter settled in Franktown, in Northampton County, and from 1869 to 1871 attended the Hampton Normal and Agricultural Institute (later Hampton University). By 10 February 1873 he had married Georgianna Mapp. They had one daughter and three sons, one of whom died in childhood.

In November 1871, with votes from many of the Eastern Shore's freedpeople, Carter won election as a Republican to Northampton County's seat in the House of Delegates. His opponent unsuccessfully contested the election. Carter was appointed to the Committees of Agriculture and Mining and on Retrenchment and Economy. He won reelection three times, and his eight-year tenure was one of the longest among nineteenth-century African American members of the General Assembly. He held the same committee assignments until his last term, when he was named to the Committee on Claims and the Committee on Militia and Police. Carter introduced bills dealing with such local concerns as taxes on oysters and boundaries of election precincts, and he attempted to correct abuse of prisoners in the state penitentiary, improve care of black deaf-mutes, and provide housing for the aged or afflicted poor in Richmond. He sought to amend antebellum laws pertaining to juries and criminal laws that discriminated between blacks and whites. Carter's bill to incorporate the Northampton Land Association, of which several black leaders were members, passed in March 1875.

A fine speaker and formidable presence, Carter quickly emerged as one of the leading African American members of the assembly. In 1872 he joined a delegation that met with President Ulysses S. Grant to solicit support of the civil rights bill pending in Congress. At the Republican State Convention that met in Lynchburg on 29 July 1873, Carter was a sergeant at arms and a vice president, and he won election to the state committee. Newspapers believed him the likely choice for a place on the state ticket, should white leaders decide to nominate an African American.

On 19 August 1875 about a hundred black delegates from more than forty counties and cities assembled in Richmond in response to a call from African American legislators. Carter served on the Committees on Address and on Resolutions and also was sergeant at arms. He acted as temporary chair and employed his gavel frequently during intense debates over education, jobs, party organization, and other issues. He introduced a resolution calling for the replacement of the state superintendent of education, and he and another delegate nearly came to fisticuffs while arguing about the state debt. Carter was appointed to a committee on labor unions, and after the convention adjourned the committee elected him treasurer of the short-lived statewide Laboring Men's Mechanics' Union Association, with proposed headquarters in Richmond.

During Carter's eight years in the General Assembly, the most divisive political issue was payment of Virginia's antebellum debt. The Funding Act passed in March 1871 committed the state to payment of the full principal and interest, but inadequate revenue required the assembly on 15 December of that year to suspend payment temporarily. Carter voted for suspension. On 5 January 1872 he voted with the majority in support of a joint resolution to discontinue the issuance of bonds for funding the public debt. Carter joined the majority on 2 March 1872 in overriding the governor's veto and passing a bill that prohibited using coupons to pay taxes and debts, thereby repealing a key provision of the Funding Act. Many white Republicans supported full funding, but many black Republicans, who with other whites came to be called Readjusters, opposed raising taxes for that purpose and feared that the new public school system would be endangered if money were diverted from education to debt service.

Although Carter represented an area that had not benefited from the expenditures on internal improvements that had created the state debt, he believed that Virginia should honor its full obligation. In December 1875 he voted with the assembly minority for Williams Carter Wickham, a former Confederate general and a Funder Republican, for the United States Senate. On 7 February 1878 Carter proposed raising taxes to pay off the debt. Acknowledging that the cost would be passed along to his own constituents, he declared, "In every way it is plain the working man—the Virginia negro—pays the additional tax. I belong to that toiling race. I am a poor man; but like my brethren, who will feel a higher tax keenly, I am ready to raise the rate and preserve the honor of the old Commonwealth." Two days later he was the only Republican to vote against the so-called Barbour bill that some regarded as a prelude to partial repudiation. Carter did not vote on 24 March 1879 when the assembly passed a bill to pay the debt in full but at a reduced rate of interest. As a Richmond newspaper observed, Carter was "no less a curiosity than a colored Funder and the only one of his race in Virginia who has ever voted in the Legislature for an increase of taxation to meet the indebtedness of the Commonwealth."

Carter was temporary chair of the Republican State Convention that met in Lynchburg in April 1876 and that named him a delegate to the national convention. In September of that year he attended the First Congressional District convention in Fredericksburg. Carter won reelection to the General Assembly in 1877, but before the next election Conservatives created a floto-

rial district consisting of Accomack and Northampton Counties in hope of defeating him. He did not seek reelection from the gerrymandered district in 1879. Instead, Carter campaigned for the seat in the Senate of Virginia representing those two counties but lost by a margin of 1,224 votes out of 2,964 cast. Even out of office, Carter remained the predominant black leader on the Eastern Shore. He controlled the county's federal patronage and enjoyed the income from his federal job as lighthouse keeper at Cherrystone Inlet. In April 1880 he was once again elected temporary chair of the Republican State Convention, sat on its Committee on Resolutions, and in June chaired the Virginia delegation to the party's national convention.

The Readjuster leader, Senator William Mahone, formed an alliance with national Republican leaders in 1881 and received a share of the state's federal patronage. Heavily courted by Mahone, Carter left the declining Republican Party, embraced coalition with the Readjusters, and was president of a committee to reconcile mainstream and Readjuster Republicans. The Republicans failed to name a ticket for the next election, and Carter, though called a traitor and accused of taking a bribe, worked tirelessly for Readjuster candidates. In November the party captured both houses of the legislature and the governorship. As a reward, the Senate of Virginia elected Carter doorkeeper on 7 December 1881.

Carter chaired the 1882 First Congressional District Readjuster convention that nominated Robert Murphy Mayo for the House of Representatives, and he campaigned for the successful Mayo throughout the far-flung district. Stumping also for Readjusters elsewhere in Virginia, he ably debated opponents "with gloves off," as he noted in a letter to Mahone. During the 1883 campaign Carter signed a circular address to the black voters of the state, recounting the benefits that they had received from the Readjusters. A riot in Danville days before the election helped Democrats seize control of the assembly and effectively terminated the existence of the Readjuster Party. Black leaders assembled in Norfolk in December, with Carter in the chair, to protest the deadly events in Danville and subsequently drafted a set of grievances.

Early in 1884 Carter served on the state Republican Central Committee and in April attended the Readjuster-Coalition state convention, which dropped the name Readjuster and proclaimed itself the Republican Party of Virginia. He was a member of the Committee on General Business. Carter also sat on the Committee on Business during the 1885 state Republican convention. During the ensuing campaign he reported attempts by Democrats to bribe him and to bribe and deceive other black voters.

Carter's political importance earned him appointment to the board of the new Virginia Normal and Collegiate Institute (later Virginia State University), and at the initial meeting on 15 February 1883 the other members elected him rector. He served for about two years. When not engaged in public life, Carter farmed the 150 acres that he owned near Franktown. He also owned several other smaller parcels of land. For a time he was a merchant and also served as a justice of the peace.

On 28 November 1882 his wife died, and on 17 July 1884 Carter married Maggie F. Treherne, of Accomack County. They had a son, William M. Carter, apparently named in honor of William Mahone. After Carter's death this son changed his name to Peter J. Carter, studied medicine at Howard University, and during the 1930s was a physician at the veterans' hospital in Tuskegee, Alabama. Peter Jacob Carter became ill while traveling by steamer from Norfolk to the Eastern Shore and died on 19 July 1886, probably of appendicitis. He was buried in the family cemetery near Franktown.

Birth and death dates from gravestone; biographies in *Richmond Daily Dispatch*, 20 Aug. 1875, Luther P. Jackson, "Peter J. Carter of Northampton County, Va.," *Norfolk Journal and Guide*, 17 Feb. 1945, and Jackson, *Negro Office-Holders*, 7, 52 (por.); family history information and documents, including discharge papers (copies in *DVB* Files), provided by grandson, Arthur Treherne Carter (2004); middle name on Student Record Index Card, Hampton University Archives; 1860 sale (age fifteen on 5 Dec. 1860) in Northampton Co. Deed Book, 36:115; Compiled Service Military Records, Records of the Adjutant General's Office, RG 94, NARA; BVS Marriage Register, Northampton Co. (1884); *Washington New Era*, 5 May 1870; *Richmond Enquirer*, 30, 31 July, 1 Aug. 1873; *Richmond Daily Dispatch*, 31 July 1873, 21, 23 Aug. 1875, 17 June 1880, 14 Dec. 1883; *New-York Times*, 22 Aug. 1875; *Lynchburg Daily Virginian*, 13, 14 Apr. 1876, 11, 12 Aug. 1881; *Fredericksburg News*, 4 Sept. 1876; *Richmond Daily Whig*, 22, 23, 26 Apr. 1880; *Richmond Southern Intelligencer*, 26 Apr. 1880 (second quotation); *The Debt Question: Speech of Hon. Peter J. Carter of Northampton County, in the House of Delegates, Va., February 7th, 1878* [1878], first quotation on 3; numerous Carter letters to William Mahone (third quotation in 16 Oct. 1882) in Mahone Papers, Duke; Northampton Co. Order Book, 47:520; Herbert Aptheker, ed., *A Documentary History of The Negro People in the United States* (1951), 1:636–637, 731–734; Brooks Miles Barnes, "Triumph of the New South: Independent Movements in Post-Reconstruction Politics" (Ph.D. diss., UVA, 1991), esp. 99–105, 125–132, 142, 166, 167, 182, 207, 208; Northampton Co. Will Book, 39:257–259; death notices and brief obituaries in *Norfolk Public Ledger*, 21 July 1886, *Norfolk Landmark*, 22 July 1886, and *Accomack Court House Peninsula Enterprise*, 24 July 1886 (reporting death "last Tuesday," 20 July 1886).

DONALD W. GUNTER

CARTER, Robert (ca. 1664–4 August 1732), land baron, Speaker of the House of Burgesses, and member of the Council, was born probably at Corotoman, his father's Lancaster County estate on the Rappahannock River. He was the son of John Carter (ca. 1613–1670) and the fourth of his five wives, Sarah Ludlow Carter. His immigrant father, a member of the governor's Council, had prospered in Virginia, and when Carter was orphaned, his elder half brother, John Carter (ca. 1653–1690), was able to educate him as their father's will directed by sending him to London about 1673 to live for six years with Arthur Bailey, a merchant and family friend. Carter gained a lifelong appreciation for the classics and a thorough knowledge of the English end of the Virginia trade.

After his return to Virginia, Carter most likely lived at Corotoman and enjoyed society. In 1688 he married Judith Armistead, of Gloucester County. Before her death eleven years later they had four daughters and one son, John Carter (d. 1742), for whom Carter later purchased the lucrative office of secretary of the colony. About 1701 Carter married Elizabeth Landon Willis, a wealthy widow who died in July 1719. Their five daughters and five sons included Charles Carter (ca. 1707–1764), who represented King George County in the House of Burgesses for many years, and Landon Carter, who represented Richmond County in the assembly. Carter inherited most of his half brother's estate following the latter's death in 1690, and he also managed his niece's estates and about the same time inherited a younger half brother's portion.

Carter began his public career not long after his elder half brother's death. He became a vestryman of Christ Church Parish in November 1690 and on 10 June 1691 took his seat as a justice of the peace in Lancaster County. Other influential positions, including commander of the militia of Lancaster and Northumberland Counties and naval officer of the Rappahannock River in charge of a customs office, added to his political and financial power. He represented Lancaster County in the House of Burgesses in the spring sessions of 1691 and 1692 and then continuously from 1695 through 1699. Carter quickly assumed a leading role in the assembly. In 1692 he became a member of the Committees for Elections and Privileges and for Examination of Propositions and Grievances, and in 1695 he may have been nominated for Speaker. During that session he chaired the Committee for Propositions and Grievances and presided over the committee of the whole; and in May the assembly appointed him to the committee to revise the laws of the colony. When the assembly convened on 25 September 1696, Carter defeated four other aspirants to win election as Speaker. He presided over the House of Burgesses during that session and the assembly session of October 1697. When the House met next, on 29 September 1698, Carter was almost certainly one of the five candidates for Speaker but was not reelected. The following year the House of Burgesses appointed him treasurer of the colony, with responsibility for the money raised by taxes that the assembly levied and expended under its authority. Carter remained treasurer until 1705.

On 14 December 1699 the Privy Council approved Governor Francis Nicholson's recommendation that Carter be appointed to the governor's Council. Carter took the oaths of office on 10 July 1700 and served on the Council until his death. He was as influential as a member of the Council as he had been in the House of Burgesses. With a majority of the councillors Carter opposed Nicholson in 1704, action that led indirectly to the governor's dismissal; and a

decade later, when Lieutenant Governor Alexander Spotswood posed a political threat to the great planters who dominated the General Assembly, Carter joined his fellow Virginians in opposing Spotswood. After Lieutenant Governor Hugh Drysdale died in the summer of 1726, Carter, who had succeeded the aged and ailing Edmund Jenings as the senior member of the Council, served as president (in effect, acting governor) from 1 August of that year until Lieutenant Governor William Gooch took office in Williamsburg on 11 September 1727. Carter was in poor health for much of that time but regularly presided over Council meetings in Williamsburg. He continued to attend through the adjournment of the General Assembly on 1 July 1732, five weeks before his death.

Accumulation of land was a lifelong passion for Carter. He purchased many properties and acquired others by foreclosing mortgages, but he obtained most of his vast landholdings by taking patents on unsettled lands in the Northern Neck Proprietary, the area between the Rappahannock and Potomac Rivers extending to their headwaters. As Virginia agent for the proprietors from about 1702 until 1711 and from 1722 until 1732, Carter used his position to have his surveyors find the best land for him to patent in his own or his children's names. At the time of his death, Carter held at least 295,000 acres of land and many other tracts of unknown size. Slaves working under the supervision of overseers provided the labor on his plantations, and senior overseers with responsibility for several farms managed those overseers. Carter was a capable and diligent administrator. He visited his properties frequently and forcefully communicated his directions to his overseers and managers. The chief cash crop was tobacco, but he also produced beans, cattle, corn, fruits, hogs, and wheat to sustain his family, servants, and slaves and occasionally for sale. Carter also earned money from such enterprises as rental of the sloops and flatboats that he owned and for acting as an agent for slave traders. He invested his earnings shrewdly in both England and Virginia and became the richest man in the colony.

Carter traveled regularly to Williamsburg on Council business or to attend board meetings of the College of William and Mary. He lived well at Corotoman and about 1725 built the largest house in the colony there, only to see it burn four years later. Carter's chief affliction was gout, and he recorded his suffering in the diary he kept for several years in the 1720s, also noting in it his reading, visitors, meals, and expenses while away from home. He was a devout member of the Church of England and late in life began construction of a splendid new brick church for Christ Church Parish. Carter's political power, great wealth, large ambitions, and imperious bearing earned him the nickname of "King" from his contemporaries. Many of his ten children who lived to adulthood married into other wealthy and distinguished Virginia families, adding to the family's wealth as well as to its political importance.

Suffering from poor health, Carter prepared his will in August 1726 and added four long codicils during the next four years. The final text contained more than 18,000 words and filled forty sheets of paper. Carter provided large landed estates for his sons and generous bequests for his daughters and grandchildren. So wealthy had he been that even after the legacies were paid and the estate settled, the division of his estate among his surviving sons made all of them among the wealthiest men in Virginia. Robert "King" Carter died at Corotoman on 4 August 1732 and was buried at Christ Church in Lancaster County.

Kukla, *Speakers and Clerks, 1643–1776*, 94–98 (por.); Carl F. Cannon, "Robert ('King') Carter of 'Corotoman' " (Ph.D. diss., Duke, 1956); Edmund Berkeley, Jr., "Robert 'King' Carter" (M.A. thesis, UVA, 1961); Berkeley, "Robert Carter—Colonial 'King,' " *Northern Neck of Virginia Historical Magazine* 12 (1962): 1116–1135; Katharine L. Brown, *Robert "King" Carter, Builder of Christ Church* (2001), several pors.; possible birth date of 18 Apr. 1662 suggested in dedicatory inscription by John Gooche in *Biblia Sacra* (1631), bound with *The Whole Booke of Psalmes* (1633), copy at VHS, reproduced in [John Melville Jennings], "Robert 'King' Carter?" Virginia Historical Society *An Occasional Bulletin* 35 (1977): 3–5; family history in Christine Jones, comp., *John Carter I of "Corotoman," Lancaster County, Virginia* (1977); Carter's letters, letter books, and diaries in Huntington Library, LVA, UVA, and VHS, and letters as president of the Council in PRO CO 5/1320 and 5/1337; Louis B. Wright, ed., *Letters of Robert Carter, 1720–1727: The Commercial Interests of a Virginia Gentleman* (1940); Berkeley, ed., "Robert Carter as Agricultural Administrator: His Letters to Robert Jones, 1727–1729," *VMHB* 101 (1993): 273–295; Berkeley, ed., "The Diary, Correspondence, and Papers of Robert 'King' Carter of Virginia, 1701–1732," online ed., UVA; Wright, "The 'Gentleman's Library' in Early Virginia: The Literary Interests of the First Carters," *Huntington Library Quarterly* 1 (1937): 3–61; Carter L. Hudgins, "The 'King's' Realm: An Archaeological and Historical Study of Plantation Life at Robert Carter's Corotoman" (M.A. thesis, Wake Forest University, 1981); Alan Simpson, "Robert Carter's Schooldays," *VMHB* 94 (1986): 161–188; appointment to Council in PC 2/77, 401–403; authenticated copy of lost original will (written in sixty-third year on 22 Aug. 1726) and estate inventory, VHS, printed in *VMHB* 5 (1897–1898): 408–428, ibid. 6 (1898–1899): 1–22, 145–152, 260–268, 365–370, ibid. 7 (1899–1900): 64–68, with variant photostatic copy, Carter Family Papers, Acc. 25840, LVA; death date in William Gooch to Commissioners for Trade and Plantations, 9 Aug. 1732, PRO CO 5/1323, fol. 55, and on gravestone (noting death at age sixty-nine); death notices in *Philadelphia American Weekly Mercury*, 7 Sept. 1732 (with death date and noting death "in the 69th Year of his Age"), and *Gentleman's Magazine* 23 (Nov. 1732): 1082; memorial poem in *Philadelphia American Weekly Mercury*, 14 Sept. 1732 (noting death "in the 69th Year of his Age").

EDMUND BERKELEY, JR.

CARTER, Robert (9 February 1728–11 March 1804), member of the Council, was the son of Robert Carter (1704–1732) and Priscilla Churchhill Carter and was born probably at Corotoman, the Lancaster County plantation of his paternal grandfather. Both of his grandfathers, the land baron Robert "King" Carter (ca. 1664–1732) and William Churchhill, of Middlesex County, served on the governor's Council. He has often been referred to as Councillor Robert Carter to distinguish him from his father, grandfather, and other near relatives of the same name, among whom only his grandfather served on the Council. Until sometime after his father's death in May 1732 he lived at the family plantation in Westmoreland County. Because Carter's father died before his grandfather, it was necessary for his guardians to obtain a special act of assembly to enable him to inherit the portion of his grandfather's estate intended for his father. The law of October 1734 entitled him to receive more than 65,000 acres of land and several hundred slaves when he reached age twenty-one.

Following his mother's marriage to John Lewis sometime during the winter of 1734–1735, Carter lived at his stepfather's Warner Hall plantation in Gloucester County until about 1737, when he entered the grammar school of the College of William and Mary. Little else is known about his youth until February 1749, when he received his patrimony and sailed for London. On 1 December 1749 Carter was admitted to the Inner Temple to study law, but he returned to Virginia in June 1751 without being admitted to the bar. An elegant portrait by Thomas Hudson dating from this period and depicting a poised young courtier attired for a costume ball does not reflect what his contemporaries saw when he arrived in Williamsburg. Several of them commented unfavorably on his lack of learning and social grace.

Carter moved into Nomony Hall (as he nearly always wrote its name, although it is usually spelled "Nomini" or "Nominy"), the Westmoreland County mansion he had inherited from his father. He learned the business of a tobacco planter and until the 1770s thereafter exported to England as many as a hundred hogsheads each year. On 2 April 1754 Carter married Frances Tasker, of Annapolis, daughter of Benjamin Tasker, longtime president of the Council of Maryland. Of their thirteen daughters and four sons, eight daughters and all four sons reached adulthood. In April 1752 Carter was appointed to the Westmoreland County Court. That same year and again in 1754 he ran for vacant seats in the House of Burgesses, but he received the smallest number of votes each time. Through the influence of his wife's uncle, Thomas Bladen, who had served in Parliament, Carter received an appointment from the king on 7 April 1758 to serve on the governor's Council. He took his seat on 18 October of that year.

During his first three years on the Council, Carter attended only about a third of the recorded meetings. In 1761 he purchased a large frame house near the Governor's Palace on the green in Williamsburg and moved there with his family. For the next fourteen years he regularly participated in Council proceedings. Carter was frequently a member of committees drafting responses to the governor's speeches to the assembly, considering amendments to proposed legislation, or examining accounts of the treasurer or the journals of the Council. He accompanied Lieutenant Governor Francis Fauquier to

New York in 1761 to discuss Indian affairs and to Georgia two years later to discuss relations with the southern Indian tribes. In 1763 Carter served on the Virginia Committee of Correspondence, and in 1766 he drafted the Council's response to the king following the repeal of the Stamp Act. Evidently trusted by both sides during the tense years preceding the American Revolution, Carter joined Richard Corbin in representing the Council early in June 1775 when it officially expressed to the royal governor its concern about rumors that British marines were to be stationed in Williamsburg. As a member of the Council, Carter was also a judge of the General Court, but because of the loss of most of the court's records little is known of his service, except that he was in the minority in 1764 when he voted to uphold John Camm's complaint against the Two Penny Act.

Carter's residence in Williamsburg brought him into frequent contact with the colony's intellectual, political, and social leaders and smoothed off some of his rough edges. He developed close friendships with such educated men as Fauquier and his successor, Governor Norborne Berkeley, baron de Botetourt, as well as William Small, who taught at the College of William and Mary, and George Wythe. Carter shared with Fauquier and Wythe's law student, Thomas Jefferson, a love for instrumental music, and Fauquier named Carter one of his executors in Virginia. Carter did not form the same bond with Botetourt's successor, John Murray, fourth earl of Dunmore, and in 1772, not long after Dunmore took office, he moved his family back to Nomony Hall.

Carter still traveled to Williamsburg on Council business but focused more on the management of his estate. He diversified crops and added manufactures such as milling, spinning, and weaving. About 1770 he purchased a one-fifth stake in a large Baltimore ironworks that his father-in-law had helped found. In 1773 and 1774 the tutor Philip Vickers Fithian recorded a fascinating intimate picture of the Carter household in the diary he kept at the plantation, and he copied into his journal a catalog of Carter's extensive library.

The Revolution concluded Carter's service on the Council, which ceased to exist in July

1776. The following summer he took an oath of loyalty to the new Commonwealth of Virginia but held no public office. British ships raided his plantations near the Potomac River, and he was plagued in the postwar period by heavy plantation expenses and a shortage of cash in a stymied economy. Carter campaigned for a seat in the Virginia Convention of 1788 as a supporter of the proposed constitution of the United States but was not elected.

A member of the Church of England from childhood, Carter became a vestryman of Cople Parish in Westmoreland County in November 1752. In June 1777 he announced his conversion to evangelical Christianity and soon allied himself with the Baptists. The next year Carter was baptized by immersion and joined Morattico Baptist Church. He regularly attended prayer meetings, provided financial support for numerous evangelical preachers, and became one of the denomination's most influential adherents in Virginia.

Carter's household was then shrinking. His daughters were marrying and leaving home, his eldest son died in 1779, and his wife died on 31 October 1787 and was buried in the garden at Nomony Hall. He sent his two younger sons to school in Rhode Island, where they could be educated free from the taint of slavery. Although Carter inherited and owned hundreds of slaves, his growing opposition to the institution echoed the antislavery sentiments of many Baptists in the 1780s. On 1 August 1791 he executed a deed of emancipation for more than 500 of his enslaved African Americans. It was probably the largest emancipation by an individual person in the United States before 1860. Because of Virginia's restrictive laws, the emancipation was gradual, and the young slaves received their freedom when they reached adulthood. Carter spent his remaining years working out the details and schedule, an effort that embroiled his agents and executors well into the nineteenth century.

In January 1788 Carter discovered and quickly embraced the theology of the Swedish mystic Emanuel Swedenborg and switched his allegiance from the Baptists to the Church of the New Jerusalem. Carter caused several of Swedenborg's writings to be reprinted in America and wrote the preface for the first American edition of *The Liturgy of the New Church*, published in Baltimore in 1792. Carter moved with two of his younger daughters to Baltimore in 1793 in order to be closer to a center of Swedenborgian worship, and three years later he divided his Virginia estate among his surviving children and grandchildren, who drew lots for their portions. He spent his last years managing his investments. Robert Carter died suddenly in Baltimore on 11 March 1804 and was buried in the garden at Nomony Hall in Westmoreland County.

Birth date derived from Land Book A:iv (stating Carter attained age twenty-one on 9 Feb. 1749), Robert Carter Papers (1760–1815), VHS; Louis Morton, *Robert Carter of Nomini Hall: A Virginia Tobacco Planter of the Eighteenth Century* (1941); John Randolph Barden, " 'Innocent and Necessary': Music and Dancing in the Life of Robert Carter of Nomony Hall, 1728–1804" (M.A. thesis, W&M, 1983); Barden, "Reflections of a Singular Mind: The Library of Robert Carter of Nomony Hall," *VMHB* 96 (1988): 83–94; Barden, " 'Flushed With Notions of Freedom': The Growth and Emancipation of a Virginia Slave Community, 1732–1812" (Ph.D. diss., Duke, 1993); Shomer S. Zwelling, "Robert Carter's Journey: From Colonial Patriarch to New Nation Mystic," *American Quarterly* 38 (1986): 613–636; Andrew Levy, *The First Emancipator: The Forgotten Story of Robert Carter, the Founding Father Who Freed His Slaves* (2005); Hening, *Statutes*, 4:454–457; *Annapolis Maryland Gazette*, 4 Apr. 1754; E. Alfred Jones, *American Members of the Inns of Court* (1924), 41; Council appointment in PRO CO 391/65, 103, 134–135, and PRO CO 324/51, 122; Hunter Dickinson Farish, ed., *Journal and Letters of Philip Vickers Fithian, 1773–1774: A Plantation Tutor of the Old Dominion* (1943); Hall, *Portraits*, por. facing 44; Carter letters, letter books, and business records at CW, Duke, LC, Maryland Historical Society, Swedenborgian House of Studies, Berkeley, Calif., VHS, and W&M; deed of emancipation in Northumberland Co. District Court Orders, Deeds, Etc. (1789–1825), 232–237, and deed and emancipation schedules in vol. 11, Robert Carter Papers, Duke; Baltimore Co., Md., Register of Wills (1802–1805), 7i:264–265; obituary in *Richmond Virginia Argus*, 21 Mar. 1804.

JOHN R. BARDEN

CARTER, Robert Randolph (15 September 1825–8 March 1888), naval officer and diarist, was born at Shirley, the Charles City County plantation of his parents, Hill Carter (1796–1875) and Mary Braxton Randolph Carter. In 1839 he and a younger brother enrolled in the first class to enter the new Episcopal High School in Alexandria. On 30 March 1842, at age sixteen, he joined the United States Navy as a midshipman and began a tour of duty that lasted six years. After initial assignment aboard the frigate *Constitution*, Carter sailed to the West Indies in August 1843 on the sloop of war *Falmouth*. During the Mexican War he served on the *Savannah* in the Pacific Squadron. Carter returned to Shirley in July 1848 and later that year entered the United States Naval School at Annapolis (in 1850 renamed the United States Naval Academy). In 1849 he graduated as a passed midshipman.

During the next decade Carter joined three naval expeditions of scientific exploration and surveying. In May 1850 he set sail as acting master aboard the brig *Rescue*, one of two ships that the New York merchant Henry Grinnell fitted out to assist the British search for Sir John Franklin, whose expedition to find the fabled Northwest Passage had not been heard from since July 1845. The navy took charge of Grinnell's expedition and prepared for its first mission to the Arctic seas. The voyage lasted about eighteen months, during which time Carter kept a private journal that is the only full, daily account of the failed rescue attempt. He was candid in his assessment of the expedition and its leadership, and his drawings further documented his experiences. The diary appeared in print in 1998.

By the autumn of 1851 Carter was safely back in New York City. Following a brief courtship he married Louise Humphreys on 6 January 1852 in Annapolis. They had two daughters. After a year's duty on the naval academy's *Preble,* Carter served from 1853 to 1855 as junior lieutenant and navigator on the flagship *Vincennes,* whose expedition exploring and mapping the China Sea, the northern Pacific Ocean, and the Bering Strait was the navy's hydrographic counterpart to Matthew Calbraith Perry's diplomatic mission to Japan. Afterward Carter returned stateside and was stationed at the Norfolk Navy Yard for two years. In 1858 he began a two-year tour of service aboard the steamer *Argentina* on an exploration of La Plata River and its tributaries in South America.

Carter was in Washington, D.C., preparing reports on the expedition along La Plata when the Virginia convention met to discuss secession from the Union. He resigned from the United States Navy on 2 April 1861 and on 10 June

joined the Confederate States Navy as a lieutenant and was assigned to the steam tender *Teaser*, an armed tug deployed at Jamestown Island on the James River. Ordered the next year to duty aboard the *Richmond*, he was promoted to first lieutenant on 23 October 1862, to rank from 2 October of that year. In April 1863 he sailed to Europe to aid Confederate agent James D. Bulloch in equipping ships and purchasing supplies and became a valued assistant. Later Carter commanded the blockade runner *Coquette*, operating between Bermuda, Nassau, and the Atlantic ports. At Bulloch's request, Carter was ordered back to England and arrived in Liverpool on 28 September 1864. He was assigned to the French-built ironclad *Stonewall* outfitted in Copenhagen, but the Civil War ended before he arrived in United States waters. The *Stonewall* surrendered to Cuban authorities, and Carter returned to England, where he obtained a British master's certificate and joined the British mercantile marine.

At the urging of his father, Carter returned to Virginia and received a presidential pardon on 22 August 1866. He assumed management of Shirley plantation and over the next two decades became a prosperous farmer. Carter was treasurer of Westover Episcopal Church and in 1884 represented the Virginia State Agricultural Society at the World's Industrial and Cotton Centennial Exposition in New Orleans. In his later years he compiled a family genealogy, published posthumously in 1951 as *The Carter Tree*. In December 1887 Robert Randolph Carter fell from a granary loft and never recovered from his injuries. He died on 8 March 1888 and was buried at Shirley.

Birth and death dates in Carter family Bible records (1732–1913), LVA; autobiographical sketch of naval career and naval, personal, and plantation papers in Shirley Plantation Collection (1650–1989), CW; expedition diary on deposit at CW and published as Harold B. Gill, Jr., and Joanne Young, eds., *Searching for the Franklin Expedition: The Arctic Journal of Robert Randolph Carter* (1998), pors.; Edward W. Callahan, *List of Officers of the Navy of the United States and of the Marine Corps from 1775 to 1900* (1901), 104, 619; *Register of Officers of the Confederate States Navy, 1861–1865* (1931), 32; *ORN*; James D. Bulloch, *The Secret Service of the Confederate States in Europe* (1884), 1:412–413, 416, 2:130, 233–237; Presidential Pardons; obituaries in *Richmond State*, 9 Mar. 1888, *Richmond Dispatch*,

10 Mar. 1888, *Southern Churchman*, 15 Mar. 1888; memorial in *Southern Churchman*, 12 Apr. 1888.

HAROLD B. GILL, JR.

CARTER, Sara Elizabeth Dougherty (21 July 1898–8 January 1979), musician, was born in Flatwoods, near Coeburn, in Wise County, and was the daughter of William Sevier Dougherty, a sometime sawmill operator, and Elizabeth Kilgore Dougherty. When she was about three years old her mother died, and she and an elder sister went to live in the Copper Creek community, in Scott County, with their childless maternal aunt Melinda Kilgore Nickels and her husband Milburn Nickels. She attended a local school. Dougherty, nicknamed Jake as a child, became interested in music and from a neighbor learned to play the five-bar autoharp. By age twelve she had purchased her own eight-bar instrument from the Sears Roebuck catalog by selling greeting cards. According to family lore, in the spring of 1914 Dougherty was singing the train-wreck ballad "Engine 143" and accompanying herself on the autoharp when a salesman, Alvin Pleasant Delaney Carter, heard her. A romance quickly blossomed, and the pair were married in Scott County on 18 June 1915. The Carters lived initially in a two-room cabin A. P. Carter built but by 1919 had moved to Maces Spring in Poor Valley. They had two daughters and one son.

For the next decade the duo performed at churches, picnics, singing conventions, and other informal gatherings. They sang their repertoire of ballads, love songs, gospel music, and comic ditties to the accompaniment of Sara Carter's autoharp. This musical blend appealed to their neighbors, and the pair performed as often as their busy family schedule permitted. In 1926 they unsuccessfully auditioned for a scout from the Brunswick-Balke-Collender Company record label who proved unenthusiastic about a woman singing the lead part and who displayed more interest in A. P. Carter's fiddling.

In March 1926 Sara Carter's first cousin, Maybelle Addington, an accomplished guitarist and vocalist, married A. P. Carter's younger brother, Ezra J. "Eck" Carter, and joined the informal singing group. Sara Carter, who never learned to read music, performed the lead vocal melody and played the autoharp, Maybelle Carter

sang tenor harmony and played the guitar, and A. P. Carter sang bass, collected and arranged songs, and promoted and managed the family group. During the summer of 1927 the trio traveled to nearby Bristol, on the Virginia-Tennessee border, in response to a newspaper advertisement in order to audition for the Victor Talking Machine Company. They impressed the talent scout Ralph Sylvester Peer, and in Victor's makeshift studios on 1 August 1927 they recorded "Bury Me under the Weeping Willow," "Little Log Cabin by the Sea," "Poor Orphan Child," and "The Storms Are on the Ocean." They returned the next day to lay down two more tracks, "Single Girl, Married Girl," and "The Wandering Boy." Thus began a recording career that lasted until 1941. Their nearly 300 songs for Victor (later RCA Victor Records), Decca, and the American Record Corporation included "Can the Circle Be Unbroken," "I'm Thinking Tonight of My Blue Eyes," "Wabash Cannonball," "Will You Miss Me When I'm Gone," "Wildwood Flower," and their signature song, "Keep on the Sunny Side."

The popularity of the Carter Family was immediate, and the trio's priorities quickly shifted to include more performing and biannual trips to Victor's recording studios in Camden, New Jersey, or to the other temporary studios that Victor set up in southern cities such as Atlanta, Louisville, and Memphis. As the group spent more time on the road, Carter's innate discomfort on the stage grew worse. The strain on the Carters' marriage increased along with their success, a situation worsened by A. P. Carter's frequent absences on song-hunting expeditions between performances. By 1932 Carter had begun an affair with her husband's first cousin, Coy W. Bays (later Bayes). Early in 1933 Carter and her husband officially separated, and she returned to Copper Creek, leaving her three children with her husband.

A. P. Carter and Sara Carter remained professional partners even after they divorced on 15 October 1936. The Carter Family, expanded to include one of their children as well as three of their nieces, began to focus on radio work. Between 1938 and 1942 they lived for several months each year in Texas and performed over ultrahigh-power Mexican border radio stations, which enabled them to reach hundreds of thousands of listeners throughout the United States and overseas. On 20 February 1939 Carter married Coy Bayes in Brackettville, Texas. Two years later, on 14 October 1941, the group had their final recording session in RCA Victor's New York studio, and in March 1943, following a several-month engagement with radio station WBT in Charlotte, North Carolina, the three original members of the Carter Family finally split.

By 1942 Sara Bayes and her second husband had settled in Angels Camp, Calaveras County, California. Except for trips back to Virginia to visit her children (all of whom remained in Southwest Virginia), she lived in California for the rest of her life. She continued to perform occasionally. Between 1952 and 1956 she, A. P. Carter, and their children Janette Carter and Joe Carter, performing sometimes as the Carter Family and sometimes as the A. P. Carter Family, recorded nearly one hundred sides for the Tennessee-based Acme Records label, a venture that proved musically successful but a commercial failure. In 1966, at the urging of Johnny Cash, Bayes reunited with Maybelle Carter for a Columbia Records album.

Interest in the Carter Family renewed following A. P. Carter's death in 1960 and the folk revival that swept through popular music circles early in the 1960s. Although somewhat overshadowed by the role of her more famous cousin, Maybelle Addington Carter, Sara Carter's status as a pioneering figure in country music increased throughout the 1960s and 1970s. In 1970 the Country Music Hall of Fame in Nashville inducted the original Carter Family. The group's 1935 Banner label recording of "Can the Circle Be Unbroken (Bye and Bye)" and 1928 RCA Victor recording of "Wildwood Flower" received Grammy Hall of Fame Awards from the National Academy of Recording Arts and Sciences in 1998 and 1999, respectively, as enduring works of historical significance. Sara Elizabeth Dougherty Carter Bayes died on 8 January 1979 in Lodi, California, and was buried in Mount Vernon United Methodist Church Cemetery in Maces Spring, two rows away from her first husband's grave. In 1985 the Maces Spring home she had shared with A. P. Carter was placed on both the Virginia Landmarks Register and the National Register of Historic Places.

John Atkins et al., eds., *The Carter Family*, Old Time Music Booklet 1 (1973); Atkins, "The Carter Family," in Bill C. Malone and Judith McCulloh, eds., *Stars of Country Music: Uncle Dave Macon to Johnny Rodriguez* (1975), 95–120; June Carter Cash, *Among My Klediments* (1979); Mark Dawidziak, "It All Began in Bristol," *Commonwealth* 48 (Feb. 1981): 17–23; Janette Carter, *Living with Memories* (1983); Irwin Stambler and Grelun Landon, *The Encyclopedia of Folk, Country and Western Music*, 2d ed. (1983), 94–97; Mary A. Bufwack and Robert K. Oermann, *Finding Her Voice: The Saga of Women in Country Music* (1993), 50–59; Ed Kahn, "The Carter Family on Border Radio," *American Music* 14 (1996): 205–217; Charles Wolfe, "Jake and Doc and May: The Carter Family Goes to the End of the World," *Bluegrass Unlimited* 34 (Feb. 2000): 22–27; Mark Zwonitzer with Charles Hirshberg, *Will You Miss Me When I'm Gone? The Carter Family and Their Legacy in American Music* (2002), pors.; Katie Doman, "Something Old, Something New: The Carter Family's Bristol Session Recordings," in Charles K. Wolfe and Ted Olson, eds., *The Bristol Sessions: Writing about the Big Bang of Country Music* (2005), 66–86; original Carter Family discography in Kip Lornell, *Virginia's Blues, Country, and Gospel Records, 1902–1943: An Annotated Discography* (1989), 35–58; *The Carter Family on Border Radio*, John Edwards Memorial Foundation 101 (n.d.), recording with brochure notes by Archie Green, William H. Koon, and Norm Cohen; *The Carter Family: In the Shadow of Clinch Mountain*, Bear Family Records 15865 (2000), including 1963 interview of Carter and Maybelle Carter conducted by Mike Seeger and Ed Kahn, discography by Tony Russell and Richard Weize, and companion book by Charles K. Wolfe (pors.); BVS Marriage Register, Scott Co. (variant first marriage date of 20 June 1915); divorce confirmed by BVS (first marriage date of 18 June 1915 on judgment of divorce); obituaries in *Richmond News Leader*, 8 Jan. 1979, and *Bristol Herald Courier*, *New York Times*, and *Richmond Times-Dispatch*, all 9 Jan. 1979; account of funeral in *Bristol Herald Courier* and *Bristol Virginia-Tennessean*, 13 Jan. 1979.

KIP LORNELL

CARTER, Stuart Barns (25 April 1906–12 June 1983), member of the House of Delegates and of the Senate of Virginia, was born in Philadelphia, Pennsylvania, and was the son of Charles Dale Carter and Sarah Strother Barns Carter, both natives of Smyth County. His father's sister married Henry Carter Stuart, Virginia's governor from 1914 to 1918. His father died in January 1907, and when Carter was about three years old his mother married John S. Pechin. Carter and his younger half brother grew up in Botetourt County, where his stepfather and other

Pechin family members owned property. Carter was educated in the public schools and at Virginia Episcopal School. He attended the University of Virginia during the 1925–1926 academic year as well as Western Reserve University, in Cleveland, Ohio, and the Cumberland University School of Law, in Lebanon, Tennessee, from which he received a law degree. Carter passed the Virginia bar examination in December 1934 and opened a law office in Fincastle. On 31 October 1934 he married Mary Shelley Pechin Sheridan, of Ossining, New York, a relation of his stepfather. They lived in Botetourt County and had one daughter and one son.

In 1949 Carter won election to the House of Delegates representing Botetourt and Craig Counties, and he was reelected in 1951 and 1953. He was a member of the Committees on Counties, Cities, and Towns, on Manufactures and Mechanic Arts, and on Public Property during all three terms, as well as the influential Committee on Finance during his first two terms and the Committee for Courts of Justice during his third. Carter was initially aligned with the dominant Democratic Party organization of Harry Flood Byrd (1887–1966), but during the 1950 legislative session he and Armistead Lloyd Boothe, of Alexandria, emerged as leaders of a group of young, reform-minded delegates called the Young Turks, most of them from Virginia's rapidly growing urban areas. They did not seek to displace the leadership of Byrd's organization but to bring in a new generation of leaders with more progressive views, especially regarding spending on public education and mental health facilities. The clash between the Young Turks and the so-called Old Guard came to a head in the 1954 session over a bill sponsored by the state senator Harry Flood Byrd Jr. (b. 1914), of Winchester. It required that all revenue that the state government collected and that the General Assembly did not appropriate be rebated to the taxpayers. Arguing that big business would benefit disproportionately from the proposal and that the money was needed for education and mental hospitals, Carter offered an amendment to keep that year's entire $7 million surplus in the treasury. Though it narrowly passed in the House, Carter's amendment met strong opposition in the Senate of Virginia. The resulting stalemate between the two chambers kept the General Assembly in session more than thirty hours past its mandated adjournment. A compromise reduced to $2.2 million the amount of the surplus to be retained in the treasury.

Carter ran for the Senate of Virginia in 1955 from the district comprising the counties of Alleghany, Bedford, Botetourt, Craig, and Rockbridge and the cities of Buena Vista and Clifton Forge. Promising to renew his battle to increase funding for education and mental health, he prevailed over Hale Collins, an organization-backed candidate, in the Democratic primary and had no Republican opponent in the November general election. Carter received routine appointments to the Committees on Agriculture, Mining, and Manufacturing, on Enrolled Bills, on Roads and Internal Navigation, and on Welfare.

Before Carter could take his seat, the prospect of racial desegregation of the public schools overshadowed the Young Turks' issues. During a special session in November 1955 Carter joined with Boothe and three other Northern Virginia delegates in opposing a referendum allowing the state to offer tuition grants to students attending private schools. In the 1956 session, in deference to his cousin Henry Carter Stuart (1893–1963), he abstained from voting on a resolution that Stuart sponsored to assert that the state could interpose its authority between the Supreme Court of the United States and the people, in effect obstructing implementation of the Court's desegregation order. At the 1956 special session called to implement the senior Byrd's Massive Resistance plan, Carter opposed closing schools that came under court orders to desegregate. He argued for protection of the public school system and obedience to the law of the land. Carter was quoted as publicly declaring, "I do conscientiously believe in integration." Fearing that immediate, large-scale desegregation would produce social turmoil, he supported a moderate, gradual desegregation plan and voted in 1956 and 1958 for the bipartisan legislation that Boothe and State Senator Theodore Roosevelt Dalton proposed. Although Carter had recently had abdominal surgery, he flew from Roanoke to Richmond to attend a special session of the assembly and on 17 April 1959 cast the tie-breaking vote in the 20–19 decision to send the governor's moderate school desegregation plan to the committee of the whole Senate, thus ensuring its passage and bringing an end to Massive Resistance. The story that Carter was carried into the chamber on a stretcher has entered the lore of modern Virginia politics. He denied that he had been carried in, though clearly his presence in the chamber was unexpected and his vote essential.

The incident had fateful political consequences for Carter's political career. As the 1959 Democratic primary approached, Byrd organization leaders began preparing Hale Collins once again to run against Carter, with the clear indication that Carter's stand on school desegregation would be the key issue. Carter recognized that in the prevailing climate among white Virginians his forthrightly expressed views on racial integration probably would not gain majority support in his district and would certainly exclude him from leadership in state politics. He therefore retired from the Senate in 1959 after one term.

Even though he was no longer a member of the assembly, Carter, who had become a member of the Democratic State Central Committee in 1948, continued to serve on that body through the 1960s, often as chair of the Sixth District Democratic Committee. In that capacity, at the 1964 state convention he helped lead a successful effort, against the wishes of the senior Byrd, to endorse the presidential candidacy of Lyndon Baines Johnson. Carter also served from 1961 to 1970 on the Botetourt County board of supervisors, part of that time as its chair, and as president of the Virginia Association of Counties. Throughout most of his adult life, he was an active member and vestryman in the Episcopal Church. Carter's wife died in October 1966. After he retired in 1975 as senior partner in the law firm of Carter, Roe, Emick, and Hontz, he spent much of his time at Topsail Island, North Carolina. Stuart Barns Carter died of cancer in a Roanoke hospital on 12 June 1983. His remains were cremated.

Morton, *Virginia Lives*, 170; family information verified by son, S. Dale Carter (2001); Stuart B. Carter interview with author, 19 Dec. 1979; BVS Marriage Register, Botetourt Co.; *Roanoke Times*, 2 Nov. 1934, 13 May 1959; *Roanoke World-News*, 2 Nov. 1934; *Richmond News Leader,* 16 Mar. 1954, 18 June 1955; *Richmond Times-Dispatch,* 19 July 1964; Benjamin Muse, *Virginia's Massive Resistance* (1961), 33 (quotation); Robbins L. Gates, *The Making of Massive Resistance: Virginia's Politics of Public School Desegregation, 1954–1956* (1962); J. Harvie Wilkinson III, *Harry Byrd and the Changing Face of Virginia Politics, 1945–1966* (1968); James R. Sweeney, "Byrd and Anti-Byrd: The Struggle for Political Supremacy in Virginia, 1943–1954" (Ph.D. diss., University of Notre Dame, 1973); James H. Hershman Jr., "A Rumbling in the Museum: The Opponents of Virginia's Massive Resistance" (Ph.D. diss., UVA, 1978); Douglas Smith, "'When Reason Collides with Prejudice': Armistead Lloyd Boothe and the Politics of Desegregation in Virginia, 1948–1963," *VMHB* 102 (1994): 18–19, 29–33, 38–39; obituaries in *Richmond News Leader*, *Richmond Times-Dispatch*, and *Roanoke Times and World-News* (por.), all 14 June 1983, *Washington Post,* 15 June 1983, and *Botetourt County News and Fincastle Herald*, 16 June 1983.

JAMES H. HERSHMAN JR.

CARTER, Thomas (24 April 1731–5 October 1803), member of the Convention of 1788, and his twin brother, Dale Carter, were born probably at the Lancaster County plantation of their parents, Peter Carter and Judith Norris Carter. In 1733 their father inherited half of their grandfather's 304-acre King George County plantation. Carter's early life is not well documented. About 1773 he, a younger brother, at least two cousins, and other relatives moved to Rye Cove in the Clinch River valley. Boundary changes during Carter's thirty-year residence there placed it in Fincastle County until 1776, in Washington County from 1776 to 1786, and in Russell County from then until the formation of Scott County in 1814. Through the Loyal Land Company, Carter obtained a survey dated 26 March 1774 for 197 acres of land on the north side of the Clinch River on Cove Creek. On 31 March 1783 he obtained a survey for an additional 1,420 acres in Rye Cove, confirmed by a grant in 1787. At the time of his death he owned more than a dozen slaves.

Probably before 1770 Carter married a woman named Mary whose maiden name may have been Morgan. They had three sons and three daughters before her death about 1781, possibly as a consequence of giving birth in that year to twin daughters. Carter later married Elizabeth Moss, who may have been the widow of Mathew Moss who died in Washington County about 1782. They had no known children.

The threat of Indian attacks was a constant feature of frontier life at the time of Carter's move to southwestern Virginia. Participating in local defense, he served in the field in 1774 for twenty-four days and later for forty-two days. Carter's name was on a list of men on duty from 1 February to 31 March 1777 at Rye Cove and again from 1 May through 30 June of that year. Surviving records probably do not reflect the full extent of Carter's militia service. In an incident much noted at the time, Indians killed and scalped his cousin Dale Carter near the Clinch River in 1774. The wife and children of another cousin were killed in an attack close to Rye Cove in 1787. As a result of the raids, Carter may have retreated for about three years to the safety of the Big Moccasin Creek area (near present-day Gate City). As late as 1792 Carter's place on Rye Cove was the site of a militia garrison and sometimes was known as Carter's Fort. On 20 April 1788 Indians abducted Carter's youngest son, Morgan Carter, then about fourteen, a cousin, Elijah Carter, and their African American companion. The details of their captivity are not known, but the return of the three boys was reported in 1793.

Carter served as justice of the peace from the first meeting of the court of the newly created Russell County on 9 May 1786 until June 1794, when increasing infirmity forced his resignation. He was a lieutenant of the county militia in 1786 and also that year was licensed to perform marriages and appointed an overseer of the poor in the lower district of the county. The county court recommended him as sheriff at least seven times before he received a commission for that office in 1803. Carter represented Russell County in the House of Delegates from 1787 through 1791. During the 1787–1788, 1790, and 1791 assemblies he served on the Committee of Propositions and Grievances, and during the 1789 and 1791 assemblies he sat on the Committee of Religion. Carter also regularly corresponded with the governor regarding Indian attacks on the frontier and recommended military deployments and responses.

Carter was one of two men elected on 18 March 1788 to represent Russell County in the convention called to consider the proposed con-

stitution of the United States. The voters probably knew that he opposed ratification. In spite of the recent abduction of his son, Carter attended all twenty-six sessions of the convention in Richmond in June, but he did not speak during the debates. He voted in favor of requiring amendment of the Constitution before ratification, and after that motion was defeated, he voted against ratification on 25 June. Two days later Carter and other antifederalists, joined by twelve delegates who had favored ratification, voted to propose an amendment limiting the new government's power of taxation.

Following a decade of poor health, Thomas Carter died, presumably at his home in Rye Cove, on 5 October 1803. He was probably buried there or nearby.

Birth date recorded by father in Book of Common Prayer owned by Thomas Carter (ca. 1630–1700), VHS; Joseph Lyon Miller, *The Descendants of Capt. Thomas Carter of "Barford," Lancaster County, Virginia . . .* (1912), 237–238; Robert M. Addington, *History of Scott County, Virginia* (1932), 97–103, 306; Rita K. Sutton, *Early Carters in Scott County, Virginia* (1981), pt. 2:1, 4–6; some correspondence in Governor's Office, Letters Received, RG 3, LVA, printed in *Calendar of Virginia State Papers*, 4:375–376, 389, 460; wives and children identified in *Joseph Jones and Wife* v. *Thomas M. Carter*, Scott Co. Ended Chancery Cause, no. 1830-017, LVA, and *Brickey* v. *Jones and Wife*, Wythe Co. Superior Court of Chancery, Pleas no. 8, 457–506; Montgomery Co. Record of Plots, A:77; Land Office Grant Book, 11:264–266, RG 4, LVA; Kaminski, *Ratification*, 9:563, 630, 10:1541, 1557, 1565; Russell Co. Will Book, 2:39–40; death date in Russell Co. Order Book, 3:278.

F. CLAIBORNE JOHNSTON, JR.

CARTER, William Richard (22 April 1833–8 July 1864), Confederate cavalry officer and diarist, was born on the Nottoway County farm of his parents, Martha Anderson Craig Gregory Carter and Sharpe Carter, a farmer, sometime schoolmaster, and charter member of the Nottoway Library Society. Carter excelled in his studies at Hampden-Sydney College from 1848 until 1852, when he graduated with high honors in chemistry. Exhibiting talent as an essayist, he served as clerk for the college's Union Literary Society and in 1850 and 1851 was elected vice president.

Recommendations from his professors led to Carter's employment in February 1853 at the Flat Rock Female Seminary in Lunenburg

County, but after two years he became restless. He inquired about buying a newspaper, but nothing came of it. Carter unsuccessfully sought the mathematics chair at Hampden-Sydney in 1856 and suffered another disappointment when Amelia Trotter ended their engagement. Discouraged and frustrated, he resorted to drink for a time before deciding to seek his fortune in the West.

By March 1858 Carter was living in Columbus, Mississippi, anxious to remove any stigma attached to his name in Virginia and optimistic about opportunities in the bustling town. He joined the Presbyterian Church and renewed contact with Amelia Trotter, who invited him to write but then rejected another marriage proposal. Soon after his arrival Carter published an essay, "Wealth *versus* Character," in the *Columbus Enquirer*. Although he had lost his taste for teaching, he took a position at the Collegiate High School run by the Independent Order of Odd Fellows and became so well regarded there that he was invited to purchase the two-story school. On 1 January 1859 he became both proprietor and principal in charge of eighty-five students and two assistants.

The demands of the school proved greater than expected and by April 1860 Carter had decided to sell the institution. Returning to Nottoway County by 15 July, he began studying law and was admitted to the bar in April 1861. Carter had hardly settled into his new Richmond practice when Virginia's secession from the Union prompted him to enlist on 27 May as a private in the Nottoway Troop. That same day he began keeping a field diary.

His unit was soon incorporated as Company E of the 3d Regiment Virginia Cavalry. Carter was captured at Big Bethel on 10 June 1861 and held at Fort Monroe until his exchange twelve days later. On 23 November he was elected first lieutenant and on 18 January 1862 was elected captain to fill a vacancy caused by death. During the Peninsula campaign the 3d Virginia was attached to Brigadier General James Ewell Brown Stuart's brigade but did not join in Stuart's celebrated ride around the Union Army of the Potomac in June or in the Catlett's Station Raid during the Second Manassas (Bull Run) campaign. Carter was absent from the Chambersburg Raid but entered a detailed description of it in his field diary. On 7 November 1862 he was promoted to major to rank from 21 October and on 18 November was elevated to lieutenant colonel, in which capacity he occasionally commanded the regiment. In a letter home that month he summed up his wartime experiences so far as "fighting, skirmishing, advancing, or retreating nearly every day."

Carter performed bravely during the Dumfries Raid in December 1862 and at Kelly's Ford in March 1863. During the Gettysburg campaign in June he fought at Brandy Station and at Aldie and joined in the controversial Gettysburg Raid, although, as his diary notes, only the sharpshooters represented his regiment in the cavalry fight on 3 July. During the army's retreat his troopers fought a rearguard action against pursuing Union forces. Carter led the regiment at Raccoon Ford in October and was captured but escaped to participate in the rout of Union cavalry at Buckland Mills, also called the "Buckland Races." In May 1864 his regiment was heavily engaged at Todd's Tavern, Yellow Tavern, and Haw's Shop. On 1 June, the eve of Cold Harbor, he wrote his father that he was ill from nearly fifty days of constant marching and fighting. Ten days later William Richard Carter was wounded at Trevilian Station, in Louisa County, and taken to the general hospital at Gordonsville, in Orange County, where he died on 8 July 1864. He was buried at his father's house, Hickory Hill (later Carter's Hall), in Nottoway County.

Carter's detailed, articulate field diary became a boon for researchers. In 1876 Sharpe Carter planned to publish it and obtained letters from former generals Fitzhugh Lee and Williams Carter Wickham testifying to his son's military skills. Henry Brainerd McClellan borrowed it while writing *Life and Campaigns of Major-General J. E. B. Stuart, Commander of the Cavalry of the Army of Northern Virginia* (1885). That same year the Southern Historical Society expressed an interest in publishing the diary in its magazine, but Carter's compelling observations did not appear in print until 1998, when editor Walbrook D. Swank published *Sabres, Saddles, and Spurs*. That edition, however, was based unknowingly on a partial transcription covering only the period from 27 July 1862 to 30 April 1864. The original field diary, kept from 27 May 1861 to 7 June 1864, no longer survives, but a complete two-volume transcription, probably made by Sharpe Carter, is preserved at Hampden-Sydney College.

Carter Family Papers (1817–1892), Acc. 33886 (including birth date in Carter to Sharpe Carter, 22 Apr. 1860, quotation in Carter to Sharpe Carter, 10 Nov. 1862, two incomplete diary transcriptions, essays, addresses, and clipping from *Columbus Enquirer*, ca. 24 Apr. 1858), and a complete microfilm diary transcription, Misc. Reel 2644, both LVA; William Richard Carter Papers (including complete transcription of original diary) and minutes of the Union Literary Society, both Hampden-Sydney College; incomplete diary published in Walbrook D. Swank, ed., *Sabres, Saddles, and Spurs* (1998); Compiled Service Records; *OR*, 1st ser., 21:732, 738, 739, vol. 25, pt. 1, 25, vol. 29, pt. 1, 471; H. B. McClellan, *Life and Campaigns of Major-General J. E. B. Stuart, Commander of the Cavalry of the Army of Northern Virginia* (1885), reissued as *I Rode with Jeb Stuart: The Life and Campaigns of Major General J. E. B. Stuart* (1958), 184, 202, 204–207, 220; Thomas P. Nanzig, *3rd Virginia Cavalry* (1989).

DONALD W. GUNTER

CARTMELL, Thomas Kemp (28 January 1838–15 May 1920), local historian, was the son of Mordecai Bean Cartmell and Eliza Campbell Cartmell and was born at his father's Frederick County home near Round Hill, several miles west of Winchester. He received an education, the details of which are not recorded, and at age twenty-two moved to Bell County, Texas, where he was an assistant United States marshal and spent much of June and July 1860 compiling the census for that county, in which he enumerated all 4,800 residents except himself.

Cartmell returned to Virginia early in 1861, evidently to serve his native state during the Civil War. He was an assistant quartermaster in the militia until the autumn of 1861, when he became assistant provost marshal at Winchester under Thomas J. "Stonewall" Jackson. Cartmell often carried dispatches to Confederate commanders in the western theater until he resigned in March 1862 after the Confederate evacuation of Winchester. He immediately enlisted as a private in Company B of the 11th Virginia Cavalry under the command of Turner Ashby. Cartmell was severely wounded at Linville Creek in Rock-

ingham County at the beginning of the following year and was on medical leave from January 1863 until April 1864, during which time his younger brother, a captain in the same company, was killed in action. After Cartmell's return to active duty, he was commissioned captain in charge of the Bureau of Information for the Shenandoah Valley.

On 22 November 1866 Cartmell married Annie Glass Baker, of Frederick County. They lived at Ingleside, the family farm south of Winchester, and had one daughter and one son, who died in infancy. After years of farming, Cartmell became deputy to the clerk of Frederick County about 1881. In March 1887 he obtained the Democratic Party nomination to succeed the clerk and was elected to that office on 26 May. Reelected twice, Cartmell served as clerk until the end of 1905, after which he worked for several more years as a deputy to his successor. That experience enabled him to become an expert on the county's history.

It is as a genealogist and historian that Cartmell is best remembered. In 1909 he published *Shenandoah Valley Pioneers and Their Descendants: A History of Frederick County, Virginia*, a compilation of nearly 600 pages of family histories and historical notes on the origin and development of economic, social, and political life in the county. The volume constituted a life's work for Cartmell, who used his free hours to rummage through public records in the clerk's office. The resulting local history contains chapters on European settlement in the Shenandoah Valley; the development of banks, churches, courts, fire companies, schools, and towns; and the emergence of such local improvements as newspapers, public utilities, and railroads. Additional chapters cover the Revolutionary War, the Civil War, and the lives of notable citizens, their families, and their residences. The book is a classic in the genre of late-nineteenth- and early twentieth-century local historical writing and has been reprinted several times.

During his working years Cartmell was instrumental in rebuilding the Opequon Presbyterian Church in Kernstown, after a fire destroyed an earlier structure. He also took a leading role in the erection of a Confederate memorial statue in front of the Frederick County courthouse in Winchester in November 1916. Cartmell lived on his farm until long after his wife died in January 1907. In poor health during his later years, he eventually moved to the Winchester home of his daughter. Thomas Kemp Cartmell died there of a cerebral hemorrhage on 15 May 1920 and was buried in Mount Hebron Cemetery, in Winchester.

Family and personal history, with birth and marriage dates, in Cartmell, *Shenandoah Valley Pioneers and Their Descendants: A History of Frederick County, Virginia* (1909), 423–424, and Quarles, *Worthy Lives*, 60–61 (por.); Thomas K. Cartmell Papers, Handley Regional Library, Winchester; BVS Marriage Register, Frederick Co.; Compiled Service Records; Richard L. Armstrong, *11th Virginia Cavalry* (1989), 129; *Winchester Times*, 26 Jan., 9 Mar., 1 June 1887; BVS Death Certificate, Frederick Co.; obituary in *Winchester Evening Star,* 15 May 1920.

WARREN R. HOFSTRA

CARUTHERS, William Alexander (23 December 1802–29 August 1846), writer, was born in Lexington and was the son of William Caruthers, a prosperous merchant and landowner, and Phebe Alexander Caruthers, a sister of Archibald Alexander, president of Hampden-Sydney College from 1797 to 1806. Caruthers attended Washington College (later Washington and Lee University) from 1817 to 1820 before entering the medical college of the University of Pennsylvania, from which he received a degree in 1823. On 30 June of that year Caruthers applied for a marriage license and early in July married Louisa Catherine Gibson, a wealthy heiress from Whitemarsh Island, Chatham County, Georgia. They had three sons and two daughters who survived childhood. The couple took up residence in Lexington, where Caruthers practiced medicine and enthusiastically engaged in various civic activities, including serving as president of a local debating society. Financial difficulties led him in 1829 to move his family to New York City, where he established a medical practice and assisted in treating victims of the 1832 cholera epidemic.

In 1834 Caruthers published his first work, *The Kentuckian in New-York; or, The Adventures of Three Southerns, by a Virginian.* A comic two-volume epistolary novel that borrowed from several genres, *The Kentuckian* narrated the intersectional travels of three young southern gentlemen through the North and Deep South and was notable for its Daniel Boone–like title character, Montgomery Damon. Caruthers demonstrated his explicit nationalistic vision in having the travelers overcome their sectional prejudices and discover newfound appreciation for the various regions of the country. His next novel, the two-volume *Cavaliers of Virginia; or, The Recluse of Jamestown. An Historical Romance of the Old Dominion* (1834–1835), combined his interest in Virginia history with historical romance and took for its subject Bacon's Rebellion. Caruthers portrayed Nathaniel Bacon (1647–1676) as the heroic leader of an insurrection mounted to preserve the liberties of the people against Virginia's oppressive royal governor, a portrait drawing on the interpretation of the historian John Daly Burk.

In 1835 Caruthers returned to Lexington, where he worked on his third and final novel, *The Knights of the Golden Horse-Shoe, a Traditionary Tale of the Cocked Hat Gentry in the Old Dominion.* Again selecting an event from Virginia's colonial past, he fashioned the first extended literary treatment of Lieutenant Governor Alexander Spotswood's 1716 expedition to the Blue Ridge Mountains. Publication was delayed when a house fire destroyed Caruthers's papers on the eve of his move to Georgia in 1837. In Savannah he practiced medicine, served two terms as a Whig on the city's board of aldermen, and became a charter member of the Georgia Historical Society. Caruthers also published short works in several periodicals including the New York–based *Knickerbocker* magazine, which in 1838 ran "Climbing the Natural Bridge," a sketch based on an incident during his college days, and the *Magnolia; or, Southern Monthly*, which serialized the reworked *Knights of the Golden Horse-Shoe* in 1841. In 1845 a small Alabama publishing house issued the novel in book form.

Early in his career Caruthers sought to establish a reputation as a writer of national scope and voice. Unlike some of his contemporaries whose regional writing inspired universal application, he was unable to transcend the genre in which he later worked. The Virginia stories evinced a strong regional pride while impressing critics as superior to his first novel, and Caruthers became identified as a sectional historian and romancer of the Old Dominion. After his death the *Southern and Western Literary Messenger and Review* observed, "He was a Virginian by birth, and in all his feelings." His literary attainments were often ignored in the decades immediately following his death, even in his native state. Modeled on the romances of Sir Walter Scott, Caruthers's second and third novels established a precedent followed by such later Virginia writers as John Esten Cooke and Mary Johnston, but it was not until 1884 that he was credited as the originator of what came to be known as the Virginia novel. Since the 1920s literary scholars have regarded Caruthers as the first significant Virginia novelist and among the earliest southern practitioners of the romantic tradition.

William Alexander Caruthers contracted tuberculosis in the spring of 1846 and died on 29 August of that year at a health resort at Kennesaw Mountain, Georgia. He was buried most likely in an unmarked grave in the cemetery of Saint James Episcopal Church, in Marietta, Georgia.

Curtis Carroll Davis, *Chronicler of the Cavaliers: A Life of the Virginia Novelist Dr. William A. Caruthers* (1953), with bibliography of manuscripts and publications; birth date in Caruthers Family Genealogical Notes, 47, UVA; Genealogical Committee of Georgia Historical Society, comp., *Marriages of Chatham County, Georgia* (1993), 1:112; Elizabeth Preston Allan, "Notes on William Alexander Caruthers," *WMQ*, 2d ser., 9 (1929): 294–297; Caruthers correspondence at Duke and edited by Davis in "Chronicler of the Cavaliers: Some Letters from and to William Alexander Caruthers, M.D. (1802–1846)," *VMHB* 55 (1947): 213–232, "Chronicler of the Cavaliers: Three More Letters from and to William Alexander Caruthers, M.D. (1802–1846)," *VMHB* 57 (1949): 55–66, and "Dr. Caruthers Confronts the Bureaucrats" and "Dr. Caruthers Aids a Lady," *Georgia Historical Quarterly* 56 (1972): 101–111, 583–587; Davis, "An Early Historical Novelist Goes to the Library: William A. Caruthers and His Reading, 1823–29," *Bulletin of the New York Public Library* 52 (1948): 159–169; Matthew Joseph Hurt, "Uniting States: Narration, Space, and Nation in Four Nineteenth-Century American Travel Novels" (Ph.D. diss., University of Illinois, Urbana-Champaign, 2000); *Southern and Western Literary Messenger and Review* 12 (1846): 764 (quotation); obituaries in *Savannah Daily Georgian* and *Savannah Daily Republican* (with death date), both 2 Sept. 1846; *Savannah Daily Republican* obituary reprinted in *Daily Richmond Enquirer* and *Richmond Times and Compiler*, both 7 Sept. 1846; memorial resolutions of Washington Literary Society in *Lexington Gazette*, 24 Sept. 1846.

Matthew Hurt

CARVER, William (d. ca. 3–6 September 1676), participant in Bacon's Rebellion, was by the mid-1650s an experienced merchant mariner of uncertain age who was master of a ship engaged in trade between the English ports of Bristol (probably his native city) and London and the colonies. His name first appears in extant Virginia records on 15 June 1659, when he patented 500 acres of land on the South Branch of the Elizabeth River in Lower Norfolk County. By then Carver was already married to a woman named Elizabeth, maiden name unknown, and father of a ten-year-old son. Carver became a justice of the peace in June 1663 and in the following summer secured renewal of his original patent and acquired 890 acres of additional land nearby.

Elected to a vacant seat in the House of Burgesses in 1665, Carter represented Lower Norfolk County until 1669. During the session that met in October and November 1666 he served on the Committee for Propositions, and on 26 September 1667 at the conclusion of the Second Anglo-Dutch War he was appointed to a committee to inquire of the governor and Council whether there was enough money available to erect a fort. Carver was a tax collector for Lower Norfolk County in 1669 and 1672, took his turns overseeing the county roads in 1669 and 1671, and was sheriff in 1670. He continued to own trading ships but by 1668 described himself as a merchant rather than a mariner. In 1667 Carver placed management of all his property in the hands of his eighteen-year-old son. His wife evidently died about that time, and he probably remarried not long thereafter to a woman whose name is unrecorded.

Carver engaged in several serious quarrels with his neighbors late in the 1660s and in the 1670s. He possessed a volatile temper and may have indulged too frequently in drink. On 25 July 1672, while suffering from severe abdominal pains and perhaps taking alcohol to relieve the symptoms, Carver stabbed to death Thomas Gilbert, who was sitting beside him at dinner. Several witnesses described Carver as behaving irrationally, and Carver later stated that he did not remember anything about the incident or the several days before and after the stabbing. A

General Court jury acquitted him of murder, presumably persuaded that he had been deranged and not responsible for his actions. Soon after Carter's return home from his trial in Jamestown, his treatment of his neighbors led the General Court to order his arrest. During a legal dispute three years later, he retaliated against his adversary by accusing the man's wife of practicing witchcraft.

In June 1676 Carver appeared in Jamestown while the assembly was in session and requested a commission from Nathaniel Bacon (1647–1676) to lead forces in a campaign against the Indians. Instead, Bacon appointed Carver and Giles Bland commanders of a naval force and in August ordered them to capture Governor Sir William Berkeley, who about that time had retreated to the Eastern Shore. The two men organized a flotilla of small boats and with several hundred men sailed into the lower Chesapeake Bay, where they captured several small vessels and ships, including Thomas Larrimore's 265-ton *Rebecca*. They found Berkeley on 1 September at Arlington, the Northampton County estate of John Custis (d. 1696). Carver went ashore with a force of more than one hundred men, leaving Bland on board the *Rebecca*. Accounts of what happened next contain inconsistencies. Carver may have negotiated with Berkeley, the governor's men may have plied Carver with wine, or both, but Berkeley suddenly found himself with the upper hand. On the next day the governor seized Carver, Bland, and the *Rebecca* and its crew. Bland and Carver apparently blamed each other for Berkeley's success, but a later commentator speculated that it was not Carver's treachery but "the ju[i]ce of the Grape" that betrayed him and Bland into Berkeley's hands and doomed the expedition. Of the event, Berkeley wrote that Carver was a "valiant stout seaman, taken miraculously."

The governor hanged Carver and four other men within three or four days, then moved swiftly to retake Jamestown, which he achieved on 8 September 1676. The five were among the first men the governor executed. Carver's burial place is not recorded. Early in November, Berkeley ordered that Carver's property be confiscated and sold and later specifically excluded him from the proclamation of pardon issued to Bacon's

lesser followers. Carver's widow reportedly died of grief shortly after he was hanged. A year later Carver's son petitioned the Crown for restitution of the estate, a part of which he recovered and sold in 1681. On that land William Craford established the town of Portsmouth in 1752.

Biographies in *WMQ*, 1st ser., 3 (1895): 163–165, and *Lower Norfolk County Virginia Antiquary* 2 (1897): 48–49 (identifying second wife as Rose Carver without documentation); affidavit of William Yeamans, 22 Dec. 1659, in Deposition Book of Bristol, 1657–1661, Bristol Record Office 04439 (3), fol. 103; Virginia Land Office Patent Book, 5:194–195 (first record in Virginia), 197, 6:583, RG 4, LVA; Lower Norfolk Co. Deed Book, 4:209; Lower Norfolk Co. Wills and Deeds, D: fols. 380, Wills and Deeds E: fols. 1, 17, 41, 94, 127–130, and Wills and Deeds E, pt. 2 (Orders, 1666–1675), fols. 22, 34, 38a, 55a, 56a, 70a, 80, 82, 84; *JHB, 1659/60–1693*, viii, 32, 36, 39, 46–47, 50; *Minutes of Council and General Court*, 210, 276, 319, 584–585, 597; Sir William Berkeley to Henry Coventry, 2 Feb. 1677, Coventry Papers, Longleat House, Wiltshire, Eng.; Berkeley's list of men hanged, in Samuel Wiseman's Book of Record, unpaginated, Pepysian Library 2582, Magdalene College, University of Cambridge (first quotation); John Cotton, "Narrative of Bacon's Rebellion" (n.d.), unpaginated, VHS (second quotation); T[homas] M[atthew], "The Beginning Progress and Conclusion of Bacons Rebellion in Virginia in the Years 1675 & 1676" (ca. 1705), Thomas Jefferson Papers, LC; Wilcomb E. Washburn, *The Governor and the Rebel: A History of Bacon's Rebellion in Virginia* (1957), 72, 77–79; James Horn, *Adapting to a New World: English Society in the Seventeenth-Century Chesapeake* (1994), 243, 271, 290, 345, 415; PRO CO 1/41, fols. 243–245, and CO 391/2, fols. 144, 146–147.

JOHN G. DEAL

CARWILE, Howard Hearnes (14 November 1911–6 June 1987), attorney and local politician, was born in Charlotte County and was the son of Willis Early Carwile and Allie Taylor Carwile, who lived on a small tobacco farm and had at least twelve children. Educated in the county's public schools, he entered the University of Virginia in 1931 but soon dropped out. Carwile spent two years at Alma White College, in Zarephath, Somerset County, New Jersey, where he washed dishes to pay his way. He completed the law course at Southeastern University, in Washington, D.C., but did not stay to receive his degree. Soon after passing the bar in Virginia late in 1938, Carwile contracted tuberculosis and spent nearly a year in the Blue Ridge Sanatorium, where he suffered a hemorrhage in one of his eyes and accused the staff of negligence and abuse. He attempted to sue the state, but the suit was dismissed under the doctrine of sovereign immunity, and he twice failed to persuade the Virginia Supreme Court of Appeals to have the suit reinstated.

Growing up poor and having to struggle for his education and livelihood, Carwile nurtured grudges against capitalists and government officials, and while in Washington he associated briefly with communists and socialists. In 1942 he was the Socialist Party candidate against the Democrat Thomas Granville Burch for the House of Representatives seat from the Fifth Congressional District running along the North Carolina border. He received less than 7 percent of the vote and two years later polled 15 percent as an unaffiliated, independent candidate for the same seat. By then Carwile had broken with the socialists and later in life was virulently derogatory about the political left.

Disqualified from military service because of his tuberculosis and poor eyesight, Carwile practiced law in Charlotte County until January 1945, when he moved to Richmond. He specialized in criminal cases and defended the poor and others whom he believed had suffered injustices at the hands of state or local government officials. Carwile gained attention in Richmond shortly after his arrival when he ran as an independent candidate for governor in 1945, while also mounting a public campaign against physical abuse in the state's prison system and public health institutions. Despite receiving only 4,023 votes out of 168,783 cast in his first statewide campaign, Carwile ran for the United States Senate the following year against Harry Flood Byrd (1887–1966). Nearly every year between then and 1980 he campaigned for a seat on the city council, in the General Assembly, in Congress, or for governor.

Combative by temperament and possessing an inexhaustible and readily activated sense of righteous indignation, Carwile took his causes directly to the public in a weekly radio program that he paid for out of his own pocket for twenty-six years. He was a severe critic of Virginia's Democratic Party leadership and during the 1940s and 1950s vehemently attacked the party leaders for supporting racial segregation and for

their policy of Massive Resistance to court-ordered desegregation of the public schools. In 1948 Carwile was arrested for sitting in a section reserved for African Americans at a segregated church revival, and afterward he taunted the city's white elites when he sold his house to a black family. Later he was equally disdainful of government programs intended to end or ameliorate the effects of segregation.

Carwile took on all issues that attracted his attention and pursued them with tenacious zeal. He was ejected from a legislative hearing on at least one occasion and more than once crossed verbal swords with judges and came close to being jailed for contempt of court. In style as well as by his eager opposition to the political leaders of the state, Carwile was uniquely obnoxious to Richmond's establishment, and he took pride in his conflicts with conservative politicians and judges. In 1960 he published *Speaking from Byrdland*, a volume of his selected radio-broadcast excoriations of Virginia politicians. Carwile's voice, famous and instantly recognizable, defied description. His speaking style was coarse and loud, colorful and rhythmical, and his voice, flexible in volume and pitch, easily adapted to the cadences of hellfire-and-brimstone preachers. His language was memorably alliterative and often personally insulting or abusive. He delighted the few who agreed with him on an issue, infuriated the others, and alternately amused and appalled nearly everybody. For decades Carwile traded colorful insults with the editors of the two daily Richmond newspapers, who never understood his motivations or his appeal. A *Richmond News Leader* editorial in June 1966 tried to characterize him and could do so only with comprehensive inexactitude: he was "a kind of special radical ultra-liberal lone-wolf back-handed conservative, whose public career has been built entirely upon his passionate opposition to the state."

Having repeatedly lost political campaigns, Carwile surprised nearly everybody in 1966 when he won a seat on the city council. His victory coincided with a large increase in black voting in Richmond, and he was reelected in 1968 and again in 1970, both times with more votes than any other candidate in the at-large race for nine council seats. Following his 1968 and 1970 victories, however, not one of his colleagues nominated him for mayor or even suggested that he should be considered for the office. Naturally, Carwile announced that he had expected the insult. Constant bickering with other members of the council, with local newspaper editors and reporters, and with citizens on a variety of issues kept Carwile's name in the papers and his voice in radio and television newscasts. In December 1969 the Virginia chapter of the American Civil Liberties Union presented him with its first Bill of Rights Award for his fights to protect the civil rights of African Americans, civil liberties of persons appearing in court, and freedom of speech.

In 1973 Carwile perplexed many of his former supporters by defeating the Democratic incumbent William Ferguson Reid, the first African American member of the House of Delegates in the twentieth century, for the floater seat representing Henrico County and Richmond in that body. He served on the Committees on Health, Welfare, and Institutions and on Militia and Police. Still independent of a party, he had become a rigid social and economic conservative. Carwile vigorously opposed court-ordered school busing, supported anti-abortion legislation, and fought ratification of the Equal Rights Amendment to the United States Constitution. He characteristically made few allies in the General Assembly and failed to get a single member of the House Committee on Privileges and Elections to support his bill to allow voters to elect members of local school boards. Carwile lost his 1975 reelection bid to Gerald Lee Baliles, who later served as attorney general and governor.

For several more years Carwile spoke out on public issues and announced new campaigns, but after 1980 his health deteriorated, and he receded from public view, though he continued to practice law. He had married Violet Virginia Talley, of Richmond, on 7 June 1948, and they had one son. Howard Hearnes Carwile died in a Richmond hospital on 6 June 1987 and was buried in Forest Lawn Cemetery. After Carwile's death his widow and son published a miscellaneous collection of recollections, newspaper articles, radio-broadcast transcripts,

letters, and anecdotes that he had assembled during his final years.

Violet T. Carwile and Howard H. Carwile Jr., eds., *Carwile, His Life and Times: An Autobiography* (1988), with pors.; Morton, *Virginia Lives*, 171; Anna Deihls Callahan, *A History of the Callaham and Carwile Families* (1976), 401; Carwile biographical file, Richmond Public Library; Howard H. Carwile Papers, including scrapbooks and audio tapes of radio broadcasts, VCU; feature articles in *Richmond News Leader*, 15 Oct. 1953, 15 (quotation), 24 June 1966, 3 June 1970, 20 Apr. 1983, *Richmond Times-Dispatch*, 23 Oct. 1953, 16 Dec. 1969, 2 Oct. 1977, 21 Apr. 1985, and *Richmond Afro-American*, 22 June 1968; obituaries in *Richmond News Leader* and *Richmond Times-Dispatch*, both 8 June 1987.

BRENT TARTER

CARY, Archibald (24 January 1721–26 February 1787), member of the Convention of 1776 and Speaker of the Senate of Virginia, was born probably in Williamsburg and was the son of the builder Henry Cary (d. by 2 March 1750) and his second wife, Ann Edwards Cary. He grew up in Williamsburg and at Ampthill, the elegant brick mansion that his father erected near the mouth of Falling Creek in the portion of Henrico County that in 1749 became Chesterfield County. Cary probably attended the College of William and Mary. He was handsome, strong, tall, and pugnacious. On 21 September 1742 his father deeded him 4,132 acres of valuable land in the part of Goochland County that in 1749 became Cumberland County. In 1744 Cary married Mary Randolph, of Turkey Island, in Henrico County. They had one son and eight daughters, several of whom died in infancy or childhood.

Cary was appointed a justice of the peace in Goochland County on 22 April 1747 and represented the county in the House of Burgesses in the two sessions of 1748 and 1749. Named to the new Cumberland County Court on 27 April 1749, he also became a vestryman of Southam Parish in December of that year. In 1750, after the death of his father, Cary moved to Ampthill and quickly became one of Chesterfield County's wealthiest and most important public men. He was appointed to the county court on 15 June 1750, on 6 November 1766 was named presiding judge, and by 22 October 1760 also had become county lieutenant, or commander of the militia. Cary erected an iron foundry near the site of the first ironworks established by the Virginia

Company of London in the seventeenth century. He built a successful flour mill and other manufacturing enterprises at the James River landing called Warwick. In 1769 the General Assembly appointed Cary a trustee of the town of Warwick, which it expanded onto his property near Ampthill, and also of Manchester, a town lying across the James River from Richmond that became an important commercial and manufacturing center. Cary led early efforts to improve navigation on the Appomattox and James Rivers and served on the committee that the assembly appointed in 1772 to attempt to extend the navigation of the upper Potomac River. He also kept a well-known stable of fine horses.

Between 1770 and 1774 Cary used his power as presiding justice of the county court to try to curtail Baptist activities. He fined or jailed Baptist exhorters who preached without a license, and after people crowded around the jail and the incarcerated ministers attempted to preach through the grated windows, Cary enclosed the jail with a brick wall. If Baptist ministers were whipped in Chesterfield County for preaching without a magistrate's permission, as some testimony suggests, it may have been with Cary's assent. In spite of, or perhaps because of, Cary's notorious persecution, the number of Baptists in the county increased rapidly during those years.

Cary represented Chesterfield County in the House of Burgesses from 1756 until the outbreak of the Revolution. Recognized as a man of ability, he took responsibility in the mid-1760s for managing the large supply of trade goods that the colony purchased in an attempt to ensure an alliance with western Indians. He became chairman of the Committee of Public Claims in November 1762 and retained that influential position through 1775. By the end of the 1760s he was routinely appointed to high-ranking positions on several of the other most important committees, including Privileges and Elections, Propositions and Grievances, and after 1769 the Committee for Religion.

Cary's rise to prominence reflected his intelligence and competence, but he was also allied through marriage and financial dealings with other leading burgesses. By the 1760s he was heavily in debt to John Robinson (1705–1766),

the Speaker of the House and treasurer of the colony, who was not only the most powerful Virginia politician of the age but also the principal in the colony's largest financial scandal. Shortly before it became publicly known that Robinson owed the colony more than £100,000, Cary had sat on a House committee that reported that Robinson's treasury records were in good order. After the scandal became public, Cary was one of the men who spent decades attempting to pay off their loans and preserve their fiscal and personal integrity.

Cary's relationship with Peyton Randolph (1721–1775), who succeeded Robinson as Speaker, and with the younger generation of burgesses was equally strong but not tinged with financial dependency. In 1765 Cary opposed Patrick Henry's resolutions condemning the Stamp Act because he deemed them too inflammatory, but never thereafter did he fail to support the most energetic Virginia protests against Parliament. Cary signed the nonimportation associations adopted later in the 1760s and early in the 1770s, and in March 1773 he was appointed to the new Committee of Correspondence that the House of Burgesses created to coordinate Virginia's actions with those of the other colonies. He was elected to each of the five Revolutionary Conventions that met between August 1774 and July 1776. During the convention in the summer of 1775 he was a member of nearly every important drafting committee and in August came within a few votes of being elected to the Committee of Safety that in effect governed Virginia for the next eleven months. Cary also served on every significant committee in the fourth convention during the winter of 1775–1776 and usually presided during debates in the committee of the whole. In the fifth convention, which assembled on 6 May 1776, he was one of the two or three most influential members. Cary regularly presided over the committee of the whole and chaired the committee appointed on 15 May 1776 to draft the Virginia Declaration of Rights and the first constitution of Virginia. The convention unanimously adopted both documents, as well as the resolution calling for independence from Great Britain.

During the Revolutionary War, Cary directed recruitment of soldiers and procurement of supplies in central Virginia, and he erected factories in Manchester and Richmond to produce gunpowder and rope. Ampthill became well known to Continental army officers who relied on Cary for advice and assistance or who stayed there while on duty in or in transit through Virginia. He was one of the commissioners named in 1779 to manage the move of the state government from Williamsburg to the new capital at Richmond, and he continued his staunch support of the Anglican Church even as the Revolution brought about its disestablishment as the official church in Virginia. Because Cary was a strongly opinionated man capable of enforcing his beliefs with violence, at least some of his contemporaries believed a story that Cary, after hearing a rumor that Patrick Henry might be appointed dictator of Virginia, swore to stab Henry to death.

In 1776 Cary was elected to the new Senate of Virginia to represent the counties of Amelia, Chesterfield, and Cumberland (and also Powhatan after 1778). At its first meeting on 7 October he was unanimously chosen Speaker, and each year thereafter through 1786 the senators reelected him to that office. The Senate's fragmentary surviving records make it uncertain whether the elections were all unanimous, but they probably were. Because of poor health Cary missed the October 1779 assembly session, when the members chose Nathaniel Harrison (1713–1791) to preside in his stead. Again in the autumn of 1781 Cary was unable to attend, and Harrison was acting Speaker.

Scarcely known at all outside Virginia, Cary was in many respects the peer of the distinguished Virginians who gained international fame in the Continental Congress or on the battlefield during the Revolutionary War. Within Virginia his eminent status was undoubted. He may have owned more than 14,000 acres of land and more than 200 slaves during the 1780s. On paper Cary was a wealthy planter with valuable commercial and manufacturing enterprises at his command, but he suffered from a variety of economic problems. His Richmond mills were destroyed during the war, he had trouble collecting money owed to him, and he could not pay his British creditors.

Because he was involved with many other men in large-scale partnerships, their similar financial situation created additional difficulties for him. In that, Cary was not in an unusual circumstance, but the range of his interests made the scale of his financial problems especially notable. As a Richmond merchant reported to Cary's close friend Thomas Jefferson after Cary's death, "no Gentleman of this Country in the memory of man ever left his affairs so distracted. The debts are immense. I had almost said innumerable. His family will be left very bare indeed."

Cary presided over the Senate of Virginia for the last time during the session that began on 16 October 1786. He served until at least 21 November, so far as extant pay records show. He then became ill and returned home, and by or on 7 December the senators chose John Jones to succeed him. Archibald Cary died at Ampthill on 26 February 1787. He may have been buried there, where a legend circulated as late as the early years of the twentieth century that his ghost occasionally appeared in the basement. No evidence of a grave was found when the mansion was moved during the winter of 1929–1930 to a site north of the James River in western Richmond.

Birth and death dates and year of marriage in Cary family Bible records, VHS; Hugh Blair Grigsby, *Virginia Convention of 1776* (1855), 90–93; Harrison, *Virginia Carys*, 91–95; Robert K. Brock, *Archibald Cary of Ampthill: Wheelhorse of the Revolution* (1937), including frontispiece por.; William M. E. Rachal, "Archibald Cary and the Revolution in Virginia" (M.A. thesis, UVA, 1938); Rachal, "Archibald Cary, Practical Politician," *Virginia Cavalcade* 1 (summer 1951): 36–38; Manarin, *Senate Officers*, 15–16; Archibald Cary Papers and Cary documents in various other collections, VHS; some Cary letters in *Jefferson Papers*, 1:249–250, 3:43–44, 75–76, 4:378–379, 463, 596–597, 6:96–98; *Revolutionary Virginia*, vols. 1–7; Senate of Virginia, Pay Vouchers, Entry 262, Auditor of Public Accounts, RG 48, LVA; Lewis Peyton Little, *Imprisoned Preachers and Religious Liberty in Virginia* (1938), 209–218, 312, 334–339, 356–363, 441–444, 447–449; David John Mays, *Edmund Pendleton, 1721–1803: A Biography* (1952), 1:176–184, 213, 360; Jeffrey M. O'Dell, *Chesterfield County: Early Architecture and Historic Sites* (1983), 278–280, 407; Hummel and Smith, *Portraits and Statuary*, 22 (por.); James Currie to Thomas Jefferson, 2 May 1787, in *Jefferson Papers*, 11:329 (quotation); will and estate inventories in Chesterfield Co. Will Book, 4:20–29, 83–97; death notice (with variant death date of 27 Feb. 1787) in *Richmond Virginia Gazette and Weekly Advertiser*, 1 Mar. 1787.

BRENT TARTER

CARY, George Booth (ca. 1802–26 February 1850), member of the House of Representatives, was born probably on the Southampton County estate of his parents, Miles Cary and his third wife, Elizabeth Booth Yates Cary, who had been a widow at the time of their marriage. His father owned three plantations in Southampton County and about seventy-five slaves when he died in the summer of 1806, leaving Cary the principal heir. Cary probably lived with his mother at the place of his birth, but she evidently died about 1815, and responsibility for overseeing his education and managing his inheritance then fell to John Stith, of Petersburg, husband of one of Cary's elder half sisters. During the interval of two or three years between his own twenty-first birthday and that of his younger sister, Cary served as her guardian.

Little is known of Cary's personal and professional life. He probably received a good education and may have practiced law as well as managing his plantations. On 1 March 1825 Cary executed a marriage bond in Southampton County and on that date or soon afterward married a young widow, Martha P. Blunt Urquhart. She died about a decade later. They had one daughter, so far as is known, who died young. About the time of his marriage Cary built a large frame house that he called Midfield, near the community later known as Capron. He was well known locally as a breeder and racer of fine horses.

Insofar as records show, Cary was not active in elective politics until April 1841, when he defeated a Whig candidate to win election to the House of Representatives from the district comprising the counties of Greensville, Prince George, Southampton, Surry, and Sussex and the city of Petersburg. He was a states' rights Democrat and an opponent of reestablishing a national bank. During the politically explosive sessions of the Twenty-seventh Congress, the Whigs expelled Cary's acquaintance, President John Tyler, from the party after he vetoed two bills to charter a new national bank. Cary took little part in the acrimonious political battle, but he endorsed and unsuccessfully tried to read into the records of the House the resolutions adopted by a public meeting in Petersburg on 20 August 1841 denouncing protective tariffs and public debt and endorsing states' rights and Tyler's first bank-veto message. Cary served on the relatively insignificant Committee on Accounts and tended to the business of his constituents. He engaged in debate on the floor only once, in January 1843, when he and another Virginian, John Minor Botts, unsuccessfully tried to persuade Millard Fillmore, chair of the Committee of Ways and Means, to bring up a Senate bill for the relief of the Petersburg Railroad Company, which sought to complete the installation of new iron rails it had already imported without having to pay the tariff imposed by a new bill. Cary's service in the House of Representatives was not distinguished, and he did not seek reelection in 1843.

Cary resumed the life of a planter after his retirement from Congress. By 1850 he owned about 4,350 acres of land in Southampton County, but much of it was regarded as of little value; and he owned about 120 slaves. On 26 February 1850 George Booth Cary committed suicide, probably at his Southampton County home and for reasons that extant records do not disclose. The place of his burial is unknown.

Harrison, *Virginia Carys*, 71, with birth year of 1803; most reference works give birth year of 1811 and death date of 5 Mar. 1850; father's will and estate inventory in Southampton Co. Will Book, 6:361–365, 419–423; Southampton Co. Marriage Bonds and Consents; *Richmond Enquirer*, 27, 30 Apr., 4 May 1841, 28 Apr. 1843; *Congressional Globe*, 27th Cong., 1st sess., 373, 3d sess., 196; *Charlotte L. Gholson et al.* v. *Administrator of George B. Cary*, Southampton Co. Chancery Causes, 1850-007, and *John H. Stith et al.* v. *Charlotte L. Gholson et al.,* Southampton Co. Chancery Causes, 1850-018 (with death date and itemized property holdings at time of death); cause of death at age forty-eight in Census, Mortality Schedule, Southampton Co., 1850.

CHRISTOPHER J. LEAHY

CARY, Henry (ca. 1650–by 1 September 1720), builder, was born in Warwick County and was the son of Miles Cary (d. 1667) and Anne Taylor Cary. His father immigrated to Virginia from Bristol, England, probably early in the 1640s and became a member of the governor's Council before mid-March 1664. After his father's death, the orphaned Henry Cary and his underage brothers inherited Warwick County plantations, his being called the Forest, and that of Miles Cary (d. 1709), surveyor general of Virginia and member of the House of Burgesses for more than twenty years, being called Richneck. By the spring of 1671 Cary had married Judith Lockey. They had three daughters and two sons, the elder of whom, Henry Cary (d. by 2 March 1750), became one of the principal building contractors in the region.

There is no evidence that Cary trained in the building trades in preparation for his career, but the loss of the Warwick County records leaves many aspects of his life poorly documented. His first recorded involvement in construction was a proposal to the governor's Council in December 1695 to build a platform for the defensive cannon at the new port of Yorktown. In 1697 Cary contracted for 28,000 pounds of tobacco to erect a new courthouse for York County on the north side of Main Street in Yorktown. He completed the work by the end of the year. Given its relatively low cost and the speed with which it was constructed, the building probably resembled other courthouses of the period, a frame structure with exterior clapboard sheathing and a few windows lit by wooden casements. The building was replaced with an arcaded brick courthouse early in the 1730s.

With this public building experience and perhaps other private commissions that have left no documentary trace, Cary seized the opportunity to secure the contract to build the colony's new Capitol after the previous statehouse in Jamestown burned in October 1698. Cary's petition to oversee construction of the new brick building in Williamsburg was granted in November 1699. During the next half-dozen years, Cary procured materials, supervised dozens of skilled and unskilled workmen, and coordinated the erection of the two-story, double-winged building at the east end of Duke of Gloucester Street. Although he was not the designer, he was able to shape many of its details. In the midst of this project, Cary also erected a prison for the colony, a one-story brick building located a few hundred yards north of the Capitol. He had completed both structures by 1705, to the satisfaction of government officials, not an insubstantial feat in a colony where public works on that scale had not before been attempted.

Cary's achievement led to his appointment in 1706 to oversee construction of the new house for the governor. He may have been responsible in part for the building's design as well. Under his direction between 1706 and 1708, the two-story, double-pile brick residence rose at the north end of what became Palace Street. Cary's success with the Capitol did not guarantee success on his second ambitious undertaking. By 1708 he had exhausted all the money appropriated for the building, his craftsmen threatened to stop work unless they received back wages, and roofing slate arrived from England so severely damaged that it proved unusable. Although the General Assembly reluctantly advanced money to keep the project from foundering, Cary was forced to move into the unfinished house to protect it from damage, an action the Council perceived as an attempt "to maintain his whole family at the publick charge." When Lieutenant Governor Alexander Spotswood arrived in Williamsburg in 1710 and discovered that his residence was an unfinished shell and that there was little money left to complete it, he turned his wrath on Cary for mismanaging the project and charged that he was incapable of the business of building. The Council complained of Cary's extravagance in April 1711 and in December ordered him to present an account of his expenses. Soon afterward Cary was dismissed from the project.

The fiasco of the governor's house ruined Cary's chances for further government work. In 1711 he proposed to supply materials for the new Bruton Parish church, but Spotswood considered the price too high and ensured that the contract went to a competitor. Recognizing that his career in Williamsburg was at an end, Cary retired to his plantation in Warwick County. Possibly he continued to work outside the capital on occasion. In 1719, for example, Richard King's agreement to erect the Swan Tavern in Yorktown allowed him to bring in Cary to appraise the building if the compensation agreed on did not cover the construction costs. Except for a fragment of the prison, all the public buildings that Cary erected in Williamsburg have been destroyed, making it difficult to judge the quality of the work that Spotswood condemned.

Henry Cary died, probably at his Warwick County plantation, on an unrecorded date before 1 September 1720, when his will was proved in the county court.

Harrison, *Virginia Carys*, 86–87, 170–171, including text of lost will; Winfree, *Laws of Virginia*, 347–349; marriage documented in *Minutes of Council and General Court*, 258–259; petitions, vouchers, and other documents in Colonial Papers, folder 18 no. 15, folder 19 no. 27, folder 20 nos. 17, 18, folder 22 no. 10, folder 24 no. 8, RG 1, LVA; numerous documents about construction and controversy with Spotswood in *Executive Journals of Council*, vols. 1–3 (quotation on 3:293), and *JHB*; Marcus Whiffen, *The Public Buildings of Williamsburg, Colonial Capital of Virginia* (1958), 40–66, 79, 89; Harold B. Gill Jr., "'building the Capitoll,'" *Colonial Williamsburg* 20 (summer 1998): 52–56.

CARL LOUNSBURY

CARY, Henry (d. by 2 March 1750), builder, was the son of the builder Henry Cary (ca. 1650–1720) and Judith Lockey Cary and was born in the mid- or late 1670s, probably at his father's Forest plantation in Warwick County. Little is known of his education or training, but he must have learned about the management of construction projects from his father, though it is unlikely that he practiced a trade.

Following in his father's footsteps, Cary became one of the leading building contractors in Virginia. The first evidence of his involvement in construction appears late in the 1710s, following his father's retirement from Williamsburg. In 1718 Cary undertook the erection of a T-shaped church for Saint Paul's Parish in the portion of New Kent County that in 1720 became Hanover County and in the following year erected a fence around the churchyard. His building career blossomed in the capital in the 1720s. In December 1720 the Council authorized Cary to complete work on the residence for the colony's governor, a project that must have given him satisfaction. His father had begun the construction but had been discharged before finishing the building because of clashes with the Council and Lieutenant Governor Alexander Spotswood. From time to time during the ensuing years when the palace required repairs, Cary often took charge of them, and he repaired the Capitol and constructed new gates for it in 1726.

It is likely, though documentation is lacking, that in 1723 Cary supervised construction of the Brafferton, a two-story, double-pile brick building southeast of the main building at the College of William and Mary. Intended to house a school for the education of American Indians, the Brafferton is one of the earliest manifestations of the "neat and plain" style that dominated late colonial Virginia architecture. Beneath a hip roof and modillion cornice, the glazed headers of the Flemish bond walls give a rich texture to an otherwise plain facade, accentuated only by rubbed corners, jambs, and arches and a pediment over the front entrance. In 1729 Cary directed construction of the chapel wing on the south side of the college building that complemented the size and compass-headed windows of the original hall wing on the north. Within a month of the dedication of the chapel in 1732, Cary began his last major project for the college, a residence for its president. Set on the north side of a forecourt originally ornamented with topiary, the president's house is a near mirror image of the Brafferton in size, materials, and details.

The absence of private papers makes the full scope of Cary's business unrecoverable, particularly his domestic work in Williamsburg and surrounding areas. Surviving examples of Cary's public work include a 1728 brick church for Elizabeth City Parish in Hampton. The building has suffered from a fire and numerous alterations, but the original plan of what is now Saint John's Episcopal Church was cruciform, the walls decorated with compass-headed windows, rubbed work, and glazed headers, details that became standard during the period. About this time Cary did some major, though unspecified, work for Stratton Major Parish in King and Queen County that required him to bring suit against the parish vestry, presumably for nonpayment. Unlike the work of his father, several of the buildings that Cary erected still survive and show high-quality craftsmanship and provide a useful guide to architectural fashion in the colony early in the eighteenth century, a style to which he contributed several important and enduring examples.

Cary was a member of the Warwick County Court, even though he resided in Williamsburg and was a churchwarden for Bruton Parish Church. He bought and sold land in the capital during the 1720s and served as keeper of the magazine there. Late in the decade he began amassing landholdings along the James River at and above the fall line. In 1730 an act of assembly enabled him to sell the Forest, the entailed family land in Warwick County, which allowed him to purchase even more land in the west. During his lifetime he acquired more than 20,000 acres.

About 1733 Cary moved to his new estate on the bank of the James River in the part of Henrico County that a few months before his death became Chesterfield County. Sometime during that decade he built a two-story brick house that he named Ampthill. During the winter of 1929–1930 the house, by then much changed, was moved to the West End of Richmond. The nearby river landing, on which he and later his son erected warehouses and manufacturing structures and where he owned an ordinary and the ferry, was called Warwick. Cary spent the remainder of his life as a country gentleman, leaving no evidence that he resurrected his contracting business. He became a member of the Henrico County Court, was sheriff of the county in 1733, and was a churchwarden of Dale Parish in 1739.

Cary married Sarah Sclater about 1710. They had two sons and one daughter, all of whom had died by the end of 1734. Following the death of his wife on an unrecorded date before 1719, he married Ann Edwards. They had three daughters and one son, Archibald Cary, who became the first Speaker of the Senate of Virginia. By the time Cary married a third time, he was a wealthy man. He executed a marriage agreement that secured his wife's financial future in the event he predeceased her and that also protected the interests of his own children. The date of that marriage has been estimated at about 1741. His third wife's given name was Elizabeth, but her maiden name is not certain. She may have been a sister or close relation of John Brickenhead, a London peruke maker. They are not known to have had any children. Henry Cary died, probably at Ampthill, during the winter of 1749–1750, perhaps not long before his will was proved in the Chesterfield County Court on 2 March 1750. The place of his burial is not recorded.

Harrison, *Virginia Carys*, 87–91; Cary family Bible records, VHS; Cary Family Papers, including original land grants, deeds, and attested copy of will, Acc. 21434, 21437, LVA; Winfree, *Laws of Virginia*, 199–201, 347–349; Marcus Whiffen, *The Public Buildings of Williamsburg, Colonial Capital of Virginia* (1958); J. E. Morpurgo, *Their Majesties' Royall Colledge: William and Mary in the Seventeenth and Eighteenth Centuries* (1976), 75–76, 90–91; Parke Rouse Jr., *A House for a President: 250 Years on the Campus of the College of William and Mary* (1983), 7, 12–16; Chesterfield Co. Will Book, 1:36–43; Chesterfield Co. Order Book, 1:34.

CARL LOUNSBURY

CARY, John Baytop (18 October 1819–13 January 1898), educator, was born probably at Elmwood, the Elizabeth City County plantation of his parents, Gill Armistead Cary and Sarah Elizabeth Smith Baytop Cary. He attended Hampton Academy and in 1839 received a B.A. from the College of William and Mary. On 23 January 1844 Cary married Columbia H. Hudgins, of Mathews County. Over the next fourteen years they had four daughters and two sons.

Cary taught at the Hampton Academy and was its principal for the last seven years before it became part of the new county public school system in 1852. He then established a boarding school, the Hampton Male and Female Academy, frequently referred to as the Hampton Academy or the Hampton Military Academy. Cary was principal and also taught ancient languages and mathematics. The academy offered instruction in ancient and modern languages, English grammar and rhetoric, mathematics, and natural science. In addition, boys studied military tactics under a series of teachers, the last being Wilfred Emory Cutshaw, subsequently a colonel in the Confederate army and afterward Richmond city engineer. The object of the academy, as stated in its publications, was to prepare students to attend a college or university and to help them develop habits of "independent thought" and to be ready "for the active pursuits of life." Cary was an effective, inspiring teacher and a strict disciplinarian. Painted on the wall of the classroom was the motto, "Order is Heaven's first Law." Several of Cary's own children attended the academy, as did William Gordon McCabe, who became a noted educator in Petersburg and Richmond after the Civil War and who married one of Cary's daughters. In 1854 Cary received an honorary M.A. from William and Mary.

Soon after Virginia seceded from the Union in April 1861, Cary, who had been an ardent defender of the South, obtained a commission as a major of artillery. He was soon involved in a pair of incidents that dramatized contrasting characteristics of the war. Surprised in May by the approach of a large Union scouting party from nearby Fort Monroe, Cary negotiated a gentleman's agreement with the commander that allowed the party to march peacefully into the heart of Hampton under Cary's escort and then return to the fort. The following day Cary called on Major General Benjamin Franklin Butler to request the return of three escaped slaves who had taken refuge behind the lines. Butler's refusal set a precedent for Union confiscation of slave property and eventual military emancipation of slaves.

Serving on the staff of Major General John Bankhead Magruder, Cary earned commendation for his conduct in the Southern victory at Big Bethel, near Hampton, on 10 June 1861. Several weeks later Cary was elected colonel of the 32d Regiment Virginia Infantry and spent nearly a year detailed to Magruder's staff and as acting provost marshal in Yorktown. When the regiment was reorganized in May 1862, the forty-two-year-old Cary failed to be reelected colonel, but he was immediately appointed a major and resumed his service as inspector general and assistant adjutant general on Magruder's staff. The general praised Cary's conduct on the field during the Seven Days' Battles near Richmond late in June 1862. Soon afterward, following Magruder's transfer to the West, Cary joined the quartermaster corps and served for the remainder of the Civil War as paymaster of troops in Richmond-area hospitals.

The war cost Cary his personal estate and his school when Confederates burned Hampton in August 1861. At the close of the war, he remained in Richmond, where for a time he held the public office of grocer for the state penitentiary. Cary then became a partner in a commission merchant business and eventually became an insurance salesman. He and his youngest son, Thomas Archibald Cary, formed a lucrative partnership as Richmond agents for Northwestern Mutual Life Insurance Company. Cary was also active in the Christian Church, which he had joined after his marriage, for many years chaired Richmond's Democratic committee, and from 1884 to 1886 served on the city school board.

In the spring of 1886 the State Board of Education appointed Cary superintendent of the Richmond public schools, the largest public school system in the state. The city's schools then had an enrollment of more than 8,300 students, employed nearly 200 teachers, and had an annual budget of approximately $102,500. Shortly after taking office Cary recommended that teachers' salaries be significantly raised and that students in the high schools be given an opportunity to demonstrate whether they had a talent for teaching so that they could be directed to the normal school curriculum. Promoting increased expenditure for education of the city's African American children, Cary proposed "to educate every child, so that he can read his Bible and the Constitution of his country in his mother tongue, and thus fit him for the privileges, the duties and the responsibility of citizenship." During Cary's two and a half years as superintendent, enrollment in the city's schools increased by more than 30 percent, and the annual budget increased by about 60 percent. Although Cary earned by far the highest salary of any public school superintendent in the state (more than $1,000 per annum), he continued to direct his profitable insurance business during that time and resigned as of 15 February 1889 to return to fulltime management of his private affairs.

On 1 July 1890 Cary began a four-year term on the city's board of aldermen. Continuing his involvement in public education, he chaired the city council's school committee and in that capacity was instrumental in transferring the former White House of the Confederacy, then being used as a public school, to the Confederate Memorial Literary Society, of which one of his daughters was an officer. The house thereupon became the Confederate Museum and later the Museum of the Confederacy. Cary was keenly interested in Confederate veterans affairs, attended reunions, and was the Virginia representative on a committee chartered in 1896 to found and erect the Confederate Memorial Institute (also known as Battle Abbey). Cary served on the board of the

College of William and Mary from 1892 until the end of the 1896–1897 academic term.

John Baytop Cary died at his home in Richmond on 13 January 1898 after suffering a month-long illness. He had predicted to a friend that he would be the last member of his family to be buried in the family cemetery near Hampton, but his body was interred in Richmond's Hollywood Cemetery. Former students served as pallbearers at the funeral. In 1906 his descendants established the nondenominational John B. Cary Memorial School of Biblical History and Literature at the University of Virginia; and, most appropriately, public schools in both Hampton and Richmond were named in his honor.

Robert A. Brock, *Virginia and Virginians* (1888), 2:774–775; Charles A. Young, *The Power of a Noble Life* (1899); Harrison, *Virginia Carys*, 74–75 (por.); *Richmond Enquirer*, 3 Feb. 1844; *Catalogue of the Hampton Male and Female Academy* (1856), first quotation on 7; Gillie Cary McCabe, *The Story of an Old Town: Hampton, Virginia* (1929), esp. 21–40; George Benjamin West, *When the Yankees Came: Civil War and Reconstruction on the Virginia Peninsula*, ed. Parke Rouse Jr. (1977), 9–10, 21–23 (motto quoted on 22); Compiled Service Records; Les Jensen, *32nd Virginia Infantry* (1990); John B. Cary Letter Book (16 May–3 Aug. 1861), and Cary's copies of *Regulations for the Army of the United States* (1857), given to him by Cutshaw, and H. W. Halleck's *Elements of Military Art and Science* (1861), which he purchased in Hampton in 1861, MOC; Richmond City Superintendent of Public Schools *Annual Reports* (1886–1889) (third quotation in 1888 report, p. 8); obituaries and editorial tributes in *Richmond Dispatch* and *Richmond Times*, both 14 Jan. 1898 (both with birth date), *Confederate Veteran* 6 (1898): 41, and *VMHB* 6 (1898): 320.

JOHN M. COSKI
RUTH ANN COSKI

CARY, Lott (ca. 1780–10 November 1828), Baptist minister and settler of Liberia, was born into slavery, most likely on the Charles City County plantation of Gideon Christian, whose 1797 estate inventory included two African American boys named Lot and Cary, each valued at £50. Some contemporaries and some later writers spelled his given name as Lot and his surname as Carey, but he consistently signed his name as Lott Cary. The names of his parents are not recorded, and many details of his life are obscured by propaganda published during his life and after his death.

Cary probably learned the fundamentals of Christianity in his youth. Beginning in 1804, his owner hired him out to labor in the tobacco warehouses of Richmond, where Cary attended a Calvinistic Baptist church and underwent a conversion experience about 1807. He married, but the name of his wife, who died about 1813, is not known. They had two children, at least one of them a daughter. Labor in tobacco warehouses earned Cary a reputation as a resourceful entrepreneur who dealt in his own stock, gathered from the wastage of other dealers. By about 1813 he had saved at least $850, enough to buy freedom for himself and his two children. In 1817 and 1818 Cary purchased a total of twenty acres of land in eastern Henrico County. He executed a marriage bond in Richmond on 6 January 1819 and on that date or soon afterward married Nancy Cary, another free African American whose possible kinship to her husband is unknown. They had one child.

Cary, who probably had broken from his predestinarian background by 1815, became a popular lay preacher among black Richmonders. His auditors recalled his preaching as eloquent, albeit unpolished; no reliable transcription of any of his sermons survives. African missions attracted Cary's attention, and in April 1815 he helped found the Richmond African Baptist Missionary Society, of which he also served as recording secretary. After the American Society for Colonizing the Free People of Color of the United States (founded late in 1816 and popularly known as the American Colonization Society) announced plans for a settlement of American freedpeople in West Africa, Cary prepared to emigrate. The Richmond missionary society and several notable white Richmonders, including the merchants Benjamin Brand and William Crane, supported Cary and other black Virginia emigrants with money and supplies. Before their departure, seven emigrants formed themselves into a Baptist church, with Cary ordained as its minister.

They sailed from Norfolk on the *Nautilus* on 23 January 1821 and landed in Sierra Leone. Cary's second wife, who had been ill with consumption before their departure, died there later that year. Early in 1822 he and the other colonists moved to an area near Cape Mesurado, a promontory soon incorporated into the new colony of Liberia. Cary and his congregation organized their church as the Providence Baptist Church and repulsed an attack by natives of the region who resisted the colonization.

In 1823 Cary was one of the settlers who challenged the American Colonization Society's agent, Jehudi Ashmun, over his austere policies, which included conserving imported provisions. Cary and Ashmun soon reconciled, in part because both were committed to the defense and economic development of the new town, which in February 1824 was named Monrovia. As new settlers continued to arrive, Cary exhibited his competence by tending to those infected with malaria, organizing a labor force from natives and captives who were removed from the control of slave traders, establishing a joint stock company to improve the harbor, and helping Ashmun extend the territory of the settlers eastward along the Saint Paul River. In 1826 and again in 1827 the settlers elected Cary vice agent of Liberia. He was elected president of the Monrovia Baptist Missionary Society in April of the latter year, and he was also responsible for a school. Cary married a daughter of Richmond Sampson, a Petersburg resident who had emigrated on the *Nautilus*, but she died on an unrecorded date before 15 October 1825. By 19 September 1827 Cary had married a fourth time, to a daughter of J. Benson, of Monrovia. No children are recorded from his third or fourth marriages.

In the spring of 1828 Cary assumed leadership of Monrovia and its outposts when Ashmun, ill with what was probably malaria, sailed for the United States. In November of that year, as Cary was preparing munitions for defense of the colony, an accidental explosion of gunpowder killed several men and mortally wounded him and others. Lott Cary died in Monrovia two days later, on 10 November 1828, and was buried there in an unmarked grave. The Liberian town of Careysburg, in Montserrado County, bears his name.

During the mid-1820s, such periodicals as the *African Repository and Colonial Journal*, the *American Baptist Magazine*, and the *Religious Intelligencer* made Cary one of the most famous black men of his day. The man who became a folk hero in the twentieth-century surge of interest in African American history was born in myth. Proponents of colonization and missionary work cast Cary as a noble and powerful man who became free through his own strenuous efforts, yet who devoutly served God and native Africans in schools and missions. William Crane's short biographical sketch published in 1825 contained some valuable information about Cary, but Ralph Randolph Gurley's longer biography, published a decade later, enlarged on and embellished the record, as did James B. Taylor's book-length biography published in 1837. Gurley's work significantly influenced most subsequent accounts of Cary and reprinted a number of writings attributed to him.

Extant writings in Cary's hand demonstrate that he shared little of the language skills or the missionary interests others attributed to him. Letters published and reports printed over his name were either extensively rewritten or composed by someone else. Cary's own writings and the early history of Liberia suggest a pragmatic man. In 1827 he mailed to Benjamin Brand in Richmond an essay that promoted immigration to Liberia and requested that Brand have it printed. Brand did not publish the document but preserved it along with a number of letters Cary had sent him. Cary's essay and the two dozen surviving letters that he and Brand exchanged, along with several other documents in which Brand and his peers commented on him, are the best sources of information on Cary's life.

Cary envisioned Monrovia as an entrepôt for American and West African goods; bacon, cloth, flour, tobacco, and whiskey from the United States would be exchanged for African raw materials, such as camwood, coffee, ivory, and palm oil. Cary planned to be the leader among the traders. He also anticipated that native African laborers would produce the raw materials to be sold in America and also would perform the onerous task of transporting materials to the harbor. American goods were to be consumed by the colonists or sold to native groups, probably to elite members. When the natives proved resistant to working on the settlers' terms, Cary, Ashmun, and others made indentured servants of the captives taken by force from Spanish slave-trading factories and of the "recaptives," those removed by the United States Navy from illegal slave ships and remanded to Monrovia. They provided the labor necessary to create new settlements, the so-called halfway farms midway between Caldwell and Millsburg. Cary's vision was commercial, not religious. Moreover, it was destined to cause discord between the natives and the settlers, who wanted the natives to provide both labor and valuable trade goods at low prices. Hostilities between settlers and natives seem to have derived less from the settlers' occupation of territory than from their treatment of native laborers and the prices settlers were willing to pay for items they shipped to the United States.

Lott Cary the folk hero was pious and vigorous, Lott Cary the man forceful and commercial. The man died in 1828; the legend survived and inspired the Lott Carey Baptist Foreign Mission Convention, which was founded in 1897 and soon afterward sent its first missionary to Brewerville, Montserrado County, Liberia.

Biographies in [William Crane], "Lott Cary," *Richmond Family Visitor*, 15 Oct. 1825 (reprinted in *African Repository and Colonial Journal* 1 [1825]: 233–236, and including first and third marriages and age as older than forty), Ralph Randolph Gurley, *Life of Jehudi Ashmun, Late Colonial Agent in Liberia* (1835), Appendix, 147–160, J. B. Taylor, *Biography of Elder Lott Cary, Late Missionary to Africa* (1837), with approximate birth year on 10, Miles Mark Fisher, "Lott Cary, The Colonizing Missionary," and Fisher, comp., "Letters, Addresses, and the Like Throwing Light on the Career of Lott Cary," *Journal of Negro History* 7 (1922): 380–418, 427–448, and William A. Poe, "Lott Cary: Man of Purchased Freedom," *Church History* 39 (1970): 49–61; Gideon Christian estate inventory, taken 31 Jan. 1797, in Charles City Co. Will Book (1789–1808), 393; Richmond City Marriage Bonds (1819); fourth marriage in William Crane to Ralph Randolph Gurley, 19 Sept. 1827, American Colonization Society Papers, 1st ser., LC; Henrico Co. Deed Book, 15:501–503, 17:605–606; Land Tax Returns, Henrico Co. (1817–1821, 1825), RG 48, LVA; Cary letters in Benjamin Brand Papers, VHS; John Saillant, ed., "Circular Addressed to the Colored Brethren and Friends in America: An Unpublished Essay by Lott Cary, Sent from Liberia to Virginia, 1827," *VMHB* 104 (1996): 481–504; conjectural por. at VBHS, reproduced in E. Lee Shepard, Frances S. Pollard, and Janet B. Schwarz, comps., "'The Love of Liberty Brought Us Here': Virginians and the Colonization of Liberia," *VMHB* 102 (1994): 98; obituary with death date in *African Repository, and Colonial Journal* 5 (1829): 10–14; inaccurate report of death on 18 Nov. 1828 in *Washington Daily National Intelligencer*, 12 Feb. 1829, reprinted in *Richmond Visitor and Telegraph*, 14 Feb. 1829, and *Religious Herald*, 27 Feb. 1829; memorials in *Religious Herald*, 24 Apr. 1829 (with eyewitness account of explosion reprinted from *Washington Daily National Intelligencer*, 16 Apr. 1829), and *The Thirteenth Annual Report of the American Society for Colonizing the Free People of Colour of the United States*, 2d ed. (1830), 4–5.

JOHN SAILLANT

CARY, Miles (bap. 30 January 1623–10 June 1667), member of the Council, was baptized in All Saints Parish, Bristol, England, on 30 January 1623. He was the son of a woolen draper, John Cary, and his second wife, Alice Hobson Cary. Both of his grandfathers had been mayors of Bristol, and as a member of a socially prominent and respected family he received a good education, the details of which are not known. The English Civil Wars divided the family, and Cary's father suffered substantial losses. Perhaps as a consequence, Cary became involved in the tobacco trade and moved to Virginia, probably early in the 1640s and certainly no later than November 1645, when a mariner deposed that "one Miles Cary, a Bristoll man" then in Elizabeth City County, had failed to deliver 250 pounds of tobacco. Copies of Virginia records that refer to him often spell his given name as Myles or Mylles and his surname as Carey.

Cary initially resided in the Warwick County household of Thomas Taylor, who may have been a kinsman, and by about 1646 he had married Taylor's daughter Anne. Before she died on an unrecorded date before June 1667, they had at least three daughters and four sons, including Henry Cary (ca. 1650–1720), who became a successful builder in Warwick County, Williamsburg, and Yorktown, and Miles Cary (d. 1709), who became an influential member of the House of Burgesses and surveyor general of Virginia. Opening a store and acting as an agent in various business transactions, Cary prospered and became a commissioner, or justice, of the peace by 1650. At that time he was still called Mr. Cary, but in 1654 when he patented 3,000 acres of land in the new county of Westmoreland he was identified as a major in the militia. When he renewed that patent three years later he was a lieutenant colonel, and by 1660 he was a colonel. He acquired more than 2,200 acres of land in Warwick County, some of which he inherited from Taylor. At the time of his death Cary also owned two lots in his native Bristol, a tract in Jamestown, and four plantations. His financial success exposed him to some criticism. In January 1650 a local woman denounced him as a "scabbed fisted knave," likened him to a "pox," and declared that if Cary could become a commissioner of the peace, "they will make Comrs of black doggs shortly."

Cary became a collector of taxes in Warwick County in 1658 and was elected to the House of Burgesses the following year. He was present in the spring of 1660 when the General Assembly elected Sir William Berkeley governor, pending receipt of a new royal commission from Charles II, and was also a member of a committee of burgesses that later in that year drafted a petition to the king requesting forgiveness for submitting to Parliament and seeking the restoration of colonial privileges. In addition the committee asked that Virginia-born children be declared denizens of England.

Cary was a burgess again from 1661 to 1663 and on 15 May 1661 became escheator general of the colony, with responsibility for taking possession for the Crown of land that was forfeit for nonpayment of quitrents. He became a member of the governor's Council on an unrecorded date before 23 March 1664. The scant surviving Council records from the period indicate that Cary participated in planning for the defense of the colony during the Second Anglo-Dutch War (1665–1667). One of his last recorded acts as a Council member was to sign a protest that the governor and Council sent to the king complaining that Maryland's governor and Council refused to join in a voluntary reduction in the production of tobacco in order to raise its price.

On 5 June 1667 at the mouth of the James River four Dutch men-of-war captured an English frigate and approximately twenty merchant vessels. Four days later Cary drew up his will. According to family tradition he was shot and killed defending against the Dutch incursion, and it is possible that he had been wounded and then prepared the will, with its two codicils, while on his deathbed. Miles Cary died on 10 June 1667 and was buried in a brick tomb on the grounds of his home at Windmill Point.

Biography and family history in Fairfax Harrison, *The Devon Carys* (1920), 2:564–669, with death date from gravestone inscription on 661; baptism (on 30 Jan. 1622 Old Style and recording name as Miles Cary) in All Saints Parish Register, Bristol Record Office, Eng.; Bristol Deposition Book (1643–1647), 92–93, Bristol Record Office (first record in Virginia and first quotation); other Cary documents in fragmentary Warwick Co. court orders (1647–1660), W&M, in *Cavaliers and Pioneers*, 1:353–354, 474, 533, and in Richard Dunn, ed., *Warwick County, Virginia: Colonial Court Records in Transcription* (2000), 18, 22, 25, 32, 33, 176; Warwick Co. Orders (1648–1651), 6 (second, third, and fourth quotations); burgess service in Hening, *Statutes,* 1:529–531, 2:31, and Jon Kukla, ed., "Some Acts Not in Hening's *Statutes*: The Acts of Assembly, October 1660," *VMHB* 83 (1975): 92–93; Council service in *Minutes of Council and General Court,* 484–488, 507 (appointed escheator general), 508, 513–514, Northampton Co. Order Book (1657–1664), fol. 190 (first record as Council member), old Rappahannock Co. Deeds, Etc., 3:257–258, and governor and Council to king, n.d. (docketed 24 June 1667), PRO CO 1/21, fols. 118–121; copy of will provided for Archibald Cary (signatures copied as Mylles Carey), Personal Papers, Acc. 21438, LVA.

KATHARINE E. HARBURY

CARY, Miles (d. 17 February 1709), member of the House of Burgesses, was the son of Miles Cary (d. 1667), a member of the governor's Council, and Anne Taylor Cary. He was born probably in the mid-1650s at his father's Warwick County plantation. At the time of his father's death, Cary was in England, where he remained to complete his education, as his father's will directed. Sometime during the 1680s Cary married Mary Milner, daughter of Thomas Milner, who was clerk of the House of Burgesses in 1682 and 1684 and Speaker from 1691 to 1693. They had no children before she died on 27 October 1700. In the spring of 1702 Cary married Mary Wilson Roscow, widow of William Roscow, of Warwick County, who had at least three sons from her first marriage. Cary and his rival in the courtship, a violent-tempered captain of an English warship, nearly fought a duel. Cary's second marriage produced two daughters and two sons.

Cary was a captain in the militia and a justice of the peace for Warwick County by 21 October 1680, but the fragmentary surviving county records do not contain the dates of his appointments. He remained on the county court as late as June 1705 and probably until his death. On 3 June 1699 he became commander of the county militia with the rank of lieutenant colonel.

Cary was elected to the House of Burgesses in November 1682 and again in 1684. Reelected in 1688, he served until 1706 with the exception of the 1695 and 1696 assemblies, to which he failed to win election, and the first part of the autumn session in 1693, which he missed. He became one of the most influential members of the General Assembly. After serving on the Committee of Propositions and Grievances during several sessions and on the Committee for Elections and Privileges in 1691 and 1692, Cary became chair of the latter in the spring of 1693 and that same year chair of the even more important Committee for Public Claims and of the Committee for Proportioning the Public Levy, committees that oversaw most of the important legislation and public spending. He retained the chairs of the Committee for Public Claims and for Proportioning the Public Levy throughout most of the remainder of his tenure in the assembly and from 1699 to 1706 frequently presided when the House resolved itself into a committee of the whole. During those years, only the Speaker wielded more power in the House of Burgesses.

Cary was senior burgess on a joint committee that from 1699 to 1705 worked on a complete revisal of the colony's laws, and he was also senior burgess on a joint subcommittee that oversaw construction of the new Capitol in Williamsburg. His elder brother Henry Cary (ca. 1650–1720) was in charge of that construction. In 1699 and again in 1700 Cary may have been a candidate for Speaker, but the House journals do not identify the unsuccessful burgesses who were nominated for that office.

In addition to being one of the most powerful men in the assembly, Cary acquired other influential and lucrative posts. From 29 October 1691 until December 1692 he was clerk of the General Court. In the autumn of the latter year he traveled to New York to represent Virginia at an intercolonial conference concerning defense against the French. Cary was register of the Virginia Court of Vice Admiralty from early in 1698 until 27 December 1700, and on 8 June 1699 the

governor and Council appointed him naval officer, a customs official, for the York River district. He held that office until his death, when the Council took special care in appointing a successor to what its members recognized was "a place of so Considerable a profite." A founding trustee of the College of William and Mary, Cary served on its board probably until his death and was rector for one-year terms beginning in 1695 and in 1704. The college's trustees controlled the office of surveyor general of Virginia, to which they appointed Cary in February 1699. He held that lucrative office until his death and for part of the time was also surveyor of Gloucester and York Counties. In November 1708 the lieutenant governor included Cary's name on a list of a dozen men qualified to fill vacancies on the governor's Council.

Cary had public interests in Elizabeth City and York Counties, but he lived in Warwick County, where he eventually controlled nearly 2,000 acres of land and was one of the county's wealthiest and most influential citizens. Miles Cary died, probably at his plantation in Warwick County, on 17 February 1709 and was buried in the family cemetery there. His widow later married Archibald Blair (d. 1733), a prominent Williamsburg physician and merchant.

Harrison, *Virginia Carys*, 100–105 (por. facing 100); undocumented birth date of 27 Oct. 1655 in Mary Selden Kennedy, *Seldens of Virginia and Allied Families* (1911), 1:262; second marriage license recorded between 13 Apr. and 3 May 1702 in Elizabeth City Co. Deeds, Wills, Orders, Settlements of Estates (1684–1699), 218; documents relating to courtship confrontation in York Co. Deeds, Orders, Wills, Etc., 12:21–23, and E. B. O'Callaghan, ed., *Documents Relative to the Colonial History of the State of New York* (1857), 4:1056; numerous references in *JHB, 1659/60–1693, 1695–1702, 1702/03–1712*, in *Executive Journals of Council*, vols. 1–3 (appointment as clerk on 1:203, appointment as naval officer on 1:449, quotation on 3:207), and George Reese, ed., *Proceedings in the Court of Vice-Admiralty of Virginia, 1698–1775* (1983); appointment as register in Sir Edmund Andros to Board of Trade, 14 Mar. 1698, PRO CO 5/1309, fols. 134–135, and commission, 30 Mar. 1698, PRO CO 5/1310, fols. 53–54; journal of committee to revise the laws in *Legislative Journals of Council*, 1518–1533; documents relating to Capitol and college in *WMQ*, 1st ser., 10 (1901): 78–83, and 1st ser., 7 (1899): 158–174, respectively; Sarah S. Hughes, *Surveyors and Statesmen: Land Measuring in Colonial Virginia* (1979), 23, 26–27, 60–63, 73, 75; death date (17 Feb. 1708 Old Style) on gravestone.

Peter V. Bergstrom

CARY, Richard (d. 13 November 1789), member of the Convention of 1776, member of the Convention of 1788, and judge of the Virginia Court of Appeals, was born early in the 1730s in Warwick County, probably at Peartree Hall, near Hampton, the residence of his parents, Miles Cary (d. 1766) and his first wife, Hannah Armistead Cary. He probably received a good education, but the details, as with many other aspects of his private life, are not known. He married Mary Cole about 1760 and had five daughters and two sons, the elder of whom, also named Richard Cary, served in the General Assembly during the 1780s and 1790s and has been confused with his father.

Cary became an attorney and by the end of the 1760s was clerk of Warwick County. In what may have been a move to increase his income and widen his acquaintance among the colony's influential gentlemen, he successfully petitioned in 1766 for the clerkship of the House of Burgesses' Committee of Trade. Three years later he also won the clerkship of the Committee for Religion, both of which he held through the House's final session that began in June 1775.

Cary signed the Virginia nonimportation association of 27 May 1774. Elected to the Warwick County Committee when it was created on 23 November 1774, he chaired the committee by the end of the following year. On 11 April 1776 he won election to the fifth and final Revolutionary Convention. Cary attended nearly every day and was almost certainly present for the three most important and unanimous votes, in favor of independence on 15 May, to adopt the Declaration of Rights on 12 June, and to approve the first constitution of the commonwealth on 29 June. He served on the Committees on Privileges and Elections and of Public Claims and on the large committee, chaired by his distant kinsman Archibald Cary, selected to draft the declaration and the constitution. He was also a member of two select committees appointed to examine accounts left over from Dunmore's War of 1774 and another committee charged with deciding what to do with several men held in the Williamsburg jail awaiting criminal trials in a court that by the summer of 1776 no longer existed.

Cary served in the House of Delegates in the October 1776 session. He sat on the Committees for Courts of Justice, on Privileges and Elections, and of Public Claims and was one of seven men named to audit the accounts of the retiring treasurer of Virginia. Cary's brief legislative career ended after the assembly on 17 December elected him one of three judges of the new Virginia Court of Admiralty. Few records of the court survive, so it is not clear how busy the docket was, but Cary was the only judge who served from its formation until the court was abolished at the end of 1788 after ratification of the United States Constitution extinguished state admiralty law. For the last three years of the court's existence, from December 1785 through December 1788, Cary was presiding judge.

As a judge of the Court of Admiralty, Cary became an ex officio member of the Virginia Court of Appeals, established in May 1779. The records of that court's work provide few details about Cary's career on the appellate bench. In two instances, however, he took part in deciding cases that raised the relatively novel question of judicial review, or whether the court could invalidate acts of assembly that were inconsistent with the state constitution. In November 1782 in *Commonwealth* v. *Caton et al.* the court accepted a case that arose under a statute that may have violated Virginia's constitution. By tacitly affirming the constitutionality of the act, Cary and the other judges implicitly recognized that they might reject unconstitutional acts of the assembly. The second case, commonly referred to as the *Cases of the Judges*, concluded in March 1789. The General Assembly had reorganized the state court system and, among other things, increased the duties of some judges without a corresponding increase in their compensation. In 1788 the judges complained to the assembly and characterized the act as a threat to the independence of the judiciary. In response, the legislature modified the law and created a new Court of Appeals whose judges were not simultaneously to be judges of any other court. The assembly declared vacant all appellate court judgeships and then appointed judges for the new Court of Appeals. Cary was not reappointed, but he and the other judges of the former court nevertheless assembled and pronounced the law an intolerable legislative interference with the judiciary and a clear violation of the Virginia constitution. In the interests of avoiding a confrontation and of putting the otherwise-welcomed new law into effect, they all then resigned from the offices that the assembly had already declared vacant.

On 13 March 1788 Cary was one of two delegates elected to represent Warwick County in the convention called to consider the proposed constitution of the United States. He sat on the Committee of Privileges and Elections. Cary did not speak during the recorded debates. He voted on 25 June 1788 with the opponents of the Constitution to demand amendments before ratification, and after that motion failed he voted against ratification.

In May 1785 Cary attended the first annual convention of the clergy and laity of the Protestant Episcopal Church of Virginia. He was a serious student of botany and during the 1780s supplied specimens to the French consul in Norfolk and also exchanged plant specimens with Thomas Jefferson, then in France. Jefferson returned the favor in 1787 when he sent Cary copies of the new English edition of *Notes on the State of Virginia* and of Erasmus Darwin's recently translated version of Carolus Linnaeus's *Systema Vegetabilium*.

On 24 December 1788, after the assembly abolished the Court of Admiralty and terminated Cary's service on the Court of Appeals, it elected him to the General Court. He took office on 9 February 1789 and presided at trials, probably in the southeastern districts, heard appeals from the county courts, and occasionally met at the capital with the other judges to hear appeals in criminal cases, the General Court being then Virginia's only criminal appellate court. Richard Cary died on 13 November 1789 at the Richmond tavern where he was staying while attending one of the sessions of the court. He may have been buried in the city, where the governor and members of the Council of State paid their respects to his remains, although family tradition records he was interred at Peartree Hall.

Biographies in (4 Call), *Virginia Reports*, 8:xxii, Hugh Blair Grigsby, *The History of the Virginia Federal Convention of 1788* (1891), 2:382, and Harrison, *Virginia Carys*, 52, 54–55 (with birth year of 1730), all of which confuse facts in Cary's life and the life of his namesake son; death date in Wynne family Bible records (1757–1909), LVA; some Cary letters in *Jefferson Papers*, 9:444, 10:226–228, 601–602, 635–636, 11:48, 228–230, 12:29, 130; *Revolutionary Virginia*, 1:98, 2:175, 4:95, 100, 5:67, 71, 6:378, 7:25, 61, 123, 143, 273, 341, 419; *Commonwealth v. Caton et al.* (1782) and *Cases of the Judges of the Court of Appeals* (1788) (4 Call), *Virginia Reports*, 8:5–21, 135–151; David John Mays, *Edmund Pendleton, 1721–1803: A Biography* (1952), 2:187–202; Mays, ed., *The Letters and Papers of Edmund Pendleton, 1734–1803* (1967), 2:426, 553–554; *Richmond Virginia Independent Chronicle*, 26 Mar. 1788, 11 Mar. 1789; Kaminski, *Ratification*, 9:615–617, 10:1444, 1539, 1541, 1557 (incorrectly identifies Cary's namesake son as delegate to the Convention of 1788); obituaries in *Richmond Virginia Independent Chronicle, and General Advertiser*, 18 Nov. 1789, and *Richmond Virginia Gazette and Weekly Advertiser*, 19 Nov. 1789.

BRENT TARTER

CARY, Virginia Randolph (30 January 1786–2 May 1852), writer, was born probably at Tuckahoe, the Goochland County plantation of her parents, Thomas Mann Randolph (1741–1794), a member of the Convention of 1776, and his first wife, Ann Cary Randolph. Her twelve siblings included Mary Randolph Randolph, author of *The Virginia House-Wife* (1824); Thomas Mann Randolph (1768–1828), who served in the House of Representatives from 1803 until 1807 and as governor of Virginia from 1819 through 1822; Judith Randolph Randolph, who as her husband's executor carried out the manumission and resettlement of more than seventy slaves; and Ann Cary "Nancy" Randolph Morris, who became embroiled in a cause célèbre when accused of adultery with her brother-in-law and infanticide in 1792. After her mother's death in 1789, Virginia Randolph lived with an aunt, but by 1791 she had joined the household of her brother and sister-in-law, Thomas Mann Randolph and Martha Jefferson Randolph, at Monticello and later at Edgehill, both in Albemarle County. Unlike her six elder sisters, who had studied with their brothers' tutors at Tuckahoe, she received no formal education, although she probably studied informally with Martha Jefferson Randolph, who later tutored her own children.

At Monticello on 28 August 1805 Virginia Randolph married her cousin Wilson Jefferson Cary, a Fluvanna County planter, justice of the peace, and leading member of the Episcopal

Church. They resided at Carysbrook, in Fluvanna County, with his grandfather Wilson-Miles Cary, a member of the Convention of 1776. Between 1806 and 1823 Virginia Randolph Cary gave birth to two sons and seven daughters, two of the latter of whom died in infancy. Cary's marriage was affectionate but financially troubled. Like many other postrevolutionary Virginia planters, Wilson Jefferson Cary inherited debts, along with land and slaves, from his grandfather. When he died in 1823, his will mandated the sale of his estate to satisfy his creditors. Though named an executor, his widow declined service. After several land sales between 1831 and 1833, Virginia Cary and her surviving children received a maintenance from a portion of the proceeds, most of which went to repay debts.

In November 1831, during antislavery debates following Nat Turner's Rebellion and at the urging of her neighbor John Hartwell Cocke (1780–1866), Cary drafted a memorial in behalf of the women of Fluvanna County calling for the gradual abolition of slavery in Virginia. The petition was neither circulated for signatures nor submitted to the General Assembly. Instead, it appeared in such periodicals as the *African Repository, and Colonial Journal* and *Niles' Weekly Register.*

During her widowhood's difficult early years Cary began writing for publication. In 1826 Carysbrook burned, and, though the house was nearly rebuilt by 1828, rheumatism and excessive opium use had debilitated its mistress. In this period Cary produced three of the four major works with which she is credited: *Letters on Female Character, Addressed to a Young Lady, on the Death of Her Mother* (1828), the first advice book written by a southern woman for the women of her region; *Mutius: An Historical Sketch of the Fourth Century* (1828), a didactic novel published by the American Sunday School Union; and *Christian Parent's Assistant, or Tales, for the Moral and Religious Instruction of Youth* (1829), which she addressed to the "Mothers of America."

Cary's first and best-known work, *Letters on Female Character*, foreshadows the patriarchal ideology of antebellum white southerners. Perhaps reflecting on her own wretched and unpro-

tected state, Cary idealized the authority of benevolent men and cited both Scripture and the laws of nature to argue that women must be subordinate to men both at home and in society. She warned that women's attempts to equal or surpass men in power or knowledge would jeopardize the nation's virtue and happiness, although she conceded that the "partial illumination" of women's minds could make them better wives and mothers.

Cary hoped to "see women highly cultivated in mind and morals, and yet content to remain within . . . the family circle." This domestic ideal presumably shaped her objectives as an educator, an occupation she first pursued in 1832, when she and her younger children moved to Norfolk to live with her sister Harriet Randolph Hackley, who operated a successful school for young women there. Inspired by Hackley's example, Cary in 1833 opened her own school in Norfolk, where, despite her earlier criticism of women's public ambitions, she plunged into religious and benevolent activities.

By April 1835 Cary had left Norfolk for Fairfax County, where she opened a school in partnership with a brother of Orlando Fairfax, who had married her daughter Mary Randolph Cary. She probably spent her remaining years in the Fairfaxes' home in Alexandria and visiting her other children, who settled in Maryland, New York, and Washington, D.C. Cary contributed poetry and short stories to various publications. She also published another novel, *Ruth Churchill; or, The True Protestant: A Tale for the Times* (1851), which urged Episcopalians to experience religious conversion, as had she herself. Like her earlier novel *Mutius*, this work appeared under the pseudonym "A Lady of Virginia."

Cary's life illustrates the significant and sometimes contradictory implications of the postrevolutionary decline of the gentry for Virginia women. At her nadir, Cary accepted the notion of women's powerlessness and became an early, active participant in constructing southern patriarchy. Yet Cary was also among the earliest southern women to write extensively for publication. Her activities as a writer and educator generated income and made her a public figure, belying the image of the submissive and dependent southern lady that her best-known work promoted. Virginia Randolph Cary died at her daughter's house in Alexandria on 2 May 1852 and was buried in the cemetery of Saint Paul's Episcopal Church in that city.

Birth and marriage dates in Cary-Page-Randolph family Bible records, LVA; Albemarle Co. Record of Marriage Bonds, 1:275 (bond dated 27 Aug. 1805); *Richmond Enquirer*, 3 Sept. 1805 (variant marriage date of 25 Aug. 1805); Cary correspondence in Carr-Cary Family Papers, Cocke Family Papers (1725–1939), Cocke Family Papers (1800–1871), and William Cabell Rives Papers, all UVA, and at VHS; other documentation in Smith Family Papers, American Philosophical Society, Philadelphia, and Edwin Morris Betts and James Adam Bear Jr., eds., *The Family Letters of Thomas Jefferson* (1966); husband's will, estate inventory, and sale in Fluvanna Co. Will Book, 3:6–7, 9–12, and Fluvanna Co. Deed Book, 10:105, 290–291, 346–347, 351–352; Cary, *Letters on Female Character, Addressed to a Young Lady, on the Death of Her Mother* (1828), quotations on v, 149; *African Repository, and Colonial Journal* 7 (1831): 310–312; *Niles' Weekly Register* 41 (1831): 273; *Alexandria Gazette*, 14 Apr. 1835; Cynthia A. Kierner, " 'The dark and dense cloud perpetually lowering over us': Gender and the Decline of the Gentry in Postrevolutionary Virginia," *Journal of the Early Republic* 20 (2000): 185–217; Patrick H. Breen, ed., "The Female Antislavery Petition Campaign of 1831–32," *VMHB* 110 (2002): 377–398; Hall, *Portraits*, 46 (por.); obituaries in *Washington Daily National Intelligencer*, 7 May 1852, and *Alexandria Gazette*, 8 May 1852.

Cynthia A. Kierner

CARY, Wilson-Miles (1733 or 1734–25 November 1817), member of the Convention of 1776, was the son of Wilson Cary and Sarah Blair Cary and was born probably in Warwick County. From 1752 to 1755 he attended the College of William and Mary, and on 25 May 1759 he married his first cousin Sarah Blair, daughter of his uncle John Blair (ca. 1687–1771), then president of the governor's Council. They had three daughters and two sons. Cary was also closely related to the influential Fairfax, Nelson, and Nicholas families, and his siblings and children married into other prosperous and powerful families, including the Amblers, Carrs, and Jeffersons. For some unrecorded reason, he hyphenated his given names.

Cary entered public life in 1757 when he was commissioned a justice of the peace in Warwick County and elected to the parish vestry. The following year he became a lieutenant colonel in the militia. Succeeding his father in 1761 to a customs post as naval officer of the lower district of the James River, he moved to Elizabeth City County early the following year and served on the court of that county for nearly forty years and also as colonel of the militia. In 1767 Cary became an Elizabeth City parish vestryman. From 1766 to 1771 he represented Elizabeth City County in the House of Burgesses, where he served on the Committee for Propositions and Grievances and the Committee for Religion.

Cary signed the nonimportation associations in 1769 and 1770 opposing British tax policies and used his post as naval officer to monitor enforcement of those agreements. After the nonimportation clauses of the Continental Association of 1774 went into effect, he obstructed the flow of banned goods. The following summer, after Cary spread news of the arrival in Virginia of a British warship, the royal governor described him as "one of the most active and virulent of the Enemies of Government." Cary closed his office in the autumn of 1775, an act that may have cost him as much as £500 a year. He was elected to the Elizabeth City County Committee that November and on 25 April 1776 was elected to the fifth and final Revolutionary Convention. A member of the Committee on Privileges and Elections, Cary also served on the ad hoc committee formed to oversee the establishment of the Virginia State Navy. He was almost certainly present for the unanimous votes for independence on 15 May 1776, to adopt the Declaration of Rights on 12 June, and to approve the first constitution of the commonwealth on 29 June.

A member of the House of Delegates during the October 1776 session, Cary again served on the Committee of Privileges and Elections. By the following year he was living temporarily in the new county of Fluvanna and was appointed to its county court and returned to the House in 1777 and 1778. He sat on the Committee for Religion during the former session and the Committees of Privileges and Elections, of Propositions and Grievances, and for Religion during the latter term. By 1780 he was living at Scotchtown, in Hanover County, which he purchased from Patrick Henry. Elected, nevertheless, to the

House of Delegates that year from Elizabeth City County, Cary was once again appointed to the Committees of Privileges and Elections and of Propositions and Grievances, but his election was ruled illegal under the Constitution of 1776 because he resided in Hanover County. By 1783 Cary had moved to Warwick County, where voters elected him to the House of Delegates for two consecutive sessions. In 1783 he chaired the Committee of Privileges and Elections, and the next year he again served on that committee, chaired the Committee for Religion, and sat on the Committee of Propositions and Grievances. Cary later returned to Elizabeth City County and was elected to the House in 1795 and 1796. During the 1795 session he chaired the Committee of Religion and served on the Committees of Privileges and Elections, of Propositions and Grievances, of Claims, and of Courts of Justice. He sat on each of these committees except Courts of Justice in the following term.

A devout, lifelong Anglican, Cary attended the first convention of the Protestant Episcopal Church of Virginia in 1785, at least two subsequent conventions during the next five years, and again in 1797. He became a staunch Federalist during the 1790s and closed his political career in March 1799 by entering his condemnation of the Virginia Resolutions, which opposed the Alien and Sedition Acts, into the Elizabeth City County records.

Cary's wife died on 28 February 1799, and not long thereafter he moved to Williamsburg, where he served on the board of the College of William and Mary. About 1802 he married Rebecca Dawson, daughter of Thomas Dawson, formerly commissary of the bishop of London and president of the college. During his final years Cary shared his house at Carysbrook, in Fluvanna County, with his grandson, his grandson's wife, the writer Virginia Randolph Cary, and their children. Once one of the wealthier men in the colony, he depended after the Revolution on the productions of his plantations, but bad crops and floods, other economic troubles, and heavy spending on hospitality to family and friends severely depleted his wealth. During the 1810s he added several codicils to his will denouncing the governmental policies of the Jeffersonian Republicans, which he blamed in part

for his financial difficulties. Wilson-Miles Cary, a respected but heavily indebted old Revolutionary nationalist, died at Carysbrook on 25 November 1817 and probably was buried there.

Harrison, *Virginia Carys*, 108–110, 179–180 (including abstracts of unlocated will and por. facing 108); Wilson Miles Cary (1838–1914), genealogical notes on the Cary family (compiled 1896–1912), VHS (with birth year of 1734 and first marriage and death dates); Cary letters in several collections in LC, LVA, UVA, and VHS; earl of Dunmore to earl of Dartmouth, secretary of state, 12 July 1775, PRO CO 5/1353, fol. 228 (quotation); *Revolutionary Virginia*; 1799 declaration in Elizabeth City Co. Deeds, 34:468; *Richmond Virginia Argus*, 5 Mar. 1799; *Richmond Virginia Gazette, and General Advertiser*, 5 Mar. 1799; obituary without date of death "in the 84th year of his age" in *Richmond Enquirer*, 4 Dec. 1817, reprinted in *Virginia Patriot, and Richmond Daily Mercantile Advertiser*, 5 Dec. 1817.

PETER V. BERGSTROM

CASKIE, John Samuel (8 November 1821–14 December 1869), member of the House of Representatives, was born in Richmond and was the son of Eliza Kennon Randolph Pincham Caskie and James Caskie, a Scottish immigrant, tobacco merchant, and longtime president of the Bank of Virginia. Educated locally, Caskie entered the University of Virginia in 1838 and after a stellar academic career graduated in 1841 with an M.A. Caskie then read law in Richmond. Never robust, he traveled with a cousin in Europe for his health during the summer of 1842. While in England, Caskie formed a brief, passionate liaison with a married British actress, Laura Seymour, which resulted in her pregnancy. Seymour never revealed the child's paternity, and Caskie appears never to have acknowledged the affair. On 26 September 1849 Caskie married Frances Jane Johnson, daughter of the celebrated horse breeder William Ransom Johnson, of Chesterfield County. The couple had one daughter and three sons.

On his return to Richmond, Caskie again took up the law. After qualifying for the bar in July 1843, he established his practice in the capital and surrounding counties. By December 1845 Judge Philip Norborne Nicholas had appointed him commonwealth's attorney for the Circuit Superior Court of Law and Chancery for Richmond and Henrico County. One of the busiest jurisdictions in Virginia, the circuit court heard both civil and criminal cases touching residents and businesses in the metropolitan area. On 14 March 1850 the General Assembly chose Caskie judge of the circuit superior court to replace Nicholas, who had died the previous August. After about eighteen months on the bench, Caskie stepped down in September 1851 in order to campaign for Congress.

As a prosecuting attorney, Caskie naturally came to public notice, but his local reputation as an orator predated his admission to the bar. Just days before he qualified in the Richmond courts, Caskie launched a parallel career as stump speaker and political organizer by addressing a large Richmond crowd on the Fourth of July 1843. A committed supporter of John C. Calhoun, he worked tirelessly for the states' rights Democrats in a region where the Whigs held significant sway. A protégé of James Alexander Seddon, who served two nonconsecutive terms in the House of Representatives and later was Confederate secretary of war, Caskie became a natural choice when his mentor suddenly withdrew from the election for the House of Representatives seat from the Sixth Congressional District late in the 1851 campaign. Caskie enthusiastically took on his opponent, the former Whig congressman John Minor Botts, and defeated him in a close race despite an abbreviated campaign. Caskie continued to win reelection to Congress for a total of four terms. He represented the Sixth District, comprising Chesterfield, Goochland, Hanover, Henrico, Louisa, and Powhatan Counties and the city of Richmond, until redistricting for the Thirty-third Congress in 1853 placed him in the Third District, comprising Caroline, Chesterfield, Goochland, Hanover, Henrico, King William, and Louisa Counties and the city of Richmond. In 1858 Caskie lost his bid for renomination to Daniel Coleman DeJarnette, as a number of independent Democrats vied for votes with their more conservative colleagues during escalating sectional tensions.

In Congress, Caskie championed traditional Democratic positions on banking, tariffs, and finance and played an important, behind-the-scenes role in 1854 in the passage of the Kansas-Nebraska Act, which allowed residents of the two territories to determine whether they should enter the Union as free or slave states. Never a

dominating figure in the legislative halls, he served on the Committee of Elections during his first term and exercised some influence as a senior member of the Committee on the Judiciary in the Thirty-third, Thirty-fourth, and Thirty-fifth Congresses.

Soon after Virginia voted for secession in the spring of 1861, Caskie joined the Richmond Fayette Artillery (Company I, 1st Virginia Artillery) on 25 April 1861 as a private. His lack of military experience, however, combined with his age and poor health, forced him to leave Confederate service on 15 June of that year. He took little part during the remaining years of the Civil War, although he may have served briefly again in local defense with Company A of the 1st Virginia State Reserves. Following the surrender at Appomattox Court House, he attempted to revive his legal career, but ill health rendered him unable to pursue his profession. John Samuel Caskie died at his Richmond residence on 14 December 1869 and was buried in Hollywood Cemetery in that city.

Biography in George L. Christian, "Reminiscences of Some of the Dead of the Bench and Bar of Richmond," *Virginia Law Register* 14 (1909): 9; birth date and full name in Caskie family Bible records (1792–1864), LVA; John S. Caskie Papers, VHS; Caskie correspondence in various collections at UVA and VHS; works include Caskie et al., *A Circular to the Former Students of the University of Virginia: Proposing the Purchase of a Painting, by Them, to Be Presented to the University* (1851), and *Speech of the Hon. John S. Caskie, of Virginia, in the House of Representatives, May 19, 1854, on Nebraska and Kansas* (1854); legal and political career documented in correspondence between Peter Vivian Daniel (1818–1889) and Richard Barnes Gooch, Gooch Family Papers, UVA; Chesterfield Co. Marriage Bonds (bond dated 25 Sept. 1849); *Richmond Enquirer*, 7, 14 July 1843, 28 Sept. 1849, 12, 26 Sept., 3 Oct. 1851; *Southern Churchman*, 4 Oct. 1849; *Richmond Semi-Weekly Examiner*, 22 Aug., 12 Sept. 1851; *JHD*, 1849–1850 sess., 398–399; *Congressional Globe*, 32d Cong., 1st sess., 1639, 33d Cong., 1st sess., 636, 1234, 1411; *Appendix to Congressional Globe*, 33d Cong., 1st sess., 1141–1145; Compiled Service Records; *Catalogue of Law and Medical Books, Embracing the Libraries of the Late Judge Jno. S. Caskie and Gustavus A. Myers, esq.* (1870); Richmond City Hustings Court Will Book, 26:491–492; obituary and Richmond bar tribute in *Richmond Daily Dispatch*, 16, 17 Dec. 1869.

E. LEE SHEPARD

CASPARI, Richard Bernard (20 April 1942–19 January 2000), orthopedic surgeon, was born in Montgomery, Alabama, and was the son of

German immigrants Frederick Caspari and Hildegard Elizabeth Wolff Caspari. His father worked as a cotton broker, and his mother established and managed the scientific library at a local factory. They divorced, and both remarried. Following high school, Caspari attended Pensacola Junior College in 1959 and 1960. He received a B.S. in chemistry from the University of Florida in 1962 and an M.D. from the same university in 1966. He married Judith Ellen Bonnett in Gainesville, Florida, on 26 February 1966. They had two daughters.

Caspari completed his internship in 1967 at Barnes Hospital at Washington University in Saint Louis, Missouri, where he trained under Fred Reynolds, the team doctor for the Saint Louis Cardinals football team. Caspari joined the United States Navy in 1968 and served as lieutenant commander aboard the nuclear-powered fleet ballistic missile submarine *Ethan Allen*, based at Rota, Cádiz, Spain. His family moved to Groton, Connecticut, for the year that he was at sea. Caspari spent the second year of his naval service in the Department of Orthopedics at the United States naval hospital in Millington, Tennessee. In 1970 he returned to Washington University and completed his residency in orthopedics there three years later.

In 1973 Caspari moved to Virginia and became a founding director of Henrico Orthopaedic Associates, Ltd. (later Tuckahoe Orthopaedic Associates), in Henrico County. During the next twenty-five years he built his practice and established himself as a pioneer in arthroscopic surgery. Caspari gained international recognition in the field to which he contributed key concepts and medical designs. In 1982 he helped found Orthopaedic Research of Virginia, an organization dedicated to teaching, research, and advancement in the field of arthroscopy and sports medicine. Caspari created numerous surgical instruments and held twenty-six patents for medical designs. His inventions included suturing instruments (especially an Arthrotek suture punch system that bears his trademarked name), shoulder traction devices, a knee joint prosthesis, thigh stabilizers, surgical cutters for arthroscopic surgery, and methods and apparatuses for knee replacement surgery.

In addition to his personal practice, Caspari was an active staff member at several hospitals in the region and served as a consultant to numerous laboratories and medical corporations throughout the United States. He was an instructor at Washington University in 1972 and 1973 and at the Medical College of Virginia from 1974 until he stepped down as clinical professor of surgery in 1999. Caspari often lectured and presented papers on arthroscopic techniques at national and international conferences, published dozens of scientific papers and chapters in reference works and textbooks, and occasionally reported his observations and demonstrated his techniques in video productions. He served on the editorial boards of several scholarly journals, including *Arthroscopy* and the *American Journal of Sports Medicine*, and as president of the Arthroscopy Association of North America for the 1990–1991 term.

Caspari was among the earliest orthopedic surgeons to offer arthroscopic surgery as an option in the Richmond area and treated several famous athletes. He removed a piece of cartilage from the knee of Mary Lou Retton six weeks before she won a gold medal in the women's gymnastics all-around competition, along with four other medals, at the 1984 Olympic Games. He treated members of the Washington Redskins football team and the journalist Ted Koppel, among many other celebrities.

Caspari was an accomplished pilot of both helicopters and fixed-wing aircraft, and he occasionally filled in for the regular morning traffic reporter for Richmond radio station WRVA. He enjoyed climbing and ascended Fuji, Kilimanjaro, and Mount Kenya. In June 1999 Caspari left his practice and MCV in order to pursue a lifelong dream of sailing around the world. He purchased a forty-eight-foot catamaran, the *Libreterre*, and began the trip accompanied by his wife and a two-member crew. Caspari sailed the Caribbean, then through the Panama Canal to French Polynesia, and from there to New Zealand. He wrote about his travels in a series of six articles for the *Richmond Times-Dispatch*.

On vacation in Vail, Colorado, before resuming his circumnavigation of the globe, Richard Bernard Caspari died of a heart attack while skiing on 19 January 2000. His remains were cremated. A memorial service was held four days later at the MartinAir/HeloAir hangar at the Richmond International Airport. In 2003 the International Society of Arthroscopy, Knee Surgery and Orthopaedic Sports Medicine created a monetary prize, the Richard B. Caspari Award, for the best paper on the upper extremities presented at its international congress.

Biographical information, including copy of 1999 curriculum vitae with complete bibliography of Caspari's writings and presentations, provided by widow, Judith Ellen Bonnett Caspari (2004); feature articles in *Richmond Times-Dispatch*, 25 Sept. 1992, 5 Nov. 1993, 4 Aug. 1994; presidential address "Arthroscopy—An Orthopaedic Surgical Subspecialty or a Technique?" in *Arthroscopy: The Journal of Arthroscopic and Related Surgery* 7 (1991): 390–393; Caspari's travel articles in *Richmond Times-Dispatch*, 1 Aug., 12 Sept., 10 Oct., 21 Nov., 5 Dec. 1999, 21 Jan. 2000; obituaries in *Vail Daily*, 20 Jan. 2000, *Richmond Times-Dispatch*, 20 (por.), 21 (editorial tribute) Jan. 2000, and *Goochland Gazette*, 29 Jan.–4 Feb. 2000; memorials in *Arthroscopy: The Journal of Arthroscopic and Related Surgery* 16 (2000): 227–229 (several pors.), and International Society of Arthroscopy, Knee Surgery and Orthopaedic Sports Medicine *Newsletter* 5 (winter 2000): 4.

MARGARET R. RHETT

CASSELL, Emma Frances Plecker (15 June 1863–8 April 1944), civic and patriotic organization leader, was born in Centerville in Augusta County and was the daughter of Jacob H. Plecker, a merchant, and Frances Burton Smoot Plecker. From 1877 until 1880 she attended Augusta Female Seminary (later Mary Baldwin College) in Staunton, where she took courses in history, Latin, mathematics, and the natural sciences. At age fifteen she began a lifetime of volunteer work by helping to organize a sewing class for Sunday school children at a Presbyterian mission church in Augusta County.

On 23 December 1884 Plecker married Julius Frederick Ferdinand Cassell, a German-born civil and mining engineer whose railroad work took the childless couple to Maryland, West Virginia, Pennsylvania, Illinois, and Indiana, where she engaged in various civic, club, and mission activities. After he retired, they returned to Staunton in 1909, in part to care for her widowed mother. While her husband managed a wholesale grocery company, Emma Cassell plunged into civic work and patriotic societies.

She joined a local circle of the International Order of the King's Daughters and Sons, which she served as secretary in 1910, and was president of the Society for Women's Work at First Presbyterian Church in Staunton. In 1913 she was recording secretary of the Florence Crittenton League of Virginia.

Although Cassell's father probably had served fewer than six months in a Confederate mounted infantry unit at the end of the Civil War, Cassell joined the J. E. B. Stuart Chapter of the United Daughters of the Confederacy and was the chapter's president in 1911. After working on several committees in the Virginia Division of the United Daughters of the Confederacy, Cassell served as custodian from 1914 until 1916 and as registrar from 1917 until 1919. Using her considerable ability to marshal people and resources, she organized the Bath County chapter of the UDC on 30 October 1912 and a local chapter of the Children of the Confederacy in Staunton on 4 April 1914. Under her direction, the Staunton Juniors had the largest enrollment in the state—650 by early in 1919, including two children admitted on the days they were born. Before the chapter disbanded in March 1919, Cassell reported to the secretary of Virginia Military Records that the Juniors were diligently "hunting up the indigent, old Veterans too old, ignorant & helpless to know how to assist themselves" and helping them apply for state pensions. The Juniors also delivered fruit baskets and pocketknives to veterans in the local almshouse and treated the residents of the R. E. Lee Camp Confederate Soldiers' Home in Richmond to cigars. Early in the twentieth century, children's patriotic and heritage societies were battlegrounds in the attempts to shape values and retreat from expanding ideals of social and political equality, and in many ways Cassell's work inculcating the principles of the Lost Cause placed her on a parallel path with her elder brother Walter Ashby Plecker, the state registrar of vital statistics who used his position to wage a fierce campaign for white racial purity.

After World War I, Cassell chaired the local committee of Fatherless Children of France, a group dedicated to soliciting funds to support war orphans. In November 1919 the National

Society United States Daughters of 1812, State of Virginia, elected her president, an office she held until resigning in 1924. She also served as the society's national curator from 1923 to 1926. In November 1919 Cassell became state chair of the Children of the American Revolution, an auxiliary group of the National Society Daughters of the American Revolution. She revitalized the virtually moribund state CAR and remained at its helm until 1939. Cassell considered the publication of a history of that organization in 1930 to be the greatest accomplishment of her tenure. "Many long, tedious hours were spent, letters written, [and] trips taken," she recalled, "trying to gather up the scattered threads of early history."

While lending her formidable energy and organizational skills to patriotic societies, Cassell continued her church work. She served as the historian for the Woman's Auxiliary of Lexington Presbytery from 1929 until 1933 and for the Woman's Auxiliary of the Synod of Virginia from 1933 until 1937. Cassell doggedly collected church histories, meeting minutes, and photographs for the Historical Foundation of the Presbyterian and Reformed Churches (later the Presbyterian Historical Society) at Montreat, in Buncombe County, North Carolina, and urged other presbyterial historians to follow her example. Working industriously in 1936 during the seventy-fifth anniversary year of the Presbyterian Church in the U.S. to collect materials for the church archives, she deposited more than 200 auxiliary histories and 200 church histories, in addition to collecting money for book repair.

Emma Frances Plecker Cassell died on 8 April 1944 at King's Daughters' Hospital in Staunton. She was buried in Thornrose Cemetery next to her husband, who had died on 4 March 1936.

Margaret Wootten Collier, *Biographies of Representative Women of the South, 1861–1925* (1925), 3:141–143 (por. facing 141); probable autobiography, 23 June 1943, supplied to Sue Ruffin Tyler for "The Women of Virginia" project, Tyler Family Papers Group D, W&M; birth date and place confirmed by BVS; Staunton Marriage Register; published works include Cassell, comp., "History of the Virginia Society, Children of the American Revolution, 1895–1930," in *History of the Virginia State Society, Daughters of the American Revolution*, comp. Jennie Thornley Grayson (1930),

with por. facing 372; Virginia Division, United Daughters of the Confederacy, *Minutes*, 1911–1921; *Confederate Veteran* 21 (July 1913): 359; ibid. 22 (June 1914): 300–301; ibid. 26 (Apr. 1918): 178; ibid. 27 (Apr. 1919): 154, 158; Cassell to Joseph V. Bidgood, 21 Feb. 1917, Department of Confederate Military Records, Correspondence, Box 2, Acc. 27684, LVA (first quotation); Daughters of the American Revolution, State Conference, *Proceedings*, 1919–1944 (second quotation in 1930 volume, p. 93); National Society United States Daughters of 1812 *News-Letter*, 1920–1924; Woman's Auxiliary of Lexington Presbytery *Minutes*, 1929–1933; Woman's Auxiliary of the Synod of Virginia, Presbyterian Church in the U.S., *Minutes*, 1933–1937; obituaries in *Richmond Times-Dispatch* and *Staunton News-Leader*, both 9 Apr. 1944, and *Richmond News Leader* and *Staunton Evening Leader*, both 10 Apr. 1944.

JENNIFER DAVIS MCDAID

CASSIDY, Harry Evans (6 January 1889–14 November 1962), document examiner, was born in Flemingsburg, Kentucky, and was the son of Alice C. Hawley Cassidy and Roger Cassidy, a farmer who later served as the town's chief of police and mayor. He worked in his father's livery and feed stable and at age eighteen became a deputy policeman and then deputy sheriff in Flemingsburg before working as a guard at the Kentucky State Reformatory at Frankfort. While there Cassidy organized the prison's fingerprint identification system and began to study handwriting after he was asked to examine threatening letters several prisoners had received. He successfully determined their authorship and became superintendent of the penitentiary's Identification Bureau. On 7 April 1909, in Fleming County, Cassidy married Elizabeth Poyntz Richardson. They had four sons.

In 1915 the family moved to Richmond. There until 1948 Cassidy worked as an inspector of special agents for the Chesapeake and Ohio Railway Company, studying anonymous letters and forged documents. He estimated that only one in ten of his cases went to trial, because offenders usually admitted their guilt after his investigation and made restitution, thus avoiding arrest. Cassidy worked for other parties as well and examined such documents as bogus wills, forged letters, and an architect's drawing bearing the alleged signature of Thomas Jefferson. During World War II he did intelligence work for the United States Army, the United States Navy, the Federal Bureau of Investigation, and other organizations. He disliked the title "expert" and once told a reporter that "It sounds presumptuous. Just because a man is a blacksmith and the only one in the neighborhood doesn't make him an 'expert,' even if he is a good blacksmith."

Cassidy gained national fame in January 1935, when he testified at the trial of Bruno Richard Hauptmann, the accused kidnapper and murderer of the twenty-month-old namesake son of the world-famous aviator Charles Augustus Lindbergh and his wife, Anne Morrow Lindbergh. The trial, held in Flemington, New Jersey, was a sensational event that drew global attention. Cassidy, one of several handwriting experts who testified for the prosecution, took the stand on 16 January. Basing his opinion on writing samples Hauptmann gave after his arrest, Cassidy decisively stated that the defendant had written the fourteen ransom notes. He pointed to consistent misspellings in the samples and the ransom demands.

Cassidy's sense of humor and Kentucky drawl amused the crowd. When the defense attorney asked if Cassidy had observed Hauptmann writing the samples, the witness drew laughter when he replied, "I wasn't present when Washington crossed the Delaware, but I got a pretty good idea he got over to the Jersey side." When the lawyer asked if he was certain that police officers had not directed Hauptmann to misspell certain words, Cassidy replied, "If you can prove it, it certainly will help your case." After another round of laughter, Cassidy stepped down. Partly as a result of the persuasive testimony of Cassidy and his fellow document examiners, Hauptmann was convicted of first-degree murder and executed in 1936.

To perform his work, Cassidy amassed a large library, a collection of cameras, enlargers, and other equipment, and his own voluminous notes on the history of typewriters, all of which he kept at his home office. He continued his work after his retirement from the C&O and move to a historic Hanover County farm he rechristened Ascoinoir. Late in the 1920s Cassidy joined an informal association of his peers, which in September 1942 officially became the American Society of Questioned Document Examiners.

One of fifteen charter members, he later served as vice president.

A chain smoker, Harry Evans Cassidy suffered from emphysema and on 14 November 1962 shot himself at his Hanover County farm. He was buried in the cemetery of the Bethlehem Presbyterian Church, near Mechanicsville, in that county.

Samuel M. Cassidy, *Cassidy Family and Related Lines* (1985), 95–102; Fleming Co., Ky., Marriage Register, 6:216; feature articles in *Richmond News Leader*, 24 Feb. 1947, and *Richmond Times-Dispatch*, 3 Dec. 1950 (first quotation); testimony at Lindbergh trial in *Richmond News Leader*, 16 Jan. 1935 (por.; second and third quotations), and *New York Times*, 17 Jan. 1935; obituaries in *Richmond News Leader*, 15 Nov. 1962, and *New York Times* and *Richmond Times-Dispatch*, both 16 Nov. 1962.

JULIE A. CAMPBELL

CATLETT, John (bap. 12 March 1626–by 17 October 1671), colonist, was born most likely in Canterbury, England, the residence of his maternal grandfather, and was christened in All Saints Parish in Kent. His father, John Catlett, sometimes identified as John Catlett the younger, had died at least five months before his birth, and his widowed mother, Sarah Hawkins Catlett, remarried in September 1626, to Lodowick Rowzee, a physician who later wrote a pamphlet on the efficacy of the waters at Tunbridge (later Royal Tunbridge Wells). Catlett probably grew up in Ashford, Kent, but details of his early life are scarce. His father's will bequeathed him properties, including two cherry gardens, in Sittingbourne Parish, Kent, following the death of his mother. Catlett married, had at least two sons, and was widowed by 1650. The name of his wife and the dates of their marriage and her death are not known. No later than the winter of 1649–1650 Catlett, one of his sons, and a half brother settled in Virginia. His other son and another half brother either traveled with him or joined him later in the colony.

On 23 May 1650 Catlett purchased part interest in 400 acres of land on the south side of the Rappahannock River just west of what became Port Royal. Near Golden Vale Creek he established a residence that remained in the family for generations. Catlett may have named Sittenburne Parish, which was created about a decade later, after the place of his father's residence in England. In 1651 the area in which he lived became part of Lancaster County and in 1656 was split off into the county of Rappahannock. Sometime before October 1659 Catlett married the twice-widowed Elizabeth Underwood Taylor Slaughter. They had at least two daughters and two sons, one of whom, also named John Catlett, served in the House of Burgesses for several terms between 1693 and 1702.

During his first fifteen years in Virginia Catlett acquired at least 12,000 acres by patent or purchase and probably owned much more property in the colony, in addition to what he owned in England. As befitted a prominent landowner and planter, he held various county offices, including tax collector in 1654 and sheriff in 1662 and 1664, and by the last year was a colonel in the county militia. Catlett also served on the county court and had become presiding judge by 1668. He worked as a land surveyor in both Virginia and Maryland during the 1660s, and in September 1663 the House of Burgesses appointed him and another man to assist the surveyor general Edmund Scarburgh in negotiating with Maryland to settle a boundary dispute on the Eastern Shore. Scarburgh appeared alone at a May 1664 meeting with the Maryland commissioners, and Catlett does not appear to have taken part in drawing the boundary line in 1668. A member of the vestry for Sittenburne Parish by 1665, he was embroiled for at least three years in a public dispute with the parish minister over religious practices. At Easter in 1668, the minister refused to administer communion to Catlett and the other justices and vestrymen with whom he disagreed. Catlett successfully appealed to the governor, who had supported the minister during the dispute, to dismiss the clergyman, who soon afterward left the parish.

As county coroner Catlett investigated the deaths of several men at the hands of Native Americans in 1661 and later complained to the governor about troubles with the Indians. After the assembly began passing laws to prohibit incursions by Maryland Indians and to hold Virginia tribes responsible for attacks on settlers, Catlett and other justices vowed to carry the fight to the Doeg Indians in Maryland and to local tribes suspected of attacking Virginia settlements.

On 20 August 1670 Catlett joined an expedition of John Lederer, a German explorer who had made two previous trips to the west looking for a passage through the mountains and who was the first European to document his explorations of the Piedmont and the Appalachian Mountains. On Lederer's third exploration he and Catlett climbed to the summit of the Blue Ridge in the vicinity of present-day Front Royal, from which they were the first recorded white men to view the Shenandoah Valley and the distant ranges of the Alleghenies.

In April and June 1670 the governor and Council named Catlett and several other men to act as surveyors and arbitrators in a series of land disputes. Catlett was evidently still engaged in that work when his name was mentioned in connection with the disputes in documents dated as late as 8 April 1671. John Catlett died between that date and 17 October 1671, when Elizabeth Catlett, described as the relict of Colonel John Catlett, executed a power of attorney for the settlement of his estate. (She married a fourth time in 1672 and died the following year.) It is not known how Catlett died. An undocumented report stated that he was killed by Indians at a fort not far from his home. His will does not survive, but it is known from other records, including his widow's 1672 marriage contract and her 1673 will, that he bequeathed 600 acres to his two daughters, to be divided between them, and that his two sons received his books. The will also made provisions for his children's education in England and their return transportation to Virginia.

Baptism in All Saints Parish, Bishop's Transcripts, DCb/BT1/41/16, Canterbury Cathedral Archives, Canterbury, Eng.; William Carter Stubbs and Elizabeth Saunders Blair Stubbs, *A History of Two Virginia Families Transplanted from County Kent, England* (1918), 1–17; Thomas Hoskins Warner, *History of Old Rappahannock County, Virginia, 1656–1692* (1965); George R. Catlett, *The Catlett Family in Virginia and Illinois and Related Families* (1982–1986), 1:3–6, 201–203, 205–209, 2:1, 7–17; Timothy Field Beard, "Catlett Family of England and Virginia," in David A. Avant Jr., ed., *Some Southern Colonial Families* (1989): 3:41–67; one Catlett letter, 1 Apr. 1664, CW; Catlett petition, 14 Oct. 1670, Colonial Papers, RG 1, LVA; second marriage by Oct. 1659 in old Rappahannock Co. Records (1656–1664),

391–392; landholdings documented in Virginia Land Office Patents, vols. 2–6 (first mention in Virginia records, 23 May 1650, on 2:224), RG 4, LVA, and old Rappahannock Co. Deeds, Etc. (1663–1668); public officeholding documented in old Rappahannock Co. Records (1656–1664), 129, 202, 223, 427; *Minutes of Council and General Court*; elements of lost will mentioned in documents concerning widow's 1672 marriage in old Rappahannock Co. Records (1671/1672–1676), 19–22, and old Rappahannock Co. Wills, Deeds (1665–1677), 136–143; widow's power of attorney, 17 Oct. 1671, in old Rappahannock Co. Records (1668–1672), 498–499.

DONALD W. GUNTER

CATTERALL, Louise Fontaine Cadot (20 November 1899–11 November 1986), preservationist, was born in Richmond and was the daughter of Clarence Percival Cadot and Louise (originally Louisa) Fontaine Meade Cadot. Descended from prominent early Virginia families, including the Beverleys, Meades, and Randolphs, she was a privileged young girl who enjoyed the benefits that her situation provided. After attending Virginia Randolph Ellett's school (later Saint Catherine's School) in Richmond, she continued her education at Bryn Mawr College. She majored in history, politics, and economics and graduated cum laude with an A.B. in 1921. The first woman in her family to attend college, she later said that she and the other graduates of Ellett's school were considered "unheard-of freaks" for selecting Bryn Mawr, but Ellett had established a relationship with the college and encouraged her best students to apply there. The well-known reformer and suffragist Lila Hardaway Meade Valentine, who was Louise Cadot's aunt, also encouraged her and offered to help finance her education.

Cadot went to New York City after graduation and received a certificate of completion from the Katherine Gibbs School of Secretarial and Executive Training in 1922. On 4 November of that year, in Richmond, she married Ralph Tunnicliff Catterall, a Chicago native and New York attorney. They moved to Richmond in 1924, where he joined a respected law firm and later became a judge of the State Corporation Commission. They had no children, and he died on 8 October 1978.

Louise Catterall was executive secretary of the Richmond League of Women Voters from 1925 to 1928 and editor of its *News Bulletin* from at least 1927 to 1930. She did research for the Medical Society of Virginia from 1928 to 1934 and was a secretary for the Richmond Academy of Medicine from 1934 to 1936, when she began her long association with the Valentine Museum (later the Valentine Richmond History Center). Catterall started as a volunteer librarian and became secretary to the board and also curator of prints and manuscripts. The collections grew under her care, as did her knowledge of Richmond history, which local historians regarded as encyclopedic. She gained a reputation as exacting and outspoken but was also generous in sharing her knowledge and detailed files with researchers and professional historians. Catterall's publication of Valentine Museum material included an introduction to the exhibition catalog *Richmond Portraits in an Exhibition of Makers of Richmond, 1737–1860* (1949), *Virginia's Capitol Square: Its Buildings and Its Monuments*, with Mary Wingfield Scott (1957), *Illustrated Guide to Richmond, the Confederate Capital*, with Eleanor Sampson Brockenbrough (1960), and *Conrad Wise Chapman, 1842–1910: An Exhibition of His Works in the Valentine Museum* (1962).

Catterall's interest in historic preservation probably developed from witnessing the decline of her childhood neighborhood in downtown Richmond. She and other like-minded women, along with local members of the Association for the Preservation of Virginia Antiquities, led the fight to preserve Richmond's architectural variety from being replaced. They were especially concerned about the historic Church Hill neighborhood, and in 1957 they formed the Historic Richmond Foundation. As one of the founding members, Catterall helped persuade the city to designate Church Hill and other areas as historic districts. She and her husband led one of the attempts in the 1960s to preserve the Gilded Age city hall and to save their former church, Monumental Episcopal Church. Through the Historic Richmond Foundation, Catterall arranged the purchase of other endangered properties in order to restore them. Her commitment of time, money, and knowledge stimulated interest in the adaptive reuse of buildings of architectural distinction and influenced the evolving appearance of Virginia's capital. In recognition of her work, the Virginia

Historical Society named her an honorary member in 1978. Despite Catterall's success in saving a number of important buildings, she could not stop urban redevelopment and believed that her preservation efforts had largely failed.

Louise Fontaine Cadot Catterall died at her home in Richmond on 11 November 1986 and was buried in the city's Hollywood Cemetery.

Who's Who of American Women (1958), 1:225; birth date in Meade family Bible records (1860–1909), LVA; BVS Marriage Register, Richmond City; *Richmond Times-Dispatch*, 5 Nov. 1922; Mrs. Ralph T. Catterall Papers, VRHC; some Catterall letters in correspondence archives and minute books, both VHS Archives; other publications include Catterall, "Books Printed in Richmond: An Exhibition," *Commonwealth* 7 (Apr. 1940): 17–18, "Old Houses Reflect Richmond's Story," *Commonwealth* 8 (Dec. 1941): 13–14, 20, "Valentine Museum: An Educational Force in Richmond and Virginia," *Commonwealth* 9 (Nov. 1942): 11–13, 23, ed., "Tabb-Hubard Letters," *VMHB* 56 (1948): 57–65, and "Reflections on an 81st Birthday," *Richmond Quarterly* 6 (fall 1983): 46–49 (quotation on 46); *Richmond News Leader*, 31 May 1963; Valentine Museum *Bulletin* (Sept. 1963), including cover por.; information provided by Anne Hobson Freeman (2002); obituaries in *Richmond News Leader*, 13 Nov. 1986, and *Richmond Times-Dispatch*, 14 Nov. 1986; memorial resolutions in VHS Minute Book, 19 Nov. 1986, VHS Archives, and *Historic Richmond Foundation News* (winter 1987), 11.

FRANCES S. POLLARD

CATTERALL, Ralph Tunnicliff (14 March 1897–8 October 1978), judge of the State Corporation Commission, was born in Chicago, Illinois, and was the son of Ralph Charles Henry Catterall, a historian who moved from the University of Chicago to Cornell University in 1902, and Helen Honor Tunnicliff Catterall, an attorney who published an important reference work on the law of slavery. Catterall grew up in Ithaca, New York, and often traveled to Europe as a child when his father did historical research. He graduated from Saint Paul's School, in Concord, New Hampshire, in 1914 and received bachelor's and law degrees from Harvard University in 1918 and 1921, respectively. During World War I he was a second lieutenant in the United States Army. After completing law school Catterall joined a law firm in New York City. He married Louise Fontaine Cadot in Richmond on 4 November 1922 and moved to that city two years later. They had no children.

For many years Catterall was both a practitioner and a teacher of the law. From 1924 until 1949 he was first an associate and subsequently a partner in a Richmond law firm. Highly regarded by his colleagues in the legal profession, he was elected president of the Richmond Bar Association in 1942. Catterall served on many committees of both the city and state bar associations. Legal education topics and professional ethics especially interested him, and he published several articles in professional journals on various aspects of the law. In 1948 the chief justice of the Virginia Supreme Court of Appeals named Catterall a member of the reorganized Judicial Council for Virginia, created to recommend improvements in the rules of procedure and practice in Virginia courts. Although Catterall formally stepped down the next year, he remained a member attending by request of the chief justice until 1968. Despite the demands of an active law practice, Catterall also taught part-time at the T. C. Williams School of Law of the University of Richmond from 1924 to 1949. He was most highly regarded for his expertise on constitutional law.

Having won a reputation for brilliance among his peers, Catterall often heard his name mentioned for judicial positions. In 1947 the Richmond Bar Association endorsed him for a municipal judgeship, but the governor did not follow its recommendation. Two years later an opening occurred on the State Corporation Commission. Catterall received numerous endorsements, including that of his friend David John Mays, a Richmond attorney who was close to the governor. The governor appointed Catterall to the commission on 14 April 1949 to fill an unexpired term. The state's dominant political figure, Senator Harry Flood Byrd (1887–1966), had been criticized for having his friends and close supporters named to important public offices, but Catterall was well qualified, had never been politically active and had not even met Byrd, and was a natural choice. In January 1950 the General Assembly elected him to a full term.

During the ensuing years the legislature reelected Catterall to consecutive six-year terms. He served until 1973 and had an enduring influence on the SCC. The three members of the commission shared duties and rotated the responsibility of chair annually but also had their specific areas of expertise. Catterall's special interest was banking, and he was the de facto director of the banking section. Although born and raised in the North, he fit in well with the prevailing conservative philosophy of Virginia's ruling elite in the 1950s and 1960s. A man of judicial temperament, Catterall was skeptical of innovation. In fact, it was said that he never even drove an automobile. Although not a reformer, he was known for his often witty dissents. Generally, however, Catterall's opinions on regulatory issues were in accord with the business community and the leadership of Byrd's political organization. If his decisions were at odds with their views, though, he could not be influenced to change his mind.

On the preeminent social issue of his time, desegregation of the public schools, Catterall strongly criticized the Supreme Court of the United States. In an essay published in the *American Bar Association Journal* in 1956 he censured the justices for abandoning judicial self-restraint in the school segregation decisions, a tendency that he believed would lead to judicial despotism. Two years later he advocated congressional passage of a law that would remove cases involving public schools from the jurisdiction of the federal courts. In 1959 Catterall joined his SCC colleagues in deciding to examine the records of organizations that asked the public for contributions, an action intended to intimidate the National Association for the Advancement of Colored People, which was deeply involved in the litigation to desegregate the public schools.

By late in the 1960s consumer advocates and their political allies were criticizing the SCC for what they perceived as its bias in favor of corporations, especially in cases involving public utilities and insurance companies. Some members of the General Assembly opposed Catterall's reelection to another six-year term in January 1968. Known for his acerbic wit and independent mind, Catterall did not have a reserve of political support among legislators. This was a major reason why he never achieved his goal of election to the Virginia Supreme Court of

Appeals. Mays, a lobbyist with excellent legislative connections, and Henry Lester Hooker, the senior judge on the commission, worked together to promote Catterall's reelection. The Democratic Party's legislative caucus renominated him by a 94–15 vote in January 1968, thereby assuring his reelection. Had a stronger opponent taken the field against him, Catterall would likely have received fewer votes. The debate in the caucus was bitter, as even some of Catterall's supporters condemned the commission for not being responsive to the public interest. These sentiments and the advanced age of the commissioners foreshadowed major changes on the SCC during the 1970s. In January 1972 Catterall announced that he would retire one year later.

After his retirement Catterall pursued interests in historical writing and historic preservation, a passion also of his wife, who was a founding member of the Historic Richmond Foundation. On 8 October 1978 Ralph Tunnicliff Catterall died at his Richmond residence after an illness of approximately two years. He was buried in the city's Hollywood Cemetery.

Biographies in *Commonwealth* 16 (May 1949): 20–21 (por.), and by Kevin V. Logan in W. Hamilton Bryson, ed., *Legal Education in Virginia, 1779–1979: A Biographical Approach* (1982), 127–131 (por. on 128), with bibliography of publications; Ralph Tunnicliff Catterall Papers, VHS; Catterall's writings include "Judicial Self-Restraint: The Obligation of the Judiciary," *American Bar Association Journal* 42 (1956): 829–833, 1091, "The State Corporation Commission of Virginia," *Virginia Law Review* 48 (1962): 139–151, and "Traitor or Patriot? The Ambiguous Conduct of Charles Lee," *Virginia Cavalcade* 24 (1975): 164–177; BVS Marriage Register, Richmond City; *Richmond Times-Dispatch*, 5 Nov. 1922, 13 Feb. 1942, 18 Oct. 1947, 15, 16 Apr. 1949, 10 Oct. 1958, 26 Oct. 1967, 24, 25 Jan. 1968; *Richmond News Leader*, 16 Apr. 1949, 24, 25 Jan. 1968, 5 Jan. 1972; *Norfolk Virginian-Pilot*, 17 Dec. 1967; David John Mays Diary, 12 Jan. 1951, 17 Sept., 5, 12 Nov. 1956, 15, 17 Nov., 7 Dec. 1967, 24 Jan. 1968, VHS; Laurence J. O'Toole Jr. and Robert S. Montjoy, *Regulatory Decision Making: The Virginia State Corporation Commission* (1984), 67–69, 72–73; obituaries in *Richmond News Leader* and *Richmond Times-Dispatch*, both 9 Oct. 1978.

JAMES R. SWEENEY

CAUDILL, Walter Cleveland (9 June 1888–18 January 1963), physician and member of the Senate of Virginia, was born in Alleghany County, North Carolina, and was the son of

Tyrrell R. Caudill, a farmer, and Caroline Fender Caudill. Educated in the local public schools, he attended Appalachian Training School for Teachers, in Boone, North Carolina, and Elk Creek Training School just across the state line in Grayson County, Virginia. Caudill and his brother, Estill L. Caudill, graduated from the Medical College of Virginia in 1913, and he served his internship at the Lewis Gale Hospital in Roanoke and at Saint Elizabeth's Hospital in Richmond. He moved to Pearisburg and practiced medicine there until September 1917, when he volunteered for service in the United States Army Medical Corps during the First World War. Caudill served in France and in July 1919 was discharged with the rank of captain.

Caudill returned to his Pearisburg medical practice and on 30 June 1920 in Bluefield, West Virginia, married Mary Ring Cornett, a teacher who had also attended the Elk Creek Training School. One of their two sons died in infancy, and the other became a physician. In 1924 Caudill and his brother founded Saint Elizabeth's Hospital, initially a twenty-bed general hospital in Pearisburg that served parts of five Virginia counties until the opening of Giles Memorial Hospital in 1950. Caudill then became the first president of the medical staff of Giles Memorial and served on the hospital's board until his death. In 1928 the brothers formed a partnership with another doctor in Elizabethton, Tennessee, and built in that town a fifty-five-room facility, also called Saint Elizabeth's Hospital (later Ivy Hall Hospital), of which Caudill was vice president.

Caudill invested in local businesses and by the mid-1930s was a director and sometime president of the Bank of Giles County and a member of the board of directors of the First National Bank of Pearisburg. Active in numerous community and service organizations, including the American Legion, he was a Freemason, a Shriner, and president of the Pearisburg Lions Club. He was the organizing president of the Pearisburg Kiwanis Club in 1954 and served as a lieutenant governor for the Capital District in 1959. Caudill was a member of the American College of Surgeons, served as president of the Southwestern Virginia Medical Society, and in 1949 was elected president of the Medical Society of Vir-

ginia for the following year. His presidential address, delivered in October 1950, extolled the virtues and social value of the medical profession in a free enterprise economy and warned that "the insidious processes of socialism" could bring disastrous consequences for health care in the United States.

Becoming chair of the Democratic Committee of Giles County in the 1920s, Caudill joined the Democratic State Central Committee in 1933. He also served on the Pearisburg town council from 1934 to 1936. In 1935 and in 1937 he won election to consecutive two-year terms in the House of Delegates representing Bland and Giles Counties. He sat on the Committees on Enrolled Bills, on General Laws, on Immigration, and on Moral and Social Welfare.

In 1939 Caudill was elected to the first of four four-year terms in the Senate of Virginia. His district comprised the counties of Bland, Giles, Pulaski, and Wythe. For sixteen years Caudill served on the Committees on Finance and on Public Institutions and Education. He became chair of the latter in 1950, when he also joined the Committee on Federal Relations, which he chaired during the special session in December 1955. He won seats on the Committees on Welfare and on Agriculture, Mining, and Manufactures in 1952. His colleagues elected him chair of the Senate Democratic caucus, or leader of the overwhelming Democratic majority, in January 1952, and on 13 January 1954 the thirty-seven Democratic senators unanimously elected him president pro tempore. (The three Republicans in the Senate did not vote.) In February of the following year Caudill announced that he would not seek reelection and thus concluded twenty consecutive years as a legislator.

Walter Cleveland Caudill continued to practice medicine in Pearisburg until his death in that city on 18 January 1963. He was buried in Birchlawn Cemetery, in Giles County.

Biographies in *Virginia: Special Limited Supplement* [to Tyler, *Encyclopedia*] (1929), 69–70 (with birth and marriage dates), Glass and Glass, *Virginia Democracy*, 3:502, 505 (por. facing 502), *Commonwealth* 16 (Dec. 1949): 43, and Manarin, *Senate Officers*, 245–246 (por. on 244); Military Service Records (with birth date); Caudill, "American Medicine Must Remain Free," *Virginia Medical Monthly* 77 (1950): 568–570 (quotation on 568); *JSV*, Jan. 1954 sess.,

21; *Richmond Times-Dispatch*, 13 Jan. 1954, 16 Feb. 1955; obituaries in *Roanoke World-News*, 18 Jan. 1963, *Roanoke Times*, 19 Jan. 1963, and *Virginia Medical Monthly* 90 (1963): 151; memorial in *Virginia Medical Monthly* 91 (1964): 90.

WILLIAM ALLEN VESELIK

CAUTHEN, Baker James (20 December 1909–15 April 1985), executive director of the Foreign Mission Board of the Southern Baptist Convention, was born in Huntsville, Texas, and was the son of James Sylvester Cauthen, a shop clerk, and Maude Baker Cauthen. The family moved to Lufkin, Texas, where he grew up and in April 1916 was baptized during a revival at the city's First Baptist Church. At age sixteen Cauthen was asked to preach at a nearby church and in November 1926 was licensed to preach. In the spring of 1927 he was ordained and accepted a second part-time pastorate.

Cauthen graduated from Lufkin High School in 1926 and from Stephen F. Austin State Teachers College (later Stephen F. Austin State University), in Nacogdoches, Texas, in 1929 and received a master's degree in English from Baylor University the following year. He continued to preach at several rural churches while attending Southwestern Baptist Theological Seminary, in Fort Worth, from which he received a Th.M. in 1933 and a Th.D. three years later. He served as pastor of Polytechnic Baptist Church, in Fort Worth, from 1933 to 1939 and from 1935 to 1939 was also acting professor of missions at the seminary. On 20 May 1934 Cauthen married Eloise Glass, whom he had met while at Baylor University. She was the daughter of Baptist missionaries in China and received her master of theology degree from the seminary a few days before they married. They had one daughter and one son.

In the summer of 1939 Cauthen and his family departed for missionary work in China. He spent a year in language training at Beijing before moving to Huangxian, his wife's birthplace in Shandong province. During World War II the Cauthens had to evacuate their home in China. They were able to return a short time later, this time going to Guilin, but they were again forced to evacuate, lost all their possessions, and eventually returned to the United States.

In October 1945 the Foreign Mission Board (later the International Mission Board) of the Southern Baptist Convention elected Cauthen its secretary for the Orient, in charge of Asian missions, effective in January 1946. He spent the first six months at the board's Richmond headquarters before moving his office to Shanghai to be nearer the missionaries. To accelerate the postwar recovery, Cauthen was determined to get the missionaries back into the areas that had suffered most during the war and focused his attention on China and Japan. He returned to Richmond in 1952.

Following the death of the incumbent Milledge Theron Rankin, the Foreign Mission Board on 14 October 1953 elected Cauthen executive secretary (after 1976 executive director). He deferred taking office until January 1954 so that he could make a final trip to China. Cauthen led the board into a period of vigorous expansion. He reorganized the administrative offices by forming three divisions, and he created new opportunities for laypeople to serve as missionaries. The defining program of the Cauthen years was Advance. Begun in 1948, this initiative sought to expand the board's reach, place 1,750 missionaries in the field, and support them with a $10 million budget. During Cauthen's tenure the board more than met the goal. The number of missionaries grew from 908 in more than thirty countries in 1954 to 2,981 in ninety-four countries by 1979, by which time the board's annual budget had risen to $76.7 million. The expansion of staff at the administrative headquarters as well as the growth in missionary opportunities throughout the world were the hallmarks of Cauthen's administration. Reflecting the enlargement of the missionary program, the board in 1959 moved into a large new headquarters in Richmond.

Cauthen had a heart attack in 1977 but scarcely slowed down until he retired in December 1979. During the academic years 1980–1981 and 1982–1983 he taught at Golden Gate Baptist Theological Seminary, near San Francisco, and during the 1983–1984 year he taught at his alma mater, Southwestern Baptist Theological Seminary. An endowed professorship of world missions at Golden Gate Seminary is named for him. Cauthen received honorary degrees from eight colleges and universities, including one in

Japan. In recognition of the Cauthens' contributions to missionary work, the board named its new training center outside Richmond the Baker James Cauthen and Eloise Glass Cauthen Missionary Learning Center. Cauthen contributed to several books, including collections of articles on missions, *Now Is the Day* (1946) and *By All Means* (1959), and a foreword and afterword to *Advance: A History of Southern Baptist Foreign Missions* (1970). He also published *Beyond Call* (1973), a collection of his addresses to new missionaries.

Baker James Cauthen suffered a stroke in 1984 and died at his Richmond home on 15 April 1985. He was buried in the city's Hollywood Cemetery.

Jesse C. Fletcher, *Baker James Cauthen: A Man For All Nations* (1977), including several pors.; feature article based on interviews with Cauthen in Martha Skelton, "The Voice of Missions," *Commission* 39 (Oct. 1979): 4–19; correspondence and records in Cauthen Collection (including Cauthen's 12 Feb. 1969 résumé with birth date) and in other collections, International Mission Board Archives and Records Center, Richmond; William R. Estep, *Whole Gospel, Whole World: The Foreign Mission Board of the Southern Baptist Convention, 1845–1995* (1994), 287–323; obituaries in *Foreign Mission News* and *Richmond News Leader*, both 15 Apr. 1985, and *New York Times* and *Richmond Times-Dispatch*, both 16 Apr. 1985; obituary, editorial tributes, and account of funeral in *Religious Herald*, 18, 25 Apr., 2 May 1985.

LAURA DRAKE DAVIS

CAYCE, Edgar (18 March 1877–3 January 1945), founder of the Association for Research and Enlightenment, Incorporated, was born in the town of Beverly, in Christian County, Kentucky, and was the son of Leslie Burr Cayce, a failed farmer then operating a dry-goods store, and Carrie Elizabeth Major Cayce. Reared in the Disciples of Christ (Christian Church), Cayce became sexton of Liberty Church in Beverly at age ten and was baptized in 1888. About two years later while in bed at home he had a vision of an angelic being, after which he began to exhibit evidence of a photographic memory, an ability to retain large volumes of printed information. About 1892 after a baseball struck him in the spine, he appeared to enter a trance state in which he diagnosed his injury and prescribed a poultice treatment.

At age fifteen Cayce left school after completing the eighth grade. He worked on an uncle's farm before returning to his family in Hopkinsville, Kentucky, where he took jobs as a bookstore clerk and as a shoe salesman. In 1898 Cayce moved to Louisville to work for a book and stationery business and then joined his father as a traveling insurance salesman. In 1900 Cayce lost his voice for about a year. Unable to continue selling insurance, he found a job with a photographic studio. The following year a Hopkinsville hypnotist, Al Layne, placed him in a trance, during which Cayce diagnosed his malady and prescribed a treatment, and he then regained the use of his voice. Cayce periodically lost his voice thereafter, but he was always able to regain it after entering a trance. Until 1903, when the medical board required him to stop, Layne used Cayce as a medical clairvoyant when treating other patients.

In 1902 Cayce moved to Bowling Green, where he worked in a bookstore. After a six-year engagement, he married Gertrude Evans, of Hopkinsville, on 17 June 1903. They had three sons, one of whom died in infancy. Cayce opened a photographic studio in 1904 but continued to explore medical clairvoyance with several Bowling Green physicians. In June 1909 he moved to Alabama, where for a time he operated photographic studios in several small cities. On a return visit to Hopkinsville, he met Wesley Harrington Ketchum, a homeopath in practice there. Ketchum tested Cayce's ability at clairvoyant diagnosis and was sufficiently impressed to report the results to a Boston medical conference. The *New York Times* picked up the story and on 9 October 1910 published an article headlined "Illiterate Man Becomes a Doctor When Hypnotized." The story was reprinted in many of the nation's newspapers and gave Cayce his first national fame. Cayce moved back to Hopkinsville and from then until 1912 ran a photographic studio while also serving in partnership with Ketchum and another man as a psychic diagnostician.

Early in 1912 Cayce returned to Alabama and set up the photographic Cayce Art Company in Selma. He eventually resumed giving psychic readings. Between 1919 and 1923 he spent much of his time in Texas. With several partners he founded the Cayce Petroleum Company in hopes of raising enough money to build a hospital, but his use of trances in oil prospecting was unsuccessful. Within two years he had begun a national lecture tour giving psychic demonstrations for the public. In September 1923 he hired Gladys Davis as his secretary, and she recorded the results of virtually all of his reading sessions for the next twenty-one years. In 1923 Arthur Lammers, a publisher in Dayton, Ohio, met Cayce and helped focus his trance readings on such subjects as Atlantis, the Great White Brotherhood, and reincarnation. Cayce moved his family to Dayton, but the partnership soon faltered.

Morton Harry Blumenthal, a young and successful New York financier, met Cayce about that time and for several years provided financial support. In September 1925 Cayce moved his family and residence to Virginia Beach, where he and Blumenthal in May 1927 jointly established the Association of National Investigators, Incorporated, a company organized to promote psychic and scientific research, with Blumenthal as president and Cayce as secretary-treasurer. In February 1929 the two men opened the Cayce Hospital to provide medical care for patients under the direction of Cayce's psychic readings. The ANI chartered Atlantic University in May 1930, with William Moseley Brown, a former professor of education and psychology at Washington and Lee University and Republican candidate for governor, as first president. The association also launched a magazine, *The New To-Morrow*, but the Great Depression and conflicts among Cayce's financial supporters led in 1931 to the closing of the Cayce Hospital, the dissolution of the association, and the bankruptcy of the university.

Cayce and his remaining supporters reorganized as the Association for Research and Enlightenment, Incorporated, in the summer of 1931 to support continuation of his work. They also created affiliated local study groups that used his readings for spiritual development. In November of that year Cayce and his wife and secretary were arrested in New York on a fortune-telling charge, but the judge dismissed the case because he declined to interfere with the beliefs of an incorporated ecclesiastical body. Cayce, along with his wife, elder son, and secretary, was arrested in Detroit in 1935 after a medical reading. Convicted of practicing medicine without a license, Cayce received probation with no fine or jail sentence.

During the next decade Cayce finally enjoyed financial stability. The growth of the ARE made it necessary to add an office, library, and fireproof vault to the Cayce residence in 1940, and two years later Norfolk Study Group Number 1 published *A Search for God*, based on group readings and years of applying the readings' lessons. In December 1942 Thomas Sugrue published a highly sympathetic biography, *There Is a River: The Story of Edgar Cayce*, to wide acclaim, which also produced a huge demand for readings. An article calling Cayce the "Miracle Man of Virginia Beach" appeared in the popular magazine *Coronet* in September 1943 and further increased Cayce's workload.

Cayce published very little during his life beyond several articles for ARE publications. A twenty-four-volume edition of most of his readings was published in the 1970s and 1980s, and in the 1990s a new edition with related correspondence appeared in CD-ROM format. The ARE Press also issued a popular paperback series of studies of different aspects of the readings. Three autobiographical accounts dating from the 1920s and 1930s appeared in 1997 under the title *The Lost Memoirs of Edgar Cayce: Life as a Seer* (reprinted in 1999 as *My Life as a Seer: The Lost Memoirs*).

During much of his residency in Virginia Beach, Cayce was a member of the Presbyterian Church, in which he taught Sunday school for many years, but his trance readings conveyed a synthesis of Theosophy, New Thought, and Protestant theology. Although medical readings retained primacy, many seekers obtained readings for dream interpretation, personal guidance, prophecy, and past-life information. The last included elaborate details about Atlantis, ancient Egypt, and early Christianity. Late in the twentieth century some of those readings became important foundation texts in the New Age movement.

Despite being warned by the readings themselves that he could undertake no more than five readings each day without serious risk to his health, Cayce yielded to public demand, exacerbated by wartime worries, and in 1943 increased his workload dramatically. Suffering from poor health, he recuperated in Roanoke, where he suffered a stroke in September 1944. Edgar Cayce returned to Virginia Beach in November and died on 3 January 1945, less than three months before his wife died of cancer. He was buried in Riverside Cemetery, in Hopkinsville, Kentucky.

His sons Hugh Lynn Cayce, who became president of the ARE, and Edgar Evans Cayce, together with other staff members, ensured that the association survived and thrived. Its worldwide membership stood at about 30,000 by the end of the twentieth century, when New Age thinking increased interest in the psychic phenomena that made Cayce nationally famous during his lifetime and even more famous and influential thereafter.

The Lost Memoirs of Edgar Cayce: Life as a Seer, ed. A. Robert Smith (1997), with several pors.; biographies include Thomas Sugrue, *There Is a River: The Story of Edgar Cayce*, rev. ed. (1945), Harmon Hartzell Bro, *A Seer Out of Season: The Life of Edgar Cayce* (1989), and Sidney D. Kirkpatrick, *Edgar Cayce: An American Prophet* (2000); K. Paul Johnson, *Edgar Cayce in Context: The Readings: Truth and Fiction* (1998); Edgar Cayce Papers, including more than 14,000 original readings, in Edgar Cayce Foundation Archives, Virginia Beach; SCC Charter Book, 143:71–73, 163:552–554; obituaries in *New York Times*, *Norfolk Ledger-Dispatch*, and *Norfolk Virginian-Pilot*, all 4 Jan. 1945, and *Washington Post*, 5 Jan. 1945.

K. PAUL JOHNSON

CAYCE, Hugh Lynn (16 March 1907–4 July 1982), business manager and president of the Association for Research and Enlightenment, Incorporated, was born in Bowling Green, Kentucky, and was the son of Edgar Cayce and Gertrude Evans Cayce. Soon after his birth the family moved to Hopkinsville, Kentucky, and in 1912 to Selma, Alabama. The accidental explosion of some photographic flash powder during a practical joke damaged Cayce's eyes when he was about six years old and rendered him temporarily blind. He attributed his recovery to treatment his father prescribed while in a trance. From 1919 to 1923, while his father spent much of his time in Texas promoting a petroleum business

and then began a national lecture tour, Cayce lived in Hopkinsville with his mother and younger brother. Later the family rejoined Edgar Cayce in Dayton, Ohio, and finally in the autumn of 1925 moved to Virginia Beach, where the senior Cayce and a financial supporter established the Association of National Investigators, Incorporated, in May 1927 to encourage research on psychic phenomena. Hugh Cayce attended public schools in Selma and Hopkinsville and in 1925 completed high school at a private school in Dayton. He attended a Norfolk business school for one year before entering Washington and Lee University, from which he graduated in 1930 with a B.A. cum laude in psychology.

In December 1929, while still in college, Cayce and his friend Thomas Sugrue began editing the Association of National Investigators' quarterly journal *The New To-Morrow*, to which Cayce also contributed articles. After graduating he returned to Virginia Beach to work with his father, who with a supporter had opened a hospital that offered patients unconventional treatments and remedies following clairvoyant diagnoses, or readings, that Edgar Cayce made while in a trance. Hugh Cayce served as librarian at the short-lived Atlantic University, which the ANI chartered in May 1930 and of which William Moseley Brown, his former psychology professor at Washington and Lee, was president.

After the effects of the Great Depression and conflicts between the senior Cayce and some of his financial supporters closed the ANI, the hospital, and the university, the Cayces organized the Association for Research and Enlightenment, Incorporated, in the summer of 1931, with Hugh Cayce as one of the original board members and business manager. Cayce, along with his parents and his father's secretary, was arrested in Detroit in 1935 after a medical reading. His father was convicted of practicing medicine without a license and placed on probation, but Cayce went free. For thirteen weeks in 1938 he moderated *Mysteries of the Mind*, a national radio program originating in New York over the Mutual Broadcasting System, in which guest experts discussed episodes of psychic phenomena dramatized in skits. Cayce became recreation director for Virginia Beach in May 1941 and later that year secretary of the new Virginia Beach Defense Service Committee, a group providing recreation for the military personnel flooding the area. On 10 October 1941 he married Sally Gregory Taylor at her family home in Stovall, Granville County, North Carolina. They had two sons. Drafted into the army in the spring of 1943, Cayce served with the 30th Special Service Company, a unit that booked entertainment and provided recreation for the troops, and was in Europe when his father died on 3 January 1945.

Honorably discharged as a sergeant on 12 November 1945, Cayce returned to Virginia Beach to continue his father's work and took charge of the Association for Research and Enlightenment. For more than thirty years he wrote, lectured both nationally and internationally, and held conferences that transformed the ARE into an influential forum for a national spiritual movement. He advocated meditation, dream interpretation, and spiritual study in small groups as safe gateways to greater spiritual awareness. Cayce's book *Venture Inward* (1964) included a skeptical section on hallucinogenic drugs under the heading, "Dangerous Doorways to the Unconscious." The Virginia Beach Junior Chamber of Commerce, in naming him First Citizen of Virginia Beach in 1964, cited this book and his work with young people. Cayce was a scoutmaster in Virginia Beach for more than twenty years and in 1958 received the Silver Beaver Award from the Boy Scouts of America Tidewater Council for distinguished service to youth.

To disseminate his father's philosophy, Cayce and his younger brother Edgar Evans Cayce chartered the Edgar Cayce Foundation in February 1948; built a library to house Edgar Cayce's works; encouraged writers to publish his views on dream interpretation, holistic health, reincarnation, the soul's journey, and other topics; and worked to revive Atlantic University, which reopened with graduate programs in 1985. The brothers described their father's clairvoyant gift and its limitations in *The Outer Limits of Edgar Cayce's Power* (1971). Hugh Cayce edited *The Edgar Cayce Reader* (1969) and published *God's Other Door* (1958), a commentary on life after death based on his father's readings; *Earth Changes Update* (1980), a commentary on Edgar Cayce's predictions of coming events; and *Faces of Fear* (1980), an explanation of the causes of fear and anxiety in the context of Edgar Cayce's readings. By the time poor health required his retirement as ARE president in 1976 in favor of his son Charles Thomas Taylor Cayce, Cayce had expanded the association into a headquarters for spiritual enlightenment with centers worldwide. Hugh Lynn Cayce chaired the ARE governing board until his death from cancer in Virginia Beach on 4 July 1982. His body was donated to the University of Virginia Hospital for medical research.

A. Robert Smith, *Hugh Lynn Cayce: About My Father's Business* (1988), including several pors.; much information in biographies of Edgar Cayce, especially Thomas Sugrue, *There Is a River: The Story of Edgar Cayce*, rev. ed. (1945), and Sidney D. Kirkpatrick, *Edgar Cayce: An American Prophet* (2000); Hugh Lynn Cayce interviews and correspondence in Edgar Cayce Foundation Archives and ARE Library, Virginia Beach; *Norfolk Virginian-Pilot*, 14 Oct. 1941; SCC Charter Book, 223:349–351; obituaries in *Norfolk Ledger-Star* and *Norfolk Virginian-Pilot*, both 5 July 1982 (pors.).

A. ROBERT SMITH

CECIL, Russell (1 October 1853–15 June 1925), Presbyterian clergyman, was born in Monticello, Kentucky, and was the son of Russell Howe Cecil and Lucy Anne Phillips Cecil. He grew up in Mercer County, Kentucky, and was educated in the local public schools. Cecil received an A.B. in 1874 from the College of New Jersey (later Princeton University) and an A.M. three years later, after returning to Kentucky for one year to teach school. Cecil graduated from Princeton Theological Seminary in 1878, following which he also studied at the Free Church College in Edinburgh, Scotland, and traveled throughout Europe and Palestine. In New York City on 19 January 1881 he married Alma Miller, of Richmond, Kentucky. They had three sons, two daughters, and another child who died in infancy.

Licensed by the Transylvania Presbytery in Kentucky in 1877 and ordained by the West Lexington Presbytery in the same state in 1879, Cecil held pastorates in Nicholasville, Kentucky (1879–1885), Central Presbyterian Church, in Maysville, Kentucky (1885–1889), and First Presbyterian Church, in Selma, Alabama (1889–1900). In 1893 he received an honorary doctorate of divinity from Southwestern Presbyterian University (later Rhodes College) and in 1895 a D.D. from Princeton Theological Seminary.

Accepting the call to Second Presbyterian Church, in Richmond, Virginia, Cecil was installed on 4 November 1900, the church's third pastor since its founding in 1845. During his twenty-five-year tenure, the church became the largest in East Hanover Presbytery and the Synod of Virginia. A popular minister and a respected clergyman in the city, Cecil preached a conservative theology. His sermons, known for their simplicity and directness, emphasized a loving and caring God. In 1919, when the evangelist Billy Sunday preached in Richmond, Cecil and other local clergy objected to his anecdotal and animated style, but Cecil noted approvingly that Sunday's sermons were straightforward and readily understood by listeners. In a period of social change, Cecil argued against the church's acting as an instrument of social and political reform. He believed that Christianity was compelling enough to move a person into morally correct actions. From 1898 to 1924 Cecil regularly contributed to the *Union Seminary Review*. He wrote two books—*Handbook of Theology* (1923) and *The Religion of Love* (1924)—and published several of his sermons and addresses.

In addition to his pastoral duties, Cecil served on church committees and as a representative of the southern branch of the Presbyterian Church in national organizations. He became a member of the Presbyterian Committee of Publication in 1901 and chaired it from 1919 until his death. Cecil served for more than twenty years on the Board of Managers of the Virginia Bible Society, chaired the Southern General Assembly's Permanent Committee of the Bible Cause, and was a member of the Advisory Council of the American Bible Society. Before leaving Alabama, he sat on the Executive Committee of Foreign Missions. Cecil was also a charter member of, and for fourteen years a representative to, the World Conference on Faith and Order. He served on the Executive Committee of the Federation of Protestant Churches of Christ in Amer-

ica (later the National Council of Churches) and represented the Presbyterian Church in the Council of Reformed Churches. Interested in education, he was a member of the boards of Columbia Theological Seminary, in South Carolina (1898–1900), of Southwestern Presbyterian University, in Clarksville, Tennessee (1893–1895), of Agnes Scott Institute (later Agnes Scott College), in Decatur, Georgia (1895–1899), and of Union Theological Seminary in Virginia, in Richmond (1918–1925). He taught a course at the Richmond seminary during the 1913–1914 academic year and also Christian theology at the General Assembly's Training School for Lay Workers (later the Presbyterian School of Christian Education) in Richmond.

Cecil favored a reunion of the various Presbyterian churches, especially the northern and southern branches, which had split in 1861, and was a member of a committee that studied a proposed plan of union presented to the church's 1920 General Assembly. He was uniquely influential in 1911, when he served simultaneously as moderator of the General Assembly of the Presbyterian Church in the U.S. (the southern church branch), the Synod of Virginia, the East Hanover Presbytery, and the Session of Second Presbyterian Church. No other Presbyterian official had achieved that distinction.

Cecil was president of the alumni association of Princeton Theological Seminary in 1912, of the Virginia Huguenot Society for twenty years, and of the Richmond Ministerial Union. For recreation he played golf, but not well. Russell Cecil died of heart disease at his home in Richmond on 15 June 1925 and was buried in Hollywood Cemetery. A memorial service held at Second Presbyterian Church on 8 November 1925 included a large number of Presbyterian clergymen. In his honor, the Woman's Auxiliary of the church purchased a memorial plaque, unveiled by Cecil's grandchildren, and vase and linen for the communion table. In 1938 the church dedicated its new educational building, named Cecil Memorial House.

Biographies in Tyler, *Encyclopedia*, 4:132–134, Joshua Kinney, *My Years of Service* (1931), 18–21, and Wyndham B. Blanton, *The Making of a Downtown Church: The History of the Second Presbyterian Church, Richmond, Virginia,*

1845–1945 (1945), 267–281 (with birth and marriage dates and por. facing 270); collections of sermons at UTS and UVA; BVS Death Certificate, Richmond City (variant birth date of 2 Oct. 1853 and variant birthplace of Mercer Co., Ky.); obituaries and editorial tributes in *Richmond News Leader* and *Richmond Times-Dispatch*, both 16 June 1925; memorials in *Minutes of the Synod of Virginia, Presbyterian Church in the United States* (1925), 369–370 (with incorrect death date of 13 June 1925), and *Memorials, Rev. Russell Cecil, D.D., Pastor Second Presbyterian Church, Richmond, Va.* (1925).

BARBARA C. BATSON

CECIL, William P. (9 April 1820–20 July 1899), member of the Convention of 1861, was the son of Samuel Cecil, a farmer, and Salley Brown Cecil and was born on the Clinch River in Tazewell County. One of the first students to attend Emory and Henry College after it opened in 1838, Cecil remained there until 1841, when he moved to Giles Court House to study law with Albert Gallatin Pendleton, later his brother-in-law and a member of the Convention of 1850–1851. On 19 April 1842 in Giles County, Cecil married Isabella A. Chapman, daughter of Henley Chapman, a member of the Convention of 1829–1830. They had one daughter.

In March 1842 Cecil qualified to practice law in Tazewell County and in June 1853 began the first of several terms as the county's commonwealth's attorney. By 1850 Cecil owned twelve slaves and real estate valued at several thousand dollars. Ten years later he possessed more than $18,000 in personal property, including twenty-five slaves, and could boast of $16,000 in real estate. In 1859 he was president of the Jeffersonville branch of the Northwestern Bank of Virginia. As a states' rights delegate to the National Democratic Convention in 1860, Cecil supported the unsuccessful presidential candidacy of John Cabell Breckinridge, of Kentucky.

In February 1861 Cecil was one of two delegates elected to represent Buchanan, McDowell, and Tazewell Counties at the convention called to debate the issue of Virginia's secession. He seldom spoke on other than routine procedural matters except for a speech supporting John Buchanan Floyd's failed bid for election to the Provisional Confederate Congress meeting in Montgomery, Alabama. Cecil favored secession both in the first vote on 4 April and in the final vote on 17 April 1861 and signed the Ordinance of Secession. On 22 August of that year he was elected captain of Company L, 51st Regiment Virginia Infantry (later Company D, 23d Battalion Virginia Infantry). Elected major on 21 May 1862 when the army reorganized, Cecil fell ill and requested reassignment to military courts in western Virginia. He was forced to resign on 5 March 1863 as a result of varicose veins in one of his legs that made marching and riding horseback painful.

After the Civil War, Cecil successfully resumed his legal practice. He increased his antebellum wealth and in 1870 possessed $20,000 in personal property and $25,000 in real estate. Cecil represented Tazewell County in the House of Delegates during the 1874–1875 and 1875–1877 assemblies. During both of his terms he served on the Committees on Propositions and Grievances and on the Chesapeake and Its Tributaries, and in the second session of the 1875–1877 term he was added to the Committee for Courts of Justice. His political audiences appreciated the wit and sarcasm he often used in debate.

Cecil moved to California about 1878 but in 1880 returned to the Giles County farm at the mouth of Walker Creek that his father-in-law had deeded to Isabella Cecil in 1863. In the mid-1880s he chaired the county Republican Party and regularly corresponded with the party leader William Mahone about local political affairs and patronage. William P. Cecil died on his Giles County farm on 20 July 1899 and was buried in the Chapman family cemetery, near Ripplemead, in Giles County.

French Biographies (variant birth date of 19 Apr. 1820); Cecil's nephew gave birth date of 9 Apr. 1820 and variant death date of 12 July 1899 in William C. Pendleton, *History of Tazewell County and Southwest Virginia, 1748–1920* (1920), 599 (por.); several secondary sources give middle name as Preston without documentation; *Semi-Centennial Catalogue and Historical Register of Emory and Henry College, Washington County, Virginia, 1837–87* (1887), 63; Giles Co. Marriage Bonds; Personal Property Tax Returns, Tazewell Co., RG 48, LVA; Reese and Gaines, *Proceedings of 1861 Convention*, 3:163, 4:144, 617–618; Compiled Service Records; Cecil letters in William Mahone Papers, Duke; *Richmond Daily Whig*, 8 Jan. 1876; Research Committee, Giles County Historical Society, *Giles County, Virginia,*

History—Families (1982), 156; obituary with birth date of 9 Apr. 1820 in *Tazewell Republican*, 27 July 1899.

JOHN G. DEAL
KEVIN T. LETT

CHAFFIN, William Womach (5 May 1868–7 May 1925), physician, was born at Poplar Camp, in Wythe County, and was the son of Sarah Ann Painter Chaffin and Alexander Chaffin, president of a local zinc lead–manufacturing company. Chaffin was tutored by a governess and then attended private schools before beginning a two-year course of study at Washington and Lee University in 1887, but he did not receive a degree. He matriculated at the Jefferson Medical College, in Philadelphia, interned at the college hospital and in New York City, and in 1893 received an M.D. Returning to Wythe County, he qualified before the State Board of Medical Examiners in October of that year and was elected to membership in the Medical Society of Virginia at its annual session. On 21 June 1893 Chaffin married Mary Clare Carroll Macgill, of Washington County. They had one daughter and later adopted another.

About 1895 Chaffin moved his family to Pulaski County, where he established both a medical practice that lasted thirty years and a reputation as one of the area's foremost citizens. By 1897 he was a member of the Pulaski County Medical Society and worked as an assistant surgeon for the Norfolk and Western Railway Company and as a surgeon for the Pulaski Iron Company. He joined the Pulaski County Board of Health, which for a number of years he served as secretary before becoming chair. From 1904 until 1908 and again from 1914 until his death, Chaffin sat on the town council and became identified with promoting the development of community resources. He was a member of the Virginia State Board of Health from 1905 until July 1908, when the governor appointed new members following the General Assembly's reorganization of the board. In April 1910 Chaffin began a four-year term on the State Board of Medical Examiners and was continuously reappointed for the rest of his life. He served on several committees, chaired the Question Committee, and was vice president from 1918 until 1925. Recognizing a need for closer coop-

eration among physicians serving the area west of Roanoke, Chaffin was a charter member of the Southwest Virginia Medical Society. At its June 1911 meeting he was elected to a single term as president of the organization and later served on the executive committee.

In 1915 Chaffin became chief surgeon of Pulaski's first hospital, a seven-bed facility located in a converted office building. Late in September 1918 the worldwide influenza outbreak struck the town. Businesses, schools, and churches closed as the epidemic spread, and the tiny hospital was quickly overwhelmed. By 7 October almost two-fifths of Pulaski's 5,000 citizens had contracted the disease, and an emergency hospital opened at the Elks Club. Several doctors fell ill, leaving only Chaffin and a handful of other physicians working around the clock. Chaffin and Mayor Ernest William Calfee appealed to the State Board of Health and the United States Public Health Service for medical assistance, which began arriving from Abingdon, Richmond, and Roanoke and from as far away as Washington, D.C., and New York City. By month's end the worst was over, but 125 county residents had died, 92 of them in the town. Many more might have perished if not for the leadership and dedication of Chaffin and other community leaders.

In addition to his private practice and his medical and administrative duties at Pulaski Hospital, Chaffin became county coroner in 1919 and the next year resumed work on the county board of health. At its October 1923 meeting in Roanoke, the Medical Society of Virginia recognized Chaffin's contributions to his profession, both locally and statewide, by electing him president. He was already suffering from debilitating heart disease, however, and the next year he was unable to preside over the annual meeting in Staunton.

Chaffin joined several fraternal organizations, including the Benevolent and Protective Order of Elks, the Freemasons, and the local Rotary Club, of which he was a charter member and president. His professional memberships included the American Medical Association, the Southern Medical Association, and the Tri-State Medical Association of the Carolinas and Virginia.

While preparing to make his rounds at Pulaski Hospital on 7 May 1925, William Womach Chaffin died of a heart attack at his office. The high regard accorded him was attested by one of the largest funerals held in the area to that time, including several truckloads of flowers, a long list of honorary pallbearers, and mourners from across and outside the state. He was buried in Oakwood Cemetery, in Pulaski.

Tyler, *Encyclopedia,* 5:583–584 (por.; variant middle name Wamach); BVS Marriage Register, Pulaski Co.; birth date and middle name in BVS Death Certificate, Pulaski Co.; some Chaffin correspondence in Mary Belle Pierce Macgill Papers, Acc. 29157, LVA; Southwest Virginia Medical Society presidential address "What Is the Doctor Worth?" in *Virginia Medical Semi-Monthly* 17 (1912): 378–380; Medical Society of Virginia *Transactions, 1913* (1914), 398; *Virginia Medical Monthly* 50 (1923): 570 (por.), 571, and 51 (1924): 506; Conway Howard Smith, *The Land That Is Pulaski County* (1981), 415–416, 424; obituaries in *Pulaski Southwest Times,* 8 (with memorial resolutions), 12 May 1925, *Richmond Times-Dispatch,* 8 May 1925, *Alumni Magazine and Summer Bulletin of Washington and Lee University* 1 (Aug. 1925): 42, *Journal of the American Medical Association* 84 (1925): 1764, and *Virginia Medical Monthly* 52 (1925): 205–206; memorial in *Proceedings of the Medical Examining Board of Virginia* (June 1925), 3.

DONALD W. GUNTER

CHAHOON, George (2 February 1840–29 July 1934), mayor of Richmond, was the son of John Chahoon, a building contractor, and Temperance Jameson Chahoon and was born in Sherburne, Chenango County, New York. A few months after his birth the family moved to Virginia and during the 1840s and 1850s lived in Botetourt County. Chahoon's childhood and education are not well documented. He probably attended one or more private schools in Virginia, and he studied law. About the time the Civil War began Chahoon moved to Washington, D.C., where by 1863 he was a clerk in the Treasury Department. Three men of his name enlisted in New York regiments during the Civil War, but it is unlikely that Chahoon ever served in the army.

Chahoon evidently went to occupied Norfolk in 1864 and practiced law for a few months before moving to Elizabeth City County, where he was elected commonwealth's attorney the following year and then became a leader of Williamsburg's Republican Party after the end of the Civil War. Late in 1866 Chahoon moved to Richmond, where in May 1867 Judge John Curtiss Underwood appointed him commissioner of the United States District Court. In July of that year local Republicans nominated Chahoon for city attorney. Although as a federal official he was ineligible, under Virginia law, for municipal office, Brigadier General John McAllister Schofield, the state's military commander, appointed him mayor to replace the longtime incumbent, Joseph Mayo. Chahoon took office on 6 May 1868 and set out to cleanse the municipal government of Confederate sympathizers. He removed ten white police officers, recommended that African Americans be appointed to replace some of them, and created a twenty-five-member special black police force and selected as its chief Benjamin Scott, an African American who in March 1865 had been named a noncommissioned officer for a black Confederate company that never took the field. Chahoon also required saloonkeepers to post their city licenses. In moves rejected by the city council, he sought to hire lamplighters to relieve policemen of that duty and requested a stiffer dog ordinance. All of those actions provoked protests from the city's police officers and native white political leaders.

Following the end of Reconstruction in Virginia, the governor declared all city council seats vacant, and on 16 March 1870 the new council members named Henry Keeling Ellyson interim mayor. Chahoon and some of the former Republican council members refused to surrender power, and for a nearly a month two city administrations and police forces struggled to oust each other. Supporters of the new council and mayor briefly besieged Chahoon and his allies in the police station, cut off the gaslights, and refused to let them have access to food and water. Chahoon finally left the building and let the courts resolve the controversy. When the Virginia Supreme Court of Appeals met in the Capitol on 27 April 1870 to deliver its opinion, the courtroom was so crowded with curious spectators and officials that the gallery collapsed and approximately sixty people died. Chahoon was injured, as were about 250 other people, some seriously. The court ruled in favor of Ellyson and against Chahoon.

In the second of two elections held in May and November 1870, both of which were marred by fraud and violence, Anthony M. Keiley, supported by the new Conservative Party, was elected Richmond's mayor. The army refused to interfere in Chahoon's behalf, and he finally relinquished his claim to the office. His political enemies then prosecuted him for forgery in connection with a case that they exploited to try to stain the reputations of other Republicans, among them the former attorney general Thomas Russell Bowden. Tried in 1870 and again in the following year, Chahoon was twice convicted and sentenced to two years in the state penitentiary. The trials involved several irregularities, and although the Supreme Court of Appeals did not vacate the second verdict, Governor Gilbert Carlton Walker, a fellow New York native, pardoned Chahoon on 16 December 1871, citing both the large number of petitions he had received supporting a pardon and the jury's recommendation of executive clemency, but reportedly on the condition that Chahoon leave the state.

After two years as one of Virginia's most controversial local political leaders and a principal in a celebrated court case that led to one of the state's most deadly accidents, Chahoon returned to New York. On 24 September 1867 he had married Mary Jane Rogers, member of a wealthy family of Black Brook, a township in Clinton County, New York, about fifteen miles south of Plattsburgh. They had two sons and one daughter. Chahoon prospered as an officer of his in-laws' enterprise, the J. and J. Rogers Company. Running a foundry and later a pulp and paper mill that his wife's family owned, he served many years as the company's vice president and eventually became president. Chahoon's namesake son (1872–1951) followed in his father's footsteps, moved to Quebec, and early in the twentieth century became one of the leading pulp and paper manufacturers in Canada.

In 1895 Chahoon won election to a three-year term in the New York Senate to represent the counties of Clinton, Essex, and Warren, and in 1898 he was reelected to a two-year term. During his first term he served on the Committees on Agriculture, on Forest, Fish, and Game Laws, on Miscellaneous Corporations, and on Railroads, and he chaired the Committee on Trades and Manufactures. During his second term he gained seats on the Committees on Banks and on Penal Institutions. Chahoon retired from electoral politics in 1900 but remained politically active until his death. He served for twenty years on the Clinton County board of supervisors, for part of that time as chair, and as a leader of the county Republican Party and a delegate to national party conventions. His career paralleled that of the rising class of Republican businessmen who achieved wealth, political office, and respectability during the Gilded Age.

Chahoon's enjoyment of life in the Adirondack Mountains and his involvement in that area's industrial development led him to publish three articles, on the Hudson River's water supply and on the birds and the bears of the Adirondacks. Following the death of his wife on 27 November 1887, Chahoon in 1898 married Christiana Van Allen. She died on 13 August 1903. George Chahoon died in Au Sable Forks, Clinton County, New York, on 29 July 1934 and was buried in Fairview Cemetery in that town.

Biographies in *Daily Richmond Whig*, 5 May 1868, and Edgar L. Murlin, *The New York Red Book: An Illustrated Legislative Manual* . . . (1897), ix (por.), 140 (with birth date); birth and death dates on gravestone; first marriage in Au Sable Forks Methodist Episcopal Church Records, Au Sable Forks, Clinton Co., N.Y.; publications include "Water-Supply of Rivers," *Popular Science Monthly* 13 (July 1878): 288–292, "The Birds of the Adirondacks," *Popular Science Monthly* 57 (May 1900): 40–47, and "The Adirondack Black Bear," *Forest, Fish, and Game Commission, State of New York, Report, 1901* (1902), 243–249; *Richmond Whig*, 28 Apr. 1865; *Richmond Daily Dispatch*, 8 May, 27 July 1867, 4, 5, 7 May 1868, 30 Apr., 28 Oct. 1870; *Richmond Mayoralty Case* (1870) (19 Grattan), *Virginia Reports*, 60:673–719; *Chahoon* v. *Commonwealth* (1871) (20 Grattan), *Virginia Reports*, 61:733–799, and (21 Grattan), *Virginia Reports*, 62:822–845; pardon recorded in Secretary of the Commonwealth, Executive Journal, 16 Dec. 1871, RG 13, LVA; George L. Christian, *The Capitol Disaster: A Chapter of Reconstruction in Virginia* (1915), 11–12; Louis Bernard Cei, "Law Enforcement in Richmond: A History of Police-Community Relations, 1737–1974" (Ph.D. diss., Florida State University, 1975), 72–82; Michael B. Chesson, *Richmond after the War, 1865–1890* (1981), 96, 104–114, 227; obituaries in *New York Times*, *Plattsburgh Daily Press* (por.), and *Richmond News Leader*, all 30 July 1934; obituary and account of funeral in *Plattsburgh Daily Republican*, 30 July, 1 Aug. 1934.

MICHAEL B. CHESSON

CHALMERS, Anna Maria Campbell Hickman Otis Mead (23 July 1809–8 December 1891), writer and educator, was born in Detroit, Michigan, and was the daughter of Harris H. Hickman, an attorney and native of Alexandria, and Ann Binney Hull Hickman, whose father was then governor of the territory. Anna Hickman's father died when she was about fifteen, and her mother took the family back to her native Massachusetts. She received an excellent private education in Georgia, where an aunt resided, and in Massachusetts, including study with William Bentley Fowle at Boston's first high school for girls.

In February 1830, in Newton, Massachusetts, Hickman married George Alexander Otis, a Boston attorney. He died of consumption (probably tuberculosis) on 18 June 1831. They had one child, George Alexander Otis, who in 1853 assisted in founding the *Virginia Medical and Surgical Journal* and later compiled the three volumes on Civil War surgery in the highly respected *Medical and Surgical History of the War of the Rebellion* (1870–1883). After a second sojourn in Georgia, Anna Otis returned to Newton and lived with her mother while writing children's books for the American Sunday School Union, of Philadelphia. In keeping with the fashion of the times, her name did not appear on the title pages. The volumes varied in length from about 35 to about 100 pages and included *The Good Resolution* (1834), *The Good Son* (1834), *The First Falsehood* (1835), *The Reformed Family* (1835), and *The Autumn Walk* (1836). Otis may also have written one entitled *The Evening Walk*.

On 25 February 1836, in Newton, Otis married a Virginia clergyman, Zacharia Mead, a graduate of Yale University and the Protestant Episcopal Theological Seminary in Virginia, who then joined the staff of Grace Episcopal Church in Boston. They had two sons and one daughter. Late in 1837 the family moved to Virginia, where he became an assistant clergyman at Monumental, Saint James's, and Saint John's Episcopal Churches in Richmond and also editor of the *Southern Churchman*. Zacharia Mead died, also of consumption, on 27 November 1840. For the next several months, until the proprietors appointed a new editor, Anna Mead, who had assisted her husband, took part in editing the *Southern Churchman*.

On 4 October 1841, with the help of several clergymen, she opened a Richmond boarding and day school for girls. For twelve years, even through the death of her only daughter in December 1843, she was principal of Mrs. Mead's School, one of the larger and better private schools in the city. She initially employed one other female teacher and two male teachers, but the success of the school was such that within two years she added other members to the faculty and in 1843 began the session with more than 130 pupils. The curriculum was demanding, comparable to the best available in academies for the sons of prominent Virginia families. The offerings included ancient and modern languages, astronomy, chemistry, history, literature, mathematics, music, philosophy, and theology, specifically including poetry with Christian messages. Mead expected her students to attend Episcopal services with her unless their parents provided a proper escort to another church.

Mead continued to write and in 1842 published a collection of short works of fiction and devotion, *A Token of Affection, or, Sketches by a Christian's Way-Side*, her first book that directly identified her as author. She added short tributes to a friend and an aunt when she published a second edition four years later with the shorter title *Sketches by a Christian's Way-Side*. Over the years Mead contributed numerous short articles to such periodicals as the *Boston Home Journal*, the *New York Churchman*, the *New York Tribune*, and the *Southern Literary Messenger*.

In October 1853, her three sons having grown to maturity, Mead no longer needed the income from the school and relinquished it to one of her former faculty members. After an extended period traveling and also visiting her family in Georgia and Massachusetts, she returned to Richmond and on 3 January 1856 married David Chalmers, a widower then age fifty-five, and moved to his Halifax County plantation, where she lived for almost twenty years. Late in 1860 she completed *Brown and Arthur: An Episode from "Tom Brown's School Days,"* containing six chapters from the second part of Thomas

Hughes's popular 1857 novel *Tom Brown's School Days*, one of the first books in the genre of stories about boys growing up and coming of age at school. Selecting episodes that she believed contained lessons equally valuable for girls, Chalmers published her edition in Richmond early in 1861.

She moved temporarily to New York in 1863, and the following year her youngest son, a lieutenant in the Confederate army, was killed in action in Georgia. After the Civil War, Chalmers raised money and established Sunday schools for Halifax County freedpeople and for several years taught them. In 1877 she formed the Southern Churchman Cot fund to support a cot, or bed, for poor children at Retreat for the Sick, a Richmond hospital.

After her third husband died on 5 March 1875, Chalmers lived with her eldest son in Washington, D.C., until his death early in 1881. Thereafter she resided in Albemarle County with her sole surviving son, Edward Campbell Mead, who later wrote a book-length memoir of her life. Anna Maria Campbell Hickman Otis Mead Chalmers died there on 8 December 1891 and was buried near the bodies of her daughter, third son, and second husband in Richmond's Shockoe Cemetery.

Edward C. Mead, *A Biographical Sketch: Anna Maria Mead Chalmers, In Memoriam* (1893), with birth date, letters, selected writings, memorials, and frontispiece por.; *Vital Records of Newton, Massachusetts, to the Year 1850* (1905), 349; first and second marriages in *Boston Columbian Centinel*, 13 Feb. 1830, 27 Feb. 1836; third marriage in BVS Marriage Register, Richmond City; numerous references in *Southern Churchman* (1837–1853); *Mrs. Mead's School. Catalogue of the Teachers and Pupils for the Scholastic Year, 1845–6* (1846); death notices in *Richmond State*, 9 Dec. 1891, *Richmond Times*, 10 Dec. 1891, and *Southern Churchman*, 17 Dec. 1891; obituary in *Richmond Dispatch*, 9 Dec. 1891.

RENEE SAVITS

CHALONER, John Armstrong (10 October 1862–1 June 1935), celebrity and writer, was born in New York City and was the son of Margaret Astor Ward Chanler and John Winthrop Chanler, a lawyer and three-term congressman. Both parents had died by 1877. Related to the Astors, Livingstons, and Stuyvesants, Chanler was closely connected to the social and economic elite of New York. After attending a military academy and studying in England, he received bachelor's and master's degrees from Columbia University in 1883 and 1884, respectively, and was admitted to the New York bar. He traveled extensively at home and abroad before settling in Paris, where he attended the Collège de France, the Ecole Libre des Sciences Politiques, and the Sorbonne. By 1888, Archie Chanler, as he was called, had a reported personal fortune of $4 million and seemed destined to live on equal terms with the nation's most powerful industrialists and politicians.

Often at odds with his family, Chanler legally changed his name to its original historical spelling, Chaloner, on 1 June 1908. Conflicts arose from both his personal and business behavior. His family disapproved of his marriage on 14 June 1888 to Amélie Louise Rives, of Albemarle County, author of *The Quick or the Dead? A Study* (1888), a daring novel in which the leading male character bore a clear resemblance to Chaloner. The marriage was unsuccessful from the beginning, and he eventually agreed to her obtaining a divorce under the lenient laws of South Dakota in September 1895. The Chanlers were shocked when he continued to reside near his former wife's Albemarle County property on an estate he enlarged and named the Merry Mills, provided her with an annual sum, and became friendly with her and her second husband. Newspapers widely reported these events, and his mortified brother, Robert Winthrop Chanler, is supposed to have characterized him as "looney."

Entering a partnership in North Carolina with another of his brothers, Chaloner was a founder of the town of Roanoke Rapids, where he built an electric power-generating station and a cotton mill. He provoked his brothers when he proposed that girls working at the mill receive education at company expense, as if he cared nothing about profits. Late in 1896 Chaloner announced his experiments with what he termed the "X-Faculty." Convinced that he was an experimental psychologist of great insight, he stated that he had discovered a new sense and that while he was in a trance and taking dictation from the faculty, it had given him a tip that netted him a tidy profit in the stock market. The faculty also predicted that his brown eyes would turn gray, erroneously led him to believe that he could carry hot coals in his hands without harm, informed him that he resembled the emperor Napoléon I, and cautioned him that with danger lurking everywhere, he should sleep with a pistol.

The family regarded those assertions as proof that Chaloner had become incurably insane and enticed him to return to New York, where they had him certified as a lunatic and on 13 March 1897 committed him involuntarily to the Bloomingdale Hospital, in White Plains. Vehemently disagreeing with his diagnosis, Chaloner regarded his family's actions as the product of a sinister desire to seize his estate and silence him about his radical experiments. He composed bitter sonnets on that and related themes while in the asylum. On 12 June 1899 a New York court declared him insane and ruled that he be permanently institutionalized.

In November 1900 Chaloner escaped and entered a private clinic, where doctors declared him competent to function in society. He began plotting a strategy to challenge the New York verdict and lunacy laws in general. His case became a cause célèbre for the nation's leading psychologists. Opponents of custodial insane asylums declared that Chaloner's behavior was rational and that his experiments were compatible with recent research into parapsychology and the subconscious. Professional psychiatrists at Bloomingdale and elsewhere declared that Chaloner suffered from a textbook case of paranoia and that little could be done to treat his systematic delusional insanity other than permanent involuntary commitment at Bloomingdale. Although a Virginia court in 1901 declared him sane, a verdict in which a North Carolina court later concurred, in New York he was still legally insane and required involuntary institutionalization.

Between 1906 and his death Chaloner published about two dozen books, largely at his own expense, that focused on his experiences at Bloomingdale Hospital, his subsequent legal battles, and the X-Faculty. The books included the sonnets composed in the asylum and plays and sonnets that the X-Faculty dictated to him, as well as legal briefs, favorable newspaper articles about his case, reviews of his other books, and his comments on the reviews, often in verse. Chaloner cast himself as a crusader against the tyranny of psychiatric power, especially in *The Lunacy Law of the World* (1906). He was far too unstable to lead a reform campaign effectively, and other men, such as Clifford Whittingham Beers, organized the reform movement that led to the creation in 1909 of the National Committee for Mental Hygiene.

Chaloner's public lectures on the X-Faculty and on his resemblance to Napoléon Bonaparte often included ranting against psychiatry and the Chanler family. He declared that through the medium of the X-Faculty he had received messages from beyond the grave from P. T. Barnum, Julia Ward Howe, Abraham Lincoln, Theodore Roosevelt, William Shakespeare, and George Washington, among others. Chaloner asserted, on no less an authority than William James, that he was the first scientific medium.

Chaloner attracted more public notice in 1909 when during a struggle he accidentally shot and killed a neighbor, John Gillard, whose wife had sought refuge at the Merry Mills after a violent domestic quarrel. A coroner's jury acquitted him of responsibility, but Chaloner suffered a nervous breakdown and required medical attention. Eventually, however, he paid for the victim's funeral and gravestone, hung a picture of Gillard and his family in his dining room, and with a silver circle marked the spot on the floor where Gillard's head had fallen.

Journalists closely followed Chaloner's colorful career and his conflicts with the Chanler family. In the summer of 1910 his brother Robert Winthrop Chanler married the opera singer Lina Cavalieri and signed over control of nearly all of his property to her. The marriage broke down almost immediately, and they obtained a divorce at the beginning of January 1912. In September 1910, after the embarrassing details about the marriage settlement became public, Chaloner wired his brother, "Who's looney now?" The phrase, which may have already had some popular currency, captured the public imagination and was ever after credited to Chaloner. The line was popularized in movie titles and written into burlesque sketches. Chaloner later pretended that a newspaper writer had coined the phrase, but he reveled in the notoriety and titled one of his many books *The Swan-Song of "Who's Looney Now?"*

After years of discord the family reconciled in 1919 and offered no opposition when Chaloner successfully petitioned a New York court to certify him as sane in that state. Yet to people in the North Carolina mill town where he owned property and the Virginia countryside where he resided, Chaloner remained more than an eccentric curiosity. His neighbors in Virginia called him "the General," and he often paid their bills and opened his house to them. Concerned throughout his life with education, he presented both the University of North Carolina and the University of Virginia with large sums of money. During the winter of 1890–1891 he established the Paris Prize Fund (after 1917 the John Armstrong Chaloner Paris Prize Foundation), which enabled select students to study art abroad. He augmented a history prize established by his father at Columbia University and endowed a research fellowship at the Mackay School of Mines, a division of the engineering school at the University of Nevada, in Reno. In his later years Chaloner developed a special interest in rural depopulation. Convinced that farmers left the countryside because it lacked amusement and entertainment, he opened a movie theater in 1920 at the Merry Mills to show educational and feature films and later operated a dance pavilion and public pool there as well.

John Armstrong Chaloner died of cancer in the University of Virginia Hospital in Charlottesville early on the morning of 1 June 1935. He was buried near his Albemarle County residence in the graveyard of Grace Episcopal Church, of which he had been a longtime trustee. Nearly every obituary summed up his life with the single phrase that seemed both to characterize his existence and reflect the controversies in which he was involved: "Who's looney now?"

Birth date in Chaloner, *The Swan-Song of "Who's Looney Now?"* Hippodrome ed. (1914), 184, 294; A. B. Tunis, ed., *Press Reference Book of Prominent Virginians, Dedicated to the Fourth Estate* (1916), 63–65 (por.); J. Bryan III, "Johnny Jackanapes, the Merry-Andrew of the Merry Mills: A Brief Biography of John Armstrong Chaloner," *VMHB* 73 (1965): 3–21 (por. facing 3 and variant birth date of 11 Oct. 1862 on 4); Lately Thomas, *A Pride of Lions: The Astor Orphans, The Chanler Chronicle* (1971), including several pors.; Carole Haber, "Who's Looney Now? The Insanity Case of John Armstrong Chaloner," *Bulletin of the History of Medicine* 60 (1986): 177–193; Roderick R. Ingram, "John Armstrong Chaloner's 'Movies for the Farmers,'" *Magazine of Albemarle County History* 53 (1995): 58–69; John Armstrong Chaloner Papers, Duke and UVA; J. Bryan Papers concerning John Armstrong Chaloner, including draft MS and research notes, VHS; Albemarle Co. Marriage License; *New York Times*, 2 June 1908; *Richmond Times-Dispatch*, 22 Nov. 1908, 11 Sept. 1910; *Washington Post*, 11 Sept. 1910; estate and bequests described in *Richmond Times-Dispatch*, 27 Nov. 1935; obituaries in *Charlottesville Daily Progress* and *Richmond News Leader*, both 1 June 1935, *New York Times* and *Richmond Times-Dispatch*, both 2 June 1935, and *Washington Post*, 2, 3 June 1935.

CAROLE HABER

CHAMBERLAINE, William (1 March 1871–9 June 1925), army officer, was born probably in Norfolk, the residence of his parents, Matilda Hughes Dillard Chamberlaine and William Wilson Chamberlaine, a former Confederate artillery officer and a banker and railroad executive in postwar Norfolk. Educated at Norfolk Academy between 1882 and 1888, Chamberlaine entered the United States Military Academy at West Point in 1888 and graduated four years later, eighteenth in a class of sixty-two. Commissioned a second lieutenant in the artillery to date from 11 June 1892, he was posted for one year to coastal garrison duty at Fort Adams, in Rhode Island, and for the following year at Fort Hamilton, in New York. In Washington, D.C., on 11 April 1894 Chamberlaine married Margaret Smith, daughter of a career artillery officer. They had no children.

In 1896 Chamberlaine graduated with honors from the artillery school at Fort Monroe, where he remained for two more years taking an advanced course and serving as an instructor. Promoted to first lieutenant on 2 March 1899, he was assigned for several months to the coastal artillery at Mobile, Alabama, and to Fort Sam Houston, in San Antonio, Texas. He then taught chemistry and electricity at West Point from 1899 to 1901, and on 1 July of the latter year he was promoted to captain in the artillery. Chamberlaine was assistant to the chief of artillery and stationed in Washington, D.C., from 1901 to 1903 and commanded a company of coast artillery from 1903 to 1906. From 1906 to 1910 he was assigned to the general staff and was stationed first in San Francisco and later in the Philippines. After returning to the United States, Chamberlaine was promoted to major on 10 December 1909. He was director of the department of artillery in the Coast Artillery School at Fort Monroe from September 1911 through August 1913 and while there published *Coast Artillery War Game* (1912). This widely used training book, designed to teach strategies employed in engagements between ships and seacoast forts, was reprinted in revised editions in 1913, 1914, 1916, and 1922. He was promoted to lieutenant colonel on 1 July 1916.

After the United States entered World War I, Chamberlaine organized the 6th Coast Artillery Corps in July 1917 and was promoted to colonel on a temporary basis on 5 August of that year. Several days later he sailed with his regiment to France. Assigned to the French Heavy Artillery Headquarters to study its organization and operation, Chamberlaine served in combat with the French during the winter of 1917–1918 and on 8 February 1918 accepted promotion (dated 17 December 1917) to brigadier general in the National Army, comprising primarily conscripted soldiers and those who had enlisted only for the duration of the war. In June 1918, as chief of artillery of the 2d Division, he participated in the Belleau Woods campaign that stopped the German advance on Paris. Following his success in that battle, Chamberlaine received command of the Railway Artillery, American Expeditionary Force, which provided important mobile firepower during the Saint-Mihiel and Meuse-Argonne campaigns by deploying large artillery pieces mounted on railway cars and served by the coast artillery. He received the Distinguished Service Medal and the French Croix de Guerre with Palm and was named an officer of the French Legion of Honor. On 10 September 1919 he was honorably discharged from the National Army.

Chamberlaine's rank as colonel in the Coast Artillery Corps was made permanent on 9 January 1919. He served as commanding officer of the Coast Artillery Training Center at Fort Monroe from 31 January to 9 September of that year and was then sent to Hawaii, where as chief of staff of that department he oversaw improvement of coastal artillery defenses. At his request, having completed thirty years of service, Chamberlaine retired effective 31 December 1922. He was particularly fond of France and visited that country several times after he retired. William Chamberlaine died there early in the morning of 9 June 1925 following a late-night taxicab collision in Paris. He was wearing his Legion of Honor decoration at the time. Chamberlaine's body was returned to the United States for burial in Arlington National Cemetery.

Biography in *NCAB*, 20:76, with birth date and variant 8 June 1925 death date (por. facing 77); Superior Court of the District of Columbia Marriage License; Arthur Kyle Davis, ed., *Virginians of Distinguished Service of the World War* (1923), 28; Robert Arthur, *The Coast Artillery School, 1824–1927* (1928), 90, 96, 113; obituaries in *New York Times*, 9 (indicating death took place very early on that date), 21 June 1925, *Norfolk Ledger-Dispatch*, 9 June 1925, and *Norfolk Virginian-Pilot and the Norfolk Landmark* (por.) and *Washington Post*, both 10 June 1925.

ROGER E. CHRISTMAN

CHAMBERLAINE, William Wilson (16 October 1836–19 October 1923), Confederate army officer and railroad executive, the son of Richard Henry Chamberlaine and Mary Eliza Wilson Chamberlaine, was born in Norfolk, where his father's family had resided for several generations. After attending Norfolk Military Academy from 1848 until 1852, he entered Hampden-Sydney College in 1852 but remained for only one year. About 1855 he became a clerk at the Norfolk bank of which his father was an officer.

Chamberlaine joined a volunteer company formed in Norfolk following John Brown's 1859 raid on Harpers Ferry and was elected a corporal. When word reached Norfolk in April 1861 that Virginia had seceded, he and his company went on duty guarding the port. Chamberlaine was elected first lieutenant and stationed at nearby Craney Island, from which the following spring he witnessed the battle between the *Monitor* and the *Virginia* (formerly the *Merrimack*). On 18 May 1862 he became second lieutenant in Company G of the 6th Regiment Virginia Infantry. Chamberlaine took part in skirmishes near Richmond and the battle on Malvern Hill. Near Antietam Creek in Maryland on 17 September 1862 he helped to activate a defective cannon and used it to delay a Union advance.

During a bombardment he was struck in the face. Bruised and bleeding, his nose fractured, Chamberlaine tended his wounds in Sharpsburg, spent the next day in a hospital, and that afternoon crossed the Potomac River. Assigned to the 2d Corps as adjutant to the chief of artillery in February 1863, he saw action at Chancellorsville. During the summer Chamberlaine was attached to the 3d Corps and was engaged at Gettysburg. Late in December 1863 he was promoted to captain and served as adjutant to the corps's artillery commander. He fought at Bristow Station, Mine Run, the Wilderness, Spotsylvania Court House, and Petersburg and served until the end of the war.

In 1864 Chamberlaine was out of action for about a month recovering from the bite of a water moccasin, and he took a brief leave of absence to marry Matilda Hughes Dillard in Franklin County on 20 April of that year. They had met early in the war while he was chasing slackers in that county. They had two daughters and one son, William Chamberlaine, a brigadier general of coast artillery during World War I.

Chamberlaine returned to Norfolk after the Civil War and in 1867 became cashier of the Citizens Bank, of which his father was then a director and later president. Chamberlaine resigned in 1877 to become secretary and treasurer of the Seaboard and Roanoke Railroad, which operated an eighty-mile line from Portsmouth to Weldon, North Carolina. Five years later the railroad began acquiring other lines or controlling interest in other lines, leading to the formation by 1889 of the Seaboard Air-Line, which also ran a steamship line with regular service between Norfolk and Baltimore. By 1894 it had expanded to become the Seaboard Air Line System and operated passenger and freight service over about 925 miles of track from Virginia to Georgia. Chamberlaine was comptroller of the Seaboard from 1894 to 1898 and in 1894 was elected to the boards of two of its affiliates, the Carolina Central Railroad and the Raleigh and Augusta Air-line Railroad. He also served as secretary of the affiliated Raleigh and Gaston Railroad in 1898 and 1899. After a new controlling interest reorganized the Seaboard Air Line System in April 1900 with two other railroads into a new corporate umbrella entity called the Seaboard Air Line Railway, Chamberlaine continued to serve as secretary of the Seaboard and Roanoke Railroad, which was his main responsibility during the five years before he retired about 1904.

Chamberlaine was also treasurer and one of the commissioners for the Norfolk City Water Department, a founder in 1884 of the Norfolk Electric Light Company, first president in 1886 of the Savings Bank of Norfolk, and a board member of at least one insurance company. An Episcopalian and a member in good standing of Norfolk's business elite, Chamberlaine moved his residence about 1900 from a prestigious older neighborhood to the fashionable new suburb of Ghent.

In 1910 or 1911 Chamberlaine moved to Washington, D.C. In 1912 he published *Memoirs of the Civil War between the Northern and Southern Sections of the United States of America, 1861 to 1865*. The modest recounting of his battlefield experiences, written in businesslike and unromantic prose, reveals him to be a bit of a dandy. He offered few comments on the causes or consequences of the Civil War and indulged in no glorification of himself or his fellow officers. A member of one of the Confederate veterans organizations in Norfolk, Chamberlaine remained active after his retirement and in 1921 was elected commander of the District of Columbia's Brigade of Confederate Veterans with the honorary rank of brigadier general. His wife died on 22 September 1922. William Wilson Chamberlaine died in Washington, D.C., on 19 October 1923 and was buried in Glenwood Cemetery in the capital.

Chamberlaine, *Memoirs of the Civil War between the Northern and Southern Sections of the United States of America, 1861 to 1865* (1912), frontispiece por.; biographies in Clement A. Evans, ed., *Confederate Military History* (1899), 3:799–800 (with birth date and variant marriage date of 21 Apr. 1864), Henry and Spofford, *Eminent Men*, 420–421 (with birth date), and *NCAB*, 42:372–373; Franklin Co. Marriage Register; Compiled Service Records; Michael A. Cavanaugh, *6th Virginia Infantry* (1988), esp. 71, 87; corporate railroad offices in annual editions of Henry V. Poor, comp., *Manual of the Railroads of the United States* (1878–1905); obituaries in *Norfolk Ledger-Dispatch*, *Norfolk Virginian-Pilot and Norfolk Landmark* (por.), and *Washington Post*, all 20 Oct. 1923; memorial in *Confederate Veteran* 32 (1924): 29.

PETER C. STEWART

CHAMBERLAYNE, Churchill Gibson (23 December 1876–3 April 1939), educator and historian, was born in Richmond and was the son of John Hampden Chamberlayne, a former Confederate artillery officer and publisher of the *Richmond State* newspaper, and Mary Walker Gibson Chamberlayne, whose brother Robert Atkinson Gibson became bishop of the Episcopal Diocese of Virginia. His father died when Chamberlayne was five. An adept student, Chamberlayne matriculated at McCabe's University School, in Petersburg, and in 1901 received a B.A. from the University of Virginia, which in 1931 elected him to membership in Phi Beta Kappa. Continuing his studies in Alexandria at the Protestant Episcopal Theological Seminary in Virginia (popularly known as the Virginia Theological Seminary), Chamberlayne graduated in 1904 with a bachelor of divinity degree. He was ordained a deacon in the Episcopal Church in that year and a priest in 1914. From 1904 to 1906 he attended the University of Halle-Wittenberg (later Martin Luther University Halle-Wittenberg), in Germany, where he earned an M.A. and Ph.D. and learned to speak fluent German, a language he later taught.

Returning to Virginia, Chamberlayne served as a missionary in Albemarle County and as chaplain to Episcopal students at the University of Virginia from 1906 until 1907 and then became teacher and chaplain at a private school for boys in Baltimore for the next four years. On 22 June 1911 he married Elizabeth Breckinridge Bolling, of Bedford County. They had two sons. Three months after his marriage, Chamberlayne opened the Chamberlayne School for Boys, in Richmond. Established on the city's western outskirts, the school began with sixteen students and two buildings, one the headmaster's residence and dining hall and the other providing classrooms, a study hall, and a gymnasium. A nearby vacant block served as the athletic field. Catering to the children of Richmond's business and political elite, the school offered classical, mathematical, scientific, technical, and general education. By the 1913–1914 academic term the number of students had more than tripled and instruction was divided into upper and lower schools, with a middle school added in 1938. In the autumn of 1914 the school, incorporated as the Chamberlayne Country School, Inc., moved far beyond the city limits to the Westhampton section of Henrico County.

In 1920 the Episcopal Church incorporated the Church Schools in the Diocese of Virginia to create a diocesan school system and that year purchased the Chamberlayne School for $75,000 and, at Chamberlayne's request, renamed it Saint Christopher's School to conform with the designations of its sister institutions in Charlottesville and Richmond. Known by his students simply as "Doctor," Chamberlayne continued to lead the school as headmaster for the remainder of his life. A devotee of the Lost Cause, he shepherded his students on daylong tours of the nearby Richmond and Petersburg Civil War battlefields, routinely awarded books on Civil War topics as prizes for academic achievement, and assigned Margaret Mitchell's *Gone with the Wind* (1936) as outside reading. His curriculum emphasized clear composition, eloquent rhetoric, and mental discipline. Valuing both the acquisition of knowledge and the building of character, Chamberlayne reminded his students on the first day of examinations that "we cannot all be scholars, but we can all be gentlemen." To recognize his achievements in education, Hampden-Sydney College awarded him an honorary LL.D. in 1926.

Along with education Chamberlayne's passion was historical research, especially in Anglican and Episcopal Church history. He transcribed for publication the vestry books of Bristol Parish, in Charles City, Dinwiddie, Henrico, and Prince George Counties (1898), Christ Church Parish, in Middlesex County (1927), Kingston Parish, in Gloucester (later Mathews) County (1929), Stratton Major Parish, in King and Queen and New Kent Counties (1931), Petsworth Parish, in Gloucester County (1933), Blisland Parish, in James City, New Kent, and York Counties (1935), Saint Peter's Parish, in James City and New Kent Counties (1937), and Saint Paul's Parish, in Hanover and New Kent Counties (1940). Chamberlayne published his father's wartime correspondence in a collection entitled *Ham Chamberlayne—Virginian: Letters and Papers of an Artillery Officer in the War for Southern*

Independence, 1861–1865 (1932) and also during the 1930s transcribed several colonial and Civil War documents that appeared in the *Virginia Magazine of History and Biography* and the *William and Mary Quarterly*.

During the last years of his life he worked to restore Saint Peter's Church, in New Kent County, and from 1931 until 1939 was a member of the executive committee of the Virginia Historical Society. Early in 1939 Churchill Gibson Chamberlayne became seriously ill with leukemia and died at his home at Saint Christopher's School on 3 April 1939. He was buried in the cemetery at Emmanuel Episcopal Church, in Henrico County.

De Witt Hankins, *The First Fifty Years: A History of St. Christopher's School, 1911–1961* (1961), with frontispiece por. and quotation on 1; BVS Birth Register, Richmond City (name recorded as Church Chamberlayne); Chamberlayne correspondence, manuscripts, and research notes in Churchill Gibson Chamberlayne Papers, Chamberlayne Family Papers, Protestant Episcopal Church in Virginia Papers, and other collections, VHS; other published works include memorial sermon for uncle Robert Atkinson Gibson in *The Shrine of the Transfiguration, Orkney Springs, Virginia* (1925), 23–33; BVS Marriage Register, Bedford Co.; BVS Death Certificate, Henrico Co. (variant birthplace of Petersburg); obituaries and editorial tributes in *Richmond News Leader*, 3 Apr. 1939, and *Richmond Times-Dispatch*, 4 Apr. 1939; memorials in Saint Christopher's School *Pine Needle*, 28 Apr. 1939.

ROBERT F. STROHM

CHAMBERLAYNE, John Hampden (2 June 1838–18 February 1882), journalist, was born in Richmond and was the son of Martha Burwell Dabney Chamberlayne and Lewis Webb Chamberlayne, a physician and founder of the medical school that became the Medical College of Virginia. Of the thirteen children in the family, he was one of only three not born deaf and one of only four to live to adulthood. His younger sister Lucy Parke Chamberlayne married the writer George William Bagby and became a noted Richmond civic leader.

After receiving his early education at home and at a private school in Richmond, Chamberlayne attended Hanover Academy for two sessions beginning in 1853. He entered the University of Virginia in 1855 and received an M.A. three years later. Chamberlayne taught one session at Hanover Academy before beginning

to read law in Richmond with Gustavus Adolphus Myers. Licensed on 16 March 1860, Chamberlayne practiced law in the city of Richmond and in Hanover and Henrico Counties until the beginning of the Civil War.

A supporter of secession, Chamberlayne enlisted on 21 April 1861 as a private in the 21st Regiment Virginia Volunteers. His company, composed of elite members of Richmond society, later became Company F, 21st Regiment Virginia Infantry. Chamberlayne resigned after receiving appointment as a lieutenant in the Provisional Army of Virginia, but he later rejoined his company and served with it during the Cheat Mountain campaign. On 4 March 1862 he transferred to Captain Cayce's Company (Purcell Artillery) and on 5 June was appointed a first lieutenant in the Confederate army and became adjutant to Colonel Reuben Lindsay Walker, chief of artillery under Major General Ambrose Powell Hill. Chamberlayne earned praise for his service during the remainder of the year in the Seven Days' campaign and at Cedar Run, Second Manassas (Bull Run), Sharpsburg (Antietam), and Fredericksburg. In January 1863 he took command of Crenshaw's Battery, Virginia Light Artillery, and ably directed it at the Battle of Chancellorsville. Chamberlayne was captured at Emmitsburg, Maryland, late in June of that year while on detached duty confiscating horses. Before being exchanged on 10 March 1864, he spent time in several prisoner-of-war camps in Delaware, Maryland, and Ohio. Promoted to captain on 10 August 1864 to date from 4 August, he assumed command of Davidson's Battery (renamed Chamberlayne's Company) and led it through the siege of Petersburg and until the end of the war.

Chamberlayne did not surrender at Appomattox Court House in April 1865 and instead joined General Joseph Eggleston Johnston's army in North Carolina. Initially he refused to surrender when Johnston capitulated, but he signed a parole on 12 May and spent the summer at an uncle's residence in Hinds County, Mississippi. Chamberlayne returned to Virginia penniless in August 1865 and attempted to support his family as a farmer in Louisa County. He moved back to Richmond early in 1867 and worked in a law office until a physical and nervous breakdown required him to be admitted to the Western Lunatic Asylum, in Staunton.

In May 1868, following his discharge from the hospital, Chamberlayne found work as a clerk for the Virginia and Tennessee Railroad, at Central Depot (later Radford). Late in 1869 he joined the editorial staff working under the future governor William Evelyn Cameron at the Democratic *Petersburg Daily Index*. Chamberlayne became co-publisher and co-editor of the newspaper early in November 1870. He and his partner sold the *Index* in July 1873, and in November of that year Chamberlayne succeeded James Barron Hope as editor of the *Norfolk Virginian*. On 18 March 1876 Chamberlayne purchased the *Richmond Evening Journal* and two days later renamed it the *Richmond State*, which he edited until his death.

While editing the *Petersburg Index* Chamberlayne became involved in politics. An early supporter of William Mahone, he aligned himself with the former Confederate general at the 1873 Democratic State Convention. While working in Norfolk, Chamberlayne earned a reputation as an effective and eloquent political speaker and used his journalistic and oratorical skills to help the Democratic candidate, John Goode, defeat the Republican James Henry Platt in the 1874 congressional election. Chamberlayne won election in 1879 to one of four seats in the House of Delegates from the city of Richmond. By then a Funder who supported payment of the state's public debt in full and an opponent of Mahone's Readjusters, he was a member of the Committees on Federal Relations and Resolutions, on the Library, on Propositions and Grievances, and on Public Property. Chamberlayne declined to seek reelection in 1881 but continued to oppose Mahone, who allied himself with African American voters and eventually became a Republican.

Chamberlayne employed his speaking skills in fields other than politics. In an address delivered on 23 June 1875 to a literary society at Randolph-Macon College and published as *Public Spirit*, he created a sensation when he frankly recognized the defects and consequences of slavery and considered the possibilities of the post–Civil War South. His popular address on Robert Edward Lee's character, delivered in Richmond on 19 January 1876, was reprinted several times. At least two speeches, at the University of Virginia in 1880 and at a reunion of Confederate veterans in Maryland in 1881, emphasized reconciliation between North and South. After the disputed presidential election of 1876, Chamberlayne publicly called for acquiescence in Rutherford Birchard Hayes's victory.

Although later characterized as an elitist and white supremacist, Chamberlayne was a mentor of George Freeman Bragg, an aspiring African American journalist who founded the *Petersburg Lancet*. Not long before his death, Chamberlayne used the *State* to raise several thousand dollars to aid the widows and children of dozens of men, most of them black, who had been killed in an explosion at a Chesterfield County coal mine. The editor of the *Richmond Star*, a black newspaper, praised him for his journalistic abilities even though they had been opposed "on all the great political battlefields of the past sixteen years."

On 15 October 1873, in Petersburg, Chamberlayne married Mary Walker Gibson, whose brother Robert Atkinson Gibson became bishop of the Episcopal Diocese of Virginia. They had three daughters and three sons, among them Churchill Gibson Chamberlayne, an educator and historian who edited and in 1932 published a volume of Chamberlayne's Civil War letters. John Hampden Chamberlayne died of pneumonia at his Richmond home on 18 February 1882, prompting an immense public outpouring of grief. The House of Delegates adjourned to attend his funeral at Saint James's Episcopal Church on 20 February, and more than sixty newspapers in Virginia and other states published tributes to his life and career. He was buried in Hollywood Cemetery.

Biography in C. G. Chamberlayne, ed., *Ham Chamberlayne—Virginian: Letters and Papers of an Artillery Officer in the War for Southern Independence, 1861–1865* (1932), including several pors.; birth, marriage, and death dates in Smith-Dabney-Chamberlayne-Bagby family Bible records, LVA; Petersburg Hustings Court Marriage Register; Compiled Service Records; Chamberlayne correspondence and other documents in Bagby Family Papers and John Hampden Chamberlayne Papers, both VHS, and William Mahone Papers, Duke; printed public addresses include *Public Spirit* (1875), "Address on the Character of General R. E. Lee," *SHSP* 3 (1877): 28–37, "Specialized Study," *Educational Journal of Virginia* 8 (1877): 481–490, and *Why Despair?*

(1880); J. Louis Campbell III, "John Hampden Chamberlayne and the Rhetoric of Southern Histories," *Southern Communication Journal* 58 (1992): 44–54; BVS Death Register, Richmond City; obituaries and accounts of funeral in *Richmond State*, 18, 21 Feb. 1882, *Richmond Daily Dispatch*, 19, 21 Feb. 1882, *Richmond Daily Whig*, 20 Feb. 1882, and *SHSP* 10 (1882): 95; editorial tributes reprinted in *Richmond Daily Dispatch*, 21 Feb. 1882, and *Richmond State*, 21–25, 27, 28 (including quotation from *Richmond Star*) Feb., 1, 3 Mar. 1882.

DALE F. HARTER

CHAMBERLAYNE, Lewis Webb (ca. 9 January 1798–28 January 1854), medical educator, was born at Windsor Shades in King William County and was the son of Edward Pye Chamberlayne and his second wife, Mary Bickerton Webb Chamberlayne. When he was seventeen he enrolled in the medical school at the University of Pennsylvania, from which he received an M.D. in the spring of 1817 after writing a thesis on intermittent fevers, a class of diseases including malaria.

Chamberlayne had begun to practice medicine in Richmond by 1820 and continued until his health failed in 1852. His patients encompassed a wide spectrum of the city's population, including slaves and free blacks, and also a few people from King William County. Like many of his contemporaries, Chamberlayne used calomel, jalap, opium, and other standard therapeutics, but unlike many of them he shunned the practice of bleeding. A generous and benevolent physician, Chamberlayne built a large practice but never amassed a large fortune. At the end of his life he owned a 429-acre plantation in Henrico County and seventeen slaves age sixteen or older.

On 11 April 1820 Chamberlayne married Martha Burwell Dabney. Of their seven daughters and six sons, only four children lived to adulthood. A fourteenth pregnancy ended in stillbirth. One of their sons, John Hampden Chamberlayne, became a leading Virginia journalist after the Civil War, and one of their daughters, Lucy Parke Chamberlayne, married the writer George William Bagby and was a prominent Richmond civic leader during the latter years of the nineteenth century and the early years of the twentieth. Most of their children were born deaf. Chamberlayne lobbied the General Assembly to create a school for deaf students, and in December 1837 he invited the Connecticut and New York educator Frederick Augustus Porter Barnard to appear before the assembly with several of his deaf pupils. Chamberlayne's efforts succeeded when the legislature created a school for the deaf, mute, and blind in 1838. The school opened in Staunton the following year, and Chamberlayne sent one of his sons there and established an award to recognize a deaf student for distinguished scholarship and deportment.

In 1837 Chamberlayne supported a petition that several other Richmond physicians presented to the board of Hampden-Sydney College requesting the establishment of a medical department in Richmond. The medical school, forerunner of the Medical College of Virginia, opened in November 1838 with Chamberlayne as professor of materia medica and therapeutics. He instructed students on the classification of medicines and their physiological effects and practical application. Chamberlayne also lectured at the infirmary and the city almshouse, of which he was resident physician. He served on various committees of the medical department to examine accounts and seek relief for interest payments due on the loan that financed construction of the school's Egyptian Building. Three times Chamberlayne was elected to represent the medical department at the annual meetings of the American Medical Association, but he never attended, not even in 1852 when the convention met in Richmond.

Chamberlayne was a charter member of the Medical Society of Virginia when it was incorporated in 1824, served on the city's common council, and wrote for the popular press. By early in the 1850s poor health limited his activities just as a controversy over faculty appointments erupted at the medical department. Chamberlayne initially opposed a faculty proposal to create a new faculty chair of physiology and medical jurisprudence, but he eventually acquiesced in his colleagues' efforts to assert their authority to select new members of the medical faculty. The relationship between the medical department and Hampden-Sydney College deteriorated during the summer of 1853, complicated by an expectation that Chamberlayne was dying. In February 1854 the medical faculty finally secured from the General Assembly a charter to form the Medical College of Virginia and formally severed ties with Hampden-Sydney College. The separation took place less than a month after Lewis Webb Chamberlayne died of a hemorrhage at his Henrico County residence on 28 January 1854. He was buried at the Brook Hill estate in that county.

Wyndham B. Blanton, "Lewis Webb Chamberlayne (1798–1854)," *Virginia Medical Monthly* 55 (1928): 192–195; Blanton, *Medicine in Virginia in the Nineteenth Century* (1933), 44, 76 (por. facing 51); "Lewis Webb Chamberlayne, 1798–1854, First Professor of Materia Medica and Therapeutics," *Medicovan* 15 (Apr. 1962): 8; birth date of ca. 9 Jan. 1798 and variant death date of 27 Jan. 1854 in C. G. Chamberlayne (grandson), ed., *Ham Chamberlayne—Virginian: Letters and Papers of an Artillery Officer in the War for Southern Independence, 1861–1865* (1932), vii; variant death date of 27 Jan. 1854 in Smith-Dabney-Chamberlayne-Bagby family Bible records, LVA; Census, Henrico Co., 1850 (age fifty-three on 11 Dec. 1850); *Richmond Commercial Compiler*, 14 Apr. 1820; Chamberlayne account book and commonplace book in Chamberlayne Family Papers, VHS; Faculty Minutes, Medical Department of Hampden-Sydney College, and Chamberlayne's lectures described in Leroy Thrasher Student Notebooks, both Tompkins-McCaw; R. Aumon Bass, *History of the Education of the Deaf in Virginia* (1949), 34, 196–199, 223–228; William T. Sanger, *Medical College of Virginia before 1925 and University College of Medicine, 1893–1913* (1973), 5, 10, 12, 17, 18; Henrico Co. Will Book, 14:278–280; BVS Death Register, Henrico Co., recording death at age fifty-six on variant date of 29 Jan. 1854; obituaries in *Richmond Daily Dispatch*, 30 (died "on Saturday morning, 28th inst., at 5 o'clock"), 31 Jan. 1854, *Richmond Daily Whig*, 1 Feb. 1854 ("died at his residence near this city on last Saturday morning"), and *Virginia Medical and Surgical Journal* 2 (1854): 427; obituary and memorial resolutions in *Stethoscope* 4 (1854): 244–245, 312–313.

JODI L. KOSTE

CHAMBERLAYNE, William (d. 2 September 1836), militia general during the War of 1812, was born probably in New Kent County about 1764 or 1765 and was the son of Richard Chamberlayne and Mary Chamberlayne, whose maiden name was probably Wilkinson. He inherited land and status derived in part from the success of his paternal grandfather, who immigrated to Virginia early in the eighteenth century and became a merchant and large-scale landowner. Chamberlayne's obituaries state that he served in the army during the American Revolution, but it is unclear whether this assertion is accurate or

the result of confusion in contemporary records and in subsequent reference works that may have mingled the facts of his life with those of his relative William Byrd Chamberlayne. If he did serve, it was most likely in a militia unit and not in the Continental army.

On 27 July 1784 Chamberlayne married Margaret Wilkinson in Henrico County. They had several children, but because existing family records are fragmentary and few New Kent County records survive, little is known about his family life. Chamberlayne became a justice of the peace in January 1789 and was a member of the vestry of Saint Peter's Parish by 1792. Commissioned a captain in the county militia on 17 May 1793, he was promoted to major on 24 January 1798 and to lieutenant colonel in command of the regiment on 5 June 1807. He then owned more than 2,000 acres of land in New Kent County, and during the 1810s, in a complicated series of transactions involving his wife's father, sister, and several other people, he acquired from his father-in-law a plantation in Henrico County that contained more than 700 acres. By 1817 Chamberlayne owned about 3,300 acres of land in eight parcels in the two counties and paid taxes on more than sixty slaves. He also owned a gristmill in New Kent County for several years, maintained a commercial fishery in season, and was prosperous enough in 1815 to enjoy a four-wheeled carriage worth $300. He gambled with friends, kept a breeding stallion, bred fighting roosters, raised more than twenty varieties of apples as well as cherries and pears in his orchard, and distilled brandy and whiskey for sale.

Elected to the House of Delegates from New Kent County in 1791, Chamberlayne won reelection through 1796. He gradually emerged as a respected member of the House and during his final year held memberships on five of the most influential standing committees, those of Claims, for Courts of Justice, of Privileges and Elections, of Propositions and Grievances, and of Religion. Chamberlayne supported Thomas Jefferson in the presidential election of 1800 and served another one-year term in the House of Delegates during the 1801–1802 session. He won election in 1805 to the first of four consecutive four-year terms in the Senate of Virginia representing the district composed of Charles City, James City, and New Kent Counties. Senate records do not indicate how influential he may have been in that body, but during the sessions of 1815–1816 and 1816–1817 he was a member of the Senate's only standing committee, that of Privileges and Elections.

On 12 December 1807 the General Assembly elected Chamberlayne a brigadier general of militia. In June and July 1813, during the second year of the War of 1812, he commanded Virginia militia between the James and York Rivers. He supervised defensive preparations at Hampton, Jamestown, and Yorktown during the failed British assault against Craney Island, near Portsmouth, on 22 June and the subsequent British capture of Hampton on 25 June. In March 1814 the governor ordered Chamberlayne to Norfolk to command the army units stationed there, but he was unable to take full charge because officers of the United States Army initially declined to serve under a general of militia. Chamberlayne also commanded militia units near Richmond from late in August until the end of November 1814 when Virginians feared a British attack on their capital. Chamberlayne was not personally engaged in any fighting. On 28 April 1815, believing that younger men than he should be entrusted with the responsibility of defending the state in the future, he resigned his commission.

Following his retirement from public life in February 1818 after two decades in the General Assembly, he resumed full-time the life of a gentleman planter. William Chamberlayne died on 2 September 1836 in Henrico County at the residence of Edward C. Mosby, owner of the property that Chamberlayne had acquired from his father-in-law many years earlier and that he had sold to Mosby in 1828. Chamberlayne's body was probably buried on that estate.

Malcolm Hart Harris, comp., *Old New Kent County: Some Account of the Planters, Plantations, and Places in New Kent County* (1977), 1:80, 97, 127–128, 2:725–726; Henrico Co. Marriage Bonds; *Richmond Virginia Gazette, or the American Advertiser*, 7 Aug. 1784; William Chamberlayne Papers, including plantation account books, VHS, with letters printed in part in *WMQ*, 2d ser., 8 (1928): 34–35; militia service documented in militia registers, Department of Military Affairs, RG 46, LVA; William Chamberlayne General Order Book, 1814, Duke; Stuart Lee Butler, *A Guide to Virginia Militia Units in the War of 1812* (1988), 24–25, 248, 296 (subject mistakenly identified as William Byrd Chamberlayne); correspondence in James Barbour and Wilson Cary Nicholas Executive Papers, RG 3, LVA, printed in part in *Calendar of Virginia State Papers*, vol. 10; obituaries in *Richmond Whig and Public Advertiser*, 6 Sept. 1836, and *Richmond Compiler*, 7 Sept. 1836, both giving death in his seventy-second year.

BRENT TARTER

CHAMBERS, Edward R. (23 May 1795–20 March 1872), member of the Convention of 1850–1851 and of the second and third sessions of the Convention of 1861, was born at Flat Rock, the Lunenburg County estate of his father, Edward Chambers, and his first wife, Martha Cousins Chambers. Among his siblings were a twin sister who died at age ten and an elder brother, Henry H. Chambers, who represented Alabama in the United States Senate in 1825 and 1826. Following his mother's death in 1810, Chambers was sent to study at Hampden-Sydney College. He attended the University of North Carolina from the academic year 1813–1814 until 1817 but during the War of 1812 interrupted his studies for thirteen days' service in the summer of 1814 as a private in a cavalry troop. On 20 October 1817 Chambers was admitted to the bar in Mecklenburg County and began building an extensive law library, valued at his death at $400.

On 11 February 1824 Chambers married Lucy Goode Tucker, of Brunswick County. They had at least ten daughters and three sons before her death on 20 May 1854. In 1825 Chambers received from his father the approximately 1,100-acre Flat Rock estate, along with thirty-five slaves, on condition that he pay his father a $1,000 annuity, but two years later financial difficulties and overextension forced Chambers to rescind the transaction. He moved his family to a property owned by his father-in-law near Boydton, in Mecklenburg County. There Chambers practiced law and on 18 May 1835 became commonwealth's attorney. He served as a trustee of Randolph-Macon College beginning in 1842 and as law professor in its newly established law school for the academic year 1842–1843. Chambers fought the college's relocation to Ashland in 1868 and, after refusing to attend board meetings at the new site, was removed as a trustee in 1871.

By 1850 he and his wife owned twelve slaves and a modest sixty-six acres of land valued at $693. In August of that year Chambers, campaigning as a reformer, won election to represent Halifax, Mecklenburg, and Pittsylvania Counties in a convention called to revise the state constitution. As one of only two Whigs among the six delegates elected from his district, Chambers favored a mixed basis of apportionment based on the white population and the value of taxable property, although he paired with another delegate who would have voted differently and therefore did not vote on a key compromise on legislative apportionment on 16 May 1851. He served on the minor Committee on Compensation of Officers and on the important Committee on the Right of Suffrage and Qualifications of Persons to be Elected, which debated the extension of the right to vote to all free white males over the age of twenty-one regardless of property qualifications. Chambers seldom spoke on the convention floor but in April 1851 moved to appoint and became chairman of a special committee to consider a constitutional provision requiring the removal of all free persons of color from the state. The committee reported a draft article mandating the deportation from the United States of most free African Virginians or their reenslavement if they chose to remain. An amended version became the basis of Article IV, Section 19 of the new constitution. Though present, Chambers did not vote on the final approval of the constitution on 31 July 1851.

Late in the spring of 1861 Chambers won election as Mecklenburg County's representative in the second and third sessions of the secession convention in place of his son-in-law Thomas Francis Goode, who had resigned in order to raise a cavalry troop for Confederate service. Chambers took his seat on 14 June 1861 and on that same day signed the Ordinance of Secession. He attended regularly, served on a committee of five to adopt an ordinance against persons disloyal to the commonwealth, and chaired a committee to investigate the expediency of completing a railroad under construction from Clarksville to Keysville.

At the close of the Civil War, Chambers, overestimating his net worth, applied for a presidential pardon, granted on 3 July 1865. Soon thereafter, on 7 September 1865, the governor appointed him judge of the Second Judicial Circuit, comprising the counties of Amelia, Brunswick, Chesterfield, Dinwiddie, Lunenburg, Mecklenburg, Nottoway, Powhatan, and Prince George and the city of Petersburg. Unanimously elected to the position by the House of Delegates on 22 February 1866, Chambers resigned and had been replaced on the bench by 1 December 1869. He returned to law practice in Boydton with his son-in-law Thomas F. Goode and partner William Baskerville Jr. and in November 1870 was elected to a three-year term as commonwealth's attorney beginning on 1 January 1871. After four months' illness Edward R. Chambers died at his home in Boydton on 20 March 1872 and was buried in the Boydton Presbyterian Church Cemetery.

Biographies in S. Bassett French Papers II, W&M, and Rose Chambers Goode McCullough, *Yesterday When It Is Past* (1957), 167–188, including birth, marriage, and death dates transcribed from family Bible and por. facing 166; Chambers correspondence at MOC and VHS; Brunswick Co. Marriage Bonds (bond dated 3 Feb. 1824); Lunenburg Co. Deed Book, 27:86–87, 408–411; *Richmond Enquirer*, 27, 30 Aug., 3, 6 Sept. 1850; *Journal of 1850–1851 Convention*, 173, 175, 177, 227, and appended "Report of the Committee on Free Negroes, &c."; *Supplement, 1850–1851 Convention Debates*, nos. 28, 30; Reese, *Journals and Papers of 1861 Convention*, vol. 1, Journal, 240, 242, 243, 246; Presidential Pardons; Richard Irby, *History of Randolph-Macon College, Virginia* (1898), 91, 168, por. facing 92; estate account in Mecklenburg Co. Will Book, 23:1–2; obituaries in *Boydton Roanoke Valley*, 23, 30 Mar. 1872, *Petersburg Index*, *Richmond Daily Dispatch*, and *Richmond Daily Enquirer*, all 26 Mar. 1872, and *Petersburg Rural Messenger*, 30 Mar. 1872.

CRAIG S. MOORE

CHAMBERS, Joseph Lenoir (26 December 1891–10 January 1970), editor, writer, and recipient of the Pulitzer Prize, was born in Charlotte, North Carolina, and was the son of Grace Singleton Dewey Chambers and Joseph Lenoir Chambers, an editor for the *Charlotte Observer* before becoming a manufacturer of machinery. He was educated in the city's public schools and at Woodberry Forest, a preparatory school in Madison County, Virginia, from which he graduated in 1910. Chambers attended the University of North Carolina, where he played varsity sports and for three years edited the campus newspaper. Elected to Phi Beta Kappa, he graduated third in his class in 1914.

Lenoir Chambers taught English and history and helped coach basketball and football for two years at Woodberry Forest. In 1916 he entered the Columbia University School of Journalism, where he was exposed not only to the metropolitan North but also to a broad diversity of literary and political thought. After the United States entered World War I in April 1917, he collaborated with a faculty member and other Columbia students to found the New Republic News Service in Washington, D.C., but the venture failed. Chambers then attended officers' training camp and was commissioned a first lieutenant in the army. In France with the 52d Infantry of the 6th Division, he briefly commanded a company in trench combat in Alsace. In letters home he recorded his observations of the freedoms that African Americans enjoyed in France and the multiracial nature of the Allied forces. Chambers entered into romantic relationships with Ruth Draper, later one of the nation's most celebrated character actors, and Cornelia "Nell" Battle Lewis, who earned fame in the 1920s as a liberal journalist with the *Raleigh News and Observer*.

After the war Chambers returned to the University of North Carolina for two years as director of the news bureau. He worked with the future university president Frank Porter Graham and other prominent faculty and administrators to organize an ambitious fund-raising campaign that helped make the university the South's foremost institution of higher education and a bastion of southern liberal thought. Chambers retained lifelong ties to his alma mater. He joined the *Greensboro Daily News* as a reporter in 1921 and served successively as city editor and associate editor for the independent-minded newspaper. He worked closely with the paper's widely respected editor, Earle Godbey, and with Gerald White Johnson, Chambers's predecessor as associate editor and later a nationally acclaimed commentator on the South. On 15 September 1928 Chambers married Roberta Burwell Strudwick Glenn, for-

merly society editor of the *Daily News*, who had a son from a previous marriage. They had one daughter.

Disgusted by a turn in his newspaper's politics and its management's support for mill owners during a bloody strike by textile workers in Marion, North Carolina, Chambers moved to Norfolk in 1929 to become associate editor of the *Norfolk Virginian-Pilot*. He worked intimately with Virginia's first Pulitzer Prize–winning journalist, Louis Isaac Jaffé, who had earned the award earlier that year for his anti-lynching editorials and who advocated and achieved distinction for his liberalism. In 1944 Chambers became editor of the city's afternoon newspaper, the *Norfolk Ledger-Dispatch*, in which he advanced an editorial philosophy similar to that of the *Virginian-Pilot*. After Jaffé died in 1950, Chambers became editor of the latter newspaper.

In spite of having grown up with his region's tradition of racial segregation, Chambers nevertheless was one of a handful of southern white editors to urge acceptance of the Supreme Court's 1954 decision in *Brown* v. *Board of Education* declaring mandatory racial segregation of public schools unconstitutional. The *Norfolk Virginian-Pilot* was the only daily newspaper in Virginia to oppose Massive Resistance, the legislative program of the state's powerful senior senator, Harry Flood Byrd (1887–1966), to prevent desegregation of the public schools. Chambers mounted an editorial campaign that lasted five years and reached a high point in the autumn of 1958 and winter of 1959, after Governor James Lindsay Almond Jr. closed Norfolk's white secondary schools, which a federal court had ordered desegregated. In an editorial on 29 September 1958 Chambers demanded that the schools be reopened and exhorted the city council, the school board, the city's members of the General Assembly, parents, and teachers to "take the lead and exert the influence in reversing this unjust and cruel policy that does not and will not accomplish even its own ends." Chambers provided crucial leadership during the crisis and exposed the sham of Massive Resistance. Early in 1959 both state and federal courts ordered the city's schools reopened.

In 1960 Chambers received the Pulitzer Prize for distinguished editorial writing for his numerous and powerful editorials against Massive Resistance. The prize committee specifically cited his editorials "The Year Virginia Closed the Schools," which ran on the first day of 1959, and "The Year Virginia Opened the Schools," which ran on the final day of the same year. In 1959 Chambers also published an admiring two-volume biography of Thomas J. "Stonewall" Jackson. The result of twelve years of reading and research, the work received critical acclaim and was nominated for the Pulitzer Prize in biography, giving Chambers the unusual distinction of being nominated in two major categories in the same year. The biography of one of the Confederacy's most celebrated commanders demonstrated that Chambers's acceptance of desegregation did not break his links to his southern identity. In 1960 the University of North Carolina awarded him an honorary doctorate.

Despite his retirement at age seventy at the end of 1961, Chambers remained active in civic and journalistic affairs. With Joseph E. Shank he wrote *Salt Water and Printer's Ink: Norfolk and Its Newspapers, 1865–1965* (1967). Joseph Lenoir Chambers died of a stroke in Norfolk on 10 January 1970 and was buried in Forest Lawn Cemetery in that city.

Alexander Leidholdt, *Standing before the Shouting Mob: Lenoir Chambers and Virginia's Massive Resistance to Public-School Integration* (1997), several pors.; Lenoir Chambers Papers, Norfolk Public Library (including manuscripts of speeches and *Salt Water and Printer's Ink*) and UNC (including several autobiographical memoranda and letters with birth date); other published works include Chambers, "History as an Avocation," *VMHB* 76 (1968): 131–135; family information supplied by daughter, Elisabeth Lacy Chambers Burgess (1990); *Greensboro Daily News*, 16 Sept. 1928; *New York Times*, 3, 8 May 1960; David Pace, "Lenoir Chambers Opposes Massive Resistance: An Editor against Virginia's Democratic Organization, 1955–1959," *VMHB* 82 (1974): 415–429; Robert Mason, *One of the Neighbors' Children* (1987), 147–161, 197–198; Leidholdt, "Virginius Dabney and Lenoir Chambers: Two Southern Liberal Newspaper Editors Face Virginia's Massive Resistance to Public School Integration," *American Journalism* 15 (fall 1998): 35–68; obituaries in *Norfolk Ledger-Star*, 10 Jan. 1970, and *New York Times*, *Norfolk Virginian-Pilot*, *Richmond Times-Dispatch*, and *Washington Post*, all 11 Jan. 1970; editorial tributes in *Norfolk Ledger-Star* and *Norfolk Virginian-Pilot*, both 12 Jan. 1970, and *Richmond Times-Dispatch*, 15 Jan. 1970.

ALEXANDER S. LEIDHOLDT

CHAMBERS, Robert Edward (24 April 1870–22 April 1932), Baptist missionary, was born in Bedford County and was the son of Robert M. Chambers and Lucy Ann Vest Chambers. Educated at first at home and then in the Lynchburg public schools, he completed high school in his father's native Baltimore, to which the family moved about 1885. Chambers worked briefly in his father's construction business before entering Richmond College (later the University of Richmond), from which he graduated in 1892. While still in college, he and a friend preached at the state penitentiary in Richmond, and in April 1892 Chambers became the first pastor of the new Barton Heights Baptist Church in the city. Later in the year he resigned to enter the Southern Baptist Theological Seminary, in Louisville, Kentucky. After about a year and a half of study, Chambers was appointed a missionary to China on 23 February 1894. He did not immediately leave for his assigned post, however, and on 27 August of that year he married Mary E. "Mattie" Hall, a Buckingham County native then living in Richmond. They had two sons and two daughters, one of whom died in infancy.

In September 1894 Chambers began work in Richmond as acting assistant secretary to the Southern Baptist Convention's Foreign Mission Board, a position he held until May 1895. From then until October of that year he was a missionary for the Baptist City Missionary Society of Richmond and Manchester. In October 1895 he and his wife sailed for China, where he lived, except for several trips back to the United States on leave, for thirty-seven years. Chambers resided in Canton (Guangzhou) and worked in the Baptist Mission Compound. Interrupting his study of Chinese in February 1899, he and other missionaries organized the China Baptist Publication Society and before the end of the year set up the first Baptist printing press in Canton. The society began publishing Sunday school lesson leaflets and *True Light*, a Chinese-language monthly magazine. In its 1903 report the Foreign Mission Board characterized the society's goals and achievements and noted that "the Publication Society, offering facilities for publishing, and the *True Light* furnishing a medium for addressing a large audience, have stimulated both the missionaries and the Chinese brethren to larger use of the pen."

The publication society under Chambers's direction moved into a larger building in Canton in August 1912. By the mid-1910s the society annually published more than 30 million pages of books, periodicals, and tracts to support Baptist missionary work in China. Chambers's missionary work in the Canton area included overseeing Chinese evangelists and country stations. He also advised or supervised other building projects for the mission. In June 1910 Richmond College awarded him an honorary doctorate of divinity.

Chambers's wife died on 28 March 1905 of complications following the birth of their fourth child several weeks earlier. On 28 February 1906 in Canton he married Julia Etta Trainham, also a native Virginian who had served with the mission in China for several years. They had two daughters (both of whom died in infancy) and one son before she died of cancer on 6 September 1917 while they were on medical leave in the United States. On 24 October 1918 Chambers married Christine Coffee, a young missionary teacher then living in Canton, in a civil ceremony in Yokohama, Japan, as required by local law, and few days later in a Baptist ceremony in Tokyo. They had two daughters and one son.

During Chambers's residence, China experienced a revolution and was frequently in political and social turmoil. In part as a consequence of unrest and strikes in Canton, the publication society moved its offices to Shanghai in 1926 and not long thereafter began constructing a large new brick headquarters, the True Light Building. Chambers became a member of the board of the University of Shanghai and during the months preceding his death reported on the Japanese invasion of China in letters published in the *Religious Herald*, a Baptist periodical. Robert Edward Chambers died of pneumonia in a Shanghai hospital on 22 April 1932 and was buried in the mission section of the city's Pahsienjao Cemetery. A memorialist for the Southern Baptist Convention's annual proceedings noted that "the news of the death of 'Stonewall' Jackson could not have meant a greater shock

to the Southern Confederacy than was the news of the death of Dr. R. E. Chambers to the Baptist cause in China."

Biographies in George Braxton Taylor, *Virginia Baptist Ministers*, 6th ser. (1935), 395–398, and Ruth Carver Gardner and Christine Coffee Chambers, *Builder of Dreams: The Life of Robert Edward Chambers* (1939), including several pors.; Bedford Co. Birth Register; BVS Marriage Register, Richmond City (1894); Chambers correspondence in Southern Baptist Historical Library and Archives, Nashville, Tenn.; reports on missionary work and publication society in Southern Baptist Convention *Annuals* (1894–1932), including 1903, p. 141 (first quotation), 1906, pp. 70–71 (second marriage), and 1919, p. 204 (third marriage); obituaries in *Baltimore Sun* and *Shanghai North-China Daily News*, both 23 Apr. 1932, *Shanghai North-China Sunday News*, 24 Apr. 1932, and *Religious Herald*, 28 Apr. 1932; memorials in *Religious Herald*, 28 July 1932, Southern Baptist Convention *Annual* (1932), 154, and (1933), 185 (second quotation), and Baptist General Association of Virginia *Minutes* (1933), 211–213.

VIRGINIA S. DUNN

CHAMBLISS, John Randolph (5 March 1809–3 April 1875), member of the Convention of 1850–1851, of the Convention of 1861, and of the Confederate States House of Representatives, was born in Sussex County and was the son of James Jarred Chambliss and Lucy Rives Newsom Chambliss. After studying law at the College of William and Mary during the 1829–1830 term, he was admitted to the bar in Greensville and Sussex Counties in June 1830. He settled in the former county and practiced in the town of Hicksford (later incorporated as part of Emporia). On 25 December 1830 he married his cousin Sarah John Rives Blow, also of Greensville County. Of their three sons and at least four daughters, one son and two daughters died in childhood.

From 1840 to 1841 Chambliss was clerk of the county and later in the decade was a county school commissioner. Appointed commissioner in chancery in 1845, he served until September 1847, when he became commonwealth's attorney. In 1850 he owned about a thousand acres of land in the county and twenty-two taxable slaves above age twelve. In August of that year Chambliss, a Whig, received the second-highest vote total of seven candidates campaigning for four seats representing Greensville, Isle of Wight, Nansemond, Southampton, Surry, and Sussex Counties in a convention summoned to revise Virginia's constitution. He served on the Committee on the Judiciary. Chambliss agreed with western reformers that property qualifications should be removed from the suffrage, but he sided with eastern delegates who insisted on a mixed formula of population and property as the basis for apportioning seats in the General Assembly and in opposition to western reformers who wanted seats allocated solely on the basis of the white population. He spoke twice on the latter subject and voted against a compromise, later adopted, that allowed eastern counties, where slave ownership was heaviest, to maintain a majority of seats in the Senate of Virginia but allocated the majority of seats in the House of Delegates to western counties, where slavery was economically less important. Chambliss also opposed westerners' demand that slaves be taxed according to their market value rather than at the lesser per capita rate established by the former constitution, and on that question he and the other eastern delegates prevailed. Chambliss voted on 31 July 1851 against the draft constitution that the convention adopted by a vote of 75 to 33 and submitted to the voters for ratification.

In 1857 Chambliss attended the Southern Commercial Convention in Knoxville, Tennessee, where he was elected one of ten vice presidents. Like many other Virginia voters in 1860, by which time he owned twenty-seven taxable slaves, he supported the Unionist candidate, John Bell, for president. After Abraham Lincoln's victory at the polls, Chambliss, believing that the slave states should remain united, changed his mind and reluctantly advocated secession as a last resort. In February 1861 he won election to represent Greensville and Sussex Counties in the convention called to craft the state's response to the secession crisis and served on the Committee on Elections. On 4 April 1861, when the convention defeated a motion for secession, he paired in favor, and on 17 April he voted with the majority to secede and submit an ordinance of secession to the voters for ratification. Chambliss continued to oppose western delegates who reintroduced the subject of taxing slaves according to their market value and voted against a constitutional amendment on that subject that the convention submitted to a referendum.

Chambliss returned to Richmond in June and November for the brief second and third sessions of the convention. During the former session he chaired a special committee to report on measures concerning the stores and machinery at the Harpers Ferry arsenal. From 5 August to 2 December 1861 he served again as commonwealth's attorney for Greensville County. On 6 November 1861 Chambliss won election to the Confederate States House of Representatives from the district comprising the counties of Greensville, Isle of Wight, Nansemond, Norfolk, Princess Anne, Southampton, Surry, and Sussex and the city of Norfolk. Between 18 February 1862 and 17 February 1864 he attended all four sessions of the First Confederate Congress. A member of the Committee on Naval Affairs and during the final weeks of his term of a special committee on the veteran soldiers' home, he introduced designs for a national flag on three occasions and offered resolutions or amendments on such topics as the navy and terms of enlistment for the army. Refugees from areas under Union occupation and tax relief for persons living in areas under occupation were among his other interests, probably because portions of his district were under Union control during part of the Civil War. In 1863 he declined to seek reelection.

Chambliss took an oath of allegiance to the United States in the summer of 1865 and petitioned for a presidential pardon, granted on 16 October of that year. He commented on Andrew Johnson's administration in a speech at Lawrenceville, in neighboring Brunswick County, at the end of September but took no further recorded part in electoral politics. He lived at Hicksford with his wife and the widow and children of his son, John Randolph Chambliss (1833–1864), who had been killed while serving as a Confederate brigadier general. After almost six months' illness John Randolph Chambliss died at his Greensville County residence on 3 April 1875 of what was described as nervous debility and was buried with Masonic honors in the family cemetery on his estate, a site in present-day downtown Emporia.

Birth and marriage dates in Chambliss family Bible records, LVA; other personal information in 1868 life insurance application and policy, Arlington Mutual Life Insurance

Company, of Virginia, Records of Piedmont and Arlington Life Insurance Company, Robert Alonzo Brock Collection, Huntington; Greensville Co. Marriage Bonds (bond dated 6 Dec. 1830); *Richmond Enquirer*, 6 Jan. 1831 (variant marriage date of 21 Dec. 1830), 10 Sept. 1850; *Journal of 1850–1851 Convention*, 59, 227, 419; *Debates and Proceedings of 1850–1851 Convention*, 292–294; *Supplement, 1850–1851 Convention Debates*, no. 32; *Petersburg Daily Southside Democrat*, 14 Aug. 1857; Reese and Gaines, *Proceedings of 1861 Convention*, 3:163, 447–449, 4:144, 542–545, 685, 690–695, 707–708; Presidential Pardons, including undated 1861 Chambliss campaign broadside "The State Convention. To my Fellow-Citizens of Sussex and Greensville Counties"; por. in private collection (2005); will and estate inventory in Greensville Co. Common Law Will Book (1824–1876), 26–27, 34–37; BVS Death Register, Greensville Co.; obituaries in *Petersburg Index and Appeal*, 5, 6, 7 (reprinting from lost issue of *Richmond Whig*) Apr. 1875, and *Richmond Daily Dispatch*, 5 Apr. 1875; Greensville Co. bar memorial resolutions in Greensville Co. Common Law Order Book, 14:156–157, and *Petersburg Index and Appeal*, 8 Apr. 1875.

BARBARA SMITH

CHAMBLISS, John Randolph (23 January 1833–16 August 1864), Confederate cavalry officer, was born near Hicksford (later incorporated as part of the city of Emporia), in Greensville County. He was the son of Sarah John Rives Blow Chambliss and John Randolph Chambliss (1809–1875), a prominent attorney and planter who served in the Conventions of 1850–1851 and 1861 and in the Confederate States House of Representatives. From July 1849 to July 1853 Chambliss attended the United States Military Academy, where he turned in an indifferent academic performance and graduated thirty-first in a class of fifty-two cadets. He returned home and on 19 September 1853 married Emeline Ann Turner. They had four daughters and two sons. Commissioned a second lieutenant and assigned to the mounted rifles, Chambliss was posted to the school for cavalry practice at Carlisle, Pennsylvania, but resigned his commission on 4 March 1854 and returned to Greensville County, where he purchased and managed a 724-acre farm. He became colonel of the 50th Regiment of the Virginia militia and was appointed a brigade inspector in March 1859 and an aide-de-camp to the governor the following November.

After Virginia seceded from the Union in April 1861, Chambliss became a major in the state's provisional army. On 12 July of that year he accepted a commission as colonel of the 41st Regiment Virginia Infantry, to date from 13 June. For the next ten months the unit was stationed near Norfolk. On 1 June 1862 Chambliss led the regiment in its first major action of the Civil War at the Battle of Seven Pines. He then was transferred to mounted duty and on 29 July became colonel of the newly formed 13th Virginia Cavalry. For the next three months Chambliss commanded this regiment and an unofficial brigade in reconnaissance missions along the Rappahannock River. On 10 November 1862 the 13th Virginia was assigned to Brigadier General William Henry Fitzhugh Lee's cavalry brigade. Chambliss led a handful of men against a larger Union cavalry troop at Beverly Ford, near Brandy Station, on 15 April 1863 and in a spirited engagement that drew praise from his commanding officer forced it to withdraw across the Rappahannock. During the Chancellorsville campaign Chambliss commanded forces in the Culpeper area protecting railroads from Union cavalry. At Brandy Station on 9 June his small force of dismounted cavalrymen helped blunt the Union advance. After Lee received a severe leg wound during the fighting, Chambliss became acting brigade commander.

When the Army of Northern Virginia invaded the North, Confederate cavalry was assigned to screen the army's movements by guarding the mountain passes. Chambliss's brigade contested the probing Union cavalry in sharp engagements at Aldie, Middleburg, and Upperville. After an arduous march through Maryland and into Pennsylvania, his brigade reached the main army at Gettysburg on 2 July. The next day Chambliss's men clashed with Union cavalry in hand-to-hand fighting that ended in a bloody draw. Following the Confederate defeat at Gettysburg, Chambliss's cavalry fought rearguard actions as the Confederate army withdrew to the Potomac River and crossed back into Virginia. Recommended by Major General James Ewell Brown Stuart as a "meritorious and most gallant officer," Chambliss was promoted to brigadier general on 19 December 1863 and became his brigade's official commander.

As the Union army thrust toward Richmond in May and June 1864, Chambliss's men monitored the location of advancing Union forces and screened the maneuvering Confederate army while also protecting supply lines and sparring with Northern cavalry. The brigade engaged Union infantry at the Battle of Spotsylvania Court House on 14 May and two weeks later fought at Haw's Shop and Hanover Court House. Operating south of Petersburg late in June, Chambliss figured prominently in the defeat of Union cavalry at Sappony Baptist Church, in Sussex County. Ordered north of the James River, elements of his brigade encountered Union forces east of Richmond on the Charles City Road, and while rallying his men John Randolph Chambliss was shot and killed on 16 August 1864. Union soldiers recovered his body, along with a detailed map of Confederate fortifications around Richmond. The next day a truce was arranged, and the body was exhumed and passed through the lines. On 21 August, Chambliss was reinterred in the family cemetery in present-day Emporia. His grave marker bears an inscribed tribute from Robert Edward Lee.

Birth date on gravestone; George W. Cullum, *Biographical Register of the Officers and Graduates of the U.S. Military Academy at West Point* (1868), 2:354; John Randolph Chambliss Jr. File, Meherrin Regional Library, Emporia; Greensville Co. Ministers Returns (1810–1859); erroneous marriage date of 15 Sept. 1853 in Greensville Co. Marriage Register; Compiled Service Records (quotation in Stuart to Samuel Cooper, 23 Oct. 1863); William D. Henderson, *41st Virginia Infantry* (1986), 5, 95; Daniel T. Balfour, *13th Virginia Cavalry* (1986), 9–10, 13–14, 16–19, 24–26, 29, 31–37; numerous references in *OR*, esp. account of death and first burial in 1st ser., vol. 42, pt. 1, 242–243; James C. Mohr, ed., *The Cormany Diaries: A Northern Family in the Civil War* (1982), 466–470; Douglas Summers Brown et al., eds., *Sketches of Greensville County, Virginia, 1650–1967, Second Edition, 1968–2000* (2000), 100, 116–117 (por. facing 185); obituaries in *Richmond Semi-Weekly Enquirer*, 19, 26 Aug. 1864.

GRAHAM T. DOZIER

CHAMPE, John (d. 30 September 1796), Continental army soldier, was born in Loudoun County in the mid-1750s and probably was the son of John Champe or Thomas Champe, the two sons and executors named in the 1763 will of John Champe, a Loudoun County farmer who bequeathed to his namesake grandson some household furnishings and utensils, a cow and calf, and a horse and saddle. The name of Champe's mother is not recorded. The Loudoun County family was related to the prominent family of that name in King George County, but the exact relationship has not been documented.

Champe was living in Loudoun County during the second half of 1776 when he enlisted as a private in the cavalry troop being raised by Captain Henry (later "Light-Horse Harry") Lee (1756–1818). One of six troops of light horse that composed the 1st Regiment of Continental Light Dragoons, Lee's troop joined George Washington's army in New Jersey in January 1777 and soon distinguished itself in scouting, foraging, and raiding actions. In April 1778 when Lee was promoted to major and given command of an independent partisan corps consisting of two light-horse troops, Champe became corporal of the 2d Troop, and on 1 January 1779, by which time Lee's corps had grown to consist of three troops, Champe was promoted to sergeant. The addition of three troops of infantry to Lee's command by the spring of 1780 transformed it into a legionary corps with an authorized strength of three hundred men, half mounted and half dismounted, capable of taking on special missions in all sorts of terrain. Sometime before the autumn of 1780 Champe apparently became the corps's sergeant major, its senior noncommissioned officer responsible for discipline, drill, and the duty roster.

Champe earned a place in history because of his attempt to capture Benedict Arnold. On 14 October 1780, soon after the discovery of Arnold's plot to surrender West Point and his escape to British-occupied New York City, George Washington asked Lee, who was then managing intelligence and reconnaissance operations in northern New Jersey, to devise a plan for abducting Arnold. About six days later Lee informed Washington that he had engaged two men for that purpose, a sergeant and a Newark inhabitant who had useful contacts with the enemy. Lee's plan was for Champe to join Arnold in the guise of a deserter and "contrive to insinuate himself into some menial or military birth about the Genls person." Champe would communicate with Lee through the intermediary in Newark until they could "seize the prize in the night, gag him, & bring him across to Bergen woods." Lee characterized the sergeant (whom he did not identify by name) as "a very promising youth of uncommon taciturnity, & inflexible perseverance. His connexions & his service in the army from the beginning of the war assure me that he will be faithful. I have instructed him not to return till he receives direction from me, but to continue his attempts, however unfavorable the prospect may appear at first. I have excited his thirst for fame by impressing on his mind the virtue & glory of the act." Lee also promised Champe a promotion. Washington approved Lee's plan on 20 October with the "express stipulation & pointed injunction" that Arnold be taken alive. Washington also warned that "the Sergeant must be very circumspect—too much zeal may create suspicion—and too much precipitancy may defeat the project."

Champe deserted from the American camp during the night of 20–21 October, and Lee reported seeing him and his civilian accomplice in Newark the next day. On 25 October, Lee wrote Washington that Champe had "accidentally met Col. Arnold in the street" and entertained "high hopes of success." Years later when writing his *Memoirs*, Lee stated that Champe had hinted vaguely to the British commanding general at the likelihood of many more American desertions and that a few days later the sergeant enlisted in the American Legion, the Loyalist corps that Arnold commanded. Lee's *Memoirs* also include a dramatic account of how Champe and his accomplice plotted to seize and gag Arnold in the garden behind his house late one night early in November, carry him like a drunken soldier through alleys and back streets to the Hudson River, and row him across to Hoboken, New Jersey, where Lee would meet them with a party of dragoons. That plan, Lee wrote, was thwarted the day before its attempted execution when Arnold unexpectedly moved his headquarters to another part of the city and ordered the American Legion, including Champe, to board transport ships for an expedition to Virginia. Lee's account cannot be substantiated in detail, however, because Arnold's expeditionary force did not embark until mid-December, by which time Lee and his corps were already on their way to join the Continental army in the Carolinas. In any event, the difficulty of abducting a man of Arnold's notoriety from a garrisoned city was so great that the chance of success could not have been very favorable.

According to Lee's *Memoirs*, Champe accompanied Arnold's expedition to Virginia, where he found an opportunity to desert from the British ranks in the spring of 1781. Traveling through the backcountry, Champe rejoined Lee's corps in South Carolina that summer. Lee introduced the sergeant to General Nathanael Greene, who promptly sent him north to General Washington. According to Lee, Washington discharged Champe from the army so that he would not run the risk of being captured and executed by the British.

Champe married in July 1783 and settled in Hampshire County. He and Phebe Champe (whose maiden name is not known) had at least four daughters and three sons before he died on 30 September 1796 while inspecting land along the Monongahela River near Morgantown. Champe's presumed gravesite is in Prickett Cemetery at Prickett's Fort State Park in Marion County, West Virginia.

William Buckner McGroarty, "Sergeant John Champe and Certain of His Contemporaries," *WMQ*, 2d ser., 17 (1937): 145–175; George F. Scheer, "The Sergeant Major's Strange Mission," *American Heritage* 8 (Oct. 1957): 26–29, 98; Peter F. Stevens, "The Strange Saga of John Champe: The Virginian Who Attempted to Kidnap Benedict Arnold," *Virginia Cavalcade* 35 (1985): 64–69; grandfather's will in Loudoun Co. Will Book, A:96–97; Henry Lee, *Memoirs of the War in the Southern Department of the United States* (1812), 2:159–187, a dramatized account that gives Champe's age as twenty-three or twenty-four in 1780, suggesting a birth date about 1756 or 1757; a fabricated account, adapted from Lee's *Memoirs* but purporting to be by Champe, was published in the Dec. 1834 issue of the British magazine *United Service Journal* and reprinted in *WMQ*, 2d ser., 18 (1938): 322–342; quotations from Henry Lee to George Washington, n.d. [ca. 20 Oct. 1780], and 25 Oct. 1780, George Washington Papers, LC, and from Washington to Lee, 20 Oct. 1780, de Coppet Collection, Princeton University; John Frederick Dorman, ed., *Virginia Revolutionary Pension Applications* (1973), 17:55–56; depositions of widow Phebe Champe, 13 Dec. 1828 (with marriage and death dates), and elder brother William Champe, 17 Dec. 1828 (also with death date), BW; John Champe file, LOMC; John Champe file, Revolutionary War Pension and Bounty-Land Warrant Application Files, RG 15, NARA (with variant marriage date of July 1782 in appended report *Phebe, Widow of John Champe*, 25th Cong., 2d sess., 17 Feb. 1838, House Rept. 568, serial 335); dedication of stone at presumed gravesite reported in *Morgantown [W.Va.] Dominion Post*, 23 Apr. 2001.

PHILANDER D. CHASE

CHANCO. See **CHAUCO.**

CHANDLER, Algernon Bertrand (12 May 1870–20 September 1928), president of the State Normal School for Women at Fredericksburg (later the University of Mary Washington), was born in Bowling Green and was the son of Algernon Bertrand Chandler (1843–1928), for many years commonwealth's attorney of Caroline County, and Julia Yates Callaghan Chandler. He was a distant cousin and near contemporary of Julian Alvin Carroll Chandler, also a Caroline County native, who became president of the College of William and Mary. After attending public and private schools in Bowling Green, Chandler received a master's degree from the University of Virginia in June 1893 and on that same day won a medal for oratory from the university's Washington Literary Society.

A. B. Chandler Jr., as he was usually known, then studied law at Washington and Lee University and was licensed in 1895. He practiced in Atlanta for two years with his brother John Washington Chandler. When he was just twenty-six, the Virginia Society of Atlanta invited him to speak at its annual meeting on the life and character of Robert Edward Lee, and that same year Chandler gave the commencement address at the Georgia Normal and Industrial College at Milledgeville (later Georgia College and State University). Chandler returned to Virginia in 1897 or 1898 and abandoned the law for education. He became principal of the public high school in Clifton Forge and then briefly taught mathematics in Caroline County. On 23 July 1902, in Richmond County, Chandler married Blanche Montgomery, of Warsaw. They had no children.

By 1901 Chandler had moved to Richmond, where he taught at Virginia Randolph Ellett's school for girls (later Saint Catherine's School) and at a private school for boys. Beginning with the 1904–1905 school year he was a principal in the city's elementary schools until 1910. From 1906 to 1910 he also taught an evening adult English course at the Virginia Mechanics' Institute in Richmond. He served on the State Board of Examiners and Inspectors in 1910 and 1911 and for three years edited the school page of the *Richmond News Leader*. In Fredericksburg in 1910 and 1911 Chandler conducted summer schools for teachers. He also contributed a section on Virginia to a 1902 edition of Alexis Everett Frye's *Grammar School Geography* textbook.

In 1911 Chandler became professor of Latin and social sciences at the recently opened State Normal and Industrial School for Women at Fredericksburg (after 1914 the State Normal School for Women at Fredericksburg and after February 1924 the State Teachers College at Fredericksburg). Three years later he was appointed dean of the school, and in May 1919 when the president resigned, he became acting president. The board appointed Chandler the school's second president on 7 June of that year. By all accounts he was an able educator and administrator. Chandler expanded the two-year normal school (with a curriculum modeled after French *écoles normales*) into a serious four-year institution of higher learning. In his first commencement address as school president, he unveiled an ambitious plan to add commercial courses, home economics, industrial arts, and music and to develop a research farm that would also produce food for the school. Chandler eliminated all high school classes and recruited "only outstanding high school graduates and first grade certificate holders as students"; he advised the "flapper type, lacking in seriousness of purpose," not to apply. Having seen the school weather the 1918 flu pandemic, Chandler was particularly concerned about student health and added health education courses to the curriculum. He even used the school's record of good health as a selling point for enrollment, announcing that no student had ever died at the school.

Although Chandler's religious faith strongly informed his philosophy of education, the curriculum promoted wholesome living but stopped short of religious indoctrination. In an article he wrote about education, Chandler proposed a personal creed and an elaborate code of ethics to guide would-be teachers and leaders. In keeping with a whole-health ideal, he enthusiastically supported the establishment of a branch of the Young Women's Christian Association on campus, and he encouraged athletics. The school's formidable basketball team won every game during the 1921–1922 season. Chandler introduced student government to the campus, encouraged school spirit, and supported the performing arts. He beautified the school grounds by adding an outdoor amphitheater and paving the paths that threaded the wooded campus.

A popular speaker on educational and historical topics, he delivered one of the addresses on 22 June 1922 in Richmond at the laying of the cornerstone for a monument to Matthew Fontaine Maury, who had been born near Fredericksburg. Algernon Bertrand Chandler suffered a stroke and died at his home in Fredericksburg on the afternoon of 20 September 1928. Following a funeral at Antioch Christian Church in Bowling Green two days later, he was buried in the Chandler family plot in Lakewood Cemetery in Caroline County. Chandler Hall on the University of Mary Washington campus was named in his honor. Fairfax House, his former residence, has served as the school's infirmary, a dormitory, and faculty offices.

Biography in Marshall Wingfield, *A History of Caroline County, Virginia* (1924), 150–154 (por.); birth and death dates from BVS Death Certificate, Spotsylvania Co., and gravestone; BVS Marriage Register, Richmond Co.; Chandler's published lectures include "The Rappahannock River Country," *Bulletin of the State Normal School, Fredericksburg, Virginia* 1 (Oct. 1915): 1–16, "Appreciation of Matthew Fontaine Maury," *Bulletin, State Normal School for Women, Fredericksburg, Va.* 8 (Jan. 1923): 3–7, "Christian Education the Hope of the World," ibid. 8 (Jan. 1923): 13–21, "The Needs of Virginia's Rural Schools," *Bulletin, State Normal School, Fredericksburg, Va.* 9 (Jan. 1924): 3–9, "Fredericksburg State Normal School," *Virginia Journal of Education* 15 (1922): 321–324, 353–354, and "Teacher-Training and Professional Ethics Among Teachers," ibid. 17 (1923): 231–234; other works include "High Lights of Fredericksburg State Normal School," *Bulletin, State Normal School for Women, Fredericksburg, Va.* 8 (Jan. 1923): 23 (quotations); Edward Alvey Jr., *History of Mary Washington College, 1908–1972* (1974), 34, 91–94, 151–153, 551–552 (por. following 338); obituaries in *Fredericksburg Free Lance-Star*, *Richmond News Leader*, and *Richmond Times-Dispatch*, all 21 Sept. 1928; editorial tributes in *Fredericksburg Free Lance-Star*, 22 Sept. 1928, and *Virginia Journal of Education* 22 (1928): 71–72 (with variant death date of 21 Sept. 1928).

LUCY SOUTHALL COLEBAUGH

CHANDLER, Alvin Duke (18 August 1902–26 May 1987), naval officer and president of the College of William and Mary, was born in Richmond and was the son of Lenore Burten Duke Chandler and Julian Alvin Carroll Chandler, superintendent of the Richmond public schools from 1909 to 1919 and president of the College of William and Mary from 1919 to 1934. Chandler was educated in the Richmond public schools and entered the College of William and Mary in 1918. The following year he won appointment to the United States Naval Academy. He graduated on 7 June 1923 and on the same day was commissioned an ensign. Chandler married Mary Louise Michaels, in Richmond, on 25 September 1926. They had no children.

Chandler served with the Atlantic fleet until 1927 and then in the destroyer fleet in the Pacific until 1930, when he was assigned to the Naval Academy for two years to teach electrical engineering and physics. He was successively electrical officer and gunnery officer on the battleship *Oklahoma* from 1932 to 1934 and then returned to the academy for two additional years teaching in the department of ordnance and gunnery. During that time he contributed to a textbook on naval gunnery. Between 1937 and 1941 Chandler served as operations officer of a battleship division, in command of his own destroyer, and on assignment in the office of the chief of naval operations. Promoted to commander on 30 June 1942 and to captain on 1 May 1943, he commanded a destroyer division during the invasion of North Africa in World War II and then a series of destroyer squadrons in the South Pacific, where he took part in the capture of Guadalcanal and in the campaigns in the Solomon Islands, the Marshall and Gilbert Islands, New Guinea, Iwo Jima, and Okinawa. From May 1945 until May 1948 Chandler served again in the office of the chief of naval operations. He oversaw the outfitting of the heavy cruiser *Des Moines* in Massachusetts and commanded the vessel when it first put to sea in February 1949. Chandler attended the Imperial Defence College (later the Royal College of Defence Studies) in London before becoming director of the logistic plans division in the chief of naval operations office in January 1951. He was promoted to rear admiral effective 1 July of that year. Offered the presidency of the College of William and Mary, Chandler accepted and was promoted to vice admiral when he retired from the navy on 1 November 1951.

Chandler became president of William and Mary in the wake of an athletics scandal that led to the resignation of the president, John Edwin Pomfret, on 13 September 1951. Seeking a leader who would be able to control a restive faculty, the board of visitors selected Chandler, who was formally installed as president of the college on 11 October. Immediately after assuming office he recommended several steps to prevent, among other things, favoritism in admission and retention of athletes. In May 1952 the board approved his new athletic policy. Chandler kept the faculty's role largely advisory and deserves credit for keeping the athletic program free of scandal during his presidency.

Early in his administration Chandler began an extensive institutional evaluation to clarify William and Mary's educational mission. Completed in October 1954, the report stated that liberal arts should remain the core of the college's program, but it also provided a rationale for maintaining a multicampus system, including William and Mary's Norfolk and Richmond divisions, to offer professional and vocational training for all of the Tidewater Virginia region. Chandler's program reprised the educational goals of his father.

Unfortunately, in gaining control of the athletic program and putting his stamp on William and Mary's educational objectives, Chandler weakened or bypassed the authority of the faculty. Accustomed to issuing commands and expecting unquestioning obedience, he had little understanding of the role that the faculty should play in college governance. Chandler's efforts to run a tight ship resulted in stormy faculty meetings, a pervasive collapse of faculty morale, an atmosphere of tension at the college, and a spate of faculty resignations. His methods also antagonized students and provoked a serious crisis in 1955 following his attempt to crack down on rowdy student behavior by issuing strict new regulations prohibiting alcoholic beverages on campus. Students staged a series of noisy protests, and the student assembly denounced him. The board backed Chandler and rejected all the complaints, but by the summer of 1955 the problems were being widely reported and led to calls for

an investigation by the governor and the General Assembly and for removal of the president.

Despite his difficulties, Chandler was a hardworking president who was deeply committed to William and Mary. He sought to raise faculty salaries and to increase the college's small endowment. He also favored an increasingly more selective admissions process and strongly supported the small law program as well as new master's degree programs in several arts and science departments. Under Chandler's leadership the college began a significant new building program, the first since the 1930s, and developed a master plan for the expanded campus, which was presented to the board in May 1960.

Throughout his presidency, Chandler did his best to have William and Mary serve the broader educational needs of Tidewater Virginia. He increased the number of extension courses that the college offered in surrounding communities, and he began an evening program in Williamsburg. In 1960 his vision of what he called the Greater College of William and Mary was substantially realized when the General Assembly enacted a measure that consolidated several campuses under the overall direction of a chancellor of the Colleges of William and Mary. The Norfolk Division (later Old Dominion University) and the Richmond Professional Institute (later Virginia Commonwealth University), which were already under the college's supervision, and two junior colleges to be established in Newport News and Petersburg all became divisions of William and Mary, subject to the control of one board of visitors. The board promptly elected Chandler to the new position of chancellor.

To replace Chandler as college president the board followed his recommendation and selected Davis Young Paschall, the state superintendent of public instruction. Chandler and Paschall assumed their new offices on 16 August 1960, but in a remarkable reversal of policy in 1962 the General Assembly abolished the system and made the Richmond and Norfolk divisions into independent universities. The two junior colleges, Richard Bland near Petersburg and Christopher Newport in Newport News, remained under William and Mary's supervision. Chandler's position as chancellor of the colleges was abolished, although he served as coordinator of the two junior colleges until mid-September 1962. The board named him honorary chancellor of the College of William and Mary, a position he held for twelve years.

Chandler received honorary doctorates from the University of Pennsylvania in 1955, Brandeis University in 1958, and William and Mary in 1963. After his retirement, he moved to Virginia Beach and served for several years as president and subsequently a trustee of William and Mary's endowment association. Alvin Duke Chandler died in a Virginia Beach hospital on 26 May 1987 and was buried in Hollywood Cemetery, in Richmond.

Susan H. Godson, "Admiral Chandler at the Helm: Running a Tight Ship," *William and Mary Magazine* 58 (winter 1991): 17–20 (pors.); Godson et al., *The College of William and Mary: A History* (1993), 2:775–805; official navy biography, 23 Nov. 1951, Naval Historical Center, Department of the Navy, Washington, D.C.; Alvin Duke Chandler Papers, including biographical data sheets with birth date, W&M; *Richmond Times-Dispatch*, 26 Sept. 1926, 4 Oct. 1959; inaugural address, 15 May 1953, in *The Inauguration of Alvin Duke Chandler as Twenty-Second President of the College of William and Mary in Virginia* (1953), and sound recording, WRVA Radio Collection, Acc. 38210, LVA; "Two Hundred and Sixty-Six Years Later: An Interview with the President," William and Mary *Alumni Gazette* 26 (Dec. 1958): 5–8, 10; obituaries in *Richmond News Leader* and *Richmond Times-Dispatch*, both 27 May 1987, *Norfolk Virginian-Pilot* and *Washington Post*, both 28 May 1987, and *New York Times* and *Williamsburg Virginia Gazette*, both 30 May 1987.

RICHARD B. SHERMAN

CHANDLER, Julian Alvin Carroll (29 October 1872–31 May 1934), president of the College of William and Mary, was born in Caroline County. The son of Joseph Alsop Chandler, a physician, and Emuella Josephine White Chandler, he was a distant cousin and near contemporary of another Caroline County native, Algernon Bertrand Chandler, who became president of the State Normal School for Women at Fredericksburg (later the University of Mary Washington). Chandler attended a private school in the county, a boys' academy, and the public schools in Bowling Green. He received a B.A. from the College of William and Mary in 1891 and an M.A. the following year. Chandler was principal of a high school in the town of Houston (later Halifax) during the 1892–1893 school

year and then entered the Johns Hopkins University, where he studied history and received a Ph.D. in 1896. While completing his graduate work he taught history at Morgan College (later Morgan State University), in Baltimore. Chandler mined his dissertation on the constitutional history of Virginia in two works, *Representation in Virginia* (1896) and *The History of Suffrage in Virginia* (1901).

For four years beginning in 1896 Chandler was dean of the faculty and taught English and pedagogy at the Woman's College of Richmond. In Portsmouth on 10 July 1897 he married another faculty member, Lenore Burten Duke. Their four sons included Alvin Duke Chandler, who served as president of the College of William and Mary from 1951 to 1960. Chandler was acting professor of history and literature at Richmond College (after 1920 the University of Richmond) from 1897 through 1901 and professor of English language and literature there from 1900 until June 1904, when the college awarded him an LL.D. After serving as acting president of the Woman's College during the 1900–1901 academic year, Chandler was dean of the Richmond Academy, a secondary school for boys that Richmond College sponsored, from 1902 to 1904. He also taught in summer teacher education sessions at the University of Virginia from 1900 to 1904, summer normal sessions in Norfolk in 1907 and 1908, and history and political science at Richmond College during the 1908–1909 term.

During the decade after receiving his doctorate, Chandler was an industrious writer. Co-author of *Virginia* (1902), a short geography text, he also collaborated with Oliver Perry Chitwood on the textbook *Makers of American History: A Beginner's Book in the History of Our Country* and wrote a companion volume, *Makers of Virginia History*, both published in 1904. In June of that year Chandler moved to New York and worked as a book editor for two years. He returned to Virginia in 1906 as chief of the division of history, education, and social economy of the Jamestown Exposition Company that was preparing the 1907 commemoration of the founding of Jamestown. Chandler contributed to *Colonial Virginia* (1907) and edited *Life in Old*

Virginia, published that same year. From 1907 to 1909 he was the first editor of the *Virginia Journal of Education*. Chandler wrote for the multivolume series *The South in the Building of the Nation*, which began publication in 1909, and was editor in chief of the state history volume in that series. With Franklin Lafayette Riley and Joseph Gregoire de Roulhac Hamilton he wrote *Our Republic: A History of the United States for Grammar Grades* (1910).

In July 1909 Chandler became superintendent of schools in the city of Richmond, where he put his strong belief in public education into practice. He pushed for adequate buildings and for the training of pupils with learning disabilities, and he made known his concern for the health of sickly children and his desire for competent teachers. The student body of Richmond doubled during his administration, and he started the junior high school system. To enable students of all ages to make a living Chandler introduced vocational work and business courses and promoted adult education and night schools. He introduced physical education and free textbooks, tried to limit class size, and built new schools for both white and black students, although spending on black schools remained far below that on white schools. Chandler exhibited strong leadership skills, but his tenure was not without controversy. He advocated higher salaries for those teachers who were well trained but showed no patience with instructors who were not interested in furthering their own education. Chandler extended the employment period of principals to ten months. The city council, the city's daily newspapers, and the school board supported him, but the teachers and his employees feared him.

During World War I and into 1919 Chandler was chief of a federal vocational education program for disabled soldiers and sailors. In the spring of 1919 the board of visitors of the College of William and Mary, by a close vote, appointed Chandler president to succeed Lyon Gardiner Tyler, who had directed the college for more than thirty years. Chandler took office on 1 July and immediately began building on Tyler's decision to make the college coeducational and attempting to realize the goal

of making the school accessible to the sons and daughters of Virginia's middle-class farmers and shopkeepers. Chandler realized that the college needed to serve the whole state, but especially the Tidewater region, by educating as many students as possible. As he had in Richmond, he believed that education should fit students to earn a living.

Chandler's wife died of cancer on 10 August 1920, and after his first year in Williamsburg he seldom entertained and often ate in the college's dining hall. The death of his wife may have affected his personality by making him more rigid and intensifying his work habits, which might later have been labeled as workaholic. Chandler's top-down management style had clearly been in evidence in the Richmond city schools, and in Williamsburg he left no doubt who was in charge. The board of visitors approved most of his major decisions after he had already made and implemented them. Chandler handled all the discipline of male students. He sat on the bench during football games and encouraged women's athletics as a way to advertise the school. For Chandler no detail was too small for his attention, as he even ordered strawberries for the college's farm and told the superintendent what to plant and when. He had a temper with a short fuse. He routinely fired staff members and was amazed when they did not come to work the next day.

Chandler consulted with other college presidents to learn what they required of their deans and faculty, but his relations with his own faculty were not good. The professors and instructors chafed under heavy workloads and did not have tenure or true academic freedom. Against his wishes faculty members formed a local chapter of the American Association of University Professors. Chandler did not want the faculty to conduct research, and he astonished them when he proposed awarding membership in Phi Beta Kappa to potential donors. Unlike some other college administrators, Chandler was not reluctant to hire women. Some of the women who joined the faculty were educators of outstanding ability, but most held lower ranks than the male faculty and received lower pay. The faculty increased from fewer than twenty when

Chandler was appointed in 1919 to approximately one hundred full professors, associate and assistant professors, and instructors during the 1933–1934 term.

A mercurial and dynamic leader, Chandler presided over a major increase in the college's enrollment from 131 students in the term before he arrived to 1,682 on the main campus during the 1931–1932 academic year, the peak level of his tenure. He sent the faculty out to recruit students from Virginia high schools, began offering evening classes, and allowed students to receive credit for war service. Chandler worked hard to make money available to assist financially needy students and wrote letters to alumni and parents seeking repayment of student loans and other money owed to the college. Chandler believed that students should be given moral as well as intellectual training. He taught Sunday school at the local Baptist church and brought religious speakers to the campus.

After taking office Chandler expanded the academic curriculum by increasing the degree requirements, offering new courses in such fields as accounting, business administration, engineering, dentistry, medicine, and nursing, and reestablishing a law program that had been dormant since the Civil War. His commitment to training competent teachers resulted in the establishment of the School of Education from the education department and expanded requirements for earning teaching certificates, as well as the development of a library science program. During Chandler's tenure these improvements enabled the college to receive accreditation from the Association of Colleges and Secondary Schools of the Southern States (1921), the Association of American Colleges and the Association of American Universities (both 1922), and the American Association of University Women (1927).

Chandler and the architects Charles Morrison Robinson and Charles Freeman Gillette outlined a new vision for the campus. The president courted wealthy donors with the help of William Archer Rutherfoord Goodwin and cooperated with Goodwin in planning for the restoration of Williamsburg. Chandler's financing of the college was remarkable. He used every trick at his disposal. He frequently began projects before the money was in hand, expecting that he could raise funds to complete them, and he used money intended for one project on another. Chandler borrowed money from banks for construction and land purchases. He had houses built that the sororities rented and that, when paid for, became college property. William and Mary carried insurance on his life, and he was in regular communication with the state auditor, who constantly wrote letters questioning his fiscal practices. During Chandler's tenure, the college renovated old structures such as the Sir Christopher Wren Building, enlarged the library, and erected new dormitories (one named for Chandler), a gymnasium, a science building, and the Phi Beta Kappa Memorial Hall.

In addition to enlarging the campus in Williamsburg, Chandler expanded the reach of the school to Newport News, Norfolk, and Richmond through extension classes that he began in 1919. At times there were classes in other locations as well. In 1925 the college took control of the Richmond School of Social Work and Public Health (forerunner of Virginia Commonwealth University) and added liberal arts classes to its offerings. The Norfolk Division (later Old Dominion University) opened in 1930. Unfortunately, Chandler either lost interest in those other schools or was too overburdened to manage them adequately.

A member of the State Board of Education from 1924 to 1929, Chandler remained a force in educational politics and successfully dealt with successive governors and legislators. He seriously considered running for governor in 1929, but lacking the support of key political leaders he withdrew his name from consideration in the spring of that year, thus leaving the way open for John Garland Pollard, professor of constitutional law and government at William and Mary, to receive the Democratic Party nomination and be elected governor that November.

The most embarrassing episode of Chandler's college presidency occurred in September 1926, when the Ku Klux Klan presented a flagpole to the college. Chandler accepted it, for which he was castigated in several quarters, but he used the occasion to give a speech on toleration. His last years as president were difficult because of declining health and financial problems imposed by the Great Depression that required him to implement such cost-cutting measures as a 25 percent reduction of faculty salaries. A critical report on his financial management embittered him. The board of visitors helped meet his medical expenses, and board member John Stewart Bryan, who succeeded Chandler as president, paid for a vacation in Europe that they hoped would restore Chandler's vigor. The board suggested that he take a long recuperative leave of absence, but he preferred to die working for William and Mary. On 31 May 1934 Julian Alvin Carroll Chandler died in a Norfolk hospital from chronic nephritis and myocarditis. He was buried in Hollywood Cemetery, in Richmond.

Biographies in *NCAB*, 24:73–74, *In Memoriam: Dr. J. A. C. Chandler, President, William and Mary College, 1919–1934* (1934), with frontispiece por., reprinted from *WMQ*, 2d ser., 14 (1934): 259–314 (including 1921 installation address on 290–294), and Solomon R. Butler and Charles D. Walters, *The Life of Dr. Julian Alvin Carrol [sic] Chandler and His Influence on Education in Virginia* (1973); BVS Birth Register, Caroline Co. (misrecorded as a daughter named Julia A. Chandler); BVS Marriage Register, Norfolk Co.; *Portsmouth Star*, 12 July 1897; J. A. C. Chandler Papers, J. A. C. Chandler Presidential Papers, Board of Visitors Minutes, Faculty Minutes, and oral history interview with Chandler in the Columbia University Oral History Tapes (1930), all in University Archives, W&M; Chandler letters in several collections, VHS; *Virginia Journal of Education* 27 (1934): 327–328, 332–335 (cover por.); Susan H. Godson et al., *The College of William and Mary: A History* (1993), 2:541–635; BVS Death Certificate, Norfolk City; obituaries in *Norfolk Ledger-Dispatch*, 31 May 1934, and *New York Times, Norfolk Virginian-Pilot and the Norfolk Landmark, Richmond News Leader, Richmond Times-Dispatch, Washington Post*, and *Williamsburg Virginia Gazette*, all 1 June 1934; editorial tributes in *Norfolk Ledger-Dispatch, Norfolk Virginian-Pilot and the Norfolk Landmark, Richmond News Leader*, and *Richmond Times-Dispatch*, all 1 June 1934, and *Williamsburg Virginia Gazette*, 8 June 1934; memorial in *Virginia Journal of Education* 28 (1934): 5–6.

SUSAN A. RIGGS

CHANDLER, Lucius Henry (20 February 1812– ca. 6 April 1876), Republican Party leader and member-elect of the House of Representatives, was the son of Chauncey Cheneny Chandler, a physician, and Louisa (or Lowicy) Miller Chandler and was born in Belfast, which then lay in Massachusetts but after 1820 in Maine. After receiving an A.B. from Waterville College (later Colby College) in Maine in 1831, he moved to Virginia to teach school at Capeville, in Northampton County. On 9 December 1833 Chandler married Susan Ann Kendall. They had four daughters and two sons. He returned to Maine in 1834 and began practicing law in Thomaston. About 1845 he moved his growing family to Boston for several years before returning to Virginia. Chandler had settled in Norfolk by October 1852, when he became licensed to practice law in the state. He was a staunch Whig throughout the 1850s, even as the national party disintegrated. Like many other Whigs, Chandler supported the American Party (Know Nothing) presidential ticket of Millard Fillmore in 1856, and four years later he was a presidential elector for John Bell, the Constitutional Union Party candidate.

As sectional tension increased in the months following Abraham Lincoln's election, Chandler continued to express his strong Unionist position. He met with the new president in March 1861 to discuss Union sentiment in the state and made several other trips to Washington, D.C., before being arrested in Yorktown as a Union spy. Following his release, Chandler considered settling his family in California. Lincoln rewarded his loyalty by appointing him United States consul at Matanzas, Cuba, late in 1861. Chandler remained at that post for just over a year.

After Union forces captured Norfolk in May 1862, Chandler returned to his adopted home and in July 1863 became the United States attorney for Virginia. In addition to prosecuting many confiscation cases, he helped defend David Minton Wright, a physician who was charged with murdering Alanson L. Sanborn, a white second lieutenant of the 1st Regiment, United States Colored Infantry, in July 1863. This high-profile case brought Chandler into contact with Lincoln once again when he and his co-counsel, United States senator Lemuel Jackson Bowden, appealed to the president to intercede. Both attorneys hoped to have their client declared insane and thereby save him from the gallows, but their efforts proved unsuccessful, and Wright was hanged in October.

In December 1863 Chandler presented his credentials to take a seat in the United States

House of Representatives from the Second Congressional District, comprising eleven counties in southeastern Virginia. He maintained that in May 1863, on the state-mandated date for federal congressional elections, he had polled 778 of 779 votes cast in Norfolk County and the cities of Norfolk and Portsmouth. Examining his application, the House Committee of Elections reported that ten counties in the district were under Confederate control during that time and thus had not participated in the election. On 25 April 1864 the committee found that Chandler was not entitled to a seat on the grounds that the votes tallied in one county could not reasonably reflect the choice of the electorate in the other counties. When the issue was brought to the House floor the following month, Chandler argued his case vociferously, but on 17 May he was denied the seat.

In 1865 Chandler was a Republican candidate for the same Second District seat in the House of Representatives. With most Virginians increasingly mindful that manifestations of continued loyalty to the Confederacy would alienate the Republican-controlled Congress, the election hinged on which candidates could successfully distance themselves from secession and subsequent Confederate service. Chandler's unblemished loyalty to the Union made him the strongest contender, and he further helped his cause by staking out conservative positions: support of President Andrew Johnson's policies and of a general pardon of former Confederates, advocacy of sectional unity, and opposition to African American suffrage. Winning just shy of 50 percent of the vote, he defeated four other candidates, including John Richardson Kilby, a member of the Convention of 1861, and John Singleton Millson, a former congressman. When the members-elect of the Thirty-ninth Congress assembled, Radical Republicans in the House refused to seat Chandler and all the other representatives elected from the former Confederate states.

Chandler remained United States district attorney for Virginia until 1868, by which time he had embraced more-radical positions, particularly the enfranchisement of African American men. That spring Republicans again nominated him for Congress in a convention marred by the exclusion of several delegates loyal to Thomas Bayne, a black dentist who had recently represented Norfolk in the Convention of 1867–1868. Outraged, Bayne announced his own candidacy and drew away many of the Second District's black voters. A heated campaign ensued during the summer of 1868 but ended after Congress did not fund the proposed state elections, which the military district commander then indefinitely postponed.

The death of Chandler's wife early in June 1868 and the disintegration of his congressional campaign may have encouraged him to move to Richmond, where he practiced law and continued his political activism. In January 1869 he worked with other conservative Republicans to convince Washington politicians to accept a proposed compromise that would end Reconstruction in Virginia. Its terms permitted the state electorate to vote separately on the ratification of the new constitution prepared by the Convention of 1867–1868 and on the clauses that would have disfranchised many former Confederates. More-radical Republicans, led by the provisional governor, Henry Horatio Wells, opposed the scheme, which they interpreted as a threat to their political strength. Despite Chandler's role in gaining widespread acceptance of the compromise, during the subsequent campaign for approval of the constitution and election of statewide officers he aligned with the Wells faction of the party in opposition to a coalition of Conservatives and less-radical Republicans. In preparation for the election, held on 6 July 1869, Chandler traveled the state with Wells and delivered speeches in behalf of the Republicans. Late in June, Chandler replaced an African American on the slate of Radical candidates to represent Richmond in the House of Delegates. Although running ahead of the other Radicals, Chandler lost, and statewide the Wells forces suffered resounding defeat. In October, Radicals in the House of Delegates nominated Chandler for a truncated term in the United States Senate, but he lost to John Warfield Johnston, the Democratic candidate, by a vote of 88 to 37.

The following spring Chandler provided legal counsel for George Chahoon in the contested Richmond mayoral election argued before the

Virginia Supreme Court of Appeals. On 27 April 1870 the case was thrown into pandemonium when the courtroom floor in the State Capitol collapsed, killing more than sixty people. Chandler suffered head injuries, which plagued him with severe headaches and periods of depression for the rest of his life. Despite these problems, he unsuccessfully sought election as Richmond commonwealth's attorney that autumn. Early in the 1870s he served as a clerk and inspector for the customs house. He returned to Norfolk in 1875 after being appointed a United States pension agent.

In 1876 Chandler suffered much distress when questions arose concerning financial management of his district attorney and pension accounts. His friend, former congressman James Henry Platt, made inquiries for him, while a government investigation cleared him of any wrongdoing. On 3 April 1876 Platt told Chandler, who was visiting Washington, D.C., that no discrepancies had been found in the accounts. Chandler returned to Norfolk the following afternoon. He spent 5 April taking care of personal business, which included conveying furniture and other household items to his daughter, an action urgent enough to require a notary public to acknowledge the document late that evening.

Lucius Henry Chandler disappeared from the home he shared with his daughter early in the morning on 6 April 1876. Eleven days later an oysterman discovered his body floating in the Elizabeth River. Because rocks weighted the pockets of his coat and pants, a coroner's jury of inquest quickly concluded that he had committed suicide. Chandler was buried in Elmwood Cemetery, in Norfolk.

Biographical materials in alumnus file, Colby College, Waterville, Maine; birth date in Alfred Johnson, ed., *Vital Records of Belfast, Maine, to the Year 1892* (1917–1919), 1:45 (name recorded as Louis Henry Chandler); Northampton Co. Marriage Bonds and Licenses; *Charleston [S.C.] Mercury*, 28 June 1861; *Norfolk Journal*, 29 Apr., 1, 20 May, 7 July 1868; *Alexandria Gazette*, 1 Nov. 1872; *OR*, 2d ser., 6:187, 233, 380; *Congressional Globe*, 38th Cong., 1st sess., 6, 12, 1854, 2311, 2317–2323, 2424–2425; *Lucius H. Chandler . . . Report*, House Committee of Elections, 38th Cong., 1st sess., 1864, House Rept. 59, serial 1206; Alan B. Bromberg, "The Virginia Congressional Elections of 1865: A Test of Southern Loyalty," *VMHB* 84 (1976): 75–98; Richard Lowe, *Republicans and Reconstruction in Virginia, 1856–70* (1991); Thomas C. Parramore with Peter C. Stewart and Tommy L. Bogger, *Norfolk: The First Four Centuries* (1994), 209–211, 219–221; accounts of disappearance, obituaries, and tributes in *Norfolk Virginian*, 8, 11–14, 18, 19 Apr. 1876, *Petersburg Index and Appeal*, 10, 20 Apr. 1876, and *Norfolk Landmark*, 18, 19 Apr. 1876.

JODI L. KOSTE

CHANLER, Amélie Louise Rives. See **TROUBETZKOY, Amélie Louise Rives Chanler.**

CHANLER, John Armstrong. See **CHALONER, John Armstrong.**

CHAPMAN, Augustus A. (9 March 1805–7 June 1876), member of the House of Representatives and member of the Convention of 1850–1851, was born at the residence of his parents, Henley Chapman, a member of the Convention of 1829–1830, and Mary Alexander Chapman, in the part of Montgomery County that became Giles County the following year. Chapman's early years and education are not well documented. With his younger brother Manilius Chapman, later a member of the Convention of 1861, he took courses in law and natural philosophy at the University of Virginia during the 1827–1828 term. On 27 October 1828 the brothers were admitted to practice before the Giles County Court. On 24 March 1830 Chapman married Mary R. Beirne, niece of the wealthy Monroe County merchant and future congressman Andrew Beirne and sister of Manilius Chapman's future wife. Chapman's other politically prominent relatives included his brothers-in-law William P. Cecil, a member of the Convention of 1861, and Albert Gallatin Pendleton, a member of the Convention of 1850–1851. Chapman moved to Union, in Monroe County, about 1832 and lived there the remainder of his life. He and his wife had at least four sons and four daughters.

A natural orator and a Jacksonian Democrat, Chapman excelled in political debate. He was elected to one-year terms representing Monroe County in the House of Delegates in 1835, 1836, and 1837 and again in 1839 and 1840. In his first year he was a member of the Committee of Roads and Internal Navigation. A strong advocate of state support for improved transportation in the western counties, Chapman probably welcomed that appointment. In the next two sessions he sat on the Committee for Courts of Justice, and during his final two terms he was named to the Committees for Courts of Justice and of Privileges and Elections. On 2 March 1840 the General Assembly elected him brigadier general of the 19th Brigade of the Virginia militia.

In April 1843 Chapman easily defeated the Whig candidate James B. Watts to win election to the House of Representatives from the large Twelfth Congressional District, comprising Alleghany, Bath, Botetourt, Floyd, Giles, Greenbrier, Logan, Mercer, Monroe, Montgomery, Pocahontas, Pulaski, and Roanoke Counties. Two years later he won reelection over an independent opponent, Fleming Bowyer Miller. During both terms Chapman was a member of the Committee of Elections and held the ranking position during his second term. Despite his oratorical abilities he did not often speak in debates on the House floor. Chapman probably surprised his fellow Democrats late in 1846 by declining to seek another term in Congress.

In August 1850 Chapman was one of three men in a four-candidate field elected to represent Giles, Mercer, Monroe, and Tazewell Counties in a convention that met from 14 October 1850 to 1 August 1851 to revise the state constitution. A member of the Committee on the County Courts, County Organization, and County Taxation, he was not an active debater during the proceedings, but he twice spoke forcefully in favor of basing representation in both houses of the General Assembly on the white population alone and not counting slave property, as most eastern delegates desired. Chapman, who owned twenty slaves at the time of the convention, also supported other western delegates' proposals to tax slaves according to their market value. He predicted that if eastern slaveholders thwarted the democratic aspirations of western residents, Virginia might ultimately split into two states. Chapman reluctantly acquiesced in the convention's compromise on the apportionment of the legislature in a key vote taken in the committee of the whole on 16 May 1851, and on 31 July he voted in favor of the final constitution, which voters ratified later that year.

Chapman was a delegate to the 1852 and 1856 Democratic National Conventions. In 1857 and 1859 he again won election to the House of Delegates, where he chaired the Committee of Roads and Internal Navigation in both sessions. During the winter of 1860–1861 Chapman became convinced that secession was necessary. Still a brigadier general in the militia, he tried to hold his part of western Virginia, which contained pockets of Union sentiment, for the Confederacy. Chapman led his men to Fayette County and in the autumn of 1861 fought at least one skirmish in that vicinity before returning to reserve duty in Monroe County. He became provost marshal for the county in January 1863 and served in that capacity until June.

After the Civil War, Chapman continued to practice law and took part in Democratic Party politics in West Virginia, although without again running for office. Augustus A. Chapman died in Hinton, West Virginia, probably of a heart attack, on 7 June 1876 while on his way to the state Democratic convention in Charleston. He was buried in Green Hill Cemetery in Union, West Virginia.

Undated biography by son-in-law with birth date in S. Bassett French Papers II, W&M; same birth date on gravestone; improbable middle name Alexandria given in *Biographical Directory of the American Congress, 1774–1949* (1950), 966, and subsequent editions; Chapman correspondence in John McCauley Papers and Stuart-Baldwin Family Papers, UVA; Monroe Co. Minister Returns (1799–1854); *Richmond Enquirer*, 28 Apr., 9 May 1843, 9, 13 May 1845, 3 Sept. 1850; *Journal of 1850–1851 Convention*, 59, 419, and Appendix, 22; *Supplement, 1850–1851 Convention Debates*, nos. 21, 48; *OR*, 1st ser., vol. 51, pt. 2, esp. 266, 273–274, and vol. 52, pt. 2, 326–327; David Scott Turk, *The Union Hole: Unionist Activity and Local Conflict in Western Virginia* (1994); Turk, *The Memorialists: An Antebellum History of Alleghany, Craig, and Monroe Counties of Western Virginia, 1812–60* (1997), por. facing 49; obituary in *Union Border Watchman*, 9 June 1876.

DAVID S. TURK

CHAPMAN, Flavius Josephus (29 June 1839–1 February 1894), hotelier and entrepreneur, was born in Roanoke County and was the son of Nancy Ann Wright Chapman and Henry Harrison Chapman, later proprietor of the original Salem Hotel. Joe Chapman, as he was known, took lessons at a local school and about age twelve became an apprentice in the *Salem*

Roanoke Beacon's printing shop. By 1860 Chapman was leasing the Roanoke Red Sulphur Springs Hotel, located ten miles north of Salem in the Catawba Valley. Two years after their father's death in 1862, he and his brother Henry Clay Chapman inherited the Salem Hotel and renamed it the Chapman Hotel. In 1867 the brother sold his half interest to Chapman, who operated the hotel for three more years before selling it.

On 7 September 1864 Chapman married Clementine Persinger. Of their eleven children, five sons and four daughters survived childhood. Though supporting secession, Chapman did not take up arms for the Confederacy. Because he held property valued at more than $20,000, following the Civil War he sought a presidential pardon, granted on 7 August 1865. As postwar conditions improved, Chapman resumed leasing and eventually purchased the Roanoke Red Sulphur Springs Hotel, and the resort became as famous for its hospitality as it was for its mineral springs. As a sideline, Chapman bottled and shipped the popular mineral waters, which he touted as relief for dyspepsia, hay fever, and lung diseases. His family continued to operate the resort until 1908, when it sold the property to the Commonwealth of Virginia, which established a tuberculosis sanatorium there.

In July 1876 Chapman opened a second resort, the three-story Lake Spring Hotel, in Salem. That same year he constructed Salem's waterworks using three lakes adjacent to his new hotel as the reservoir. A persistent drought undermined the project, however, and several years later the town took over the operation. Chapman experimented with telephone service and was one of the first in the area to use telegraph lines, connecting the Roanoke Red Sulphur Springs Hotel, the Lake Spring Hotel, and the Central Hotel, managed by his brother Orlando B. Chapman. By 1881 he owned the Hampton House. Although Chapman sold the Lake Spring Hotel at public auction, he regained control of that resort in 1883. He also operated Chapman's Mill and was one of the area's principal farmers.

Southerners seeking refuge from yellow fever and northerners fleeing urban congestion made Virginia's medicinal springs a popular destination. The construction of railroads and the large mineral deposits in the region promised huge profits, and land speculation rose precipitously. In 1884 Chapman and other leading residents formed a citizens' executive committee that published 10,000 copies of *Salem and The Roanoke Valley: A Circular of Information*, a seventy-page promotional book designed to attract investors, tourists, and new residents. It advertised both Chapman's resorts and the numerous properties for sale by his real estate business, F. J. Chapman and Company.

During the 1870s and 1880s Chapman developed mining operations in Bedford and Roanoke Counties and others extending from Big Lick (after 1882 Roanoke) westward into Giles and Pulaski Counties. In 1879 he was a charter member of the Virginia Mineral and Gypsum Railroad Company (later the Virginia Iron Trunk Railroad Company). By 1882 he was associated with the prominent Roanoke businessman Ferdinand Rorer, owner of Rorer Iron Mines. Operating as F. Rorer and Company, the two men engaged in numerous land and mineral-rights transactions and built a branch line from the Shenandoah Valley Railroad to the Cloverdale mines in Botetourt County.

Fully participating in the Roanoke Valley speculation and land boom, Chapman in 1890 sold the Lake Spring Hotel to the Lake Spring Land Company, of which he was a director, while continuing to oversee its daily operations. That same year he gained control of yet another hotel when his wife and son purchased the Duval House, which Chapman renamed the Hotel Lucerne. In 1891 he closed a $132,000 deal with the Dixie Land Company and built a handsome brick residence near the Lake Spring property. The next year, however, fire destroyed the Lake Spring Hotel, which was not fully insured. Other financial reverses followed as Chapman's real estate and iron production operations proved especially vulnerable during the panic of 1893. He was forced to sell his new home, and the Lucerne reverted to its previous owner. Praised by the mining engineer and publisher Jedediah Hotchkiss for having done more than anyone else to bring prosperity to the greater Roanoke County region, Flavius Josephus Chapman might have rebounded from his losses, but he died unexpectedly on 1 February 1894 while conducting business at the Hotel Lucerne. He was buried in East Hill Cemetery, in Salem.

Biographies in *South-West Virginia and the Valley* (1892), 155–156 (por.), and William McCauley, ed., *History of Roanoke County, Salem, Roanoke City, Virginia, and Representative Citizens* (1902), 552–553; birth and death dates on gravestone; variant birth date of 29 June 1829 in Nancy Wright Chapman Shanks and Lula E. J. Parker, comps., ancestral chart of Flavius Josephus Chapman, n.d., Salem Museum and Historical Society; BVS Marriage Register, Roanoke Co.; Presidential Pardons; numerous references in Roanoke Co. Chancery Causes and Roanoke Co. Deed Books; Jedediah Hotchkiss, ed., *The Virginias, A Mining, Industrial and Scientific Journal* 3 (1882): 56, 57, 145, 153; *Salem Times-Register*, 14 Mar. 1890, 27 May 1938, 2, 16 Feb. 1984; *Roanoke Times*, 17 June 1892; Martha Whitehurst Chapman, "Summers Long Ago," *The Roanoker* 9 (Aug. 1982): 28–31 (por. on 31); Norwood C. Middleton, *Salem, a Virginia Chronicle* (1986), 110–111, 121–122, 136, 144, 163, 327; "Hotels, Taverns, Enrich City's Past," *A Guide to Historic Salem* 2 (summer 1996): 1, 5, 6; "Local Spas Cured Ailments Galore," *A Guide to Historic Salem* 4 (summer/fall 1998): 1, 4–5; information provided by Helen Chapman Cobbs (2002); obituary and funeral accounts in *Roanoke Times*, 2–4, 6 Feb. 1894, and undated, unidentified Salem newspaper clipping, Salem Museum and Historical Society.

DONALD W. GUNTER

CHAPMAN, Harry Powell (26 November 1888–1 June 1952), editor of the *Roanoke Times*, was born in Portsmouth and was the son of Elizabeth Powell Chapman and James Harry Chapman. Before becoming a banker, Chapman's father had briefly operated the Roanoke Red Sulphur Springs Hotel in Roanoke County, of which his father, the hotelier and entrepreneur Flavius Josephus Chapman, was the proprietor. When Chapman was eleven, the family moved to Salem. He attended the local public schools and then Roanoke College, which granted him a bachelor's degree in 1908 and a master's in 1909. In college Chapman won the Declaimer's Medal and was the final orator for the Demosthenean Literary Society.

Although he had expected to study law after graduating, H. Powell Chapman taught at and was principal of the Cedar Bluff school in Tazewell County during the 1909–1910 academic year. At the end of the term he took a job as reporter for the *Lynchburg News* and a short time later moved to Roanoke as sports writer and city editor of the *Roanoke Times*. By the autumn of 1913 he was living in Savannah, Georgia, and working as news editor for the *Morning Newspaper*. On 4 October 1913 Chapman married Josephine Mann Koehler, of Roanoke. They had one son and one daughter.

Chapman returned to Roanoke in 1915 as associate editor of the *Roanoke Times* and a few months later became editor of the newspaper. During most of his thirty-seven years in that influential position, the *Times* had the widest circulation of any daily paper in the southwestern region of Virginia and earned the nickname the Southwest Virginia Bible. Chapman's daily editorials reached as many as 200,000 people. Politically he was a conservative Democrat and usually supported the dominant faction of the Virginia party, under the leadership of Harry Flood Byrd (1887–1966). Chapman maintained his independence, however, and publicly differed with Byrd on relaxing restrictions on the franchise. He often used sports language in his editorials and was noted for his dry humor. Chapman's editorials won praise from other editors for their high quality. His best-known and most moving editorial, "Our 'Knight in Shining Armor,'" was published on 9 November 1943, two weeks after his namesake son, a naval aviator, died in a plane crash in the Pacific Ocean during a combat mission. The *Times* printed extra copies to meet the demand, and the editorial was widely reprinted in national publications.

Chapman was an enthusiastic fan of local and regional baseball and football teams, and he was active in the community and throughout southwestern Virginia. He served as president of the Roanoke Kiwanis Club and district lieutenant governor of the Kiwanis, president of the Roanoke Executives Club, director and president of the Roanoke Chamber of Commerce, and a national counselor of the United States Chamber of Commerce. Chapman was vestryman of Saint John's Episcopal Church and a member of the Shenandoah Club in Roanoke, of the National Press Club, and of the National Conference of Editorial Writers. He also sat on the board of the Comas Machine Company, of Salem. A popular after-dinner speaker, Chapman during the 1940s was a commentator on the Roanoke radio stations WDBJ and WSLS.

Harry Powell Chapman also helped raise money for Roanoke College and had just returned home from the college's baccalaureate service when he suffered a heart attack and died on 1 June 1952. He was buried in East Hill Cemetery, in Salem.

Biography in *Roanoke Times*, 26 Nov. 1961; birth date of 26 Nov. 1888 on gravestone and in Roanoke newspaper obituaries; BVS Birth Register, Portsmouth (name registered as Harry Powell Dillard Chapman, with variant birth date of 25 Nov. 1888); BVS Marriage Register, Roanoke City; *Roanoke Times*, 4 Oct. 1913; family information provided by daughter, Sophie Chapman Ingles, and by cousin Helen Chapman Cobbs (2004); obituaries and editorial tributes in *Roanoke Times* (por.) and *Roanoke World-News*, both 2 June 1952, *Richmond Times-Dispatch*, 2, 3 June 1952, and *Richmond News Leader*, 3 June 1952.

GEORGE A. KEGLEY

CHAPMAN, Henley (28 March 1779–8 April 1864), member of the Convention of 1829–1830, was born in the valley of the New River, where his parents, John Chapman and Sallie Abbott Chapman, had been among the earliest settlers. He grew up in that part of Virginia, but almost nothing is known about his youth or education before 2 June 1801, when he was admitted to practice law in Montgomery County. On 16 September 1803 Chapman married Mary Alexander in neighboring Monroe County. Their three daughters and two sons included Augustus A. Chapman, who served in the House of Representatives and in the Convention of 1850–1851, and Manilius Chapman, who was a member of the Convention of 1861. One son-in-law, Albert Gallatin Pendleton, was elected to the Convention of 1850–1851, and another, William P. Cecil, represented Buchanan, McDowell, and Tazewell Counties in the secession convention.

Chapman lived on a prosperous plantation known as Mount Prospect, in the part of Montgomery County that in 1806 became Giles County. Following his initial purchase of 160 acres on the west side of the New River in 1802, he acquired more than 6,000 acres in Giles County by 1860, when his real estate was valued at $25,000. Chapman was the first commonwealth's attorney for Giles County. Elected in 1812 to the Senate of Virginia for a four-year term from the sprawling fourteen-county district that encompassed much of present-day southwestern Virginia and southern West Virginia, he served on the Committee to Inspect the Manufactory of Arms in the assemblies of 1812–1813 and 1813–1814. During the 1815–1816 session his district expanded to include an additional county, and he served on the important Committee on Privileges and Elections.

Although never a leading figure in state politics, Chapman evidently retained the respect of his region's voters, who in the spring of 1829 elected him one of four delegates from the counties of Giles, Grayson, Montgomery, and Wythe to the convention that met in Richmond from 5 October 1829 to 15 January 1830 to revise the state constitution. As one of the experienced legislators from southwestern Virginia, Chapman was a member of the committee appointed on the third day to advise the convention on the most expedient way to consider amendments proposed during the proceedings. He also served on the Committee on the Legislative Department. Though he seldom spoke in the debates, he was present for nearly all of the crucial votes and usually sided with advocates of democratic reform. Chapman supported loosening the property qualifications for the franchise. He favored apportioning representation in the General Assembly on the basis of the white population alone, not counting slaves or property as eastern delegates desired, but like other western delegates he opposed the convention's compromise on reapportionment because the eastern part of the state would still control the legislature. Chapman successfully proposed a clause to prohibit one house of the assembly from adjourning for more than three days while the other house was in session, arguing that senators had been known to obstruct the legislative process by not meeting. During the debate on the judiciary in January 1830, he offered an amendment to dock the salaries of judges who without good cause failed to hold court as scheduled, but his proposal was not adopted. Along with many other western delegates who sought democratic reforms, Chapman voted against the new constitution, which the electorate ratified later that year.

Chapman withdrew from elective politics after the convention. He continued to practice law and in September 1834 was one of the commissioners the Giles County Court appointed to oversee the building of a new courthouse. Chapman also managed his vast landholdings and invested in real estate. The 1830 census indicates that he owned twenty-seven slaves. He was an active land trader from the 1830s until his death, but his greatest acquisition, about 1850, was Mountain Lake, one of only two natural lakes in Virginia. In March 1856 Chapman and three partners incorporated the Mountain Lake Company to exploit the sulfur springs and develop the property into a resort. How much involvement Chapman had in the construction of the hotel there is unclear, but he probably did not supervise the resort's daily operations.

Chapman's wife died on 13 July 1837. Thereafter Chapman sometimes lived alone and sometimes with his younger son. The 1860 census enumerator identified him as a "retired Gentleman." Henley Chapman died on 8 April 1864 and was buried probably in the Chapman family cemetery, near present-day Ripplemead, in Giles County.

Birth date in French Biographies; family history in Research Committee, Giles County Historical Society, *Giles County, Virginia, History—Families* (1982), 3, 9 (death date), 36, 73, 225; Monroe Co. Minister Returns (1799–1828), 9; Montgomery Co. Deed Book, C:574; Giles Co. Deed Book, Q:3–6; Land Tax Returns, Montgomery Co. (1805), Giles Co. (1806–1863), RG 48, LVA; Census, Giles Co., 1830, 1850, 1860 (quotation); *Richmond Enquirer*, 5 June 1829; *Journal of 1829–1830 Convention*, 10, 21, 297; *Proceedings and Debates of 1829–1830 Convention*, 799, 800–801, 803, 859–862; Catlin, *Convention of 1829–30* (por.); *Lynchburg Daily Virginian*, 19 July 1855; Patricia Givens Johnson, *Mountain Lake Resort* (1987), 6, 11, 17–23; Virginia Finnegan Roberts, *Mountain Lake Remembered* (1994), 13–24; estate settlement in Giles Co. Order Book (1860–1868), 189.

DARA A. BAKER

CHAPMAN, Hunter Boyd (24 March 1866–18 May 1942), member of the Convention of 1901–1902, was born in Winchester and was the son of Daniel Chapman, a farmer, tavern keeper, and wagoner, and Cornelia Swartz Chapman, who held a house and two adjoining town lots under deeds of trust to protect the property from being used to settle her husband's debts. After his father died in 1875, Chapman continued to

live with his mother until about 1884, when he moved to Mount Jackson, in Shenandoah County, as a night agent for the Baltimore and Ohio Railroad. In April 1885 he became the railroad line's station agent at Woodstock, a position he held for more than forty years, and also served initially as the telegraph operator. Chapman successfully lobbied for a modern depot to replace the shabby building then being used for both passengers and freight, and in 1888 the railway completed a new, ornate limestone facility. He also farmed and became a partner in George R. Geary and Company, a retailer of bark, coal, fertilizer, grain, and agricultural equipment. On 23 April 1888 Chapman married Carrie Lee Stine, a Clarke County native. They had seven sons, including one set of twins.

In 1899 Chapman unsuccessfully sought the Democratic nomination for clerk of Shenandoah County. In March 1901 two rival factions of the county's Democratic Party united to nominate Chapman for a seat in a convention called to revise the state constitution. In the election on 23 May he defeated the Republican nominee, Charles A. R. Moore, by a vote of 1,988 to 1,408. Chapman served on the Committee on Accounts and Expenditures of the Convention. He seldom spoke on the convention floor but introduced two resolutions, the first requiring the counties to pay 75 percent of the expense of prosecuting accused criminals and the second concerning commissioners of revenue. Neither resolution became part of the new constitution. Chapman was not present on 4 April 1902 for the vote on restrictive suffrage measures designed to reduce the number of black and poor white voters. On 29 May he broke with the Democratic majority and opposed proclaiming the constitution in effect without submitting it to the electorate. Chapman voted on 6 June 1902 to approve the final version of the constitution.

Chapman enlarged his farming operation in August 1902 by purchasing the 510-acre Laurel Hill estate and an adjoining 21.5-acre tract three miles southeast of Woodstock. H. B. Chapman and Company, a coal, feed, and grain partnership, prospered as well. Chapman served two terms as captain of the local fire company and on 22 May 1902 won election as mayor of Woodstock by a vote of 188 to 53. During his second term as mayor, he and his wife donated land for a town reservoir and the right of way to reach it and permitted the water mains to connect across their property. In August 1905 Chapman tried to resign as mayor effective immediately. Too few councilmen attended the session, so his resignation was declined and tabled until the next meeting. He remained in office until the spring of 1906.

Woodstock received its first electric streetlights late in 1903, and electricity for general use arrived in the town four or five years later. In September 1909 Chapman bought approximately 194 acres on the North Fork of the Shenandoah River south of Woodstock, and in January of the following year he and his partners received a charter for the Valley Light and Power Company. Completed by the autumn of 1910, the power plant supplied electricity to parts of Shenandoah County. By 1915 the company's lines extended from Strasburg to Edinburg. Chapman sold his interest sometime before August 1925, when the company consolidated with three others to form the Shenandoah River Power Company.

In the autumn of 1921 Chapman and a partner bought the approximately 120-acre Neff Orchard Company farm and orchards near Mount Jackson with the intent of developing the property, particularly the underlying cave discovered late in the nineteenth century. The Shenandoah Caverns formally opened to the paying public on 30 May 1922. Soon a pavilion for dancing and a building at the cave's entrance with tearoom, office, and restrooms awaited visitors. Chapman bought out his partner in February 1925 and incorporated the caverns, which he advertised as the "Grotto of the Gods." He opened a new hotel over the cavern entrance and completed facilities for campers. Chapman and his wife moved to the caverns that same year.

Three of Chapman's brothers died violently. One, a brakeman for the Baltimore and Ohio Railroad, died in March 1876 when a railway trestle south of Woodstock collapsed under the weight of a cattle train and fell more than a hundred feet into a creek bed. The second, a baggage master for the same railroad, was robbed and murdered near Brunswick, Maryland, in Sep-

tember 1907 and then thrown on the railroad tracks, where he was run over by perhaps as many as a dozen trains. Another brother was fatally shot in July 1908 at his store in Hampshire County, West Virginia. Hunter Boyd Chapman died of a heart attack at his home at the Shenandoah Caverns on 18 May 1942. He was buried in Mount Hebron Cemetery, in Winchester.

Birth date in Pollard Questionnaires; biography in *Richmond Times*, 12 June 1901 (por.); BVS Marriage Register, Winchester; *Woodstock Shenandoah Herald*, 27 Apr. 1888, 31 Mar., 7 Apr. 1899, 29 Mar., 28 June, 6 Sept., 18 Oct. 1901, 14 Mar., 23, 30 May 1902, 11 Aug. 1905, 4 Nov. 1921, 26 May 1922, 13 Feb., 17 July 1925; *New Market Shenandoah Valley*, 3 Nov. 1921, 16 Feb., 1, 29 June 1922; *Strasburg Northern Virginia Daily*, 19 Dec. 1941; SCC Charter Book, 71:70–72, 132:136–138; *Journal of 1901–1902 Convention*, 51, 504, 535; *Resolutions of 1901–1902 Convention*, nos. 73, 212; *Convention of 1901–1902 Photographs* (por.); *Shenandoah Caverns, Valley of Virginia* (1928), quotation on 3; obituaries in *Harrisonburg Daily News-Record*, *Richmond Times-Dispatch*, and *Winchester Evening Star*, all 19 May 1942, and *Woodstock Shenandoah Herald*, 22 May 1942.

EMILY J. SALMON
STACY G. MOORE

CHAPMAN, James Archer (8 January 1885–1 March 1956), president of Ferrum Training School and Junior College (later Ferrum College), was born in the town of Omega, in Halifax County, and was the son of James Jackson Chapman and Rosa Archer Blount Chapman. His younger brother Oscar Littleton Chapman, who moved to Colorado as a young man, was secretary of the interior from 1949 to 1953. From childhood Chapman intended to enter the Methodist ministry. He attended Bedford Academy and in 1912 graduated with a B.A. in political economy from Randolph-Macon College, where he was captain of the football team. Two years later he received a divinity degree from Vanderbilt University.

From 1914 to 1916 Chapman was a minister on trial at Ridgeway, in Henry County. During the 1916–1917 academic year he taught history and Bible classes at the Methodist Church's small Ferrum Training School, in Franklin County, while serving as a field representative for the school. Chapman returned to the ministry in 1917 as pastor of Park View Methodist Church, in Portsmouth. He served from 1918 to 1922 at High Street Methodist Church, in the town of Franklin, from 1922 until 1927 at Grace Methodist Church, in Cambridge, Maryland, from 1927 to 1930 at Colonial Avenue Methodist Church, in Norfolk, and from 1930 to 1935 at First Methodist Church, in Hampton. He undertook postgraduate study at Union Theological Seminary, in New York, during the 1931–1932 term, and Randolph-Macon awarded him an honorary D.D. in June 1935.

On 15 July 1935 Chapman returned to Ferrum Training School as its third president. He proposed reinstating the junior college curriculum, which had been discontinued after a trial period in the 1920s. Insisting that a junior college curriculum was in greater demand than the high school curriculum that the school then offered, Chapman persuaded the board to offer junior college courses during the 1936–1937 school year. In 1939 the Methodist Board of Missions and Church Extension gave Ferrum officials permission to seek junior college accreditation from the State Board of Education. Achieving this status, however, required substantial improvements in the school's facilities and financial prospects. In June 1940 Chapman and the school's board of trustees launched the Ferrum Advance campaign to raise $100,000 for improvements. The board changed the name of the school to the Ferrum Training School and Junior College in that same year and won accreditation in July 1941. Having achieved success in elevating the standing of the school and with the fund-raising campaign working toward its goals, Chapman submitted his resignation on 6 June 1943 in order to resume the ministry.

During his presidency, Ferrum's annual budget rose from $20,000 to $66,000 and its endowment from $11,000 to $34,000. The campus nearly doubled in size from 360 to 700 acres, and the school erected six new major structures, including library and music buildings, a faculty apartment, and an infirmary. Under Chapman's leadership, enrollment steadily increased from a Great Depression–era low of slightly more than 100 students during the 1935–1936 term to more than 250 students in the 1939–1940 academic year. By the 1942–1943 term, however, enrollment had contracted again to about 100 students

as a result of military enlistments during the Second World War and expanded employment opportunities in wartime industries.

Chapman was pastor at Larchmont Methodist Church, in Norfolk, in 1943 and 1944 and superintendent of the Eastern Shore District of the Virginia Conference from the latter year until October 1950. Returning to the pulpit once again, he served as pastor of Trinity Methodist Church, in Petersburg, until 1952 and of Trinity Methodist Church, in Smithfield, from then until he retired on 1 September 1955.

On 25 December 1912 Chapman married Gertrude Leigh Sams, of Pittsylvania County. They had three sons before her death from cholecystitis on 2 May 1929. He married Mary Margaret Willis, of Norfolk, on 1 July 1930. They had one son. Chapman published *Catechism* (1918), a small instruction book for children preparing to join the Methodist Church, and four volumes of sermons, *Launching Out into the Deep, and Other Sermons* (1925), *The Royal Road to Friendship* (1929), *The Neglected Service* (1935), and *The First Families of the Old Testament* (1952). James Archer Chapman died in a Suffolk hospital on 1 March 1956 and was buried in Forest Lawn Cemetery, in Norfolk. A student residence hall at Ferrum, built in 1964, bears his name.

Biographies in Elmer T. Clark, ed., *Who's Who in Methodism* (1952), 128, and Arthur L. Stevenson, *Native Methodist Preachers of Norfolk and Princess Anne Counties, Virginia* (1975), 20–21; BVS Marriage Register, Pittsylvania Co. (1912), Norfolk City (1930); Frank Benjamin Hurt, *A History of Ferrum College: An Uncommon Challenge, 1914–1974* (1977), 42, 77–86 (por. on 78); Carolyn Pilla Nolen, "The History of Ferrum College from a Mission School to a College" (Ed.D. diss., VPI, 1996), 97–100; obituaries in *Norfolk Ledger-Dispatch and Star*, *Norfolk Virginian-Pilot*, and *Suffolk News-Herald*, all 2 Mar. 1956, and *Smithfield Times*, 8 Mar. 1956; memorial with birth date in Virginia Conference of the Methodist Church *Annual* (1956), 221–222.

LAURA DRAKE DAVIS

CHAPMAN, John Gadsby (11 August 1808–28 November 1889), painter, was born in Alexandria. The son of Charles Thomas Chapman, a bank cashier, and Margaret Sarah Gadsby Chapman, he was named in honor of his maternal grandfather, John Gadsby, the proprietor of

Gadsby's Tavern in Alexandria. Chapman attended the Alexandria Academy with a son of Eleanor "Nelly" Parke Custis Lewis, a friendship that awakened an interest in George Washington and gave him valuable contacts with the Custis and Washington families. He began drawing at an early age, and his first attempts at oil painting about 1824 received encouragement from the artists George Cooke and Charles Bird King. During the winter of 1824–1825 Chapman attended school in Harford County, Maryland, where he painted at least seven portraits. The next year, at the urging of his father, he began studying law in Winchester, probably with Henry St. George Tucker (1780–1848).

Never truly interested in a legal career, Chapman worked hard in Winchester to improve his painting skills. In 1828 he sought advice from Thomas Sully, who recommended that he study in Philadelphia with Pietro Ancora, an émigré from Naples. Ancora in turn urged Chapman to continue his studies in Europe. Chapman returned to Virginia to paint portraits and take orders for copies of Old Master paintings in order to finance his trip. In 1828 he arrived in Paris and spent several weeks in the Musée du Louvre studying and copying well-known paintings. He then traveled to Rome, where he continued his education in the galleries and polished his skills by reproducing the work of famous artists. He also attended an art class and created an original composition, *Hagar and Ishmael Fainting in the Wilderness* (1830), reproduced later that year in *Giornale de Belle Arti*, an Italian art journal. Chapman devoted much of his time to exploring the Italian countryside on various sketching expeditions. Early in 1831 he arrived in Florence, where he joined a circle of other American artists that included Thomas Cole, Horatio Greenough, and Samuel Finley Breese Morse. Rembrandt Peale visited about this time, and Chapman may have renewed his acquaintance with the novelist James Fenimore Cooper, who in Rome had commissioned Chapman to paint a copy of Guido Reni's *Aurora*. After trips to Bologna, Milan, and Venice, Chapman returned to Virginia later in 1831.

On 20 November 1832 Chapman married Mary Elizabeth Luckett in Martinsburg and then settled in Alexandria. Of their children, only one daughter and two sons survived infancy. Their younger son, Conrad Wise Chapman, named for his father's law school friends David Holmes Conrad and Henry Alexander Wise, also became an artist well known for his Civil War paintings. Chapman opened a studio in Washington, D.C., painted portraits, including *The Family of Mrs. John Augustine Washington of Mount Vernon*, two of David "Davy" Crockett, and one of James Madison (1751–1836), and established a reputation for small canvases of scenes and important events in Virginia history. His painting of the ruins of Jamestown's seventeenth-century church, completed in 1834, is owned by the Virginia Historical Society. In 1836 Chapman rendered several dramatic scenes from the earliest days of the Virginia colony, *The Coronation of Powhatan*, *The Warning of Pocahontas*, and *Pocahontas Saving the Life of Captain John Smith*.

Hoping to advance his career as an illustrator, Chapman moved to New York City in 1834 to take advantage of the city's burgeoning publishing business. A series of his paintings of sites and landscapes connected to George Washington illustrated James Kirke Paulding's *Life of Washington* (1835). Other Chapman engravings appeared in Jared Sparks's multivolume edition of *The Writings of George Washington* (1834–1837), and he was the sole illustrator of Paulding's *Christmas Gift from Fairy Land* (1838) and John Keese's poetry anthology *The Poets of America, Illustrated by One of Her Painters* (1840). A popular and gregarious man, Chapman was one of the founders of the Century Club and an active member of the National Academy of Design, of which he served as secretary from 1845 to 1848.

In February 1837 Henry Wise, then a member of the House of Representatives, helped Chapman win one of the four prestigious and lucrative commissions for new paintings for the Rotunda of the United States Capitol. Chapman had lobbied for such a commission since 1832 and originally planned an epic depiction of John Paul Jones's capture of the British ship *Serapis* in 1779. Within a month of securing the commission, however, he chose an alternative subject from the founding of Jamestown and sailed to England for research on appropriate historical costumes, furniture, and settings. His *Baptism of Pocahontas*, unveiled three years later, was not greeted with enthusiasm and failed to establish his reputation as a muralist. In 1846 he received the commission to model in wax a bas-relief portrait bust of President James Knox Polk for use on an Indian peace medal.

During the mid-1840s Chapman completed two ambitious publishing ventures. Between 1843 and 1845 he provided wood engravings for more than 1,400 illustrations in *Harper's Illuminated and New Pictorial Bible* (1846). In 1847 he published *The American Drawing-Book: A Manual for the Amateur, and Basis of Study for the Professional Artist*, an instructional guide he hoped would find acceptance in America's schools. Although popular and reprinted several times before his death, the book did not rescue Chapman from financial distress. He was plagued by debt and by illness brought on in part by the physical demands of his work and the pressure of stringent deadlines.

In 1848 Chapman auctioned off his artwork and household furnishings to pay his creditors and moved his family to Europe. This hiatus to concentrate on his painting turned into a stay lasting more than thirty years. After stopovers in London, Paris, and Florence, in 1850 the family settled into a studio-apartment in the heart of Rome's international art community. During the next decade Chapman enjoyed the society of other expatriate artists and earned enough income for his family to live in modest comfort. He and his sons, whom he trained, specialized in depictions of Italian peasants and picturesque scenes in Rome and the surrounding countryside. His softly realistic and somewhat sentimental work found a ready market among the many tourists who visited Rome. The American Civil War proved to be a financial and emotional hardship on the Chapman family when American tourism declined and Conrad Chapman left Italy to fight in the Confederate service. After the war the family reunited and resumed painting souvenirs for tourists. Specializing in large-scale landscapes, Chapman completed some of his finest compositions during this period but never fully recovered financially. His last years, when his artistic output slowed and his style fell out of favor, were lean ones.

Chapman's wife died in 1874. He returned to the United States in 1884 and lived first with his elder son in Brooklyn and then for a short time in Mexico City with his younger son. Shortly after returning to New York City, John Gadsby Chapman died on Staten Island on 28 November 1889 and was buried in an unmarked grave. In 1903 Conrad Wise Chapman moved his remains to Brooklyn's Green-Wood Cemetery and the following year donated many of his and his father's works to the Virginia State Library (later the Library of Virginia), which later placed them in the collections at the Valentine Museum (later the Valentine Richmond History Center), in Richmond. The National Gallery of Art and the Library of Virginia mounted exhibitions of Chapman's works in 1962 and 1998, respectively.

Biographies in William Dunlap, *A History of the Rise and Progress of the Arts of Design in the United States* (1834), 2:436–438 (with birth date of 11 Aug. 1808 probably provided by Chapman; 1918 ed., 3:244–246, gives birth date of 8 Dec. 1808 in a footnote without documentation), and Henry T. Tuckerman, *Book of the Artists: American Artist Life* (1867), 216–222; William P. Campbell, *John Gadsby Chapman: Painter and Illustrator* (1962); Georgia Stamm Chamberlain, *Studies on John Gadsby Chapman: American Artist, 1808–1889* (1963), frontispiece self-por.; William M. S. Rasmussen and Robert S. Tilton, *Pocahontas: Her Life and Legend* (1994), 15–16, 18–19, 23–26; Tilton, *Pocahontas: The Evolution of an American Narrative* (1994), 99–131; Ben L. Bassham, *Conrad Wise Chapman: Artist and Soldier of the Confederacy* (1998), esp. 1–54; partial chronology of works in New-York Historical Society, *National Academy of Design Exhibition Record, 1826–1860* (1943), 1:74–78; Chapman correspondence and documents in Chapman Family Correspondence at University of California, San Diego, at VHS, at VRHC, and in privately held Kemble Papers, Bedford Hills, N.Y. (1998), and Robert B. Mayo Collection, Gloucester, Va. (1999; available on LVA microfilm); several Chapman copperplates of engravings and scrapbook of designs on wood, LVA; published writings include Chapman, "Drawing in Public Schools," *The Crayon* 6 (Jan. 1859): 1–4; *Alexandria Phenix Gazette*, 28 Nov. 1832; obituaries in *Brooklyn Daily Eagle*, 29, 30 Nov. 1889, *Alexandria Gazette*, *New York Times*, and *Washington Post*, all 30 Nov. 1889, and *Harper's Weekly*, 14 Dec. 1889; memorial of National Academy of Design printed in *Bulletin of the Virginia State Library* 12 (1919): 77–78.

BEN L. BASSHAM

CHAPMAN, Manilius (14 October 1806–3 October 1883), member of the Convention of 1861, was born on the Giles County estate of his parents, Henley Chapman, a member of the Convention of 1829–1830, and Mary Alexander Chapman. He and his elder brother Augustus A. Chapman, who later served in the House of Representatives and in the Convention of 1850–1851, studied natural philosophy and law together at the University of Virginia during the 1827–1828 academic year. Both were admitted to the practice of law in the Giles County Court on 27 October 1828. About the time he entered the university, Chapman purchased land from his father and began his lifelong occupation of farmer. On 27 July 1837 in Monroe County he married Susan P. Beirne, a sister of his brother's wife and niece of Andrew Beirne, an Irish-born merchant elected to two terms in the House of Representatives. They had two daughters and three sons. Chapman's politically prominent kin network also included his brothers-in-law William P. Cecil, who represented Buchanan, McDowell, and Tazewell Counties at the secession convention, and Albert Gallatin Pendleton, a member of the Convention of 1850–1851.

In 1838 and 1839 Chapman was elected to one-year terms in the House of Delegates, representing Giles and Mercer Counties. In the 1838 session he served on the Committee of Schools and Colleges and in the 1839 session on the Committee for Courts of Justice. Chapman returned to Richmond in 1853 for a four-year term representing Giles, Mercer, Monroe, and Tazewell Counties in the Senate of Virginia. The state senate met twice while he was a member, and in both sessions he sat on the Committee on Agriculture and Commerce and the Committee for Courts of Justice.

Chapman devoted most of his time to farming, not politics. He owned about two dozen slaves in 1850 but only three in 1860. In the latter year Chapman estimated that his real estate was worth about $7,000 and his personal property about $38,000. Chapman's pro-secession views were clearly known to Giles County voters, who early in February 1861 elected him by a narrow margin over Charles D. Peck, also a slave owner but a strong Unionist, to represent the county in the state convention called to consider the secession question. Chapman did not serve on any standing committees and never

spoke on the floor during the recorded debate, but the advocates of secession could count on his vote. On 4 April 1861 he was one of forty-five delegates who voted for secession, when the motion failed. Thirteen days later, following the firing on Fort Sumter and Abraham Lincoln's call for troops to suppress the rebellion, Chapman was in the majority when the convention voted in favor of secession.

After the convention adjourned, Chapman returned to Giles County and managed his farm. Manilius Chapman died on 3 October 1883 and was buried in the Chapman family cemetery, near present-day Ripplemead, in Giles County.

French Biographies; birth and death dates from gravestone, transcribed in Research Committee, Giles County Historical Society, *Giles County, Virginia, History—Families* (1982), 156; Monroe Co. Marriage Bonds; Census, Slave Schedules, Giles Co., 1850, 1860; Reese and Gaines, *Proceedings of 1861 Convention*, 3:163, 4:144; David E. Johnston, *A History of Middle New River Settlements and Contiguous Territory* (1906), 186; some estate accounts and documents in Giles Co. Will Book, 5:304–307, 476.

JOHN G. SELBY

CHAPPELEAR, John Willis (3 February 1929–6 April 1986), architect, was born in High Point, North Carolina, and was the son of John Willis Chappelear and Floyce Goodson Chappelear. After graduating from Hugh Morson High School, in Raleigh, in June 1945, he enrolled in the North Carolina State College of Architecture and Engineering of the University of North Carolina (later North Carolina State University). Following six months of service in the United States Navy early in 1946, Chappelear returned to North Carolina State College and in 1949 completed his architectural training in the School of Design. He married Betty Jean Hooker in Covington, Virginia, on 25 November 1948. They had two daughters and two sons.

Chappelear worked as a designer and draftsman in Henderson, North Carolina, from 1949 to 1953. In the latter year he moved to Roanoke and became an associate and project architect for the architectural firm of Frantz and Addkison. He obtained certification as an architect in 1955 and in 1966 formed a new partnership with Randolph Frantz. Chappelear became a member of the Virginia Chapter (after 1975 the Virginia

Society) of the American Institute of Architects (AIA) in 1957 and three years later was a founding member of its southwest section, of which he was president in 1963 and 1964. He served as treasurer of the Virginia Chapter in 1967, as secretary from 1968 to 1969, as vice president from 1970 to 1971, and as president in 1972.

In 1960 Chappelear began two decades of public service in the civic promotion of architecture and master planning. He served as chair of the Roanoke Junior Chamber of Commerce Civic Center Committee from then until 1964. A member of the Roanoke City Board of Zoning Appeals from 1964 to 1980, he chaired that body from 1966 to 1974. As president of Downtown Roanoke, Inc., from 1965 to 1966, Chappelear led an effort to preserve the character of the downtown business area and what became the Roanoke City Market Historic District. He served two terms, from 1970 to 1978, on the Virginia Art Commission, the last three years as president.

Chappelear's skills in articulating the need for architectural collaboration and civic planning enabled him to secure several important commissions. He worked closely with the Roanoke architectural firm of Smithey and Boynton to prepare the 1967 master development plan for Virginia Western Community College. The Roanoke Civic Center, dedicated in 1971, marked the culmination of Chappelear's efforts in master planning, public relations, fund-raising, and project direction. He received a Distinguished Service Award from the Virginia Society of the American Institute of Architects in 1981 for his achievements in architecture and his involvement in local and state civic programs.

Chappelear's architectural designs frequently reflected the influence of Frank Lloyd Wright, the architect he most admired. He designed the Thomas Engleby House in Roanoke in 1962 in the simple rectilinear Usonian form that Wright employed for residences for a decade after World War II. The Chappelears lived in that house from 1971 to 1986. One of his last commissions, the quarter-round semidetached addition to the Roanoke City Public Library, completed in 1984, drew on Wright's design for the Solomon R. Guggenheim Museum in New York City. Perhaps Chappelear's most successful institutional building was the Charles A. Dana Science Building for Hollins College (later Hollins University), completed in 1967. Designed by Frantz and Chappelear, along with the firm of Douglas Orr, de Cossy, Winder and Associates, of New Haven, Connecticut, the square, brick, two-story building with prominent external supports received a national Award of Merit from the AIA.

A private, quiet man, Chappelear enjoyed woodworking, gardening, gourmet cooking, and surf fishing. He suffered from chronic bronchitis and emphysema during the last five years of his life. John Willis Chappelear died of congestive heart failure in Roanoke on 6 April 1986 and was interred in the city's Evergreen Burial Park.

John F. Gane, ed., *American Architects Directory*, 3d ed. (1970), 150; John Willis Chappelear Family Papers, in possession of widow, Betty Jean Hooker Chappelear, Roanoke (2003); family information furnished by Betty Jean Hooker Chappelear and son Donald Eugene Chappelear; *Covington Virginian*, 26 Nov. 1948; *Roanoke Times*, 12 Feb. 1967; [W. L. Whitwell, ed.], *Roanoke Architecture* (1969), 35, 42–43; "A Science Building—Contemporary Yet Sedate—for an Old Southern College," *Architectural Record* 147 (1970): 110–111; Frances J. Niederer, *Hollins College: An Illustrated History* (1973), 197–199; Roanoke City Library Addition, 1982–1984, clipping file, Virginia Room, Roanoke Public Library; obituary in *Roanoke Times and World-News*, 7 Apr. 1986 (por.).

JOHN R. KERN

CHAPPELL, John Taylor (18 May 1845–27 September 1915), labor leader, was the son of Samuel Chappell, a Richmond butcher, and Eliza B. Gentry Chappell. Before his fifteenth birthday he began an apprenticeship to a coachmaker. The Civil War intervened, and in May 1861, against his mother's wishes, Chappell enlisted in Company H of the 23d Regiment Virginia Infantry, also known as the Richmond Sharpshooters. He took part in the Rich Mountain and Cheat Mountain battles in western Virginia before being discharged on 12 October 1861. Early the next year he joined Company A of the 10th Virginia Cavalry and fought in the Peninsula campaign. Chappell also served in the Confederate States Navy aboard the ironclad *Virginia II* late in 1864 and as first sergeant in Company D of the 1st Regiment Naval Brigade. He surrendered in North Carolina and was paroled at Greensboro on 1 May 1865.

Chappell returned to Richmond, became a carriage painter, and resided at the corner of Twenty-second and Clay Streets on Union Hill, a community of laboring men, artisans, and shopkeepers who lived in modest frame houses. On 14 October 1866 he married Martha Virginia Scherer. Of their four children, one daughter and one son reached adulthood. Chappell owned a large library from which he educated himself. His grandson, Samuel Warren Chappell, who became a nationally recognized book illustrator and typographer, fondly recalled his grandfather, who lived with the extended family, and his grandfather's meetings at their home, where his progressive friends and comrades discussed philosophy, society, and socialism.

Chappell joined the Independent Order of Odd Fellows and taught in a Baptist Sunday school. His experiences as a laboring man in a time of corporate and industrial consolidation combined with his socialist beliefs to lead him into working-class activism. Chappell joined the Knights of Labor, organized and served as master workman of Union Assembly No. 3545, and became a leader in Richmond's District Assembly 84. Also one of the organizers of the Knights of Labor Building Association in the city, he won election on 19 January 1886 as a trustee and director representing Union Assembly. In November of that year he was elected secretary.

Despite simmering class antagonism, a lack of working-class solidarity had defeated strikes by Richmond ironworkers and bricklayers in the 1870s and early in the 1880s. Breaking this pattern, the Knights organized workers across skill, racial, and even gender divides. Richmond's working-class people boycotted flour produced in the local Haxall Mills because it used convict labor and eventually forced the giant mill to capitulate. Arguing that local quarries should provide the stone and employ organized labor, the Knights in May 1886 also organized protests against the contracts to construct a new city hall.

The national leadership of the Knights of Labor had long eschewed overt politics as an avenue for implementing change, but as the movement gathered strength, local leaders in many communities turned to the political arena. As working-class activism in Richmond increased, both the Democratic and Republican Parties co-opted the movement. In July 1885 several Knights won election to the Democratic Party's ward committees. Chappell received a seat on the seven-member committee representing Jefferson Ward. The Knights of Labor held a convention in Richmond in May 1886 and nominated a slate of reform candidates for city offices. Later that month the reformers won election in five of the city's six wards. Some, including Chappell, who became one of three aldermen from Jefferson Ward, were veteran labor men, and others were Republicans and Democrats pledged to reform.

Chappell served on the bicameral Richmond city council for four years and sat on the committees on the streets, on the first market, on retrenchment and reform, and on the fire alarm and police telegraph. He chaired the committee on the second market in 1888. The victory of the reformers quickly proved illusory. Even before the new council's first meeting, the reform caucus fell into bitter feuds regarding policy and patronage. Democrats elected under the reform banner backed away from their campaign commitments, especially after the council's African American members demanded that blacks receive a share of the city's jobs. Chappell and the remaining eleven members of the caucus, all white trade unionists and labor and political reformers, turned to the six African American councilmen for support. The reformers remained a marginalized minority, however. They were attacked for their progressive views and effectively shut out of major decisions.

Despite these setbacks, Chappell and other white progressives made common cause with a powerful black popular movement that increasingly associated its interests with those of the Knights of Labor. The hundreds of black fraternal orders that flourished in postwar Richmond provided thousands of recruits who were attracted by the Knights' fraternal ritual and structure and its acceptance of black working people, albeit in segregated local assemblies. White radicals increasingly allied themselves with black aspirations as well. Chappell was instrumental in opening membership in the Knights' building association to African Americans. When the

Knights of Labor held its national convention in Richmond in October 1886, he served as a key organizer for a series of events that brought thousands of black Richmonders into the streets. On 11 October he was a marshal for a parade of black and white laboring men that made its way to the fairgrounds for sporting events, fireworks, and a grand ball.

While Chappell and other white labor leaders drew closer to the black popular movement in 1886, the national meeting of the Knights exposed an opposite tendency among Richmond's white workingmen. Many declared their anger when some northern delegates to the convention flouted racial conventions in the city, and a dispute about the role of a black delegate in the meeting's program also caused consternation. The massive participation of African Americans in public events at the convention and the black community's agenda, which went well beyond workplace reforms, gave white trade unionists pause. Such splits along lines of race, occupational skill, and religion contributed to the eventual decline of the Knights both nationally and locally, divisions that Democratic and Republican Party leaders eagerly exploited.

The waning of the Knights did not deter Chappell and his comrades from continuing to organize workingmen and to advocate transformations of society. In January 1888 he attended a state convention of wage-workers in Staunton. There Chappell introduced resolutions asking the General Assembly to restrict child labor and to adopt the secret ballot. The convention attempted to unite the labor movement with farmers and advocated such familiar reforms as restriction of convict labor but had no practical result. In April 1895 Chappell held a meeting at his Union Hill home to organize the Altrurian Assembly of a new, or reformed, Knights of Labor. The organization became Local Union No. 1 of the Cooperative Commonwealth of Virginia. Because the members preferred to spend their dues on local projects, on 7 February 1898 the local withdrew from the national organization and renamed itself the Socialist Educational Club of Richmond. From its inception, it sought to educate the people of Richmond about socialism, and the members sponsored lectures and distributed literature on social and labor topics.

For the organization's second meeting, Chappell prepared a short paper entitled "What Is Socialism." In it, he explicitly rejected the notion that socialism was derived from a Christian basis, although he admitted that Christian ethics were perfectly compatible with socialist teaching. Chappell's views may have been a reaction to the overtly Christian symbolism and language employed by the Knights of Labor and other Christian Socialists. Chappell asserted that socialism sprang from basic human necessities of a materialistic character, notably adequate clothing, food, and shelter. He had put those views into practice as an officer in the Knights of Labor Building Association. Chappell and his contemporaries believed that many of the difficulties facing the working class were the result of rents and other sources of economic dependence, a key tenet of early Jeffersonian Republicanism and American artisan protest. According to his grandson, Chappell's unusual views on society and religion were the probable cause of his removal as a Sunday school teacher and expulsion from his church.

Chappell's socialist worldview did not deter him from honoring the memory of his fellow Confederates. As master workman of Union Assembly No. 3545, Knights of Labor, he presented to the city council a petition signed by many of his neighbors asking that the proposed equestrian statue of Robert Edward Lee be placed in Marshall Park on Church Hill rather than at the site that was eventually selected on the western outskirts of the city. Chappell's postwar writings suggest that he learned different lessons from the Civil War than had many other Confederate veterans. In a series of unpublished reminiscences written in the 1890s, he recounted some of his wartime experiences in a decidedly nonheroic style, focusing instead on the common soldier and the irony of war. His writings include a poignant account of a young soldier's death at Cheat Mountain and his own small part in the blunders of his unit at the Battle of Malvern Hill. Chappell also wrote about the career and death of a member of Richmond's all-Irish Montgomery Guard who had been a childhood playmate. Because the soldier was not "born with a silver spoon in his mouth, and there being no one sufficiently interested to trace his pedigree back to some family of English ari[s]tocracy, the fount from which must flow all human perfection," his memory was fleeting, like that of "a meteor which causes exclamations of wonder and admiration, when coursing its way through the heavens, [but] is forgotten as soon as its trail of fire fades from view." Chappell's sympathy, as always, was with the common man. Indeed, when asked why he had fought for the Confederacy, he stated that he went to war because he did not want to leave his friends. After the Civil War, Chappell became a pacifist.

John Taylor Chappell died suddenly of an aneurism on 27 September 1915 at the Gross Carriage Works in Richmond and was buried in the city's Oakwood Cemetery.

Birth date on BVS Death Certificate, Richmond City; family history by grandson Samuel Warren Chappell in *Something about the Author: Autobiography Series* 10 (1990): 57–59 (por. on 59); marriage date and other information in pension application of widow Martha Virginia Chappell, filed on 29 Dec. 1922, Confederate Pension Rolls, Veterans and Widows, Department of Accounts, RG 6, LVA; John Taylor Chappell Papers, including unpublished MSS, among them "From Yorktown to Williamsburg" (quotation), VHS; Chappell Family Papers, including MS "What is Socialism" and John Taylor Chappell Notebook with organization minutes, UVA; Compiled Service Records; Robert J. Driver Jr., *10th Virginia Cavalry* (1992), 18, 101; *ORN*, 2d ser., 1:311; *Richmond Labor Herald*, 8, 22, 29 May 1886; *Staunton Vindicator*, 20, 27 Jan. 1888; Peter Jay Rachleff, "Black, White, and Gray: Working-Class Activism in Richmond, Virginia, 1865–1890" (Ph.D. diss., University of Pittsburgh, 1981), esp. 858–860, 1,082–1,083; Gregg D. Kimball, "The Working People of Richmond: Life and Labor in an Industrial City, 1865–1920," *Labor's Heritage* 3 (Apr. 1991): 53–55 (por. on 54–55); obituaries in *Richmond News Leader*, 28 Sept. 1915 (por.), and *Richmond Times-Dispatch*, 29 Sept. 1915.

GREGG D. KIMBALL

CHAPPELL, Samuel Warren (9 July 1904–26 March 1991), illustrator and typographer, was born in Richmond. He was the son of Samuel Michael Chappell and Mary Lillian Hardie Chappell and the grandson of John Taylor Chappell, a Richmond coach-painter committed to socialist and labor activities. Chappell attended John Marshall High School, where he was a member of the cadet corps, edited the monthly *John Marshall Record*, and in his senior year was arts edi-

tor and assistant business manager of the yearbook. After graduating in 1922, he matriculated at the University of Richmond and studied biology and economics. Chappell was president of the Omicron Delta Kappa leadership honor society and edited the university's annual. He graduated in 1926 and moved to New York to study etching, woodcutting, and wood engraving with Allen Lewis at the Art Students League. On 27 August 1928 Chappell married Lydia Anne Hatfield, whom he had met when she was a student at Westhampton College of the University of Richmond and a fellow member of the university's theatrical group. They had no children and lived initially in Brooklyn Heights, New York.

Warren Chappell served on the Board of Control at the Art Students League from 1927 to 1930. For Christmas 1928 the Chappells collaborated with Allen Lewis and George Grady to produce Honoré de Balzac's *Jésus Christ en Flandre*. Lydia Chappell translated the text, Lewis provided the illustrations, and Chappell designed the book. For Grady, editor and owner of Strawberry-Hill Press, Inc., Chappell also designed and illustrated editions of Geoffrey Chaucer's *Prioress's Tale* (1929), using the pseudonym Georg Hansen, and of James Russell Lowell's *Vision of Sir Launfal* (1930). Grady helped Chappell find a position in promotional advertising at *Liberty Magazine*.

In 1931 the Chappells went to Germany, where he studied calligraphy, type design, and hand punch-cutting with Rudolf Koch in Offenbach am Main and she studied bookbinding, weaving, and tapestry embroidering. Returning to New York the following year, Chappell worked as a freelance illustrator and taught at the Art Students League. They moved in 1935 to Colorado Springs, where Chappell worked with Boardman Robinson to establish the Colorado Springs Fine Arts Center. The Chappells returned to New York in September 1936 and moved to Norwalk, Connecticut, in 1951.

By 1955 Chappell had designed, decorated, or illustrated more than 120 books. For about thirty years, beginning in the mid-1940s, he served as a design consultant for the Book-of-the-Month Club and from November 1947 designed its monthly newsletter. He illustrated titles in the Collier series of Junior Classics for children beginning in 1936 and from 1940 until the 1970s was a regular designer and illustrator of classics, music books, and cookbooks for Alfred A. Knopf, Inc., and of titles for Random House and other publishers.

Chappell wrote several books on printing and typography, including *The Anatomy of Lettering* (1935) and *The Living Alphabet* (1975), as well as articles on design and illustration. The American Institute of Graphic Arts named *The Anatomy of Lettering* one of the fifty best books of the year, and nine of his other books, including an edition of *Don Quixote* (1939) for which he did the illustrations, received the same distinction. In 1947 the Chappells collaborated a second time on *A Gallery of Bible Stories*. Chappell published *A Short History of the Printed Word* in 1970 and had an exhibition at Gallery 303 of the Composing Room in New York that displayed forty years of his work. He received praise as an illustrator for the clarity of his drawings and his ability to complement narratives.

As a typographer, Chappell considered the white space of a letter as important as its black form. From Koch he learned that punch-cutting was a sculptural process that taught the designer to simplify. Chappell designed Lydian, a typeface named for his wife. In 1939 American Type Founders cut the face, which was the first broadpen letter in roman, italic, and cursive by an American designer. Chappell also designed Trajanus, cut in 1940 by the D. Stempel Foundry in Frankfurt, Germany. In 1970 Chappell gave the Frederic W. Goudy Lecture at which he received the Goudy Award. His lecture warned against complacency in modern electronic typesetting and photographic composition and echoed what he had written in *A Short History of the Printed Word*— "A good page of letterpress printing *is* an original. It is not a picture of a page of type." In a privately printed pamphlet, *My Life with Letters* (1974), issued by the Typophiles, Chappell admitted that he was "hopelessly dedicated to letterpress, and the authority of an impression into paper."

Chappell received an honorary doctorate of fine arts from the University of Richmond in 1969. Nine years later he became artist-in-residence at the University of Virginia, and the Chappells moved to Charlottesville. He received a bequest from a friend in 1984 and in his name established the Charles Locke Fund for purchasing books on drawing and printing for the university's libraries. Samuel Warren Chappell died in Charlottesville on 26 March 1991 and was cremated. Lydia Hatfield Chappell died in that city on 25 June 2001.

Autobiography with birth and marriage dates and bibliography of publications in *Something about the Author: Autobiography Series* 10 (1990): 57–74 (pors.); Mark Lutz, "Warren Chappell, '26: Distinguished American Artist," University of Richmond *Alumni Bulletin* 5 (Mar. 1941): 1 (self-por.), 20; Norman Kent, "Warren Chappell, Pen Draughtsman," *American Artist* 8 (Oct. 1944): 19–23; Paul A. Bennett, "Designer, Artist, Illustrator: Warren Chappell," *Publishers' Weekly* 168 (1 Oct. 1955): 1586–1590; Warren Chappell Papers and Warren Chappell Oral History Interview, 1978, both UVA; other publications include "The Woodcut in Book Decoration," *League* 6, no. 1 (1934): 10–13, "The Anatomy of Printing," *Virginia Quarterly Review* 17 (1941): 574–588, "Illustration in These United States," *Dolphin* 4 (1941): 174–184, "Artist vs. Craftsman?" *Printing and Graphic Arts* 4 (1956): 1–8, and "Bench Marks for Illustrators of Children's Books," *Horn Book* 33 (1957): 413–420; Frederic W. Goudy Lecture published as *Forty-Odd Years in the Black Arts* (1970); Chappell, *A Short History of the Printed Word* (1970), first quotation on 244; Chappell, *My Life with Letters* (1974), second quotation on 2; *Richmond Times-Dispatch*, 7 Apr. 1946, 30 Oct. 1949, 9 June 1969, 30 Aug. 1982; *New York Times Book Review* (6 Dec. 1970), 90; information provided by Weston Hatfield, Lydia Hatfield Chappell's nephew (2002); obituaries in *Charlottesville Daily Progress*, *Richmond News Leader*, and *Richmond Times-Dispatch*, all 28 Mar. 1991.

BARBARA C. BATSON

CHARITY, Ruth LaCountess Harvey Wood (18 April 1924–26 April 1996), attorney and civil rights activist, was born in Danville and was the daughter of Charles Clifton Harvey, a Baptist minister, and Annie Elizabeth Lovelace Harvey, a teacher. She was educated in the racially segregated Danville public schools and finished high school at the Palmer Memorial Institute in Sedalia, Guilford County, North Carolina, known for its leadership training for African American women. She received an A.B. from Howard University and in June 1949 graduated from its law school. After working for the federal government for about a year, she was admitted to the Virginia bar in 1951 and on 30 June of that year married the Danville attorney Harry Inman

Wood. They opened a joint practice in Danville, and she retained her maiden name professionally. They had no children and divorced on 4 November 1964. On 24 February 1968 she married Ronald Karl Charity, formerly of Richmond, an accomplished tennis player and coach who had helped train Arthur Robert Ashe. He had one son whom the Charitys raised in their Danville home. After her second marriage, she was known as Ruth Harvey Charity.

As president of the Howard University chapter of the National Association for the Advancement of Colored People in 1944, Ruth Harvey led a sit-in at a segregated restaurant in Washington, D.C. Civil rights advocacy was a constant theme of her professional career. In 1960, as sit-ins in nearby Greensboro, North Carolina, drew national attention and galvanized the direct-action phase of the civil rights movement, she protested segregation in Danville's public library and parks. In the spring of 1963 local black ministers affiliated with the Southern Christian Leadership Conference organized the Danville Movement to combat segregation and discrimination in all aspects of the city's public and economic life. When the Danville Movement collided in June of that year with a city government determined to maintain segregation, Harvey became deeply involved in defending civil rights activists.

As one of a small group of attorneys—some local, some from elsewhere in Virginia, and ultimately some nationally known—she defended the members of the movement against intense legal attack. Faced with an increasing number of demonstrations, the Danville judge Archibald Murphey Aiken issued a sweeping injunction banning most forms of public protest. While enforcing Aiken's blanket ban, Danville police officers assaulted a group of nonviolent protestors on 10 June 1963; using nightsticks and fire hoses, they injured forty-eight people. The city council passed ordinances reinforcing Aiken's injunction, and a special grand jury indicted movement leaders under an antebellum state law making it a felony to incite the black population to insurrection against whites. Local protestors, augmented by representatives from the Student Nonviolent Coordinating Committee, defied the city's ban on demonstrations, an action that resulted in more than 600 arrests on 1,200 charges. During the complicated appeals in state and federal courts that followed, attorneys from the NAACP and nationally known civil rights lawyers, including Arthur Kinoy and William M. Kunstler, assisted with the initial appeals, but after 1964 the work fell mostly on Harvey and a few African American lawyers in Danville.

The Danville demonstrations briefly gained national news coverage and contributed to the rising sentiment in favor of civil rights legislation, but the costs were high for the demonstrators, in fines and jail time, and for Harvey, in having her legal practice dominated by financially nonlucrative civil rights work. After a break for the first round of appeals, Aiken resumed his heavy-handed trials of the demonstrators in 1966. He issued contempt citations to Harvey and a local white business executive who criticized his courtroom conduct. The trials and appeals lasted until 1973, two years after Aiken's death. The Virginia Supreme Court of Appeals ultimately overturned more than two hundred of the convictions. Through that long legal process Ruth Harvey Charity became Danville's best-known civil rights lawyer and one of the best-known black women in the state. Her skill also attracted clients among low-income whites who began to turn to her as a legal advocate for the poor.

Charity directed her civil rights activism into politics. In 1967 she lost a runoff primary vote for a seat in the Virginia House of Delegates and mounted an unsuccessful write-in campaign in the November election. The next year she unsuccessfully sought election to the House of Representatives as an independent candidate, and in 1969 state civil rights leaders recommended her for appointment to the Virginia Supreme Court of Appeals. She supported the statewide campaigns of Henry Evans Howell Jr., a maverick Democrat from Norfolk elected lieutenant governor in 1971. Charity won enough support from both black and white voters in 1970 to come in fourth in a field of sixteen candidates in a race for four city council seats, thus becoming the first black woman in Danville's history elected to the city council. She served only one four-year term on that body, but she held other political party offices, including two terms, from 1972 to 1980, as one of four Virginia members of the Democratic National Committee. Her husband managed her campaigns for office and shared her political activism. They also had several business ventures in public relations, including the promotion of a national beauty and scholarship pageant for African American teenage girls. She served on the boards of several educational institutions, including Howard University, and in 1967 was president of the Old Dominion Bar Association.

Personal misconduct brought an unfortunate end to Charity's legal career. In 1984 the Danville commonwealth's attorney prosecuted her for embezzling more than $51,000 from the estates of two of her clients. She was convicted and sentenced to eight years' incarceration. The sentence was suspended on the condition that she serve three years on probation, perform 400 hours of community service, and restore the stolen money. She also lost her license to practice law. In 1985 Charity moved to Alexandria and worked for the Fairfax Human Rights Commission. Governor Lawrence Douglas Wilder restored her voting rights in June 1990. On the following 14 April her husband died in Charlotte, North Carolina, where he had been residing.

On 5 February 1996 Charity collapsed while waiting for a bus in Washington, D.C., and fell into a coma. Taken to a nursing home in Greenbelt, Maryland, Ruth LaCountess Harvey Wood Charity died there on 26 April 1996 and was buried in Oak Hill Cemetery, in Danville.

Dawn Bradley Berry, *The 50 Most Influential Women in American Law* (1996), 191–193; birth, marriage, and divorce dates verified by BVS; family information provided by Louise F. Harris, Danville (2002); Charity oral history interview, 29 Aug. 1970, Ralph J. Bunche Oral History Collection, Moorland-Spingarn Research Center, Howard University; Danville Corporation Court 1963 Civil Rights Case Files (1963–1973), including Dictabelt sound recordings, Acc. 38099, LVA; *Danville Commercial Appeal,* 15 June 1970; *Richmond News Leader*, 29 Jan. 1991; *Richmond Times-Dispatch*, 30 Jan. 1991; Len Holt, *An Act of Conscience* (1965); James W. Ely Jr., "Negro Demonstrations and the Law: Danville as a Test Case," *Vanderbilt Law Review* 27 (1974): 927–968; Ruth Harvey Charity, Christina Davis, and Arthur Kinoy, "Danville Movement: The People's Law Takes Hold," *Southern Exposure* 10 (July/Aug. 1982): 35–45; Mary King, *Freedom Song: A Personal Story of the 1960s Civil Rights Movement* (1987), 79–119; obituaries in *Danville Register and Bee,* 27 Apr. 1996 (por.), *Richmond Free Press,* 9–11 May 1996 (por.), and *Richmond Times-Dispatch,* 10 May 1996.

JAMES H. HERSHMAN JR.

CHASE, Richard Thomas (15 February 1904–2 February 1988), writer and folklore collector, was the son of Robert Collier Chase and Emma Florence Chase Chase. He was born near Huntsville, Alabama, where his family operated a profitable nursery. A gifted but rebellious and troubled youth who never satisfied his father's strict demands, he fondly remembered the African American servant who appeared to love him and his siblings more than their parents did. Educated at several schools including a private one in Tennessee, Chase attended Vanderbilt University for the academic year 1920–1921 and then Harvard University for the academic years 1921–1922 and 1923–1924. In 1929 he received a B.S. in botany from Antioch College, in Yellow Springs, Ohio. On 1 December 1929 in Arden, New Castle County, Delaware, he married Katherine Gay Stout in a Quaker ceremony. They had one daughter before they divorced on 17 March 1950. Much later in life, Chase privately defended love between men and cited ancient and modern writers who acknowledged what he called Greek love or Greek friendship.

Following their marriage Chase and his wife spent several years traveling in Europe. After their return he settled in Chapel Hill, North Carolina, where he worked at the Institute of Folk Music in the mid-1930s. His interest in traditional music had been sparked in 1924, when he had hitchhiked from Boston to Kentucky to visit the Pine Mountain Settlement School, where he heard children sing the ballad "Merry Golden Tree." A second turning point in Chase's life occurred in 1935, when Marshall Ward, a teacher attending one of his North Carolina folk-song workshops, introduced him to folktales about a boy named Jack. Ward and his relatives in the Hicks-Harmon family of storytellers in the Beech Mountain area of Avery and Watauga Counties, North Carolina, were major sources for Chase and other researchers who collected folklore that their ancestors had brought from Europe.

Chase immersed himself in both informal and academic study of southern mountain folklore. He taught about folklore and participated in re-creation workshops and festivals, joined and organized dance and music societies, and visited hundreds of libraries and schools. He emulated humble rural singers and storytellers, as well as such professionals as Cecil James Sharp, the English folklorist who had published ballads collected in the American South. Chase made field recordings at the White Top Folk Festival, in Grayson County, in 1935 and the next year became a director of the festivals, held annually through 1939 and cancelled in 1940 because of flooding. There he presented programs derived from his folklore research and in cooperation with John Powell and others. They used the festivals to foster music and musicians whom they believed were preserving an authentic Appalachian folk-music culture.

About 1938 Chase moved to Richmond, where he taught school and worked for the Works Progress Administration. He had moved to Glade Spring, in Washington County, by 1940. In 1941 he visited James Taylor Adams, another collector of folklore, who lived in Wise County, and the next year Chase moved to the Albemarle County town of Proffit, where he prepared a volume of Wise County tales for publication by the WPA's Virginia Writers' Program. The WPA ceased operation in 1942, however, and the following year Houghton Mifflin published Chase's book as *The Jack Tales*. Chase's research papers were later destroyed when his house in North Carolina burned, but Adams kept thousands of typescript pages of their southwestern Virginia correspondence and unpublished folklore. The Chase and Adams collections provided scholars and storytellers a wealth of material after being rediscovered in the 1970s.

Chase also recorded songs and tales for archives and journals in the 1930s, but it was his publication of books during the next two decades that brought him fame and earned royalties. *Grandfather Tales: American-English Folk Tales* (1948) combined a frame story about a folklorist visiting mountain families with comic and adventurous tales of male and female heroes, including three shoats attacked in their houses by a fox and Ashpet, an Appalachian Cinderella. His volumes, especially *American Folk Tales and Songs,*

and Other Examples of English-American Tradition as Preserved in the Appalachian Mountains and Elsewhere in the United States (1956), continue to number among the most popular collections of American folktales. *The Jack Tales* and other of Chase's books have remained in print, including *Hullabaloo and Other Singing Folk Games* (1949), republished in 1967 as *Singing Games and Playparty Games*. Chase published three picture books for children, *Jack and the Three Sillies* (1950) and *Wicked John and the Devil* (1951), both adapted from the tales, and *Billy Boy* (1966), adapted from the song of that name. In 1987 the Children's Literature Association named *The Jack Tales* a "Touchstone" of children's literature. Many of his songs and tales were featured on audio and video recordings, in which Chase collaborated with other performers and in some instances provided narration or played the harmonica. Like the Brothers Grimm, Chase acknowledged that he combined and edited oral sources. He earned praise for making the tales accessible to family audiences but received criticism from scholars for distorting the folklore record and dialect of his informants.

Chase compiled and wrote an introduction for a 1955 edition of Joel Chandler Harris's *Complete Tales of Uncle Remus*. Although he was best known, and sometimes criticized, for promoting the revival of ancient Anglo-Saxon folk traditions as vital to the heritage of all Americans, his knowledge and appreciation of African American and Native American traditions were extensive. Chase emphasized the blending of cultural traditions throughout American history. He taught English Morris dances, sword dances, puppetry, folk dramas, and rituals and also urged his audiences and students to collect folklore from their own families. He advertised his services as a master storyteller, sometimes billing himself as "Uncle Dick." His countless public appearances, often wearing Indian necklaces and berets with feathers, inspired many descriptions of his eccentric attire and personality. Cantankerous and impatient if students or colleagues were slow to respond, he was also a performer and teacher who made everyone laugh, sing, and dance with him.

From the mid-1950s to the mid-1960s Chase lived in the Beech Mountain area of North Carolina. He held afternoon folk festivals in nearby Boone and conducted summer school classes at Appalachian State Teachers College (later Appalachian State University). Sometime after 1963 he moved to California and in 1970 received an award from the Southern California Council on Literature for Children and Young People for distinguished contributions to folklore. The Los Angeles Renaissance Pleasure Faire honored him in 1971 and 1973. In September 1972 the governor of Virginia hosted a dinner in Richmond for thirty-five living Virginians distinguished in the arts, at which Chase, one of those honored, attracted attention with his flowing cape and walking stick.

Chase had moved to the Hendersonville area of North Carolina by 1978 and in Macon County on 1 May 1981 attended a public school folk festival called Richard Chase Day. Arthritic and legally blind by 1978 and in and out of wheelchairs during the final decade of his life, he continued to travel and give enthusiastic lectures and performances into the 1980s. He relied on assistants and relatives to take dictation. His compilations evolved for more than fifty years into a huge unfinished anthology of world literature on life, love, peace, and mythology. By 1984 Richard Thomas Chase had moved back to Huntsville, Alabama, where he died in a nursing home on 2 February 1988. His body was donated for medical research.

Autobiographies in Muriel Fuller, ed., *More Junior Authors* (1963), 43–45, with birth date and por., and undated résumé (post-1972), Ferrum College; David E. Whisnant, *All That Is Native and Fine: The Politics of Culture in an American Region* (1983), chap. 3; Nina Mikkelsen, "Richard Chase's *Jack Tales*: A Trickster in the New World," in *Touchstones: Reflections on the Best in Children's Literature*, vol. 2: *Fairy Tales, Fables, Myths, Legends, and Poetry* (1987), 40–55; Charles L. Perdue Jr., ed., *Outwitting the Devil: Jack Tales from Wise County, Virginia* (1987), 91–119; Perdue, "Is Old Jack Really Richard Chase?" *Journal of Folklore Research* 38 (2001): 111–138 (pors. on 115, 120); Richard Chase Papers, W. L. Eury Appalachian Collection, Appalachian State University, including audio and video tapes; other Chase materials in James Taylor Adams Collection, Ferrum College and University of Virginia's College at Wise; Chase file, Archive of Folk Culture, LC; Richard Gaither Walser Papers, UNC; bibliography of Chase's publications and recordings in Tina L. Hanlon and Judy A. Teaford, eds., "AppLit: Resources for Readers and Teachers of Appalachian Literature for Children and Young Adults," online ed., Ferrum College; marriage and divorce dates confirmed by BVS; other family information provided by daughter, Anne Gay Chase (2004); feature stories in *Charlotte [N.C.] Observer*, 22 July 1957, 1 Jan. 1978, *Los Angeles Times*, 9 Dec. 1957, and *Richmond News Leader*, 25 Sept. 1972; death notice in *Huntsville Times*, 2 Feb. 1988, obituaries in *Richmond News Leader*, 4 Feb. 1988, and *School Library Journal* 35 (June/July 1988): 28.

TINA L. HANLON

CHASE, Roland Ephriam (14 August 1867–14 September 1948), attorney and member of the Senate of Virginia, was born on the Holly Creek (later Clintwood) farm of his parents, John Perry Chase and Nannie Luemma Dunbar Chase. His father, a Confederate veteran, served two terms in the House of Delegates late in the 1870s and early in the 1880s. Chase graduated from Gladeville College, in Wise, and in 1888 received a law degree from the National Normal University, in Lebanon, Ohio. He returned to Clintwood, was admitted to the bar on 14 September 1888, and practiced law there until his death. On 19 May 1890 Chase married a cousin, Mary Louemma Chase, in Letcher County, Kentucky. They had four daughters and three sons, one of whom died in infancy. Chase's wife died on 18 November 1929, and on 1 November 1934, in Lebanon, Ohio, he married a widow, Elizabeth Randolph Smith.

Chase's law practice flourished, and within less than two decades he was able to build one of the largest houses in Clintwood. A Freemason and a member of the Independent Order of Odd Fellows, he served on the board of the Odd Fellows Home for children in Lynchburg for more than fifty years. He was a steward and trustee of the Clintwood Methodist Church, which had been organized in the home of his maternal grandparents. His father donated the land for building the church. In 1893 Chase joined Frank Monroe Beverly in editing and publishing the short-lived *Dickenson County News* in Clintwood. He had strong interests in such civic matters as improvement of roads and schools (including free textbooks for elementary school students), workers' compensation laws, and public facilities for the disadvantaged.

A lifelong Republican, Chase earned a presidential appointment as postmaster of Clintwood on 2 March 1892. He served until 8 May 1893, when a Democrat replaced him. Chase was not a candidate for a seat in the constitutional convention of 1901–1902, but he took part in the preliminary debates and argued that when the General Assembly apportioned the seats in the convention it had slighted several Virginia regions, including the southwestern districts. In Chase's own district, Republicans did not nominate a candidate for the convention, which allowed a former state attorney general and Democrat, Rufus Adolphus Ayers, to win the seat unopposed.

In 1907 Chase won election to a four-year term in the Senate of Virginia representing Buchanan, Dickenson, Russell, and Tazewell Counties. As a new Republican member of a body with a large Democratic majority, he was appointed to the lowest-ranking seats on the Committees on Enrolled Bills, Executive Expenditures, and General Laws. In 1917 he was elected to the House of Delegates to represent Dickenson and Wise Counties and was named to the Committees on Enrolled Bills, Officers and Offices at the Capitol, and Privileges and Elections. He was reelected to a second two-year term in 1919 and appointed to the Committees on Claims, for Courts of Justice, and on Labor and the Poor. Chase supported laws requiring that commissioners of the revenue be elected and prohibiting judges from giving peremptory instructions to juries. As a lawyer specializing in chancery matters he advocated making authenticated stenographic reports of trials sufficient as a bill of exceptions on appeal. Although such a proposal did not become law, the case for such a change was so strong that the Virginia Supreme Court of Appeals later adopted it as a procedural rule during the 1930s. Chase also took, and in his district received, some credit for improvement in the region's highways.

Reentering elective politics a decade after retiring from the House of Delegates, Chase in 1931 was elected to the Senate of Virginia from the Dickenson and Wise district. He served on the Committees on Finance, to Examine the Treasurer's Office, and on General Laws. In 1932, after a botched assembly attempt to redraw Vir-

ginia's congressional district lines forced all candidates for the state's nine seats in the House of Representatives to run at-large, Chase was one of six Republican candidates for Congress, but all of them, including one incumbent, lost in the Democratic landslide on 8 November of that year. In 1935 Chase lost his campaign for reelection to Robert Randolph Parker, although he carried Dickenson County. Citing irregularities and unlawful acts relating to absentee ballots, Chase contested the results. An investigation by the Committee on Privileges and Elections found no evidence of wrongdoing, and the Senate upheld Parker's victory.

Noted for his expertise in land law as well as in chancery causes, Chase during his career at the bar was often engaged in complicated cases involving land and coal interests. When a corporation attempted to evict several Buchanan County citizens under the authority of some old land grants, Chase successfully defended their property in federal court in *Virginia and West Virginia Coal Company* v. *Charles* (1918). He also argued and won several cases in the Virginia Supreme Court of Appeals that set legal precedents. The 1896 case *Cool* v. *Commonwealth* established the principle that if a criminal statute has been often changed, an indictment must specify the particular time in which a crime was committed. *Powers* v. *Carter Coal and Iron Company* (1902) clarified the power of a court to enter a *nunc pro tunc* order, and *Charles* v. *Big Sandy and Cumberland Railroad Company* (1925) clarified when a litigant may resort to the courts in eminent domain proceedings. Chase had to argue an unusually complex case of *Yukon Pocahontas Coal Company* v. *Ratliff* twice before the court was able to decide in 1943 on the merits of a dispute concerning implied rights under a coal deed.

Because Dickenson was the last county to be created in Virginia, Chase regarded his family as among its pioneers, even though people had lived for generations in the parts of Buchanan, Russell, and Wise Counties that in 1880 became Dickenson County. He encouraged his uncle Ephriam A. Dunbar to write down his recollections of settling in the Clintwood area in the middle of the nineteenth century. Dunbar's letters, eventually published in 1984 in

Chase

the compilation *Pioneer Recollections of Southwest Virginia*, offer an unusually personal reflection on the earliest settlements in the area at the time when Chase's parents and grandparents lived there.

Chase concluded his public career by completing another man's term as commonwealth's attorney for Dickenson County from July 1946 through December 1947. Roland Ephriam Chase died at his Clintwood home on 14 September 1948, probably of a heart attack, sixty years to the day after his admission to the bar. He was buried in Clintwood Cemetery (later Phipps Memorial Cemetery).

NCAB, 48:236–237; Bruce, Tyler, and Morton, *History of Virginia*, 6:353–354; Records of Appointment of Postmasters, Virginia, Dickenson Co., Post Office Department, RG 28, NARA; *Richmond Times*, 3 Mar. 1901; *Roanoke Times*, 22 June 1921; *Norton Crawford's Weekly*, 5, 12 Nov. 1932; 1935 contested election in *JSV*, 1936 sess., 78–79, and Contested Election in the Senate of Virginia, Committee on Privileges and Elections, Acc. 29185, LVA; *Virginia and West Virginia Coal Co.* v. *Charles* (1918), *Federal Reporter*, 254:379–391; Chase's cases that set precedents include *Cool* v. *Commonwealth* (1896), *Virginia Reports*, 94:799–803, *Powers* v. *Carter Coal and Iron Company* (1902), *Virginia Reports*, 100:450–458, *H. G. Charles* v. *Big Sandy and Cumberland Railroad Company* (1925), *Virginia Reports*, 142:512–528, *Yukon Pocahontas Coal Company, a Corporation, et als.* v. *F. M. Ratliff, et als.* (1940), *Virginia Reports*, 175:366–372, and *Yukon Pocahontas Coal Company, et als.* v. *F. M. Ratliff, et als.* (1943), *Virginia Reports*, 181:195–206; Associated Press obituary with some inaccuracies in *Richmond Times-Dispatch* and *Roanoke Times*, both 15 Sept. 1948; obituaries in *Norton Coalfield Progress,* 16 Sept. 1948, and *Clintwood Dickensonian*, 17 Sept. 1948; memorial in *Virginia State Bar Association Proceedings* (1949), 129–132 (por.).

JAMES T. EDMUNDS

CHAUCO (fl. 1622–1623), one of several Native Americans who saved the lives of English colonists by warning of Opechancanough's plans to attack their settlements on 22 March 1622, is named in no more than two known documents, leaving details about his parentage, birth, death, and tribal affiliation unknown. It is possible that he was the person referred to in 1624 as Chacrow, an Indian who a decade earlier had lived with an English colonist and knew how to use a gun.

All surviving contemporaneous sources report that several Indians alerted colonists to the imminent danger in 1622, but surviving documents from that year do not name any of them. English and colonial writers described the informants as men or boys, presumably from one of the Powhatan tribes and sometimes referred to as converts to Christianity. The assigned motive for informing was usually a feeling of friendship or gratitude toward a particular colonist. In the first and only official publication about the uprising, *A Declaration of the State of the Colony and Affaires in Virginia* (1622), Edward Waterhouse, the secretary of the Virginia Company of London, summarized what was then known and wrote that the attack might have achieved the Indians' purpose of "utter extirpation, which God of his mercy (by the meanes of some of themselves converted to Christianitie) prevented."

Waterhouse's account described "one of them alone which was made a Christian" as an Indian "belonging to" one of the colonists (possibly William Perry) and living with Richard Pace, across the James River from Jamestown. That Indian's brother told him that they had received orders to kill Perry and Pace as part of the coordinated attack throughout the colony on Friday morning, 22 March. During the night of 21 March, according to Waterhouse, "*Perries* Indian rose out of his bed and reveales it to *Pace*, that used him as a Sonne." Pace prepared the defenses of his own house and before daybreak rowed the three miles to Jamestown "and gave notice thereof to the Governor." Thus, "the rest of the Colony that had warning given them, by this meanes was saved." Subsequent published narratives by Captain John Smith and others followed Waterhouse's account almost word for word, added no new information, and did not identify any informant.

The only extant document to name any informant is a seventeenth-century transcription in the Library of Congress of a letter, dated 4 April 1623, that the governor and Council sent to the Virginia Company about routine business and to inform the company officers of steps taken to keep the peace during the winter and spring following the 1622 uprising. Negotiations for the release of some captives had been carried on by two Indians, "one of which Called (Chauco) who had lived much amo[ng]st the English, and by revealinge that pl[ot] To divers upon the day of

188

Massacre, saved theire lives." The letter does not indicate that Chauco had converted to Christianity or had lived with Pace, and it does not state which colonist or colonists he had warned. Another seventeenth-century transcription of the same letter, this one dated 3 April 1623, is in the British Public Record Office. It does not include the two words, "Called (Chauco)." The original letter does not survive.

In August 1622 company officials recommended that the governor treat "those Indians whom God used as instruments of revealing and preventinge the totall ruine of you all" with "a good respect and recompence" and suggested that they be given "a good and carefull education." At the company's Preparative Court held in London on 26 April 1624, William Perry presented "an Indian Boy . . . for whome a motion was made for some Contribution towards his mayntenance, wherby to bring him up in Christianitie and some good course to live by." The record does not name him or identify him as one of the informants. It is highly unlikely that Chauco, the presumably adult negotiator in April 1623, was the "Boy" who accompanied Perry to London in the spring of 1624.

The first historian to give a name to Pace's informant and Perry's Indian boy was William Stith, who in his *History of the First Discovery and Settlement of Virginia* (1747) repeated the essence of Waterhouse's account of the uprising. Perhaps having access to other documents since lost or perhaps misreading the 4 April 1623 transcription, Stith wrote that "Chanco" was responsible for saving "*James-Town*, and all such Plantations, as could possibly get Intelligence in time." Subsequent generations of writers, including many historians, uncritically repeated and embellished Stith's version, and in some instances conflated all the references to the informants and the boy who traveled to London in 1624.

The story has become one of the most popular Virginia legends and appears in scholarly histories and school textbooks. Community organizations and land developers have used the name Chanco, and in the twentieth century tablets honoring Chanco were placed in Surry County, near where Richard Pace lived, and in the wall of the reconstructed church on Jamestown Island. Many Americans have embraced the story of a Christian Indian who, like Pocahontas, helped the Virginia colonists survive the hostilities of their own people, to serve the national belief in providential support for a superior culture that conquered a continent and continues to police the world, convinced of its manifest destiny to do so. It is ironic that the real Chauco, who liked the English with whom he lived, has been forgotten, even though his actions did, indeed, save some of the English from death on 22 March 1622.

Edward Waterhouse, *A Declaration of the State of the Colony and Affaires in Virginia* (1622), quotations on 13, 18, 20, 21; phrase "Called (Chauco)" in copy of governor and Council to Virginia Company of London, 4 Apr. 1623, Records of the Virginia Company, Thomas Jefferson Papers, LC; copy of same letter but dated 3 Apr. 1623 and without phrase "Called (Chauco)," PRO CO 1/2, fol. 128; Kingsbury, *Virginia Company*, 2:532 (1624 quotation), 3:611–615, 673 (Aug. 1622 quotation), 4:98 (printing phrase "Called [Chauco]"); Chacrow mentioned in *Minutes of Council and General Court*, 28; William Stith, *History of the First Discovery and Settlement of Virginia* (1747), quotations on 212.

J. FREDERICK FAUSZ

CHEATHAM, Benjamin Franklin (20 May 1867–2 December 1944), army officer and preservationist, was born in Coffee County, Tennessee, and was the son of Anna Bell Robertson Cheatham and Benjamin Franklin Cheatham (1820–1886), a Confederate major general. The younger Cheatham attended the Sewanee Military Academy in 1883 and 1884 and the University of the South from 1884 to 1886. He did not complete a degree, but in 1930 the university awarded him an honorary doctorate of civil law. Cheatham began a career in civil engineering, but the outbreak of the Spanish-American War in 1898 changed the course of his life. He served as a major in the 1st Regiment Tennessee Infantry and the 37th Regiment United States Volunteers during the Philippine Insurrection and was promoted to colonel in the latter service on 10 April 1900. Deciding on a military career, he joined the United States Army with the rank of captain in April 1901, thus beginning a thirty-year association with the Quartermaster Corps. Between 1901 and 1917 Cheatham served at stations in the Philippines, Indianapolis, San

Francisco, Washington, D.C., and Honolulu. He was promoted to major in 1908 and lieutenant colonel in 1914.

When the United States entered World War I, Cheatham was sent to France with the Quartermaster Corps. He requested combat service and participated in the Meuse-Argonne offensive, for which he later received the Distinguished Service Medal. After a year at the General Staff School at Fort Leavenworth, Kansas, and another at the Army War College in Washington, D.C., he received promotion to colonel. In January 1926 Cheatham was appointed and confirmed to a four-year term as quartermaster general with the rank of major general. In this post he oversaw the continued demobilization of the army while trying to ensure the country's military preparedness in the event of future emergencies. His department also planned the first government-sponsored pilgrimage of mothers and widows to visit the graves of American soldiers who had died in Europe during the war, and Cheatham personally accompanied at least one tour of Gold Star Mothers in 1930.

In 1925 Congress authorized the restoration of Arlington House, the Greek Revival mansion in Arlington County constructed by George Washington Parke Custis early in the nineteenth century that was also Robert Edward Lee's home before the Civil War. Occupied by Federal troops during the war, the estate was designated Arlington National Cemetery in 1864 and fell under the jurisdiction of the War Department. After Congress appropriated funds for the project in 1928, the renovation became the responsibility of the quartermaster general's office at a time when the government had little experience in historic preservation. Cognizant of the national significance of the renovation, Cheatham consulted local and national experts on the best ways to restore the house and its furnishings to the Custis and Lee periods. He supervised the early stages of removal of post–Civil War additions to the mansion, restoration of the structure, acquisition of appropriate furnishings, and the property's transformation from cemetery headquarters into a house museum. Cheatham also moderated sensitive historical issues associated with Arlington House, including the proper name of the man-

sion and the replacement of a flagpole anachronistic to the Lee era but beloved by local veterans.

Cheatham retired from the military in January 1930, with a temporary return to active duty from May to September of that year, but his connection to the Lees and historic preservation continued. In June 1932 the Robert E. Lee Memorial Foundation (later the Robert E. Lee Memorial Association) invited him to become the first resident superintendent of Stratford Hall, in Westmoreland County. The organization planned to restore and open as a museum this Lee family plantation, the birthplace of Robert E. Lee and boyhood home of the brothers Francis Lightfoot Lee and Richard Henry Lee, both signers of the Declaration of Independence. Cheatham accepted the position, provided that the estate also operate as a producing colonial farm. Armed with an interest in southern heritage, childhood experiences of farm life, and his background in engineering, procurement, and military efficiency, Cheatham transformed Stratford Hall's long-neglected grounds. He implemented plans for growing crops and raising livestock for use on the farm and for the education of visitors and developed a series of plantation-made products to help fund restoration efforts. As resident superintendent for twelve years Cheatham also supervised the renovation of the great house, suggested changes based on his own research, and served as a liaison between operations at Stratford Hall and the foundation directors. Newspaper editors lauded Cheatham's hands-on dedication and his ability to maintain restoration efforts during the Great Depression.

On 7 December 1901 Cheatham married Mary Warren Denman, of San Francisco, later a national leader of the Girl Scouts of the USA. They had two sons and one daughter. In August 1944 he took a leave of absence from Stratford Hall and traveled to Denver for medical treatment. Benjamin Franklin Cheatham died in an army hospital there on 2 December 1944 and was buried in Arlington National Cemetery.

Biographies in *NCAB*, 35:476–477 (por. facing 476), and Christopher Losson, *Tennessee's Forgotten Warriors: Frank Cheatham and His Confederate Division* (1989), 280–281; *San Francisco Chronicle*, 8 Dec. 1901; Compiled Military Service Records, Spanish-American War, Philippine Insurrection, Records of the Adjutant General's Office, RG 94, and Records of the Office of the Quartermaster General, RG 92, NARA; correspondence as superintendent in Robert E. Lee Memorial Association, Stratford Hall; Charles B. Hosmer Jr., *Preservation Comes of Age: From Williamsburg to the National Trust, 1926–1949* (1981), esp. 473–474, 995–996; Charles W. Snell, *Historic Structure Report, Historical Data Section: Arlington House, the Robert E. Lee Memorial, Virginia . . .* , vol. 1: *1802–1933* (National Park Service report, 1985); obituaries in *Nashville Banner*, *New York Times*, *Richmond News Leader* (includes editorial tribute), *Richmond Times-Dispatch*, and *Washington Post*, all 4 Dec. 1944.

MICHELLE A. KROWL

CHEEK, Leslie (28 October 1908–6 December 1992), museum director, was born in Nashville, Tennessee, and was the son of Leslie Cheek, a wealthy businessman whose family created the Maxwell House coffee brand, and Mabel Wood Cheek. The family's affluence and his mother's love for the arts enabled him to visit museums, enjoy the theater in New York, and accompany his parents on art-collecting trips to many parts of the world. Cheek attended Nashville preparatory schools and an Indiana military academy. Choosing not to follow his father into business but to gratify his own and his mother's inclinations, he switched from engineering studies to fine arts at Harvard University, from which he graduated in 1931. Four years later he received a BFA in architecture from Yale University, where he also studied stage, costume, and lighting design.

Leslie Cheek Jr., as he continued to identify himself even after his father's death, joined the faculty of the College of William and Mary as an instructor in fine arts in 1935 and became chair of the Department of Fine Arts the following year. He renovated an old campus dormitory to house the department, exhibited the work of such modern artists as Georgia O'Keeffe, brought Frank Lloyd Wright to Williamsburg to speak at an exhibition borrowed from the Museum of Modern Art, and designed theatrical productions to show his students the wider applications of art. Cheek served on the Virginia Art Commission from 1938 until he left the state the following year. Under a tight deadline, he revised Virginia's design for its exhibition at the 1939 World's Fair in New York. The commission in charge of the exhibition had selected a plan through an open competition but then repudiated it, in

part because the design focused too much on the restoration of the colonial capital at Williamsburg but perhaps also because the commissioners learned that the designer, the Hampton Institute architect William Henry Moses, was an African American. Cheek made free use of unique features of Moses's plan for the Virginia room and accepted full credit for its success.

On 3 June 1939 Cheek married Mary Tyler Freeman, daughter of the journalist and historian Douglas Southall Freeman. A Richmond civic leader and philanthropist, she helped found the Richmond Better Housing Coalition. They had three sons and one daughter. On 1 September 1939 Cheek became director of the Baltimore Museum of Art. There he staged inventive exhibitions and incorporated modern design into the museum's new theatrical offerings. Cheek also designed a modern house, Faraway Farm, in the mountains of North Carolina, where for more than a decade his family spent part of each year. In 1940 he took a leave of absence to prepare an exhibition on American civilization for the Museum of Modern Art in New York, but the prohibitive cost of mounting the show during World War II led to its cancellation. Cheek resigned from the Baltimore Museum in the spring of 1942 to work for the Army Corps of Engineers camouflage school at Fort Belvoir, and for several months in 1945 he worked in Washington, D.C., for the Office of Strategic Services. He moved to New York during the summer of 1945 and until April 1947 was an associate editor of the monthly magazine *Architectural Forum*. For several months in 1947 he wrote on architecture for *House Beautiful*.

Cheek moved to Richmond after succeeding Thomas Clyde Colt as director of the Virginia Museum of Fine Arts on 1 July 1948. One of the first state art museums in the country, the Virginia Museum was a small institution that relied on donations and membership dues for most of its acquisitions and programming. Cheek energetically raised money, solicited donations of artworks, enlarged the museum and its cultural offerings, and introduced exciting but sometimes controversial innovations. He experimented with dramatic lighting techniques, used recorded sound in the galleries, and treated furniture and architecture as art. He acquired and exhibited paintings, sculpture, and decorative arts from different world cultures and different periods, ranging from antiquity to contemporary art. In giving the museum's collections a more cosmopolitan character, he reduced the institution's early focus on the work of Virginia artists.

Creativity and controversy were the hallmarks of Cheek's career. In the spring of 1950 he mounted a major exhibition of modern American art that drew strong condemnation from Virginians with conservative artistic tastes and generated a bitter public debate about the exhibition and about modern art that attracted comment in the *New York Herald Tribune* and the *New York Times*. After the museum began construction of a new wing in 1954, Cheek raised money to create the Virginia Museum Theatre (later TheatreVirginia). Drawing visitors to the museum for the performing arts as well as for the fine arts was part of Cheek's plan to expand the museum membership and reputation, and he hoped that visitors who attended for one purpose would stay to enjoy the other cultural offerings. In 1960 he created *Arts in Virginia*, a thrice-yearly illustrated magazine that disseminated information about Virginia artists and showcased the museum's collections. He made imaginative use of publicity opportunities and carefully monitored the museum's press coverage.

Cheek's passionate determination to introduce ordinary people to fine art was perhaps best demonstrated in 1953 when he initiated the Artmobile, a traveling museum housed in a large tractor trailer fitted out with works of art and educational materials. The first such program in the country, the Artmobile won national attention, and the museum added three more units during the 1960s. By the last year of Cheek's administration the Artmobiles had attracted nearly 130,000 visitors, and through the museum's affiliation with local arts councils and the formation of Virginia Museum chapters in many communities, the museum's programs reached 755,000 Virginians in all parts of the state. The Artmobile program continued until conservation concerns and operating costs forced termination of the service in 1994.

Cheek was an imaginative artist and a man of formidable talent. He was also a demanding manager and was never shy about borrowing ideas from other people or taking full credit for work to which other people had contributed significantly. Staff turnover during his administration was high, a rate attributable in part to low state salaries for the professional staff but also a consequence of the difficulty some people had in working with Cheek. He had as many vigorous critics as appreciative supporters. One admiring insider echoed the praise of Cheek as a "genius, pioneer, innovator, brilliant fund-raiser, charming host, untiring perfectionist" but acknowledged he could also be "a whip-cracker, a tyrant, an autocrat." A *Richmond News Leader* editorial after one public dispute in 1959 proclaimed what many people had come to believe, that Cheek was "a virtuoso in the art of controversy."

Neighborhood clashes, such as disputes with the United Daughters of the Confederacy in 1954 and 1958 over the museum's plans to acquire adjoining property, strained Cheek's relationship with the community and with some board members, and early in 1958 he submitted his resignation as director. Less than a month later, however, he and the board patched up their differences and agreed that he should remain. In 1959 he unsuccessfully endorsed placing the headquarters building of the Civil War Centennial Commission in the Confederate Memorial Park adjacent to the Virginia Museum, even though the modern, domed structure would have harmonized poorly with the neighborhood architecture. In a major disappointment for Cheek, in March 1967 the Virginia Arts Commission rejected the museum's architectural plans for a new north wing because it deemed the modern design incompatible with the original building.

Cheek's creativity increased the museum's high reputation, and his achievements proved more durable than the many controversies that surrounded them. The Richmond-area chapter of the Public Relations Society of America presented Cheek its Thomas Jefferson Award for Public Service in 1966, and in 1985 the Virginia Society of the American Institute of Architects awarded him its architecture medal. He received honorary degrees from the University of Richmond in 1955 and from the College of William and Mary in 1967.

Cheek retired as director at the end of October 1968. During his two decades in charge, the museum staff increased from about 25 to 150, and its membership grew from little more than 1,000 to more than 11,000. The museum more than doubled the value of its art holdings and more than tripled its floor space. State appropriations for operating the museum rose from $47,000 per annum in 1948 to more than $700,000 in 1968, while expenditures on operations and acquisitions rose from about $68,000 per year to more than $1,000,000.

During the first years of his retirement, Cheek operated a Christmas tree farm on Nelson County land for which he also designed and constructed Skylark, a vacation house that he and his wife deeded to Washington and Lee University in 1977. During the 1970s he assisted in designing the interpretive center at Stratford Hall, the Westmoreland County plantation of the Lee family. In 1985 the College of William and Mary mounted a major retrospective biographical exhibition, "Cheek and the Arts," in conjunction with the publication of Parke Rouse Jr.'s laudatory illustrated biography. The college also created the Cheek Award in the arts. Arthritis that put crippling pressure on Cheek's spinal cord increasingly incapacitated him after the 1970s and eventually confined him to his Richmond home. Leslie Cheek died there on 6 December 1992 and was buried in Hollywood Cemetery.

Davidson Co., Tenn., Birth Certificate D-360255 (delayed); personal and family information verified by widow, Mary Tyler Freeman Cheek McClenahan (2003); autobiographical essay in David H. Stevens, ed., *Ten Talents in the American Theatre* (1957), 183–197; Parke Rouse Jr., *Living by Design: Leslie Cheek and the Arts: A Photobiography* (1985), with several pors.; K. Richmond Temple, *Designing for the Arts: Environments by Leslie Cheek* (1990), with several pors.; Mary Tyler Freeman Cheek McClenahan, *Southern Civility: Recollections of My Early Life* (2003), 95–119; feature stories quoting Cheek extensively include *Nashville Tennessean Magazine*, 17 June 1956, *Richmond Times-Dispatch*, 19 May 1957, 24 Sept. 1967 (first and second quotations), 5 Dec. 1971, 13 Sept. 1981, 4 Apr. 1982, *The Diplomat* (July 1957), 20–21, 52, and *Richmond News Leader*, 24 Jan. 1979, 11 Dec. 1985; major collections of Cheek's papers, drawings, and other personal and professional material in Archives of American Art, Smithsonian Institution (including 1982 oral history interview), Washington, D.C., in Museum of

Modern Art, New York, in Queens Museum of Art, New York, in Robert E. Lee Memorial Association, Stratford Hall, in Virginia Museum of Fine Arts (including 1981 oral history interview and museum publicity scrapbooks), Richmond, in VHS, in W&M, and in Virginia Museum of Fine Arts, Director's Office (including 1965 oral history interview), RG 34, LVA; *Southern Workman* 68 (1939): 14–18, 102–105; *Richmond News Leader*, 18 Nov. 1959 (third quotation); J. Carter Brown, "The Virginia Museum of Fine Arts: An Essay" (1960 typescript, New York University Institute of Fine Arts), copy in Virginia Museum of Fine Arts, Richmond; Mary Tyler Cheek, "'An Island of Quiet in an Ocean of Noise': The Virginia Room at the 1939 World's Fair," *Virginia Cavalcade* 35 (1985): 30–37; obituaries in *Richmond Times-Dispatch*, 7, 8 Dec. 1992, *New York Times*, 8 Dec. 1992, and *Richmond Style Weekly*, 15 Dec. 1992; memorial in Virginia Museum of Fine Arts *Bulletin* 53 (Mar./Apr. 1993): 1.

BRENT TARTER

CHEEK, Mary Tyler Freeman. See **McCLENAHAN, Mary Tyler Freeman Cheek.**

CHEESMAN, Edmund (d. by 10 February 1677), participant in Bacon's Rebellion, was born in Virginia, probably in what is now York County and probably a year or two after the marriage in the mid-1640s of his father, Edmund Cheesman (d. by 24 February 1674), to a widow, Mary Lilley, whose maiden name is not known. She had at least one son at the time of the marriage. Contemporaries spelled his surname in a variety of ways, the most common being Chisman, and some records mistakenly refer to Cheesman and his father by the given name Edward. His father and two uncles, including John Cheesman (d. by 2 May 1665), who served on the governor's Council, emigrated from England and patented land on Poquoson Creek and what was later known as Chisman Creek in York County. In spite of a decree the General Assembly had issued, in 1661 Cheesman's mother apparently involved her husband, "his said negroes & whole family" in an illegal Quaker meeting.

Cheesman married late in the 1660s and had one son, who died at age ten. His wife's given name was Lydia, and her maiden name may have been Farloe or Farlow. Her stepfather was probably a Quaker, and it is possible that she also followed that religion. Cheesman patented about 200 acres of land in York County on 8 July 1670 and on 25 July became a justice of the peace. He attended court sessions regularly, was a captain in the York County militia by 1672, and four years later became a major. When Bacon's Rebellion began in the summer of 1676, Cheesman supported Nathaniel Bacon (1647–1676). His father had marched against the Pamunkey Indians in 1644, and Cheesman may have embraced Bacon's plans to make war on Virginia's Indians, but his wife later asserted that she bore responsibility for his choice. His wife's uncle also supported the rebellion and later was hanged.

Cheesman's role in Bacon's Rebellion is sparsely documented, but he was described as one of the principal actors. Captured in York County in November 1676, about a month after Bacon's death, Cheesman was accused of treason. His wife contrived to be present when Governor Sir William Berkeley questioned him, and she pleaded with the governor to spare her husband's life on the grounds that "if he had not bin influenc'd by her instigations, he had never don that which he had don." On "her bended knees" she begged the governor "that shee might be hang'd, and he pardon'd." Her eloquence and bravery failed to persuade the governor to release or spare him, but before his trial could take place, Edmund Cheesman "dyed in prisson, of feare, Greife, or bad useage." The date of his death is not recorded. Berkeley's proclamation of pardon, issued on 10 February 1677, exempted several men, including Cheesman, who were already dead and declared that they were to be adjudged convicted and attainted of high treason as though they had been tried. In April 1678 Lydia Cheesman claimed her husband's estate, which consisted of 250 acres in York County, six laborers (five black, one white), livestock, and household furnishings. She married Thomas Harwood in June of that year and lived until the spring of 1695.

Adventurers of Purse and Person, 1:570–571; Lyon G. Tyler, "Maj. Edmund Chisman, Jr.," *WMQ*, 1st ser., 1 (1892): 89–97; York Co. Deeds, Orders, and Wills, 3: fol. 125 (first quotation); John Cotton, "Narrative of Bacon's Rebellion" (n.d.), unpaginated, VHS (all other quotations); Berkeley's pardon, PRO CO 1/39, fols. 64–65; Hening, *Statutes*, 2:366–377; estate inventory, stating natural death, in PRO CO 5/1371, fols. 238–239.

VIRGINIA BERNHARD

CHEESMAN, John (ca. 1598–by 2 May 1665), member of the Council, was born in England, but the date and place of his birth and the names of his parents are not known. Contemporaries spelled his surname in a variety of ways, the most common being Cheesman and Chisman. Families with those names resided in the county of Kent and elsewhere near London, and it is likely that he was a member of one of them. He may have been the John Cheesman who married Anne Willett in the parish of Saint Saviour's, Southwark, in Surrey, on 24 June 1616. He became a merchant and probably established connections with other merchants before he traveled to Virginia in 1621 aboard the *Flyinge Hart*. He settled initially at Kiccoughtan (later Elizabeth City County), where he and two brothers resided. When Cheesman patented 200 acres of land near there in September 1624, he was identified as a gentleman and not long afterward as a lieutenant, classifications that suggest he arrived in Virginia with his social rank already established.

Cheesman married a second time, possibly in Virginia during the 1620s. The maiden name of his second wife, Margaret, is not recorded. They had at least one son. Through his marriage and the marriages of his brothers, Cheesman became related to other Virginia families that were prominent during the second quarter of the century, notably the Mason and Matthews families. He engaged in commerce between Virginia and England during the 1620s and moved to Charles River County (after 1643 York County) soon after that part of the colony was opened to settlement in 1630. Cheesman acquired more than 1,000 acres of land and lived on a 600-acre tract on what became known as Chisman Creek. He may have used his connections to other merchants to acquire the workers of African origin or descent who labored on his plantation alongside the white indentured servants.

Cheesman was one of the first commissioners, or justices, of the peace for Charles River County and was a captain in the militia by 1637 and a lieutenant colonel by April 1652. He also served as a tobacco viewer in the county on 6 January 1640 and a tobacco collector in November 1648. Cheesman represented York County in the General Assembly that met on 2 March 1643, when for the first time burgesses and Council members met separately, and thus had the distinction of being a member of the first House of Burgesses. Incomplete records do not disclose whether that was his only service in the assembly before 30 April 1652, when the two houses elected him to the governor's Council after the colony surrendered to Parliament following the conclusion of the English Civil Wars. It is possible that Cheesman received the appointment because of his support of Parliament, his standing in York County, his mercantile connections, or some combination of the three. The scant surviving records do not reveal how long he served on the Council.

Cheesman returned to England, possibly after learning of the restoration of King Charles II in May 1660. He and his wife resided across the Thames River from London, in the parish of Saint Mary Magdalen, Bermondsey, in the county of Surrey. In August 1661 Cheesman executed a power of attorney authorizing Lawrence Smith, of York County, to lease his land in that county to his younger brother, Edmund Cheesman (d. by 24 February 1674). In December 1663 Cheesman wrote a new will, leaving his English properties and his York County land to his wife and his land in Gloucester County to his young granddaughter, with a proviso that if she died without heirs, the land would descend to his nephews, one of whom, Edmund Cheesman (d. by 10 February 1677), was a participant in Bacon's Rebellion. John Cheesman died on an unrecorded date before 2 May 1665, when his will was proved in the Prerogative Court of Canterbury. Thirteen years later his widow authorized a relative in Virginia to manage the York County property she had inherited from her husband. She died before 21 July 1680.

Lyon G. Tyler, "Maj. Edmund Chisman, Jr.," *WMQ*, 1st ser., 1 (1892): 89–90; *Adventurers of Purse and Person*, 1:58 (age twenty-seven in muster on 7 Feb. 1625), 568–570; *Cavaliers and Pioneers*, 1:7, 35, 37, 53, 69, 74, 88, 122, 127–128, 232, 262, 263, 419, 469, 2:69; *Minutes of Council and General Court*, 35, 56, 182, 300; York Co. Deeds, Orders, and Wills, 1:9, 17, 24, 34, 53, 152, 2:430, 3: fols. 162–163, 6:61; election to Council in Hening, *Statutes*, 1:371–372; will in Prerogative Court of Canterbury, Hyde 46, abstracted in *VMHB* 14 (1906): 86; wife's will in Prerogative Court of Canterbury, Bath 92, abstracted in Henry F. Waters, ed., *Genealogical Gleanings in England* (1901), 1:691–692.

JULIE RICHTER

CHENERY, Christopher Tompkins (16 September 1886–3 January 1973), public utilities executive and horse breeder, was the son of James Hollis Chenery, a merchant, and Ida Burnley Taylor Chenery. His five siblings included William Ludlow Chenery, who edited *Collier's Weekly* from 1925 to 1943, and the writer Blanche Chenery Perrin. Born in Richmond, he grew up in Ashland. When he was not working odd jobs to augment the family's limited finances, he rode horses belonging to a cousin, Bernard Doswell, at a Caroline County farm a few miles away. Chenery was educated in local public schools and attended Randolph-Macon College from 1902 to 1903, when he surrendered his place to a brother, who in return gave Chenery his job surveying for a railroad in West Virginia. The brothers sent part of their salaries to their family to pay for an indoor bathroom and other improvements to their Ashland residence. Chenery entered Washington and Lee University in 1907 and graduated with a B.S. in engineering in 1909. During his final year he taught engineering to undergraduate students.

From 1909 to 1914 Chenery was an engineer in Alaska (where he surveyed the interior for potential rail routes), Oregon, and Washington. He worked for the United States Commission on Industrial Relations from 1914 to 1915 and then became an executive engineer with a Chicago firm. On 18 January 1917 he married Helen Clementina Bates, of Forest Grove, Oregon, a graduate of Smith College who died in November 1967. Their two daughters and one son included Hollis Burnley Chenery, an economist who was vice president for development at the World Bank from 1970 to 1983.

Stationed at the officers' training camp at Camp A. A. Humphreys (later Fort Belvoir), Virginia, during World War I, Chenery taught riding to cavalrymen. From 1919 to 1920 he worked in Washington, D.C., where he conducted a study of the organization of the federal government's engineering and construction work. He returned to the Chicago engineering firm in 1920 and then worked as an independent engineer in New York City from 1923 to 1926.

In June 1926 in New York City, Chenery founded the Federal Water Service Corporation (after 1941 the Federal Water and Gas Corporation) and served as president and chairman of the board until 1948. The holding company, incorporated in Delaware, originally comprised water companies from several states, including Alabama, California, New York, Pennsylvania, and West Virginia, but later specialized in gas interests. After Chenery and other directors purchased preferred stock on the open market in order to retain control of the company during a reorganization, the Securities and Exchange Commission refused to approve the reorganization plan and argued that the principals should not have been acquiring stock during the negotiations. The case of *Securities and Exchange Commission* v. *Chenery Corporation* was twice argued before the Supreme Court of the United States and ultimately decided in 1947 in favor of the SEC.

In September 1948 the Federal Water and Gas Corporation was superseded by the Southern Natural Gas Company, which operated a natural gas pipeline in the South. Chenery was chairman of the board until 1965 and then chairman emeritus until 1968. From 1948 to 1956 he also served as chairman of the board of the Southern Production Company, Inc., which produced oil, natural gas, and gas distillates. In 1954 he formed the Offshore Company, a Southern Production Company subsidiary conducting deepwater drilling in the Gulf of Mexico. He was chairman of the board and chief executive officer until 1965.

Chenery's passion was breeding thoroughbreds. He helped found the Greater New York Association in 1955 to promote racing and remained a driving force in the Jockey Club, the National Museum of Racing, the National Steeplechase and Hunt Association, and the Thoroughbred Owners and Breeders Association. In 1936 Chenery bought the Caroline County farm that had once belonged to his Doswell relatives, lovingly restored the property, and established the Meadow to raise and train racehorses. He chose blue-and-white racing silks to honor his alma mater, Washington and Lee University. Among his many fine horses were the blind broodmare Hildene, whose colt Hill Prince won the Preakness Stakes and was the 1950 Horse of

the Year; Hildene's colt First Landing (named for the 350th anniversary of Jamestown), who sired another Chenery horse, Riva Ridge, winner of the 1972 Kentucky Derby and Belmont Stakes; and the broodmare Imperatrice, who gave birth to Somethingroyal, dam of Sir Gaylord, another leading stallion. Between 1939 and 1972 horses Chenery raced won more than $8.5 million on the track.

In 1965 Chenery entered an unusual business arrangement with Arthur "Bull" Boyd Hancock, proprietor of the Claiborne Farm, in Paris, Kentucky, and Gladys Livingston Mills Phipps, owner of the famed racehorse Bold Ruler (which stood at Claiborne). Each year Chenery would send two Meadow broodmares to Claiborne for breeding with Bold Ruler. The first mating would usually produce two foals, and the second mating soon after their birth would result in two more foals within a year. After the birth of the first pair but before the birth of the second, Phipps and Chenery would flip a coin. The winner received first choice of the first pair, while the loser had first choice of the second. By 1968 the ailing Chenery had ceded many of the Meadow's business operations to his daughter Helen Bates "Penny" Chenery Tweedy. She sent Somethingroyal and other mares to Claiborne for breeding to Bold Ruler. In 1969 Tweedy lost the coin toss with the Phipps family and ended up with Somethingroyal's yet-to-be-born second foal.

At the Meadow on 30 March 1970, Somethingroyal gave birth to a big chestnut colt with three white feet and a white star on his face. Chenery's secretary, Elizabeth Ham, suggested his official Jockey Club name, Secretariat. Of forty-one races in less than two years, the colt won twenty-one and placed second in sixteen, third in three, and fourth in one. He won more than $1.3 million and was named 1972 and 1973 Horse of the Year. In the latter year he won the Triple Crown (the Kentucky Derby, the Preakness Stakes, and the Belmont Stakes), set blistering records (including victory at the Belmont by an astonishing thirty-one lengths), appeared on three national magazine covers in the same week, and gained international celebrity. Even before completing the Triple Crown, the stallion was syndicated to stud for the then-record sum of $6.08 million to offset inheritance taxes on Chenery's estate. Late in 1973 Secretariat retired from racing to Claiborne Farm, where he stood at stud until his death on 4 October 1989.

Chenery divided his time among the Meadow, Pelham Manor in New York, and Palm Beach, Florida. He chaired Washington and Lee University's bicentennial celebration in 1948–1949 and served on the university's board of trustees from 1950 until 1970, when he became a trustee emeritus. Randolph-Macon College awarded him an honorary LL.D. in 1964. Christopher Tompkins Chenery suffered from Alzheimer's disease in his last years and died at a hospital in New Rochelle, New York, on 3 January 1973, four months before Secretariat won the Kentucky Derby. He was buried in Woodland Cemetery, in Hanover County. In 1985 he was inducted into the Virginia Sports Hall of Fame. The Atlantic Rural Exposition, Inc. (later the State Fair of Virginia), purchased the Meadow in 2003, with plans to use it as the new site of the annual fair and to preserve the farm's history.

NCAB, 58:410–411 (por.); BVS Birth Register, Richmond City; family and racing information provided by daughter Penny Chenery (2004); W&L *Alumni Magazine* 3 (Aug. 1927): 39 (por.); *W&L* 48 (Sept. 1973): 5; ibid. 60 (May 1985): 16; *Securities and Exchange Commission* v. *Chenery Corporation et al.* (1943), *United States Reports*, 318:80–100, and (1947), 332:194–218; Blanche Chenery Perrin, "Time Out of Mind: A Memoir" (undated typescript), Blanche Chenery Perrin Papers, UVA; Chauncey Durden, "Home Ground of Great Thoroughbreds: Virginia's Meadow Farm," *Commonwealth* 29 (Aug. 1962): 19–22; William Nack, *Secretariat: The Making of a Champion* (2002); obituaries in *New York Times*, *Richmond News Leader*, *Richmond Times-Dispatch*, and *Washington Post*, all 5 Jan. 1973, and *Spur of Virginia* 8 (winter 1973): 23.

JULIE A. CAMPBELL

CHESTERMAN, Aubrey (17 June 1875–28 January 1937), architect, was born in Richmond. He was the son of Edwin Bruce Chesterman, a journalist, and Cannie Mitchell Chesterman and a first cousin of the popular Richmond journalist Evan Ragland Chesterman, who also chaired the Virginia State Board of Censors. Probably educated in the city's public schools, Chesterman showed promise in drawing and design, although rendering perspective continued to be a weakness throughout his career. He worked as a draftsman for about five years for the Richmond architect Marion Johnson Dimmock and engaged in a systematic and comprehensive study of the history and principles of architecture. On 25 June 1896 Chesterman married Helena Hampton Booker, a native of Cumberland County. They had one son and two daughters before her death on 15 July 1915.

Chesterman was a draftsman in the Richmond architectural firm of William Churchill Noland and Henry Eugene Baskervill from 1899 to 1901, when he moved to Lynchburg and formed a partnership with the well-established Lynchburg architect Edward Graham Frye. They may have practiced separately as well as in partnership during the next few years and remained partners until 1921. About 1913 they moved to Roanoke. After working there and in Danville between 1913 and 1917, Chesterman returned to Lynchburg, where he remained until his death.

Chesterman was a prominent and prolific architect. Working alone or in one of the two partnerships in which he was associated, he executed about 170 completed commissions, about one-third of them in Lynchburg and one-third in Danville. The remaining third was divided among Farmville, Roanoke, and other Virginia locales. During his partnership with Frye, Chesterman participated in the design of a number of significant Lynchburg buildings, including the Piedmont Club (1901–1902), the municipal aviary (1902), the Academy of Music (1905), the Young Men's Christian Association Building (1905), the City Market House and Auditorium (1908–1910), and Lynchburg High School (1909–1910). Frye and Chesterman employed a modified Beaux-Arts style for many of their early municipal buildings. The firm designed buildings for Randolph-Macon Woman's College, including Science Hall (1904), two dormitories (1905 and 1909), and a gymnasium (1908–1909). Frye and Chesterman made a significant and lasting contribution to Lynchburg's fashionable Rivermont neighborhood, including a fire station in the Classical Revival style (1904), a school (1905), and the Beaux-Arts–style George M. Jones Memorial Library (1905–1908), as well as several notable residences in the increasingly popular Georgian Revival style.

Among the most important Frye and Chesterman works outside Lynchburg are two designs for the Virginia Military Institute—the Administration Building, later the Chemistry Building (1903–1905), and the Mess Hall (1905)—and Roanoke's city hall and jail (1913–1916). The most visible product of the partnership was its participation, along with the Noland and Baskervill and the John Kevan Peebles firms, in the enlargement, restoration, and repair of the State Capitol in Richmond between 1904 and 1906 and in the design of the new legislative wings for the building.

Within a year of returning to Lynchburg, Chesterman formed a new partnership with J. Bryant Heard that by 1919 was designated Heard and Chesterman. With offices in Lynchburg and Danville, the productive firm completed more than fifty commissions in Danville alone. In addition to numerous private residences, Heard and Chesterman designed such institutional structures as auxiliary buildings at the Riverside and Dan River Cotton Mills (1919), the Danville Municipal Building (1925–1927), and the Danville Post Office and Courthouse (1931–1932). The partners also completed a gymnasium for Randolph-Macon Academy, in Bedford (1921), and a gymnasium, auditorium, and dormitory for Chatham Training School (later Hargrave Military Academy), in Chatham (1921).

Chesterman was a member of the Court Street Methodist Church, in Lynchburg, the Ancient, Free and Accepted Masons, and the Benevolent and Protective Order of Elks. Aubrey Chesterman died in Lynchburg of heart disease on 28 January 1937 and was buried in Fairview Cemetery, in Roanoke.

Biography in Tyler, *Encyclopedia*, 5:581 (por. facing 581 and variant birth date of 7 June 1875); BVS Birth Register, Richmond City; BVS Marriage Register, Henrico Co.; some Chesterman architectural drawings at George M. Jones Memorial Library, Lynchburg, and at LVA; advertising brochure *Selections from the Work of Heard & Chesterman, Architects, Danville, Virginia* (ca. 1930), photocopy at Virginia Department of Historic Resources, Richmond; Royster Lyle Jr. and Pamela Hemenway Simpson, *The Architecture of Historic Lexington* (1977), 232–234; S. Allen Chambers Jr., *Lynchburg: An Architectural History* (1981); W. L. Whitwell and Lee W. Winborne, *The Architectural Heritage of the Roanoke Valley* (1982), 128–129; Charles E. Brownell et al., *The Making of Virginia Architecture* (1992), 336–339; Jeni Sandberg, "Edward Graham Frye and the Jones Memorial Library" (M.A. thesis, UVA, 1994); Wells and Dalton, *Virginia Architects*, 83–84, 157–161, 189–192; Calder Loth, ed., *The Virginia Landmarks Register*, 4th ed. (1999), 284, 285, 287; BVS Death Certificate, Lynchburg (variant birth date of 7 June 1874); obituaries in *Lynchburg News*, 29 Jan. 1937, and *Roanoke Times*, 30 Jan. 1937.

BRYAN CLARK GREEN

CHESTERMAN, Evan Ragland (20 May 1870–22 February 1931), journalist and chair of the Virginia State Board of Censors (later the Division of Motion Picture Censorship), was born in Richmond. He was the son of William Dallas Chesterman and Mildred Victoria Davis Chesterman and a first cousin of the Danville and Lynchburg architect Aubrey Chesterman. From 1865 until his death in 1904, his father wrote for or edited a series of Richmond newspapers, including the *Southern Opinion*, the *Richmond Enquirer*, the *Richmond Examiner*, and after 1874 the *Richmond Dispatch*, of which he became vice president and managing editor. After a merger created the *Richmond Times-Dispatch* in 1903, the elder Chesterman was one of its first editors. He also wrote two widely reprinted guidebooks, *The James River Tourist* (1878) and *Guide to Richmond and the Battlefields* (1881).

Educated in Richmond public schools, Evan R. Chesterman attended Richmond College (later the University of Richmond) from 1886 to 1889, was the editor of its first college annual, and received diplomas of graduation in English, French, and Latin and modern languages. He worked briefly for the Richmond Chamber of Commerce and then became a city reporter for the *Richmond Dispatch*, of which his father was then managing editor. Chesterman honed his writing style, which bristled with humor and featured a rich vocabulary. He accompanied his father to Europe in 1892, and two years later, because of his writing skills and connection to the pro-Democratic and influential *Dispatch*, became private secretary to Governor Charles Triplett O'Ferrall. Chesterman worked for the governor during his term in office, from 1894 to 1898, and may have ghostwritten O'Ferrall's autobiography, *Forty Years of Active Service* (1904).

While working for O'Ferrall, Chesterman studied law at Richmond College. In 1895 he earned a certificate of proficiency in constitutional and international law and the next year received a bachelor of laws degree. On 10 November 1896 he married Ellie Douglas Frayser, of Richmond, who in 1918 started Camp Okahahwis, a Rockbridge County camp for girls that she operated for more than thirty-five years. They had two daughters and one son. In August 1896 Chesterman published his first independent work, a short story entitled "The Devil's One Good Deed," in *Lippincott's Monthly Magazine*. He also began writing a column, "Letters of An Idle Reporter," in the Sunday edition of the *Richmond Dispatch*, in which he offered a witty view of everyday Virginia life. In 1912 he published a 152-page compilation of the columns as *Things Mundane*.

After practicing law from 1898 to 1902, Chesterman resumed his journalism career, first as a news editor for the *Richmond Dispatch* and then as assistant city editor of the *Richmond News Leader* from 1903 to 1905. In the latter year he joined the staff of the *Richmond Evening Journal* as a reporter. He covered in detail several sensational murder cases and trials, among them those of James Samuel McCue in 1904 and Henry Clay Beattie in 1911. He and Joe F. Geisinger published a *History of the McCue Case* (1904), and Chesterman also compiled a series of columns he had written for the *Evening Journal* under the title *Duels and Duelists of Bygone Virginia Days* (1908–1909).

Chesterman became secretary to the State Board of Education in January 1913. The job required that he take minutes for the board, act as chief clerk to the superintendent of public instruction, answer correspondence, and write reports. One of the reports he prepared, *Illiteracy in Virginia: Some Facts Which Cannot Be Overlooked* (1914), contained a strong denunciation of Virginia's high illiteracy rate with suggestions for improvement. Suffering from arthritis, Chesterman resigned in November 1916, but he continued to write. Under the publisher's stock nom de plume Elliott Whitney he produced three works of juvenile literature for the Boys Big Game series, *The Bobcat of Jump Mountain* (1920), *The Crazy Elk of Terrapin Swamp* (1921), and *The Lady Dragon of Dancing Point* (1922). These novels drew on his own life for inspiration and are very much period pieces.

In April 1922 the governor appointed Chesterman to the new three-member State Board of Censors, responsible for screening and licensing all motion pictures shown in Virginia and for requiring such changes as the members deemed necessary. Elected chair at the board's initial meeting, Chesterman was a staunch opponent of films that appeared to him to breach the rigid code of racial segregation then in force in Virginia and those that showed a laxity in moral conduct. In 1925 he reported to the governor that the board "scrutinized with peculiar care all films which touch upon the relations existing between whites and blacks" and had demanded deletion of all scenes that might produce "friction." Perceptions of obscenity or immorality accounted for the greatest number of demanded cuts or changes, and Chesterman closely reviewed subtitles for double entendres. Comedies were particularly suspect in the board's eyes. A section of the board's 1927 annual report appeared under the headline "Comedies Demand Scrutiny" and asserted that such films "for the most part preserve and emphasize the primitive types of vulgar slap-stick farce with correspondingly coarse and suggestive subtitles." From 1922 to 1929 the board ordered deletions of offensive scenes and subtitle dialogue in almost 10 percent of the films it reviewed.

After an administrative reorganization of the state government, in 1927 Chesterman became director of the Division of Motion Picture Censorship. His workload increased, and the advent of talking pictures presented the board with new administrative and technical problems that Chesterman lamented. In 1928 and 1929 the board was forced to license films without proper review because it lacked the technology with which to synchronize sound and image, a failure that embarrassed Chesterman. Although the board had not been inaugurated with profit in mind, it charged a fee for reviewing films, initially $1 before being raised to $2 in 1923. The increasing number of films requiring review late in the 1920s produced a significant revenue stream, and in 1928 Chesterman reported a profit of more than $7,000.

Advanced rheumatoid arthritis required Chesterman to use a wheelchair during his last years, but he continued working in spite of the infirmity. Between 1929 and 1930 he wrote some reminiscences of his boyhood in Richmond for serialization in *Richmond* magazine. He also acted as a mentor to younger writers, and his home became something of a literary salon late in the 1920s. Evan Ragland Chesterman died in Richmond on 22 February 1931 and was buried in the city's Hollywood Cemetery.

Middle name and birth date in Davis family Bible records (1791–1965), LVA; variant birth date of 20 May 1871 in BVS Death Certificate, Richmond City, in funeral contract, 23 Feb. 1931, L. T. Christian Funeral Home Records, Acc. 34483, LVA, and in obituaries; middle name erroneously given as Rayland in some author authority records; BVS Marriage Register, Richmond City; Chesterman scrapbooks, VHS, and some letters in Mary Frayser Papers, Winthrop University, Rock Hill, S.C.; other published writings include memorial of Charles Triplett O'Ferrall in *Virginia State Bar Association Proceedings* (1906), 51–57; Division of Motion Picture Censorship Papers, Acc. 26515, RG 5, LVA; annual *Report of the Virginia State Board of Censors* (1922–1932), esp. 1925, p. 2 (first quotation), and 1927, p. 5 (second quotation); *Richmond Times-Dispatch*, 30 Apr. 1922 (feature article with birth date of 20 May 1870), 11 Jan. 1931; obituaries, editorial tributes, and account of funeral in *Richmond News Leader*, 23 Feb. 1931 (por.), and *Richmond Times-Dispatch*, 23 (por.), 24 Feb. 1931.

MINOR T. WEISIGER

CHEVALLIÉ, Peter Joseph (15 May 1791–21 February 1837), flour manufacturer, was born in New York. His father, Jean Auguste Marie Chevallié (who later anglicized his name to John Augustus Chevallié), had visited Virginia at the end of the Revolutionary War to secure full payment for supplies the French playwright Pierre-Augustin Caron de Beaumarchais had sold to the state. In 1790 he married Sarah Magee, a sister of Mary Magee Gallego, whose husband, Joseph Gallego, owned a large flour mill in Richmond. Peter Joseph Chevallié's mother died five days after his birth, and his father sent him to live with the Gallego family. Chevallié's father soon returned to Richmond, married again, and prospered as a French consul, as Gallego's partner, and as an investor in land and in commercial and manufacturing enterprises.

Educated in Richmond and in Paris, Chevallié served for twenty-seven days as a corporal in a Richmond militia company during the War of 1812. He married Elizabeth Green Gilliam on 23 November 1815. They had at least four sons and three daughters. In January 1817 he published *Claim of Beaumarchais' Heir against the United States*, a forty-two-page pamphlet on the legal action that had first brought his father to Virginia. In 1818 Chevallié inherited the bulk of Gallego's estate, because the miller's wife and adopted daughter had died in the 1811 Richmond Theatre fire. Chevallié's inheritance included the Gallego Mills, a large flour mill on the banks of the James River near Richmond, and Gallego's mansion, Moldavia, where he lived until 1825.

Chevallié became one of Richmond's leading industrialists. He operated cornmeal-, lumber-, and tobacco-manufacturing enterprises and directed the Gallego Mills, by 1831 the largest in the city and whose flour was regarded as the best. Richmond was then the leading flour-producing and -exporting city in the South. Operating under the style of P. J. Chevallié and Company, the mills produced between 45,000 and 50,000 barrels of flour a year, most of which was exported to London and South America.

On 6 February 1833 the Gallego Mills burned. Chevallié then purchased a lot on Twelfth Street between Cary and Canal Streets in downtown Richmond and erected a huge new water-powered flour mill that he described as larger than any other in the United States. The new mill, operating by mid-1834, contained twenty-four pairs of grinding stones, four times the number in the first mill. Milling capacity increased to 900 barrels of flour a day, significantly more than the Haxall mill, which was the next-largest milling operation in the city. The Gallego mill was one of many successful industries in Richmond that used both free and enslaved laborers. Chevallié took his son-in-law Abraham Warwick into the business about the time the new mill opened.

In January 1834 Chevallié incorporated and collected subscriptions for the Gallego Manufacturing Company, a proposed cotton mill and iron-, paper-, and wool-manufacturing enterprise, but he did not form the authorized venture. At about the same time a House of Delegates committee rejected his petition to incorporate the Gallego Milling Company. On 14 December 1835 Chevallié sold all of his inherited property, except the Gallego Mills and a lease for the land and water for operating it, for $85,000.

Peter Joseph Chevallié died in Richmond, without having made a will, on 21 February 1837 and was buried in Shockoe Cemetery. Warwick formed a partnership with William J. Barksdale to operate the Gallego Mills, which was then one of the largest in the United States and remained the largest flour miller in the South until the end of the Civil War, when the mill burned in the evacuation fire. Warwick and Barksdale built another mill and continued flour production.

Biography in Valentine Museum, *Richmond Portraits in an Exhibition of Makers of Richmond, 1737–1860* (1949), 39 (por.); birth and death dates from gravestone; Henrico Co. Marriage Bonds; Peter Joseph Chevallié Journal (1825–1831), LVA; Chevallié letters and documents in various collections, VHS; commercial and residential properties described in various Mutual Assurance Society Declarations, LVA; Chevallié petitions, 3, 5, 31 Dec. 1833, 16 Feb. 1836, Legislative Petitions, Richmond City, RG 78, LVA; Thomas S. Berry, "The Rise of Flour Milling in Richmond," *VMHB* 78 (1970): 387–408; obituaries in *Richmond Enquirer*, 23 Feb. 1837, *Alexandria Gazette*, 27 Feb. 1837, and *Charles Town Virginia Free Press*, 2 Mar. 1837.

AMANDA MORRELL

CHEW, Roger Preston (9 April 1843–16 March 1921), Confederate artillery officer, was the son of Roger Chew, a magistrate and farmer, and Sarah West Aldridge Chew and was born in Loudoun County. About 1846 his family moved to Jefferson County. He attended the Charles Town Academy and late in July 1859 entered the Virginia Military Institute. The following December, R. P. Chew, as he usually signed his name, and some of his fellow cadets traveled with their professor Thomas J. Jackson to Charles Town to stand guard at the hanging of the abolitionist John Brown.

Soon after Virginia's secession in April 1861 Chew and other cadets left VMI for Richmond to serve as drill instructors for volunteer troops. In May he and a classmate were sent to Harpers Ferry to serve under Lieutenant Colonel Jackson. Their stay was brief, however, because Jackson ordered them back to Lexington that same month for visiting nearby relatives without a furlough. Chew then went to Richmond seeking a permanent army position but, because of his youth and inexperience, was rebuffed. He obtained temporary assignment to the Lee Battery of the Virginia Light Artillery and served as acting lieutenant from 15 July until September 1861. Because of the disruption of the Civil War, Chew's VMI class was declared graduated in December 1861, at which time he finished eighth in a class of thirty-five.

In November 1861 Chew helped organize and was commissioned a captain of a horse artillery company, the first of its type in Civil War Virginia. Known as Chew's Battery, this unit went into the field in December and served in Turner Ashby's brigade in the Shenandoah Valley and in western Virginia. It won accolades as a model for a swift-moving artillery company. In May and June 1862 the battery participated in Thomas J. "Stonewall" Jackson's Shenandoah Valley campaign, during which Ashby was killed. Over the next twelve months it operated in the Valley, east of the Blue Ridge Mountains, and in western Virginia and fought at Crampton's Gap during the Antietam (Sharpsburg) campaign.

By mid-1863 Chew's unit had joined the Stuart Horse Artillery Battalion, an organization created to feature the mobile batteries that fought with the cavalry branch. His artillery arrived just in time to see action at Brandy Station in June and subsequently participated in engagements at Hagerstown, Culpeper Court House, the Wilderness, Spotsylvania Court House, and Trevilian Station. As the Army of Northern Virginia equipped even more horse artillery batteries, Chew won promotion. His commission as major of horse artillery dated from 27 February 1864, and he became lieutenant colonel on 18 February 1865. The latter appointment made Chew the chief of the Stuart Horse Artillery commanding approximately forty guns, although he was not yet twenty-two years old.

Considered one of the finest commanders of horse artillery during the Civil War, Chew managed to keep his artillery in the field during the final year of the war despite increasing shortages of equipment and horses. He and some of the Army of Northern Virginia's other horse artillerists avoided the surrender at Appomattox

Court House and pushed southward to North Carolina, where they hoped to join General Joseph Eggleston Johnston's Confederate army. An impassable river forced Chew to bury his remaining cannon, and on 26 April 1865 he surrendered with Johnston at Greensboro.

After the war Chew returned to Charles Town, where he capitalized on his war record to forge successful careers in business, politics, and Confederate veterans' affairs. He was president both of the Charles Town Mining, Manufacturing, and Improvement Company and of the Goshen Land and Improvement Company, a director of the Northern Virginia Power Company, and an organizer of the Charles Town Water Company. Beginning in 1885 Chew, a Democrat, represented Jefferson County in the West Virginia House of Delegates. During his three terms he chaired the Committee on Taxation and Finance and, for the 1885–1886 term, the Committee on Immigration and Agriculture as well. From at least 1902 until 1913 Chew's financial expertise earned him a seat on the depositing committee that held the Virginia Deferred Certificates during the continued wrangling over the settlement of West Virginia's portion of Virginia's antebellum public debt. Chew commanded his local camp of United Confederate Veterans, which paid for and erected about two dozen stones to mark Civil War sites in Jefferson County. As president of the Lee Memorial Association he delivered the main address at the unveiling of the monument to his former instructor Stonewall Jackson at the Virginia Military Institute in 1912.

On 15 August 1871 Chew married Louisa Fontaine Washington, daughter of John Augustine Washington (d. 1861), the last private owner of Mount Vernon. Of their three sons and three daughters, two sons and one daughter did not reach adulthood. After more than a year of failing health, Roger Preston Chew died in Charles Town on 16 March 1921 and was buried there in the cemetery of Zion Episcopal Church.

Death date from gravestone; biographies in *Charles Town Spirit of Jefferson*, 14 Oct. 1890, Thomas Condit Miller and Hu Maxwell, *West Virginia and Its People* (1913), 3:1088–1089, and Millard Kessler Bushong, *Historic Jefferson County* (1972), 408–409; Roger Preston Chew alum-nus file, VMI; Compiled Service Records; Chew papers at Jefferson County Museum, Charles Town, W.Va., and West Virginia and Regional History Collection, WVU; published works include *Military Operations in Jefferson County, Virginia (and West Va.), 1861–1865* (1911), *Stonewall Jackson: Address of Colonel R. P. Chew, Chief of Horse Artillery, Army of Northern Virginia, Delivered at the Virginia Military Institute, . . . June 19, 1912* (1912), and *Letters and Papers Relating to Services of Lieutenant-Colonel R. P. Chew, C.S.A.* (n.d.); Avis Mary Custis Cauley, "The Confederacy in the Lower Shenandoah Valley as Illustrated by the Career of Colonel Roger Preston Chew" (M.A. thesis, University of Pittsburgh, 1937); Robert H. Moore, *Chew's Ashby, Shoemaker's Lynchburg and the Newtown Artillery* (1995), esp. 93, 96 (pors.), 102; Robert J. Trout, *Galloping Thunder: The Story of the Stuart Horse Artillery Battalion* (2002); obituaries in *Winchester Evening Star*, 16 Mar. 1921 (noting death "at 4 o'clock this morning"), *Charles Town Farmer's Advocate*, 19 Mar. 1921 (noting death "Tuesday night," that is, 15 Mar. 1921), and *Charles Town Spirit of Jefferson*, 22 Mar. 1921 (noting death "last Tuesday night"); obituary and memorial resolutions in *Confederate Veteran* 30 (1922): 149 (with variant death date of "Tuesday night, March 14, 1921").

ROBERT E. L. KRICK

CHEYNE, Christopher Ethelbert (5 July 1867–14 August 1943), photographer, was born in Brampton, Ontario, Canada, and was the son of Luther Cheyne, a farmer and sometime real estate and insurance salesman, and Mary Jane Switzer Cheyne. He attended the local primary and secondary schools but terminated his formal education early to begin working for the London Oil Company, a coal and wood dealer. After three years he decided to indulge his artistic interests instead. A talented portrait painter, Cheyne dabbled in the photography business in Buffalo, New York, and Indianapolis, Indiana, before moving to Cincinnati, Ohio, where he apprenticed himself to a leading photographer. He paid the studio $5 a week to learn the art of retouching and printing images. In the meantime he supported himself by playing the flute in the local orchestra.

After several years in Cincinnati, Cheyne struck out on his own in New Orleans but found the climate so oppressive he quickly abandoned the city. A trip to Hampton, Virginia, to visit a former fellow musician from the Cincinnati orchestra persuaded Cheyne to try his luck there. On 10 June 1894 he opened a photography studio, the only such establishment in Hampton at that time and one of the first on the Peninsula. After moving his studio several times, C. Ethelbert Cheyne, as he called himself professionally, settled in a downtown building on East Queen Street. He maintained his photography studio on the second floor and, until 1930, also operated on the first floor a music store selling musical instruments, phonograph players, radios, and records. Cheyne married Emily Louise Couch, a Hampton schoolteacher, on 13 July 1897. They had two daughters and one son, William Ethelbert "Happy" Cheyne, who took over his father's business in the 1930s and managed the studio until he sold it in 1966.

During seventy years of continuous operation, the Cheyne Studio documented people, places, and events of the Hampton area. Approximately 4,000 images, taken between 1894 and 1945, are preserved at the Hampton History Museum. In addition to studio portraits of individuals and families, including his own, Cheyne also captured images of local residents at work, members of area organizations and sporting teams, and such events as baseball games, parades, and the aftermath of a 1933 hurricane. He photographed numerous Hampton residences, businesses, hotels and seaside resorts, institutions, schools, and modes of local transportation, thereby preserving a record of his community from the turn of the twentieth century through World War II. Cheyne published fifteen plates taken for the National Home for Disabled Volunteer Soldiers, Southern Branch, in *National Home, D.V.S., Hampton, Va.: Photogravures* (1900) and other work in the sixteen-leaf *Rapid Transit in Virginia: Old Point Comfort, Hampton, Williamsburg and Historical Points: Photo-Gravures* (1905). An exhibition and sale of about 1,200 Cheyne images at the Hampton City Hall in November 1985 raised $17,000 in two days for what became the Virginia Air and Space Center. The success of this fund-raising venture spurred development of the Hampton History Museum Association, which mounted another exhibit of approximately 160 Cheyne photographs at its Information Center in July and August 1997.

Cheyne served as president of the Photographers' Association of Virginia and the Carolinas. A member of several local fraternal organizations, including the Benevolent and Protective Order of Elks, Kiwanis, Knights of Pythias, and Royal Arch Masons, he was also a director and vice president of the Hampton branch of the Young Men's Christian Association and a trustee of the First Methodist Church. Having suffered a prolonged period of poor health, Christopher Ethelbert Cheyne died on 14 August 1943 in a Hampton hospital and was buried in the cemetery of Saint John's Episcopal Church in that city.

Biographies in Tyler, *Encyclopedia*, 4:482–483, and *Who Is Who in Hampton Kiwanis* (ca. 1936), including por., birth date, and variant birthplace of Toronto; BVS Marriage Register, Elizabeth City Co.; *Newport News Times-Herald*, 19 Dec. 1958 (por.), 25 May 1966; *Newport News Daily Press*, 13 July 1997; obituaries and accounts of funeral in *Newport News Times-Herald*, 14 (with birthplace), 16 Aug. 1943, and *Newport News Daily Press*, 15, 16 Aug. 1943.

ELIZABETH M. GUSHEE

CHICHELEY, Sir Henry (1614 or 1615–5 February 1683), lieutenant governor of Virginia and member of the Council, was the son of Sir Thomas Chicheley and Dorothy Kempe Chicheley, of Wimpole, Cambridgeshire, England. Descended from a well-to-do family and assured of a privileged upbringing, he matriculated at University College, University of Oxford, at age seventeen on 27 April 1632 and received a B.A. three years later. A Royalist during the English Civil Wars, Chicheley became a lieutenant colonel before King Charles I knighted him about 1644. Complicity in a plot against Parliament landed him in the Tower of London, but in the spring of 1650 the Council of State paroled him and allowed him to sail to Virginia on the condition that he "do nothing prejudicial to the State and present government thereof."

Chicheley found safe haven in the household of Ralph Wormeley (d. 1651), where he befriended other Royalist refugees, one of whom introduced him to Governor Sir William Berkeley. Sometime after 31 May 1652 Chicheley married Wormeley's widow, Agatha Eltonhead Stubbins Wormeley, whose sister Eleanor Eltonhead married first William Brocas, a member of the governor's Council, and then John Carter (ca. 1613–1670), also a member of the Council, and whose sister Alice Eltonhead Burnham married Henry Corbyn, another member of the Council.

The union not only set Chicheley on the top rung of Virginia society but also gave him control of Wormeley's considerable properties. Chicheley resided at Wormeley's estate, Rosegill, in the part of Lancaster County that in 1669 became Middlesex County. He acquired additional land elsewhere in the Rappahannock River basin, all of which, because he had no children, eventually passed to his widow's son, Ralph Wormeley (d. 1701), later a president of the Council.

An early convert to Berkeley's schemes for diversifying the colony's economy, Chicheley experimented with sericulture. His success ranked him in a group of great planters who, like Berkeley, established mulberry orchards, tended silkworms, and made silk in profitable quantities that found ready markets in England. Chicheley also followed Berkeley's lead by advocating restrictions on tobacco cultivation to raise its price and as a means of fostering diversification.

Chicheley represented Lancaster County in the House of Burgesses in 1656 and not long thereafter, in violation of his parole, returned to England, where he made contact with supporters of Charles II who paved the way for the return of the king in 1660. Chicheley was still in London when Berkeley arrived in 1661 on a mission to extract royal blessings for his diversification plans and worked tirelessly in the lobbying campaign that won much of what Berkeley sought. Chicheley stayed behind when the governor left for Virginia in the autumn of 1662 and with other Virginians pressed the Privy Council for curbs on tobacco production. The failure of the negotiations sent him back to America, where a grateful Berkeley heaped generous rewards on him. The governor appointed him to the Council in April 1670, made him a lieutenant general of the militia in July 1672, and arranged for the king early in 1674 to name him lieutenant, or deputy, governor. Chicheley's influence with the royal master general of the ordnance, his brother Sir Thomas Chicheley, resulted in the dispatch of some much-needed great guns and ammunition during the Third Anglo-Dutch War (1672–1674).

During the frontier unrest that preceded Bacon's Rebellion, Berkeley gave Chicheley command of a force that was supposed to attack marauding Indians, but Chicheley never took the field because Berkeley countermanded the order. Berkeley's sudden change of heart was one in a series of missteps that inspired Nathaniel Bacon (1647–1676) to revolt. Chicheley and others tried without success to compose the disagreements between the governor and Bacon, and when the rebellion began, Chicheley stood by Berkeley. The Baconians branded him a traitor and held him hostage until the insurgency fell to pieces.

On 30 December 1678 Chicheley succeeded Herbert Jeffreys as acting governor, and from that moment until his death, Chicheley was a man in a tight spot. No Virginia politician was more alarmed than he by the Crown's aggressive attempt to regain control of the colony, though few shared his cautious disposition as he awaited the coming of Berkeley's replacement, the dilatory Thomas Culpeper, second baron Culpeper of Thoresway, who finally arrived and took up his duties on 10 May 1680, only to depart on 11 August of the same year. It fell largely to Chicheley to steer the colony through a troubled period of political and economic readjustment. Commandments from Charles II prevented him from using the General Assembly in the spring of 1682 to improve tobacco prices by limiting crop size. In response to falling prices, gangs of frustrated planters went about the countryside cutting down tobacco seedlings on more than 200 plantations. Prompt action by local officials prevented the plant-cutting riots from spreading beyond Gloucester, Middlesex, and New Kent Counties. Unlike Culpeper, who returned for another short administration from December 1682 to May 1683, Chicheley regarded the plant cuttings as comparatively insignificant, and most of the offenders were only lightly punished. His instinct for circumspection kept the riots from turning into a major insurrection and spared the colony further intervention from London.

Quelling the plant cutters was Chicheley's last important act as deputy governor. On the whole he acquitted himself better than might have been expected. Culpeper erred with his wickedly cutting characterization of Chicheley as "that Lumpe, that Masse of Dulnesse, that worse then nothing." Sir Henry Chicheley died on 5 February 1683, probably at Rosegill, several weeks after Culpeper's second arrival. He was buried "neare the Comunion Table" in the chancel of Christ Church, in Middlesex County.

Joseph Foster, *Alumni Oxonienses* (1891–1892), 1:270 (age seventeen on 27 Apr. 1632); biography in *VMHB* 17 (1909): 144–146; G. Melvin Herndon, "Sir Henry Chicheley, Virginia Cavalier," *Virginia Cavalcade* 16 (summer 1966): 10–15; *VMHB* 17 (1909): 133 (first quotation); Sainsbury, *Calendar of State Papers, Colonial Series, 1574–1660*, 337, 338; Chicheley letters in PRO CO 1/18, fols. 311, 313, CO 1/30, fol. 113, CO 1/49, fols. 98–99, 100–101, CO 5/1355, 360–362, CO 5/1356, fols. 65–69, in Coventry Papers, Longleat, Wiltshire, Eng., and in William Blathwayt Papers (also including Culpeper to William Blathwayt, 20 Mar. 1683 [second quotation]), CW; appointments in *Minutes of Council and General Court*, 205, 494, 515, 522; Wilcomb E. Washburn, *The Governor and the Rebel: A History of Bacon's Rebellion in Virginia* (1957), 24, 70, 71; Stephen Saunders Webb, *The Governors-General: The English Army and the Definition of the Empire, 1569–1681* (1979), 115, 347, 364, 391, 404–406, 410, 420, 509; Warren M. Billings, John E. Selby, and Thad W. Tate, *Colonial Virginia: A History* (1986), 83–84, 103–108; Billings, *Sir William Berkeley and the Forging of Colonial Virginia* (2004); death date in *The Parish Register of Christ Church, Middlesex County, Va., from 1653 to 1812* (1897), 7 (third quotation).

WARREN M. BILLINGS

CHICHESTER, Richard Henry Lee (18 April 1870–3 February 1930), judge of the Virginia Supreme Court of Appeals, was born in Fairfax County and was the son of Daniel McCarty Chichester, a county court judge, and his second wife, Agnes Robinson Moncure Chichester, daughter of Richard Cassius Lee Moncure (1805–1882), longtime president of the Supreme Court of Appeals. Chichester was educated in the Fairfax County schools and later at Saint John's Academy, in Alexandria. He attended the University of Virginia during the 1889–1890 academic year and completed one year at its law school in the 1891–1892 term. Illness rendered him unable to continue study in an academic setting, but he read law at Fairfax Court House with Robert Walton Moore, later a member of the House of Representatives. In July 1892 Chichester received a license to practice in Fairfax County. He married Virginia Belle Wallace, of Stafford County, on 11 June 1895. They had two sons and one daughter.

Chichester established his own law office in Stafford County. In May 1895 he was elected commonwealth's attorney for the county and held that position until the General Assembly elected him judge of the courts of King George and Stafford Counties in December 1897. He served from January 1898 until 1904, when those courts were abolished. Chichester then practiced law with his brother for six years until December 1910, when the governor appointed him a justice for the Fifteenth Judicial Circuit, composed of Caroline, Hanover, King George, Spotsylvania, and Stafford Counties. The next session of the General Assembly in January 1912 confirmed the appointment.

In 1915 Samuel P. Powell, a one-term delegate representing Fredericksburg and Spotsylvania County, brought charges of political corruption against Chichester in the House of Delegates. Among other accusations he asserted that in those localities Chichester had inappropriately appointed electoral board members in an attempt to manipulate elections, was politically motivated in naming local officials, displayed bias in adjudicating cases, and had engaged in nepotism. After investigating the charges a special subcommittee of the Committee for Courts of Justice absolved him, finding that politics had not influenced his actions on the bench and that he had behaved impartially when conducting the business of the court. The assembly confirmed its confidence in Chichester by reelecting him judge of the Fifteenth Judicial Circuit in 1918.

To alleviate the crowded docket of the Supreme Court of Appeals, the General Assembly in 1924 created a Special Court of Appeals. On 18 June of that year the Supreme Court of Appeals selected Chichester and four other judges from the circuit and city court benches for the temporary court. On 16 April 1925 the governor appointed Chichester to the Supreme Court of Appeals to fill the vacancy caused by the death of Joseph Luther Kelly. Chichester took his seat in June and on 16 February 1928 won election to a full term on the bench, where he served until his death less than two years later. Characterized as a fair jurist of integrity and ability, he wrote thoughtful, carefully researched opinions sometimes numbering dozens of pages.

Chichester had many interests outside his profession. On Glencairne, his farm near Falmouth, in Stafford County, he raised purebred Guernsey cattle that won prizes at many livestock and state fairs along the Atlantic seaboard. In 1900 Chichester formed the Star Printing and Publishing Company with himself as president and purchased the two *Fredericksburg Star* newspapers. Two years later he became president of the newly incorporated Free Lance-Star Publishing Company, which published both the local *Free Lance* and *Daily Star* newspapers (merged in 1926 as the *Fredericksburg Free Lance-Star*), to which he occasionally contributed editorials. In 1908 Chichester was appointed to a four-year term on the board of trustees for the State Normal and Industrial School for Women at Fredericksburg (later the University of Mary Washington). A lifelong Episcopalian, he served on the vestry of Saint George's Episcopal Church in Fredericksburg from 1901 until 1919 but later transferred his membership to Aquia Episcopal Church in Stafford, where he also served on the vestry. Richard Henry Lee Chichester died of chronic nephritis at a Fredericksburg hospital on 3 February 1930. He was buried in the family cemetery at Glencairne.

Biographies in *Fredericksburg Free Lance*, 23 Dec. 1910 (por.), Henry Winston Holt, "Richard Henry Lee Chichester," *Virginia State Bar Association Proceedings* (1930), 204–206 (por.), and Daniel M. Chichester, "Judge Richard Henry Lee Chichester: A Short Biography," *Northern Neck of Virginia Historical Magazine* 25 (1975): 2780–2783; BVS Marriage Register, Stafford Co.; *Fredericksburg Free Lance*, 14 June 1895, 3 Feb. 1914, 19 Jan. 1926; *Fredericksburg Daily Star*, 2 June 1920, 1 Mar. 1921, 16, 17 Apr., 2 June 1925; Fairfax Co. Minute Book (1892–1895), 66; judicial appointments in *JHD*, 1912 sess., 66, *JHD*, 1918 sess., 100, *JHD*, 1926 sess., 49, 69, *JHD*, 1928 sess., 390, Special Court of Appeals Order Book, 4:1, RG 107, LVA, and Supreme Court of Appeals Order Book, 39:330, RG 100, LVA; political corruption investigation in *JHD*, 1915 extra sess., 407–410, 466–467, *JHD*, 1916 sess., 24–27, and Proceedings Relevant to the Investigation of Charges against Judge R. H. L. Chichester (1915), Virginia House of Delegates, Committee for Courts of Justice, Acc. 25523, LVA; BVS Death Certificate, Fredericksburg; obituaries in *Fredericksburg Free Lance-Star* and *Richmond News Leader*, both 3 Feb. 1930, and *Richmond Times-Dispatch*, 4 Feb. 1930.

ELIZABETH TERRY LONG

CHILDRESS, Robert Walter (19 January 1889–16 January 1956), Presbyterian minister, was born in the portion of Patrick County known as the Hollow. He was the son of Columbia Francis Smith Childress and James Anderson Childress, a farmer, timber cutter, and failed distiller of whiskey. Bob Childress, as he was known, grew up in a large family living in extreme poverty. He recalled taking his first drink of whiskey when he was not quite three years old. In 1896, against his mother's wishes, Childress followed an elder brother's advice and entered a local school operated by a Quaker missionary from North Carolina. Childress left school about 1904 and returned in 1911, but after a few months he quit again to live as he chose. His drinking and fighting earned him a reputation as "The Heller of the Hollow."

On 12 January 1912 Childress married Pearl Ayers. They had one son and one daughter. Childress became a farm laborer and helped out in a blacksmith shop. Later in 1912 he joined a posse to track down members of the Floyd Allen family after the notorious courthouse shootout in neighboring Carroll County. The degrading comments about violent and illiterate mountain people that appeared in press coverage of that event persuaded Childress to give up drinking and violence and focus on a better life. He and his wife attended a succession of Methodist, Quaker, and Primitive Baptist churches before she died on 21 November 1918 after giving birth to their third child, who also died. Following her death Childress opened his own blacksmith shop and in June 1919 became deputy sheriff of Patrick County.

On 3 August 1919 Childress married Mamie Lelia Montgomery, also of Patrick County. They had four sons and two daughters. He began teaching Sunday school and eventually decided to enter the ministry. Childress also taught beginning students at a local school and led church services at the Free Union Church, a nondenominational congregation he helped found, and at a small African American community chapel. He and his family were baptized and joined the Presbyterian Church.

Childress resumed his own education and returned to high school late in 1921, the same time that his eldest son started the first grade. He completed the tenth grade in one month and in September 1922 moved his family to North

Carolina so that he could attend Davidson College. While in school Childress sold apples to support his family and earned extra money as a substitute teacher in a local elementary school. His professors arranged for him to become a student pastor at Mayberry, in western Patrick County, and he also began leading services at nearby Vesta. He acquired a portable pulpit and preached against the drinking and shooting life that he had once led. Childress occasionally lost his temper with a congregation's behavior during revival services and once pitched a chair down the center aisle in order to run Satan out of the church. His rough but dramatic method succeeded, and seventeen people converted that evening.

After one year at Davidson College, Childress borrowed $100 from a brother and in 1923 moved his family to Richmond, where he was permitted to attend classes at the Union Theological Seminary in Virginia (later the Union Theological Seminary and Presbyterian School of Christian Education). After his successful first semester, the school president offered him two scholarships and a house on campus. He also received financial assistance from the city's First Presbyterian Church. Childress did not complete a bachelor of divinity degree but did receive a diploma for finishing the full English course in 1926. During his studies he continued as pastor of the Mayberry Presbyterian Church and with the help of the congregation erected a school in the town. The Roanoke Presbytery licensed and ordained him in the autumn of 1924.

Childress accepted a call to preach at Buffalo Mountain, a southern Floyd County community then without an organized church, and early in June 1926 moved there. He opened Buffalo Mountain School with three mission teachers. He helped erect Buffalo Mountain Presbyterian Church using stone and timber from the local mountains and labor, horses, and oxen provided by local residents. Completed in 1929, it was the first of six churches that Childress erected during his ministry. He simultaneously made an effort to improve the local economy so that residents would not resort to running moonshine. Childress experimented with different types of livestock, including goats, swine, and Brahma cattle that he acquired in South Car-

olina. With an anonymous $200 donation he purchased and operated a sawmill, which provided much-needed jobs during the Great Depression. In the 1930s Childress lobbied for public money to improve and build new roads and bridges in Carroll and Floyd Counties. He then used the roads to facilitate his own travel to the eight churches at which he preached each week.

During parts of his career Childress served as many as fourteen rural churches simultaneously. Three of his sons also became Presbyterian ministers, as did one grandson. In August 1950 Childress suffered a stroke that partially paralyzed his right arm and leg. He had so many visitors at the hospital that his doctor sent him to Florida to recuperate in a hospital there. Once recovered, Childress ignored his physician's advice to reduce his church visits and continued to preach at as many as nine churches each week. After his stroke he began encouraging racially integrated fellowship and communion between members of an African American church where he sometimes preached and white congregants of several of the other churches he served.

Robert Walter Childress suffered a second stroke in December 1955 and died in a Roanoke hospital on 16 January 1956. He was buried in the cemetery at Buffalo Mountain Presbyterian Church. His enduring regional fame and his accomplishments resulted in articles about him appearing in regional periodicals during subsequent decades, publication of a biography, a proposal to produce a film about his career, and the staging in Floyd County in 2002 of a play based on his life.

Birth date from BVS Birth Register, Patrick Co.; gravestone inscription, family tradition, and several reference works with 1890 birth year; Census, Patrick Co., 1900, with birth date of Jan. 1891; E. C. Scott, comp., *Ministerial Directory of the Presbyterian Church, U.S., 1861–1941: Revised and Supplemented, 1942–1950* (1950), 121 (with birth date of 19 Jan. 1890); Richard C. Davids, *The Man Who Moved a Mountain* (1970), with birth date of 19 Jan. 1890 and several pors.; Rodger Doss, "The Man Who Moved a Mountain," *Blue Ridge Country* 6 (Sept./Oct. 1993): 44–49, including excerpts from unpublished memoirs in possession of Childress family (2002); BVS Marriage Register, Patrick Co. (1912, 1919); information supplied by grandson Stewart Childress (2002); obituaries in *Roanoke World-News*, 17 Jan. 1956, *Roanoke Times*, 17, 18 Jan. 1956, and *Hillsville*

Carroll News, 26 Jan. 1956; memorial in *Minutes of Montgomery Presbytery* (1956), 152–153 (with birth date of 19 Jan. 1890).

AMANDA MORRELL

CHILDS, James Rives (6 February 1893–15 July 1987), diplomat and writer, was born in Lynchburg and was the son of John William Childs, an insurance broker, and Lucy Howard Brown Childs, a public school teacher and principal. He graduated from a Lynchburg high school in 1908, attended the Virginia Military Institute from 1908 to 1910, earned a B.A. from Randolph-Macon College in 1912, and received an M.A. in literature from Harvard University in 1915. Before attending Harvard, Childs taught school in Charlotte County. In 1915 and 1916 he worked as a private tutor in Illinois and Colorado and for the 1916–1917 academic year as assistant master at a New Jersey preparatory school.

J. Rives Childs volunteered to serve in France with the American Field Service in 1915. Two years later when the United States entered World War I, he joined the army and was commissioned a second lieutenant. After training in Virginia, Washington, D.C., and Illinois, Childs returned to France as a cryptanalyst at the American general headquarters, where he served as liaison officer of radio intelligence with the French and British. During the last year of the war, in cooperation with the French, he achieved notable success reading German military ciphers. Childs worked briefly in radio intelligence during the peace conference at Versailles and imbibed the heady exuberance of postwar Paris. To avoid being posted home, he joined Herbert Hoover's American Relief Administration distributing food and medicine in the Kingdom of the Serbs, Croats, and Slovenes (after 1929 Yugoslavia).

Childs returned to the United States late in 1919 and tried newspaper work in Washington, D.C. Finding it unrewarding, he rejoined the American Relief Administration in 1921. For two years he worked as an assistant supervisor and then district supervisor in the Kazan District in the Soviet Union. In Petrograd (formerly Saint Petersburg and later Leningrad) Childs met and married Georgina Pavlovna de Brylkine, daughter of a French woman and a Russian naval officer, in a civil ceremony witnessed only by a Red Army soldier and a sailor. A few weeks later, on 13 August 1922, they were married in Saint Isaac's Cathedral. They had no children.

Childs resigned from the American Relief Administration in 1923 after Soviet customs officials caught him trying to send his mother-in-law's collection of eighteenth-century gold snuffboxes out of the country. He returned to the United States for another try at journalism, but later that year he took and passed the examination for the consular service. His first post at the consulate in Jerusalem lasted a year and a half and introduced him to the Muslim world, where he spent most of his diplomatic career. From a professional perspective, it was not a happy time for Childs, largely because he was at cross-purposes with his superior. Transferred to the consulate in Bucharest, Romania, in 1925, he was passed over for promotion for several years. In 1930 the Department of State nominated Childs second secretary to the legation in Cairo, Egypt. Three years later he was transferred to Tehran, Iran, with the same rank, before being returned to Cairo.

Finally promoted in February 1937, Childs worked in the State Department's Division of Near Eastern Affairs and remained in Washington for almost four years. During World War II he held the sensitive post of chargé d'affaires at the American legation in Tangier, Spanish Morocco, from February 1941 to June 1945, which he considered his most important assignment. In 1946 Childs was appointed concurrently minister to Saudi Arabia and Yemen. He served as ambassador to Saudi Arabia in 1949 and 1950 and to Ethiopia from 1951 to 1953.

Believing himself unappreciated in the State Department and disappointed at not receiving a European assignment, Childs resigned in 1953. He left diplomacy as he had begun, on a sour note, unwilling to stifle his independent opinions when they differed from official policy. His early sympathetic view of the Soviet Union had raised eyebrows, and his years in the Middle East later led him to support Arab opinion against what he saw as the unwarranted pro-Israeli position of the government. In retirement, Childs liked to project the image of an outspoken nonconformist. He was a bit of a crank, albeit an urbane and erudite one, but it would be wrong to think him mismatched for diplomacy. He showed the instincts to represent his government well, often in awkward circumstances and usually with the right blend of steel and aplomb. The War Department awarded Childs the Medal of Freedom in 1946.

Having spent more years abroad than in the United States, Childs made Nice, France, his retirement home. He devoted his time to writing, traveling, and voraciously collecting books. Throughout his diplomatic career he had written on a variety of topics. In 1932 Childs published *Before the Curtain Falls*, a novel that drew on his experiences in Europe during and after World War I. Two autobiographical novels, *The Pageant of Persia* (1936) and *Escape to Cairo* (1938), appeared under the pseudonym Henry Filmer, a name borrowed from a seventeenth-century Virginia colonist and ancestor. Childs also published a family history, *Reliques of the Rives (Ryves)* (1929), and several supplementary articles and smaller publications of genealogical interest. He edited portions of the diary of his great-grandfather, the Methodist bishop John Early, for publication in the *Virginia Magazine of History and Biography* between 1925 and 1932. In 1939 his article "The Evolution of British Diplomatic Representation in the Middle East" appeared in the *Journal of the Royal Central Asian Society*, and in 1948 he published *American Foreign Service*, a well-received textbook.

Childs also compiled *Restif de La Bretonne: Témoignages et Jugements, Bibliographie* (1949), an annotated bibliography of the works of the eighteenth-century French writer Nicolas-Edme Restif. He became the world's leading authority on and collector of works by and about Giovanni Giacomo (Jean-Jacques) Casanova. Childs published a monumental bibliography, *Casanoviana: An Annotated World Bibliography of Jacques Casanova de Seingalt and of Works Concerning Him* (1956), which he supplemented in scholarly journals from time to time, and two biographies, *Casanova: A Biography Based on New Documents* (1961) and *Casanova: Die grosse Biographie* (1977), which shifted the focus of Casanova studies from his amatory exploits to his scientific and literary achievements. Childs also collected the

works of Henry Miller, whose early publications were suppressed in the United States because they were deemed indecent. Childs championed Miller's literature, and the men's extended correspondence was published in book form in 1968.

After his wife died in Nice on 23 November 1964, Childs returned permanently to Virginia. He lived in Richmond and in addition to *Diplomatic and Literary Quests* (1963) wrote three more autobiographical volumes, *Foreign Service Farewell: My Years in the Near East* (1969), *Vignettes, or, Autobiographical Fragments* (1977), and *Let the Credit Go: The Autobiography of J. Rives Childs* (1983). Childs assisted the editors of the modern edition of the *Papers of James Madison* in decoding encrypted correspondence that Madison exchanged with Thomas Jefferson in 1783; and doing his own translation, he published "French Consul Martin Oster Reports on Virginia, 1784–1796" in the January 1968 issue of the *Virginia Magazine of History and Biography*.

For more than a decade after he returned to Virginia, Childs served as scholar in residence at Randolph-Macon College, where he deposited his celebrated collections of Casanova books and manuscripts and his correspondence with Henry Miller. James Rives Childs died in a Richmond nursing home on 15 July 1987. His body was cremated and the ashes buried in the Childs family section of Spring Hill Cemetery, in Lynchburg.

James Rives Childs, *Reliques of the Rives (Ryves)* (1929), 545–546 (por. by Nicolai Ivanovich Fechin facing 547); Nancy Hugo, "Rive[s] Childs: Reprobate in Good Standing," *Richmond* 3 (Mar. 1978): 17–20; Childs, *Let the Credit Go: The Autobiography of J. Rives Childs* (1983), several pors.; Childs letters are in many of the world's libraries, the major collections at Randolph-Macon College and UVA; Richard Clement Wood, ed., *Collector's Quest: The Correspondence of Henry Miller and J. Rives Childs, 1947–1965* (1968); obituaries in *Richmond News Leader*, 15 July 1987, *New York Times* and *Richmond Times-Dispatch*, both 16 July 1987, *Lynchburg News and Daily Advance* and *Washington Post*, both 17 July 1987, and U.S. Department of State *State*, no. 303 (Aug./Sept. 1987): 77; editorial tribute by Virginius Dabney in *Richmond Times-Dispatch*, 18 July 1987; memorials in *Tributes to Amb. J. Rives Childs at a Memorial Service, January 5, 1988, at Randolph-Macon College's Washington and Franklin Hall* (1988).

NELSON D. LANKFORD

CHILDS, Lucy Howard Brown (31 December 1854–5 November 1947), educator, was the daughter of James Leftwich Brown, a Lynchburg tobacco merchant, and Mary Virginia Early Brown. Probably born late at night in Lynchburg or Campbell County, she may have celebrated her birthday on 1 January. Her mother died in July 1864, and her father, who had lost most of his property during the Civil War, died in August 1872. She lived for at least part of her childhood in the Lynchburg household of her maternal grandfather, John Early, a retired Methodist bishop whose death in 1873 reinforced the necessity that Brown find work to support herself.

Shortly after graduating from high school in Lynchburg in 1874, Brown began teaching in the Seventh Street Primary School. For twelve years she taught in the city's grammar schools. During that time she won two pay raises and increased her income from $40 per month to $60. In July 1886 Brown received another raise to $75 per month and became supervising principal in charge of all the city's grammar and primary schools for white children. She was the first woman in the city to have such large supervisory responsibility and no teaching duties, although she was not the first woman principal as later reported. In 1888 Brown became principal of the Biggers School but retired shortly before her marriage on 9 October 1890 to her cousin John William Childs, then an investor in Buena Vista real estate and afterward a Lynchburg life insurance agent and director of the Traders Bank. They had one daughter who died on the day of her birth and two sons, the elder of whom, James Rives Childs, became a diplomat and author.

The failure of Traders Bank in Lynchburg created a time of financial hardship for the family, and in 1898 Childs returned to work as a teacher. Her first assignment was in the Jackson Street Colored High School, Lynchburg's only black high school. Although she was not the first white woman to teach in a black school in that city, her social background drew attention, and she was later described as a pioneer. Childs was principal of Monroe School, one of the city's white schools, from 1901 until early in 1926,

when she transferred to Frank Roane School. After several months there she retired in mid-1926. While heading Monroe School she took classes and attended teacher training institutes at Randolph-Macon Woman's College and the University of Virginia, and during the summer of 1913 she studied elementary education and school administration at Cornell University.

In addition to her long career in Lynchburg's public schools, Childs was a member of various patriotic societies and charitable organizations. She taught Sunday school at a local Methodist church and served on its board of home and foreign missions. Childs was a founder of the Lynchburg branch of the Woman's Christian Temperance Union and initiated a fund-raising drive for the first school library in the city. She helped found the Associated Charities of Lynchburg (later the Lynchburg Family Welfare Society) and in 1894 assisted in organizing the Open Door Home, a rescue mission for unmarried mothers that in 1897 became the local affiliate of the National Florence Crittenton Mission. Childs became president emerita of the chapter when she stepped down in April 1944, at which time the organization created the Lucy B. Childs Memorial Fund in her honor.

After her husband died on 15 September 1930, Lucy Howard Brown Childs lived alone in Lynchburg until her own death from heart failure on 5 November 1947. She was buried in Spring Hill Cemetery in that city.

WPA Biographies, based in part on author M. M. Jones's interview with Childs; BVS Birth Register, Campbell Co.; variant birth dates include 1 Jan. 1858 in James Rives Childs, *Reliques of the Rives (Ryves)* (1929), 529, and 29 Jan. 1852 on BVS Death Certificate, Lynchburg; Childs materials, including certificates and diplomas, in J. Rives Childs Papers, UVA; BVS Marriage Register, Rockingham Co.; employment history in Lynchburg City School Board Minute Books (1872–1926); *Lynchburg News*, 27, 29 Apr. 1944; Otto Wilson, *Fifty Years' Work with Girls, 1883–1933: A Story of the Florence Crittenton Homes* (1933), 342–346; J. Rives Childs, *Let the Credit Go: The Autobiography of J. Rives Childs* (1983), 1–3; obituaries and editorial tributes in *Lynchburg Daily Advance*, 5, 6 Nov. 1947 (por.), and *Lynchburg News*, 6, 7 Nov. 1947.

MARGARET R. RHETT

CHILES, Walter (bap. 20 March 1609–after 6 July 1653), member of the Council and Speaker of the House of Burgesses, was probably the son of Walter Chiles (also Childs or Childes) and was born in Bristol, England, where his father was a textile merchant. His mother's name is uncertain. Baptized in the church of Saint Mary Redcliffe, in Bristol, on 20 March 1609, Chiles entered the textile trade there, married a woman named Elizabeth, whose maiden name may have been Sanders, and had at least two sons.

Chiles made his first recorded trip to Virginia in the service of the merchants William Harris and Nicholas Jolly aboard the *Blessing*, probably in 1636. By 1638 Chiles had fitted out his own ship and returned to the colony with his wife and sons. During the next few years he patented about one thousand acres of land in Charles City County and regularly traveled between Virginia and England transporting merchandise and immigrants. In hope of expanding his business, Chiles joined three other men in June 1641 in petitioning the General Assembly for permission to "undertake the discovery of a new river or unknowne land bearing west southerly from Appomattake river." The assembly granted them a license in January 1642 and renewed it in 1643, but the Anglo-Powhatan War of 1644–1646 temporarily halted exploration and closed trading opportunities in the west. They did not attempt to obtain another license.

Chiles was elected a burgess from Charles City County for the assembly that met on 12 January 1642 and signed a declaration against a revival of the Virginia Company of London. He represented the county again in 1643 and took part in the last meetings of the General Assembly as a unicameral body and the first sessions of the House of Burgesses as a separate branch of the legislature. About that time the county court unsuccessfully recommended him to the governor for appointment as sheriff of Charles City County. Chiles then moved to James City County, which he represented in the assemblies that began on 20 November 1645, 5 October 1646, and 10 October 1649. It is possible that his absence from some of the intervening legislative sessions was a consequence of trips to England.

On 23 March 1650 Chiles purchased from Sir William Berkeley the brick house in Jamestown where governors had resided for more than a decade. Owning one of the largest and finest dwellings in the colony and acquiring a new title of lieutenant colonel, Chiles had clearly become a man of importance, and the governor appointed him to the Council. Because most of the Council's records for the period are lost, almost nothing is known about his tenure. The only surviving documents recording his attendance at Council meetings are dated 21 May and 20 September 1651. Chiles did not remain a councillor after Virginia surrendered to Parliament in March 1652, perhaps because he was not in Virginia at that time.

Chiles was still engaged in trade. He owned his own ships and may have carried messages between the governor and the Crown and, after the future king Charles II fled England for the Netherlands, between the government in Virginia and the court in exile. Late in January 1652 Chiles sailed for Rotterdam in his ship the *Fame of Virginia*. Five months later he returned and anchored off the Eastern Shore. As the ship was departing for Jamestown on 13 June, a local militia captain detained it for violating Parliament's Navigation Act, which forbade unauthorized trade with the Netherlands. Chiles informed the county court that the terms of Virginia's surrender to Parliament exempted Virginians from that interdiction of trade, but faced with a new charge that Dutch merchants were the real owners of the ship, he remained fearful that his property might still be lost. Eastern Shore taxpayers worried that because a county militia officer had attempted to confiscate the ship, they might have to pay Chiles for the *Fame of Virginia*. The following summer Chiles embraced an opportunity to preserve his investment by agreeing to exchange one vessel for another. For £400 he acquired another ship that had been seized for violating the law, the larger *Leopoldus of Dunkirk*, and its valuable cargo.

The resulting legal complications and their political and commercial ramifications required the General Assembly to intervene. When the assembly met on 5 July 1653, Chiles was a burgess from James City County and also a candidate for Speaker. Governor Richard Bennett, anxious not to add another complication to an already difficult situation, advised the burgesses not to choose Chiles. The burgesses, jealous of the right to elect their own officers without executive interference, elected Chiles Speaker of the House anyway and so notified the governor. The next day Chiles resigned, citing the impropriety of presiding over the House of Burgesses while it settled the question of who owned the *Fame of Virginia*. Preconcerted or not, these acts of political theater enabled the House of Burgesses to preserve the right to elect the Speaker, Chiles received the honor of being elected, and by resigning he made it possible for the governor and other members of the assembly to resolve the controversies and seal the deal that gave him the *Leopoldus of Dunkirk*. The episode was important in preserving the independence of the House of Burgesses as a powerful parliamentary body during a time of political uncertainty, and it led to a peaceful solution of most of the problems.

Walter Chiles's name drops from documents relating to public affairs with the conclusion of the assembly session about a week later, and it is probable that he died not long thereafter. Dutch documents place a "Walter Chiels, merchant, living in the Virginias" in Amsterdam in August 1654 and indicate that he intended to sail for New Netherland the following month. The wording of an order of the Charles City County Court on 17 December 1655 indicates that Chiles might have still been alive then, but on 5 November of that year, when a deed he had executed in 1652 was recorded in James City County, a witness authenticated the document, suggesting that Chiles might have been dead by that date. The widow of his namesake son stated on 20 November 1673 that Walter Chiles had died in or about 1653.

Biography in Kukla, *Speakers and Clerks, 1643–1776*, 49–52; Arden H. Brame Jr. II, "The English Birth and Ancestry of Walter Chiles (1609–1653) of Jamestowne, Virginia," *Augustan Society Omnibus* 7 [1987]: 102–109, citing research in incomplete Bristol and Somerset Co. parish records; baptism confirmed by Bristol Record Office, Eng.; Virginia family history (some identifying Chiles's father, bap. 1572, as the Speaker) treated in Joanne Chiles Eakin, *Walter Chiles of Jamestown* (1983), 1–10, Virginia Lee Hutcheson Davis, *Tidewater Virginia Families* (1989), 209–222, and Patricia W. Lockwood, *From Jamestown to Tahlequah: The Virginia Ancestors of Judge John Martin* (1994), 1:2–128 (printing many Chiles documents in facsimile); Hening, *Statutes*, 1:236 (misidentified as Mathew Chiles), 239, 262 (first quotation), 298, 322, 358, 377, 378, 382–383; Warren M. Billings, *A Little Parliament: The Virginia General Assembly in the Seventeenth Century* (2004), 129–130; Northampton Co. Deeds, Wills, Etc., 4:22, 49, 126–129, 183; deposition of 24 July 1637 (age twenty-nine, clothworker, of Bristol), PRO HCA 13/111 no. 301, printed in Dorothy Olivia Shilton and Richard Holworthy, eds., *High Court of Admiralty Examinations (MS. Volume 53), 1637–1638* (1932), 127–128; 23 Mar. 1650 and 20 Nov. 1673 deeds in Ambler Family Papers, LC; 1654 Dutch documents printed in Henry B. Hoff, "Some Records of Walter Chiles, Virginia Merchant, in the Netherlands," *Virginia Genealogist* 43 (1999): 218–219 (second quotation); 5 Nov. 1655 deed and 17 Dec. 1655 order in Charles City Co. Orders, Deeds, Depositions (1655–1665), 18–19, 23.

DAPHNE GENTRY

CHILTON, Edward (9 March 1658–by 26 July 1707), attorney general of Virginia and coauthor of *The Present State of Virginia, and the College* (1727), was born in Little Wilbraham Parish, Cambridgeshire, England, and was the son of Edward Chilton and Katherine Chilton, whose maiden name is unknown. He entered Trinity College, Dublin, on 24 April 1674 and on 12 January 1676 was admitted to Saint John's College, University of Cambridge, as a sizar, a student receiving financial aid in return for work. By that time his father had died. If his father was the E. Chilton who had been a clerk in the Principal Probate Registry as late as 16 June 1675 and who was acquainted with persons who had Virginia connections, that might help account for Chilton's first appointment in Virginia. The date and circumstances under which Chilton moved to Virginia are otherwise unknown.

Chilton's name first appeared in Virginia records in April 1682 as clerk of the governor's Council and concurrently as clerk of the General Assembly. As salary for the latter office he received 10,800 pounds of tobacco in the spring of 1684, about half the annual sum that the governor had recommended. His duties included preparing formal documents for the Council, acting as intermediary in official communications between the two houses of the assembly, recording land patents, and carrying out other clerical responsibilities. Chilton gained an intimate understanding of the workings of the colony's political and legal systems and how its land laws were administered. On two occasions he helped preserve the public records of Virginia. On 10 November 1682 the assembly voted to pay Chilton 20,000 pounds of tobacco "for his care and paines in settling and alphabetting the Records in the Secretaries office & for Recording many publique letters and papers and Proclamations and all other publique Services to this day." On 27 October 1686 he presented to the assembly his transcription of two volumes of land patent books. Chilton's name appeared as clerk for the last time on 17 November 1686.

Chilton acquired a significant amount of land, beginning with two acres in Jamestown in the spring of 1683. During the next two years in partnership with other men he obtained grants for more than a thousand acres of land in New Kent County, and in 1686 he patented more than a thousand acres in Surry County. He also acquired and sold other tracts elsewhere and practiced law. In referring a client to Chilton in January 1691, the planter and lawyer William Fitzhugh (d. 1701) described Chilton as a better lawyer than himself. Chilton also appeared as attorney for the former Speaker of the House of Burgesses and Council member Edward Hill (d. 1700), who by 1693 was his father-in-law. The date on which Chilton married Hannah Hill is not recorded. They acquired 2,717 acres of land from her father and are not known to have had any children.

On 20 October 1691 Chilton took office as attorney general of Virginia, succeeding Edmund Jenings, who had become a member of the Council on 4 June of that year. In the following April, Council members weighed the possibility that Jenings might resume the office, but they abandoned the idea on the grounds that Chilton's name had already been forwarded to England for confirmation by the Crown. The loss of the records of the General Court leaves information concerning his service as attorney general scarce. Copies of two of his opinions survive in manuscript. One, issued on 30 October 1691, specified procedures that the Middlesex County justices should follow in a case involving a slave, and the other, dated 23 June 1692, limited the authority of justices of the peace to admit to bail persons charged with major felonies. While he was attorney general, Chilton also served once as clerk of the House of Burgesses's Committee for Elections and Privileges and three times as clerk of the Committee for Propositions and Grievances.

With his service in a high office in the government of the colony, a marriage that connected him to its leaders, and possession of a growing landed estate, Chilton appeared well established in Virginia, but on 8 January 1694 he registered a power of attorney authorizing his father-in-law to take charge of his property in Virginia and Maryland. In April the Council swore in William Randolph (d. 1711) as attorney general, "Edward Chilton Esqr late Attorney Genll being gon for England and that place thereby become Vacant."

Chilton probably intended to return to Virginia but never did. He gained admission to the Middle Temple on 13 April 1694, soon after returning to England, and was called to the bar on 22 May 1696. Chilton became a successful London barrister and has been identified as the Edward Chilton who edited a fifth edition of Sir Henry Hobart's *Reports* (published in 1724) and also as the author of marginal references in a 1697 French edition of Sir Edward Coke's *Reports*.

In May 1696, within two years of Chilton's arrival in England, Parliament established a new regulatory body, the Lords Commissioners of Trade and Plantations, often called the Board of Trade. Its mission was to strengthen control over the colonial governments and regulate their commerce in order to restrict illegal trade. When the board began to investigate affairs in Virginia in the summer of 1696, its members turned to Chilton and Henry Hartwell, an even more recent arrival from Virginia who had also once been clerk of the Council and had served both in the House of Burgesses and on the governor's Council. Testifying before the commissioners in July and August 1696, Chilton condemned members of the Council for claiming exemption from common law actions. He also reported that members failed to take an oath of office before sitting as judges in the General Court.

In the autumn of 1695 Edward Randolph, surveyor general of royal customs in the colonies, had completed a plan for restricting illegal trade in the colonies by establishing a new system of admiralty courts with their own judges and advocates, or prosecutors, to be appointed by the English government. For a district that embraced five colonies from West Jersey southward through

North Carolina, he nominated Chilton late in the summer of 1696 to serve as advocate as soon as he returned to Virginia.

The Board of Trade resumed its investigation of Virginia in August 1697, spurred by one of its members, the political philosopher John Locke, who had developed a strong interest in the colony. The panel of Virginia experts had acquired a new member with the arrival earlier that summer of James Blair, who was president of the College of William and Mary, commissary of the bishop of London, and a suspended member of the Council. Blair sought support for the college and removal of the incumbent governor, but once in England he quickly established a rapport with Locke and became a willing participant in the effort to reform Virginia. In a flurry of activity in August and September 1697, Blair testified before the board and at Locke's urging prepared an initial written statement on needed changes in the governance of the colony. Hartwell made written responses to a series of thirty-seven inquiries that Locke prepared, and late in September Chilton appeared before the commissioners and answered questions regarding irregularities in land policy, such as grants of excessively large blocks of land, failure to develop land, and avoidance of the payment of quitrents. Chilton also criticized the functioning of the Virginia courts.

The commissioners asked the three Virginians to submit a full written account of conditions in the colony. By 20 October 1697 they had presented a collaborative report, signed by each and described as a true account of the present state of Virginia. About 18,500 words in length, its twelve sections provided both a comprehensive description of the colony and an agenda for significant reforms. Board members gave the document a brief review and agreed to consider it later but never did. The report disappeared into the board's archives and was seldom consulted thereafter. One important exception, however, occurred when Robert Beverley (d. 1722) examined the manuscript and copied parts of it into his *History and Present State of Virginia, In Four Parts*, published in 1705. Chilton and his fellow authors did not see their extensive effort produce the reforms they had recommended.

By February 1698 Chilton had been appointed advocate of an admiralty court for Virginia and North Carolina and was expected to return to Virginia, although he did not take his post. Instead, later that year he left England for Barbados and in April 1699 petitioned to be appointed attorney general of that colony. Chilton's commission required him to reside in Barbados and "to execute the said office in his own person, except in case of sickness or other incapacity." He took the oath of office on 16 January 1700 and faced a difficult time in the turbulent politics of the island. Late in July 1701 two men assaulted him; he was injured and one of the men killed. Chilton asked for a one-year leave of absence in September 1704 to recover his health and settle his personal business, but even though the Crown approved his request, he apparently remained in Barbados. In 1705, during the political turmoil that characterized the administration of Governor Sir Bevil Granville, the governor suspended Chilton from office, had him tried and found guilty of high misdemeanors, fined, and imprisoned. The governor identified Chilton's offenses as uttering scandalous words against the governor, suppressing evidence, and advising two defendants to flee. Granville later wrote, "I have found him here a very troublesome fellow, and a very great knave."

Chilton returned to England in the autumn of 1705 to defend himself against Granville's accusations. He was still in London in the autumn of the following year when he supported a successful effort of Barbadian merchants to secure disallowance of a paper money bill, although he did not in that instance identify himself as attorney general. On 7 July 1707 Chilton was in Portsmouth, England, probably waiting to board a ship to return to Barbados. Falling sick, he dictated a will, which he was too ill to sign. Edward Chilton died in that city on an unrecorded date between 20 and 26 July 1707. On the latter date the queen appointed a new attorney general of Barbados, "in the roome of Mr. Chilton, deceased."

Chilton had been dead for two decades when the 1697 report that he had helped prepare appeared in print. A London printer issued it early in 1727 under the title *The Present State*

000

of Virginia, and the College. Its three authors were named on the title page and the contents little altered except for the inclusion of the 1693 royal charter of the College of William and Mary as an appendix. Almost certainly James Blair, who was in London at the time, was responsible for the work's appearance. The belated publication of the report made the name of Edward Chilton more famous to students of Virginia's history than did his service as clerk of the Council and attorney general.

Birth date in Little Wilbraham Parish Register, Cambridgeshire Record Office, Eng.; George Dames Burtchaell and Thomas Ulick Sadleir, eds., *Alumni Dublinenses* (1935), 149; John Venn and J. A. Venn, comps., *Alumni Cantabrigienses* (1922), 1:333; Sir Henry F. MacGeagh and H. A. C. Sturgess, comps., *Register of Admissions to the Honourable Society of the Middle Temple* (1949), 1:234; marriage mentioned in R. T. Barton, ed., *Virginia Colonial Decisions* (1909), 2:B179–B180; *Legislative Journals of Council*, 13 (first mention in Virginia); numerous references in *JHB, 1659/60–1693* (first quotation on 174), *Executive Journals of Council* (second quotation on 1:308), and *Cavaliers and Pioneers*, vol. 2; numerous references in Sainsbury, *Calendar of State Papers, Colonial Series*, esp. *1699* (appointment as attorney general of Barbados and third quotation on 172), *1704–1705* (fourth quotation on 619), and *1706–1708* (date of appointment of successor on 508 and fifth quotation on 523); 30 Oct. 1691 and 23 June 1692 legal opinions in Colonial Papers, RG 1, LVA; 1694 power of attorney in Charles City Co. Deeds, Wills, Etc. (1692/93–1694), 183–184; Henry Hartwell, James Blair, and Edward Chilton, *The Present State of Virginia, and the College*, ed. Hunter Dickinson Farish (1940); original MSS of book in PRO CO 5/1309, fols. 83–122, and contemporary copy in British Library, Add. MSS 27382, fols. 196–228; Robert A. Bain, "The Composition and Publication of *The Present State of Virginia, and the College*," *Early American Literature* 6 (1971): 31–54; Jon Kukla, "Robert Beverley Assailed: Appellate Jurisdiction and the Problem of Bicameralism in Seventeenth-Century Virginia," *VMHB* 88 (1980): 419–421, 426; will and authentication in Prerogative Court of Canterbury, Poley 161.

THAD W. TATE

CHILTON, Robert Hall (ca. March 1816–18 February 1879), Confederate army officer, was born in Loudoun County and was the son of William Orrick Chilton and Sarah Powell Chilton. Appointed in 1833 from Winchester to the United States Military Academy, he graduated on 1 July 1837, ranked forty-eighth out of fifty cadets and with a commission as brevet second lieutenant in the 1st United States Dragoons. Chilton spent the next nine years at various frontier posts. On 21 February 1842 he was promoted to first lieutenant. In 1845 he traveled to New York City, where on 25 September he married Laura Ann Thomson Mason. They had two daughters and one son.

During the Mexican War, Chilton served as captain and assistant quartermaster on Brigadier General John E. Wool's staff from 11 May to 6 December 1846, when he was appointed captain in the 1st Dragoons. On 23 February 1847 he won a brevet promotion to major for bravery at the Battle of Buena Vista. After the war he resumed frontier duty. Promoted to major and assigned to duty as a paymaster on 25 July 1854, he served until 1861 at several locations, including San Antonio, Texas, where he and his family struck up a friendship with a fellow Virginian, Lieutenant Colonel Robert Edward Lee.

On 29 April 1861, shortly after Virginia seceded from the Union, Chilton resigned his commission in the United States Army and on the same day secured appointment as lieutenant colonel of volunteers in the Provisional Army of Virginia. By 19 May he had been promoted to colonel of cavalry. On 20 May he was appointed a lieutenant colonel in the Confederate States Army, to rank from 16 March. For the next fifteen months he served in Richmond as an assistant adjutant general on the staff of General Samuel Cooper, the adjutant and inspector general of the Confederate army.

On 4 June 1862 Chilton reported to the Army of Northern Virginia as an assistant adjutant and inspector general, and the commanding general, R. E. Lee, introduced him as his new chief of staff. The title was not an official designation, although Lee probably intended that Chilton serve as the army's chief administrative officer. President Jefferson Davis nominated Chilton for promotion to colonel on 13 October 1862, but the Confederate States Senate postponed consideration of the appointment until its next session. In addition to his duties as chief of staff, Chilton on 28 October 1862 also became inspector general of the army.

Although Chilton handled routine administrative tasks satisfactorily, he did not fully develop into the sort of staff officer that Lee required. His performance at critical moments on the march or in battle was sometimes disappointing. On several occasions, most notably during the Seven Days' Battles and at Chancellorsville, he created confusion by drafting poorly written orders or passing on misunderstood verbal instructions. After Chilton made an obvious error in positioning an artillery battery at Fredericksburg, an irritated Lee observed, "Colonel Chilton takes a lot upon himself." Concluding that Chilton was ill-suited for the position, the historian Douglas Southall Freeman described him as "somewhat of a misfit, more than an aide but less than a chief of staff." Lee gradually came to act as his own chief of staff and continued to rely on his longtime adjutant, Walter Herron Taylor. Chilton gained some notoriety as the author of Special Orders Number 191, which outlined Confederate plans for the Sharpsburg (Antietam) campaign and became known as "the Lost Order" after a copy fell into Union hands. The officer responsible for losing the order was never identified, although Chilton is sometimes mentioned as a possible culprit.

Despite Chilton's uneven performance, Lee recommended him for promotion to brigadier general after regulations opened that grade to chiefs of staff. Jefferson Davis nominated Chilton on 5 March 1863, but the Confederate States Senate rejected the appointment on 11 April. The defeat of the nomination stemmed from an earlier incident following the Seven Days' Battles, when Chilton had criticized Major General John Bankhead Magruder's behavior and leadership to Cooper and thus delayed Magruder's appointment to the Trans-Mississippi Department. When Chilton's bid for promotion came before the Senate, Magruder's supporters killed the appointment. Instead the Senate confirmed Chilton's appointment as colonel, to rank from the date of Davis's original nomination. Stung by his rejection, Chilton requested a court of inquiry to investigate his conduct and received an endorsement from Lee calling him "zealous and active" in discharging his duties. The court exonerated Chilton that autumn.

Davis nominated Chilton a second time on 21 December 1863, and the Senate confirmed his appointment as brigadier general on 16 Feb-

ruary 1864, to rank from 21 December 1863. Believing, however, that he had been treated badly by the Senate and unhappy with the date his new rank became effective, Chilton resigned his commission on 1 April 1864 and left the Army of Northern Virginia. He reverted to his previous grade of colonel and served for the rest of the war as the senior assistant adjutant general of the Confederate army. He was paroled at Greensboro, North Carolina, about 1 May 1865. He returned to Richmond and on 14 June swore a loyalty oath to the United States and applied for a presidential pardon.

After the war Chilton moved to Muscogee County, Georgia, and late in the 1860s became president of the Columbus Manufacturing Company, a large textile mill on the Chattahoochee River. Robert Hall Chilton died of a stroke in Columbus, Georgia, on 18 February 1879. A contingent of Columbus militia accompanied his body to Richmond, where the Virginia governor and several former Confederate generals attended his funeral and burial in Hollywood Cemetery.

Biography by Robert K. Krick in William C. Davis and Julie Hoffman, eds., *The Confederate General* (1991), 1:184–185 (por.); Ezra J. Warner, *Generals in Gray: Lives of the Confederate Commanders* (1959), 49, gives birth date as 25 February 1815, citing Adjutant General's Office, Washington, D.C., but United States Military Academy records give age at admission on 1 July 1833 as seventeen years, four months; Fauquier Historical Society *Bulletin*, 1st ser. (June 1923), 329; George W. Cullum, *Biographical Register of the Officers and Graduates of the U.S. Military Academy . . .* (1891), 1:695–696; Francis B. Heitman, *Historical Register and Dictionary of the United States Army . . .* (1903), 1:299; marriage date and place confirmed by Gunston Hall Plantation, Mason Neck, Va., from privately held family Bible records; correspondence and commissions in Robert H. Chilton Papers, LVA, and in several collections, MOC; Compiled Service Records, including R. E. Lee to Chilton, ca. 22 Apr. 1863 (third quotation); *Journal of Confederate Congress*, 1:495, 2:489, 3:136, 281, 490, 574, 779; many references in *OR*, in Douglas Southall Freeman, *R. E. Lee: A Biography* (1934–1935), esp. 2:235 (second quotation), 443 (first quotation, citing an eyewitness interview), and in Freeman, *Lee's Lieutenants: A Study in Command* (1942–1944); Kenneth H. Williams, "Prince without a Kingdom: The Recall of John Bankhead Magruder," *Civil War History: A Journal of the Middle Period* 41 (1995): 5–21; Presidential Pardons; obituaries and accounts of funeral in *Columbus [Ga.] Daily Times*, 19, 20 Feb. 1879, and *Richmond State*, 20–22, 24 Feb. 1879.

J. TRACY POWER

CHILTON, Samuel (7 September 1805–7 January 1867), member of the House of Representatives and of the Convention of 1850–1851, was born in Fauquier County. A birth date of 7 September 1804 recorded later in the nineteenth century appears in many reference works, but his age as he reported it to census enumerators in 1850 and 1860 indicates that he was born in 1805. His parents, Stephen Chilton and Susan Turner Chilton, later moved to Missouri with several of their other children. Chilton read law with a Winchester judge and returned to his native county to practice. In Falmouth, Stafford County, on 16 February 1832 he married Isabella R. Brooke, whose younger brother James Vass Brooke read law with Chilton and later served in the second and third sessions of the Convention of 1861. They had at least four sons and one daughter, and Chilton's widowed mother-in-law joined the household as well.

On 31 March 1843 the Ninth Congressional District convention of the Whig Party nominated Chilton for the House of Representatives on the second ballot. He pledged unconditional support for Henry Clay's presidential candidacy in 1844 and campaigned on a platform advocating a liberal interpretation of the Constitution, immediate establishment of a third Bank of the United States, circulation of a national paper currency with uniform value and convertible to specie at will, tariff both to raise revenue and to protect domestic industry, and equitable distribution among the states of proceeds from the sales of public land. John M. McCarty, who had finished second to Chilton at the nominating convention, remained in the race. Changes in the district boundaries had removed some traditional Democratic counties from the district and added several Whig counties, and despite the split among the Whigs, Chilton narrowly defeated William "Extra Billy" Smith (1797–1887), the Democratic incumbent, in the April election. Representing the counties of Culpeper, Fairfax, Fauquier, Loudoun, Prince William, Rappahannock, and Stafford, Chilton served on the Committee for the District of Columbia, spoke occasionally on procedural matters, and advocated abolishing imprisonment for debt. He did not seek reelection in 1845.

On 22 August 1850 Chilton, finishing third in a five-candidate field, won election as one of three delegates representing Fauquier and Rappahannock Counties in a convention that met from 14 October 1850 until 1 August 1851 to revise Virginia's constitution. Characterizing himself as a conservative reluctant to abandon the checks and balances of republican government for a more pure form of democracy, he debated Henry Alexander Wise in February 1851 on the definitions of conservatism in a running display of quicksilver wit and oratorical skills that informed the convention debates for several days. A critic described Chilton as "one of the ablest, most indolent, and finest looking men in the convention" who "possessed great power in debate: yet it was that of a gun of heavy calibre difficult to wield or bring to bear on any point."

Chilton sat on the Committee on the Legislative Department of the Government and also on an eight-member special committee appointed on 12 May 1851 to report on apportionment of the General Assembly. Chilton, who at the time of the convention paid taxes on three slaves, had initially supported calculating legislative representation on a mixed basis of population and property holding, but by then he was willing to compromise with western delegates who opposed considering property in apportioning representation. The special committee reported a plan that gave western counties a majority of seats in the House of Delegates but left eastern counties in control of the Senate of Virginia until 1865. When adoption of the plan faltered in the committee of the whole, Chilton on 16 May 1851 proposed options for the required legislative reapportionment in 1865. If the General Assembly could not then agree on bases for reapportionment, the governor would offer voters alternatives based on the number of qualified voters, on the total white population, on taxation, or on a combination of white inhabitants and taxation. Voters also could choose whether to apportion the two houses using the same or different methods. After several attempts to derail or gut Chilton's proposal failed, this key compromise that shifted the balance of power in the assembly away from slaveholding easterners passed by a vote of 55 to 48. On 31 July Chilton voted with the majority in favor of the final version of the constitution that won ratification in a referendum later that year.

By 1853 Chilton had moved to Washington, D.C., but he retained his town lot in Warrenton, valued at $3,000. He joined the American (Know Nothing) Party and in a Fourth of July oration delivered in Fredericksburg in 1855 likened the partisanship prevailing in national politics to the Jacobinism of the French Revolution. His successful law practice and reputation as an able, eloquent advocate led to his being added to the legal team representing John Brown in his treason trial following the 1859 raid on Harpers Ferry. Chilton appeared before the Jefferson County circuit court in Charles Town on 29 October 1859 and with Hiram Griswold, of Cleveland, Ohio, represented Brown for the final two days of the trial. In his summation on 30 October, Chilton argued that by definition Brown could not have committed treason against Virginia because he was not a citizen of the commonwealth. After the jury returned a guilty verdict, Chilton requested an arrest of judgment on the grounds of errors in the verdict and because Brown had been tried for a crime not enumerated in the grand jury record. He and the prominent Culpeper County lawyer William Green prepared Brown's petition to the Virginia Supreme Court of Appeals for a writ of error, which the court denied on 19 November 1859. Chilton submitted to the governor more than a dozen affidavits from Ohio citizens with an unsuccessful plea for a postponement of Brown's scheduled execution so that his counsel could secure a hearing on their client's sanity. The following January, Chilton testified before a select committee of the United States Senate investigating the raid on Harpers Ferry about the circumstances surrounding his hiring and who had paid his fees.

Chilton reportedly declined an appointment in Abraham Lincoln's administration and returned to Warrenton. In the spring of 1861 he addressed crowds in Alexandria at the recruitment of volunteers for Confederate service but probably because of his age took no other recorded part in the Civil War. Samuel Chilton wrote his will in May 1864 and died in Warren-

ton on 7 January 1867, possibly after suffering a stroke. As a past master of the Mount Carmel Lodge, he was interred with Masonic honors in the Warrenton Cemetery.

French Biographies (with birth date of 7 Sept. 1804 and erroneous death date of 14 Jan. 1867); Charles Lanman, *Biographical Annals of the Civil Government of the United States*, 2d ed. (1887), 92 (birth year of 1804 and death date of 14 Jan. 1867); Annie G. Day, *Warrenton and Fauquier County, Virginia* (1908), 29 (por.); Census, Fauquier Co., 1850 (age forty-five on 30 Oct. 1850), Washington, D.C., 1860 (age fifty-four on 5 July 1860); several Chilton letters and accounts, broadsides, and receipts in various collections, VHS; *Fredericksburg Virginia Herald*, 22 Feb. 1832; *Alexandria Gazette*, 10, 29 Apr., 1, 2 May 1843; *Richmond Daily Whig*, 29 Apr., 1, 3 May 1843; *Richmond Enquirer*, 27 Aug., 3, 10 Sept. 1850; *Fredericksburg News*, 9 July 1855; *The Liberator*, 2 Dec. 1859; *Congressional Globe*, 28th Cong., 1st sess., 592, 2d sess., 15; *Journal of 1850–1851 Convention*, 59, 216, 226, 419, Appendix, 17–19, 22; *Debates and Proceedings of 1850–1851 Convention*, 139–144, 160–163, 210–218; *Supplement, 1850–1851 Convention Debates*, nos. 40, 69, 72, 78; John P. Little, "History of Richmond," *Southern Literary Messenger* 18 (June 1852): 334 (quotation); Robert M. De Witt, *The Life, Trial and Execution of Captain John Brown . . .* (1859), esp. 90–91; *Court of Appeals of Virginia, Richmond. Commonwealth v. Brown* (1859); Chilton's testimony, 30 Jan. 1860, in *Report [of] the Select Committee of the Senate Appointed to Inquire into the Late Invasion and Seizure of the Public Property at Harper's Ferry*, 36th Cong., 1st sess., 1860, Senate Rept. 278, serial 1040, 137–140; Fauquier Co. Will Book, 30:367; Fauquier Co. Death Register (1866, death date "not given"); obituaries, editorial tributes, and memorial resolutions in *Warrenton True Index*, 12 (died on "the 7th inst., after a lingering illness, in the sixty-first year of his age"), 19 Jan. 1867, *Leesburg Mirror*, 16 Jan. 1867 (death date of 7 Jan. 1867), *Staunton Valley Virginian*, 23 Jan. 1867 (death date of 21 Jan. 1867), and *The American Annual Cyclopædia and Register of Important Events of the Year 1867* (1870), 552 (reporting death at age sixty-two on 14 Jan. 1867).

SARA B. BEARSS
AMANDA MORRELL

CHINN, Joseph William (16 November 1798–8 December 1840), member of the House of Representatives, was born on the Lancaster County estate of his parents, Elizabeth Griffin Chinn and Joseph Chinn, a prominent attorney who served in the House of Delegates and the Senate of Virginia in the 1790s. After attending the Northumberland Academy, Chinn enrolled in 1817 at Union College, in Schenectady, New York, was elected to Phi Beta Kappa, and in 1819 graduated with a B.A. He returned to Virginia, studied law with Creed Taylor at Needham, in Cumberland County, and on 5 November 1821 received a license to practice in Richmond County. Chinn executed a marriage bond on 7 January 1822 and most likely on 12 January married Marianna Smith, of Richmond County. They had one son and one daughter. A grandson, Joseph William Chinn (1866–1936), was a judge of the Virginia Supreme Court of Appeals.

Chinn enjoyed a reputation as an effective lawyer, and his successful practice allowed him to build Wilna, a house in Richmond County on a 593-acre tract that straddled the Lancaster and Richmond County line. In 1835 he owned thirteen taxable slaves age twelve or older. Chinn won election to the House of Delegates in 1826 for the first of two consecutive one-year terms representing Lancaster County. During the 1826–1827 session he sat on the Committee of Claims and during the 1827–1828 assembly on the Committee of Propositions and Grievances. In 1829 the voters of King George, Lancaster, Northumberland, Prince William, Richmond, Stafford, and Westmoreland Counties elected Chinn to a four-year term in the Senate of Virginia. He served on a joint committee to examine the treasurer's accounts in the 1829–1830 session and on the Committees of General Laws and to Examine the Library in the 1830–1831 session.

Chinn resigned from the state senate on 4 June 1831 and in August of that year defeated the incumbent John Taliaferro for the Thirteenth District seat in the House of Representatives from King George, Lancaster, Northumberland, Richmond, Stafford, and Westmoreland Counties. Serving during the Twenty-second Congress (1831–1833) on the Committee for the District of Columbia, Chinn, a Jacksonian Democrat, rarely spoke on the floor.

Following a redistricting that added Prince William County to his constituencies, Chinn narrowly defeated Taliaferro and won reelection in 1833 representing the new Tenth District. Appointed chair of the Committee for the District of Columbia, Chinn during his second term frequently introduced routine legislation and engaged in debate, sometimes vigorous, over matters relating to the nation's capital. He sponsored several bills to charter banks and insur-

ance companies and opposed discussing petitions calling for the abolition of slavery in Washington. He promoted legislation for such internal improvements as bridges, canals, public buildings, and roads in the District of Columbia and northern Virginia. His campaigning hampered by illness, Chinn lost his 1835 reelection bid to Taliaferro and was the only Democratic incumbent congressman in the state not returned to office. He resumed practicing law, chiefly in Richmond County.

Joseph William Chinn died at Wilna on 8 December 1840 and was buried in the family graveyard on his estate. In his will he reserved all his law books for his son's future study, but he bequeathed all the volumes he had received while in Congress to the Northumberland Academy.

Birth and death dates on gravestone; biographies in Marguerite Relyea Lewis, comp., *The Chinn Book* (1972), 35–39, and Walter Neal Chinn, Jr., *An Autobiography of Walter Neal Chinn, Jr., His Relatives and Friends* (1976), 84–91 (with marriage date and variant place of death of Tappahannock on 85); Richmond Co. Order Book, 25:208; Richmond Co. Marriage Bonds; Chinn to governor, 4 June 1831, John Floyd Executive Papers, RG 3, and Chinn to Robert Wormeley Carter, 24 Feb. [ca. 1832–1835], Acc. 40351, both LVA; congressional election returns in *Fredericksburg Virginia Herald*, 3, 6, 13, 17, 24 Aug. 1831, and *Richmond Enquirer*, 30 Aug., 20 Sept. 1831, 23 Apr., 7 May 1833, 10, 24 Apr., 12 May 1835; *Congressional Globe*, 23d Cong., 1st sess., 122, 173, 430, 2d sess., 112, 199, 208, 251; Richmond Co. Will Book, 10:344–346; estate settlement in Richmond Co. Order Book (1837–1844), 241, 325, 343; obituary and memorial in *Richmond Enquirer*, 22 (with variant death date of "Monday last," 7 Dec. 1840), 31 Dec. 1840, respectively; county court and bar memorial in Richmond Co. Order Book (1837–1844), 234, printed in *Richmond Enquirer*, 14 Jan. 1841.

WADE SHAFFER

CHINN, Joseph William (15 February 1866–16 August 1936), judge of the Virginia Supreme Court of Appeals, was born in Tappahannock and was the son of Joseph William Chinn (1836–1908) and his first wife, Gabriella Brockenbrough Chinn. His parents were members of socially and politically prominent families. His father, a Richmond County lawyer and Confederate veteran, served as superintendent of Richmond County schools early in the twentieth century; his paternal grandfather, Joseph William Chinn (1798–1840), served in the House of Representatives; and his mother's uncle, William

Brockenbrough, was a judge of the Virginia Supreme Court of Appeals.

Educated in Tappahannock public schools and a private school in King and Queen County, Chinn taught in Louisiana and South Carolina and then from 1889 to 1890 studied law at the University of Virginia. Admitted to the bar in the latter year, he practiced law in Warsaw and in 1891 won election as commonwealth's attorney for Richmond County. A Democrat, he was regularly reelected and served until 1915. Chinn was a vestryman at Saint John's Episcopal Church, in Warsaw, where on 14 December 1899 he married Sarah Fairfax Douglas. They had three daughters and two sons.

A leader in both civic and business life, Chinn became president and a director of Warsaw's new Northern Neck State Bank in 1909 and served in those capacities for many years. Beginning in 1919 he was also president and a director of the Northern Neck Telegraph and Telephone Company. During World War I, Chinn was a member of the county draft board and chaired the Fourth Liberty Loan Campaign for Richmond County. In 1914 the governor appointed him to the board of visitors of the University of Virginia, but he resigned the following year when he was elected to fill an unexpired term as judge of the Twelfth Judicial Circuit, comprising Essex, Lancaster, Northumberland, Richmond, and Westmoreland Counties. Elected to a full term in January 1916, he earned high praise from other members of the legal profession and served on the circuit court until 1930, when he became head of the Virginia Commission of Fisheries.

On 3 June 1925 the Virginia Supreme Court of Appeals appointed Chinn to a vacant seat on the Special Court of Appeals that the General Assembly had created in 1924 to aid in clearing the congested docket of the Supreme Court of Appeals. He continued to serve on the circuit court while he was a member of the Special Court from 22 September 1925 until 24 June 1926 and of a second Special Court that met from 19 July 1927 until its mandate expired on 18 December 1928. The governor on 28 November 1931 appointed Chinn to a vacancy on the Supreme Court of Appeals. Chinn took his seat on 3 December of that year, won election to a full twelve-year term from the General Assembly, and served until his death.

During his tenure on the Special Court and the Supreme Court, Chinn wrote ninety-six opinions and seldom dissented from majority opinions. After Chinn's death, Henry Winston Holt, who served with him on both courts, wrote that Chinn "was modest in conference and weighed with consideration the sometimes divergent views of his associates, but he was unyielding when principles were involved and without heat stood steadfast for right and justice as he saw it." Chinn's wife died on 14 December 1932, and Joseph William Chinn died of bronchopneumonia on 16 August 1936 at a sanitarium in Battle Creek, Michigan, where he was receiving medical treatment for chronic heart and kidney disease. He was buried in the cemetery of Saint John's Episcopal Church, in Warsaw.

Biography in Bruce, Tyler, and Morton, *History of Virginia*, 6:275–276, with por. facing 275 and birth date of 15 Feb. 1866 provided by Chinn; Elizabeth Lowell Ryland, ed., *Richmond County, Virginia: A Review Commemorating the Bicentennial* (1976), 163, 414, 415, 416, 420; BVS Marriage Register, Richmond Co.; *Warsaw Northern Neck News*, 15 Dec. 1899; judicial appointments in *JHD*, 1916 sess., 43–49, Supreme Court of Appeals Order Book, 39:481, RG 100, LVA, Special Court of Appeals Order Book, 4:65, 135, RG 107, LVA, and *Richmond Times-Dispatch*, 29 Nov. 1931; Michigan Department of Health Death Certificate, Calhoun Co., with variant birth date of 13 Feb. 1866 provided by son; obituaries, editorial tributes, and accounts of funeral in *Richmond Times-Dispatch* and *Richmond News Leader*, both 17, 18 Aug. 1936, and *Warsaw Northern Neck News*, 21 Aug. 1936; memorials in *Virginia State Bar Association Proceedings* (1937), 205–209 (por. facing 205), and *Virginia Reports* (1938), 169:v–vii (quotation on vii).

HARRY L. CARRICO

CHISWELL, John (d. 15 October 1766), mine operator, was the son of Esther Chiswell, whose maiden name is not recorded, and Charles Chiswell, a land speculator, sometime clerk of the General Court, and part owner of a Spotsylvania County iron mine. References to the family as "Chissell" or "Chizzell" suggest the name's pronunciation. The date and place of Chiswell's birth are not known, but he grew up at Scotchtown, the Hanover County plantation that his father built about 1719 and that Patrick Henry later owned. On 19 May 1736 Chiswell married

Elizabeth Randolph, whose prominent family included her father William Randolph (1681–1742) and brother Peter Randolph (1717–1767), both members of the governor's Council, and her cousin Peyton Randolph (1721–1775), who was attorney general of Virginia when Chiswell died. They had four daughters, among them Elizabeth Chiswell, who married Charles Carter (1732–1796), a member of the Council of State, and Susannah Chiswell, the third wife of John Robinson (1705–1766), Speaker of the House of Burgesses and treasurer of Virginia.

Chiswell inherited Scotchtown following his father's death in 1737, and by 1738 he had become a colonel in the Hanover County militia. Throughout his life he was a tobacco planter and land speculator, and he accumulated tens of thousands of acres in central and western Virginia. By 1751 he had moved to Williamsburg. The next year he and George Gilmer, a local physician, purchased the Raleigh Tavern in Williamsburg, and by the mid-1750s Chiswell was operating an ordinary in James City County.

Late in the 1750s Chiswell discovered a lead deposit in the part of western Virginia that later became Wythe County. About 1760 he formed a partnership with Robinson, William Byrd (1728–1777), a member of the Council, and for a time Francis Fauquier, then lieutenant governor of Virginia, to mine and smelt the lead. Chiswell ran the daily operations, while the others provided capital and political support. The initial mining operation was unprofitable, but in 1762 Chiswell traveled to England to have the ore analyzed and to hire experienced miners. After his return the following year the mine began producing lead using hired miners and slave labor. The mine provided lead for the colonial militia during the frontier fighting early in the 1760s and later during the American Revolution. Chiswell also was part owner of copper mines in Albemarle and Augusta Counties.

In 1760 Byrd, then colonel in command of one of the Virginia regiments during the French and Indian War, housed hundreds of militiamen at an abandoned homestead on a tributary of the New River. He named it Fort Chiswell, for his friend and partner in the nearby lead mine. The

fort was an important military post during the American Revolution. The surrounding area became known as Fort Chiswell and consisted of a storage facility for lead from the mines and a successful trading post that capitalized on westward expansion. For a time the fort served as the courthouse for Montgomery County, created in 1776.

Like many other businessmen, especially ones with important family connections, Chiswell entered public service to advance and protect his wealth and property holdings. On 27 April 1737 the Council appointed him a justice of the peace for Hanover County. He represented the county in the House of Burgesses from 1742 to 1755 and served on the Committees on Privileges and Elections and of Propositions and Grievances. Following his move to Williamsburg, he represented the city during the 1756–1758 sessions and again sat on the Committees on Privileges and Elections and of Propositions and Grievances. Chiswell was one of the commissioners named in 1752 to oversee the clearing of the Pamunkey River and during the 1750s and 1760s was appointed to committees to allocate public money for militia guarding the western frontier and to manage trade between the colony and the Indians.

Chiswell was a man of stature in colonial Virginia. He had a temper and reacted violently to perceived slights. On 3 June 1766 he stabbed and killed Robert Routledge, a Prince Edward County merchant, at a tavern in Cumberland County. Accounts of the incident vary. A conversation between the two became an argument, and a drunken Routledge seems to have provoked Chiswell, who may or may not have been drinking. Chiswell reportedly insulted him as "a fugitive rebel, a villain who came to Virginia to cheat and defraud men of their property, and a Presbyterian fellow." Chiswell was arrested, and the county court sent him to Williamsburg for trial before the General Court. Three judges of that court, John Blair (ca. 1687–1771), William Byrd, and Presley Thornton, allowed Chiswell to go free on bail. The legality and propriety of the judges' bailing a man accused of murder was hotly debated for weeks in the Williamsburg newspapers.

John Chiswell died in his Williamsburg home on 15 October 1766 on the eve of his trial. He may have committed suicide, but physicians swore that his death was caused by "nervous fits, owing to a constant uneasiness of the mind." His recently widowed daughter, Susannah Chiswell Robinson, arranged for him to be buried at Scotchtown, which John Robinson had purchased in 1760.

William Hendy Shephard, "Colonel John Chiswell, Chiswell's Lead Mines, Fort Chiswell" (M.A. thesis, UVA, 1936); marriage date in Chiswell family Bible records (1736–1739), LVA; John Chiswell Daybook (1751–1757), Frederick's Hall Plantation Records, UNC; Land Office Patents and Grants, LVA; York Co. Deeds, 5:493–494; Mary A. Stephenson, "Chiswell-Bucktrout Historical Report, Block 2 Building 17 Lot 253–254" (1959 typescript report; 1990 microfiche ed.), CW; Martha W. McCartney, *History of Fort Chiswell, Wythe County, Virginia* (1976); Mary B. Kegley and F. B. Kegley, *Early Adventurers on the Western Waters* (1980–1995), vols. 1, 3; death of Routledge and bail controversy in Cumberland Co. Order Book (1764–1767), 253, *Williamsburg Virginia Gazette* (Purdie and Dixon), 20 June–10 Oct. 1766 (first quotation in 18 July 1766 issue), Carl Bridenbaugh, "Violence and Virtue in Virginia, 1766: or, The Importance of the Trivial," *Proceedings of the Massachusetts Historical Society* 76 (1964): 3–29, J. A. Leo Lemay, "Robert Bolling and the Bailment of Colonel Chiswell," *Early American Literature* 6 (1971): 99–142, William E. White, "Charlatans, Embezzlers, and Murderers: Revolution Comes to Virginia, 1765–1775" (Ph.D. diss., W&M, 1998), 242–265, and Alan Pell Crawford, "The Upstart, the Speaker, the Scandals, and Scotchtown," *Colonial Williamsburg* 23 (winter 2001–2002): 14–21; George H. S. King, ed., "Will of Colonel John Chiswell (c. 1710–1766), with some Genealogical Notes," *Virginia Genealogical Society Quarterly Bulletin* 7 (1969): 77–83; death reported in *Williamsburg Virginia Gazette* (Purdie and Dixon), 17 Oct. 1766 (second quotation), and *Annapolis Maryland Gazette*, 30 Oct. 1766.

JOHN G. DEAL

CHRISMAN, Arthur Bowie (16 July 1889–by 21 February 1953), recipient of the John Newbery Medal, was born near White Post, in Clarke County, on the farm of his parents, Isaac Arthur Chrisman and Mary Louisa Bryarly Chrisman. As a child he delighted in spinning animal adventure stories to entertain his siblings. Educated at a local one-room school, Chrisman developed a passion for Edgar Allan Poe's works. He studied electrical engineering at the Virginia Agricultural and Mechanical College and Polytechnic Institute (later Virginia Polytechnic Institute and State University) from 1906 to 1908 but left at the end of his sophomore year without taking a degree. He never married.

Chrisman worked at various times as a draftsman, farmer, lecturer, schoolteacher, and head of a kindergarten. In the 1910s the lure of the new motion picture industry drew him to Los Angeles, where he earned some money as a movie extra and knocked about the state on foot. A Chinese shopkeeper whom he met during his California sojourn awakened Chrisman's interest in Chinese culture and literature and helped him develop his distinctive voice as a storyteller. By about 1918 Chrisman had begun writing humorous, superficially Chinese fairy and folk tales, a mixture of authentic Chinese elements with sly American storytelling in the tall-tale tradition, including characters with such pseudo-Chinese names as Ah Mee, Ah Tcha, and Hai Low. Chrisman sold several stories to the serials *North American* and *What to Do*, and in 1925, after his return to farming at White Post, he published *Shen of the Sea: A Book for Children*, a collection of sixteen Chinese tales illustrated by the Danish silhouette artist Else Hasselriis. The next year the American Library Association awarded *Shen of the Sea* the fifth annual John Newbery Medal for the most distinguished contribution to American children's literature during 1925. A second compilation of Chinese yarns, *The Wind That Wouldn't Blow: Stories of the Merry Middle Kingdom for Children, and Myself* (1927), again illustrated by Hasselriis, followed. Chrisman's success spurred him to move to Manhattan about 1930, but soon he returned again to the family farm at White Post, where he enjoyed sitting under his favorite walnut tree and telling stories to his nieces and their friends. In 1931 he considered but never undertook a collection of American folktales. The Clarke County Centennial Commission engaged its nationally recognized local author to write the thirty-page centennial history *Clarke County, 1836–1936* (1936). Chrisman's final book, *Treasures Long Hidden: Old Tales and New Tales of the East*, appeared in 1941.

Respiratory problems caused Chrisman to move to Stone County, Arkansas, ostensibly to study Ozark folklore, about 1943 and then in

1946 to Van Buren County in that state. In his later years, although he had several thousand dollars deposited in two banks, he seldom left his primitive one-room cabin in the Shirley community near Clinton, and he ceased contact with his family. Two local men discovered his body in the cabin on 21 February 1953 after the reclusive author missed one of his regular trips into town to purchase groceries. The county coroner estimated that he had been dead for about a week. Arthur Bowie Chrisman's remains were returned to White Post for burial in the cemetery of Meade Memorial Episcopal Church.

Autobiography in Stanley J. Kunitz and Howard Haycraft, eds., *The Junior Book of Authors* (1934), 87–89, with birth date and por.; biographies in Dilly Tante [Stanley J. Kunitz], ed., *Living Authors: A Book of Biographies* (1931), 70–71 (por.), and Bertha Mahony Miller and Elinor Whitney Field, eds., *Newbery Medal Books: 1922–1955* . . . (1955), 39–43; variant birth date of 18 July 1889 in BVS Birth Register, Clarke Co.; family information provided by nieces Ethel R. Chrisman and Louise Chrisman (2003); *New York Times*, 5 Oct. 1926; *Washington Post*, 12 Nov. 1934; obituaries in *Winchester Evening Star*, 23, 24 Feb. 1953, *Richmond News Leader*, 24 Feb. 1953, *Richmond Times-Dispatch* and *Washington Post*, both 25 Feb. 1953, and *Clinton [Ark.] Van Buren County Democrat*, 27 Feb. 1953.

VERONICA ALEASE DAVIS

CHRISTIAN, Annie Henry (d. 4 May 1790), pioneer, was born in Hanover County, probably late in the 1730s or early in the 1740s. She was the daughter of Sarah Winston Syme Henry and her second husband, John Henry, a Scottish immigrant. Her siblings included Patrick Henry, orator and governor of Virginia, and Elizabeth Henry Campbell Russell, a Methodist lay leader in Washington County.

The good education Henry received from her parents enabled her to compose during the 1770s and 1780s a series of informative letters written in a clear, steady hand and characterized by the straightforward tone and easy narrative flow of one comfortable with the written word. Sometime between mid-January and mid-March 1768 she married William Christian, who later briefly served on the Council of State. Between 1770 and 1785 they had five daughters and one son. In the first year of their marriage, the Christians lived in the Roanoke River Valley in that part of Augusta County that was organized in 1770 as Botetourt County, where Annie Henry Christian became close to her sister-in-law, Anne Christian Fleming, who lived nearby. In 1770 the Christians moved to Mahanaim in Dunkard's Bottom, thirty-five miles to the southwest in the area that in 1772 became Fincastle County, and Christian began a correspondence with her sister-in-law that continued for the rest of her life.

Christian was not one of the women politicized by the American Revolution, even though in 1776 she accompanied her husband to Williamsburg, where he was serving as lieutenant colonel and then colonel of the 1st Virginia Regiment. Later that year while he commanded an expedition against the Cherokee on the southwestern frontier of Virginia, she complained to her brother the governor about her husband's frequent absences from home and the consequent inattention to his own business affairs.

In the spring of 1785 the Christian family, including their children, and an undetermined number of slaves moved to Kentucky, but William Christian's widowed mother turned back before reaching Cumberland Gap. Christian's letters to her sister-in-law chronicled the trek along the Wilderness Road and her early months in Kentucky and contain the best first-person accounts of that portion of the westward movement that survive from the pen of any woman. Her letters, which her sister-in-law preserved, strongly influenced later generations' understandings of the effects on women of the westward movement and life on the frontier.

By August 1785 the Christians had settled on Beargrass Creek, near the site of present-day Louisville, Kentucky. Her husband sent some of the slaves to work in his saltworks, known as Bullitt's Lick or Saltsburg, near present-day Shepherdsville, Kentucky, before he was killed on 9 April 1786 while participating in an expedition against the Indians north of the Ohio River. Christian retreated southeast to near Danville, Kentucky, where she stayed with a sister-in-law, Rosanna Christian Wallace, and her husband Caleb Wallace. Christian settled at Cove Spring, near Danville, in the autumn and moved her five youngest children there. Deciding she would prefer to rent a plantation because it would be less expensive than having to stock and supply her own, she moved again in September 1787. Christian managed the family's financial affairs with two goals in mind: protecting her children's inheritances and returning to Virginia.

In September 1788 Christian and five of her children, together with a few slaves, returned to Virginia. Her daughters eventually moved back to Kentucky, but it is not certain whether she intended to go back. In the spring of 1789 Christian became ill with consumption, probably tuberculosis. She wrote a will in October of that year, providing for her children, and then sailed to the West Indies in order to recover her health. She apparently spent the winter on the island of Antigua and returned to Virginia in the spring. Annie Henry Christian died in Norfolk on 4 May 1790, shortly after she landed. Family tradition provides contradictory evidence about the place of her burial; in his will her son set aside £400 for erecting a fine tombstone over the grave of his parents at Beargrass Creek.

Gail S. Terry, "Family Empires: A Frontier Elite in Virginia and Kentucky, 1740–1815" (Ph.D. diss., W&M, 1992), 132–133, 191–204, 247, 254–255, 298–305; principal collections with Christian letters include Draper MSS 2U140, Bullitt Collection (including plantation accounts), Filson Historical Society, Louisville, Ky., Breckinridge Family Papers, LC, William Fleming Papers, W&L, and Hugh Blair Grigsby Papers, VHS; approximate marriage date in William Wirt Henry, *Patrick Henry: Life, Correspondence, and Speeches* (1891), 1:122, and Augusta Co. Deed Book, 14:312–313; Prince Edward Co. Will Book, 2:103–104; account of illness and death in Eliza Ramsey (husband's niece) to Lyman C. Draper, 22 Feb. 1843, Draper MSS 8ZZ4; death notices in *Norfolk and Portsmouth Chronicle*, 8 May 1790, and *Richmond Virginia Independent Chronicle, and General Advertiser*, 12 May 1790 (with date).

GAIL S. TERRY

CHRISTIAN, Frank Patteson (18 November 1858–6 June 1933), judge of the Special Court of Appeals, was born in Lynchburg and was the son of Edward Dunscomb Christian, a prominent attorney, and Cornelia Burton Christian. His younger brother, William Asbury Christian, was a Methodist minister who wrote histories of Lynchburg and Richmond. Educated in private and public schools in Lynchburg but unable to afford a college education, Christian worked as a messenger for a telegraph company and taught for several years in the Lynchburg public schools.

He studied law in his father's office and attended two sessions of the law school at the University of Virginia before beginning his practice in Lynchburg in 1887.

On 28 January 1890 Christian married Mary Lucretia Dearing, whose father, James Dearing, had been a Confederate brigadier general. Christian invested in local businesses, sat on the boards of three coal companies, and became a director of the First National Bank of Lynchburg. For many years he taught a Sunday school class at the Court Street Methodist Church and was active in the temperance movement and in local Democratic Party politics. By 1894 he chaired the Lynchburg Democratic Executive Committee. In 1897 Christian built a large Romanesque-style house on fashionable Madison Street, where with a small staff of domestic servants he and his wife raised their four sons and one daughter and also provided a home for his mother-in-law and later a son-in-law, a daughter-in-law, a grandchild, and a niece.

Christian was elected commonwealth's attorney of Lynchburg in 1890 and won reelection two years later. In 1894 the General Assembly elected him city judge of Lynchburg. After a revisal of the city charter in 1896, his title became judge of the corporation court. The legislature's Democratic majority reelected him without opposition in 1900, 1906, 1914, 1922, and 1930.

In the spring of 1924 the assembly created a Special Court of Appeals to sit for two years in order to alleviate a backlog of cases that the Supreme Court of Appeals could not rule on expeditiously. To serve on the new court the Supreme Court of Appeals selected four circuit court judges and Christian, the only municipal court judge chosen. The judges took their oaths of office on 24 June 1924, and by the time they completed their work on 25 June 1926, they had decided 124 cases. The following spring the assembly re-created the Special Court of Appeals, and the Supreme Court of Appeals reappointed the members of the earlier court. Christian arrived one day late for the second court and did not take his seat until 20 July 1927. He and the other judges rendered 105 decisions and cleared their docket before the court's statutory authority expired on 18 December 1928. In all the cases for which the judges of the two Special Courts issued written opinions, the workload of writing for the majority was evenly distributed, but Christian filed nineteen dissents, nearly twice the number of all of the other judges combined.

Frank Patteson Christian continued to serve as judge of the corporation court of Lynchburg throughout his years on the Special Court of Appeals and was the senior municipal court judge in Virginia when he died of influenza in a Lynchburg hospital on 6 June 1933. He was buried in the city's Spring Hill Cemetery.

Biographies in *Men of Mark*, 5:65–66, and Bruce, Tyler, and Morton, *History of Virginia*, 5:351 (por. on 350); birth date in Christian family Bible records (1842–1887), VHS; BVS Marriage Register, Lynchburg; some letters in Dearing Family Papers, VHS; W. Asbury Christian (brother), *Lynchburg and Its People* (1900), 386, 403, 416, 422, 428; S. Allen Chambers Jr., *Lynchburg: An Architectural History* (1981), 337–339; *Lynchburg Daily Virginian*, 29 Jan. 1890; *Lynchburg News*, 22 Apr. 1892, 20 Apr. 1894; Special Court of Appeals Order Book, 4:1, 133, 135, 136, 218, RG 107, LVA; opinions of Special Court of Appeals printed in *Virginia Reports*, vols. 139–144, 146–151; obituaries, editorial tributes, and accounts of funeral in *Lynchburg Daily Advance*, 6, 8 June 1933, and *Lynchburg News*, 7, 9 June 1933.

BRENT TARTER

CHRISTIAN, George Llewellyn (13 April 1841–26 July 1924), defender of the Lost Cause, was the son of Edmund Thomas Christian and Tabitha Rebecca Graves Christian. He was born in Charles City County, where his father was clerk of the county court and where he attended private academies. On 14 August 1861 Christian joined the 1st Virginia Artillery (popularly known as the Richmond Howitzers) as a private. He was promoted to corporal in 1862 and to sergeant the following year. Christian fought in several major battles, including at Seven Pines, Fredericksburg, and Gettysburg. On 12 May 1864, during the Battle of Spotsylvania Court House, a cannon shot severed his left foot and the heel of his right. The wounds required the amputation of the lower part of his left leg and caused him much pain for the remainder of his life. Six years later, he was injured again when the courtroom floor in the State Capitol collapsed, killing more than sixty people.

Christian enrolled as a law student at the University of Virginia in the autumn of 1864. When Union forces threatened Charlottesville the following February, he fled to Richmond, where he witnessed the city's burning, surrender, and initial occupation. He remained in Richmond, was admitted to the bar in 1867, and on 7 April 1869 married Ida Morris. They had two sons and one daughter before she died of consumption on 27 January 1879. He married a cousin, Emma Christian, on 25 November 1881. They had three sons.

Christian rose steadily in the ranks of Richmond's legal profession. From 1873 to 1878 he was clerk of the Virginia Supreme Court of Appeals, and in 1877 he and his cousin Frank Wood Christian founded the *Virginia Law Journal*. The monthly periodical published major appellate court decisions and other federal and state cases of interest, as well as original articles on legal topics, some of which the editors wrote. Christian edited the *Virginia Law Journal* through 1882 and in 1909 serialized in the *Virginia Law Register* his 1908 address before the Bar Association of the City of Richmond under the title "Reminiscences of Some of the Dead of the Bench and Bar of Richmond."

Christian represented Clay Ward on the Richmond common council from 1874 to 1878. He chaired the Committee on Ordinances, and in December 1877 the biracial council unanimously elected him president. Three months later Christian resigned from the council and from his clerkship after the General Assembly elected him judge of the Hustings Court of Richmond. His judicial responsibilities included hearing criminal cases as well as appeals from the city's police court, impaneling grand juries, ruling on the constitutionality of all city ordinances, and appointing voter registrars and election commissioners for each of Richmond's wards. A conservative Democrat, Christian supported paying the state's funded prewar debt in full. After Readjusters, who advocated reducing the amount of the principal to repay, cemented control of the General Assembly in 1881, they removed him and many other public officials from office.

Judge Christian, as he was almost always known thereafter, and his cousin then formed a legal partnership, initially known as Christian and Christian, which developed a largely corporate clientele. In 1888 he was president of the Bar Association of the City of Richmond and in 1910 was elected to a one-year term as president of the Virginia State Bar Association. His presidential address on Chief Justice Roger Brooke Taney focused on issues of state sovereignty and limited federal government authority. Like many other prominent attorneys, Christian also had other business interests. He was president of the National Bank of Virginia from 1893 to 1902 and president of the Virginia State Insurance Company, which specialized in fire insurance, from 1903 until 1919. He won election in 1892 to the first of three one-year terms as president of the Richmond Chamber of Commerce, which successfully pushed for the reorganization of the State Board of Health as part of an effort to lower the city's high mortality rate. The chamber also advocated improvement of the James River and the expansion of the port of Newport News in order to counter the economic influence of northern ports. It supported repeal of the purchasing clause of the Sherman Anti-Trust Act and lobbied for the creation of a national department of commerce. Christian was a Presbyterian lay leader and favored making Richmond the home of Union Theological Seminary in Virginia, of which he was a trustee from 1898 until his death.

The abiding concern of Christian's later life was inculcating in Virginia's youth an appreciation for the Confederacy. Beginning in the 1890s he helped orchestrate the efforts of the history committee of Virginia's Grand Camp Confederate Veterans. Christian and his compatriots policed the content of history textbooks and successfully pressured schools to use only books that rejected pro-Northern interpretations and that defended the justice of the Confederate cause. In a series of widely distributed speeches and pamphlets, many of which he and Hunter Holmes McGuire published in the joint compilation entitled *The Confederate Cause and Conduct in the War Between the States* (1907), Christian expounded a hard-line defense of the Confederacy. He argued that secession had been constitutionally justified, that slavery had not been a cause of the Civil War, that the North had been the aggressor, and that Union armies had committed numerous war crimes against the South while Confederate forces had behaved admirably. A second edition of the book published in 1913 included as an addendum Christian's 1909 lecture on Abraham Lincoln, whom he characterized as a *"coarse, secretive, cunning man and wily politician, and one of the greatest tyrants of any age."*

Christian received much praise for his advocacy of the Lost Cause. When he announced his candidacy in 1901 to represent Richmond in the state constitutional convention that met later that year, his loyalty to the South was a chief recommendation, but he failed to win election. In 1903 Christian became grand commander of Virginia's Grand Camp, and four years later his interpretation of the Civil War was incorporated into the official report of the United Confederate Veterans' reunion.

Christian never wavered in his advocacy of a properly Confederate view of history. "Are we so debased and cowed by the results of the conflict," he once asked, "that we must remain silent" in the presence of alternative interpretations "for the sake of political expediency or material gain, and not tell our children *the truth*?" In 1915 he published a small book, *The Capitol Disaster: A Chapter of Reconstruction in Virginia*, including contemporary accounts of the 1870 accident in which he had been injured. In his narrative, he overtly assigned blame for the event to the politics of Reconstruction and extended his defense of Virginia against Northern interference into the postwar period. Although Christian remained active in other professional and civic endeavors (for example, he chaired the Virginia Association for Local Self-Government, which opposed statewide prohibition), historical activities consumed much of his attention. He was at various times treasurer, vice president, and acting president of the Confederate Memorial Association, while his wife served as treasurer of the board of lady managers. Christian served on the executive and publication committees of the Southern Historical Society, routinely contributed addresses and recollections to its *Southern Historical Society Papers*, and for the last five years of his life was president of the society.

George Llewellyn Christian died at his Richmond home on 26 July 1924 and was buried in the city's Hollywood Cemetery.

Biographies in Tyler, *Encyclopedia*, 4:273–275, and *NCAB*, 20:321; BVS Marriage Register, Richmond City (1869, 1881); Compiled Service Records; Lee A. Wallace, Jr., *The Richmond Howitzers* (1993), 138; 1884 Artificial Limb Application, Confederate Disability Applications and Receipts, Auditor of Public Accounts, RG 48, LVA; *Richmond Dispatch*, 15 June 1894; some Christian letters and documents in various collections at LVA and VHS; presidential address in *Virginia State Bar Association Proceedings* (1911), 167–192; other published works include address in *A Souvenir of the Unveiling of the Richmond Howitzer Monument at Richmond, Virginia, December 13th, 1892* (1893), 88–98, *Charles City: Some of Its Noted Places and People and Personal Recollections of Some of These* (1910), "Some Recollections of the Evacuation of Richmond on April 3, 1865," in *Richmond Evening Journal*, 17 July 1912, *Confederate Memories and Experiences* (1914), *Sketch of the Origin and Erection of the Confederate Memorial Institute at Richmond, Virginia* (1921), and "A Comparatively Unknown Incident in the Life of Daniel Webster," *SHSP* 44 (1923): 209–214; Hunter McGuire and George L. Christian, *The Confederate Cause and Conduct in the War Between the States*, 2d ed. (1913), Addenda, 29 (first quotation), 31 (second quotation); Fred Arthur Bailey, "Free Speech and the Lost Cause in the Old Dominion," *VMHB* 103 (1995): 237–266; Hall, *Portraits*, 49–50 (por. by Edith Leeson Everett); BVS Death Certificate, Richmond City; obituaries and editorial tributes in *Richmond Times-Dispatch*, 27, 28 July 1924, and *Richmond News Leader*, 28 July 1924; memorials in Chamber of Commerce magazine *Richmond* 11 (Aug. 1924): 3, 15, *Virginia State Bar Association Proceedings* (1924), 88–92 (por.), and by W. W. Moore in *Union Seminary Review* 36 (1924–1925): 6–25.

WILLIAM BLAND WHITLEY

CHRISTIAN, Israel (d. by 1 October 1784), county leader and merchant, immigrated to Virginia from the British Isles during the first half of the 1740s, but the exact date is not known, nor are the date and place of his birth, the names of his parents, or the date of his marriage to Elizabeth, whose maiden name was probably Starke. Most likely married before he arrived in Virginia, Christian had four daughters, three of whom married into leading families in the Valley of Virginia, and one son, William Christian, who became a colonel in the Continental army during the American Revolution and later a member of the Council of State. Christian's name first appears in Virginia records on 6 January 1746 when the surveyor of Augusta County recorded laying off a tract of 120 acres of land for him. By then he had probably opened a store in the county, where he became a prominent merchant.

Christian exemplified the late colonial frontier entrepreneur and the rise of a new class of reliable leaders of orderly expansion in late colonial and Revolutionary Virginia. He kept an ordinary, was a merchant in Staunton, acted as a vendor of indentured servant contracts, traded with the region's Native Americans, planted hemp, and owned a gristmill. He was commissary for the campaign that William Byrd (1728–1777) led in 1761 against the Cherokee while simultaneously supplying British troops on the Monongahela River. He owned about 3,240 acres of land in eighteen separate tracts by the end of the 1760s, and his laborers included at least twelve slaves at one time. Like other frontier leaders, Christian moved frequently in search of land to develop.

Commissioned a captain in the Augusta County militia in 1754, Christian patrolled the area during the Seven Years' War. From 1758 to 1765 he represented the county in the House of Burgesses, where he served on the Committees of Public Claims and of Trade. He drafted four bills, a modest achievement typical of the area's burgesses of the time. Christian became a justice of the peace on 20 March 1758 and the following year was named a member of the Augusta Parish vestry. He and many other western vestrymen were in fact Presbyterians, not members of the Church of England, but vestries had important social responsibilities, such as providing for the poor and for orphans, in addition to managing the ecclesiastical affairs of the parish. In November 1769 the other members removed Christian from the vestry after he refused to subscribe to the doctrines of the Church of England.

The General Assembly in November 1761 named Christian a trustee of the new town of Staunton. Late in 1764 he moved to the southern part of Augusta County that in 1770 became the new county of Botetourt. He was one of the first justices of the peace for Botetourt County and with unabashed self-promotion aspired to more. Christian maneuvered unsuccessfully to have his son appointed county surveyor. For himself he sought appointment as the county's first sheriff and lobbied so vigorously that the governor's Council rebuked him for disrespectful behavior. He eventually won approval for the county courthouse to be built on his land, which increased the value of his property, and in 1771 he became the county's second sheriff. This office, and helping to establish the town of Fincastle the following year on land he had once owned, capped his record of public service.

Western Virginia's growth soon produced another partition, the creation of Fincastle County out of Botetourt County in 1772. That division marked Christian's retirement from the county bench. He also resigned the remainder of his two-year sheriff's appointment and in 1773 moved with his wife into the new county. They returned to Botetourt County the following year and most likely lived with one of their daughters. By 1784 the aging Christian had moved to Montgomery County, where on 12 July he signed his will. Stating that he was in poor health, he named his wife and son executors of his estate and divided among his wife, children, and grandchildren about 12,000 acres of land, including parcels in Bedford, Fayette, Jefferson, Kentucky, and Washington Counties. Israel Christian died on an unrecorded date before 1 October 1784, when his widow began receiving a designated £100 annuity from his estate. His will was proved at the November session of the county court. The place of his burial is not recorded.

Biographies in *Fincastle Herald*, 18 June 1874 (giving age at death as about seventy), copy in Draper MSS 5ZZ104–105, and in Stoner, *Seed-Bed*, 285–287; Augusta Co. Surveyors Record, 1:10 (first record in Virginia); land acquisitions documented in Virginia Land Office Patents, RG 4, LVA, and in deed books of Augusta and Botetourt Counties; Augusta Parish Vestry Book, LVA, esp. 265, 431, 464; Christian to governor, 16 Oct. 1770, Colonial Papers, RG 1, LVA; *Executive Journals of Council*, 6:171, 243, 371–372, 436; Hening, *Statutes*, 8:616; Mary B. Kegley and F. B. Kegley, *Early Adventurers on the Western Waters* (1980–1995), vols. 1–3; will and estate inventory in Montgomery Co. Deeds and Wills, B:66–68.

TURK MCCLESKEY

CHRISTIAN, James Samuel (26 October 1918–29 December 1982), member of the House of Delegates, was born in Richmond and was the son of Estelle Jasey Christian and James Samuel Christian, a postal worker and a founder of the National Baptist Deacon's Convention of America. Christian graduated from Armstrong High School in Richmond. While attending Virginia Union University, he supported himself with a series of jobs, including highway maintenance work and as doorman and assistant manager at a movie theater. Soon after the United States entered World War II, Christian suspended his studies and volunteered for the Army Air Corps. He was the first African American from Richmond to report for flight training at the Tuskegee Army Air Base in Alabama. On 11 July 1943 in Jamaica, New York, he married a Richmond teacher, Margaret Constance Olphin. They had no children.

A few weeks after his wedding, Christian and his aviation unit were sent to Livorno, Italy. He was promoted from sergeant to first lieutenant in January 1944. For his service during World War II as pilot of an observation plane and for part of the time as personal pilot for General Mark Wayne Clark, Christian received the Air Medal with four oak leaf clusters and was recommended for the Silver Star for gallantry. He remained in the reserves after the war and became a postal worker in Richmond. Recalled to active duty during the Korean War, he commanded an anti-aircraft battery of the New York National Guard.

By 1954 Christian had returned to Richmond and resumed his job with the post office. Resuming his education as well, he took accounting courses at Virginia Union University and government courses at the Richmond Professional Institute (later Virginia Commonwealth University). In 1963 he opened an accounting and bookkeeping business in Richmond's Jackson Ward neighborhood. Christian began a four-year term on the city planning commission in 1972 and became vice chair in 1975. When in September 1976 he was named chair of the commission, his stated agenda called for revitalizing the city's downtown, encouraging development along the James River, increasing employment, and reforming land-use policies to solve some of the city's housing problems. He was also a member of the Capital Region Area Airport Commission and of the Richmond Regional Planning District Commission.

In March 1975 Christian campaigned for the Democratic Party nomination for one of five seats representing Richmond in the House of Delegates. He received endorsements from two influential African American political organizations, the Richmond Crusade for Voters and the Peoples Political and Civic League, and also from the Virginia State AFL-CIO. Christian finished seventh in a field of eight candidates in the June primary. Two years later he again sought and this time won the party nomination. Spending only $5,000 on his campaign and relying heavily on support from the black community, he was one of two African American men elected in November 1977 to represent Richmond in the House of Delegates for a two-year term. He served on the Committees on General Laws and on Nominations and Confirmations. A quiet man, Christian did not sponsor any bills during his first term in the General Assembly but instead preferred to sign on as co-patron of bills other members introduced. He supported ratification of the proposed Equal Rights Amendment to the United States Constitution and also a measure to ensure that women could receive Medicaid payments for an abortion if the pregnancy jeopardized her life. He backed pari-mutuel betting on horse races and voted for a bill to provide financial aid for cities that could not legally annex land in adjacent counties.

Christian won reelection in 1979. He sat on the Committees on Corporations, Insurance, and Banking, on General Laws, and on Nominations and Confirmations. He opposed the state sales tax on food because he believed that it imposed undue financial hardships on the state's poor. His bill that would have allowed local governments to give real estate tax breaks to the elderly and disabled was defeated. Christian received credit for helping to enact a law that permitted voter registrars to go into the residences of elderly and handicapped people in order to register them. He won election to a third term in 1981, after the city had been divided into single-member districts. Christian's primary objective continued to be the repeal of the state sales tax on food. He served on the Committee on General Laws during the 1981 session and on Committees on Conservation and Natural Resources, on Cor-

porations, Insurance, and Banking, on Finance, and on Nominations and Confirmations.

Back spasms that resulted from a collapsed vertebra in his lower back forced Christian to miss part of the 1982 legislative session. It was widely expected that at the next session he would become chair of the House Committee on Nominations and Confirmations, which would have made him only the second African American to preside over a House of Delegates committee in the twentieth century. Diagnosed with advanced bone cancer, James Samuel Christian died at the Medical College of Virginia Hospital on 29 December 1982, a few weeks before the start of the 1983 legislative session. Following a funeral service at Fourth Baptist Church in Richmond, he was buried in the city's Mount Olivet Cemetery. In 1996 a monument to honor Christian, featuring a portrait and a figure of a boy playing with a toy airplane, was erected at the intersection of P Street, Oakwood Avenue, and Chimborazo Boulevard in Richmond.

Birth date in Richmond City Department of Public Health Birth Records; biography in Elizabeth R. Herbener and Jon Kukla, eds., *The General Assembly of Virginia, 11 January 1978–27 April 1989* (1990), 82; feature articles in *Richmond Times-Dispatch*, 5 Sept. 1976, 27 Feb. 1982, and *Richmond Afro-American and Planet*, 27–31 Dec. 1977; transcript of oral history interview, 30 Sept. 1982, for Church Hill Oral History Project, Virginia Black History Archives, VCU (with birth date of 26 Oct. 1918); New York City Certificate of Marriage Registration (with variant birth date of 26 Oct. 1917); *Richmond Afro-American*, 11 Sept. 1943; *Richmond Times-Dispatch*, 1 Apr. 1996; Flora Crater et al., comps., *The Almanac of Virginia Politics* (1977–1983); obituaries in *Richmond News Leader* and *Richmond Times-Dispatch*, both 30 Dec. 1982, and *Richmond Afro-American and Planet*, 8 Jan. 1983 (all with pors.); editorial tributes in *Richmond News Leader*, 30 Dec. 1982, *Richmond Times-Dispatch*, 1 Jan. 1983, and *Richmond Afro-American and Planet*, 8 Jan. 1983; memorial resolution in *JHD*, 1983 sess., 1:281–282.

HAROLD MARSH

CHRISTIAN, John Beverly (ca. 1793–21 February 1856), member of the Council of State, was born at Cedar Grove, the New Kent County plantation of his parents, Mary Browne Christian and Robert Christian, a planter and six-term member of the House of Delegates. His sister, Letitia Christian, married John Tyler (1790–1862), later president of the United States. Christian attended the College of William and Mary and practiced law in Williamsburg and the surrounding counties. As a young man he owned fine racehorses. On 11 March 1822 Christian married Martha Eliza Semple, of Williamsburg. They lived for several years in New Kent County before settling in Charles City County. About 1835 they moved to Williamsburg, but Christian continued to own land in Charles City for the rest of his life. He and his wife had three sons and one daughter before her death on 10 February 1838.

Christian won election to the House of Delegates in 1820 representing New Kent County and was reelected each year through 1824. During his first term he served on the Committee of Privileges and Elections and on a committee to examine the land register's office. In 1821 he gained a seat on the Committee for Courts of Justice, which he retained throughout his service in the assembly. He was also a member of a committee to examine the disbursement of public money in the 1823–1824 assembly and of a committee to examine the auditor's office for two sessions. In 1825 Christian replaced Tyler, who had been elected governor, in the House of Delegates from Charles City County and was reelected to four more consecutive terms. He served on the Committee of Schools and Colleges during the 1825–1826 and 1829–1830 assembly sessions and also during the latter session on a committee to examine the auditor's office.

On 19 January 1830, early in his tenth term, the General Assembly elected Christian to fill a vacancy on the Council of State. He took his seat four days later and attended about half the sessions of the governor's advisory board during the relatively uneventful months before it ceased to exist at the end of March 1831, when the new state constitution replaced the eight-member body with a three-member Council.

Christian continued to practice law while serving as a delegate and a councillor and after the conclusion of his Council service. On 16 September 1835 the governor named him to succeed his father-in-law, James Semple, on the General Court, and on 18 December the General Assembly elected him to fill the vacancy. Christian presided at civil and criminal trials in the large Second Judicial District, which included much of Tidewater Virginia and the Eastern Shore. Occasionally he met with other General Court judges as the state's only court of appeals in criminal cases. Few of Christian's opinions in the latter capacity were published. Those that were suggest that he was a common-sense judge who seldom indulged in long, learned decisions but made his rulings with precision and clarity.

Christian spent time in Washington, D.C., in the summer and autumn of 1841 after his brother-in-law became president. On 2 April 1844 Tyler nominated him as judge of the United States District Court for the Eastern District of Virginia. By the time the Senate took up the nomination on 15 June, Whigs who were furious at Tyler were rejecting the president's appointments wholesale, including on that day two nominees for the Supreme Court of the United States and a secretary of the treasury. By a vote of 24 to 20 the Senate refused to confirm Christian, and when Virginia senator William Segar Archer moved to reconsider the nomination later in the day, the motion failed by a vote of 23 to 16.

The Constitution of 1851 abolished the General Court and created a new system of circuit courts. It also made all judicial offices in Virginia elective. In the May 1852 election Christian was a candidate for judge of the Sixth Judicial Circuit, consisting of Williamsburg and the counties of Charles City, Elizabeth City, Gloucester, Henrico, James City, Mathews, Middlesex, New Kent, Warwick, and York. He lost by a large margin to another General Court judge, John Bacon Clopton.

Christian served on the vestry of Bruton Parish in Williamsburg and in 1844 became a member of the board of visitors of the College of William and Mary. A descendant described him as "a genial, hospitable, generous man, a faithful friend, and a 'good hater.'" John Beverly Christian died in Williamsburg on 21 February 1856 and was buried in the family cemetery at Cedar Grove, in New Kent County.

George L. Christian, "Judge John Beverly Christian," *Virginia Law Register* 6 (1900): 205–210, with birth year of 1796, por. facing 205, and quotation on 209; death date at age sixty-three on gravestone; *Richmond Enquirer*, 26 Mar. 1822, 8 June 1852; *Washington Daily National Intelligencer*, 17 June 1844; some Christian letters in John Tyler Papers, LC, and several collections, VHS; elections to Council and to General Court in *JHD*, 1829–1830 sess., 94, and 1835–1836 sess., 31; Council of State Journal (1829–1831), 17, RG 75, LVA; published General Court opinions include *Gwatkin* v. *Commonwealth* (1839) (9 Leigh), *Virginia Reports*, 36:681–683, *Williams* v. *Commonwealth* (1845) (2 Grattan), *Virginia Reports*, 43:568–571, and a dissent in *Pitman* v. *Commonwealth* (1843) (2 Robinson), *Virginia Reports*, 41:846–853; *Journal of the Executive Proceedings of the Senate of the United States of America from December 6, 1841, to March 20, 1845, Inclusive* (1887), 6:252, 314, 341–342; estate accounts in Williamsburg Will Book, 1:4–8; obituaries in *Virginia Gazette [and] Richmond, Norfolk and Williamsburg Advertiser*, 28 Feb. 1856, *Richmond Daily Dispatch*, 1 Mar. 1856, *Richmond Enquirer*, 11 Mar. 1856, and *Petersburg Daily Express*, 12 Mar. 1856 (all repeating death occurred "in the 63d year of his age").

BRENT TARTER

CHRISTIAN, Joseph (10 July 1828–29 May 1905), judge of the Virginia Supreme Court of Appeals, was born in Middlesex County and was the son of Elizabeth Robinson Steptoe Christian and Richard Allen Christian, a physician who later became a Baptist minister. His younger brother, William Steptoe Christian, was a Confederate army officer and a leader of the temperance movement in Virginia. Educated by tutors as a child, Christian attended Columbian College (later George Washington University), in Washington, D.C., and received an A.B. in 1847, a master's degree in 1853, and an honorary LL.D. in 1872. He read law in Middlesex County and in Staunton and on 27 April 1849 was admitted to the bar in Middlesex. Christian executed a marriage bond on 25 June 1850 and between that date and the end of the month married Maria Augusta Healy. They had three daughters and one son before her death on 28 July 1885.

Christian practiced law in Middlesex County and in 1859 was elected to a four-year term in the Senate of Virginia representing Gloucester, Mathews, and Middlesex Counties. He sat on the Committee for Courts of Justice and during several sessions chaired the Joint Committees on the Library and to Examine the Bonds of Public Officers. Named to a special committee charged with overseeing legislation to regulate oyster harvesting, Christian vehemently opposed efforts to tax oystermen. During the presidential election of 1860 he stumped the Eighth Congressional District as an elector for the Consti-

tutional Union ticket, which won the state's electoral votes. He opposed secession, but after President Abraham Lincoln called for Virginia troops to help suppress the rebellion in April 1861, Christian supported the Confederate cause. He remained in the state senate during the Civil War and was appointed to the Committee on Confederate Relations during the 1862 session. He also sat on the Committee on Finance and Claims and beginning in 1863 chaired the Committee on Public Institutions of the State.

On 22 February 1866 the House of Delegates elected Christian a judge of the Sixth Circuit, which comprised the counties of Charles City, Elizabeth City, Gloucester, Henrico, James City, Mathews, Middlesex, New Kent, Warwick, and York and the city of Williamsburg. In 1868 he adjudicated the James Jeter Phillips case, in which circumstantial evidence led to the conviction of a young man for the murder of his wife. The trial attracted widespread attention and helped establish Christian as an expert on the use of circumstantial evidence in criminal cases. After being removed from the bench under a federal law that required replacement of all Mississippi, Texas, and Virginia officials who had supported the Confederacy, Christian moved to Richmond in 1869, practiced law, and campaigned for the statewide Conservative Party ticket that won election in July 1869. A general order of the First Military District removed his legal and political disabilities at the end of that year.

On 23 March 1870 the General Assembly elected Christian a judge of the Virginia Supreme Court of Appeals for a twelve-year term. Present a month later when the court convened at the State Capitol on 27 April to announce its decision in the contested election for Richmond's mayor, he narrowly escaped injury when the courtroom floor collapsed and killed approximately sixty people. Christian applied his conservative philosophy to civil and criminal cases as well as to knotty public policy issues. In *Bailey* v. *Bailey* (1871) he upheld a divorce (the first ever adjudicated in the Supreme Court of Appeals) but warned that the current social and political turmoil threatened the sanctity of marriage. Christian defended the local knowledge that informed jury decisions and ruled in *Blosser*

v. *Harshbarger* (1871) that only an obvious deficiency in the evidence presented could be used to overturn a decision and not the possibility that another jury might reasonably have reached a different conclusion. His opinion in *Dean* v. *Commonwealth* (1879) applied the same respect for local juries and clarified his views on circumstantial evidence in upholding a murder conviction.

During the debt controversy of the 1870s, Christian, like most of his fellow Conservatives on the court, defended the cause of the Funders, who advocated paying the state's antebellum public debt in full. In *Clarke* v. *Tyler, Sergeant* (1878) he ruled unconstitutional any efforts to outlaw the use of bond receipts in the payment of municipal fines. One of Christian's most important decisions, known by the consolidated title *The Homestead Cases* (1872), further indicated his commitment to the rights of creditors. He ruled that the retroactive enactment of homestead exemptions passed by the 1870 General Assembly violated the United States Constitution's mandate to uphold contracts. As senior member, Christian acted as president of the court from 1 December 1881, when President Richard Cassius Lee Moncure became too ill to attend, through 31 December 1882.

The Readjusters, who supported partial repudiation of the state's debts, gained control of the state government early in the 1880s, and when his term expired at the end of 1882, the General Assembly did not return Christian to the court. He represented the city of Richmond in the House of Delegates during the 1883–1884 session and was ranking member of the Committees for Courts of Justice, on Counties, Cities, and Towns, and on Federal Relations and Resolutions. He also chaired the Committees on the Chesapeake and Its Tributaries and on the Library. He maintained his legal practice in Richmond until declining health restricted his activities. Joseph Christian died of chronic nephritis at the Retreat for the Sick in Richmond on 29 May 1905 and was buried in Hollywood Cemetery.

Biographies in William Cathcart, ed., *The Baptist Encyclopædia* (1881), 1:221–222 (por.), and Tyler, *Encyclopedia*, 3:19; some Christian correspondence at Huntington and VHS and printed in *Virginia Law Journal* 14 (1890): 253–254, and William M. E. Rachal, ed., "The Capitol Disaster, April 27, 1870: A Letter of Judge Joseph Christian to his Wife," *VMHB* 68 (1960): 193–197; Middlesex Co. Marriage Bonds; Middlesex Co. Ministers' Returns; *Speech of Joseph Christian on the "Oyster Fundum" Bill, . . . February 8th, 1860* (1860); *JHD*, 1865–1866 sess., 392–393, 1869–1870 sess., 236–237, 1881–1882 sess., 394–395; *Richmond Daily Dispatch*, 11 July 1868; *Petersburg Index*, 6 July 1869; *General Orders and Circulars, Headquarters First Military District, 1869* (1870), General Orders no. 144, 31 Dec. 1869; *Bailey* v. *Bailey* (1871) and *Blosser* v. *Harshbarger* (1871) (21 Grattan), *Virginia Reports*, 62:43–59, 214–219; *The Homestead Cases* (1872) (22 Grattan), *Virginia Reports*, 63:266–301; *Clarke* v. *Tyler, Sergeant* (1878) (30 Grattan), *Virginia Reports*, 71:134–165; *Dean* v. *The Commonwealth* (1879) (32 Grattan), *Virginia Reports*, 73:912–928; obituaries in *Richmond News Leader*, 29 May 1905, and *Richmond Times-Dispatch*, 30 May 1905 (por.).

WILLIAM BLAND WHITLEY

CHRISTIAN, Langdon Taylor (26 May 1853–13 November 1935), funeral director, was born in New Kent County and was the son of William Edmund Christian, a farmer, and Ann E. Taylor Christian. When he was five, his family moved to a farm in Charles City County. Orphaned by the deaths of his mother in 1863 and his father two years later, Christian received abbreviated formal schooling of only four months. After laboring on a farm in Charles City County, he moved to Richmond in 1870 and found employment with Scott and Clarke, a tobacco-stemming factory. Two years later he went to work for John A. Belvin, a lumber and furniture dealer. Like many other cabinetmakers, Belvin also provided undertaker services. Christian mastered this trade and after Belvin's death in 1880 took over his funeral business. On 5 October 1881 Christian married Belle Beverley Brown, daughter of a Fredericksburg merchant. They had one daughter and one son.

Christian entered the funeral business at a time of transformation. From a sideline performed by undertakers who often did not preserve the deceased's body or take steps to stop the spread of disease, preparing the dead for burial evolved into a commercial enterprise carried out by funeral directors performing arterial embalming in handsomely appointed parlors and fully equipped offices. As part of this transition, a part-time sideline of barbers, furniture dealers, and livery stable proprietors became a full-time specialized profession requiring education and regulation. In June 1883 Christian traveled to

Cincinnati to attend the organizational meeting of the National Funeral Directors Association.

Moving to the forefront of Virginia efforts to professionalize and standardize his industry, Christian joined four colleagues in calling a meeting of all white undertakers in Virginia on 20 September 1887 for the purpose of forming a state professional organization. At the initial meeting of the Undertakers of Virginia (soon thereafter renamed the Virginia Funeral Directors Association), Christian was elected secretary and served in that office until his retirement in 1920. At the association's annual meeting in 1893, he served on a three-man committee that drafted legislation requiring the state licensing of funeral directors. In response to such calls for regulation within the funeral industry, the next session of the General Assembly created a five-member State Board of Embalming of Virginia, on which Christian served as secretary from its first meeting in July 1894 until his death. He was the fourth Virginia funeral director and the first Richmonder to be licensed by the board.

Christian earned national recognition among his professional colleagues. He was unanimously elected first vice president of the National Funeral Directors Association for the 1904–1905 term and defeated an opponent to win election as president for the 1905–1906 term. Christian also served as president of the Joint Conference of Embalmers Examining Boards and State Boards of Health (later the International Conference of Funeral Service Examining Boards, Inc.) from 1907 through 1908. Among his particular national concerns was the regulation of the transportation of human remains by public carriers. Christian called for greater cooperation among funeral directors in the United States and Canada and to increase the standing of his profession urged his colleagues to disassociate themselves from fraternal burial societies. He also condemned the insensitivity of manufacturers of embalming chemicals and apparatus who advertised with photographs of their clients' preserved bodies.

A Democrat, Christian represented Jefferson Ward on Richmond's common council from 1888 through 1891 and Madison Ward on the board of aldermen from 1914 through 1917. He was one of five delegates representing the city

of Richmond in the House of Delegates for the long 1901–1904 term. He served on the Committees on Counties, Cities, and Towns, on Executive Expenditures, and on Manufactures and Mechanic Arts. Early in 1903 Christian successfully lobbied to reenact the 1894 legislation establishing the State Board of Embalming with an amendment making it illegal to embalm a corpse when foul play was suspected without first securing the coroner's permission.

Known in Richmond as Major Christian, he was especially proud of his twenty-six years of service in the state militia. After enlisting in 1872 in the 1st Regiment Virginia Infantry, he became quartermaster with the rank of first lieutenant of the 1st Battalion Cavalry in 1887 and was elected captain of the Walker Light Guard, 1st Regiment, three years later. He was appointed assistant inspector general of the 1st Brigade, Virginia Volunteers, with the rank of major, on 25 February 1895 and retired on 16 April 1898. An avid outdoorsman, Christian enjoyed hunting and fishing, avocations that led him into organized efforts to protect migratory birds and other wildlife. As a high-ranking Freemason he joined many Masonic relief charities and was a longtime president of the governing board of the Masonic Home of Virginia.

L. T. Christian Funeral Home flourished and in October 1921 relocated from downtown Richmond to larger offices in the burgeoning western part of the city. Christian's namesake son (1893–1975) succeeded him as director of the family business and also served as president of the Virginia Funeral Directors Association for the 1940–1941 term. Christian's wife died on 12 January 1928. Three months later, on 19 April 1928, he married the twice-widowed Catherine Emerson DuBose Wallace, a New Orleans native. They had no children. She died of uterine and bladder cancer on 2 October 1935, and a few weeks later, after suffering a cerebral hemorrhage, Langdon Taylor Christian died at his Richmond home on 13 November 1935. He was buried in Hollywood Cemetery.

Biographies in Tyler, *Encyclopedia*, 4:247–249, and Bruce, Tyler, and Morton, *History of Virginia*, 4:85–86 (por. facing 85); BVS Marriage Register, Richmond City (1881, 1928); L. T. Christian Funeral Home Records, Acc. 34483, LVA; Virginia Board of Funeral Directors and Embalmers Minutes,

RG 37, LVA; *Virginia Funeral Directors' Association Proceedings* (1893), 12–14, 31–32; presidential election and address in *National Funeral Directors Association Proceedings* (1905), 165–166, 172–173; [L. T. Christian], *Golden Anniversary, 1880, 1930* (1930), pors.; Gladys B. Clem, *Seventy-Five Years of the Virginia Funeral Directors Association* (1963); Joann Peery McElmurray, *A Journey—From Then to Now: The History of the Virginia Funeral Directors Association, 1888–1988* [1988]; BVS Death Certificate, Richmond City; obituaries in *Richmond News Leader*, 13 Nov. 1935, and *Richmond Times-Dispatch*, 14 Nov. 1935.

SARA B. BEARSS

CHRISTIAN, William (ca. 1742–9 April 1786), Continental army officer and member of the Council of State, may have been born in Augusta County. He was the son of Israel Christian, an immigrant from the British Isles who became a prominent merchant and county leader, and Elizabeth Christian, whose maiden name probably was Starke and who may have been responsible for the unusually good education that he and his sisters received. The sisters married into enterprising and influential families in western Virginia. Early in the 1760s Christian commanded a company of men in an expedition against the Cherokee Indians on the southwestern frontier, and later in the decade he read law in Hanover County with Patrick Henry. Sometime between mid-January and mid-March 1768 he married Henry's sister, Annie Henry. They had five daughters and one son.

In March 1769 Christian obtained a certificate of good character from the Augusta County Court in preparation for qualifying to practice law, but there is no evidence that he ever did. Early in his marriage he lived in a house his father provided in the southern portion of Augusta County, which in 1770 was organized as Botetourt County. In 1770 he moved to Mahanaim, in Dunkard's Bottom, in the region that in 1772 became Fincastle County. Although the efforts of his father to have him appointed surveyor of Botetourt County failed, Christian sat on that county court and became a justice of the peace of Fincastle County in January 1773. He won election to the House of Burgesses in 1773 and 1774 and was a member of the Committee of Public Claims in the sessions that met in May 1774 and June 1775 and of the Committee of Propositions and Grievances in 1774. At one of the final meetings of

the burgesses in June 1775, he was one of four members, and the only junior member and only representative from a southwestern county, appointed to complain to the governor about his flight from the capital and the removal of the public arms from the governor's palace.

Christian was a member and sometime chair of the Fincastle County Committee during 1775 and 1776 and also attended the second and third of the five Revolutionary Conventions. He missed the first probably because of the need to bring the militia into the field in preparation for Dunmore's War, in which he commanded a company in the autumn of 1774. The third Virginia Convention on 17 August 1775 elected Christian lieutenant colonel of the newly created 1st Virginia Regiment, stationed in Williamsburg for defense of the capital. In February 1776 the Continental Congress took the Virginia regiments into the new Continental army and renewed the appointment of field officers. After Christian's brother-in-law Patrick Henry declined to continue as colonel, Congress promoted Christian to that rank on 18 March 1776, but he resigned the appointment during the summer, perhaps in order to accept from the governor's Council command of an expedition to attack the Cherokee on the southwestern frontier. After Christian and his men had destroyed Cherokee towns along the Little Tennessee and Tellico Rivers, he negotiated a peace treaty during the winter.

In the summer of 1776 Christian was reportedly elected to the new Senate of Virginia to represent the counties of Botetourt and Fincastle, but because he was in the field commanding the expedition he did not attend. During and after the Revolutionary War he remained active in the militia defending the frontier and supporting the campaign in the southern states. Christian made one or more trips to Kentucky, including one in 1781 and 1782 to negotiate a treaty with Indians in the Ohio Valley.

Christian served for a time as a trustee of Liberty Hall Academy (later Washington and Lee University). He won election to a four-year term in the Senate of Virginia in 1780 representing Botetourt, Greenbrier, Kentucky, Montgomery, and Washington Counties. In November of that year Kentucky County became extinct, and beginning with the 1781 session Christian's district included the new counties of Fayette, Jefferson, and Lincoln. Before his term ended, the General Assembly elected him to the Council of State on 27 November 1783. Christian took his seat on 23 December but attended few meetings between then and 18 March 1784. When the assembly voted on 17 November of the latter year to replace two members, as the constitution required, he lost his seat. By then Christian was planning to move to the West, where he had been acquiring land for a decade.

In 1785 Christian sold Mahanaim and moved his wife, their six children, and an unrecorded number of his more than forty slaves to Beargrass Creek, near the site of present-day Louisville, Kentucky. Two sisters and their families already lived in Kentucky, and Christian's widowed mother set out with her son but found the journey too strenuous and turned back. Christian put some of his slaves to work in his saltworks, known as Bullitt's Lick or Saltsburg, near present-day Shepherdsville, Kentucky. One of the more experienced military men in the West, William Christian commanded an expedition across the Ohio River the following spring and was killed in a fight with Wabash Indians on 9 April 1786 near the site of present-day Jeffersonville, Indiana. His body was buried on his property at Beargrass Creek.

Hugh Blair Grigsby, "Colonel William Christian," *Washington and Lee University Historical Papers* 2 (1890): 52–56, with death date from gravestone inscription on 55; approximate birth year in Eliza Ramsey (niece) to Lyman C. Draper, 22 Feb. 1843, Draper MSS 8ZZ1; approximate marriage date in William Wirt Henry, *Patrick Henry: Life, Correspondence and Speeches* (1891), 1:122, and Augusta Co. Deed Book, 14:312–313; Christian letters in Draper MSS, in Campbell-Preston-Floyd Papers, LC, in Hugh Blair Grigsby Papers, VHS, and in Patrick Henry, Thomas Jefferson, Thomas Nelson, and Benjamin Harrison Executive Papers, all RG 3, LVA, the last printed in part in *Calendar of Virginia State Papers*, 2:24–25, 199–200, 349, 540–541, 572, 3:331–333, 398, 406–408, 424–425; numerous references in *Revolutionary Virginia* and *Journals of Council of State*; election to and removal from Council in *JHD*, Oct.–Dec. 1783 sess., 65, and 1784–1785 sess., 24; will in Miscellaneous Papers, Filson Historical Society, Louisville, Ky.; accounts of death in Samuel McDowell to Patrick Henry, 18 Apr. 1786, and John May to Patrick Henry, 19 Apr. 1786 (the latter abstracted in *Virginia Journal and Alexandria Advertiser*, 25 May 1786), both Patrick Henry Executive Papers, RG 3, LVA.

GAIL S. TERRY

CHRISTIAN, William Asbury (8 January 1866–1 May 1936), Methodist minister and writer, was born in Lynchburg and was the son of Cornelia Burton Christian and Edward Dunscomb Christian, a prominent lawyer. An elder brother, Frank Patteson Christian, served on two Special Courts of Appeals in the 1920s. After attending private schools and Lynchburg High School, Christian worked for four years in a Lynchburg railroad office. Entering Randolph-Macon College in 1886, he graduated with an A.B. in Latin in 1890. He received a B.D. from Vanderbilt University in 1892. Although most biographies note that Christian received a master's degree and an honorary doctorate of divinity, and although he was usually addressed as Doctor Christian, neither Randolph-Macon nor Vanderbilt record awarding him such higher degrees. On 18 October 1893 he married Anna Edith McMullan, of Madison County. They had two daughters.

In 1892 W. Asbury Christian joined the Virginia Conference of the Methodist Episcopal Church South. He was pastor of Richmond's Washington Street Methodist Episcopal Church for three years and the city's Asbury Methodist Church for one year and then served as minister at Centenary Methodist Church in Lynchburg until 1900 and at Berkley-Memorial Methodist Church in Norfolk from then until 1904. After pastorates at High Street Methodist Church in Petersburg (1904–1906) and Trinity Methodist Church in Newport News (1906–1908), Christian became presiding elder of the Richmond District in 1908. After four years in that office, he served as minister of Richmond's Union Station and Branch Memorial Methodist Church from 1912 to 1916.

As a clergyman, Christian vigorously championed traditional morality but welcomed innovative church policies. An outspoken advocate of prohibition, he held important committee positions in the Anti-Saloon League of Virginia for more than three decades. Before World War I, Christian deplored football as dangerous, condemned new dances as immodest, and later advocated state censorship of motion pictures. Believing that a woman's place was in the home, he denounced woman suffrage. By contrast,

Christian promoted social services at Richmond's Broad Street Methodist Church. He supported interdenominational cooperation among Richmond Protestants and in 1925 voted at the Virginia Conference for an unsuccessful plan to unify the two branches of the Methodist Church, which had split before the Civil War. Christian served on numerous boards and committees of the Virginia Conference (including two terms as president of the Board of Missions for 1907–1908 and 1908–1909 and as secretary of the Joint Board of Finance between 1914 and 1918). Several times he was a delegate to the quadrennial General Conference of the Methodist Episcopal Church South.

Christian made his most enduring mark with two books, *Lynchburg and Its People* (1900) and *Richmond: Her Past and Present* (1912). The books shared notable strengths and weaknesses. Filling a historical void for each city, the volumes long served as standard accounts of their communities. Christian recounted major events in a chronological framework and described such occasions as parades, conventions, mass meetings, and public funerals that were common in the nineteenth century. Admittedly favoring a historical approach that identified achievements and recognized heroic deeds, he repeatedly recited episodes of business and political success yet did not ignore human foibles or institutional failures. Christian often quoted primary documents at length and also depicted such community tragedies as epidemics, floods, and fires. Largely confining his accounts to facts, he praised individual character, acts of collective generosity, technological improvements, and evidence of community progress, and he occasionally attempted to characterize the corporate mood of each city during specific historical periods.

By addressing social, economic, and political developments, Christian intended to write comprehensive histories of the two cities, but he devoted little attention to women, African Americans, ethnic groups, and industrial workers. Reflecting the racism of his time, he characterized Native Americans as savages and endorsed segregation of whites and blacks. He offered little explanation or analysis in enumerating important episodes. Though clearly based on extensive research, both of his urban histories lacked notes and bibliographies. Despite these flaws, *Lynchburg and Its People* and *Richmond: Her Past and Present* contain valuable information and remain useful resources. A similar statement cannot be made about Christian's *Marah: A Story of Old Virginia*, a melodramatic historical novel published in 1903. Preoccupied with celebrating Virginia's antebellum social order, Christian created a convoluted, sentimental plot to illustrate the perceived social and political horrors of the Civil War and Reconstruction.

In 1916 Christian began his career as an educator by accepting the position of Richmond commissioner for Emory University. Two years later his Anti-Saloon League ally, James Cannon, selected Christian to succeed him as president of Blackstone Female Institute, a secondary school and junior college. Christian allowed a new student council to acquire significant responsibility over student behavior and social events, and the college reached an unprecedented level of enrollment. Two devastating fires, in 1920 and 1922, requiring reconstruction of large buildings, dealt blows to the school's financial health, but it nevertheless won accreditation from the State Board of Education and in 1922 amended its charter under a new name, the Blackstone College for Girls. In 1920 Cannon began complaining of Christian's performance as president, and early in 1924 he let it be known that the president had lost his support, reportedly because he was insufficiently industrious at raising money. Later that year Christian resigned.

Resuming his ministry, Christian was pastor of Richmond's Barton Heights Methodist Church from 1924 to 1928, followed by one year at Monumental Methodist Church in Portsmouth, one year at the Martinsville Methodist Church, and one year at Berryman Methodist Church in Richmond. A conference evangelist between 1932 and 1934, he retired sometime after the Virginia Conference's annual meeting in October 1934. William Asbury Christian died in Richmond on 1 May 1936 and was buried in Spring Hill Cemetery, in Lynchburg. On 2 June 1937 his family had his body reinterred in Richmond's Hollywood Cemetery.

Biographies in John J. Lafferty, *Sketches and Portraits of the Virginia Conference, Twentieth Century Edition* (1901), 391, 393 (por. on 246), Bruce, Tyler, and Morton, *History of Virginia*, 5:59, and Bernard J. Henley, "W. Asbury Christian: Minister-Prohibitionist-Historian," *Richmond Quarterly* 4 (winter 1981): 51–52; birth date in Christian family Bible records (1842–1887), VHS; BVS Marriage Register, Madison Co.; David W. C. Bearr, *Scholars for Blackstone* (1992), 33–37 (por. on 32); Bearr, *Blackstone College History* (1994), 28–32; BVS Death Certificate, Richmond City; obituaries in *Lynchburg Daily Advance* and *Richmond News Leader*, both 1 May 1936, *Lynchburg News, New York Times*, and *Richmond Times-Dispatch*, all 2 May 1936, and *Richmond Christian Advocate*, 14 May 1936; editorial tributes in *Richmond Times-Dispatch*, 2 May 1936, and *Lynchburg Daily Advance*, 4 May 1936; memorial in Virginia Methodist Conference *Annual* (1936), 67–68.

SAMUEL C. SHEPHERD JR.

CHRISTIAN, William Steptoe (26 December 1830–10 December 1910), Confederate army officer and temperance organization leader, was born in Middlesex County and was the son of Elizabeth Robinson Steptoe Christian and Richard Allen Christian, a physician who in 1838 became a Baptist minister. His elder brother Joseph Christian served on the Virginia Supreme Court of Appeals. Christian attended local preparatory schools and in 1848 received an A.B. from Columbian College (later George Washington University), in Washington, D.C. He graduated from Jefferson Medical College, in Philadelphia, in 1851 and returned to Middlesex County, where he began practicing medicine at Urbanna. On 11 January 1853 in Halifax County, North Carolina, Christian married Helen Elizabeth Steptoe, a cousin a few years older than he. They had two daughters and four sons, two of whom died in infancy, before her death on 6 December 1898. Christian married Alice Taylor Woodward, of Middlesex County, on 10 July 1900. They had no children.

In 1859 Christian raised a cavalry company, known as the Middlesex Light Dragoons, which became Company C of the 55th Regiment Virginia Infantry. He proved to be a courageous soldier and effective officer, as demonstrated by his promotions—to captain on 2 June 1861, to major on 1 May 1862, to lieutenant colonel on 18 March 1863 (to rank from 23 June 1862), and to colonel in command of the regiment on 23 June 1863 (to rank from 2 May). He was wounded in the right thigh at Frayser's Farm on 30 June 1862, and at Chancellorsville on 2 May 1863, a rifle ball broke his upraised sword and drove the tip into his body.

Christian had recovered sufficiently from the latter wound to participate in the Army of Northern Virginia's advance into Pennsylvania that summer. A letter written to his wife from camp, dated 28 June 1863 and later found on the battlefield at Gettysburg, described the foraging expeditions of the Confederate invaders, including the capture of terrified African Americans to be sent to Virginia and enslavement. The text of his recovered letter was published in a collection of war documents in 1864, and historians regularly cite it in books about the Gettysburg campaign.

During the army's retreat, Christian and many under his command were captured in Maryland on 14 July 1863 and imprisoned at Johnson's Island, Ohio. There Christian worked long hours as the superintendent of the prison's hospital and, as a physician, persuaded the authorities to permit prisoners to secure clean drinking water from Lake Erie. While there he composed a long poem, entitled "The Past," describing in rhyme his life and his love for his wife and family. Christian was exchanged on 3 March 1864 and returned to his command.

Lingering effects from his wounds and his desire to serve in the army's medical department led Christian to resign his commission in March 1865. Soon thereafter he joined his wife and children in North Carolina, where they had sought safety as refugees. Christian practiced medicine there for eighteen months and rebuilt his finances before returning to Malvern Hill, his house in Middlesex County. Affectionately known as Doctor Billy, he was a highly respected local physician who took pride in his moniker as a country doctor.

A teetotaler Baptist and Sunday school superintendent, Christian joined the Independent Order of Good Templars, an international organization advocating total abstinence from alcohol. He represented his local lodge at the 1876 session of the Grand Lodge of Virginia and to his surprise was elected Grand Worthy Chief Templar, or state head of the order. Membership increased during his tenure, but few who joined remained for long, a circumstance that forced the state organization to devote much of its energies and resources to organizing and reorganizing lodges. More than half of the 600 lodges established in Virginia between 1867 and 1886, including Christian's lodge in Middlesex, had closed by the latter year.

Christian headed the Virginia organization through 1881, which were years of controversy within the larger order. Many northern and British members believed the order's inclusive principles mandated admitting African Americans, a notion white southern Good Templars resisted. Attempting to smooth over the controversy in Virginia, Christian emphasized the order's nonpolitical character and worked effectively with George White Hawxhurst, a onetime Radical Republican who was the Virginia order's longtime Grand Worthy Secretary. Christian backed the compromise, segregated Dual Grand Lodge instituted in Richmond on 4 October 1880. Although he was one of the Virginia representatives to the 1878 meeting in Minneapolis of the Right Worthy Grand Lodge of the World, he played no part in the schism over race and did not long remain active in the organization, which the Prohibition Party supplanted.

Christian became a member of the Medical Society of Virginia in 1886 and was selected as the society's orator in 1888 and 1903. He did not attend the medical society's meeting in 1904 because he was caring for an ill relative, but the society waived its unwritten rule that candidates for office had to be present and unanimously elected him president. The next year, the society marked his fifty-four years in medical practice by naming him an honorary member. In 1909 he was secretary of Middlesex County's board of health.

A member of the United Confederate Veterans, Christian served at least one term as commander of the veterans' camp at Saluda. Probably at the 1907 veterans' reunion in Richmond, he recounted to James Dinkins, of New Orleans, a story about thirteen slave body-servants who had stayed with their masters at the Johnson's Island prison camp. Dinkins subsequently quoted Christian's recollection in articles that asserted the loyalty of the slaves to the Confederacy, a story that latter-day partisans have kept alive.

In 1890 Christian became superintendent of Middlesex County's public schools and served, except for a portion of one term, until 1909. William Steptoe Christian died at Malvern Hill on 10 December 1910 and was buried by the Urbanna Masonic Lodge, of which he was a past master, at the family cemetery at Hewick, an estate north of Urbanna.

William Christopher Hight, "Dr. William Steptoe Christian," in Jessie M. DeBusk et al., comps., *Family Histories of Middlesex County, Virginia* (1982), 71–73 (including por. and reprint of memorial by Walter H. Ryland, editor of the *Urbanna Southside Sentinel*); first marriage in David B. Gammon, *Marriage Records of Halifax County, North Carolina, 1817–1868* (1997), 15; second marriage in Middlesex Co. Marriage Register, 3:204; Compiled Service Records; Richard O'Sullivan, *55th Virginia Infantry* (1989), with incorrect death date of 15 Dec. 1910 on 112; letter to wife, 28 June 1863, published in Frank Moore, ed., *The Rebellion Record: A Diary of American Events* (1864), 7:325; Christian, "The Past," VHS; Grand Lodge of Virginia of the Independent Order of Good Templars, *Proceedings* (1879), 4–10, 30–31; ibid. (1880), 4–7; ibid. (1889), 53; ibid. (1892), 15, 35; presidential address "The Country Doctor" in Medical Society of Virginia, *Transactions, 1905* (1906), 9–20; James Dinkins, "The Negroes as Slaves," *SHSP* 35 (1907): 62–64; obituaries in *Richmond Times-Dispatch*, 12 Dec. 1910, *Fredericksburg Free Lance*, 13 Dec. 1910, *Virginia Medical Semi-Monthly* 15 (1911): 431–432, *Confederate Veteran* 19 (1911): 350, and Medical Society of Virginia, *Transactions, 1911* (1912), 236–237.

JOHN T. KNEEBONE

CHRYSLER, Jean Esther Outland (15 September 1921–26 January 1982), art collector, was born in Norfolk and was the daughter of Lida Ann Maddox Outland and Grover Cleveland Outland, an insurance salesman who later served in the House of Delegates. Educated in Norfolk's public schools, she received a B.S. from the College of William and Mary in 1942 and then taught physical education at the Norfolk branch of William and Mary (later Old Dominion University). In Norfolk on 13 January 1945 she married Walter Percy Chrysler, the divorced namesake son of the founder of the Chrysler Corporation who as a lieutenant junior grade in the United States Naval Reserve had been stationed in Norfolk. They had no children. The Chryslers divided the first years of their marriage between a residence in New York City and a large estate near Warrenton known as North Wales. There they raised thoroughbred horses for the remainder of the decade, and Jean Chrysler began breeding prize Chihuahuas.

Chrysler shared her husband's enthusiasm for the visual arts, especially sculpture, fine glass, and paintings. She purchased contemporary works by such artists as Frank Auerback, Milton Avery, Michael Goldberg, and Wolf Kahn and eventually gave her collection to the College of William and Mary, where it became part of the holdings of the Muscarelle Museum of Art. In 1963 Chrysler donated forty-two modern paintings and sculptures to the Norfolk Museum of Arts and Sciences as a tribute to her parents and in 1965, 1967, and 1973 made additional gifts to that institution. After Walter Chrysler established a museum in Provincetown, Massachusetts, in 1958 to house his growing art collection, she helped to organize and catalog the extensive holdings of books, exhibition catalogs, and clippings that became the foundation of the museum's reference library. Her childhood love of books blossomed in this role, and later, when the collection moved to Norfolk, she sharpened her bibliographic skills with further study at William and Mary. Working part-time over about twenty years with the reference collection in both Provincetown and Norfolk, she arranged and cataloged approximately 44,000 titles.

Chrysler and her husband had placed a large number of artworks with the Norfolk Museum on long-term loan by November 1967, and Walter Chrysler's decision in 1970 to transfer his extensive collection of paintings, sculpture, decorative arts, and art glass from the Provincetown museum to the Norfolk Museum, which was renamed the Chrysler Museum at Norfolk (and later the Chrysler Museum of Art), represented a seminal event in the city's cultural history. Jean Chrysler's influence and fondness for her native city reportedly proved decisive in the relocation of the collection. Although the Chryslers continued to maintain a residence in New York City, they spent an increasing amount of time at their house in Norfolk.

Chrysler worked to enhance the cultural and intellectual life of her hometown. She served on the board of trustees of the Chrysler Museum from 1977 until her death, and she became a devoted supporter of the Virginia Opera. Tireless in her efforts at fund-raising and securing innovative new productions, she served on the board of trustees of the Virginia Opera Association, Inc., and was secretary of its executive committee. She once noted that she thought she could help Norfolk improve its quality of life by putting her "energies into the opera and museum because I believe that these two organizations are doing most to bring local respect and national recognition to the city." Although her efforts to establish a collection of books, magazines, and recordings focusing on opera were cut short by her death, her most visible and lasting personal legacy was the art research library that bears her name at the Chrysler Museum. Growing to include more than 80,000 volumes by the end of the twentieth century, the library comprises art books, exhibition and auction catalogs, and historic and current periodicals, as well as the renowned art library of the London art dealer M. Knoedler and Company. The library also contains important archival material documenting the early commercial history of Norfolk and the region. An integral part of the museum, the Jean Outland Chrysler Library has been recognized repeatedly as one of the top such facilities in the South.

After suffering a stroke, Jean Esther Outland Chrysler died in a Norfolk hospital on 26 January 1982. She was buried in the Chrysler family mausoleum in Sleepy Hollow Cemetery, in Tarrytown, New York, where her husband's remains were also buried after his death on 17 September 1988.

Biography in *Norfolk Virginian-Pilot*, 29 Jan. 1982 (por.); biographical information in vertical file and video documentary at Chrysler Museum of Art, Norfolk; personal information provided by brother Grover Cleveland Outland, sister Nancy Outland Chandler, and Edythe C. Harrison (all 2003); *Norfolk Virginian-Pilot*, 11, 14 Jan. 1945; *An Exhibition of the Jean Outland Chrysler Collection, February 26–March 26, 1963, Norfolk Museum of Arts and Sciences* (1963), including cover por. by Christopher Clark; Vincent Curcio, *Chrysler: The Life and Times of an Automotive Genius* (2000), esp. 117, 454–455, 623–624, 635, 644, 658–661; obituaries in *Norfolk Ledger-Star, Norfolk Virginian-Pilot, Richmond News Leader*, and *Richmond Times-Dispatch*, all 27 Jan. 1982, and *Washington Post*, 31 Jan. 1982; editorial tribute in *Norfolk Ledger-Star*, 30 Jan. 1982 (quotation); memorial in *Chrysler Museum* 12 (Mar. 1982): 1.

WILLIAM S. RODNER

CHRYSLER, Walter Percy (27 May 1909–17 September 1988), art collector, was born in Oelwein, Iowa, and was the son of Walter Percy Chrysler and Della Viola Forker Chrysler. In 1912 the family settled in Flint, Michigan, where his father entered the burgeoning automotive industry. They moved again in 1920 to New York, and five years later the elder Chrysler founded his eponymous automobile company, which he quickly built into one of the largest corporations in the United States. Chrysler received his education at private schools in New York and Connecticut. As a child he developed an interest in collecting, moving from toy banks to stamps, coins, and eventually fine art. While attending the Hotchkiss School, in Lakeville, Connecticut, he made his first major purchase, a Pierre-Auguste Renoir watercolor featuring a small female nude, which his outraged dormitory master destroyed. Interested in the aesthetics of books, Chrysler printed four titles at age fifteen under the imprimatur of the York Publishing House.

Walter P. Chrysler Jr., as he was known even after the death of his father, matriculated at Dartmouth College in the autumn of 1929 but left without declaring a major at the end of his sophomore year. In the spring of 1930 he joined Nelson Aldrich Rockefeller in publishing a limited-edition arts magazine entitled *The Five Arts*. In September of that year Chrysler founded Cheshire House, Inc., a short-lived publishing concern that won the prestigious Grolier Award for its finely crafted editions of classic works by Dante, Shakespeare, and Virgil. Chrysler then toured Europe, where he purportedly met many avant-garde artists. After his return to the United States, he joined the family corporation as director of the newly created Airtemp division, which manufactured air-conditioning for buildings and Chrysler automobiles. Between 1935 and 1953 he also served as president of the Chrysler Building in New York. In that city on 29 April 1938 he married Marguerite Price Sykes. They separated the following year and divorced in Reno, Nevada, on 4 December 1939.

During the 1930s Chrysler began to amass a significant collection of European and American modern art, including works by Henri-Émile-Benoît Matisse and Pablo Picasso. He also became involved with building the collections of the Museum of Modern Art and was the first chair of the museum's library committee. His father's death in 1940 left him with a multi-million-dollar inheritance and enabled him to pursue his collecting on an even grander scale.

Chrysler's initial ties to Virginia date from 1941, when he purchased North Wales, a sprawling estate near Warrenton, on which to start raising thoroughbred horses. That same year the Virginia Museum of Fine Arts mounted the first public exhibition of his entire collection, which caused a stir among conservative Richmonders unaccustomed to the formal experimentation characteristic of much modern art. After the United States entered World War II later that year, Chrysler worked for the Department of Commerce for several months before joining the United States Naval Reserve. Commissioned a lieutenant junior grade in April 1942, he was stationed in Norfolk and in Key West, Florida, before resigning in December 1944. On 13 January 1945 Chrysler married Jean Esther Outland, a Norfolk teacher whom he had met while stationed there. They had no children. Jean Chrysler shared her husband's enthusiasm for art collecting and horses, although his involvement in breeding and racing waned by the end of the decade. The Chryslers divided their time between an apartment in New York City and their North Wales estate.

In the postwar years, Chrysler's collecting expanded with forays into antiquities, Old Masters, non-Western art, art nouveau and art deco decorative arts, and glass. He purchased and sold works, sometimes from unscrupulous dealers and without professional advice, more with an eye toward their potential rather than prevailing value. Shrewdly, he realized that critical tastes were subject to change and that underappreciated artists often came to be viewed in a more favorable light, given enough time. "I have been fortunate in being able to have the time and the desire to make my own decisions as a collector," Chrysler stated in 1980, "and I have based my decisions on my own understandings and my own response to the artist's total *oeuvre*."

Chrysler sold North Wales in 1957 and by deaccessioning selected pieces to finance the venture purchased an abandoned Protestant church in Provincetown, Massachusetts, the following year for use as a museum to exhibit and store his collection. He donated part of his collection to his new museum outright but kept many works in his personal possession. The Chrysler Art Museum began to garner widespread attention, not all of it favorable. In 1962, when the collection of 187 paintings traveled to the National Gallery of Canada, in Ottawa, the newly formed Art Dealers Association of America charged that many of the works were misattributed and given questionable provenances. In a separate controversy earlier that year, Picasso had identified two works from the Chrysler collection as inauthentic before a major retrospective exhibition of the artist's work. Undaunted, Chrysler continued acquiring works for himself and the museum and befriended many younger, emerging artists, including Andy Warhol.

Increasingly dissatisfied with Provincetown's lack of support for the museum, Chrysler negotiated in 1970 to donate its contents, but not his personal collection, to the Norfolk Museum of Arts and Sciences. His wife had made several gifts to her hometown museum beginning in 1963, and he had lent approximately seventy-five paintings since 1967 and served on the board of trustees since 1969. In exchange for Chrysler's donation, the institution was renamed the Chrysler Museum at Norfolk (later the Chrysler Museum of Art), the museum committed to construct a new wing to house the expanded collection, and a recently completed municipal performing arts facility in downtown Norfolk was christened Chrysler Hall. To cement his new relationship with the city, Chrysler and his wife took up residence in a house near the museum. He served as the museum's director from 1971 to 1976 and afterward chaired the board of trustees until 1984, when he became chairman emeritus. The transition during his early tenure was not smooth. Several museum trustees and staff members raised concerns about the authenticity and value of the donation during the initial negotiations, and strife with museum trustees continued for several years. After retiring as director, Chrysler remained involved in the museum's day-to-day affairs. The Metropolitan

Arts Congress of Tidewater Virginia, Inc., named him its First Citizen of the Arts in 1980, and in 1985 Old Dominion University recognized his contributions to the region and state by awarding him an honorary doctorate.

Chrysler produced or bankrolled several Broadway plays, including *New Faces of 1952*, the musical revue in which Eartha Kitt scored her first major success, and the film *The Joe Louis Story* (1953). In 1980 Chrysler founded in Norfolk the Music Library and Musical Instruments Museum, a research collection of 10,000 volumes and 400,000 recordings donated to the Virginia Opera Association, Inc., at his death and then broken up. He eventually gave many artworks from his personal collection to the Chrysler Museum, but a will that would have bequeathed much of the remaining art and most of his personal fortune and family trust monies as well was left unsigned at the time Walter Percy Chrysler died of cancer in a Norfolk hospital on 17 September 1988. He was buried in the family mausoleum at Sleepy Hollow Cemetery, in Tarrytown, New York, with his wife, who had died on 26 January 1982. Chrysler had no children, and his personal collection, then valued at about $15 million, passed to a nephew and subsequently was dispersed at auction.

Chrysler's legacy to the commonwealth is enormous. Through his collecting, he brought modern art to the serious attention of many Virginians for the first time. His largesse catapulted Norfolk's local museum into national and international prominence. Moreover, his interest in baroque art, nineteenth-century French academic paintings, art nouveau and art deco artworks, and glass of all types and periods proved to be prescient. Though mixed during his lifetime, Chrysler's reputation has since undergone a steady rehabilitation, and after his death he was acknowledged as a true art collector.

Biographical information in Vincent Curcio, *Chrysler: The Life and Times of an Automotive Genius* (2000), esp. 117, 443, 454, 623–624, 644, 658–661, and in vertical files at Chrysler Museum of Art, Norfolk; 5 Sept. 1964 interview in Archives of American Art, Smithsonian Institution, Washington, D.C.; *New York Times*, 10 Sept. 1930, 30 Apr. 1938, 5 Dec. 1939, 11 Aug. 1991; *New Yorker* (28 May 1932), 12; *Norfolk Virginian-Pilot*, 14 Jan. 1945, 27, 28 Aug. 1970, 9, 10 Feb., 10 Mar. 1971; *Life* (2 Nov. 1962), 80–87 (pors.);

ArtNews 75 (Feb. 1976): 56–62; *American Artist* 44 (Nov. 1980): 12, 92 (quotation); *Norfolk Virginian-Pilot and Ledger-Star*, 9 Apr. 1989; *Collection of Walter P. Chrysler, Jr.* (1941); obituaries in *Norfolk Virginian-Pilot and Ledger-Star*, 18 Sept. 1988, and *New York Times, Norfolk Virginian-Pilot, Richmond News Leader, Richmond Times-Dispatch*, and *Washington Post*, all 19 Sept. 1988; editorial tribute in *Norfolk Virginian-Pilot*, 20 Sept. 1988; memorial in Chrysler Museum *Bulletin* 18 (Oct. 1988): 1–2 (cover por.).

ROBERT WOJTOWICZ

CHURCH, Merton Elbridge (14 February 1858–16 September 1931), business and civic leader, was born in the town of Derby Line in Orleans County, Vermont, and was the son of Joshua Church and Mary Elizabeth Cobb Church. His father, a native of Quebec, served in Company H of the 15th Regiment Vermont Infantry and died during the Civil War. Until his mother married George S. Spofford about 1870, Church lived with various relatives in Quebec, Vermont, and Massachusetts. As a schoolboy, he worked at a variety of trades from farming to operating a magic lantern at temperance lodges, and about 1880 he completed an apprenticeship in a drugstore in Fitchburg, Massachusetts.

Church's mother and stepfather moved to Fairfax County about 1876, and he followed in 1880. He and his stepfather opened a drugstore, Spofford and Church, in Herndon in the latter year and another in Falls Church in 1886. Known throughout his residence in Virginia as Doctor Church, he was president of the Virginia Pharmaceutical Association in 1892. Church represented Virginia at the National Pure Food Congress in March 1898 and sat on the conference's executive committee and Committee on Credentials.

Church married Carrie Belle Northrup, a New Jersey native, on 11 February 1884. They had one son and one daughter. His wife's father owned the Eagle House Hotel and an undertaking business in Falls Church, to which town he moved after his marriage. Church's name then began to appear on county deeds as a title examiner or notary public. He had entered the real estate business by 1889 and two years later was one of ten men who purchased Home Hill, a valuable ten-acre property in the center of Falls Church. About the same time Church joined a group of men in developing the nearby Sherwood subdivision. On land he acquired from his in-laws in 1910 he also developed an African American community on the outskirts of the segregated town. As part of his real estate ventures, he engaged in insurance and loan enterprises.

In 1888 Church joined other town residents in establishing a community telephone service and added telegraph service when he signed a contract with Western Union to serve nearby Camp Alger during the Spanish-American War. The Falls Church Telephone and Telegraph Company, with Church as president and general manager, served localities in Arlington, Fairfax, and Loudoun Counties by 1925. He was also president and director of the Arlington Electric Company, created on 4 April 1911 to provide electricity to Falls Church and parts of Alexandria (after 1920 Arlington) and Fairfax Counties. Church was a director and secretary of the Falls Church and Potomac Railway Company, and he became president of the Arlington and Fairfax Railway Company, from which he retired a few months before his death. In the 1920s he was a director of the Lee Highway Association, which promoted and raised funds to construct a highway from Washington, D.C., to San Diego, California.

By the 1920s Church was at the center of nearly every important local enterprise. He had become an officer in several banks, including the National Bank of Fairfax, the Arlington Trust Company, and the Falls Church Bank and Trust Corporation, of which he was first vice president. He published the *Falls Church Monitor* from late in the 1890s until he sold the Republican newspaper in January 1901, and he was founding president of the Fairfax County Chamber of Commerce in 1925. A member of Crossman Methodist Episcopal Church, of which he was a Sunday school superintendent, Church was also active in the Methodist organization Temperance, Prohibition, and Public Morals and became its treasurer in 1929.

Merton Elbridge Church was an honorary president of the Virginia Pharmaceutical Association when he died of pernicious anemia at his son's home in Falls Church on 16 September 1931. He was buried in Oakwood Cemetery, in Falls Church. He made bequests of $1,000 each to his church, the Methodist temperance organization, and the Council of Religious Education in Virginia and of $7,000 to American University, in Washington, D.C., of which he had been a board member since 1922.

Biographies in *A Virginia Village: Historical Sketch of Falls Church and the Old Colonial Church* (1904), 89–92 (por. on 89), and Bruce, Tyler, and Morton, *History of Virginia*, 6:198–199; birth and death dates from BVS Death Certificate, Falls Church; BVS Marriage Register, Fairfax Co.; Merton Elbridge Church Papers at Mary Riley Styles Public Library, Falls Church (including autobiographical notes with birth date), and at UVA; Melvin Lee Steadman Jr., *Falls Church by Fence and Fireside* (1964); Nan Netherton et al., *Fairfax County, Virginia: A History* (1978); *Falls Church Historical News and Notes* (1993); Bradley E. Gernand and Nan Netherton, *Falls Church: A Virginia Village Revisited* (2000); Fairfax Co. Will Book, 14:17–20; obituaries in *Herndon News-Observer* and *Washington Post*, both 17 Sept. 1931, *Fairfax Herald* and *Richmond Times-Dispatch*, both 18 Sept. 1931, and *Virginia Pharmacist* 15 (1931): 231.

RUTH PRESTON ROSE

CHURCH, Randolph Warner (9 March 1907–20 December 1984), librarian, was born in Lynchburg and was the son of Samuel Robbins Church, an attorney and former Washington, D.C., judge, and Mildred Hannah Parker Church, whose interest in literature and poetry may have influenced her son's choices in education and career. Church graduated from the city's E. C. Glass High School and in 1929 earned a B.S. from the University of Virginia, where he made the dean's list while working part-time in the library. He received a master's degree from the university's English department in 1932. In a thesis entitled "The Alcoholism and Opiumism of Edgar A. Poe," Church contended that the poet had not written his greatest works while under the influence of drink or drugs. After receiving a B.A. in library science from Emory University in 1933, he returned to the University of Virginia, where he worked in the library's reference department and taught in its summer library school.

On 11 January 1934 in Charlottesville, Church married Elizabeth Lewis Gochnauer. They had three sons and one daughter. In September 1934 he moved to Richmond to become assistant state librarian. Church arrived during a stressful time for the Virginia State Library (later the Library of Virginia). Severe budget problems during the Great Depression placed strains on the library and its limited resources, as did reduced staffing during World War II and increased demands for research resources. Church played a major role in planning for the construction of a new state library building, which began in 1938. He also assisted with the simultaneous restructuring of the staff and responsibilities of the library's component divisions in preparation for the move into the new building two years later. Church explained the lessons learned during the process to the community of professional librarians in articles published in the *American Archivist* in 1943 and *College and Research Libraries* in 1944.

On 1 January 1947 Church became acting state librarian after Wilmer Lee Hall asked to step down to direct the library's new publications division. Appointed state librarian effective 1 March, Church served for twenty-five years. Widely respected, he was president of the Southeastern Library Association for the 1956–1958 term. Church retained his interest in Poe, significantly improved the library's holdings of Poe imprints and works on the poet, and took pride in the agreement the library had with the Poe Museum in Richmond to house the museum's collection of Poe's works.

The state library grew significantly during Church's long association with it. The staff consisted of about twenty members and had an annual budget of approximately $41,000 in 1934. When Church retired almost thirty-eight years later, the staff numbered more than one hundred, the budget was more than $3,000,000, and the collection had grown in size from about 273,000 to more than 500,000 volumes. Manuscript and archival records increased tenfold in number and were estimated in 1972 at about 15,000,000 items. Of principal importance was the acquisition of new books and materials useful for genealogical research. During the decades before and after World War II the library acquired one of the country's finest collections of English local history. The state library's staff assisted localities in establishing and improving public libraries, and by the time of Church's retirement nearly 90 percent of Virginia's population had access to public library services. Church and the State Library Board offered space and support for William James Barrow's pioneering research, sponsored by the Council on Library Resources, Inc., into the causes and prevention of book-paper deterioration. Church edited the resulting research reports, which the library published in two volumes. The library also formed a film collection and in 1962 began showing and lending educational films to public and school libraries in Virginia. During the 1950s and 1960s the library cooperated with the Virginia Colonial Records Project to survey European repositories and obtain microfilm of manuscripts and archival records pertaining to the colonial period of Virginia's history. Perhaps the most conspicuous achievement of Church's tenure, aside from the addition of four floors to the top of the state library building in 1971, was his creation in the summer of 1951 of *Virginia Cavalcade*, a quarterly illustrated magazine of Virginia history and culture.

During the 1960s the library's publications program languished, organizational and personnel problems vexed the board members, and once-amiable working relationships between Church and some of the library's senior staff members deteriorated as he became increasingly prickly and difficult to work with. Reports also circulated that some board members were impatient with Church's reluctance to expand the library's role in the distribution of federal aid to Virginia public libraries. In October 1971 the State Library Board set the retirement age for the state librarian and other senior administrators at sixty-five, and early in the following year Church announced his retirement effective 30 June 1972. It was well known that Church did not wish to retire, and he continued to work in the library for several years preparing an annotated calendar of more than 1,700 petitions submitted to the General Assembly during the American Revolution. The library published the volume in 1984.

Church served on Richmond's school board from August 1944 to June 1952 and became chair in 1946 after the city council reorganized the school administration. He was president of the Virginia Association of School Trustees

for the 1947–1948 term and helped produce a manual for school board members. In 1952 Church was elected to Richmond's city council. He served one two-year term but did not seek reelection.

Elizabeth Gochnauer Church died on 22 July 1976, and Randolph Warner Church died in a Richmond nursing home on 20 December 1984. They were buried in the University of Virginia Cemetery, in Charlottesville.

Feature articles in *Richmond News Leader*, 21 Apr. 1948, 28 Sept. 1961, 30 June 1972, and *Virginia Librarian* 18/19 (fall–winter 1971/spring 1972): 1, 10–11 (the latter also printed in *Virginia State Library News* 4 [May 1972]: 1–2); BVS Marriage Register, Charlottesville; biographical files, Richmond Public Library; official Virginia State Library correspondence (including Church's school board and city council papers) and Publicity Scrapbooks, RG 35, LVA; principal professional publications include Church, "The Relationship Between Archival Agencies and Libraries," *American Archivist* 6 (1943): 145–150, "A Library Reorganizes through Building," *College and Research Libraries* 5 (1944): 315–321, 334, and *Virginia Legislative Petitions: Bibliography, Calendar, and Abstracts from Original Sources, 6 May 1776–21 June 1782* (1984); State Library Board activities, 1962–1969, documented in C. Sterling Hutcheson Papers, Acc. 32432, LVA; retirement tribute by John Melville Jennings in *Virginia Cavalcade* 22 (summer 1972): 4–5 (por.); Sandra Gioia Treadway and Edward D. C. Campbell, Jr., eds., *Common Wealth: Treasures from the Collections of the Library of Virginia* (1997), 36–46 (por. on 42); obituaries in *Richmond News Leader* and *Richmond Times-Dispatch*, both 22 Dec. 1984.

BRENT TARTER

CHURCHHILL, William (bap. 2 December 1649–November 1710), member of the Council, was baptized (and probably born) in the parish of North Aston, Oxfordshire, England. He was the youngest of eleven children of John Churchill and Dorothy Churchill (whose maiden name is not recorded), but little else is known of his family, early years, or education. Autographs indicate that he spelled his surname with a double *h*. Churchhill immigrated to Virginia, possibly when he was a young adult and in the capacity of a factor, or agent, for an established merchant. His name appears in Virginia records for the first time on 1 February 1675, when he witnessed a document in Middlesex County. On 1 November of that year Churchhill was appointed an undersheriff of the county. He held that office again in 1677.

Churchhill practiced law in the colony. He may have continued to operate as a factor for London merchants for as long as a decade after arriving in Virginia, but he also hired his own factor to assist in collecting debts that other county residents owed him. His business consisted largely of importing merchandise and servants and exporting tobacco. His success in commerce led him into public office. Churchhill became a justice of the peace on 14 October 1687 and remained a member of the Middlesex County Court until 1705. He was placed on a committee in 1691 to acquire land for a courthouse in the proposed town of Urbanna and the next year purchased a half-acre lot there. Twelve years later, having firmly established his own trade connections, he opposed developing the new town. Within a decade after his arrival in Virginia, Churchhill began acquiring land in the lower end of Middlesex County and by the end of the century numbered among those with the largest landholdings in the county. In 1704 he owned 1,950 acres in Middlesex County, and at the time of his death he owned 2,280 acres in Richmond County as well. His Middlesex County plantation was known later, and perhaps during his lifetime, as Bushy Park. The inventory of his estate, returned four years after his death, recorded sixty-one slaves. Unlike some of his contemporaries who held slaves, Churchhill had some of his slaves' children baptized.

Churchhill married at least twice. A 1683 document records his wife's first name, Mary, but not her maiden name. Churchhill's wife was mentioned but not named in a document relating to an event in November 1693. It is not clear whether that instance referred to Mary Churchhill or to a second wife whose existence is not otherwise known; nor is it certain that later assertions that Churchhill had two daughters during the seventeenth century are correct. On 5 October 1703 Churchhill married Elizabeth Armistead Wormeley after executing a detailed marriage contract to secure the property that she and her children had inherited from her father, John Armistead, formerly a member of the governor's Council, and her first husband, Ralph Wormeley, of Rosegill in Middlesex County, who had also been a member of the Council and sec-

retary of the colony when he died in 1701. Their one son and two daughters included Priscilla Churchhill, who married first the namesake son of the land baron Robert "King" Carter and then John Lewis, a member of the Council. Following his marriage, Churchhill undertook the management of Rosegill, and his influence in the county and colony increased through his alliances with these prominent Virginia families.

Churchhill won election to the House of Burgesses for the sessions that met in the springs of 1691 and 1692. He took part in drafting several bills and petitions, including a petition to the Crown for chartering a college in the colony, and served on the important committee that apportioned the public levy. Churchhill was elected to the House again in the spring of 1704 to fill a vacancy for the sessions that met in the spring of that year and in the spring of the following year. On 20 April 1705, noting a recommendation from Governor Francis Nicholson, officials in London added Churchhill's name to the list of Council members in the commission of the new governor, Edward Nott. Churchhill took his seat on 15 August 1705 when Nott was sworn in as governor. Churchhill had a good attendance record as a member of the Council. He attended his last meeting in Williamsburg on 27 October 1710, shortly before his final, fatal illness.

By 1706 Churchhill was a colonel in the county militia. He became a vestryman of Christ Church Parish, in Middlesex County, on 2 June 1684 and several times was appointed warden for the chapel in the lower part of the county. When he wrote his will, Churchhill left £100 to Christ Church Parish with the stipulation that the ministers preach quarterly sermons against atheism, irreligion, swearing, cursing, fornication, adultery, and drunkenness and concluded, "This I would have done forever." He made another bequest to support the parish and two £10 bequests for the benefit of the poor in his native North Aston Parish and in Christ Church Parish in London.

William Churchhill dated his will on 8 November 1710 and died about two weeks later. Lieutenant Governor Alexander Spotswood reported on 15 December that Churchhill had by then been dead for about three weeks. Churchhill's will directed that he be buried without conspicuous ceremony. If his fatal illness, which he may have contracted while attending Council meetings in the capital, prevented him from returning home, he may have been buried in Williamsburg; otherwise he was probably buried at his residence in Middlesex County. At the beginning of his will and also in the body Churchhill quoted 2 Kings 20:1: "Set thine house in Order for thou Shall Dye and not Live."

Baptism in North Aston Parish Register, Oxfordshire Record Office, Eng., abstracted in *WMQ*, 2d ser., 4 (1924): 285; autograph letters dated 29 Aug. 1693 and 26 Aug. 1706 in Colonial Papers, RG 1, LVA; some family history in Charles Timothy Todhunter, *The Churchill Family Genealogy* (1988), 1:11–12, 16, 29, 32–35, and Roberta Churchill Crosby and Zelda Churchill Jackson, eds., *The History of the Churchill Family of Richmond County, Virginia* (1995), 1–4; Darrett B. Rutman and Anita H. Rutman, *A Place in Time: Middlesex County, Virginia, 1650–1750* (1984), 207–209, 217–224; first wife or wives mentioned in Middlesex Co. Deeds, Etc. (1679–1694), 125, and 5 Mar. 1694 document in Middlesex Co. Wills, Etc. (1675–1798), pt. 1 (pages not sequentially numbered); marriage to Elizabeth Armistead Wormeley in Christ Church Parish Register and Miscellaneous Material (1653–1821), 78, with marriage contract in Middlesex Co. Deed Book (1703–1720), 1–6; numerous references in Middlesex Co. Deed and Order Books (first reference in Virginia in Middlesex Co. Order Book, 1: fol. 27) and Christ Church Parish Vestry Book; appointment to Council in PRO CO 391/17, 364, and *Executive Journals of Council*, 3:23–24; will and estate inventory in Middlesex Co. Will Book, A:247–249 (quotations on 247), B:16–17; death reported in Alexander Spotswood to Board of Trade, 15 Dec. 1710, PRO CO 5/1316, fol. 238.

NANCY D. EGLOFF

CLAIBORNE, Augustine (3 April 1787–30 June 1839), member of the Convention of 1829–1830, was born in Brunswick County and was the son of Thomas Claiborne (1747–1811), later a member of the House of Representatives, and his first wife, Mary Clayton Claiborne. Among his six elder brothers were John Claiborne, a physician who served in the House of Representatives from 1805 until his death in 1808, and Thomas Claiborne (1780–1856), who from 1817 to 1819 represented a Tennessee district in Congress. Probably privately educated, Claiborne began practicing law in Brunswick and Greensville Counties in 1809 and by that year had moved to Greensville County, where

he was one of three attorneys holding licenses to practice before the Superior Court of Law. He handled a variety of routine legal cases involving land disputes and occasionally acted as court-appointed attorney. In September 1831 he successfully defended a slave charged with an unspecified felony.

In 1811 in Northampton County, North Carolina, Claiborne married Jane Eppes Fraser Blunt, a widow with one daughter. They had two daughters and four sons. During the War of 1812 Claiborne was commissioned captain of a cavalry troop and stationed at Norfolk in April and May 1814. On 18 May of the latter year he became lieutenant colonel of the 50th Regiment Virginia militia. Claiborne resigned his commission on 8 February 1819. He served from May 1818 until December 1821 as a Greensville County school commissioner.

In May 1829 Claiborne won election in a fourteen-candidate field to the third of four seats representing the counties of Greensville, Isle of Wight, Prince George, Southampton, Surry, and Sussex in a convention summoned to revise the state constitution. Probably because of his legal background, he was named to the Committee on the Judicial Department. A fellow delegate characterized him as an untalented lawmaker elected at the behest of religious men but who nevertheless vigorously defended his county's interests. On 29 December 1829 Claiborne unsuccessfully tried to gut a resolution removing from the bench all judges sitting at the time the new constitution went into effect, but otherwise he seldom spoke on the floor save on procedural matters. Voting consistently with the conservatives and against advocates of democratic reform and a more equitable distribution of power between the eastern and western sections of Virginia, he favored retaining the Council of State and opposed efforts to enlarge the suffrage. On 14 January 1830 he voted with the convention majority in favor of the final version of the new constitution, which his constituents overwhelmingly approved by a vote of 1,214 to 63 in a referendum later that year.

Following the convention, Claiborne represented Greensville County for a single term in the House of Delegates in the session that met from 6 December 1830 until 19 April 1831. He sat on the prestigious Committee of Privileges and Elections and as a member of the Committee for Courts of Justice debated requiring each county to establish a fund for paying jurors and defraying court costs.

During the 1830s Claiborne maintained a prominent law practice and was a trustee of the Methodist Episcopal church in Hicksford (later incorporated as part of Emporia). At the time of his death he owned 816 acres of land in Greensville County, 573 acres in Brunswick County, half interest in a mill, twenty-four taxable slaves twelve years of age or older, and several blooded racehorses. Augustine Claiborne died on 30 June 1839 in Greensville County and most likely was buried there on his plantation. In his memory the Greensville bar asked that its members wear black armbands for thirty days and issued joint resolutions with local court officials in surrounding counties lamenting his death. His widow and several of their children moved to Tipton County, Tennessee.

Biography in Dorman, *Claiborne of Virginia*, 293–295 (variant marriage date of 24 Nov. 1812 on 293); birth date and marriage year in Claiborne family Bible records, dated 1859, Acc. 24288, LVA; otherwise undocumented middle initial *C.* in Personal Property Tax Returns, Greensville Co. (1812), RG 48, LVA, and *Richmond Enquirer*, 30 Aug. 1839; several 1814 and 1816 Claiborne letters in Militia Commission Papers, Office of the Governor, RG 3, LVA; Land and Personal Property Tax Returns, Brunswick Co. (1820–1839), Greensville Co. (1809, 1816–1839), RG 48, LVA; *Richmond Enquirer*, 2 June 1829; *Journal of 1829–1830 Convention*, 22, 296; *Proceedings and Debates of 1829–1830 Convention*, 767–768; Hugh Blair Grigsby Commonplace Book (1829–1830), 67, Hugh Blair Grigsby Papers, VHS; *JHD*, 1830–1831 sess., 241; Catlin, *Convention of 1829–30* (por.); will and estate inventory (recorded 1860) in Greensville Co. Will Book, 5:470–471, 8:308–310; obituary in *Watchman of the South*, 25 July 1839; memorial resolutions in Greensville Co. Order Book, 10:27–28, and *Richmond Enquirer*, 23 July, 16, 30 Aug. 1839.

STUART LEE BUTLER

CLAIBORNE, Herbert Augustine (20 February 1886–30 April 1957), contractor and preservationist, was born in Richmond and was the son of Herbert Augustine Claiborne, an insurance executive who died in 1902, and his third wife, Katherine Hamilton Cabell Claiborne, who later married the former Confederate brigadier general and North Carolina congressman William Ruffin Cox and for many years was a state leader in the National Society of the Colonial Dames of America and in the Association for the Preservation of Virginia Antiquities. Privately educated in Richmond and Radford, Claiborne graduated from the University of Virginia in 1908 with a degree in civil engineering. He lived and practiced in Richmond, from 1908 to 1910 with Allen Jeter Saville, a former classmate at the University of Virginia, and from 1911 to 1913 by himself. On 4 December 1912 Claiborne married Eleanor Hazard Lindsey and then spent about a year in Panama during construction of the isthmian canal. After he returned to Richmond, his wife had a son and soon afterward died, on 21 April 1915. During World War I, Claiborne was a lieutenant in the Army Air Service and from March 1918 until May 1919 served in France. Returning again to Richmond, he married Virginia Watson Christian on 19 February 1920. They had one son and two daughters.

Saville and Claiborne, Incorporated, received its charter in February 1915 and designed and constructed water systems in various Virginia localities, including at Camp Lee, a mobilization and division-training camp near Petersburg. Saville left the partnership in 1920, and in October of that year Claiborne rechartered the company in partnership with Henry Taylor. As Claiborne and Taylor, Inc. (later Taylor and Parrish, Inc.), the business attracted increasingly substantial commercial and industrial projects, but of special significance was its growing popularity for expensive residential commissions.

Early in the 1920s several Virginia organizations promoted the construction of new houses that drew on the aesthetic appeal as well as the historical associations of colonial American architecture. This Colonial Revival style enjoyed national currency among those who prized the Anglo-Protestant origins of America's colonial heritage. To many Virginians this attitude and its architectural manifestation seemed appropriately respectful, as well as emblematic, of early Virginia's exemplary contributions to American history. No group more enthusiastically endorsed Colonial Revival domestic design than the new

Garden Club of Virginia, and the talented William Lawrence Bottomley, of New York, unofficially became the architect of choice for the organization's members. Claiborne's mother-in-law was a forceful leader of the Garden Club, and he became the preferred contractor for Bottomley's Virginia commissions. By 1930 Claiborne and Taylor had attained a reputation for success in the building of fine Colonial Revival houses.

Claiborne's professional standing and his family's connections to the National Society of the Colonial Dames brought him an invitation to move Wilton, a large colonial house that had been built by the Randolph family between 1750 and 1753 in Henrico County on a site overlooking the James River and that was threatened by impending development. To save it, the Virginia chapter of the Colonial Dames engaged Claiborne in 1933 to dismantle Wilton and reassemble it on a similar site west of Richmond. The project involved the most drastic measures Claiborne was ever required to take, but important work at other colonial Virginia sites followed his successful completion of the relocation in 1934.

Between 1933 and 1942 the Claiborne and Taylor firm was the contractor for the restoration of Stratford Hall, the Lee family's Westmoreland County mansion, built between 1738 and 1742. Working under the direction of Fiske Kimball, the most prominent and respected restoration architect in America, Claiborne kept his own notes and sketches for the project. He often annotated and sometimes challenged Kimball's interpretations of the architectural evidence. The two men also collaborated on a comprehensive restoration of Gunston Hall, George Mason's Fairfax County residence, built between 1755 and 1759. In addition to these major restoration projects, Claiborne and Taylor undertook projects of varying scale at other historic sites, including Brandon in Prince George County, Mount Vernon in Fairfax County, old Saint Luke's Church in Isle of Wight County, Christ Church in Lancaster County, Westover Parish Church in Charles City County, and the King William County courthouse.

An able and successful member of Virginia's building industry, Claiborne was also as thoughtful and observant as any restoration specialist in

the first generation of professionals who devoted serious attention to the materials, forms, and details of early Virginia architecture. He is most widely remembered for his restoration projects and his published discussions of historic sites and materials. Claiborne's *Some Paint Colors from Four Eighteenth-Century Virginia Houses* (1948) was among the first discussions to note that aging might have altered the hues and tones of historic pigments. The posthumously published *Comments on Virginia Brickwork before 1800* (1957) remained a significant guide to colonial masonry for many decades. Texts of several of Claiborne's speeches also preserve his explanations of the evolution of colonial Virginia houses through the descriptive strategies of the antiquarian and the classificatory schemes of the connoisseur. His presentations often promoted these houses as tangible links with the past that deserved protection from what he termed the advancing "mechanical wilderness of the modernistic house."

Herbert Augustine Claiborne was well known throughout Virginia as a respected restoration expert by the time he died at his Richmond home on 30 April 1957. He was buried in the city's Hollywood Cemetery.

Brief biographies in *Taylor and Parrish Incorporated: General Contractors, Richmond, Virginia* [ca. 1965], including frontispiece por., and Dorman, *Claiborne of Virginia*, 602–603 (por.); BVS Birth Register, Richmond City; BVS Marriage Register, Richmond City (1912, 1920); Herbert Augustine Claiborne Papers (including book manuscripts, research notes, architectural drawings, and quotation in Claiborne, "Eighteenth Century Colonial Virginia Houses," undated MS of speech delivered at Tuckahoe plantation), VHS; Military Service Records; SCC Charter Book, 86:482–484, 109:406–408; Constance Hooper Wyrick, "Restoration Precis" (unpublished report, Oct. 1975, Robert E. Lee Memorial Association, Stratford Hall); William B. O'Neal and Christopher Weeks, *The Work of William Lawrence Bottomley in Richmond* (1985); obituaries in *Richmond News Leader* and *Richmond Times-Dispatch*, both 1 May 1957, and University of Virginia *Alumni News* 45 (June/July 1957): 27; editorial tribute in *Richmond Times-Dispatch*, 3 May 1957.

CAMILLE WELLS

CLAIBORNE, John (26 January 1778–9 October 1808), member of the House of Representatives, was born in Brunswick County and was the son of Thomas Claiborne (1747–1811) and his first wife, Mary Clayton Claiborne. His younger brother Thomas Claiborne (1780–1856) served in the House of Representatives from Tennessee, and another younger brother, Augustine Claiborne, was a member of the Convention of 1829–1830. Little is known of John Claiborne's early education, but he studied medicine with Benjamin Rush at the University of Pennsylvania and in 1798 received an M.D. after completing a thesis entitled *An Inaugural Essay on Scurvy.* On 14 September 1798 Claiborne posted a marriage bond in Brunswick County and on that day or soon afterward married a cousin, Sally Clayton. They had one son before her death on 1 October 1805.

By December 1799 Claiborne had moved his family to Raleigh, North Carolina, where he helped organize the North Carolina Medical Society and served as its vice president in 1799 and 1800. He soon returned to Virginia and sat on the Brunswick County Court from 28 July 1800 until his resignation on 28 November 1803. By March 1805 his father was completing the last of his five nonconsecutive terms in the House of Representatives, and in April of that year voters of the Seventeenth Congressional District, comprising Brunswick, Lunenburg, and Mecklenburg Counties, elected Claiborne to succeed his father. He took his seat in the Ninth Congress on 2 December 1805.

Claiborne was appointed to the three-member Committee of Revisal and Unfinished Business and did not speak on the House floor. A Jeffersonian Republican like his father, he did not always vote along party or even regional lines. A letter Claiborne circulated among his constituents at the close of the first session demonstrates that he carefully examined the implications of each bill before casting his vote and just as carefully explained, but did not apologize for, his choices.

In the spring of 1807 Claiborne was reelected without opposition. Probably because of ill health that had plagued him for several years, he did not take his seat in the Tenth Congress until 8 March 1808, more than four months late. John Claiborne died in Brunswick County of consumption, probably tuberculosis, on 9 October 1808. He was buried in the Dinwiddie County family graveyard of his uncle, the Episcopal clergyman Devereux Jarratt.

Biography in Dorman, *Claiborne of Virginia*, 286; birth date and variant marriage year of 1797 in Claiborne family Bible records, dated 1859, Acc. 24288, LVA; Brunswick Co. Marriage Bonds; *Richmond Enquirer*, 30 Apr. 1805; *National Intelligencer and Washington Advertiser*, 25 May 1807; Cunningham, *Circular Letters of Congressmen*, 1:457–462; Brunswick Co. Will Book, 7:302; death noted in *Annals of Congress*, 10th Cong., 2d sess., 470; obituaries in *Charles Town [Va.] Farmer's Repository* and *Richmond Enquirer*, both 21 Oct. 1808, and *Raleigh Star*, 3 Nov. 1808.

MARION CHRISTINA NELSON

CLAIBORNE, John Herbert (10 March 1828–24 February 1905), physician, was born in Brunswick County and was the son of John Gregory Claiborne and his first wife, Mary Elizabeth Weldon Claiborne. Educated at private academies in Virginia and North Carolina, he graduated from Randolph-Macon College in 1848 and received an M.D. from the University of Virginia the following year. He completed his medical training in Philadelphia and in 1850 received both an M.D. from the Jefferson Medical College (later part of Thomas Jefferson University) and a certificate from a Philadelphia obstetrics institute. Claiborne opened a successful medical practice in Petersburg the following year and with two colleagues established the short-lived Petersburg Primary Medical School to give private instruction in medicine. On 3 May 1853 in Louisburg, North Carolina, he married Sarah Joseph Alston. They had four daughters and one son, John Herbert Claiborne (1861–1922), who became a successful New York physician and published a biography of their immigrant ancestor, *William Claiborne of Virginia, with Some Account of His Pedigree* (1917).

In 1855 Claiborne, formerly a Whig, won election as a Democrat to represent Petersburg in the House of Delegates. He was a member of the Committee on Finance. At the completion of his two-year term, Claiborne was elected to a four-year term representing Petersburg and Prince George County in the Senate of Virginia, where he served on the Committees on Finance and Claims and on Roads and Internal Improvements. He also chaired the Committee to Examine the Lunatic Asylums of the Commonwealth. In February 1858 he unsuccessfully advocated establishing a Board of Medical Examiners for the Commonwealth to oversee the licensing of physicians. Not long after Virginia seceded from the Union on 17 April 1861, Claiborne joined the 4th Battalion Virginia Volunteers, initially as assistant surgeon with the rank of captain and from 5 May as surgeon. When the battalion entered Confederate service in July as the 12th Regiment Virginia Infantry, he became a major. Reelected to the Senate in May 1861, Claiborne resigned his seat on 25 December of that year and the following 17 February was commissioned a surgeon. That summer he opened a military hospital in Petersburg, one of seven of which he was executive officer and chief surgeon during the siege of 1864–1865. He was captured a few days before the Confederate surrender at Appomattox Court House.

After the Civil War, Claiborne resumed his Petersburg medical practice and specialized in women's diseases. He sought to embody the virtues of a gentleman of his profession by sharing the benefits of his education and experience through service to the poor and lectures to medical students and to such organizations as the Merchants Benevolent Association, the Sons of Temperance, and the Young Men's Christian Association. His appointment as health officer for Petersburg in 1875 terminated after only a year, during which his report on the measures necessary to combat epidemic disease and improve sanitation caused a rift with the city council.

Claiborne belonged to the American Medical Association, the American Public Health Association, and the Tri-State Medical Association of the Carolinas and Virginia and was a fellow-elect of the Victoria Institute of Great Britain, a fellow of the Southern Surgical and Gynecological Society, and a corresponding member of the Gynecological Society of Boston. A founding member of the Medical Society of Virginia, Claiborne became its president in 1877. In his presidential address, delivered on 23 October 1878, he argued that scientific advances in modern medicine placed a responsibility on physicians to impress public officials with the need to take preventive public health measures, but he lamented the poor state of Virginia's public health laws. Long an advocate of the necessity of regulating the practice of medicine, Claiborne was an original member of the State Medical

Examining Board (later the State Board of Medical Examiners), established in November 1884.

Claiborne published numerous articles in medical journals, and his *Clinical Reports from Private Practice* (1873) was well received. He also wrote about his experiences in the Civil War and about his hometown. In 1895 Claiborne published a lecture entitled *The Old Virginia Doctor*, which presented an idealized reminiscence of the antebellum practice of medicine. Shortly before his death he published *Seventy-Five Years in Old Virginia* (1904), a lively, incisive autobiography that vividly depicts Petersburg and its citizens in the 1850s and during the Civil War.

Claiborne's wife died on 3 February 1869, and on 3 November 1887 he married Annie Leslie Watson, of Petersburg. They had one daughter and one son. John Herbert Claiborne died in his home in Petersburg on 24 February 1905 and was buried in Blandford Cemetery.

John Herbert Claiborne, *Seventy-Five Years in Old Virginia* (1904), frontispiece por.; biographies in Howard A. Kelly and Walter L. Burrage, eds., *Dictionary of American Medical Biography* (1928), 226 (with variant birth date of 16 Mar. 1828), Mary Grace Hawkins, "John Herbert Claiborne, M.D.," *Virginia Medical Monthly* 88 (1961): 617–621, and Dorman, *Claiborne of Virginia*, 705–709; birth and marriage dates in Claiborne family Bible records (1763–1979), LVA; John Herbert Claiborne Papers, UVA; some Claiborne letters in William Mahone Papers, Duke; published speeches include *Speech of John Herbert Claiborne of Petersburg, on the Bill Asking a Charter for an Air Line Railroad between the Cities of Richmond and Lynchburg* (1856), *Address of John Herbert Claiborne, of Petersburg and Prince George, to His Constituents of the Sixth Senatorial District* (1861), and *Personal Reminiscences of the "Last Days of Lee and his Paladins," . . . 6th of March 1890* (1890); *JSV*, 1857–1858 sess., 339, 348, 570; "Communication Enclosing Resignation of John H. Claiborne, the Senator from Sixth District," 6 Jan. 1862, Doc. 11 appended to *JSV*, 1861–1862 sess.; Compiled Service Records; presidential address in *Medical Society of Virginia Transactions* 2 (1879): 333–343; obituaries in *Petersburg Daily Index-Appeal*, *Petersburg Daily Progress*, *Richmond News Leader*, *Richmond Times-Dispatch*, and *Washington Post*, all 25 Feb. 1905, *Journal of the American Medical Association* 44 (1905): 728, and *Virginia Medical Semi-Monthly* 9 [renumbered 31] (Mar. 1905): 552; editorial tribute in *Petersburg Daily Index-Appeal*, 25 Feb. 1905.
HEIDI M. HACKFORD

CLAIBORNE, Katherine Hamilton Cabell.
See **COX, Katherine Hamilton Cabell Claiborne**.

CLAIBORNE, Nathaniel Charles (15 February 1822–1 February 1889), member of the Convention of 1850–1851, was born on the Franklin County farm of his parents, Elizabeth Archer Binford Claiborne and Nathaniel Herbert Claiborne, who served on the Council of State during the War of 1812 and in the House of Representatives from 1825 to 1837. His uncle William Charles Cole Claiborne was a Tennessee congressman, territorial and state governor of Louisiana, and United States senator from Louisiana. He attended Washington College (later Washington and Lee University) for the 1837–1838 session. For several years Claiborne traveled in the West and supported himself by working on steamboats, but by 1846 he had returned to Franklin County and begun to practice law. On 13 June 1849 he married Mildred Kyle Morris, of Buckingham County. They had one son and two daughters.

Claiborne attended the Democratic National Convention in 1848 and that year also won election to the House of Delegates for the first of two one-year terms representing Franklin County. He served on the Committee for Courts of Justice in both sessions and during the 1848–1849 term on special committees to present swords or medals to Virginia soldiers who had fought with distinction in the Mexican War and to formulate the state's response to the Wilmot Proviso, an unsuccessful congressional attempt to ban slavery in the new territories acquired from Mexico. The attorney John Hazlehurst Boneval Latrobe, a cousin by marriage for whom Claiborne named his son, credited Claiborne's eloquence, enthusiasm, and charisma with securing House approval of Thomas Crawford's design for an equestrian statue of George Washington to be erected on Capitol Square. During the 1849–1850 session Claiborne chaired the Committee of Schools and Colleges and served on special committees to consider calling a constitutional convention, on the Wilmot Proviso (which he chaired), and on Richmond citizens' desire to elect their city officers. He occasionally supported internal improvements despite the fact that the community he represented opposed them.

In August 1850 Claiborne polled the second-highest number of votes among ten candidates campaigning for three seats representing Franklin, Henry, and Patrick Counties in a convention summoned to revise the state's constitution. He supported reapportioning representation in the General Assembly on a mixed basis of population and property holding and favored state encouragement of internal improvements. He declared on one occasion that as long as the convention delegates brought a railroad line to Franklin's county seat, he would vote for almost any guarantee for affixing the basis of representation they required. As a member of the Committee on the Executive Department and Ministerial Officers he favored allowing the governor to serve more than one term and argued that the hope of reelection was the highest inducement for an official to be honest, faithful, and industrious. On 16 May 1851 Claiborne voted for the final compromise on legislative reapportionment that established a western majority in the House of Delegates but retained an eastern majority in the Senate of Virginia. He left the convention on 30 July 1851 and did not vote the next day on final approval of the constitution.

In 1852 Claiborne won election to a four-year term as commonwealth's attorney of Franklin County. He served as one of five delegates from the Third Congressional District to the 1852 Democratic National Convention. After attending the state Democratic convention in November and December 1854 and vowing to support the Democratic candidate for governor, he agreed to run for Congress as a Know Nothing (American Party) candidate against Thomas Salem Bocock, the Democrat who had held the seat since 1847. The *Lynchburg Republican* decried Claiborne's perfidy and accused him of having not bad political principles, but no political principles whatsoever. In public debates Bocock savaged Claiborne for writing him letters supporting his candidacy while simultaneously declaring himself a candidate for the same congressional seat. A Richmond newspaper reported a Franklin County debate "with contending feelings of pain and pleasure—pain in witnessing the remorseless cruelty which Mr. Bocock displays in cutting up and mangling a human body; pleasure at the just chastisement of a wretched traitor." The revelation of Claiborne's equivocal position may have led some Know Nothings to consider seeking a replacement candidate. In the final tally in June 1855, Claiborne lost by about 1,700 votes of more than 10,000 cast.

Early in 1857 Claiborne moved with his family to Kansas City, Missouri, where he practiced law and operated a hotel. He served in the Missouri delegation to both sessions of the 1860 Democratic National Convention and as an alternate to the 1864 convention in Chicago. He won election to the Missouri House of Representatives for the sessions of 1860, 1868, and 1871. As secretary of the Missouri State Senate in 1861, Claiborne moved to Saint Louis about that time and approximately five years later opened a lucrative law practice with his brother. Admired for his oratorical abilities, he reportedly declined several requests to run for governor and remained a respected criminal attorney. Nathaniel Charles Claiborne died at his Saint Louis home of uremia and acute bronchitis on 1 February 1889 and was buried in Oak Hill Cemetery, in Saint Louis.

Biographies in *Richmond Standard*, 28 Aug. 1880, *Biographical Dictionary and Portrait Gallery of Eminent and Self-Made Men: Missouri* (1878), 1:383–385, A. J. D. Stewart, ed., *The History of the Bench and Bar of Missouri* (1898), 123, Nathaniel Claiborne Hale, *Roots in Virginia: An Account of Captain Thomas Hale, Virginia Frontiersman* . . . (1948), 125, and Dorman, *Claiborne of Virginia*, 481–483 (por. on 482); birth and marriage dates in Claiborne family Bible records (1720–1913), LVA and VHS; *Richmond Enquirer*, 30 Aug., 3, 13 Sept. 1850, 10 Apr., 5 June 1855; *Lynchburg Republican*, n.d., quoted in *Richmond Enquirer*, 6, 17 (quotation) Apr. 1855; *Debates and Proceedings of 1850–1851 Convention*, 180–182; *Journal of 1850–1851 Convention*, 59, and Appendix, 22; *Supplement, 1850–1851 Convention Debates*, nos. 20, 34, 47, 48; James P. Hambleton, *A Biographical Sketch of Henry A. Wise, with a History of the Political Campaign in Virginia in 1855* . . . (1856), 345–347; John E. Semmes, *John H. B. Latrobe and His Times, 1803–1891* (1917), 447; undated, unidentified obituary clipping, including por., in Nathaniel Herbert Claiborne Journal and Diary (1824–1831), Acc. 28698, LVA; obituaries and accounts of funeral in *Saint Louis Evening Chronicle*, 2, 4 Feb. 1889, and *Saint Louis Post Dispatch*, 3, 4 Feb. 1889; Saint Louis County Bar Association memorial in *Saint Louis Republic*, 3 Feb. 1889.

EMILY J. SALMON

CLAIBORNE, Nathaniel Herbert (1 February 1775–15 August 1859), member of the Council of State and of the House of Representatives, was born in Sussex County and was the son of

first cousins William Claiborne and his first wife, Mary Leigh Claiborne. His uncle Thomas Claiborne served five terms in the House of Representatives. Claiborne's father suffered financial reverses during and after the Revolutionary War and by 1782 had moved the family to Manchester, opposite Richmond. He engaged in trade and remarried about a year after his wife died in April 1782. Nathaniel Herbert Claiborne received a classical education at a Richmond academy and by March 1798 had moved to Lee County and was practicing law. By the spring of 1801 he had settled in Franklin County, where on 4 May of that year he became commonwealth's attorney and in November 1803 a captain in the militia. Between 1802 and 1806 he bought more than 800 acres of land north of the Blackwater River on which he built Claybrook, his home for the rest of his life. On 17 May 1815 he married Elizabeth Archer Binford, of Goochland County, whom John Quincy Adams once toasted as the most beautiful woman he had ever seen. Their six daughters and five sons included Nathaniel Charles Claiborne, a member of the Convention of 1850–1851.

Claiborne resigned as commonwealth's attorney on 2 April 1810 after winning election to the first of two one-year terms in the House of Delegates representing Franklin County. He served on the Committee for Courts of Justice during both the 1810–1811 and 1811–1812 sessions. During his first term he objected to the numbers of and salaries for the judges of the Virginia Court of Appeals and also the length of time it took to adjudicate cases. He preferred county courts "as the sacred barriers between the multitude and oppression." He voted to instruct Virginia's congressional delegation to do all in its power to prevent renewal of the charter of the Bank of the United States, but he approved a new bank in Lynchburg.

On 7 January 1812 the General Assembly elected Claiborne to the Council of State, which shared executive powers with the governor during the War of 1812. The Council proceedings record few dissents by Claiborne to actions the governor and Council took. He regularly attended Council meetings through 1814, but after his marriage in May 1815 his attendance became sporadic. He resigned on 1 April 1817 after having missed about three weeks in February and March and ceasing to attend altogether after 13 March.

During the War of 1812 Claiborne wrote "The Crisis," a series of articles and commentaries on political and military affairs. In 1819 he published several of those essays in *Notes on the War in the South; with Biographical Sketches of the Lives of Montgomery, Jackson, Sevier, the Late Gov. Claiborne, and Others*, an account of Andrew Jackson's campaign against the Creek Indians and of the Battle of New Orleans. He also included a short biography of his elder brother William Charles Cole Claiborne, a Tennessee congressman, territorial and state governor of Louisiana, and United States senator.

In 1818 the governor appointed Claiborne one of twenty-four commissioners authorized to determine a location for the new University of Virginia. Meeting at Rockfish Gap beginning on 1 August of that year, Claiborne voted with the majority to select Albemarle County as the home for the proposed institution and also declined a professorship at the university.

In April 1821 voters in the counties of Franklin, Henry, Patrick, and Pittsylvania elected Claiborne to the Senate of Virginia for a four-year term. During the 1821–1822 assembly he served on a committee concerning separate elections in Patrick County, but after 31 January 1822 he took a leave of absence for the rest of the session. In the 1822–1823 and 1823–1824 sessions he sat on the Committee of Privileges and Elections. Claiborne also served on a committee on enrolled bills in the 1822–1823 session and on the Committees of Claims and of General Laws in the 1823–1824 and 1824–1825 assemblies. Although he believed that the states, rather than Congress, should be responsible for financing internal improvements, he voted against most of the improvements bills that came before the Senate during his four years' service.

In April 1823 Claiborne sought the Seventh Congressional District seat in the House of Representatives but lost the tainted contest to Jabez Leftwich, of Bedford County. Each county within a congressional district set its own dates for voting, and usually the running tally was public knowledge before the election ended. Leftwich lagged Claiborne by 814 votes after every county except Bedford had conducted its poll. Bedford County election officials held the voting precincts open for several additional days, and as a result Leftwich outpolled Claiborne 1,180 to 47 there, for a 319-vote overall victory. Claiborne campaigned again in 1825, and again the Bedford polls remained open longer than proper. This time, however, Claiborne's lead held up, and he defeated the incumbent Leftwich by 78 votes.

Reelected five times, Claiborne represented Bedford, Franklin, Henry, and Patrick Counties from 1825 to 1837. He usually supported the policies of President Andrew Jackson until 1832, when he began to vote with the anti-Jackson faction. Appointed to the Committee of Elections in the second session of the Nineteenth Congress (1825–1827), Claiborne chaired that committee from 1833 to 1837. He seldom made formal remarks during his congressional service and routinely opposed most proposals, including internal improvements at national expense and increased protective tariffs. He also voted against most pension and relief bills because he believed "we have no right to be generous and charitable with the money of other people."

Claiborne delivered a major speech against the tariff of 1828 because he favored free trade and opposed any tariff that benefited one region to the detriment of the southern or western economies. Without recording his reasons, he supported the tariff bill of 1832 that pushed South Carolina to nullification, as well as Henry Clay's compromise tariff of 1833, while opposing the Force Bill. In July 1832 Claiborne voted against rechartering the second Bank of the United States but broke with Jackson over other fiscal policy, particularly the president's removal of public money deposited with the bank. In May of that year Claiborne attended an anti-Jackson Republican convention in Baltimore gathered to choose a vice presidential candidate. He lost his reelection bid in May 1837 to Archibald Stuart and retired to his farm near Rocky Mount. Nathaniel Herbert Claiborne died at Claybrook on 15 August 1859 and was buried in the family cemetery there.

Birth date in Gertrude R. B. Richards, trans. and ed., *Register of Albemarle Parish, Surry and Sussex Counties, 1739–1778* (1958), 119; autobiographies in Nathaniel Herbert Claiborne Journal and Diary (1822–1831), Acc. 28698, LVA (variant birth date of 1 Feb. 1780 suggested by statement, p. 4, that Claiborne "entered my forty third year" on 1 Feb. 1822), and *Richmond Standard*, 28 Aug. 1880; biographies in Nathaniel Claiborne Hale, *Roots in Virginia: An Account of Captain Thomas Hale, Virginia Frontiersman . . .* (1948), 119–120, Dorman, *Claiborne of Virginia*, 459–465 (por. on 462), and John S. Salmon and Emily J. Salmon, *Franklin County, Virginia, 1786–1986: A Bicentennial History* (1993), 101; Claiborne family Bible records (1720–1913), LVA and VHS; Goochland Co. Marriage Register; published speeches include *Sketch of a Speech, Delivered in Session of the House of Delegates, 1810, by N. H. Claiborne, Esq., Member from Franklin, in Opposition to a Bill Concerning the Court of Appeals* (1810), including first quotation on 3, *Nathaniel H. Claiborne's Address to the Electors of the Senatorial District, Composed of the Counties of Franklin, Patrick, Henry, and Pittsylvania, January 1825* (1825), and "Circular: To the Electors of Franklin, Patrick, Henry, and Bedford" (9 Feb. 1827), copy at Duke; appointment to Council in *JHD*, 1811–1812 sess., 68; Council of State Journal (1812–1813), esp. 123–127, 138–143, and (1816–1817), 115, RG 75, LVA; *Richmond Enquirer*, 6, 9 May 1823, 15, 22 Apr., 6 May 1825; *Register of Debates*, 20th Cong., 1st sess., 1789–1797, 21st Cong., 1st sess., 575–576 (second quotation), 22d Cong., 1st sess., 1669–1673; Franklin Co. Will Book, 11:209–210; Franklin Co. Death Register (age at death eighty-three, suggesting birth in 1776); obituaries in *Lynchburg Daily Virginian*, 1 Sept. 1859 (died "in his 83d year," suggesting birth in 1777), and *Baltimore Sun*, 24 Sept. 1859 (died "in the 83d year of his age"); memorial resolutions in Franklin Co. Order Book (1855–1860), 466, printed in *Richmond Daily Whig*, 13 Sept. 1859.

JOHN S. SALMON
EMILY J. SALMON

CLAIBORNE, Thomas (1 February 1747–1811), member of the House of Representatives, was born in Dinwiddie County and was the son of Hannah Ravenscroft Poythress Claiborne and her second husband, Burnell Claiborne. Little is known about his early years, but on 19 January 1772 he married Mary Clayton in Dinwiddie County. Their seven sons included John Claiborne, who served in the House of Representatives from 1805 until his death in 1808, Thomas Claiborne (1780–1856), who from 1817 to 1819 represented a Tennessee district in Congress, and Augustine Claiborne, a member of the Convention of 1829–1830. His nephew Nathaniel Herbert Claiborne served on the Council of State and for six terms in the House of Representatives, and another nephew, William Charles Cole Claiborne, was a Tennessee congressman and later territorial and state governor of Louisiana. By 1773 Claiborne had moved to Brunswick County. During the Revolutionary War he was captain of the county militia and as a county impressment officer provided supplies for local troops and for the Continental army.

Although at one time Claiborne owned substantial property, his land- and slaveholding declined during the 1780s and 1790s. In 1787 he owned 1,504 acres of Brunswick County land and 36 slaves and held a license to keep an ordinary. A decade later he owned only 424 acres and 26 slaves over age twelve, and by the time he left the county in 1805 he held 506 acres of land and 10 adult slaves.

Beginning in 1783 Claiborne represented Brunswick County in the House of Delegates for five consecutive one-year terms. During the 1785–1786 session he served on the Committees of Propositions and Grievances and of Claims. The following session he was returned to the Committee of Propositions and Grievances and also named to the Committee for Religion. The latter assignment probably held special significance for Claiborne because in 1785 he had been a lay delegate at the Richmond convention called to organize the Protestant Episcopal Church's diocese in Virginia. Later that year he voted against the bill to establish religious freedom. Reappointed during his final term in October 1787 to the Committees of Propositions and Grievances and of Claims, he left the House in November after receiving a commission as sheriff of Brunswick County, a post he held until 1789. Claiborne returned to the General Assembly in 1790, representing Brunswick, Greensville, Lunenburg, and Mecklenburg Counties in the Senate of Virginia for a single four-year term. During the 1791 session he served on a committee to examine enrolled bills and during the following session sat on a committee charged with examining the treasurer's accounts.

Claiborne was elected to the House of Representatives from the Eighth District, comprising Brunswick, Greensville, Lunenburg, and Mecklenburg Counties, for three consecutive terms from 1793 to 1799 and an additional term from 1801 to 1802. After a redistricting, he represented the Seventeenth District, consisting of the counties of Brunswick, Lunenburg, and Mecklenburg, for a final term from 1803 until 1804. Not an influential member, Claiborne strongly favored a separation of powers and aligned himself with the Republicans. He opposed the Jay Treaty with England and in June 1798 called the Alien and Sedition Acts "fitter for the code of Algiers than of America." He was an election commissioner for the presidential election in 1800 and three years later defended his acquaintance Thomas Jefferson against charges that he was hostile to religion.

After Claiborne's wife died on 4 June 1802, he expressed regret that he had left her alone for so many years while pursuing a political career and serving his country. He contemplated running for another term in Congress in 1805 but ultimately decided not to seek reelection. Instead, the voters of the Seventeenth District elected his son John Claiborne to replace him in that office. On 15 August 1805 Claiborne married Ann Driver, a widow with four children. Settling in Suffolk, where his new wife owned property, they suffered financial setbacks and could not pay their debts. Thomas Claiborne died in Suffolk on an unrecorded date in 1811.

Biography in Dorman, *Claiborne of Virginia*, 282–284; birth, first marriage, and death dates in Claiborne family Bible records, dated 1859, Acc. 24288, LVA, also giving otherwise undocumented middle initial *B.* and naming mother as Georgianna Ravenscroft Poythress Claiborne; second marriage in *Petersburg Intelligencer*, 23 Aug. 1805; fragmentary material in Fillmore Norfleet Papers, Acc. 33180, Box 4, LVA; Claiborne letters in *Calendar of State Papers*, 4:616–617, 9:131–132; *Journals of Council of State*, 4:168; *Annals of Congress*, 5th Cong., 2d sess., 1116–1117, 1924–1925, 1944, 1999 (quotation), 2055–2056, 2131, 2133; circular letters to constituents in *Virginia Gazette and Petersburg Intelligencer*, 20 May 1796, *Republican and Petersburg Advertiser*, 21 Dec. 1802, and *Petersburg Republican*, 8 Mar., 28 Oct. 1803; *National Intelligencer and Washington Advertiser*, 21 June 1802; *Petersburg Republican*, 22 Mar., 2 Apr. 1805; Ellen G. Miles, *Saint-Mémin and the Neoclassical Profile Portrait in America* (1994), 270 (por.).

JOHN C. PINHEIRO

CLAIBORNE, William (bap. 10 August 1600–by 25 August 1679), member of the Council and secretary of the colony, was born probably in Crayford Parish, in Kent, England, where he was baptized on 10 August 1600. He was the son of Sara Smyth James Cleyborne and her sec-

ond husband, Thomas Cleyborne, a merchant and former mayor of King's Lynn in the county of Norfolk; Sir Roger James, a shareholder in the Virginia Company of London, may have been his elder half brother. Contemporaries wrote Claiborne's surname with a variety of phonetic variants, and during his first decades in Virginia he sometimes spelled his name Claybourne, but in later years he signed as Claiborne. He entered Pembroke College, University of Cambridge, on 31 May 1617. Four years later, perhaps on his half brother's recommendation, the Virginia Company appointed Claiborne surveyor of the colony at a salary of £30 per annum and also offered him an assistant, 200 acres of land, and a convenient house, presumably in Jamestown.

Claiborne traveled to Virginia in the retinue of Governor Sir Francis Wyatt and arrived in October 1621. His first task was to survey the New Town section of Jamestown, but he was soon involved in Virginia's politics and was one of the company's officers who in 1622, following the deadly Powhatan Uprising, requested that the king take over management of the colony. By the spring of 1623 Claiborne was a member of the governor's Council, in which office James I confirmed him in August 1624 when appointing Wyatt the first royal governor of Virginia. Surveying allowed Claiborne to accumulate a considerable amount of land, including property in Elizabeth City County. After 1640 he lived at Romancoke, near the confluence of the Mattaponi and Pamunkey Rivers, in the part of York County that in 1654 became New Kent County and in 1701 King William County. In the mid-1630s he married Elizabeth Boteler, or Butler. They had four sons and two daughters.

Late in the 1620s Claiborne explored trading opportunities in the upper part of the Chesapeake Bay and for much of the 1630s operated a lucrative trading post on Kent Island, which put him in conflict with successive Lords Baltimore, who maintained that the island was within the charter boundaries of Maryland. Eventually expelled from the island and losing perhaps as much as £10,000, Claiborne harbored a long and intense animosity toward Maryland and the Calvert family. Beginning with tobacco and fur, Claiborne built a profitable and influential commercial network that connected the Chesapeake Bay with London. His closest Virginia associates included Samuel Mathews (d. 1657), another merchant, land magnate, and member of the governor's Council, and his initial London associates were William Cloberry and Maurice Thompson, two of the most successful merchants in that city. In 1638 Claiborne received a grant of an island off the coast of Honduras and may have intended to set up a trading post there.

Claiborne made several voyages across the Atlantic to advance his commercial interests and protect his political connections. Growing wealth and influence made him a leader of Virginia's emerging political elite. In 1626 Claiborne became secretary of the colony, an office that ranked second only to the governor in political weight. He and Mathews led a dominant faction of Council members whose quest for land and influence produced clashes with Governor Sir John Harvey. In May 1635, while Claiborne was at Kent Island, the faction evicted Harvey from office. Claiborne initially emerged from that feud a much stronger politician, and when Sir Francis Wyatt returned to Virginia as governor in November 1639, he handled Claiborne gingerly.

Claiborne yielded the secretary's lucrative office to his rival Richard Kemp, who in 1634 arrived with a royal appointment, and when Harvey returned to Virginia for a second term as governor in 1637 Claiborne lost his seat on the Council. In 1640 he scored a victory over Kemp by obtaining royal permission to found a signet office for the purpose of validating public records, providing the Council consented, which it did. The new office reduced Kemp's influence and income because the great seal of Virginia and its attendant fees were transferred from him to Claiborne. Not long thereafter Wyatt relinquished the office of governor to Sir William Berkeley. Claiborne acted as an intermediary, and in 1642 the new governor reappointed Claiborne to the Council and named him treasurer of the colony.

The two dominant figures in Virginia, Claiborne and Berkeley contested for leadership of the planter elite. They differed over trade policy, with Claiborne opposing Dutch traders whose presence in Virginia threatened his own connections with London. They disagreed over how to prosecute the Anglo-Powhatan War of 1644–1646, during which Claiborne commanded some of the Virginia militia and made an attempt to recover Kent Island. They also took different positions on the issues that led to the English Civil Wars. Claiborne readily accommodated himself to the Puritans and was one of the commissioners Parliament appointed to bring Virginia and Maryland under its dominion. In that capacity he helped negotiate the terms by which Berkeley surrendered Virginia to Parliament in March 1652. Claiborne and his fellow commissioner Richard Bennett, who succeeded Berkeley as governor of Virginia, appointed a new Council in Maryland, action that precipitated two years of intermittent warfare between competing factions in that colony.

In the spring of 1652 the House of Burgesses elected Claiborne senior member of the Council and secretary of the colony. He and Berkeley remained on civil terms, despite their differences, and Claiborne eased Berkeley's return to the governorship in March 1660. Berkeley retained him in office for a few months, but Claiborne was too deeply implicated in the parliamentary cause to continue as a Council member and secretary after Charles II returned to England as king. Claiborne retired from public life in March 1661 and lived quietly and in relative obscurity at Romancoke. Berkeley threw a few crumbs in his direction by appointing two of his sons to the county court, and one of Claiborne's sons sat in the House of Burgesses. Claiborne remained loyal to the governor during Bacon's Rebellion in 1676, suffered significant property losses in the process, and may have sat on some of the courts-martial that sentenced several rebels to death, although it is possible that Claiborne's namesake son took on that responsibility. On 13 March 1677 Claiborne petitioned the Crown to recoup financial losses he had incurred when he was expelled from Kent Island forty years earlier. The following 16 July a Colonel Claiborne, who may have been the father, the son, or an unrelated person, boarded the royal naval ship *Bristol* to collect eight barrels of shot for use by the county militia.

The date and place of William Claiborne's death are not known, nor is the place of his burial.

He died on an unrecorded date before 25 August 1679, when his son Thomas Claiborne was identified in a York County record as executor of the estate of "Coll William Clayborne Decd."

Baptism recorded in Crayford Parish Register, Bexley Local Studies and Archive Centre, Bexleyheath, Kent, Eng.; Clayton Torrence, "The English Ancestry of William Claiborne of Virginia," *VMHB* 56 (1948): 328–343, 431–460; Nathaniel C. Hale, *Virginia Venturer: A Historical Biography of William Claiborne, 1600–1677* (1951); Dorman, *Claiborne of Virginia*, 1–6; two pors. of uncertain authenticity in Hummel and Smith, *Portraits and Statuary*, 24, and frontispiece (with discredited 1587 birth date) in John Herbert Claiborne, *William Claiborne of Virginia, with Some Account of His Pedigree* (1917); John Venn and J. A. Venn, comps., *Alumni Cantabrigienses* (1922) 1:350; Kingsbury, *Virginia Company*, 1:483–484, 494 (appointment as surveyor), 3:477, 486, 580–581, 4:69–70, 501–504 (appointment to Council), 551–574; numerous references in *Minutes of Council and General Court* and in William Hand Browne et al., eds., *Archives of Maryland* (1883–1972), vols. 1–5; *William Claiborne* v. *William Cloberry et al.*, PRO HCA 13/243, printed in "Claiborne *vs.* Clobery et als. in the High Court of Admiralty," *Maryland Historical Magazine* 26 (1931): 383–404, ibid., 27 (1932): 17–28, 99–114, 191–214, 337–352, ibid., 28 (1933): 26–43, 172–195, 257–265; Erich Isaac, "Kent Island," *Maryland Historical Magazine* 52 (1957): 93–119, 210–232; J. Frederick Fausz, "Merging and Emerging Worlds: Anglo-Indian Interest Groups and the Development of the Seventeenth-Century Chesapeake," in Lois Green Carr, Philip D. Morgan, and Jean B. Russo, eds., *Colonial Chesapeake Society* (1988), 47–98; Warren M. Billings, *A Little Parliament: The Virginia General Assembly in the Seventeenth Century* (2004); Timothy B. Riordan, *The Plundering Time: Maryland and the English Civil War, 1645–1646* (2004); 13 Mar. 1677 petition enclosing documents relating to Kent Island, PRO CO 1/39, fols. 110–169, printed in part in *Archives of Maryland*, 5:157–239; HMS *Bristol* log, 16 July 1677, PRO Adm 51/134; York Co. Deeds, Orders, Wills, Etc., 6:114 (quotation).

Warren M. Billings

CLAPHAM, Josias (d. by 12 September 1803), member of the Convention of 1776, was born, reportedly, in Wakefield, Yorkshire (later West Yorkshire), England. Little is known about his early life, including the names of his parents, his date of birth, or where he was educated. The uncle for whom he was named had settled in Virginia by 1735 and acquired land in Goochland County and property along the Potomac River in the part of Prince William County that in 1742 became Fairfax County. In his will, dated 29 October 1744 and proved on 27 December 1749, he bequeathed the property to his nephew, who

was probably then a young man, with the stipulation that he immigrate to Virginia.

It is not certain when Clapham arrived in the colony. With the 1,500 or more acres of land that he inherited, he quickly established himself as a respectable landowner, slaveholder, planter, and merchant. In April 1757 the House of Burgesses granted him a license to operate a public ferry across the Potomac River, something his uncle had failed to accomplish in several attempts. Clapham operated the ferry until 1778, when the General Assembly repealed his license. After the same assembly session that granted him the ferry license created Loudoun County out of Fairfax County, the governor named Clapham to the new county court, which met for the first time on 12 July 1757. Clapham served as a justice of the peace through 1763 and again from 1767 to 1786. Very active in local affairs during the county's formative years, he was a captain in the county militia by 1758 and also served at various times as coroner, surveyor, sheriff, trustee for the towns of Leesburg and Georgetown, and vestryman and churchwarden of Shelburne Parish. About 1 August 1761 Clapham married Sarah Eltinge, a widow from Frederick County, Maryland, whose maiden name is not recorded. They had at least one son and two daughters.

Clapham won election to the House of Burgesses to fill a vacant seat for the session that met for a few days in July 1771. He was elected again in the summer of 1774 and attended the final meeting of the burgesses in June 1775, when he served on the Committees for Courts of Justice and of Trade. On 24 June 1775 the House appointed him one of the commissioners to settle the accounts of the volunteers who had served in Dunmore's War the previous year. As an elected burgess, Clapham was eligible to sit in the first Revolutionary Convention that met in August 1774, but he did not attend. On 25 March 1775 during the second Revolutionary Convention, Clapham was named to a committee to encourage manufacturing, and on 26 May of that year he took his seat on the Loudoun County Committee. He sat in the third and fourth conventions, and despite riots resulting from a shortage of salt and deteriorating economic conditions, the Loudoun County voters elected him on 8 April 1776 to the fifth and final Revolutionary Convention. Present for the entire session that met from 6 May to 5 July 1776, Clapham was a member of the Committees of Propositions and Grievances and of Public Claims. The convention unanimously voted for independence on 15 May, adopted the Declaration of Rights on 12 June, and approved the first constitution of Virginia on 29 June.

During the Revolutionary War, Clapham was a colonel in the county militia, formed a company of volunteers, operated a gun manufactory, and was one of several men who looked after the families of the county's soldiers and provided supplies to local militia companies and rations for prisoners of war held in Loudoun County. He represented the county in the House of Delegates for three terms from October 1776 until December 1778. During the 1776 term he served on the Committees of Propositions and Grievances and of Public Claims, and he sat on the latter committee again in 1777. Although not elected to the assembly in 1779, he won election to fill a vacancy and had taken his seat by 3 December. He was elected again for one-year terms in 1780 and in 1787 and in the latter year served on the Committees of Commerce, of Propositions and Grievances, and for Religion.

On 16 June 1786 the governor appointed Clapham escheator for Loudoun County, but he did not present his commission to the county court until 9 April 1793 and did not take office until 12 March 1794. In November 1787 he became a trustee for the new town of Middleburg. The following year Clapham was a candidate for one of two seats representing the county in a convention called to consider the proposed constitution of the United States. A supporter of ratification, he lost an acrimonious election with a four-candidate field.

Josias Clapham dated his will on 8 July 1803 and died between then and 12 September 1803, when the will was proved in the Loudoun County Court. The place of his burial is not recorded. In 1997 a building on the site of Clapham's Ferry in Leesburg was added to the National Register of Historic Places.

Yorkshire origin reported in *Journal of Nicholas Cresswell, 1774–1777* (1924), 185; uncle's will in Fairfax Co. Will Book, A:309–311; approximate marriage date in Frederick Co., Md., chancery records of John Thompson estate, 22 Sept. 1787, Maryland State Archives, Annapolis; Hening, *Statutes*, 7:126, 9:62, 586; *Journals of Council of State*, 3:561; local appointments and service in Loudoun Co. Deed Books and Order Books; Land and Personal Property Tax Returns, Loudoun Co. (1782–1803), RG 48, LVA; numerous references in *Revolutionary Virginia*; 1788 campaign in Robert Conrad Powell, *A Biographical Sketch of Col. Leven Powell, Including His Correspondence during the Revolutionary War* (1877), 6; Harrison Williams, *Legends of Loudoun: An Account of the History and Homes of a Border County of Virginia's Northern Neck* (1938), esp. 121–122, 134–136; Charles Preston Poland Jr., *From Frontier to Suburbia* (1976), 10, 18, 19, 32, 35, 51, 53, 61; James Chapin Bradford, "Society and Government in Loudoun County, Virginia, 1790–1800" (Ph.D. diss., UVA, 1976), 25, 69–70, 121, 128, 297–298; will in Loudoun Co. Will Book, G:92–95.

JOHN G. DEAL

CLARK, Adèle Goodman (27 September 1882–4 June 1983), painter and woman suffrage activist, was born in Montgomery, Alabama, and was the daughter of Robert Clark and Estelle Goodman Clark. During her childhood her family moved several times, to Virginia, to Mississippi, back to Alabama, and then to Louisiana. After her family settled in Richmond about 1894, she enrolled in Virginia Randolph Ellett's school (later Saint Catherine's School). She graduated in 1901, studied art privately with Lily M. Logan and at the Art Club of Richmond, and in 1906 received a scholarship to the Chase School of Art (later the New York School of Art and eventually the Parsons School of Design), where she studied with William Merritt Chase and Robert Henri.

Clark returned to Virginia and taught classes in illustration at the Art Club of Richmond and was an instructor at the Richmond Training School for Kindergartners. About 1916 she and the Richmond artist Nora Houston established the Atelier. Their studio became a training ground for a generation of Virginia artists, including Theresa Pollak, who later founded the art program at the University of Richmond and the art school at Virginia Commonwealth University. Intending to revive the long-moribund eighteenth-century Academy of Sciences and Fine Arts, Clark and Houston in 1919 founded the Virginia League of Fine Arts and Handicrafts, which later merged with the Atelier and became part of the Richmond Academy of Arts. A painter primarily of portraits, landscapes, and religious scenes, Clark exhibited canvases at the Carnegie Institute, in Pittsburgh, and at Richmond's Valentine Museum. Her oil painting *Cherry Tree* (ca. 1920–1930), depicting a shimmering impression of a tree blooming in her garden, is in the permanent collection of the Virginia Museum of Fine Arts.

Clark's life exemplified the crucial role women played in the social reform movements of the twentieth century. She applied her sharp intellect, artistic skills, and determination to champion women and the arts. Her interest in the woman suffrage movement began in 1909. On 27 November of that year Clark and other civic-minded women held a meeting to establish a statewide suffrage organization. Many of them wanted the vote in order to work more effectively for the passage of health, education, and child labor laws.

Clark was elected recording secretary at that first meeting of the Equal Suffrage League of Virginia but resigned the office the following March. Her first paying job in Richmond, as a stenographer for the Chamber of Commerce, provided useful experience. She enlisted her mother and sister in the suffrage cause, helped direct legislative initiatives, designed and drew postcards, organized suffrage rallies, and went on speaking tours that helped establish league chapters throughout the state. In 1912 Clark debated the antisuffrage leader Molly Elliot Seawell in various Richmond newspapers. Clark opened with "If Women Were to Vote" on 8 February in the *Richmond Virginian*, Seawell answered with "Why Women Should Not Vote" on 25 February in the *Richmond Times-Dispatch*, and Clark shot back in the *Times-Dispatch* on 11 March with "The Suffragist Movement: A Reply to Miss Molly Elliot Seawell," a detailed explanation of why women should have the vote. Clark's second article was so persuasive that the Equal Suffrage League distributed an expanded version as an educational booklet entitled *Facts vs. Fallacies: Anti-Suffrage Allegations Refuted* (1912). That same year Clark organized the screening of a suffrage film at the state fair, where the league also distributed suffrage buttons and yellow "Votes for Women" flags. The women often held their meetings in public places, such as Capitol Square, and Clark sometimes set up her easel and began drawing chalk sketches to lure people to suffrage speeches. "It reached the point," she recalled, "where I couldn't see a fireplug without beginning, 'Ladies and gentlemen.'"

Through canvassing, distributing leaflets, and public speaking, members of the Equal Suffrage League intended to educate Virginia's citizens and legislators and win their support for woman suffrage. Despite the fact that the league was one of the most vital suffrage organizations in the South, the General Assembly defeated woman suffrage resolutions in 1912, 1914, and 1916. Virginia suffragists thereafter directed their work primarily toward the passage of an amendment to the Constitution of the United States. By the time Congress submitted the Nineteenth Amendment to the states in June 1919, the league boasted 30,000 members. Clark chaired the league's ratification committee in 1919 and 1920. Nevertheless, Virginia was one of the nine southern states that refused to approve the amendment, and the commonwealth did not ratify the Nineteenth Amendment until 1952.

Within a few weeks of the national ratification of the Nineteenth Amendment in 1920, the Equal Suffrage League disbanded, and its successor, the Virginia League of Women Voters, began work to make the new vote an informed one. Clark chaired the organization committee to establish the league, was the first chair of the league in 1920, and served as president from 1921 to 1925 and again from 1929 to 1944. With fellow suffragist Naomi Silverman Cohn, Clark in 1923 founded the Virginia Women's Council of Legislative Chairmen of State Organizations (later the Virginia Council on State Legislation) to monitor bills of special interest to women. Her work involving social issues and governmental efficiency expanded in 1924 when she was elected to the board of the National League of Women Voters (later the League of Women Voters of the United States) as director of the third region, which included Washington, D.C., Virginia, and several other southern states. From

1925 to 1928 she was second vice president of the national league. In that capacity she traveled to and spoke at conventions in twenty-four states, including an address before the platform committee at the 1928 Democratic National Convention. In 1927 she chaired the Lila Meade Valentine Memorial Association, which sought to place a tablet or bust honoring the Richmond suffragist in the State Capitol.

In 1922 the governor appointed Clark to the Commission on Simplification and Economy of State and Local Government, on which she served for almost two years as secretary. In 1928 the next governor appointed her to a nine-member commission, of which she also became secretary, to study the feasibility of establishing a new liberal arts college for women at one of the state teachers' colleges. From March through September 1926 Clark was acting social director of women at the College of William and Mary, which had become coeducational in 1918.

Beginning in 1933 Clark was a field supervisor in Virginia for the National Reemployment Service, and from 1936 to 1942 as the state director of the Federal Art Project (after 1939 the Federal Art Program) of the Works Progress Administration (after 1939 the Work Projects Administration) she sought to provide employment opportunities for artists in Virginia. Under her direction, artists produced murals for public buildings and executed hundreds of paintings for display in local and state tax-supported institutions. During Clark's tenure several new art galleries were established, including the Federal Art Gallery at Big Stone Gap. In 1938 Clark chaired the Virginia committee for the exhibition of southern art at the 1939–1940 World's Fair in New York. She served in 1941 on the Virginia executive committee for National Art Week.

Clark was active in the Richmond community for decades. After converting to Catholicism in 1942 (her mother had been Jewish, her father raised in the Church of England in his native Ireland), she helped organize the Richmond Diocesan Council of Catholic Women and shape its legislative program. She spoke for desegregated schools and against the poll tax. In December 1967 Clark received a brotherhood citation from the Richmond chapter of the National Confer-

ence of Christians and Jews (later the National Conference for Community and Justice). In the 1940s she taught art to Richmond children who were disabled or convalescing from illness. She also worked with the city school board and the Virginia Society for Crippled Children and Adults. Clark offered instruction in painting and modeling, along with making masks, puppets, marionettes, and block prints. She continued to support the city's art community and was instrumental in establishing Virginia's Art Commission, of which she was a member from 1941 to 1964. Clark never married and for many years lived with her companion and first cousin, the bohemian fashion designer, artist, and writer Willoughby Ions.

On 2 February 1973 Clark's photograph appeared on the front page of the *Richmond Times-Dispatch* with the skeptical headline, "Beginning of an ERA?" The ninety-year-old Clark and 800 other people had attended a public meeting to express their opinions of the proposed Equal Rights Amendment. As usual, Clark did not mince words. "This is an appalling amendment," she told an audience that included citizens, legislators, the president of the National Association of Women Lawyers, and prominent ERA opponent Phyllis Schlafly. "It reflects the thinking of fifty years ago. They are fighting a battle that has already been won." Adèle Goodman Clark, who had been fighting the battles from the beginning, died in a Richmond retirement community on 4 June 1983 and was buried in Emmanuel Episcopal Church Cemetery, in Henrico County.

Biography in Valentine Museum, *Catalogue: Three Generations of Richmond Artists: William Ludwell Sheppard, Nora Houston, Adele Clark, Edmund Minor Archer* (1957); Adèle Goodman Clark Papers (1849–1978), including several autobiographical memoranda and questionnaires (two with birth date), VCU, and Adèle Clark Papers, VHS; other Clark letters in LVA, VRHC, VHS, and Virginia Museum of Fine Arts, Richmond; transcription of 1964 oral history interview, VHS; Equal Suffrage League of Virginia Records (1909–1935) and League of Women Voters of Virginia Scrapbook (1920–1923), both LVA; Federal Art Project Records of Adèle Clark (1931–1963) and Clark interview, 16 Nov. 1963, both Archives of American Art, Smithsonian Institution, Washington, D.C.; feature articles (most with pors.) in *Richmond Times-Dispatch*, 10 July 1932, 5 Feb. 1943 (first quotation), 27 Dec. 1944, 3 July 1949, 16 Sept. 1956, 6 Dec. 1967, 2 Aug. 1971, 13 Aug. 1978, 26 Jan., 22 June 1979, 20

Apr. 1980, 12 June 1983, *Richmond Catholic Virginian*, 21 Sept. 1956, and *Richmond News Leader*, 16 Dec. 1964, 18 Apr., 4 June 1969, 24 Sept. 1982; *Richmond Times-Dispatch*, 20 Apr. 1929, 2 Feb. 1973 (second quotation); Cynthia Kennedy-Haflett, "To 'Raise Oneself to a Higher Plane': The Political Activism of Adele Clark, 1909–1930" (M.A. thesis, University of Richmond, 1989); Amanda Garrett, "Adele Clark: Suffragist and Women's Rights Pioneer for Virginia" (honor thesis, University of Richmond, 1999); principal publications include "If Women Were to Vote," *Richmond Virginian*, 8 Feb. 1912, "The Suffragist Movement: A Reply to Miss Molly Elliot Seawell," *Richmond Times-Dispatch*, 11 Mar. 1912, *Facts vs. Fallacies: Anti-Suffrage Allegations Refuted, A Reply to Miss Molly Elliot Seawell* (1912), "Address before the Conference on Citizenship Education at the University of Virginia, April 22, 1920," *Proceedings of School of Citizenship*, University of Virginia Record, Extension Series (1920), 46–49, *Atelier of the Virginia League of Fine Arts and Handicrafts*, with Nora Houston (1921), "The Ideals of the League of Women Voters," *Institute of Citizenship and Government*, University of Virginia Record, Extension Series (1923), 64–67, "A Critical Analysis of State Administrative Reorganization," *Virginia Institute of Citizenship and Government*, University of Virginia Record, Extension Series (1927), 145–163, "Academy Square, Richmond, Virginia," Medical College of Virginia *Bulletin* 25 (Nov. 1928): 9–13, a tribute to Lila Hardaway Meade Valentine in *Richmond Times-Dispatch*, 10 May 1931, reprinted in *Richmond Literature and History Quarterly* 2 (fall 1979): 33–35, Virginia Capital Bicentennial Commission, "Art," *Sketches of Societies and Institutions, Together with Descriptions of Phases of Social, Political and Economic Development in Richmond, Virginia* (1937), pt. 6, and "Robert Terrill Gills, Artist and Illustrator," in *It Happened at Appomattox: The Story of an Historic Virginia Village* (1948), 41–42; obituaries in *Richmond Times-Dispatch*, 5 June 1983, *Richmond News Leader*, 6 June 1983, and *Richmond Catholic Virginian*, 20 June 1983.

JENNIFER DAVIS MCDAID

CLARK, Amanda Virginia Thomas (January 1869–26 May 1952), educator and civic leader, was born in Smithfield. Her parents, George Washington Thomas, a lighthouse keeper, and Adeline Boykin Thomas, both had been born into slavery, but they achieved a measure of economic success after the Civil War and instilled in their six children a strong desire for education. At age thirteen Amanda Thomas entered the Virginia Normal and Collegiate Institute (later Virginia State University). After receiving a teaching certificate from the normal department in 1887, she taught for three years in Isle of Wight County public schools. During the 1890–1891 academic year Thomas instructed elementary students at the Twenty-second Street Public School in the booming shipbuilding town of Newport News. She held lessons for several grades in an upstairs room of the principal's house.

Thomas returned to Smithfield in 1891 and there on 27 April 1892 married Norris Berkley Clark, a native of Alexandria and graduate of Hampton Normal and Agricultural Institute (later Hampton University). The following year they moved to Newport News, where he became a respected attorney, educator, business leader, civic activist, and the first African American member of the city school board. She returned to teaching at the Twenty-second Street Public School, but in 1896, soon after Newport News incorporated as a city, the school board ruled that only single women could teach in the public schools. Consequently, from 1897 until 1911 Clark concentrated on her family. She had five sons, two daughters, and two other children who died young; she also raised one foster son. Clark became involved in numerous educational and civic organizations. She persuaded the city to increase the number of schools for African American children, improve streets around those schools, and incorporate vocational training into the public school programs for African Americans.

After the school board changed its rule in 1911 and again allowed married women to teach, Clark returned to the classroom and taught at John Marshall School, an elementary school for black children that at its opening in 1899 was the first school for the city's African American elementary students. Clark taught at John Marshall until she retired in 1941. In the meantime she continued with her own education. Completing summer courses at Hampton and extension courses at Virginia Normal and Industrial Institute, Clark received a second teaching certificate from her alma mater in August 1924 and a B.S. in elementary education in 1933, one year after her youngest surviving child graduated from the same college.

Her own experience made Clark keenly aware of the importance of parental involvement in the education of children. With financial assistance from the wife of the owner of the Newport News shipyard, she organized the Mothers' Clubs, from which the Parent-Teacher Association emerged. In 1918 she and seven other women organized the Women's Leisure Hour Club to encourage middle-class African American women in the constructive use of their leisure time through civic, religious, and social activity. Using the motto "Through Leisure to Deeper Culture," the club organized programs of panel discussions, speakers, book reviews, and self-improvement efforts.

Imbued with a tradition of service, Clark was a committed community leader and assisted in founding organizations throughout the broader Hampton Roads area. She was a member of the Federation of Colored Women's Clubs, which formed a Hampton chapter in 1908. An alliance of several women's groups, the federation attracted women primarily from the middle and educated classes who had some financial resources and leisure time to devote to community service. At a meeting of the Hampton chapter in Clark's home, members made plans to create a school for wayward girls. Initially named the Industrial Home School for Colored Girls and later the Virginia Industrial School for Colored Girls, it opened in Hanover County in 1915 under the direction of Clark's friend and fellow chapter member, Janie Porter Barrett. Clark, Barrett, and other members also established a chapter of the Negro Organization Society, which helped coordinate the work of several groups interested in improving health, schools, and neighborhoods and in addressing civic concerns of African Americans in Virginia. Clark also became a charter member of other service organizations, such as the local chapter of the United Order of Tents.

Clark and her husband were active members of Saint Paul African Methodist Episcopal Church in Newport News. She organized the church's first choir, and he served as the church clerk and chaired the trustee and steward boards. Devoted to music, she was the organist at Saint Paul A.M.E. Church, A.M.E. Zion Church, and the Presbyterian Church. Clark's husband died on 29 July 1940. After an extended illness that confined her to her home for several years, Amanda Virginia Thomas Clark died on 26 May 1952 at Whittaker Memorial Hospital in Newport News. She was buried in Holly Grove Cemetery in Hampton following a well-attended funeral service.

Biography (with variant birth year of 1872) in Virginia Iota State Organization of Delta Kappa Gamma Society, *Adventures in Teaching: Pioneer Women Educators and Influential Teachers* (1963), 160–163; variant birth date of 16 Jan. 1875 provided by BVS; Census, Isle of Wight Co., 1880 (age eleven on 4 June 1880), Warwick Co., 1900 (birth date of Jan. 1869), 1910 (age forty on 27 Apr. 1910), 1920 (age forty-seven on 19 Jan. 1920), 1930 (age fifty-five on 16 Apr. 1930); Isle of Wight Co. Marriage Register (age twenty-three on 27 Apr. 1892); Virginia State Federation of Colored Women's Clubs, Inc., *History of the Virginia State Federation of Colored Women's Clubs, Inc.* (1996), 87; husband's obituaries in *Newport News Daily Press* and *Newport News Times-Herald*, both 31 July 1940, and *Norfolk Journal and Guide*, 3 Aug. 1940; obituaries in *Newport News Times-Herald*, 28 May 1952, *Newport News Daily Press*, 29 May 1952, and *Norfolk Journal and Guide*, 7 June 1952 (por.).

CASSANDRA L. NEWBY-ALEXANDER

CLARK, Christopher Henderson (ca. 1768–4 November 1828), member of the House of Representatives, was probably the son of Robert Clark and Susan Henderson Clark and may have been born in Goochland County. If so, he was an elder brother of James Clark, who moved with their parents to Kentucky, returned to study law with Christopher Clark, and then went back to Kentucky, where he became governor and served five nonconsecutive terms in Congress. Christopher Clark attended Liberty Hall Academy (later Washington and Lee University). He studied law, settled in Bedford County (where his father had become a justice of the peace), and was admitted to the bar on 26 May 1788. On 24 November of that year the county court recommended that he be appointed commonwealth's attorney for the county, in which post he served until September 1803. If Clark had not yet reached the age of twenty-one when he began to practice law, that was unusual but not unprecedented. As an adult he seldom used his middle name or initial and was almost always referred to as Christopher or Chris Clark, and his contemporaries frequently added a terminal *e* to his surname.

On 24 April 1790 Clark married Elizabeth Hook, daughter of John Hook, a Franklin County merchant. They had at least one daughter and probably had two sons. About the time of his marriage Clark won election to the House of Delegates for the session that met from October to

December 1790 and served on the Committee for Courts of Justice and the Committee of Propositions and Grievances. Even though he was a new member and a very young attorney, he was also named to a select committee to draft amendments to the Virginia law governing descent of property. Clark was appointed a lieutenant in the county militia in August 1791 and promoted to captain in June 1794, but he resigned his commission the following year.

Whether Clark actively engaged in elective politics during the remainder of the decade is uncertain, but in 1800 he supported Thomas Jefferson for president. In the summer of 1804 Clark won a special election to succeed John Trigg, who had died, in the House of Representatives from the district composed of the counties of Bedford, Franklin, Henry, and Patrick. Clark took his seat on 5 November 1804 and was elected to a full term shortly thereafter. For a new member he spoke fairly often, and he appears to have impressed other members with his abilities or perhaps with his loyalty to Jefferson, because on 28 January 1805 the House named him one of the managers to prosecute the impeachment of Associate Justice Samuel Chase in the United States Senate. Not so active as the other managers, Clark made only one speech during the proceedings, to explain the Virginia law that Chase should have applied when presiding over the 1800 trial of the acerbic Richmond journalist James Thomson Callender, one of the cases that Chase was accused of trying improperly. Clark also reportedly attempted to engineer the appointment of John Randolph of Roanoke as minister to Great Britain, but whether Clark thought that Randolph deserved the prestigious diplomatic post or wanted to help get one of Jefferson's sometime critics out of Congress is unclear.

Clark probably surprised his colleagues when he resigned from Congress early in August 1806 to resume the full-time practice of law in Bedford County. Among his clients were his father-in-law, the wealthy Callaways of Bedford and Franklin Counties, and Jefferson, whose Poplar Forest estate was near Clark's Mount Prospect, where he lived for about a decade beginning in 1805. Clark's wife died about 1810, and in 1812

he contemplated giving up the law in favor of agriculture and sought advice on farm management from Jefferson. They occasionally discussed points of law, and Clark may have transacted legal business for Jefferson in Bedford County for several more years. Clark probably continued his practice. His other interests included the New London Academy, of which he was probably a board member in 1817.

On 8 July 1815 Clark purchased the Grove, a 1,050-acre Campbell County estate adjacent to Jefferson's Bedford County property. Two days later Clark married Mary Norvell, of Campbell County. Whether they had any children before her death sometime after 15 October 1819 is unclear. Details of Clark's family life are sketchy and contradictory. During the winter of 1818–1819 his two sons were boarding with neighbors, but they were probably the children of his first wife.

The death of Clark's second wife came almost simultaneously with financial disaster. As a responsible party in the settlement of the large and complicated Hook and Callaway estates, Clark was entangled in a web of debts and lawsuits. Following the panic of 1819 he had to borrow money, sell property at a loss, convey other property to his creditors at a discount, and finally on 20 July 1820 sign over everything he owned, including nearly sixty slaves, to his creditors. The anonymous author of a fulsome obituary later reported that these events "proved more than he could bear. The energies of his mind gave way and could never be rallied." Christopher Henderson Clark lived the remainder of his life in a debilitated, destitute condition and died at a private residence near New London on 4 November 1828.

Catalogue of the Officers and Alumni of Washington and Lee University (1888), 50 (with incorrect death year of 1825); Christopher Henderson Clark Papers, Duke; some Clark letters in various other collections at Duke, in Thomas Jefferson Papers, LC, and in Coolidge Collection of Thomas Jefferson Manuscripts, Massachusetts Historical Society, Boston; Bedford Co. Order Book, 9:163 (full name given), 202, 10:107, 315, 11:15, 13:40, 22:211; numerous entries in Bedford and Campbell Co. Deed Books; Franklin Co. Marriage Bonds (1790); Campbell Co. Marriage Bonds and Consents (1815); children identified in Bedford Co. Marriage Bonds (bond for daughter dated 21 July 1814), and in estate accounts of John Dabney, returned 11 Sept. 1820,

Campbell Co. Will Book, 4:273; *Annals of Congress*, 8th Cong., 2d sess., cols. 353–354, 678, 1019; resignation from Congress in William Armistead Burwell to Thomas Jefferson, 7 Aug. 1806, Thomas Jefferson Papers, LC, and Clark to William H. Cabell, 9 Aug. 1806, William H. Cabell Executive Papers, RG 3, LVA; Gerard W. Gawalt, ed., "'Strict Truth': The Narrative of William Armistead Burwell," *VMHB* 101 (1993): 117, 121; Nora A. Carter, "Mount Prospect" (typescript dated Nov. 1937), in Works Progress Administration, Virginia Historical Inventory, LVA; obituaries giving death date "in the 61st year of his age" in *Lynchburg Virginian*, 20 Nov. 1828 (quotation), and *Richmond Enquirer*, 25 Nov. 1828.

BRENT TARTER

CLARK, David Henderson (25 February 1899–3 September 1982), naval officer and executive director of the Virginia State Ports Authority, was born in Henderson, Kentucky, and was the son of David Clark, a tobacco farmer, and Julia Ballard Dixon Clark. He attended the Henderson public schools and the United States Naval Academy Preparatory School in Annapolis, Maryland. Clark entered the United States Naval Academy in 1915, lettered in basketball and lacrosse, and graduated with a B.S. in 1918. Commissioned an ensign in June 1918, Clark performed convoy escort duty until the end of World War I and during the next decade served as a staff or engineering officer on board several destroyers and battleships. He was promoted to lieutenant junior grade in September 1918 and lieutenant four years later. From 1923 to 1924 he attended the Naval Postgraduate School and in 1925 graduated from Columbia University with an M.S. in electrical engineering. On 2 July 1927 in Woodbury, New Jersey, he married Catharine Angelica Hutchinson, an amateur golfer who won the Virginia state championship in 1932 and the Mid-Atlantic states championship two year later. They had two sons and one daughter.

Clark served as an engineer at the Philadelphia Navy Yard from November 1928 to September 1930 and then returned to sea duty for the next two years as executive officer on the destroyer *Dupont*. He was promoted to lieutenant commander in 1932 and assigned to an afloat command in Norfolk from 1932 to 1933. Clark made Virginia his permanent residence in 1935 when he built a house in Arlington County. That same year he requested engineering duty and

served as the officer in charge of naval and aeronautical engineering postgraduate training at the Naval Postgraduate School from 1936 to 1938. In the latter year he was promoted to commander. For the next two years Clark was a naval personnel officer, first with the Bureau of Engineering and then, after its creation in 1940, with the Bureau of Ships. During the early years of the country's involvement in World War II he served as fleet engineering officer on the staff of the commander in chief of the Pacific fleet and as assistant fleet maintenance officer. Promoted to captain in 1942, Clark the next year became a planning officer for the Boston Navy Yard. For his war service he received the Legion of Merit.

Promoted to rear admiral in 1946, with rank to date from 24 July 1943, Clark was named commanding officer of the Naval Engineering Experiment Station at Annapolis. From 19 March 1947 to 1 February 1949 he commanded the Norfolk Naval Shipyard, where the Atlantic fleet was serviced and repaired. The most important assignment in Clark's naval career came in 1949, when he became the chief of the Bureau of Ships, the office responsible for the design, construction, and maintenance of the navy's vessels as well as the management of naval shipyards and several large research and development laboratories. Clark served until 1951. In that year he was elected to a one-year term as president of the American Society of Naval Engineers but held office only four months before resigning on 28 April 1951. He concluded his military career with a second tour of duty as commander of the Norfolk Naval Shipyard from 15 February 1951 until his retirement on 30 June 1953.

Clark then began a second career as the first executive director of the Virginia State Ports Authority, created by the General Assembly in 1952 to develop and promote the commonwealth's ports and waterborne commerce. Elected by the board of commissioners on 2 April 1953, he formally took the position on 1 July. During his thirteen-year tenure Clark educated members of the legislature on the importance of ports to the state's economy and attracted national and international trade to Virginia. The volume of the state's waterborne commerce increased from about 41 million tons in 1953 to 71 million tons in 1964, while the value of cargo shipping increased from about $1.1 billion to $1.8 billion during the same period. From 1953 to 1964 civilian employment in Virginia related to waterborne commerce increased from about 47,000 to more than 53,000, and wages in this sector rose from about $160 million to more than $300 million. State and local tax revenue generated by goods shipped from Virginia's ports more than doubled from $12.5 million in 1953 to $30.7 million in 1965.

While Clark was the executive director, the Virginia State Ports Authority established branch offices in New York and Chicago, was the first transport agency to open full-time offices in Europe, and was one of the first port authorities on the East Coast to set up an office in Tokyo to promote trade in Asia. The agency also became involved in issues related to truck and railroad freight rates as well as cargo terminal charges. Clark oversaw the construction of modern cargo terminals and supported harbor and channel improvement projects. He retired from the Virginia State Ports Authority on 31 December 1966. David Henderson Clark died in a Virginia Beach hospital on 3 September 1982 and was buried in that city's Eastern Shore Chapel Cemetery.

Résumé, Mar. 1953, Virginia State Ports Authority Recommendations folder, John Stewart Battle Executive Papers, RG 3, LVA; Morton, *Virginia Lives*, 186–187; published works include Clark, *Activities of the Virginia State Ports Authority in the Development of Hampton Roads Ports* (1963); *Norfolk Ledger-Dispatch*, 19 Mar. 1947, 18 Jan. 1949, 15 Feb. 1951; *Norfolk Virginian-Pilot*, 20 Mar. 1947, 3 Apr., 2 July 1953; *Portsmouth Star*, 2 Apr. (por.), 1 July 1953; *Newport News Daily Press*, 3 Apr. 1953; *Norfolk Ledger-Star*, 16 Nov. 1966; Board of Commissioners of the Virginia State Ports Authority, *Annual Reports* (1954–1967); William Shands Meacham, "Hampton Roads: A Rising Tide in Harbor Planning," *Commonwealth* 32 (Oct. 1965): 33–35; obituary in *Norfolk Virginian-Pilot*, 4 Sept. 1982 (por.).

ROGER E. CHRISTMAN

CLARK, Emily Tapscott (8 September 1891–2 July 1953), editor and writer, was the only child of William Meade Clark, an Episcopal minister, and his second wife, Nancy Douglas Tapscott Clark. She was born in Raleigh, North Carolina, and grew up in Fredericksburg and then in Richmond, where her father became rector of Saint James's Episcopal Church in 1896 and edited the *Southern Churchman*. After her mother's death in 1894, her father married Mary Alice Peirce on 7 December 1899. Emily Clark was close to her stepmother and continued to live with her after her father died on 29 April 1914.

While a student at Virginia Randolph Ellett's school (later Saint Catherine's School) in Richmond, Clark joined the editorial staff of *Frills and Frizzes*, the student literary yearbook, to which she contributed poems and essays. Later she began writing for the *Richmond Evening Journal's* book review page, the demise of which in 1920 prompted Clark and three other Richmonders—Margaret Waller Freeman (later James Branch Cabell's second wife), Hunter Taylor Stagg, and Mary Dallas Street—to begin their own literary magazine, *The Reviewer*. First appearing in February 1921 as a fortnightly publication (and later becoming a monthly and then a quarterly journal), *The Reviewer* quickly attracted the attention of James Branch Cabell, Joseph Hergesheimer, and H. L. Mencken, who helped shepherd the editors through their early issues.

Created just after Mencken's essay "The Sahara of the Bozart" had decried the southern literary wasteland, *The Reviewer* sought to encourage the burgeoning renascence in southern literature. In addition to providing breezy, gossipy book reviews, Clark served as the enthusiastic acquisitions editor who employed flattery and sometimes flirtation to attract both established national writers and southern authors just beginning their careers. Contributors included Maxwell Bodenheim, John Galsworthy, Ellen Glasgow, Paul Green, DuBose Heyward, Mary Johnston, Amy Lowell, Henry Read McIlwaine, Gertrude Stein, Julia Peterkin, Allen Tate, and Amélie Louise Rives Troubetzkoy, all of whom wrote for payment "in fame not specie," as a notice on the subscription page declared. Despite its shoestring budget, *The Reviewer* garnered favorable notice from the *New York Herald* and *New York Times* but received scant attention in the southern press.

Carl Van Vechten described the carroty-haired Clark as looking "like the child of Sarah Bernhardt by a yellow panther." Her buckteeth and speech impediment frequently made her difficult to understand, but she displayed enough charm, vivacity, and biting wit to create a place for herself at the Algonquin Round Table. While editing *The Reviewer* gratis, she worked as a staff writer for the *Richmond News Leader* from 1920 to 1923. In the latter year Clark attracted the attention of the widower Edwin Swift Balch, an attorney, author, and explorer thirty-five years her senior whom she described in a letter to Hergesheimer as "rich and fat and aristocratic, and rather nauseating at times." Balch pulled *The Reviewer* out of debt by purchasing the magazine's stock and putting it in Clark's name. Clark married him in Richmond on 1 November 1924, one month after editing her last issue of *The Reviewer*. Emily Clark Balch moved to her husband's home in Philadelphia, while *The Reviewer* took up residence at the University of North Carolina, where it ceased publication in 1925. The Balches had no children, and Edwin Balch died on 15 March 1927.

Remaining in Philadelphia, Emily Clark Balch made her home a salon for writers and artists. She continued writing reviews for the *American Mercury*, the *Saturday Review of Literature*, and the *Smart Set*, using her maiden name, until 1934. Mencken encouraged Clark to complete *Stuffed Peacocks*, a series of thirteen barely disguised character sketches that provided a scathing satire of Richmond society, and helped her find a publisher for the collection in 1927. That volume, as well as her catty letters to Joseph Hergesheimer, published after her death as *Ingénue among the Lions* (1965), left feathers ruffled in Richmond for decades. In 1931 Clark published the less controversial *Innocence Abroad*, an account of the founding of *The Reviewer* along with biographical essays on thirteen literary colleagues, and dedicated it to her stepmother.

Emily Tapscott Clark Balch died at her home in Philadelphia on 2 July 1953. She was buried the following day in Hollywood Cemetery in Richmond. The *Virginia Quarterly Review* established the Emily Clark Balch Prizes in poetry and short stories in 1955 with a bequest left by Clark to the University of Virginia to encourage appreciation and creation of American literature.

Maurice Duke, "Ingénue Among the Richmonders: Of Emily Clark and Stuffed Peacocks," *Ellen Glasgow Newsletter* 3 (Oct. 1975): 5–9; Elizabeth S. Scott, " 'In fame, not specie':

The Reviewer, Richmond's oasis in 'The Sahara of the Bozart,' " *Virginia Cavalcade* 27 (1978): 128–143 (por. on 141); Scott, "Emily Clark: Ingénue or Super Shrew?" *Richmond Quarterly* 6 (fall 1983): 16–21; Benjamin E. Wise, " 'An Experiment in Southern Letters': Reconsidering the Role of *The Reviewer* in the Southern Renaissance," *VMHB* 113 (2005): 146–178; birth year 1891 in Census, Richmond City, 1900 (name given as Emily D. T. Clark), 1920; variant birth date of 8 Sept. 1892 in funeral contract, 2 July 1953, L. T. Christian Funeral Home Records, Acc. 34483, LVA; Richmond City Marriage Records (giving age as thirty-three on 1 Nov. 1924); *Richmond News Leader*, 3 Nov. 1924; Clark, *Innocence Abroad* (1931), 8 (first quotation), 132 (second quotation); Clark correspondence in various collections at UVA and printed in *Ingénue among the Lions: The Letters of Emily Clark to Joseph Hergesheimer*, ed. Gerald Langford (1965) (third quotation on 187); prospectus for *The Reviewer*, 1921, reproduced in *Ellen Glasgow Newsletter* 6 (Mar. 1977): 13–15; Clark, "Postscript," *The Reviewer* 4 (1924): 405–408; Maurice Duke, "*The Reviewer*: A Bibliographical Guide to a Little Magazine," *Resources for American Literary Study* 1 (spring 1971): 58–103; *Virginia Quarterly Review* 31 (autumn 1955): xcv; obituaries in *Richmond News Leader*, 2 July 1953, *Philadelphia Inquirer*, 3 July 1953 (confuses Clark's career with that of Balch's first wife), *Richmond Times-Dispatch*, 3 July 1953, and *New York Times*, 4 July 1953.

MARY CARROLL JOHANSEN

CLARK, George Rogers (19 November 1752–13 February 1818), member-elect of the Convention of 1776 and Revolutionary War officer, was the son of John Clark and Ann Rogers Clark. He was born near Charlottesville in Albemarle County and grew up on the family's small farm in Caroline County. Little is known about his early life or education, but in the 1760s he may have briefly attended Donald Robertson's well-known school in King and Queen County. Clark was not studious, but he possessed an aptitude for mathematics and by age nineteen had become a surveyor. He developed an interest in history, geography, and natural phenomena and acquired a large library. He never married. His much-younger brother William Clark was also born in Virginia but lived his eventful life in the West, where he became governor of the Missouri Territory after he and Meriwether Lewis led a successful expedition of discovery across North America.

Between the summer of 1772 and the spring of 1774 Clark explored the upper Ohio River Valley and claimed land about 130 miles downriver from Fort Pitt. The plans in which he participated to establish a settlement in Kentucky were delayed when fighting broke out between settlers and western Indian tribes. On 2 May 1774 Clark became a militia captain and in October of that year took part in the campaign that defeated Cornstalk at Point Pleasant. By the treaty that terminated Dunmore's War the Indians relinquished hunting grounds south of the Ohio River, thus leaving Kentucky open to settlement. The following spring Clark joined other surveyors working for the Ohio Company of Virginia, one of several competing western land companies that claimed rights to Kentucky land. Chief among its rivals was the Transylvania Company of Richard Henderson, of North Carolina. In June 1776 Clark was one of two men whom western settlers elected to represent them in the last of the Revolutionary Conventions then meeting in Williamsburg, but the convention adjourned long before they reached the capital. The district had not been authorized to elect representatives, and in October the House of Delegates declined to seat them, but the General Assembly created Kentucky County and thus scotched Henderson's proposed western colony.

During the winter of 1776–1777 Clark returned to Kentucky with a supply of gunpowder and a major's commission, which made him the ranking militia officer of the new county. Seeking to curb enemy Indian raids by striking at British-controlled outposts in the West, he dispatched spies to Vincennes and Kaskaskia, on the Mississippi River, and prepared a report for Virginia's governor. In December 1777, with the governor's cooperation, the assembly provided resources for a western expedition but carefully concealed Clark's plans. Clark, in Williamsburg at the time, was promoted to lieutenant colonel and on 2 January 1778 received the governor's confidential orders to organize the expedition.

Operating in secrecy made recruiting difficult, and when Clark's flatboats departed down the Ohio River on 12 May 1778 only about 150 men were on board. His Illinois Regiment, augmented to about 175 men by the latter part of June, began the 120-mile march to Kaskaskia, where on 4 July they slipped across the river, broke into the fort, and seized the commander. After reassuring the French inhabitants of their safety and securing their loyalty, Clark dispatched

troops to occupy Cahokia and Vincennes and by 20 July had secured their allegiance as well. He also established cordial relations with Spanish officials at Saint Louis, who offered him military aid. Clark's dramatic expedition reinforced Virginia's claim, and hence the claim of the United States, to the region north of the Ohio River.

The British reacted quickly. On 17 December 1778 a British force seized the fort at Vincennes. Clark counterattacked two months later with a force estimated at from 127 to 200 men. They marched 180 miles to Vincennes under exceptionally harsh winter conditions, forded a flooded plain five miles wide, with shallows three feet deep, and seized Fort Sackville on 25 February 1779. Following Clark's daring victory the General Assembly created Illinois County north of the Ohio River and east of the Mississippi.

Clark repeatedly planned to attack the British at Detroit, but even with the support of Virginia's governor he had too few men and supplies and had to postpone planned expeditions in 1779 and 1780. Instead, he defended against British attempts to recapture the Illinois country. The British made wide-ranging raids on key American positions and, after Spain declared war on Great Britain, attacked outposts at Saint Louis and elsewhere. Clark quickly moved to repulse British forces and led a punishing campaign against the Shawnee at Chillicothe. He became a brigadier general of Virginia troops on 22 January 1781 but was still not able to recruit and equip a force adequate to attack Detroit. As he wrote later that year, "I have lost the object that was one of the principal inducements to my fatigues & transactions for several years past— my chain appears to have run out."

Fighting in the East largely ceased late in 1781, but military disasters in the West in 1782 so demoralized Kentuckians that Clark undertook a retaliatory expedition, in part at his own expense, and destroyed six Shawnee towns. His militia commission was rescinded after the signing of the Treaty of Paris in 1783, but the treaty acknowledged American ownership of the vast region north of the Ohio River and east of the Mississippi River. The Northwest Territory, as it came to be known, belonged to the United States by virtue of Clark's military leadership.

Clark spent much of the remainder of his life attempting to put his military accounts in order and to secure compensation for expenses he had incurred or money that he had paid out of his own pocket. Virginia owed him nearly £3,400 in back pay and out-of-pocket expenses, which was to be paid with military certificates and warrants instead of cash, but he was held liable for unpaid wartime debts made in the state's name. Auditors in Richmond lost many of his vouchers, which complicated his personal finances for years. Several thousand of his unpaid vouchers were discovered in the State Capitol in 1913.

In 1783 Clark was named a trustee for Transylvania Seminary (later part of Transylvania University) and was certified as a surveyor by the College of William and Mary. The following year he became the principal surveyor of bounty lands that the state had set aside to compensate Virginia officers and soldiers. Clark also served on a board that supervised the distribution of lands in the Illinois grant. After Virginia ceded to the United States its claim to the Northwest Territory in March 1784, Congress appointed him one of the commissioners to manage negotiations with the Indians. He was present at Fort Macintosh in January 1785 when the tribes signed over most of their lands north of the Ohio River, and a year later he concluded a treaty with the Shawnee that granted the United States sovereignty over all lands ceded by Great Britain. Despite rumors of excessive drinking, Clark in 1786 was chosen to lead an expedition against the Wabash Indians. His inadequately supplied troops mutinied, and he returned to Vincennes, where he established a garrison outfitted with provisions seized from Spanish merchants. The United States and Spain were then locked in a dispute about use of the Mississippi River, and Clark's enemies used this incident against him. Accused of drunkenness, he found himself repudiated by the state government and his reputation in tatters. Believing that the facts spoke for themselves, Clark declined to defend himself. He lived with his father in Louisville, where he devoted much of his time to writing his memoirs.

Virginia still owed Clark nearly $12,000. He was not able to sell the large tracts of land that he owned in the West, and in 1791 the assembly rejected his claim for reimbursement for money that he had borrowed on his own credit and spent during the war in support of his military operations. To Spanish officials he offered his services in founding a colony in the Mississippi Valley, but unable to agree on conditions, he became involved in an abortive attempt to establish an independent colony between the American and Spanish settlements. In 1792 Clark proposed to help France wrest Louisiana from Spain and received a military commission. During a visit to Philadelphia in 1798 he was threatened with arrest and warned to resign as brigadier general in the French army or give up his American citizenship. He eventually escaped to Saint Louis.

In 1799 Clark returned to Louisville, where he depended on one of his brothers for support. He moved to a small cabin across the Ohio River from Louisville in 1803 and ran a gristmill. Impoverished and increasingly frail, he unsuccessfully petitioned Congress for financial relief. Clark had a stroke in 1809 and, after his infected right leg was amputated, lived with a sister at nearby Locust Grove, in Jefferson County, Kentucky. In 1812 the Virginia General Assembly finally granted him an annual pension of $400 and awarded him a sword. George Rogers Clark suffered a debilitating stroke the next year and died at Locust Grove on 13 February 1818 following another stroke. He was buried at Locust Grove, but in 1869 his remains were moved to Cave Hill Cemetery, later renamed Cave Hill National Cemetery, in Louisville. The George Rogers Clark National Historical Park, established in 1966 in Vincennes, Indiana, commemorates Clark's capture of Fort Sackville in 1779.

Biographies include James Alton James, *The Life of George Rogers Clark* (1928), John Bakeless, *Background to Glory: The Life of George Rogers Clark* (1957), Lowell H. Harrison, *George Rogers Clark and the War in the West* (1976), and Kenneth C. Carstens and Nancy Son Carstens, eds., *The Life of George Rogers Clark, 1752–1818: Triumphs and Tragedies* (2004), with several pors.; birth date of 19 Nov. 1752 in Draper MSS 1J40; miscalculated Old Style birth date of 9 Nov. 1752 on modern gravestone; family history documents, military records, and memoirs in George Rogers Clark Papers in Draper MSS, J series; many essential documents from British Library, LC, and LVA printed in James, ed., *George Rogers Clark Papers, 1771–1781* (1912), with quotation from Clark to Thomas Nelson, 1 Oct. 1781, on 608, and

George Rogers Clark Papers, 1781–1784 (1926); *Revolutionary Virginia*, 7:518–520, 565–567; financial records in Auditor of Public Accounts, RG 48, and correspondence in Office of the Governor, RG 3, both LVA; Virginia State Library *Annual Report, 1912–1913* (1914), 14; obituaries in *Lexington Kentucky Gazette*, 21 Feb. 1818, and *Washington Daily National Intelligencer*, 12 Mar. 1818.

DONALD W. GUNTER

CLARK, Matt (b. ca. 1844), member of the House of Delegates, was born into slavery in Halifax County and was the son of Mathew Clark and Chaney Clark. Contemporary public records occasionally expand his name to Mathew or Matthew Clark, and sometimes add a terminal *e* to his surname, but he signed his name as Matt Clark, and his name appeared in that form in the official proceedings of the House of Delegates. The name of his owner and the circumstances under which he secured his freedom are not known. By 1870 Clark had married Elizabeth Betts, could both read and write, was a farm laborer, and lived in the Mount Carmel district of Halifax County, near the North Carolina border. On 6 October 1870 he paid $154.12 for thirty-four acres of land located at or near the township of Black Walnut, where on 22 May 1873 he was elected justice of the peace.

In November 1873 Clark received just six fewer votes than the leading candidate in a six-man race that pitted three Republicans against three Conservatives in a contest for Halifax County's three seats in the House of Delegates. One of two black Halifax Republicans elected to serve in the sessions that met from 1 January to 30 April 1874 and from 2 December 1874 to 31 March 1875, he sat on the Committee on Asylums and Prisons. Clark seldom spoke on the House floor, even on routine procedural matters, and introduced only a few bills and resolutions, including a resolution supporting the improvement of living conditions at the Central Lunatic Asylum in Petersburg and a bill authorizing Halifax County residents to vote on establishing a free bridge at South Boston either by purchasing the existing toll bridge there or erecting a new bridge.

Virginia's public debt was one of the most contentious political issues during the 1870s. The controversy split the dominant Conservative Party into Funders, who wanted to preserve the state's honor and financial rating by paying off the debt in full, and Readjusters, who advocated refinancing at a lower interest rate or repudiating a portion of the debt and using the remaining revenue to support the new public school system and other public programs. Clark's House term coincided with a lull in the struggle between the opposing camps. Black Republicans generally supported readjustment, and it is likely Clark joined his colleagues in opposing Funder policies. On 25 March 1875 he voted with the minority against a bill authorizing payment of the interest on the debt.

A split also developed within the Republican Party. African Americans grew dissatisfied with white party leaders who favored raising taxes to fund the debt and who withheld the best federal patronage offices for themselves. Frustrated, black legislators called in March 1875 for an election of delegates to a special convention to be held in Richmond beginning on 19 August. About one hundred representatives from more than forty counties and cities attended the three-day meeting. Clark, one of five Halifax County representatives at the convention, was appointed to the Committee on Rules. Delegates discussed a range of subjects including job scarcity and the wretched condition of black schools. The convention established the Laboring Men's Mechanics' Union Association, a short-lived statewide grassroots organization designed to further black economic and political interests.

Clark did not stand for reelection in 1875. In September 1878 he put his land and house in a deed of trust to secure a debt. Clark was unable to pay off the debt, and in March 1882 creditors forced the sale of his property at public auction. Two years later his personal property, consisting of a cow, two hogs, a clock, household furniture, and at least one weapon, was valued at $40. Clark and his wife had at least three sons and at least two daughters. His wife died of dropsy on 13 April 1876, and on 30 December 1879 Clark married nineteen-year-old Nannie Walker, also of Halifax County. They had at least two daughters and one son. The date and place of Matt Clark's death are not known. His last appearance in the Halifax County public record is in the personal property tax list for 1892, when he owned a cow, three hogs, a watch, a clock, and a sewing machine with an aggregate value of $58.

Jackson, *Negro Office-Holders*, 8; signatures in Treasury Office Receipt Book (1872–1874), RG 12, LVA; Census, Halifax Co., 1870 (age twenty-eight on 20 Oct. 1870), 1880 (age forty on 12 June 1880); Halifax Co. Marriage Register (age thirty-five on 30 Dec. 1879); Land and Personal Property Tax Returns, Halifax Co., RG 48, LVA; Halifax Co. Minute Book, 23:308; Halifax Co. Deed Book, 62:123, 66:474–475, 71:308–309; Election Records, no. 411, RG 13, LVA; *JHD*, 1874 sess., 41, 71, 236, 1874–1875 sess., 56, 92, 201, 393; *Richmond Enquirer*, 5, 7 Nov. 1873, 20–22 Aug. 1875; *Richmond Daily Dispatch*, 20, 21 Aug. 1875.

DONALD W. GUNTER

CLARK, Pendleton Scott (21 February 1895–25 October 1975), architect, was born in Lynchburg and was the son of John Robert Clark, a tobacco dealer, and Bessie Pendleton Scott Clark. He attended Lynchburg public schools and graduated from the Augusta Military Academy in 1912. Clark began working as a draftsman for a Lynchburg architectural firm in 1914 and the following year entered the University of Pennsylvania, where he undertook a special two-year course in architectural studies and received a certificate of proficiency in 1917. After the United States entered World War I, he joined the United States Navy and served in the Atlantic fleet on the USS *Missouri* and then in troop transport service aboard the USS *Huron.* Having earned a Victory medal with one star, he was discharged with the rank of ensign in 1919. Clark returned to Lynchburg, for a brief time worked as a traveling salesman, and on 26 October 1922 married Alice Thornhill Fleming. They had one son and two daughters.

Shortly after beginning his professional practice early in the 1920s, Clark formed a partnership with Walter Rogers Crowe under the name Clark and Crowe. Clark's work designing both residential and commercial structures demonstrated an appreciation for the Piedmont's vernacular heritage, as seen in his own farmhouse-styled residence (1930). The firm also worked on large-scale projects, most notably at Sweet Briar College with the Boston architect Ralph Adams Cram. The Clark and Crowe firm dissolved in 1936 during the lean years of the Great Depression, and Clark continued to prac-

tice under his own name. In 1938 he designed Glen Alpine, a Bedford County house that the National Register of Historic Places later included in the Cifax Rural Historic District. Following the Japanese attack on Pearl Harbor, Clark joined the United States Naval Reserve as a lieutenant commander in 1942. He served with the Seabees in both the European and Pacific theaters of operation and was discharged in 1945 with the rank of commander. He received a Naval Reserve Medal and a Bronze Star for his service in the Philippines.

After World War II, Clark resumed his architectural practice in Lynchburg and formed a succession of partnerships there and in Norfolk. His most significant associate, Walter Rowbottom Nexsen, moved to Norfolk in 1954 to operate a second branch of the firm, Clark, Buhr, and Nexsen, and also became a partner in the Lynchburg branch, Clark, Nexsen, and Owen. In these partnerships, Clark earned a reputation for ambitious institutional and public projects in the region. Named campus architect at Sweet Briar College after Cram's death in 1942, Clark subsequently completed buildings for Lynchburg College, Mary Baldwin College, Virginia Military Institute, and Washington and Lee University. One exemplary project was Lynchburg's E. C. Glass High School (1950–1953), in which Clark employed a modernistic design that made creative use of inner courtyards and natural light. His other major commissions included the Coca-Cola Bottling Company Building (1938) in Danville and the Lynchburg General Hospital (1955), in addition to numerous churches, commercial buildings, health care facilities, hotels, residences, and theaters.

Clark was a director of the Lynchburg Historical Society in 1934 and two years later helped the city prepare for its sesquicentennial celebration by co-chairing a history committee of 150 members. He chaired Lynchburg's City Planning Commission from 1934 to 1938 and was a director of the city chamber of commerce from 1935 to 1936 and again from 1953 to 1955. Clark served the Virginia Chapter of the American Institute of Architects as secretary-treasurer for the 1932–1933 term, vice president from 1934 to 1936, and president in 1937. He was named to the AIA's exclusive College of Fellows in 1952 and the following year chaired the AIA's legislative committee. In September 1974 the Virginia chapter of the AIA conferred on Clark its highest honor, the William C. Noland Award, bestowed to recognize a distinguished body of work. At the time of his death he was writing a history of Lynchburg architects. Pendleton Scott Clark died on 25 October 1975 and was buried in Spring Hill Cemetery, in Lynchburg. Following his death the Lynchburg and Norfolk branches of his firm formally merged as Clark Nexsen, still at the beginning of the twenty-first century a prominent architectural firm with offices in Virginia and North Carolina and commissions in dozens of foreign countries.

Birth date provided by Clark in George S. Koyl, ed., *American Architects Directory* (1955), 97; Clark's surviving drawings and papers in several collections in the Lynchburg Architectural Archives, George M. Jones Memorial Library, Lynchburg; writings include "Society Will Restore Landmark" in *Lynchburg News*, 24 June 1934, and "A Brief History of Architects Practicing in Lynchburg, Virginia and Vicinity from 1800 to 1942" (1975), copy at Jones Memorial Library; Lynchburg Marriage Register; *Lynchburg News*, 1 Oct. 1974 (por.); *Lynchburg Daily Advance*, 2 Oct. 1974; S. Allen Chambers, *Lynchburg: An Architectural History* (1981), 373, 432, 459, 461, 467, 470–474, 477–478; Wells and Dalton, *Virginia Architects*, 87–89; obituaries and editorial tributes in *Lynchburg News*, 26, 28 Oct. 1975, and *Lynchburg Daily Advance*, 27, 30 Oct. 1975.

RYAN K. SMITH

CLARK, Samuel Harris (11 April 1885–25 June 1979), labor leader, was born in the town of Vicker in Montgomery County and was the son of a farmer, Charles E. Clark, and his second wife, Julia Lewis Clark. At the age of eleven he joined the New Hope Baptist Church, thus laying the foundation of faith that guided his life's work. After completing his education in the county's public schools, Clark attended Hampton Normal and Agricultural Institute (later Hampton University) before taking his first job on the railroad. On 25 October 1911 in Montgomery County he married Millie Virginia Nichols, who died on 27 June 1961. Their one son and four daughters included Alma Bernice Clark, who married Samuel Lee Gravely, the first African American to achieve flag rank in the United States Navy.

In 1913 Clark went to work in Roanoke as a brakeman for the Norfolk and Western Railway Company. Later he joined the Association of Colored Railway Trainmen and Locomotive Firemen (ACRT&LF), which had been founded in 1912 as the Colored Association of Railroad Employees. The union was one of several that represented African Americans, who were excluded from such unions as the Brotherhood of Locomotive Firemen and Enginemen (BLFE), which admitted only white members. Clark rose to the presidency of the Roanoke local in the 1930s, and in 1939 he was elected Grand President of the ACRT&LF at the union's convention in Bluefield, West Virginia. He served as president until his retirement from the Norfolk and Western in July 1958. During most of his tenure the union consisted of a small number of locals in southern railroad centers.

When elected, Clark promised that he would work to end racial discrimination in American railroading. In 1939 he approached the noted civil rights attorney Charles Hamilton Houston for help in protecting the railroad workers' rights. With Houston serving as the association's chief counsel, Clark led the organization through a number of landmark legal decisions that upheld the rights of black railroad workers. The first victory came in 1940 when the union negotiated a settlement for better wages, hours, and benefits for the black car-riders who worked on the coal piers of the Virginian Railway in Norfolk.

Clark, Houston, and the ACRT&LF then turned their attention to discrimination against black firemen. The union joined with the all-black International Association of Railway Employees to combat an agreement that the Southeastern Carriers' Conference had reached in 1941 that permitted the BLFE and twenty-one railroads to replace black firemen, who could not be promoted under union rules, with white firemen who could be promoted. In 1944 the Supreme Court of the United States ruled in the combined cases of *Steele* v. *Louisville and Nashville Railroad Co. et al.* and *Tunstall* v. *Brotherhood of Locomotive Firemen and Enginemen et al.* that because the BLFE was the recognized bargaining agent for railway employees, it could not discriminate against black firemen.

As in many other early civil rights cases, difficult as it sometimes was to establish a legal precedent, it was often even more difficult to enforce it. In 1958 Clark himself successfully sued the Norfolk and Western after the railroad employed similar discriminatory measures in deciding which brakemen could apply for promotion to higher-paying jobs as retarders.

Clark's dedication to public service, labor rights, and racial equality extended beyond his work with the ACRT&LF. He was a deacon at Roanoke's Jerusalem Baptist Church and sat on the board of Burrell Memorial Hospital, also in Roanoke. After he retired, Clark moved to Christiansburg, but he did not resign himself entirely to his favorite pastimes, gardening and fishing. He volunteered much of his time and served several terms as president of the Montgomery County chapter of the National Association for the Advancement of Colored People. As a leader of the NAACP and of a local senior volunteer program, he encouraged people to register and vote. Samuel Harris Clark died in a Blacksburg hospital on 25 June 1979 and was buried in the city's Schaeffer Memorial Community Cemetery.

Samuel H. Clark Papers, LC; BVS Marriage Register, Montgomery Co.; Genna Rae McNeil, *Groundwork: Charles Hamilton Houston and the Struggle for Civil Rights* (1983), 156–158, 162–163, based in part on a 1972 interview with Clark and on Clark's personal papers; Eric Arnesen, *Brotherhoods of Color: Black Railroad Workers and the Struggle for Equality* (2001), 149, 181, 227; *Steele v. Louisville and Nashville Railroad Co. et al.* (1944), and *Tunstall v. Brotherhood of Locomotive Firemen and Enginemen* (1944), *United States Reports*, 323:192–209, 210–214; *Norfolk Journal and Guide*, 19 Oct. 1946, 18 Aug. 1962 (both with pors.); *Norfolk and Western Magazine* (Nov. 1958), 609; obituaries in *Blacksburg-Christiansburg News Messenger* (with birth date) and *Roanoke Times and World-News*, both 27 June 1979; death notice in *Norfolk and Western Railway Company Magazine* (15 Oct. 1979), 27.

EVAN P. BENNETT

CLARK, William John (5 January 1877–17 June 1956), president of Virginia Union University, was born in Albion, Nebraska, and was the son of Stephen Clark and Edna Maria Gould Clark. In 1889 he joined the Baptist Church. His family moved to Madera, California, where he completed high school in 1899. Clark graduated from California College, in Oakland, in June 1903 with a B.A. and three years later received a B.D. from Newton Theological Institution (later Andover Newton Theological School), in Massachusetts. On 23 August 1906 he married Daisy Belle Peck in Morrisville, Vermont. They had one daughter and four sons, one of whom died in infancy.

On 11 December 1905 the American Baptist Foreign Mission Society appointed Clark to Maubin, a station in the Irrawaddy Division, Burma (later the Union of Myanmar), with about two dozen churches and 1,100 church members. Ordained a missionary on 14 October 1906 in Madera, he arrived in Burma with his wife on 7 November of that year and took up his post at the Pwo Karen Mission. During the first year he studied the Burmese language and organized a new church with about two dozen members.

Clark and his wife returned to the United States on 30 June 1909. He served as pastor at Enosburg, in Franklin County, Vermont, until 1912 and then at Saint Cloud, Florida, until September 1913, when he became professor of church history and biblical introduction at Virginia Union University, an African American junior college and seminary in Richmond operated by the American Baptist Home Mission Society. In addition to teaching theology and later English literature courses, he also was the school's librarian until 1923. Clark assumed the president's duties in January 1919, after George Rice Hovey resigned, and in March of that year Virginia Union's board of trustees formally appointed him president of the university.

Under Clark's guidance Virginia Union reopened its summer school for teachers in 1922 and began offering four-year education-degree programs that also fulfilled state requirements for obtaining professional teaching certificates. Extension programs established in Richmond and the Northern Neck provided educational opportunities for working teachers. In March 1924 the Virginia State Board of Education accredited the university as a standard four-year college. A federal government committee appointed to review the institution in 1928 found that under Clark's leadership it had rendered valuable service in training leaders and teachers. In 1932 Hartshorn Memorial College merged with Virginia Union University to establish a women's division of the institution. One of the few black colleges that adopted a classical liberal arts curriculum, the university received the highest accreditation from the Southern Association of Colleges and Secondary Schools in 1935. That same year the Norfolk Unit of Virginia Union University opened to provide junior college classes for students in the Norfolk-Portsmouth area. The Norfolk unit operated cooperatively with Hampton Institute and in March 1942 was separately chartered as the Norfolk Polytechnic College (after 1944 the Norfolk Division of Virginia State College and after 1979 Norfolk State University).

In 1940 Clark oversaw the acquisition of the Belgian Pavilion, an International Style building valued at $700,000 erected to house the Belgian exhibit at the New York World's Fair of 1939–1940. World War II prevented the shipping of the structure to Belgium as originally planned, so the Belgian government gave the pavilion, with its tower, art deco murals, and ceramic sandstone bas-reliefs depicting scenes in the Belgian Congo, to Virginia Union University. The pavilion was dismantled, shipped to Richmond, and reconstructed on the campus. Known as the Belgian Friendship Building, it housed the library, gymnasium, and science laboratories for decades. It was placed on the Virginia Landmarks Register in 1969 and on the National Register of Historic Places the following year.

During Clark's tenure the school's endowment increased from about $100,000 to more than $800,000, despite the financial difficulties generated by the Great Depression, and enrollment increased from about 300 to more than 600 students. Clark almost tripled the number of faculty members and worked to raise their salaries, and he expanded the library's holdings and services. He also brought in John Malcus Ellison, a former student, to teach social science. Ellison, later appointed executive vice president, succeeded Clark and became Virginia Union University's first black president. In 1927 Clark received an honorary doctorate of divinity from the college.

By late in the 1930s university administrators and supporters were voicing concern that Clark was losing his ability to manage the school effectively and to raise funds adequate for its operation and growth. Agreeing that it was time for a change in the administration, he submitted his resignation as president in April 1941, to become effective on 15 June. Naming him president emeritus, the board of trustees noted how Clark had transformed the university, and Ellison highlighted the role Virginia Union had played in developing African American leaders during Clark's tenure. Clark continued to teach in the theology department for several years. At the school's fiftieth anniversary celebration in 1950 the library was renamed in Clark's honor. A wing of the Belgian Friendship Building, William J. Clark Hall served as the university's library until 1997. William John Clark died at his Richmond home on 17 June 1956. He was buried in Westhampton Memorial Park, in Henrico County.

Autobiographical information, including birth and marriage dates, in Newton Theological Institution questionnaire, completed 1 Dec. 1941, Andover Newton Theological School, Newton Centre, Mass., and American Baptist Missionary Union Missionary Register, American Baptist Historical Society, Valley Forge, Pa.; biographies in "A Century of Service to Education and Religion: Virginia Union University, 1865–1965," *Virginia Union Bulletin* 65 (June 1965): 26–30 (por. on 27), and Cecil Raynard Taliaferro, "Virginia Union University, The First One Hundred Years—1865–1965" (Ph.D. diss., University of Pittsburgh, 1975), 68–72; annual reports, board minutes, correspondence, and photographs in Records of the President's Office, Virginia Union University; Clark and Virginia Union University documents in General Education Board Archives, Rockefeller Archive Center, Sleepy Hollow, N.Y.; *Watchman Examiner: A National Baptist Paper* 29 (2 Jan. 1941): 6 (cover por.); *Richmond News Leader*, 30 Apr., 1 May 1941; *Richmond Times-Dispatch*, 30 Apr. 1941; obituaries in *Richmond News Leader* and *Richmond Times-Dispatch*, both 18 June 1956, and *Norfolk Journal and Guide* and *Richmond Afro-American*, both 23 June 1956; memorial in *Virginia Union Bulletin* 57 (Aug. 1956): 1.

VONITA WHITE FOSTER

CLARKE, John (24 April 1766–17 May 1844), architect and arms manufacturer, was the son of Marianne Salle Clarke and Charles Clarke, an emigrant from Surrey, England. He was born probably at his father's plantation in the part of Cumberland County that in 1777 became Powhatan County. Little is known about his education, but his writing, in the form of reports, letters, and design proposals, reflects an advanced level of achievement. On 15 October 1791 Clarke executed a marriage bond in Chesterfield County and soon afterward married Elizabeth H. Moseley. They had three daughters before she died on 11 July 1806, after an extended period of poor health.

By the 1790s Clarke had become a millwright and before the end of the decade had constructed several mills near Richmond. In 1797 the Council of State requested that he select a suitable location for the future Virginia Manufactory of Arms, which would supply cannon, muskets, small arms, and swords to the state militia. He recommended a site just west of Richmond between the James River and the canal, which could provide water to operate the machinery. His plan accepted, Clarke visited northern foundries and armories where he observed production techniques and hired skilled artisans. On 8 August 1798 the Council appointed Clarke to oversee the construction of the manufactory. The first of several buildings completed was the armory, which had a neoclassical facade more than three hundred feet long, consisting of two wings connected by an arched entrance over which rose a domed belfry with a cupola.

On 9 March 1799 Clarke was appointed to oversee the building of the Virginia State Penitentiary, on which construction had begun two years earlier. He made several changes to the design of the original architect, Benjamin Henry Latrobe. Clarke strengthened the upper galleries with arched masonry supports and moved the keeper's quarters to a position over the front gate. He also raised the height of the facade walls and pierced them with three large grilled arches on each side of the central gateway. These features heightened security while ensuring that fresh air could reach the interior open court of the large horseshoe-shaped complex, which began receiving inmates in 1800. Clarke also had responsibility for constructing public warehouses around Richmond and for maintenance of the State Capitol. In 1801 he was charged with finding a public building in which to store arms for the militia. He chose the attic of the Capitol and had a lunette window installed in the south portico of the building to admit light and air.

By the time the manufactory had begun producing arms about 1802, Clarke was its super-intendent with responsibility for managing all of its operations. In this capacity he became major commandant of the Independent Corps of Artificers, a militia unit comprising the manufactory's workers. Because the artisans considered themselves civilian gunsmiths and refused to cooperate, the establishment of a military organization there was ultimately unsuccessful. Clarke, however, used his title throughout his life, and it appears on his gravestone.

In 1806 the Council asked Clarke to design a commemorative sword for presentation to Lieutenant Presley Neville O'Bannon in gratitude for his actions in the war against the Barbary pirates. Clarke submitted a letter describing his design, along with presentation drawings by an unknown artist. The finished sword was a much simplified version of Clarke's proposal, but his letter and the accompanying drawings provide a rare example of a complete design program for an early nineteenth-century ornamental weapon.

The following year a committee investigated the Virginia Manufactory of Arms for producing poor-quality weapons but found no fault with Clarke's administration. The charge that some arms were defective led the Council and the General Assembly in 1808 to inquire more closely into the manufactory's management and finances. In a series of letters printed in the *Richmond Enquirer*, Clarke vehemently denied the accusations against him. Although ultimately vindicated, he resigned his position in mid-February 1809. Clarke did not completely sever his government connections, however, and in 1816 the Council asked him to prepare a plan to improve the grounds of the Capitol Square. His unsuccessful proposal recommended including commercial buildings at the base of the hill, improving the springs on the property, adding a fountain, and landscaping lawns and wooded areas.

After quitting the manufactory, Clarke began to develop his Chesterfield County property into a foundry with his partner William Wirt, a prominent lawyer and later attorney general of the United States. Named Bellona Furnace for the Roman goddess of war, the facility, which had begun production by the spring of 1816, manufactured cannon for the War Department as well as machinery, iron fencing, and other products.

In 1815 the federal government made plans to establish a military arsenal and garrison in Virginia. At Clarke's suggestion, the Bellona Arsenal was completed in 1817 on land adjacent to his foundry.

In 1832 the arsenal began scaling back its operation, and the next year the garrison transferred to Fort Monroe, although it continued until at least 1840 to store cannon cast at Clarke's foundry. For several years beginning in 1837 the arsenal's buildings were leased as a cocoonery to raise silkworms. Clarke also ventured into the mid-Atlantic sericulture craze and erected an unusual round brick building at his Keswick residence. The structure contained a central chimney with three fireplaces, and the interior of the building consisted of a single circular room with five windows around its circumference. Local tradition has designated the building a slave quarter, but it seems more probable that Clarke designed it for silkworms. This structure was his last known architectural work. John Clarke died at his Powhatan County home on 17 May 1844 and was buried in the family graveyard at Keswick.

Biographies in Richard T. Couture, *Powhatan: A Bicentennial History* (1980), 111–118 (with incorrect death date), and Elizabeth Johnson Barnett, "John Clarke (1766–1844): Richmond Architect and Industrialist" (M.A. thesis, VCU, 2001); birth date from gravestone transcribed in Catherine Lynn Nowery and Sharon Lee Nowery, *Tombstone Inscriptions of Powhatan County, Virginia* (1966), 1:137; Chesterfield Co. Marriage Bonds; Virginia Manufactory of Arms Records, Auditor of Public Accounts, RG 48, LVA; Virginia Manufactory of Arms Record Book (1802–1815) and Letter Book (1804–1808), RG 49, LVA; O'Bannon sword design letter and presentation drawings in William H. Cabell Executive Papers, RG 3, LVA; *Richmond Enquirer*, 21, 28 Feb., 24 Mar., 7 Apr., 19, 23 May 1809; William H. Gaines Jr., "Guns, Silkworms, and Pigs," *Virginia Cavalcade* 3 (fall 1953): 32–37; David C. Poteet, "The Armory Scandal," ibid. 15 (spring 1966): 38–43; Giles Cromwell, *The Virginia Manufactory of Arms* (1975), 11–17 (por. by Charles Balthazar Julien Fevret de Saint-Mémin), 110–111; will and estate inventory in Powhatan Co. Will Book, 12:261–264, 359–367; obituary in *Richmond Whig and Public Advertiser*, 28 May 1844.

ELIZABETH J. BARNETT

CLARKE, Joseph Calvitt (30 June 1887–17 July 1970), founder of the Christian Children's Fund, Incorporated, was born in Brooklyn, New York, and was the son of Joseph Calvitt Clarke, a stockbroker, and Ella Hamilton Clarke. A sickly child, he grew restless at the age of fourteen and dropped out of school. Following a brief time at a Manhattan publishing house, Clarke worked for three years at the Presbyterian Mission Board, also in Manhattan. From 1906 to 1910 he attended the Mount Hermon School for Boys (later Northfield Mount Hermon School), in Massachusetts, and Doane Academy, a secondary school connected to Denison University, in Ohio.

Having decided to enter the ministry, J. Calvitt Clarke, as he was known, attended Meadville Theological Seminary (later Meadville Lombard Theological School), a Unitarian institution in Chicago, during the 1912–1913 academic year and then moved to Pittsburgh to train as a Presbyterian minister. There he married Helen Caroline Mattson on 8 December 1913. They had one son, Joseph Calvitt Clarke (1920–2004), who served as judge of the United States District Court for the Eastern District of Virginia from December 1974 through July 1991, and one daughter, Helen Jeanne Clarke Wood, international director of the Richmond-based relief organization Children, Incorporated. School records and various reference works for which Clarke provided information contain discrepancies about his graduate studies and degrees. Routinely addressed as Doctor Clarke, he reported that he had received a doctorate of divinity at Oskaloosa College (later Iowa Christian College). Western Theological Seminary (later Pittsburgh Theological Seminary) awarded him a bachelor of sacred theology degree in 1919.

During World War I, Clarke joined a Young Men's Christian Association mission in Europe and ministered to Russian troops stranded in France as a result of the politics surrounding the Bolshevik Revolution. After about a year he returned to Pittsburgh, where he expected to settle down as a Presbyterian minister. Instead, in 1919 he began an eleven-year stint as a campaign organizer for Near East Relief, an organization that sought to alleviate the suffering of refugees in the disintegrating Ottoman Empire. Starting in Harrisburg as director for central Pennsylvania, Clarke held a series of posts with Near East Relief: campaign consultant for the north-central region, state director in Ohio, and assistant regional director for the Middle Atlantic states. In 1926 he became director of the nine-state southern region and moved to its Richmond office. As part of his work, Clarke surveyed famine conditions in Armenia, Greece, the Russian Caucasus, and Turkey in 1920 and traveled to Armenia and Palestine in 1924. His experiences overseas allowed him to draw graphic portraits in the many speeches he delivered before churches and civic groups. Clarke became a master fund-raiser and later described his method as a departure from traditional solicitations: "I never ask for gifts. I only tell the real conditions and needs."

After the dissolution of Near East Relief, Clarke remained in Richmond and worked for several social welfare agencies. From 1931 to 1933 he was national secretary and southern director for the Golden Rule Foundation. He helped found the American branch of the Save the Children Federation and was its southern director from 1934 to 1937. Later he raised funds for the National Foundation for the Blind. Also during this period Clarke published novels and short stories under his own name and under the pseudonym Richard Grant. Titles included *Melissa* (1934); *The True Light*, *Castles in the Sand*, and *Eurasian Girl* (all 1935); *Dream No More* (1937); *Shoot Your Enemies* (1948); and *The Slaves of Ishtar* and *Lives in a Box* (both 1951).

Relief work remained Clarke's primary calling. Disturbed by the large numbers of children orphaned by the Japanese invasion and occupation of China in 1937, he decided to launch an aid organization. With the assistance of his wife, in October 1938 he founded China's Children Fund, Incorporated, in Richmond. Over the next few months, Clarke assembled a board consisting largely of Richmond businesspeople, developed a 450-member national committee, and began sending checks to Chinese orphanages. China's Children Fund grew rapidly as a result of Clarke's fund-raising innovation, individual sponsorship. Inspired by the Save the Children Federation's strategy, which asked groups and individual benefactors to sponsor some of its supported institutions, Clarke had donors "adopt" specific children. Providing a personal link between donor and recipient proved a successful fund-raising technique and became the backbone of

the organization's efforts. By November 1944 China's Children Fund helped support forty-five orphanages throughout China.

The organization maintained its rapid growth after World War II and expanded beyond China into other battered and impoverished areas in Asia. Clarke and his wife continued to act as the organization's public faces and principal fundraisers. Their flexible management allowed innovations at individual orphanages to flourish. On a tour of the fund's orphanages in 1946 Clarke witnessed the success of a Cantonese home that had incorporated industrial education into its program, and he pushed for the adoption of similar strategies throughout the fund's network of homes. Later the organization helped found two postsecondary schools in Japan, Izumi College and Clarke Junior College, which trained social workers and signaled the comprehensive approach that increasingly characterized China's Children Fund. Reflecting the expansion of its work beyond Asia, the organization changed its name in February 1951 to the Christian Children's Fund, Incorporated, and within a decade had established itself as one of the most recognizable and significant private relief agencies in the world. By the end of Clarke's twenty-five-year tenure as executive director, the CCF provided more than $3 million annually to its various programs. Clarke received a series of honors from some of the many countries he had helped, including the Cultural Merit Medal from the Republic of Korea, the Order of Brilliant Star with Cravat from Nationalist China, and induction into Japan's Order of the Sacred Treasure, fourth class.

Many staff members and CCF international workers began to chafe under the Clarkes' commitment to funneling the organization's aid through missions and orphanages, as well as at their failure to update the Richmond headquarters. Preferring a new approach that would distribute aid directly to families and community development projects, the CCF board encouraged the Clarkes to step down on 10 December 1963. Disappointed by their reduced role, the Clarkes helped their daughter found Children, Incorporated, in 1964 and assisted with its management during their remaining years. Helen

Mattson Clarke died on 25 October 1967. Joseph Calvitt Clarke died in a Richmond hospital on 17 July 1970 and was buried in Hollywood Cemetery.

Edmund W. Janss, *Yankee Si! The Story of Dr. J. Calvitt Clarke and His 36,000 Children* (1961), including frontispiece por. and quotation on 2; John C. Caldwell, *Children of Calamity* (1957); Larry E. Tise, *A Book about Children: Christian Children's Fund, 1938–1991* (1992); *Richmond News Leader*, 31 May 1946, 6 June 1957 (por.), 6 Mar. 1961, 29 Mar. 1962; *Richmond Times-Dispatch*, 18 July 1946, 15 Mar. 1962; obituaries in *Richmond News Leader*, 17 July 1970, *New York Times* and *Richmond Times-Dispatch*, both 18 July 1970, and *Washington Post*, 19 July 1970.

WILLIAM BLAND WHITLEY

CLARKE, Mary Ellen Pollard (22 August 1862–30 July 1939), woman suffrage activist, was born in King and Queen County and was the daughter of John Pollard, minister at a Middlesex County Baptist church, and Virginia Bagby Pollard. In 1870 the family moved to Baltimore, where from 1877 to 1880 Pollard attended the city's Female High School and earned near-perfect marks in each of her subjects of study. Her family returned to Virginia in 1880, when her father became pastor of Leigh Street Baptist Church in Richmond. Between 1886 and 1901 he taught English at Richmond College (later the University of Richmond). An ardent proponent of education for women and an early devotee of the Social Gospel, John Pollard encouraged his seven daughters and two sons to study art and literature and instilled in them the idea that Christian morality demanded progressive reforms in public policy. Mary Pollard's brother, John Garland Pollard, aligned himself with the state's progressive Democrats early in his political career and later served as attorney general and governor of Virginia. Her other brother, Edward Bagby Pollard, a Baptist minister, advocated suffrage for women, and several of her sisters held office in women's organizations. On 15 November 1882 Mary Pollard married George Harvey Clarke, a Richmond hardware merchant. They had three daughters and two sons.

Despite an eye disorder that occasionally prevented her from reading for weeks at a time, Clarke pursued a life of study and self-improvement. Like many other educated middle-class American women, she found an outlet for her scholarship in women's literary societies. A founder in 1889 of the Every Tuesday Club, which soon changed its name to the Every Monday Club, Clarke wrote and presented an impressive variety of essays on history, literature, and religion during her more than thirty years of membership. She was also a member of the Woman's Club of Richmond from 1916 to 1930. The city's most prestigious literary organization for women, the club became increasingly involved in community reform projects, particularly in the realms of child welfare, education, labor law, and public health. By 1922 Clarke was active in the Virginia Federation of Women's Clubs, and, serving that year on the Resolutions Committee at the federation's annual convention, she helped produce a document that called for legislative protection for women in industry, the establishment of kindergartens and public libraries, and a variety of measures to strengthen public education. In 1923 she chaired the federation's Special Committee on Illiteracy. Clarke and her contemporaries in the woman's club movement asserted that their femininity endowed them with a finely tuned sense of morality as well as a special interest in childcare and thus gave them an indispensable role in shaping public policy.

Clarke worked for many years to improve public education in Richmond. As early as 1904 she was a member of the Richmond Education Association, organized in 1900 to generate public interest in school reform. For the 1911–1912 term she chaired the Press Committee, after which she served at least five consecutive terms as secretary. Clarke publicized the association's goal of securing a free public library for the city by writing letters to the editors of Richmond's major newspapers in which she argued that no city could prosper without investing in such an institution. Also affiliated with the Co-Operative Education Association of Virginia, organized in 1904, she volunteered in 1915 to speak to local community groups in order to spark interest in improving schools, health, roads, and home conditions throughout the state. The State Board of Education recognized Clarke's work on behalf of literacy and education by appointing her to two five-year terms on the State Library Board beginning in 1922. The first female member, she was part of the initial wave of women who obtained positions on state government advisory boards after adoption of the Nineteenth Amendment.

Clarke's talent as a writer and her dedication to community reform combined most powerfully in her decade of work as a woman suffrage activist. By 1911 she had joined the Equal Suffrage League of Virginia, founded in 1909 to educate and organize Virginians during the struggle to secure voting rights for women. As the league's press secretary and editor-in-chief of its publication *Virginia Suffrage News* in 1914, as press chair in 1915, and as chair of the Committee on Political Study and Research between 1916 and 1920, Clarke disseminated the league's message throughout the state. In letters to Richmond newspaper editors and in her own editorials, she asserted that it was God's will that women, endowed with a special moral compass, find a voice in government and contribute to the improvement of humanity. Clarke appealed to Virginians' patriotism by arguing that true patriot-mothers had a broad interest in public welfare that extended beyond their own homes and that the nation would benefit from their ability to influence legislation. League resolutions called for such reforms as the abolition of child labor, compulsory education for children, an eight-hour workday, and the prohibition of alcohol. In 1916 the league appointed a chair for each of the state's congressional districts to organize constituents and place political pressure on Virginia congressmen. Clarke became chair of the Third District, comprising Richmond, Williamsburg, and the surrounding counties.

About 1915, to counter the widespread idea that a national constitutional amendment enfranchising women would infringe on states' rights, Clarke wrote *Human-Rights Not in Violation of States' Rights: An Appeal to the Men of Virginia*, in which she contended that women's eligibility to vote would not affect each state's ability to restrict the franchise through literacy tests and poll taxes. In "Equal Suffrage and the Negro Vote," a broadside published probably the following year, she addressed fears that the enfranchisement of women would threaten white supremacy. Clarke asserted that female suffrage would augment white political power and render the state "secure from negro domination."

Simultaneously a member of the Equal Suffrage League of Richmond, to which her husband, a daughter, and a son also belonged, Clarke planned the local organization's meetings as chair of the Program Committee, led the Church Committee for at least two years, and served as third vice president for four years. Despite the Equal Suffrage League's vigorous campaigns and growing membership, the General Assembly defeated resolutions for women's voting rights in 1912, 1914, and 1916. Nonetheless, Virginia women won the franchise in 1920 through the federal amendment.

To prepare women for the duties of citizenship, about 1920 Clarke wrote *Studies in Citizenship for the Virginia Woman* and *Facts of Government Every Virginia Woman Should Know*, which guided readers through the study of civics. The Equal Suffrage League disbanded that year and was succeeded by the Virginia League of Women Voters, which held registration drives, educated new voters, and advocated social welfare legislation. Clarke immediately became a member of the league, sat on the board of the Richmond branch, and chaired the state league's Committee on Research and Data beginning in 1921. That year she was one of four delegates representing Virginia at the Regional Conference of the National League of Women Voters, and the following year she chaired the Virginia league's Bureau of Information Committee.

Clarke's husband died on 1 November 1931. The expiration of her second term on the State Library Board in 1932 ended her public activism. Mary Ellen Pollard Clarke died of kidney disease on 30 July 1939 at her daughter's Henrico County home. She was buried in Hollywood Cemetery, in Richmond.

Biographical information in Maud Pollard Turman (sister), *John Garland Pollard, 1871 1937: An Informal Biography with an Appendix on the Family of John Pollard and Virginia Bagby and Their Descendants* (1960), esp. Appendix, v; diary (with birth date on 61, entry for 22 Aug. 1894), letters, newspaper clippings, and scrapbook in Clarke Family Papers, VHS; BVS Marriage Register, Richmond City; Equal Suffrage League of Virginia Records (1909–1935), LVA;

some correspondence in John Garland Pollard Papers, W&M; quotation in broadside "Equal Suffrage and the Negro Vote" (ca. 1916), copy at VHS; other publications include "Christopher Robinson, One of the First Trustees of William and Mary College: His Home, 'Hewick on the Rappahannock,'" *WMQ*, 2d ser., 1 (1921): 134–136, and "The Will of Joseph Pollard of King and Queen County, Virginia," ibid. 2 (1922): 162–166; *Roanoke World-News*, 6 Nov. 1914 (por.); *Richmond News Leader*, 2 Oct. 1916; *Richmond Times-Dispatch*, 20 Sept. 1922; BVS Death Certificate, Henrico Co. (death date of 30 July 1939); obituaries in *Richmond News Leader*, 31 July, 1 Aug. 1939, and *Richmond Times-Dispatch*, 1 Aug. 1939 (all with variant death date of 31 July 1939).

JENNIFER R. LOUX

CLAY, Charles (24 December 1745–8 February 1820), member of the Convention of 1788, was the son of Charles Clay and Martha Green Clay and was born probably in the part of Goochland County that in 1749 became Cumberland County. His younger brother Green Clay also served in the Convention of 1788, representing Madison County, and another brother Matthew Clay served in the House of Representatives. Their father's brother was grandfather of the Kentucky senator Henry Clay. Likely some combination of family instruction, local preparatory schooling, and private tutoring constituted Clay's education and preparation for the Anglican ministry, but there is no evidence of where or when or by whom he was instructed. Nor is there any clue what motivated his choice of vocation, though late in the colonial period the ministry proved attractive to dozens of native Virginians.

Clay traveled to England, where the bishop of London ordained him as a deacon on 21 May 1769 and as a priest on 7 June of that year, and on the latter date also licensed him to serve in Virginia. The vestry of Saint Anne's Parish, in Albemarle County, received him as its rector when he returned to the colony. The surviving vestry records for the years 1772–1785 testify to Clay's vigorous and committed ministry. His service in Saint Anne's is of special and continuing interest because it provided the occasion for his friendship with the parish's most notable resident, Thomas Jefferson. Youth, integrity, and a shared zeal for the patriot cause may partially account for the mutual attraction. Whatever the basis, the friendship surmounted at least one substantial hurdle. Clay was theologically orthodox and evangelical in his Christian faith and thus a pole apart from his neighbor and friend.

Clay's promising labors in Saint Anne's Parish had ended on a sour note by 1784. The American Revolution dismantled the Anglican establishment and parish system, and disputes with the vestry over repairs to the glebe and his unpaid salary led Clay unsuccessfully to seek redress through the county court and by petitioning the House of Delegates. He then moved to a farm in Bedford County, near Jefferson's Poplar Forest estate. Clay served as a justice of the peace in Bedford County from 1782 to 1785, when he accepted appointment as rector of Manchester Parish, in Chesterfield County. He represented that parish at the 1785 convention that organized the Protestant Episcopal Church's Virginia diocese and also at the convention held the following year. By 1787 he again had abandoned the ministry, this time for good, and returned to his farm in Bedford County.

In 1788 Clay was one of two men elected to represent that county in the convention called to consider ratification of the proposed constitution of the United States. Along with his brother and his colleague from Bedford County, he voted on 25 June to require amendment of the Constitution before ratification. He voted against ratification and two days later voted in favor of a proposal to reduce the taxation power of Congress. Clay's disappointment at the outcome did not prevent him from offering himself as a candidate for the House of Representatives in 1790 and again in 1792. Defeated on both occasions, he thereafter let his political aspirations go the same way as his religious vocation.

Clay spent the final three decades of his life as a farmer residing at Petty Grove in Bedford County. On 4 July 1796 he married Editha Landon Davies. They had four sons, among them Odin Green Clay, later president of the Virginia and Tennessee Railroad Company. Charles Clay died in Bedford County on 8 February 1820 and was buried in the family cemetery on his farm. A huge mound of rocks marks the site believed to be his grave. One story has it that the mound was intended to prevent the building of a road over his burial site, but family tradition states that the stones accumulated into a mound because

Clay required his sons to throw a rock on the pile for each wrongful act they committed. Clay's will made his wife and sons beneficiaries of town lots in Lynchburg, sizable tracts of land in Amherst, Bedford, Buckingham, and Campbell Counties, stock in the Farmers Bank of Virginia, his numerous slaves, and "my Small Silver Cane presented me by my very honble Friend Thomas Jefferson," all signs that he had made a very comfortable life for himself and his family.

Clay family Bible records (1745–1873), with birth, marriage, and death dates, LVA; Clay Family Genealogical Notes, Acc. 32301, LVA; Zachary F. Smith and Mary Rogers Clay, *The Clay Family* (1899), 76–77, 84–88; biographies in Meade, *Old Churches*, 2:48–50 (with erroneous 1824 death date), and Katharine L. Brown, *Hills of the Lord: Background of the Episcopal Church in Southwestern Virginia, 1738–1938* (1979), 134–136; Clay Family Papers, including account books, letters, and sermons, VHS; Clay letters in Coolidge Collection of Thomas Jefferson Papers, Massachusetts Historical Society, Boston, in UNC, and in Jefferson Papers, UVA, and printed in *Jefferson Papers*; Fulham Papers, Lambeth Palace Library, London, Eng., 25:121–131 (with variant birth date of 4 Jan. 1745), 34:255, 38:7; Saint Anne's Parish Vestry Book (1772–1785), LVA; G. MacLaren Brydon, "A Sketch of the Early History of Saint Anne's Parish in Albemarle County, Virginia," in Elizabeth Coles Langhorne, *A History of Christ Church, Glendower, with an Account of the Early Days of St. Anne's Parish* (1957), 33–35, 49–54; Brydon, notes on Charles Clay, in Papers Relating to the History of the Protestant Episcopal Church in Virginia, VHS; numerous references in James A. Bear Jr. and Lucia C. Stanton, eds., *Jefferson's Memorandum Books: Accounts, with Legal Records and Miscellany, 1767–1826* (1997); John K. Nelson, *A Blessed Company: Parishes, Parsons, and Parishioners in Anglican Virginia, 1690–1776* (2001), 202, 307, 428, 460–461; Kaminski, *Ratification*, 9:907, 10:1294, 1298, 1538, 1540, 1557, 1565; por. believed to be of Clay in possession of Sara Phillips, Raleigh, N.C. (2002); Bedford Co. Will Book, 5:171–172 (quotation), 180–181.

JOHN K. NELSON

CLAY, Green (14 August 1757–31 October 1828), member of the Convention of 1788, was the son of Martha Green Clay and Charles Clay, whose brother was a grandfather of the Kentucky senator Henry Clay. He was born in the portion of Cumberland County that in 1777 became Powhatan County. His elder brothers included Charles Clay (1745–1820), also a member of the Convention of 1788, and Matthew Clay, a member of the House of Representatives. Like many other young men of his generation, Clay heard of Daniel Boone's western exploits and in 1777 set

out for Kentucky, where he served in the militia but took no major role in the Revolutionary War. He apprenticed as a surveyor and by 1781 had been appointed deputy surveyor of Lincoln County. Displaying a remarkable memory for property lines, Clay soon became one of the most sought-after surveyors in western Virginia. As was common at the time, he acquired many valuable tracts of land for himself and quickly became one of the largest-scale landowners and one of the richest men in Kentucky. On one of his tracts in Madison County he built Clermont, later renamed White Hall.

Clay cultivated tobacco but did not use it nor allow his family to do so, because he suspected it to be addictive and harmful. He built and operated a resort at Estill Springs near White Hall, drilled artesian wells for pure water, and also owned several ferries in central Kentucky. On 14 March 1795 Clay married Sally Lewis. Their four daughters and three sons included Cassius Marcellus Clay, later a prominent abolitionist, early member of the Republican Party, and United States minister to Russia during the Civil War. The naming of another son Brutus Junius Clay suggests that Green Clay's undocumented education had given him a strong foundation in classical history.

Clay was more interested in financial matters than in public service, but in 1787 he won election to the first of three consecutive one-year terms in the House of Delegates representing Madison County. New to legislative procedures, he obtained and annotated a copy of the rules of the House early in his first term. In each of his first two years he was a member of the Committee of Propositions and Grievances, in his second term he sat on the Committee for Courts of Justice, and in his final term he was appointed to the Committee of Claims.

In the spring of 1788 Clay was one of two men elected to represent Madison County in the convention called to consider the proposed constitution of the United States. He was not active in the debates, although on several occasions when the role of the militia was under discussion he asked questions or provided comments based on his frontier experience. On 25 June 1788 Clay voted, as did nearly every other member from western Virginia, to require amendment of the Constitution prior to ratification. After the opponents of the Constitution lost that vote, he voted against ratification, and two days later he supported a proposed amendment to reduce the taxing power of the new government.

Clay became a justice of the peace in Madison County at the end of 1793 and that same year won election to the lower house of the Kentucky legislature. He served for two years before being elected in 1795 to the Kentucky Senate for a four-year term. At the Kentucky convention of 1799 he assisted in drafting the state's second constitution. Clay returned to the state senate in 1802 and served until 1808, when he was elected Speaker. After an unsuccessful campaign for governor in that year, he retired from elective politics. In 1807 the legislature named the newly formed Clay County for him.

Clay joined trustees of Transylvania University in 1802 in trying to lure James Madison (1751–1836) to its presidency, and six years later, as Speaker of the Kentucky Senate, he led the legislative caucus that nominated Madison for president of the United States. A major general in the Kentucky militia during the War of 1812, Clay in the spring of 1813 led a contingent of 1,500 militiamen to relieve William Henry Harrison's force under siege at Fort Meigs, in Ohio. After a combined force of British soldiers and Native Americans, the latter under the command of Tecumseh, failed to draw Clay out of the fort and into an ambush, the enemy withdrew, and Clay and his regiment returned home.

Remaining interested in land until the end of his life, Clay published a pamphlet, *To the People of Kentucky and of the United States* (1825), concerning disputed legal title of land in the Tennessee River Valley. After suffering several years from face cancer, Green Clay died at his home in Madison County, Kentucky, on 31 October 1828 and was buried in the nearby family cemetery.

Birth and death dates from gravestone; biographies in Lewis Collins, *Historical Sketches of Kentucky* (1847), 243–245 (with incorrect death date of 31 Oct. 1826, copied in many secondary sources), Cassius Marcellus Clay, *The Life of Cassius Marcellus Clay: Memoirs, Writings, and Speeches* (1886), 1:17–18, 20, 22, 37–46 (engraving of por. by Chester Harding facing 44), and Jonathan Truman Dorris, *A Glimpse at Historic Madison County and Richmond, Kentucky* (1934),

23–24; Zachary F. Smith and Mary Rogers Clay, *The Clay Family* (1899), 76–77, 87–88; letters in Cassius Marcellus Clay Papers (including draft biography of Green Clay, with birth and marriage dates), Green Clay Papers, and Sidney Payne Clay Papers, all Filson Historical Society, Louisville, Ky., in Clay Family Papers and Green Clay Papers, University of Kentucky, Lexington, and in Green Clay Papers, including 1813 orderly book, New York Public Library; C. Frank Dunn, "Gen. Green Clay in Fayette County Records," *Register of the Kentucky State Historical Society* 44 (1946): 146–147; Kaminski, *Ratification*, 9:904, 10:1269, 1274, 1288, 1294, 1296, 1298, 1506, 1539, 1541, 1557, 1565; death notice in *Lexington Kentucky Reporter*, 19 Nov. 1828.

BRIAN McKNIGHT

CLAY, Matthew (25 March 1754–27 May 1815), member of the House of Representatives, was the son of Martha Green Clay and Charles Clay, whose brother was grandfather of the Kentucky senator Henry Clay. He was born probably in the part of Cumberland County that in 1777 became Powhatan County. Nothing is known for certain about Clay's schooling, but his brothers Charles Clay (1745–1820) and Green Clay, who both served in the Convention of 1788, were well educated. In 1776 he enlisted as an ensign in the 9th Virginia Regiment and probably fought in the New Jersey and Pennsylvania campaigns during the next year and a half, but he was not present at the Battle of Germantown in October 1777 because he was on detached duty. Clay won promotion to second lieutenant in May 1778, about four months before his depleted regiment became part of the 1st Virginia Regiment, and at the end of that year he became regimental quartermaster. Clay was lucky in not being sent south where his new regiment was captured when Charleston surrendered in May 1780. In February 1781 he was reassigned to the 5th Virginia Regiment, a unit that existed only on paper, until it was dissolved and he was discharged early in January 1783. As a result of his Revolutionary War service, he was entitled to more than 2,660 acres of western bounty land.

Clay worked in Richmond for a few years as a clerk for the state solicitor general before moving to a Pittsylvania County farm that he had inherited from a brother. He farmed and practiced law there for the remainder of his life and on 4 December 1788 married Mary Williams of that county. They had two sons and two daughters. She died as a consequence of childbirth on

25 March 1798. On 18 June 1803 Clay married Ann Saunders, of Buckingham County, who had one daughter before her death on 10 July 1806.

In 1790 Clay was elected to the first of five consecutive one-year terms representing Pittsylvania County in the House of Delegates. A member of the Committee of Propositions and Grievances for all of his terms, he served also on the Committee for Religion in 1791, on the Committees for Courts of Justice and of Privileges and Elections from 1791 to 1794, and on the Committee of Claims from 1792 to 1794. In 1790 the General Assembly named him a commissioner to improve the upper regions of the Roanoke River for commercial navigation and the following year head of a commission to determine whether millworks and dams on the Banister River should be removed to allow the upstream passage of fish. Clay voted in December 1792 for a compromise that had it become law would have given the Episcopal Church a chance to retain some of the parish glebe lands that Baptists and other dissenting denominations in Virginia had begun to demand be sold for the benefit of the public.

Clay had a combative personality and a self-righteous style of debate. During the 1791 legislative session he got into a heated public argument with another assembly member, whose brother was one of Clay's political adversaries in Pittsylvania County. The two delegates accused each other of improprieties, and Clay had to apologize formally to the House for his conduct.

Clay's political opinions made him a natural ally of Thomas Jefferson, and like Jefferson he supported revising the Virginia constitution to expand the suffrage to all white men who owned property or were liable to bear arms in defense of the state. "It is not fair," Clay declared in 1806, "that a part of the community should be compelled to pay taxes, to support a government, and bear arms to defend it, when they have no part, nor lot, in the making of the laws."

In 1793 Clay sought election to the House of Representatives from the district of Campbell, Halifax, and Pittsylvania Counties, but he lost to Isaac Coles. Four years later he defeated Coles and was reelected seven consecutive times, until 1813. In some sessions Clay arrived after the

initial appointment of the standing committees and therefore did not receive high-ranking seats on influential committees in those years. In 1801 he was a member of the Committee of Revisal and Unfinished Business and in 1803, 1807, and 1808 of the Committee of Elections, of which he became ranking member in 1809. Clay opposed the Alien and Sedition Acts of 1798 and favored paying off the public debt, repeal of the Judiciary Act of 1801, purchase of Louisiana in 1803, adoption of the embargo on trade with Great Britain in 1807, and an end to the first Bank of the United States in 1811. His devotion to states' rights and strict interpretation of the Constitution sometimes allied him with Jefferson's Republican critics such as John Randolph of Roanoke and John Taylor of Caroline, but Clay spoke against divisions among the Republicans. Although he favored James Monroe over James Madison (1751–1836) for president in 1808, he reluctantly agreed that Monroe should not challenge Madison and risk splitting the party.

As chair of the Committee on the Militia in 1807 and 1808, Clay argued forcefully for strengthening the militia and for fixing the terms of militia service. Though not usually associated with the so-called War Hawks, he supported increased taxes and some increased military spending immediately preceding the War of 1812. He did not vote when the House of Representatives passed a declaration of war on 4 June 1812, but he endorsed the war and advocated seizing all of Canada from the British.

In the spring of 1813 Clay lost his congressional seat to another Republican, John Kerr, who had unsuccessfully challenged him in 1811. Personal differences or local factionalism, rather than opposition to the war, probably account for Clay's loss in 1813, and those differences characterized the campaign two years later, when in April 1815 he defeated Kerr. Matthew Clay would have resumed his place in Congress later that year, but he died suddenly at Halifax Court House on 27 May 1815. He may have been buried in the family vault in Pittsylvania County, with the remains of his first wife and at least one of his children.

In addition to more than 3,000 acres of land he owned in Kentucky, at the time of his death

Clay owned more than 1,800 acres and at least thirteen slaves in Pittsylvania County. His will named his two sons as executors of the estate and directed them to provide a fourteen-year-old boy named William Penn with a horse, bridle, saddle, suit of clothes, and $1,000 when he reached age twenty-one. The will also named three mixed-race girls about eight years old and directed the executors to emancipate them from slavery, transport them out of Virginia, maintain and educate them until they reached age eighteen, and at that time give each of them a good new suit of clothes and $500. Extant documents do not disclose the relationship between Clay and these four children.

Lawrence W. Williamson, "Matthew Clay: Old School Republican" (M.A. thesis, VPI, 1984); Zachary F. Smith and Mary Rogers Clay, *The Clay Family* (1899), 77, 86 (with birth date); Matthew Clay Papers, including circular letters to his congressional constituents, Mississippi Department of Archives and History, Jackson; some Clay letters in James Monroe Papers, LC, Stuart Family Papers, VHS, and Executive Communications, Records of the House of Delegates, RG 79, LVA; BW; LOMC; Pittsylvania Co. Marriage Bonds (fragment, 1788); first wife's gravestone inscription with family data in Maud Carter Clement, *The History of Pittsylvania County, Virginia* (1929), 202–203; *JHD*, Oct. 1791 sess., esp. 74–75, 78, 82, 101, 105; *Richmond Virginia Argus*, 25 June 1803, 19 July 1806; congressional career documented in *Annals of Congress*, 5th–12th Cong.; Cunningham, *Circular Letters of Congressmen*, 1:462–465 (quotation on 465), 3:1555; Ellen G. Miles, *Saint-Mémin and the Neoclassical Profile Portrait in America* (1994), 271 (por.); Pittsylvania Co. Deeds and Wills, 11:405–406; death notices with death date in *Richmond Virginia Argus*, 7 June 1815, and *Richmond Enquirer*, 10 June 1815.

JOHN R. VAN ATTA

CLAY, Odin Green (5 May 1801–17 January 1883), president of the Virginia and Tennessee Railroad Company, was born at Petty Grove, the Bedford County farm of his parents, Editha Landon Davies Clay and Charles Clay, a former Anglican minister and member of the Convention of 1788. His uncles Green Clay and Matthew Clay served in the Convention of 1788 and in the House of Representatives, respectively. Classically educated by his father and with access to books from the extensive library of Thomas Jefferson, who owned the nearby Poplar Forest plantation, Clay became a Campbell County planter and investor. He owned several large tracts of land and a gristmill on Tomahawk Creek and was part owner of the Lynchburg company of Clay and Wilkes. By 1850 Clay's Campbell County land was worth $55,500, and ten years later he held sixty-four slaves. On 9 October 1822 he married a cousin, Ann Clayton E. Davies. They had at least six sons and three daughters before she died on 26 October 1848.

Clay became a justice of the peace in Campbell County on 15 July 1828 and the following year won election to the House of Delegates representing Campbell County and Lynchburg. He was a member of the Committee of Privileges and Elections and after winning reelection in 1830 was appointed to the Committee of Claims, the Committee of Roads and Internal Navigation, and a committee to examine the second auditor's office. Campbell County voters returned Clay, by that time a member of the Whig Party, to the House of Delegates for the 1835–1836 session. He served on the Committee of Finance and a joint committee to examine the Bank of Virginia and the Farmers Bank of Virginia. On 16 December 1835 Clay presented a petition from Lynchburg citizens seeking to charter an independent bank in the town with capitalization of $1 million. He was president of the first Central Agricultural Society exhibition and fair held in Lynchburg on 26 October 1837. In a special election held 13 December 1847, Clay was returned to the House of Delegates to fill a vacant seat. On 22 March 1848 the assembly elected him brigadier general of the Twelfth Brigade of the Virginia militia. Thereafter he was usually referred to as General O. G. Clay. Running in 1855 as a Democrat against a Know Nothing (American Party) candidate, Clay unsuccessfully sought the seat in the Senate of Virginia representing Appomattox and Campbell Counties.

As early as 1831 citizens of Lynchburg and surrounding counties began efforts to construct a railroad from Lynchburg to eastern Tennessee. During his final year in the General Assembly, Clay promoted the incorporation of the Lynchburg and Tennessee Railroad Company. At the first meeting of stockholders, on 19 August 1848, he was elected president, and in his first annual report he emphasized that the completed railroad would revive the economy and reputation of the state and also "tend more to harmonize the jarring interests of Eastern and Western Virginia, than any mere political scheme that can be adopted." Clay engaged and directed the engineers who surveyed the route from Lynchburg to Bristol, on the Tennessee border. Renamed the Virginia and Tennessee Railroad Company in March 1849 and with the state government owning a large portion of the stock, the company began construction on 16 January 1850.

Clay and the chief engineer, Charles Fenton Mercer Garnett, announced that local resources would be used when possible, although a plan to lay rails produced in Lynchburg had to be abandoned. Joseph Reid Anderson, in charge of the Tredegar Iron Company in Richmond, supplied locomotives in exchange for stock in the company. In addition to the original route, Clay planned a branch line to Cumberland Gap and also another line along the New River to connect with a proposed railroad to the Ohio River. He and other company officers saw the Virginia and Tennessee as the crucial segment of a national railroad network linking the mid-Atlantic states with Memphis and New Orleans. In January 1852 Clay attended the Southern and Western Rail-Road Convention in New Orleans, where more than 600 delegates from eleven states endorsed construction of a railroad along a southern route from the lower Mississippi valley to California. The Virginia and Tennessee Railroad would have been an essential eastern link in the proposed transcontinental network.

Citing poor health, Clay retired from the presidency on 4 November 1852, but he remained an active board member. Four years later the company completed construction of the 204 miles of track between Lynchburg and Bristol, and by 1860, when connecting rail lines north and south of the Virginia and Tennessee Railroad opened, speedy mail and passenger service became possible between such eastern cities as Norfolk and Washington on the one hand and such western cities as Memphis and New Orleans on the other. In part fulfilling Clay's predictions, the railroad stimulated economic growth in the region and promoted an increase in population and stronger economic and political ties with eastern Virginia.

Clay was a founding member of the Central Southern Rights Association, organized in Richmond in 1851 by opponents of the Compromise of 1850 and dedicated to fostering southern economic independence of northern capital. Following the association's revival in the wake of John Brown's raid on Harpers Ferry in 1859, Clay became one of its vice presidents. In 1859 he was elected one of three members of the Board of Public Works, which oversaw the state's investments in and promotion of such internal improvement projects as canals, railroads, and turnpikes. Representing the district that included all the counties in the southern part of the state, he continued to sit on the board until he resigned on 31 January 1864. During the Civil War the board had responsibility for facilitating transportation for the Confederate armies, and in June 1862 Clay arranged for improvements to navigation on the New River so that batteaux could transport military stores from Central Depot (later Radford) to the mouth of the Greenbrier River. In 1863 the General Assembly gave the board responsibility for producing and distributing salt in Virginia, a task made easier by the recent construction of a short line connecting the Virginia and Tennessee Railroad to production facilities in Saltville, in Smyth County. The railroad was one of the most important supply routes in the Confederacy and the object of several attacks by Union forces during the war.

Because of his Confederate service and wealth, Clay petitioned for a presidential pardon on 18 July 1865 (granted on 29 July of that year) and for the remainder of his life managed his estates. Still financially interested in the Virginia and Tennessee Railroad Company, he was probably a mere spectator after the war when William Mahone gained control and consolidated it with the South Side and the Norfolk and Petersburg Railroads to form the Atlantic, Mississippi, and Ohio Railroad, predecessor of the Norfolk and Western Railway Company. Odin Green Clay died in a Lynchburg hotel late on 17 January 1883 and was buried beside his wife's grave near his house in Campbell County.

Biography in Ruth Hairston Early, *Campbell Chronicles and Family Sketches, Embracing the History of Campbell County, Virginia, 1782–1926* (1927), 374–377; birth date in *Lynch-*

burg News, 19 Jan. 1883 (agrees with age given elsewhere); variant birth date of 5 May 1802 in Clay family Bible records (1745–1873), LVA; Zachary F. Smith and Mary Rogers Clay, *The Clay Family* (1899), 112–113; Bedford Co. Marriage Bonds; Clay's legal, land, and business records in Clay Family Papers, VHS; Clay letters and official reports in Virginia and Tennessee Railroad Company Records (1848–1871), Norfolk and Western Railway Archives, VPI, and Board of Public Works Papers, RG 57, LVA; printed annual *Reports* of the president of the Lynchburg and Tennessee Railroad Company (1848) (quotation on 7), and Virginia and Tennessee Railroad Company (1849–1852); Norfolk and Western Railway Company, *Lynchburg's First Railway: The Virginia & Tennessee* (1936); Elizabeth Dabney Coleman, "Southwest Virginia's Railroad: Lynchburg Started It; Virginia Built It; The Yankees Wrecked It," *Virginia Cavalcade* 2 (spring 1953): 20–27; Central Southern Rights Association Record Book (1850–1860), VHS; Presidential Pardons; por. in Norfolk and Western Historical Photograph Collection, VPI, from original in possession of Sara Phillips, Raleigh, N.C. (2002); Campbell Co. Will Book, 16:58–61; obituaries in *Lynchburg Daily News*, 19 Jan. 1883, and *Lynchburg Virginian*, 19, 20 Jan. 1883.

MARTIN STAKES LANE

CLAYTON, John (1656 or 1657–23 September 1725), Anglican minister and naturalist, was born near Preston, in Lancaster County, England, and was the son of Robert Clayton and Elianor Atherton Clayton. He was distantly related to John Clayton (ca. 1666–1737), who later became Virginia's attorney general. On 17 July 1674 at age seventeen Clayton matriculated at the University of Oxford's Saint Alban Hall. Later he transferred to Merton College, where he received a B.A. in January 1678 and an M.A. in 1682. On an unrecorded date he was ordained to the priesthood in the Church of England.

Like many other clergymen, including John Banister (ca. 1650–1692), who was in Virginia when Clayton arrived, Clayton had a keen interest in the natural sciences and is known at least as much for his scientific experiments and observations as for his career in the church. He experimented with a "digester," a precursor to the pressure cooker, studied the weights of liquids, and is credited by some authors with discovering gas lighting no later than 1687. Clayton recorded his observations of numerous natural phenomena, including subjects as diverse as the anatomy of English fowl and Virginia's animals, geology, native peoples, plants, and weather. He presented accounts of his observations to the Royal Society of London for Improving Natural Knowledge, of which he was elected a fellow on 30 November 1688.

Clayton traveled to Virginia early in 1684 to become rector of James City Parish in Jamestown, a posting that afforded him an opportunity to serve the church and further his scientific pastime in a part of the world few European scientists had the occasion to visit. He collected numerous bird specimens, built a distillery and tried his hand at distilling various native plants, asserted he had discovered hundreds of herbs then unknown in Europe, made detailed investigations of the colony's flora and fauna, and answered a long questionnaire on the colony's natural life for Sir Robert Boyle. So thorough and impressive were Clayton's accounts of Virginia that John Brickell plagiarized his works for his own *Natural History of North-Carolina* (1737). Clayton made perceptive observations of the colony's settlers as well. One valuable document that he acquired was the journal that Thomas Batte and Robert Hallom kept on an exploratory march to the New River and beyond the Appalachian Mountains in 1671. Misspellings of the principals' surnames in the copy that Clayton presented in 1688 to the Royal Society in London led to their later misidentification in published accounts as Batts and Fallam. Clayton doubtless would have engaged in other serious scientific investigations while in Virginia had the vessel on which he shipped his reference books and scientific instruments to the colony not been lost at sea.

Clayton's reputation as a preacher preceded him to Virginia. Shortly after arriving he received an invitation from the governor and Council to preach to the General Assembly. He joked: "I must mind my hits to preserve that blooming repute I have got. I have had the happinesse to be cried up farr beyond my deserts." Clayton's learned sermons, full of references to the church fathers and church history and buttressed with numerous Latin footnotes, probably appealed to the better-educated Virginians, among whom he made friends, however members of the assembly received them.

When Clayton was in Virginia, Henry Compton was bishop of London and had jurisdiction over the church in the North American colonies. The fortunes of the Church of England, which was the established church in the colony, were looking up. Until then, the church and the Crown had failed to take an adequate interest in Virginia's religious life. As a result, many parishes were without ministers, and ministers lacking proper ordination filled some pulpits. The clergy was unsupervised, holy days were not celebrated, and wealthy members of the laity preferred burial in their gardens rather than the churchyard. Among the steps Compton took to improve Virginia's religious life was to send qualified ministers, such as Clayton, to Virginia parishes. On an unrecorded date, probably not long after Clayton arrived in Virginia, the governor at Compton's request nominated Clayton to become the colony's first commissary, or personal representative of the bishop. Although new to the colonies, this administrative position was common in England and provided for the administration of the bishop's episcopal authority without requiring his formal presence, thus making it the perfect means of establishing the Church of England's ecclesiastical authority in North America.

As commissary, Clayton took part in the Anglicization of Virginia. He later stated that he had "Setled the Service of our Church very Regularly" and been the first minister in Jamestown to wear a surplice. He took pride in his ability to convert dissenters. In order to help both conformists and dissenters better understand the Church of England's set liturgies, he offered regular afternoon lectures on the Book of Common Prayer and by this means, as he put it, "brought over many Dissenters to be very affectionate to our Church Service." Clayton also baptized enslaved blacks and readily accommodated himself to planters' needs by helping "to take off one grand Obstruction that had Obtain'd, *Viz.* a Notion, that Negroes being Baptiz'd were immediately Free."

Clayton left Virginia in May 1686, and consequently his leadership as commissary may have left little mark on the colony's established church. After returning to England, he became rector of the Church of All Saints in Crofton, Yorkshire, in 1687 and sometime before the end of 1694 married Juliana Edmundson. They had three daughters and two sons, one of whom became a bishop. In 1697 Clayton accepted the position of rector at Saint Michan's Church, in Dublin, and moved to Ireland at a time when relations between Catholics and Protestants remained tense. His three extant published sermons contain elements of anti-Catholic polemic. In the preface to a 1701 discourse he described his ministry in Virginia. John Clayton was elected dean of Kildare in 1708, in which office he was still serving when he died in Dublin on 23 September 1725. He was buried three days later in Saint Michan's Church in that city.

Biographies in Walter T. Layton, *The Discoverer of Gas Lighting: Notes on the Life and Work of the Rev. John Clayton, D.D., 1657–1725* (1926), and Edmund Berkeley and Dorothy Smith Berkeley, eds., *The Reverend John Clayton: A Parson with a Scientific Mind: His Scientific Writings and Other Related Papers* (1965); Joseph Foster, *Alumni Oxonienses* (1891), 1:287 (giving age seventeen at matriculation on 17 July 1674 and including death date but with incorrect identification of parents); family relationships in Sir William Dugdale, *The Visitation of the County Palatine of Lancaster, Made in the Year 1664–5*, ed. F. R. Raines (1872), 84–85; Billings, *Effingham Papers*, 219, 459–460; John Clayton to Dr. [Edmond Borlase?], 24 Apr. 1684, Sloane 1008, British Library (first quotation); Clayton's scientific writings in Royal Society of London and British Library; Marcus B. Simpson Jr. and Sallie W. Simpson, "The Reverend John Clayton's Letters to the Royal Society of London, 1693–1694: An Important Source for Dr. John Brickell's *Natural History of North-Carolina, 1737,*" *North Carolina Historical Review* 54 (1977): 1–16; nonscientific publications include *A Sermon Preach'd at St. Michan's Church in Dublin, February the 23d 1700. Upon Receiving into the Communion of the Church of England, the Honble Sir Terence Mac-Mahon, Knt & Barnet and Christopher Dunn, Converts from the Church of Rome* (1700), *The Defence of a Sermon, Preach'd Upon the Receiving into the Communion of the Church of England, the Honourable Sir Terence Mac-Mahon Baronet, and Christopher Dunn: Converts from the Church of Rome* (1701) (all other quotations from preface), *Christ Crucified: The Power of God, and the Wisdom of God. A Sermon Preach't at St. Margaret's Westminster, November 11th, 1705* (1706), and *Dean Clayton's Letter, to One of the Common Council of the City of Dublin: Relating to the Means of Reconciling the Present Difficulties of the Said City* (1713).

EDWARD L. BOND

CLAYTON, John (ca. 1666–18 November 1737), attorney general of Virginia, was the son of Alice Bowyer Buggins Clayton and her second husband, Sir John Clayton, both of whom came from well-connected families of Buckinghamshire and Middlesex County, England. He may have been born at his paternal grandmother's Parson's Green estate in Middlesex, as were at least two of his younger siblings, but the place and date of his birth are not recorded. Clayton attended Eton College and then Trinity Hall, University of Cambridge, but he did not take a degree. On 16 June 1682 he entered the Inner Temple, of which his father was a member, to study law. He was called to the bar on 24 May 1691 and began practicing in London. The date and place of Clayton's marriage are not known, nor is the maiden name of his wife, whose given name was Lucy. By 1702 they had three sons, one of whom was John Clayton (1695–1773), often known as John Clayton the botanist.

Clayton's wife may have died not long after the birth of their third child, and that event could have contributed to his decision to travel to Virginia, where he was secretary to his acquaintance Edward Nott, governor of the colony from August 1705 until his death on 23 August 1706. Clayton remained in Williamsburg to settle Nott's estate and expanded his acquaintances among the influential families into a lucrative law practice. He was attorney for William Byrd (1674–1744) for more than a decade. Widely liked and evidently a good companion over a glass of wine or at the gaming table, Clayton earned a reputation as an able and honest lawyer.

On 23 January 1706 Clayton became register of the Virginia Court of Vice Admiralty. Late the following year he assisted the attorney general in a murder trial, and in 1712 he assisted again in the trial of several Indians and African Americans charged with treason or rebellion. Active in a variety of the colony's affairs, Clayton was elected to the board of the College of William and Mary on 25 April 1710, traveled to North Carolina in 1711 at the order of the lieutenant governor to adjust a dispute, and served from 1712 to 1714 as the paid clerk of the Committee of Propositions and Grievances for the House of Burgesses. He helped oversee the surveying of Williamsburg's streets during that decade and was one of the men who directed repairs to the Capitol in the 1710s and again during the 1720s. Twice, in 1716 and in 1732, Clayton was appointed to a board to devise methods

for judging the qualifications of men to practice law. He became presiding judge of the James City County Court on 13 August 1717.

Elected to the House of Burgesses from Jamestown in 1715, Clayton became chair of the Committee of Propositions and Grievances on his first day as a member and regained the post in 1720, when he was elected from James City County. He won reelection to the assembly that met from 1723 to 1726 and again served on the Committee of Propositions and Grievances. Clayton represented Williamsburg in the assembly that met from 1728 to 1734. He chaired the Committee for Courts of Justice in 1728 and in 1732 and 1734 served again as chair of the Committee of Propositions and Grievances. Late in the 1710s Clayton, John Holloway, and William Robertson prepared a collection of Virginia statutes in force, and Clayton took part in revising that edition, which William Parks published in 1733. Clayton obtained the permission of the burgesses in 1718 to procure a marble statue of Edward Nott for erection in the churchyard in Williamsburg but for reasons not recorded was unable to fulfill the commission. When the city of Williamsburg was chartered in 1722, Clayton was named recorder, or chief legal officer, in which post he served until he died.

Soon after the death early in February 1714 of Attorney General Stephens Thomson, Lieutenant Governor Alexander Spotswood appointed Clayton to the office and affirmed to the Board of Trade that Clayton was "an English Gentleman and a Barrister at Law, who has as fair a Character as anyone I ever knew of that profession." The Crown confirmed the appointment, and in April 1721 Clayton was also commissioned judge of the Virginia Court of Vice Admiralty, a joining of offices that each subsequent attorney general held until the American Revolution. Clayton served in both offices until his death, although in April 1726 he obtained a leave of absence in order to return to England to settle family and personal business. He selected John Randolph (later Sir John Randolph) to serve as acting attorney general during his absence, which lasted until late in 1727 or early in 1728.

A few days after his appointment as attorney general, Clayton arranged for a woman who was suspected of beating to death one of her slaves to be indicted and tried for murder before the General Court, even though the Isle of Wight County Court, of which her husband was a member, had declined to indict her. She was acquitted. After Clayton learned that political opponents of the lieutenant governor accused him of illegally prosecuting the woman as part of an alleged scheme by Spotswood to persecute his adversaries, Clayton took full responsibility for bringing the case before the General Court after the county court had refused to act.

The routine business of the attorney general's office was not so time-consuming that Clayton initially had to give up his private practice, but in 1733 he petitioned treasury officials in London for an addition to his £100 annual salary. The colony's courts had experienced a large proliferation in criminal business as a result of the many convicts sentenced to serve their time as servants in Virginia. The lords of the treasury increased his salary by £40.

Clayton occasionally suffered from gout and his step slowed as he aged, but his health was generally good until he reached the age of seventy. John Clayton died at his Williamsburg home early in the morning of 18 November 1737. He was buried in the city without much ceremony or a funeral sermon, as he had specified in his will.

"The Clayton Family," *Virginia Historical Magazine* 1 (1891): 25–29; Edmund Berkeley and Dorothy Smith Berkeley, *John Clayton, Pioneer of American Botany* (1963), 10–21; Inner Temple Admissions Register, ADM/2/1 and BAR/4/1, Archives of the Honourable Society of the Inner Temple, London, Eng.; numerous references in Louis B. Wright and Marion Tinling, eds., *The Secret Diary of William Byrd of Westover, 1709–1712* (1941), and *The London Diary (1717–1721) and Other Writings* (1958); public offices documented in *Executive Journals of Council*, vols. 3–4, and *JHB*; Alexander Spotswood to Board of Trade, 9 Mar. 1714, PRO CO 5/1316, fols. 503–506 (quotation on 506); murder trial described and letter Clayton wrote as attorney general on 18 Feb. 1714 mentioned in PRO CO 5/1318, fols. 95–98; salary increase in PRO T 29/27, 198, and T 54/32, 42–43; copy of will, Acc. 29679, LVA; obituary (reporting death "in the 72d Year of his Age") and account of funeral in *Williamsburg Virginia Gazette*, 18, 25 Nov. 1737.

BRENT TARTER

CLAYTON, John (August 1695–15 December 1773), botanist, was born in England, possibly in Fulham, Kent, and was the son of John Clayton (ca. 1666–1737), who became attorney general of Virginia early in 1714, and Lucy Clayton, whose maiden name is not known. He may have attended Eton College and the University of Cambridge, and like his father he might have studied law, but little is known for certain about his education. Clayton may have traveled to Virginia as early as 1715, but his name appears in extant colonial records for the first time on 7 October 1720 when he was identified as clerk of Gloucester County. He had probably worked as a deputy to Peter Beverley, who relinquished the position in 1719 or 1720, but the loss of the county records makes it impossible to determine for how long. Early in the 1720s Clayton married Elizabeth Whiting, daughter of Henry Whiting, a former member of the governor's Council. Their three daughters and five sons included William Clayton, who became clerk of New Kent County and a member of the Conventions of 1776 and 1788.

As clerk of Gloucester County for more than fifty years, Clayton recorded deeds, land surveys, wills, and other documents and attended the county court sessions. He owned a 450-acre plantation, on which he raised tobacco and livestock, and eventually acquired more than thirty slaves. Clayton's duties were not so onerous as to prevent him from devoting much of his energy to the study of botany. He provided Mark Catesby, a noted naturalist who had resided in Williamsburg off and on from 1712 to 1719, with at least one ornithological specimen and several plants, which Catesby mentioned in his *Natural History of Carolina, Florida and the Bahama Islands* (1731–1743). By 1735 Clayton had begun sending dried plant specimens to John Frederick Gronovius, a botanist of Leiden, in the Netherlands, often by way of Catesby. Initially Clayton asked Gronovius to identify the plants he sent, but Clayton soon began making his own identifications and was the first to name the genus *Agastache*, a group of perennial, woody herbs with spiked flowers. Gronovius shared Clayton's specimens with Carolus Linnaeus, a Swedish botanist who developed the modern system of binomial nomenclature. In 1737 Linnaeus named the genus *Claytonia*, wildflowers of the Portulacaceae family, in Clayton's honor.

During the 1730s Clayton traveled around Virginia collecting seeds and plants and began compiling for Gronovius a *Catalogue of Herbs, Fruits, and Trees Native to Virginia*, based on the new Linnaean system of classification. Without asking permission or informing Clayton of his intentions, Gronovius in 1739 translated the catalog into Latin and published it as *Flora Virginica*, a 128-page book describing about six hundred plant species. Clayton continued to identify and send specimens to Gronovius, who in 1743 published the second part of *Flora Virginica*, containing about three hundred additional species.

Clayton's name became well known in American and European botanical circles, and by the 1740s he had begun a correspondence with the Pennsylvania botanist John Bartram that lasted for more than twenty years. They exchanged seeds and advice about the cultivation of native plants, many of which Clayton raised in his extensive garden, which Bartram described as one of the best he had seen in Virginia. In 1743 Bartram included Clayton, whom he considered a "worthy, ingenious man," as a member of the American Philosophical Society, organized that year for the study of sciences and humanities. Clayton probably did not attend any of its meetings. On 3 May 1747, on the recommendation of Linnaeus, the Swedish Royal Academy of Science elected Clayton to membership.

Clayton continued collecting and in 1746 went to Canada and about 1747 or 1748 may have traveled as far west as the Mississippi River. About that time he began corresponding with Peter Collinson, an English horticulturalist and member of the Royal Society of London for Improving Natural Knowledge. They exchanged plant samples, and in the 1750s Clayton experimented with growing wheat from seed that Collinson provided. Collinson occasionally presented Clayton's letters on scientific topics to the Royal Society and published one in the *Gentleman's Magazine* in 1752 and another in 1755.

Known for the accurate detail of his plant descriptions, Clayton began compiling his own *Flora Virginica* during the mid-1750s and in 1758 sent Collinson a copy for publication. The volume was to include illustrations by Georg Dionysius Ehret, one of the foremost botanical artists of the period. Before Clayton's illustrated version could be published, however, Gronovius's son published a new edition of *Flora* in 1762, which apparently precluded any need for the new book. Clayton's own copy was probably lost in 1787 when fire destroyed the clerk's office in New Kent County, where his son had stored the botanist's papers for safekeeping. The editions of Clayton's *Flora Virginica* were the first, and for more than two hundred years the only, such compilation of Virginia's native plants.

About 1769 Clayton hired John James Beckley, later clerk of the House of Representatives and librarian of Congress, to assist with the work in the county clerk's office. Although his eyesight was failing, Clayton visited Orange County on a collecting expedition in the autumn of 1772, and his enthusiasm was such that he reportedly offered rewards to people who discovered native plants not yet known to him. In May 1773 he was elected the first president of the new Virginian Society for the Promotion of Usefull Knowledge, in effect a Virginia chapter of the American Philosophical Society.

John Clayton was in poor health when he wrote his will in October 1773, and he died, probably at his residence in Gloucester County, on 15 December of that year. His death was reported without comment in one of the Williamsburg newspapers three weeks later. In keeping with instructions, he was buried without ceremony or sermon next to the bodies of his wife and two of his children, probably at his plantation. In 1794 the English naturalist Sir Joseph Banks acquired hundreds of the specimens that Clayton had sent to Gronovius. They form the John Clayton Herbarium, part of the Natural History Museum in London.

Biographies in Benjamin Smith Barton, "Memorandums of the Life of Mr. John Clayton, the Celebrated Botanist of Virginia," *Philadelphia Medical and Physical Journal* 2 (1805): 139–145 (with death date, probably from family sources, and recording death "in his eighty-eighth year"), and Edmund Berkeley and Dorothy Smith Berkeley, *John Clayton: Pioneer of American Botany* (1963); Clayton correspondence in John Norton and Sons Papers (age seventy-seven in John Clayton to John Norton, 31 Aug. 1772, enclosure, and also in Clayton to Norton, 2 Aug. 1773), CW, printed in part in Frances Norton Mason, ed., *John Norton and Sons:*

Merchants of London and Virginia (1937), 155, 197–198, in William Darlington, *Memorials of John Bartram and Humphry Marshall* (1849), 406–412 (quotation on 224), in *VMHB* 7 (1899): 172–174, and in *WMQ*, 2d ser., 4 (1924): 246–248, ibid. 6 (1926): 317–325; C. G. Chamberlayne, ed., *The Vestry Book of Petsworth Parish, Gloucester County, Virginia: 1677–1793* (1933), 154 (first mention in Virginia); Caroline Heath Tunstall, "A Virginian in Dutch Eyes: John Clayton of Virginia and Frederick Gronovius of Holland," *Virginia Cavalcade* 28 (1979): 149–153; *Williamsburg Virginia Gazette* (Purdie and Dixon), 13 May 1773; copy of will in Jenings Family Papers, VHS; death notice without death date in *Williamsburg Virginia Gazette* (Purdie and Dixon), 6 Jan. 1774.

MARIANNE E. JULIENNE

CLAYTON, William (d. by 14 December 1797), member of the Convention of 1776 and of the Convention of 1788, was born most likely in Gloucester County and was the son of John Clayton (1695–1773) and Elizabeth Whiting Clayton. His father was clerk of Gloucester County for more than fifty years, president of the Virginian Society for the Promotion of Usefull Knowledge, and a renowned botanist. The date of Clayton's birth is not recorded, but he had an elder brother born about 1725 and therefore was born probably late in the 1720s or early in the 1730s. Little is known of his youth, but his father appears to have educated his sons well. In the 1750s Clayton married a woman whose first name was Elvira but whose maiden name is not known. They had two daughters and one son.

It is possible that Clayton's father arranged for him to work as an assistant to the clerk of New Kent County, just as Clayton's younger brother did in Gloucester County for their father. Clayton became clerk of New Kent County about 1756. The county courthouse burned in March 1775, but because the county's records were stored in a separate clerk's office, no valuable papers were lost. In 1787, however, a man burned the clerk's office in order to destroy incriminating documents kept there. The fire destroyed all the county's public records as well as some of the scientific papers of Clayton's father, which he had housed in the clerk's office for safekeeping.

In 1758 Clayton became a vestryman of Saint Peter's Parish. Appointed church warden in 1769, he remained active in parish affairs through at least 1779. Clayton was also a colonel in the militia and from 1766 to 1771 represented the county in the House of Burgesses. He served on the Committee for Courts of Justice in 1766 and 1769 and in the latter year also on the Committee of Propositions and Grievances and the Committee to Proportion the Public Levy.

Clayton signed the nonimportation association of 1769 in protest of Parliament's taxes on the colonies, a second association dated 22 June 1770, and a third on 27 May 1774, in which former burgesses proposed a congress of the colonies. He was clerk of the New Kent County meeting on 12 July 1774 that condemned Parliament and instructed the county's delegates to the first of Virginia's Revolutionary Conventions. On 11 April 1776 Clayton was elected to the fifth and last of the conventions. He served on the Committees of Privileges and Elections and of Public Claims and attended nearly every day from 6 May through 5 July. Clayton was undoubtedly present for the three most important, unanimous votes, on 15 May to instruct the Virginia delegates in the Continental Congress to move a resolution of independence, on 12 June to adopt the Declaration of Rights, and on 29 June to approve Virginia's first constitution.

A member of the House of Delegates in the autumn of 1776, Clayton served on the Committee for Courts of Justice, the Committee of Privileges and Elections, and the Committee of Public Claims. He retained his position as clerk of New Kent County during the American Revolution and was also county lieutenant, or commander of the county's militia. He attempted, when requested, to recruit horses, men, and supplies for the defense of Virginia. Clayton did not return to the General Assembly or take part in elective politics, so far as is known, until the spring of 1788, when the county's voters elected him to the convention called to consider the proposed constitution of the United States. He did not speak during the debates. Clayton voted on 25 June 1788 against requiring prior amendments to the Constitution and then voted for ratification. Two days later he voted against a proposed amendment to limit congressional taxing authority.

Clayton's home at East Greenwich, in New Kent County, was known as Chestnut Hill. A visiting Methodist minister who held a large meeting on Clayton's plantation in 1791 described it as very beautiful. In 1782 Clayton owned 728 acres of land in the county and by 1788 had acquired another tract of 1,080 acres. He paid taxes on two dozen slaves in 1797. William Clayton dated his will on 10 June 1797 and died on an unrecorded date between then and 14 December 1797, when the will was proved in court. He may have been buried on his property at Chestnut Hill.

Malcolm Hart Harris, *Old New Kent County: Some Account of the Planters, Plantations, and Places in New Kent County* (1977), 1:161–162; numerous references in C. G. Chamberlayne, ed., *The Vestry Book and Register of St. Peter's Parish, New Kent and James City Counties, Virginia, 1684–1786* (1937); *Revolutionary Virginia*, 1:76, 83, 98, 147–149, 2:319, 6:377, 380–381, 7:24, 28, 78; Kaminski, *Ratification*, 10:1539, 1540, 1557, 1565; some letters in Thomas Jefferson, Thomas Nelson, and Benjamin Harrison Executive Papers, all RG 3, LVA; Land Tax Returns, New Kent Co. (1782, 1788), and Personal Property Tax Returns, New Kent Co. (1797), both RG 48, LVA; abstract of lost will in William Armstrong Crozier, ed., *Williamsburg Wills* (1906), 19.

MARTHA J. KING

CLAYTOR, Gertrude Harris Boatwright (1 October 1888–21 August 1973), poet, was born in Staunton and was the only child of James Sampson Boatwright and Gertrude Floyd Harris Boatwright. When she was young, her family moved to Roanoke, where she attended a private school and her father worked as business manager and later treasurer of Virginia College, a school for young women founded in 1893 by her maternal grandfather, William Anderson Harris. After Harris's death in 1895, Boatwright's mother served as vice president and her aunt, Mattie Powell Harris, as president of the college. Boatwright's love of poetry began when she discovered the English Romantic poets at age twelve, and soon she was composing verse herself. She graduated from Virginia College in 1907 and broadened her education with a European tour in the company of her aunt.

On 19 February 1908 Boatwright married William Graham Claytor (1886–1971), an engineer at the Roanoke Railway and Electric Company (later Appalachian Electric Power Company). Of their five sons, only three reached adulthood, including William Graham Claytor (1912–1994), who settled in Washington, D.C.,

and was secretary of the navy from 1977 to 1979, deputy secretary of defense, acting secretary of transportation, and president of Southern Railway and of the National Railroad Passenger Corporation (Amtrak), and Robert Buckner Claytor, president of the Norfolk and Western Railway Company and later chief executive officer of the Norfolk Southern Corporation. While Claytor focused on raising and educating her children, her husband's career advanced rapidly, and in 1923 the family moved to Philadelphia and three years later to New York City.

Claytor had set poetry aside while her sons were young, but by late in the 1920s she was writing in earnest. In 1929 the first of her published poems appeared in the Roanoke-based magazine *The Lyric*. In 1932 "Indian Wife" won first prize in the Poetry Society of America's annual contest, and two years later the Virginia State Commission on Conservation and Development inscribed one of her poems on a marker placed at Swift Run Gap to commemorate Lieutenant Governor Alexander Spotswood's 1716 expedition to the Shenandoah Valley. From 1937 to 1939 Claytor pursued postgraduate work at Columbia University, including study at the Poetry Workshop with the Pulitzer Prize–winning poets William Rose Benet and Leonora Speyer.

A lyric poet, Claytor worked in a tradition that emphasized intense personal emotion and musical language, elements that appealed to general readers but contrasted sharply with the obscurantism characteristic of abstract modern poetry. She was preoccupied thematically with "earth's undertow," her term for the irresistible connection to the natural world and to homeland that inspired her meditations on nature and on Virginia's past. Claytor's best verse lacked sentimentality and featured an authentic voice and artfully constructed lines that resonated with insight. One of her poems was published in *Columbia Poetry, 1938* (1938), and over time others appeared in such periodicals as the *Carolina Quarterly*, *Florida Magazine of Verse*, *Georgia Review*, *New York Times*, *Poetry Chap-Book*, *Prairie Schooner*, *Saturday Review of Literature*, and *Voices*.

In 1938 Claytor met Edgar Lee Masters, author of *Spoon River Anthology* (1915). The two remained close friends until his death in 1950, after which Claytor presented her collection of signed first editions, manuscript poems, photographs, and other materials that Masters had given her, including dozens of his letters, to Princeton University. In 1952 she wrote a vivid portrayal of the aged poet and biographer, "Edgar Lee Masters in the Chelsea Years," for the *Princeton University Library Chronicle*, and two years later she spoke at Hollins College on his life and career.

Claytor published two poetry collections, *Sunday in Virginia and Other Poems* (1951), which quickly went into a second edition, and *Mirage at Midnight and Other Poems* (1960). A 1958 article in a Virginia journal placed her among the state's poets who were winning national attention. Claytor's poetry received favorable reviews in the Richmond newspapers, the *Los Angeles Times*, and the *New York Times* and appeared in several compilations, including *The Poetry Society of America Anthology* (1946), the *Gold Medal Treasury of American Verse* (1953), the second volume of *Lyric Virginia To-Day* (1956), *The Golden Year: The Poetry Society of America Anthology (1910–1960)* (1960), and the Poetry Society of Virginia's *Golden Anniversary Anthology of Poems by Member Poets* (1974).

Claytor joined *The Lyric*'s advisory board in 1953 and four years later became an advisory editor, a position she retained until her death. About this time she was also named an advisory editor of the Borestone Mountain Poetry Awards, service that brought her into contact with the work of emerging poets and established writers nationwide. A member of the International Association of Poets, Playwrights, Essayists, Editors, and Novelists (PEN), the Academy of American Poets, and the Virginia Writers Club, Claytor was also vice president of the Craftsman Group for Poetry and president of the New York Women Poets. She sat on the Poetry Society of America's executive board for three years.

In September 1961 Claytor moved to Washington, D.C. She and her husband divided their time between that city and Claytor Lake, in Pulaski County, until his death on 28 February 1971. She served on the advisory board of the Poetry Society of Virginia from 1963 until 1970 and worked on annual Borestone Mountain Poetry Award anthologies until she resigned in March 1967. Gertrude Harris Boatwright Claytor died in a Salem hospital on 21 August 1973 and was interred in Roanoke's Evergreen Burial Park. For several years after her death the Poetry Society of America offered a poetry prize in her name.

NCAB, 57:512 (variant birth year of 1889); WPA Biographies; *Who's Who of American Women* (1964/1965), 195; BVS Birth Register, Staunton; BVS Marriage Register, Roanoke Co.; Gertrude Boatwright Claytor Papers, UVA; correspondence in Gertrude Claytor Collection of Edgar Lee Masters, Princeton University; *Roanoke World-News*, 3 Dec. 1932; *Richmond Times-Dispatch*, 17 Apr. 1952; poetry reviewed in *Richmond Times-Dispatch*, 11 Mar. 1951, *New York Times*, 14 Oct. 1951, and *Washington Post*, 31 Aug. 1952; Harry M. Meacham, "The Virginia Poets and Their Poetry," *Commonwealth* 25 (July 1958): 24; obituaries in *Roanoke World-News*, 21 Aug. 1973 (por.), and *Roanoke Times* and *New York Times*, both 22 Aug. 1973.

DONALD W. GUNTER

CLAYTOR, Robert Buckner (27 February 1922–9 April 1993), president of the Norfolk and Western Railway Company and chief executive officer of the Norfolk Southern Corporation, was born in Roanoke and was the son of William Graham Claytor (1886–1971), an electric company executive, and Gertrude Harris Boatwright Claytor, a lyric poet. His elder brother, William Graham Claytor (1912–1994), settled in Washington, D.C., and became secretary of the navy, deputy secretary of defense, acting secretary of transportation, and president of Southern Railway and of the National Railroad Passenger Corporation (Amtrak). His parents moved the family to Philadelphia about a year after his birth and then to New York in 1926. Educated at a military boarding school in Gainesville, Georgia, and at an academy in Mercersburg, Pennsylvania, Claytor studied economics at Princeton University and received an A.B. in 1943 after completing a thesis on silver and United States monetary policy. During World War II he served stateside as a first lieutenant in the field artillery. On 25 September 1943 in Princeton, Claytor married Frances Tice, a native of Roanoke then enrolled at the Westminster Choir College. They had two sons and one daughter. Following his tour of duty, Claytor attended Harvard University Law School and in 1948 received an LL.B. He was admitted to the state bars of Massachusetts, New York, and Virginia in 1948, 1949, and 1952, respectively.

Claytor first practiced law at the New York headquarters of the American Telephone and Telegraph Company. In 1951 he became a solicitor in the Norfolk and Western Railway Company's law department in Roanoke. Well-versed in government regulations affecting the transportation industry, Claytor gained increasing executive responsibility. He received promotion to vice president of law in 1964, senior vice president and member of the board of directors in 1968, and executive vice president in 1970.

Claytor's dedication and personal passion for the railroad earned him the nickname "Red Baron." During a railroad clerks' strike in 1978 the Norfolk and Western kept its trains running by having management personnel take over strikers' duties. For three months Claytor kept office hours in Roanoke and then in the evenings donned overalls to work as a freight train engineer on the route from Roanoke to Norfolk. Ignoring union work rules calling for a four-man crew and a shift change halfway to Norfolk, he regularly drove the nearly 300 miles assisted by only one crewman.

In October 1980 Claytor was named president of the Norfolk and Western Railway Company and the following October became its chief executive officer. During this time the Seaboard Coast Line Railroad and the Chessie System, Inc., merged to form the CSX Corporation, the country's largest railroad, and Congress passed the Staggers Act (1980), which ended the regulations that had governed the freight-hauling industry. In response, Claytor oversaw the merger on 1 June 1982 of the Roanoke-based Norfolk and Western Railway Company and the Southern Railway Company, headquartered in Washington, D.C., to form the Norfolk Southern Corporation, a railroad system with more than 18,000 miles of tracks in twenty-one states and Canada, more than 41,000 employees, and assets totaling almost $7 billion.

Appointed chairman and chief executive officer, Claytor was credited with engineering a positive merger for shareholders, management, and employees. He balanced the corporate culture and distribution of power of each rail system within the new company. One of his most important decisions was to establish the corporate headquarters in Norfolk, a neutral location, so that neither railroad could claim an advantage. Despite the merger, the Norfolk Southern was still smaller than its rival CSX, and as a consequence, Claytor spent two years pursuing the Consolidated Rail Corporation (Conrail) for another merger. The deal could have made the Norfolk Southern the nation's largest railroad network, but Congress blocked the merger. In June 1985 the corporation did expand with the acquisition of North American Van Lines, Inc., for more than $375 million.

Claytor stepped down as chairman and CEO on 1 March 1987 but continued to serve on the board and as chair of its executive committee until he retired in 1992. The Norfolk Southern became one of the largest and most influential companies in the region. His legacy also included historic preservation. After the corporation restored the J-611, the last American steam locomotive built, Claytor engineered the train on its inaugural run from Roanoke to Norfolk. In 1981 he donated the Norfolk and Western's corporate papers to Virginia Polytechnic Institute and State University and three years later added the archives of the Southern Railway. Throughout his career he also supported the National Railway Historical Society.

Dedication to the arts, education, and industry in Virginia was a constant theme in Claytor's life. He sat on the boards of many businesses, clubs, and service organizations, including the Eastern Virginia Medical Foundation, the Future of Hampton Roads, Inc., the General Douglas MacArthur Foundation, the Greater Norfolk Corporation, and Piedmont Airlines. Chancellor of the Episcopal Diocese of Southwest Virginia from 1969 to 1975, he was elected to a five-year term as trustee at large of the Protestant Episcopal Theological Seminary in Virginia (popularly known as Virginia Theological Seminary), in Alexandria, in 1985 and reelected to another in 1990, although he resigned the following year. Under his leadership the Norfolk Southern donated funds to the Chrysler Museum of Art, the Cultural Alliance of Greater Hampton Roads, the Roanoke Symphony Orchestra, the Southwest Virginia Center for the Arts and Sciences, and the Virginia Opera Company.

Claytor was chair and trustee of the Virginia Foundation for Independent Colleges, regent and board chair of his alma mater Mercersburg Academy, and visitor and vice rector of Virginia Polytechnic Institute and State University's board of advisers. A trustee of Hollins College for twenty-two years, he chaired the college's board for a decade. In 1982 Hollins awarded him an honorary doctorate of humane letters and in 1990 the Algernon Sydney Sullivan Award for leadership. Robert Buckner Claytor died of cancer on 9 April 1993 at his Norfolk home. His remains were cremated and placed in the columbarium at Saint John's Episcopal Church, in Roanoke, with those of Frances Tice Claytor, who had died on 19 June 1989.

Norfolk Southern Corporation, "Robert B. Claytor: A Life in Railroading," *Portrait* 20 (2002), 24–26 (pors.); *Who's Who in America* (1992/1993), 625; information provided by son-in-law, Samuel Webster (2003); business and personal correspondence (including typescript speech, 10 Dec. 1959, to the National Railway Historical Society) in Robert B. Claytor Papers, and corporate records in Norfolk and Western Railroad Company Records, both VPI; *Roanoke Times*, 26 Sept. 1943; *Roanoke Times and World-News*, 18 Oct. 1981; *U.S. News and World Report* 99 (22 July 1985): 52; James A. Bacon, "Bob Claytor's Conrail Quest," *Virginia Business* 1 (Mar. 1986): 46–52 (pors.), 68; *Norfolk Southern Focus* 3 (winter 1986–1987): 10–11; Norfolk and Western Railway Company *Annual Reports*; Norfolk Southern Corporation *Annual Reports*; obituaries in *Norfolk Virginian-Pilot*, *Richmond Times-Dispatch*, *Roanoke Times*, and *Washington Post*, all 10 Apr. 1993; editorial tributes in Norfolk Southern Corporation *Annual Report* (1993), 48, and *Norfolk Virginian-Pilot*, 14 Apr. 1993.

JENNIFER GUNTER KING

CLAYTOR, Samuel (6 October 1794–15 September 1831), member of the Convention of 1829–1830, was born in Bedford County and was most likely the son of John Claytor and Charlotte Leftwich Claytor. Little is known about his early life. By 1822 Claytor had moved to Lynchburg, where he became a prosperous tobacconist. On 22 January 1822 he married Rosanna Eliza Murrell, the only daughter of one of Lynchburg's leading merchant families. They had one

son and two daughters. Emerging as one of the growing town's prominent citizens, Claytor was a member of the arrangements committee for the marquis de Lafayette's visit in 1824. He also served on a committee to petition the General Assembly for internal improvements and assisted in raising money for the construction of the town's waterworks.

In May 1829 Claytor polled the second-highest number of votes among the dozen candidates for four seats representing Bedford, Buckingham, and Campbell Counties in the state constitutional convention scheduled to begin meeting the following October. Like many of his western Piedmont colleagues, he agreed with reformers that the western region of Virginia was underrepresented in the General Assembly. They hoped to reapportion the legislature based on the state's white population and to extend the suffrage to all white men. As a member of the Committee on the Executive Department, Claytor advocated the election of the governor by the qualified voters rather than by the General Assembly as was done under the existing constitution. A measure, based in part on Claytor's resolution, to establish formally the executive office of lieutenant governor and to provide for direct election of the governor and lieutenant governor for three-year terms failed in a tie vote among the committee's twenty-four members.

Claytor consistently sided with western reformers and submitted several resolutions on expanding the suffrage and reapportioning the legislature. Verbally sparring with conservative opponents, he occasionally became so zealous that the chair was forced to call him to order. When the convention passed a constitution with minimal revisions on 14 January 1830, Claytor joined the reformers who voted against it because the document did not implement their goals. His district constituents, however, voted 1,620 to 103 to ratify the document, which also won approval statewide.

Claytor returned to his tobacco business in Lynchburg, where he continued to flourish. At the time of the convention, he owned town lots, including a residence previously known as the Mansion House and later designated the Miller-Claytor House, as well as five slaves and 160 acres of land in Bedford County. Samuel Claytor died in Lynchburg on 15 September 1831 following a long illness. He was buried in the city's Presbyterian Cemetery.

W. Asbury Christian, *Lynchburg and Its People* (1900), 81, 87, 93–95, 109; birth date on gravestone; Lynchburg Marriage Register (variant marriage date of 21 Jan. 1822); Land Tax Returns, Bedford Co. and Lynchburg (1830, 1831), and Personal Property Tax Returns, Lynchburg, (1822, 1830, 1831), both RG 48, LVA; marriage date in *Lynchburg Press*, 25 Jan. 1822; *Richmond Enquirer*, 2, 5 June, 15, 20 Oct. 1829; *Proceedings and Debates of 1829–1830 Convention*, 22–23, 42, 575, 808–811, 854, 882, 903; Bruce, *Rhetoric of Conservatism*, 37; Catlin, *Convention of 1829–30* (por.); por. miniature, attributed to George Catlin, in private collection (1986); obituary in *Lynchburg Virginian*, 19 Sept. 1831.

TRENTON E. HIZER

CLAYTOR, William Graham (20 December 1886–28 February 1971), electric company executive, was born in Bedford, the county seat of Bedford County, and was the son of Marion Orville Bell Claytor and William Graham Claytor (1852–1903), a lawyer, state senator, and writer. He was educated at local public schools before studying electrical engineering from 1902 to 1905 at Virginia Agricultural and Mechanical College and Polytechnic Institute (later Virginia Polytechnic Institute and State University). In 1906 and 1907 Claytor worked as a student engineer for the General Electric Company, of Lynn, Massachusetts. In 1907 he took a sales position with the Roanoke Railway and Electric Company and the following year became an electrical engineer.

Claytor married Gertrude Harris Boatwright in Roanoke County on 19 February 1908. His wife became a distinguished lyric poet and published two collections, *Sunday in Virginia and Other Poems* (1951) and *Mirage at Midnight and Other Poems* (1960). They had five sons, but only three reached adulthood, including Robert Buckner Claytor, who became president of the Norfolk and Western Railway Company and chief executive officer of the Norfolk Southern Corporation, and William Graham Claytor (1912–1994), who settled in Washington, D.C., and became secretary of the navy, deputy secretary of defense, acting secretary of transportation, and president of the Southern Railway and of the National Railroad Passenger Corporation (Amtrak).

The Roanoke Railway and Electric Company appointed Graham Claytor, as he was known, superintendent of its lighting and power departments in 1910 and four years later promoted him to general superintendent of the corporation, which by then included the Lynchburg Traction and Light Company. In 1918 and 1919 he served as a captain in the United States Army Quartermaster Corps in Brunswick, Georgia, where he helped supervise the construction of an ordnance plant. After World War I, Claytor returned to his position with the Roanoke Railway and Electric Company, by then renamed the Appalachian Electric Power Company. The American Electric Power Company, the owner of Appalachian and headquartered in Philadelphia, named him its chief engineer in 1923 and three years later promoted him to general manager. Claytor moved his family to Philadelphia in 1923 and in 1926 to New York City, after the New York–based American Gas and Electric Company acquired American Power and appointed him operating vice president of the company's numerous subsidiaries, including Appalachian Electric Power of Roanoke.

In 1937 American Gas and Electric elevated Claytor to vice president of its new Service Corporation and placed him on that subsidiary's board of directors. For the next two years he supervised construction of the company's 75,000-kilowatt hydroelectric dam on the New River in Pulaski County. On its completion in August 1939 the dam and the resulting 4,500-acre lake both were named in Claytor's honor, and in 1951 the Commonwealth of Virginia established the adjoining Claytor Lake State Park. From 1943 to 1954 Claytor served as vice president of American Gas and Electric, from 1944 to 1962 sat on its board of directors, and from 1951 to 1962 was a member of its executive committee. He retired in 1954 but returned from 1960 to April 1962 as executive vice president of the company, then called American Electric Power. He served as president of the Richardson-Wayland Electrical Corporation, of Roanoke, from 1959 until he died.

Claytor was a fellow of the American Institute of Electrical Engineers and also served on the board of governors of the Railroad and Machinery Club of New York. An enthusiastic amateur radio operator, he ran licensed radio station W2MYL from his house in Greenwich Village while he lived in New York and later operated W4HYE at his summer cottage at Claytor Lake. After retiring, Claytor split his time between homes in Washington, D.C., and at Claytor Lake. He sat on the board of directors of VPI's alumni association from 1941 until his death. In 1951 Claytor delivered the university's commencement address, and in 1959 he received a citation as a distinguished alumnus. William Graham Claytor died in a Roanoke hospital on 28 February 1971 and was interred in that city's Evergreen Burial Park. After his death, his family and members of the VPI alumni association established the Graham Claytor Memorial Scholarship to benefit students who demonstrated financial need and academic achievement.

Birth date on gravestone; biographies in *NCAB*, 57:211–212 (por.), Ellsworth Marshall Rust, *Rust of Virginia: Genealogical and Biographical Sketches of the Descendants of William Rust, 1654–1940* (1940), 304, and *VPI Old Guard Who's Who: 1888 through the Class of 1912* (1962), 14; BVS Marriage Register, Roanoke Co. (variant birthplace of Botetourt Co.); 1933, 1940, and 1951 autobiographical statements (all with birth date of 20 Dec. 1886 and birthplace of Bedford), business correspondence, speeches, and alumni association files in W. Graham Claytor Papers, VPI; *Iron Worker* 12 (fall 1949): 1, 12–14; VPI *Techgram*, 15 June 1951; *Commonwealth* 21 (Sept. 1954): 27 (por.); obituaries in *New York Times* (variant birth date of 29 Dec. 1886), *Richmond News Leader*, *Richmond Times-Dispatch*, *Roanoke Times* (variant birth date of 29 Dec. 1886), *Roanoke World-News*, and *Washington Post*, all 1 Mar. 1971, and *Virginia Tech Techgram* (May 1971), 7 (variant birth date of 29 Dec. 1886).

RAND DOTSON

CLEMENS, Sherrard (28 April 1820–30 May 1880), member of the House of Representatives and of the Convention of 1861, was born in Wheeling and was the son of James Walton Clemens, a physician, and Eleanor Sherrard Clemens. He was a distant cousin of Samuel Langhorne Clemens (Mark Twain). Educated at home, Clemens entered the United States Military Academy at West Point in 1836. He resigned after six months and then attended his father's alma mater, Washington College (later Washington and Jefferson College), in Washington, Pennsylvania. Clemens graduated with a law degree in 1840 and returned to Wheeling, where he continued to study law and in 1843 was admitted to the bar.

A Democrat noted for his brilliant oratory, Clemens was elected to the House of Representatives in 1852 to fill a vacancy caused by the resignation of George Western Thompson. Clemens served in the second session of the Thirty-second Congress from 6 December 1852 to 3 March 1853, representing the Fifteenth District counties of Brooke, Marion, Marshall, Monongalia, Ohio, Preston, Randolph, and Tyler, which had strong economic and social connections to Ohio and Pennsylvania. He also took Thompson's seat on the Committee on Private Land Claims. Clemens did not seek a full term in 1853, but in May 1857 he was again elected to Congress and served two terms representing the Tenth District, comprising Brooke, Hancock, Marion, Marshall, Monongalia, Ohio, Pleasants, Preston, Taylor, Tyler, and Wetzel Counties. During the Thirty-fifth Congress (1857–1859) he sat on the Committees on Manufactures and on Revolutionary Pensions and during the Thirty-sixth Congress (1859–1861) on the Committee on Commerce. He spoke often during the House proceedings and on 18 February 1858 deplored the unrest in Kansas. Clemens kept an alphabetical list of his constituents so he could quickly update them about political events. He was not a candidate for reelection in 1860.

In 1856 Clemens was a presidential elector for James Buchanan. Two years later, his support of John Letcher in Virginia's gubernatorial race led to a duel with Obediah Jennings Wise, an editor of the *Richmond Enquirer*. After Clemens announced in the *Enquirer* that John White Brockenbrough, a federal district court judge and supporter of southern rights who was Letcher's rival for the nomination, did not want to run for governor, Wise wrote a scathing editorial accusing him of treachery toward Brockenbrough. Clemens responded by challenging Wise to a duel. The two men met on 17 September 1858 near the Fairfield Race Course, in eastern Henrico County. On the fourth volley, Wise shot Clemens in the right thigh, breaking the bone. The injury prevented Clemens from attending the second session of the Thirty-fifth

Congress. In August 1859 he underwent an operation in Pennsylvania to remove part of the bone in his thigh that had become detached, but he continued to suffer from the effects of the wound for the rest of his life. On 8 June 1859 Clemens married Catherine Elizabeth Dawson Groves, a widow with two daughters, at her plantation in Madison Parish, Louisiana. They had at least two sons and one daughter.

A Unionist and a supporter of Stephen Arnold Douglas during the presidential election of 1860, Clemens condemned the secession of South Carolina and did not think that Abraham Lincoln's election was grounds for such action. Along with other Unionist congressmen from Virginia, Clemens believed the best chance for preserving the Union would come if the border states did not secede. He did not oppose slavery and in 1860 owned at least two slaves, probably domestic servants at his Wheeling home, and many more worked his wife's Louisiana plantation. In a public letter to his Wheeling constituents in November 1860, he promised to oppose secession but offered to resign if they wanted him to support that course of action. Clemens addressed a Unionist audience in Wheeling on 14 December 1860 and made a major speech in the House on 22 January 1861 advocating union and reconciliation between North and South.

On 4 February 1861 Ohio County voters elected Clemens and another Unionist to represent them in the Virginia convention called to consider the issue of secession. He spoke frequently during the debates and served on the Committee on Federal Relations. He was not present on 4 April for the first vote on secession, but on 17 April he voted with the minority against leaving the Union. Before casting his vote, Clemens argued that the convention had no right to pass an ordinance of unconditional secession and maintained that only the people of the state could pass such an ordinance. Clemens left Richmond and did not return for the subsequent two sessions held during the summer and autumn of 1861. Charging him with disloyalty to Virginia and the Confederacy, the convention expelled him.

Early in March 1861 Clemens and a delegation of other Virginians traveled to Washington, D.C., to meet with Lincoln. Writing to a friend afterward, Clemens stated that he was not impressed by Lincoln and predicted that the president would force Virginia and other slave states to secede. A group of Wheeling citizens used Clemens's remarks against him when they wrote to the president on 16 March 1861 to complain that Clemens, whom they characterized as an enemy of the Republican Party, was trying to control political patronage in the area in order to promote his own reelection to Congress.

After returning to Wheeling in 1861, Clemens maintained his Unionist stance. During a review of two Ohio regiments in Wheeling on 18 June 1861, he spoke in support of the soldiers and in opposition to Virginia secessionists. In March 1862 he asked that the United States secretary of war appoint him as an aide to a Union general. Lincoln endorsed the request, but Clemens never received an appointment. In 1863 he refused a possible nomination for Congress representing the new state of West Virginia.

Immediately after the Civil War, Clemens was an agent of President Andrew Johnson in investigating the theft and confiscation of cotton by United States Treasury officials in Arkansas, Louisiana, Mississippi, and Tennessee. He eventually returned to West Virginia and resumed his law practice. By 1870 Clemens was living in Union Township, Marshall County, but he soon moved to Saint Louis, Missouri. There he became a respected member of the bar and campaigned for Democratic candidates in 1874 and 1876.

Increasingly ill in his later years, in part as a result of the wound he had suffered in his duel with Wise, Clemens finally became so incapacitated that he could no longer continue his once-lucrative law practice. Estranged from his sons, who were then working as laborers in Mississippi, he was destitute for a year or more before his death and depended on friends for his basic needs. Sherrard Clemens died from the effects of dropsy on 30 May 1880 at a Saint Louis hospital and was buried in Calvary Cemetery in that city. The community of Sherrard, in Marshall County, West Virginia, is named in his honor.

Birth date on gravestone; biographies in Atkinson and Gibbens, *Prominent Men*, 269 (with variant birth date of 28 Apr. 1826 and incorrect death year of 1874), and Henry Clay

McDougal, *Recollections: 1844–1909* (1910), 119–120; *Congressional Globe*, 32d Cong., 2d sess., 6, 35th Cong., 1st sess., 777–782; *Appendix to the Congressional Globe*, 36th Cong., 2d sess., 103–106; *Richmond Enquirer*, 31 Aug., 7, 14, 21, 24 Sept. 1858; *New York Times*, 24 Sept. 1858, 30 Aug. 1863; *Richmond Whig and Public Advertiser*, 17 June 1859; *Wheeling Daily Intelligencer*, 23 Nov., 15 Dec. 1860; Reese and Gaines, *Proceedings of 1861 Convention*, 1:38, 95–100, 142–147, 4:108–110, 144; *Report of the Committee of Elections, on the Cases of Sherrard Clemens, Caleb Boggess and Benjamin Wilson*, printed in Reese, *Journals and Papers of 1861 Convention*, vol. 3, Doc. 38; obituaries in *Saint Louis Post-Dispatch*, 31 May 1880, and *New York Times*, 3 June 1880 (reporting death in his fifty-ninth year).

DALE F. HARTER

CLEMENTS, Edwin Manie (15 October 1862–7 March 1920), journalist, was born in Petersburg three months after his father, Edwin Reuben Clements, a grocer's clerk, died of pneumonia while serving as a corporal in the 16th Regiment Virginia Infantry. Raised by his mother, Mary T. Edwards Clements, who married William H. Gentry in 1870, he attended school in Petersburg until 1874, when he went to work in a tobacco factory. Clements subsequently learned the printers' trade in the composing room of the *Petersburg Index-Appeal*. He converted to Catholicism and on 8 October 1889 married Mary Teresa Tierney, daughter of an Irish immigrant and Petersburg grocer, in a double ceremony with the bride's sister at Saint Joseph's Catholic Church in Petersburg. Clements and his wife had two sons and one daughter.

On 6 August 1888 Clements began publishing a weekly newspaper, the *Petersburg Progress*, and within weeks converted it to an afternoon daily. He was the sole proprietor except for a period in 1891 and 1892 when he had a partner. The newspaper was a reliable supporter of the Democratic Party during the decades that the party regained and solidified its control over Virginia politics. Too few issues survive from the nineteenth century to assess whether the *Petersburg Progress* was as relentlessly partisan as Richard Pannell Barham's morning *Petersburg Index-Appeal*. Clements's newspaper especially attracted local readers because it emphasized city news and advocated in editorials anything that would benefit Petersburg.

In November 1889, in one of the last elections in the city in which Republicans mounted a serious challenge to Democrats, Clements won election to one of Petersburg's two seats in the House of Delegates. He was reelected without opposition in 1891. During his first term he sat on the Committees on Federal Relations and Resolutions, on Militia and Police, on Officers and Offices at the Capitol, and on Printing. In his second term he served on the Committees on Claims and on Labor and the Poor, was ranking member of the Committees on Manufactures and Mechanic Arts and on Militia and Police, and chaired the three-member Committee on Printing. He did not seek renomination or reelection in 1893.

Active in the Petersburg business community, Clements served on the boards of the Petersburg Insurance Company, Incorporated, and the Petersburg Savings and Trust Company. He was also Grand Knight for Petersburg Council 694 of the Knights of Columbus. By January 1903 Clements had renamed his newspaper the *Petersburg Daily Progress*, and in March of that year he formed the E. M. Clements Publishing Company, with himself as president. Clements sold his interest in the *Daily Progress* to the Petersburg Progress Publishing Company, Incorporated, in mid-1917. As secretary of the company, he continued to manage the daily operations of the newspaper until September 1917, when he retired. At that time the daily circulation of his newspaper in Petersburg was more than 6,000 copies, while that of the morning *Index-Appeal* was fewer than 5,000. During World War I, Clements became the city's fuel administrator overseeing energy conservation. Beginning in December 1917, Petersburg residents were prohibited from using electric lights on Thursday and Sunday evenings, and "heatless Mondays" closed many businesses once a week beginning in January 1918.

Edwin Manie Clements sought treatment for a kidney ailment at the Johns Hopkins University Hospital in Baltimore, but when it became evident that he could not be cured, he returned home to Petersburg, where he died on 7 March 1920. He was buried in the cemetery at Saint Joseph's Catholic Church in that city.

James H. Bailey, *A Compilation of the Descendants of William Fenton* (1955), 33–35; birth date of 15 Oct. 1862 on BVS Death Certificate, Petersburg; Petersburg Marriage

Register; *Petersburg Daily Index-Appeal*, 9 Oct., 6 Nov. 1889, 4 Nov. 1891; SCC Charter Book, 51:516–517; Arthur Kyle Davis, ed., *Virginia Communities in War Time*, 2d ser. (1927), 175, 184, 195; obituaries, editorial tributes, and pors. in *Petersburg Evening Progress* (incorrect birth date of 13 Oct. 1863) and *Petersburg Index-Appeal* (incorrect birth date of 13 Oct. 1853), both 8 Mar. 1920; obituary in *Richmond News Leader*, 9 Mar. 1920.

L. DIANE BARNES

CLEMENTS, James H. (January 1831–16 August 1900), member of the Convention of 1867–1868, was born in Washington, D.C., and was the son of Eliza B. Clements (whose maiden name may have been Banks) and John Thomas Clements, a carpenter originally from Maryland. Little is known about his early life and education, but by 1850 he was a machinist living in Baltimore. By 1860 Clements had moved to the city of Norfolk, where he continued working as a machinist, and on 15 August of that year he married Margaret Catherine Jarvis. They had at least seven sons and five daughters, but six of their children did not live to adulthood. Clements remained loyal to the Union during the Civil War and may have been the same James Clements who served with the 2d Dragoons of the regular army or the 1st Battalion, District of Columbia militia.

In the years immediately after the war Clements became a moderate Republican and attended party meetings in Portsmouth, where he then resided. He became friends with James Dennis Brady, another Republican who later served in the United States House of Representatives. In federally mandated elections held on 22 October 1867 to select delegates for a convention called to draft a new constitution for Virginia, the support of African Americans, eligible to vote for the first time, helped Clements and two others win election to represent Norfolk County and Portsmouth. He chaired the Committee on Taxation and Finance and was ranking member on both the Committee on the Elective Franchise and Qualifications for Office and the Committee on Printing. Clements presided over the convention several times and spoke often on such issues as the language in the constitution's preamble and the Bill of Rights, adherence to procedural rules, and close examination of printing costs. He favored uni-

form taxation of property and called for limiting business license taxes imposed by the General Assembly.

A self-proclaimed Radical, and characterized as such by Brigadier General John McAllister Schofield, commander of the Virginia military district, Clements voted with reformers on most issues, including universal manhood suffrage, expansion of public schools, and democratizing state government. His moderate beliefs emerged, however, as he voted with Conservatives in defeating measures calling for the integration of public schools and disfranchising whites who had voted for secessionist delegates to the Convention of 1861. On 17 April 1868 he joined the majority in approving the constitution, which voters ratified in July 1869.

Republicans expected that the federal government would authorize statewide elections. In May 1868 they met in Richmond and elected Clements president of the state nominating convention. Republicans chose Henry Horatio Wells, whom Schofield had appointed provisional governor of Virginia the previous month, and Clements as candidates for governor and lieutenant governor, respectively. For political reasons relating to that year's presidential race and the pending adoption of the new constitution, however, Congress did not allow Virginia to hold elections that year.

In March 1869 Republicans gathered in Petersburg, once again to select candidates for statewide office. This time the moderate Clements battled the increasingly radical Wells for the party's gubernatorial nomination. Amid political maneuvering, fistfights, and accusations of bribery, Wells became the candidate for governor, but the convention split the party, and he was defeated in the general election by a moderate Republican, Gilbert Carlton Walker. Despite Clements's loss, his party affiliation and political contacts secured his appointment on 8 April 1869 as postmaster of Portsmouth, although he also continued to work as a machinist. Reappointed four years later, he served until February 1876. The following year Clements began working as a United States pension agent. In this capacity he traveled to such cities as

Baltimore, Boston, Knoxville, Vicksburg, and New Orleans, where in January 1882 he wrote his will.

From late in the 1870s to the mid-1880s Clements regularly corresponded with William Mahone, leader of the Readjusters and a United States senator. The two men had met in October 1868, and during the 1869 gubernatorial contest Richmond newspapers had reported that Mahone supported Clements in his fight with Wells. In an effort to curry favor, Clements wrote to Mahone on subjects relating to state politics, especially in southeastern Virginia, and of Clements's efforts to help Republicans and Readjusters in Portsmouth and Norfolk County elections.

Clements eventually grew weary of the travel demanded of a pension agent, and in March 1881 he sought Mahone's endorsement for reappointment as postmaster in Portsmouth. Denied that post, Clements by July 1883 had been appointed a clerk in the division of special examinations of the federal pension office, and four years later he became a clerk in the principal examiner's office. He was reappointed for another two years in July 1899. These jobs required him to move to Washington, D.C., but he maintained a residence in Portsmouth, where he owned four town lots, two with buildings having a combined value of more than $4,000. James H. Clements died at his residence in Washington, D.C., on 16 August 1900 and was buried three days later in Oak Grove Cemetery, in Portsmouth.

Birth date in Census, Washington, D.C., 1900; BVS Marriage Register, Norfolk City; Election Records, no. 427, RG 13, LVA; Richard Lowe, *Republicans and Reconstruction in Virginia, 1856–70* (1991), 138, 149, 156, 165, 199; Lowe, "Virginia's Reconstruction Convention," 347; Hume, "Membership of Convention of 1867–1868," 481; *Debates and Proceedings of 1867–1868 Convention*, 22, 60, 122, 359–360, 391–393, 406–409, 649–651, 668–671; *Journal of 1867–1868 Convention*, 28, 41, 389; *Richmond Daily Enquirer and Examiner*, 22 Feb., 7 May 1868, 9–12 Mar. 1869; *Norfolk Journal*, 9, 13, 15 Mar. 1869; *Norfolk Virginian*, 12 Mar. 1869; Record of Appointment of Postmasters, Virginia, Portsmouth, RG 28, NARA; appointments to pension office in *Official Register of the United States, Containing a List of the Officers and Employees in the Civil, Military, and Naval Service* . . . (1883–1899); some Clements correspondence in William Mahone Papers, Duke; Norfolk Co. Will Book, 11:24–25 (will probated 6 Nov. 1911); death notices in *Portsmouth Star* and *Washington Post*, both 17 Aug. 1900.

JOHN G. DEAL

CLEMONS, William Harry (9 September 1879–30 August 1968), librarian, was born in Corry, Pennsylvania, and was the son of Henry Dwight Clemons and Harriet Eliza Barber Clemons. His mother died when he was about eleven years old. Clemons received a B.A. from Wesleyan University, in Middletown, Connecticut, in 1902 and studied and taught English at Princeton University from 1904 to 1906 and again during the 1907–1908 school term. He received M.A. degrees from both Princeton and Wesleyan in 1905. Clemons attended the University of Oxford as a Porter Ogden Jacobus University Fellow in English during the 1906–1907 academic year. After 1910 he was known professionally as Harry Clemons.

Clemons worked in the Wesleyan library in 1902 and 1903 as a student assistant. His lifelong devotion to librarianship was solidified at Princeton, where he was a reference librarian from 1908 to 1913. His love of literature and interest in Chinese literature and culture served him well from 1913 to 1920, when he was a professor of English at the University of Nanking (later Nanjing University) in China. Clemons was the university librarian from 1914 to 1927. His time in China was interrupted from November 1918 to May 1919, when he served as the American Library Association's representative developing library service for the American Expeditionary Force in Siberia, and again in 1922, when he worked in the Chinese section of the Library of Congress. On 21 May 1918 Clemons married Jeannie Cooper Jenkins, a New Jersey native. They had one daughter and one son, who became a test pilot and was killed on 31 July 1943.

Clemons and his wife were forced to leave China in the spring of 1927 following street fighting and attacks on foreigners in Nanjing, in which a vice president of the university was killed and Clemons narrowly escaped injury. He returned to the United States and in July accepted the position of librarian at the University of Virginia. Before assuming his duties in September, he took a summer course in library administration at the Columbia University School of Library Service.

Clemons was the University of Virginia's tenth librarian and the first to be granted rank as a professor. During his twenty-three-year tenure, the university's library engaged in an unprecedented expansion. The library increased the number of volumes it owned fourfold, to about 600,000; its manuscript collections grew from a few thousand items to approximately 3,500,000; and its map collection expanded from a few hundred to 73,000. The budget grew from $26,000 to $273,000 and the fulltime staff from nine to sixty-eight. In 1930 Clemons appointed the historian Lester Jesse Cappon as the university's first archivist. He also created a regional collection of historical source materials and established a department of rare books. During that time the library acquired such special collections as the Tracy W. McGregor Library of American History, the Elizabeth Cocke Coles Collection of Virginia books, the Stone library on the history of printing, the Streeter collection of material on southeastern railways, the Sadleir-Black Collection of gothic novels, the Taylor Collection of bestselling American novels, and the Paul Victorious Collection on evolution. Seeking to remove the book collection from the Rotunda where it had been housed since the university's founding, Clemons planned and campaigned for construction of a new library. Named for the former university president Edwin Anderson Alderman, the new library opened in 1938.

Clemons was president of the Virginia Library Association for the 1931–1932 term and a member of the State Board for the Certification of Librarians from 1936 to 1948. He was also a member of Phi Beta Kappa and the American Library Association and a fellow of the American Geographical Society and the Virginia Academy of Science. Wesleyan University awarded him a doctorate of letters in 1942. Among other honors, Clemons was elected to the University of Virginia's Raven Society and in 1956 received the university's coveted Thomas Jefferson Award. A witty man who nurtured the talented junior members of the staff, he had few outside interests other than baseball and boxing, seldom took a vacation, and kept a peculiar schedule. Clemons worked two six-hour sessions each day, six days a week, beginning at 8:00 A.M. and 8:00 P.M. Between sessions he slept for a few hours. On Sunday mornings he attended a Presbyterian church service, the only routine variation in his schedule.

Throughout his career and in retirement Clemons wrote and published. While at Princeton he prepared a twenty-six-page *Essay Towards a Bibliography of the Published Writings and Addresses of Woodrow Wilson, 1875–1910* (1913) and with Morris William Croll edited John Lyly's *Euphues: The Anatomy of Wit; Euphues and His England* (1916). The American Library Association issued a forty-seven-page booklet, *The A.L.A. in Siberia: Letters Written by Harry Clemons, Representative of the American Library Association War Service, With the A.E.F. in Siberia* (1919). While he was in Charlottesville, Clemons compiled *A Survey of Research Materials in Virginia Libraries, 1936–37* (1938), and he wrote *The Home Library of the Garnetts of "Elmwood"* (1957), *Notes on the Professors for Whom the University of Virginia Halls and Residence Houses Are Named* (1961), and his longest volume, *The University of Virginia Library, 1825–1950: Story of a Jeffersonian Foundation* (1954). The book includes a long foreword that Clemons did not commission, in which the distinguished Jeffersonian historian Dumas Malone praised his accomplishments at the University of Virginia. A review in the *William and Mary Quarterly* characterized the book as "a literate and sophisticated contribution to the neglected field of American university library history."

Clemons retired on 30 June 1950 and was named librarian emeritus in October 1957. Six years after the death of his wife, William Harry Clemons died in Charlottesville on 30 August 1968 and was buried in the University of Virginia Cemetery. In April 1982 a new university library building for undergraduates was dedicated and by a 1978 order of the board of visitors was named the Harry Clemons Library.

Biography in Bohdan S. Wynar, ed., *Dictionary of American Library Biography* (1978), 81–83; information provided by daughter, Emily Barber Clemons Vest (2003); personal and professional papers in Papers of the University Librarian, UVA; some Clemons correspondence in Virginia Library Association Records, LVA; feature articles in *Richmond Times-Dispatch*, 2 July 1950, *Virginia Library Bulletin*, 15 Sept. 1950, *Commonwealth* 17 (Oct. 1950): 23, and UVA *Alumni News* 44 (May 1956): 17–18 (por.) and 93 (summer 2004): 98; William S. Dix review in *WMQ*, 3d ser., 12 (1955):

368 (quotation); obituaries in *Charlottesville Daily Progress*, 30 Aug. 1968 (por.), *Richmond Times-Dispatch*, 31 Aug. 1968, *Washington Post*, 1 Sept. 1968, and UVA *Alumni News* 57 (Dec. 1968): 38; memorial by Dumas Malone in *Virginia Librarian* 15 (winter 1968): 17–18.

MICHAEL PLUNKETT

CLENDINEN, George (ca. 1746–by 18 May 1797), member of the Convention of 1788, may have been born in the region of Augusta County known as the Borden Grant, to which his parents, Charles Clendinen and Mary Patterson Clendinen, had immigrated from Ireland early in the 1740s. During the 1760s his father and uncle moved their families westward to the Greenbrier River, but Indian opposition forced the evacuation of the settlements. Little is known of Clendinen's youth or education. He may have taught school on the Greenbrier River in 1773 and 1774. In the latter year he and his three brothers participated in Dunmore's War against the Shawnee and on 10 October fought in the Battle of Point Pleasant. On 2 February 1779 Clendinen married Jemima McNeill. They had three daughters.

Clendinen was living in the western portion of Botetourt County in 1777, when he was one of the men who petitioned the General Assembly for the creation of Greenbrier County. He became a militia captain in the new county in 1780, a justice of the peace in 1786, and county lieutenant, or commander of the militia, in 1787. From 1781 through 1789 Clendinen inconspicuously represented Greenbrier County in the House of Delegates. His main concerns proved to be frontier defense and construction of a road westward to the Ohio River. He served on the Committees of Claims and of Propositions and Grievances in the 1786 session and returned to those two committees and sat also on the Committee for Courts of Justice in the 1788 session.

Clendinen spent some of his time in Richmond engaged in western land speculation for himself and for others. In 1787 he made his most important purchase, a 1,030-acre tract of land at the confluence of the Elk and Great Kanawha Rivers that later became the site of Charleston. By the end of the decade Clendinen owned or was partner in the ownership of about 30,000 acres of land. During the 1780s he acted as a land agent for John James Beckley, who acquired large tracts in western Virginia, and for a brief time early in the 1790s he was also land agent in the Kanawha Valley for George Washington, who was trying to secure short-term leases for some of his large landholdings.

In the spring of 1788 Greenbrier County voters elected Clendinen to one of two seats representing the county in the state convention that met in Richmond in June to consider the proposed constitution of the United States. He did not speak during the debates but like all but one of the other northwestern Virginia delegates voted on 25 June 1788 against requiring amendments prior to ratification and then voted for ratification of the Constitution. Clendinen either was not present or chose not to vote two days later when the convention defeated a motion to insist on a reduction in the taxing power of Congress.

After serving in the convention Clendinen moved his family and several neighbors to the mouth of the Elk River, where he built Fort Lee. The following year he was instrumental in establishing Kanawha County, and his settlement became the county seat. Two of his brothers sat on the county court, and Clendinen became county lieutenant and served as clerk. In April 1794 he also became a member of the court. That year he sponsored legislation to create the town of Charlestown (later Charleston) on his land, and he named the future capital of West Virginia for his father.

Militia activities against the Indians, sometimes marked by virulent strife with political rivals, occupied Clendinen for several years before, during, and after his election to the House of Delegates in 1791 from Kanawha County. With the exception of the 1792 term, he served until December 1795. Clendinen's legislative service remained unremarkable, as he concentrated on land speculation and local defense.

After the Battle of Fallen Timbers (1794) and the federal Treaty of Greenville (1795) removed the immediate threat to Virginia's western settlements posed by Indians in the Northwest, the governor ordered Clendinen to discharge his scouts from Fort Lee. Snarling that "a wink is as good to a blind horse as a nod," Clendinen resigned as county lieutenant in mid-November

1795 and moved west again the following year to the east bank of the Ohio River between Leading Creek and Eight Mile Island. George Clendinen reportedly died on an unrecorded day in April 1797 while visiting one of his daughters in Marietta, Ohio Territory. On 18 May of that year an indictment for perjury that had been brought in the district court for the counties of Botetourt, Greenbrier, Kanawha, and Montgomery abated by reason of his death. Nothing is known about the circumstances that produced the indictment, but legal actions involving the settlement of his estate occupied his widow and descendants for several years. Clendinen may have been buried in the community cemetery in Marietta, from which some bodies were later moved to Mound Cemetery and others to Oak Grove Cemetery, both in that city.

John Edmund Stealey III, "George Clendinen and the Great Kanawha Valley Frontier: A Case Study of the Frontier Development of Virginia," *West Virginia History* 27 (1966): 278–295; John F. Clendenen and Harriet M. Clendenen, *Charles Clendinen of Virginia* (2000–2001), 1:31–32, 2:74–144, abstracting many documents concerning Clendinen and with estimated birth year based on birth order among siblings on 2:74; John Alderson Marriage Register, VBHS, printed in *WMQ*, 2d ser., 8 (1928): 195; numerous Clendinen letters in George Washington Papers, LC, and in Patrick Henry, Edmund Randolph, Beverley Randolph, Henry Lee, and Robert Brooke Executive Papers, all RG 3, LVA, printed in part in *Calendar of Virginia State Papers*, vols. 4–8 (quotation in Clendinen to Brooke, 8:313); Kaminski, *Ratification*, 10:1539, 1540, 1556–1557, 1565; Roy Bird Cook, *The Annals of Fort Lee* (1935), with date and place of death and burial on 109; estate appraisal in Kanawha Co. Will Book, A:273.

JOHN E. STEALEY III

CLINE, Patsy (8 September 1932–5 March 1963), singer, was born Virginia Patterson Hensley, in a Winchester hospital. Her parents, forty-three-year-old Samuel Lawrence Hensley, a blacksmith, and his second wife, sixteen-year-old Hilda Virginia Patterson Hensley, had married six days before the birth. Until 1937 Hensley lived on her paternal grandparents' farm near Elkton and with her maternal grandparents in Gore, just outside Winchester in Frederick County. The Hensley family moved nineteen times in sixteen years to various towns in the Shenandoah Valley, including Lexington, and during World War II to Portsmouth. They had returned to Winchester by 1948, when Samuel Hensley deserted his wife and three children. Hensley quit school shortly after her sixteenth birthday and to help support her family began working, first in a poultry plant and then later at a bus depot and as a soda clerk at a drugstore. She also began singing professionally at night and on weekends to supplement the money her mother made as a seamstress.

During the next few years Hensley won amateur contests, sang both country and western tunes and popular standards on local radio stations, and performed with a number of bands. She auditioned in Nashville for the Grand Ole Opry but was deemed too young. In September 1952 Hensley auditioned for the country bandleader Clarence William "Bill" Peer, who had a radio show on a station in Martinsburg, West Virginia. Peer liked what he heard, hired her full-time to sing with his Melody Boys and Girls on the Maryland, Northern Virginia, and Washington music circuit, and gave her the stage name of Patsy. On 7 March 1953 she married Gerald E. Cline, the divorced son of a wealthy contractor from Frederick, Maryland. Virginia Patterson Hensley thereafter became known as Patsy Cline.

In September 1954 Cline signed a contract with the 4 Star Record Company, Inc., and the following June recorded her first songs in Nashville, "Hidin' Out," "Honky-Tonk Merry-Go-Round," "Turn the Cards Slowly," and "A Church, a Courtroom, and Then Goodbye." Her first record, released in July 1955 on the Coral Records label, was unsuccessful, although it was produced by the former bandleader Owen Bradley, who was helping create what became the Nashville Sound, a synthesis of country and popular music designed to attract a mass audience. Cline initially resisted his attempts to tone down her "hillbilly" sound with pop arrangements for which he thought her voice was better suited. In 1954 Cline began a series of guest appearances on *Town and Country Time*, the half-hour daily music-variety television program of Connie Barriot Gay, the premier country music promoter in the Washington area. Usually she performed on the regionally broadcast program as the female vocalist with Jimmy Dean and the

Texas Wildcats. This exposure won Cline a booking on *Arthur Godfrey's Talent Scouts*, and on 21 January 1957 she won the competition by singing "Walkin' After Midnight." The publicity from this appearance increased sales of the Bradley-produced song, recorded for the Decca Records label on 8 November 1956, and by March "Walkin' After Midnight" held the second spot on *Billboard*'s country music chart and twelfth place on the popular music chart.

In October 1955 Cline broke both professionally and personally with Peer, with whom she had been having an affair. Gerald Cline, jealous of his wife's success and frustrated that she did not stay at home like a traditional housewife, separated from Patsy Cline, and the childless couple divorced in Maryland on 28 March 1957. Cline had met Charles Allen Dick, a linotype operator for the local newspaper, at a Berryville dance in April 1956. They married on 15 September 1957 and had one daughter and one son. Dick was serving in the United States Army at Fort Bragg, and without a hit to follow "Walkin' After Midnight" and with an infant to care for, Cline was back to scraping by as a regional performer. A few months after Dick was mustered out of the army in February 1959, the couple moved to Nashville.

Cline, who had appeared several times as a guest in the mid-1950s, joined the Grand Ole Opry as a regular cast member in January 1960. She began to record more songs and performed to supplement the income from her husband's printing job. The couple struggled until January 1961, when Decca released "I Fall to Pieces." This Cline-Bradley masterwork topped the country chart and reached the twelfth spot on the pop chart. In June, Cline was critically injured in an automobile accident but had returned to the studio by August, when she recorded "Crazy," a song written by Willie Nelson that rose to second place on the country chart and ninth place on the pop chart. In December 1961 she recorded "She's Got You," which became her second number-one country hit.

Achieving newfound success, Cline won several outstanding female country singer awards during the next two years. Beginning in January 1962 she frequently appeared as the second-billed performer in a concert tour organized by Johnny Cash that also featured June Carter and George Jones. Her touring schedule included television performances on *American Bandstand* and the *Tennessee Ernie Ford Show* as well as concerts at Carnegie Hall, the Hollywood Bowl, and the Mint Casino in Las Vegas. By early in 1963 she had recorded more than one hundred songs. Her well-controlled, instantly recognizable voice wrung the last drop of emotion from every lyric.

On 5 March 1963, while flying home to Nashville after a benefit concert in Kansas City, Missouri, in a plane piloted by her manager, Patsy Cline and the country music luminaries Lloyd Estel "Cowboy" Copas and Harold Franklin "Hawkshaw" Hawkins died in a crash near Camden, Tennessee. After a prayer service in Nashville, her remains were returned to Winchester, where her funeral attracted the news media and thousands of fans. She was buried in Shenandoah Memorial Park just outside the city.

In the decades following her death, Cline became a musical icon. In 1973 she was the first solo woman performer to be elected to the Country Music Hall of Fame in Nashville, and in 1981 she was inducted into the Virginia Folk Music Association's Virginia Country Music Hall of Fame. Her recordings have sold millions of copies, and she has been the subject of numerous biographies, several musicals, a tribute album, and a feature film, *Sweet Dreams* (1985). The National Academy of Recording Arts and Sciences recognized Cline with a Lifetime Achievement Award in 1995 and with Grammy Hall of Fame awards in 1992 and 2001 for "Crazy" (1961) and "I Fall to Pieces" (recorded 1960, released 1961), respectively. At the end of the twentieth century, her recording of "Crazy" remained the song most often played on jukeboxes. Cline has fan clubs around the world, a United States commemorative postage stamp, and a star on the Hollywood Walk of Fame (although she never made a movie). In Winchester there is a bell tower erected in her memory at Shenandoah Memorial Park, an annual Labor Day celebration of her life, and the Patsy Cline Memorial Highway (Route 522) and Patsy Cline Boulevard. Her soulful interpretations of lyrics and her unmistakable voice continue to win admirers across musical genres and to inspire generations of vocalists, from Loretta Lynn and Dolly Parton to Linda Ronstadt and k. d. lang.

Melvin Shestack, *The Country Music Encyclopedia* (1974), 44–46 (por.); Joli Jensen, "Patsy Cline's Recording Career: The Search for a Sound," and Don Roy, "The Patsy Cline Discography," *Journal of Country Music* 9, no. 2 (1982): 34–46, 47–115; Mary A. Bufwack and Robert K. Oermann, *Finding Her Voice: The Saga of Women in Country Music* (1993), 240–242 (por.), 251–259; Ellis Nassour, *Honky Tonk Angel: The Intimate Story of Patsy Cline* (1993); Margaret Jones, *Patsy: The Life and Times of Patsy Cline* (1994), including discography; Mark Bego, *I Fall To Pieces: The Music and the Life of Patsy Cline* (1995); Cindy Hazen and Mike Freeman, eds., *Love Always, Patsy: Patsy Cline's Letters to a Friend* (1999); *Washington Evening Star*, 18 Mar. 1956; *Winchester Evening Star*, 4 Apr., 16 Sept. 1957; obituaries in *Richmond News Leader* and *Winchester Evening Star*, both 6 Mar. 1963, and *Nashville Tennessean*, 7 Mar. 1963; account of funeral in *Winchester Evening Star*, 11 Mar. 1963.

DOUGLAS GOMERY

CLOPTON, Abner Wentworth (24 March 1784–20 or 21 March 1833), Baptist minister and temperance advocate, was born in Pittsylvania County and was the son of Robert Clopton, a farmer, and Frances Anderson Clopton. After some local schooling, Clopton clerked in a country store for four years beginning about 1800. He married Sally B. Warwick, of Campbell County, on 24 September 1803, but they immediately separated after he discovered that she was pregnant with another man's child. Six years later he petitioned the General Assembly for a divorce, which it granted in January 1810. The act of divorce did not give Clopton the right to remarry.

In despair over his failed marriage, Clopton turned his attention to scholarship. In 1804 he began to study languages at Banister Academy in Pittsylvania County and then at a private school in Guilford County, North Carolina. In 1806 he moved to South Carolina, where he taught school until 1808. He enrolled at the University of North Carolina, in Chapel Hill, received an A.B. in 1809, and then tutored at the school for a year. Deciding to pursue a career in medicine, Clopton returned to Virginia and worked with a doctor in Halifax County before entering the University of Pennsylvania in 1811. A serious illness soon forced him to withdraw, and he moved back to Chapel Hill, where he received an A.M. from the University of North Carolina in 1812. He practiced medicine for a time and also served from 1812 until the end of 1819 as principal of the grammar school associated with the university. From 1820 through 1822 he was head of a female academy in Milton, Caswell County, North Carolina.

Although Clopton made a comfortable living as an educator, at several times during his career he seriously considered becoming a minister. His illness in 1811 was accompanied by an intense religious experience, and he was subsequently baptized in August 1812 at Shockoe Baptist Church in Pittsylvania County. Recurring illnesses in 1815 and 1821 deepened Clopton's conviction that he should abandon his worldly endeavors for the church. At first he acted as a lay preacher but then sought formal ordination in 1816 and became a full-time minister in 1823.

In the latter year Clopton took the pulpits at Ash Camp (later Keysville) and Mossingford Baptist Churches in Charlotte County, and in 1825 he added the new Chaney's Chapel (later Shiloh Baptist Church) to his ministry. He served these congregations and itinerated widely until his death. Clopton had a strong and immediate influence among Charlotte County's Baptists. He asserted control over his new flocks by insisting on strict discipline and closed communion. Seeking to revitalize the Appomattox Baptist Association, he wrote widely distributed circular letters on church discipline in 1824 and on ministerial ordination in 1827. He later preached against the sectarian efforts of Alexander Campbell and in 1830 and 1831 published a series of writings on the subject in the *Columbian Star, and Christian Index* (after 1831 the *Christian Index*), to which Campbell responded in the *Millennial Harbinger*. Clopton became clerk of the Appomattox Baptist Association as early as 1825 and in 1827 of the Baptist General Association of Virginia.

In 1826 Clopton assumed what was probably his most important public role outside the pulpit when he and several other ministers formed the Virginia Society for the Promotion of Temperance. He wrote the constitution for the society, served as its corresponding secretary, and in February 1833 became its second vice president. Clopton organized the Charlotte County Temperance Society and similar associations at his three churches. With Eli Ball he compiled and published in Philadelphia a collection of temperance tracts entitled *Wisdom's Voice to the Rising Generation: Being a Selection of the Best Addresses and Sermons on Intemperance* (1828). The temperance movement that Clopton helped found and promote spread rapidly. Within two years there were more than 40 local societies in Virginia, the largest number in any southern state, and after a decade there were perhaps 250.

Clopton was appointed in 1827 to be the Georgia state fund-raising agent for Columbian College (later George Washington University), which had fallen into serious financial trouble. Success in that role led to his appointment as a member of the board of trustees by 1829 and as general agent for the college in December 1832. He quickly set to work on a plan to reverse the financial woes of the school, but his death intervened before his ideas could be implemented. Abner Wentworth Clopton died of pleurisy at his home in Charlotte County during the night of 20–21 March 1833 and was buried in the family cemetery in Pittsylvania County. Early in the twentieth century, probably not long after Virginia enacted prohibition legislation in 1916, a tablet honoring his work was placed in the Keysville Baptist Church.

Jeremiah B. Jeter, *A Memoir of Abner W. Clopton, A.M.* (1837), with birth date and reprinting some personal and pastoral letters; biographies in James B. Taylor, *Virginia Baptist Ministers*, 2d ser. (1859), 388–400, William B. Sprague, *Annals of the American Baptist Pulpit* (1860), 657–663, William Cathcart, ed., *The Baptist Encyclopædia* (1881), 233–234, and Gene H. McKinney, "A. W. Clopton: A Dedicated Minister of the Gospel," *Southsider* 5 (1986): 42–50 (por. on 43); Campbell Co. Marriage Bonds and Consents (bond dated 23 Sept. 1803); marriage date in petition of Abner W. Clopton, presented 19 Dec. 1809, Legislative Petitions, Campbell Co., RG 78, LVA; *Acts of Assembly*, 1809–1810 sess., 60; some Clopton correspondence in Stephen Chapin Papers and Luther Rice Papers, both George Washington University; C. C. Pearson and J. Edwin Hendricks, *Liquor and Anti-Liquor in Virginia, 1619–1919* (1967), 57–60, 64–69; death date of 20 Mar. 1833 on gravestone, transcribed in Virginia–North Carolina Piedmont Genealogical Society, *Cemetery Records of Pittsylvania County, Virginia* (1982), 2:47; obituaries in *Religious Herald*, 29 Mar. 1833, *Christian Index*, 30 Mar. 1833 (printing letter from neighbor Thomas Read, dated 22 Mar. 1833 and reporting death "last night precisely at 1 o'clock"), and *Richmond Enquirer*, 5 Apr. 1833 (with death date of 20 Mar. 1833); memorials in *Christian Index*, 13 Apr. 1833 (noting death "Wednesday night the 20th of March"), *Religious Herald*, 26 Apr. 1833 (memorial not extant in microfilm copy), and Mossingford Baptist Church Minute Book, 13–28, Acc. 28981, LVA.

JEWEL L. SPANGLER

CLOPTON, John (7 February 1756–11 or 12 September 1816), member of the House of Representatives and of the Council of State, was born in New Kent County and was the son of Elizabeth Dorrall Ford Jones Clopton and her second husband, William Clopton. Initially tutored at home, he matriculated at the College of Philadelphia (later the University of Pennsylvania) in August 1774 and graduated in June 1776. He joined the Pennsylvania militia during the summer of 1775. After abortive attempts to raise a company in Williamsburg during the spring of 1777, Clopton volunteered for service in a Pennsylvania artillery unit, and his exemplary performance at the Battle of Brandywine on 11 September 1777, when he received a serious wound, earned him recommendation for a commission. After returning to New Kent County, he practiced law.

Clopton married Sarah Bacon on 15 May 1784. They had three sons and two daughters. A member of the Church of England as a young man, Clopton joined the Baptist Church about 1790. In 1789 he won election to the first of three consecutive one-year terms in the House of Delegates representing New Kent County. He served on the Committees of Claims and of Propositions and Grievances in all three terms and became a member of the Committee of Religion in 1791.

On 16 March 1795 Clopton defeated Burwell Bassett (1764–1841) for the seat in the House of Representatives from the counties of Charles City, Hanover, Henrico, James City, and New Kent. Bassett unsuccessfully contested the election. Clopton won reelection in 1797. He spoke infrequently in the House, perhaps because of poor health, but the record of his speeches, as well as his circular letters to his constituents, affirm his "warm attachment to republican principles." A reliable Jeffersonian, he opposed the Alien and Sedition Acts of 1798. Clopton ran for a third term against John Marshall, whom George Washington had recruited to run for the seat. In the course of the campaign, a Federalist newspaper in October 1798 accused Clopton of seditious libel for charging that President John Adams was a traitor who had tried to bribe Congress. The secretary of state began seeking evidence against Clopton in order to indict him, but Clopton successfully rebutted the accusation by producing a certificate from the alleged recipient of the libelous letter, who denied ever having received such a missive. After Patrick Henry endorsed Marshall's candidacy, Clopton lost the April 1799 election.

On 12 December 1799 the General Assembly elected Clopton to the Council of State. After taking his seat on the following 31 May, he was regular in attendance, and following the revelation of Gabriel's Conspiracy in the autumn of 1800 he advised the governor on securing Richmond and apprehending the slave Gabriel and other suspected insurrectionists. In 1801 Clopton was elected to the House of Representatives, and political opponents pressured the governor into seeking the state attorney general's opinion on whether Clopton could remain on the Council until he formally took his seat in Congress. The attorney general ruled in Clopton's favor. He attended his final Council meeting on 28 November 1801 and by 10 December had resigned his seat.

Clopton won reelection to Congress seven more times, beginning in 1803 representing the district comprising the city of Richmond and Charles City, Hanover, Henrico, and New Kent Counties. He was unrelenting in his strict approach to constitutional questions. Even after other Jeffersonian Republicans accepted the legitimacy of the Bank of the United States, he continued to argue that Congress had no constitutional power to charter a bank. He applied his strict constitutionalism to both broad issues and narrow questions, such as whether Congress could levy a tax on personal carriages. In December 1806 Clopton proposed an unsuccessful amendment to narrow the range of congressional

action allowed under the "necessary and proper" clause of the Constitution. He favored repealing the Judiciary Act of 1801 and all internal taxes in 1802. Although he noted with "peculiar satisfaction" the progress made in reducing the public debt, he enthusiastically welcomed the Louisiana Purchase in 1803. He supported the president's embargo on trade with the British in 1807 and in June 1812 voted to declare war on the United Kingdom.

Because of poor health, Clopton considered not seeking reelection in 1815, but he won a tenth term. On 11 or 12 September 1816 John Clopton died at Roslin, his estate in New Kent County, and probably was buried there. He had hoped his elder surviving son would succeed him in the House of Representatives, but in a special election that November John Bacon Clopton (later a member of the Convention of 1829–1830 and circuit court judge) lost a three-man race to John Tyler (1790–1862).

Margaret Stevenson Poos, "A Biography of John Clopton of Virginia" (M.A. thesis, Duke, 1948); Clopton Family Papers, Duke (including birth and marriage dates in MS Clopton biography and genealogy by unidentified Wallace family descendant); thirteen letters in Cunningham, *Circular Letters of Congressmen*, esp. 1:154 (first quotation), 382 (second quotation); *Annals of Congress*, 4th Cong., 1st sess., 253, 265–266, 7th Cong., 1st sess., 958–971, 8th Cong., 1st sess., 376–377, 422–425, 490–495, 9th Cong., 1st sess., 852–862, 2d sess., 131–148, 10th Cong., 1st sess., 1901–1904, 2053–2055, 2d sess., 591–594, 1452–1460, 12th Cong., 2d sess., 1029–1033, 13th Cong., 1st sess., 422–428, 3d sess., 496, 976–987, 14th Cong., 1st sess., 1217–1219; 1799 congressional election in Nancy M. Merz, "The XYZ Affair and the Congressional Election of 1799 in Richmond, Virginia" (M.A. thesis, W&M, 1973), and *Marshall Papers*, 3:496–502; *Richmond Virginia Gazette, and General Advertiser*, 9, 16 Oct. 1798; *Richmond Examiner*, 7 Apr. 1801; obituaries with death date of 11 Sept. 1816 in *Washington Daily National Intelligencer*, 17 Sept. 1816, *Richmond Enquirer*, 18 Sept. 1816, and *Norfolk American Beacon and Commercial Diary*, 20 Sept. 1816; obituaries with death date of 12 Sept. 1816 in *Virginia Patriot, and Richmond Daily Mercantile Advertiser*, 14 Sept. 1816, and *Richmond Virginia Argus*, 21 Sept. 1816 ("died on the morning of the 12th inst. . . . in the 64th year of his age").

STEVEN L. DALLE MURA

CLOPTON, John Bacon (12 February 1789–29 March 1860), member of the Convention of 1829–1830, was born in Richmond and grew up at Roslin, the New Kent County plantation of his parents, John Clopton and Sarah Bacon Clopton. His father later served in the House of Representatives and on the Council of State. Tutored at home, Clopton attended the College of William and Mary and may have read law in Richmond with Edmund Randolph. He received a license to practice in May 1810 and that year also mounted an unsuccessful campaign for election to the House of Delegates representing New Kent County. During the War of 1812 Clopton was a sergeant in a New Kent County infantry company called into service from 28 June to 13 July 1813. His father had hoped that he would succeed him in Congress, but in November 1816 Clopton lost the special election to fill his father's vacant seat in the House of Representatives, and he did not seek the office in the regular election held the next spring.

In December 1821 Clopton was elected by a narrow margin to fill a vacant seat in the Senate of Virginia representing the cities of Richmond and Williamsburg and the counties of Charles City, Elizabeth City, Henrico, James City, New Kent, Warwick, and York. During his two four-year terms he served on the important Committee of Claims for the 1823–1824 and 1827–1828 sessions, on the Committee of Internal Improvement from 1825 through 1829, on the Committee to Examine the Treasurer's Accounts for the 1826–1827 session, and on the Committee of General Laws for the 1827–1828 and 1828–1829 sessions. After his mother's death in 1824, Clopton became embroiled in a dispute with two of his sisters over the distribution of slaves and stock dividends from their parents' estate. In 1829 he owned 613 acres of land in New Kent County and twenty taxable slaves age twelve or older.

In May 1829 Clopton, John Marshall, Philip Norborne Nicholas, and John Tyler (1790–1862) won election in a nine-candidate field to represent the cities of Richmond and Williamsburg and the counties of Charles City, Elizabeth City, Henrico, James City, New Kent, Warwick, and York at a convention called to revise Virginia's constitution. Clopton sat on the Committee on the Bill of Rights. His proposed amendment describing the advisory nature of the Council of State, reducing its membership from eight to

three and fixing their terms of service, and defining the senior member of the Council as lieutenant governor became Article IV, Section 5, of the new constitution. Clopton's fellow delegate Hugh Blair Grigsby characterized him as "a reformer in every vein and artery of his system," but Clopton believed he was duty-bound to represent his conservative constituency, even when he disagreed with its views, and much of the time voted against democratic reform. He chaired the three-man select committee that superintended the engrossing of the draft and on 14 January 1830 voted to approve the constitution.

After the convention and end of his term in the Senate, Clopton intended to retire from public life. In February 1834 the General Assembly elected him judge of the Circuit Superior Court of Law and Chancery for the Seventh Judicial Circuit, comprising Chesterfield, Goochland, Hanover, Henrico, and Powhatan Counties. The severing of Henrico County and the city of Richmond from his circuit in February 1837 caused the auditor, on his own authority, to reduce Clopton's salary by $300. Clopton appealed for the restoration of his full salary of $1,800 and won a favorable ruling by the Virginia Supreme Court of Appeals in *Commonwealth* v. *Clopton* (1837). Clopton heard both civil and criminal cases and in 1846 presided over the sensational murder trial of Thomas Ritchie (d. 22 May 1854), who had killed the Whig newspaper editor John Hampden Pleasants in a duel.

In 1852, after a constitutional revision reorganized the court system and made judges elective, voters of the city of Williamsburg and the counties of Charles City, Elizabeth City, Gloucester, Henrico, James City, Mathews, Middlesex, New Kent, Warwick, and York elected Clopton judge of the Sixth Judicial Circuit. He remained on the bench until his death. From 1 January 1855 until his death Clopton was also, by virtue of the circuit judgeship he held, one of five judges of the Special Court of Appeals that met in Richmond for a few weeks beginning in January of each year to hear cases that the Supreme Court of Appeals was ineligible to decide.

Beginning in the 1830s Clopton moved several times, from Manchester, across the James River from Richmond, to Henrico County, and then to Williamsburg. He also owned a fourteen-room mansion near Old Point Comfort in Elizabeth City County. Clopton was a founding member of the Virginia Historical and Philosophical Society, its first corresponding secretary, and in 1835 its vice president. He amassed a large private library of approximately 1,800 books and 350 pamphlets on criminal trials, geography, history, literature, philology, theology, and travel, offered at auction in New York City in 1861. A family tradition that maintains Clopton failed in 1840 by a single vote in the Virginia caucus to win the Whig nomination for vice president appears in some local secondary literature but is undocumented.

On 4 May 1820 Clopton married Maria Gaitskell Foster, a former Richmond mayor's daughter who had attended a Moravian female seminary in Pennsylvania. Valuing her judgment, Clopton often sought her counsel and on one occasion exhorted her when reviewing some of his writing "to be a critic, a sound, severe, judicious yet friendly one." During the Civil War she chaired a ladies' defense committee to raise funds for building an ironclad and opened her house to wounded Confederate soldiers. Of the Cloptons' five sons and seven daughters, four children died in infancy or early childhood. John Bacon Clopton died from the effects of gout at his residence in Elizabeth City County on 29 March 1860 and was buried in a family cemetery near Richmond.

Biographies in *Biographical Sketches of Distinguished American Lawyers* (1852), 78–81 (with birth date and place, probably provided by Clopton), *Virginia Law Register* 6 (1900): 505–511 (por. facing 505), *Richmond Times-Dispatch*, 23 July 1905, and Lucy Lane Erwin, *The Ancestry of William Clopton of York County, Virginia* . . . (1939), 162–163; Clopton Family Papers, Duke (including marriage date in Clopton family Bible records and second quotation in Clopton to Maria Gaitskell Foster Clopton, 31 Aug.–2 Sept. 1834); John B. Clopton Papers, Acc. 27133, LVA; Clopton broadsides, "To the Freeholders of New Kent," 20 Feb. 1810, and "To the Freeholders of the Congressional District Composed of the Counties of Hanover, Henrico, New-Kent, Charles City and the City of Richmond," 9 Oct. 1816, both LVA; Henrico Co. Marriage Bonds (bond dated 22 Apr. 1820); *Richmond Enquirer*, 6, 23 Nov. 1816, 22, 26 May, 5 June 1829; *Journal of 1829–1830 Convention*, 22, 295–296; *Proceedings and Debates of 1829–1830 Convention*, 822, 849, 855–856; Catlin, *Convention of 1829–30* (por.); Hugh Blair Grigsby Commonplace Book (1829–1830), 31 (first quotation), Hugh Blair Grigsby Papers, VHS; Bruce, *Rhetoric of Conservatism*, 36; *JSV*, 1833–1834 sess., 155; *Commonwealth* v. *Clopton* (1837) (9 Leigh), *Virginia Reports*, 36:109–118; some Clopton opinions in John M. Patton Jr. and Roscoe B. Heath, eds., *Reports of Cases Decided in the Special Court of Appeals of Virginia, Held at Richmond* (1856–1857); *Administrator's Sale: Catalogue of the Large and Important Private Library of the Late Hon. John B. Clopton, (Who Was One of the Judges of Virginia)* (1861); Census, Mortality Schedule, Elizabeth City Co., 1860; obituaries in *Richmond Enquirer*, 30 Mar. 1860, and *Norfolk Southern Argus*, 2 Apr. 1860; memorial resolutions in *Norfolk Southern Argus*, 3 Apr. 1860.

AMI PFLUGRAD-JACKISCH

CLOSE, James Titus (14 April 1829–30 August 1869), member of the Second Wheeling Convention of 1861 and of the Restored Senate of Virginia, was the son of Diana Titus Close and Slawter Close, a farmer and insurance agent. He was born in Broadalbin Township in that section of Montgomery County, New York, reorganized in 1838 as Fulton County. Sometime between 1845 and 1850 Close moved to Virginia, where in Fairfax County on 1 April 1851 he married Ann Eliza Sherman, a Connecticut native. They had five daughters and at least four sons. In July 1854 Close was living in or near the city of Alexandria, where he served on the board of directors of the Southern Protection Insurance Company and as actuary and general agent for the firm. In January 1861 he resigned to become an agent for the Northern Assurance Company.

During the secession winter of 1860–1861 Close's allegiance remained with the Union. After voters approved the Ordinance of Secession in the May 1861 referendum, Unionists elected Close one of two men to represent Alexandria County (after 1920 Arlington County) in the Second Wheeling Convention, which met from 11 to 25 June and from 6 to 21 August 1861. Close was added to the Committee on Business on 13 June, immediately after that committee had presented "A Declaration of the People of Virginia," demanding the reorganization of Virginia's government and proclaiming all state offices in Richmond vacated. The following day the committee called for the convention to elect a new governor, lieutenant governor, and advisory council. It also proposed that members of the House of Delegates elected in May 1861 and the state senators already holding office were, after affirming their loyalty to the Union, to constitute the legislature of the Restored government at Wheeling. The convention unanimously approved the Declaration on 17 June, and two days later Close voted with the majority to adopt the ordinance to reorganize state government. On 24 June he introduced a resolution condemning the secession convention in Richmond and appealing to the government of the United States for protection against "these foreign and domestic traitors." At the convention's adjourned session on 20 August, Close voted against a proposal to establish the state of Kanawha from thirty-nine Virginia counties, with the possibility of later adding seven more. He complained to the Restored governor that Virginians would "sell their birthright" for a new state comprising too few counties that were nothing more than a "*Pan* handle and a couple of Huckle Bury patches."

On 2 July 1861 Unionists in Alexandria chose Close to represent Alexandria and Fairfax Counties in the eight-man Restored Senate of Virginia that convened in Wheeling from 1 to 26 July. He arrived on 6 July and was added to the Committees on Banks and on Courts of Justice and General Laws. Condemning the Southern supporters who headed the Alexandria businesses and courts, Close introduced legislation in the Restored state senate to scrutinize the operations of two city banks operated by Confederate sympathizers. He also forced the "vile secessionist" mayor and members of the police department from their positions. Close appealed to the Restored governor to vacate other local offices so that loyal citizens could fill the posts and lobbied the governor to appoint him as an aide and thus boost his credentials. He asked permission to organize several military units but had little success persuading recruits to serve outside their counties and expressed dismay at the lack of patriotism in Alexandria County. In April 1862 he accepted a commission as adjutant of the 175th Regiment of Virginia militia.

In August 1862 Close approached the secretary of war about raising a regiment and on 25 September received a commission as colonel of the 16th Regiment Virginia (later West Virginia) Infantry Volunteers, which was mustered into service on 25 October 1862 and served in the

defenses of Washington, D.C. The appointment angered a rival Unionist leader, Lewis McKenzie, mayor of Alexandria and later a United States congressman, who complained to the Restored governor that Close was one of the most unpopular men in Alexandria and unfit for command. The volunteer regiment never recruited sufficient numbers to meet requirements, and Close resigned his commission on 19 May 1863 in order to accept a presidential appointment as United States provost marshal for the Eastern District of Virginia.

Close won reelection to the state senate that met in Wheeling between 2 December 1861 and 5 February 1863. He served on the Committee on Finance and Claims and on a committee to examine the auditor's office, treasurer's accounts, and bonds of public officers. Nominated for brigadier general of the 6th Brigade of the state militia on 9 May 1862, he lost the election to McKenzie. After Congress agreed to admit West Virginia as a new state, Close introduced a Senate resolution on 11 December 1862 to move the capital of the Restored government to Alexandria and was appointed to a joint committee to study the proposal. That month he also mounted a campaign as an independent Union candidate for the congressional seat representing Alexandria and Fairfax Counties, but his name did not appear on the ballot. Close resigned his Senate seat in May 1863 when he became United States marshal for the Eastern District of Virginia. He was removed from the latter office by 5 October of that year. After the Civil War he and other Unionists joined with Confederate veterans, including a former major general, to sponsor a tournament and ball at Fairfax Court House in September 1865.

Close engaged in a variety of business and civic activities. In 1862 he was a director of the Washington and Alexandria Turnpike Company. By 1865 he was operating a foundry and machine shop in Washington, and the next year he formed an attorney, claims agent, and real estate partnership in that city. Close was a general agent for the National Capital Insurance Company in 1868. He joined a local temperance society and also the Potomac Fruit Growers Association. In July 1869 James Titus Close won election in a nine-candidate field to represent Alexandria County in the House of Delegates, but before the General Assembly convened he died at his Closeville residence on 30 August 1869. A newspaper reported the cause as stomach cancer, but an autopsy revealed his liver was three times the normal size. Funeral services took place at his home. Close owned several plots in the Ivy Hill Cemetery in Alexandria, but his burial site is not recorded.

Biography in Lewis R. Close, "Lewis Gile Close: Ancestors and Descendants" (1955 typescript), 14–15 and Appendix D, Johnstown Public Library, Johnstown, N.Y.; birth, marriage, and death dates in widow's Federal Pension Application File, Records of the Veterans Administration, RG 15, NARA; Close correspondence in *Calendar of the Francis Harrison Pierpont Letters and Papers in West Virginia Depositories* (1940), 104, 146–147, 213, 216, in Francis Harrison Pierpont Executive Papers, RG 3, LVA (including Close to Pierpont, 20 Aug. [fourth quotation], 7 Sept. [second and third quotations] 1861), and *Calendar of Virginia State Papers*, 11:370–372; *Alexandria Gazette*, 25 July 1854, 27 Dec. 1862, 16 Jan., 7 Apr., 9 May, 5 Oct. 1863, 1, 6 Sept. 1865; *Journal of Second Wheeling Convention*, 10, 18, 24, 32 (first quotation), 67; *JSV (Wheeling)*, July 1861 sess., 18, 19, May 1862 sess., 9, 19, 21, Dec. 1862–Feb. 1863 sess., 27, 29; Close's resignation from Senate in Executive Journal, 16 May 1863, Francis Harrison Pierpont Papers, Restored Government of Virginia, Secretary of the Commonwealth, RG 13, LVA; Compiled Service Military Records, Records of the Adjutant General's Office, RG 94, NARA; *General Orders and Circulars, Headquarters First Military District, 1869* (1870), "Returns of Election of July 6, 1869," 3, 4; Nan Netherton et al., *Fairfax County, Virginia: A History* (1978), 323–324, 332, 340, 385; death notices (both with variant death date of 31 Aug. 1869) in *Alexandria Gazette*, 31 Aug. 1869, and *Washington Evening Star*, 1 Sept. 1869.
DONALD W. GUNTER

CLOYD, Gordan (19 March 1771–4 May 1833), member of the Convention of 1829–1830, was the son of Mary Gordon Cloyd and Joseph Cloyd, a Revolutionary War militia commander and merchant. He may have been born on Back Creek in the western part of Botetourt County that in 1772 became Fincastle County, in 1776 Montgomery County, and in 1839 Pulaski County. Cloyd received a solid education in reading, writing, and arithmetic from a tutor his father hired. On 13 February 1798 in Wythe County he married his first cousin Elizabeth McGavock, who died in September 1830. Of their two sons and four daughters, only two daughters survived to adulthood.

Cloyd became deputy sheriff of Montgomery County in November 1790. He surveyed the boundary line between Montgomery and Wythe Counties during the summer of 1792 and in July of the following year became the surveyor for Montgomery County. Cloyd used his position to patent and purchase thousands of acres of land in Montgomery and the surrounding southwestern Virginia counties, including a one-third share of 80,000 acres in what became Giles County. He prospered buying and selling livestock and as a merchant. Cloyd established his home, Springfield, on Back Creek, adjacent to his father's property, and also built a gristmill there. In June 1796 he became a justice of the peace on the Montgomery County Court.

At age sixteen Cloyd was appointed an ensign in the Montgomery County militia. In April 1793 he became a lieutenant and three years later received a commission as captain of a new cavalry company. The General Assembly elected Cloyd a brigadier general of militia on 7 January 1814, and during the last year of the War of 1812 he commanded the 19th Brigade, comprising militia units from Giles, Monroe, Montgomery, and Wythe Counties. Elected major general of the 5th Division of the militia on 11 February 1822, he held that commission until his death eleven years later.

In May 1829 Cloyd received the most votes of the six candidates vying for four seats representing Giles, Grayson, Montgomery, and Wythe Counties in the constitutional convention that met in Richmond from 5 October 1829 to 15 January 1830. Like other delegates from western Virginia, he supported expanding suffrage to all white males and reapportioning the legislature based on the white population. A member of the Committee on the Executive Department, Cloyd spoke little in the recorded convention debates. While in Richmond, he wrote one of his brothers providing details of the convention proceedings, but he tended to be more concerned with his various business interests. In the final vote on the constitution taken on 14 January 1830, Cloyd sided with his fellow trans-Allegheny delegates in voting against the new document because they thought its reforms did not extend far enough. In the subsequent statewide referendum, the counties he represented confirmed his opposition by voting against the constitution in overwhelming numbers.

Cloyd returned to his Montgomery County plantation and resumed raising and selling livestock. At the time of his death he owned several hundred head of cattle, hogs, and sheep, as well as sixty-one slaves. He bequeathed most of his estate, valued at $40,364, to his two surviving daughters and made lesser bequests to other relatives and friends. Gordan Cloyd died in Montgomery County on 4 May 1833 and was buried in the family cemetery on Back Creek, in present-day Pulaski County.

Biographies in A. D. Cloyd, *Genealogy of the Cloyd, Basye and Tapp Families in America* (1912), 74–75 (including birth date), and Mary B. Kegley, *Early Adventurers on the Western Waters*, vol. 2: *The New River of Virginia in Pioneer Days, 1745–1800* (1982), 270–274 (por. on 269); Robert Gray, *The McGavock Family* (1903), 16–17 (variant marriage date of Mar. 1797); Gordan Cloyd Daybook (1803–1852), Acc. 39678, LVA; Cloyd correspondence and business documents, including signatures with spelling of first name, in Cloyd Family Papers and Edmundson Family Papers, both VHS; Wythe Co. Miscellaneous Marriage Records; Land Office Patents and Grants, RG 4, LVA; Montgomery Co. Order Book, 1:281, 5:57, 6:13, 83, 107, 118, 9:153–154, 169; *JSV*, 1813–1814 sess., 15, 1821–1822 sess., 95; *Richmond Enquirer*, 12, 26 May, 2, 5 June 1829; *Journal of 1829–1830 Convention*, 22, 297; *Proceedings and Debates of 1829–1830 Convention*, esp. 22, 882, 903; Catlin, *Convention of 1829–30* (por.); will and estate inventory and appraisal in Montgomery Co. Will Book, 5:161–164, 252–253; death notice in *Richmond Enquirer*, 14 May 1833.

TRENTON E. HIZER

CLOYD, Joseph (10 June 1744–31 August 1833), county leader, was the son of David Cloyd and Margaret Campbell Cloyd and may have been born in Pennsylvania. His paternal grandfather, and perhaps his father, too, had been born in Ireland of Scottish ancestry. At the time of Cloyd's birth, his father owned land in Chester County, Pennsylvania, and in New Castle County, Delaware. In May 1745 Cloyd's father purchased land on a tributary of the Roanoke River in Virginia, where the family was residing in March 1764 when his mother and one brother were killed during an Indian raid on their farm.

Cloyd married Mary Gordon probably late in the 1760s. Their one daughter and three sons included Gordan Cloyd, a member of the Con-

vention of 1829–1830. By February 1772 Cloyd had moved to Back Creek in the western part of Botetourt County that later that year became Fincastle County, in 1776 Montgomery County, and in 1839, six years after his death, Pulaski County. He settled on a 632-acre portion of James Patton's Springfield tract. From that choice location Cloyd extended his own landholdings to the east and west by obtaining numerous tracts of land and buying property from people who were leaving the community. His Back Creek farm contained 1,870 acres of land, his property on Falling Spring another 3,000, and the westernmost portion of Springfield and adjoining tracts 1,000 acres more. Most of the choice farming and grazing land in what became Pulaski County belonged to Joseph Cloyd or his sons.

One of many immigrants or descendants of Scots-Irish immigrants in that portion of Virginia, Cloyd rose steadily into positions of local leadership and responsibility. He was a captain in the Fincastle County militia in 1774 and that year commanded a company on frontier patrol during Dunmore's War. Cloyd was elected to the Fincastle County Committee in November 1775 and during the ensuing years took part in securing Virginia's southwestern frontier, controlling local Loyalists, and recruiting men for the regiments that the state was raising. In September 1779 he became a major in the Montgomery County militia, and during the Revolutionary War he fought in several engagements in western North Carolina. At Wetzell's Mills on 6 March 1781, a few days before the larger and more important Battle of Guilford Court House, Cloyd saved the life of his friend, neighbor, and commanding officer, William Preston. He was promoted to lieutenant colonel on 6 November 1781 and appointed colonel on 6 March 1782.

The county court recommended in 1779 that Cloyd be named a justice of the peace and renewed the recommendation again in 1782, when the governor and Council of State added his name to the list for Montgomery County. The order books for the period are incomplete but record Cloyd's first appearance on the county court in November 1785. Elected to the House of Delegates in 1786 and 1787, Cloyd arrived too late after the opening of the 1786 session to be appointed to a standing committee, but in 1787 he sat on the Committees of Claims and of Propositions and Grievances. In 1792 he became one of the trustees of the new town of Christiansburg. He concluded his public officeholding by taking the oath as sheriff of Montgomery County on 3 December 1793.

Cloyd built a mill in 1790 and by early in the 1790s also operated a lucrative store near the town of New Dublin, for a time one of the few mercantile houses in the large county and therefore of significant local importance. His store offered manufactured goods purchased from as far away as New York and Philadelphia, and he dealt in local commodities, including slaves. He also profited from lending money or extending credit to his neighbors. On his farm, Cloyd erected a large stone barn, resembling the barns that descendants of German immigrants constructed in the Pennsylvania farm country where he may have once lived. About 1790 he employed the noted local builder John Swope to construct a commodious brick house there. The imposing residence, among the largest houses in the region at the time, symbolized Cloyd's prosperity and prominence. It still stands and in 1975 was listed on the Virginia Landmarks Register and the National Register of Historic Places.

Throughout his residence at Back Creek, Cloyd and his family were closely associated with New Dublin Presbyterian Church, which had been established about five years before he arrived. According to family tradition, Cloyd's wife required of him as a condition of moving to the then-remote site a promise that he would erect a Presbyterian church there. He set aside a forty-nine-acre tract for the New Dublin meetinghouse.

Cloyd's wife died on an unrecorded date before he completed his will on 22 May 1823. At that time he owned nearly forty slaves and more than 9,000 acres of land in Montgomery and several neighboring counties. Joseph Cloyd died on 31 August 1833 and was buried in the family cemetery near his house at Back Creek farm, in present-day Pulaski County.

Biography in Mary B. Kegley, *Early Adventurers on the Western Waters*, vol. 2: *The New River of Virginia in Pioneer Days, 1745–1800* (1982), 265–269, quoting gravestone and privately owned family Bible records for birth and death dates, with age at death on gravestone suggesting variant birth year of 1742; A. D. Cloyd, *Genealogy of the Cloyd, Bayse and Tapp Families in America* (1912), 63–67, 71–72; Conway Howard Smith, *The Land That Is Pulaski County* (1981), 49, 73–74, 126–129, 148–162; *Revolutionary Virginia*, 4:484, 5:375, 6:130, 136, 327, 7:440–441; business accounts and other documents in Cloyd Family Papers, VHS; some Cloyd correspondence in Draper MSS 3QQ17, 3QQ49, 5QQ115, and 5QQ116; Montgomery Co. Will Book, 5:190–191.

MARY B. KEGLEY

CLUVERIUS, Thomas Judson (10 August 1861–14 January 1887), principal in a criminal case, was the son of Beverly W. Cluverius, a farmer, and Mary A. Walker Cluverius. Born in King William County, he was tutored at home and attended local schools. After his family moved to King and Queen County in the mid-1870s, he continued his education at several rural schools until a wealthy aunt's beneficence allowed him to earn a law degree from Richmond College (later the University of Richmond) in June 1882. Cluverius (pronounced "Klu'-veers") practiced law in King and Queen and King William Counties.

On 14 March 1885 a young, pregnant woman was found drowned in Richmond's reservoir. Marks of a struggle found nearby suggested that her death was a murder. Three days later the body was identified as Cluverius's cousin, Fannie Lillian Madison. Police arrested him on 18 March and charged him with murder. Cluverius came from a family with a good reputation and had been a Baptist Sunday school teacher in King and Queen County, and the evidence against him was circumstantial. Several people testified that they had seen Cluverius and Madison together at various times and places on the day of her death. A watch key found at the site of the murder was reported to be his, but he and his family denied it. Cluverius might have been the father of Madison's unborn child, as some letters that implied a possible intimacy suggested, but this accusation, like so much in the case, remained open to argument. The mystery and indeterminacy in the case against a seemingly upright young man quickly made it Richmond's all-absorbing topic.

The celebrity of both legal teams added to the drama of Cluverius's trial, which lasted from

5 May to 4 June 1885. Charles Vivian Meredith, later a member of the Convention of 1901–1902, presented the prosecution's case, assisted by William Roane Aylett, longtime commonwealth's attorney of King William County. Three of the most prominent lawyers in the region defended Cluverius: William Wood Crump, a former Richmond judge, Andrew Brown Evans, a Middlesex County lawyer, and Henry Robinson Pollard, then commonwealth's attorney for King and Queen County and a member of the House of Delegates. Crump's son, Beverley Tucker Crump, later a member of the State Corporation Commission and president of the Special Court of Appeals, assisted the defense. The prosecutors made Cluverius out to be a fiend, a calculating predator who acted civilized but lured his cousin into sin and then killed her in order to free him to marry another woman. Defense counsel emphasized his good reputation and the weakness of the circumstantial evidence. They suggested that Madison had probably killed herself, an argument bolstered by her own words and self-destructive behavior in the weeks before her death. After brief deliberations, the jury rendered a verdict of guilty on 4 June, and on 19 June the judge sentenced Cluverius to death.

The case remained before the public for another year and a half as Cluverius's lawyers appealed to the Virginia Supreme Court of Appeals. His counsel compiled and printed a 383-page argument, including much trial testimony, and the prosecution's printed argument, in which Attorney General Rufus Adolphus Ayers became lead counsel, was 95 pages long. Both documents dealt extensively with the circumstantial evidence. On 6 May 1886, by a vote of four to one, the court ruled against Cluverius. Reflecting the controversy's complexity, the court's opinion by Thomas Turner Fauntleroy, a concurring opinion by Benjamin Watkins Lacy, and a dissent by Drury Andrew Hinton filled more than a hundred pages.

The murder, trial, and appeals created a long-running sensation in Richmond. Contemporary diaries and later memoirs mention it prominently, and the press covered each step in detail. The *Richmond Dispatch*, for instance, printed stories in more than 170 separate editions of the paper. The national press also followed the story. The *New York Times* published 37 stories on the case, many of them on the front page, and articles appeared in such other periodicals as *Frank Leslie's Illustrated Weekly* and the *National Police Gazette*. A Richmond newsstand sold photographs of Cluverius and Madison for twenty-five cents each.

Many observers at the time and since have questioned Cluverius's guilt. More than 2,700 Virginians, including many lawyers, legislators, and even members of the trial jury, signed petitions requesting that the governor commute the death sentence. Two fictional versions of the case published about the same time emphasized its sensational and unresolved nature by arguing that Cluverius was innocent.

In December 1886 the governor decided not to intervene in the case. Thomas Judson Cluverius was hanged with a silk rope on gallows erected in the Richmond city jail a few minutes after one o'clock on the afternoon of 14 January 1887. He was buried on family land in King and Queen County. In violation of recent Virginia laws that had specified that capital punishment was to be carried out in private, several hundred people crowded into the jail yard to witness the hanging, hoping in vain to hear a confession. Many thousands more gathered outside the jail and on housetops and hillsides overlooking the jail's walls. Some purchased from enterprising hawkers copies of Cluverius's memoirs, written while he was in jail awaiting execution. The *Richmond Daily Times*, the *Richmond Dispatch*, and the *Richmond State* all covered the hanging in great detail.

Thomas J. Cluverius, *Cluverius: My Life, Trial, and Conviction* (1887), with birth date; George A. Booker, *The Virginia Tragedy: Trial and Conviction of Thomas J. Cluverius for the Murder of Lillian Madison, March 13, 1885* (1885); original trial transcripts and other documents, Meredith Family Papers, VHS, printed in heavily edited version in John D. Lawson, ed., *American State Trials* (1914–1936), 17:379–506; testimony quoted at length in appellate briefs, *In the Supreme Court of Appeals of Virginia, Richmond: Thomas J. Cluverius vs. the Commonwealth* [1885], *In the Supreme Court of Appeals of Virginia: Thomas J. Cluverius v. the Commonwealth: Brief for the State* [1885], and *In the Supreme Court of Appeals of Virginia: Thomas J. Cluverius vs. The Commonwealth: Petition for Rehearing* [1886]; petitions to the governor in Secretary of the Commonwealth, Executive Papers, RG 13, LVA; *Cluverius* v. *The Commonwealth* (1886), *Virginia Reports*, 81:787–899; Michael Ayers Trotti, "Murder and the Modern Sensibility: Sensationalism and Cultural Change in Richmond, Virginia, from the Victorian Era to the Age of Ragtime" (Ph.D. diss., UNC, 1999), 20–71; Trotti, "Murder Made Real: The Visual Revolution of the Halftone," *VMHB* 111 (2003): 379–384 (several pors.); earliest fictional works include *"Cousin Tommie!" A Parody by a Richmond Lady* (1885), Phillip Leigh, *Lillian's Marriage and Murder* (1887), and *Old Man Bruce, the Richmond Detective: or "Piping" the Reservoir Mystery* (1888); hanging reported in *Richmond Dispatch* and *Richmond State*, both 14, 15 Jan. 1887, *Richmond Daily Times*, 15 Jan. 1887, and *National Police Gazette*, 29 Jan. 1887.

MICHAEL AYERS TROTTI

COALE, Charles B. (d. 3 January 1879), journalist, was born in Maryland, possibly in or near Bel Air, in Harford County, where he attended school, delivered newspapers, and worked in the *Bond of Union and Weekly Advertiser* office, run by a printer who was probably a relative. The ages he reported to census enumerators in 1850, 1860, and 1870 suggest that he was born between 1807 and 1809, and the age at death on his gravestone indicates that he was born in 1806 or 1807. The names of his parents are not known, but the Coale family included several Maryland printers and booksellers. On 14 July 1831, while temporarily residing in Washington, D.C., Coale married Julia Ann Sanford, who died on 4 December 1875. They are not known to have had any children. His mother was a Quaker, and in March 1841 Coale, who may have been a Baptist, converted to Methodism.

Coale may have been engaged in journalism as a young man, but not until November 1839 can his whereabouts can be established. In that month he and John W. Lampkin formed a partnership in Abingdon and began publishing the *South-Western Virginian*, of which Coale was also sometimes editor. On 4 September 1841 Coale entered a new partnership with George R. Barr, and they continued to edit and publish the weekly newspaper, later retitled the *Abingdon Virginian*, from then until January 1873, when they sold it. Through the paper Coale supported the Whig Party, and he took part in a variety of community affairs. In the 1850s he promoted construction of the Virginia and Tennessee Rail-

road, which linked Lynchburg with Bristol on the Tennessee border and passed through Abingdon. A charter member of the McCabe Lodge No. 56, Independent Order of Odd Fellows, Coale worked with it to establish Martha Washington College, in Abingdon. He served on its board of trustees from 1858 until his death, for part of that time as secretary. Coale also joined the Freemasons and promoted the building of the order's Saint John's Orphan Asylum. In addition to serving on the examining committee of nearby Emory and Henry College, he earned money publishing its catalogs, and for a time during the Civil War he sold insurance for the Lynchburg Hose and Fire Insurance Company.

Like a majority of other Washington County residents, Coale, who owned no slaves, was opposed to secession until Virginia left the Union in April 1861. His newspaper consistently thereafter supported the Confederacy, even though the people of the area had divided loyalties. The *Abingdon Virginian* continued to appear almost every Friday through 9 December 1864, though it occasionally missed an issue because of a lack of paper. Union forces entered Abingdon on the evening of 14 December and destroyed the newspaper's office and press. Not until after Coale and Barr received material support from Charles William Button, editor of the *Lynchburg Virginian*, were they able to resume publication on 8 December 1865.

In the autumn of 1875 Coale won election to the House of Delegates as one of two men representing Washington County. During the campaign he recommended reducing the amount of the principal of the antebellum public debt to be paid off to an amount that the state's taxpayers could afford. Coale's two-year term was unremarkable. He sat on the relatively inconsequential Committees on Printing and on Retrenchment and Economy. He introduced an unsuccessful bill to incorporate the Abingdon fire department and a successful bill to amend a section of the town's charter. Coale failed to win a second term in 1877.

Having published a weekly newspaper for more than thirty years, an unusually long time in a relatively small city, Coale resumed his connection with journalism three years after selling his interest in the *Abingdon Virginian*. He joined forces with Findlay Harris in 1876 to begin another newspaper in Abingdon, the *Standard*. Between December 1869 and March 1870 Coale published a series of fifteen personal reminiscences in the *Abingdon Virginian* and the *Bel Air Aegis and Intelligencer*. In 1878 he completed and published *The Life and Adventures of Wilburn Waters, the Famous Hunter and Trapper of White Top Mountain*, a biography of a legendary character from the early, formative years of southwestern Virginia.

Charles B. Coale died near the town of Emory in Washington County on 3 January 1879 and was buried in Sinking Spring Cemetery, in Abingdon. No copies of local newspapers survive from the time of his death to give a fully informed assessment of his long career in Abingdon. The inventory of his personal estate compiled several months after his death identified no property other than his library of 361 books.

Biography in Lewis Preston Summers, *History of Southwest Virginia, 1746–1786, Washington County, 1777–1870* (1903), 786 (por. and birth date of 1807), with other information on 495–504, 527–528, 565, 569, 570, 588–589; Census, Washington Co., 1850 (age forty-two on 9 Oct. 1850), 1860 (age fifty-one on 13 Aug. 1860), and 1870 (age sixty-two on 15 Aug. 1870); death date at age seventy-two on gravestone; personal reminiscences in *Abingdon Virginian*, 3 Dec. 1869, *Bel Air [Md.] Aegis and Intelligencer*, 17 Dec. 1869–25 Mar. 1870, and Hunter C. Sutherland, ed., "'Glimpses from the Past': Character Recollections of Charles B. Coale," *Harford Historical Bulletin* 14 (fall 1982): n.p.; *Washington Daily National Intelligencer*, 29 July 1831; *Abingdon Virginian*, 8 Dec. 1865, 12 Jan. 1866, 24 Jan. 1873, 19, 26 Mar., 9 July, 5 Nov. 1875; Claude D. Curtis, *Three Quarters of a Century at Martha Washington College* (1928), 12; John Cook Wyllie and Randolph W. Church, eds., *Virginia Imprint Series, Number 1: Preliminary Checklist for Abingdon, 1807–1876* (1946), 29–31; Martha Washington College Board of Trustees Minutes, Historical Society of Washington County, Virginia, Abingdon; estate inventory in Washington Co. Will Book, 20:225–226; obituaries in *Lynchburg Daily News*, 6 Jan. 1879 (with death date at age seventy-two), and *Knoxville Holston Methodist*, 18 Jan., 1 Feb. 1879.

ROBERT J. VEJNAR, II

COALTER, John (20 August 1769–2 February 1838), judge of the Virginia Court of Appeals and member of the Convention of 1829–1830, was born in the portion of Augusta County that in 1778 became Rockbridge County. When he was about nine years old, his parents, Michael

Coalter and Elizabeth Moore Coalter, moved the family to a plantation near Staunton. Coalter intermittently attended common schools before entering Liberty Hall Academy (later Washington College and still later Washington and Lee University), where he received a rudimentary classical education. At age eighteen he left home to seek employment, and after making the acquaintance of St. George Tucker, a well-known legal scholar and later a judge of the Court of Appeals, he decided to study law. Coalter spent about three hours a day teaching Tucker's children in exchange for board and the use of Tucker's library, first in Chesterfield County and then in Williamsburg. Tucker arranged for him to attend the College of William and Mary to study law under George Wythe.

After completing his legal education in 1790, Coalter began his practice in Augusta County, where he was admitted to the bar on 15 March 1791 and by September 1793 had become clerk of the court for the district that included Augusta, Bath, Pendleton, Rockbridge, and Rockingham Counties. He returned to Williamsburg in the autumn of 1791 and married Maria Rind, who had worked in the Tucker household. Personal tragedy and professional advancement marked the next several years of Coalter's life. His wife died in the autumn of 1792 after giving birth to a child who also died. On 15 February 1795 he married Margaret Davenport, of Williamsburg, but she died within a year or two as well. They had no surviving children, but her mother lived with Coalter until her death early in 1816, throughout the years of his third marriage. On 5 June 1802 Coalter married one of St. George Tucker's daughters, Ann Frances Bland Tucker. They had two daughters, one of whom died young, and one son.

Coalter's education and connections eventually paid handsome professional dividends. By the time of his third marriage he had prospered and made a name for himself. He was a member of the board of Washington College from 1798 until 1830. Coalter became commonwealth's attorney for Augusta County in 1803 and rented Elm Grove, a 900-acre plantation near Staunton. The General Assembly elected him to the General Court on 7 February 1809. Coalter presided over courts in a circuit consisting of the counties of Botetourt, Cabell, Greenbrier, Kanawha, Mason, and Monroe and from time to time met with other General Court judges in Richmond to hear appeals in civil cases and to act as the court of last resort in criminal cases. During his many absences on legal business, which strained relations between him and his wife, Frances Tucker Coalter managed the plantation and its enslaved laborers. She died of consumption (probably tuberculosis) on 12 September 1813.

On 11 May 1811 the governor named Coalter to the seat on the Virginia Court of Appeals left vacant by the resignation of his father-in-law, St. George Tucker. A bitter dispute with Spencer Roane had led Tucker to resign, and he attempted to dissuade Coalter from taking the position and even chastised his son-in-law for disobedience. Coalter nevertheless accepted the appointment, and the General Assembly elected him on 6 December 1811. Coalter took his seat on the state's highest court on 1 June 1811 and three or four years later moved to a Henrico County farm on the outskirts of Richmond. He served on the court for two decades, during which he compiled a solid but unspectacular record. Coalter arrived during a period of transition on the court, as the judges increasingly acceded to the leadership of Roane and began to issue a larger proportion of rulings in short, unanimous opinions. Coalter delivered one of his most notable opinions in *Asbury Crenshaw and Thomas B. Crenshaw* v. *The Slate River Company* (1828), in which he joined the other judges in declaring unconstitutional a state law that authorized a company formed to improve the navigation of a watercourse to require such expensive modifications to mill owners' property as to threaten economic ruin to the mill owners. Coalter confirmed the traditional common-law understanding of eminent domain, which required just compensation for property taken for a public purpose.

While he was a member of the Court of Appeals, Coalter also served on a five-member commission that the General Assembly created early in 1817 to prepare a comprehensive report on which laws should be revised or repealed.

Before the end of the year the members compiled and published a report of nearly 450 pages.

On 14 February 1822 Coalter married Hannah Harrison Jones Williamson, a Stafford County widow who had one daughter. They had no children. In 1825 her father transferred to him the deed to Chatham, a large, venerable brick house on the north bank of the Rappahannock River overlooking Fredericksburg, and the next year Coalter sold his Henrico County residence and moved to Chatham. Always known for his gentility and conviviality, Coalter, along with his fourth wife, took an active role in the social life of the community. Among the valuable properties he acquired by virtue of his fourth marriage was land in Orange County near where deposits of gold had been found, and for a time he anticipated profiting from mining gold on his own land.

On 23 November 1829 three delegates representing King George, Lancaster, Northumberland, Prince William, Richmond, Stafford, and Westmoreland Counties in the constitutional convention then meeting in Richmond selected Coalter to fill a vacancy in their ranks following the resignation of John Taliaferro, the fourth delegate from the district. Coalter entered immediately into the work of the convention and participated in the debates beginning on the day that he was selected and took his seat. He spoke several times against proposals to allow the state to increase its indebtedness and against eliminating or reducing property ownership as a qualification for the franchise. Coalter also opposed allowing voters, rather than the General Assembly, to elect the governor. He summed up his objections to most suggested innovations in a formal prepared speech to the convention on 1 December. In spite of his many reservations, Coalter voted in favor of the new constitution that the convention approved on 14 January 1830 and submitted to the voters, who later in the year ratified it.

Coalter resigned from the Court of Appeals on 23 March 1831 and lived in retirement at Chatham, where five or six years later he suffered a stroke. Following a partial recovery from his paralysis, John Coalter died at Chatham on 2 February 1838 and was buried in Saint George's Episcopal Church Cemetery, in Fredericksburg.

His estate, valued at more than $100,000, included 133 slaves, most originally the property of his fourth wife.

John Stewart Bryan, "John Coalter," *Virginia State Bar Association Proceedings* (1929), 460–468 (por. facing 460); autobiographical fragment with birth date published as "Copy of a Sketch of John Coalter in His Own Hand Writing," *Augusta Historical Bulletin* 4 (fall 1968): 17–19, together with his daughter Elizabeth Tucker Coalter Bryan's "Some Further Account of John Coalter" (ca. 1840), which includes information on first three marriages and children (ibid., 20–24); fourth marriage reported in *Richmond Commercial Compiler*, 18 Feb. 1822; Coalter letters in St. George Tucker Grinnan Papers, LVA, and Brown-Coalter-Tucker Papers, W&M, and numerous other collections at Duke, LVA, UVA, VHS, and W&M; court appointments in *JHD*, 1808–1809 sess., 105, Council of State Journal (1810–1811), 143, RG 75, LVA, and *JHD*, 1811–1812 sess., 14; *Asbury Crenshaw and Thomas B. Crenshaw v. The Slate River Company* (1828) (6 Randolph), *Virginia Reports*, 27:245–284, with Coalter's opinion on 278–284; John Coalter to John Floyd, 23 Mar. 1831, John Floyd Executive Papers, RG 3, LVA; *Proceedings and Debates of 1829–1830 Convention*, 431, 440–441, 453–455, 482–484, 516–519, 882; Catlin, *Convention of 1829–30* (por.); Ralph Happel, *Chatham: The Life of a House* (1984), 28–33, 82–83; Phillip Hamilton, *The Making and Unmaking of a Revolutionary Family: The Tuckers of Virginia, 1752–1830* (2003); will and estate inventory in Stafford Co. Deed Book, LL:172–175, 202–205; obituaries in *Fredericksburg Political Arena* and *Richmond Enquirer*, both 6 Feb. 1838.

TIMOTHY S. HUEBNER

COBB, Nathan Fosque (15 December 1797–20 March 1881), founder of the Cobb Island resort, was born in Eastham, Massachusetts, on the east coast of Cape Cod. He was the son of Elkanah Cobb and Jerusha Foster Cobb and as a young man joined his father and brothers in the whaling and shipbuilding business. On 25 December 1820 he married Nancy Doane. They had four daughters and four sons, one of whom died in infancy. According to family traditions published in the 1890s, Cobb's wife was diagnosed with tuberculosis, and her physician suggested that she move to a warmer climate. Following the birth of their last child, Cobb divested himself of his interest in the family business, packed his furniture, tools, and lumber, and sailed south. A storm off the Virginia coast forced the family into the small fishing town of Oyster, in Northampton County.

It is possible that Cobb may have already been familiar with the Eastern Shore. The date of his settlement there is not known with certainty, but their last child was born in August 1838, and Cobb's name appears in the county's records for the first time on 7 December of that year, when he paid a $7.91 license fee to operate a retail business. Three days later the county court authorized him to sell alcohol at the store. To supplement his income, Cobb organized some of his neighbors in a wrecking and salvage business, removing freight from wrecked ships near the coast. Oyster was several miles from the open ocean, and in order to be closer to the sea, Cobb on 11 March 1839 purchased for $150 (not $100 plus 50 bushels of salt, or a wagonload of salt, as later stated) eighty-six acres of land called Great Sand Shoal Island, part of the chain of barrier islands between the Atlantic Ocean and the Eastern Shore. The little island was separated from much larger Prout's Island by a narrow channel that later silted up and connected Cobb's island to the larger island. It was a perfect location for conducting salvage operations, and he erected a house there and opened a tavern.

Cobb's wife died soon thereafter, on 1 January 1840, and was buried on the mainland at nearby Glenair. On 13 September 1842 Cobb married Esther Carpenter Fletcher, a widow with one son and one daughter. She had lived on Hog Island, another of the barrier islands. They had at least two daughters before her death on an unrecorded date after 3 July 1860. Cobb's sons also married local women and lived with their wives and growing families on the island.

The salvage business was lucrative, and the Cobbs salvaged at least thirty-seven vessels and saved numerous lives. Stranded captains had little bargaining power if they wished to preserve any of their freight, and Cobb was known to drive a hard bargain, although he reportedly charged no fees for rescuing passengers and crew members. Because the salvage business was dependent on accidents, he was naturally left with much free time. Cobb furnished his table with fish and game that were abundant on the islands, and he and his sons engaged in commercial hunting of migratory birds in the spring and late summer and of waterfowl in the winter. The Cobbs were excellent shots and in a day often killed more than 150 wildfowl, which they plucked, packed into barrels, and loaded into one of their boats for shipment to northern markets.

Stories of the extraordinary number of wild-fowl that were being shipped from the Virginia island began to make the rounds of the northern sporting community, and sportsmen contacted Cobb and offered to pay for the opportunity to hunt on what they soon began calling Cobb's island. He realized that there was more financial certainty in entertaining wealthy sportsmen than in waiting for ships to founder, and he began putting up guests in his house. Before the Civil War he had erected guest cottages and later built a large hotel that could accommodate two hundred guests at a time. By the 1870s his initial $150 for the purchase of the island had proved a profitable investment. The Cobbs catered to hunters and fishermen as well as to people looking for a remote spot to spend their summer vacations. He purchased a farm on the mainland and built a mill to help feed the customers. Local employees cooked and cleaned in the hotel and acted as guides in the field. Cobb's sons carved decoys to attract waterfowl into shooting range, and he arranged for his guests to have their game packed for shipment home. The island became one of the most famous resorts of its type on the East Coast. In 1868 it provided guests a bowling alley, a billiard room, and musicians to entertain them. Cultivating his reputation, Cobb became a local celebrity about whom visitors told tall tales after they returned to their homes.

Cobb owned two slaves in 1856. It appears that he and his sons remained loyal to the United States during the Civil War. On 5 July 1866 Cobb married a widow, Nancy Roberts Richardson. They had no children. A few days before his third marriage he sold the two main guest lodgings to his three adult sons, who paid $4,000 for the resort and operated it at least until 1894. In July 1880 Cobb sold half an acre of his island to the United States government, which for the next half century operated a life-saving station on the treacherous coastline. Nathan Fosque Cobb died at his residence on his island on 20 March 1881 and was buried in the cemetery there. Storms destroyed Cobb's residence and resort during the 1890s, and all that remain are a few photographs, descriptions by visitors, and the collectible decoys that his sons carved. In November 1893 the United States Board on Geographic Names officially designated the island where Cobb lived as Cobb Island.

Family history, including birth and death dates, middle name, and first marriage date from 1833 sampler worked by eldest daughter, in *Saint Louis Missouri Republican*, 2 Dec. 1886 (reprinted in *Onancock Eastern Shore News*, 4 Dec. 1952), and *Richmond Dispatch*, 23 Aug. 1896; Northampton Co. Marriage Bonds and Licenses (1842); BVS Marriage Register, Northampton Co. (1866); Northampton Co. Deed Book, 31:66–67, 32:79–80 (second marriage contract), 36:611–613, 616–619 (third marriage contract); *Accomac Court House Peninsula Enterprise*, 13 Nov. 1897; *Eastville Eastern Shore Herald*, 30 Jan. 1932; James E. Mears, "Cobb's Island," misdated *Onancock Eastern Shore News* clipping, in James Egbert Mears Scrapbooks, 4:55–56, Acc. 36083, LVA; Amine Kellam, "The Cobb's Island Story," *Virginia Cavalcade* 23 (spring 1974): 18–27; Brooks Miles Barnes and Barry R. Truitt, eds., *Seashore Chronicles: Three Centuries of the Virginia Barrier Islands* (1997), 72–84, 116–129; Kessler Burnett, "Cobb's Island," *Chesapeake Life Magazine* (Jan./Feb. 2000): 84–91; will in Northampton Co. Will Book, 39:221–222; obituary in *Forest and Stream*, 14 Apr. 1881 (with variant death date of 26 March 1881).

DENNIS R. CUSTIS

COBB, William Lewis (13 September 1850–31 August 1909), member of the Convention of 1901–1902, was born in Caroline County and was the son of James E. Cobb, a farmer, and Maria L. Cobb. After his education in the public schools of Caroline County, he acquired a farm there called Woodlawn, adjoining Polecat Creek. Later describing himself as a self-made businessman who "had to work my way from the plow by my own exertions," Cobb farmed and prospered as the proprietor of sawmills at a variety of Caroline locations centering on the adjoining postal districts of Penola and Ruther Glen. On 25 November 1869 he married Bettie C. Thomas, of Louisa County. Of their one daughter and five sons, only one son reached adulthood. Bettie Cobb died in childbirth on 30 August 1881, and on 19 June 1882 Cobb married Landonia A. Flippo, of Caroline County. Two of their three daughters survived childhood.

Cobb held no public office until he won election on 23 May 1901 to represent Caroline County in a convention called to revise the state's constitution. His Democratic opponents withdrew in advance of the nomination meeting, but his response to a questionnaire circulated before the general election observed that some "sore head" Democrats were backing Samuel E. Pitts, his Republican opponent and the incumbent representing Caroline in the House of Delegates. In one of the election's few close contests, Cobb defeated Pitts by 1,284 to 1,128 votes.

Stating that he had no special interest in any particular branch of the constitution, Cobb was placed in low-ranking seats on the Committee on the Journal, the Committee on Public Institutions and Prisons, and the Committee on Agricultural, Manufacturing, and Industrial Interests and Immigration. During an unusually long convention that met in Richmond from 12 June 1901 to 26 June 1902, Cobb seems never to have spoken on the floor. He missed a significant number of roll-call votes but was present to support the majority when it passed a key provision on 4 April 1902 narrowly restricting the franchise so as effectively to end voting by African Americans and many poor whites. Cobb backed the decision on 29 May to proclaim the constitution in effect without subjecting it to a popular referendum, and on 6 June 1902 he voted for the Constitution of 1902 as finally adopted.

William Lewis Cobb returned to his business concerns in Caroline County and after several months of illness died at his home there on 31 August 1909. He was buried in the family cemetery near Ladysmith.

Birth date and variant death date of 30 Aug. 1909 on gravestone; birth month and year confirmed in Pollard Questionnaires (quotations); middle name recorded in entry for daughter Alma Belle Cobb in BVS Birth Register, Caroline Co. (1872); BVS Marriage Register, Louisa Co. (1869), Caroline Co. (1882); Caroline Co. Deed Book, 58:65–68; Election Records, no. 47, RG 13, LVA; *Richmond Dispatch*, 25 May 1901; *Richmond Times*, 25 May, 12 June 1901 (por. and variant birth date of 5 Sept. 1850); *Journal of 1901–1902 Convention*, 50–51, 94, 487, 504, 535; *Convention of 1901–1902 Photographs* (por.); will in Caroline Co. Will Book, 37:344; Caroline Co. Fiduciary Account Book, 3:397–398; obituaries in *Fredericksburg Daily Star*, 1 Sept. 1909 (noting death "early Tuesday morning," 31 Aug. 1909), and *Fredericksburg Free Lance*, 2 Sept. 1909.

J. JEFFERSON LOONEY

COCHRAN, Herbert Green (15 April 1885–17 November 1969), judge of the Norfolk Juvenile and Domestic Relations Court, was born in Farm-

ington, Kent County, Delaware, and was the son of Frederick J. Cochran and Dora Bell Hoffecker Cochran. He grew up in Delaware and on the Eastern Shore of Maryland, where his father, a Methodist minister, held pastorates. He attended the Wilmington Conference Academy (later Wesley College), in Dover, Delaware, before enrolling in Dickinson College, in Carlisle, Pennsylvania, where he was elected to Phi Beta Kappa and in 1908 received a B.A. Cochran read law from 1908 to 1911 as a Rhodes Scholar at the University of Oxford before attending the law school at the University of Virginia for one year. He was admitted to the bar in 1912 and began practicing law in Norfolk. Cochran served as a public defender from 1916 to 1917 before leaving for service in France during World War I. Following his return to Norfolk after the war, he became a special assistant city attorney and in April 1919 began rewriting Norfolk's city code, which the city council adopted the following year.

Cochran joined a prominent law firm in 1921 and the following year established a partnership with Norfolk's mayor, Albert L. Roper. In 1925 Cochran became substitute judge for the Norfolk Juvenile and Domestic Relations Court, after William Wadsworth Dey took a leave of absence beginning on 31 March 1925. Dey submitted his resignation in December of that year, effective on 5 January 1926, and Cochran was appointed to fill the vacancy.

Described as intelligent and tireless, Cochran also was controversial during three decades on the bench. He believed that the welfare of defendant juveniles was paramount and that the court's mission was to salvage lives rather than simply imposing punishments. In adjudicating cases Cochran emphasized individual treatment of defendants and examined their personal characteristics and social relationships instead of focusing strictly on their offenses. Believing that confinement in prisons did little to rehabilitate inmates and make them productive members of society, he argued that incarceration contributed to recidivism. He was one of the first Virginia judges who used probation and family counseling programs to resolve cases.

Cochran and his counterparts in Richmond and Roanoke, James Hoge Ricks and Odessa

Pittard Bailey, respectively, were allies in firmly establishing the juvenile court movement in Virginia. Ricks and Cochran were equally prominent on the national level. Cochran served on the board of directors of the National Probation Association from 1928 through 1943, and he joined Ricks on the association's committee that in 1943 revised the Standard Juvenile Court Act, which became a model statute for many states' juvenile codes, including the one Virginia adopted in 1950.

Active in many state and national legal organizations, Cochran was a fellow of the American Law Institute, sat on the advisory council of the Association of Juvenile Court Judges of America, helped establish the Virginia Council of Juvenile Court Judges and served on its executive committee, and influenced legislative policy as a member of the Juvenile Court and Delinquency Committee of the Virginia Advisory Legislative Council. In 1936, as a member of a special legislative commission that studied Virginia jails, he urged that prisons be used for temporary detention only, and not as places in which criminals served long sentences, because prisoners were not being rehabilitated. Cochran also served the local community and the state in social causes as president of the Norfolk Council of Social Agencies and the Virginia Conference of Social Work. He sat on the boards of the Norfolk Community Fund and the Virginia League for Planned Parenthood and was a member of the Virginia Interracial Commission.

Cochran enjoyed a national and international reputation. He assisted Massachusetts in modernizing its juvenile laws. He was a fellow of the American Academy of Political and Social Science, a member of the International Council on Social Welfare, and a participant in the 1930 White House Conference on Child Health and Protection. He often spoke at conferences on juvenile justice issues and social work. On 30 April 1954 poor health forced Cochran to begin a six-month leave of absence from the bench, after which he retired. He continued to live in Norfolk with his wife Jeannette Payne Todd Cochran, a widow whom he had married on 5 April 1941 in Louisville, Kentucky. Herbert Green Cochran died in a Norfolk hospital on 17 November 1969 and was buried in Lakeside Cemetery, in Dover, Delaware.

Bruce, Tyler, and Morton, *History of Virginia*, 5:514, with birth date provided probably by Cochran; Kentucky Marriage License, Jefferson Co.; writings include Cochran, "Mental Cases and the Court," *Probation* 7 (Oct. 1928): 3, "Old Crime and New Methods of Dealing with It," National Probation Association *Proceedings* (1928), 62–88, "Probation, Its Uses and Potentialities," National Probation Association *Year Book* (1929), 12–17, "The Child and the Home," *Probation* 13 (Oct. 1934): 3–4, 14, "The Child and the Law," National Probation Association *Year Book* (1934), 23–36, and "Should Virginia Have a State-Wide System of Probation and Parole?" *Virginia State Bar Association Proceedings* (1935), 288–309 (por. facing 288); *Virginian-Pilot and Norfolk Landmark*, 6 Jan. 1926; *Richmond News Leader*, 16 Nov. 1936; Virginia Legislative Jail Commission, *The Virginia Jail System, Past and Present: A Program for the Future* (1937); Norfolk Juvenile and Domestic Relations Court Historical Commission, *Juvenile and Domestic Relations Court, Norfolk, Virginia: Fifty Year History, 1919 to 1969* (1969), vii (por.), 4–8; Robert E. Shepherd Jr., "Pursuing a Dream: The Juvenile Court Movement in Virginia," *Virginia Lawyer* 47 (Feb. 1999): 8–14, 16; obituaries and editorial tributes in *Norfolk Ledger-Star*, 18 Nov. 1969, and *Norfolk Virginian-Pilot*, 18, 19 Nov. 1969; memorial in *Virginia State Bar Association Proceedings* (1971), 299–300.

ROBERT E. SHEPHERD JR.

COCKACOESKE, also known as Cockacoeweske (d. by 1 July 1686), Pamunkey chief, was a descendant of Opechancanough, brother of the paramount chief Powhatan. Little is known about her life before she succeeded her husband, Totopotomoy, chief of the Pamunkey from about 1649 until he was killed during 1656 while assisting the colonists in frontier defense against Indian foes. She was usually referred to as the queen of Pamunkey. By the time Cockacoeske commenced her rule, the ancient Powhatan chiefdom had disintegrated, and the Indians of Virginia's coastal plain were no longer subordinate to a paramount leader. The Pamunkey, like other native subscribers to the Treaty of 1646, were tributaries to the English Crown.

Early in the summer of 1676 Cockacoeske appeared before a committee of burgesses and Council members in Jamestown. She entered the room with regal bearing, flanked by her interpreter and by her son John West, whose father was an English colonel. The queen's head was crowned with a broad woven band of beaded black and white wampum and peake shells, and she wore a full-length deerskin mantle with edges cut to resemble deep, twisted fringe. With "grave Courtlike Gestures and a Majestick Air," she took a seat at the Council table and refused to speak except through her interpreter, even though the committee members believed that she understood English. When asked how many warriors she could provide to defend the colony against frontier tribes, Cockacoeske disdainfully fell silent. Pressed further, she became agitated and delivered a quarter-hour speech during which she cried out, "Tatapatamoi Chepiack," meaning, "Totopotomoy is dead," to remind the committee members that her husband and a hundred of his warriors had perished while fighting alongside the colonists and that the Pamunkey had never received any compensation for their loss. Reluctantly, she eventually agreed to provide a dozen men, a small fraction of the number under her command. Conflict and disease had reduced the Native American population since 1607, but the number of Pamunkey warriors was then probably about 150.

Although the Pamunkey signed a treaty with the colony in March 1676, a few months before the outbreak of Bacon's Rebellion, the insurrection's leader, Nathaniel Bacon (1647–1676), and his followers attacked them, took captives and plunder, and killed some of Cockacoeske's people. To save her own life, the queen abandoned her goods and possessions, including bags of wampum, peake, and roanoke, and retreated to the depths of the Dragon Swamp, where she nearly starved to death. The following February, Cockacoeske asked the General Assembly for the release of Pamunkey who had been taken captive and for the restoration of Pamunkey property. The burgesses were unresponsive, but the royal commissioners whom the king had sent to quell the rebellion and investigate its origins concluded that Cockacoeske should be rewarded for her notable loyalty to the English. At their suggestion, authorities in England ordered that a jeweled coronet, other jewelry, and a suit of regal attire be presented to the queen of Pamunkey, her son, and her interpreter.

Cockacoeske was an astute leader and skillful politician. On 29 May 1677 when the Treaty of Middle Plantation was signed, at her request several tribes were reunited under her authority, and she signed the treaty on behalf of all the tribes under her subjection. Afterward, the Chickahominy and Rappahannock, having been free of Powhatan domination since 1646, stubbornly refused to become subservient to her or to pay tribute, and in the summer of 1678 Cockacoeske directed her interpreter Cornelius Dabney to compile a list of grievances, which she sent to the governor. She also had him dispatch to England a letter in which she professed her loyalty to the Crown and complained about the tribes that disobeyed her orders. The letter, signed "Cockacoeske Queen of Pamunkey," included her signature mark, the same W-like symbol that she had affixed to the Treaty of Middle Plantation.

Cockacoeske was unsuccessful in re-creating the chiefly dominance enjoyed by her people's leaders during the first half of the seventeenth century, but she continued to rule the Pamunkey until her death. Cockacoeske, the queen of Pamunkey, died on an unrecorded date before 1 July 1686, when her interpreter George Smith reported to the governor's Council that she was "lately dead." She was succeeded by a niece, as was customary in the matrilineal society. Whether the niece, called Betty, was the predecessor of or the same person as Ann, who was queen of the Pamunkey by 1706, is not known.

Martha W. McCartney, "Cockacoeske, Queen of Pamunkey," Association for the Preservation of Virginia Antiquities Annual Report, *Discovery* 17 (1984): 3–6; McCartney, "Cockacoeske, Queen of Pamunkey: Diplomat and Suzeraine," in Peter H. Wood, Gregory A. Waselkov, and M. Thomas Hatley, eds., *Powhatan's Mantle: Indians in the Colonial Southeast* (1989), 173–195; T[homas] M[athew], "The Beginning Progress and Conclusion of Bacons Rebellion in Virginia in the Years 1675 & 1676" (ca. 1705), 28–33 (first and second quotations), Thomas Jefferson Papers, LC; copies of 1677 treaty in Thomas Jefferson Papers, ser. 8, 14:226–233, LC, and in Samuel Wiseman's Book of Record, unpaginated, Pepysian Library 2582, Magdalene College, University of Cambridge; "A list of the Names of those Worthy Persons . . . most deserving of his Majesties Royal Remark," PRO CO 5/1371, fol. 181; Commissioners' Report, PRO CO 5/1371, fols. 185, 199; "Agrieveances of the Queen of Poemonkey and her Sonn: Capt. John West," docketed 5 June 1678, PRO CO 1/42, fol. 177; Cockacoeske to Francis Moryson, 29 June 1678, PRO CO 1/42, fol. 270; *JHB, 1659/60–1693*, 89; gifts itemized in Lord Chamberlain's Wardrobe Accounts, PRO LC 5/108, 8, and 9/275, fols. 264–267; report of death in *Executive Journals of Council*, 1:79 (third quotation).

MARTHA W. MCCARTNEY

COCKE, Allen (d. by 9 December 1780), member of the Convention of 1776, was born probably in the mid-1740s and was the son of Benjamin Cocke, a Surry County merchant, and Katherine Allen Cocke, a daughter of Elizabeth Bray Allen Smith Stith. Through her first marriage his maternal grandmother became mistress of the seventeenth-century residence in Surry County then known as Allen's brick house and later as Bacon's Castle, and through her second and third marriages she preserved it and a large estate for the Allen family. Allen Cocke inherited his grandmother's house after her death in 1774 and earlier had inherited an interest in land in Albemarle, Buckingham, Goochland, and Surry Counties following his father's death in 1763. He married Nancy Kennon, of Charles City County, and had at least three sons and two daughters.

A young man of property and good connections, Cocke was appointed to the Surry County Court in May 1770 and elected to the House of Burgesses late the following year. He attended the assembly that met from February to April 1772 but missed the next session that convened in March 1773. In the last two meetings of the House of Burgesses, in May 1774 and May 1775, he served on the Committee of Propositions and Grievances. A consistent supporter, so far as extant evidence shows, of colonial interests during the years immediately preceding the American Revolution, Cocke chaired the Surry County Committee and attended all five of the Revolutionary Conventions that met between August 1774 and July 1776. Winning unanimous election to the fifth convention in April 1776, he served on the Committee of Privileges and Elections and was almost certainly present for the three most important and unanimous votes, in favor of independence on 15 May, to adopt the Virginia Declaration of Rights on 12 June, and to approve the first constitution of Virginia on 29 June 1776.

As a result of his election to the fifth convention, Cocke was a member of the House of Delegates that met in October 1776 and retained his seat on the Committee of Privileges and Elections. He was elected to the General Assembly again for one-year terms in 1779 and 1780 and

also served on the Committee of Privileges and Elections, but he did not complete his second term. Allen Cocke dated his will on 20 November 1780 and about two weeks later died, probably at his Surry County residence. The *Williamsburg Virginia Gazette* reported his death in its issue of 9 December 1780.

Family history in James C. Southall, "The Cocke Family of Virginia," *VMHB* 4 (1897): 324–325, and 5 (1897): 72–73, and Leonie Doss Cocke and Virginia Webb Cocke, *Cockes and Cousins*, vol. 1: *Descendants of Richard Cocke (c. 1600–1665)* (1967), 8, 17, 37; Stephenson B. Andrews, ed., *Bacon's Castle* (1984), 8–9; *Revolutionary Virginia*; will and partial estate inventory in Surry Co. Deeds, Wills, Etc., 11:183–184, 217–221; death notice without date in *Williamsburg Virginia Gazette* (Clarkson and Davis), 9 Dec. 1780.
BRENT TARTER

COCKE, Charles Francis (10 June 1886–3 February 1971), president of the American Bankers Association, was born in Roanoke and was the son of Lucian Howard Cocke, a former mayor of Roanoke and lawyer for the Norfolk and Western Railway Company who served as president of the Virginia State Bar Association in 1918–1919, and his first wife, Lelia Maria Smith Cocke, a portraitist. His paternal grandfather, Charles Lewis Cocke, was a longtime superintendent of Hollins Institute (later Hollins University). After the death of his mother in 1899, Cocke lived in Charlottesville with his maternal grandparents, Francis Henry Smith, a professor of natural philosophy at the University of Virginia, and Mary Stuart Harrison Smith, a writer. Cocke entered the University of Virginia in 1903 and received a B.A. in 1908, followed by two years at the law school. Admitted to the bar in 1910, he left school without graduating and practiced law in Roanoke with a series of partners. Eventually he became senior partner in the firm of Cocke, Hazlegrove, and Shackleford. As a young attorney he helped represent Sidna Allen, one of the men convicted of the shootout at the Carroll County courthouse in 1912, but his practice was mostly civil, not criminal.

On 1 October 1914 C. Francis Cocke, as he was known professionally, married Francis Tilghman Mingea, of Abingdon. They had one daughter. During World War I, Cocke served at several aviation and signal corps stations in the United

States. In 1919 he chaired the organizational meeting of the Virginia Department of the American Legion. Cocke became a director of the First National Exchange Bank of Roanoke in 1927 and ten years later became executive vice president. He served as president from January 1938 until 1956, when he was elected chairman of the board. Cocke won recognition for implementing innovations in the tradition-bound banking business, thereby greatly increasing the success and size of his bank. At a time when savings and loan associations advanced most real estate loans, he pushed his bank into the residential mortgage field. Banks had been primarily oriented to serve business customers, but he expanded consumer and installment lending. Taking advantage of his bank's regional prominence, Cocke established correspondent relationships with nearly every bank in southwestern Virginia and secured for his bank a leading position in western Virginia.

An active member of both the Virginia Bankers Association and the American Bankers Association, Cocke was president of the former for the 1948–1949 term. His presidential address, with its warnings against excessive regulation of private banking, placed him squarely in line with most other Virginia business leaders. Cocke chaired the American Bankers Association's Committee on Federal Legislation from 1946 to 1950, when he became the association's vice president. In October 1951 he won election to a one-year term as president. He traveled throughout the United States and in Mexico during his term and spoke out on issues relating to regulation of banking, public and private credit, and federal deficit spending.

Cocke retired in 1964. He published five books during the 1960s, one of them a memoir of his father-in-law and another a history of Saint Mark's Episcopal Church in the town of Fincastle. The other three treated the historic parishes of the Episcopal Church in Virginia and were published by the Virginia State Library (later the Library of Virginia), of which he was a board member from 1944 to 1954, the final year as chair. Cocke supported the development and publication of the library's quarterly illustrated magazine, *Virginia Cavalcade*. He was a member of Saint John's Episcopal Church in Roanoke and was chancellor of the Episcopal Diocese of Southwestern Virginia from its creation in 1919 to 1961. A trustee of Hollins College from 1929 until his death, Cocke served as chairman of the board from 1938 to 1968.

A member of the boards of the Chesapeake and Potomac Telephone Company of Virginia, the Lawyers Title Insurance Corporation, and the Peoples Federal Savings and Loan Association of Roanoke, Cocke served on numerous other public boards, including those of the Barter Theatre, in Abingdon, the Medical College of Virginia, the Roanoke Historical Society (later the Historical Society of Western Virginia), the Roanoke Memorial Hospital Association, the Roanoke Public Library, the Virginia Museum of Fine Arts, and the VPI Educational Foundation (later the Virginia Tech Educational Foundation). Charles Francis Cocke died at his Roanoke home on 3 February 1971 and was buried in the Cocke family cemetery at Hollins College.

NCAB, 56:260–261 (por. facing 260); William B. Bagbey, "Cocke Family History" (typescript, ca. 2000), 7–8 (copy in *DVB* Files); BVS Birth Register, Roanoke City; BVS Marriage Register, Washington Co.; feature articles in *Banking* 43 (Nov. 1950): 47, and 44 (Oct. 1951): 40–43, 135, 138, in *Commonwealth* 18 (Nov. 1951): 20–21, and 23 (Aug. 1956): 8, 10, 45, 48, and in *Virginia and the Virginia County* 6 (Aug. 1952): 6–8, 20–21, 24–26 (several pors., including cover por.); presidential address in Virginia Bankers Association *Yearbook* (1949), 20–27; principal publications include Cocke, *Parish Lines, Diocese of Southwestern Virginia* (1960), *Parish Lines, Diocese of Southern Virginia* (1964), *Parish Lines, Diocese of Virginia* (1967), *Recollections of Wilton Egerton Mingea, 1855–1938* (1965), and *St. Mark's Episcopal Church, Fincastle, Virginia: Two Centuries of the Church in Botetourt County* (1969); obituaries in *Richmond News Leader* and *Roanoke World-News*, both 3 Feb. 1971, and *Roanoke Times*, 4 Feb. 1971.

GILBERT E. BUTLER, JR.

COCKE, Charles Lewis (21 February 1820–4 May 1901), educator, was born at Edgehill, the King William County plantation of his parents, James Cocke and Elizabeth Fox Cocke. He spent his early years studying at local schools, working on the family farm, and developing his religious beliefs at nearby Beulah Baptist Church. In 1836 Cocke entered the Virginia Baptist Seminary (later the University of Richmond). Two years later the school's principal advised him to continue his education at Columbian College (later George Washington University), in Washington, D.C., where Cocke received an A.B. in 1840 and A.M. in 1844. During this time his religious commitment deepened, and he was baptized in the Potomac River. He also decided to devote his life to the higher education of southern women.

On 31 December 1840 Cocke married Susanna Virginia Pleasants, of Henrico County. They had six daughters and three sons. That same year he returned to the Virginia Baptist Seminary, about the time it was incorporated as Richmond College, as assistant professor of mathematics and manager of the dining hall. After a successful tenure at the school, Cocke in 1846 accepted an appointment as principal of the Valley Union Seminary, at Botetourt Springs in Roanoke County.

He took charge of an institution on the verge of collapse and used $1,500 of his own money to pay creditors. The original buildings of the school were those of a resort hotel built near the healing springs in the 1820s. The hotel had failed and in 1839 came to house Edward William Johnston's ultimately unsuccessful Roanoke Female Seminary. The Baptist clergyman Joshua Bradley established the Valley Union Seminary at the site in 1842. He, also, was unable to make the venture succeed, and the trustees hired Cocke to operate the school.

The Valley Union Seminary was a coeducational institution until 1851, when enrollment outstripped the school's physical capacity. Cocke, acting on his early educational intent, urged that the boys' department be dropped, even though it had doubled the enrollment, in order to establish a female seminary. Consequently the board of trustees discontinued the department of study for boys and reopened the school for the 1852–1853 session as the Female Seminary at Botetourt Springs. Cocke sought funding for the seminary and found generous donors in John Hollins and Ann Halsey Hollins, of Lynchburg. In 1855 the seminary was renamed Hollins Institute in their honor.

During the half century he was superintendent at the institution, Cocke increased enrollment from 81 students in 1852 to 236 in 1901, as well as steadily raising the level of academics.

He shared the belief of his time that women should work in a limited sphere of society but maintained that they required the same mental training given to young men. Cocke saw himself as a father figure and protector of the young women at Hollins and believed that parents wanted their daughters to learn the graceful values of the antebellum South. As a result he limited the social, intellectual, and economic freedom of his charges and made Hollins one of the more restrictive women's schools in the region.

Operating a female seminary proved challenging, even though the school was unscathed by the Civil War. In difficult financial times Cocke did not require the trustees to pay his stipulated salary. Despite his generosity, by 1882 Hollins had incurred so much debt that the trustees leased the school to Cocke. By 1900 the debt had increased to more than $150,000, and the trustees deeded Hollins Institute to him. Along with his son, daughter, and other relatives, Cocke reincorporated the school early in February 1901. Although he had not started the institute, in 1898 the trustees established Cocke's birthday as Founder's Day.

Cocke published several articles on female education in the *Educational Journal of Virginia* and aided in establishing both the short-lived Alleghany College, in Blue Sulphur Springs, Greenbrier County, founded in 1859, and Alleghany Institute, in Roanoke, a preparatory school for boys that operated from 1886 to 1897. Never straying from his religious roots, he taught Sunday school regularly and helped organize the Enon Baptist Church near Hollins in 1855. A humble man, he declined an honorary LL.D. from Richmond College.

Several months after moving to Roanoke to live with his son, Charles Lewis Cocke died there on 4 May 1901. He was buried in the family cemetery on the grounds of Hollins Institute (later Hollins University). His daughter Martha Louisa Cocke succeeded him as head of Hollins and became Virginia's first woman college president. In 1908 the Charles L. Cocke Memorial Library opened at the college. Later renamed the Cocke Memorial Building, the structure housed the office of the president and other Hollins administrators.

Biographies in W. R. L. Smith (son-in-law), *Charles Lewis Cocke: Founder of Hollins College* (1921), including frontispiece por. and marriage date on 15, Hollins College Endowment-Improvement Fund, *A Great Virginian, a Noble Ideal, a Notable Achievement* [1927], Bruce, Tyler, and Morton, *History of Virginia*, 5:508–510 (por. facing 507), and *NCAB*, 29:452–453; birth and death dates on gravestone; Charles Lewis Cocke Papers, Hollins University Archives; published addresses include Cocke, *Valedictory: Closing Remarks of the Superintendent, to the Young Ladies of Hollins Institute, June 26, 1872* (1872), "Discipline and Training of Girls," *Educational Journal of Virginia* 10 (1879): 385–393, "Woman's Opportunity: Advice by Which every Aspiring Woman may Profit," ibid. 19 (1887): 377–390, and *Christian Evangelism by the Baptists of Virginia: An Address by Prof. Chas. L. Cocke before the Baptist General Association of Virginia, at Norfolk, November 12th, 1891* (1892); Dorothy S. Vickery, "Hollins College in Virginia," *VMHB* 50 (1942): 97–107; Donna Marie Packard, "Conservative Progress in the Higher Education of Southern Women: Hollins Institute, 1855–1901" (B.A. thesis, Princeton University, 1979); Frances J. Niederer, *Hollins College: An Illustrated History*, 2d ed. (1985), 9–11; Albert K. Cocke, *Family Reunion: Descendants of Charles L. Cocke, Founder of Hollins College* (1992); Nancy C. Parrish, *Lee Smith, Annie Dillard, and the Hollins Group: A Genesis of Writers* (1998), esp. 15–16, 21–27; obituary, account of funeral, and editorial tribute in *Roanoke Times*, 5, 7 May 1901; obituary in *Washington Post*, 5 May 1901; *In Memoriam: Charles Lewis Cocke, 1820–1901* (1901).

NANCY C. PARRISH

COCKE, Edmund Randolph (25 March 1841–19 February 1922), Populist party leader, was born at Oakland, one of two Cumberland County plantations owned by his parents, William Armistead Cocke and Elizabeth Randolph Preston Cocke. In 1856 he matriculated at Washington College (later Washington and Lee University). Intellectually gifted but shy and sometimes indolent, Cocke ranked near the bottom of his class during the first of his two years at that institution. Nevertheless, in 1858 the College of New Jersey (later Princeton University) accepted him as a transfer student with sophomore standing.

During the secession crisis Cocke abandoned his studies, returned to Virginia, and on 23 April 1861 enlisted in the Black Eagle Rifles, a Cumberland County militia unit that mustered into Confederate service as Company E of the 18th Regiment Virginia Infantry. Elected second lieutenant in June 1861, he became first lieutenant in mid-1862 and captain in January 1863. The Black Eagle Rifles performed with distinction at the First Battle of Manassas (Bull Run) and

fought in most of the Army of Northern Virginia's early campaigns. During George Edward Pickett's charge at the Battle of Gettysburg, Cocke suffered a superficial wound, but more than one-third of the men in his command were killed, including one of his brothers. The shattered company saw only limited action in the remaining years of the Civil War. Cocke served in 1865 as major of the 18th Virginia, without formal promotion to that rank. On 6 April 1865 he was captured during the Battle of Saylers Creek. Briefly confined in Washington, D.C., he spent two months in the prisoner-of-war camp at Johnson's Island, Ohio. On 9 June he swore allegiance to the United States and was paroled.

Emancipation and the accompanying collapse of land values severely reduced the Cocke family's wealth. The makeshift sharecropping and day-labor arrangements that replaced slavery arguably generated more frustration than income, and the Cockes' dark tobacco cash crop began to encounter serious competition from the newly popular bright leaf of Pittsylvania County and North Carolina. By 1880 his brothers had abandoned plantation life for other pursuits, but Captain Cocke, as he was customarily known, remained at Oakland for almost six decades after the Civil War, initially as the estate's heir and farm manager and then, after his mother's death in 1889, as its owner. On 17 October 1871 Cocke married his cousin Phoebe A. Preston, of Rockbridge County. They had two daughters before her death on 5 August 1873 following childbirth. On 6 May 1878 Cocke married another cousin, Lucia Cary Harrison, of Charles City County. Three of their four sons and three of their six daughters lived to adulthood.

After 1865 Cocke staunchly supported the Democratic Party and its low-tariff, white-supremacist creed. African American voters gave Republican candidates a decisive edge in Cumberland County, but in 1884, 1888, and 1890 the overwhelmingly Democratic General Assembly named Cocke chair of Cumberland's electoral board, a three-member panel that oversaw voting arrangements and appointed polling-place officials in county precincts. The local Readjusters' and GOP's continued victories during his seven-year tenure suggest that he fulfilled the obligations of the post without fraud or excessive partisanship. Even so, Cocke's private correspondence indicates that he harbored bitter antagonism toward the Republicans' policies, especially their support of black suffrage. He urged repeal of the Fifteenth Amendment and wrote that because of his intense hatred for Republicans, who "contaminate, debauch and putrefy every thing they touch," he could not "in sincerity pray for their Salvation."

Cocke's stint on Cumberland's electoral board coincided with his emergence as a noted figure in the state's farm organizations—and also with his first significant deviations from the Democratic Party's laissez-faire economic principles. Service on the Virginia State Agricultural Society's executive committee from 1883 to 1885 enhanced his contacts with Robert Beverley (1822–1901), Mann Page (1835–1904), and other independent-minded patricians who shared his concerns about deflationary trends in crop prices and land values. In 1884 and 1885 Cocke joined these activists in establishing the Farmers' Assembly of the State of Virginia, a broadly based group that soon demonstrated marked willingness to challenge the status quo. Signaling his support for a reform agenda that ranged from state railroad regulation to federal aid for public schools, Cocke between 1885 and 1889 represented the Cumberland farm club in at least three of the assembly's conferences.

In 1889 the Farmers' Assembly was absorbed into the National Farmers' Alliance and Industrial Union, a more radical group that had expanded into Virginia from the cotton states. An enthusiastic convert, Cocke was particularly attracted by the Alliance's demand for the free coinage of silver, a price-raising initiative that he viewed as tailor-made to alleviate the Southside's difficulties. He was also receptive to the organization's controversial subtreasury scheme, which would have allowed farmers to use tobacco and other nonperishable crops as collateral for low-interest, government-funded loans.

To Cocke's chagrin, his fellow Democrats did not share his view that the deflationary gold standard would inexorably reduce rural landowners to serfdom. Vexed by the state legislature's passage of a watered-down railroad regulatory bill early in 1892, and appalled by the party's nomination of Grover Cleveland, an avowed proponent of the gold standard, as its presidential candidate in June of that year, Cocke joined the front ranks of agrarian political insurgency and attended the first state convention of the Alliance-sponsored People's Party of Virginia (also known as the Populists). In the summer of 1892 he traveled to Omaha, Nebraska, as a delegate to the national convention of the People's Party. It soon became apparent, however, that Populism commanded little popular support in the Old Dominion. In November 1892 only about 12,000 Virginians voted for the presidential ticket that Cocke had helped nominate—a total dwarfed by the turnout for the victorious Democrats and even by that for the badly beaten Republicans. Meanwhile, the state Alliance's membership began to plummet, undercut by the collapse of many of the group's cooperative agribusiness ventures and by rank-and-file resistance to third-party activism. Cocke chaired the troubled organization's executive committee in 1892 and 1893, but his conscientious performance failed to halt the decline.

At the Populist state convention in August 1893 Cocke drafted much of the party platform, which championed free silver and called for radical reforms in Virginia's fraud-stained election procedures. After endorsing the platform committee's handiwork, the delegates put aside concerns about Cocke's staid, lackluster oratorical style and unanimously selected him as the party's gubernatorial nominee. Help from an unexpected quarter gave Cocke at least some chance for an upset victory. Demoralized by a ten-year succession of defeats, Virginia's GOP leaders decided not to field candidates for statewide office in 1893—a choice that, in effect, encouraged Republican voters to cast their ballots for the People's Party ticket. Unfortunately for Cocke, the emergence of this de facto coalition prompted an aggressive and vitriolic response from the Democrats, who lambasted the Populists as ne'er-do-well purveyors of communistic doctrines and, worse yet, as Republicans in all but name. Democratic newspapers assailed Cocke as an inexperienced political nonentity; as a rich, silver-spoon aristocrat who had never done a day's work in his life; and as a turncoat hypocrite whose allegations about vote fraud were belied by his own extended (and presumably honorable) tenure as a Democratic election official in Cumberland County. Backed by only 37.6 percent of the electorate, Cocke lost to congressman Charles Triplett O'Ferrall by a margin of 46,701 votes of 216,154 cast. The bulk of Cocke's support came from Republicans, black and white, who had cared little for him, his platform, or his party.

On 23 August 1894 Cocke served as temporary chair of the Populist state convention and, according to press reports, proclaimed that anyone who denied the need for reform in Virginia belonged in a lunatic asylum. That same day a Tenth District caucus nominated him for the United States House of Representatives. The November election brought yet another landslide defeat, this time at the hands of the incumbent Democratic congressman, Cocke's cousin Henry St. George Tucker (1853–1932).

During the next two years Cocke's public activities mirrored the erratic course of the third-party movement. In August 1895 he attended the Honest Election Conference in Petersburg at which he helped devise plans for a coordinated campaign by Populists and Republicans in the autumn legislative races. By contrast, the next year he served on a committee orchestrating a cooperative campaign of Virginia Populists and Democrats, and as a delegate to the People's Party convention in Saint Louis, Missouri, he endorsed the candidacy of the Democratic presidential nominee William Jennings Bryan, an outspoken champion of the free-silver cause.

In July 1897 the Populists nominated Cocke for lieutenant governor and, fielding no candidates for the other statewide offices, urged the Democrats to give him the second spot on their ticket and thus produce a fusion slate acceptable to both parties. Southside Democrats were receptive to this plan, but at their party's state convention in August, only one-fifth of all the delegates voted for Cocke. The Democratic nomination for lieutenant governor went instead to Edward Echols, a conservative machine politician from Staunton. Stung by this perceived insult, Populist leaders encouraged Cocke to con-

tinue his futile third-party candidacy, even though they lacked the resources to mount anything more than a token campaign on his behalf. The 7,429 votes that he polled in November constituted only 4.6 percent of the 162,770 votes cast and signaled the demise of Populism as even a minor influence in Virginia.

Private misfortunes accompanied public defeats. On 31 March 1898 Cocke's wife died of childbirth complications that also claimed the life of her newborn infant. In August 1900 fire destroyed his cherished ancestral home at Oakland. Indicative of Cocke's reduced circumstances, a remodeled outbuilding that had once served as the plantation's business office became the family residence. Beset by cash shortages, he began selling off parts of Oakland in the 1880s, sold another 792 acres in 1900, and later attempted to alleviate concerns about his children's financial prospects by designating the former state Alliance president Mann Page as trustee of the Cocke estate. A less rational response to accumulating adversities emerged as well. Family tradition records that Cocke began to practice the pseudoscience of alchemy. No stranger to lost causes, he devoted countless hours to gold-making experiments that ruined an array of kettles and tubs but failed to transform Oakland into El Dorado.

Preoccupied with this eccentric pursuit, the erstwhile champion of free silver displayed little interest in the reform crusades of the Progressive era. Cocke had no sympathy with the Prohibition movement and in 1919 lashed out against the state's machine Democrats and their newfound enthusiasm for "dry" principles. "There are a few gentlemen in Virginia still," he archly observed, "and they are not dominated by Methodist preachers." Edmund Randolph Cocke died at Oakland of kidney failure on 19 February 1922 and was buried in the family graveyard a short distance from his home.

Birth and death dates on BVS Death Certificate, Cumberland Co.; biography in *Richmond Times*, 5 Aug. 1893; family information provided by grandnephew, Thomas Preston Cocke, and Oakland's former caretaker, Linda Bryant Smith (both 2002); Cocke correspondence in Tucker Family Papers, UNC (including first quotation in Cocke to Henry St. George Tucker, 9 June 1890), Beverley Family Papers (including second quotation in Cocke to Robert Beverley, 29 Jan. 1919) and Henry Thweatt Owen Papers, both VHS, and Armistead-Cocke Family Papers, W&M; BVS Marriage Register, Rockbridge Co. (1871), Charles City Co. (1878); Compiled Service Records; *Southern Planter* 44 (1883): 94–97, and 46 (1885): 620; *Richmond Dispatch*, 24 June 1892, 24 Aug., 21 Sept. 1893, 24 Aug. 1894, 29, 30 July 1897; *Petersburg Index-Appeal*, 4 Aug. 1893; *JHD*, 1893–1894 sess., 65, and 1897–1898 sess., 70; *People's Party of Virginia: For Lieutenant-Governor, Edmund R. Cocke, of Cumberland* (1897); William DuBose Sheldon, *Populism in the Old Dominion: Virginia Farm Politics, 1885–1900* (1935), with frontispiece por.; Marie K. Frazee, "Oakland" (typescript dated 7 July 1936), in Works Progress Administration, Virginia Historical Inventory, LVA; obituaries in *Richmond Times-Dispatch* and *Richmond News Leader*, both 20 Feb. 1922, and *Confederate Veteran* 30 (June 1922): 226.

JAMES TICE MOORE

COCKE, John Hartwell (25 November 1749–9 February 1791), member of the Convention of 1788, was born in Surry County and was the son of Hartwell Cocke, a prominent planter, and Anne Ruffin Cocke. Little is known of his childhood or education, but as the oldest of nine children he inherited the bulk of the family estate after his father's death in 1772 and managed the interests of his minor siblings. On 28 November 1773 Cocke married Elizabeth Kennon, of Chesterfield County. Of their six daughters and two sons, four daughters and one son lived to adulthood, including John Hartwell Cocke (1780–1866), a well-known agricultural reformer and temperance advocate.

As was customary for gentlemen of local prominence, Cocke throughout the 1770s and 1780s frequently served as executor of neighbors' wills and guardian of orphaned children and also held bonds of considerable sums from various persons. He was elected to the Surry County Committee in 1775 and 1776 and during the Revolutionary War helped supply provisions to the local militia. Commissioned a captain in the militia on 27 June 1775, he was promoted to major on 26 June 1781. Cocke became a colonel on 24 May 1785 and on 31 March 1787 county lieutenant, or commander of the militia, a post he occupied until his death. The bulk of his local service, however, took place on the Surry County Court. Sworn in as a justice of the peace on 24 February 1778, he attended court regularly until late in 1790, just before his death.

In 1777 Surry County voters elected Cocke to a single term in the House of Delegates for the sessions that met from 5 May through 28 June 1777 and from 20 October 1777 through 24 January 1778. Late in December 1777 he was one of several members taken into custody by the House sergeant at arms, escorted to the General Assembly, and fined for nonattendance. Probably because of his late arrival he did not serve on any major standing committees, but the following January he was named to a ten-member committee to apportion the public levy.

On 25 March 1788 Cocke and John Allen (d. 1793) were elected to represent Surry County in the Virginia convention called to consider ratification of the proposed constitution of the United States. Cocke attended all twenty-six sessions of the convention in Richmond, but there is no record that he spoke during the debates. He voted against requiring prior amendments before approving the Constitution and for ratification on 25 June 1788. Two days later he supported an unsuccessful resolution limiting the taxing power of Congress.

After the convention Cocke retained his commissions as justice of the peace and commander of the local militia and resumed the life of a wealthy, prominent planter. By 1791 he owned three major plantations in Buckingham, Fluvanna, and Surry Counties serviced by about 130 slaves, as well as other property in Brunswick and Halifax Counties and 1,100 acres in Bourbon County, in what became the state of Kentucky. John Hartwell Cocke died on 9 February 1791 and was buried at Mount Pleasant, his Surry County estate.

Birth dates of 25 Nov. 1747 and 25 Nov. 1749 and death date on family monument erected by son and grandson at Mount Pleasant, printed in *WMQ*, 1st ser., 15 (1906): 87–88; marriage date and variant birth date of 26 Nov. 1749 in family prayer book, printed in *VMHB* 5 (1897): 76–78; Cocke family Bible records (1688–1861), UVA; *Revolutionary Virginia*, 2:291, 6:58; 7:587; Militia Commission Papers, Office of the Governor, RG 3, LVA; *JHD*, 1777–1778 sess., 91, 106; Kaminski, *Ratification*, 10:1540, 1557, 1565; Hugh Blair Grigsby, *The History of the Virginia Federal Convention of 1788* (1891), 2:381, 382, mistakenly conflates the brothers Hartwell Cocke and John Hartwell Cocke; Surry Co. Will Book, 12:289–291; estate inventory in Cocke Family Papers, UVA.

CHERYL COLLINS

COCKE, John Hartwell (19 September 1780–24 June 1866), planter and reformer, was born in Surry County and was the son of John Hartwell Cocke (1749–1791) and Elizabeth Kennon Cocke. His father, a member of the Convention of 1788, owned three large plantations in as many counties and about 130 slaves. Cocke's parents died when he was ten years old. Between about 1794 and 1800 he attended grammar school and college at William and Mary, where he absorbed the Enlightenment and antislavery ideals then ascendant among the faculty. At age twenty-one Cocke inherited the bulk of his father's estate and on 25 December 1802 married Ann Blaws Barraud, of Norfolk. They lived in Surry County until 1809, when they moved permanently to Bremo, a 3,100-acre Fluvanna County plantation Cocke had inherited. Their three sons included Philip St. George Cocke, an agricultural reformer and Confederate brigadier general, and their three daughters included Ann Blaws Cocke, who married Nathaniel Francis Cabell, a writer of religious and agricultural treatises.

Self-disciplined and industrious, Cocke embraced life as a planter and became one of the South's foremost agricultural innovators. He denounced the exhaustive, wasteful style of cultivation that had stifled eastern Virginia's productivity and advocated scientific farming to reinvigorate the state's economy. On his own land, worth approximately $110,000 in 1823, he experimented with terracing, applying marl and manure to worn-out fields, cultivating silkworms, and developing methods of pest control. Cocke corresponded with other agricultural reformers, including Edmund Ruffin, and on 5 May 1817 chaired the founding meeting of the Agricultural Society of Albemarle. He frequently dispensed agricultural advice at that influential organization's meetings and held office intermittently as first and second vice president. The *American Farmer*, a Baltimore journal established in 1819, published more than ten of Cocke's essays and letters to the editor in its first series. His essays appeared in the *Cultivator* and the *Southern Planter* as well.

Cocke designed a variety of outbuildings for his plantations, noteworthy for their innovative stone and pisé construction, and he contributed significantly to the plans for Bremo's striking stone barn and Palladian mansion, recognized by architectural historians as among the finest plantation structures in the nation. He divided the property into three sections and redesigned and added to two more mansions, Lower Bremo and Bremo Recess. Cocke's participation in the design of such Fluvanna County buildings as the church and temperance hall at Fork Union and the county jail and courthouse extended his architectural legacy beyond his own estate. He became a justice of the peace on 21 September 1810 and a captain in the artillery on 19 January 1810. During the War of 1812 Cocke commanded troops at Camp Carter and Camp Holly, outside Richmond, and became a brigadier general on 7 January 1814, a commission he resigned in January 1829.

Unlike many of his social equals, Cocke considered politics a corrupt and irrational pursuit and after a defeat in 1800 for election to the House of Delegates did not again seek public office, even as a means to implement desired reforms. He did, however, accept appointments from the governor and General Assembly to serve on state boards that shared his interest in modernizing Virginia's society and economy. A lifelong proponent of education who established a school for boys at Bremo, Cocke was appointed in 1816 to the board of the new Central College, predecessor of the University of Virginia. During thirty-five years of service on the board, he was deeply involved in the university's early development, supervised the construction of its campus with Thomas Jefferson, and pushed for an emphasis on Christianity and agricultural education in the curriculum. Cocke also promoted construction of a canal system to decrease the danger and expense of transporting crops to market. The General Assembly elected him on 1 February 1823 to the state Board of Public Works, from which he resigned in 1829, and he served on the board of directors of the James River and Kanawha Company from 1835 until 1841.

The death of Ann Blaws Barraud Cocke on 27 December 1816 led Cocke to embrace evangelical Christianity, which quickly became the guiding principle of his life. He married Louisa

Maxwell Holmes, a Norfolk widow whose brother William Maxwell was later president of Hampden-Sydney College, on 19 July 1821. A devout Presbyterian who aided Bible, missionary, and colonization organizations, she shared in Cocke's spiritual and philanthropic pursuits until her death on 16 May 1843. They had no children. Committed to spreading the influence of Christianity, Cocke became a member of the New York–based American Tract Society before its first annual meeting in 1826 and remained a member until his death. He also joined the Boston-based American Board of Commissioners for Foreign Missions in 1826 and was a longtime vice president of the American Bible Society, headquartered in New York. Through these associations Cocke became familiar with the North and its residents, whose piety and industry he often praised.

In a private letter in 1843, Cocke identified temperance, the eradication of tobacco cultivation in central Virginia, and the colonization of former slaves in Africa as "the three objects nearest my heart in this life." One of the South's most prominent temperance activists, he regularly invoked the will of God in his denunciations of alcohol, which he deemed "the most prolific source of evil on earth" because it diverted men's attention from Christ and led to crime, illness, and the disintegration of families. Cocke opposed the James River and Kanawha Company board's decision in 1838 to provide ardent spirits to its laborers, and he erected a Greek Revival temple over a spring along the canal at Bremo to encourage bargemen to consume water. He also established an antiliquor society for local black residents, including his own slaves. Cocke joined the Virginia Society for the Promotion of Temperance after its founding in 1826, became vice president in 1830, and was elected president in 1834, by which time the organization was known as the Temperance Society of Virginia. In 1834 Cocke also presided at the first Temperance Convention of Virginia, which met in Charlottesville. A member of the American Temperance Society, he became a leader in the national movement when he assumed the presidency of its successor organization, the American Temperance Union, from 1836 to 1843.

In an 1856 letter he condemned the use of intoxicating wine in communion services as a desecration of the sacrament.

With similar zeal, Cocke combated the cultivation and use of tobacco, one of Virginia's agricultural staples. Having inherited several large tobacco plantations, he continued to grow the crop until 1840, when for economic and moral reasons he ceased planting tobacco. He detailed his objections between 1858 and 1860 in a forceful six-part *Southern Planter* article, later issued as a pamphlet, *Tobacco, the Bane of Virginia Husbandry* (1860). Virginia could not prosper, Cocke asserted, as long as planters remained entranced by a crop that exhausted the land and diverted labor and time from the production of food and clothing. Cocke declared that the physical deterioration of people who used tobacco was an affront to God, and he likened self-indulgent addiction to the intoxicating substance to idolatry in that it diverted time and money from Christ's service and prevented the return of His kingdom on earth. Cocke circulated anti-tobacco tracts in southern Virginia and distributed medals to boys who promised never to use the weed.

Cocke hoped that the decline of tobacco cultivation would eliminate planters' reliance on slavery, an institution he criticized for decades. As a college student he resolved to emancipate the slaves he had inherited, but further reflection convinced him that they were morally and intellectually unprepared for independence and that free blacks and whites could never coexist peacefully. Although Cocke considered slavery inconsistent with God's long-term vision for humanity and pronounced the institution a curse to the enslaved, to their masters, and to the nation's economy, he owned and paid taxes on 89 slaves age twelve or older in 1816 and 107 age twelve or older in 1830, and he reported 135 bondsmen in Alabama and Virginia to the census enumerator in 1860. Like Jefferson, he believed that the South must gradually extricate itself from the slave system, but he deplored abolitionism, which he feared would spark social upheaval. Convinced that the removal of free blacks was a crucial component of any emancipation scheme, Cocke became an enthusiastic promoter of the

American Society for Colonizing the Free People of Color of the United States (popularly known as the American Colonization Society), served as a vice president between 1819 and 1866, and also founded a Fluvanna colonization society in 1825. He believed that his slaves possessed immortal souls and natural rights and had been rendered unfit for liberty only by "the debasing influence of their bondage," and he considered it his responsibility to educate, evangelize, and deport them.

At Bremo, Cocke's second wife instructed the slaves in reading and in religious matters during the 1820s. He later hired teachers from the North to conduct a more formal school for the slaves, although his wife resumed her duties when Virginia outlawed the employment of teachers for blacks in 1831. Among the few slaves Cocke deemed qualified for freedom were his stonemason, Peyton Skipwith, and his family, who described their experiences in a series of letters to Cocke after he dispatched them to Liberia in 1833. Cocke's boldest experiment began early in the 1840s, when he purchased an Alabama cotton plantation and sent a contingent of slaves there to learn the skills necessary for success in the African colony. During an 1841 visit to his new property he advised the slaves of his intention to emancipate each one who earned his value through labor, behaved honestly and obediently, renounced alcoholic drinks, and kept the plan a secret. Despite providing for their intellectual and spiritual education, Cocke had identified only fourteen slaves who met his standards for freedom by 1860, when he reported eighty-two slaves to the Alabama census enumerator.

Though Cocke had for decades criticized some of the most salient features of Southern society, he accepted Virginia's secession in 1861 and sympathized with the Confederacy. Deeply disillusioned by his Alabama experiment and convinced that reckless abolitionists had forced the nation into war, he reevaluated his opinion of slavery during the 1860s and concluded that slavery was "of Divine Origin" and that God intended blacks to remain enslaved. A gradual emancipationist who had come of age late in the eighteenth century, Cocke had foreseen the cataclysm slavery was capable of producing, attempted creatively but unsuccessfully to avert it, and believed he had no choice but to defend the slave system just as it finally crumbled. After the Civil War, Cocke applied for a presidential pardon, required because the value of his property exceeded $20,000, and he took the amnesty oath on 1 August 1865. John Hartwell Cocke died on 24 June 1866 and was buried near the remains of his two wives in the family plot at his Bremo Recess plantation in Fluvanna County.

William Cabell Moore, "Gen. John Hartwell Cocke of Bremo, 1780–1866: A Brief Biography and Genealogical Review with a Short History of Old Bremo," *WMQ*, 2d ser., 13 (1933): 143–154; M. Boyd Coyner Jr., "John Hartwell Cocke of Bremo: Agriculture and Slavery in the Ante-Bellum South" (Ph.D. diss., UVA, 1961); Randall M. Miller, ed., *"Dear Master": Letters of a Slave Family* (1978), pors. on 24, 26, 30; birth date and genealogical information, including records from family prayer book, in *VMHB* 5 (1897): 76–78; first marriage in Cocke family Bible records (1688–1861), UVA, and *Norfolk Herald*, 28 Dec. 1802; Norfolk City Marriage Returns (1821); John Hartwell Cocke Papers, UVA (first quotation in Cocke to William Brent Jr., 20 Nov. 1843; third quotation in Cocke Diary [1851–1852], 7 Sept. 1851; fourth quotation in Cocke Diary [1863–1864], 77–78); Cocke letters at Duke, LC, LVA, UVA, VHS, and W&M; Cocke Family Papers (including Louisa Maxwell Holmes Cocke's diaries), UVA; Cocke to Edward C. Delavan, 20 Nov. 1856, in *Letter to General John H. Cocke, of Virginia* (1856), 7–8 (second quotation); agricultural essays and letters to the editor in *American Farmer* 1 (1819–1820): 295–296, 331, 350, ibid. 2 (1820–1821): 92–93, 274–275, ibid. 3 (1821–1822): 157, ibid. 4 (1822–1823): 71–72, 324–325, ibid. 5 (1823–1824): 118, 241–242, ibid. 6 (1824–1825): 71–72, ibid. 7 (1825–1826): 109–110; anti-tobacco essay in *Southern Planter* 18 (1858): 716–719, ibid. 19 (1859): 129–133, 264–266, 482–483, 659–664, ibid. 20 (1860): 22–24; Clement Eaton, *The Mind of the Old South* (1964); Ellen Miyagawa, "John Hartwell Cocke's Architectural Legacy to Fluvanna County," *Bulletin of the Fluvanna County Historical Society* 40 (1985): 3–46; will and estate inventory and sale in Fluvanna Co. Will Book, 10:55–58, 67–70, 158–163; Fluvanna Co. Death Register; death notice and obituary in *Daily Richmond Whig*, 3, 4 July 1866; obituary and funeral sermon in *Religious Herald*, 12 July, 2 Aug. 1866.

JENNIFER R. LOUX

COCKE, Lelia Maria Smith (18 March 1859–5 April 1899), portraitist, was born in Pavilion V at the University of Virginia, where her father, Francis Henry Smith, was a professor of natural philosophy. Her mother, Mary Stuart Harrison Smith, later wrote *Lang Syne, or The Wards of Mount Vernon, a Tale of the Revolutionary Era*

(1889) and edited several collections by Virginia women, including the *Virginia Cookery-Book* (1885) and *From Virginia to Georgia: A Tribute in Song* (1895). Smith was tutored at home as a young girl and early in the 1870s attended the Wesleyan Female Institute, in Staunton. Her parents encouraged her desire to pursue art as a profession, and in September 1875, at age sixteen, she entered the Female Art School of the Cooper Union for the Advancement of Science and Art, in New York City. There in 1877 Smith received a First Grade Certificate in drawing and engraving, the first prize—$30 in gold—for drawing from cast, and also an honorable mention in object drawing. The following year she won the second prize for portrait drawing and graduated with a certificate in drawing. Smith also studied privately with the painter Wyatt Eaton, who introduced her to such colleagues as the sculptor Augustus Saint-Gaudens and who included one of her drawings among the student artwork he sent to a Paris exposition in 1878.

After returning to Charlottesville in the summer of 1878, Smith divided her time between painting and teaching there and continuing art studies in New York. During the winter of 1881–1882 she began studying with the muralist and illustrator Will H. Low. Clay modeling-techniques she learned in the studio of the Brooklyn art teacher Caroline V. Sanborn, a former classmate at Cooper Union, led to exhibition in 1883 of a plaque by Smith at the New York Society of Decorative Art.

In July 1883 Smith left the United States to pursue studies in Berlin, Germany, where her brother was serving as United States vice consul. She worked for several months with the German painter Karl Gussow until illness forced her to stop her lessons. In August 1884 Smith qualified as a copyist at the Königliche Gemäldegalerie, in Dresden, noted for its stringent requirements for and careful supervision of copyists.

Smith returned to Charlottesville in October 1884 and painted on commission for private clients and for the University of Virginia. Her noted works included portraits of the classicist and philologist Basil Lanneau Gildersleeve and of the geologist William Barton Rogers, her father's predecessor at the university. On 17 September 1885 at the University of Virginia she married Lucian Howard Cocke, an attorney and former mayor of Roanoke. Their two daughters and two sons included the attorney and banker Charles Francis Cocke. The family lived in Roanoke, where Lelia Smith Cocke continued to undertake commissions.

Cocke's canvases appeared in several state and national venues after her marriage. Her full-length portrait of John Albert Broadus, commissioned for presentation to Richmond College (later the University of Richmond), was exhibited at the 1888 Virginia Agricultural, Mechanical, and Tobacco Exposition. In 1893 at least two of her works, including portraits of her children, hung in the Virginia Pavilion of the World's Columbian Exposition in Chicago. Two years later the Virginia Room of the Cotton States and International Exposition in Atlanta, Georgia, featured several of her works, including a full-length portrait of her father-in-law, Charles Lewis Cocke, longtime superintendent of Hollins Institute (later Hollins University), which had commissioned the likeness. In 1962 Hollins mounted an exhibition of thirty-nine of Cocke's paintings, sketches, and studies. Her portraits hang in private collections and at Hollins University, the University of Virginia, and the Virginia Baptist Historical Society.

In addition to her professional artistic commitments, Cocke maintained an active civic life in Roanoke. In February 1894 she helped found the Margaret Lynn Lewis Chapter of the National Society Daughters of the American Revolution. The DAR staged a benefit performance of Cocke's four-scene play *A Rose of Albemarle* at the Roanoke Academy of Music in November 1895 to raise funds for rebuilding the Rotunda at the University of Virginia, which had burned the month before.

Cocke once again traveled to New York City late in 1898 in order to learn techniques of painting miniatures. After being ill for several months, Lelia Maria Smith Cocke died at her Roanoke residence on 5 April 1899 and was buried in the Cocke family cemetery at Hollins Institute. In 1903 her widower, who later served as general counsel of the Norfolk and Western Railway Company and as president of the Virginia State Bar

Association, married Sarah Cobb Johnson Hagan, a writer who became the first president of the Woman's Civic Betterment Club in Roanoke.

[Ulysse Desportes, comp.], *An Exhibition of Paintings and Drawings by Lelia Maria Smith Cocke* (1962), including self-por.; Lydia Taylor Pitman, "The Founder of the Margaret Lynn Lewis Chapter of the National Society of the Daughters of the American Revolution" (typescript, 1955), and William B. Bagbey, "Lelia Maria Smith Cocke: Artist from the Lawn" (typescript, ca. 1992), both in *DVB* Files; Albemarle Co. Birth Register; Albemarle Co. Marriage Licenses; Cocke correspondence and commissions in possession of William B. Bagbey (2005), in Hollins University Archives, in Southern Baptist Theological Seminary, Louisville, Ky., and in Papers of the Tucker, Harrison, and Smith Families, UVA; *Roanoke Times*, 23 Nov. 1895; obituaries in *Roanoke Times*, 6, 8 Apr. 1899, *Charlottesville Daily Progress*, 6 Apr. 1899, and *Richmond Dispatch* and *Richmond Times*, both 7 Apr. 1899; editorial tribute in *Roanoke Times*, 7 Apr. 1899; memorial by Sarah Ann Brock Putnam and William Henry Pleasants essay "Mrs. Cocke as an Artist" in Hollins Institute *Spinster* (1899), 23–24, 25–29.

MARY LYNN BAYLISS

COCKE, Martha Louisa (9 October 1855–15 August 1938), president of Hollins College (later Hollins University), was born in Roanoke County and was the daughter of Charles Lewis Cocke and Susanna Virginia Pleasants Cocke. Her father had been superintendent since 1846 of the Valley Union Seminary, which became the Female Seminary at Botetourt Springs in 1852 and in the year of her birth Hollins Institute. Matty Cocke, as she was always known, lived at Hollins for her entire life and received her education there. An older sister was her first tutor, and at age ten she began taking classes in the seminary's preparatory department. In 1866 Cocke entered the collegiate department, from which she earned departmental diplomas in English language and literature, French, history, Latin, mathematics, and natural science. She and one other student received full diplomas in 1874.

After graduating, Cocke, who never married, provided secretarial assistance to her father, and beginning in 1876 she also taught English, French, German, and mathematics. In 1884 she became registrar and school librarian. The years 1899 and 1900 were a turning point for Cocke. Three of her siblings died unexpectedly during that time, including her elder brother Charles Henry Cocke, who was business manager of the

institute and the obvious choice to succeed their father as superintendent. In his will, dated 16 June 1900, Charles Lewis Cocke named Matty Cocke, her brother Lucian Howard Cocke, and two of her nephews as trustees of his estate, including Hollins, which the school trustees had deeded to him earlier that year to cover money they owed him. He left it to his heirs to choose the institute's new president. After her father's death on 4 May 1901, they elected Cocke.

Miss Matty, as she was known on campus, did not fit the image of college president. Born and educated on the campus, she was somewhat insulated from the world and also a modest and retiring person who initially found it difficult to preside over faculty meetings. Not comfortable in public, Cocke made few speeches and seldom attended academic functions. Although she overcame her initial difficulties, she continued to rely heavily on the advice of her brother and nephews in decision-making. After assuming the presidency, Cocke announced that Hollins would continue to operate "upon the same lines of conservative progress that have characterized its history for more than half a century," by which she meant that she would insist on retaining the school's traditional high academic standards.

Cocke was the first woman college president in Virginia, preceding Mary Kendrick Benedict, who became president of Sweet Briar College later that decade. Hollins experienced tremendous growth during Cocke's thirty-two-year tenure, not in the number of students, which averaged about 250 each term (the largest proportion from Virginia but with about two dozen other states represented in 1933), but in faculty and facilities. The faculty and staff increased from about forty (three with doctorates) in 1901 to more than sixty (seven with doctorates) in 1933, and the school erected at least a dozen new buildings and renovated and enlarged others. Artists, musicians, and writers of note visited the campus to enrich the students' educational experience. In 1903 Hollins began awarding the A.B. degree, and in February 1911 the school changed its name to Hollins College, Incorporated. At the end of the 1918–1919 academic year it discontinued the preparatory department, and by the time of Cocke's retirement it had adopted a four-year college curriculum. On 1 August 1932 Cocke transferred ownership of the college to a public board of overseers. At the end of that year the Southern Association of Colleges and Secondary Schools fully accredited Hollins.

Conservative progress required a successful balancing of traditions with the changing social climate. Students took advantage of Cocke's willingness to allow change, and initiatives flourished. A theater and gymnasium ranked low among the administration's priorities, but the students wanted them and helped raise much of the money to erect the necessary new buildings. A student government association began functioning during the 1910–1911 academic year, and a campus newspaper began publishing in 1928. Believing that such organizations divided the campus, the students voted in 1929 to disband sororities. Hollins students named a short-lived literary society for Cocke and in 1930 began a tradition of singing to her every year on her birthday.

Roanoke College awarded Cocke an honorary LL.D. in 1926. Once Hollins became a fully accredited college, she retired in 1933 at age seventy-eight. Martha Louisa Cocke died in her sleep at her residence at Hollins College on 15 August 1938 and was buried in the family cemetery on the campus. In tribute, an alumna wrote, "So closely was she to be identified with the school that as the years went by she was to become for Hollins girls all over the country the living symbol of their Alma Mater and the personal actuality of their ideals for educated womanhood."

Biography in *NCAB*, 29:453–454 (por.); birth date and middle name provided by nephew Charles Francis Cocke on BVS Death Certificate, Roanoke Co.; Charles Lewis Cocke Papers and Matty L. Cocke Papers, both Hollins University Archives; oral history interview, 20 May 1938, Virginia Works Projects Administration Files, UVA; WPA Biographies; Hollins Institute *Annual Register* (1900–1901), 3 (first quotation); Dorothy Scovil Vickery, *Hollins College, 1842–1942: An Historical Sketch* (1942), 43–67; Frances J. Niederer, *Hollins College: An Illustrated History*, 2d ed. (1985), 56–62 (several pors.); obituaries in *Richmond News Leader*, *Richmond Times-Dispatch*, *Roanoke Times*, and *Roanoke World-News*, all 16 Aug. 1938; editorial tributes in *Richmond News Leader* and *Roanoke World-News*, both 16 Aug. 1938, and *Richmond Times-Dispatch* and *Roanoke Times*, both 17 Aug. 1938; memorials in *Hollins Alumnae Quarterly* 13 (fall 1938): 4–14 (second quotation on 4), 18.

BETH S. HARRIS

COCKE, Philip St. George (17 April 1809–26 December 1861), planter and Confederate army officer, was born in Surry County and was the son of John Hartwell Cocke (1780–1866), a planter and reformer, and his first wife, Ann Blaws Barraud Cocke, who died in December 1816. He attended the University of Virginia for the 1825, 1827, and 1827–1828 sessions before entering the United States Military Academy on 1 July 1828. After graduating sixth in a class of forty-five in 1832, Cocke served as a second lieutenant of artillery in the United States Army and was stationed at Charleston, South Carolina, during the Nullification Crisis. On 1 April 1834 he resigned his commission, and on 4 June of that year in Surry County he married Sally Elizabeth Courtney Bowdoin. They had seven daughters and four sons.

Cocke inherited and acquired great wealth, including extensive agricultural holdings in Virginia and Mississippi. He bought several properties in Powhatan County, including Belmead, where he built a mansion overlooking the James River to serve as his family home. By 1860 Cocke owned more than 27,000 acres of land and more than 610 slaves in the two states and reckoned his net worth at more than $1,000,000. His widely scattered plantations required management through overseers, and he compiled detailed manuals for directing the work. Cocke gained renown as a leading advocate of agricultural interests. He built an extensive library of more than 600 titles, including a wide array of volumes on agriculture and plantation management. As president of the Virginia State Agricultural Society from 1853 to 1856, he promoted the cause of agricultural education. Attempting to establish a program of agricultural studies at the University of Virginia, Cocke pledged $20,000 in bonds to help endow a professorship. After that plan failed, he proposed developing a school of agriculture at the Virginia Military Institute. Cocke served on VMI's board from 1846 to 1852 (from June 1851 through June 1852 as president) and from 1858 until his death, again as board president. His second plan for agricultural education died during the Civil War.

Cocke was enamored of Gothic architecture and sponsored the New York architect Alexander

Jackson Davis, who worked in that style. Under Cocke's patronage, Davis designed Belmead and Emmanuel Episcopal Church in Powhatan County, where Cocke and members of his family worshiped, as well as Gothic Revival structures for the Virginia Military Institute. Cocke also engaged Davis to prepare a Greek Revival design for the Powhatan County courthouse.

In response to John Brown's raid on Harpers Ferry, Cocke organized a Powhatan cavalry troop that drilled in 1860. In April of the following year he became a brigadier general of volunteers and was ordered to Alexandria, where he initially commanded the defenses in northern Virginia. He issued a call to arms to the men of central Virginia. A few weeks later, when the volunteers were folded into the Confederate army, Cocke was commissioned a colonel, a reduction in rank that deeply offended him. In a flurry of letters he complained bitterly about what he regarded as shameful treatment. Cocke commanded the 5th Brigade at the First Battle of Manassas (Bull Run) in July 1861, but he felt insulted afterward when he believed that General Pierre Gustave Toutant Beauregard insufficiently praised his achievements.

Cocke possessed a strong impulse to public service and an equally strong sense of self-importance and high opinion of his own abilities as a military commander. Proud and temperamental, he was easily affronted and quick to perceive malice in others' treatment of him. In October 1861 Cocke was promoted to brigadier general but too late to salve his wounded pride. His manner became distracted, and one colleague feared he was no longer of sound mind. On 26 December 1861, in a state of despondency and mental anguish over what he regarded as poor treatment by General Robert Edward Lee and others, Philip St. George Cocke committed suicide at Belmead by shooting himself in the head with a pistol. He was buried on his estate, but in 1904 his remains were reinterred in Hollywood Cemetery, in Richmond.

Biographies in Charles W. Turner, *Virginia's Green Revolution (Essays on the Nineteenth Century Virginia Agricultural Reform and Fairs)* (1986), 37–55 (por. facing 54), and Albert K. Cocke and A. Robert Kuhlthau, "VMI's Forgotten Benefactor: Philip St. George Cocke," *VMI Alumni Review* 68 (spring 1992): 13–17 (por. on 13); birth, marriage, and death dates in Cocke family Bible records (1688–1861), UVA; Surry Co. Marriage Register (bond dated 3 June 1834); *Norfolk American Beacon and Virginia and North Carolina Gazette*, and *Richmond Enquirer*, both 10 June 1834; Cocke Family Papers, UVA; Philip St. George Cocke Papers, VHS (including Beldale and Belmead plantation records) and Florida State University, Tallahassee; Cocke correspondence in Superintendent's Records, VMI; major publications include *Address of Philip St. Geo. Cocke at the Third Annual Meeting of the Virginia State Agricultural Society* (ca. 1855), *Report of the President of the Virginia State Agricultural Society* (1856), and "Agricultural Associations and Universities," *De Bow's Review* 22 (1857): 495–505; Compiled Service Records; *OR*, 1st ser., 2:477, 500, 776–777, 785, 804–805, 823, 824, 828, 832, 836–837, 845–847, 51:24–32; *Catalogue Auction Sale of Valuable Miscellaneous Books, the Library of General Philip St. George Cocke, . . . Embracing Rare Historical, Agricultural, Military, and Other Miscellaneous Volumes* (1892); Royster Lyle Jr. and Pamela Hemenway Simpson, *The Architecture of Historic Lexington* (1977), 210–223, 234, 240; Richard T. Couture, *Powhatan: A Bicentennial History* (1980), 240–257, 266–267, 278–283; copies of will in VHS and Powhatan Co. Will Book, 15:557–563; BVS Death Register, Powhatan Co.; obituaries in *Daily Richmond Enquirer* and *Daily Richmond Whig*, both 28 Dec. 1861.

KENNETH E. KOONS

COCKE, Richard Ivanhoe (13 August 1820–30 August 1873), member of the Convention of 1850–1851, was born at Clover Pasture, the Powhatan County estate of his parents, Ann Waller Ronald Cocke and John Feild Cocke. His father commanded a Powhatan cavalry company during the War of 1812 and inspired the character "Captain Macon" in Marion Harland's novel *Judith: A Chronicle of Old Virginia* (1883). One of his parents must have had a literary bent; to match his storybook name, he had a younger sister named Rowena. Cocke attended the University of Virginia for the 1836–1837 session and studied law and senior politics at the College of William and Mary during the 1838–1839 school year. Like his father an ardent Whig, Cocke displayed a flair for oratory, and two of his addresses before literary societies at William and Mary appeared in pamphlet form. On 4 May 1848 he married Frances Allan Ellis, daughter of a deceased Richmond merchant. They had two sons and after the death of his sister in March 1861 also raised his two orphaned nieces. Cocke's marriage tied him to several influential brothers-in-law, including Charles Ellis, president of the Richmond and Petersburg Railroad Company during the Civil War and Reconstruction, George Wythe Munford, longtime clerk of the House of Delegates and secretary of the commonwealth, and Nathaniel Beverley Tucker (1820–1890), United States consul in Liverpool and Confederate diplomatic agent to Canada.

In May 1842 Cocke was admitted to practice law in Fluvanna County, and in October 1849 he defeated an opponent by a margin of more than two to one to become commonwealth's attorney for the county. At mid-century he owned four adult slaves, probably domestic servants. On 22 August 1850 Cocke, finishing third in a ten-candidate field, won election as one of three delegates representing the counties of Fluvanna, Goochland, and Louisa in a state convention that met from 14 October 1850 until 1 August 1851 to revise Virginia's constitution. Appointed to the Committee on the Judiciary, he spoke occasionally on routine procedural matters and to clarify actions taken by the General Assembly then also in session. Cocke had been elected on a radical ticket and therefore presumably favored such reforms as extension of white male suffrage rights regardless of property holding, reapportionment of representation in the General Assembly, and popular election of most state officials. Like his two Democratic colleagues from his district, however, he voted on 16 May 1851 against a key compromise on reapportionment of the state legislature that shifted the balance of power away from slaveholding easterners and on 31 July against the final version of the constitution, which won ratification later that year.

Simultaneously with his service in the Convention of 1850–1851, Cocke represented Fluvanna County in the House of Delegates in the session that met from 2 December 1850 until 31 March 1851. He served on the Committee for Courts of Justice. Returning to Fluvanna County and his law practice, Cocke won reelection as commonwealth's attorney in July 1852. Increasingly, however, he spent his time farming at his Powhatan County birthplace, and by April 1856 he had moved back there after three incidents of suspected arson in a four-month period destroyed his Fluvanna property. Though no longer a county resident, Cocke defeated an opponent to

win election in June 1856 as commonwealth's attorney of Fluvanna. Chosen by the voters again in June 1860, he took the requisite constitutional and antidueling oaths but resigned immediately.

After Virginia seceded from the Union in the spring of 1861, Cocke, with Willis Jefferson Dance, recruited for Confederate service a company of artillery, later designated Captain Dance's Company (Powhatan Artillery). Elected a lieutenant, Cocke accepted a commission for one year on 16 July 1861, but the next month he was absent on furlough for unspecified reasons, and by 31 October of that year he had resigned.

By the will of Cocke's father, in 1856 Cocke's wife inherited a tract of land on the Ohio River in Ballard County, Kentucky, opposite the busy port of Cairo, Illinois. Before the Civil War, Cocke and one of his brothers-in-law licensed timber removal and a steam ferry there and began planning to transform the property into a transportation hub by attracting an extension of the Mobile and Ohio Railroad Company. In the postwar years they still hoped, according to another brother-in-law, to found a great city and become millionaires, and they continued to lobby two other Illinois railways to extend a rail line onto their land. Early in 1871 Cocke moved his family to Ballard County, Kentucky, so that he could better oversee his commercial interests. Malaria in the muggy river bottoms undermined his health, and Richard Ivanhoe Cocke moved to Blandville, in Ballard County, Kentucky, where he died on 30 August 1873.

French Biographies; Virginia Webb Cocke, *Cockes and Cousins*, vol. 2: *Descendants of Thomas Cocke (c. 1639–1697)* (1974), 51, 93, with birth date, citing family Bible records; Richmond City Marriage Bonds (bond dated 3 May 1848); Cocke correspondence in Ellis Family Papers and Powhatan Ellis Papers, VHS; Cocke, *An Oration Delivered before the Franklinian Society of William and Mary College: On the 17th of January, 1839* (1839), and *An Address Delivered before the Licivyronean Society of William and Mary College, 15th May 1847 . . .* (1847); *Richmond Whig and Public Advertiser*, 12 May 1848, 27, 30 Aug. 1850; *Richmond Enquirer*, 27 Aug., 3, 6 Sept. 1850; *Journal of 1850–1851 Convention*, 419, and Appendix, 22; Cocke broadside "To the Voters of Fluvanna," 25 Apr. 1856, VHS; Compiled Service Records; Powhatan Artillery Muster Roll, p. 421, in Record, Powhatan Troop (1861–1865), Powhatan Co. Records; variant death date of 20 Aug. 1873 and variant place of Wickliffe, Ky., in M. Juliette Magee, *Vital Statistics: Never before Published Records of Far Western*

Kentucky (1977), 30; obituary and editorial tribute in *Richmond Daily Whig*, 8 Sept. 1873, with death date of 30 Aug. 1873 and death place of Blandville, Ballard Co., Ky.

SARA B. BEARSS

COCKE, Sarah Cobb Johnson Hagan (7 February 1865–20 January 1944), civic leader, was born in Selma, Alabama. Her father, John Milton Johnson, was a physician from Kentucky who served as a post surgeon with the Confederate army, and her mother, Mary Willis Cobb Erwin Johnson, was a sister of Howell Cobb, a former Speaker of the House of Representatives, secretary of the treasury, and Confederate major general. It was the second marriage for both, and the family settled in Atlanta, Georgia, after the Civil War. Sarah Johnson received her primary education in a schoolroom set up by her mother in their home. Because Johnson's father was in his fifties when she was born, she maintained he treated her more as a granddaughter than as a daughter and encouraged her in all pursuits, even those not typical for a girl at the time. In the autumn of 1879 Johnson went to Washington, D.C., to attend Waverly Seminary. She graduated from Lucy Cobb Institute, in Athens, Georgia, in 1883.

While visiting New York City, Johnson met Hugh Hagan, a medical student from Richmond, Virginia. They married on 26 October 1887 and lived in New York while Hagan continued his studies. In the spring of 1889 they moved to Vienna, Austria, where for about a year he studied neurology with leading physicians. After returning to the United States, they settled in Atlanta, where Sarah Hagan raised their two sons and became involved in local civic activities. Her cousin founded the Atlanta chapter of the National Society Daughters of the American Revolution, and in February 1892 Hagan attended the DAR's first national conference in Washington, D.C. After delivering a well-received speech to the other delegates, she was elected a vice president general. In 1895 she chaired the Ways and Means Committee of the Board of Women Managers who organized the Cotton States and International Exposition in Atlanta. In the autumn of that year Hagan was elected treasurer of the new Atlanta Woman's Club, although she soon resigned. She was enjoying her success as a public figure when her husband suffered a stroke and died on 22 March 1898. Her mother died the following year, and Hagan felt that her life was drifting. At the suggestion of friends she turned to writing short stories based on tales told by her childhood African American nurse, one of which, "Phillis Tells about Her Visit to Michigan," was published in the December 1902 issue of *Century Magazine*.

In 1903 a friend invited Hagan and her sons to the Homestead in Hot Springs, Virginia. During their stay Hagan met Lucian Howard Cocke, a former mayor of Roanoke who later served as general attorney for the Norfolk and Western Railway Company and as president of the Virginia State Bar Association. They married on 30 October 1903. They had no children, but they raised her two sons and his two sons and two daughters from his first marriage to Lelia Maria Smith Cocke, a portraitist who had died in 1899. Moving to Roanoke, Sarah Cocke was surprised to discover a frontierlike railroad center where expansion had outpaced civic improvements. Violence, drunkenness, and prostitution marred the crowded downtown. Poor sanitation resulted in many deaths from cholera, dysentery, malaria, tuberculosis, and typhoid fever. Attracted by the railroad boom, rail officials and other prominent business professionals from major urban areas moved to Roanoke. Their wives, many accustomed to the luxury of larger cities and unhappy with their husbands' apathy and with city officials' negligence, resolved to improve conditions in Roanoke.

With the assistance of Willie Brown Walker Caldwell, among others, Cocke established the Woman's Civic Betterment Club, chaired its organizational meeting on 7 December 1906, and was elected its first president. The organization promoted health and cleanliness in the city and began petitioning Roanoke's board of aldermen on such issues as acquiring land for public parks. As one of her first acts Cocke organized a two-week fall festival to raise money for beautification and revitalization efforts. The festival brought in $5,000 to pay for a sanitation study of Roanoke and a development and remodeling plan by John Nolen, a landscape architect from Massachusetts. Although city officials did not implement Nolen's comprehensive plan, the club's efforts improved the city in many other ways. A boycott of unprotected meat and produce sold at the city market impelled farmers to store and package their foods correctly. The women also raised money for construction of two schools, one for black and one for white children, and for the creation of playgrounds and parks. They pressed for the installation of sanitary drinking fountains, lobbied for more and better paved streets, offered cash prizes for the most improved yards, organized a parent-teacher association, and worked to establish a juvenile court. Largely as a result of Cocke's efforts, Roanoke created a department of public health.

Cocke was active in other organizations as well. She chaired the Roanoke chapter of the Society of the Colonial Dames in the State of Virginia (later the National Society of the Colonial Dames of America in the Commonwealth of Virginia) and at the organizational meeting of the Virginia Federation of Women's Clubs in 1907 was elected second vice president. Cocke favored woman's suffrage with educational and property qualifications. Beginning in the mid-1920s she served on the city planning commission.

After her second marriage, several of Cocke's friends encouraged her to pursue her writing hobby more seriously, and in 1911 E. P. Dutton and Company published a series of her short stories in a collection entitled *Bypaths in Dixie: Folk Tales of the South*, which was reissued in 1926 as *Old Mammy Tales from Dixie Land*. Her stories, inspired by real people and events in her life and written in stereotyped black and "cracker" dialects, continued to appear in such periodicals as the *Saturday Evening Post*. After spending time with a cousin in northern Georgia, Cocke wrote *The Master of the Hills: A Tale of the Georgia Mountains* (1917), based on the moonshiners she met there. The success of her stories led to speaking engagements at various institutions, including Columbia University. Between 1929 and 1933 she wrote her memoirs, which were adapted and published in 2002 under the title *A Woman of Distinction: From Hoopskirts to Airplanes, a Remembrance*.

Sarah Cobb Johnson Hagan Cocke died at her home in Roanoke on 20 January 1944 and was buried in the Cocke family cemetery at Hollins College (later Hollins University).

Family and personal information in J. Hayden Hollingsworth, ed., *A Woman of Distinction: From Hoopskirts to Airplanes, a Remembrance* (2002); biographies in Bruce, Tyler, and Morton, *History of Virginia*, 5:508 (por. between 508 and 509), and Margaret Wootten Collier, *Biographies of Representative Women of the South, 1861–1929* (1929), 5:147–151; *Roanoke Times*, 8, 13 Dec. 1906, 9 Nov. 1907, 20 May 1937 (por.); writings include 1908 speech to the Woman's Civic Betterment Club and MS memoir "From Hoopskirts to Airplanes" (copy), both Roanoke City Public Library, "The Woman's Civic Betterment Club of Roanoke," *Virginia Realtor* 1 (Sept. 1926): 35–36, and "History of the Woman's Club of Roanoke," *Virginia Club Woman* 1 (Mar./Apr. 1929): 3–4; obituaries in *Roanoke World-News*, 21 Jan. 1944, and *Roanoke Times*, 22 Jan. 1944.

KELLEY M. EWING

COCKE, William (1672–22 October 1720), secretary of the colony and member of the Council, was born in Sudbury, Suffolk County, England, and probably was the son of William Cocke and Susan Cocke, whose maiden name is not known. He attended Felsted School near London and in March 1688 entered Queens' College, University of Cambridge, from which he received a medical degree in 1693. Before November 1700 he married Elizabeth Catesby, also of Sudbury, without her father's consent. They had two sons and at least three daughters.

In the spring of 1710 Cocke traveled to Virginia as personal physician to Lieutenant Governor Alexander Spotswood. They arrived in June of that year, and within a few days Cocke chanced to meet William Byrd (1674–1744), with whom he had attended Felsted School. Byrd's diaries record that Cocke was a frequent visitor at Westover and that Byrd regularly met Cocke in Williamsburg. Conflicting political loyalties during the tumultuous early years of Spotswood's administration might have strained their friendship, but they evidently remained on good terms until Cocke died. Cocke resided in or near Williamsburg, perhaps as a member of Spotswood's household, until his wife, two of their children, and his wife's younger brother, the naturalist Mark Catesby, arrived in April 1712. Cocke purchased eight lots and a house in the capital, and Catesby lived with them for about seven years while beginning his botanical and zoological collecting trips in Virginia and the West Indies.

Perhaps one of the few university-trained doctors in Virginia, Cocke practiced medicine with some success. Without any known administrative or political experience, he also moved rapidly into the upper ranks of Virginia officialdom. In April 1711 Spotswood unsuccessfully tried to arrange his election to the board of visitors of the College of William and Mary, but the following year he engineered a deal whereby Cocke replaced Edmund Jenings (d. 1727), who was temporarily returning to England, as secretary of the colony. Cocke took the oaths of office at the Capitol in Williamsburg on 10 June 1712. On the recommendation of Spotswood and Governor George Hamilton, earl of Orkney, the Privy Council in August 1713 approved Cocke's appointment to a vacant seat on the governor's Council. Cocke was one of three Council members who in November 1714 with members of the House of Burgesses drafted the colony's address to George I congratulating him on assuming the throne. Spotswood appointed Cocke county lieutenant, or commander of the militia, of Elizabeth City and Warwick Counties in 1715.

Except when he was in England from the summer of 1716 to the spring of 1718, Cocke regularly attended meetings of the Council, which was also the upper house of the General Assembly and the General Court, the colony's highest court, which met twice a year. Few records exist to characterize what effect he had on the secretary's office, but in 1716 Spotswood reported that Cocke "applyed himself to the reforming sundry abuses" in the office. Because Cocke continued to practice medicine both in and out of Williamsburg, it is possible that he left the day-to-day business of issuing writs, managing land office records, and commissioning county clerks to a skilled deputy, who collected and kept a portion of the many lucrative fees to which the secretary was entitled.

Whether Cocke's two-year absence from Virginia was occasioned by personal or official business in England is not known, but Spotswood provided him with a letter of introduction praising his dedication and skill and employed him to deliver official documents to the Board of Trade and to explain the need for a new colonial seal. At that time, Spotswood and most members of the Council were at loggerheads over proposed changes in the collection of quitrents and whether the lieutenant governor could appoint anyone other than a Council member to the semiannual courts of oyer and terminer. On 15 November 1717 both Byrd, an opponent of Spotswood, and Cocke, who remained loyal to the lieutenant governor, appeared before the Board of Trade, which was considering the complaints that Council members and Spotswood had filed against one another. While in London, Cocke was authorized to oversee the printing of a new compilation of Virginia statutes in force and also advised the Board of Trade that a Virginia law concerning debts and another preventing the assembly of Quakers were both contrary to the laws of England. He warned that the latter might banish "numbers of Industrious Inhabitants" from Virginia.

Cocke and his family appear to have lived comfortably in Virginia. In addition to his town lots, house, and other buildings in Williamsburg, he owned forty acres of land in James City County and with several partners patented tracts of 6,000 and 4,000 acres in Essex County. He entertained friends, regularly engaged in games of chance, owned a coach, had servants, and may have owned slaves. Cocke never came close to the imprisonment for debt that his skeptical father-in-law had predicted at the time of his marriage, but there is evidence that he lived beyond his means. His medical practice brought in a respectable £200 annually and the secretary's office even more, although he had to share that income with Jenings and had to pay his deputies. Cocke was noted for his generosity to friends and his reluctance to accept payment from them for his medical services. He eventually mortgaged his Williamsburg home and his land in James City County, which were sold to satisfy the debt they secured. After his death, his widow was left with few resources, and she was forced to come to an arrangement with her eldest son and married daughter to provide for the other children.

On 22 October 1720 while attending a session of the General Court, William Cocke "was struck with a fit of an apoplexy and died immediately," collapsing onto William Byrd. The lieutenant governor, Council members, and other dignitaries attended Cocke's funeral two days later. He was buried under the floor near the altar in Bruton Parish Church, in Williamsburg. In 1724 Cocke's widow married John Holloway, Speaker of the House of Burgesses. About thirty years later, Cocke's son ordered for the church an inscribed tablet that recorded Cocke's birth, public services, and death.

Birth year from memorial stone, transcribed in *Bruton Parish Churchyard and Church: A Guide to the Tombstones, Monuments, and Mural Tablets* (1976), 87; family history in L. H. Jones, *Captain Roger Jones, of London and Virginia* (1891), 117–143, and George Frederick Frick and Raymond Phineas Stearns, *Mark Catesby: The Colonial Audubon* (1961), 4, 11–16, 92–93; John Venn and J. A. Venn, eds., *Alumni Cantabrigienses* (1922), 1:362; Cocke letters in PRO CO 5/1318, fols. 118–119 (second quotation on 118), and CO 5/1337, fols. 50–51; Junius Rodes Fishburne Jr., "The Office of Secretary of State in Colonial Virginia" (Ph.D. diss., Tulane University, 1971), 333–346; numerous references in *Executive Journals of Council*, vol. 3 (taking office as secretary on 317 and as Council member on 350), in R. A. Brock, ed., *The Official Letters of Alexander Spotswood* (1882–1885), including first quotation on 2:163, and in Louis B. Wright and Marion Tinling, eds., *The Secret Diary of William Byrd of Westover, 1709–1712* (1941), including first arrival in Virginia on 194, and *William Byrd of Virginia: The London Diary (1717–1721) and Other Writings* (1958), including third quotation and date of death on 465; some estate and family records in Roger Jones Family Papers (1649–1896), LC.

LINDA H. ROWE

COCKE, William Horner (12 September 1874–9 June 1938), superintendent of the Virginia Military Institute, was born in Prince George County and was the son of Henry Teller Cocke, a merchant, and Elizabeth Welsh Horner Cocke. After his father died in 1888, his mother moved the family to Augusta County. Cocke graduated from a Staunton high school in 1890 and entered the Virginia Military Institute that autumn. During his four years at VMI he excelled in the demanding military and academic environment. In 1894 he graduated first in his class of thirty with a B.S. in civil engineering and was awarded a Jackson-Hope Medal for academic achievement.

Immediately after graduating Cocke became commandant and mathematics teacher at a military school in Boonville, Missouri. After three years he resigned to enter the Washington University Law School, in Saint Louis. Just short of completing his law studies, Cocke volunteered at the outbreak of the Spanish-American War for service with the 4th Missouri Infantry, United States Volunteers. He was commissioned a first lieutenant and served as a battalion adjutant. Cocke returned to civilian life early in 1899, was admitted to the Missouri bar, and entered a partnership in Saint Louis. On 20 December 1905 he married Anne Jeanette Owen, a native of Saint Joseph, Missouri. They had no children. Cocke joined the Sterling Price Camp Number 145 of the Sons of Confederate Veterans and in 1910 served as camp commander.

In 1906 Cocke left his law practice. He established and in January 1908 incorporated in Illinois the Commercial Acid Company, which manufactured sulfuric, muriatic, and nitric acid and various other chlorides and sulfates. By 1916 the company's two plants in Arkansas and Illinois and its sulfur mill in Texas produced net sales of more than $2.9 million a year. Cocke sold his main East Saint Louis plant to the Monsanto Chemical Works in 1918 for a half-million-dollar profit but stayed on as president of the renamed Southern Acid and Sulphur Company.

Having maintained his commission in the Missouri National Guard after the Spanish-American War, Cocke again volunteered beginning in August 1917 for active military service during World War I. Commissioned a major of infantry, he served as adjutant of the 69th Infantry Brigade, 35th Division. He was stationed in Europe from May 1918 to March 1919, during which time his division fought in the Saint Mihiel and Meuse-Argonne offensives. While in Langres, France, Cocke completed the course at the Army General Staff College. By then a wealthy man, he directed that his army salary be donated to the American Red Cross for the entire time he was on active duty. He returned to Saint Louis after the war.

In April 1924 Cocke's alma mater, Virginia Military Institute, recruited him to become its fourth superintendent. Appointed to the post on 31 July, he formally took office on 1 October.

Along with leadership of the school, Cocke assumed the state rank of brigadier general. During his five-year administration he inaugurated a number of far-reaching reforms and policies. Determined to end the notorious hazing of new cadets, Cocke established a zero-tolerance policy that caused the senior class to boycott courses and petition for his resignation. As a result of his efforts, the General Assembly in 1928 made hazing a crime. Cocke encouraged, and in a number of instances personally funded, faculty members' pursuit of advanced degrees. He secured admission of VMI into the Association of Colleges and Secondary Schools of the Southern States.

In December 1927 the *Report of the Commission to Survey the Educational System of Virginia* (popularly known as the Barton Report) recommended that Virginia sever VMI from the state education system or convert it to vocational training because the school's citizen-soldier model was obsolete. Cocke responded with a fourteen-page report, *The Virginia Military Institute and Higher Education in Virginia* (1928), which highlighted the merits of the institution and its contribution to the state, and he led a successful effort to convince legislators to reject the Barton Report's findings. Cocke took particular interest in the VMI physical plant and donated most of the funds to build a gymnasium that bears his name. In 1928 his wife donated the adjacent Memorial Garden.

Failing health forced Cocke's resignation in March 1929, to be effective on 30 June. Within six months he had been appointed to the VMI board of visitors, on which he served until 1935. After leaving VMI Cocke and his wife retired to Claremont Manor, their newly purchased home in Surry County. Cocke remained active in the Democratic Party, was an aide to Governor John Garland Pollard, and in 1931 was president of the Virginia division of the Association against the Prohibition Amendment. He also served on the board of the Virginia Museum of Fine Arts. In 1929 Washington and Lee University awarded him an honorary LL.D. After a long illness William Horner Cocke died of heart disease at a Richmond hospital on 9 June 1938. He was buried in the cemetery at Saint John's Episcopal Church, in Hopewell. Attilio Piccirilli's statue *Spirit of Youth* (1939) in the Memorial Garden at VMI honors him.

Biographies in *NCAB*, 27:451–452 (por.), *The V.M.I. Alumni News* 1 (May 1924): 2, William Couper, *One Hundred Years at VMI* (1939), 4:302–304, Henry A. Wise, *Drawing Out the Man: The VMI Story* (1978), 116–119 (por. on 117), 129–130, 479, James M. Morgan, *The Jackson-Hope and the Society of the Cincinnati Medals of the Virginia Military Institute: Biographical Sketches of All Recipients, 1877–1977* (1979), 66–67, Eve S. Gregory, *Claremont Manor: A History* (1990), 83–85, and *The 1995 Register of Former Cadets of the Virginia Military Institute* (1995), xxi, 86; biographical information, letters, and newspaper clippings in William H. Cocke personal file, VMI Archives; BVS Birth Register, Prince George Co.; *Richmond Times-Dispatch*, 9 Apr. 1924, 14 Mar. 1929; *Lexington Gazette*, 23 Apr. 1924, 12, 19 Mar. 1929; BVS Death Certificate, Richmond City; obituaries and editorial tributes in *Richmond News Leader*, 10, 22 June 1938, *Richmond Times-Dispatch*, 10, 11 June 1938, and *Lexington Gazette*, 17 June 1938.

KEITH ERIC GIBSON

COFFMAN, Samuel (20 August 1781–26 November 1841), member of the Convention of 1829–1830, was born in Rockingham County and was the son of David Coffman and Anna Lionberger Coffman. Little is known about his early life, and he appears to have had limited formal education. On 22 June 1807 he married Margaret Gore. Their six daughters and five sons included Samuel Augustus Coffman, who served in the secession convention. Their daughter Maria Coffman married Green Berry Samuels, a member of the House of Representatives and judge of the Virginia Supreme Court of Appeals. By 1810 Coffman had established himself as a merchant in New Market and began acquiring land and speculating in real estate in Rockingham and Shenandoah Counties. His wife died on 21 March 1832, and on 26 February 1833 Coffman married Mary Moore. They had no children.

In February 1817 the General Assembly named Coffman a trustee of New Market Academy. Seeking to develop a Shenandoah Valley turnpike, he accepted a commission in 1817 to take subscriptions in New Market for funding a turnpike from Winchester to Salem. After this project stalled, Coffman received another commission early in 1828 to take subscriptions for a proposed turnpike from Winchester to Stony Creek, in Shenandoah County. In March 1834 the General Assembly incorporated the Valley Turnpike Company and authorized Coffman to receive subscriptions in New Market. He and one of his sons were among the few individuals holding a large number of shares in the company in 1839, although they liquidated their shares the next year. He consistently opposed the tariff and restrictions on commercial trade.

In May 1829 Coffman polled the second-highest number of votes among nine candidates vying for four seats representing Rockingham and Shenandoah Counties in a convention called to revise the state constitution. He sat on the Committee on the Executive Department but said little in the recorded convention proceedings. Coffman, a Democrat, aligned with the majority of the other western delegates and voted to broaden the suffrage for white men, to oppose representation based on slave ownership and to secure a greater representation of western counties in the General Assembly, to support popular election of the governor and local officials, and to abolish the Council of State. His fellow delegate Hugh Blair Grigsby, who befriended Coffman at the convention, described him as a "sober sensible dutchman" and "as sound a republican as ever breathed." Because the convention produced few reforms to satisfy western demands, on 14 January 1830 Coffman voted with the minority against passage of the constitution, which the electorate subsequently ratified.

Coffman's great-grandfather and grandfather were Mennonite ministers, but his own ties to the Mennonites may have been loose. His eldest daughter married in a ceremony performed by a Lutheran minister. Mennonites generally opposed slave ownership, but Coffman owned six slaves in 1830 and twenty slaves a decade later. Coffman's life suggests that participation in the commercial economy of the Valley may have encouraged some Mennonites to forsake their principles for profits. About 1837 he moved from New Market to Mannheim, an old limestone house of German construction possibly built by his father, near Linville Creek in Rockingham County. Samuel Coffman died on 26 November 1841 and was buried in a nearby family plot later incorporated into the cemetery of Lindale Mennonite Church.

Birth and death dates on gravestone; biographies in Charles Fahs Kauffman, comp., *A Genealogy and History of the Kauffman-Coffman Families of North America, 1584 to 1937* (1940), 550–552 (with otherwise undocumented middle initial L., variant birth year of 1784, variant first marriage date of 22 June 1804, and variant second marriage date of 22 Feb. 1833), and Agnes Kline, *Stone Houses on Linville Creek and Their Communities: Rockingham County, Virginia* (1971), 45–46; Gore family Bible records (1765–1864), LVA; Gore-Coffman Family Papers, LVA; Shenandoah Co. Marriage Register (1807); Rockingham Co. Marriage Register (1833); John W. Wayland, *A History of Shenandoah County, Virginia* (1927), 13, 250, 262, 263, 469, 594–595; *Acts of Assembly*, 1816–1817 sess., 137–138, 146–147, 1827–1828 sess., 69, 1833–1834 sess., 171–172; *Richmond Enquirer*, 19 May 1829; *Journal of 1829–1830 Convention*, 21, 296; Bruce, *Rhetoric of Conservatism*, 37; Hugh Blair Grigsby Diary, 86 (entry for 18 Oct. 1829), and Commonplace Book (1829–1830), 35 (quotations), both in Hugh Blair Grigsby Papers, VHS; Catlin, *Convention of 1829–1830* (por.).

KENNETH W. KELLER

COFFMAN, Samuel (2 June 1822–28 August 1894), Mennonite bishop, was born in Greenbrier County and was the son of Christian Coffman, a farmer, and Anna Wenger Coffman. He had no formal education but learned how to read and write English and probably to read German, and he became quite proficient in arithmetic. On a trip to Rockingham County he met Frances Weaver, whom he married on 8 November 1847. They resided near Burketown in Augusta County before moving to Rockingham County. They lived first near Spring Creek in that county, then at Dale Enterprise, and finally on a farm on the west bank of Dry River near Rushville. Of their five sons and six daughters, Mary Alice Coffman married Lewis J. Heatwole, later a Mennonite bishop.

In July 1852 Coffman was ordained a Mennonite minister and on 11 May 1861 was selected bishop of the Middle District of the Virginia Mennonite Conference. On 26 June of the latter year he applied for and received an exemption from military duty with Virginia troops fighting for the Confederacy. Coffman staunchly maintained Mennonite doctrine and counseled young men not to fight on either side in the Civil War. He received threats from Confederate military officials and may have considered taking his family north. He likely traveled alone to Pennsylvania for several weeks in 1862, and later he and his family suffered the devastating effects of Union raiders in the Shenandoah Valley.

Some members of the Virginia Conference opposed both Sunday schools and evangelistic meetings. Coffman was progressive in advocating Mennonite Sunday schools, and later he approved when his son, John Samuel Coffman, became a pioneer evangelist in the Mennonite Church. Coffman either helped to establish or permitted the formation of a mission committee, which allowed laypersons to have a part in proselytizing work. He may also have endorsed publishing a Mennonite Church hymnal. He often rode horseback into the highlands of West Virginia for preaching appointments and was famous for always remembering the names of the people he had met.

An able speaker, Coffman sometimes trembled and wept in the pulpit. Some Mennonites criticized his recruitment of young ministers, but he showed leniency in his administration of the church, which increased in membership during his long tenure as bishop. Coffman carried a heavy burden of responsibilities and in his last years requested assistance by another bishop. After contracting typhoid fever in the summer of 1894, Samuel Coffman died at his home in Rockingham County on 28 August of that year. His funeral attracted a large crowd, and he was buried at the Bank Mennonite Church.

Nellie Coffman, "A Short Biography of Samuel Coffman," *Mennonite Historical Bulletin* 19 (Jan. 1958): 1 (por.), 4, 6, 8; Jonas G. Wenger, Martin D. Wenger, and Joseph H. Wenger, *History of the Descendants of Christian Wenger . . .* (1903), 26, 35–36 (por. facing 56), with birth date and variant marriage date of 11 Nov. 1847; Lewis J. Heatwole, C. H. Brunk, and Christian Good, comps., *A History of the Mennonite Conference of Virginia and Its Work* (1910), with birth date on 4 provided by son-in-law; Rockingham Co. Marriage Register (1791–1852), 222; Coffman letters and other information in Samuel Coffman, L. J. Heatwole, and Samuel M. Burkholder Collections, Eastern Mennonite University Archives, Harrisonburg, and John S. Coffman Collection, Historical Committee and Archives of the Mennonite Church, Goshen, Ind.; numerous references in Harry Anthony Brunk, *History of Mennonites in Virginia* (1959–1972), vol. 1, and in Samuel Horst, *Mennonites in the Confederacy: A Study in Civil War Pacifism* (1967); obituaries in *Rockingham Register*, 31 Aug. 1894, and *Chicago Herald of Truth*, 1 Oct. 1894.
GERALD R. BRUNK

COFFMAN, Samuel Augustus (9 March 1824–8 February 1885), member of the Convention of 1861, was born in Shenandoah County and was the son of Samuel Coffman (1781–1841), a New Market merchant who represented Rockingham and Shenandoah Counties at the Convention of 1829–1830, and his first wife, Margaret Gore Coffman, who died in 1832. His elder sister Maria Coffman married Green Berry Samuels, a member of the House of Representatives and judge of the Virginia Supreme Court of Appeals.

After attending the University of Virginia for the 1844–1845 academic year and then Jefferson Medical College, in Philadelphia, during the next academic year, Coffman returned to Shenandoah County and practiced medicine in Mount Jackson. On 19 October 1847 he married Catharine Ann Bear, of Lexington. They had one daughter and two sons, the elder of whom was paralyzed and unable to care for himself by 1865 and the younger of whom, DeWitt Coffman, retired from the United States Navy as a vice admiral at the end of World War I. Coffman Cove, on Prince of Wales Island, Alaska, and a World War II destroyer-escort vessel were named for him. Samuel A. Coffman's wife died of consumption (probably tuberculosis) on 7 October 1855, and on 19 October 1858, in Lexington, Coffman married her sister, Fannie M. Bear. No children were recorded from his second marriage.

In 1851 Coffman and his four brothers acquired control of Mannheim, their father's Rockingham County farm about seven miles north of Harrisonburg on the west side of Linville Creek. Coffman made substantial changes to the old limestone house while living and practicing medicine there. Eventually he moved into Malmaison, a brick house on the opposite side of the creek from Mannheim. In 1863, after selling his interest in Mannheim, he purchased the Inglewood farm, located two miles northwest of Harrisonburg.

In 1859 Coffman represented John Thomas Harris, an independent candidate for Congress, in at least three debates during the latter's successful campaign in Rockingham and Shenandoah Counties. During the secession crisis, Coffman asked Harris to arrange a meeting for him and several Lexington men with Abraham Lincoln in order to discuss Virginia's position and possible response. They met with the president-elect on 2 or 3 March 1861 at Willard's Hotel, in Washington, D.C.

On 4 February 1861 Coffman polled the most votes in a six-candidate field and won election to one of three seats representing Rockingham County in a state convention called to consider secession. A Harrisonburg newspaper characterized him as a conservative Unionist, although he believed in the right of secession and owned three slaves outright and at least twenty more jointly with family members. He served on the Committee on Compensation of Officers. Although Coffman voted against secession on 4 April 1861, he soon came to believe that secession was the only honorable course to avoid what he called degradation, disgrace, and humiliation, and he was the only delegate from Rockingham County to vote for it on 17 April. He seldom spoke formally during the convention. On 16 April Coffman opposed a proposition calling for a referendum on secession. Ten days later he presented a petition from Rockingham County businessmen asking that banks be authorized to issue notes in denominations of less than $5. On 29 April he opposed the nomination of his friend John T. Harris to represent Virginia in the Confederate Congress because he believed Harris did not reflect the majority views in his district.

After John C. Woodson resigned from the House of Delegates, Coffman polled 393 votes in an unopposed election to fill the vacancy representing Rockingham County. He took his seat on 16 September 1862 and served for the remaining sessions of the General Assembly that concluded on 31 March 1863. Late in May 1863 Coffman won election in a four-candidate race to a four-year term representing Pendleton and Rockingham Counties in the Senate of Virginia. He served on the Committee on Finance and Claims and the Joint Committee on Executive Expenditures, which he chaired for the session that met from December 1864 through March 1865. Because he was a physician, Coffman was exempt from Confederate military service.

During the Civil War, Coffman suffered a substantial loss of property, including a grain-filled barn burned by Union troops. In 1865 he estimated that the value of his estate had declined to $25,000. Stating that he had been "a Union man before the war & resisted disunion until swept away by the Tornado produced by hostilities," Coffman took the amnesty oath on 12 June 1865 and later that month applied for a presidential pardon.

In 1866 Coffman represented the Sixth Congressional District at the Democratic State Convention in Richmond and at the national convention in Philadelphia. He helped organize the federally chartered First National Bank of Harrisonburg in August 1865 and served on the bank's board of directors from that date until June 1870. Coffman, a director of the Manassas Gap Railroad Company in 1862, chaired a meeting in January 1866 of Rockingham County citizens seeking to construct a branch of the Baltimore and Ohio Railroad between Harrisonburg and Salem, and in October 1868 he represented Rockingham County at a commercial convention in Norfolk.

In addition to practicing as a physician after the war, Coffman farmed and with his brother, Michael D. Coffman, and Jason N. Bruffy owned a Harrisonburg mercantile company known as Coffmans and Bruffy. By 1870 the business had failed, leaving Coffman with large debts. He declared bankruptcy and was forced to sell Inglewood to pay his creditors. Samuel Augustus Coffman moved to Belle Grove, a nearby farm, where he died of typhoid fever on 8 February 1885. He was buried in Woodbine Cemetery, in Harrisonburg.

Biographies in John W. Wayland, *A History of Shenandoah County, Virginia* (1927), 595, and Agnes Kline, *Stone Houses on Linville Creek and Their Communities: Rockingham County, Virginia* (1971), 46–47; birth date in Gore family Bible records (1765–1864), LVA; Gore-Coffman Family Papers, LVA; Rockbridge Co. Marriage Bonds (1847); Rockbridge Co. Marriage Licenses (1858); *Lexington Gazette*, 21 Oct. 1847; *Lexington Valley Star*, 28 Oct. 1858; *Harrisonburg Rockingham Register and Advertiser*, 25 Jan., 8 Feb. 1861, 5 Sept. 1862, 8 May 1863, 19 Jan. 1866; *Daily Richmond Examiner*, 5 Apr. 1861; *Staunton Vindicator*, 12 Apr. 1861; Reese and Gaines, *Proceedings of 1861 Convention*, 4:57–58, 144, 497–499, 591; Presidential Pardons (quotation); *E. Coffman &c. v. Charles Moore's Ex'or &c.*, Rockingham Co. Chancery Causes, 1876, Box B76, Acc. 40981, LVA; obituary in *Rockingham Register*, 12 Feb. 1885.

DALE F. HARTER

COHEN, Jacob I. (ca. 1744–9 October 1823), merchant and civic leader, was born in Oberdorf, Bavaria, and was the son of Joshua Cohen and

Peslah Cohen, whose maiden name is unknown. According to family tradition, his middle initial did not stand for anything but simply served to distinguish him from others with the same name. Cohen immigrated to America about 1773. He settled in Lancaster, Pennsylvania, where he received a license to trade with the Indians. Approximately three years later he moved to Charleston, South Carolina. During the American Revolution he joined a unit of Charleston militia popularly known as the Jew Company. His commander noted his courage at the Battle of Beaufort (Port Royal Island) on 3 February 1779. Claims that Cohen was captured and imprisoned on the British ship *Torbay* seem unlikely.

By 1781 Cohen was in Richmond and had formed a partnership with Isaiah Isaacs, a silversmith and fellow veteran. Together the two men, the city's earliest-known Jewish residents, engaged in a wide range of commercial activities. Cohen and Isaacs speculated in land warrants, and in December 1781 Daniel Boone contracted to survey 10,000 acres in Kentucky on their behalf.

In the spring of 1782 Cohen went to Philadelphia in order to acquire goods. There he advanced £50 to his fellow Virginian, James Madison (1751–1836), who was short on funds. Cohen applied to join Philadelphia's Congregation Mikveh Israel in March 1782 and also fell in love with the recently widowed and impoverished Esther Mordecai. She had been born Elizabeth Whitlock in England but had changed her name when she converted to Judaism before marrying Moses Mordecai, with whom she had three sons. Jewish law forbade Cohen, as a descendant of priests, from marrying a convert. Following a stormy internal debate, Mikveh Israel prohibited its *hazzan*, or reader, from conducting the marriage or even mentioning the couple's name within the synagogue. In defiance, the congregation's leading member and two other well-respected members of the Jewish community privately conducted and witnessed the wedding ceremony late in August 1782.

Cohen soon returned to Richmond and continued to prosper operating the highly successful mercantile company of Cohen and Isaacs, often known as "the Jews Store." Its customers included Edmund Randolph, governor of Vir-

ginia, and Carter Braxton, a former member of the Continental Congress. The two entrepreneurs also owned the Bird in Hand, an inn and tavern operated for a time by Cohen's stepson, Jacob Mordecai. Cohen and Isaacs successfully speculated in land and owned several slaves. The business was one of the four largest contributors to a campaign in 1785 to erect public buildings on Shockoe Hill. Cohen and Isaacs amicably dissolved their partnership in 1792, and Cohen continued in business on his own.

Active in Richmond civic life, Cohen won election to the common hall, or city council, in January 1795, and that year he also served on a committee charged with assessing which quarantined ships would be permitted to proceed up the James River to Richmond. In 1801 he became an inspector of the penitentiary. Cohen was a Freemason and served as master of his lodge from 1805 to 1806. He also joined the Silver Greys, a volunteer company that prepared to protect Richmond during the uncertainties following the British seizure of deserters from the American frigate *Chesapeake* in June 1807. As perhaps the wealthiest and most prominent member of Richmond's small Jewish community, Cohen in August 1789 helped found Kahal Kadosh Beth Shalome, Virginia's first synagogue and the sixth Jewish congregation established in the United States. He composed a special prayer for the country recited before the congregation in November 1789 on a national day of thanksgiving that George Washington had proclaimed.

Cohen's wife died on 22 August 1804, and within several years he had returned to Philadelphia, where on 3 November 1807 he married Rachel Jacobs Polack, a widow. He served as *parnas*, or president, of Congregation Mikveh Israel in Philadelphia from 1810 to 1811 and later presided over its Hebrew Society for the Visitation of the Sick and Mutual Assistance. Although he had no children of his own, Cohen was close to his nephews and nieces in Baltimore. Jacob I. Cohen died in Philadelphia on 9 October 1823 and was buried in the Mikveh Israel Cemetery on Spruce Street in Philadelphia. He bequeathed much of his estate to his wife and Baltimore relatives, but he also provided money to friends as well as their widows and children. In his will he directed that five slaves, along with their families, be freed and given $25 each. Cohen also donated considerable sums to Jewish congregations in New York, Philadelphia, and Richmond.

Biographies in Herbert T. Ezekiel and Gaston Lichtenstein, *The History of the Jews of Richmond from 1769 to 1917* (1917), 15–20, Aaron Baroway, "The Cohens of Maryland," *Maryland Historical Magazine* 18 (1923): 359–362 (with birth date of 2 Jan. 1744 from unspecified family records), Harry Simonhoff, *Jewish Notables in America, 1776–1865: Links of an Endless Chain* (1956), 107–111 (por.), and Jonathan D. Sarna, "Jacob I. Cohen and the 350th Anniversary of American Jewish Life," Beth Ahabah Museum and Archives *Generations* 11 (May 2005): 1, 3, 8, 12, 14; age thirty-five in 1782 list of Richmond inhabitants in *Heads of Families at the First Census of the United States . . . ; Records of the State Enumerations: 1782 to 1785, Virginia* (1908), 115; age eighty-six on 7 June 1822 on list dictated to nephew Joshua I. Cohen, printed in Leon Hühner, "Some Additional Notes on the History of the Jews of South Carolina," *Publications of the American Jewish Historical Society* 19 (1910): 153; Myron Berman, *Richmond's Jewry, 1769–1976: Shabbat in Shockoe* (1979), 4–11 (por. on 5); Malcolm H. Stern, comp., *First American Jewish Families: 600 Genealogies, 1654–1988*, 3d ed. (1991), 32, 234; Melvin I. Urofsky, *Commonwealth and Community: The Jewish Experience in Virginia* (1997), 10–12, 14, 22, 24–26, 29, 35; *Calendar of Virginia State Papers*, 4:64, 347, 358, 439, 8:305, 9:328, 548; appointment as penitentiary inspector in American Jewish Historical Society, New York, N.Y. (photocopies in Cohen Family Papers [1794–1840], LVA); other Cohen documents printed in Jacob Rader Marcus, ed., *American Jewry: Documents, Eighteenth Century* (1959), 120–124, 144–148, 441–442; photographic collection at Jacob Rader Marcus Center, American Jewish Archives, Cincinnati, Ohio; Richmond City Hustings Court Wills, Inventories, and Accounts, 8:431–438; obituary in *Richmond Enquirer*, 17 Oct. 1823 (died "in the 80th year of his age," suggesting birth in 1743 or 1744), reprinted in *Norfolk American Commercial Beacon and Norfolk and Portsmouth Daily Advertiser*, 20 Oct. 1823.
JONATHAN D. SARNA

COHEN, Zipporah Michelbacher (13 December 1853–20 August 1944), association and civic leader, was born in Richmond and was the daughter of Maximilian Joseph Michelbacher, the first religious leader of Congregation Beth Ahabah, and his second wife, Miriam Angle Michelbacher. She was educated at her father's synagogue school and at a school for girls, probably in Richmond. On 25 February 1875 she married Samuel Cohen, director of the Cohen Company, a Richmond department store his family had founded. They had three sons before his death on 11 September 1916.

As a child she undoubtedly had assisted her mother in caring for wounded Confederate soldiers in their home, and she continued to follow her mother's example of service to the needy. In 1880 Cohen became the treasurer of the Richmond Eye, Ear, Nose and Throat Infirmary, a clinic for those who could not afford medical care. She served in that office until at least 1917 and possibly until the infirmary closed in the mid-1920s. In January 1902 Cohen joined the board of the newly formed Instructive Visiting Nurses Association, which provided financial support for the Nurses' Settlement, an organization founded by several Richmond nurses to help indigent patients. The IVNA's board consisted of representatives from Richmond's various religious denominations and through area congregations raised money for the settlement's work. Cohen represented the Jewish community on the IVNA board for forty-two years, until her death. She often served as a vice president of the board between 1906 and 1933, was treasurer from 1923 to 1924, and was a longtime member of the executive, financial, and nursing committees.

In addition to her work with the IVNA, Cohen was the longest-serving president of the Ladies' Hebrew Benevolent Association (later Jewish Family Services). Her father founded the Ladies' Chebrah, a beneficial membership organization, in 1849, and by 1890 it had become an entirely charitable organization and changed its name to the Ladies' Hebrew Benevolent Association. It is unclear exactly when Cohen became involved with the LHBA because its early records are incomplete, but in 1903 she served as vice president and in January 1904 was elected president, an office she held until her retirement in 1938. The association primarily helped Jewish immigrants recently arrived in Richmond, and its members provided financial assistance, fuel, medicine, and clothing to needy families. Much of the LHBA's attention focused on victims of tuberculosis, a constant and significant problem in poor immigrant communities. The association made annual contributions to the IVNA for its nurses to care for hundreds of tubercular patients identified by the LHBA's executive committee. During Cohen's presidency, the association began to expand its efforts beyond material relief to offer advice to its clients on ways to improve their situations, and in 1937 the LHBA hired its first professional social worker. Throughout her long tenure Cohen was a tireless advocate for the LHBA. She worked to increase membership, created funds to encourage greater giving, and instituted an annual New Year's appeal for contributions.

In January 1905 Cohen attended a meeting called to organize the Richmond section of the National Council of Jewish Women. The new group named her to its board of directors in February of that year, and she later served on the budget committee from the 1920s to the 1940s. In 1908 she represented the Richmond branch at the National Council's triennial convention. Like its parent organization, the Richmond branch aided recent immigrants and provided religious and vocational education. Cohen chaired the group's immigration committee and supported the Council Neighborhood House, a community center offering entertainment, classes, a library, and a place for boys and girls to gather rather than remaining on the streets.

In addition to her work with charities, Cohen served on the board of Congregation Beth Ahabah from 1930 to 1934 and was first vice president for more than twenty years of what became the Beth Ahabah Sisterhood. She served on the executive committee of the local Red Cross for many years and also chaired Beth Ahabah's Red Cross committee during the First World War. She sat on the board of the Richmond Exchange for Women's Work, was a trustee for the Crippled Children's Hospital, and was active in the Richmond Tuberculosis Association.

"Aunt Zip," as Cohen was known, was greatly admired and respected for her extensive community work, and in 1933 many Richmonders turned out to pay tribute at her eightieth birthday party. The Ladies' Hebrew Benevolent Association created the Zipporah Cohen Fund in her honor and in 1937 sponsored a testimonial luncheon to acknowledge her long service as its president. After her retirement the following year, Zipporah Michelbacher Cohen remained the LHBA's honorary president until her death at her Richmond home on 20 August 1944. She was buried in the city's Hebrew Cemetery.

Biography in Gaston Lichtenstein, "History of the Jews of Richmond: Their Progress and Prospects," *Reform Advocate* (8 Mar. 1913), 20 (por.); birth date recorded in family Bible, reproduced in Beth Ahabah Museum and Archives *Generations* 5 (Apr. 1993): 6; BVS Marriage Register, Richmond City; Instructive Visiting Nurses Association Minute Books (1902–1944) and *Annual Reports* (1903–1923), in IVNA Papers, Tompkins-McCaw; Ladies' Hebrew Benevolent Association *Annual Reports* (1903–1938) and National Council of Jewish Women (Richmond Section) Papers, both in Congregation Beth Ahabah Museum and Archives, Richmond; *Richmond News Leader*, 13 Dec. 1933; *Richmond Times-Dispatch*, 26 Jan. 1937 (por.), 29 Mar. 1940; Herbert T. Ezekiel and Gaston Lichtenstein, *History of the Jews of Richmond from 1769 to 1917* (1917), 210; Peter K. Opper, *"Like a Giant Oak": A History of the Ladies Hebrew Benevolent Association and Jewish Family Services of Richmond, Virginia, 1849–1999* (1999); obituaries in *Richmond News Leader* and *Richmond Times-Dispatch*, both 21 Aug. 1944; editorial tribute in *Richmond Times-Dispatch*, 22 Aug. 1944.

MARIANNE E. JULIENNE

COHN, Naomi Silverman (15 April 1888–20 October 1982), civic leader, was the daughter of Harri Silverman and Sadie Silverman (maiden name unknown), who both emigrated from Poland with their children in 1886 and settled in Bristol, Pennsylvania. Her father found employment as a crockery peddler, and her elder sisters worked in a dry goods store and as yarn spinners in the local mill. She attended school and may have trained to be a teacher. For her first twenty years she gave her name on official documents as Mayme Silverman.

On 30 March 1909 Silverman married the Richmond lawyer Jacob Saul Cohn at her parents' home. The couple lived in Richmond, where Jacob Cohn had practiced law since graduating from the University of Richmond in 1904. They had two daughters and one son, and she later also raised orphaned twin nephews. Despite the demands of her young family, Cohn plunged into a whirl of civic activity. About 1911 she joined the Richmond section of the National Council of Jewish Women, a group that assisted newly arrived immigrants, and later chaired its legislative committee. A charter member of the Richmond League of Women Voters, Cohn served in the 1930s as the organization's treasurer and at various times on the state level as vice president, secretary, and chair of the legislative committee of the Virginia League of Women Voters. Beginning about 1922 she sat on the industrial committee of the Young Women's Christian Association. With fellow suffragist Adèle Goodman Clark, Cohn in 1923 founded the Virginia Women's Council of Legislative Chairmen of State Organizations (later the Virginia Council on State Legislation) to monitor bills of special interest to women and later became treasurer and president. After the Virginia Consumers' League formed in 1936 to work for legislation improving conditions of the state's laborers, she became its executive secretary.

Cohn was an outspoken advocate of women's political involvement and social advocacy. "Women can find time to do other things than raising children and attending bridge parties," she told a *Richmond Times-Dispatch* reporter in 1943. "The mothers are the ones who should be interested in the Legislature, because in this way they can make Virginia a better place for their children." Cohn spent a lifetime exercising the right to vote secured through the Nineteenth Amendment and never tired of encouraging others to do the same.

The "Virginia Honor Roll of 1938," published in the *Richmond Times-Dispatch* on New Year's Day 1939, praised Cohn for her role in the passage of a state law restricting a woman's work week to forty-eight hours. Before enactment of the law, Virginia women could work ten hours a day and as much as seventy hours a week. The new legislation limited women's labor to no more than nine hours a day and forty-eight hours a week in most occupations outside domestic and agricultural work, although legislative special interests secured exemptions for such occupations as bookkeepers, stenographers, and florists and for women stemming tobacco, shelling peanuts, shucking oysters, and canning and packing fruits and vegetables. Earning a reputation as a one-woman lobby, Cohn spent up to thirteen hours each day at the State Capitol as an unpaid advocate, interviewing delegates and senators and depositing reading material in their offices. She once explained to a reporter that her passion for helping working women and children came from witnessing the plight of mill hands in her hometown of Bristol, but she failed to mention that her sisters had also worked in the mills. Cohn's volunteer work in behalf of

working women and children became a paying job in 1939, when she joined the Virginia Department of Labor and Industry's Division of Women and Children as an inspector of factories and mercantile businesses. She also was the division's director until 1942, when she began working for the Office of Price Administration in Richmond.

In 1947 Cohn as vice chair of the Richmond charter campaign successfully fought for a new city charter to replace the bicameral city council with a single nine-person body and to weaken the mayor's power by implementing a city-manager system. She broke new ground in 1950 when she was the only woman among the twenty-three candidates for the at-large seats on the city council. Citing her interest in civic affairs and her longstanding involvement in the Richmond Citizens Association (which, ironically, did not endorse her candidacy), Cohn ran as an independent, though the Richmond Democratic League, an umbrella organization for more than a dozen black interest groups, placed her name on its slate. Cohn advocated a new juvenile detention home, more schools, a study of local crime, and a slum-clearance program. She finished eighteenth with 3,553 votes.

Naomi Silverman Cohn died on 20 October 1982 in Milwaukee, Wisconsin, where she had moved in the mid-1970s to live with her elder daughter, Sarah A. Cohn Ettenheim, board president of the Settlement Cook Book Company and former president of the Federation of Jewish Women's Organizations of Milwaukee. Her cremated ashes were buried in Hebrew Cemetery in Richmond, next to her husband, who had died of cardiac failure on 15 November 1938. In 1993 the Virginia Federation of Business and Professional Women's Clubs named Cohn among the first thirty honorees on the Women of Virginia Historic Trail. The plaque commemorating her contributions is located at Congregation Beth Ahabah, in Richmond.

Biographies in *Richmond Times-Dispatch*, 1 Jan. 1939 (por.), 26 July 1971, and Virginia Women's Cultural History Project, Acc. 32425, LVA; birth date from Social Security application, Social Security Administration, Office of Earnings Operations, Baltimore, Md.; variant birth date of Apr. 1886 and variant birthplace of Poland in Census, Bucks Co., Pa., 1900;

Cohn correspondence in Adèle Clark Papers, VCU, and National Consumers' League Papers, LC; Bucks Co., Pa., Marriage Application and Marriage Register; *Bucks County Gazette*, 2 Apr. 1909; *Richmond News Leader*, 8 June 1936, 5 June 1950, 25 Nov. 1957; *Richmond Times-Dispatch*, 17 Jan. 1943 (quotations and por.), 15 Apr., 17 May, 4, 6, 14 June 1950; Landon R. Y. Storrs, *Civilizing Capitalism: The National Consumers' League, Women's Activism, and Labor Standards in the New Deal Era* (2000); obituaries in *Richmond News Leader* and *Richmond Times-Dispatch*, both 21 Oct. 1982.

JENNIFER DAVIS MCDAID

COKE, Richard (16 November 1790–31 March 1851), member of the House of Representatives, was born in Williamsburg and was the son of Rebecca Lawson Shields Coke and her second husband, John Coke. Throughout his life he referred to himself as Richard Coke Jr. His namesake nephew represented Texas in the United States Senate from 1877 to 1895. He may have been the Richard Coke who during the War of 1812 served from 28 May to 2 June 1814 with the 99th Regiment Virginia militia. Coke received an A.B. from the College of William and Mary in 1815, read law, and then began practicing in Williamsburg and Gloucester County. Sometime before 1824 he married Mary Willing Byrd. Before her death on 7 October 1831, they had at least one daughter. Coke married Eglantine Cochran, of Washington, D.C., on 6 January 1848. No children are recorded from his second marriage.

In the spring of 1829 Coke announced his candidacy for the House of Representatives in the Eighth Congressional District, consisting of Accomack, Gloucester, James City, Mathews, Northampton, Warwick, and York Counties and the city of Williamsburg. The incumbent, Burwell Bassett (1764–1841), had earlier announced his retirement from Congress but reentered the race after many prominent local Democrats had already pledged their support for Coke. In the April election Coke received 647 votes and defeated both Bassett, with 582 votes, and Carter Moore Braxton, with 323 votes. During the Twenty-first Congress (1829–1831), Coke did not serve on any standing committees. He aligned himself with congressmen who supported Andrew Jackson and opposed legislation, such as internal improvements measures, that would increase the power of the federal government. Coke supported a claim submitted by an impoverished James Monroe seeking compensation for expenses he had incurred while serving as a diplomat. Coke also defended John Randolph of Roanoke, then minister to Russia, from assaults by administration critics.

In his bid for reelection in 1831, Coke again faced Braxton, who withdrew from the contest and left Coke unopposed. During his second term (1831–1833) Coke served on the Committee on Private Land Claims. Continuing to argue that the federal government already possessed more powers than should have been ceded to it, he spoke against legislation on colonization of free blacks and on the promotion of silk culture and argued that each measure required an unwarranted increase in the power of the federal government. During the commemoration of the centennial of George Washington's birth, Coke opposed removing Washington's remains from Mount Vernon and reinterring them in the United States Capitol, although he approved of plans to move the remains to Richmond. He voted against rechartering the second Bank of the United States in 1832, but he split with the administration during the Nullification Crisis by joining the minority opposed to the Force Bill, the president's revenue collection bill designed to carry out the federal tariff law in South Carolina. Coke voted for Henry Clay's adjusted tariff measure early in 1833 that averted a confrontation between the federal government and South Carolina.

Labeled a nullifier during his reelection campaign in 1833 and facing Henry Alexander Wise, who had been recruited for the race by pro-administration politicians, Coke led in the polling heading into Accomack County but lost in Wise's birthplace by a wide margin, 83 to 834, and consequently lost the congressional election by 401 votes. Rancor simmering between the two political foes finally boiled over on 22 January 1835, when Coke and Wise fought a duel after Wise accused his opponent of campaigning on both sides of the nullification issue in different areas of the congressional district. Coke received a wound in the shoulder and never fully recovered the use of that arm. He sought to regain his House seat from Wise in 1835, but apparently realizing that another close election hinged again on Accomack County, he withdrew from the race shortly before the polling.

Coke resumed his lucrative legal practice in Gloucester County and in Williamsburg. He also became a successful planter at Abingdon, his 279-acre Gloucester County plantation. At the time of his death he owned 43 taxable slaves and 1,119 acres of land. Richard Coke died on 31 March 1851 at his Gloucester County estate and was buried there.

Birth and death dates on gravestone, in Association for the Preservation of Virginia Antiquities, Joseph Bryan Branch, *Epitaphs of Gloucester and Mathews Counties in Tidewater Virginia through 1865* (1959), 18; undocumented marriage year of 1817 in Pecquet du Bellet, *Virginia Families*, 1:157; Coke letters in several collections, VHS; *Richmond Enquirer*, 14, 17, 21, 24 Apr., 5, 12 May 1829, 16, 19 Aug., 9 Sept. 1831, 23, 30 Apr., 7 May 1833, 8 May 1835, 14 Jan. 1848; *Register of Debates*, 21st Cong., 2d sess., 392, 503–507, 510, 22d Cong., 1st sess., 1425, 1628–1630, 1785–1786, 3018, 3092–3093, 2d sess., 890; Craig M. Simpson, *A Good Southerner: The Life of Henry A. Wise of Virginia* (1985), 11–12, 18; obituary in *Richmond Enquirer*, 2 May 1851 (variant death date of 30 Mar. 1851).

TRENTON E. HIZER

COLDSMITH, James Wesley (16 June 1929–10 March 1990), journalist and civic leader, was born in Parsons, Kansas, and was the son of Charles Irwin Coldsmith, a Methodist minister, and Sarah Ethel Willett Coldsmith. He grew up in southeastern Kansas and attended public schools in Baldwin (later Baldwin City). Coldsmith received a B.A. from Baker University, in Baldwin, in 1950 and an M.S. from the Medill School of Journalism at Northwestern University, in Evanston, Illinois, in 1951. He served in the United States Army during the Korean War and was posted to Tokyo as a news editor for the Pacific *Stars and Stripes*. After his discharge from the army, Coldsmith remained in Tokyo as a news editor for the Associated Press and later took AP jobs in Denver and Chicago. For two years in Chicago he worked as assistant editor at the World Book Encyclopedia. On 24 April 1954 he married Anne Anker in Baldwin. They had two daughters and one son before they divorced on 17 January 1979.

In 1966 Coldsmith became director of information services for the Greater Washington Edu-

cational Television Association, Inc., which operated an educational television station for the Washington, D.C., area and secured a license to establish an FM radio station as well. After stepping down he worked briefly on the staff of the National Association of Educational Broadcasters on membership development. In 1967 Coldsmith purchased an Alexandria community advertising flyer and turned it into a weekly newspaper, the *Alexandria Journal*. The next year he and an Alexandria business partner purchased controlling interest in the Journal Newspapers, Inc., which published the weekly *Alexandria Journal*, *Alexandria Journal-Standard*, *Arlington Journal*, and *Fairfax County Journal-Standard* newspapers, with a combined circulation of 35,000 copies each week. Coldsmith became president and publisher and also bought Weadon Printing Service, Inc. He sold the Journal Newspapers, Inc., in 1971 to the Army Times Publishing Company, of Washington, D.C., and resigned as editor in September 1972. For several years he wrote a humorous syndicated column, "Through the Wry."

From August 1976 until August 1984 Coldsmith was editor and publisher of the *Alexandria Port Packet*. Under his leadership, the weekly newspaper included a greater number of substantive articles on major community issues, such as housing policies, a scandal in the sheriff's office, and the need for a mass transit system. "We've defined our market," Coldsmith noted. "If an atom bomb hit Washington, we wouldn't cover it unless there was fallout or refugees coming down the Potomac." Late in 1982 the *Port Packet* lost a libel suit brought by a couple whose infant son's accidental death the paper had mentioned in a two-part series on child abuse. The total verdict of $150,000 was five times the *Port Packet*'s net worth, a potential calamity compounded because Coldsmith had inadvertently allowed the paper's libel insurance to lapse. The Supreme Court of Virginia upheld the compensatory damage award of $50,000 but dismissed the additional $100,000 in punitive damages, and the Supreme Court of the United States let that ruling stand on appeal in July 1985.

In December 1984 Coldsmith became editor in chief and publisher of the financially strapped *Alexandria Gazette*, founded in 1784. He focused more tightly on local news and devoted fewer editorials to national issues. Casual in tone and management style, he declared at his initial staff meeting, "My name is 'Jim.' This is probably the last time you'll see me with my tie tightened." Following the sale of the *Gazette* to a group of local businessmen in the autumn of 1986, Coldsmith stepped down as president and publisher, but he remained senior editor, even after the *Port Packet* and *Gazette* merged as the twice-weekly *Alexandria Gazette Packet* in July 1987. Over the years he won several awards for excellence in journalism from the Virginia Press Association, including a citation for editorial writing in 1971. Generous in sharing his skills, Coldsmith taught courses in editing, layout, and newspaper management during the 1970s and 1980s as an associate professional lecturer at George Washington University. He provided entry-level jobs for many aspiring journalists and offered invaluable professional experience. From 1986 to 1989 he was a director of the Virginia Press Association.

A moderate Republican, Coldsmith ran unsuccessfully for Alexandria's city council in 1973 and 1976 and served with a number of local organizations, including the board of Alexandria Hospital, the Alexandria Police Boys and Girls Clubs, the local Rotary Club, and the city's Chamber of Commerce, which honored him with its George Washington Leadership Award in February 1990. Many Alexandrians best knew Coldsmith as "Mr. Bicentennial," following his appointment as chair of the Alexandria Bicentennial Commission in 1971. As the nation approached its two-hundredth anniversary, he successfully lobbied the Virginia Independence Bicentennial Commission to select Alexandria as the host of a tourist center for the bicentennial celebration and then helped secure $500,000 in state funds to restore the nineteenth-century Greek Revival–style city Lyceum for use as the George Washington Northern Virginia Bicentennial Center. When the Alexandria Art League needed a new home, Coldsmith suggested converting a rundown government building on the waterfront where torpedoes had once been assembled into the Torpedo Factory Art Center.

He also proposed a system of parks and history-related walkways along the waterfront. Coldsmith helped to create the Alexandria Third Century Scholarship Fund, which assisted students interested in local government. He served on the Jamestown Foundation (after 1976 the Jamestown-Yorktown Foundation) from 1976 through 1983.

A tall and affable man, Coldsmith once gave his height as five feet, seventeen inches. He enjoyed restoring houses and office buildings and had a second career as a real estate investor. He continued to write occasional weekly columns for the *Alexandria Gazette Packet* even during his final illness, when from his hospital bed he researched and prepared an obituary of Armistead Lloyd Boothe, an Alexandria politician who in the 1950s had led the progressive wing of the state's Democratic Party. James Wesley Coldsmith died of leukemia at his Alexandria home on 10 March 1990. His remains were cremated. In January 1991 the Lyceum's changing exhibition gallery was renamed the James Coldsmith Gallery in his honor.

Feature article in *Washington Post*, 3 July 1975 (por.); family information provided by brother Donald E. Coldsmith and daughter Janet E. Coldsmith (both 2004); career information provided by Philip Brooks, Lawrence Laurent, Julie Perry, and Marian Van Landingham (all 2004); marriage and divorce dates confirmed by BVS; Alexandria Bicentennial Commission Records, Alexandria Archives and Records Center; published writings include introduction to Nettie Allen Voges, *Old Alexandria: Where America's Past Is Present* (1975), 10–12; *Alexandria Journal-Standard*, 18 Apr. 1968; *Washington Post*, 29 Dec. 1972, 17 Dec. 1975, 6 May 1981 (first quotation), 16 Mar. 1983, 30 Dec. 1984, 2 July 1985; *Alexandria Journal*, 12 Apr. 1973, 22 Apr. 1976; *Alexandria Port Packet*, 26 Aug.–2 Sept. 1976, 30 Aug.–5 Sept. 1984; *Alexandria Gazette*, 28 Dec. 1984 (por. and second quotation); obituaries in *Washington Post*, 11 Mar. 1990, and *Alexandria Journal*, 12 Mar. 1990; obituary and editorial tribute in *Alexandria Gazette Packet*, 15 Mar. 1990.

JAMES C. MACKAY

COLE, Fred Carrington (12 April 1912–6 May 1986), president of Washington and Lee University, was born near Franklin, Texas, and was the son of Robert Wiley Cole and Elizabeth Taylor Cole. He grew up on the family's 11,000-acre Duck Creek ranch, where he worked as a saddle hand during the summers. After graduating from Franklin High School, Cole enrolled in the Louisiana State University and Agricultural and Mechanical College, where his brother taught political science. He received a B.A. in 1934, an M.A. in 1936, and a Ph.D. in 1942, the last after completing a dissertation on the nineteenth-century agricultural writer Thomas Affleck. While a student he supported himself by waiting tables, managing a boarding house, and teaching at a Baton Rouge high school for the 1934–1935 academic year. Cole served as an editorial associate of the *Journal of Southern History* from 1936 to 1941 and then as managing editor in 1941 and 1942. He was the history editor at Louisiana State University Press from 1938 to 1942 and also, with Wendell Holmes Stephenson, coeditor of the press's Southern Biography Series from 1938 to 1945. Cole married Lois Ferguson, an Arkansas native who taught at Belhaven College in Mississippi, on 22 August 1937. They had three sons and one daughter.

During World War II, Cole enlisted in the United States Naval Reserve and saw sea duty as a gunnery officer with the rank of lieutenant junior grade. He later supervised the revision of the navy's *Manual of the Medical Department*, for which he was honored with a special commendation from the navy's surgeon general. After completing active military duty, he spent a year as an editor, writer, and historian for the United States Army Air Force. In 1946 Cole joined the Tulane University faculty as associate professor of history. Within a year of his arrival, he was promoted to full professor and began a distinguished career as a university administrator as dean of the College of Arts and Sciences, a position he held until assuming the post of academic vice president in 1954. He was an associate editor of the *Mississippi Valley Historical Review* (later the *Journal of American History*) from 1946 to 1953. Cole took a leave of absence from Tulane during the 1954–1955 academic year to serve as a special consultant to the Ford Foundation in New York City.

In June 1959 Washington and Lee University's board of trustees chose Cole as president to succeed Francis Pendleton Gaines. Faculty members later recalled Cole's leadership style as unobtrusive, but the list of his achievements was impressive. He guided the university in Lexington through several building and major renovation projects, including a new science facility, a new home for the Department of Journalism and Communications, a new university radio station, the installation of a modern electronic language laboratory, and the renovation of a faculty residence as a new alumni house. Cole obtained a $370,000 grant from the Ford Motor Company to renovate and restore the Lee Chapel, where Robert Edward Lee, the school's president from 1865 to 1870, is buried. Early in his administration, he recognized the importance of computer technology and data processing and guided the university in the creation of a computer center. Cole increased faculty salaries and tripled the amount of available student financial aid. He also implemented a creative program that funded undergraduate participation in faculty research.

Cole helped Washington and Lee University chart a course to move beyond its history as a segregated institution. During the autumn of 1961 a student Christian group asked Martin Luther King Jr. to speak on campus, but the board of trustees rescinded the invitation. A vigorous champion of academic freedom, Cole aided the faculty in making a strong statement supporting the free exchange of diverse ideas on campus. In 1963 he became a trustee of the Prince Edward Free School Association, a biracial board responsible for reopening the Prince Edward County schools, which had closed rather than integrate. The next year President Lyndon Baines Johnson named Cole to the national Citizens Committee for Community Relations, established to resolve issues arising from the Civil Rights Act of 1964. Under Cole's leadership, Washington and Lee in 1964 dropped its racial barriers to admission and two years later began admitting African American students. In a quiet and gentle manner, Cole led by example rather than rhetoric.

A man of incredible energy, Cole found time for service on numerous boards dedicated to the advancement of learning. He chaired the advisory committee on foreign affairs for the Southern Regional Educational Board and the southern section of the Fund for the Advancement of Education's faculty fellowship program. In 1959 Cole became a director of the George C. Marshall Foundation and also a trustee of the

College Entrance Examination Board, which he later chaired. From 1964 to 1967 he served as president of the Virginia Foundation for Independent Colleges. Cole chaired the army's Historical Advisory Committee and the Advisory Council on Research of the Office of Education. He also represented the United States at international conferences on education in 1965 and 1966.

Cole submitted his resignation as president of Washington and Lee in May 1967, to be effective on 1 September. In June he was elected president of the Council on Library Resources, Inc., an organization based in Washington, D.C., and dedicated to developing resources and services for the nation's libraries. Washington and Lee honored Cole in 1968 with an honorary doctorate of laws for his work as an educational administrator and for his many contributions to the university. He retired from the council in 1977 and the following year moved to Chapel Hill, North Carolina. Fred Carrington Cole died at his home there on 6 May 1986 and was buried in Chapel Hill Memorial Cemetery.

Biographies in *Commonwealth* 26 (Sept. 1959): 55–56 (pors.), and *Richmond Times-Dispatch*, 8 May 1960 (with marriage date); Cole Presidential Papers, RG 3, and some correspondence in Lewis F. Powell Jr. Papers, both W&L; *Richmond News Leader*, 12 June 1959; *Lexington Gazette*, 17 June 1959; *Richmond Times-Dispatch*, 23 May 1967; *Lexington News-Gazette*, 24, 31 May 1967; W&L *Alumni Magazine* 34 (summer 1959): 2–3; ibid. 35 (July 1960): 2–4; ibid. 42 (Aug. 1967): 3–9, 14–15 (pors.); *Commonwealth* 27 (June 1960): 26, 68–69; published works include Cole, "Research Projects in Southern History," *JSH* 4 (1938): 544–558, *International Relations in Institutions of Higher Education in the South* (1958), "Universities and Athletics: An Address," W&L *Alumni Magazine* 36 (May 1961): 4–5, and "Comments on the Function of a University," *Journal of Medical Education* 36 (1961): 883–887; obituaries in *Richmond News Leader* and *Richmond Times-Dispatch*, both 8 May 1986, *Washington Post*, 11 May 1986, *Lexington News-Gazette*, 14 May 1986, *W&L* 61 (Aug. 1986): inside cover, and *JSH* 53 (1987): 152–153.

THEODORE C. DE LANEY

COLE, George William (d. after 10 June 1880), member of the House of Delegates, was born in Athens, Georgia, late in the 1840s. The record of his 1879 marriage identified his parents, William Cole and Martha Cole, as freedpersons,

but little else is known of his youth. By early in the 1870s he was living in Chattanooga, Tennessee. Inspired perhaps by his parents or by the heady events of emancipation and Reconstruction, Cole developed a desire for education and self-improvement. In 1872 he enrolled in the junior class of the Hampton Normal and Agricultural Institute (later Hampton University). Having earned promotion to the middle class, Cole left the school during the 1873–1874 academic year. By 1879 he had made his way to Essex County, where he found work as a teacher and probably also farmed. On 21 April 1879 Cole married Edith Banks, a native of the county. They had at least one daughter.

Cole must have impressed natives of Essex as a reliable and promising figure. A black-majority county that had previously elected several Republicans, white and black, to the General Assembly, Essex possessed no shortage of viable African American politicians. Although more-stringent suffrage restrictions passed in 1876 had allowed Essex Conservatives to triumph in the election of 1877, blacks remained a potent political force. Complicating matters was the escalating conflict over the state debt, which split white Conservatives into two factions: Funders, who believed that the state's honor and future ability to secure capital depended on paying off the antebellum debt and its accrued interest in full, and Readjusters, who favored restructuring the debt in order to allow the state to sustain and perhaps improve the funding of various programs, particularly education. Out of this tense political environment Cole emerged in 1879 as the Republican candidate for the county's seat in the House of Delegates.

It is uncertain on which side of the debt issue Cole campaigned. Republicans had generally supported full funding of the debt. Conservative newspaper accounts of the race called Cole a Funder, cited him as a supporter of the McCullough Act (the Funders' solution), and used his victory as evidence that Readjusters had not won a majority in the General Assembly. Most black voters, however, had begun to favor restructuring, if not repudiating, the debt. Cole's victory over the Conservative candidate

John R. Motley by a vote of 803 to 635 in a county that favored the Readjuster position suggests that Cole probably expressed at least an openness to restructuring the state debt.

In the House of Delegates, which opened its session on 3 December 1879, Cole joined fifteen other Republicans (ten of them African American) who formed a wedge between virtually equal numbers of Funders and Readjusters. Both of the latter groups jockeyed for the support of Republicans. After brokering satisfactory agreements with Readjuster leaders, Cole and the other black Republicans sided with the Readjusters and gave them a comfortable voting majority. The new coalition immediately voted in its slate of House officeholders, including a few African Americans, who replaced Confederate veterans in minor functions. Cole supported legislation lowering the tax on vendors of malt liquor, spirits, and wine and also a proposed constitutional amendment to repeal the poll tax as a prerequisite for voting. He voted to elect the Readjuster chief William Mahone to the United States Senate and for the so-called Riddleberger Bill, which, although vetoed, became the basis of the Readjusters' successful restructuring of the state debt in the next legislative session. During his one term Cole did not propose any major legislation. He served on the relatively insignificant Committee on Labor and Poor, which may offer some indication of his policy interests.

Nothing certain is known about Cole's life after his term in the House ended on 9 March 1880. Later that year the census enumerator in Essex County listed him as a farmer. There is no indication in the land and tax records that he owned any property in the county, so if he did farm, he probably rented or worked as a tenant. Cole does not seem to have sought political office in Essex again and appears in no subsequent county records. Most likely he left the county to pursue other opportunities, but it is not known where he might have gone. Records from Washington, D.C., identify several men named George W. Cole, but although their ages and occupations offer plausible possibilities, no evidence ties any of them directly to the former Virginia legislator. Whatever his fate,

George William Cole's significance lay in his brief role in one of the most important political movements in nineteenth-century Virginia.

Essex Co. Marriage Register (including full name, birthplace, and parents' names and status and giving age as thirty on 21 Apr. 1879); Census, Essex Co., 1880 (age thirty-three on 9–10 June 1880); Election Records, no. 14, RG 13, LVA; *Richmond State*, 6 Nov., 9 Dec. 1879, 2 Mar. 1880; *Richmond Daily Dispatch*, 7, 15 Nov. 1879, 2 Mar. 1880; *JHD*, 1879–1880 sess., 30, 59–63, 97, 381–386, 389–394, 398–399, 401–404.

WILLIAM BLAND WHITLEY

COLE, William (1638 or 1639–4 March 1694), member of the Council and secretary of the colony, was born probably in Warwick River County (after 1643 Warwick County). He was most likely the son of William Cole, who arrived in Virginia from Essex County, England, in 1618 and in 1629 represented Nutmegg Quarter in the General Assembly. The name of his mother is uncertain, but she may have been the Francis (or Frances) Cole who came to the colony aboard the *Susan* in 1616. Nothing is known about Cole's early life or education, but he studied law and was representing clients before the General Court by October 1670. By the spring of 1672 he was a lieutenant colonel in the county militia. In April 1671 Cole purchased from Frances Culpeper Stephens Berkeley and her second husband, Governor Sir William Berkeley, 1,350 acres of land in Warwick County, an estate later known as Boldrup or Bolthrope. Cole eventually acquired more than 2,400 additional acres in Elizabeth City, Warwick, and York Counties.

On 3 March 1675 the governor appointed Cole and three other men, including Nathaniel Bacon (1647–1676), to the governor's Council. Cole took the oath of office three days later. When Bacon's Rebellion began in the summer of 1676, he criticized Bacon's treatment of the Indians but acted as an intermediary between the governor and the rebel in June. The next month Cole joined the governor when he withdrew to the Eastern Shore, and Bacon subsequently enumerated Cole on his list of "wicked, and pernitious Councollors, aiders, and Assisters against the Commonalty." The royal commissioners sent to suppress the rebellion and investigate its causes confirmed Cole's loyalty and his position on the

Council. In March 1677 Cole was one of six witnesses to Berkeley's will.

On 4 May 1683 Cole and other Council members signed a letter recommending that the Lords Committee for Trade and Plantations improve the governance of the colony by restricting trade with the Indians to a few persons to be designated by the governor, accurately defining Virginia's borders to cut off encroachments by Maryland and North Carolina, providing a sixty-man garrison for security, redirecting certain quitrents to the colonial government's use, limiting tobacco production, and permitting a tobacco levy. Twice in the 1680s Cole assisted in the suppression of piracy. In June 1682 the Council ordered him to impress a vessel and collect a crew to pursue a pirate ship that had been raiding along the York River. Cole took testimony in June 1688 from Edward Davis and three other men for trial before the General Court in the last recorded piracy case before the formation of a court of vice-admiralty in the colony.

Cole augmented his income with the lucrative post of customs collector for the upper district of the James River, which he held until the summer of 1686, when the governor transferred him to the lower district. Three marriages also advanced his status and bound him more firmly into the tangled kinship networks of the colonial elite. With his first wife, whose name is unknown but to whom he was married by 1674, he had at least one daughter, who married Dudley Digges (d. 1711), a member of the Council and brother of Cole's second wife. Sometime after the death of his first wife, Cole married Ann Digges, daughter of Edward Digges, who was governor in 1655 and 1656. They had at least two sons before her death on 22 November 1686. By mid-1689 Cole had married Martha Lear, daughter of the Council member John Lear. They had at least two daughters and two sons. After Cole's death, his widow married Lewis Burwell (d. 1710), a Gloucester County planter.

On 18 October 1689 the president of the Council appointed Cole to the vacant office of secretary of the colony, an important and profitable post responsible for maintaining the official correspondence of the governor and Council, drawing up and recording all public documents,

reporting the General Assembly's proceedings, keeping the seal of the colony, and naming the county clerks. The king and queen granted him the office on 17 January 1690. Cole was one of four councillors appointed in May 1691 to a committee to accept a royal charter for a college in the colony. The second man named in the charter of 8 February 1693 establishing the College of William and Mary, Cole was a founding visitor, or trustee, of the institution.

By that time, however, Cole had blundered and toppled from power. Without the knowledge of the other councillors, in April 1691 he sent an indiscreet letter to Governor Francis Howard, baron Howard of Effingham, then in England, in which he "very highly taxed and abused his Honor the Lieut Govr," Francis Nicholson. On 23 June 1692 Nicholson produced a copy of the letter during a Council meeting and confronted Cole, who immediately submitted his resignation as councillor, secretary, and customs collector. In an effort to save face, he cited not his embarrassment but rather his rapidly declining health, "as he is lately much decayed in his body & Strength, and by reason of a deepe Melancholly that hath Seized him." William Cole died on 4 March 1694 and was buried at his Boldrup plantation in Warwick County.

Family relationships in *Adventurers of Purse and Person*, 1:714–715; landholdings in Hening, *Statutes*, 2:321–325, and Patent Book, 7:336, 8:168–169, RG 4, LVA; PRO C 66/3333, no. 6 (grant of secretary's office); PRO CO 1/65, fols. 100–101; PRO CO 1/37, fol. 128 (first quotation); PRO CO 5/1371, fol. 179v; PRO IND 6818, entries for Jan. 1689/90 and Feb. 1692/93; Cole letters in PRO CO 5/1305, fols. 63–65, and PRO CO 5/1356, 175–187; numerous references in *Minutes of Council and General Court* (appointment to Council on 401), *Executive Journals of Council*, esp. 1:249–251 (second and third quotations on 249, 250), 521 (appointment as secretary), and Billings, *Effingham Papers*; gravestone transcription in *WMQ*, 1st ser., 1 (1893): 142, and 14 (1906): 165, with death date "in the 56th, year of his age."

MARIANNE E. JULIENNE
SARA B. BEARSS

COLEMAN, Asa (d. after 24 February 1893), member of the House of Delegates, was born into slavery early in the 1830s, probably in North Carolina. The names of his parents are not known. He grew up on a Person County farm owned by William Bailey, who later sold him to Joseph Pointer, another county farmer who owned sixty-seven slaves in 1860 and who may have brought him to Virginia. Coleman learned to read but not to write. He was married, probably by 1858, to a woman named Amanda, a Tennessee native, born about 1839, whose maiden name is not recorded. They had at least one son. It is not known when or under what circumstances Coleman secured his freedom nor when he came to Virginia. His name first appears in the Halifax County tax records in 1869, and by the next year he was working as a carpenter. In June 1872 he bought at public auction 150 acres of land, for which he paid $982.50. The county court approved the deed and conveyed it to him in March 1875.

In 1871 Coleman finished second in a field of seven candidates and won election as one of three Radical Republicans representing Halifax County in the House of Delegates. Serving in three sessions from 6 December 1871 to 2 April 1873, he sat on the Committee on Asylums and Prisons. Coleman supported an unsuccessful attempt to repeal an 1870 act that authorized chain gangs and voted with the minority to sustain a bill to prevent punishment by whipping. He sponsored a bill authorizing Halifax County residents to vote on purchasing a local bridge in order to eliminate its tolls, introduced a resolution petitioning Congress to set aside public lands for the education of African Americans living in the South, and proposed that the Committee on Schools and Colleges admit to white public schools all children of white fathers. In 1872 Coleman and other black legislators traveled to Washington, D.C., where they met with the president and sought his support for a civil rights bill then in Congress.

Of major concern to Coleman and the other House members was the crushing state debt created during the antebellum period to finance internal improvements. Conservatives were divided on how to pay the debt. One faction, called Funders, advocated full payment to preserve the state's honor and credit rating, while Readjusters proposed paying only a portion and funneling remaining resources to distressed sectors of Virginia society. The controversial Funding Act, passed in March 1871 to remedy the fiscal crisis, only deepened the state's financial woes. Coleman was on authorized leave when the House voted on 15 December 1871 to suspend the act, but on 5 January 1872 he voted with the majority in favor of a joint resolution to discontinue the issuance of bonds for funding the public debt. He voted with the majority on 2 March to override the governor's veto and pass a bill prohibiting the use of bond coupons to pay taxes and debts, thereby repealing a key provision of the Funding Act. Coleman did not stand for reelection in 1873. In November of that year he sat on a Halifax jury.

In August 1875 Coleman served on the Resolutions Committee at a Richmond convention called by black legislators to address the lack of jobs. About one hundred African American delegates from across the state formed a short-lived Laboring Men's Mechanics' Union Association, adopted a resolution supporting readjustment of the state debt, and called for better educational opportunities for black children. In November 1875 Coleman unsuccessfully ran for another term in the House of Delegates but finished fourth in a field of six candidates. He did not again seek a seat in the General Assembly.

Although Coleman apparently did not hold any county offices, he remained politically active. Like many other African Americans, he abandoned the declining Republican Party and joined the Readjusters. Led by the former Confederate general William Mahone, the Readjusters broke with Conservatives, formed their own party, and at an 1884 convention declared themselves the new Republican Party of Virginia. Coleman was elected chair of the Halifax County Republican Party, and on 11 May 1888 he attended a meeting of Sixth District Republicans at Liberty (later Bedford City), in Bedford County. He campaigned on behalf of Patrick Henry McCaull, the district's nominee for the House of Representatives, and corresponded with Mahone on how best to manage party affairs, but McCaull lost the November election.

In June 1883 Amanda Coleman died of consumption (probably tuberculosis), and by April 1888 Coleman had married a woman named Mary, whose surname is undocumented. As a

Coleman last appears in the public record on 24 February 1893, when he deeded to his wife and his other heirs his remaining eighty-nine acres, his house, furniture, all personal property, and a cow and a calf. The date and circumstances of his death are not known. He was buried in the Coleman family cemetery near Virgilina, in Halifax County, but his grave marker is no longer legible.

Biographies in *Richmond Daily Dispatch*, 20 Aug. 1875 (age given as forty-four), Jackson, *Negro Office-Holders*, 8 (with birth year of 1845), and Eric Foner, *Freedom's Lawmakers: A Directory of Black Officeholders during Reconstruction*, rev. ed. (1996), 48 (variant birthplace of South Carolina); Census, Halifax Co., 1870 (age thirty-eight on 2 Sept. 1870), 1880 (age forty-seven on 17 June 1880); Personal Property Tax Returns (1869–1883) and Land Tax Returns (1876–1882), Halifax Co., RG 48, LVA; Halifax Co. Deed Book, 64:272; Halifax Co. Minute Book, 23:380; Election Records, nos. 4 (1871), 10 (1875), RG 13, LVA; *JHD*, 1871–1872 sess., 32, 63, 124, 170, 389, 1872–1873 sess., 37, 155, 207, 249; *Richmond Daily Whig*, 9 Nov. 1871; *Richmond Daily Dispatch*, 21 Aug. 1875; Coleman to William Mahone, 8 Sept. 1888, Mahone Papers, Duke; Herbert Aptheker, *A Documentary History of the Negro People in the United States* (1951), 1:636–637 (mistakenly identified as A. C. Coleman); 1893 deed in Halifax Co. Deed Book, 84:419–420.

DONALD W. GUNTER

COLEMAN, Claude C. (21 July 1879–9 January 1953), neurosurgeon and medical educator, was born in Caroline County and was the son of Henry Frank Coleman, a farmer, and Jane Moffett Patrick Coleman. He was educated in local public schools and occasionally by private tutors before enrolling at the College of William and Mary in the autumn of 1894. Awarded his licentiate certificate in 1897, Coleman also won the R. Walton Moore Medal that year for his essay on civil law. For about five months during each of the next two years he taught on the Eastern Shore in order to fulfill the obligations of his college scholarship and to save money for medical school. Coleman matriculated at the Medical College of Virginia in October 1900 and received an M.D. in May 1903. He accepted a summer appointment as the physician for Warm Springs and then settled in Buena Vista, where he opened a general practice. While maintaining his private practice in Virginia, he served a brief internship at a New York City hospital as well as an apprenticeship with John Shelton Horsley, a noted Richmond surgeon.

By 1910 Coleman had moved to Richmond and established a general surgical practice. Two years later he received a faculty appointment at the Medical College of Virginia as professor of the principles of surgery. When the faculty was reorganized in 1913 following the merger of MCV with the University College of Medicine, Coleman had to accept a junior appointment in surgery, although he was simultaneously elected professor of oral surgery and anesthesia within the school of dentistry. He continued his dual teaching assignments while pursuing an interest in oral and plastic surgery until the United States entered World War I. Coleman was commissioned a major in the United States Army Medical Corps in 1918 and assigned to the division of head surgery in the Office of the Surgeon General. He directed the brain surgery school in the Medical Officers Training Camp at Fort Oglethorpe, Georgia, where he worked closely with the noted neurologist Stanley Cobb. He later served with the pioneer neurosurgeon Charles Harrison Frazier at United States Hospital No. 11 in Cape May, New Jersey, before his discharge on 4 August 1919.

Following his return to civilian life, Coleman decided to confine his surgical practice to the developing specialty of neurosurgery. He became one of the first full-time neurosurgeons in the United States and the only such specialist in Virginia. Coleman incorporated neurosurgical principles and techniques in his instruction at MCV when he resumed his teaching assignments in 1919. By 1924, when he received an appointment as professor of neurological surgery at MCV, he had established the neurosurgical service at Memorial Hospital, served briefly as its medical director, and initiated a residency program, one of the first four approved neurosurgery specialty programs in the country. Coleman's successful practice and his reputation enhanced the standing of the medical school in the period before World War II. He consulted throughout Virginia and North Carolina and frequently left Richmond in order to perform emergency surgery on patients who had sustained brain injuries. The energetic and often restless Coleman took great personal satisfaction in teaching and guiding young surgeons in his residency program, and he considered the dozens of neurosurgeons he trained as his most significant achievement.

In 1937 the dean of the School of Medicine at the University of Virginia asked Coleman to establish a neurosurgical service there. While continuing his programs and practice in Richmond, Coleman developed the division of neurosurgery in Charlottesville. He served as the clinical professor of neurological surgery until the division became a separate department in 1941. Coleman's teaching responsibilities at both of Virginia's medical schools did not keep him from active membership in a number of medical and surgical associations. He was one of the earliest members of the Society of Neurological Surgeons. On the local level, Coleman served as president of the Richmond Academy of Medicine in 1925 and later headed the Committee on the Cost of Medical Care. The recommendations of this influential committee led in 1934 to the formation of a group hospitalization insurance plan. As a director of the American Board of Neurological Surgery from 1946 to 1952, he helped certify specialists.

Throughout his career Coleman contributed to the medical literature and presented papers at professional meetings. He earned acclaim for his work on the treatment of compound skull fractures, peripheral nerve injuries, and brain abscesses. Coleman wrote chapters for several surgical texts, including the fourth edition of Horsley and Isaac A. Bigger's *Operative Surgery* (1937), and a section on the treatment of gunshot wounds in the head for the surgeon general's official history of the medical department in World War I. He also found time to serve on the board of visitors of the College of William and Mary from 1941 to 1950. In recognition of his service and support, the college awarded Coleman an honorary doctorate of science in 1946. The Medical College of Virginia similarly recognized him at the time of his retirement in June 1951.

A quick wit and raconteur, Coleman could charm patients and colleagues alike. These characteristics may have appealed to the three women he married. On 28 April 1917 Coleman married Julia Langhorne Cone. They had three daughters and one son before her death on 4 January 1926. Coleman married Ruth Threadcraft Putney, a widow, on 16 June 1931. They had no children, and she died on 26 February 1945. Coleman married Constance Gooding Cardozo, with whom he also had no children, on 31 December 1948. The couple spent their honeymoon in Arizona hoping that the arid climate would help the ailing surgeon's lungs. A long-time heavy smoker, he battled emphysema during the last years of his life. Claude C. Coleman died on 9 January 1953 at the MCV Hospital where he had operated many times as Virginia's pioneer neurosurgeon. He was buried in Hollywood Cemetery, in Richmond.

Biography in Tyler, *Men of Mark*, 2d ser. (1936), 89–91 (por. opposite 89 and birth date of 21 July 1879 supplied by Coleman); BVS Birth Register, Caroline Co. (variant birth date for Baby Coleman of 27 July 1879); BVS Marriage Register, Richmond City (1917), Gloucester Co. (1931); *Richmond Times-Dispatch*, 1 Jan. 1949; personal information and some correspondence in Richmond Academy of Medicine Membership Files, William T. Sanger Papers, and Sanger Historical Files, all Tompkins-McCaw; publications include "Late Treatment of Gunshot Wounds of the Head" in M. W. Ireland, *The Medical Department of the United States Army in the World War* (1927), vol. 11, pt. 1, 804–840, and "Some Observations on the Practice of Medicine," *Journal of Southern Medicine and Surgery* 103 (1952): 163–167, 189–193, 243–244; *Richmond Times-Dispatch*, 6 Dec. 1924, 31 May, 1 June 1949, 5 June 1951; obituaries and editorial tributes in *Richmond News Leader*, 9 Jan. 1953, *Richmond Times-Dispatch*, 9, 10, 12 Jan. 1953, *Journal of the American Medical Association* 151 (28 Feb. 1953): 756, *Journal of Neurosurgery* 10 (1953): 327–329, *Transactions of the Southern Surgical Association* 65 (1953): 400–402, and *Virginia Medical Monthly* 80 (1953): 125–126, 241–243.

JODI L. KOSTE

COLEMAN, Cynthia Beverley Tucker Washington (18 January 1832–24 October 1908), preservationist, was born in Saline County, Missouri, and was the daughter of Nathaniel Beverley Tucker (1784–1851), writer, judge, and well-known advocate for states' rights, and his third wife, Lucy Ann Smith Tucker. She was christened Cynthia Smith Tucker, but her middle name was later changed to Beverley. The family moved to Williamsburg in 1834 when her father became law professor at the College of William and Mary. She briefly attended a Loudoun County boarding school but otherwise was educated at home and by her cousin Elizabeth Tucker Coalter Bryan in Gloucester County. On 8 July 1852 Tucker married Henry Augustine Washington, a professor at William and Mary and later editor of the nine-volume *Writings of Thomas Jefferson* (1853–1854). They had two daughters, both of whom died young, before her husband's death on 28 February 1858 in Washington, D.C., of a gunshot wound through the eye.

On 29 October 1861 she married Williamsburg native Charles Washington Coleman, a surgeon in the Confederate army. During the Civil War, Coleman nursed injured soldiers and presided over a local sewing society at the college hospital, although by the spring of 1863 she had sought refuge in North Carolina. Afterward she returned to Williamsburg, where her husband practiced medicine. Coleman attempted to open a school for girls late in the 1860s, but her plans never advanced beyond lessons for a handful of day students. Part of the reason might have been her growing family. Between 1862 and 1874 the Colemans had four sons and two daughters, of whom one son was stillborn and one daughter died in childhood. Another son, Charles Washington Coleman (1862–1932), published poetry in such magazines as *Century* and surveyed "The Recent Movement in Southern Literature" for *Harper's New Monthly Magazine* in May 1887, and a third son, George Preston Coleman, served as state highway commissioner for nine years beginning in December 1913.

After the death of her younger daughter, Catharine Brooke Coleman, in September 1883, Coleman looked for a way to memorialize her. The following February she organized her daughter's friends into a benevolent association known as the Catharine Memorial Society. They made small items to sell for the benefit of Bruton Parish Church and gathered ivy and early daffodils for sale in New York City's flower markets. Coleman's eloquent fund-raising letters appeared in newspapers and the *Southern Churchman*. The group of children, spearheaded by Coleman and several other local women, pulled weeds and cleaned the crumbling tombstones in the church's graveyard. They also raised considerable sums of money to repair the gravestones, wall, and main building. After an escalating altercation with the rector about the use of their donations, Coleman transferred her focus from the church to other historic structures in Williamsburg.

Concerned about what she perceived as a moral crisis in the United States as modern society appeared to abandon its cultural traditions, Coleman became interested in creating a women's historical association to protect the visible symbols of Virginia's illustrious past. In 1888 she met Mary Jeffrey Galt, a Norfolk resident who was organizing a group to preserve the state's colonial structures. Coleman held the first official meeting of the Association for the Preservation of Virginia Antiquities at her house on 4 January 1889, and the group received its charter on 13 February. Coleman became director of the Williamsburg chapter, known as the Colonial Capital Branch, and concentrated her efforts in that city, while Galt's Norfolk Branch focused on preserving Jamestown Island. The two formidable leaders did not get along, and the branches operated separately within the organization. To defuse tensions between the cofounders, Ellen Bernard Fowle Lee, the governor's wife, agreed to serve as the APVA's first president.

Coleman's ties to Virginia society through her friendships and familial connections helped the infant association thrive. In 1889 the APVA acquired the powder magazine in Williamsburg, from which the colony's last royal governor had removed the gunpowder in April 1775 in hopes of thwarting the Virginia patriots. The Colonial Capital Branch preserved the decaying structure and opened it as a small museum. The branch also raised funds to provide memorial tablets for various other Williamsburg structures. Coleman successfully obtained the donation to the APVA of the site of the colonial Capitol, of which only brick foundations remained. She served as branch director until her resignation in December 1899. She was a vice president of the APVA from 1889 until 1905, when she became an honorary vice president, and was the association's historian from 1898 to 1900. She also traveled around the state organizing other local chapters and making speeches. Recognized by the APVA as one of its most enthusiastic leaders, Coleman withdrew from her work as a result of poor health in the months before her death.

In 1892 Coleman became a charter member of the Society of the Colonial Dames of America in the State of Virginia (later the National Society of the Colonial Dames of America in the Commonwealth of Virginia). She served as the Virginia society's historian from 1893 to 1894 and again from 1895 to 1898 and was a vice president from 1904 to 1907. In her later years Coleman wrote vignettes of Virginia and southern history. None of her work seems to have been published, although her stipulation that her name be removed before any of her creations appeared in print makes identification difficult. Her second husband died on 15 September 1894. Cynthia Beverley Tucker Washington Coleman died at her Williamsburg residence on 24 October 1908 and was buried in the graveyard at Bruton Parish Church, where the preservation impulse had first led her to work.

Birth, marriage, and death dates in Coleman family Bible records (1820–1902), LVA; *Richmond Whig and Public Advertiser*, 16 July 1852; BVS Marriage Register, Williamsburg (1861); Coleman correspondence in several collections, VHS; biographical information, correspondence, and other materials in Association for the Preservation of Virginia Antiquities, Colonial Capitol Branch Records (1898–1980), Brown-Coalter-Tucker Papers (1839–1929), and Tucker-Coleman Papers, all W&M; APVA *Yearbook* (1896–1908); Janet C. Kimbrough, "The Early History of the Association for the Preservation of Virginia Antiquities: A Personal Account," *Virginia Cavalcade* 30 (1980): 68–75; James M. Lindgren, "'Whatever Is Un-Virginian Is Wrong': The APVA's Sense of the Old Dominion," *Virginia Cavalcade* 38 (1989): 112–123; Lindgren, *Preserving the Old Dominion: Historic Preservation and Virginia Traditionalism* (1993), including por. on 138; Will Molineux, "The Memory of a Little Girl and Williamsburg's Restoration," *Colonial Williamsburg* 23 (spring 2001): 26–35; Carol Kettenburg Dubbs, *Defend This Old Town: Williamsburg during the Civil War* (2002), por. on 217; obituaries in *Richmond News Leader*, 24 Oct. 1908, *Richmond Times-Dispatch*, 25 Oct. 1908, and *Williamsburg Virginia Gazette*, 31 Oct. 1908.

EMMA L. POWERS

COLEMAN, Frederick William (3 August 1811–24 December 1860), educator, was born in Caroline County and was the son of Thomas Burbage Coleman and Elizabeth Lindsey Coghill Coleman. Educated at Concord Academy, his father's school in the county, he entered the University of Virginia in 1832 at age twenty-one and studied ancient languages, chemistry, mathematics, moral philosophy, and natural philosophy. Several of his professors, including Charles Bonnycastle, John Emmet, Gessner Harrison, and George Tucker, commented that he was an intellectually industrious student who did not engage in unruly behavior. After receiving an M.A. in 1835, Coleman joined two of his brothers as a director of Concord Academy, which occupied a three-story brick building on the family's plantation along the Mat River. James D. Coleman soon left, however, and Atwell C. Coleman moved to Alabama within a few years. Frederick Coleman, who never married and who affectionately was referred to as "Old Fred," remained the academy's sole director until his nephew, Lewis Minor Coleman, joined him and became an assistant master in 1846.

Under Coleman's direction, Concord Academy quickly gained a reputation as one of the most stringent preparatory schools for young men who wanted to attend the University of Virginia. Devoting all his time and energy to the success of his school, Coleman devised a rigorous course of instruction that included a general preparation in languages and sciences. He did not use Latin and Greek grammars but instead required students to learn these languages by reading Livy's historical works on Rome and the *Hecuba* of Euripides in complete texts without notes. Former students recalled Coleman as an autocratic authority who relied not on written rules and regulations to enforce discipline, but rather on his students' own sense of honor and honesty. He held classes on an erratic schedule, varied their lengths, and often summoned his charges for impromptu late-night lectures with the cry, "Sophocles with your candles, gentlemen." Despite the loose organization, his students revered him and his colleagues admired him as a scholar. Concord Academy attracted as many as fifty students a year from around Virginia and from as far away as Florida and Louisiana. Desiring to pursue other interests, Coleman closed the school in 1850, and Lewis Minor Coleman went on to establish Hanover Academy in the neighboring county.

Coleman became postmaster of the office at Concord Academy on 27 January 1849 and held that post until the office closed in May 1851. At mid-century he owned 221 acres of land and nine slaves age twelve or older. After closing his school, he engaged in various business activities. At the annual meeting of the Fredericksburg and Gordonsville Railroad Company in June 1854, Coleman was nominated as the company's president but did not win the election. Two months later he represented Fredericksburg at a convention at White Sulphur Springs, in Greenbrier County, called to discuss internal improvements. Fredericksburg's mayor included Coleman's name among the delegates to represent the city at the Southern Commercial Convention, held in Knoxville, Tennessee, in August 1857.

Coleman, a Democrat also backed by the American Party (Know Nothings), was elected to the Senate of Virginia in February 1856 to replace William A. Moncure, who had resigned. Representing the counties of Caroline and Spotsylvania, Coleman took his seat on 22 February but did not receive any standing committee assignments. In May 1857 he won election without opposition to a full four-year term. During the sessions of 1857–1858 and 1859–1860 he sat on the Committee on Banks and the Committee on Finance and Claims.

Coleman enjoyed the company of women and had a passion for fine horses and for good food and drink. Herculean in build, he became obese later in life. Frederick William Coleman died in Fredericksburg on 24 December 1860, perhaps of food poisoning. He was buried in Hollywood Cemetery, in Richmond.

Biographies in W. Gordon McCabe, *Virginia Schools Before and After the Revolution, with a Sketch of Frederick William Coleman, M.A., and Lewis Minor Coleman, M.A.* (1890), 40–53 (with birth date), Edward S. Joynes, "Old Concord Academy," and responding letters to the editor, in UVA *Alumni Bulletin* 3 (1896–1897): 25–32 (quotation on 28), 74–75, 105–106, Paul Brandon Barringer, James Mercer Garnett, and Rosewell Page, eds., *University of Virginia* (1904), 1:367–368, and Marshall Wingfield, *A History of Caroline County, Virginia* (1969), 121–127 (incorrect death date of Nov. 1860); *Fredericksburg Virginia Herald*, 28 Nov. 1835; *Fredericksburg News*, 11, 18, 21 Feb. 1856, 16 Apr., 1 June 1857; *JSV*, 1855–1856 sess., 293; Caroline Co. Will Book, 30:681; death notice in *Richmond Daily Dispatch*, 25 Dec. 1860; editorial tributes and memorials in *Richmond Daily Dispatch*, 27 Dec. 1860, *Fredericksburg News*, 28 Dec. 1860 (variant birth year of 1812), 4 Jan. 1861, and *JSV*, 1861 sess., 50–51.

TERRY L. STOOPS
JENNINGS L. WAGONER, JR.

COLEMAN, George Preston (4 May 1870–17 June 1948), civil engineer, was born in Williamsburg and was the son of Cynthia Beverley Tucker Washington Coleman, a founder of the Association for the Preservation of Virginia Antiquities, and her second husband, Charles Washington Coleman, a physician. His maternal grandfather Nathaniel Beverley Tucker (1784–1851) was a longtime professor of law at the College of William and Mary. Educated at private schools in Williamsburg and at the College of William and Mary, Coleman in 1890 embarked on a career as a civil engineer that took him to Georgia, Mississippi, and West Virginia. From 1901 to 1906 he was city engineer in Winona, Minnesota. He married Mary Haldane Begg, of Campbell County, on 21 February 1900. They had two daughters, one of whom, Janet Haldane Coleman Kimbrough, became a physician and helped to preserve the historical records of Williamsburg.

Coleman returned to his native state in 1906 as an assistant commissioner of the new State Highway Commission. The governor appointed him commissioner in December 1913. Serving in that capacity until January 1923, Coleman led the fight to improve Virginia's public roads, which were so woefully inadequate that critics urged travelers to bypass the state. He proposed construction of better roads using modern equipment and high-quality materials and sat with state senator Harry Flood Byrd (1887–1966) on the legislative commission that recommended creating a state highway system. In 1918 the General Assembly endorsed the recommendations and established such a highway system for Virginia.

Coleman's reputation as a road builder was recognized nationwide. He was an organizer and president for one term (1916–1917) of the American Association of State Highway Officials and as chair of its executive committee for ten years helped draft the Federal Aid Road Act of 1916, which provided the first federal money for a national highway system. He also chaired the American Road Builders Association in 1920. Coleman was president of the Virginia Road Builders' Association in 1915, a vice president of the Southern Appalachian Good Roads Association, and a founder and three-term president of the Virginia Good Roads Association. During World War I he was a member of the Virginia Council of Defense and directed highway transportation in the state.

Coleman's efforts to build a statewide network of primary roads with borrowed money precipitated a struggle with Byrd, who favored greater emphasis on constructing county roads to be paid for with gasoline taxes—the pay-as-you-go method. Byrd also preferred that a businessman rather than an engineer serve as highway commissioner. In the 1922 session of the General Assembly, he accused Coleman of inefficiency and waste. The assembly restructured the highway commission, and Governor Elbert Lee Trinkle appointed Henry Garnett Shirley as the five-member board's new chair. This action represented a demotion for Coleman, who retained his title as highway commissioner for engineering functions only.

The struggle continued in 1923 during public debate whether to build roads with money raised through the sale of bonds or by a tax on gasoline. Coleman resigned as highway commissioner in January to lead the bond forces. He opposed many of the Democratic Party's leaders and accused them of engaging in petty politics and demagoguery. Reflecting the division in the state, a special session of the General Assembly passed a gasoline tax and authorized a November referendum on a $50 million bond issue. Byrd's well-funded and well-organized anti-bond group overwhelmed Coleman's allies and won a substantial victory that solidified Byrd's leadership of the state's Democratic Party.

The bond referendum terminated Coleman's career as a road builder but not his life of public service. In March 1924 he completed eleven years on the board of the College of William and Mary, of which he had been vice rector since 1918. Coleman returned to Williamsburg, where he was mayor from 1929 to 1934, reportedly the sixth in his family to hold that office. He invested in and served on the boards of several local and regional banks and during the 1930s was president of the Peninsula Bank and Trust Company and of Nolting First Mortgage Corporation. He sat on the board of Eastern State Hospital from 1933 to 1937 and of the State Hospital Board

from the latter year until his death. Living in the historic Tucker house, Coleman in 1929 deeded both it and the site of the first theater in America, which had stood on his property, to the Williamsburg Holding Corporation (later the Colonial Williamsburg Foundation). He published a small pamphlet, *The Flat Hat Club and the Phi Beta Kappa Society: Some New Light on Their History* (1916), and *In His Own Country, and Other Poems* (1942), a volume of the collected poetry of his elder brother, Charles Washington Coleman (1862–1932). Coleman's wife wrote a biography of his great-grandfather, *St. George Tucker: Citizen of No Mean City* (1938), and she also published two smaller historical books in 1934 and 1935.

George Preston Coleman died in Williamsburg of a heart attack on 17 June 1948 and was buried in the churchyard at Bruton Parish Church. The editors of the *Richmond News Leader* and the *Williamsburg Virginia Gazette* published long editorials praising him as the recognized father of Virginia's modern state highway system. The editor of the *Richmond Times-Dispatch* concluded, "He was a man of ability, imagination and force, who could glimpse a future for the State which few of his contemporaries were wise enough to envision." The George P. Coleman Bridge, erected across the York River at Yorktown in 1952, bears his name.

Biographies in Duval Porter, *Official Virginia: A Composition of Sketches of the Public Men of Virginia at the Present Time* (1920), 41–43, and Tyler, *Men of Mark*, 2d ser. (1936), 167–169 (por. facing 167); birth date of 4 May 1870 in Coleman family Bible records (1820–1902), LVA; variant birth date of 8 Mar. 1870 in BVS Birth Register, Williamsburg; Campbell Co. Marriage Register; some records in Department of Highways and Transportation, RG 45, LVA; State Highway Commissioner *Annual Report*s (1914–1921); *Addresses of the Hon. G. P. Coleman, State Highway Commissioner, and D. B. Ryland, Secretary of the Chamber of Commerce of Lynchburg, Va., at the Convention of the Virginia Good Roads Association, held in Richmond, Virginia, January 14, 15 and 16, 1919* (1919); *Richmond Times-Dispatch*, 17 Nov. 1921, 19 Jan., 1 Feb. 1923, 3 Sept. 1925; *Richmond News Leader*, 18, 19 Jan. 1923; Stanley Willis, "'To Lead Virginia out of the Mud': Financing the Old Dominion's Public Roads, 1922–1924," *VMHB* 94 (1986): 425–452; Ronald L. Heinemann, *Harry Byrd of Virginia* (1996), 32–36, 39–42; obituaries in *Williamsburg Virginia Gazette*, 11–18 June 1948, and *Richmond News Leader* and *Richmond Times-Dispatch*, both 18 June 1948; editorial tributes in *Richmond News Leader*, 18 June 1948, *Richmond*

Times-Dispatch, 19 June 1948 (quotation), and *Williamsburg Virginia Gazette*, 18–25 June 1948; memorials in *Virginia Highway Bulletin* 14 (Aug. 1948): 1–8.

RONALD L. HEINEMANN

COLEMAN, John Phillips (21 January 1903–21 August 1993), banker, was born in Roanoke and was the son of John William Coleman, a Norfolk and Western Railway Company engineer, and Sarah Alice Phillips Coleman. He attended local public schools and as a teenager worked in a Roanoke bank, where he rose from messenger to night bookkeeper. Coleman received a B.S. in commerce, with an emphasis on banking and accounting, from the University of Virginia in 1926. He soon accepted a position in New York City at Bankers Trust Company. Over the next five years he was promoted several times, from credit investigator to head investigator to assistant credit manager. In 1931 J. Phillips Coleman, as he was known in the banking profession, received a special assignment as the bank's southern representative. He traveled throughout the region examining loans, interviewing customers, and acquiring new clients. As assistant treasurer beginning in 1934, he administered loans for the bank's eastern and southern districts. In Saint Johns County, Florida, on 14 April 1934 he married Jewell Bowles, a Jacksonville native whom he had met at a banking convention. They had no children.

In 1936 Coleman became the loan officer for Bankers Trust Company and managed its business for the southeastern United States. He moved to Richmond early in 1938 when he took the position of assistant vice president with First and Merchants National Bank of Richmond. The bank's management sought to modernize its operations and had become familiar with Coleman's abilities during his travels throughout the South. He was assigned the task of increasing new business, especially in Virginia, West Virginia, North Carolina, and South Carolina. He also expanded the bank's hiring practices beyond the state and region and brought in young men who had obtained their education and experience in the North.

Promoted to vice president in 1942, Coleman spearheaded a training program after World War II to hire recent college graduates, keep them with the company for the long term, and prepare them for management positions later in their careers. In 1950 First and Merchants hired its first professional personnel associates in order to relieve senior managers of some of these responsibilities. In 1952 Coleman became senior vice president and a member of the board of directors. He was appointed executive vice president in 1961 and the following year became president and chief administrative officer. Early in 1966 Coleman succeeded Robert Thornton Marsh Jr. as chairman and chief executive officer of First and Merchants National Bank. Age restrictions at the bank forced Coleman to retire on 1 February 1968, not long after he turned sixty-five. He remained honorary chairman of the board until 1969.

Coleman was a progressive banker during his tenure at First and Merchants. While older, more conservative bankers such as John M. Miller, the bank's president during the 1920s and 1930s, had eschewed advertising and promotions as vulgar and undignified, Coleman considered banking like any other business and believed that it should focus on selling itself to prospective customers. He strongly believed that banks should not only cater to corporations and wealthy clients, but also seek small depositors. Worrying that finance and insurance companies would step into the void left by an inactive banking industry, Coleman stressed the need for banks to grant term loans of three to five years to small businesses.

During his thirty years at First and Merchants, bank loans and discounts increased from $13 million to $368 million, deposits expanded from $65 million to more than $610 million, and capital and profits rose from $6.5 million to $49 million. At the time of Coleman's retirement, fifty-six branches operated throughout the state. Although driven in part by the introduction of innovative banking practices, these increases occurred also because of aggressive mergers during the 1950s and 1960s. In order to reach new markets, First and Merchants merged with other banks in Ashland, Lynchburg, Newport News, Petersburg, Richmond, Staunton, and Waynesboro. As a result of its expansion from a local city bank to a leading statewide institution, it removed the Richmond designation from its name in 1963 to become officially First and Merchants National Bank.

Active in many social and service organizations, Coleman served as president of the Commonwealth Club, as a director of the Virginia Board of Health, and as a trustee for the Virginia Supplemental Retirement System. He was a treasurer of the United Negro College Fund in Virginia and helped lead a campaign to raise funds for the expansion of Saint Mary's Hospital, in Henrico County. He was a director of the Richmond Chamber of Commerce and such businesses as American Filtrona Corporation and Union Life Insurance Company.

Following his retirement from First and Merchants, Coleman and his wife moved to their vacation home in Atlantic Beach, Carteret County, North Carolina. She died at a local hospital on 4 October 1990. John Phillips Coleman died at home on 21 August 1993 after a long illness. Their remains were donated to the medical school at East Carolina University and later cremated, and the ashes were scattered in the Atlantic Ocean.

Frances Leigh Williams, *A Century of Service: Prologue to the Future, A History of the First and Merchants National Bank* (1965), 115, 126, 132–140 (por. on 135); feature articles in *Richmond News Leader*, 19 Mar. 1956 (por.), 19 Jan. 1968; some correspondence in Samuel Merrifield Bemiss Papers and Archibald Gerard Robertson Papers, both VHS; *Richmond News Leader*, 13 Jan. 1938, 23 Jan. 1952, 24 Jan. 1968; *New York Times*, 14 Jan. 1938, 28 Jan. 1966; obituary in *Richmond Times-Dispatch*, 24 Aug. 1993; death notice in *Carteret County [N.C.] News-Times*, 25 Aug. 1993.

JOHN G. DEAL

COLEMAN, Reuben Turner (d. 14 February 1909), entrepreneur, was born in the latter half of the 1840s and was the son of Samuel A. Coleman, a Cumberland County farmer, and Mary Coleman, his enslaved mistress. Coleman's brothers-in-law included Shed Dungee, who served in the House of Delegates from 1879 through 1882. It is not certain when Coleman and his brothers and sisters gained their freedom. That he was economically independent, and that his financially pressed father owed him at least $426 in January 1866, suggests that his father probably freed him and provided him with financial resources before the end of the Civil War.

R. T. Coleman, as he was generally known, may have received only basic education and training as a child, but he used his keen financial sense and strong kinship connections with white Coleman family members in the area to become an independently successful investor and entrepreneur. He began buying and selling land in the spring of 1866 and operated a general store in Cumberland County throughout the 1870s and 1880s. Coleman also owned a hotel and before 1873 was licensed to sell alcohol there. In that year, believing that he was being illegally taxed on his business, he lodged a successful complaint with the county court. If, as happened in 1887 concerning disputed ownership of a buggy, he lost a court case, Coleman did not hesitate to appeal, although in that instance his suit failed.

By the mid-1880s Coleman was also one of the county's principal farmers. A large tract of land that he owned a few miles north of the county courthouse contained about three dozen mineral springs. He developed the property into his largest and most profitable business venture, which increased his community prestige and social standing. On 29 December 1891 he incorporated the Colemanville Mineral Springs Company, of which he became principal stockholder and president, to oversee and manage the springs. He had the water bottled and shipped to stores in several cities. The company also sold town lots and summerhouses to vacationing northerners and southern city-dwellers who bathed in the pools and drank from the mineral springs. People without summer homes could stay in the Colemanville Hotel. The town had its own post office (of which Coleman was postmaster from June 1876 until July 1881), bank, a newspaper entitled the *Central Call*, and horse stables. Although the town was called Colemanville during the heyday of the Colemanville Mineral Springs Company, the post office was established as Lucyville, named for a daughter who had died. The management company failed in the early years of the twentieth century, and the post office closed about the same time.

Coleman helped found Mount Olive Baptist Church in 1875 and provided it with a two-acre tract of land. He was also the church's founding minister, and in June 1882 the county court licensed him to perform marriages. Coleman was pastor of the church until he died. On 27 February 1882 the county court named him to fill a vacancy as justice of the peace. He won election to a full two-year term in May 1883 and served, probably without interruption, for approximately eighteen years. In 1901 the governor appointed him to a four-year term as notary public. Coleman was probably the last African American to hold public office in Cumberland County during the decades after Reconstruction.

Descendants described Coleman as tall and handsome and sometimes as arrogant and haughty. His prosperity allowed him to live in a large, well-furnished house, and his connections with respectable local white businessmen and attorneys helped him insulate himself from the deteriorating political condition of African Americans at the end of the nineteenth century.

Coleman tested the limits of black freedom by marrying three white women in violation of Virginia law. At least twice he wed in Washington, D.C., where interracial unions were legal. On 21 April 1868 Coleman married Martha Catherine Anderson. Following her death on an unrecorded date between 29 February and 23 October 1876, the county court appointed a white male guardian for their two daughters and one son. (A third daughter had died in infancy.) The legal necessity for that court action is unclear, unless the questionable legality of the marriage impaired Coleman's capacity as father to retain custody of his children. On 30 May 1878 Coleman married Mary Catherine Anderson, who may have been closely related to his first wife. In April 1879 a grand jury issued a presentment against his second wife and alleged that the marriage was unlawful. Perhaps because of his local connections and the power of the Coleman family in Cumberland County, the commonwealth's attorney, who was probably a relative, dropped the charges. Coleman's wife died within a few years and without having any children. Coleman later married Willie F. Whitlow, another local white woman, probably about 1889 and certainly before 29 March 1892. She may have lived for part of the time in a separate house a short distance from his, although the 1900 census enumerator recorded them as residing in the same household. They had one daughter.

Reuben Turner Coleman suffered a stroke in 1908 and died on 14 February 1909. He was buried on his estate.

Biographies and family history in *Cumberland County, Virginia, and Its People* (1983), 26–27, 95, and Marilyn Mildred White, "'We Lived on an "Island"': An Afro-American Family and Community in Rural Virginia, 1865–1940" (Ph.D. diss., University of Texas at Austin, 1983), 56–91 (with birth year of 1844 on 59), 238 (death date of 14 Feb. 1909 from family sources), 291–304, 340–342; Census, Cumberland Co., 1870 (age twenty-six on 24 July 1870), 1880 (age thirty-three on 1–2 June 1880), 1900 (age fifty on 17 June 1900, with birth date of June 1849, and with third marriage in 1889); District of Columbia Marriage Licenses Register (1868); District of Columbia Marriage Records (1878); Jackson, *Negro Office-Holders*, 62; public offices documented in Cumberland Co. Order Books and land transactions in Cumberland Co. Deed Books; Records of Appointment of Postmasters, Virginia, Cumberland Co., Post Office Department, RG 28, NARA; Colemanville Mineral Springs Company prospectus in *Richmond Planet*, 16 Feb. 1895; estate administrator appointed on 13 Mar. 1909 in Cumberland Co. Order Book (1906–1934), 55.

ALEXANDER H. LORCH III

COLEMAN, William D. (9 October 1837–2 October 1901), principal in a criminal case, was born in Danville and was the son of Sarah Leland Rawlins Coleman and Thompson Coleman, a postmaster of Danville and merchant who was in constant financial trouble. Coleman entered the Virginia Military Institute in February 1854 but was dismissed on 3 January 1855 in punishment for a malicious prank. He was reinstated on 15 January but resigned in July because the family could not pay his expenses. He eventually settled his accounts in 1863. Coleman never married.

In August 1858 Coleman and Hartshorne Miller purchased the *Danville Semi-Weekly Transcript*. Coleman bought out Miller early in 1860 and merged the *Transcript* with the *Danville Republican* to form the *Democratic Appeal*, the first issue of which appeared on 1 February. He was appointed postmaster at Danville on 14 September 1860, but after Abraham Lincoln was elected president he submitted his resignation effective on inauguration day. On 23 April 1861 Coleman joined the Danville Blues, which became Company A of the 18th Regiment Virginia Infantry, and served as a first sergeant until 28 September, when the Confederate secretary of war appointed him postmaster of Danville. He resumed publication of his newspaper in May 1863 and soon thereafter began a daily edition called the *Bulletin*, the first daily newspaper published in Danville. Coleman sold his interest in the *Appeal* in November 1863 and in the *Bulletin* about September 1864. The following March he attempted to become commander of a proposed Confederate troop of African American soldiers. He relinquished the postmaster's position to a United States Army officer at the end of the Civil War.

On 13 July 1865 Coleman received a presidential pardon and soon thereafter moved to Richmond. When the *Richmond Enquirer* resumed publication on 30 October of that year, he was its junior editor. Several months later he and the senior editor, Nathaniel Tyler, exchanged angry editorials with Henry Rives Pollard, editor of the *Richmond Examiner*, about the contract for public printing. On 5 January 1866 the three had a confrontation in the rotunda of the State Capitol, during which four shots were fired. Coleman and the others were tried before the House of Delegates on a charge of breech of privileges but were not convicted.

After Tyler left the *Enquirer* in March 1866, Coleman published the paper with a partner until 1867, when Coleman purchased the *Examiner*. He overextended himself buying stock in the combined *Richmond Enquirer and Examiner* and in 1867 failed to pay off other debts that he had contracted in 1863. As a result, on 16 November 1867 his house and lot in Danville were sold at public auction.

On 16 March 1870 Governor Gilbert Carlton Walker appointed Coleman executive clerk. Walker arranged Coleman's election as secretary of the Board of Public Works effective 1 July 1871 and the following month made him secretary of the Commissioners of the Sinking Fund. The economy-minded governor convinced Coleman to accept the second position without an increase in salary. The Funding Act of 1871 that created the Sinking Fund pledged the state to pay off a large antebellum debt at high interest and allowed taxpayers to remit coupons from

state bonds in payment of taxes. Tax revenues swiftly fell to less than half the sum required to operate the government as people sent coupons instead of cash to the treasury. A surplus in the state treasury suddenly became a large deficit. In 1872 the General Assembly passed a new funding act that disallowed the use of coupons as payment for taxes, but in December of that year the Virginia Supreme Court of Appeals, in the case *Antoni* v. *Wright*, declared that act unconstitutional. By then, the state treasurer, Joseph Mayo (1834–1898), had already begun issuing new bonds, which within a short time were selling for as much as 5 percent higher than the original bonds.

With Mayo's approval, Coleman allowed some brokers to exchange old bonds for new ones before the difference in price impaired the value of the bonds in the Sinking Fund account, and early in 1873 the two men permitted some brokers to exchange other bonds in the Sinking Fund. Mayo and Coleman pocketed some of the profit from the second exchange and shared the rest with other members of the state's finance offices. In February 1874 the practice came to light when Governor James Lawson Kemper learned that Coleman was drinking and gambling with state bonds at Richmond faro houses. During the subsequent investigation, Coleman found and corrected a mistake in the Sinking Fund records and then erased the correction. He was arrested and charged with forgery and theft of $10,000 in state bonds. Coleman was tried in the Richmond Hustings Court in March 1874, convicted, and sentenced to a four-year term in the penitentiary. Mayo, who was admittedly intoxicated when he testified, told the jury that Coleman had confessed to changing the entry in the warrant book.

On 30 March a General Assembly investigating committee issued a report on the Sinking Fund that disclosed a deficiency of $15,939.89 in the state's bonds and another of $3,201, the difference in value between the two classes of bonds. Of the latter amount Mayo had pocketed $1,851 and Coleman $1,350. Mayo was soon removed from office and on 3 April declared insane. He entered Western Lunatic Asylum for treatment. Coleman's attorneys then appealed his conviction and sentence on the grounds that Mayo had been insane when he testified and that the warrant book that Coleman had altered was not a document that the law required the secretary to maintain and therefore was not a public record as defined by the forgery laws. On 28 April 1874 the Virginia Supreme Court of Appeals ruled against Coleman on both counts. The court found that the judge had lawfully permitted Mayo's testimony, which was clear and intelligent, and that the warrant book was a public record even though the law did not specifically require that it be kept. The second part of the court's opinion was cited as precedent in 1974 when the United States District Court for the District of Columbia declared that the secret audiotape recordings that Richard Milhous Nixon had made in the White House were public records.

Coleman entered the state penitentiary on 6 May 1874, spent his sentence working in the weaving shop, and was released early, for good behavior, on 26 October 1877. Hoping to win a new trial, he published an account of his actions in a 110-page pamphlet, *The Case of William D. Coleman* (1878). Kemper, whom Coleman suspected of holding a grudge against Walker and his allies, three times refused applications to remove Coleman's civil disabilities that resulted from his conviction, but on 25 June 1878 Governor Frederick William Mackey Holliday restored Coleman's full rights. Coleman returned to Danville, edited the *Danville News* for a time, and in 1879 received a license to practice law. In 1881 and 1885 he was commissioned a notary public in Danville, and he served as a United States commissioner for the Western District of Virginia for about nine years beginning on 31 July 1889. In spite of his almost lifelong personal financial problems, Coleman was also a referee in federal bankruptcy for the same district from 1898 until his death. William D. Coleman died of heart failure in Danville on 2 October 1901 and was buried in the city's Green Hill Cemetery. His inability to pay his debts followed him beyond the grave. A month after his death the local court sold his residence to its previous owner, Coleman having defaulted on the deed of trust with which he had purchased the property.

Emily Anne Croom, *Coleman Kin: A History of Cumberland County Virginia Colemans and Related Families*, 2d ed. (1996), 16; Sherrianne Coleman Nicol, *The Coleman Family of Mobjack Bay, Virginia* (1998), 2:534, 593; William D. Coleman Papers, UVA; Coleman alumnus files and Coleman letters to Francis Henney Smith (1856–1870), VMI; Compiled Service Records; Presidential Pardons; W. D. Coleman, application for removal of political disabilities, 25 June 1878, Secretary of the Commonwealth, Executive Papers, RG 13, LVA; *Richmond Daily Dispatch*, 10 Feb., 24–27 Mar., 1–3 Apr. 1874; *Report of the Joint Committee of Investigation into the Affairs of the Sinking Fund*, Doc. 6 appended to *JHD*, 1874 sess.; *Coleman* v. *Commonwealth* (1874) (25 Grattan), *Virginia Reports*, 66:865–886; *Richard M. Nixon* v. *Arthur F. Sampson et al.*, 44 (74-1518) (DC Dist. 1974); Michael B. Chesson, "'Editors Indulging in Double-leaded Matter': The Shoot-out at the Capitol in 1866," *Virginia Cavalcade* 30 (1981): 100–109; obituaries in *Richmond Dispatch*, 3 Oct. 1901, *Lynchburg News*, 4 Oct. 1901 (with birth date), and *Petersburg Daily Index-Appeal*, 4 Oct. 1901 (variant death date of 3 Oct. 1901).

EMILY J. SALMON

COLES, Isaac (2 March 1747–2 June 1813), member of the Convention of 1788 and of the House of Representatives, was born in Richmond and was the son of Mary Winston Coles and her first husband, John Coles, a prominent Irish-born merchant who died seven months after his son's birth. He attended the College of William and Mary in 1768 and on 1 April 1771 married Elizabeth Lightfoot, whose sister was the wife of Coles's elder brother. They had one daughter, who died as an infant, and two sons before her death on 27 July 1781. Known for his quick wit, penetrating mind, buoyant spirit, and integrity, Coles resided for most of his adult life on his Halifax County plantation at Coles Ferry on the Staunton River, where in 1787 he owned 3,896 acres of land, sixty-six slaves, twenty-four horses, mares, colts, and mules, and ninety-seven cattle.

From July 1770 until at least July 1788 Coles was a justice of the Halifax County Court. He served as a tax commissioner in 1780 and later that year declined appointment as sheriff. He represented the county in the House of Burgesses from 1772 to 1774 but attended only the session that met in May 1774, when he was added to the Committees of Propositions and Grievances and of Public Claims. On 27 May of that year Coles joined eighty-eight of his colleagues in calling for the nonimportation of British goods until Parliament addressed the colonists' grievances. He was eligible to attend the first Revolutionary Convention, which met during the first week of August 1774, but his presence cannot be documented. Coles represented Halifax County in the House of Delegates during the 1780–1781 session and from 1783 to 1788, when he consistently was named to the Committee of Propositions and Grievances and also sat at various times on the Committees of Privileges and Elections and of Claims.

On 24 March 1788 Halifax County voters elected Coles, along with his niece's husband George Carrington (1758–1809), to the Virginia convention called to consider ratification of the proposed constitution of the United States. Like his first cousin Patrick Henry, with whom he later owned shares of the Virginia Yazoo Company, Coles supported addition of a bill of rights and on 25 June voted to require amendment of the Constitution before ratification. After that motion failed, he voted against ratification.

By a narrow margin Coles won election from the predominantly anti-Federalist Sixth Congressional District, consisting of Bedford, Buckingham, Campbell, Charlotte, Franklin, Halifax, Henry, Pittsylvania, and Prince Edward Counties, to the first House of Representatives, which met from 4 March 1789 to 3 March 1791. An inconspicuous member of that body, he neither served on one of two standing committees nor addressed his colleagues from the floor. His uniformly anti-Federalist voting record included opposition to an excise on distilled liquor and to the federal government's assumption of the states' Revolutionary War debts. Coles supported the removal of the seat of government to a site on the Potomac River and a constitutional amendment forbidding Congress to levy direct taxes unless its requests for state funds had gone unheeded. During the First Congress he met Catharine Thompson, a New York native and sister-in-law of Elbridge Gerry. They married in New York on 2 January 1790 and had three daughters, one of whom died in infancy, and six sons, including Walter Coles, later a member of the House of Representatives. Also during this period Coles may have introduced his niece, Dolley Payne, to her future husband, James Madison (1751–1836).

Although Coles apparently neither attended the third session of the First Congress nor stood for reelection in 1791, he returned to the House in 1793 by defeating Matthew Clay in the redrawn Sixth District, comprising Campbell, Halifax, and Pittsylvania Counties, and won reelection two years later. Not appointed to any standing committees during the Third and Fourth Congresses, Coles favored the construction of a naval force to protect American commerce from the Barbary pirates, congressional oversight of presidential diplomacy, and restriction of trade with Great Britain until that country had fulfilled its obligations under the 1783 Treaty of Paris and granted restitution for the illegal seizures made by British naval forces and privateers. He opposed raising taxes on carriages, paper, sugar, tobacco, and other items, increasing the size of the military, appropriating funds for the construction of a naval yard, additional pay for high government officials and legislators, increased funds for the presidential household, a provision that foreigners applying for citizenship had to free their slaves, and the 1795 Jay Treaty with Great Britain. Coles joined eleven other congressmen in opposing the House's address of 15 December 1796, which was generally complimentary of President George Washington and contained an explicit approbation of his administration's policies.

Coles's defeat at the hands of Matthew Clay in the election of 1797 marked the end of his political career. Soon thereafter he moved his family to Pittsylvania County, where he owned more than 6,000 acres of land and paid taxes in 1812 on forty-eight slaves. In January 1800 Coles attended a meeting to choose Republican candidates for the ensuing election, and in July of that year he was appointed a Pittsylvania County election commissioner for the upcoming presidential race. He seems to have played little other role in state or local politics after leaving Congress. Having long suffered from weakness of the lungs, Isaac Coles died on 2 June 1813 and was buried in the family graveyard in Pittsylvania County.

Birth and death dates on gravestone (incorrectly transcribed in Maud Carter Clement, *The History of Pittsylvania County, Virginia* [1976], 201–202); biographies in Clarence Winthrop Bowen, ed., *The History of the Centennial Celebration of* the *Inauguration of George Washington as First President of the United States* (1892), 84 (pors., one by James Peale, facing 111), William B. Coles, *The Coles Family of Virginia: Its Numerous Connections, from the Emigration to America to the Year 1915* (1931), 57–64, Linda Grant De Pauw et al., eds., *Documentary History of the First Federal Congress of the United States of America, March 4, 1789–March 3, 1791* (1972–1998), 14:893–895, and Alice Clement Coles, "The Coles Family of Pittsylvania Co., Virginia" (unpublished MS, 1997), 17–19 (por. on 17), copy in *DVB* Files; marriage dates in *VMHB* 21 (1913): 203; *Revolutionary Virginia*, 1:98, 221; Kaminski, *Ratification*, 9:907, 10:1539, 1541; *Calendar of Virginia State Papers*, 9:80, 86, 125; Pittsylvania Co. Deeds and Wills, 11:380–382; obituary in *Richmond Enquirer*, 13 July 1813 (with variant death date of 4 July 1813).

ROBERT F. HAGGARD

COLES, Russell Jordan (31 December 1865–22 November 1928), ichthyologist, was born at Coles Hill, the Pittsylvania County estate of his parents, Walter Coles (1825–1914) and Lavinia Catherine Jordan Coles. His paternal grandfather, Walter Coles (1790–1857), served five terms in the House of Representatives. Educated at Prince Edward Academy in Worsham, and at Kenmore University High School in Amherst Court House, Coles entered the Virginia Military Institute in 1883 but left after two years without graduating. He studied medicine privately for a time, but, as a journalist later reported of his choice of careers, he "decided to let his possible victims live" and did not seek a medical degree. Coles lived in Danville, where he was a successful dealer in leaf tobacco with Edward G. Moseley in Russell J. Coles and Company. He never married.

Interested in hunting and fishing from his youth, Coles became known during the 1890s as a deep-sea fisherman. For decades he spent several months each year fishing at various locations off the American and Canadian coasts, and he maintained a houseboat at Morehead City, North Carolina. During a major storm off Cape Lookout, North Carolina, in July 1908, Coles aided a lifesaving crew in rescuing a boat and its crew after a tiring, protracted struggle. Troubled to discover that the lifesaving station was poorly equipped and having learned that local congressmen were unable to take appropriate action, Coles wrote to President Theodore Roosevelt, who immediately took steps to rectify the situation.

Coles was an energetic exemplar of the many well-to-do amateurs who made modest but valuable contributions to biological knowledge. Over a period of years, his wealth from the tobacco business enabled him to contribute a number of valuable deep-sea specimens and useful scientific data to the American Museum of Natural History, in New York, the Smithsonian Institution and the United States Bureau of Fisheries (later the United States Fish and Wildlife Service), both in Washington, D.C., the British Museum of Natural History (later the Natural History Museum), in London, and the Muséum d'Histoire Naturelle (later the Muséum National d'Histoire Naturelle), in Paris. Coles collected specimens of many species of sharks and rays and published scientific articles, some jointly with other authors, in the *Bulletin of the American Museum of Natural History* and other journals. His accounts of sharks and rays in the Atlantic Ocean were still being quoted in studies of sharks published more than fifty years later. Coles was also sometimes quoted in the popular press, as when *New York Times* and *Washington Post* articles early in the 1910s cited his authority on electrical properties of several species of fish.

Coles collected an unusually large specimen of devilfish (*Manta birostris*), the largest of the rays, for the American Museum of Natural History and published a dramatic account of the capture in the *American Museum Journal* of April 1916. In the autumn of that year, after Roosevelt read the article, the former president wrote to Coles, who invited Roosevelt the following spring on a monthlong fishing expedition off the Florida Gulf coast. The impending entry of the United States into World War I forced Roosevelt to shorten the trip to one week, but he caught one fine specimen of devilfish and in September 1917 published an account of his expedition in *Scribner's Magazine*. The narrative, reprinted in the 1926 edition of Roosevelt's *Book-Lover's Holidays in the Open*, gave extra publicity to Coles and his work. Roosevelt soon found a way to express his gratitude. He ordinarily declined offers of honorary degrees, but he agreed to accept one from Trinity College, in Hartford, Connecticut, in June 1918 on the condition that

Coles be similarly honored. They received honorary doctorates of science. After Roosevelt's death seven months later, Coles was one of a select number of sportsmen appointed to a commission that the Republican National Committee formed to erect a national memorial to Roosevelt.

During World War I, Coles suggested that ocean fish be exploited as a food source and recommended that sharks be harvested for their meat and leather. Coles also tried to redeem the reputation of sharks. "There is not a fish in the ocean more maligned than the shark," he told a *New York Times* reporter, and added that with a few exceptions the shark "is well meaning and leads an exemplary life." Coles retired from the tobacco business about 1920 and spent part of each year at his vacation home in Nova Scotia. In 1925 two Pittsylvania County chapters of the National Society Daughters of the American Revolution published an honor roll of distinguished county citizens, on which Coles was the lone scientist. Russell Jordan Coles suffered from heart disease in his later years and on 22 November 1928 died at Coles Hill of a heart attack during a bout of influenza. He was buried in the family cemetery on the estate.

Birth date on BVS Death Certificate, Pittsylvania Co.; *Washington Post*, 3 Aug. 1906, 2 July 1911, 23 May 1915, 18 June 1916, 24 Mar., 26 Aug. 1917, 28 May 1921; *New York Times*, 29 June 1913, 22 May 1915 (first quotation), 2 (second quotation), 30 Sept. 1917, 18 June 1918; *Danville Register*, 10 May 1925; principal publications include: with Eugene Willis Gudger, *Natural History Notes on Some Beaufort, N.C., Fishes, 1910–11. No. III. Fishes New or Little Known on the Coast of North Carolina* (1913), "My Fight with the Devilfish," *American Museum Journal* 16 (1916): 217–227, "The Large Sharks of Cape Lookout, North Carolina. The White Shark or Maneater, Tiger Shark and Hammerhead," *Copeia* 69 (7 May 1919): 34–43 (extracts reprinted in *Forest and Stream* 89 [1919]: 346–347, 383), and several articles in the *Bulletin of the American Museum of Natural History*: "Observations on the Habits and Distribution of Certain Fishes Taken on the Coast of North Carolina," 28 (1910): 337–348, with Louis Hussakof, "Notes on the Embryos of Several Species of Rays: With Remarks on the Northward Summer Migration of Certain Tropical Forms Observed on the Coast of North Carolina," 32 (1913): 29–35, with Louis Hussakof, "On Two Ambicolorate Specimens of the Summer Flounder, Paralichthys dentatus, with an Explanation of Ambicoloration," 33 (1914): 95–100, with John T. Nichols, "A New Scorpaena and a Rare Ray from North Carolina," 33 (1914): 537–538, with John T. Nichols, "A New Gymnachirus from North Carolina," 35 (1916): 71–72, and "Natural History Notes on the Devilfish, Manta birostris (Walbaum) and Mobula olfersi (Müller)," 35 (1916): 649–657; Theodore Roosevelt, "Harpooning Devilfish," *Scribner's Magazine* 62 (1917): 293–305 (por. on 295); *American Museum Journal* 17 (1917): 290 (por.); obituaries in *Danville Bee*, 22 Nov. 1928, and *Danville Register*, *New York Times*, *Richmond Times-Dispatch*, and *Washington Post*, all 23 Nov. 1928.

KEIR B. STERLING

COLES, Walter (8 December 1790–9 November 1857), member of the House of Representatives, was born in Halifax County and was the son of Isaac Coles, a member of the Convention of 1788 and of the House of Representatives, and his second wife, Catharine Thompson Coles. When he was about seven years old, he moved with his family to Pittsylvania County. He attended Hampden-Sydney College, where he joined the debating society, and Washington College (later Washington and Lee University), in Lexington. On 6 July 1812 he became a second lieutenant in the 2d Regiment Light Dragoons and during the War of 1812 served on the northern front near the Canadian border. Promoted to captain on 17 March 1814 and given a company command in the 3d Rifle Regiment, he was honorably discharged on 15 June 1815.

After his father's death early in June 1813, Coles inherited nine slaves and 1,240 acres of land in Pittsylvania County. Naming his estate Coles Hill, he focused his energies after the war on developing his lands and also began constructing a large Georgian-style brick mansion, undoubtedly meant as a statement of his wealth and prominence in the county. Like many other residents of south-central Virginia, Coles wanted to improve the region's access to markets, and in 1819 he helped survey the Roanoke River for the Roanoke Navigation Company, which sought to extend the navigability of the river and its many tributaries. On 4 April 1821 he executed a marriage bond in Charlotte County and most likely on the following day married Lettice Priscilla Carrington, a daughter of Paul Carrington (1733–1818), who had been a member of the Conventions of 1776 and of 1788 and a judge of the Virginia Court of Appeals. They had five daughters and two sons.

Coles represented Pittsylvania County in the House of Delegates during the 1817–1818 and 1833–1834 sessions, when he sat on the

Committees for Courts of Justice and to Examine the First Auditor's Office, respectively. He gained a reputation in the assembly as a hardworking, conscientious member. In April 1835 Coles narrowly defeated the Whig incumbent, Thomas Davenport, for the seat in the House of Representatives from the Sixth Congressional District, comprising the counties of Campbell, Halifax, and Pittsylvania. He won reelection four consecutive times, often in close contests and often without carrying his home county. During his final term he represented the reapportioned Third Congressional District, composed of Franklin, Halifax, Henry, Patrick, and Pittsylvania Counties.

A Democrat, Coles cherished the memory of Thomas Jefferson, abhorred the growing power of the federal government, idealized the agrarian lifestyle, and condemned bankers, speculators, and stockjobbers. Perhaps because of his service during the War of 1812 and a continuing interest in army affairs, he devoted much of his attention to military issues. During his five terms Coles sat regularly on either the Committee on Military Affairs or the Committee on the Militia and held the ranking position on the former by his second term. He dealt with such issues as army administration, military pay, government pensions for veterans and widows, and funding monuments to Revolutionary War heroes. Southern Virginia's tobacco-based economy induced Coles also to focus on agriculture. In the Twenty-fourth Congress (1835–1837) he was ranking member of a select committee appointed to examine the high rates of duty foreign governments imposed on American tobacco, and during the Twenty-sixth Congress (1839–1841) he sat on another select committee relating to the tobacco trade. He opposed excessive tariffs and called for free trade in order to encourage the export of Virginia's major cash crop.

Although Coles often reported committee action and presented constituents' petitions, he rarely spoke on issues. His growing frustration with the partisan quarrels that characterized national politics during the Jacksonian era spurred him to introduce resolutions and make speeches urging the House to adopt a measure to table without further action any petition related to the abolition of slavery or the buying, selling,

trading, and transportation of slaves. He reasoned that debating these divisive questions tied up too much time and that his amendment would preserve the peace among the representatives. In an address on 2 February 1841 he supported a government proposal to issue $5 million in treasury notes but argued that the issuance of such notes, with its potential for abuse, should be only a temporary measure in anticipation of incoming revenue.

After completing five terms, Coles did not seek reelection in 1845. He returned to Coles Hill, where he concentrated on his family and agriculture. By 1850 he owned 2,239 acres in Pittsylvania County. Walter Coles died of pneumonia at Coles Hill on 9 November 1857 and was buried in the family cemetery there.

Biographies in George W. Dame, *Historical Sketch of Roman Eagle Lodge, No. 122, A.F. and A.M., 1820–1895* (1895), 96–97, William B. Coles, *The Coles Family of Virginia: Its Numerous Connections, from the Emigration to America to the Year 1915* (1931), 145–158 (including marriage date on 145), and Alice Clement Coles, "The Coles Family of Pittsylvania Co., Virginia" (unpublished MS, 1997), 2–3, 19–21 (por.), copy in *DVB* Files; Mabel Moses, "Coles' Family Burying Ground at 'Coles Hill'" (including birth and death dates on tombstone) and "Miscellaneous Relics and Documents—Walter Coles" (typescripts dated 3 Feb. 1937), both in Works Progress Administration, Virginia Historical Inventory, LVA; Maud Carter Clement, *The History of Pittsylvania County, Virginia* (1976), 204–205, 214, 236–237; Charlotte Co. Marriage Bonds (bond dated 4 Apr. 1821); *Congressional Globe*, 26th Cong., 1st sess., 93, 122–123, 2d sess., 139, 146, 27th Cong., 2d sess., 20, 28th Cong., 1st sess., 455; speech on the treasury note bill in *Congressional Globe*, 26th Cong., 2d sess., Appendix, 386–392, published as *Speech of Mr. Coles, of Virginia, on the Treasury Note Bill. Delivered in the House of Representatives, February 2, 1841* (1841); Pittsylvania Co. Will Book, 2:252–255; obituary in *Danville Republican*, 19 Nov. 1857.

PHILLIP HAMILTON

COLLEY, Richard (ca. 1793–16 March 1858), legendary frontier character, was born in the Reeds Valley section of Russell County and was the son of Thomas Colley, a veteran of the Battle of Kings Mountain during the Revolutionary War, and his second wife, Judith Colley, whose maiden name may have been Fields. Colley's father died in 1800, and his mother later remarried. About 1810 Colley became caretaker of Andrew Heburn's 6,100 acres of undeveloped property in the Sandy Basin, a large area of mountain land in the western portion of Russell County that in 1856 became part of Wise County, in 1858 part of Buchanan County, and in 1880 part of the new county of Dickenson. Colley erected a primitive cabin on the Sand Lick Branch of the Russell Fork of the McClure River in the untouched wilderness, twenty or thirty miles by narrow animal trails from any neighbor. He resided at Sand Lick, often alone, until about 1816, when he moved his wife, Lucretia Christina Counts Colley, whom he reportedly had married on 17 May 1813, and their first son to his Sandy Basin cabin. Colley and his wife lived in the Sandy Basin for the remainder of their lives and had at least two more sons and four daughters.

Colley was a skilled woodsman and lived self-sufficiently and happily alone with his family. They cultivated potatoes, cabbage, and turnips near his cabin and later planted an orchard. They also kept horses and a few cattle in nearby pastures and brought them in at night for protection from predators. Colley furnished bear, venison, turkey, and assorted game for the table. An occasional trek across Sandy Ridge to the gristmills on the Clinch River provided supplies and cornmeal for bread. The family made most of its clothing from wool, flax, animal skins, and domestic goods.

Colley was an unusually strong and fearless man with a quick temper and was said never to have lost a fight. Often referred to as Fighting Dick Colley, he became the principal in many durable regional legends involving fistfights, hunting and shooting exploits, and killing a bear with his hands. In one instance, Colley in 1817 was convicted and fined $2.50 "for assaulting & beating" a man. His many exploits in the field and the fights in which he engaged became part of the legendary history of southwestern Virginia, tales rooted in reality but resembling those told elsewhere about such other frontier characters as Daniel Boone and David "Davy" Crockett.

Colley was a member of a Russell County militia company that was called to duty in February 1815 at the close of the War of 1812 but that probably did not remain in the field very long. In spite of his early reputation for rough exploits, he became a respectable and responsible citizen. Encouraging the economic develop-ment of the western portion of Russell County, he was said to have operated one of the first mills in the Sandy Basin, and several times beginning in the 1840s the county court appointed him a surveyor of roads, in which office he directed the marking and clearing of several of the county's first roads. Modern Highway 80, which passes through Breaks Interstate Park, follows the route that he suggested to link the Clinch Valley with Pike County, Kentucky. In 1845 Colley supervised a special election held at his residence, which then became or already was the polling place for the Sand Lick District of Russell County. He was elected a justice of the peace in 1852 but did not serve.

Colley and his wife never owned land of their own, although their children purchased large parcels of Sand Lick land. His wife died late in 1855. Richard Colley died on 16 March 1858 at the residence of a son on Grassy Creek near the Kentucky border and was buried near his son's house. Even though his residence had for two years been in the new county of Wise, it was the Russell County Court that appointed three men to appraise his estate, which was sold at auction. Consisting largely of livestock, agricultural implements, and the guns, axes, and other objects that hunters owned, his estate also included cooking utensils, bedding, household furniture, and one umbrella.

Biography in Elihu Jasper Sutherland, *Some Sandy Basin Characters* (1962), 49–66; family history in Joye Boardman, comp., *Thomas Colley Family* (2001), 10–11, 364–365, and Hetty Swindall Sutherland, comp., *Some Descendants of John Counts of Glade Hollow (Southwest Virginia)* (1978), 155–156; collected family history sources and folklore in Pearle Goode, "Legends of the Colley Family" (typescript dated 23 May 1936), in Works Progress Administration, Virginia Historical Inventory, LVA, and in Elihu Jasper Sutherland and Hetty Swindall Sutherland, eds., *Pioneer Recollections of Southwest Virginia* (1984), esp. 54–55, 64–68, 81–82, 128–130, 147, 155–156, 236, 284–285, 329–332; Census, Russell Co., 1850 (age fifty-seven on 23 Aug. 1850); Russell Co. Law Order Book, 5:388 (quotation), 398; Register of Justices and County Officers (1852–1860), Acc. 36076, LVA; estate inventory and accounts in Russell Co. Will Book, 7:187–190, 214–215; BVS Death Register, Russell Co. (wife's death on 6 Dec. 1855); wife's death date of 8 Nov. 1855 and Colley's death date in John Colley family Bible records, Dickenson Co. Historical Records Survey, Bible Records, C:130, Jonnie B. Deel Memorial Library, Clintwood.

BEVERLY REPASS HOCH

COLLEY, William Washington (12 February 1847–24 December 1909), Baptist missionary and a founder of the Baptist Foreign Mission Convention, was the son of William Washington Colley, a white resident of Prince Edward County, and Selina, a neighbor's slave. After the Civil War, Colley identified his mother as Selina Colley, although it is unlikely that his parents were ever legally married. Even later, Colley's widow described his parents as a Scottish clergyman and a Native American woman. Nothing is known of Colley's childhood, early education, or when or how he gained his freedom. From the autumn of 1870 until 1874 he was a student at the Richmond Theological School for Freedmen (popularly known as the Richmond Theological Institute or the Colver Institute and later part of Virginia Union University). He preached in Louisa County during the summers of 1871 and 1872 and in Norwich, Connecticut, during the summers of 1873 and 1874.

In May 1873 Colley was ordained a minister in Alexandria. The following year he requested assignment to Africa as a missionary. He sailed for west Africa on 8 January 1875 under appointment of the Foreign Mission Board of the Southern Baptist Convention. In cooperation with the Virginia Baptist State Convention, to which many African American Baptist churches in Virginia belonged, the board sent Colley and a white minister, from Mississippi, to the area then known as Yorubaland and later as Nigeria. They began their work in Lagos in October, but Colley soon became disappointed with how white missionaries treated the local population and with the restrictions that his colleague and other white leaders of missionary work placed on the activities of African American missionaries. He returned to the United States in November 1879 and resigned.

Colley and the Virginia Baptist State Convention immediately began to lay the groundwork for a national organization of Baptists to support missionary work in Africa. Named official ambassador of the state convention in January 1880, he worked tirelessly throughout that year to organize a national convention, writing many letters and traveling throughout the Southeast to solicit black Baptist support. When about 150 delegates gathered in Montgomery, Alabama, in November 1880, Colley opened the proceedings as temporary presiding officer. His role in founding the Baptist Foreign Mission Convention (BFMC) was pivotal. In addition to its importance to black Americans as an instrument to conduct missionary work in Africa, the conference was one of three major African American Baptist organizations that merged in 1895 to form the National Baptist Convention, the largest and most-enduring national association of African American Baptists.

In the year following the creation of the BFMC, Colley's work was instrumental in setting the organization on sound footing. Elected corresponding secretary and one of five Virginians to serve on the first executive board, he corresponded widely and traveled extensively, to Baptist conventions and both black and white Baptist churches. Though Colley strongly supported independent black Baptist mission work in Africa, he did not oppose participation of white Baptists, many of whom shared his conviction that African American Christians had a providential role as leaders in evangelizing Africans.

On 1 November 1883 Colley married Georgie Carter, of Portsmouth, a twenty-five-year-old Baptist lay leader and public school teacher. In consenting to be his wife, she fully understood and accepted the challenge of mission work as a co-laborer with her new husband. Shortly after they married, the Colleys journeyed to Liberia with several other missionaries as part of the BFMC's first major mission operation, with a goal of establishing the Bendoo station among the Vai people of western Liberia. Foreign missions were a challenge for white Christians and even more so for African American organizations whose memberships were poorer. In addition to the difficulty of raising money, the BFMC faced the sad reality that among its first group of missionaries several died and others returned home ill. Tragedy hit the Colleys twice. One of their seven children, who was born during their three years in Africa, died there. (They also had four daughters and two sons.) In addition, Colley, when firing a gun in an attempt to frighten away a mentally ill man, accidentally killed an African boy. Local officials and the testimony of witnesses to the incident exonerated him of wrongdoing. Grieving, ill, and already planning to return to the United States, Colley was recalled for investigation. The BFMC formally accepted his explanation and assigned him domestic leadership responsibilities, but he was no longer one of the organization's most conspicuous leaders.

Colley spent the remainder of his career laboring for the cause of African missions, delivering addresses on African peoples and customs, and helping to write religious tracts. In 1889 the BFMC recommended that the president of the United States offer him an appointment as consul to the Congo Free State. William Washington Colley resided in Harrisonburg in 1900 and died in Winston-Salem, North Carolina, on 24 December 1909, having contributed immensely to the mission programs of the Virginia Baptist State Convention and the Baptist Foreign Mission Convention.

Biographies in H. A. Tupper, *The Foreign Missions of the Southern Baptist Convention* (1880), 427–428 (with birth date), and Charles H. Corey, *A History of the Richmond Theological Seminary, with Reminiscences of Thirty Years' Work among the Colored People of the South* (1895), 143–144; parents identified on 8 Nov. 1870 application (no. 2143), Freedmen's Savings and Trust Company Records, RG 101, NARA; 1840s relationship of parents documented in Melvin Patrick Ely, *Israel on the Appomattox: A Southern Experiment in Black Freedom from the 1790s through the Civil War* (2004), 305, 573; Portsmouth Marriage Register (with full name); L. A. Scruggs, *Women of Distinction: Remarkable in Works and Invincible in Character* (1893), 228–231; Lewis G. Jordan, *Negro Baptist History U.S.A., 1750–1930* (1930), 114–115 (pors. facing 24 and 56, death date and place facing 56); C. C. Adams and Marshall A. Talley, *Negro Baptists and Foreign Missions* (1944), 32–35; J. H. Jackson, *A Story of Christian Activism: A History of the National Baptist Convention, U.S.A., Inc.* (1980), 32–34; Walter L. Williams, *Black Americans and the Evangelization of Africa, 1877–1900* (1982), 17–18, 66–69, 185, 189; Sandy D. Martin, *Black Baptists and African Missions: The Origins of a Movement, 1880–1915* (1989); missionary career, including Colley's reports and letters from the field, documented in Baptist Foreign Mission Convention annual *Minutes* (1881–1891).

SANDY DWAYNE MARTIN

COLLIER, Charles Fenton (16 September 1827–29 June 1899), member of the Confederate States House of Representatives, was born in Petersburg and was the son of Mary Ann Davis Collier and Robert Ruffin Collier, a lawyer and later a state senator. Collier attended local schools and perhaps prepared for college at a Brunswick County boarding school. From 1844 to 1845 he attended the University of Virginia and Washington College (later Washington and Lee University). He then entered Harvard University and in 1848 received a law degree. On 14 March of that year he married Arabella E. Gee, of Surry County. They had no children.

In the spring of 1848 Collier established a law practice in Petersburg. He soon moved to Shellbanks, a Prince George County farm once owned by the agricultural reformer Edmund Ruffin, to try his hand at planting. In a special election held in 1852 to fill a vacancy caused by the death of the incumbent, Collier won a seat in the House of Delegates representing Prince George and Surry Counties. He was appointed to the Committee of Schools and Colleges. The following year he won election to a full term and secured seats on the Committees for Courts of Justice and of Propositions and Grievances.

About 1857 Collier moved back to Petersburg in order to practice law with his father. In May 1859 Petersburg voters returned him to the House of Delegates representing the city. He sat on the Committees for Courts of Justice and on Finance. A Democrat who opposed secession, Collier supported Stephen Arnold Douglas for president in 1860 and may have introduced him that summer at a Petersburg campaign stop. On 9 January 1861 Collier voted in the minority against calling a convention to consider Virginia's secession from the Union and introduced an unsuccessful amendment calling for a referendum on whether such a convention should be summoned. After the Civil War began, he served as an aide to Major General Walter Gwynn. Collier used the rank of colonel in operations around Norfolk, but his service was short-lived. Reelected on 23 May to another term in the House, he once again sat on the Committees for Courts of Justice and on Finance. He occasionally acted as the Speaker pro tempore and resigned from the assembly on 10 May 1862.

Early in May 1862 Collier narrowly defeated two other candidates in a special election to fill Virginia's vacant Fourth District seat in the

Confederate States House of Representatives. Representing the city of Petersburg and the counties of Amelia, Chesterfield, Cumberland, Dinwiddie, Goochland, Nottoway, Powhatan, and Prince George, Collier took his seat on 18 August 1862 and served through 17 February 1864 in the remaining three sessions of the First Confederate Congress. At various times he sat on the Committees on Commerce, on Naval Affairs, and on the War Tax. He also served on a five-member committee to investigate fraud in railroad transportation. Collier often spoke on exceptions to the Confederacy's draft laws and supported exemptions for coal miners, postal workers, and men older than forty years of age. Twice he offered designs for the Great Seal of the Confederate States of America, and in February 1863 he proposed that all African Americans captured while in the service of the United States should become the slaves of their captors.

In his May 1863 bid for reelection, Collier lost a close contest to Thomas Saunders Gholson by 29 votes of 4,261 cast. Collier asked for a recount, which he discontinued in May 1864. He returned to Petersburg and volunteered with the militia when it repulsed Union troops in June 1864. As a member of Petersburg's common council, he was one of three local leaders appointed to surrender the city to Union forces following the Confederate evacuation during the night of 2–3 April 1865.

Collier took an oath of allegiance to the United States on 28 June 1865 and petitioned for a presidential pardon, which after several follow-up letters he received on 1 February 1867. Elected mayor of Petersburg on 7 May 1866, he resigned on 25 March 1868 as federal officials began clamoring to remove former Confederates from office. The previous week, on 18 March, Collier became president of the Petersburg Railroad Company, which operated between the city and Weldon, North Carolina, and in 1868 carried almost $112,800 in debt. Within four years he had eliminated the deficit and ensured net assets of more than $31,850. Despite his success, the board of directors, citing its desire to channel more business into the city, replaced him on 20 March 1872. In appreciation of his service, employees presented Collier with a gold-headed cane.

Collier defeated the Republican Stith Bolling in the election for mayor in May 1888. He won four more consecutive two-year terms. After losing the Democratic primary by five votes in April 1898, he unsuccessfully sought a recount. Also active in the Tabb Street Presbyterian Church, he headed its Sunday school and represented the East Hanover Presbytery at national assemblies four times.

Collier's wife died on 7 May 1890. The sixty-three-year-old widower married twenty-year-old Mary Epes Jones on 24 June 1891. They had no children. Charles Fenton Collier, who had been ill for several years and also suffered from insomnia, shot himself in the head with a Colt revolver on 29 June 1899 in his house in Petersburg and died instantly. He was buried in Blandford Cemetery.

Henry and Spofford, *Eminent Men*, 427–429; French Biographies; Surry Co. Marriage Register (bond dated 28 Feb. 1848); BVS Marriage Register, Petersburg (1891); *Petersburg Republican*, 17 Mar. 1848; *Richmond Daily Enquirer*, 12 May 1862; *Petersburg Daily Index*, 26, 27 May 1868; *Petersburg Daily Express*, 9 July 1868; *Petersburg Rural Messenger*, 6 Apr. 1872; *Petersburg Daily Index-Appeal*, 25 May 1888, 8 May 1890, 27 May 1892, 29 May 1896, 8 Apr. 1898; *JHD*, 1852 sess., 489, 1861 sess., 16; *OR*, 1st ser., vol. 46, pt. 1, 1048, vol. 51, pt. 2, 45, 46; *Journal of Confederate Congress*, 5:295, 305, 6:23, 37–38, 51, 74, 88–89, 95, 129, 146, 292, 7:85; Presidential Pardons; Collier letters published in George S. Bernard, comp., *War Talks of Confederate Veterans* (1892), 137–138, and *Richmond Dispatch*, 12 June 1894; obituary in *Petersburg Daily Index-Appeal*, 30 June 1899 (with birth date).

G. W. POINDEXTER

COLLINS, Charles (17 April 1813–10 July 1875), president of Emory and Henry College, was born in the part of North Yarmouth that in 1822 became Cumberland, which at the time of his birth lay in Massachusetts but after 1820 in Maine. The son of Joseph Warren Collins and Hannah Sturdivant Collins, he grew up within a devout family for whom daily life centered on worship in a Congregational church, Bible study, and hard farmwork. In 1827 Collins entered the Maine Wesleyan Seminary (later Kents Hill School), at Readfield, in Kennebec County. While there, he joined the Methodist Episcopal Church, and after he graduated in 1832, he enrolled in the new Wesleyan University, at Middletown,

Connecticut. There Collins excelled in all his subjects and graduated in August 1837 as class valedictorian and with Phi Beta Kappa honors. He received an M.A. from the university in 1840. On 13 July 1841 Collins married Harriet Newell Hart. They had five daughters and five sons.

His brilliant record at Wesleyan made him a favorite of the university's first president, Wilbur Fisk, whose advice and assistance shaped the course of Collins's career. Collins began work in August 1837 as principal of the high school in Augusta, Maine. The following January, Creed Fulton, whom the Holston Conference of the Methodist Episcopal Church had appointed to lead efforts to establish a four-year college in southwestern Virginia, sought Fisk's help in recruiting Emory and Henry College's first president from among the graduates of Wesleyan University. Fisk recommended Collins to Fulton early in February 1838, and the college trustees formally elected Collins on 28 February. Winter travel and consultations with Fisk delayed Collins's arrival in Washington County until late in the spring. On 25 May 1838 he delivered his inaugural address as Emory and Henry's president and set to work leading and teaching in the new institution, which opened with sixty full-time students.

Initially Collins was the only professor at Emory and Henry. He taught moral and mental science and organized the college curriculum on the Wesleyan model. He established six academic departments: moral science and belles lettres, mathematics and natural philosophy, natural science, ancient languages, modern languages, and agricultural chemistry and scientific farming. Other than the addition of several new courses, the educational program that he created, which emphasized generalized study and traditional methods of learning, remained a defining feature of Emory and Henry until about 1900, when the college began to embrace the trend toward academic specialization. At different times throughout his presidency, Collins taught every subject except farming and became especially renowned for his erudition in mathematics, natural sciences, and modern and ancient languages. At its founding, the college also had a manual labor system for all students who enrolled—a nineteenth-century agricultural version of student work-study—but the experiment proved both unpopular and impractical and was abandoned within a few years. As enrollment grew, Collins hired tutors and with Fisk's help recruited two additional Wesleyan graduates as permanent faculty members.

An energetic man of robust health and astounding intellectual vigor and brilliance, Collins was also authoritarian, uncompromising, humorless, and arbitrary as an administrator. He was a strict disciplinarian whom students and colleagues held more in respect than in affection. Late in the 1840s he enhanced his prestige, and by extension Emory and Henry's growing reputation, by successfully defending Methodism against the theological attacks of a prominent Calvinist proselytizer. Frederick Augustus Ross, a leading Presbyterian minister, preached a series of sermons in southwestern Virginia and northeastern Tennessee hostile to Methodism. After several Emory and Henry students heard Ross at Glade Spring Presbyterian Church early in May 1848, they begged Collins to reply in behalf of Methodism. In a tour de force at the same church on 21 May, he preached without interruption or respite for about seven hours and enthralled a crowd of 2,000 with an erudite address described as a literary, doctrinal, and oratorical masterpiece. Later that year Collins delivered a similar address, published as *Methodism and Calvinism Compared: A Discourse Preached at the Dedication of the Methodist Episcopal Church, Marion, Virginia, December 24, 1848* (1849). So devastating was Collins's rebuttal to the Presbyterian's attacks that Ross ceased further assaults and the controversy subsided.

Collins kept Emory and Henry operating through an infancy of serious financial uncertainty. The college received a charter from the General Assembly in March 1839 and benefited from a public loan the state eventually forgave in 1852. Emory and Henry's enrollment grew steadily apace with its reputation. The college also prospered culturally and intellectually under Collins's leadership. In 1851 he founded the *Southern Repertory and College Review*, a literary journal that Emory and Henry published and to which he contributed articles on such subjects as the Convention of 1850–1851 and salt manufacturing in southwestern Virginia. That same year Collins's success earned him the unusual distinction of three honorary doctorates—from Masonic College in Missouri, Centenary College in Louisiana, and Dickinson College in Carlisle, Pennsylvania. By 1851 he had turned down several offers of other college presidencies, including the Greensboro Female College, in North Carolina, but he began seriously to consider leaving Emory and Henry. As president, Collins had clashed with individual trustees, notably former governor David Campbell, and with the board, over various issues and policies. He also believed that some trustees sought improperly to interfere in or to control the administration of the college. Matters came to a head in 1850 when Collins was unjustly accused of profiting excessively from the sale of books and supplies to the students, in his capacity as manager of the college bookstore. Although a board review vindicated Collins, suspicions among members of the college community continued to fester. He resigned on 14 July 1852 to become president of Dickinson College, where the trustees had already elected him to the office on 7 July.

At Dickinson College, Collins wrestled with many of the same problems he had at Emory and Henry—student discipline, uncertain finances, and difficult relations with trustees. He also made permanent improvements to Dickinson's academic facilities, built a new observatory, and continued a financial drive to secure an endowment for the college. The endowment campaign fell short of its goal and then failed disastrously after Collins pushed to invest the funds in high-risk western speculative ventures that collapsed. When Collins resigned on 12 July 1860 to become president of the State Female College in Memphis, Tennessee, Dickinson's finances remained precarious and persisted as a problem for his successors.

Chartered in 1858 as a private corporation by a group of leading citizens in Memphis, the State Female College quickly became a successful institution, prosperous and strong enough to survive the Civil War. Closed in 1862 during the Union occupation of Memphis and then used as barracks by United States troops, the school reopened in the autumn of 1865, when Collins once again applied his energies and experience to building a viable, prestigious educational institution. For the last ten years of his life, he was both president and proprietor of the State Female College.

Charles Collins fell ill early in July 1875, during a yellow fever epidemic, and within a week died at his Memphis home, on 10 July 1875, from the effects of severe dysentery. He was buried in Elmwood Cemetery, in Memphis. His widow succeeded him as president and proprietor of the State Female College and continued to operate the school for about nine years. On the Emory and Henry College campus, Collins House, originally built as the president's house and after 1965 used as a residence hall, honors him.

Biographies in *Alumni Record of Wesleyan University, Middletown, Conn.*, 3d ed. (1883), 15, 554–555 (including marriage date and selected bibliography of publications), *Semi-Centennial Catalogue and Historical Register of Emory and Henry College, Washington County, Virginia, 1837–87* (1887), 38–39, R. N. Rice, *Holston Methodism: From Its Origin to the Present Time* (1903–1914), 4:118–124 (por. on 120), James Henry Morgan, *Dickinson College: The History of One Hundred and Fifty Years, 1783–1933* (1933), 301–310, and George J. Stevenson, *Increase in Excellence: A History of Emory and Henry College* (1963), 68–84; Charles Collins Family Papers, including diaries (with birth date in genealogy following entry for 22 Dec. 1849, p. 65), diplomas, and sermons, Dickinson College, Carlisle, Pa.; Emory and Henry College Archives and Holston Conference Archives, both Emory and Henry College, Emory, Va.; Emory and Henry College inaugural address in Slemp and Preston, *Addresses*, 115–131; other published addresses include *An Address Delivered before the Calliopean and Hermesian Societies of Emory and Henry College, January 10, 1849* (1849); published writings include "Disfranchisement of the Clergy,—The Constitutional Convention of Virginia," *Southern Repertory and College Review* 1 (1851): 41–56, "Industrial Resources of S.W. Virginia" and "The Salt and Salt Manufacture of Southwestern Virginia," ibid. 4 (1852): 228–232, 239–250, "Christian Biography" and "Rev. Charles Nisbet, D.D., First President of Dickinson College," *Ladies' Repository* 13 (1853): 361–363, 529–532, "The Law Student," ibid. 15 (1855): 284–286, and "Dickinson College," ibid. 16 (1856): 449–453; *Southwestern Christian Advocate*, 19 July 1838; *Ladies' Repository* 20 (1860): 385; death notices in *Daily Memphis Avalanche* and *Memphis Daily Appeal*, both 11 July 1875; obituaries in *Abingdon Virginian*, 23 July 1875, and *Knoxville Holston Methodist*, 31 July 1875.

CHARLES W. SYDNOR, JR.

COLLINS, Johnson (August 1847–3 November 1906), member of the House of Delegates, was born in Virginia, probably into slavery. Information about him is scarce, and the scattered documents that mention him often contain inconsistencies or suggest that those who recorded the information may not have known much about him. It is possible, but by no means certain, that he was a Norfolk native who married Rebecca Fuller in that city on 11 July 1866. A marriage license identifies the groom on that occasion as John H. Collins, a twenty-one-year-old student and son of Margaret Collins. What is certain is that in the summer of 1870 Johnson Collins, Rebecca Collins, and their sons, ages three and one, were living near his brother, a tanner, in Brunswick County. He and his wife later had two other children who died in infancy or childhood. Collins worked as a laborer, but so far as land and tax records show, he never owned any real estate. He may occasionally have used only his surname. The census enumerator in 1870 listed him as Collin Collins and his younger son, who was thereafter usually called Johnson Collins Jr., as Collin Collins Jr.

In November 1879 Collins narrowly won a three-way race for a seat representing Brunswick County in the House of Delegates. He defeated two white men, the Republican incumbent who favored paying off the antebellum state debt in full and a Readjuster who wanted to reduce the amount of the debt to be paid and to refinance the balance at a lower interest rate. Two voters cast ballots for Collin Johnson, suggesting continued confusion about his name or that he was not well known in some parts of the county.

Identified in one newspaper as a Republican and in another as a Readjuster, Collins served in the General Assembly that met from 3 December 1879 through 9 March 1880. He was appointed to a low-ranking seat on the Committee on Federal Relations and Resolutions and to the lowest-ranking seat on the relatively inconsequential Committee on Public Property. At the opening of the session Collins voted with the dominant coalition of Republicans and Readjusters to elect the Speaker, clerk, and other House officers and again two weeks later when the assembly elected the Readjuster leader William Mahone to the United States Senate. Collins supported a proposed constitutional amendment to eliminate the poll tax as a prerequisite for voting and another measure that the Readjusters favored to reduce the tax on vendors of malt liquor, spirits, and wine. On 1 March 1880 he voted for a bill to reduce the principal of the public debt by about 40 percent and to refinance the remainder at 3 percent interest. Called the Riddleberger Bill, after its sponsor, state senator Harrison Holt Riddleberger, it passed, but the governor vetoed the measure, and the Senate of Virginia sustained the veto.

In June 1880, when Collins gave information about his family to the census taker, who recorded his name correctly this time, he identified himself as a literate laborer and added, perhaps with pride, that he was a member of the state legislature, a fact the enumerator carefully recorded. Collins did not seek reelection in 1881 but received six votes anyway. Sometime during the next half-dozen years he and his family moved to Washington, D.C., where he worked as a watchman for about two decades. Johnson Collins died of heart disease in Washington on 3 November 1906 and was buried in the city's Columbian Harmony Cemetery.

Birth date in Census, Washington, D.C., 1900 (age fifty-three on 18 June 1900); Norfolk City Marriage License (age twenty-one on 11 July 1866); Census, Brunswick Co., 1870 (as Collin Collins, age twenty-four on 22 July 1870), and 1880 (age thirty-four on 15 June 1880); Election Records, nos. 14, 17, RG 13, LVA; *Richmond Daily Dispatch*, 7, 15 Nov. 1879, 2 Mar. 1880; *Richmond State*, 7 Nov., 9 Dec. 1879, 2 Mar. 1880; *JHD*, 1879–1880 sess., 5–6, 30, 59–60, 386, 401–404; James Tice Moore, *Two Paths to the New South: The Virginia Debt Controversy, 1870–1883* (1974), 63–68; Paul E. Sluby Sr., ed., *Records of the Columbian Harmony Cemetery, Washington, D.C.* (1996), 5:15, with death date.

BRENT TARTER

COLLINS, Lewis Preston (25 December 1896–20 September 1952), lieutenant governor of Virginia, was born in Lynchburg and was the son of Lewis Preston Collins, a businessman, and Ella Bolling Moorman Collins. Soon after his birth, the family moved to Marion, in Smyth County, where he attended public schools and in 1914 graduated from Marion High School. Collins enrolled in Washington and Lee

University, but in May 1917, after the United States entered World War I, he joined the Washington and Lee ambulance unit (later designated Section Sanitaire Unie 534) and served with the 12th French Division. After his discharge in mid-1919, he returned to Washington and Lee and in 1920 received a bachelor of arts degree. Collins then studied for one year at the Yale University Law School before returning to Washington and Lee for a second year of study. Admitted to the bar in July 1922, he opened a law practice in Marion. Collins married Pauline Hull Staley in that town on 2 January 1926. They had one son.

L. Preston Collins, or Pat Collins, as he was familiarly known, was secretary of the Smyth County Electoral Board from 1925 to 1929, after which he was appointed commissioner of accounts of the Smyth County Circuit Court. During his residence in Marion he was at various times president of the Marion National Bank and of the Mountain Empire Broadcasting Corporation, and he owned and operated a department store. Collins served as president of the Marion Kiwanis Club and as vice president of the Marion Chamber of Commerce. He was also commander of Marion's American Legion post and was a member of the Veterans of Foreign Wars.

A Democrat, Collins won election in 1935 to the first of two two-year terms representing Smyth County in the House of Delegates. He was a member of the Committees on Appropriations, on Militia and Police, on Privileges and Elections, and on Retrenchment and Economy. He became a spokesman for the dominant faction of the Democratic Party then under the leadership of Harry Flood Byrd (1887–1966). In 1939 Collins lost his seat to a Republican, Quincy A. Calhoun, but he remained active in the Democratic Party and in 1940 served as state Democratic campaign manager. In 1941 Smyth County voters returned Collins to the House of Delegates, where he sat on the Committees on General Laws, on Militia and Police, on Mining and Mineral Resources, and on Public Property. Reelected in 1943, he retained his seats on the Committees on Militia and Police and on Mining and Mineral Resources and received appointments to the Committees on Courts of Justice and on Finance. One of the party's better orators, Collins gave the keynote address at the Democratic State Convention in July 1944.

Collins sought the party nomination for lieutenant governor in 1945. The other candidates were Charles Rogers Fenwick, of Arlington County, who was also a supporter of Byrd, and Leonard Gaston Muse, of Roanoke, who was an opponent. Many Byrd organization members urged the party leader to endorse Collins or Fenwick rather than split the vote of Byrd's supporters and risk nominating his adversary, but Byrd refused and remained neutral. Late in the campaign, rumors circulated that Byrd had in fact sent orders to his supporters to vote for Fenwick, and Fenwick's backers spread that word throughout the party. On 7 August, Fenwick defeated Collins in the primary by the narrow margin of 572 votes out of more than 135,000 cast. Muse finished a distant third.

Two weeks later Collins and twenty-one Wise County citizens filed a petition in the Richmond City Circuit Court charging widespread voting irregularities in mail ballots and complaining that the Hamilton precinct in Wise County did not hold an election. They also charged that in the Bond Mill and Pound precincts the number of votes recorded exceeded the number of people who voted more than four times over. When Collins's lawyers attempted to review the Wise County poll books and election records, county officials denied them access. After the court ordered the county officials to allow lawyers for Collins to examine the poll books, they discovered that twenty-five of the twenty-seven poll books had disappeared and that the ballot boxes for the two precincts contained fewer ballots than election officials had certified. Fenwick's supporters counterattacked by charging that in several Southside counties that Collins had carried by large margins his supporters had improperly used Virginia's War Voters' Act to cast ballots for people who did not go to the polls. The investigations of Fenwick's assertions uncovered no substantial misconduct, but the irregularities in Wise County were the most serious in any modern statewide campaign. Judge Julien Gunn, although reluctant to overturn the election, declared that he was convinced that "political crooks and ballot thieves" had corrupted the pri-

Collins

mary election in Wise County. With the Wise County vote disallowed, Gunn awarded the nomination to Collins.

Collins easily won the November 1945 general election and was reelected with less controversy four years later. He took office on 16 January 1946 and as president of the Senate of Virginia chaired the powerful Committee on Rules. During his first year in office, Collins cast the tiebreaking vote to kill an amendment that would have made it easier to cast absentee ballots. Two years later he endorsed Governor William Munford Tuck's proposal to amend the state election law in order to keep the name of President Harry S. Truman off the Virginia ballot in 1948, but the House of Delegates watered down the measure and diffused the original intent. Midway through his second term, on 20 September 1952, Lewis Preston Collins suffered a fatal heart attack while he was being introduced as the speaker at the dedication of a new elementary school near Austinville in Wythe County. He was buried in Roselawn Cemetery, in Marion.

Biographies in Glass and Glass, *Virginia Democracy*, 2:352–354, and Manarin, *Senate Officers*, 157–158 (por. on 156); BVS Birth Register, Lynchburg; Lewis Preston Collins Papers, at UVA and UVA Law Library; *Marion News*, 7 Jan. 1926; campaign statement in *Virginia Journal of Education* 38 (1945): 374, 379; information on 1945 primary in James Howe Latimer Papers, Acc. 37623 (including notes and draft for Latimer, "'Tis strange': 1945 Election Challenge in Wise Found Poll Books Gone," *Richmond Times-Dispatch*, 17 Dec. 1989), LVA, in Thomas R. Morris, *Virginia's Lieutenant Governors: The Office and the Person* (1970), 50–52, and in *Richmond News Leader* and *Richmond Times-Dispatch*, Aug.–Sept. 1945, with judge's full opinion and quotation in *Richmond Times-Dispatch*, 30 Sept. 1945; obituaries in *Bristol Herald Courier and Bristol Virginia-Tennessean*, 21 Sept. 1952, *Richmond Times-Dispatch*, 21, 22 Sept. 1952, and *Richmond News Leader*, 22 Sept. 1952; obituary and reprints of editorial tributes from twelve Virginia newspapers in *Marion Smyth County News*, 25 Sept. 1952.

GERALD P. GAIDMORE II

COLLINS, Mary Elizabeth "Toddy" (11 May 1868–30 December 1947), Methodist missionary, was born in Wisbech, Cambridgeshire, England, and was the daughter of Emma Elizabeth May Collins and George William Collins, a hotel owner and amateur horticulturalist. She attended a local school and reportedly greeted Queen Victoria when the queen visited. Her mother died

in June 1875, and about 1880 her father moved the family to Carteret County, North Carolina, where he acquired a farm, remarried in August 1883, and had six more children. Collins suffered from malaria and asthma in their new home and, much to her disappointment, was no longer able to attend school. To alleviate her health problems she moved to Richmond, Virginia, by 1900 and worked for a time in local flour mills and as a domestic servant.

Collins became interested in mission work, and a Richmond Methodist church helped her to attend a missionary training school operated by the Christian and Missionary Alliance in Nyack, New York. Planning to travel to South America as a missionary, she studied Spanish. Soon, however, she became aware of the need for missionaries in the Appalachian coalfields, where various religious denominations hoped to improve the lives of mountain residents as well as to evangelize, and after her graduation in 1904 she decided to join a group of fellow students headed for southwestern Virginia.

By March 1906 Collins had arrived in Wise County with less than a dollar in her pocket. She immediately went to work in the recently constructed coal town of Roda, one of the collieries of the Stonega Coke and Coal Company. Collins began holding church services and Sunday school in her home, where she also offered sewing classes to miners' wives and daughters and ran a school for the children. Stonega provided her with a five-room house and a food allowance at the company store and eventually paid her a small salary in the interest of providing a more pleasant environment for its employees. Such strategies were typical of the region's coal companies, which often adopted a paternalistic attitude toward the miners as a way to retain their labor.

Toddy Collins, as she was known in Roda and the surrounding area, was an integral part of the community for the next forty years. She continually gave away her food, her supplies, and even her furniture to those whom she thought needed them more. She helped the company doctors during epidemics by visiting the sick, distributing food, and administering medicine. In addition to ministering to the educational and religious needs of the area's children, Collins

381

also offered them such entertainments as candy pulls and fishing trips. She persuaded the coal company to build a small school for Roda and in 1921 convinced Stonega to construct a new church in the community. Annual homecomings, which began at the church in 1939, became a way for the community and former residents from around the country to honor Collins, and in 1940 the Board of Missions and Church Extension of the Methodist Church awarded her life membership for her many years of unselfish service. Collins never married, but she legally adopted two young girls as her daughters and provided a home for another girl and a boy.

In a 1939 interview with a Works Projects Administration fieldworker Collins stated that she had come to Roda "on a faith mission" and that she "enjoyed the work and plan[ned] to continue until the end," which she did despite her continuous battle with poor health. Mary Elizabeth "Toddy" Collins died on 30 December 1947 in the Norton hospital and was buried in Glencoe Cemetery, in Big Stone Gap. A month and a half after her death the *Saturday Evening Post* featured an article on "The Angel of Happy Hollow," and later that year the Southwest Virginia Museum, in Big Stone Gap, opened with a display of her Bible, her songbook, and an umbrella and handmade black bag she had always carried.

Birth and death dates on gravestone; WPA Biographies (quotations on 13–14); John Maloney, "The Angel of Happy Hollow," *Saturday Evening Post* 220 (14 Feb. 1948): 30–31 (pors.), 97–99; Ann Goode Cooper, *Gathering up Memories: A Collection of Appalachian Stories* (2003), 130–160 (pors.); activities documented in *Big Stone Gap Post*, 1906–1948; obituaries in *Norton Coalfield Progress* and *Big Stone Gap Post*, both 1 Jan. 1948; editorial tribute in *Big Stone Gap Post*, 12 Feb. 1948.

MARIANNE E. JULIENNE

COLLINS, Thomas Jasper (28 August 1844–5 October 1925), architect, was born in Washington, D.C., and was the son of William Collins, an architect and builder, and Nancy Hutchens Collins. Little is known about his education or early years, but he probably apprenticed with his family's architecture and construction business in the nation's capital. Collins enlisted in September 1862 as a private in the 1st Regiment District of Columbia Infantry. From January 1864 until June 1865 he was attached to the United States War Department as a messenger. He held an engineering position with the post office from 1867 until 1883, although during the 1870s and 1880s he also worked as a carpenter and architect. On 22 April 1867 Collins married Genevive M. Minn. They had at least four sons before her death in December 1878. Collins married Sophie Cecelia Barrett, of Philadelphia, on 5 January 1881. They had three sons and two daughters and possibly two other children who died young.

After leaving the postal service, Collins established a building company with his nephew Samuel Gaskins. The move proved disastrous when Gaskins mismanaged funds and lost the contract for a federal building in Kentucky. Financially ruined and forced to seek employment elsewhere, Collins answered an 1890 advertisement for a draftsman with the Staunton Development Company and moved to Staunton. After this company failed, Collins worked briefly as an architect for the Staunton Building Company in 1891 before joining with William T. Hackett later that year to form the architectural firm of Collins and Hackett. Hackett left the partnership in 1894, the same year that one of Collins's sons joined the business. In 1906 another son joined T. J. Collins and Sons, which continued operating in Staunton into the twenty-first century.

From 1891 until his retirement following a stroke in 1911, Collins single-handedly reshaped Staunton's architectural appearance by designing or remodeling nearly two hundred of its buildings. Although he worked primarily in the city and surrounding Augusta County, he was also responsible for notable structures in Harrisonburg, Lexington, Luray, Orange County, Waynesboro, and Harpers Ferry, West Virginia. Collins's projects ranged from remodeling homes to designing dozens of commercial, industrial, institutional, and religious buildings. Among his major commissions were Tucker Hall (1898–1900) for Washington and Lee University, the Chesapeake and Ohio Railway Company Depot (1904–1905) in Staunton, and the main barracks for the Augusta Military Academy (1915) in Fort Defiance. Many of his residential commissions are located in Staunton's Gospel Hill Historic

District. One of Collins's earliest jobs was an 1891 Romanesque-style addition to the residence of the prominent Staunton banker Arista Hoge. Known as Kalorama Castle, the house was added to the National Register of Historic Places in 1982. As president of Thornrose Cemetery, Hoge later commissioned Collins to design that burial ground's stone walls, gatehouse, and bridge.

Influenced by the eclectic architectural styles of the late Victorian period, Collins experimented with a number of popular forms, including Gothic, Renaissance Revival, Queen Anne, Second Empire, and Châteauesque. Many of his early residences employed such elements, as did one of his most prominent buildings, the Rockingham County courthouse (1896), in Harrisonburg. Although Collins did not belong to any professional organizations, he kept up with current trends through trade journals and produced designs in more modern styles. He used the classically inspired Beaux Arts style for structures built at the turn of the century, including the Augusta County courthouse (1900–1901) and the National Valley Bank Building (1903), both in Staunton. He employed the low, horizontal style of the Prairie School, popularized by Frank Lloyd Wright, in some of his twentieth-century house designs and used design elements adapted from Louis Henry Sullivan in his commercial buildings.

Affectionately known as "Pop," Collins belonged to the Knights of Columbus and was an active member of Saint Francis of Assisi Catholic Church, whose 1895 building he designed in the Gothic style. Thomas Jasper Collins died of pneumonia at his Staunton home on 5 October 1925 and was buried in Thornrose Cemetery.

William T. Frazier, "T. J. Collins: A Local Virginia Architect and His Practice at the Turn of the Century" (M.A. thesis, UVA, 1976); Wells and Dalton, *Virginia Architects*, 93–96; T. J. Collins and Sons Architectural Drawing Collection, R. R. Smith Center for History and Art, Staunton; family information provided by grandson, Joseph Johnson (2003); *Washington Evening Star*, 25 Apr. 1867; *Washington Post*, 6 Jan. 1881; Albert E. Walker, ed., *The Dispatch and News: Historical and Industrial Number, 1761–1906, Staunton, the Queen City* (1906), 15; David J. Brown, ed., *Staunton, Virginia: A Pictorial History* (1985), 47, 54 (por.), 55, 62, 74; BVS Death Certificate, Staunton; obituary in *Staunton News-Leader*, 6 Oct. 1925.

NANCY TAYLOR SORRELLS

COLONNA, Charles Jones (27 August 1849–20 February 1920), marine railway operator and shipbuilder, was born in Accomack County and was the son of John Watson Colonna and his second wife, Margaret Jones Colonna. His father farmed, operated a general merchandise store, and at one time owned a ship. Colonna attended the county's free schools until about the time the Civil War ended, when he went to sea for two years before the mast of a commercial schooner. He then enlisted as a ship carpenter in the Coast and Geodetic Service and worked aboard a survey steamer for eighteen months. Afterward, Colonna was a ship carpenter for a Chicago company that also employed him in Canada, Michigan, and Virginia.

In Norfolk, Colonna worked for the marine railway that William A. Graves owned. A device used in ship repair and operated by horse or steam power, a marine railway pulled a large cradle, into which a vessel had been maneuvered, from water into a dry dock. In 1875 Colonna started his own business on property that he leased in Berkley, across the Eastern Branch of the Elizabeth River from downtown Norfolk. He built a marine railway with a capacity of about 40 tons, and in 1881 he purchased a small piece of land that allowed him to increase his capacity to 500 tons. Colonna's business steadily grew, and in 1899 he acquired a competitor's marine railway. Three years later he bought the adjoining shipyard that Graves had owned. Although Colonna concentrated on repairing ships, he also constructed transportation barges and built and for a time operated an ocean steamer.

By the time that Colonna retired from managing the business in 1907, shortly after the city of Norfolk annexed Berkley, he was operating five marine railways and repairing an average of 650 vessels each year. Incorporated as Colonna Marine Railway Corporation in April of that year and directed by his sons, the company thrived during World War I. It repaired warships, army transports, and vessels operated by the War Shipping Board, as well as commercial ships. In December 1921 the company acquired Marine Iron Works, of Norfolk, and was renamed Colonna's Shipyards, Inc. The third generation of the family then took command. The company was still operating a century and a quarter after Colonna founded it, reportedly one of the largest and oldest family-owned shipyards in the United States.

On 20 March 1877 Colonna married Margaret Okeson Dunston, of Norfolk. They had six sons and one daughter before her death from pneumonia on 18 July 1892. He married Fannie Cornick Fentress, also of Norfolk, on 30 January 1902. They had one son. Charles Jones Colonna died at his Norfolk home of kidney failure related to diabetes on 20 February 1920 and was buried in the city's Elmwood Cemetery.

Biographies in Tyler, *Men of Mark*, 2:78–80 (por. facing 78 and birth date of 27 Aug. 1849), and W. W. Colonna Jr., comp., *Colonna Papers: Histories Involving Colonna Family, Mainly Tidewater Area, State of Virginia, U.S.A.* (2000), vol. 2, nos. 1–3 (pors.); variant birth date of 28 Aug. 1849 in 1985 typescript of Colonna family Bible records (1701–1941), LVA; family and company history in Rogers Dey Whichard, *The History of Lower Tidewater Virginia* (1959), 3:16–20 (with incorrect death date of 3 Mar. 1920); SCC Charter Book, 63:186–187, 100:342–343, 114:502–505; BVS Marriage Register, Norfolk City (1877, 1902); BVS Death Certificate, Norfolk City (with birth date of 27 Aug. 1849 and father's name as John Wilkins Colonna); obituaries in *Norfolk Ledger-Dispatch* and *Virginian-Pilot and Norfolk Landmark*, both 21 Feb. 1920.

JIM GREVE

COLSON, Edna Meade (7 October 1888–17 January 1985), educator, was born in Petersburg and was the daughter of James Major Colson and Kate Deaver Hill Colson. The family belonged to the town's black middle class, having been property-owning members of the free black community at the beginning of the nineteenth century. Her great-grandfather, William Nelson Colson, was a Petersburg merchant who traded with Liberia. The family was also among the educated black elite. Her father was a founding faculty member of Virginia Normal and Collegiate Institute (later Virginia State University) in nearby Ettrick, and her mother was one of the first African American teachers in Petersburg's public schools and for one year served as principal of the normal preparatory department at the institute.

Colson graduated from Peabody High School in Petersburg in 1904 and from Fisk University's normal school in 1908. She taught for one year at Saint Augustine's School (later Saint Augustine's College), in Raleigh, North Carolina, and then returned to the Petersburg area as an instructor in the academic department at the renamed Virginia Normal and Industrial Institute from 1909 to 1912. Colson continued her education at Fisk University and received a B.A., magna cum laude, in 1915. She returned to the Virginia Normal and Industrial Institute as an assistant in pedagogy. In 1919 the institute appointed her director of the new department of education. Until her retirement in 1953 Colson continued to guide the program as it grew into a division of education in 1929 and the school of education early in the 1950s. In the meantime, she attended Teachers College, Columbia University, and received a B.S. in 1923, an M.A. in 1924, and a Ph.D. in 1940. Teachers College published her dissertation, entitled *An Analysis of the Specific References to Negroes in Selected Curricula for the Education of Teachers* (1940), in its Contributions to Education series. She was one of the first two women on the institute faculty to hold doctoral degrees.

Colson had to pursue her graduate work outside Virginia because there was no graduate education available to African Americans in the state's segregated universities. Virginia provided tuition grants to black graduate students to study in other states—an estimated 376 grants in the years 1930–1935. After receiving authorization from the State Board of Education and approval from its own board, Virginia State College for Negroes, as it had been renamed in 1923, began to offer graduate courses in the summer of 1937. Colson chaired the committee on graduate study to implement the new program.

Long an advocate of equality for women, Colson and seven other faculty members were among the first African American women to register to vote after ratification of the Nineteenth Amendment in 1920. They had a photograph taken to commemorate the event. Colson was a charter member of the Delta Omega chapter of the Alpha Kappa Alpha Sorority, Incorporated. The chapter, founded on 6 February 1921, was the first in the mid-Atlantic region and the fourth graduate chapter of the sorority in the nation. Colson became a life member of the American

Teachers Association in 1935 and of the National Education Association in 1954. She received an outstanding alumna award from Fisk University and served on the executive board of its alumni association. In 1950 Colson was the first black Virginia woman to become a life member of the National Association for the Advancement of Colored People. Eight years later the Virginia State Federation of Colored Women's Clubs, Inc., of which she was a member, named her Woman of the Year.

Colson retired in 1953 after serving Virginia State College, as it was renamed in 1946, for more than forty years. One educator estimated at the time of her retirement that at least half of all the African American teachers employed in Virginia's public schools had once been her students or had graduated from the college's department of education. Colson Auditorium in Harris Hall, erected in 1970 as headquarters of the education department, was named in her honor.

Colson never married. With her longtime companion Amaza Lee Meredith, an architect and colleague from the college's department of fine arts, she owned and resided in Azurest South, an International-style house that Meredith designed and built in 1939 on the college campus. Colson traveled regularly to Azurest North, an enclave of vacation homes for elite African Americans in Sag Harbor, Long Island, New York, where she also jointly owned a house. Edna Meade Colson died in a Colonial Heights nursing home on 17 January 1985, a year after the death of her companion. After a funeral at Gillfield Baptist Church, of which she had been a lifelong member, Colson was buried in Eastview Cemetery, in Petersburg.

Biography with birth date and incorrect middle name of Mae in Martha Short Dance, *Peabody High School, a History of the First Negro Public High School in Virginia* (1976), 46–48; "The Colson Family," *Negro History Bulletin* 10 (1946): 3–9, 20–21; Colson-Hill Family Papers and voting registration photograph in Evie Spencer DeCosta Papers, both Virginia State University, Ettrick; numerous references and several pors. in Edgar Toppin, *Loyal Sons and Daughters: Virginia State University, 1882 to 1992* (1992); publications include Colson, "The Negro Teachers' College and Normal School," *Journal of Negro Education* 2 (July 1933): 284–298, and "The Division of Education," *Virginia State College Gazette* 9 (Dec. 1934): 21–30; *Virginia Education Bulletin* 33 (Oct.

1953): cover por.; obituaries in *Petersburg Progress-Index*, *Richmond News Leader*, and *Richmond Times-Dispatch*, all 18 Jan. 1985.

LAURANETT L. LEE

COLSON, James Major (15 October 1855–22 May 1909), educator, was born in Petersburg and was the son of Fannie Meade Bolling Colson and James Major Colson, a prosperous shoemaker whose family had been free for at least three generations. His grandfather, William Nelson Colson, was a merchant who traded between Liberia and the United States. After his mother taught him to read, Colson attended a local private school established for black children. In 1868 the city of Petersburg, with additional money from the Bureau of Refugees, Freedmen, and Abandoned Lands and the Peabody Education Fund, established segregated public schools. Colson received instruction at Elementary School Number 1 (also called the Harrison Street School) and beginning in January 1870 at the new Colored High School (forerunner of Peabody High School).

In 1872 Colson left school to become an apprentice in his father's shop. Setting out on his own, he traveled to Danville, where he worked part-time as a cobbler and also taught in nearby Henry County. Determined to resume his education and with assistance from an uncle living in Middleborough, Massachusetts, Colson enrolled in high school there in the autumn of 1877. After graduating in June 1879, he matriculated at Dartmouth College, where he was elected to Phi Beta Kappa and in 1883 received an A.B. His diaries from the period reveal an introspective, self-critical student longing for improvement and advancement. Later in life he reported that he had received an A.M. from Dartmouth in 1893, but the college has no record of awarding him that degree.

Colson returned to Petersburg in 1883 and worked briefly as a clerk in the United States Internal Revenue office. He secured an appointment as instructor at the new Virginia Normal and Collegiate Institute (after 1902 the Virginia Normal and Industrial Institute and after 1979 Virginia State University) and on 20 September 1883 became a member of the school's founding faculty. After the head of the school resigned,

Colson served as acting principal from 10 September to 31 December 1885, at which time John Mercer Langston became the college's first president.

On 3 February 1886 Colson married Kate Deaver Hill, assistant principal at the Petersburg Colored High School. In 1887 she joined her husband at the Virginia Normal and Collegiate Institute, where she served for one year as principal of the normal preparatory department. Their three sons and two daughters included Edna Meade Colson, who also became an influential Petersburg-area educator.

Colson taught various subjects, including Latin. Credited with establishing the school's science program, he was elected chair of the Department of Natural Science in 1887. That year he also organized Kappa Gamma Chi, the school's honor society, which held its initial exercises in June. Colson urged the college administrators to add agricultural education to the curriculum. He contacted state and federal agencies in an effort both to develop his own understanding of the subject and to build a library of information on modern farming methods. Colson invited outside lecturers to his classes and appealed to the college to provide him with an appropriate classroom, adequate supplies, a plot of land for experimental cultivation, and an assistant. He believed that the institution should be a resource for black farmers in adjacent counties and provide them with services that they could not obtain elsewhere.

Colson's interests extended beyond the Ettrick campus. He was a founder and first secretary of the African American chapter of Petersburg's Young Men's Christian Association. In May 1898 he traveled to Atlanta University and at the third in a series of conferences on the Study of Negro Problems presented a paper entitled "Organized Efforts of the Negro for Social Betterment in Petersburg, Virginia." At the recommendation of W. E. B. Du Bois, on 28 December 1899 Colson was elected a member of the American Negro Academy, which invited him to read a paper before the membership in January 1901. A regular participant in the annual Hampton Negro Conference, he served on its executive committee and chaired the Commit-

tee on General Statistics in 1902 and the Committee on Charities and Corrections in 1903 and 1904.

Unable to realize his plans for an agricultural program at the underfunded normal school, Colson resigned in 1904 to become superintendent of the John A. Dix Industrial School, at Dinwiddie, in Dinwiddie County. His wife joined him as the school's matron and housekeeper. A modest facility with a single unfinished building and one instructor on opening day in 1900, the school (under Colson's guidance renamed the Dinwiddie Agricultural and Industrial School) by 1908 boasted a faculty of twelve and a student body of 114. In February 1908 its main building burned at a loss of about $20,000, but several smaller buildings were saved.

Colson held Farmers' Conferences at the school in 1904 and in 1906. In the latter year he delivered an address on "The Education Element in Agriculture" at the annual meeting of the Virginia State Teachers Association at Hampton Normal and Agricultural Institute. Colson was treasurer of the National Association of Colored Teachers (in 1907 renamed the National Association of Teachers in Colored Schools) from 1906 until his death. He served as president of the Dinwiddie County Colored Teachers Association, of the Negro School Improvement League of Dinwiddie County, and in 1908 and 1909 of the Virginia State Teachers Association. James Major Colson died of stomach cancer at his Petersburg home on 22 May 1909 and was buried in Eastview Cemetery. On the Virginia Normal and Industrial Institute campus, Griffin House was renamed Colson Hall in his honor. A new science building, erected on the same site and dedicated in 1940, became the James Major Colson Science Hall.

Alumnus file and necrology, Dartmouth College Archives, Hanover, N.H.; "The Colson Family," *Negro History Bulletin* 10 (1946): 3–7 (por. on 4), 9; Colson family Bible (with birth and marriage dates), diaries, autobiographical information, and correspondence in Colson-Hill Family Papers, Virginia State University, Ettrick; BVS Marriage Register, Petersburg; Luther P. Jackson, *A History of the Virginia State Teachers Association* (1937), 50–52; Edgar Toppin, *Loyal Sons and Daughters: Virginia State University, 1882 to 1992* (1992), 17, 22–25 (por. on 23), 29; obituaries in *Petersburg Daily Index-Appeal*, 23 May 1909, and *Dartmouth Alumni Magazine* 1 (1909): 319; memorial in *Hampton Bulletin* 5 (1909): 11–12.

DONALD W. GUNTER

COLSON, William Nelson (1805–12 November 1835), merchant, was born in Petersburg and was the son of James Colson, a barber, and either his first wife, whose name is not known, or his second, whose given name was Eliza. Colson's father was one of about fifteen free African Americans who owned real estate in the city early in the nineteenth century. The exact date of Colson's birth is not known, but when he registered as "a free man of Colour" on 23 August 1825, he gave his age as nineteen and his profession as barber. The clerk who recorded the registration described him as five feet, eleven inches tall with a light complexion, a small mole under his right eye, and a scar on the back of his head near the hairline. On 2 March 1826 Colson married Sarah Herreck Elebeck, also a member of a free black property-owning Petersburg family. They had three sons and two daughters. One of their grandsons, James Major Colson, was an original member of the faculty of Virginia Normal and Collegiate Institute (later Virginia State University).

Colson formed a commercial partnership before or during 1829 with other local free blacks, including Joseph Jenkins Roberts. The firm of Roberts, Colson, and Company acquired a schooner, the *Caroline*, and began to trade between Liberia and the United States. Roberts moved to Liberia to head the partnership's African base of operations, and Colson initially remained in Virginia to manage the American side of the business. Roberts, Colson, and Company became an important commercial connection between the United States and Liberia, but because no company ledgers have survived, its financial success cannot be measured. The company's few existing records indicate that its American clients included several large partnerships in New York and Philadelphia. From Liberia the company shipped to the United States such items as camwood for cabinetmaking, ivory, and palm oil, and it sent a variety of merchandise to Liberia, including cider, clothing, metal implements, wine, and such fancy goods as feather fans and silks. In 1835 the company purchased a second vessel, the schooner *Margaret Mercer*.

Colson lived a more prosperous life than most other free blacks in early nineteenth-century Virginia. For example, in July 1835 he paid a total of $191 for a half year of his daughter's education and to cover his wife's traveling expenses. When his estate was inventoried after his death, the contents of his house and shop were valued at almost $300. In addition, he owned a half interest in the modest contents of a barber shop in Petersburg and a part of Roberts, Colson, and Company. Colson's library included books on biography, history, poetry, and religion. Probably self-educated, he was a careful man of business and kept detailed records. The inventory of the wardrobe that he took on his voyage to west Africa in 1835 suggests his economic status and identification of himself as a successful professional man. It lists new linen and fine cotton shirts, several silk vests, silk handkerchiefs, four pairs of kid gloves, 250 Spanish cigars, and more than twenty-five religious books.

Colson began his trip to Africa in the summer of 1835. He intended to remain about a year and perhaps serve as a missionary as well as become personally acquainted with the African side of his business. He arrived in Liberia about the beginning of October, toured several settlements, and contracted an unspecified fever. William Nelson Colson died in Monrovia on 12 November 1835, three days after staying up all night while ill and writing business letters. The place of his burial in Monrovia is not recorded. Colson's death led to the dissolution of one of the first African American transatlantic shipping companies, but his partner remained in Liberia and in 1848 became the first president of the new independent republic.

Luther Porter Jackson, "Free Negroes of Petersburg, Virginia," *Journal of Negro History* 12 (1927): 372–378; Jackson, *Free Negro Labor and Property Holding in Virginia, 1830–1860* (1942), 144–149, 169–170; "The Colson Family," *Negro History Bulletin* 10 (1946): 3–6 (with variant birth year of 1806), 20–21; *Norfolk Journal and Guide*, 1 Mar. 1947; full name in Petersburg Hustings Court Deed Book, 8:174; Petersburg Hustings Court Register of Free Negroes and Mulattoes (1819–1832), no. 1381 (quotation); Petersburg Marriage Bonds (bond dated 28 Feb. 1826); Petersburg Marriage Register; Colson-Hill Family Papers (including Roberts, Colson, and Company records and death on 12 Nov. 1835 reported in Joseph Jenkins Roberts to Sarah Elebeck Colson, 1 Jan. 1836), Virginia State University,

Ettrick; company business reported in *African Repository, and Colonial Journal* 11 (1835): 178, and 12 (1836): 23, 33, 47; estate inventory and accounts in Petersburg Hustings Court Will Book, 3:107–113, and Petersburg Hustings Court Account Book, 3:187–189; obituary (with death on 11 Nov. 1835 at age thirty, probably from lost issue of *Intelligencer and Petersburg Commercial Advertiser*) in *African Repository, and Colonial Journal* 12 (1836): 103.

ROBERT C. KENZER

COLSTON, Edward (25 December 1786–23 April 1851), member of the House of Representatives, was born probably in Frederick County and was the son of Rawleigh Colston, a lawyer and land speculator, and Elizabeth Marshall Colston, sister of John Marshall, later chief justice of the United States. Soon after graduating from the College of New Jersey (later Princeton University) in 1806, Colston began practicing law in Berkeley County, where his father had settled on a large estate called Honeywood. During the War of 1812 he served as a private in a Berkeley County militia company, although the governor later commissioned him a lieutenant of artillery. On 2 May 1814 Colston executed a marriage bond in Fauquier County and on that date or soon afterward married his cousin Jane Letitia Marshall. She died during childbirth on 5 March 1815, followed a few days later by the infant.

In 1812 Colston, a Federalist, was elected to the House of Delegates representing Berkeley County. During nine nonconsecutive one-year terms over the following twenty-three years he served at various times on the standing Committees for Courts of Justice, of Privileges and Elections, and of Roads and Internal Navigation. Colston also sat on joint committees to examine the state treasury and the state library. In January 1817 he supported reapportioning seats in the General Assembly in order to provide more-equitable representation for the residents of western counties.

In April 1817 Colston won a three-man race by 251 votes of 1,123 cast for a seat in the House of Representatives from the Second Congressional District, comprising Berkeley, Hampshire, Hardy, and Jefferson Counties. He served on the Committee on the Post Office and Post Roads during the first session of the Fifteenth Congress and on the Committee for the District of Columbia in the second. He spoke infrequently in the recorded proceedings but argued in favor of pensions for soldiers who had fought in the Revolutionary War and supported federal construction of roads and canals for the country's common defense under the provisions of the Constitution's "necessary and proper" clause. Colston made a long speech in January 1819 criticizing Andrew Jackson for exceeding his authority in Florida during the First Seminole War by confronting Spanish troops, who were then in their own country's territory. Although Colston was not a candidate for reelection in 1819, he sought election to the Nineteenth Congress in April 1825 but lost that race to William Armstrong by 262 votes of 1,838 cast.

In May 1818 Colston was commissioned a justice of the peace for Berkeley County, and in January 1844 he was appointed sheriff. Following his father's example of land speculation, he and a partner patented 777 acres of land in Morgan County in 1835 and another 1,891 acres in Berkeley. Although Colston owned twenty-one slaves in 1850, he had long been a proponent of colonization of freed slaves. In 1831 he traveled to Ohio with William Meade, then the assistant bishop of the Episcopal Diocese of Virginia, in order to lobby for colonization, and in 1835 he served as a vice president of the Virginia Colonization Society. At its annual meeting, held in Richmond in January of the latter year, Colston sponsored a resolution to assure slave owners that the society did not intend to interfere with their property rights or to support abolition. He donated money to the society and in 1829 manumitted a family of six slaves with the provision that they settle in Liberia.

On 28 May 1825 Colston married Sarah Jane Brockenbrough, daughter of William Brockenbrough, later a judge of the Virginia Supreme Court of Appeals, and sister-in-law of Willoughby Newton, who served one term in the House of Representatives. They had five daughters and three sons. Colston also served as the American guardian of his brother's French-born adopted son, Raleigh Edward Colston, who became a brigadier general in the Confederate army. Edward Colston died of apoplexy in his library on 23 April 1851. He was interred probably in the family burial vault at Honeywood.

Biographies in W. M. Paxton, *The Marshall Family* (1885), 105–106 (with birth date and variant second marriage date of 2 May 1825), and F. Vernon Aler, *Aler's History of Martinsburg and Berkeley County, West Virginia* (1888), 164–168 (variant birth year of 1788); J. E. Norris, ed., *History of the Lower Shenandoah Valley Counties of Frederick, Berkeley, Jefferson and Clarke* (1890), esp. 639–641; Fauquier Co. Marriage Bonds and Returns, 3:228; Brockenbrough family Bible records printed in *Hanover County Historical Bulletin* 30 (June 1984): 7–8; some Colston correspondence in American Colonization Society Papers, 1st ser., LC, and Robinson Family Papers, W&M; *Calendar of Virginia State Papers*, 10:219–220; *Annals of Congress*, 15th Cong., 1st sess., 480–481, 492, 1262, 1278–1282, 1669, 2d sess., 824–831; Land Office Northern Neck Grants, D:397–401; Census, Slave Schedule, Berkeley Co., 1850; *Charles Town Farmer's Repository*, 1 May 1812, 23, 30 Apr. 1817; *Martinsburgh Gazette*, 23 Mar. 1815; *Richmond Enquirer*, 25 Jan. 1817, 31 May 1825 (with second marriage date of 28 May 1825); *Richmond Constitutional Whig*, 3 May 1825; *African Repository, and Colonial Journal* 4 (1829): 380; ibid. 7 (1831): 208; ibid. 11 (1835): 91; death notices and obituaries in *Washington National Intelligencer*, 28 Apr. 1851, *Richmond Whig and Public Advertiser*, 29 Apr. 1851 (died in his sixty-fifth year), *Winchester Virginian*, 30 Apr. 1851, and *Stryker's American Register and Magazine* 6 (1851): 229 (died at age sixty-three).

G. W. POINDEXTER

COLSTON, Raleigh Edward (31 October 1825–29 July 1896), Confederate army officer, was born in Paris, France. His biological parents are unidentified, although at the end of his life various romanticized accounts reported that he was the son of a poor French army officer or of a woman who worked as his nurse. If the latter is true, his name at birth may have been Victor Boucher. His adoptive father, Raleigh Travers Colston, was a Virginia-born physician who lived in France. His adoptive mother was Thérèse Gnudi, an Italian whose marriages to an Italian count and to François-Étienne Kellermann, one of Napoleon I's cavalry generals, had been dissolved. Colston likely thought his adoptive parents were his birth parents until he was nearly grown. After completing his early education in Paris, he came to the United States in 1842 and lived in Berkeley County with his adoptive father's brother, Edward Colston, a former member of the House of Representatives.

Colston entered the Virginia Military Institute as a pay cadet in 1843. Attaining the rank of cadet captain, he graduated in July 1846 fourth in a class of fourteen and first in chemistry, drawing, French, and English. On 20 August 1846,

in Lexington, Colston married the twice-widowed Louisa Meriwether Bowyer Brown Gardner. They had three daughters, one of whom died as a child. Following his graduation he became an assistant professor of French at VMI; also taught military history and strategy, modern history, and political economy; and served as the school's treasurer. During the 1840s Colston wrote and published a forty-nine-page pamphlet entitled *The Problem of Free Society*, about the working class in Great Britain. By 1854 he had become the first graduate of VMI to reach the standing of full professor at the institute.

In December 1859 Colston served as adjutant of a VMI detachment sent to Charles Town for the hanging of John Brown. After Virginia seceded from the Union, the governor appointed Colston a colonel in the Provisional Army of Virginia on 2 May 1861. He was assigned to duty in Norfolk and given command of the 26th Regiment Virginia Infantry, a unit redesignated the 16th Regiment Virginia Infantry when it mustered into Confederate service on 1 July of that year. Colston remained in command of the regiment until he was promoted to brigadier general on 24 December 1861, although the Confederate States Senate did not confirm his appointment until 19 February 1864.

Along with Colston's promotion came an assignment to command the First Brigade, Department of Norfolk, from January to April 1862, when his brigade was transferred to the Peninsula to reinforce the Yorktown line. Colston commanded a brigade under Major General James Longstreet during battles at Williamsburg and Seven Pines. In June 1862 he contracted "Peninsular" fever, jaundice, and malaria and was placed on leave. Colston did not return to duty until December, when he received command of a brigade of Virginia units in the Petersburg-Blackwater District. After several months he took command of the entire district.

After serving temporarily in Major General George Edward Pickett's division, Colston on 4 April 1863 took command of a brigade in Lieutenant General Thomas J. "Stonewall" Jackson's corps. With Major General Isaac Ridgeway Trimble absent because of illness, temporary command of his division devolved on Colston during the Battle of Chancellorsville. He returned to his own brigade shortly afterward.

General Robert Edward Lee relieved Colston of brigade command on 28 May 1863, ostensibly because soldiers in two North Carolina regiments objected to being commanded by a Virginian but more likely because he had moved Trimble's division into position too slowly on the second day at Chancellorsville. Colston was assigned to attend examinations at VMI. Denied other requested military assignments at least five times during the next several months, he remained in Lexington until ordered on 21 September 1863 to report for temporary duty in the Department of South Carolina, Georgia, and Florida. Assigned to the District of Georgia on 17 October 1863, Colston was given command of a brigade in Savannah and defenses on Saint Augustine Creek. He was relieved on 16 April 1864.

On 15 May 1864 Colston took command temporarily of the First Military District, Department of North Carolina and Southern Virginia. Headquartered in Petersburg, he held this post for two weeks until he was placed in temporary command of the Petersburg garrison on 9 June. That day, along with Major Fletcher Harris Archer, he helped lead a group of invalids, old men, and young boys in a successful defense of the city from a surprise Union attack. On 6 July 1864 Colston received his final assignment as commandant of the post at Lynchburg, where he constructed extensive fortifications to protect the city. He was paroled on 22 May 1865, signed the amnesty oath on 7 July, and received a presidential pardon on 19 August. Colston returned to Lexington, but financial difficulties forced him to sell his house and property there. To earn money he lectured about his friend and former VMI colleague Stonewall Jackson, and from 1866 to 1873 he was a principal at two North Carolina military schools.

After accepting a colonel's commission from the khedive of Egypt, Colston arrived in Cairo in the spring of 1873. Although originally recruited to teach geology at an Egyptian military college, he became an explorer for the Egyptian army and conducted topographical, botanical, and geological expeditions. During the winter of 1873–1874 Colston took part in a surveying mission to Berenice, on the Red Sea. Beginning in December 1874 he helped lead the first phase of a two-year scientific survey expedition from Cairo to central Africa, where he contracted a debilitating and unexplained illness that caused him great pain, rheumatism, and paralysis. Although a doctor advised him to return to Cairo, Colston refused to abandon the expedition and remained in command until September 1875. For his services the khedive inducted him into the Osmanie Order of the Ottoman Empire.

Colston returned to the United States late in 1878 but lost his savings through poor investments. In order to earn income he gave lectures and wrote articles on his Egyptian experiences. He unsuccessfully sought appointment to the faculty of the Virginia Agricultural and Mechanical College (later Virginia Polytechnic Institute and State University) and in 1881 served as commandant at a New York military academy. Colston enlisted the support of several former Union and Confederate generals, including United States senator William Mahone, in securing permanent employment. In August 1882, while living in Petersburg, he received an appointment as a clerk and translator with the War Department and moved to Washington, D.C.

Colston's wife died on 13 November 1882 in Raleigh, North Carolina, after years of mental illness. On 27 June 1883, in Washington, D.C., he married Laura Eunice Collier Mitchell, a widow. They soon separated. She charged Colston with desertion, and they divorced on 1 May 1889.

Colston translated a French novel published in New York under the title *A Tragedy in the Imperial Harem at Constantinople* (1883) and later reissued as *A Tragedy at Constantinople* (1888). He also wrote *The War in the Soudan for the Rescue of "Chinese Gordon"* (1885) for the American Geographical Society. Colston remained ill constantly and even tried fasting for several weeks in December 1886 to relieve his condition. The Confederate Veterans' Association of Washington and the Ladies' Southern Aid Society helped to take care of him physically, while friends supported him financially. By 1891 he was confined to his home, but he continued at least nominally to work for the War Department until he was dismissed in the spring of 1894.

In September 1894 Colston entered the R. E. Lee Camp Confederate Soldiers' Home, in Richmond. Paralyzed from the waist down, he gradually lost the use of his hands as well. Raleigh Edward Colston died at the soldiers' home on 29 July 1896 and was buried in Hollywood Cemetery. Streets in Lexington and Petersburg bear his name.

Biographies in James Grant Wilson and John Fiske, eds., *Appletons' Cyclopædia of American Biography* (1887–1900), 7:72–73, *NCAB*, 12:122–123, and Benjamin H. Trask, *16th Virginia Infantry* (1986), 62 (por.), 81 (with variant birth date of 25 Oct. 1825); birth name of Victor Boucher suggested in W. M. Paxton, *The Marshall Family* (1885), 113; Raleigh E. Colston Papers (including *Report on the Northern and Central Kordofan* [1878]), alumnus file (including letter from daughter Louise Colston Byrne Ragland to J. R. Anderson, 7 Nov. 1923, with birth date), superintendent's files, and cadet files, all VMI Archives; military and personal correspondence in Raleigh Edward Colston Papers, UNC, and in William Mahone Papers, Duke; Compiled Service Records; *OR*; Presidential Pardons; District of Columbia Superior Court Marriage Records (1883); *Washington Post*, 28 June 1883, 2 May 1889; obituaries in *Richmond Dispatch*, *Lexington Rockbridge County News*, and *Washington Post*, all 30 July 1896; memorial in *SHSP* 25 (1897): 346–353.

DALE F. HARTER

COLT, Thomas Clyde (20 February 1905–6 March 1985), museum director, was born in Orange, New Jersey, and was the son of Thomas Clyde Colt, a prominent businessman and owner of the *Orange Dispatch*, and his second wife, Florence Clery Colt. He attended Blair Academy in Blairstown, Warren County, New Jersey, from 1920 to 1922 and graduated from Dartmouth College with a B.S. in 1926. Colt then attended classes at Columbia University and at King's College, University of Cambridge, and traveled in Europe. After returning to New York City, he wrote book reviews for the *New York Times* and tried unsuccessfully to publish two novels. From 1927 to 1929 he was associated with the Frank K. M. Rehn Galleries, where he came into contact with noted artists, art dealers, and collectors from around the country.

Thomas C. Colt Jr., as he continued to identify himself even after his father's death, joined the United States Marine Corps Reserve in August 1929. He served on active duty as a naval aviator and in 1930 was commissioned a second lieutenant. By December 1931 he had been placed on inactive duty and had moved to Richmond, where he became director and vice president of Cavalier Air Service. On 17 June 1933 he married Martha Belle Patterson Willingham. They had two sons and one daughter. Active in Richmond's art community, Colt served from 1933 to 1935 as trustee of the Richmond Academy of Arts. He assembled exhibitions for the academy, published articles in the *Academy News* and the *Four Arts*, and in 1933 participated in a conference at which Virginia's various art groups unified into a single statewide alliance. He was secretary of the resulting Virginia Art Alliance from 1934 to 1935.

In 1932 John Barton Payne, chair of the American Red Cross, presented Virginia with $100,000 for the construction of an art museum, and on 27 March 1934 the General Assembly established the Virginia Museum of Fine Arts. A large number of artists and art organizations expected Thomas C. Parker, director of the Richmond Academy of Arts, to become curator of the new institution, but John Garland Pollard, president of the museum board's executive committee and a former governor, wanted Colt. A bitter dispute ensued. Colt's detractors considered him "unsuited and unworthy," but his advocates detected a broad worldview and an adventuresome spirit and also valued the contacts he had cultivated while in New York. On 13 April 1935 the museum's executive committee appointed Colt as curator (a title soon changed to director), and the controversy escalated. In May the Richmond Academy of Arts trustees voted to support the museum's decision, but the membership continued its opposition. Colt was able to pacify several art groups, and shortly thereafter the Virginia Art Alliance pledged full cooperation with the museum, effectively ending the quarrel.

The museum opened on 16 January 1936 with an exhibition that surveyed the major trends of American painting from its beginnings to 1910 and featured about 150 paintings lent by museums and collectors from across the country. Colt arranged for Henry P. Strause's collection of European furniture, Georgian silver, antique clocks, and English paintings to be placed in the museum on long-term loan and also organized a show by the sculptor Paul Manship. He initiated a lecture series and symphony concerts, developed an art library, and organized traveling exhibitions for rural areas. By year's end, attendance averaged more than 5,000 per month, and the value of the art collection had quadrupled.

The next year Colt featured an exhibition of sculpture by Malvina Hoffman, followed in 1938 by a memorial exhibition of paintings by Gari Melchers. Colt continued the annual (later biennial) Virginia Artists' Exhibition, initiated the Virginia Artists' Series, and held children's art classes and night openings. The First Biennial Exhibition of Contemporary American Paintings, which opened on 12 March 1938, showcased 183 paintings by artists at home and abroad. This ambitious project prompted the noted art critic Leila Mechlin to announce that the museum had become one of the region's leading institutions. In 1941 *Life* magazine praised the museum as the "vitalizing force in Virginia's new art era."

Colt returned to active duty during World War II and in May 1942 was recommissioned a first lieutenant. Promoted to captain in April 1943, he became officer in charge of the bombardier and gunnery school at the Marine Corps Air Station in El Centro, California. Colt was promoted to major in February 1944 and served that year and in 1945 as a group operations officer in the Marshall Islands and at Iwo Jima and Okinawa. He returned to the Virginia Museum late in 1945 determined to acquire works that represented the scope of American art and the important periods in the history of art. Colt established a studio for African American children, a weekly program of lectures, concerts, and discussions, and a weekly radio show. He also arranged two significant bequests, the Lillian Thomas Pratt Collection of jeweled objects by Peter Carl Fabergé and the Thomas Catesby Jones Collection of modern art.

In April 1948 Colt announced his resignation and on 1 July left the museum to become director of the Portland Art Museum in Oregon. His first marriage ended in divorce, and on 4 April 1950 he married Priscilla Crum, a former staff member at the Virginia Museum of Fine Arts who had joined him at the Portland museum.

They had two daughters and one son. Colt remained in the Marine Corps Reserve, became a lieutenant colonel in 1954, and retired in 1959.

In Portland, Colt continued to pursue his vision and applied the methods that he had embraced in Virginia with great success. His inaugural exhibition of Northwest Coast Indian art signaled his desire to fashion a progressive institution, and he spearheaded the formation of the state's thirty-six art groups into a single alliance. His exhibit of Walter Percy Chrysler's collection drew record crowds and enhanced the museum's prestige. Colt had showcased regional artists and expanded the museum's collections, as well as increasing visitation, staff, and budget, by the time he stepped down in 1956.

Colt became director of the Dayton Art Institute in Ohio on 1 June 1957. During another successful tenure he mounted major exhibitions, increased revenues and the endowment, and expanded an art school. Colt increased the museum's holdings and tripled their value, and in the process he also created one of the country's most important European Baroque collections. He helped organize the Ohio Arts Council in 1965 and served on its executive committee until 1970. In 1972 he received the council's award for excellence in art administration.

Throughout his career Colt contributed to various magazines, including *Art Digest*, *Art News*, and *Commonwealth*, and he was an advisory editor for the *Journal of Aesthetics and Art Criticism* from 1951 to 1953. His publications included *C. S. Price (1874–1950): A Memorial Exhibition Initiated by the Portland Art Museum and the Walker Art Center* (1951), *Handbook of the Samuel H. Kress Collection: Paintings of the Renaissance* (1952), *Prehistoric Stone Sculpture of the Pacific Northwest* (1952), and *Fifty Treasures of the Dayton Art Institute* (1969). He was a member of the Association of Art Museum Directors and served as president of the Intermuseum Conservation Association from 1968 to 1970. He retired on 31 August 1975 and spent much of his time gardening and working on his father's memoirs, which he published in 1979. Thomas Clyde Colt died on 6 March 1985 in a Dayton hospital following a heart attack. His remains were cremated.

Autobiographical information, including birth and marriage dates, in Sept. 1945 war service record and in Mar. 1974 résumé in Dartmouth College Alumni Records Office, Dartmouth College Archives; subject vertical files, Virginia Museum of Fine Arts, Richmond; Thomas Clyde Colt Papers (1853–1979), Archives of American Art, Smithsonian Institution, Washington, D.C.; writings include Colt, "The Principles and Work of the Virginia Museum of Fine Arts," *Four Arts* 2 (June 1935): 11, 15, "Old Dominion Biennial," *Commonwealth* 5 (Mar. 1938): 15, 33, and "'The Calling' of the Artist," *Art Digest* 27 (1 Mar. 1953): 5; BVS Marriage Register, Richmond City (1933); Virginia Museum of Fine Arts Minute Book (1934–1942), LVA; Virginia Museum of Fine Arts, *Museum Bulletin* (1941–1948); "Virginia Art Sprouts at Richmond's Spring Show," *Life* 10 (26 May 1941): 66 (second quotation); *Dayton Journal Herald*, 5 Sept. 1975 (por.); *Richmond Times-Dispatch*, 17 Mar. 1985 (first quotation and por.); obituaries in *Dayton Daily News*, 6 Mar. 1985, *Dayton Journal Herald*, *Richmond News Leader*, and *Richmond Times-Dispatch*, all 7 Mar. 1985, and *New York Times*, 9 Mar. 1985.

CATHERINE T. MISHLER
DONALD W. GUNTER

COLTON, Samuel (d. 7 March 1841), member of the Council of State, was born in the mid-1780s, probably in Elizabeth City County, and was the son of Job Colton, a physician, and Ann Brough Colton. After his father died in 1796, he remained with his mother in Elizabeth City County under the tutelage and protection of her family, from whose members he received financial assistance, including land and slaves. He most likely was educated privately, and he may have been apprenticed to a local physician.

Colton began practicing medicine in Hampton before the War of 1812. He was present at the time the British sacked the town on 25 June 1813 and rendered invaluable aid to the Virginia authorities, not only as a surgeon with the 115th Regiment, Virginia militia, but also as an eyewitness to the British atrocities. Colton provided Brigadier General Robert Barraud Taylor with important information about the actions of the British forces during the capture of the town. He also treated frightened and wounded residents with the meager medical supplies that remained after the British had ransacked his house. Colton continued to serve the Virginia militiamen stationed at Hampton as an acting surgeon from 15 August 1813 until the end of the war.

On 22 November 1815 Colton was appointed a justice of the peace for Elizabeth City County. In the autumn of 1820 county voters elected him to the House of Delegates. He won reelection three times and served through March 1824. Colton sat on the Committee of Claims during the 1820–1821 and 1821–1822 sessions. He also served on a committee to examine enrolled bills in the 1821–1822 session and on a joint committee to examine the treasurer's accounts in the 1822–1823 and 1823–1824 sessions. During his fourth term he was appointed to the Committee of Schools and Colleges.

The General Assembly elected Colton to the Council of State on 17 January 1824, but he did not take his seat until 18 June of that year. He voted with the majority most of the time but registered two dissents, both concerning the propriety of awarding money in state contracts. He missed about twenty days each year during his time on the Council, probably as a result of poor health. The General Assembly, required by the state constitution to remove two members of the Council every third year, voted on 6 January 1830 to remove Colton, who continued to attend Council meetings until 28 May.

In 1825 Colton attempted to secure a federal appointment as a customs collector at Norfolk. Although those recommending him for the position, including a former member of Congress and a judge of the Virginia Court of Appeals, described him as a friend of John Quincy Adams's administration and as a "gentleman of unblemished integrity," the effort proved unsuccessful. On 19 March 1829 Colton married Lelia Frances Grigsby, a Norfolk resident and sister of Hugh Blair Grigsby, a member of the Convention of 1829–1830 and later a noted historian. Before her death on 21 June 1833, she and Colton had one son and one daughter who died as children, as well as a third child who also died young.

In 1840 Colton was elected to a one-year term in the House of Delegates representing the counties of Elizabeth City and Warwick. He served on the Committee to Examine the Lunatic Asylums of the Commonwealth. On 7 March 1841, while in Richmond attending the House of Delegates, Samuel Colton died at his lodging. The place of his burial is not known. He provided in his will for the eventual emancipation of his slaves.

Compiled Service Military Records, War of 1812, and Manuscript File, War of 1812, both Records of Adjutant General's Office, RG 94, NARA; Walter Lowrie and Matthew St. Clair Clarke, eds., *American State Papers: Military Affairs* (1832), 1:379–381; *JHD*, 1823–1824 sess., 120, 1829–1830 sess., 68; Council of State Journal (1823–1824), 139, and (1829–1831), 71–72, RG 75, LVA; *Clay Papers*, 4:895, 904, 906 (quotation); several Colton references in Hugh Blair Grigsby Diaries, 1828 and 1829, in Hugh Blair Grigsby Papers, VHS; Norfolk City Marriage Bonds; *Norfolk and Portsmouth Herald*, 20 Mar. 1829; Elizabeth City Co. Wills (1701–1859), no. 601; death noted in *JHD*, 1840–1841 sess., 178; obituary in *Richmond Whig and Public Advertiser*, 9 Mar. 1841.

STUART LEE BUTLER

COLVIN, Robert Mason (13 May 1845–28 July 1938), leader of Confederate veterans' organizations, was born in Campbell County, near Lynchburg, and was the son of Lucy Lee Andrew Colvin and Robert Colvin. His father was an overseer and operated a tobacco farm, on which Colvin worked before the Civil War. Colvin joined the Lynchburg Public Guard (Lieutenant Royal Bosher's Company, Virginia Local Defense) in March 1862 as a corporal and served with his father, who was a second sergeant. He remained in that unit until 15 April 1864, when he enlisted as a private in Company E, 11th Regiment Virginia Infantry. Captured on 21 May 1864 at Milford, in Caroline County, Colvin and two of his brothers were sent as prisoners of war to Point Lookout, in Saint Mary's County, Maryland. One brother died there. Colvin and his surviving sibling were exchanged near Richmond on 14 March 1865 and paroled at Lynchburg in April of that year. On 20 June 1866, in Lynchburg, he married Lelia Susan Reynolds, a native of Bedford County who died on 4 August 1904. They had one daughter.

After the war Colvin became a fireman for the Virginia and Tennessee Railroad Company. On 1 April 1868 he joined the Baltimore and Ohio Railroad operating out of Grafton, West Virginia. Promoted to engineer in 1870, Colvin worked on trains running between Clarksburg and Washington, D.C. In December 1883 he transferred to the railroad's Harrisonburg office and worked as an engineer on trains operating between that city and Lexington until he retired on 13 May 1910.

After his retirement, Colvin became a prominent figure in Virginia's Confederate memorial activities. In 1913 he joined the S. B. Gibbons Camp, No. 438, the United Confederate Veterans camp for Harrisonburg and Rockingham County. On 7 November 1914 his fellow veterans unanimously elected him commander of the Gibbons Camp, a post he held for more than fifteen years. For the 1922–1923 term he was commander of the Grand Camp, Confederate Veterans of Virginia, a group organized in 1888 that later merged with the United Confederate Veterans. Because his father had served during the Civil War, Colvin also joined the Sons of Confederate Veterans and in August 1922 led a successful effort to revive and reorganize Harrisonburg's SCV unit, Turner Ashby Camp No. 10, as the D. H. Lee Martz Camp. Colvin held various offices in the SCV's Virginia division, including assistant color sergeant and commissary. From 1931 to 1934 he served as the state commander and on stepping down in the latter year became an honorary life commander of the state division. Colvin was possibly the only veteran to lead state divisions of both the SCV and a veterans' organization.

Colvin was not a figurehead leader but instead traveled around the state working to strengthen the organization of the veterans' camps, to arrange meetings, and even to assist in printing bulletins. His work as SCV divisional commander earned praise in *Confederate Veteran* magazine. Crediting Colvin with reviving interest in state Confederate organizations, an SCV memorial noted that he had "done more than any other Son of a Confederate Veteran to keep alive and promote the organizations of Sons of Confederate Veterans" in Virginia.

On 14 September 1925 Colvin helped organize the Battlefield Markers' Association, Western Division, to raise money to erect monuments on Virginia battlefields. A director and vice president of the association, Colvin solicited funds to purchase bronze tablets and arranged their placement on bases erected by various memorial associations at battlefields and other historic sites. He supervised the erection of more than a dozen such monuments and often spoke at their unveiling ceremonies. He was elected a vice president of the Longstreet Memorial Association, formed to recognize the military achievements of Confederate general James Longstreet.

At a time when many of his fellow veterans were either dying or becoming too feeble to participate in reunions or in such organizations as the United Confederate Veterans, Colvin rarely missed meetings or the annual state and national reunions that the various veterans' organizations sponsored. At the celebration of the seventy-fifth anniversary of the First Battle of Manassas (Bull Run) on 21 July 1936, a *Washington Post* photographer recorded him enthusiastically executing the Rebel yell. Colvin also attracted much attention among the fewer than 2,000 veterans able to attend the last reunion of Confederate and Union veterans at Gettysburg in June and July 1938.

Colvin was a Freemason, a member of the Independent Order of Odd Fellows, and an elder of the Harrisonburg Presbyterian Church. His community activities earned him the moniker in Rockingham County of the Grand Old Man. While awaiting intestinal surgery at a Harrisonburg hospital, Robert Mason Colvin died on 28 July 1938, only weeks after attending the last reunion of Civil War veterans at Gettysburg. He was buried with Masonic rites in Woodbine Cemetery, in Harrisonburg.

Biographies in Bruce, Tyler, and Morton, *History of Virginia*, 4:241–242 (with marriage date and por. facing 241), *Confederate Veteran* 30 (1922): 397, and John W. Wayland, *Men of Mark and Representative Citizens of Harrisonburg and Rockingham County, Virginia* (1943), 393; published works include Colvin, "A Visit to Point Lookout Prison," *Confederate Veteran* 22 (1914): 544; Compiled Service Records; Virginia Confederate Pension Application, May 1926, Department of Accounts, RG 6, LVA; official correspondence in Sons of Confederate Veterans Records (1896–1964), Acc. 38059, and United Confederate Veterans Records (1893–1938), Acc. 38060, both LVA; *Washington Post*, 22 July 1936 (por.); BVS Death Certificate, Rockingham Co.; obituaries in *Harrisonburg Daily News-Record* and *Richmond Times-Dispatch*, both 29 July 1938; funeral accounts in *Harrisonburg Daily News-Record*, 30 July, 1 Aug. 1938; SCV memorial resolutions, voted in Columbia, S.C., Aug.–Sept. 1938, in United Confederate Veterans Records (1893–1938), Acc. 38060, LVA (quotation).

DALE F. HARTER

COMBS, Everett Randolph (18 January 1876–5 January 1957), Democratic Party leader, was born in Russell County and was the son of John William Combs and Ladora Jane Kiser Combs. His father, a farmer and stockman, died in 1880, and two years later his mother married his uncle, Fielding Combs. Ebbie Combs, as his friends knew him, received a public school education and attended Tazewell College in Bluefield during the 1896–1897 academic year. According to an early published account of his life, he received a teaching certificate at age eighteen and taught school for six years before serving for three years as principal of a graded school in Russell County. He also farmed and raised livestock until 1911. Combs married Ladora Zimenia Yrassa Candler, also of Russell County, on 22 March 1897. They had six daughters and three sons, as well as two daughters who died young and one stillborn infant.

About the time that Combs bought a large house in the county seat of Lebanon, he defeated the incumbent by about 600 votes and won election as clerk of the Russell County Circuit Court in 1911. Demonstrating the careful, thorough planning for which he became known, he was said to have traveled the county on horseback to visit many voters in their homes. The election placed Combs at the center of the courthouse ring of elected and appointed county officials who were the foundation of the Democratic Party organization that United States senator Thomas Staples Martin directed. Southwestern Virginia was then a fiercely contested partisan region. Extralegal campaign practices flourished as Democrats and Republicans battled for control of the Ninth Congressional District, which included most of the counties south and west of Roanoke.

Combs refined his skills as a political organizer and tactician. He saw to it that loyal voters were registered, had their poll taxes paid, and voted. A political pragmatist, he invariably recruited and backed the strongest candidate and worked to minimize factional strife within the party. Combs further enhanced his reputation as a county leader in the successful 1914 statewide referendum to prohibit the sale and consumption of alcohol, among other local and statewide campaigns. In 1922, as chair of the Ninth District Democratic Committee, he directed the congressional campaign of George Campbell Peery, who was later elected governor. During the successful campaign Combs worked closely with Harry Flood Byrd (1887–1966), the state party chair and a member of the Senate of Virginia. The following year Combs delivered the Ninth District vote in a statewide referendum in support of Byrd's pay-as-you-go principle and against financing road construction by bonds.

In 1925 Combs seriously considered running for state treasurer but did not enter the race. In that year Byrd was elected governor, and Combs was instrumental in his receiving a large majority in the Ninth District. Late in 1927, as Byrd was consolidating his control of the state bureaucracy and the Democratic Party organization, he appointed Combs state comptroller. For the next quarter of a century Combs functioned as the de facto chief of staff of the Byrd organization. As Byrd's principal troubleshooter, strategist, intelligence-gatherer, and informal spokesman, Combs became even more important after Byrd's term as governor ended in 1930. Byrd's elevation to the United States Senate in 1933 made Combs's presence in Richmond even more essential as the middleman between Byrd and the many local and state officials who were the heart of the party organization.

As state comptroller, Combs was responsible for overseeing all transactions in public funds, and he enforced the conservative fiscal policies that Byrd supported. In 1931 the Virginia Bureau of Research, Incorporated, a private company funded by former governor Westmoreland Davis, a Byrd opponent, criticized the comptroller's practices, which led Combs to reform and tighten procedures. Two years later Combs resigned to become manager of the Reconstruction Finance Corporation for the District of Columbia, Maryland, Virginia, and West Virginia, which gave him a raise in pay and made him the chief dispenser of federal relief money in Virginia. In June 1934, after about six months, he returned to state service as comptroller and solidified his position of influence shortly thereafter when he became chair of the new State Compensation Board, which set the salaries and controlled the expenses of many local government officials. He was therefore strategically placed to ensure that officeholders remained loyal to the party orga-

nization and its candidates. Critics never proved that Combs engaged in any impropriety, but his influence was not doubted. As one editorial writer later remarked, "Mr. Combs has walked softly, but he has carried a mighty big stick."

In 1938 Governor James Hubert Price, a Byrd critic, removed many Byrd loyalists from office, and Combs lost both of his posts. He worked briefly for the Virginia Sky-Line and the Virginia Airship Companies in Richmond. The clerk of the Senate of Virginia died suddenly in January 1940, and Byrd organization leaders in the Senate elected Combs to the position and placed him once again at the center of power. He directed the shredding of Price's legislative proposals during that session of the General Assembly and later in the year was elected one of Virginia's representatives to the Democratic National Committee. One of the first acts of Governor Colgate Whitehead Darden Jr. after he took office early in 1942 was to reappoint Combs to his former post as chair of the Compensation Board.

The Chief, as Combs came to be called, retained the Senate clerk's office and was once again firmly entrenched as Byrd's alter ego in Richmond. Large of frame and with a generous head of white hair, he was courtly and soft-spoken. Credited with "the generalship of Hannibal and the wiles of Machiavelli," he was the political overseer of the organization. He dispensed advice and patronage, collected information, and kept officials from governors to game wardens in line as the organization faced new challenges from a younger generation of more-progressive Democrats. Combs helped stage-manage a 1945 constitutional convention that allowed members of the armed services to vote without paying a poll tax while not jeopardizing the Byrd organization's continued reliance on the poll tax to restrict the electorate to a small proportion of Virginia's white adults.

Combs's resignation from the Democratic National Committee in 1948 in part reflected the organization's distaste for Harry S. Truman's administration. The following year Combs played a key role in the nomination of Byrd stalwart John Stewart Battle in a contentious four-way gubernatorial primary. Combs was attacked during that campaign for using his powers at the

Compensation Board to silence and discipline officeholders. On 13 December 1949 Combs's wife died, and in October of the following year, as a consequence of heart disease, he resigned from the Compensation Board. Combs retained the Senate clerkship but for the remaining years of his life was less politically active. He spent time in Florida even during assembly sessions.

For three decades Combs played a unique role in Virginia politics as the managing partner of one of the most durable political organizations in the country. Peerless as an adviser, organizer, strategist, tactician, conciliator, and enforcer, he was essential to the endurance and dominance of Byrd's machine. Combs helped ensure that the fiscally and racially conservative philosophy that he and Byrd shared remained in force during a period of upheaval and change on the national scene. Combs and other organization leaders were appalled at the 1954 Supreme Court decision that declared mandatory racial segregation of public schools unconstitutional, and he urged Byrd to resist all efforts at desegregation. Everett Randolph Combs had a heart attack and died in a Richmond hospital on 5 January 1957. He was buried in Westhill Cemetery, in Lebanon.

Biographies in Bruce, Tyler, and Morton, *History of Virginia*, 6:354 (variant marriage date of 24 Mar. 1897, probably provided by Combs), Glass and Glass, *Virginia Democracy*, 3:198–201 (with por. on 200 and variant marriage date of 24 Mar. 1897), Minor Tompkins Weisiger, "E. R. Combs: Chief of the Byrd Organization" (M.A. thesis, UVA, 1979), and Manarin, *Senate Officers*, 331–332; family information in Lucy Paddison Combs, Combs family genealogical notes (1974), compiled by son Carleton Everett Combs, UVA; Harry Flood Byrd (1887–1966) Papers and Everett R. Combs Papers, both UVA; Harry Flood Byrd Executive Papers, RG 3, LVA; published writings include Combs, "Present Problems in State Finance," *Commonwealth* 1 (Sept. 1934): 7, 23–24; Russell Co. Marriage Register; public career in Ronald L. Heinemann, *Harry Byrd of Virginia* (1996) and Richmond newspapers, with quotations from *Richmond News Leader*, 25 Oct. 1950; obituaries in *Bristol Herald Courier and Bristol Virginia-Tennessean*, *Richmond Times-Dispatch*, and *Roanoke Times*, all 6 Jan. 1957, and *Charlottesville Daily Progress* and *Richmond News Leader*, both 7 Jan. 1957; editorial tributes in *Richmond News Leader*, 7 Jan. 1957, *Richmond Times-Dispatch* and *Roanoke World-News*, both 8 Jan. 1957, and *Washington Post and Times Herald*, 13 Jan. 1957.

MINOR T. WEISIGER

COMBS, Morgan LaFayette (11 June 1892–25 October 1955), president of Mary Washington College (later the University of Mary Washington), was born in Buchanan County. His parents, LaFayette Combs, a physician and farmer, and Emily Frances Whitt Thompson Combs, were both in their second marriages. Combs was educated in the public schools of Buchanan and Russell Counties and at Richmond Academy, a secondary school sponsored by Richmond College (later the University of Richmond), from which he withdrew after his father died. He taught in Buchanan County between 1908 and 1912 while living with his mother and her third husband. Combs resumed his education and graduated from Richmond College in 1917. On 9 June of that year he married Eulalia P. Hilliard, of Richmond. They had two sons.

Combs was superintendent of Buchanan County schools from 1917 until the end of November 1922. From then until 1926 he resided in Richmond and served first as assistant state supervisor of secondary education and beginning in August 1923 as state supervisor. He received an A.M. from the University of Chicago in 1923, an Ed.M. from Harvard University in 1926, and an Ed.D. from Harvard the following year. Combs taught at Boston University during the 1926–1927 academic year, at the College of William and Mary in the summer of 1927, and at George Washington University, in Washington, D.C., in the summer of 1928. From 1927 through the end of 1928 he again lived in Richmond and was state director of research and surveys for the State Board of Education. The board published his doctoral dissertation, "Efficiency in Relation to Size of High Schools in Virginia," in its March 1928 *Bulletin* and his educational survey of Gloucester County in the August issue of the same year.

On 7 December 1928 the board of the State Teachers College at Fredericksburg elected Combs the school's president to succeed Algernon Bertrand Chandler, who had died in September. Combs took up his duties on 3 January 1929 and the following year secured the college's accreditation by the Association of Colleges and Secondary Schools of the Southern States (later the Southern Association of Colleges and Secondary Schools), which had previously withheld its approval because of low salaries and an inadequately trained faculty. During his twenty-six-year tenure, student enrollment more than doubled, and the number of faculty members tripled to nearly 100, of whom about 45 percent held doctorates, a higher percentage than at most state colleges. Under Combs's direction the college raised its admission and academic standards and in 1935 began offering a general liberal arts curriculum. The General Assembly changed the school's name to Mary Washington College in 1938, and in 1944 the college became a women's branch of the University of Virginia, which at that time offered only all-male undergraduate programs. Combs oversaw extensive expansion of the campus and added new residence halls and classroom buildings, a fine arts center, a library, and a student center. A new science building, completed in 1959, was named for him.

Combs was one of five American presidents of teachers colleges who in 1935 studied the methods of teaching foreign languages in German-speaking countries. He traveled widely and visited Canada, Central and South America, Europe, North Africa, and the West Indies. In 1952 Combs received an honorary LL.D. from the University of Richmond in recognition of his achievements, and at the observance two years later of the twenty-fifth anniversary of his appointment as president, he received high praise from leading educators for his role in directing the college's growth and development.

Combs's supporters saw him as decisive and firm, but his detractors regarded him as arrogant, overbearing, and stubborn. Described as a perfectionist, he was not accustomed to having his decisions questioned. Expensive renovations of the president's house carried out between 1946 and 1948 raised eyebrows in 1950, and in November 1953 the latent perception of an autocratic administration intensified when Combs ordered students who waited tables at the dining hall to wear uniforms. They objected that they had no time to change in and out of uniforms three times a day and that wearing uniforms was demeaning. The students, the student body president, and some of the professional staff united in opposing Combs's order. He reacted with such anger—dismissing students

who failed to support his order, threatening others, and firing a dormitory house mother—that the University of Virginia's board of visitors intervened. In February 1954 it reinstated the house mother (who had continued to serve during the controversy), rescinded the student suspensions, and divided all the president's responsibilities between the college bursar and dean. Although Combs initially acquiesced, the following winter a long mimeographed vindication of the president circulated on campus and around Fredericksburg asserting that he had been the victim of a conspiracy and demanding his reinstatement. He made essentially the same charges in person to a committee of the board, leading many to conclude that he had circulated the vindication. The full board again intervened. On 8 April 1955 it unanimously dismissed him from the presidency of Mary Washington College.

A few days later Combs unexpectedly announced his candidacy for the House of Delegates. Although he was forced to abandon the campaign within weeks of being hospitalized with leukemia, he nevertheless received the second-highest number of votes during the July primary. Morgan LaFayette Combs died in a Richmond hospital on 25 October 1955 and was buried in Oak Hill Cemetery, in Fredericksburg.

Biographies in Glass and Glass, *Virginia Democracy*, 2:98–101, *Commonwealth* 11 (Mar. 1944): 18, and Carrol H. Quensel, "Morgan L. Combs: Friend of the Growing," *Virginia and the Virginia County* 7 (Apr. 1953): 10–11; Combs used birth date of 11 June 1892 in such reference works as Robert C. Cook and Eleanor Carroll, eds., *Who's Who in American Education*, 16th ed. (1953/1954), 256, but BVS Birth Register, Buchanan Co., gives 3 June 1892; BVS Marriage Register, Richmond City; publications include Combs, "Efficiency in Relation to Size of High Schools," State Board of Education *Bulletin* 10 (Mar. 1928): 1–124, "Gloucester County, Virginia: Educational Survey Report," ibid. 11 (Aug. 1928): 1–83, and "Fredericksburg State Teachers College," *Commonwealth* 3 (Sept. 1936): 30–31; *Richmond Times-Dispatch*, 11 June 1917; *Fredericksburg Free Lance-Star*, 10–14 Dec. 1953, 11–13, 16–18 Feb. 1954, 23–24 Mar., 7–9 Apr. 1955; controversy documents and letters in Thomas Bahnson Stanley Executive Papers, RG 3, LVA; Edward Alvey Jr., *History of Mary Washington College, 1908–1972* (1974), esp. 155–158, 335–340, 353–358 (several pors. following 338); obituaries in *Fredericksburg Free Lance-Star*, *Richmond News Leader*, and *Richmond Times-Dispatch*, all 26 Oct. 1955; editorial tribute in *Richmond News Leader*, 27 Oct. 1955.

BRENT TARTER

COMMODORE, Aaron (1819 or 1820–24 June 1892), member of the House of Delegates, was born into slavery, probably in Essex County, but the exact date of his birth and the names of his parents are not recorded, nor are the circumstances under which he became free. Census enumerators in 1870 and 1880 recorded his age as fifty-one in the former year and sixty in the latter, identified him in both years as a shoemaker, and listed him as unable to read or write. His surname appears in public documents variously as Comadore, Commadore, and Commodore; records of the General Assembly consistently used the first spelling while his son preferred the last. At some time before emancipation Commodore married Lettie, or Letty, Garnett, although Virginia law did not recognize marriages between enslaved people. They had at least two daughters and one son. By 1870 Commodore had married Katherine, or Catherine, Williams, who died in June 1887. They are not known to have had children.

On 1 January 1872 Commodore paid $300 for a lot and one or more buildings on East Queen Street in Tappahannock, where he lived and worked for the remainder of his life. When the seller's executrix confirmed the sale by a deed executed on 3 June 1875, Commodore made his mark. In April and August of that year he was a member of the county grand jury.

In spite of having little or no formal education, Commodore was a man of recognized leadership qualities and in full command of spoken English. An acquaintance's recollection, recorded many years later but with an incorrect date and not verifiable in many details, testifies to the strong initial impression that he made. According to the anecdote, Chief Justice Salmon P. Chase, before a session of the federal court scheduled to be held during the first years after the Civil War, asked that some respectable African Americans be summoned for service on the grand jury. A white man in Essex County suggested Commodore, who accordingly traveled to Richmond and arrived after court had convened. When Commodore entered the courtroom, the chief justice interrupted the proceedings. Commodore was a striking, very large man, weighing perhaps 250 pounds, wearing work clothes, and having a large wen on his neck. He

explained that he had brought a load of timber to Richmond for shipment to a man in Maine and that although he was willing to serve on the jury, he had nobody to manage his business in the meantime. The judge excused Commodore from service and had to press him to accept payment for his time and travel expenses because Commodore declined to be paid for merely appearing and not serving. The judge and the United States marshal, who later wrote about the event, were clearly impressed with Commodore's bearing, intelligence, and eloquence.

Commodore presided over the Essex County Republican convention in 1873 and powerfully defended the party against Democratic criticism. Two years later the county's Republicans nominated him for a seat in the House of Delegates, and in the November election he defeated Albert R. Micou, of Tappahannock, a Democrat and editor of the *Tidewater Index*, by a close vote of 689 to 660. Micou filed a challenge to the election, but the House of Delegates dismissed it. The official records document little about Commodore's service in the General Assembly sessions that met from December 1875 to March 1876 and from December 1876 to April 1877. He and another first-term African American Republican, Miles Connor, from Norfolk County, were appointed to the lowest-ranking seats on the relatively inconsequential Committee on Militia and Police. On important partisan issues, such as elections for Speaker and a United States senator, Commodore voted with the Republican minority.

Commodore was not the Republican nominee for the assembly in 1877, but he remained active and chaired the party in Essex County at the time of the 1883 election, after which some prominent local Democrats asserted that African Americans had been armed with swords at the polling place in Tappahannock. In the *Richmond Daily Whig* of 31 July 1884 Commodore published a strong denial. Either he had become literate during the ensuing decade or he told a literate person what to write.

A member of the First Baptist Church, in Tappahannock, Aaron Commodore died, probably in that town, on 24 June 1892. His place of burial is not recorded.

Jackson, *Negro Office-Holders*, 8; Lillian H. McGuire, *Uprooted and Transplanted: From Africa to America* (1999), 36, 171–172; Census, Essex Co., 1870 (age fifty-one on 18 June 1870), 1880 (age sixty on 26 June 1880); Essex Co. Deed Book, 52:834; Essex Co. Law Order Book, 4:354, 358; Election Records, no. 10, RG 13, LVA; *Fredericksburg Ledger*, 10 Oct. 1873; *Richmond Daily Dispatch*, 4, 6 Nov. 1875; *Richmond Daily Whig*, 31 July 1884; David B. Parker, *A Chautauqua Boy In '61 and Afterward* (1912), 152–155; death date in "Record of the 1st Baptist Church of Tappahannock Va. Commencing January 1st 1888," First Baptist Church, Tappahannock.

LILLIAN H. MCGUIRE

CONN, Notley (d. by 19 November 1798), member of the Convention of 1788, was born most likely in the mid-1760s and probably in Frederick County, Maryland. Occasionally he signed his first name using the variant spelling Notly. Sometime between 1768 and 1771 his father, an Irish immigrant named Thomas Conn, and his mother, Sarah Maddox Conn, moved their family to Virginia. His father and other in-laws acquired land in Culpeper County, where Conn most likely received his education. In 1784 the family moved to Kentucky, and Conn's father purchased land in what the following year became Bourbon County. Conn later acquired a small portion of that property from his father. It is not recorded that he married or had children.

In the spring of 1788 Conn was elected one of the two delegates to represent Bourbon County in the convention called to consider ratification of the proposed constitution of the United States. He traveled to Richmond for the June convention but did not speak during the debates. Conn was absent on 25 June when the convention voted to ratify the Constitution and also on 27 June when it approved a long list of suggested amendments. Contemporaries believed that he, as did most of the other delegates from the Kentucky region, opposed ratification.

Conn represented Bourbon County in the House of Delegates for three consecutive one-year terms beginning in 1788. He was a member of the Committee of Propositions and Grievances in 1789 and of the Committee for Courts of Justice in 1790. In the former year he was one of the founding trustees of the town of Hopewell (later Paris) in Bourbon County.

Soon after Kentucky obtained statehood in 1792, Conn was one of Kentucky's first presidential electors, all of whom voted for George Washington for president and Thomas Jefferson for vice president. Conn became a member of the Bourbon County Court that same year, and in May 1793 he won election to the Kentucky House of Representatives. During that year's session he served on the Committees for Courts of Justice and on Propositions and Grievances. Conn retained those two assignments in 1794 and also sat on the Committee on Claims. On several occasions he presided as chair of the committee of the whole. Although he may not have owned any slaves, in November 1794 he voted against a proposal to ban the introduction into Kentucky of slaves imported into the United States after 1788. Little else is known about Conn's political career, other than that he mounted an unsuccessful campaign for Congress in 1796.

A major in the militia, Conn commanded a company of mounted volunteers in 1794 at the Battle of Fallen Timbers, one of a series of defeats for Native American tribes north of the Ohio River. In 1796 he patented 1,000 acres of land on the north bank of the Ohio River near the town of New Richmond. Conn was listed in the 1797 tax lists for Bourbon County as owning three horses and two parcels of land. The date and place of Notley Conn's death are not recorded. When the Bourbon County Court met on 19 November 1798, it issued to Conn's father letters of administration for "the estate of Notley Conn deceased."

Some family data in Elise Greenup Jourdan, *Early Families of Southern Maryland* 9 (2000): 238; Kaminski, *Ratification*, 9:899–900, 10:1513, 1565, 1670, 1675–1676; local government service documented in Bourbon Co., Ky., Order Book A; legislative service documented in *JHD*, June 1788 sess., Oct.–Dec. 1788 sess., 1789 sess., 1790 sess., and in *Kentucky House of Representatives Journals*, 1793 sess., 1794 sess.; *Lexington Kentucky Gazette*, 7 July 1792, 11 May 1793; *Madison: Congressional Series*, 16:396; Murtie June Clark, *American Militia in the Frontier Wars, 1790–1796* (1990), 12, 42–43; Bourbon Co., Ky., Tax Books (1787–1797); Bourbon Co., Ky., Order Book, B:656 (quotation), 663.

KATHARINE E. HARBURY

CONN, Raphael M. (13 November 1805–31 March 1887), member of the Convention of 1861, was born in Jefferson County and was the son of Richard Isaacs Wilkes Conn and Priscilla Morgan Conn. Little is known of his early life and education, except that his father died when he was six years old. Conn executed a marriage bond in Page County on 23 February 1835 and on that date or soon thereafter married Ann Eliza Almond, who died on 30 October 1836. They had one daughter. On 24 June 1841 Conn married Sibelia A. J. Ladd, of Henrico County. Of their four sons and two daughters, only two sons and one daughter survived childhood. Sibelia Conn died of bronchial consumption, probably tuberculosis, on 31 December 1853, and on 8 December 1859 Conn married Mary E. Russell, of Frederick County. They had one son before she died on 6 July 1871.

Conn lived near Mount Jackson, in Shenandoah County, and in 1831 inherited two tracts of land in Page County from the paternal uncle for whom he had been named. Conn's long public career began with an appointment as deputy sheriff of Shenandoah County on 12 March 1832. The following year he was both deputy sheriff and deputy coroner. Conn served as an officer in the 13th Regiment of the Virginia militia, by September 1832 until August 1833 as major, from 12 August 1833 to 11 April 1835 as lieutenant colonel, and after that date as colonel. Offended by the General Assembly's promotion of the regiment's much-younger and less-experienced lieutenant colonel to command of the brigade, Conn resigned his commission on 21 January 1854.

Between 1838 and 1841 Conn represented Shenandoah County for four consecutive one-year terms in the House of Delegates, where he sat at various times on the Committees on Agriculture and Manufactures, on Militia Laws, on Trade and Mechanic Arts, to Examine the Enrolled Bills, and to Examine the Public Armory. He became a Shenandoah County justice of the peace on 13 January 1842 and served consecutive two-year terms as sheriff beginning in June 1852. Conn was a founding director and superintendent of the Mount Jackson Manufacturing Company, a woolen manufactory incorporated in 1848 and also authorized to cast farming tools, ironware, machinery, and stoves. He paid taxes on four slaves in 1850 and a decade later owned one, a sixteen-year-old male slave whom he probably hired out.

Campaigning as a secessionist who believed prompt action was required to protect Virginia's rights, Conn won election by a large majority on 4 February 1861 as one of two delegates representing Shenandoah County in the state convention called to debate the issue of secession. He spoke only once on the convention floor, to seek clarification of a procedural question. Conn voted for secession on 4 April and again on 17 April, signed the Ordinance of Secession, and returned to Richmond for the second and third sessions in June and November 1861. He delivered a compelling speech at Columbia Furnace, near Woodstock, in May 1861 while trying to raise a volunteer company for Confederate service. On 11 June he received a gubernatorial appointment as colonel in the Provisional Army of Virginia. Conn's command, the 43d Regiment Virginia Volunteers, was stationed at Winchester on 30 September of that year, but none of its muster rolls or other records survive. He had begun serving as Shenandoah County clerk by October 1863 and the following year was elected to fill the post for a term ending on 1 July 1870, but he stepped down in 1865.

After the Civil War, Conn farmed approximately 310 acres in Shenandoah County and served as trustee of the Green Hill Academy. The absence of his name from local records after 1880 suggests he may have left the county to live with one or more of his children. Raphael M. Conn died at the Warren County residence of his daughter on 31 March 1887. He was buried in Green Hill Cemetery, in Luray, Page County.

Birth date and incorrect death date of 1 Mar. 1887 on gravestone, in Duane L. Borden, *Tombstone Inscriptions: Page County Virginia* (1986), 140; John W. Wayland, *A History of Shenandoah County, Virginia* (1927), 27, 296–297, gives middle name as Morgan and variant death date of summer 1887; Page Co. Marriage Register (1835); second marriage in *Richmond Enquirer*, 29 June 1841; Frederick Co. Marriage Bonds (1859); Militia Commission Papers, Office of the Governor, RG 3, LVA; *Acts of Assembly*, 1847–1848 sess., 300–301; *Richmond Daily Dispatch*, 7 Feb. 1861; *Staunton Vindicator*, 8 Feb. 1861; Reese and Gaines, *Proceedings of 1861 Convention*, 3:163, 4:144; *Calendar of Virginia State Papers*, 11:149; *OR*, 1st ser., 5:821, 4th ser., 1:630; obituaries in *Luray Page Courier*, 7 Apr. 1887 (giving age at death as "82 years, 4 months and 13 days"), and *New Market Shenandoah Valley*, 15 Apr. 1887.

CRAIG S. MOORE

CONNOR, Miles (d. 28 June 1893), member
of the House of Delegates, was born into slavery early in the 1830s, probably in Norfolk
County. His parents were Richard Connor and
Matilda Connor. Little is known about his early
life, but he may have worked as a valet and house
servant and been taught to read by his owners.
The circumstances under which he secured his
freedom are unknown. By November 1866 Connor was working as a laborer and was married
to Lucy Fisher Connor. They had at least two
sons and two daughters. Connor first reported
personal property in 1870, when he owned four
hogs valued at $10 and furniture worth $50. He
farmed and early in the 1870s also harvested
oysters. His wife had died by mid-September
1870, and on 27 October of that year Connor
married Joanna Watts. They had at least seven
daughters and three sons, including Miles Washington Connor, who became the first president
of Coppin State Teachers College (later Coppin
State University), in Baltimore, Maryland.

After the Civil War, Connor emerged as a
leader in the African American community in
the Western Branch area of Norfolk County,
where he helped to organize churches and fraternal organizations and held several local offices.
On 26 May 1870 Connor was elected a justice
of the peace for Western Branch and two years
later was reelected to a three-year term. In February 1874 a county grand jury indicted the officers of Western Branch for malfeasance relating
to financial disbursements. Connor and others
answered these charges before the county court
in April, at which time the court dismissed the
indictment. On 28 May he was elected supervisor of Western Branch. By virtue of this office he
took a seat on the Norfolk County board of supervisors in July and was appointed to the Committees on Auditing Accounts, Contingent Expenses
and Claims, and Roads and Bridges. He won
reelection to a two-year term in May 1875.

On 14 October 1875 Norfolk County Radicals chose Connor on the third ballot to be the
Republican Party's candidate for a seat in the
House of Delegates. The following November,
African American voter strength in the county
enabled Connor to defeat the white Conservative John Richard Lewellen, a former Confed-

erate army officer and newspaper publisher, by
1,852 to 1,454 votes, despite the latter's endorsement by the *Norfolk Landmark* and the *Norfolk
Virginian*. Appointed to a low-ranking seat on
the Committee on Militia and Police, Connor
rarely spoke during his two-year term and did
not introduce any legislation. He did not seek
reelection in 1877, and the Republicans did not
field any candidates for the General Assembly
from his district.

In October 1882 Connor paid $900 for fifty
acres of land on Hodges Ferry Road in Norfolk
County, which he purchased from Stephen B.
Carney, a local Conservative political leader.
Connor helped establish the Churchland Grove
Baptist Church, where in March 1886 he became
a trustee and helped acquire land on which to
build a sanctuary. He also served as a minister
to the congregation. In the spring of 1887 he was
once again elected a justice of the peace for Western Branch for a two-year term, and he mounted
a successful reelection campaign two years later.
His second wife died of heart disease on 31
December 1889. Miles Connor died of asthma
on 28 June 1893. His funeral took place at the
Churchland Grove Baptist Church, but the place
of his burial is not recorded.

Jackson, *Negro Office-Holders*, 8–9; BVS Marriage Register, Norfolk Co. (1870), with age given as thirty-nine; Census, Norfolk Co., 1870 (age thirty-nine on 23 Sept. 1870),
1880 (age fifty on 28 June 1880); Personal Property Tax
Returns, Norfolk Co. (1870–1883), and Land Tax Returns
(1883–1887), both RG 48, LVA; Norfolk Co. Deed Book,
116:293–294; Norfolk Co. Minute Book, 36:485, 37:368,
38:124, 323, 44:287, 45:355, Norfolk Co. Order Book,
15:602; *Norfolk Virginian*, 28 Feb., 21 Apr., 3 June, 10 July
1874, 3 Nov. 1875; *Norfolk Landmark*, 15 Oct. 1875; Election Records, no. 10, RG 13, LVA; BVS Death Register,
Norfolk Co. (age given as sixty); obituary in *Norfolk Virginian*, 29 June 1893 (age given as sixty-two).

SILVER PERSINGER

CONQUEST, Edwin Parker (19 October
1894–10 May 1966), chair of the Richmond
Regional Planning and Economic Development
Commission, was born in Richmond and was
the son of Pleasonton Laws Conquest and Emma
Parker Conquest. Ranking third in his class at
the Virginia Military Institute, he graduated with
a B.S. in 1914. Conquest then spent one year as
assistant commandant of cadets at Sewanee Mil-

itary Academy, a Tennessee preparatory school affiliated with the University of the South. He returned to Richmond in 1915 to organize and train cadets at John Marshall High School. That summer he enlisted in the Richmond Light Infantry Blues. Soon commissioned a captain, Conquest commanded a Virginia National Guard signal corps company sent to patrol the border with Mexico in 1916. After the United States entered World War I, he was among the soldiers of the 29th Division activated in July 1917 for service in Europe. Conquest spent about two years in England and France as a captain of field artillery and fought in the Meuse-Argonne offensive. He briefly studied at the University of Oxford before returning to the United States in July 1919.

Conquest remained in the Virginia National Guard and in 1925 won promotion to lieutenant colonel. In February 1941 he assumed command of the 176th Infantry Regiment during the military buildup preceding the United States' entry into World War II and was promoted to colonel in May 1941. Conquest was relieved of that command early in 1942. The next year he commanded the 366th Infantry Regiment, a black unit, while it trained at Fort Devens in Middlesex County, Massachusetts, but he did not accompany the regiment to its assignment in Italy. Conquest left active duty in 1945. Two years later he retired from the Virginia National Guard with the rank of brigadier general.

Conquest worked in his father's lumber business from 1919 until 1923. In the latter year he joined the contracting company of J. R. Jones, Incorporated, as secretary-treasurer. The company became J. R. Jones and Conquest, Incorporated, in December 1924 and Conquest, Moncure and Dunn, Incorporated, in April 1941. Conquest was president of the latter construction and engineering company, which undertook numerous projects in Richmond and elsewhere in Virginia. He also served for a time as secretary of the Yorktown Sesquicentennial Association, Incorporated, one of the groups that in 1931 organized the celebrations of the 150th anniversary of the American victory during the Revolutionary War.

In January 1955 the Richmond city council appointed Conquest to the city planning commission. At his first meeting he was elected chair, a responsibility he held for the next eight years. Conquest viewed the Richmond metropolitan area as a single community and advocated governmental changes that reflected this perspective. Often his proposals proved controversial. Henrico County voters rejected an effort to merge Richmond with the county, and Conquest's attempt to establish a regional park authority received little support. During his tenure, Conquest supervised the revision of the city's zoning map and preparation of a new traffic plan.

Conquest's most important achievement was his leadership in establishing a regional planning commission for the metropolitan area. In July 1955 officials from Richmond and from Chesterfield and Henrico Counties agreed in principle to create an advisory commission that would focus on problems that transcended jurisdictional boundaries, such as land use and transportation. A steering committee was formed in December to draft an agreement, but progress was slow. Conquest kept pushing the issue, however, and in January 1957 the city and county governments formally established the Richmond Regional Planning and Economic Development Commission. At its organizational meeting on 26 March 1957, Conquest, one of three Richmond representatives named to the commission, was elected its first chairman. He also continued to chair the Richmond planning commission.

Dissatisfied with the purely advisory authority of the new commission, Conquest soon created a controversy by suggesting a single governing body for the entire metropolitan area. He declared, "The corporate limits are not a Chinese wall from which you can divide off the city people from the county." One city council member responded by calling for Conquest's resignation from both commissions and argued that he had irreparably harmed metropolitan cooperation. Conquest retained the chair of the regional planning commission until 1961 and of the city planning commission until 1963. A *Richmond Times-Dispatch* editorial about his impending retirement from the latter body praised his dedication to duty, his exemplary attendance record, and his sincerity and enthusiasm. While pointing out that the city's professional planners revered him, the editors also noted that Conquest could be brusque and impatient with drawn-out deliberations, qualities they attributed to his military experience.

Even in retirement, Conquest remained concerned about the quality of Richmond's local government. He joined with several other prominent citizens late in 1963 to establish Richmond Forward, an organization dedicated to the promotion of sound government. The association became a potent force in local politics, and Conquest chaired its board of trustees from 1963 until his death. The Richmond First Club recognized his civic and community service in 1956 when it presented him with its Good Citizenship Award.

On 29 June 1927 Conquest married Eugenia Tennant Fairfax, a Loudoun County native. They had two sons. Edwin Parker Conquest suffered a heart attack and died on 10 May 1966 while traveling to a local hospital for a medical examination. He was buried in Hollywood Cemetery. His estate, estimated at more than $1.4 million, included bequests of $10,000 each to John Marshall High School, Saint James's Episcopal Church, the Virginia Military Institute, and a fund supporting the First Virginia Regiment. In 1972 his widow, sons, and nephew, the nationally prominent financial broker James Clifton Wheat (1920–1992), established the Edwin P. Conquest Chair in the Humanities at VMI in his honor.

Birth date in Military Service Records; biography in *Virginia Military Institute Alumni Review* 48 (spring 1972): 56–57 (pors.); *The 1995 Register of Former Cadets of the Virginia Military Institute* (1995), 109; BVS Marriage Register, Richmond City; some Conquest correspondence in Samuel Merrifield Bemiss Papers, VHS; SCC Charter Book, 124:255–256, 130:448–449, 198:41–42; *Richmond News Leader*, 23 Jan. 1942, 8 Feb. 1943, 8, 11 Jan. 1955, 27 Mar. 1956, 2 Apr. 1957 (quotation); *Richmond Times-Dispatch*, 25, 26 Mar. 1955, 27–29 Mar., 25 Apr., 26 June 1956, 27 Mar., 3 Apr. 1957, 14 Jan., 13 Nov. 1963; Richmond City Will Book, 86:288–295; death notice in *Virginia Military Institute Alumni Review* 43 (fall 1966): 41; obituaries and tributes in *Richmond News Leader*, 11 May 1966, and *Richmond Times-Dispatch*, 11 (por.), 13, 14 May 1966.

MICHAEL P. BROOKS

CONRAD, Currence B. (29 January 1812–22 October 1897), member of the Convention of 1861, was the son of John Conrad and Elizabeth Currence Conrad and was born in Bulltown in the part of Harrison County that in 1816 was organized as Lewis County and in 1836 became part of Braxton County. His early life is undocumented, but he learned to read and write and cultivated an interest in history. Conrad particularly enjoyed narratives of frontier life and later sampled such works as Thomas Babington Macaulay's essays, a translation of Jean-Henri Merle d'Aubigné's history of the Reformation, and David Hume's history of England. In November 1830 he received a commission as an ensign in the 125th Regiment of the state militia and in April 1833 was elected captain. After the formation of the 165th Regiment, Conrad became lieutenant colonel on 7 October 1843 and on 30 May 1846 was placed in command of the regiment.

On 27 March 1833 Conrad married Ann Haymond, also of Lewis County. They had nine daughters and two sons. He moved with his family to Sand Fork in 1834, took up farming, and by 1838 owned more than 3,600 acres of land and by 1845 more than 4,000 acres in the county. On 8 September 1840 he was appointed a justice of the peace for Lewis County and served in that capacity until 1845, when the area in which he lived became part of Gilmer County. Commissioned a county justice on 10 February 1845, Conrad took his seat on the court on 24 March at a meeting at which he was also appointed a school commissioner. Influential in moving the county seat to Glenville, a settlement that he is credited with naming, he also helped arrange contracts for constructing the county courthouse, jail, and clerk's office and supervised the work. In 1847 he served as county commissioner of revenue. Conrad continued as a justice until July 1852, when he was elected clerk of the county court, an office he held until June 1861.

On 28 April 1860 Conrad was commissioned a brigadier general of the 20th Brigade, consisting of eleven militia regiments from nine northwestern counties. In December of that year he chaired a meeting of Gilmer County residents who assembled to address concerns about the mounting sectional crisis. Conrad appointed a committee that in January 1861 produced several resolutions blaming the Republican Party and Northern abolitionists for instigating the hostility between the North and South and instructing the county's representatives in the General Assembly to vote in favor of holding a convention to consider Virginia's response to Abraham Lincoln's election.

A special session of the legislature on 19 January authorized a state convention, and on 4 February Conrad won election to represent Calhoun, Gilmer, and Wirt Counties in the convention, which met in Richmond in three sessions between 13 February and 6 December 1861. He seldom spoke during the debates. Conrad opposed secession in both the vote on 4 April and the final vote on 17 April. His Calhoun and Gilmer County constituents ratified the Ordinance of Secession in the statewide referendum on 23 May (although Wirt County did not), and on 12 June Conrad changed his vote on secession to the affirmative and two days later signed the Ordinance.

On 19 April Conrad was added to the convention's Committee on Military Affairs and that month also was given command of the 26th Virginia Brigade, but it is doubtful that he served, and he may have resigned his commission. During the Civil War he devoted his time to farming, reportedly remained aloof from the conflict, and ever afterward was remembered in county annals as a loyal Union man.

Conrad won election as clerk of the circuit court and took office on 1 January 1871. Sometime later he moved to Glenville. An avid hunter and a busy surveyor, he remained robust as he grew older and visited the Philadelphia centennial exhibition in 1876 and the 1893 World's Columbian Exposition in Chicago. On 31 December 1896, after twenty-five years of continuous service, he retired as circuit court clerk. Currence B. Conrad died on 22 October 1897 and was buried in the family cemetery near Sand Fork beside his wife, who had died on 23 April 1878.

Biographies in *Hardesty's Historical and Geographical Encyclopedia, Illustrated: Containing . . . Histories of Braxton and Gilmer Counties* (1883), 390, in J. Archie Langford, "The People: Memories of Colonel Conrad" (typescript dated 11 Dec. 1940), WPA Writers Project, Gilmer Co., West Virginia and Regional History Collection, WVU, in Jim Comstock, ed., *West Virginia Heritage Encyclopedia* (1976), 5:1088–1090, in Gilmer County Historical Society, *Bicentennial Biographies: Gilmer County, West Virginia* (1976), 31

(gives middle name as Benjamin without documentation), and in Gilmer County Historical Society, *History of Gilmer County, West Virginia, 1845–1989* (1994), 3, 4, 5, 12, 78–79 (por. on 78); birth and death dates from gravestone transcription in Wes Cochran, *Gilmer County, WV, Cemeteries* (1994), 2:64; Militia Commission Papers, Lewis Co., and appointment as brigadier general in John Letcher Executive Papers, both RG 3, LVA; service as county official provided by Gilmer Co. Clerk's Office, Glenville, W.Va.; resolutions adopted 1 Jan. 1861, printed in *Barbour Jeffersonian*, n.d., and presented 21 Jan. 1861, Legislative Petitions, Gilmer Co., RG 78, LVA; Reese and Gaines, *Proceedings of 1861 Convention*, 3:163, 4:144; Reese, *Journal and Papers of 1861 Convention*, vol. 1, Journal, 168, 231, 235, 240; Gilmer Co., W.Va., Will Book, 1:220–229.

DONALD W. GUNTER

CONRAD, Holmes (31 January 1840–4 September 1915), attorney, was born in Winchester and was the son of Robert Young Conrad, a prominent attorney who served in the Convention of 1861, and Elizabeth Whiting Powell Conrad. Educated in local primary schools and at Winchester Academy, he enrolled at the Virginia Military Institute in 1854 but left after one year. Conrad taught school for a time and then attended the University of Virginia during the 1858 and 1859 academic terms. He interrupted his study of the law on 19 April 1861, two days after Virginia seceded from the Union, and volunteered as a sergeant for Company A of the 1st Virginia Cavalry. The following January, Conrad transferred to the 17th Virginia Battalion (Cavalry), which was eventually folded into the 11th Virginia Cavalry. He gained some renown in June 1862 for capturing a British adventurer who was fighting for the Union. During much of the Civil War, Conrad served as a staff officer. He was promoted to first lieutenant and adjutant of the 17th Battalion on 20 November 1862, to rank from 2 October, but he resigned on 7 November 1863 following a period of illness and a disagreement with a superior officer. On 19 April 1864 Conrad volunteered as a private in Company D of the 11th Virginia Cavalry. Once again distinguishing himself in the field, he was promoted to captain on 29 April and to major in the autumn of 1864. He served for the rest of the war as a commissary and assistant inspector general.

Major Conrad, as he was usually addressed after the war, returned to Winchester and resumed his legal studies. He was admitted to the bar in

January 1866 and joined his father's law firm. Conrad developed a reputation as a sharp-tongued courtroom litigator and a serious legal thinker. Preferring broad precedents to narrow technicalities, he viewed law as a means of reinforcing concepts of justice, constitutional tradition, and obligations, precepts that dominated his public statements. His traditionalist outlook notwithstanding, Conrad embraced modern economic and industrial trends and worked with other local leaders to attract northern capital to Winchester. He was a close friend of John Handley, a wealthy resident of Scranton, Pennsylvania, who frequently visited Winchester. In 1890 they joined in organizing the Equity Improvement Company, which pursued a range of civic and industrial projects in the Winchester area. After Handley's death in 1895, Conrad became president and legal counsel of the board of Handley's trustees, who assumed control over the property that the company owned and over Handley's large bequest to the city.

Conrad's legal career and civic involvement served as a platform for his political ambitions. A conservative advocate of full payment of Virginia's antebellum public debt, he unsuccessfully sought the Democratic nomination for a seat in the House of Representatives in 1880, and in the following year he won election to represent Frederick County and Winchester in the House of Delegates. Conrad served on the Committees of Propositions and Grievances, Manufactures and Mechanic Arts, and Federal Relations and Resolutions. He took an active hand in efforts to thwart the Readjusters, who supported reducing the principal to be paid on the public debt and refinancing the remainder at a lower rate of interest. Perhaps considered too patrician and aloof, Conrad was never elected to another office, but Democrats often called on his forceful speaking skills to promote the party's candidates and positions. Three Democratic governors named him to the board of the University of Virginia, on which he served from 1876 to 1890 with one four-year interruption. As a mouthpiece for the conservative Democratic program, Conrad in 1883 debated John Sergeant Wise, a close friend and Readjuster congressman.

Conrad was a presidential elector for Grover Cleveland in 1892. As a consequence of Conrad's work on behalf of the campaign, Cleveland appointed him an assistant attorney general of the United States on 13 June 1893. Conrad's skill in arguing cases before the Supreme Court impressed observers, and on 7 February 1895 the president named him solicitor general of the United States, the official with primary responsibility for representing the government in federal courts. Conrad served through the end of Cleveland's second administration and the early months of William McKinley's first. Conrad continued to reside and practice law in Washington, D.C., for the rest of his life, but on weekends he regularly returned to his house in Winchester, where he taught a Presbyterian Sunday school class. Despite his strong Democratic connections, both McKinley and Theodore Roosevelt retained him for two high-profile cases. McKinley appointed him to represent the government in *Morris* v. *United States* (1899), more commonly known as the Potomac Flat cases, a complicated property dispute involving the boundary between Virginia and Maryland. Roosevelt named him one of two special prosecutors in a celebrated postal fraud case. Arguing the case before the jury, Conrad won convictions of all four defendants.

During the last two decades of his life, Conrad appeared repeatedly before the Supreme Court of the United States. Most important was his representation of Brown Brothers and Company, fiscal agents for Virginia's bondholders, who joined forces with the Commonwealth to force West Virginia to assume responsibility for a portion of the outstanding antebellum debt. Bringing Conrad full circle to the issue on which he had cut his political teeth, the case was not fully resolved until shortly before his death. He helped win a decision that obligated West Virginia to assume payment of more than $12,000,000 and earned him a reported $250,000 in legal fees.

Conrad participated in a range of professional and civic activities. A founding vice president of the Virginia State Bar Association, he chaired the committee that drafted its code of ethics and urged its members to resist trends that he feared were unduly commercializing the profession. Like many other prominent attorneys, he was drawn into the orbit of the railroad system and served as director for the Washington, Ohio, and Western and the Cumberland Valley and Martinsburg Railroad Companies. Conrad became a leading figure in the community of white southerners in the District of Columbia. He frequently delivered addresses in honor of the Confederacy and served as commander of the Henry Heth chapter of the United Confederate Veterans and as vice president of the Southern Society of Washington. Beginning in 1901 Conrad taught courses on the history of the law in the Georgetown University School of Law. Despite his strengthening connections to the District, he remained a prominent figure in Virginia and often spoke at Confederate memorial ceremonies and at the unveiling of Winchester civic projects.

Conrad married Mary Ellen Magruder, of Shenandoah County, on 7 July 1864, but she died about a year later. On 2 January 1868 he married Georgia Bryan Forman at her family's plantation in Cecil County, Maryland. They had four daughters and three sons. Holmes Conrad died on 4 September 1915 at the same Winchester mansion in which he had been raised and was buried in the city's Mount Hebron Cemetery.

Biographies in *NCAB*, 16:399, Quarles, *Some Worthy Lives*, 72–74, and Paul Brandon Barringer et al., *University of Virginia: Its History, Influence, Equipment and Characteristics* (1904), 1:435–436 (por.); BVS Marriage Register, Shenandoah Co. (1864); Cecil Co., Md., Circuit Court Marriage Licenses (license dated 1 Jan. 1868); variant second marriage date of 2 Jan. 1869 in *Winchester Evening Star*, 10 Feb. 1925; Holmes Conrad Papers, VHS, and Holmes Conrad Collection, Handley Regional Library, Winchester; publications include addresses printed in *New Market Day at V.M.I.* (1903), 24–45, *Ceremonies and Addresses Attending the Presentation of a Statue of Hunter Holmes McGuire* (1904), 17–30, and "The Old County Court System of Virginia: Its Place in History," *Virginia State Bar Association Proceedings* (1908), 323–350; Compiled Service Records; Richard L. Armstrong, *11th Virginia Cavalry* (1989), 132; *Morris* v. *United States* (1899) and *Commonwealth of Virginia* v. *State of West Virginia* (1907), *United States Reports*, 174:196–291, 206:290–322; *Washington Post*, 8 Feb. 1895, 26, 27 Feb. 1904, 6 June 1911; *Richmond Times-Dispatch*, 22 Apr. 1906; BVS Death Certificate, Winchester (with birth date); obituaries in *New York Times*, *Richmond Times-Dispatch*, and *Washington Post*, all 5 Sept. 1915, *Richmond News Leader* and *Winchester Evening Star*, both 6 Sept. 1915, and *Confederate Veteran* 24 (1916): 30; editorial tributes in *Richmond Times-Dispatch*, 6 Sept. 1915, and *Winchester Evening Star*, 7, 8 Sept. 1915; memorial in *Virginia State Bar Association Proceedings* (1916), 101–106 (por. facing 101).

WILLIAM BLAND WHITLEY

CONRAD, Robert Young (27 December 1805–5 May 1875), member of the Convention of 1861 and member-elect of the House of Representatives, was born in Winchester and was the son of Daniel Conrad, a physician, and Rebecca Holmes Conrad. He entered the United States Military Academy at West Point in 1819 but as a result of poor academic performance was discharged in 1821. Conrad studied law, most likely with Henry St. George Tucker (1780–1848), and became a prominent attorney in Winchester. On 10 December 1829 he married Elizabeth Whiting Powell, of Loudoun County. Their two daughters and seven sons included Holmes Conrad, who became assistant attorney general of the United States and later solicitor general.

During the antebellum years Conrad's influence expanded throughout the community. He helped organize the Bank of Winchester and Mount Hebron Cemetery and also headed the board of trustees of his local alma mater, Winchester Academy. He held stock in two turnpike companies and a shoe manufactory. A Whig, Conrad won election in 1840 to a four-year term in the Senate of Virginia representing Clarke, Frederick, and Jefferson Counties. He served on the Committee of Courts of Justice for all four years, on the Committee of Privileges and Elections during the 1841–1842 session, and on the Committee of General Laws for the 1842–1843 and 1843–1844 sessions. After returning to Winchester at the end of his term, Conrad practiced law with John Randolph Tucker (1823–1897) until 1857, when Tucker became attorney general of Virginia.

Conrad owned about a dozen slaves in 1860. He approved of the Virginia authorities' response to John Brown's raid on Harpers Ferry and early in 1860 was captain of the Home Guards of Winchester. A Unionist nevertheless, he was openly expressing his attachment to the United States Constitution by the end of the year while insisting that the North cease hostile action against slavery.

Conrad was one of two Unionists elected on 4 February 1861 to represent Frederick County in a state convention called to consider secession. On the convention's third day, he proposed establishing the important Committee on Federal Relations, which he chaired. In a major speech delivered on 15 March, Conrad persuaded the convention to meet as a committee of the whole in order to debate his committee's fourteen resolutions that favored maintaining the Union but that also confirmed states' rights, supported slavery, condemned federal coercion, and recognized the right of secession. He voted against secession on 4 April when the measure failed and again on 17 April when the convention approved secession following President Abraham Lincoln's call for troops to put down the rebellion.

In May 1861 Conrad ran for one of Frederick County's two seats in the House of Delegates. Voters rejected him almost as soundly as they embraced disunion, which they approved with 80 percent of the poll. Conrad subsequently signed the Ordinance of Secession and attended the later sessions of the convention in June and November 1861.

Five of Conrad's sons fought for the Confederacy, and during the Civil War he supported the Southern cause in Winchester. His civic leadership made him a target of Union troops who frequently occupied the town. Conrad often endured detention, arrest, and other restrictive measures that Union officers in Winchester imposed. He was imprisoned in Maryland during the latter part of the war. After hostilities ended in April 1865, Conrad advocated unity and in June took the oath of allegiance. That autumn he sought election to the House of Representatives from the Seventh District, comprising Alexandria, Clarke, Fairfax, Fauquier, Frederick, Loudoun, Prince William, Shenandoah, and Warren Counties. His chief opponent among the five other candidates was Lewis McKenzie, a former mayor of Alexandria who had served in the United States Congress for a few weeks in 1863. In the bitterly fought election, Conrad received 4,854 of the 6,786 votes cast. Through manipulating the organizational roll call of members-elect of the Thirty-ninth

Congress, Radical Republicans in the House of Representatives denied Conrad and all the other members elected from the former Confederate states their seats.

Conrad resumed his law practice and served as Winchester's mayor from 1865 until 1868. In the latter year he was a state delegate to the Democratic National Convention in New York City. His wife died on 12 July 1872. Robert Young Conrad died in Winchester of typhoid pneumonia on 5 May 1875 and was buried in Mount Hebron Cemetery.

Birth date on gravestone; biographies in J. E. Norris, ed., *History of the Lower Shenandoah Valley Counties of Frederick, Berkeley, Jefferson and Clarke* (1890), 571–573, and Quarles, *Some Worthy Lives*, 74–75 (por.), both with variant birth date of 5 Dec. 1805; David F. Riggs, "Robert Young Conrad and the Ordeal of Secession," *VMHB* 86 (1978): 259–274 (por. on 263); family and business correspondence, speeches, and other personal papers in Robert Young Conrad Papers (including certified 1865 polling results) and in Holmes Conrad Papers, both VHS; legal career documented in Conrad Account Book and Conrad and Tucker Day Books, Handley Regional Library, Winchester; Loudoun Co. Marriage Record (1794–1850), 80; *Richmond Enquirer*, 16 Mar. 1861; Reese and Gaines, *Proceedings of 1861 Convention*, 1:38, 701–716, 3:163, 4:144; Election Records, no. 423, RG 13, LVA; *Winchester Journal*, 15, 22 Sept. 1865; *Alexandria Gazette*, 18 Oct. 1865; Alan B. Bromberg, "The Virginia Congressional Elections of 1865: A Test of Southern Loyalty," *VMHB* 84 (1976): 75–98; BVS Death Register, Winchester; obituary in *Leesburg Mirror*, 13 May 1875.

DAVID F. RIGGS

CONRAD, Thomas Nelson (1 August 1837–5 January 1905), Confederate spy and president of Virginia Agricultural and Mechanical College (later Virginia Polytechnic Institute and State University), was born in Fairfax Court House and was the son of Nelson Conrad and Lavinia M. Thomas Conrad. He attended Fairfax Academy and Dickinson College, which awarded him a bachelor's degree in 1857 and a master's degree in 1860. Conrad became a lay Methodist preacher and taught at a private school in Georgetown, District of Columbia, before establishing the Georgetown Institute, a boys' school there.

After the Civil War began, Conrad made no effort to conceal his Confederate sympathies, which had attracted the attention of United States government authorities even before the institute's commencement exercise in June 1862, when his students made fiery pro-Confederate speeches, and he ordered the band to play "Dixie," to uproarious applause. On 2 August he was arrested on charges of communicating with the enemy and recruiting students for the Confederate army. Conrad was locked up in Old Capitol Prison and later paroled pending exchange. Many years afterward he wrote that during that time he plotted to assassinate the former commanding general of the United States Army, Winfield Scott, whom he considered a traitor to his native Virginia, but that Confederate officials refused to allow him to proceed.

Conrad provided Confederates with information on Major General George B. McClellan's army in 1862 during the Peninsula campaign. On 16 October 1863 Conrad became chaplain of the 3d Virginia Cavalry, with the rank of captain dating from 30 September of that year, but he was repeatedly detached on espionage assignments. According to his later accounts, he returned to Washington at least six times and set up a secret line of communication through southern Maryland into Virginia. Conrad received a personal letter of thanks from Jefferson Davis in May 1864 for the valuable intelligence he had provided on Major General Ambrose E. Burnside's corps during the Wilderness campaign. Arrested that year in southern Maryland, Conrad was imprisoned at Point Lookout, where he feigned illness and then escaped. Late in 1864 he and two associates schemed to kidnap Abraham Lincoln and hold him for political ransom, a plan they abandoned as impractical because the president traveled with an armed cavalry escort. Conrad wrote to Davis in January 1865 stating that he wished to resign his chaplaincy and devote himself to the Confederate secret service. After Lincoln was assassinated in April 1865, Conrad was arrested and threatened by an angry crowd because he resembled the assassin John Wilkes Booth. Released, Conrad was arrested again in Virginia, but he leaped from a moving train and fled to the mountains until the postassassination furor had passed.

On 4 October 1866 Conrad married Emma T. Ball, of King George County. They had three daughters and four sons, one of whom died in childhood. From 1866 to 1868 Conrad taught at Upperville Academy, in Fauquier County, and from then until 1871 at Rockville Academy in Maryland. In the latter year he became principal of the Preston and Olin Institute, a Methodist boys' school in Blacksburg. When that school was absorbed in 1872 into the new Virginia Agricultural and Mechanical College, Conrad unsuccessfully sought its presidency. He then became editor of the weekly *Montgomery Messenger*, in which he criticized the management of the college and supported the Readjusters, a new, biracial political party that advocated increasing public support for education and reducing the principal and interest rate to be paid on the antebellum state debt. Conrad wrote frequently to William Mahone, the Readjuster leader, offering political advice and reporting on political events in southwestern Virginia. Conrad became a professor of English at the college in 1877 and after the Readjusters gained control of the General Assembly was appointed president in February 1882.

Described as the most colorful and controversial president in the first century of the school, Conrad made significant, lasting changes. The college began awarding bachelor's degrees for literary and scientific studies as well as in civil and mining engineering. He organized the college into four academic departments (agricultural, business, literary and scientific, and mechanical), converted the school to summer instead of winter vacations, significantly increased spending on the library, made the school's farming operation financially successful for the first time, and continued to reorganize its military program in the pattern of Virginia Military Institute's. Conrad became a Republican after Mahone joined that party. He was criticized for continuing his political activity, and after the Readjusters lost control of the state government, he was dismissed as president effective 30 June 1886.

One of Conrad's sons died while attending Virginia Agricultural and Mechanical College during Conrad's tenure as president. For three months in 1882 and one month in 1887 Conrad served as mayor of Blacksburg. In August 1887 he moved to Maryland to teach at Maryland Agricultural College (later the University of Maryland at College Park), and then about 1890 he moved to Washington, D.C., to become a statistician for the United States census. A few years later Conrad bought a farm near Dumfries, in Prince William County, to which he retired.

In 1892 Conrad published a ghostwritten reminiscence of his espionage exploits, *A Confederate Spy: A Story of the Civil War,* based on articles he had written for a Philadelphia newspaper in May 1887. He also published a revised edition entitled *The Rebel Scout: A Thrilling History of Scouting Life in the Southern Army* (1904). His wife died in 1900, and Thomas Nelson Conrad died on 5 January 1905 in Washington, probably at his son's residence, of what was described as acute indigestion. He was buried in the Westview Cemetery in Blacksburg. The Virginia Tech Corps of Cadets honored him in 1972 by naming its new equestrian military team first Conrad's Troopers and then the Conrad Cavalry.

Biographies in *Hardesty's Historical and Geographical Encyclopedia, . . . Special Virginia Edition* (1884), 406 (with birth date probably provided by Conrad), and M. Clifford Harrison, "A Fighting Confederate Chaplain Spy," *Virginia Cavalcade* 12 (spring 1963): 18–22 (por. on 19); family history information provided by descendant Erik P. Conard (2003); BVS Marriage Register, King George Co.; Compiled Service Records; Haskell M. Monroe Jr. et al., eds., *The Papers of Jefferson Davis* (1971–   ), 10:439, 11:40, 331, 368; numerous Conrad letters in William Mahone Papers, Duke, and some in Adie Family Papers, VHS; *Rebel Scout* MS at VPI; *Washington Evening Star,* 28 June, 4 Aug. 1862; *Washington Post,* 13 Dec. 1892, 18 Jan. 1893; Duncan Lyle Kinnear, *The First 100 Years: A History of Virginia Polytechnic Institute and State University* (1972), 110–120; obituaries in *Washington Evening Star,* 5 Jan. 1905, *Washington Post,* 6 Jan. 1905, *Roanoke Times,* 8 Jan. 1905, and *Confederate Veteran* 13 (1905): 220 (por.).

ERNEST B. FURGURSON

CONVERSE, Amasa (21 August 1795–9 December 1872), Presbyterian minister and publisher, was born in Lyme, Grafton County, New Hampshire, and was the son of Joel Converse and Elizabeth Bixby Converse. He attended local public schools and worked on the family farm until age nineteen. He spent three months teaching school in Bradford, Orange County, Vermont, and three months studying Latin at an academy in Meriden, New Hampshire, before entering Phillips Academy in Andover, Massachusetts, in 1816. Influenced by a Congregationalist layman,

Converse joined the Andover Congregational Church. In September 1818 he matriculated at Dartmouth College, which granted him an A.B. in 1822 and an A.M. by vote of its board of trustees in 1825. After receiving his bachelor's degree, he taught school in Chelsea, Vermont, and in Ashfield, Franklin County, Massachusetts.

Converse enrolled in Princeton Theological Seminary in 1823, but financial difficulties and poor health interrupted his studies. He returned to Ashfield, where he was licensed to preach in the Congregational Church. Back at the seminary and still in poor health, Converse followed the advice of a professor who recommended that he move to a warmer climate. He traveled to Virginia in 1824, taught school in Nottoway County, and preached occasionally at a local church that had no minister. The following year Converse accepted an invitation from the Young Men's Missionary Society of Richmond to work as an evangelist in Amelia and Nottoway Counties, and on 7 May 1826 he was ordained an evangelist by the Presbytery of Hanover. He married Flavia Booth, a Massachusetts native who was teaching in Brunswick County, on 16 December 1828. They had at least one daughter and six sons, three of whom became Presbyterian ministers.

Unable to find a congregation to support him, Converse in February 1827 became coeditor of two religious periodicals then published in Richmond, the weekly *Visitor and Telegraph* and the monthly *Literary and Evangelical Magazine.* In the summer of the following year he purchased the publishers' interests in the magazines and became their sole editor. Converse discontinued the *Literary and Evangelical Magazine* in December 1828 in order to concentrate on the *Visitor and Telegraph,* which in January 1830 he renamed the *Southern Religious Telegraph.* Employing agents to sell subscriptions, he increased circulation and paid off his debts. Converse and the *Telegraph* became widely known and controversial in the 1830s when Presbyterians split during the so-called Old School–New School dispute. Many leading Virginia Presbyterians adhered to the Old School theology and led in the expulsion from the denomination of more than 500 New School congregations. Converse initially tried to remain neutral, but after the expulsion he sided with the New School congregations and wrote editorials arguing that expulsion was a violation of the church constitution. William Swan Plumer, the influential pastor of First Presbyterian Church in Richmond, opposed Converse and began a rival journal in Richmond, the *Watchman of the South*. The outcome of the controversy and a decline in *Telegraph* subscriptions were undoubtedly factors in Converse's decision to leave Richmond after nearly fifteen years in Virginia.

Converse moved to Philadelphia in January 1839 and united the *Telegraph* with the prestigious but financially troubled *Philadelphia Observer*, the oldest Presbyterian newspaper then in publication. In 1840 he renamed it the *Christian Observer*. In July 1843 Mississippi College awarded Converse an honorary doctorate of divinity. During the 1840s and 1850s he became involved in a disagreement in the Presbyterian Church over slavery. As a young man Converse had believed that slavery violated Christian principles, but he later changed his mind, perhaps while residing in Virginia. His shift of opinion placed him in opposition to the increasingly antislavery New School Presbyterians of Philadelphia. The *Observer* office caught fire and burned in 1854. Converse, without insurance, lost everything except his subscription books. Interpreting it as a sign of providence that his lists were saved, he rejected offers to purchase his newspaper and persevered in the face of competition from Presbyterian periodicals critical of slavery.

Late in 1860 Converse bought the *Knoxville Presbyterian Witness* and on 3 January 1861 began publishing the *Christian Observer* in both Richmond and Philadelphia, with one of his sons serving as the Richmond editor. During the secession crisis, Converse hoped that the Union would be preserved but maintained that the Southern states had a right to secede. The United States Post Office refused to deliver mail to the Confederate States after 31 May 1861, but Converse retained Richmond in his paper's masthead until 1 August, when he finally bowed to political pressure and pledged to close the Richmond office. On 22 August a federal marshal and six deputies seized Converse's office and property in Philadelphia and stopped publication of the *Christian Observer*.

Considering the suppression of his paper to be improper government censorship of the press, Converse successfully protested and had the case against him dropped. On 17 October 1861 he received permission to continue publishing the paper, but by then he had returned to Richmond, where on 24 October he resumed publication of the *Christian Observer*. The paper lost much of its circulation after the closure of the Philadelphia office, and Converse dropped the paper's claimed neutrality. During the Civil War he wrote and preached in support of the Confederacy and visited wounded soldiers in hospitals. Publication of the *Observer* was suspended for several months after the war ended in April 1865. Its office escaped the evacuation fire that destroyed much of Richmond's commercial section, and the paper was one of the first weekly periodicals in the South to resume publication. Virtually bankrupt and in shock over the Confederate defeat, Converse issued the paper only irregularly during the next four years.

In 1869 Converse accepted an invitation to merge the *Christian Observer* with the *Free Christian Commonwealth*, published in Louisville, Kentucky. He moved to that city and soon made the *Christian Observer* into one of the most widely read religious newspapers in the South and the primary publication of the southern branch of the Presbyterian Church, officially known as the Presbyterian Church in the United States. By 1870 the editor had more influence than at any other time in his life. Converse was able to pay off his debts, and he left the publication of the prosperous and influential paper to his wife and sons. Amasa Converse died of pneumonia at his home in Louisville, Kentucky, on 9 December 1872 and was buried in Cave Hill Cemetery in that city.

L. P. Yandell, *A Biographical Sketch of the Late Amasa Converse, D.D.* (1873); *The Biographical Encyclopædia of Kentucky* (1878), 227–228; Alfred Nevin, ed., *Encyclopædia of the Presbyterian Church in the United States of America* (1884), 155 (por.); numerous references in Ernest Trice Thompson, *Presbyterians in the South* (1963–1973), vol. 1, and 2:438–439; Arnold Shankman, "Converse, *The Christian Observer*, and Civil War Censorship," *Journal of Presbyterian History* 52 (1974): 227–244; Amasa Converse Papers (including 1861 MS autobiography with por. and dates of birth and marriage, and clippings of obituaries from many papers, photocopy in VHS) and Converse Family Papers, both Presbyterian Historical Society, Montreat, N.C.; excerpts from "Autobiography of the Rev. Amasa Converse," *Journal of Presbyterian History* 43 (1965): 197–218, 254–263; Brunswick Co. Marriage Bonds; Presidential Pardons; death notice in *Daily Louisville Commercial*, 11 Dec. 1872; obituaries in *Richmond Daily Dispatch*, 10 Dec. 1872, and *Christian Observer*, 11, 18 Dec. 1872.

ROBERT BENEDETTO

CONWAY, Edwin (ca. 1682–3 October 1763), member of the House of Burgesses, was the son of Edwin Conway and his first wife, Sarah Walker Conway, and was born probably in the portion of old Rappahannock County that in 1692 became Richmond County. When he was about sixteen, his father died and left him a plantation and a few slaves in neighboring Lancaster County, as well as unspecified mathematical instruments and books. Conway married Anne Ball before February 1708 and after her death married Ann Hack, who died on 28 August 1747, but the date of neither marriage is known. He had at least two sons and at least five daughters, one of whom, Milicent Conway, was the first wife of the prominent Lancaster County planter and diarist James Gordon (d. 1768).

A tobacco planter in Lancaster County and owner at one time of a tobacco warehouse, Conway may have begun his public career as a surveyor, and he eventually became an attorney, justice of the peace, and colonel of militia. He was well known to several families of regional consequence, among them the Balls, Beverleys, Carters, Robinsons, and Wormeleys. An opinionated and vocal man, Conway had a large measure of personal pride and when annoyed or contradicted spoke his mind plainly and forcefully. In 1732 he wrote three letters to the governor in four days to complain about the conduct of the local tobacco inspector, but the governor and Council dismissed them as unsupported and essentially frivolous.

Conway was elected to represent Lancaster County in the House of Burgesses in 1710 and served with only two interruptions through the spring session of 1752, one of the longest tenures of any burgess during the first half of the century. He rose quickly to a position of leadership during the politically tempestuous 1710s. Conway was appointed to the Committee of Propo-

sitions and Grievances in 1711 and the following year joined the committee that apportioned the public levy among the colony's counties and in effect oversaw the colony's budget. He served on the latter committee, often as chair, throughout most of his career. Conway frequently sat on committees appointed to draft bills on estates and inheritances and on county and parish boundaries, and by 1715 he regularly received high-ranking appointments to the Committees of Privileges and Elections or of Propositions and Grievances. Conway was defeated in the 1720 election and unsuccessfully challenged the result on the ground that not all potential voters had received notice of the election. He regained his seat in 1723 and was reelected at every subsequent poll until 1748.

An experienced and respected legislator by the 1730s, Conway was allied with some of the most influential leaders. He often served on the select committees that crafted the burgesses' replies to the governor's messages and occasionally presided over the committee of the whole. He nominated Sir John Randolph for Speaker of the House of Burgesses on 5 August 1736, and on the next day the new Speaker rewarded him with the chairmanship of the Committee of Privileges and Elections. Conway may have pleased his colleagues by reporting fully on the substance and outcome of the numerous contested election cases and breaches of the privileges of the House that arose during his ten years as committee chair; he certainly earned the gratitude of later historians who relied on his reports to understand eighteenth-century electoral politics.

Following Randolph's death, Conway was one of three men nominated for Speaker of the House in November 1738. John Robinson (1705–1766) was elected Speaker, and Conway then played a key part in enabling Robinson to become the most powerful legislative leader in the colony's history. Making effective use of Conway's competence and experience, the Speaker appointed him chair of the Committee of Privileges and Elections, ranking member of Propositions and Grievances, and a member of nearly every important select committee. Robinson often designated Conway to preside during debates in the committee of the whole, a move that allowed the Speaker to make maximum use of his personal and parliamentary skills without having to worry about unfavorable rulings from the chair. During the years that Robinson consolidated his power, Conway was perhaps his most influential colleague.

After the March 1747 assembly session, Conway retired and was succeeded by his son, Peter Conway. Five years later he replaced his son and took his seat as a burgess for the last time in February 1752. Conway regained the chairmanship of the Committee of Privileges and Elections and was second in seniority on the Committee on Propositions and Grievances, although he no longer presided over the committee of the whole or the committee on the public levy. In his seventies by then, Conway evidently did not return to Williamsburg for the assembly sessions of 1753, 1754, or 1755 and did not stand for reelection in 1756.

Not only was Conway one of the most influential burgesses of his generation, but he also took the unusual step of explaining his opinions to the public. An early and consistent supporter of having William Parks print the assembly's journals and statutes, Conway occasionally published statements in Parks's *Williamsburg Virginia Gazette* to refute his opponents or to explain his views on tobacco inspection laws (which he opposed), the career of Alexander Spotswood (which he criticized), and proposals to move the capital out of Williamsburg (which he ridiculed).

Conway outlived two wives, both of his sons, and several of his daughters. At the time of his death he owned fifteen slaves and lived in a well-furnished house with an upper chamber and a new room, a cider house, dairy, kitchen, tobacco house, and "sellar." Edwin Conway died, probably at his Lancaster County home, on 3 October 1763 and was most likely buried there.

Family history in Hayden, *Virginia Genealogies*, 231, 238–243, with death date at age eighty-one from family Bible records of son-in-law James Gordon; numerous references in Gordon's journal, printed in *WMQ*, 1st ser., 11 (1902–1903): 98–112, 195–205, 217–236 and 12 (1903): 1–11; legislative career documented in *JHB*; Conway to William Gooch, 9, 10, 12 Oct. 1732, Colonial Papers, RG 1, LVA; *Executive Journals of Council*, 4:287–288; *Williamsburg Virginia Gazette*, 22 Apr. 1737, 24 Nov., 1, 22 Dec. 1738, 29 May 1746, 17 Apr. 1752; will (giving age as seventy-nine on 27 July 1762) and estate inventory in Lancaster Co. Deeds and Wills, 17:30–32.

BRENT TARTER

CONWAY, Eustace (17 September 1820–20 May 1857), member of the Convention of 1850–1851, was born in Stafford County and was the son of John Moncure Conway, longtime county clerk, and Catherine Storke Peyton Conway. His nephew Moncure Daniel Conway became an expatriate Virginia writer, reformer, and abolitionist. Remembered by contemporaries as dark and handsome, Eustace Conway read law in Stafford County with his brother-in-law Richard Cassius Lee Moncure, later a member of the Convention of 1850–1851 and president of the Virginia Supreme Court of Appeals, and by January 1843 he was practicing law in Fredericksburg. He enjoyed a successful legal career and in 1850 owned four taxable slaves and two town lots valued at $4,900. On 27 June 1842 Conway executed a marriage bond in Northumberland County and on that date or soon thereafter married Maria Tayloe Tomlin. They had three sons (one of them born after Conway's death) and two daughters, and at the time of his death he was also the guardian of two young male kinsmen.

Conway served as secretary of a Fredericksburg meeting in April 1841 to mark the death of William Henry Harrison and may have had Whig leanings at the beginning of his political career, but he became an ardent Democrat. In 1847 he won election to the first of three consecutive one-year terms representing Spotsylvania County in the House of Delegates. During the 1847–1848 session Conway served on the Committees of Privileges and Elections and of Schools and Colleges, and during the 1848–1849 session he sat on the Committee of Roads and Internal Navigation and chaired the Committee on the Banks of the Commonwealth.

During Conway's second term, sectional divisions deepened as Congress debated whether to exclude slavery from the territories the United States had acquired during the Mexican War. In response to the Wilmot Proviso, an unsuccessful amendment twice introduced in Congress that would have barred slavery from the Mexican Cession, Conway moved that the General Assembly declare that Congress had no power to legislate respecting slavery, that the territories belonged equally to all the states, that citizens could not be prevented from immigrating there with their chattel property, and that the southern states would view any attempt by Congress to abolish slavery or the slave trade in the District of Columbia as a direct attack. After a select committee of which Conway was a member amended and reported his resolutions, he defended them on 13 January 1849 in a speech in the House of Delegates. Arguing that southerners were entitled to equal protection under the Constitution, he declared that Congress could not prohibit masters from taking their slaves into the territories "any more than they can exclude the Yankee with his wooden clocks, nutmegs or other traps." Conway's resolutions passed the House seven days later by a 117 to 13 vote.

Conway maintained his high profile during the revision of the Code of Virginia that summer. He served on one conference committee and chaired another to hammer out differences between the House and Senate. As floor manager he moved several sections of the Code revision through the House. Conway's role in modifying the judicial sections of the Code earned him a place on the Committee for Courts of Justice during the 1849–1850 session.

Campaigning on the regular Democratic ticket in August 1850, Conway finished third of eleven candidates vying for five seats representing the district of Caroline, Hanover, King William, and Spotsylvania Counties at a convention that met from 14 October 1850 until 1 August 1851 to revise the state constitution. He served on the important Committee on the Basis and Apportionment of Representation. Conway supported some reforms, such as popular election of the governor and allowing the governor to seek a second term, but opposed two key reforms advocated by western delegates to extend the suffrage to all white males regardless of property qualifications and to reapportion the General Assembly. His opposition derived from his Calhounite belief that the highest goal of government was to secure individual rights and protect the minority from the tyranny of the majority. Conway missed thirty-two days of the convention

and did not vote in the committee of the whole on 16 May 1851 on a key compromise on reapportionment of the legislature that shifted the balance of power away from slaveholding easterners. He opposed the legislative compromise on 21 May and on 31 July voted with the minority against the final version of the constitution, which won ratification later that year.

In 1852 Conway attended the Democratic National Convention in Baltimore. Some insiders credited him with suggesting to the Virginia delegation the name of Franklin Pierce, ultimately the successful candidate, after the thirty-fourth ballot. That November, Conway chaired a committee that invited James Buchanan to Fredericksburg to celebrate the Democratic victory. He also attended the 1856 Democratic National Convention in Cincinnati.

Conway lost a bid for election to the Fredericksburg city council in March 1855 when the American (Know Nothing) Party swept all twelve council seats, although he received the most votes of any Democrat in the race. Often a member of local groups that promoted the city's economic development, Conway was a director of the Fredericksburg Water Power Company in 1854 and president of the city's branch of the Bank of Virginia from 1854 until his resignation early in 1857. In 1849 he began several years of service on the board of visitors of the College of William and Mary. At age fourteen Conway had experienced religious conversion at a Prince William County camp meeting. Later he taught the Sabbath school at Fredericksburg's Methodist Episcopal church for many years. In 1850 he chaired the building committee for the erection of a new church. Also a leader of the Young Men's Christian Association of Fredericksburg, Conway bequeathed that organization $20 per annum for five years to help educate the town's indigent male youths.

On 19 February 1857 Conway won election over five other declared candidates to succeed John Tayloe Lomax as judge of the Eighth Judicial Circuit, comprising the counties of Caroline, Essex, Hanover, King and Queen, King George, King William, Lancaster, Northumberland, Richmond, Spotsylvania, and Westmoreland. Within weeks of holding his first court in

Caroline County on 2 March, he began to suffer from an excruciating and disfiguring soft cancer in his left cheek. Treatment in Baltimore, which may have included removal of a portion of his upper jaw, did not alleviate the condition, and Eustace Conway died at his Fredericksburg home on 20 May 1857. He was buried in Fredericksburg City Cemetery and honored within the month by a lithographic portrait, engraved by the artist John Adams Elder and sold in local stores for $1 each.

Birth date on gravestone; biographies by nephew Peter Vivian Daniel Conway in *Fredericksburg Daily Star*, 26 July 1899 (with birth dates of 14 and 17 Sept. 1820), and in *Fredericksburg Free Lance*, 1 Aug. 1899 (with birth date of 17 Sept. 1820), by L. S. Marye in *Fredericksburg Daily Star*, 14 Sept. 1915, and in W. Preston Haynie, "Portraits in the Courts Building: A Link to the Past," *Bulletin of the Northumberland County Historical Society* 39 (2002): 33–34 (por.); variant birth date of 19 Sept. 1820 in French Biographies, LVA, and S. Bassett French Papers II, W&M, copied in most secondary sources; Northumberland Co. Marriage Bonds; *JHD*, 1848–1849 sess., esp. 136–138, 140, 171–175, and appended Doc. 43; *Remarks of Mr. Conway, of Spottsylvania, on the Subject of Slavery in the Territories and in the District of Columbia, in Reply to Mr. Scott, of Fauquier, Made on the 13th January, 1849* (1849), quotation on 12; *Richmond Enquirer*, 27 Aug., 3, 13 Sept. 1850; *Debates and Proceedings of 1850–1851 Convention*, 178–179; *Journal of 1850–1851 Convention*, 227, 419; *Supplement, 1850–1851 Convention Debates*, no. 16; *Fredericksburg Virginia Herald*, 22 Mar., 3 May 1855; *Fredericksburg News*, 25 Dec. 1856, 23, 26 Feb. 1857; *Fredericksburg Weekly Advertiser and Chronicle of the Times*, 28 Feb., 7 Mar., 15 Aug. 1857; will and estate accounts in Fredericksburg Corporation Court Will Book, F:261–263, 384–403; obituaries in *Daily Richmond Enquirer* (reprinting in part no longer extant *Fredericksburg Democratic Recorder*, 20 May 1857) and *Richmond Daily Dispatch*, both 22 May 1857; obituaries and memorial resolutions in *Fredericksburg Weekly Advertiser and Chronicle of the Times*, 23 (with birth date of 15 Sept. 1820), 30 May 1857, and *Fredericksburg News*, 25 May 1857.

SARA B. BEARSS

CONWAY, Martha Bell (24 July 1917–9 November 1997), attorney and secretary of the commonwealth, was born in Raleigh, North Carolina. When she was about six months old, her parents, Elijah James Conway and Cora Henderson Conway, moved to Richmond, where her father was manager of the city's Public Employment Bureau until his death in September 1923. The precocious Conway skipped several grades and graduated from Thomas Jefferson High School one month before her fifteenth birthday. She studied psychology at the Richmond Division of the College of William and Mary (later Virginia Commonwealth University) from 1933 until 1936, when for financial reasons she withdrew to become a secretary at a blueprint company. A business law course with the attorney David John Mays awakened in Conway the understanding that law permeated everyday life, and she enrolled in the T. C. Williams School of Law at the University of Richmond. Graduating with an LL.B. in June 1939, she passed the state bar examination in December of that year. Women lawyers were still enough of a rarity that hanging out her shingle merited a feature story in the evening newspaper. Conway later recalled, "I really didn't know I wasn't supposed to be doing all these things, so I did."

Conway practiced law privately and from 1943 until 1951 was commissioner in chancery in the Hanover County Circuit Court. In 1945 she became a registered patent attorney and the next year purchased controlling interest in the Lawyers Publishing Company, Inc. (after 1955 the Lawyers Printing Company, Inc.), which specialized in legal briefs. Conway worked from 1951 to 1955 as a real estate broker and from 1951 to 1952 as eastern district counsel for the Office of Price Stabilization.

While building her legal practice, Conway also became active in Democratic Party politics. In 1943, 1945, and 1947 she campaigned for one of Richmond's seven seats in the House of Delegates. She favored greater state support for public education, including increased pay for teachers, repeal of the poll tax as a prerequisite for voting, allowing Richmonders to determine their form of city government, forest conservation, expansion of workmen's compensation to cover occupational diseases, and passage of a boiler safety bill. Though defeated in the primary each time, Conway gained enough stature among party regulars that she was one of five women the governor named in 1947 to the Commission on Reorganization of State Government.

On 23 August 1952 Governor John Stewart Battle appointed Conway secretary of the commonwealth to replace the retiring Thelma Young Gordon. The second woman to hold the post,

Conway took office on 3 September. Her responsibilities included keeping the governor's journal and the state seals, certifying extraditions, pardons, and proclamations, compiling and issuing the annual public report (popularly known as the blue book), commissioning and regulating notaries public, and registering lobbyists. Reappointed by four successive Democratic governors, Conway was for much of her eighteen-year tenure the highest-ranking and most visible woman in the state government, the only woman department head in Virginia, and in 1952 one of only six female secretaries of state in the country. She did not consider herself a feminist but in the 1970s supported passage of the Equal Rights Amendment. In a 1958 interview she stated that "I think many more women belong in public office, because the major functions of government concern health, welfare and education, and these are the fields in which women are most interested."

In 1958 the General Assembly directed Conway to compile all the interstate compacts to which Virginia was then a party. She published the work, also including the texts of several compacts no longer in effect and a discussion of compacts for which the state was eligible, under the title *The Compacts of Virginia* (1963). For about a decade Conway sat on the State Commission on Interstate Cooperation. In 1965 she chaired Virginia's Commission on the Status of Women and the next year issued a descriptive report and conservative recommendations. She was secretary of the National Association of Secretaries of State in 1963, treasurer in 1964, vice president in 1965, and president in 1966.

When in January 1970 Abner Linwood Holton Jr. became Virginia's first Republican governor of the twentieth century, he declined to reappoint Conway as secretary of the commonwealth. Rather than resume her law practice, on 1 April 1970, the day she left office, she became director of grants and contracts at Virginia Commonwealth University. During her eleven years as administrator, the university's annual grants and contracts increased from $6 million in 1970 to more than $25 million in 1979. In 1972 Conway was secretary-treasurer of the Southern Regional Section of the Society of Research

Administrators, and in December of that year she became the first woman elected to the board of directors of the Richmond National Bank. She retired from Virginia Commonwealth University in July 1981.

Conway never married. She lived with her mother until the latter's death in 1975 and also owned a vacation house on the North Carolina coast. Her professional achievements and volunteer services led the Young Women's Christian Association of Richmond to honor her in 1980 as one of the city's outstanding women. Martha Bell Conway died in a Richmond retirement community on 9 November 1997 and was buried in Queens Creek United Methodist Church Cemetery, in Hubert, Onslow County, North Carolina. The Coastal Carolina Community College Foundation offers a memorial scholarship in her honor.

Morton, *Virginia Lives*, 203–204; feature stories in *Richmond News Leader*, 8 Jan. 1940 (por.), 24 Jan. 1958 (second quotation), 2 Mar. 1970, and *Richmond Times-Dispatch*, 31 Aug. 1980 (first quotation); Conway biographical file, Richmond Public Library; published works include Conway, "The Commonwealth's Coat-of-Arms," *Virginia Journal of Education* 53 (Sept. 1959): 26–27, 53, and *Status of Women: Report of the Commission on the Status of Women to the Governor and the General Assembly of Virginia*, published as *JHD*, 1966 sess., House Doc. 20; *Richmond Times-Dispatch*, 4 Feb., 1 Aug. 1943, 7 Aug. 1945, 24 Aug. 1952, 16 Jan. 1970, 13 Dec. 1972; *Richmond News Leader*, 4 May 1945, 19 Mar., 3 Sept. 1952, 12 Oct. 1963, 17 Feb. 1965, 13 Feb. 1970; Peter Wallenstein, "'These New and Strange Beings': Women in the Legal Profession in Virginia, 1890–1990," *VMHB* 101 (1993): 212, 213 (por.); obituary in *Richmond Times-Dispatch*, 11 Nov. 1997.

SARA B. BEARSS

CONWAY, Moncure Daniel (17 March 1832–14 or 15 November 1907), reformer and writer, was born at Middleton, the Stafford County estate of his parents, Walker Peyton Conway, a planter, entrepreneur, and presiding judge of the Stafford County Court, and Margaret Eleanor Daniel Conway, a self-taught homeopathic doctor. From both parents he inherited prestigious names and powerful connections. His great-uncle Peter V. Daniel (1784–1860) was an associate justice of the Supreme Court of the United States, and his uncle Raleigh Travers Daniel later served as Virginia's attorney general. In 1832 no one could have envisioned this son of the Virginia slavocracy as an abolitionist and abettor of fugitive slaves, a racial egalitarian and feminist, and a leading religious radical on two continents. Yet Conway was all these things. His significance for Virginia history lies not merely in the breathtaking dimensions of his apostasy, nor in his regurgitation from the state for abolitionist activism; most fundamentally it lies in the ways in which Virginia helped create him. Virginia repudiated Conway only after Virginians had helped produce him.

In 1834 the Conway family moved to Inglewood, a plantation two miles from Falmouth, and four years later to a house in Falmouth that was the family's residence for the remainder of Conway's youth. His father concentrated his attention on Conway's elder brother; the major influence on Conway was his dynamic, outspoken mother, who encouraged his love of music and literature and without crushing his inner nature urged him to do his duty. Although not an abolitionist or a formal supporter of woman's rights, Margaret Conway imparted to her son a suspicion of arbitrary power, the key to all his later radical commitments. She expressed moral reservations about slavery, as did other female relatives. Two paternal aunts were chastised in their father's will for their antislavery views, and a cousin became the model for a fiercely antislavery southern woman in Conway's novel *Pine and Palm* (1887).

After attending a Fredericksburg academy, Conway joined his brother at Dickinson College, in Carlisle, Pennsylvania, chosen for its affiliation with Methodism. Trying to embrace the politics of his male relatives, he sent the *Richmond Examiner*—edited by his cousin John Moncure Daniel—articles lambasting northern ways. After graduating in July 1849, Conway studied law, dutifully but unhappily, in Warrenton with a family acquaintance. In April 1850 he read about Ralph Waldo Emerson, whose emphasis on self-reliance and personal authenticity energized Conway. He began corresponding with Emerson, whom he met in 1853 and with whom he maintained a fond friendship until the older man's death.

Conway became interested in public education and advocated establishing a statewide system of public schools. All his male relatives

disapproved. Senator James Murray Mason personally rebuked him and warned that public education would unleash "the entire swarm of Northern 'isms.'" In the autumn of 1850 Conway wrote and published a self-financed pamphlet entitled *Free-Schools in Virginia: A Plea of Education, Virtue and Thrift, vs. Ignorance, Vice and Poverty*. He blamed Virginia's economic decline on educational backwardness, not on slavery. Conway sent a copy to each delegate to the state convention then meeting to revise the constitution; they ignored it and the issue.

Disillusioned, struggling to meet expectations, yet increasingly determined to live an autonomous and not arbitrary life, Conway late in 1850 abandoned legal studies to become a Methodist minister. Beginning in April 1851 he rode the Rockville circuit in Maryland. For several months he threw himself into Methodist orthodoxy, but his calling had been artificially created and did not last. Paternal pressure intensified with the death of Conway's elder brother in March 1852. Conway escaped by applying to the Harvard Divinity School in order to prepare for the Unitarian ministry. He spent about two interim months in Falmouth and Fredericksburg, where his religious and political unorthodoxy had become well known. While he drew closer to the women of the family, his father was icy, and his uncle Eustace Conway, a member of the Convention of 1850–1851, threatened to have him drummed out of town. On 1 January 1853 Conway witnessed the annual hiring-out of slaves. The sight drove home "how much *hatred* I had of the Institution—and how much contempt for the persons engaged in it." On 14 February he left for Massachusetts, never to live in Virginia again.

Conway received a B.D. in 1854. He reveled in the literary and artistic life of Boston and Cambridge. Conway befriended Theodore Parker, whose politically conscious ministry became a model for his own. He declared himself a radical abolitionist during a notorious fugitive slave case, when in May 1854 Anthony Burns, of Stafford County (whom Conway apparently had met), was marched in manacles through angry Boston crowds and returned to slavery in Virginia. Conway watched the procession with a group of abolitionists including William Lloyd Garrison. At the famous Fourth of July Framingham rally at which Garrison burned a copy of the Constitution, Conway told the crowd of his exultation at the opportunity to speak freely, because "in Virginia, they not only had slaves, but every man with a conscience, or even the first throbbings of a conscience, is a slave." He urged his listeners to resist the heightened demands of the slavocracy lest they become slaves too.

In September 1854 Conway became a Unitarian minister in Washington, D.C. His support for the emerging Republican Party and a series of widely publicized antislavery sermons caused his dismissal in 1856, but a more-compatible congregation in Cincinnati immediately hired him. There on 1 June 1858 he married Ellen Davis Dana, daughter of a Unitarian businessman of Massachusetts lineage. They had three sons and one daughter. They closed their honeymoon in Falmouth, which Conway last had seen in January 1855, when almost immediately local toughs had forced him to decamp. The honeymoon visit was a fiasco as well and collapsed in acrimony after Ellen Conway kissed a four-year-old slave girl at a neighbor's farm and thus (recalled a former slave) "set the magazine on fire." Conway's wife never visited Virginia again.

In 1859, after Conway announced that he had ceased to believe in miracles or the divinity of Jesus, one-third of his Cincinnati congregation seceded. But the cosmopolitanism of his renamed "Free Church" attracted still more members and positioned Conway as a leading figure in American free thought, as he groped toward a theism compatible with an individualistic and scientific age. In 1860 he founded and edited the *Dial*, a short-lived monthly magazine that disseminated his liberal Unitarian views to a national audience.

During the Civil War, two of Conway's brothers served in the Confederate army, and his father was a Confederate supporter living at a Richmond boardinghouse. His mother spent much of the war in Pennsylvania with her married sister. Conway initially supported the war for reunion, provided it became explicitly about abolition and not mere conquest. On lecture tours and in two books—*The Rejected Stone: or, Insurrection vs.*

Resurrection in America (1861) and *The Golden Hour* (1862)—he argued that only unconditional emancipation could justify or win the war and consistently urged compassion, not hatred, for the slavery-maddened South.

In the summer of 1862 Conway learned that about thirty of his father's slaves had escaped to Washington, D.C. At great risk to himself he rushed to escort them to Ohio and posed for a time as their owner in the slave city of Baltimore. He helped to resettle the freedpeople on donated land near Yellow Springs. Conway's activity so impressed Boston abolitionists that they hired him as coeditor, with Franklin Benjamin Sanborn, of a new antislavery weekly, *The Commonwealth*. Conway moved to Concord, Massachusetts, and the paper debuted on 6 September 1862.

Yet Conway grew disillusioned by what he saw as Abraham Lincoln's timidity, disappointed that the Emancipation Proclamation left many people enslaved, and depressed by the war's ravaging of his native region. In April 1863 he left the country for a speaking tour in Great Britain. Though known to few but himself, Conway's intention was to stay away. He soon wrote to his wife beseeching her to move the family to England. Conway also wrote to the unreceived Confederate emissary in London, James Murray Mason, asserting that abolitionists would stop supporting the war if the Confederacy freed its slaves—a last, naive effort to achieve abolition and peace simultaneously. Shrewdly, Mason published Conway's unauthorized letter in the pro-Confederate *Times*. A firestorm of rebuke resulted, and most abolitionists repudiated Conway. He also was drafted, a move probably politically motivated; he paid the commutation fee. The abolitionist outcry sealed his exile. Unable to end the fratricide honorably, he felt justified in staying away from it honorably. His family sailed for London in August 1863.

In London, Conway published *Testimonies Concerning Slavery* (1864), recounting his experiences in slaveholding Virginia, attacking ethnic prejudice, and recommending interracial marriage as one step toward a better society. He also began a literary and journalistic career, during which he wrote for both British and American audiences, played a major role in popularizing Walt Whitman in England, and acted as literary agent for Louisa May Alcott and Mark Twain.

In 1864 Conway became minister at South Place Chapel, the most distinguished center of liberal religion in England. Serving there for a quarter of a century (1864–1885, 1893–1897), he made it even more a bastion of unfettered religious exploration and debate. (It continues as the South Place Ethical Society, meeting at Conway Hall in Red Lion Square.) By the 1870s Conway had become agnostic (although he never used that term) and saw comparative religious study as a way of uniting disparate people, facing life's urgent mysteries, and challenging the mind. He published noteworthy works on spiritual topics, including *Demonology and Devil-Lore* (1879) and *The Sacred Anthology: A Book of Ethnical Scriptures* (1874), a pioneering compilation of excerpts from the world's sacred books. In 1883 Conway lectured in Australia and traversed India. He recounted the journey in his last book, the sensitive and thoughtful *My Pilgrimage to the Wise Men of the East* (1906).

In 1875 and 1880 Conway lectured in the United States and visited Virginia, where family wounds were staunched if not healed. From 1885 to 1892 the family lived in Brooklyn Heights and Manhattan, where Conway buttressed his reputation as a man of letters. His literary output included a sympathetic account of Edmund Randolph (1888), an insightful biography of Nathaniel Hawthorne (1890), and *Barons of the Potomack and the Rappahannock* (1892), romanticized anecdotes about the colonial Virginia gentry. The crowning achievement of this period was his biography of fellow transatlantic radical Thomas Paine (1892). In that year Dickinson College awarded him an honorary doctorate of humane letters.

After a second sojourn in London, in 1897 Conway and his wife returned to New York, where Ellen Conway died on Christmas Day. A few months later Conway, denouncing the war with Spain and terror tactics against southern blacks, left the country. Unwilling to resettle in imperialist Britain, he chose France, where he believed independent thinkers had more influence. There Conway wrote one of the most sig-

nificant autobiographies by a nineteenth-century American. Eventually acquiring another home in New York's Greenwich Village, he commuted between continents so often that the crew of the *New York* called him their mascot.

Despite long expatriation, Conway always regarded himself as American, southern, and Virginian. He named his first child after his proslavery uncle Eustace Conway and the only house he ever built (Inglewood, in Bedford Park, London) after the Stafford County plantation of his earliest memories. Conway always respected his father and similar Virginians for their commitment to honor, duty, and hard work. But he believed them bewitched by slavery and white supremacy, driven into unintended, unnoticed daily barbarities. Leaving Virginia, he rejected not these people but the moral blinders that shackled them.

Conway retained values gained from other Virginians: generosity and forgiveness from enslaved men and women whom he knew and respected, compassion and toleration from free women who mightily influenced him. He came to envision and advocate a community infused by humane toleration, rejection of arbitrary power and easy violence, and respect for each person's autonomy. His life's "pilgrimage"—his favorite word—was a quest for these things. "Strike out the word *white* and the word *male* from our laws," he wrote in *The Commonwealth* in 1865, "and we shall reach the noblest transformation." His battles with dogma—political, social, religious—gave coherence and meaning to a dizzying, stunningly unusual life, one that requires broadening the definition of what nineteenth-century Virginia was, and what a nineteenth-century Virginian could be.

Moncure Daniel Conway was researching a biography of John Calvin when he died of a stroke, alone in his Paris apartment, during the night of 14–15 November 1907. His body was cremated at Père-Lachaise Cemetery, and his ashes were buried at Kensico Cemetery, in Valhalla, Westchester County, New York.

Conway, *Autobiography: Memories and Experiences of Moncure Daniel Conway* (1904), with frontispiece por.; Eustace Conway, ed., *Moncure D. Conway: Addresses and Reprints, 1850–1907* (1909), with selected bibliography of writings on 437–444; Mary Elizabeth Burtis, *Moncure Conway, 1832–1907* (1952), including selected bibliography of writings on 242–254; John d'Entremont, *Southern Emancipator: Moncure Conway, The American Years, 1832–1865* (1987), pors. and selected bibliography of writings on 271–273; Moncure Daniel Conway Papers (including fourth quotation from former slave Dunmore Gwinn to Conway, 10 Nov. 1891), Columbia University, New York, N.Y.; Moncure Daniel Conway Family Papers, including diary, 1851–1853 (second quotation in entry for 1 Jan. 1853), and copy of will, Dickinson College, Carlisle, Pa.; Conway, *Testimonies Concerning Slavery* (1864), 32–33 (first quotation); *The Liberator*, 14 July 1854 (third quotation); *Boston Commonwealth*, 22 Apr. 1865 (fifth quotation); *Fredericksburg Free Lance-Star*, 2, 9 Feb. 2002; *Yellow Springs [Ohio] News*, 12 June 2003; obituaries in *New York Times*, *Richmond Times-Dispatch*, and *Washington Post*, all 17 Nov. 1907, *London Times*, 19 Nov. 1907, and *Fredericksburg Free Lance*, 21 Nov. 1907.

JOHN D'ENTREMONT

COOK, Fields (ca. 1817–21 January 1897), Baptist minister and Republican Party leader, was born into slavery in King William County. The names of his parents and the name of the family who owned him are not known, nor is it clear when or under what circumstances he acquired or took his surname. He was described several times as being of mixed-race ancestry. On 23 January 1847 Fields, as he then identified himself, began writing a narrative of his life, one of the longest manuscripts known to have been composed by an enslaved Virginian. The first thirty-two pages of the memoir survive and in 1902 were deposited in the Library of Congress. He recorded that he spent his youth in the Virginia countryside, where his relationship with his master's family was close and complex. His dearest boyhood companion, the son of his master, delivered the most cutting blow of his young life when he abruptly began treating Fields as a slave. Years later the two reconciled and the white boy gave him two priceless gifts, an introduction to Christianity and literacy. Fields's criticism of slavery in his memoir was subtle, unlike his condemnation of Nat Turner for provoking a wave of terror against unoffending slaves in his region.

After a failed romance, Fields requested and received permission about 1834 to live and work in Richmond, where he presumably participated in the illegal but common system of self-hiring. He found work, arranged his own room and board, and kept any money he earned in excess of the fees he paid to his owner. Six feet tall, literate, personable, and industrious, Cook prospered in Richmond. Within a few years of arriving in the city he married Mary, an enslaved domestic servant, was baptized and joined the First Baptist Church, and became the father of at least two sons and one daughter. It is possible that Cook wrote his life story about the time that he gained his freedom, which he had secured by 1850. In that year he was working as a leech doctor, and by 1860 he had managed to free his wife and to purchase and free at least two of his children. In 1852 he bought the first of several city lots and houses in Richmond. The house and lot where he lived on North Ninth Street in 1865 were then valued at $1,700. His brother Jim Cook was a well-known Richmond cook and caterer in the years immediately after the Civil War. Inasmuch as Fields Cook was listed in the 1860 census as a waiter and identified five years later as manager of the bar and restaurant in the Ballard House Hotel, it is likely that they were engaged in business together.

After the Civil War, Cook became a Baptist minister and for several months was pastor at a church in the Chesterfield County coalfields under the auspices of the American Baptist Home Mission Society. Through his position he emerged as one of the most important African American leaders in Richmond. Late in May 1865 federal military authorities imposed pass and curfew restrictions on freedpeople and expelled hundreds from Richmond. At the same time, they reinstated the wartime municipal police force, which, together with provost guards, handled African Americans roughly. Cook and several other church leaders collected evidence of military and civilian misbehavior and called a mass meeting in June. That gathering approved a memorial detailing their grievances, informing the larger public that they alone had been steadfast in their loyalty to the Union, and arguing that the policies of the city's ruling authority harkened back to a discredited past rather than heralding a new era of liberty. Cook chaired the delegation chosen at that mass meeting to present their case to the governor and on 16 June 1865 to the president of the United States.

Cook represented the city in the first state convention of African Americans, which met in Alexandria in August 1865. The convention named him a vice president and asked him to write its address to the public. Cook argued powerfully that African Americans deserved full civil and legal equality and must have the vote for their own protection. He also wrote that Virginia's prosperity depended on harmony between the races and required a productive working relationship based on the equality of rights, duties, and protections. Cook's thoroughly radical vision was wildly at variance with the pledge of protection based on obedience and subservience that the state's white leaders offered. It was a vision that only the Radical wing of the Republican Party then embraced, but it also squared with Cook's own experience as a self-made, self-emancipated man who knew that he was anyone's equal in God's sight. As he had prospered after becoming free, so too should large numbers of his race, provided they were given opportunity, choice, and protection.

In January 1869 Cook attended the National Convention of the Colored Men of America in Washington, D.C., and was elected to the national executive committee. Late that same year he took part in the convention of the Colored National Labor Union. Cook saw no contradiction between religious leadership and political activism. Indeed, he believed that sound religious teachings, good schooling, and principled politics were all necessary for the elevation of his race and the transformation of society.

From 1867 to 1869 Cook worked tirelessly for the Republican Party. An effective organizer frequently sent into the countryside to rally rural freedmen, he engaged in important battles over strategy that put him at odds with many influential Republicans. His dream of full political freedom for blacks made him seem a natural ally of the Radical Republicans, but his inclusive view of the party often brought him into conflict with the Radical leaders. Cook favored an alliance with former Whig Unionists if they were willing to join the great mass of freedmen in the Republican Party and work to modernize the state. He argued that the party should disavow land confiscation and even make room in the

leadership for Whigs who had supported the Confederacy. During the summer of 1867, party rank and file instead heeded the strident voice of James Wesley Hunnicutt, the radical editor of the *Richmond New Nation*. After the election for the constitutional convention in October of that year demonstrated that most white Virginians opposed the Republican Party, Cook could not resist criticizing Hunnicutt and his followers for alienating potential influential allies. Although finding fault with some Republican leaders and policies, Cook continued to serve on the party's ward and executive committees, and he was secretary of the congressional district convention in May 1868. He supported the regular state Republican ticket in the watershed election of 1869, but in an unsuccessful campaign as an independent candidate for a seat in Congress that year he received less than 1 percent of the vote.

In 1870 Cook and his wife moved to Alexandria, where for a time he was an agent for the local Freedman's Savings and Trust Company bank. He lived in that city for the rest of his life and in 1872 sold his Richmond house. Cook was pastor of the Third Baptist Church until early in 1883, when he left following several disputes within the congregation. He later became pastor of the city's Ebenezer Baptist Church, in which post he served until his death. As prominent in Alexandria as he had been in Richmond, Cook also remained active politically. During the 1880s he supported the Readjusters and criticized African American voters who rejected that party's offer of a biracial coalition against the Democrats, who were regaining domination of the state government.

Cook did not live to see his native state take the final steps in stripping African American men of the franchise that he had fought for and claimed as a right and necessity for three decades. Fields Cook died at his Alexandria home on 21 January 1897 and was buried probably in the city's Douglass Memorial Cemetery, of which he was a founder.

"Fields's Observations," LC, printed in Mary J. Bratton, ed., "Fields's Observations: The Slave Narrative of a Nineteenth-Century Virginian," *VMHB* 88 (1980): 75–93; brief biographies in *New York Anglo-African*, 19 Aug. 1865 (age about forty-five), and *Richmond Southern Opinion*, 17 Aug. 1867 (age fifty); Census, Richmond City, 1850 (age thirty-six on 2 Dec. 1850), 1860 (age forty-three on 1 Aug. 1860), Alexandria City, 1880 (age fifty on 15 June 1880); *New-York Daily Tribune*, 17 June 1865; *New York Anglo-African*, 12 Aug. 1865; *Richmond Daily Dispatch*, 19 Apr., 1–3 Aug., 5 Oct., 4 Dec. 1867, 19 Jan., 20 Apr., 28 May, 9, 17 June, 5 July 1869; *Richmond Daily Enquirer and Examiner*, 8 Oct. 1867, 6 May 1868; *Daily Richmond Whig*, 7 Dec. 1867; *Washington Post*, 23, 28 Oct., 13 Dec. 1882, 12, 13 Jan., 18, 27 Oct. 1883, 18 Aug. 1886, 10 Jan. 1889, 24 Feb., 29 Dec. 1891, 25 Sept. 1894; several letters in William Mahone Papers, Duke; Peter J. Rachleff, *Black Labor in the South: Richmond, Virginia, 1865–1890* (1984), 41, 45, 52; Philip S. Foner and George E. Walker, eds., *Proceedings of the Black National and State Conventions, 1865–1900* (1986), 1:350, 352–353, 354, 365, 391; John Thomas O'Brien Jr., *From Bondage to Citizenship: The Richmond Black Community, 1865–1867* (1990); obituaries in *Alexandria Gazette*, 21 Jan. 1897, *Washington Evening Star* (with place of birth and death at age seventy-nine) and *Washington Post*, both 22 Jan. 1897, and *Richmond Planet*, 23 Jan. 1897.

JOHN T. O'BRIEN

COOK, George Major, also known as Wahunsacook or Wahansunacoke (23 October 1860–16 December 1930), Pamunkey chief, was born on the Pamunkey Reservation in King William County. His father, Major Cook, died in 1861, and his mother, Caroline Bradby Cook, raised him with the help of her father and brother. Members of the Colosse Baptist Church before the Civil War, the Bradby and Cook families numbered among the many Pamunkey who formed Pamunkey Indian Baptist Church after the war. Cook's mother brought him up as a member of the church, and, like most Pamunkey, the Cooks remained a devoutly religious family. In 1901 he was the first delegate from the church to the Baptist General Association of Virginia.

In 1870, when the first statewide system of public schools in Virginia was created, the census enumerator listed Cook as already able to read and write, although the state government did not establish a grammar school on the reservation until 1882 and may have excluded Indians from the public schools until that time. On 9 March 1887 Cook married Theodora Octavius Dennis, who had been born in Petersburg and who was also a member of the tribe and of Pamunkey Indian Baptist Church. She was the tribe's midwife for many years and had ten children, of whom four sons and three daughters lived to adulthood.

Cook was listed on several census returns as a fisherman and farmer, but tribal duties kept him busy much of the time. By 1888 he was one of the headmen of the tribe and was so identified on a letter that the Pamunkey Council addressed to the president of the United States requesting him to permit Indians to take higher education classes at Hampton Normal and Agricultural Institute (later Hampton University). Cook performed in theatrical programs, including the well-known Pocahontas and John Smith story, that the Pamunkey presented in order to enhance recognition of the tribe.

Elected chief in 1902, Cook served until his death and continued to shape public perception of the Pamunkey. For many years he collected tribal artifacts, which became the basis for the Pamunkey Indian Museum on the reservation. He was convinced that education was essential to the development of Pamunkey tribal life and pressed for better conditions at the tribal grammar school and for improved secondary education. Cook also led a short-lived attempt early in the 1920s to organize cooperation with other Powhatan tribes.

To develop a higher profile for the Pamunkey, Cook moved the traditional date of paying symbolic tribute to the state to the autumn, during deer season, in order to draw media coverage with the presentation of a large game animal. The event dovetailed nicely with remembrances in local schools and churches of the Pilgrim-Indian first Thanksgiving. In 1917 Cook precipitated a definitive reaffirmation of the Pamunkeys' status as wards of the state when he obtained rulings from the state attorney general that Virginia had no right to tax Indians on the reservation or to draft members of the tribe for military service. One of the chief's sons, Ottigney Pontiac Cook, had challenged the legality of his draft notice, and the tribe appealed the case to the United States Army, which ruled in Cook's favor. Having won their point, O. P. Cook and several other young Indian men then enlisted in the army.

During the 1920s Cook took the lead in opposing Walter Ashby Plecker, director of the state Bureau of Vital Statistics, who believed that all Virginia Indians were of African American as well as Native American descent. Plecker and other white supremacists were anxious to protect the elite white race from what they perceived as racial dilution or degeneration, a goal they achieved in March 1924 with the passage of the Virginia Act to Preserve Racial Integrity. The statute officially classified all Virginians in rigid categories of white and colored and subjected all nonwhite citizens to the racial segregation laws. Passage of the law took the Indian communities by surprise, and focused dissent did not begin until the following year, when a strongly worded letter from Cook appeared in the *Richmond News Leader* on 8 July 1925. Thereafter, in speeches, newspaper articles, letters to the editor, visits to successive governors, and appearances before legislative committees, Cook argued for the right of Virginia's Indians to maintain their distinct heritage and be correctly labeled as Indians.

The General Assembly defeated attempts to strengthen the statute in 1926 and 1928 but adopted an amendment to the racial integrity act after an epic fight in the 1930 legislative session. The amendment specified that any ascertainable amount of African American blood officially rendered a person Negroid. Known as the one-drop clause, the amendment enabled Plecker to classify hundreds of Virginia Indians as Negroes. Cook led opposition to a proposal to exempt from that classification the Indians living on the two state reservations. Enlisting assistance from the tribe's attorney, Hill Montague, and Chief George F. "Thunder Cloud" Custalow of the Mattaponi, he publicly denounced the exemption because it did not protect Pamunkey and Mattaponi living off the reservations. On 1 February 1930 Cook made an impassioned speech during a legislative committee hearing and concluded with the peroration: "We were the men who trusted you, who welcomed you and saved you from the famine of [1607]. You have taken our land. You have destroyed our hunting ground. You have left us for our support only a 300-acre sandspit and some swamp. You have taken our land, taken our forests, taken our fishing grounds—and now with one last stroke of the pen you are trying to take our very name."

It was the last public campaign for the sixty-nine-year-old chief. Cook's longtime friend, the University of Pennsylvania anthropologist Frank G. Speck, wrote that the progressive and canny chief was "sensitive, ideal but discouraged by social adversity, like many artists and composers." The teacher at the Pamunkey Indian School reported to the governor in January 1930 that the "continual harassing will kill Chief Cook. He was sick enough to be in bed to-day." George Major Cook suffered from heart disease for several years, had a heart attack in the summer of 1930, and died following another heart attack at his home on the reservation on 16 December 1930. He was interred in the Pamunkey Indian Baptist Church burial ground.

Birth and death dates from BVS Death Certificate, King William Co.; variant birth date of 21 Oct. 1860 in Mrs. Fred Pfaus, *Our Indian Neighbors* [1949], 2 (with cover por.), copy of Dover Baptist Association pamphlet at LVA; BVS Marriage Register, King William Co.; Frank G. Speck, *Chapters on the Ethnology of the Powhatan Tribes of Virginia* (1928), 238, 239 (por.), 302–303; Helen C. Rountree, *Pocahontas's People: The Powhatan Indians of Virginia through Four Centuries* (1990), 216–217; J. Douglas Smith, "The Campaign for Racial Purity and the Erosion of Paternalism in Virginia, 1922–1930: 'Nominally White, Biologically Mixed, and Legally Negro,'" *JSH* 68 (2002): 65–106; *Richmond News Leader*, 27 Nov. 1913, 5 June 1923, 8 July 1925, 30 Jan. 1928, 1 Feb. 1930 (first quotation); *Richmond Times-Dispatch*, 25 Nov. 1915, 21 Aug. 1917, 4 Feb. 1928; *New York Times Magazine*, 13 May 1923; letters in Indian affairs folders of several Virginia governors' Executive Papers (including Julia S. Kyle to John Garland Pollard, 31 Jan. 1930, with third quotation), all RG 3, LVA; second quotation from undated caption on photograph labeled Pamunkey (#6), Frank G. Speck Collection, American Philosophical Society, Philadelphia, Pa.; obituaries in *Richmond News Leader* and *Richmond Times-Dispatch* (por.), both 17 Dec. 1930.

PATRICIA FERGUSON WATKINSON

COOK, George Smith (23 February 1819–27 November 1902), photographer, was born in Stratford, Connecticut. The names of his parents are not known. He was orphaned at an early age and grew up in Newark, New Jersey, under the care of his maternal grandmother. At age fourteen Cook traveled to the Ohio River and during the next several years worked his way south along the Mississippi River. He had arrived in New Orleans by early in 1838 and there began painting portrait miniatures. Following the invention of the daguerreotype in 1839, Cook studied the technique of capturing photographic images on copper plates and began managing a gallery early in the 1840s. He returned to Newark in 1845, continued to work as a daguerreotypist, and in September 1846 married Elizabeth Smith Francisco. They had one son and one daughter. Embarking with his family on a three-year trek through the South, Cook set up temporary studios in a succession of towns in Missouri, Mississippi, Alabama, and Georgia. In most places he trained successors to take charge of the studios, to which he continued to sell photographic supplies and through which he fostered a network of contacts across the region.

In October 1849 Cook settled his family in Charleston, South Carolina, where he established a permanent studio and earned a reputation as one of the country's leading photographers. He finished his photographs with pencil to lend flesh tones to his subjects and brighter hues to his backgrounds. Cook retained his northern ties, and during the summer of 1851 Mathew B. Brady invited him to manage his New York gallery while he traveled in Europe. Cook purchased his own competing gallery at the same time, but after Brady's return in May 1852 Cook went back to Charleston. A successful and compelling portraitist, he also enjoyed a lucrative business selling supplies out of his King Street studio. Cook learned the new wet-plate process of photography during the 1850s and by 1855 was producing photographs, stereographs, and cartes de visite, many of which were purchased and widely sold by E. and H. T. Anthony and Company of New York. He opened studios in Chicago and Philadelphia and often traveled to both cities between 1857 and 1860, but he closed these galleries in the latter year partly as a result of the growing conflict between the North and South.

During the Civil War, Cook served in the home guard and continued to practice his craft. He successfully smuggled supplies through the blockade and accepted payment for his work only in gold. Cook produced numerous images of troops, prisoners, military installations, battles, and the resulting destruction in the vicinity of Charleston, especially at Fort Sumter. His carte de visite of the fort's Union commander, photographed in February 1861, sold by the thousands that spring. During the battle in Charleston Harbor in September 1863 Cook set up his camera on a parapet at Fort Sumter and took pictures under hostile fire. His image of an exploding shell became one of his best-known photographs (though it was likely the result of significant retouching), and he was the first to photograph Union ironclad gunboats in action.

Early in 1864 Cook moved his family to what he hoped would be a safer location near Columbia, where his wife died that April. He stored much of his equipment, along with negatives and records, in a temporary gallery in that city but lost them all in the fire that destroyed Columbia in February 1865. Soon after the end of the war Cook returned to Charleston and reopened his studio. He resumed his trips to Newark to visit family members and there on 24 September 1866 married Lavinia Elizabeth Pratt, his first wife's niece. They had one daughter and one son, Huestis Pratt Cook, who also became a well-known photographer. Cook opened and briefly ran a gallery in New York City in 1873–1874 while continuing to operate his Charleston studio through the 1870s.

On 30 April 1880 Cook purchased for $3,500 David H. Anderson's Virginia photographic studio, equipment, decorative backdrops, and about 20,000 glass-plate negatives, including Anderson's wartime portraits of Confederate officers and officeholders. Cook moved to Richmond soon afterward and opened for business on East Main Street. He eventually settled his family in Bon Air, Chesterfield County, just across the James River from Richmond. Again he mastered a new technique, the recently developed dry-plate process for making photographs. Known as a careful photographer, Cook offered his clients three sittings for a portrait and refused payment until the sitter was satisfied with the result. He sought out and purchased collections of negatives from other city studios, most significantly those of the Lee Gallery and of Vannerson and Jones, which he preserved, cataloged, and occasionally published. In August 1890 Cook was recognized at the annual convention of the Photographers' Association of America, held in Washington, D.C. The following year he closed his Charleston studio, which his elder son had been managing, and turned over the day-to-day operation of the family business in Richmond to his younger son, although Cook continued to spend time in the studio until his death.

George Smith Cook died at his Bon Air home on 27 November 1902, two days after suffering a stroke. He was buried in Richmond's Hollywood Cemetery. Cook's images have appeared in numerous books, exhibitions, and documentaries, beginning with Francis Trevelyan Miller's ten-volume *Photographic History of the Civil War* (1911). In 1946 and 1954 the Valentine Museum (later the Valentine Richmond History Center) purchased the vast Cook Collection of photographs and negatives, representing Cook's work and that of his sons George LaGrange Cook and Huestis Pratt Cook, as well as the historical images they had acquired from other studios. The collection remains an unparalleled source of images documenting the Civil War and the history of the Richmond region from the 1860s through early in the twentieth century.

Biographies in A. Lawrence Kocher and Howard Dearstyne, *Shadows in Silver: A Record of Virginia, 1850–1900, in Contemporary Photographs taken by George and Huestis Cook with Additions from the Cook Collection* (1954), 3–15, Conley L. Edwards III, "'The Photographer of the Confederacy,'" *Civil War Times Illustrated* 13 (June 1974): 27–33, Thomas J. Peach, "George Smith Cook: South Carolina's Premier Civil War Photojournalist" (M.A. thesis, University of South Carolina, 1982), and Jack C. Ramsay, Jr., *Photographer . . . Under Fire: The Story of George S. Cook (1819–1902)* (1994), with birth and marriage dates and other family information from Cook documents in private collection and several pors.; George S. Cook Papers, LC and VRHC; Richmond City Chancery Court Deed Book, 116A:301–302; *Washington Post*, 7 Apr. 1882; *Richmond Times-Dispatch*, 28 Nov. 1952; *New York Times*, 7 Dec. 1952; *Richmond News Leader*, 14 Oct. 1954; A. D. Cohen, "George S. Cook and the Daguerrean Art," *Photographic Art-Journal* 1 (May 1851): 285–287; "How Business Is, and What of It," *Philadelphia Photographer* 17 (Feb. 1880): 34–35; Francis Trevelyan Miller, ed., *The Photographic History of the Civil War* (1911), esp. 1:24, 99–101, 3:169–174, 6:267, 8:131; Bob Zeller, "September 8th, 1863: A Momentous Day in the History of Photography," *Military Images* 19 (Nov./Dec. 1997): 8–16, 37; Harvey S. Teal, *Partners with the Sun: South Carolina Photographers, 1840–1940* (2000), esp. 22–26, 43–48, 88–94, 270–271; death notice in *Washington Post*, 28 Nov. 1902; obituaries in *Richmond Dispatch* and *Richmond Times*, both 28 Nov. 1902.

JACK C. RAMSAY, JR.

COOK, Giles (22 June 1812–29 September 1891), member of the Convention of 1850–1851, was born at Willow Brook, in Front Royal, and

was the son of William Cook, a merchant and justice of the peace, and Elizabeth Baker Cook. Educated in the Frederick County schools, he attended the prestigious Winchester law school conducted by Henry St. George Tucker (1780–1848) and was admitted to the bar in March 1831 at age eighteen. After practicing law in Winchester for a short time, Cook returned to Front Royal, where on 14 November 1839 he married Elizabeth Lane. They had at least three sons and two daughters. In 1850 Cook owned a town lot and three slaves over age twelve. A devout Presbyterian, he served his church as ruling elder for thirty years.

In 1836, when Warren County was formed from parts of Frederick and Shenandoah Counties, Cook became Warren County's first commonwealth's attorney and commissioner in chancery, offices he held for much of his career. In June 1850 he announced his candidacy as a Democrat for one of four seats representing the counties of Hardy, Shenandoah, and Warren in a convention called to revise the state constitution. Supporting many reforms favored by westerners, including universal white manhood suffrage, reapportionment of representation in the General Assembly based on the white population, popular election of state officers including judges, and reorganization of the state treasury, Cook won election with the third-largest number of votes of the seven candidates in the polling on 22 August. He attended the convention only intermittently and did not participate in the debates. It is unclear whether he took part in drafting the report of the Committee on the Judiciary, to which he was appointed. Although Cook voted on various routine procedural motions, he did not vote on 21 May 1851 on the crucial decision on apportionment of representation in the legislature and on 31 July did not vote on final approval of the constitution.

Warren County appointed Cook to represent its stock in the Front Royal Turnpike Company in 1854 and 1855, and in 1849, 1855, and 1863 he served as an election commissioner. Cook's two elder sons fought in the Confederate States Army. On 22 August 1865 Cook took an oath of amnesty before the county court in order to continue his county service and legal practice. In

1870 the Democratic legislative caucus considered him for appointment to the reconstituted Supreme Court of Appeals. Two years later Cook joined with ten other men to found the Bank of Warren, and in 1888 he was a county judge pro tempore for his namesake son.

Cook told the Shenandoah Valley historian Thomas Kemp Cartmell the traditional story of how Front Royal got its name from a militia captain's order to his unit to "about face and front the Royal Oak," a tale Cook had learned from his father, an eyewitness. Giles Cook died at his Front Royal home early on the morning of 29 September 1891 and was buried in Prospect Hill Cemetery.

French Biographies; T. K. Cartmell, *Shenandoah Valley Pioneers and Their Descendants: A History of Frederick County, Virginia* (1909), 235 (quotation), 431; William Carter Stubbs and Elizabeth Saunders Blair Stubbs, *Descendants of Mordecai Cooke . . .* (1923), 155–170 (por. on 160), with family history provided by sons Giles Cook Jr. and George Wythe Cook; Laura Virginia Hale, *Supplement to the Centennial History of the Bank of Warren: From Saddlebags to Computers, 1872–1972* (1972), 22; Warren Co. Marriage Register; county offices documented in Warren Co. Minute Book, vols. A–F; *Woodstock Tenth Legion*, 27 June, 4, 11 July, 1, 29 Aug. 1850; *Richmond Enquirer*, 3 Sept. 1850; *Journal of 1850–1851 Convention*, 59; Warren Co. Wills, Etc., AA:129; obituary in *Winchester Times*, 7 Oct. 1891.

CHERYL COLLINS

COOK, Huestis Pratt (13 July 1868–1 August 1951), photographer, was born in Charleston, South Carolina, and was the son of George Smith Cook, a successful portrait photographer known primarily for his Civil War images, and his second wife, Lavinia Elizabeth Pratt Cook. Both Cook and his much-older half brother George LaGrange Cook trained and worked in their father's photographic studio. Their father purchased the Richmond photographic gallery of David H. Anderson in April 1880, left his elder son in charge of the Charleston studio, and moved to Richmond and then to Bon Air, in Chesterfield County, with the rest of the family. In the new Richmond studio Huestis Cook assisted his father in developing and printing photographs and by 1889 was the studio's clerk.

Family tradition records that Cook began his career as a field photographer while a teenager when he used a borrowed plate camera to photograph several African Americans picnicking near his home. At the request of Mary Virginia Hawes Terhune, who wrote under the pseudonym Marion Harland, Cook began photographing plantations late in the 1880s in order to help her research a novel on William Byrd (1674–1744), published as *His Great Self* (1892). Several of his images appeared, uncredited, in Harland's later book, *Some Colonial Homesteads and Their Stories* (1897). This assignment led to other Virginia authors, including Mary Newton Stanard, commissioning Cook for similar photographs to illustrate their publications. His images are often the only pictures of the plantations and their buildings made before they were altered or demolished. Cook's clientele grew to include businesses, churches, civic organizations, state and local governments, the Richmond newspapers, and other periodicals. The resulting assignments produced a massive collection of images documenting many aspects of life and work in Virginia. His photographs appeared in such promotional works as *City of Richmond, 1905, of Historic Fame, of Great Commercial Prestige* (1905).

Cook is perhaps most noted as an unsentimental chronicler of African Americans, whether in domestic service, picking cotton or peanuts, butchering hogs, flushing rabbits, shopping, attending church, or being baptized. Although he inherited his father's keen eye for interesting, evocative faces, he often photographed his subjects not in the confines of the studio, posed against painted backdrops, but on their own porches, skating, shooting marbles, or playing musical instruments.

While Cook was in the field, his father continued making portraits in the Richmond studio. Cook became manager and principal photographer at the studio after his father went into semi-retirement in 1891. His half brother moved to Richmond in order to operate the business, an arrangement that permitted Cook to continue concentrating on fieldwork. In addition to producing and preserving their own photographs, the Cooks, father and sons, also purchased collections from other Richmond studios, including the Lee Gallery and Vannerson and Jones. The combined collection created one of the largest and most complete visual records of nine-teenth-century Richmond in existence.

Francis Trevelyan Miller brought national attention to George Smith Cook's photographs in 1911, when he used several examples of his work in the ten-volume *Photographic History of the Civil War*. This publication generated such a demand for Cook collection photographs that Huestis Cook began neglecting his own photography in order to curate and reproduce the collection.

Cook married Mary Manning Latimer on 14 September 1915. They had one daughter and one son. Cook retired from the studio in 1946 and in that year sold about 500 of his historic Richmond photographs to the Valentine Museum (later the Valentine Richmond History Center). He began collaborating with Alfred Lawrence Kocher and Howard Dearstyne on a historical picture compilation entitled *Shadows in Silver: A Record of Virginia, 1850–1900, in Contemporary Photographs taken by George and Huestis Cook with Additions from the Cook Collection* (1954) but died before its publication. The collaboration inspired "Southern Exposures," a 1952 exhibition at the Virginia Museum of Fine Arts that showcased about 300 of the Cook studio's photographs. A joint exhibition by the Museum of the Confederacy and the Valentine Museum mounted in 1983 and 1984 also highlighted the collection.

Huestis Pratt Cook died of lung cancer at his Richmond home on 1 August 1951 and was buried in Hollywood Cemetery. In 1954 his widow sold the rest of the Cook collection of photographs, glass plates, and negatives to the Valentine Museum.

Birth and marriage dates recorded in diary of half brother George LaGrange Cook, printed in Jack C. Ramsay, Jr., *Photographer . . . Under Fire: The Story of George S. Cook (1819–1902)* (1994), 119, 135; A. Lawrence Kocher and Howard Dearstyne, *Shadows in Silver: A Record of Virginia, 1850–1900, in Contemporary Photographs taken by George and Huestis Cook with Additions from the Cook Collection* (1954), pors. on 11, 211; biographical materials in Huestis Pratt Cook and Cook Collection subject files, VRHC; *Richmond News Leader*, 25 Apr. 1946, 14 Oct. 1954; *Richmond Times-Dispatch*, 23 Nov. 1952 (pors.); *Commonwealth* 34 (Oct. 1967): 22; exhibition brochure *Old Times Here: The South as Depicted in the Collections of the Valentine Museum and the Museum of the Confederacy* (1983); obituaries in *Richmond News Leader*, 1 Aug. 1951, and *Richmond Times-Dispatch*, 2 Aug. 1951 (variant birth date of 3 July 1868).
MELINDA D. GALES

COOKE, Giles Buckner (13 May 1838–4 February 1937), Confederate army officer, educator, and Episcopal minister, was born in Portsmouth and was the son of John Kearns Cooke, a prosperous lumber merchant and sometime postmaster of the city, and Fannie Bracken New Cooke. Educated in schools in Portsmouth, Norfolk, and King and Queen County, he entered the Virginia Military Institute in 1855. Cooke was court-martialed on 18 June 1857 for striking a fellow cadet and threatening him with a pistol. He was acquitted but two weeks later was dismissed for intoxication. Cooke was reinstated and disciplined again the following year for being absent overnight from the barracks. He graduated on 4 July 1859, ranked twenty-second in a class of twenty-nine.

Cooke wanted to study law, but rather than accept an uncle's offer to join his practice in Saint Louis, Missouri, he moved to Petersburg and taught school while reading law with Roger Atkinson Pryor, a member of the House of Representatives and one of Virginia's most ardent secessionists. During the winter of 1860–1861 Cooke also advocated secession, and on the day that Virginia seceded from the Union, he enlisted in the state forces at Norfolk and participated in the capture of the Norfolk Navy Yard. On 21 April 1861 he joined the staff of Brigadier General Philip St. George Cocke, who commanded the Virginia forces in Alexandria. Cooke survived a spell of camp fever in July and was promoted to captain and assistant adjutant general on 29 October 1861. After Cocke's suicide, Cooke transferred the following January to the staff of General Pierre Gustave Toutant Beauregard and on 1 April 1862 became assistant adjutant general to Major General Braxton Bragg in the Army of the Mississippi, during which service he fought at the Battle of Shiloh.

On 20 August 1862 Cooke transferred to the headquarters of Major General Samuel Jones in the Department of Western Virginia and on 10 December became assistant adjutant and inspector general on Jones's staff. He was promoted to major on 30 April 1863, to date from 19

December of the previous year. On 12 February 1864 Cooke was assigned to Brigadier General William Montgomery Gardner, commander of the District of Florida. On the following 2 April, Cooke became assistant adjutant and inspector general under Beauregard, briefly in the Department of South Carolina, Georgia, and Florida and then beginning on 23 April in the Department of North Carolina and Southern Virginia. In the latter capacity, Cooke returned to Virginia and participated in the fighting around Richmond that summer. He was appointed assistant adjutant and inspector general of the Army of Northern Virginia on 8 October 1864 and served on the staff of Robert Edward Lee for the rest of the war. In his diary, which Cooke began when he entered the army, he described the siege of Petersburg, including the Battle of the Crater and the collapse of the Confederate defenses in March and April 1865. His writing is especially vivid in describing the final days of the Petersburg campaign and the retreat to Appomattox Court House. During the retreat, Cooke was wounded just below his right knee by an exploding shell at Saylers Creek. He was paroled on 9 April 1865.

In the early years of the Civil War, Cooke vowed that if he survived he would spend the remainder of his life in God's service. His diary records his baptism on 7 July 1861 in Centreville and reflects his increased concern with spiritual matters. After the war, he returned to Petersburg, in partnership with Thomas Hume opened a school for boys, and began studying for the ministry. Concerned with the educational plight of the former slaves and believing that they needed to be prepared to carry out the responsibilities of citizenship, Cooke in 1867 became head of a Sunday school for blacks at Saint Paul's Episcopal Church in Petersburg. That and a like Sunday school at Grace Episcopal Church provided the impetus in 1868 for founding Saint Stephen's Episcopal Church, the first African American congregation of that denomination in the city.

Petersburg created a system of public schools before the establishment of a statewide system in 1870. By 1868 the city school board, with assistance from the Bureau of Refugees, Freedmen, and Abandoned Lands and the Peabody Education Fund, had opened several public schools serving African American children. Cooke was appointed principal of one of them, Elementary School Number 1 (also called the Harrison Street School), reportedly the first public school for black children in Virginia and the forerunner of Peabody High School. It later moved to a larger building and added high school classes, including algebra, French, and Latin. Cooke resigned at the end of the 1871 school term and organized the Big Oak Private School, also for African Americans, and served as its principal until 1873.

Cooke was ordained a deacon in the Protestant Episcopal Church in 1871 and a priest in 1874. On 10 May 1873 he became the second rector of Saint Stephen's Church. Cooke merged his Big Oak School with the church's school to form a normal school. With the addition in 1878 of a divinity school, it became Saint Stephen's Normal and Industrial School, and in November 1884 it received a state charter as the Bishop Payne Divinity and Industrial School. Although it was nominally a branch of the Protestant Episcopal Theological Seminary in Virginia (popularly known as the Virginia Theological Seminary) in Alexandria, the seminary provided no funding, and Cooke spent several summers in northern states raising money.

The divinity school's first student was James Solomon Russell, a Mecklenburg County native who became the founding president of Saint Paul's Normal and Industrial School, in Lawrenceville. In his autobiography, Russell described Cooke as "a very exact man and a stickler for punctuality, but he was very human and wholeheartedly devoted to the right and the worthy." Another divinity school student, whom Cooke expelled in 1879 for lack of humility, was George Freeman Bragg, later a well-known Episcopal minister and founder of the *Petersburg Lancet*, one of the first African American newspapers published in Virginia. Cooke was proud of and won praise for his educational work among the freedpeople, but he may have shared with other white southerners some low opinions of African Americans generally. In undated notes for an address, he described former slaves as "ignorant, credulous, superstitious, deceitful, emotional, religious, grateful." Cooke intended his educational work to change that characterization.

On 1 October 1885 Cooke resigned as rector of Saint Stephen's to take a similar position at All Faith Parish in Charlotte Hall, Saint Mary's County, Maryland. He transferred to the Diocese of Kentucky on 9 January 1886 in order to work with black congregations in Louisville. Four years later Cooke returned to Maryland as rector of Saint Mary's Whitechapel, in Caroline County. From 1892 to 1904 he was rector of North Elk Parish (also called Saint Mary Ann Parish), in Cecil County, and in 1898 he was appointed dean of the Northern Convocation.

In February 1904 Cooke became principal of Saint John's Academy and rector of churches in Corbin and Middlesboro, Kentucky, but in September of that year he returned to Virginia to serve as rector of Kingston Parish in Mathews County. Eleven years later he moved to Portsmouth, where for two years before he retired in 1917 he was rector of All Saints Episcopal Church.

During his retirement Cooke lived in Mathews County and was active in several Confederate veterans' organizations. He attended many reunions, served as assistant chaplain general of the United Confederate Veterans, and was chaplain of both the Stonewall Camp in Portsmouth and the Lane-Diggs Camp in Mathews County. He was also chaplain general of the Confederate Memorial Association and a life member of the Confederate Memorial Literary Society, both headquartered in Richmond. As he aged, Cooke became increasingly aware of his own importance as one of the last living links with Robert E. Lee. In correspondence with veterans, writers, and others, he excoriated Abraham Lincoln and extolled Lee. By 1920 he was the last living member of Lee's wartime staff, an appellation he proudly carried for the rest of his life.

Both Cooke and his diaries became important historical sources. One obituary described his Mathews home as "a Mecca for historians and students of the War Between the States, who came to talk with him and to consult his diaries." Douglas Southall Freeman used the diaries and interviewed Cooke when writing his biography of Lee.

On 19 October 1870 in Portsmouth, Cooke married a widow, Martha Frances Mallory

Southall, who died on 2 January 1894. They had no children. On 27 April 1898 he married Sarah Katharine Grosh, of Cecil County, Maryland. Their one daughter and two sons included John Warren Cooke, who served as Speaker of the Virginia House of Delegates from 1968 to 1979. Giles Buckner Cooke died at his home in Mathews County on 4 February 1937 and was buried at Ware Episcopal Church two days later.

Unpublished MS biography by nephew Giles Buckner Palmer, VHS (including second marriage date); published biographies include *Washington Star*, 8 May 1932 (por.), *Mathews Journal*, 14 May 1936, and *Tyler's Quarterly* 19 (1937): 1–10, 87–94; Giles Buckner Cooke Papers, including diaries (with birth date) and undated draft address (second quotation), VHS; Giles Buckner Cooke Papers, Acc. 17042, LVA, including 1922 narrative of military and church service; published writings include Cooke, *Just Before and After Lee Surrendered to Grant* (1922) and, with others, *Confederate Leaders and Other Citizens Request the House of Delegates to Repeal the Resolution of Respect to Abraham Lincoln, the Barbarian . . .* (1928); Compiled Service Records; BVS Marriage Register, Portsmouth (1870); George F. Bragg Jr., *The Story of Old St. Stephen's, Petersburg, VA* (1906), 25–49; James S. Russell, *Adventure in Faith: An Autobiographic Story of St. Paul's Normal and Industrial School, Lawrenceville, Virginia* (1936), 17–25 (first quotation on 18); Martha Short Dance, *Peabody High School—A History of the First Negro Public High School in Virginia* (1976), 21–23; Odell Greenleaf Harris, *The Bishop Payne Divinity School, Petersburg, Virginia, 1878–1949* (1980), 1–3; *Petersburg Virginia Lancet*, 3, 10 Oct. 1885; death notice and account of funeral in *Mathews Journal*, 4, 11 Feb. 1937; obituaries (all with pors.) in *New York Times*, *Richmond News Leader* (third quotation), *Richmond Times-Dispatch*, and *Washington Post*, all 5 Feb. 1937, and *VMI Alumni News* 13 (spring 1937): 14; editorial tribute by Douglas Southall Freeman in *Richmond News Leader*, 5 Feb. 1937.

WILLIAM B. OBROCHTA

COOKE, Jack Kent (26 October 1912–6 April 1997), media entrepreneur and sports franchise owner, was born Jack Kenneth Cooke in Hamilton, Ontario, Canada. He was the son of Ralph Ercil Cooke, a salesman who had emigrated from Melbourne, Australia, and Nancy Jacobs Cooke, who had emigrated from Johannesburg, South Africa. He attended public schools in Toronto and avidly played sports. Because he did not graduate from high school, he could not accept an offered hockey scholarship to attend college. Proficient in playing several musical instruments, Cooke late in the 1920s formed Oley Kent and His Bourgeois Canadians, a twelve-man orchestra that played in local clubs. He married Barbara Jean Carnegie in Toronto on 5 May 1934, followed ten days later by an Anglican church wedding. They had two sons.

During the 1930s Cooke sold such diverse goods as Bibles, encyclopedias, and household cleaning products and spent a year as a runner at the Toronto stock exchange. Early in 1937 he became a radio station manager in Stratford, Ontario. He soon formed a partnership with the station's owner, Roy Herbert Thomson, who later acquired the *London Times* and became an English baron. The two began purchasing radio stations and bought a magazine, and Cooke established a radio syndication service of his own. By 1956, no longer working with Thomson, Cooke purchased a Canadian publishing house, two plastics factories, and an aluminum foundry. Indulging his love of sports, Cooke in July 1951 bought the Toronto Maple Leafs, a minor-league baseball team. He quickly turned the team into a successful pennant-winning franchise, and *Sporting News* named him minor-league executive of the year in 1952. During this period he began calling himself Jack Kent Cooke, possibly to differentiate himself from other local businessmen with similar names.

In the 1950s Cooke began trying to acquire media outlets in the United States. He financed his purchases of a New York record company and an advertising sales agency through his brother, who was an American citizen. In order to expand his business ventures, Cooke applied to Congress for citizenship, granted by a special act in 1960. He had moved to Los Angeles in 1959, and with citizenship in hand he began selling most of his Canadian assets. In the autumn of 1964 he started purchasing cable television systems and four years later sold them to H&B American Corporation for 1.6 million shares of its stock. The corporation merged with TelePrompTer in 1970 to become one of the nation's premier cable television providers. As its largest individual stockholder, Cooke elected a majority of the board of directors in January 1972. Concerned about TelePrompTer's lingering legal difficulties and falling earnings, Cooke in October of the next year named himself chief executive officer of the company, which through-

out the decade controlled more than one hundred North American cable systems, Muzak, and electronic surveillance systems. He sold TelePrompTer to Westinghouse Electric Corporation in 1981 for about $650 million.

Having sold his minor-league Canadian baseball team, Cooke looked to acquire sports franchises in his new home country. In September 1965 he purchased the Los Angeles Lakers, a National Basketball Association team, for more than $5 million, a record amount for an NBA team at that time. Frustrated that the team had not managed to win a title, Cooke signed center Wilt Chamberlain to a lucrative contract in 1968. The strategy paid off in 1972, when Chamberlain led the Lakers to their first championship since their move to Los Angeles. In 1966 Cooke was awarded a National Hockey League franchise that he named the Los Angeles Kings. The Lakers and the Kings played their home games at Cooke's newly constructed Great Western Forum, which opened in December 1967. Cooke bankrolled the Muhammad Ali–Joe Frazier heavyweight championship fight in 1971 at Madison Square Garden, in New York, televised as one of the first pay-per-view cable events.

On 20 October 1977 Cooke and his wife divorced, and she received a then-record settlement estimated to be more than $40 million. A year and a half later he sold the Forum, the Kings, and the Lakers for $67 million and in the autumn of 1979 purchased a fifty-acre Virginia estate near Upperville, in Fauquier County. He soon bought additional property in the area, including a cattle ranch, and about 1983 he moved to Kent Farms, his 641-acre estate near Middleburg, in Loudoun County. On 31 October 1980 Cooke married Jeanne Maxwell Williams Wilson, a widowed sculptor from Las Vegas, where he had lived briefly before moving to Virginia. They formally separated the following July and were divorced on 28 August 1981.

Cooke had moved to Northern Virginia in order to be close to the Washington Redskins, a National Football League team in which he and a partner had acquired 25 percent ownership in April 1961. He soon bought out his partner and several years later purchased an additional 13 percent of the franchise. Continuing to accumulate shares of the team, he owned about 40 percent by 1973 and 86 percent by 1976. Cooke controlled the team's operations by 1980. Placing his trust in the team's general manager, he agreed to hire Joe Gibbs as head coach and did not hesitate to use his fortune for the team's benefit, such as signing a number of talented players and constructing a state-of-the-art training facility in Loudoun County. In 1983 the Redskins won their first Super Bowl, the franchise's first championship since 1942. The following year the team returned to the Super Bowl but lost. Early in 1985 Cooke became the sole owner of the Redskins, who went on to two more Super Bowl victories in 1988 and 1992.

In addition to his media enterprises, Cooke was a real estate entrepreneur. He purchased the Chrysler Building, in New York City, in August 1979, an office building and hotel complex in Phoenix in 1983, and Elmendorf, a 540-acre thoroughbred farm in Kentucky the following year. Cooke attempted to acquire Multimedia Incorporated, a newspaper and broadcasting chain, in mid-1985, but the company rejected his takeover bid. That December he fulfilled a long-held desire to own a newspaper by acquiring the *Los Angeles Daily News* for $176 million. In 1987 he purchased First Carolina Communications Incorporated and the cable division of McCaw Communications Companies, which together owned more than sixty cable systems nationwide, but he sold them two years later. *Forbes* magazine ranked Cooke among its 400 wealthiest Americans, and *Virginia Business* consistently included him in its annual list of the state's ten richest entrepreneurs. In 1990 his wealth was estimated as high as $1.2 billion.

Cooke married Suzanne Elizabeth Szabados Martin in Alexandria on 24 July 1987. They separated four weeks later, after he discovered that she had failed to get an abortion he had insisted on as a condition of their marriage. In October Cooke filed for divorce, which was granted on 14 October 1988. He initially did not acknowledge paternity of the daughter born after their separation, and a series of bitter child-support hearings dragged on for more than five years. Eventually he established a trust for his daughter's support. On 5 May 1990 Cooke married Marlena Leonora V. Ramallo Miguens Chalmers, a twice-married Bolivian immigrant with two sons. He declared their union invalid on 8 February 1994 because she had not been legally divorced from her second husband. Cooke and Chalmers married again on 15 July 1995 at his Fauquier County estate.

Beginning late in the 1980s Cooke unsuccessfully sought to build a new, larger stadium for the Redskins in Northern Virginia or Washington, D.C. Finally he acquired land in Prince George's County, Maryland, where the stadium opened in September 1997. Jack Kent Cooke did not live to see the completed stadium, which briefly bore his name. After suffering congestive heart failure, he collapsed at his home in northwest Washington, D.C., on 6 April 1997 and was taken to the George Washington University Hospital, where he was pronounced dead. His remains were cremated and memorial services held at Trinity Episcopal Church, in Upperville. In his will he established the Jack Kent Cooke Foundation to provide funds for scholarships and other educational purposes. Headquartered in Loudoun County, the foundation offers some of the country's largest awards for high school and college students.

Birth date from birth certificate cited in Adrian Havill, *The Last Mogul: The Unauthorized Biography of Jack Kent Cooke* (1992), including pors., and *Jack Kent Cooke Report*, 86th Cong., 2d sess., 1960, House Rept. 1506, serial 12250; variant birth date of 25 Oct. 1912 in many other biographical reference works; Rick Reilly, "Larger Than Life," *Sports Illustrated* 75 (16 Dec. 1991): 118–126 (pors.); feature articles in *Washington Post*, 17–19 July 1988; business career documented in *New York Times*, *Wall Street Journal*, and *Washington Post*; obituaries in *Los Angeles Daily News*, *Los Angeles Times*, *New York Times*, *Richmond Times-Dispatch*, *Toronto Star*, and *Washington Post*, all 7 Apr. 1997; editorial tributes in *Los Angeles Daily News* and *Los Angeles Times*, both 7 Apr. 1997, *Richmond Times-Dispatch* and *Washington Post*, both 8 Apr. 1997, and *Loudoun Times-Mirror*, 9 Apr. 1997.

JOHN G. DEAL
MARIANNE E. JULIENNE

COOKE, James Edward (26 August 1856–26 September 1926), journalist and mayor of Waynesboro, was born in Orange County and was the son of James Madison Cooke and Anne Elizabeth Hawkins Cooke. Educated at home and in private schools, at age seventeen he taught for one academic term before taking a job with the Chesapeake and Ohio Railroad Company. Cooke worked as a brakeman on the run from Staunton to Hinton, West Virginia, for three years and then as yardmaster at Cannelton, in Fayette County, West Virginia, and at Richmond for about a decade. He left the Chesapeake and Ohio to become a yardmaster in Bluefield, West Virginia, for the Norfolk and Western Railroad. On 27 September 1884 in Washington, D.C., Cooke married Medora Lee Payne, an Orange County native. They had three daughters and another child who died young.

The physical strain of railroad work compelled Cooke to resign from the Norfolk and Western. By 1892 he had moved to Waynesboro, in Augusta County, and joined his brother, John T. Cooke, in establishing the *Waynesboro Sentinel*. With the exception of a brief period in 1894, the brothers published the newspaper until 1895. In 1896 J. E. Cooke founded the weekly *Waynesboro Valley Herald*. About 1901 he renamed it the *Valley Virginian*, borrowing the title of defunct newspapers published in Clifton Forge and Staunton.

Having unsuccessfully run for mayor of Waynesboro in 1896, Cooke was elected to the office in June 1906 and served three two-year terms. Under his leadership the town council installed water pipes, streetlights, sidewalks, and paved streets. He declined to run for reelection in 1912, and a 1914 campaign to regain the mayor's office failed. Cooke continued to support public improvements through forceful editorials. His newspaper also encouraged efforts to merge the town's government with that of Basic City, an industrial town on the opposite side of the South River. An Augusta County judge ordered referenda on the issue in both towns on 7 August 1923. The *Valley Virginian* reported the towns' majorities in favor of the consolidation as a tongue-in-cheek wedding announcement. The merged town was initially called Waynesboro-Basic, but the General Assembly simplified the name to Waynesboro when it changed the town charter in 1924 to reflect the consolidation.

Cooke's wife died in 1905, and about four years later he married a woman named Margaret, surname unknown, who according to census returns was not living with Cooke in 1920. Cooke served on the executive committee of the Virginia Press Association in 1914. Declining health forced him to sell the *Waynesboro Valley Virginian* in June 1925, but his daughter Marion Marshall Cooke stayed on as local editor. The *Valley Virginian* combined with another local paper in 1929 to become the *Waynesboro News-Virginian*, a daily newspaper that continued serving the community into the twenty-first century. James Edward Cooke died at his home on 26 September 1926 and was buried in Riverview Cemetery, in Waynesboro.

Biography in Bruce, Tyler, and Morton, *History of Virginia*, 4:573–574 (por. facing 573), including birth date provided by Cooke; BVS Birth Register, Orange Co. (variant birth year of 1855); Census, Augusta Co., 1900, 1910, 1920; District of Columbia Marriage Record Book, 19:271; Waynesboro Town Council Minutes, vols. 2, 3, Waynesboro Public Library; *Staunton Dispatch and News*, 13 June 1906; *Staunton Spectator*, 12 June 1908; *Staunton Daily Leader*, 17 June 1910; *Waynesboro Valley Virginian*, 28 July 1911, 22 June, 20 July, 10 Aug. 1923, 1 Feb. 1924, 26 June, 3 July 1925; *Staunton Spectator and Vindicator*, 14 June 1912; *Washington Post*, 24 June 1914; *Waynesboro News-Virginian*, 19 Sept. 1967, 20 June 1974; BVS Death Certificate, Augusta Co. (with birth date); obituaries in *Richmond News Leader* and *Richmond Times-Dispatch*, both 27 Sept. 1926, and *Harrisonburg Daily News-Record*, 28 Sept. 1926; editorial tribute in *Waynesboro Valley Virginian*, 1 Oct. 1926.

TERRY C. SHULMAN

COOKE, John Esten (3 November 1830–27 September 1886), writer, was born in Winchester and was the son of Maria W. Pendleton Cooke and John Rogers Cooke (1788–1854), an attorney and member of the Convention of 1829–1830. His twelve siblings included the poet Philip Pendleton Cooke, and he was also a cousin of the writer and Maryland congressman John Pendleton Kennedy. Cooke spent his early childhood at Glengary, his family's Frederick County farm. After the house burned late in the 1830s, the family moved to Charles Town, in Jefferson County, and shortly thereafter to Richmond, where Cooke lived until the Civil War. He hoped to attend the University of Virginia, but he repeatedly had to defer his plans because his father— perpetually in debt—could not afford the tuition. Although Cooke studied law with his father and began to practice in 1851, he was, in his own words, "dragged by literature," and he read voraciously works by Thomas Carlyle, Sir Walter Scott, Alfred Lord Tennyson, Ralph Waldo Emerson, and Washington Irving, among other British and American writers.

Cooke became friends with John Reuben Thompson, who in November 1848 published Cooke's poem "Avalon" in the *Southern Literary Messenger*. Thereafter Cooke's stories and essays regularly appeared in southern as well as northern periodicals, including *Harper's New Monthly Magazine* and *Putnam's Monthly* magazine. In 1854 Harper and Brothers published anonymously the first of his many historical romances, *Leather Stocking and Silk; or, Hunter John Myers and His Times*, a novel with title and characters inspired by James Fenimore Cooper and set in the Shenandoah Valley early in the nineteenth century. Cooke also anonymously wrote *The Youth of Jefferson; or A Chronicle of College Scrapes in Virginia, A.D. 1764* (1854). A few months later the New York publishers D. Appleton and Company brought out *The Virginia Comedians: or, Old Days in the Old Dominion*, a historical romance set in pre-Revolutionary Virginia chronicling the romantic pursuits of Champ Effingham, an aristocrat and sometime cad. The widely praised novel went through several printings during Cooke's lifetime and continues to be considered his best work.

Cooke's literary successes allowed him to abandon his moderately successful law practice in the mid-1850s. He published three more novels, *Ellie: or, The Human Comedy* (1855), an experiment with the contemporary social-problem novel; *The Last of the Foresters: or, Humors on the Border; A Story of the Old Virginia Frontier* (1856); and *Henry St. John, Gentleman, of "Flower of Hundreds," in the County of Prince George, Virginia* (1859), a sequel to *The Virginia Comedians*. Even though modern critics view his 1850s fiction as romanticizing colonial gentry and perpetuating the myth of the Virginia cavalier, Cooke saw himself as a critic of aristocracy. As at least one literary historian has pointed out, however, Cooke's view of the aristocracy was conflicted. Champ Effingham, who at the novel's beginning stalks the actress Beatrice Hallam and acts dishonorably, has been rehabilitated by the end.

Cooke joined the Richmond Howitzers, a unit raised at the time of John Brown's raid on Harpers Ferry in 1859. He became a sergeant after the unit mustered into Confederate service as Captain R. M. Anderson's Company, Virginia Light Artillery (1st Company Richmond Howitzers), but he was discharged on 31 January 1862. That spring Cooke served as a volunteer aide-de-camp to Brigadier General James Ewell Brown Stuart, who had married Cooke's first cousin. Cooke received a commission as first lieutenant of artillery on 19 May 1862, joined Stuart on his celebrated ride around the Union army on 12–16 June, and won promotion to captain on 8 August, to rank from 25 July. He became chief of ordnance for Stuart's cavalry division later that year. Stuart may have recommended Cooke for promotion to major, but Cooke remained a captain until the end of the war. In October 1863 he was temporarily assigned to duty in the adjutant general's department of Stuart's command, and beginning in May 1864 he served as assistant inspector general of the Army of Northern Virginia's artillery corps. Cooke was paroled at Appomattox Court House on 9 April 1865.

While fighting in the major eastern campaigns from the First Battle of Manassas (Bull Run) to Appomattox Court House, Cooke continued to write prolifically. His Civil War diaries fill four notebooks, and his war dispatches appeared under the pseudonym Tristan Joyeuse, Gent., in Richmond's *Southern Illustrated News*, among other periodicals. Later he collected and edited these accounts for *Wearing of the Gray* (1867). In 1863 Cooke published *The Life of Stonewall Jackson*, which he later revised and issued as *Stonewall Jackson: A Military Biography* (1866).

After the Civil War, Cooke moved to Clarke County. The war had temporarily shifted his literary focus from colonial Virginia to the recent past and to the northern literary market. Cooke's three Civil War novels—*Surry of Eagle's-Nest; or The Memoirs of a Staff-Officer Serving in Virginia* (1866), *Mohun; or, the Last Days of Lee and His Paladins* (1869), and *Hilt to Hilt; or, Days and Nights on the Banks of the Shenandoah in the Autumn of 1864* (1869)—mixed imaginative scenes with historical military figures. A compilation of his articles on Virginia battles appeared as *Hammer and Rapier* (1870). Cooke's war experience also inspired his biography *A Life of Gen. Robert E. Lee* (1871). Although he is recognized as one of the first writers to treat the Civil War in fiction, critics lament that he did not exploit his war experiences to explore the subject in more depth and forthrightness.

On 18 September 1867 in Millwood, in Clarke County, Cooke married Mary Francis Page, who died on 15 January 1878. Their one daughter and two sons included Robert Powel Page Cooke, a physician who participated in Walter Reed's experiments to determine the cause of yellow fever. The family lived at the Briars, their Clarke County estate, where Cooke wrote, entertained, and farmed. His new agricultural knowledge informed the plot of one of his best novels from the postbellum years, *The Heir of Gaymount* (1870). The productive Cooke published more than a dozen other novels and novellas, including *Fairfax: or, The Master of Greenway Court* (1868), *Doctor Vandyke* (1872), *Her Majesty the Queen* (1873), *Justin Harley: A Romance of Old Virginia* (1875), *Canolles: The Fortunes of a Partisan of '81* (1877), *Professor Pressensee, Materialist and Inventor* (1878), *The Virginia Bohemians* (1880), and *My Lady Pokahontas: A True Relation of Virginia* (1885). He also wrote two historical works, *Stories of the Old Dominion From the Settlement to the End of the Revolution* (1879) and *Virginia: A History of the People* (1883), as well as many essays for various periodicals. He was an early member of the American Historical Association.

Cooke's work holds a significant place in Virginia's literary history and in nineteenth-century American literary culture. He was arguably the most famous Virginia writer of his period, a skilled historical romancer in the tradition of Walter Scott, James Fenimore Cooper, and William Gilmore Simms who repeatedly turned to Virginia's past as his inspiration for fiction. Although sometimes viewed as derivative and careless, and especially faulted for inadequate revision, Cooke's writings embraced a breadth of subject matter, from colonial Virginia history to class in contemporary Richmond, in a wide variety of genres that gives his work enduring interest. In part because of his success in gaining recognition from northern editors and readers, his career illustrates connections between northern and southern publishing in the nineteenth century.

John Esten Cooke died, probably of typhoid fever, at the Briars on 27 September 1886. He was buried in the Old Chapel Cemetery, in Clarke County.

Hennig Cohen, ed., "Autobiography of John Esten Cooke," *American Literature* 30 (1958): 234–237 (quotation on 235); John O. Beaty, *John Esten Cooke, Virginian* (1922), including bibliography of published writings on 164–168; Oscar Wegelin, *A Bibliography of the Separate Writings of John Esten Cooke, 1830–1886*, 2d ed., rev. (1941); Jay B. Hubbell, "The War Diary of John Esten Cooke," *JSH* 7 (1941): 526–540, and "John Esten Cooke," in *The South in American Literature, 1607–1900* (1954), 511–521; Richard Barksdale Harwell, "John Esten Cooke, Civil War Correspondent," *JSH* 19 (1953): 501–516; I. B. Cauthen Jr., "John Esten Cooke on Publishing, 1865," *Studies in Bibliography* 8 (1956): 239–241; William Edward Walker, "John Esten Cooke: A Critical Biography" (Ph.D. diss., Vanderbilt University, 1957); Lucy Gaylord Starnes, "Scribe of the Old Dominion," *Virginia Cavalcade* 13 (autumn 1963): 32–37 (pors.); Mary Jo Jackson Bratton, "John Esten Cooke: The Young Writer and the Old South, 1830–1861" (Ph.D. diss., UNC, 1969); Ritchie Devon Watson, Jr., *The Cavalier in Virginia Fiction* (1985), 131–144; Jack C. Wills, "John Esten Cooke," *Antebellum Writers in the South* (2001), 75–85; Cooke correspondence in various collections at Duke, LC, LVA, UVA, VHS, and WVU; Clarke Co. Marriage Register, 1:41; Compiled Service Records; *Washington Post*, 17 Oct. 1886; *Richmond News Leader*, 26 Sept., 27 Oct. 1936; obituaries in *New-York Times* and *Richmond Dispatch*, both 28 Sept. 1886, *Winchester Times*, 29 Sept. 1886, and *Literary World*, 2 Oct. 1886.

EMILY B. TODD

COOKE, John Rogers (17 June 1788–15 December 1854), member of the Convention of 1829–1830, was born on Bermuda and was the son of Stephen Cooke, a physician, and Catherine Esten Cooke. His younger brother Philip St. George Cooke was a career army officer and became a Union brigadier general during the Civil War. Their father moved the family to Grand Turk Island in the Bahamas (later the Turks and Caicos Islands), to Alexandria, Virginia, in 1791, and then to Loudoun County by 1801. Family tradition states that Cooke studied at the College of William and Mary or the College of New Jersey (later Princeton University), but neither school has records of his attendance. He may have served in a militia unit raised in response to the British warship *Leopard*'s attack on the American frigate *Chesapeake* in 1807, and during the War of 1812 he participated in the defense of Norfolk for several months in 1813 as a private in a Berkeley County artillery company attached to the 67th Regiment Virginia militia.

Cooke began practicing law on 9 January 1809 in Martinsburg, Berkeley County, and quickly rose to prominence at the bar and in society. His marriage on 18 November 1813 to Maria W. Pendleton, the daughter of a prominent Martinsburg family, secured his social status in the community. Of their thirteen children, only two daughters and four sons survived childhood, among them Philip Pendleton Cooke and John Esten Cooke, both of whom became prominent writers. Cooke represented Berkeley County in the House of Delegates for the session that met from October 1814 to January 1815 and sat on the Committees for Courts of Justice and of Propositions and Grievances. After his single term ended, he continued his successful law practice in Martinsburg until mid-April 1824, when he moved to Winchester. Cooke established a reputation as one of the leading attorneys in western Virginia.

Along with other prominent citizens in the Valley of Virginia and the trans-Allegheny region, Cooke came to believe that the state constitution was inequitable to the growing West. He helped organize a reform convention that met in Staunton in 1816, although he did not serve as a delegate, and in July and August 1825 he represented Frederick County at another reform convention that again met in Staunton. Cooke anonymously published two pamphlets, *The Constitution of '76* (1825) and *The Convention-Question in 1827* (1827), both of which argued for reapportioning the General Assembly based on Virginia's white population only and eliminating property qualifications for suffrage. After state voters approved calling a constitutional convention, Cooke wrote *An Earnest Appeal to the Friends of Reform in the Legislature of Virginia* (1828), in which he urged the General Assembly to apportion the convention on the basis of the

white population and predicted that an apportionment favoring eastern conservatives might encourage reformists to pursue more radical strategies, including holding their own elections, drafting a reform constitution, and essentially establishing a parallel state government. Despite such strong sentiments, Cooke accepted the legislature's apportionment plan, which benefited opponents of reform by basing representation in the convention on the existing state senate districts. He easily garnered the most votes among the fourteen candidates vying for the four seats representing Frederick and Jefferson Counties at the convention, which met in Richmond from 5 October 1829 through 15 January 1830.

Cooke, who owned six taxable slaves at the time, was one of the convention's leading spokesmen for reform. In the Committee to Consider the Legislative Department of the Government, he and Philip Doddridge ardently advocated apportioning both the House of Delegates and the Senate of Virginia solely on the basis of the commonwealth's white population. They succeeded in securing a recommendation for a white basis for the House in the committee's report to the convention but were unable to overcome a 12–12 tie on the basis of apportionment of the Senate. On the convention floor Cooke frequently articulated the reform positions of reapportionment and expansion of voting rights to all white males. Although he often sparred with the conservative defenders of the existing constitution, he showed a willingness to compromise on apportionment and finally came to support a readjustment that slightly increased western representation in the General Assembly and slightly extended the suffrage by reducing but not eliminating property qualifications.

Cooke was one of seven members of the select committee to draft the new constitution. In the final vote on 14 January 1830 he, alone of all the reformers from the Valley and the trans-Allegheny region, voted for the new document. Other westerners accused Cooke of having deserted their cause; he rebutted the charge in a series of public letters to his Frederick and Jefferson County constituents published in various Virginia newspapers in the months after the convention adjourned. Arguing that the Valley had few political ties with the trans-Allegheny region, but rather shared political interests with the western Piedmont counties, he contended that the final compromise on reapportionment favored Valley citizens and came close to delivering the reformers' goal. Many of Cooke's constituents apparently agreed. Jefferson County overwhelmingly approved the new constitution in the spring referendum, 243 to 53, while Frederick County supported it by a much closer margin, 451 to 438.

Cooke resumed practicing law in Winchester and in 1832 moved to his newly built home, Glengary, in Frederick County. Soon, however, his political and financial fortunes collapsed. In 1835 Cooke, running as a Whig, lost election to the House of Representatives from the Fifteenth Congressional District, comprising Berkeley, Frederick, Hampshire, Jefferson, and Morgan Counties, to the incumbent Democrat by a vote of 1,971 to 1,849. Despite his lucrative practice as one of Virginia's leading attorneys, Cooke fell deeply into debt. Responsible for paying off the debts of his father's estate, he was often too generous with his money, and he endorsed many notes that signatories defaulted on after the panic of 1837. Investments in a coal mine and in Texas lands failed. A further financial blow fell when Glengary burned late in the 1830s, forcing Cooke to resettle his family in Charles Town, Jefferson County, and then in Richmond. The income from his still-successful legal practice began to decline by 1845, in part because he began to suffer recurrent, debilitating fevers that may have been malaria. He spent the rest of his life struggling to pay his debts while providing for his family. John Rogers Cooke died in Richmond on 15 December 1854 and was buried in Shockoe Cemetery.

Biography in F. Vernon Aler, *Aler's History of Martinsburg and Berkeley County, West Virginia* (1888), 101–104; Berkeley Co. Marriage Bonds, 3b:276 (bond dated 17 Nov. 1813); John Rogers Cooke Diary (including birth date in entry for 2 Jan. 1823 and marriage date in entry for 8 Jan. 1833), VHS; correspondence in John Esten Cooke Papers, Duke, and in Cooke Family Papers and James Ewell Brown Stuart Papers, both VHS; Cooke to Philip Clayton Pendleton, 11 May 1825, LVA; *Daily Richmond Whig*, 2 Jan., 10 Apr. 1829; *Richmond Enquirer*, 8, 10 Jan., 26 May 1829, 2, 13 Feb., 2 Apr. 1830, 21, 28 Apr., 5, 8 May 1835; *Charlestown Virginia Free Press and Farmers' Repository*, 8, 10, 17 Feb., 7, 14 Apr. 1830, 16, 23 Apr., 7, 14 May 1835; *Proceedings and Debates of Convention of 1829–1830*, 22, 54–62, 432–435, 495–496, 542–543, 678–680, 690–699, 777, 863–870, 882, 903; Catlin, *Convention of 1829–30* (por.); Hall, *Portraits*, 54–55, plate 7 (por. by Cephas Thompson); death notices in *Richmond Daily Whig* and *Daily Richmond Enquirer*, both 16 Dec. 1854; memorial resolutions in *Richmond Whig and Public Advertiser*, 8 Jan. 1855.

TRENTON E. HIZER

COOKE, John Rogers (9 June 1833–10 April 1891), Confederate army officer, was born at Jefferson Barracks, in Saint Louis County, Missouri, and was the son of Rachel Wilt Hertzog Cooke and Philip St. George Cooke, a native Virginian and career army officer. He shared his name with an uncle (1788–1854) who served prominently in the Convention of 1829–1830. His younger sister Flora Cooke married James Ewell Brown Stuart, later a Confederate major general, and became principal of a female preparatory school in Staunton after the Civil War. His first cousins Philip Pendleton Cooke and John Esten Cooke both achieved national fame as writers.

Cooke took preparatory courses at the University of Missouri in Columbia from 1845 through 1847 and then spent about a year enrolled in school in Carlisle, Pennsylvania, where his father was post commander. He attended school in Alexandria, Virginia, for a time and then studied civil engineering at Harvard University's Lawrence Scientific School during the 1851–1852 academic year but did not graduate. Cooke worked on railroad construction in Ohio and Missouri before his father secured him a commission as a second lieutenant in the United States Army on 22 July 1856 (to date from 30 June 1855). He served with the 8th Infantry in New Mexico Territory and Texas.

Cooke was promoted to first lieutenant on 29 March 1861, to date from 28 January. During the secession crisis, he returned to Missouri, and after the Civil War began, he resigned his commission and traveled to Virginia in order to join the Confederate States Army, actions that caused a bitter division with his father, who remained in the regular army and became a Union brigadier general later that year. Named a first lieutenant, Cooke was assigned to Brigadier General Theophilus Hunter Holmes's staff. Following the First Battle of Manassas (Bull Run),

Cooke raised a company of light artillery, which he commanded until February 1862, when he was promoted to major and became chief of artillery in the Department of North Carolina.

In April 1862 Cooke was elected colonel of the 27th Regiment North Carolina Infantry. During the Antietam campaign his regiment participated in the seizure of Loudoun Heights overlooking Harpers Ferry. At Sharpsburg (Antietam) on 17 September, Cooke was ordered to lead his men and an Arkansas regiment in an exposed attack on a Union line of defense. The attack failed after the Confederate units exhausted their ammunition. Reassuming their original positions, Cooke's troops, without benefit of shot, held their line against repeated Union counterattacks. Cooke was promoted to brigadier general on 1 November 1862. At the Battle of Fredericksburg in December he fought at the stone wall on Marye's Heights. Two of his regiments suffered heavy casualties, while he sustained a serious wound just above his left eye.

Cooke recovered sufficiently to resume command of his brigade early in 1863. His troops, stationed for a time in South Carolina, saw little action until they fought at Bristoe Station, in Prince William County, Virginia, in October 1863. The brigade sustained heavy casualties, and Cooke received another severe wound that kept him out of action for the remainder of the year. On 5 January 1864 in Richmond he married Nannie Gordon Patton. They had five daughters and three sons.

Cooke returned to the battlefield in the spring. His North Carolinians performed admirably at the Battle of the Wilderness in May 1864. After receiving a leg wound at Spotsylvania Court House, Cooke became incensed when a superior presumed to assume command of his troops and lead them in an attack while Cooke stayed in the field. He fought at the Battle of Reams's Station, in Dinwiddie County, on 25 August 1864. His brigade remained at Petersburg until the Union army breached the Confederate defenses early in April 1865. During the retreat Cooke successfully extricated his troops from Sutherland Station, in Dinwiddie County. On 9 April 1865 he surrendered the 560 men left under his command at Appomattox Court House.

After the war Cooke worked in Richmond briefly as a route agent for a company that handled business along several area railways and then for about four years managed a large agricultural and stock-raising operation in King William County. By 1877 he had established himself as a Richmond grocery merchant. Active in local and civic affairs, Cooke was a member of the city's Democratic Committee and served as president of the board of directors of the state penitentiary. Remaining devoted to the Confederate cause, he was the third commander of the R. E. Lee Camp, No. 1, Confederate Veterans, and helped found and served as manager of the R. E. Lee Camp Confederate Soldiers' Home, in Richmond. Cooke was a member of the Association of the Army of Northern Virginia and sat on the executive committee of the Southern Historical Society. He acted as chief of staff at the laying of the cornerstone for Richmond's Robert Edward Lee monument in 1887 and at the unveiling of the bronze equestrian statue sitting atop it three years later.

Late in the 1880s Cooke reconciled with his father and ended the estrangement that had separated them since the beginning of the Civil War. John Rogers Cooke died of pyaemia, a form of blood poisoning, at his Richmond residence on 10 April 1891. He was buried in Hollywood Cemetery.

Biographies in R. A. Brock, *Virginia and Virginians* (1888), 2:777–778, and Ezra J. Warner, *Generals in Gray: Lives of the Confederate Commanders* (1959), 61 (por.); *Richmond Daily Dispatch*, 7 Jan. 1864; John Rogers Cooke Papers, including MS biography by sister Flora Cooke Stuart (with birth date), correspondence, scrapbooks, and newspaper clippings, and Cooke Family Papers, both VHS; correspondence, military commissions, and memorial resolutions in Philip St. George Cooke Papers and Cooke Family Papers (1855–1871), both LVA; Compiled Service Records; *OR*, esp. 1st ser., vol. 19, pt. 1, 150, 840, 913–918, 21:554–555, 570, 625–630, vol. 29, pt. 1, 426–427, 430–432, vol. 42, pt. 2, 1270–1275; BVS Death Register, Richmond City; obituaries, memorials, and account of funeral in *Richmond Dispatch* and *Washington Post*, both 10, 11 Apr. 1891, and *SHSP* 18 (1890): 322–327 (with variant birth date of 10 June 1833).
BRIAN S. WILLS

COOKE, Philip Pendleton (26 October 1816–20 January 1850), poet, was born in Martinsburg. The eldest surviving child of Maria W.

Pendleton Cooke and John Rogers Cooke (1788–1854), an attorney and member of the Convention of 1829–1830, he was also the elder brother of the writer John Esten Cooke and a cousin of the novelist and Maryland congressman John Pendleton Kennedy. The family lived in Martinsburg until 1824, when they moved to Winchester. Cooke attended an academy there before enrolling at the College of New Jersey (later Princeton University) in 1831. After being suspended for fighting with another student and then reinstated, he graduated in 1834 and returned to Winchester, where he studied law with his father. Cooke was admitted to the bar in 1837 and on 1 May of that year married Williann Corbin Tayloe Burwell, niece of a wealthy Clarke County landowner who disapproved of the union. They had four daughters and one son.

Cooke's legal practice suffered from competition with his two passions, hunting and poetry. As a young teenager, he had contributed verse to the *Winchester Virginia Republican*, and while in college he published three pseudonymous poems in the *Knickerbocker; or New York Monthly Magazine*. After Cooke returned to Virginia, he began a long association with the *Southern Literary Messenger* under the pseudonym Larry Lyle. In 1835 and 1836 he contributed several poems and a critical essay on "English Poetry." Cooke's poetry, with its emphasis on lost love, the natural world, and exoticism, placed him firmly within the romantic movement; his criticism marked him as extraordinarily well-read for someone living in a relatively rustic environment.

Financial difficulties dogged Cooke. Caught between his unsteady and unsuccessful attempts to establish himself as a lawyer and his preference for gentlemanly hunts, he wrote little during the latter 1830s. Only the intervention of Edgar Allan Poe, who initiated a correspondence with Cooke in 1839, jolted him from his literary seclusion. Cooke contributed two poems to *Burton's Gentleman's Magazine*, which Poe helped edit. "Florence Vane" (1840), a lament of lost love that particularly pleased Poe, became Cooke's most famous poem. Newspapers throughout the country reprinted it, composers set it to music, and anthologizers, most notably

Rufus Wilmot Griswold, included it in their collections. Having settled in Martinsburg and intensified his efforts at the law, however, Cooke did little to follow up on his success. In 1843 he published two poems, "Life in the Autumn Woods" and "The Power of the Bards," in the *Southern Literary Messenger*, but these alone constituted his output for the first half of the decade.

Cooke's personal and professional situation improved in 1845. He moved his family to the Vineyard, a Clarke County estate of about 340 acres owned by his wife's uncle. Poe revived interest in Cooke's poetry by singling out "Florence Vane" for praise during a lecture on American poetry. At Poe's urging, Cooke published an appreciation of Poe, intended as a sequel to James Russell Lowell's memoir of the poet, in the January 1848 issue of the *Southern Literary Messenger*. Cooke resumed contributing poems to several magazines and in 1847 published *Froissart Ballads, and Other Poems*, his only book. The collection elicited positive reviews but sold poorly. Determined to achieve financial success through writing, Cooke redirected his energies to prose. The *Messenger* published several of his critical essays on contemporary literature and four novelettes, including "John Carper, The Hunter of Lost River" (1848), a frontier tale similar to the work of James Fenimore Cooper, and "The Crime of Andrew Blair" (1849), a romantic saga of an aristocrat with a dark past. At the time of his death Cooke was serializing *The Chevalier Merlin*, a historical romance based on the adventures of the Swedish king Charles XII.

Cooke's literary reputation rests largely on the widely anthologized "Florence Vane" and on *Froissart Ballads*, which was reprinted in 1972 as part of a series on the American romantic tradition. His talent for portraying nature, best represented in "Life in the Autumn Woods" (1843) and "The Mountains" (1845), and his unconventional departures from standard meter may have augured an original poetic vision. Latter-day critics have also taken interest in the potential for rich characterization and sharp plotting demonstrated in Cooke's fiction as well as its illumination of western Virginia society. "The Turkey-Hunter in His Closet" (1851), Cooke's last prose work, shared some affinities with the writing of southwestern humorists and demonstrated a willingness to tweak the heroic conventions of romantic literature.

Having contracted pneumonia after fording an icy stream in search of game, Philip Pendleton Cooke died at his home on 20 January 1850 and was buried in the Old Chapel Cemetery, in Clarke County.

Biographies in "Recollections of Philip Pendleton Cooke," *Southern Literary Messenger* 26 (1858): 419–432, David K. Jackson, "Philip Pendleton Cooke: Virginia Gentleman, Lawyer, Hunter, and Poet," in David Kelly Jackson, ed., *American Studies in Honor of William Kenneth Boyd* (1940), 282–326, John D. Allen, *Philip Pendleton Cooke* (1942), with frontispiece por. and bibliography of manuscripts and publications, and Edward L. Tucker, "Philip Pendleton Cooke," *Virginia Cavalcade* 19 (winter 1970): 42–47; birth date from tombstone inscription in Stuart E. Brown Jr., Lorraine F. Myers, and Eileen M. Chappel, *Biographical and Genealogical Record of Persons Buried at Old Chapel* (1987), 78; *Richmond Whig and Public Advertiser*, 19 May 1837; Cooke correspondence in John Esten Cooke Papers, Duke, in several collections at VHS, and published in James A. Harrison, *Life and Letters of Edgar Allan Poe* (1903), 2:49–51, 262–264, John Ward Ostrom, ed., *The Letters of Edgar Allan Poe* (1966), 2:313–315, 327–330, 686–688, and Edward L. Tucker, "Philip Pendleton Cooke and *The Southern Literary Messenger*: Selected Letters," *Mississippi Quarterly* 27 (winter 1973–1974): 79–99; death notices in *Winchester Virginian*, 23 Jan. 1850, and *Richmond Enquirer*, 29 Jan. 1850; editorial tributes in *Southern Literary Messenger* 16 (1850): 125–126, and *International Magazine of Literature, Art, and Science* 4 (1 Oct. 1851): 300–303 (por.), reprinted in *Southern Literary Messenger* 17 (1851): 669–673.

WILLIAM BLAND WHITLEY

COOKE, Philip St. George (13 June 1809–20 March 1895), army officer, was born in Loudoun County and was the son of Stephen Cooke, a physician, and Catherine Esten Cooke. He attended a local school and for two years studied at a Martinsburg academy while living with a much-older brother, John Rogers Cooke (1788–1854), a prominent attorney and member of the Convention of 1829–1830. At age fourteen Cooke entered the United States Military Academy at West Point. On 1 July 1827 he graduated twenty-third in a class of thirty-eight. Commissioned a second lieutenant, he reported to the 6th Regiment United States Infantry at Jefferson Barracks, in Saint Louis County, Missouri.

After two years of frontier duty beginning in 1828, Cooke was ordered to Cantonment Leavenworth (later Fort Leavenworth), where he met and on 28 October 1830 married Rachel Wilt Hertzog. Their one son and three daughters included Flora Cooke, who married James Ewell Brown Stuart, later a Confederate major general, and who after his death became principal of a Staunton female preparatory school renamed Stuart Hall in her honor.

During the Black Hawk War, Cooke fought at the Battle of Bad Axe in Michigan Territory (later Wisconsin) in August 1832 and became adjutant of the 6th Regiment. Assigned to the new 1st United States Dragoons, he was promoted to first lieutenant on 10 May 1834. Cooke fell ill during a cavalry foray into the unorganized Indian Territory and after he recovered was sent east on a recruiting mission. He was licensed to practice law in Virginia in 1835 and before the Supreme Court of the United States in 1850. Cooke returned to the frontier in 1835 and on 1 July of the next year won promotion to captain. While serving on patrol duty and as regimental drillmaster, he displayed a grasp of tactics that led in 1843 to independent command protecting caravans from marauding Texans and Indians. Cooke gained valuable experience escorting settlers along the Oregon Trail and intervening between warring tribes. Few soldiers had greater knowledge of the frontier inhabitants and trails leading west from Fort Leavenworth.

At the beginning of the Mexican War, Cooke joined the Army of the West and helped accomplish the surrender of Santa Fe in August 1846. Then as a temporary lieutenant colonel he led a battalion of Mormon volunteers on a hazardous three-month trek from Santa Fe to San Diego, California. Promoted to major in the 2d United States Dragoons on 17 February 1847, Cooke returned to Fort Leavenworth that summer. He was summoned to Washington, D.C., where during the winter of 1847–1848 he was a chief witness against John Charles Frémont at a court-martial that convicted the explorer of failing to obey orders in California. Cooke left in March 1848 for Mexico City. From October of that year until October 1852 he served as post commander and superintendent of cavalry recruiting at Carlisle Barracks, in Cumberland County,

Pennsylvania. He was brevetted lieutenant colonel in March 1849 in recognition of his service in California.

Cooke reported to Texas late in November 1852 and the following year was ordered to New Mexico Territory, where during the winter of 1853–1854 and the spring he led expeditions against the Jicarilla Apache. He won promotion to lieutenant colonel on 9 February 1854. Cooke helped subdue the Brulé Sioux in the fight at Blue Water Creek in Nebraska Territory on 3 September 1855. As commander of Fort Riley in Kansas Territory in 1855 and 1856, he helped restore order after the bloody clashes between proslavery and free-soil factions. In 1857, as part of an expedition against the Mormons in Utah Territory, Cooke commanded dragoons on a brutal thousand-mile march from Fort Leavenworth to Salt Lake City. He was promoted to colonel on 17 June 1858.

Cooke wrote a memoir, *Scenes and Adventures in the Army: or, Romance of Military Life* (1857). While on leave of absence in the East in 1858 he began writing a cavalry manual especially for American horse soldiers, based in part on changes in French tactics. As part of his research he traveled to Europe in 1859 to observe Napoléon III's Italian campaign, which had concluded by the time he arrived. *Cavalry Tactics, or Regulations for the Instruction, Formations, and Movements of the Cavalry of the Army and Volunteers of the United States* (1861) established Cooke as an authority on the subject and went through several editions. In August 1860 he took command of the Department of Utah. From his remote posting at Fort Crittenden, Cooke watched the Union fracture. He resisted family entreaties to join the Confederacy. In a letter to the editor of a Washington newspaper written on 6 June 1861 he condemned Virginia's secession and declared, "I owe Virginia little; my country much. She has entrusted me with a distant command; and I shall remain under her flag as long as it waves."

Secession divided Cooke's family. One son-in-law commanded a New York regiment in the Union army, but the other two served the Confederacy. Cooke's son, John Rogers Cooke (1833–1891), resigned his commission in the United States Army and late in 1862 became a Confederate brigadier general. Of Cooke's loyalty to the Union J. E. B. Stuart wrote, with mortification, "He will regret it but once & that will be continually."

Cooke became brigadier general of volunteers in November 1861 and soon thereafter a brigadier in the regular army. He was assigned to the Washington defenses and commanded the reserve cavalry during the Peninsula campaign. The press and some other officers made Cooke a scapegoat after he failed to check Stuart's ride around the Union army in mid-June 1862. A controversial cavalry charge at Gaines's Mill during the Seven Days' Battles near Richmond further tarnished his reputation, and he left the Army of the Potomac, whose commanders he believed inept. Assigned to courts-martial for about thirteen months, Cooke from 8 October 1863 to 20 April 1864 commanded the District of Baton Rouge. From 24 May 1864 until 19 March 1866 he was posted to New York as superintendent of the regular army's recruiting service. Cooke was brevetted major general on 27 July 1866 for his wartime service.

Cooke commanded the Department of the Platte from 1 April 1866 until 9 January 1867. His service during the opening months of Red Cloud's War was lackluster, and the Fetterman massacre in December 1866 sparked a controversy that led to Cooke's reassignment to special duty in Louisville, New York, and Philadelphia and then as commander of the Department of the Cumberland for a year beginning on 1 May 1869. He commanded the Department of the Lakes from 5 May 1870 until 29 October 1873, when he retired. Cooke settled in Detroit, Michigan, where he wrote *The Conquest of New Mexico and California: An Historical and Personal Narrative* (1878) and several magazine articles, including one in *Century Magazine* in 1885 in which he defended his conduct at Gaines's Mill. The University of Michigan awarded him an honorary M.A. in 1883. Late in the 1880s he reconciled with his son, from whom he had been estranged since the beginning of the Civil War. Philip St. George Cooke died at his Detroit home on 20 March 1895 and was buried in Elmwood Cemetery in that city.

George W. Cullum, *Biographical Register of the Officers and Graduates of the U.S. Military Academy at West Point, N.Y.* (1868), 1:317–318; William H. Powell, *Powell's Records of Living Officers of the United States Army* (1890), 142–146; Philip St. George Cooke Papers and Cooke Family Papers (including signed commissions and law licenses), VHS, and Philip St. George Cooke Papers and Cooke Family Papers (1855–1871), including second quotation in James Ewell Brown Stuart to John Rogers Cooke (1833–1891), 18 Jan. 1862, LVA; Otis E. Young, *The First Military Escort on the Santa Fe Trail, 1829: From the Journal and Reports of Major Bennet Riley and Lieutenant Philip St. George Cooke* (1952); Young, *The West of Philip St. George Cooke* (1955); Hamilton Gardner, "Romance at Old Cantonment Leavenworth: The Marriage of 2d Lt. Philip St. George Cooke in 1830," *Kansas Historical Quarterly* 22 (1956): 97–113 (por. facing 112); "Cooke's Journal of the March of the Mormon Battalion, 1846–1847," in Ralph P. Bieber and Averam B. Bender, eds., *Exploring Southwestern Trails, 1846–1854* (1938), 65–240; *Notes of a Military Reconnoissance, from Fort Leavenworth, in Missouri, to San Diego, in California, Including Part of the Arkansas, Del Norte, and Gila Rivers*, 30th Cong., 1st sess., 1847, Exec. Doc. 7, serial 505; *Report from the Secretary of War, Communicating . . . a Copy of the Official Journal of Lieutenant Colonel Philip St. George Cooke, from Santa Fé to San Diego, &c.*, 31st Cong., special sess., 1849, Senate Doc. 2, serial 547; *Report of Secretary of War, Communicating . . . a Copy of the Report of Lieut. Col. Cooke of the Part Taken by His Command in the Action at Bluewater, Nebraska Territory, September 3, 1855*, 34th Cong., 3d sess., 1857, Exec. Doc. 58, serial 881; *Saint Louis Missouri Republican*, 16 Nov. 1830; *Washington Daily National Intelligencer*, 21 June 1861 (first quotation); *Century Magazine* 30 (Sept. 1885): 777–779; obituaries in *New-York Times* and *Richmond Times*, both 21 Mar. 1895, and *Detroit Free Press*, 21, 24 Mar. 1895.

EDWIN C. BEARSS

COOKE, Richard Dickson (29 April 1880–10 October 1958), civic leader and mayor of Norfolk, was born in Norfolk and was the son of Mary Elizabeth Dickson Cooke and Merritt Todd Cooke, a businessman who served several nonconsecutive terms in the House of Delegates. He attended preparatory schools, including the Norfolk Academy, and in 1902 received a B.L. from the University of Virginia. Admitted to the state bar that year, Cooke joined a Norfolk law office and in 1909 became a partner in the firm. He married Fannie Webb Royster on 15 April 1909. They had two sons and one daughter.

Throughout his life Cooke worked for the betterment of the city. He was a founder, president, and trustee of the Norfolk Community Fund and sat on the boards of the Mary F. Ballentine Home for the Aged, the First Presbyterian Church, Norfolk General Hospital, the Virginia Seashore State Park Association (of which he was also a vice president), and the Navy Young Men's Christian Association. He served on the governing board of Mary Baldwin College and on the advisory committee of the local Young Women's Christian Association. During World War II, Cooke chaired the Norfolk United War Fund campaign and the local United Service Organizations management committee, both of which arranged recreational activities for military personnel and civilians. For his services to the community, the Norfolk Cosmopolitan Club presented him its First Citizen Award for 1942. When accepting the award, Cooke said with his trademark modesty, "I wish I could have done more."

World War II precipitated a population boom in Norfolk that led to dire shortages in housing, transportation, and commodities. Federal assistance helped alleviate some problems, but after government funding ended, as expected, at the conclusion of the war, the Norfolk city council late in 1945 slashed spending and cancelled several planned improvements. The business community protested, and the city manager, Charles Barney Borland, resigned. As citizens clamored for a change in leadership, Cooke announced his candidacy in the 1946 Norfolk council race.

Cooke campaigned on the independent People's Ticket with Joshua Pretlow Darden, an automobile dealer and brother of former governor Colgate Whitehead Darden Jr., and John Twohy II, a local contractor. Promoting a progressive platform, they pledged to rid the city of wartime vice and corruption and to break the political machine that had controlled local government since the Great Depression. The three candidates vowed to transform Norfolk from a city run by politicians to one managed by experienced businessmen. To relieve fears that they would seize power, they pledged to serve only one four-year term. In June 1946 a record voter turnout of almost 17,000 decisively carried the People's Ticket to victory.

After taking office on 2 September, Cooke was elected president of the council and ex officio mayor of Norfolk. He promised to serve only two years as mayor, but in September 1948, when the council reorganized following its biennial election, he was persuaded to remain in office and was unanimously reelected. On 15 February 1949 declining health and improved conditions in the city convinced Cooke to resign as mayor. He remained on the city council until his term concluded in September 1950. As they had promised during their 1946 campaign, Cooke, Darden, and Twohy did not seek reelection to the council.

During Cooke's four-year term on the city council, he helped plan and implement projects that served as a blueprint for Norfolk's development for many years. His administration revived the Elizabeth River Tunnel Commission, which constructed and in May 1952 opened the downtown Norfolk-Portsmouth Bridge-Tunnel. As mayor, Cooke oversaw expansion and redefinition of the Norfolk Redevelopment and Housing Authority's mission. Originally created in 1940 to eradicate downtown slums but diverted during World War II into providing housing for the influx of defense workers, the newly invigorated authority took charge of redevelopment throughout the city. The council appropriated funds for a planning study and authorized the implementation of a minimum housing code, one of the first in the nation. During Cooke's term as mayor, Norfolk hired more than seventy new policemen, including the first six African Americans, and reorganized the city police department in order to weed out a longstanding nucleus of graft and corruption.

Although not a trial attorney, Cooke was recognized for his skilled legal advice to clients and to other lawyers in his firm. His peers elected him president of the Norfolk and Portsmouth Bar Association for the 1946–1947 term. In his later years, even as his health deteriorated, he continued to go regularly to his law office and served on the board of the National Bank of Commerce. Richard Dickson Cooke died at his Norfolk home on 10 October 1958 and was buried in Elmwood Cemetery.

NCAB, 44:477; BVS Birth Register, Norfolk City; BVS Marriage Register, Norfolk City; *Norfolk Virginian-Pilot*, 16 Apr. 1909, 12 June, 3 Sept. 1946, 16 Feb. 1949; *Norfolk Ledger-Dispatch*, 15 Dec. 1942, 29 Jan. 1943 (quotation); *Commonwealth* 10 (Jan. 1943): 12; Forrest R. White, *Pride and Prejudice: School Desegregation and Urban Renewal in Norfolk, 1950–1959* (1992), 5–6, 30, 88, 221; Thomas C. Parramore with Peter C. Stewart and Tommy L. Bogger, *Norfolk: The First Four Centuries* (1994), 348–350; obituaries in *Norfolk Virginian-Pilot* and *Norfolk Ledger-Dispatch and Portsmouth Star*, both 11 Oct. 1958; editorial tribute in *Norfolk Virginian-Pilot and Portsmouth Star*, 12 Oct. 1958; memorial in *Virginia State Bar Association Proceedings* (1961), 136–137 (por.).

MARGARET HAILE MCPHILLIPS

COOPER, Byron Nelson (19 August 1912–26 March 1971), educator and geologist, was born in Plainfield, Indiana, and was the son of Frank Landers Cooper, a printer, and Stella P. Lynch Cooper. His mother died when he was about thirteen years old. His father remarried and died several years later. Cooper received an A.B. at DePauw University in 1934 and both an M.S. and Ph.D. in geology at the University of Iowa in 1935 and 1937, respectively. He married Willie Elizabeth Doyne in Prince Edward County, Virginia, on 31 August 1935. They had one son and one daughter, both of whom became educators.

Cooper began working as a junior geologist for the United States Geological Survey in 1937 but soon left to take a position as assistant professor of geology at the Municipal University of Wichita (later Wichita State University), in Wichita, Kansas, where he taught from 1937 to 1942. He was associate geologist of the Virginia Geological Survey from 1942 to 1945 and then an associate curator in paleontology at the United States National Museum (later the National Museum of Natural History) in 1945 and 1946. Cooper returned to teaching on 1 April 1946 as associate professor of geology and chair of the geological sciences department at Virginia Polytechnic Institute (after 1970 Virginia Polytechnic Institute and State University). He was promoted to professor the following year. During the next quarter of a century, he increased the department staff from two to sixteen full-time faculty members and developed an internationally recognized program.

Cooper viewed effective teaching as a balanced interaction between fieldwork research and classroom instruction. He looked to his students as sources of learning and enthusiasm and often practiced his mischievous sense of humor and quick-witted punning on them. He believed the geology department should employ faculty members with diverse research interests who were also open to new scientific ideas. Cooper emphasized that a successful program needed humble educators willing to sacrifice time working on their own research in order to assist students. He served as acting director of graduate studies in 1950 and as acting associate dean of engineering during the 1951–1952 academic term. Cooper's support of the Presbyterian Campus Ministry at VPI led that organization in 1970 to name its building in his honor.

A prolific researcher and author, Cooper wrote or collaborated on more than seventy articles and books, with an emphasis on the geology and mineral resources of the Appalachian Mountains in southwestern Virginia. He was both a member of the editorial board and geology section editor of the *Virginia Journal of Science* from 1950 to 1953 and from 1958 to 1960 edited the *Mineral Industries Journal*, an eight-page quarterly issued by several departments at VPI. Early in his career Cooper examined the Max Meadows fault breccias of Tennessee and Virginia and underscored their origins and magnitude in the development of the Appalachian Mountain system. Challenging a venerable theory that erosion cycles had produced the surfaces in the Appalachians, he argued instead that these mountain surfaces were continually forming and that the type and structure of the rock formations shaped them. Later he advocated a theory that ascribed the development of the Appalachian and Blue Ridge mountain chains to concurrent deformation and sedimentation, rather than to a terminal event at the end of the Paleozoic Era.

Cooper placed great emphasis on the practical applications of geology. He was a consultant and adviser for various government and private-industry projects, including the Advisory Council on the Virginia Economy (1958–1963) and the Governor's Advisory Committee on Geology (1960–1962). He also wrote articles in nonscientific magazines on such topics as the need for responsible oil and natural gas exploration west of the Blue Ridge Mountains. As a recognized authority in his field, Cooper was a prominent member and officer of many state,

regional, and national scientific and geological associations, including the American Association for the Advancement of Science, the Geological Society of America, the National Research Council, and the Virginia Academy of Science. From 1958 to 1964 he was a National Science Foundation visiting lecturer, and in 1960 he represented Virginia at the Twenty-first International Geological Congress in Copenhagen, Denmark.

Byron Nelson Cooper died of a heart attack in his campus office on 26 March 1971. According to his wishes, his ashes were scattered in the mountains on a friend's property near Mountain Lake, in Giles County. A VPI geological sciences fellowship is named in Cooper's honor, and two years after his death the *American Journal of Science* published a special volume dedicated to him.

Biographies in Morton, *Virginia Lives*, 205, *American Men of Science: A Biographical Directory*, 11th ed. (1965), 978, and Patricia Ann Cooper, "Dr. Byron Nelson Cooper, Department Head, 1946–1971: Recollections by His Daughter," *Virginia Tech Department of Geological Sciences Newsletter* (spring 2002), 6–7; information provided by children John Doyne Cooper and Patricia Ann Cooper (2003); BVS Marriage Register, Prince Edward Co.; correspondence, lectures, and other materials in Byron Nelson Cooper Papers, VPI; publications include Cooper, *Geology of the Draper Mountain Area, Virginia* (1939), *Geology and Mineral Resources of the Burkes Garden Quadrangle, Virginia* (1944), "The Search for Oil and Gas in Virginia," *Commonwealth* 16 (Dec. 1949): 28–30, 73–76, *Trilobites from the Lower Champlainian Formations of the Appalachian Valley* (1953), "Research and Effective Teaching in the Geological Sciences," *Journal of Geological Education* 6 (1958): 15–18, and *The Geology of the Region Between Roanoke and Winchester in the Appalachian Valley of Western Virginia* (1960); *Washington Post*, 5 Mar. 1946; obituaries in *Washington Post*, 27 Mar. 1971, *Richmond Times-Dispatch*, 28 Mar. 1971, *Christiansburg-Blacksburg News Messenger*, 30 Mar. 1971 (por.), and *Blacksburg Sun*, 31 Mar. 1971; memorial in Lynn Glover III and Paul H. Ribbe, eds., *The Byron N. Cooper Volume: A Special Volume of the American Journal of Science in Memory of Byron Nelson Cooper, 1912–1971* (1973), vii–viii (por. on vi).

MARGARET R. RHETT

COOPER, Esther Georgia Irving (28 November 1881–7 February 1970), civil rights activist, was born in Cleveland, Ohio, and was the daughter of William Irving and Katherine Harris Irving. Her mother's family, who had secured their freedom before the Civil War, arrived in Ohio from North Carolina in the 1850s. Nothing is known of Esther Irving's education. She began working for Harry Clay Smith, the first African American member of the Ohio legislature and editor of the *Cleveland Gazette.* Early in the 1910s, in Louisville, Kentucky, she assisted Nannie Helen Burroughs, then corresponding secretary of the Woman's Convention Auxiliary of the National Baptist Convention, in raising funds for Burroughs's recently opened National Training School for Women and Girls (later the National Trade and Professional School for Women and Girls), located in Washington, D.C.

After moving to Washington in 1913 to work as a stenographer in the Forest Service of the United States Department of Agriculture, Irving met George Posea Cooper, a Tennessee native and veteran of the Philippine Insurrection then serving as a technical sergeant in the Quartermaster Corps at Fort Myer in Alexandria County (after 1920 Arlington County). They married on 10 September 1913 and had three daughters. The family highly valued books and education and according to one daughter acquired an encyclopedia set before they had electricity or indoor plumbing. Cooper resigned from government service in the mid-1920s, but she continued part-time work teaching classes in English, shorthand, and typing at the National Training School for Women and Girls. In 1934 and 1935 she conducted business classes in the adult education program of the Arlington County Public Schools as part of the Federal Education Rehabilitation Act. After her husband died on 23 October 1937, she sought unsuccessfully to regain full-time government employment.

Cooper devoted much of her time to improving educational opportunities for African American children. Dissatisfied with the inferior facilities and textbooks offered in the black schools in Arlington County, she sent her own daughters to Washington, D.C., for their secondary education. They lived with an uncle during the week and returned home to Arlington for weekends. Cooper joined the Kemper School Parent-Teacher Association and served as its president for several years. As secretary of the education committee of the Hoffman-Boston School in 1935, she began lobbying Arlington school officials to establish an accredited junior

high school in the county. In 1940 Cooper organized and became first president of the Arlington County branch of the National Association for the Advancement of Colored People. Two years later she joined the executive board of the Virginia State Conference of the NAACP. In collaboration with state NAACP leaders and lawyers, the Arlington branch initiated a court case challenging inequalities in the county's high school facilities. Their efforts culminated in *Carter* v. *School Board of Arlington County* (1950), in which the Fourth Circuit Court of Appeals ruled that the county's separate high schools constituted unlawful racial discrimination.

As NAACP branch president during the 1940s, Cooper linked her local community to the broader statewide and national efforts to achieve voting rights and equal treatment for African Americans. She supported initiatives to abolish the poll tax and wrote letters to Arlington officials protesting segregation on public transportation and in public facilities. A member of the Southern Conference for Human Welfare, an interracial organization founded in 1938 to focus on social and economic problems in the South, Cooper served as president of the SCHW's Arlington chapter and chaired the Eighth District Committee for Virginia. She also supported the activities of the Southern Negro Youth Congress, a civil rights group advocating improvements in education, employment, and health care for African Americans. Among the organizers of the SNYC in Richmond in 1937 were her daughter, Esther Victoria Cooper, an editor of *Freedomways* from 1961 to 1985, and her future son-in-law, James Edward Jackson (b. 1914), later a prominent Communist Party activist. In 1947 Cooper ran for a seat on Arlington County's Democratic Executive Committee, but she was one of six progressive candidates disqualified from appearing on the primary ballot for allegedly failing to comply with party regulations. She retired as president of the county NAACP branch in 1951 but remained active as its president emerita.

Cooper participated in numerous community improvement organizations. She joined Saint John's Baptist Church in 1914 and served as president of the Baptist Young People's Union.

A charter member of Arlington County's chapter of the Virginia Council of Church Women, she was for many years a vice president of the Lott Carey Foreign Mission Society. During the mid-1940s she lobbied on behalf of the Citizens Committee for School Improvement. Cooper helped organize the Jennie Dean Community Center Association, a women's group that raised money to purchase land for a recreation center open to African Americans. The association acquired several lots and in 1947 donated them to the Veterans Memorial Branch of the Young Men's Christian Association. As secretary of the Butler Holmes Citizens Association, Cooper registered voters and sought to end the poll tax as a prerequisite for voting. She continued working on political campaigns and at polling places through the 1964 presidential election.

Esther Georgia Irving Cooper suffered cardiac arrest and died at her Arlington County home on 7 February 1970. She was buried next to her husband's grave in Arlington National Cemetery.

Birth date confirmed by BVS; Larissa M. Smith, "Esther Cooper and the Struggle for Racial Equality in Virginia, 1930–1955," paper delivered on 9 Nov. 2002 at Southern Historical Association Annual Meeting, Baltimore, Md.; Esther Georgia Irving Cooper Papers, Moorland-Spingarn Research Center, Howard University, Washington, D.C.; Cooper materials in Arlington County NAACP branch files, Group II, Box C203, Papers of the NAACP, LC; *Arlington Daily*, 11 July 1947; *Washington Post*, 19, 22 July 1947; *Arlington Northern Virginia Sun*, 18 May 1965 (por.); *Washington Afro-American and the Washington Tribune*, 22 May 1965; Paulina Cooper Moss, "At Home and at War, 1917–1919," *Negro History Bulletin* 45 (1982): 43–45 (with marriage date); Esther Cooper Jackson and James Jackson, "Memories of the Southern Negro Youth Congress," interview by James V. Hatch, 5 Apr. 1992, Hatch-Billops Collection, New York, N.Y.; Esther Cooper Jackson recollections in Camille O. Cosby and Renee Poussaint, eds., *A Wealth of Wisdom: Legendary African American Elders Speak* (2004), 193–195; obituaries in *Washington Post* (por.) and *Northern Virginia Sun* (por.), both 10 Feb. 1970.

LARISSA M. SMITH

COOPER, Robert Weldon (12 November 1906–16 May 1996), university administrator, was born in Kirbyville, Jasper County, Texas, and was the son of Robert J. Cooper and Eliza J. Bean Cooper. He graduated from Abilene Christian College (later Abilene Christian University) in 1926 with a B.A. On 6 June 1930 Weldon

Cooper, as he was known both personally and professionally, married Julia Allen, an Arkansas resident who had also graduated from Abilene Christian College. They had no children.

After receiving an M.A. from the University of Texas at Austin in 1932, Cooper worked as a research assistant at the school's Bureau of Research in the Social Sciences from 1933 to 1935. He served as assistant director of the university's Bureau of Municipal Research in 1936, taught government courses, and published *The Texas Municipal Civil Service* (1936). By 1938 Cooper had moved to the University of Alabama as assistant director of the Bureau of Public Administration and assistant professor of political science. The University of Chicago awarded him a Ph.D. in public administration in 1939, after he completed a dissertation published as *Municipal Police Administration in Texas* (1938). He was promoted to associate professor of political science in 1941.

Cooper served during World War II as an organization and methods examiner for the United States Bureau of the Budget in Washington, D.C. He returned to the University of Alabama after the war and in 1946 was appointed professor of public administration. Cooper wrote *Municipal Government and Administration in Alabama* (1940), *Metropolitan County: A Survey of Government in the Birmingham Area* (1949), and, with Rowland Andrews Egger, *Research, Education, and Regionalism: The Bureau of Public Administration of the University of Alabama, 1938–1948* (1949).

In the autumn of 1947 Cooper became associate director of the University of Virginia's Bureau of Public Administration and also professor of political science (beginning in the 1965–1966 academic year professor of government). In 1956 he was appointed director of the bureau, which in 1964 was renamed the Institute of Government. Cooper was active in many areas of the University of Virginia and is credited with having an important behind-the-scenes influence on its development. He served on a six-member committee in 1957 that planned the university's growth for the next decade. From 1957 to 1973 Cooper edited the *University of Virginia News Letter*, an Institute of Government publication that featured articles on governmental administration and public policy. In its pages he often included his own research relating to local government in Virginia, financial issues, and state government reorganization. For the institute he co-edited *Virginia Government and Politics: Readings and Comments* (1976), a compilation of previously published writings on state and local governments, the judiciary, and Virginia politics.

From October 1958 until 1969 Cooper served as secretary to the university's board of visitors. He oversaw the creation of a manual for the trustees and introduced the practice of formally recording minutes of board meetings. Cooper advised the university rectors and presidents on such issues as desegregation, coeducation, and faculty development. From 1959 to 1967 he also was administrative assistant to President Edgar Finley Shannon. As secretary of a board of visitors' special search committee, he played a central role in the selection of Frank Loucks Hereford as the university's president in 1973.

Cooper's position as director of the Institute of Government led him into other service opportunities. During a leave of absence beginning in October 1950 he was an executive assistant to Governor John Stewart Battle, charged with directing governmental reorganization studies. After he completed his first report, on increasing production on state-operated farms, Cooper resigned in November 1951 to return to the university. His membership on state committees included the Governor's Commission for Legislative Redistricting in 1961, the Virginia Metropolitan Areas Study Commission in 1966, and the Virginia Urban Assistance Incentive Fund, which he chaired in 1969. Cooper also frequently lectured to civic groups and participated in panel discussions on state and local government issues. His expertise was not confined to Virginia. As a special consultant to the Alaska constitutional convention in December 1955, he drafted the state charter, widely respected for its brevity and clarity as a constitutional document.

Cooper retired from the Institute of Government in 1973. That year the governor recognized his devotion to Virginia and his contributions to strengthening state and local governments.

Cooper continued to teach and in 1974 was named the Robert Kent Gooch Professor of Government and Foreign Affairs, a chair he held until retiring from the University of Virginia in 1977. Following the death of his wife in October 1978, Cooper married Mildred Ellis Martin, a widowed Texas native with one son, in Charlottesville on 21 October 1981. The university's board of visitors honored him in 1994 by renaming the institute he had headed for more than a quarter of a century the Weldon Cooper Center for Public Service. Robert Weldon Cooper died in Charlottesville on 16 May 1996 and was buried in the University of Virginia Cemetery.

Biographies in Morton, *Virginia Lives*, 206 (with first marriage date provided by Cooper), and *Celebration of the Life of Weldon Cooper, 1906–1996* (1996); Texas Birth Index, Jasper Co.; second marriage date confirmed by BVS; Weldon Cooper Papers, oral history interview dated 15 July 1977, and correspondence in Francis L. Berkeley Jr. Papers, Gerald Langford Papers, and Secretary of the Board of Visitors Papers, all UVA; *Richmond Times-Dispatch*, 19 Oct. 1950, 18 June 1973; *Richmond News Leader*, 1 Jan., 2 May, 28 Nov. 1951; obituaries in *Charlottesville Daily Progress* (por.) and *Richmond Times-Dispatch*, 17 May 1996; editorial tribute in *Charlottesville Daily Progress*, 21 May 1996.

KENNETH W. THOMPSON

COOPER, Samuel (12 June 1798–3 December 1876), United States and Confederate army officer, was born in New Hackensack, Dutchess County, New York, and was the son of Mary Horton Cooper and Samuel Cooper, a businessman who had served as a Continental army officer. Cooper entered the United States Military Academy in May 1813 and graduated on 11 December 1815 with a commission as brevet second lieutenant of light artillery. He served at various New England posts for almost three years and then in the adjutant general's office in Washington, D.C., from 1818 to 1825, during which time he was promoted to first lieutenant on 6 July 1821. He was stationed at Saint Augustine, Florida, for one year, and at the artillery school at Fort Monroe, Virginia, from 1826 to 1828. In the District of Columbia on Analostan Island (popularly called Mason's Island and later Theodore Roosevelt Island) on 4 April 1827 Cooper married Sarah Maria Mason, granddaughter of George Mason (1725–1792), the Revolutionary-era statesman and member of the

Convention of 1788. Her well-connected siblings included James Murray Mason, later a member of the United States Senate and Confederate diplomat, and Anna Maria Mason, who married Robert Edward Lee's elder brother Sydney Smith Lee. The Coopers had two daughters and one son, as well as two other sons who died in infancy.

In 1828 Cooper became aide-de-camp to Alexander Macomb, the commanding general of the army, a plum assignment that over the next eight years revealed his talent for administration. He prepared *A Concise System of Instructions and Regulations for the Militia and Volunteers of the United States* (1836), an influential and widely used manual of tactics and administration. Following his promotion to captain on 11 June 1836, Cooper briefly directed the army's clothing bureau and from 1837 to 1838 served as chief clerk of the War Department. Brevetted major on 7 July 1838 and named senior assistant adjutant general, he worked for the next three years in the office of the secretary of war. He left Washington, D.C., in 1841 for staff duty in Florida during the Second Seminole War (1835–1842). Cooper was chief of staff for Generals Edmund Pendleton Gaines and Stephen Watts Kearny from 1842 to 1846. Reassigned to the War Department in the latter year, Cooper made good use of his administrative skills during the Mexican War, which necessitated rapid increases in troop levels and complicated deployments. In recognition of his efforts, he was brevetted colonel on 30 May 1848. Two years later he was posted as an assistant inspector general and charged with inspecting army garrisons in the West.

On 15 July 1852 Cooper was promoted to colonel and appointed adjutant general. As the chief administrative officer of the army he worked closely with two successive southern-born secretaries of war, Jefferson Davis and former Virginia governor John Buchanan Floyd. His close friendship with Davis, who relied on Cooper's experience and sound judgment, proved a productive partnership that brought about expansion of the army and changes in the West Point curriculum. Cooper's administrative prowess allowed Davis between 1853 and 1857 to pursue successfully such initiatives as conducting surveys of likely transcontinental railroad routes, expanding westward the army's chain of forts, improving harbor and coastal defenses, beginning projects to enlarge the United States Capitol and construct the Washington Aqueduct, adopting the rifled musket, increasing army pay, and dispatching to the Crimean War the nation's first official military observers of a foreign conflict.

Cooper's marriage into a prominent Virginia family, his ownership of land in Fairfax County, and his friendship with Davis connected him to the South as sectional discord increased. He resigned his commission on 7 March 1861, before the Civil War began, and offered his services to Davis, newly elected president of the Confederate States of America. On 16 March of that year Davis made Cooper adjutant and inspector general, with a rank of brigadier general. He was appointed general on 31 August 1861, to date from 16 May, making him the senior general and highest-ranking officer in the Confederate States Army.

Cooper's chief contributions to the fledgling nation were organizational, as he instituted and supervised procedures, forms, and personnel in establishing the new army. Although he was a consummate bureaucrat, his influence on military policy was negligible. Cooper was criticized for his dependence on regulations and antiquated protocols and for neglecting his role as inspector general, but he had a powerful ally in Davis, who closely defended the venerable adjutant general's prerogatives. The Confederate president viewed Cooper as more than a transmitter of instructions and inquiries for the secretary of war; he saw the adjutant general as a chief of staff for the whole army.

Early in April 1865 Cooper left Richmond with Davis and the Confederate cabinet, as well as more than eighty boxes of government records, mostly from the Confederate War Department. Surrendering in Charlotte, North Carolina, Cooper turned over these archival documents to Union army officers for preservation. He was paroled in May 1865. Retiring to Cameron, his devastated estate in Fairfax County, he took up farming. Samuel Cooper died at his residence on 3 December 1876 and was buried in the cemetery of Christ Episcopal Church in Alexandria.

Matthew Brian Veatch, "The Education of a Staff Officer: The Life and Career of Samuel Cooper, 1798–1852" (M.A. thesis, University of Missouri–Kansas City, 1989); William C. Davis, "General Samuel Cooper," in Gary W. Gallagher and Joseph T. Glatthaar, eds., *Leaders of the Lost Cause: New Perspectives on the Confederate High Command* (2004), 101–131; George G. Kundahl, *Alexandria Goes to War: Beyond Robert E. Lee* (2004), 31–49; *Washington Daily National Intelligencer*, 9 Apr. 1827; George W. Cullum, *Notices of the Biographical Register of Officers and Graduates of the U.S. Military Academy at West Point . . .* (1868), 158; official papers in Records of the Adjutant General's Office, RG 94, Records of the Office of the Secretary of War, RG 107, and War Department Collection of Confederate Records, RG 109, all NARA; Compiled Service Records; *OR*; Grace E. Heilman and Bernard S. Levin, eds., *Calendar of Joel R. Poinsett Papers in the Henry D. Gilpin Collection* (1941); Haskell M. Monroe Jr. et al., eds., *The Papers of Jefferson Davis* (1971–   ), vols. 5–11, with short biography on 1:108; career reminiscences and correspondence in Samuel Cooper Papers, UNC; family memoir (ca. 1878), genealogical notes, correspondence, copy of will, and other materials in Samuel Cooper (1756–1840) Papers, UVA; correspondence, petitions, and draft reports in Cooper Family Papers, VHS; correspondence in Daniel Harvey Hill Papers and Robert Edward Lee Papers, both LVA, and in several other collections at UVA and at VHS; pors. in A. Lawrence Kocher and Howard Dearstyne, *Shadows in Silver: A Record of Virginia, 1850–1900, in Contemporary Photographs taken by George and Huestis Cook with Additions from the Cook Collection* (1954), 252, and William C. Davis and Julie Hoffman, eds., *The Confederate General* (1991–   ), 2:28–29; BVS Death Register, Fairfax Co.; obituaries in *Alexandria Gazette* and *Baltimore Sun*, both 4 Dec. 1876, and *Richmond Daily Dispatch* and *Richmond Enquirer*, both 5 Dec. 1876; memorials by Fitzhugh Lee and Jefferson Davis in *SHSP* 3 (1877): 269–276.

LYNDA LASSWELL CRIST

COOPER, Susannah Sanders (d. after 9 June 1751), principal in a cause célèbre, was born probably late in the 1690s or early in the 1700s. It is likely, though by no means certain, that she was the Susannah Sanders, daughter of William Sanders, who was baptized in Saint Peter's Parish in New Kent County on 24 February 1703. The name of her mother may have been Elizabeth.

Sanders married Isles Cooper, a York County widower, in 1717. Within three years of their marriage, her husband had deserted her and their young son and perhaps a daughter. It was probably this action that spurred his father to disinherit him early in October 1719. Isles Cooper

disappeared from York County records in that year. He lived in Norfolk County for a time, eventually settled in Currituck County, North Carolina, and illegally married at least twice more. Susannah Cooper asserted that during the few years of their cohabitation, her husband squandered most of the assets she had brought to the marriage. After his departure, his creditors seized what remained of her estate in order to satisfy the many debts he had contracted. For a time Cooper relied on friends and family for support. During the next twenty years "by her own industry," as she proudly recorded, she purchased land and several slaves (at least some of whom she had baptized) and engaged in business under her own name. She operated a New Kent County ordinary that provided food, lodging, and stableage, purchased forms for making out bills of exchange, and sold goods such as almanacs.

Although Cooper's predicament could have remained her own private misfortune, the issue of her control over her property became a test case determining a married woman's rights. More than twenty years after her abandonment, Cooper petitioned the House of Burgesses to protect her hard-earned estate from her husband and his creditors and to secure her rights to sue and be sued, to make contracts as if she had never married, and to bequeath her property to her son. She carefully documented the details of her marriage and abandonment. The burgesses and governor's Council passed authorization for Cooper to dispose of her property as a *feme sole*, or unmarried woman, in September 1744. In transmitting the private bill to London for the Crown's review, Lieutenant Governor William Gooch urged speedy approval because "should her Husband return before this Bill is confirmed by His Majesty, all that she has, with great Industry and Honesty gott, since he left her, will be forced from her." The Privy Council dawdled for almost a decade and finally, on the advice of the king's legal counsel in February 1754, either rejected the bill outright or allowed it to die on the grounds that an act of assembly could not without out a husband's consent remove the rights he held in the personal estate of his wife.

Although recourse to the General Assembly provided one solution for deserted wives trying to regain control of property, an earlier generation within Isles Cooper's family found an informal resolution to marital breakdown. In 1675 his grandfather, Thomas Isles, acknowledged he had fathered a child outside wedlock. Rather than turn to the legislature, as Susannah Cooper later did, Elizabeth Isles, the wronged wife, petitioned the York County Court to regain control of her property for the good of herself and her children, demanded that her husband relinquish half the family's property to her, and insisted that Thomas Isles post a bond to leave her alone. The Isleses' case demonstrates that a family could resolve issues arising from marital division, even when coverture remained in effect. In the 1744 bill, Cooper and the Virginia government sought a more sweeping resolution than had her grandmother-in-law.

Cooper continued to conduct business in New Kent County under her own name until 1751. On 9 June of that year Isles Cooper sold all the property at her New Kent County Court House plantation (including slaves, livestock, household goods, furniture, and bonds) to John Cooper, his son from one of his subsequent illegal marriages. Merchants' account books that had listed Susannah Cooper's business in her own name before 1751 began to render her accounts under the name of John Cooper. The assets may have supported Cooper in her old age, as she wished, but her stepson had the final word on how the money and property were managed and disposed of.

Isles Cooper wrote his will in July 1762 and had died in Currituck County, North Carolina, by July of the following year. Susannah Sanders Cooper, who tested Anglo-American restraints on married women's property ownership in Virginia for more than thirty years, disappeared from New Kent County records after 9 June 1751. Her fate, death date, and place of burial are not known.

Baptism in National Society of the Colonial Dames of America in the State of Virginia, *The Parish Register of Saint Peter's, New Kent County, Va., from 1680 to 1787* (1904), 36; Hening, *Statutes*, 5:294–296 (first quotation on 295); William Gooch to Board of Trade, 21 Dec. 1744, PRO CO 5/1326, fols. 53–54 (second quotation); PRO CO 5/1328, fol. 81; PRO CO 5/1366, 377; Norfolk Co. Deed Book, 15:78–80; business accounts in William Bassett Account Book in Bassett Family Papers and William Massie Account Book, both VHS, Francis Jerdone Balance Book and Journals in Francis Jerdone Papers, Acc. 20939, 21655, and 21656, LVA, and Francis Jerdone Account Book, W&M; Isleses' separation in York Co. Deeds, Orders, Wills, 5:9, 94, 119; Isles Cooper disinherited in York Co. Orders, Wills, Etc., 15:598–599; Marylynn Salmon, *Women and the Law of Property in Early America* (1986), 55; Linda L. Sturtz, *Within Her Power: Propertied Women in Colonial Virginia* (2002), 58–59, 62–70.

Linda L. Sturtz

COOPER, Thomas (d. by 13 February 1796), member of the Convention of 1788, was born probably in the 1730s or early in the 1740s, possibly in North Carolina. Poorly documented family histories suggest that he may have been the son of Benjamin Cooper and Elizabeth Kelly Cooper, natives of Pennsylvania who moved to Virginia in the 1720s and later to Kentucky. It is more likely that he was one of a trio of men who bought and sold land between 1765 and 1774 in the western part of Halifax County, which became Pittsylvania County in 1767 and Henry County a decade later. The others were Joseph Cooper and Thomas Cooper Sr., the latter of whom was identified in some documents as a resident of Virginia and in others recorded at different times as a resident of North Carolina. One of them may have been the father of the man who in the record of those property transfers was called Thomas Cooper Jr.

Cooper married Sarah Anthony, possibly on 6 February 1762. They had five daughters and at least four sons. During the mid-1770s Cooper acquired 1,163 acres of land near Beaver Creek in Henry County, where Cooper's Creek and Cooper's mill were then recognized landmarks and where the two Thomas Coopers had owned land previously. Another man of the same name also lived in Henry County and was a soldier during part of the Revolutionary War. His relationship to Cooper is not documented, but his presence and army career further confused the family history and led to incorrect assertions that Cooper was an army officer during the American Revolution. Neither Cooper nor his namesake son, who was probably too young to participate in the war, served in the army, and it is not certain that either ever became an officer in the county militia. The county court appointed

Cooper an overseer of the poor in 1783, and five years later he became a justice of the peace. A prosperous but not a wealthy man, he paid taxes on eight slaves in 1782 and owned seven horses and thirty-one cattle in that year. During that decade he nearly doubled his landholdings.

In 1787 Cooper was a candidate for one of the two seats in the House of Delegates representing Henry County. The election was held at the courthouse on 9 April 1787 and irregularly held open for a time on the following day. When the sheriff finally closed the poll, John Marr had 223 votes, Abraham Penn 220, and Thomas Cooper 217, but the eligibility of more than 40 voters was disputed. At the assembly session that autumn, Penn requested that a committee investigate, and on 26 October 1787 the House declared that Cooper had been legally elected and should be seated in place of Penn. The following day the Speaker appointed "Mr. *Cowper*" to the Committee of Claims. Reelected in each of the succeeding three years, Cooper received no appointment to a standing committee in 1788 or 1789, but in 1790 he was a member of the Committees of Claims, of Propositions and Grievances, and for Religion.

In March 1788 Cooper was one of two men elected to represent Henry County in the convention called for June to consider the proposed constitution of the United States. He did not speak during the debates and left only his roll-call record as evidence of his opinions. Cooper voted on 25 June to require amendment of the Constitution before ratification, and after that motion failed he voted against ratification. He supported a proposal to reduce the taxing power of Congress. His record matched that of nearly every other delegate from the southern Piedmont and was consistent also with that of all the delegates from the neighboring North Carolina counties at the first ratification convention held in that state the following month.

In 1790 and 1791 Cooper sold more than 1,600 acres of his Henry County property, including the mill. He purchased at least two tracts containing a total of 575 acres of land and possibly another with 287 1/2 acres in the portion of Greene County, Georgia, that in 1793 became Hancock County, near where one or more of his

sons and members of his wife's family had already settled. Cooper moved there probably in 1791, acquired an additional 1,130 acres, and in 1793 sold the remaining 656 acres of his Virginia holdings. Thomas Cooper died in Hancock County, Georgia, on an unrecorded date before 13 February 1796, when his will was proved in the Hancock County Court. He was buried probably on his land in that county.

Inaccurate and internally inconsistent family history in Murphy Rowe Cooper, *The Cooper Family History and Genealogy, 1681–1931* (1931), 3–5, 8–9, 89–90, 98–100; undocumented birth year of 1733 in Mark Cooper Pope III and J. Donald McKee, *Mark Anthony Cooper, the Iron Man of Georgia: A Biography* (2000), 2–3, 6–7; marriage date in *VMHB* 9 (1901–1902): 220, 328–331, citing family Bible records; identity of wife apparently verified in Henry Co. Will Book, 1:120–121; numerous references in deed books of Pittsylvania Co. (1767–1774), Henry Co. (1777–1793), and Greene Co., Ga. (1791–1793); Land Tax Returns, Henry Co. (1782–1791), and Personal Property Tax Returns, Henry Co. (1782–1790), both RG 48, LVA; 1787 election poll recorded on six unnumbered pages at back of Henry Co. Deed Book, vol. 3; *JHD*, Oct. 1787 sess., 11–14 (quotation on 14); Kaminski, *Ratification*, 10:1539, 1541, 1557, 1565; brief credit report (ca. 1800–1803) in PRO T 79/87, 33; will, estate inventory, and accounts in Hancock Co., Ga., Miscellaneous Estate Records, A:82–84, and Book AA:40–41, 105–108.

BRENT TARTER

COOPER, William Edward (16 February 1909–13 February 1987), forester, was born in Youngsville, Franklin County, North Carolina, and was the son of Edward A. Cooper and Lola Cooper (whose maiden name is unknown). His family moved several times during his early years, to Missouri, to Georgia, and back to North Carolina, before they settled in Kane, Pennsylvania, where Cooper graduated from high school in 1927. He later credited his lifelong interest in forestry to growing up in the timberland area of Kane, near what became Allegheny National Forest. Cooper entered the Pennsylvania State Forest Academy at Mont Alto, in Franklin County. After his first year the school merged with Pennsylvania State College (later Pennsylvania State University), and Cooper, along with many other members of his class, transferred to the forestry program at North Carolina State College of Agriculture and Engineering (later North Carolina State University). He graduated with a B.S.

in forestry in 1932. He married Vivian Shaw, a resident of Raleigh, North Carolina, in July 1934 in Gettysburg, Pennsylvania. They had one son.

It was difficult to find forestry work during the early years of the Great Depression, and Cooper worked for about a year as a telegraph lineman and toy salesman until the creation of the Civilian Conservation Corps in 1933. Soon employed as a forester with the Pennsylvania Department of Forests and Waters at a camp in Potter County, he subsequently served as a subdistrict forester for the Tennessee Valley Authority in Florence and Huntsville, Alabama, and then worked for the United States Forest Service in Lufkin and San Augustine, Texas. In 1938 Cooper moved to South Carolina, where for the next eight years he held a series of increasingly responsible forester positions in several federal and state agencies and ultimately served as assistant state forester overseeing public relations and forest management.

On 1 May 1946 Cooper became executive director of Virginia Forests, Incorporated (later the Virginia Forestry Association), a nonprofit organization headquartered in Richmond and dedicated to conserving, developing, and protecting the forest resources of Virginia. James Leonidas Camp (1895–1983), a lumber and paper manufacturer, and others who recognized the need to conserve the state's forests and to ensure a continuing supply of pine and hardwoods had established the organization of farmers, foresters, landowners, lumbermen, paper companies, and furniture manufacturers in 1943. When Cooper took the position, Virginia Forests had only seventy-eight members and a budget of less than $10,000. Under his leadership it expanded rapidly and by 1956 boasted more than 700 members and a $40,000 annual budget.

One of Cooper's first actions as director was to begin publishing *Virginia Forests*, the organization's official journal for which he served as editor and principal writer. Originally published six times a year, the periodical became a quarterly in 1958 and in the spring of 1966 began appearing under the title *Virginia Forests Magazine*. In the 1946 premier issue Cooper described the goals of the organization: to develop a unified forestry program for Virginia, to strengthen existing state forestry agencies, to obtain industry and landowner cooperation, to publicize the value of the forests, to secure better cutting practices, to enact supporting legislation, to prevent forest wildfires, to improve game resources, to reforest idle acres, and to educate youth. As longtime editor of *Virginia Forests Magazine* Cooper published articles on all aspects of Virginia forestry and tirelessly promoted the organization's objectives.

During Cooper's tenure as executive director, Virginia Forests became one of the most active forestry associations in the country. He organized and promoted many programs and projects to raise public awareness of forest conservation issues. His most notable efforts included Keep Virginia Green, a program that featured an annual statewide poster contest for school-age children and the distribution of millions of bookcovers featuring those posters; Plant More Trees, a project that resulted in 96 million seedlings being planted in the state from 1955 to 1957; and the establishment of the Virginia Forests Educational Fund, a permanent endowment that provided money for the organization's educational activities and for freshman forestry scholarships.

Cooper was a senior member of the Society of American Foresters and chaired its Appalachian section in 1974. A charter member of the Council of Forestry Association Executives (by 1965 the National Council of Forestry Association Executives), he served as president from 1952 to 1953 and again from 1966 to 1967 and as vice president for the 1955–1956, 1956–1957, and 1965–1966 terms. Cooper was governor of the Civitan International's Chesapeake district, comprising clubs in Maryland, New Jersey, Pennsylvania, Virginia, and Washington, D.C., in 1959 and 1960 and also helped to establish the organization's newsletter, the *Chesapeake Pilot*. He retired from Virginia Forests and from editing *Virginia Forests Magazine* on 30 June 1974. William Edward Cooper died in a Richmond hospital on 13 February 1987 and was buried in Forest Lawn Cemetery, in Henrico County.

Autobiography with birth date in *Virginia Forests* 2 (Nov./Dec. 1947): 5 (por.), 13; family information provided by son, William Edward Cooper Jr. (2003); feature article in *Richmond News Leader*, 16 July 1959; major publications include Cooper, "Virginia Stands Out in Practice of Good Forestry," *Commonwealth* 16 (June 1949): 41, 106–107, 109, and "Virginia Forests, Inc.—and how it grew!" *Virginia Forests Magazine* 22 (winter 1967–1968): 8–26, ibid. 23 (spring 1968): 16–24, ibid. 23 (summer 1968): 12–22, ibid. 23 (fall 1968): 10–14, ibid. 23 (winter 1968–1969): 14–15, 20–24, ibid. 24 (spring 1969): 12–16; *Virginia Forests* 1 (Sept./Oct. 1946): 2; *Virginia Forests Magazine* 29 (spring/summer 1974): 10–11, 22; obituaries in *Richmond News Leader* and *Richmond Times-Dispatch*, both 14 Feb. 1987; memorial in *Virginia Forests Magazine* 43 (spring 1987): 25–26 (por.).

Jo L. Byrd

COOPER, William Mason (22 November 1892–12 August 1979), educator, was born in Elizabeth City County and was the son of William Cooper, a merchant and fisherman, and Mittie Ann Mason Cooper, a secretary for the Hampton division of the Grand Fountain United Order of True Reformers, an African American mutual-benefit association. After attending a private school for two years, he enrolled in a school operated by Hampton Normal and Agricultural Institute (beginning in July 1930 Hampton Institute and after 1984 Hampton University). Cooper entered Hampton as a freshman in September 1908. He became secretary of his senior class, completed his coursework with a tinsmith certificate in 1912, and graduated on 28 May 1913 with a teaching diploma.

Cooper served as principal of Vineland School in Whiteville, North Carolina, from 1913 to 1916 and as principal of Smithfield Training School (later Johnston County Training School), also in North Carolina, from 1916 to 1923. He remained in North Carolina as director of extension at an Elizabeth City normal school (later Elizabeth City State University) from 1925 until 1928 and then as dean of instruction at that institution during the 1928–1929 academic year. Concurrently he continued his studies at Teachers College, Columbia University, where he received bachelor's and master's degrees in education in 1925 and 1929, respectively, and began working toward a doctorate.

In the autumn of 1929 Cooper returned to Virginia and joined the faculty of Hampton Normal and Agricultural Institute as director of its reorganized Extension Department, an adult education service that provided classes for teachers;

assisted communities in securing funds for buildings, textbooks, and transportation; obtained teaching materials for distribution to localities; and worked with businesses to develop jobs for African Americans. The department also established garden clubs throughout the state to beautify homes, churches, schools, and neighborhoods. Cooper sought to improve interracial cooperation through scheduling conferences and special programs featuring speakers and musical performances. He edited *Virginia's Contribution to Negro Leadership* (1937) and the *Directory of Negro Businesses in Virginia* (1940), both published by the Extension Department.

From 1939 until 1952 Cooper added the directorship of the summer school program to his other responsibilities at Hampton Institute. He became the college's registrar in 1950 and then in 1955 an assistant in the public relations office. Cooper left Hampton in 1958 to serve as associate professor of guidance and placement at the Norfolk Division of Virginia State College (later Norfolk State University). There he directed a successful training program early in the 1960s. Unskilled black laborers received a stipend while they learned such trades as automotive mechanics, electronics, and masonry. He retired in 1973.

Throughout his administrative career Cooper also led various community, state, and national associations relating to African American adult education. During his years in North Carolina he helped blacks register to vote, and from 1914 to 1924 he promoted community extension and in-service training programs. In 1935 Cooper chaired the Virginia Better Homes Committee for Negroes and also served on the executive committee of the Virginia Commission on Interracial Cooperation. That year the Federal Emergency Relief Administration appointed him as a district supervisor of adult education for African Americans, responsible for organizing adult classes in twenty eastern Virginia counties. Under the auspices of the United States Office of Education in 1936 he surveyed Virginia's black vocational education programs.

Cooper was the only African American included on the *Richmond Times-Dispatch*'s inaugural New Year's Day Honor Roll in 1938. Later that year he helped organize and host at Hampton a three-day conference on "Adult Education and the Negro." Cooper served as executive secretary of the Negro Organization Society of Virginia in 1930s and 1940s and as president of the Virginia State Teachers Association from 1940 to 1942. In the latter year he became a senior field representative for the Office of War Information. He was executive secretary of the National Conference on Adult Education and the Negro by 1946, when he also served as associate director of an Office of Education project to improve literacy among adult African Americans throughout the country.

One of twenty-six members of the revived National Advisory Committee on the Education of Negroes in 1948, Cooper was also appointed to an advisory panel coordinating the country's participation in the adult education work of the United Nations Educational, Scientific, and Cultural Organization. He began serving in 1952 on the executive committee of the Adult Education Association for the United States of America. In 1961 Cooper was the first African American elected to the Hampton city school board, of which he later became vice chair. He served on Virginia's Commission on the Status of Women, which issued conservative recommendations in 1966. Schools in Clayton, North Carolina, and Hampton were named in Cooper's honor in 1940 and 1975, respectively. He also received the Hampton Institute Centennial Medallion in 1969 for his lifetime of educational service.

On 28 December 1914 in Columbia, South Carolina, Cooper married Hattie Catharine Booker, who died in April 1925. They had one daughter. He married Ednora Mae Prillerman, a West Virginia native, on 11 August 1926. She taught home economics at Hampton, and they had one son. After his second wife's death on 3 January 1960, he married Audrey Boone on 28 December 1965. William Mason Cooper died in a Hampton hospital on 12 August 1979 and was buried in the Hampton Institute Cemetery (later Hampton University Cemetery).

Biography in *Who's Who in Colored America* 7 (1950): 121–122; BVS Birth Register, Elizabeth City Co.; William Mason Cooper Student Records (including marriage dates), Hampton University Archives; family information provided by widow Audrey Boone Cooper (2004); writings include Cooper, "Hampton Institute's Work for the Masses through Its Extension Department," *Southern Workman* 67 (1938): 120–124, and presidential message in *Virginia Teachers Bulletin* 18 (Nov. 1941): 3 (por.); *Richmond Times-Dispatch*, 2 Jan. 1938; *Washington Post*, 9 Nov. 1940, 4 Nov. 1942, 8 Aug. 1946, 26 Dec. 1948, 16 Nov. 1963; *Norfolk Journal and Guide*, 23 Dec. 1961 (por.), 15 Feb. 1969; obituaries in *Newport News Daily Press* and *Newport News Times-Herald*, both 14 Aug. 1979.

VANESSA D. THAXTON-WARD

COOPER, William Pope (26 July 1825–17 September 1880), member of the third session of the Convention of 1861, was born in New York State and was the son of Enoch Cooper, a New Hampshire native, and Maranda Cooper. Details of his early life are not known. By 1850 he was living in Mifflintown, Juniata County, Pennsylvania, and was married to Margaret F. Cooper, whose maiden name is not recorded. They had four sons and three daughters.

On 1 December 1848 Cooper purchased the *Mifflintown Pennsylvania Register and Juniata Advertiser*. In his first issue, published on 2 February 1849, he declared his support for the Democratic Party. Beginning on 4 May of that year the paper appeared as the *Mifflintown Juniata Register*. Cooper published his last issue on 4 September 1851, sold the newspaper, and moved his family to Clarksburg, Virginia, where he acquired the *Clarksburg Register*. The first weekly issue of *Cooper's Clarksburg Register* appeared on 12 November of that year. His editorial announcing the new publication proclaimed the paper's allegiance to the Democratic Party and praised the recently ratified state constitution, particularly its adoption of universal white manhood suffrage. Despite the failures of previous attempts to establish newspapers in Clarksburg and predictions that his own efforts would go unrewarded, the *Register* prospered and a year later moved its offices into a new brick building. Cooper acquired a partner in 1857 and continued to publish the *Register* until the beginning of the Civil War.

In 1853 Cooper became a charter member of the Mechanics Association of Clarksburg and helped draft its constitution and bylaws. He was elected one of Clarksburg's trustees on 30 June 1856 and from that group was chosen the town president (a designation later changed to mayor).

On 27 August 1857 Cooper won election as clerk of the Harrison County Court. He ran for the office again in May 1858 but lost by six votes and contested the result. Another election was scheduled, and during the interim he was appointed clerk pro tempore. A rancorous campaign ensued, pitting Democrats against American (Know Nothing) Party adherents. Despite the efforts of former governor Joseph Johnson to rally support for Cooper, he was again defeated, this time by a larger margin. In November 1858 Harrison County Democrats met to select delegates to the party's convention in Petersburg. Cooper served as secretary and then attended the December gathering that nominated candidates for the upcoming statewide elections. As the likelihood of war increased, he and other Clarksburg secessionists began conducting military drills in January 1861, and he was elected lieutenant of the volunteer unit.

On 17 April 1861 the state convention meeting in Richmond voted to secede from the Union. In Clarksburg on 26 April, Cooper served as a secretary for a gathering of secessionists who applauded the actions of the convention and decried Abraham Lincoln as a military despot. Late in May, Cooper led Harrison County volunteers to a rendezvous with other troops sympathetic to the Southern cause, after which he and his men were organized as Company C in what soon became the 31st Regiment Virginia Infantry. He was promoted to first lieutenant on 1 July 1861. During the next six months his regiment took part in operations in the Allegheny Mountains, including the failed Cheat Mountain campaign in September.

In June 1861 the state convention in Richmond expelled twelve northwestern delegates who had opposed disunion and had abandoned their seats. The governor ordered special elections to be held at military encampments to fill these vacancies. On 24 October 1861 Cooper, standing unopposed for the Harrison County seat forfeited by John Snyder Carlile, received all forty-three votes cast by his regiment at Camp Bartow, in Pocahontas County. He took his seat in the third session of the convention on 20 November 1861. Before the session concluded on 6 December, Cooper signed the Ordinance of Secession.

After the close of the convention, Cooper returned to his regiment. He became a captain on 1 May 1862, and in the ensuing weeks the 31st Virginia suffered heavy casualties in Major General Thomas J. "Stonewall" Jackson's Valley campaign. Cooper won promotion to major on 5 December 1863, to rank from 1 August of that year. Twice wounded, he commanded the 31st Virginia on several occasions, including at Appomattox Court House when the regiment surrendered its arms. He led the remnants of his command back through the mountains to West Virginia, where in Clarksburg on 14 June 1865 he signed the loyalty oath.

Remaining in Clarksburg after the war, Cooper had by 9 March 1866 established the *Clarksburg Conservative*, a newspaper in which he routinely sparred with the Republican editors of the *Clarksburg Weekly National Telegraph*. He had sold the paper by 11 September 1868, and by July 1870 he had moved his family to Parkersburg, where he continued to work as a publisher and printer. Within four years Cooper was residing in Marion County, where on 21 February 1874 he published the first issue of the *Fairmont Index*. A fire destroyed much of his office in 1876, and he sold what little survived of the paper.

William Pope Cooper died at his Fairmont residence on 17 September 1880 and was buried in Fairmont Cemetery. His remains and those of his wife, who died in April 1881, were moved to Woodlawn Cemetery, in Fairmont, on 31 August 1913.

Birth and death dates in Kathleen Mahaffey Bogdan, comp., *Marion County Death Records: Fairmont, West Virginia* (1985), 3:74 (giving age at death as fifty-five years, one month, and twenty-three days); George A. Dunnington, *History and Progress of the County of Marion, West Virginia* (1880), 108–109; Dorothy Davis, *History of Harrison County, West Virginia* (1970), 173–174, 184, 219, 287, 825, 830; Harrison Co. Order Book (1857), 153, and (1858), 127, 129; *Mifflintown Pennsylvania Register and Juniata Advertiser*, 2 Feb. 1849; *Cooper's Clarksburg Register*, 12 Nov. 1851, 6 July, 3 Nov. 1853, 9 May, 4 July 1856, 4 June, 23 July, 13 Aug., 10 Sept., 12 Nov. 1858; *Clarksburg Conservative*, 9 Mar. 1866; *Clarksburg Weekly National Telegraph*, 11 Sept. 1868; *Fairmont Index*, 21 Feb. 1874; Election Records, Convention of 1861, RG 93, LVA; Reese, *Journals and Papers of 1861 Convention*, 1:334, 336; Compiled Service Records; John M. Ashcraft, *31st Virginia Infantry* (1988), 122; death notice in *Morgantown Weekly Post*, 9 Oct. 1880 (reporting death "last week").

Donald W. Gunter

COPELAND, Joseph (d. after 22 April 1691), pewterer, was born probably in London late in the 1640s or early in the 1650s. His father, Thomas Copeland, was a London spectacle-maker. It is possible but not certain that he was the Joseph Copeland, a son of Thomas Copeland and Anne Copeland, who was born in the parish of Saint Gregory by Saint Paul's on 15 February 1649 and baptized at Saint Augustine Watling Street, in London, on 18 February of that year. According to records of the Worshipful Company of Pewterers, on 17 May 1666 Copeland was apprenticed to John Mann for seven years. There is no record that Copeland took his freedom in the company, action required of those wishing to practice the craft in England. He may have sailed for Virginia, where he could work without restriction, soon after completing his apprenticeship in 1673. Copeland had settled in the colony in Isle of Wight County by 1675. He may have been a nephew or other close relation of John Copeland, an emigrant from Yorkshire who was a landowner in Isle of Wight County and a prominent member of the Chuckatuck Friends Meeting.

Copeland was the first documented practicing pewtersmith in Virginia. (An earlier pewterer, John Lathbury, died in 1655 shortly after arriving in the colony and is not known to have practiced his trade there.) A soft alloy mostly of tin and lead, pewter was a mark of gentility in colonial America that could be reused and refashioned into newer forms. During excavation of the site of Jamestown in the mid-1930s, archaeologists recovered in the area of Structure 21, a frame cottage with brick foundation, a spoon bowl and a trifid spoon handle with Copeland's touchmark, reading "Ioseph Copeland / 1675 / Chuckatuck." That inscription makes the spoon handle the earliest datable surviving piece of Virginia-made pewter. As a result of the discovery, similar examples found in the vicinity are often designated Copeland or Chuckatuck spoons. The estate of Nicholas Smith, of Isle of Wight County, inventoried on 5 June 1696, included "6 doz: of Virginia pewter spoons," a tantalizing hint that perhaps Copeland filled orders for patrons.

On an unrecorded date Copeland married a woman named Mary, maiden name unknown, whose death on 27 May 1678 the Chuckatuck Friends Meeting recorded. On 18 January 1685 "Joseph Copeland Pewterer," of Isle of Wight County, purchased 150 acres in Surry County for £50 sterling. Among the witnesses to the deed, recorded on 4 May 1686, was Thomas Taberer, whose daughter Elizabeth Taberer became Copeland's second wife, although the date of their marriage is not known. They had several children, at least one of them a son. Copeland may also have owned land in James City County; a land patent dated 21 April 1690 describes property in that county granted to William Edwards as bounded from "Joseph Copelands Great Gum on James river side." On 12 May 1688 the House of Burgesses entrusted "the Severall utensills & Ornaments belonging to this house" to Copeland for cleaning and safekeeping. He submitted a petition on 22 April 1691 seeking payment for his work as custodian.

There is no record of Joseph Copeland, pewterer, after 22 April 1691. Most likely he died between that date and 14 January 1692, when his father-in-law wrote a will that bequeathed property to Copeland's minor namesake son but allowed the child's uncle free use of the estate until he came of age. When Copeland's namesake son died in 1726, the inventory of his Isle of Wight County estate included a pair of "old Spoon Molds" and thirty-eight and a half pounds of pewter, perhaps remnants of his father's craft.

Birth date and baptism in Saint Augustine Watling Street Parish Records, confirmed by Guildhall Library, London; Worth Bailey, "Joseph Copeland, 17th-Century Pewterer," *Antiques* 33 (Apr. 1938): 188–190 (including photographs of spoon fragments and touchmark); Bailey, "Notes on the Use of Pewter in Virginia during the Seventeenth Century," *WMQ*, 2d ser., 18 (1938): 227–241; John L. Cotter, *Archeological Excavations at Jamestown, Colonial National Historical Park and Jamestown National Historic Site, Virginia* (1958), 59, 189; Ledlie Irwin Laughlin, *Pewter in America: Its Makers and Their Marks* (1969), 70–73; Charles F. Montgomery, *A History of American Pewter* (1973), 158, 161, 218; Nicholas Smith's estate inventory in Isle of Wight Co. Will Book, 2:358–364 (first quotation); Surry Co. Deeds, Wills, Etc., 3: fols. 50–51 (second quotation); Land Office Patent Book, 8:42 (third quotation); *JHB, 1659/1660–1693*, 325 (fourth quotation), 340 (last record); father-in-law's will, proved 9 Feb. 1694, in Isle of Wight Co. Will Book, 2:350–354; son's will and estate inventory in Isle of Wight Co. Will Book, 3:8–10, 62–63 (fifth quotation).

BARBARA C. BATSON

COPELAND, Walter Scott (14 March 1856–24 July 1928), journalist, was born in Jackson, North Carolina, and was the son of a physician, Winfield Scott Copeland, and Katharine E. Randolph Copeland. After receiving his early education at a Jackson academy, he attended the University of Virginia from 1874 to 1876 but left without receiving a degree.

Copeland began his newspaper career with the *Petersburg Index-Appeal* before moving to the *Norfolk Virginian*, of which he was city editor. He established the *Petersburg Mail* early in 1883 and ran it for approximately a year. In 1884 Richard Lewellen sold Copeland an interest in the *Danville Register*. After the deaths of Lewellen in 1886 and his wife in 1887, Copeland and two partners assumed full ownership of the Danville newspaper. From December 1888 to March 1890 Copeland and one of his partners also owned the *Roanoke Times*. He remained associated with the renamed *Danville Daily Register*, for much of the time as editor, until about 1893, when he sold his stake in the paper and moved to Richmond in time to play a leading role in the consolidation of that city's newspaper business. He purchased an interest in the *Richmond State* but sold it in 1896 and joined the editorial staff of the *Richmond Times*. Copeland helped owner Joseph Bryan establish the *Evening Leader* as an afternoon companion to the *Times* and became editor of the evening paper in 1897 while still working on the morning paper. In 1901 and 1902 Copeland participated in negotiations that culminated in the merger of four Richmond newspapers into one morning newspaper, the *Richmond Times-Dispatch*, and one afternoon paper, the *Richmond News Leader*. In January 1903 he became the first editor of the *Times-Dispatch*.

Copeland married Mary Augustina Christian, of Petersburg, on 13 October 1885. They had one daughter before his wife's death in 1902. On 25 April 1906 he married Grace Beale Cunningham, of Richmond. They had one daughter and one son. Copeland resigned as chief editorial writer of the *Times-Dispatch* in 1908 and purchased the *Newport News Times-Herald*. Three years later he added the *Newport News Daily Press* to his holdings and by 1913

was president of the Daily Press, Incorporated, and editor and publisher of both newspapers. Held in high esteem by his journalistic peers, he served four terms as president of the Virginia Press Association, in 1902, 1906, 1907, and 1925.

While in Richmond, Copeland aligned himself with the city's leading Progressive-era reformers. He worked throughout the first decade of the twentieth century to improve educational and welfare institutions in the city and the state. To that end, Copeland lent personal and editorial support to the Co-Operative Education Association of Virginia, the Richmond Education Association, the Southern Education Board, and the Virginia Conference of Charities and Corrections. In particular, he supported increased state funding for education, longer school terms, creation of school libraries, compulsory attendance laws, and enhanced state involvement in the running of charities, asylums, prisons, and reformatories. Like his colleagues on these boards, Copeland approached reform from an essentially paternalistic and conservative point of view, envisioning it as necessary for social peace and stability.

Although reform advocates such as Copeland recognized the necessity of improving the lives of black Virginians, educational and welfare improvements in the state accrued disproportionately to white Virginians. Progressivism was, in this sense, for whites only. Nevertheless, some of Copeland's editorial stances dovetailed with the interests of black citizens. When the Ku Klux Klan made inroads in the 1920s, Copeland denounced the organization and supported a city-wide ban on the wearing of masks in public. In addition, he served for about a decade as a state curator for land-grant funds at Hampton Normal and Agricultural Institute (later Hampton University). In that capacity he and his wife regularly came into contact with the students and faculty of the school, particularly at commencement exercises and entertainment functions.

One such performance led to a series of events that sullied Copeland's legacy in later years. In February 1925 his wife attended a dance recital at Hampton's Ogden Hall. Arriving late and unaccompanied by her husband, she was seated next to a group of black patrons. Three weeks later, Copeland launched a blistering attack on Hampton officials in which he accused them of teaching and practicing social equality between the white and black races. The school denied the charges and insisted that seating practices at Ogden Hall did not promote social equality. Copeland's diatribe particularly shocked the editor of the state's largest black newspaper, Plummer Bernard Young (1884–1962), of the *Norfolk Journal and Guide*, who had considered Copeland a moderating influence in racial matters.

Copeland joined forces with John Powell, a famed composer and pianist who in 1922 helped found the Anglo-Saxon Clubs of America, a Richmond-based organization grounded in the eugenics movement and devoted to maintaining the racial and cultural purity of whites. In 1924 Powell and his supporters had persuaded the General Assembly to pass the Virginia Act to Preserve Racial Integrity, a draconian statute that prohibited whites from marrying anyone who could not prove that his or her ancestry did not include any individuals considered nonwhite. Powell remained unsatisfied and argued that only the strictest physical separation of blacks and whites would prevent racial intermixing. Fully cognizant of Copeland's standing among Virginia journalists, Powell embraced Copeland's editorial crusade against mixed seating at Hampton Institute as an opportunity to further his own agenda. For his part, Copeland enthusiastically reiterated Powell's dire message of racial vulnerability. Spurred at least in part by his wife, who was a childhood friend and admirer of Powell, Copeland used the editorial pages of his newspapers to demand that state authorities take action. In 1926 the assembly passed the so-called Massenburg Bill, a measure sponsored by Delegate George Alvin Massenburg requiring complete racial segregation in all places of public assemblage. It was the most far-reaching statute of its kind in the nation.

On 24 July 1928 Walter Scott Copeland died of heart failure at his home in Newport News. He was buried in Hollywood Cemetery, in Richmond. In 1949 his family established the W. S. Copeland Memorial Award for Community Service (later the W. S. Copeland Award for Jour-

nalistic Integrity and Community Service), the highest honor bestowed by the Virginia Press Association. In 2000, after articles in the *Richmond Times-Dispatch* chronicled for a later generation of journalists Copeland's fierce advocacy on behalf of the Massenburg Bill, the Virginia Press Association removed his name from the award.

Birth date in Copeland family Bible records, VHS; BVS Marriage Register, Petersburg (1885) and Richmond City (1906); Walter Scott Copeland Papers, UVA; Richard B. Sherman, "The 'Teachings at Hampton Institute': Social Equality, Racial Integrity, and the Virginia Public Assemblage Act of 1926," *VMHB* 95 (1987): 275–300; Sherman, "'The Last Stand': The Fight for Racial Integrity in Virginia in the 1920s," *JSH* 54 (1988): 69–92; J. Douglas Smith, *Managing White Supremacy: Race, Politics, and Citizenship in Jim Crow Virginia* (2002), chap. 4; *Richmond Times-Dispatch*, 23 July 2000; BVS Death Certificate, Newport News; obituaries (all with pors.) in *Newport News Daily Press*, *Newport News Times-Herald*, *Richmond News Leader*, and *Richmond Times-Dispatch*, all 25 July 1928; editorial tributes in *Richmond News Leader*, 25 July 1928, *Richmond Times-Dispatch*, 26 July 1928, and *Bulletin of the Virginia Press Association* (Aug. 1928), 6–7.

J. DOUGLAS SMITH

COPENHAVER, Laura Lu Scherer (29 August 1868–18 December 1940), Lutheran lay leader and founder of Rosemont Industries, was born in Columbus, Texas, and was the daughter of John Jacob Scherer (1830–1919), a native Virginian and Lutheran minister, and Elizabeth Katharine Killinger Scherer. Her siblings included John Jacob Scherer (1881–1956), a Lutheran minister and president of the Virginia Synod. The family returned to southwestern Virginia in 1871, and two years later her father founded Marion Female College (later Marion College), in Smyth County. At about age ten Laura Scherer began teaching Sunday school classes and was soon writing plays that the college produced. She graduated from Marion Female College in 1884 and two years later joined the faculty. For more than twenty years Scherer taught English and occasionally courses in mathematics and astronomy. On 26 August 1895 she married Bascom Eugene Copenhaver, who for many years served as the superintendent of Smyth County schools. They had four daughters and one son.

Copenhaver wrote fiction, poetry, and dozens of pageants for the United Lutheran Church in

America (later the Evangelical Lutheran Church in America), which by the first decade of the twentieth century had begun publishing her work. Many of the pageants, such as *The Striking of America's Hour: A Pageant of Christian Liberty* (1919), *The Way: A Pageant of Japan* (1923), and *The Way of Peace: A Pageant* (1924), she wrote in collaboration with her younger sister, Katharine Killinger Scherer Cronk, also a prominent Lutheran lay leader. One of Copenhaver's poems, "Heralds of Christ," was set to music and became a well-known hymn included in various denominational hymnals.

Interested in missionary work since her childhood, Copenhaver became a member of the executive committee of the Women's Home and Foreign Missionary Society of the Evangelical Lutheran Synod of Southwestern Virginia in 1916. By the summer of 1920 she had been elected to fill an unexpired term on the Literature Committee of the Women's Missionary Society of the United Lutheran Church in America. The committee published periodicals, textbooks, devotional booklets, and other materials for distribution throughout the country. Elected chair in 1928, she remained in that office after the committee became the Education Department in 1937.

On 27 September 1922 Copenhaver addressed the biennial convention of the Women's Missionary Society on the need to minister to the people of Appalachia. Her speech inspired the society to create a committee to conduct mission work in southwestern Virginia. Also as a result of her efforts, the Women's Missionary Society established the Konnarock Training School, which opened in Smyth County in 1925. A public elementary school with a private boarding division, it provided academic and religious education as well as practical training for boys and girls who did not have access to other public schools. Copenhaver continued giving lectures and attending Lutheran and interdenominational missionary conferences around the country during the 1920s and 1930s.

In addition to her teaching and missionary work, Copenhaver advocated strategies for developing the region's agricultural economy. By the spring of 1921 she had joined the Marion-based Virginia Farm Bureau Federation as its director of information. Copenhaver addressed farmers' meetings on such topics as improving the financial conditions of family farms and developing rural churches, homes, and schools. At the annual meeting of the Southwest Virginia Cooperative Exchange in December 1922 she emphasized the importance of cooperative marketing of farm products in order to improve the standard of living for farm families.

Copenhaver had already begun practicing such cooperative strategies by facilitating the production of textiles out of her home, Rosemont. She hired women to produce coverlets based on traditional patterns and using local wool. What became known as Rosemont Industries advertised in national newspapers and women's magazines and expanded its offerings to include a wide variety of rugs, bed canopies and fringes, and other household items. The women themselves created some of the designs, while they adapted others from antique rugs, paintings, and even designs Copenhaver copied from the Metropolitan Museum of Art. Although many of the items were hand-woven, -knitted, or -crocheted, others were manufactured on machines operated by men. Copenhaver was primarily concerned that Rosemont produce textiles "worth owning" while also providing women with profitable employment. Rosemont's textiles quickly became popular around the country and also attracted customers from Asia, Europe, and South America.

Recognized for her civic work, Copenhaver was encouraged to become a candidate for the House of Representatives early in the 1920s, after women gained the right to vote. Writing anonymously in the November 1922 issue of *Atlantic Monthly*, she contemplated the idea but decided that she could not leave her family for politics. Copenhaver had a lifelong interest in education and in 1925 served on the district committee for southwestern Virginia in a statewide campaign emphasizing improvements in education. She was also active in such organizations as the Marion Woman's Club, of which she served as president in 1926.

About this time Copenhaver met the writer Sherwood Anderson, who had recently settled in the area and acquired two Marion newspapers. They became close friends, and until her death he often turned to her as a critic and editor of his work. Through this friendship he met and in 1933 married her eldest daughter, Eleanor Gladys Copenhaver, a leader of the Young Women's Christian Association. Copenhaver continued to write. Her work appeared in such periodicals as *Scribner's Magazine*, which in June 1928 published her article on Elizabeth Henry Campbell Russell, a Methodist lay leader.

During the last several years of her life Copenhaver suffered increasingly poor health. She fretted to her son-in-law that a fulsome 1937 biography written for the Works Progress Administration made her sound like a "smug uplifter," and she hoped it would be "buried for good." Laura Lu Scherer Copenhaver died at Rosemont on 18 December 1940. She was buried in Round Hill Cemetery, in Marion. Her sister, Minerva May Scherer, longtime dean of Marion College, headed Rosemont Industries for two decades. In September 1960 some of Copenhaver's children incorporated the business as Laura Copenhaver Industries, Inc., which continued to manufacture traditional textiles into the twenty-first century.

Birth date on BVS Death Certificate, Smyth Co., in undated letter from sister Minerva May Scherer in Copenhaver materials, ULCA Biographical Files, Evangelical Lutheran Church in America Archives, Elk Grove Village, Ill., and in Hilbert H. Campbell, ed., *The Sherwood Anderson Diaries, 1936–1941* (1987), 316 (entry for 29 Aug. 1940); variant birth date of 28 Aug. 1868 in Mildred Manton Copenhaver and Robert Madison Copenhaver Jr., comps., *The Copenhaver Family of Smyth County, Virginia* (1981), 107; WPA Biographies; some biographical material in Sue Ruffin Tyler research assembled for "The Women of Virginia" project, Tyler Family Papers Group D, W&M; Smyth Co. Marriage Register; correspondence in Sherwood Anderson Papers, Newberry Library, Chicago (including second and third quotations in Copenhaver to Anderson, n.d., but after Sept. 1937); *Marion News*, 19 Oct., 21 Dec. 1922; *Marion Democrat*, 17 Jan. 1928; *Marion Smyth County News*, 19 Jan. 1928; Anne Ruffin Sims, "Rosemont Workers," *Commonwealth* 4 (Feb. 1937): 12–13 (first quotation); [Laura Copenhaver], *Rosemont: Marion, Virginia* (n.d.); Thomas W. West, *Marion College, 1873–1967* (1970), 22 (por.), 29–30; Margaret Ripley Wolfe, "Sherwood Anderson and the Southern Highlands: A Sense of Place and the Sustenance of Women," *Southern Studies*, new ser., 3 (1992): 253–275; James E. Gay, *Konnarock Training School: Its Spirit Lives On* (1998), 4–5, 31; obituaries in *New York Times, Richmond News Leader, Richmond Times-Dispatch,* and *Marion Smyth County News,* all 19 Dec. 1940; tribute in *Lutheran Woman's Work* 34 (1941): 38 (por.).

MARIANNE E. JULIENNE

COPPAGE, Samuel Francis (25 January 1886–26 February 1977), civic leader and civil rights activist, was born in Perquimans County, North Carolina, and was the son of John T. Coppage and Letitia Nixon Coppage, both former slaves. In 1892 the family moved to Norfolk, where his father worked as a jack-of-all-trades and his mother as a seamstress. Frank Coppage, as he was usually known, graduated from Norfolk Mission College, the only area high school for African Americans, in 1909. Fired from his job waiting tables at a whites-only club after announcing his intention to become a dentist, he nevertheless enrolled in the dental school at Howard University, where he played quarterback on the football team and received a D.D.S. in 1912. Coppage married Eunice Marion Ganey, a Norfolk native, on 18 June 1914, but she died on 5 September 1916 during childbirth, along with their only child. On 28 December 1943 he married Constance Elizabeth Jordan. They had one son.

Coppage established a dental practice in Norfolk that lasted more than sixty years. In 1913 he helped organize the Old Dominion Dental Society and in 1927 served as its president. Initially Coppage shared offices with two other physicians, but soon he moved to another location where as part of his practice he conducted a free clinic for needy children. The city of Norfolk later took over the service. Many of Norfolk's black residents lived in dilapidated rental housing in overcrowded, segregated neighborhoods. The city provided few services and no access to libraries, parks, and other recreational facilities. Coppage numbered among the young educated African Americans who recognized the need for local voluntary organizations to provide resources for the black community.

As a member of the Tidewater Colored Hospital Association, Coppage in 1915 helped establish the twelve-bed Tidewater Hospital, Norfolk's first hospital devoted to the care of, and staffed by, African Americans. It became Drake Memorial Hospital, in honor of one of its deceased founders, in 1930 and two years later was renamed Norfolk Community Hospital and expanded to a thirty-bed facility. In 1939 it reopened on Corprew Avenue in a new sixty-five-bed building funded through the Public Works Act. Coppage sat on the hospital's board of directors and executive committee and at one time served as its president.

During World War I, Coppage chaired the Liberty Club Committee, affiliated with the federal War Camp Community Service, and also served as committee chair of the Red Circle Clubs, which provided reading materials to servicemen. As secretary of one of the Norfolk draft boards during World War II, he refused to forward draft names unless the other board members treated black and white medical and dental students equally. Coppage worked with other African American leaders to pressure the city to provide a United Service Organizations club for black servicemen. He strongly supported associations dedicated to providing recreational and educational programs, including the Norfolk Sports Club and the local African American chapters of the Boy Scouts of America and of the Young Men's Christian Association. Beginning in 1951 Coppage was president for many years of the Community Boys' Club of Norfolk, Virginia, an association designed to groom young African American men for future leadership in civic affairs.

Along with other prominent black leaders, Coppage protested racial discrimination and segregation through helping to found the Virginia Conference of the National Association for the Advancement of Colored People. He was treasurer of the state conference in 1948 and became a life member of its executive board. Although a Norfolk NAACP chapter had been established in 1917, he refused to join until the 1930s because its president, Plummer Bernard Young (1884–1962), publisher of the Norfolk Journal and Guide, pursued an accommodationist strategy rather than directly challenging racism and segregation.

Coppage served as treasurer of the Norfolk Christian Leadership Conference (formerly the Tidewater Christian Leadership Conference), an affiliate of the Southern Christian Leadership Conference. In October 1958 the Norfolk conference organized a mass meeting at which participants rededicated themselves to ending racial discrimination through nonviolent resistance. Early in the 1960s the organization challenged Norfolk Redevelopment and Housing Authority projects that replaced slums with low-rent housing, wider streets, and commercial development without providing replacement housing for many displaced residents. Under Coppage's leadership the chapter advocated eliminating the poll tax, supported the Voting Rights Act of 1965, established working relationships with local and state agencies, and brought attention to the poor conditions and lack of jobs in the city. Through the SCLC, Coppage joined the national Poor People's Campaign and in 1968 led the local affiliate in initiating its own Poor People's March in Norfolk.

Coppage was a staunch advocate of the Democratic Party after 1928. He battled segregationists in the party and as president of the Community Democratic Club of Norfolk, Virginia, Inc., during the 1940s helped bring about a realignment of precincts that increased the number of black representatives. Coppage fought against local voter apathy and worked to secure equal opportunities for all through the Virginia Citizens Political Action Committee. In 1946 he was one of the first African American delegates selected to attend the Democratic State Convention. As a member for almost twenty years of the Tidewater chapter of the Frontiers International and as its sometime president, he sought to elect politicians who supported improving conditions for African Americans in Virginia.

Coppage received citizenship and humanitarian awards from Omega Psi Phi Fraternity in 1947 and from Alpha Phi Alpha Fraternity, Inc., in 1975. The Norfolk Journal and Guide named him to its 1948 honor roll for his achievements in politics and civil rights. Despite his efforts and successes, Coppage was not optimistic that the changes wrought were more than window-dressing. In a 1971 interview he noted that conditions in Norfolk had not changed much since his arrival in 1892. Undaunted, he remained professionally and politically active in the community until the end of his life. Samuel Francis Coppage died in a Norfolk hospital on 26 February 1977 and was buried in the city's Calvary Cemetery.

Feature articles in *Norfolk Journal and Guide*, 11 Sept. 1971, and *Norfolk Virginian-Pilot*, 13 Dec. 1973 (por.); family information provided by widow Constance Jordan Coppage and son Samuel Francis Coppage Jr. (2005); Samuel Francis Coppage Papers, Virginia Black History Archives, VCU; BVS Marriage Register, Norfolk City (1914); *Norfolk Journal and Guide* (home ed.), 1 Jan. 1944, 1 Jan. 1949 (por.); obituaries in *Norfolk Virginian-Pilot*, 1 Mar. 1977, and *Norfolk Journal and Guide* and *Richmond Afro-American*, both 5 Mar. 1977.

CASSANDRA L. NEWBY-ALEXANDER

CORBIN, Francis (1759 or 1760–23 May 1821), member of the Convention of 1788, was born probably at Laneville, the King and Queen County plantation of his parents, Richard Corbin, for many years a member of the governor's Council and deputy receiver general of the colony, and Betty Tayloe Corbin, daughter of another member of the Council, John Tayloe (1687–1747). His much-older brother, Gawin Corbin, later served on the governor's Council as well, and his sister Elizabeth Corbin married Carter Braxton, who signed the Declaration of Independence. In 1773 Corbin's family sent him to England for his education. He may have attended schools at Canterbury and Cambridge, and he was admitted to study law at the Inner Temple on 23 January 1777. Unable to return home during the American Revolution, Corbin petitioned the king in 1779 for funds to pay his debts because his Loyalist father could no longer provide assistance.

After returning to Virginia in 1783, Corbin settled in Middlesex County and in the spring of 1784 was elected to represent the county in the House of Delegates. Reelected for ten consecutive one-year terms through 1794, he served on the Committee of Propositions and Grievances in 1784, 1786–1788, and 1791–1794 and chaired the committee in 1792. Corbin also sat on the Committees of Commerce (during two sessions designated the Committee of Trade) in 1784 and 1786–1788, for Courts of Justice in 1784, 1786, 1789, and 1791–1794, for Religion in 1786, of Privileges and Elections in 1787–1789 and 1791–1794, and of Claims in 1793 and 1794.

When the General Assembly met in October 1787, Corbin introduced a resolution calling for a state convention to consider ratification of the proposed constitution of the United States. After some debate a similar resolution was adopted unanimously, and the following spring Corbin was one of two delegates elected to represent Middlesex County in the convention. He served on the Committee of Privileges and Elections. A strong supporter of the Constitution, he ably supported James Madison, John Marshall, and Edmund Randolph in promoting its passage. On 7 June 1788 Corbin delivered a detailed rebuttal of Patrick Henry's objections to the Constitution. He spoke at length on the necessity of adopting a new framework for a federal government and argued that only through a strong union could the country survive. On 25 June, Corbin voted against requiring prior amendments to the Constitution and then voted with the majority to approve the Constitution, after which he was named to a five-member committee to prepare a form of ratification. Two days later he joined the minority in voting to prevent the states from limiting the taxing power of Congress. Declaring himself "no enemy to general amendments," Corbin worked to ensure that in 1791 the House of Delegates ratified the first ten amendments to the Constitution.

In January 1789 Corbin declared himself a candidate for the new House of Representatives from the Seventh District but lost to John Page (1743–1808). He also ran unsuccessfully in the congressional elections held in September 1790 and March 1793. One of three candidates in October 1792 to replace Richard Henry Lee in the United States Senate, Corbin received only about 20 percent of the votes cast in the General Assembly.

Corbin's increasingly poor health led him to move to Caroline County about 1795. Other than a quixotic attempt to curry support for the federal government during the controversy over the Alien and Sedition Acts in 1798, he retired from public life and focused on managing the Reeds, his plantation that by 1811 had expanded to more than 3,700 acres. At the time of his death Corbin was paying taxes on seventy slaves age twelve or older, but for much of his adult life he objected to slavery on both moral and economic grounds and frequently expressed anxiety about a future rupture of the Union over the issue. In 1797 he confided to his friend Madison that he was considering moving his family to Connecticut or Rhode Island as a consequence of his aversion to the institution.

Corbin was elected to the board of visitors of the College of William and Mary in 1788 and served as rector in 1790. He volunteered his services to George Washington as a secretary or regimental officer in July 1798 when it was rumored that the former president would become head of the army during the Quasi-War against France, but Washington declined his offer because Corbin lacked field experience. In April 1816 President James Madison named Corbin one of the commissioners to oversee subscriptions to constitute the capital of the Second Bank of the United States, and at the time of his death Corbin was a director of the bank's Richmond branch.

On 3 December 1795 Corbin married Ann Munford Beverley, daughter of the Essex County planter Robert Beverley (ca. 1740–1800). They had two daughters and seven sons. Francis Corbin died suddenly of gout at his Caroline County plantation on 23 May 1821 and most likely was buried there.

Biography, with erroneous death date of 18 June 1821, in *VMHB* 30 (1922): 315–318; PRO AO 13/28; Corbin correspondence in James Madison Papers, LC (including age at death of sixty-one on 23 May 1821 in son Robert B. Corbin to James Madison, 1 May [June] 1821), in Harold C. Syrett et al., eds., *The Papers of Alexander Hamilton* (1961–1987), 16:611–613, in *Madison: Congressional Series*, esp. vols. 14 and 16, and in *Washington: Retirement Series*, 2:389–391, 430–431; Kaminski, *Ratification*, esp. 8:112–115, 9:1007–1015, 10:1391–1397, 1538–1541, 1556–1557; Merrill Jensen et al., eds., *The Documentary History of the First Federal Elections: 1788–1790* (1976–1989), 2:267–269, 353–355 (quotation on 354); marriage recorded in *The Parish Register of Christ Church, Middlesex County, Va., from 1653 to 1812* (1897), 302; *Richmond Virginia Gazette, and General Advertiser*, 6 Jan. 1796; por. privately owned (2005); death notice in *Richmond Daily Mercantile Advertiser*, 25 May 1821 (died "on Tuesday last," 22 May 1821); obituary written by James Madison in *Washington Daily National Intelligencer*, 9 June 1821 (with death on 23 May 1821 at age sixty-two), reprinted in *Richmond Enquirer*, 15 June 1821.

MARY A. HACKETT

CORBIN, Gawin (15 December 1739–19 July 1779), member of the Council, was the eldest son of Betty Tayloe Corbin and Richard Corbin, later a member of the governor's Council and deputy receiver general with close ties to many of the colony's leading families. He grew up at the Laneville plantation in King and Queen County and received an education intended to prepare him to take his own place at the apex of Virginia's elite. Corbin attended a private school in England, enrolled in Christ's College, University of Cambridge, on 26 January 1756, and on 11 February of that year entered the Middle Temple to study law. He was admitted to the bar on 23 January 1761 and returned to Virginia soon thereafter. On 17 November 1762 Corbin married a cousin, Joanna Tucker, of Norfolk. They had five daughters and one son and resided at Buckingham, his paternal grandfather's plantation in Middlesex County.

Rather than practice law, Corbin became a gentleman planter. Appointed a justice of the peace soon after settling in Middlesex County, he became county lieutenant, or commander of the militia, in December 1767. He won election to the House of Burgesses in the autumn of 1764 and served through June 1770. Corbin was usually a member of the Committee of Propositions and Grievances and in May 1769 became a member of the Committee for Religion. There is no indication that he attended the session of July 1771, for which he was eligible, and he did not make a rapid move into the ranks of the House leaders. In the mid-1760s his father lobbied unsuccessfully to secure for him the lucrative post of collector of customs for the district of the upper James River, but from 8 September 1767 until 10 October 1775 Corbin was comptroller for the York River customs district.

Early in the 1770s Corbin or members of his family began pressing for his appointment to the governor's Council, the highest office to which a Virginian could normally aspire. It was undoubtedly his family's prominence and devotion to the Crown, not his record of public service, that convinced officials in London to comply when a vacancy occurred at a critical time. On 21 February 1775 the king signed the royal warrant of appointment, giving Corbin and his father the rare distinction of serving together on the Council. That service, however, was extremely brief, consisting of about three and a half dramatic weeks beginning on 1 June 1775 when the Council and House of Burgesses met together for the last time as the General Assembly of the colony.

The Corbins were loyal to the Crown during the American Revolution, but family members suffered little overt harassment and had no legal impediments imposed on their private lives. Corbin's father even retained the respect of the new political leadership of Virginia. Among Gawin Corbin's younger brothers, John Tayloe Corbin was briefly detained at the beginning of the war, Thomas Corbin served in the British militia in the mother country and later procured a commission in the regular British army, and Francis Corbin, later a member of the Convention of 1788, spent the Revolutionary years in England completing his education. Early in the Revolution the family's Loyalism cast a shadow over their sister's husband, Carter Braxton, who signed the Declaration of Independence. Gawin Corbin apparently lived quietly and undisturbed at his estate in Middlesex County until he died on 19 July 1779. His family proudly had his appointment to the Council recorded on his gravestone. In 1941 the surviving family gravestones at the Buckingham plantation were moved to Christ Episcopal Church, in Middlesex County.

Birth, marriage, and death dates and children identified in Gawin Corbin family Bible records, LVA; J. A. Venn, comp., *Alumni Cantabrigienses*, pt. 2 (1944), 2:136 (variant birth date of 29 Dec. 1738 and death date of 10 July 1779); Sir Henry F. MacGeagh and H. A. C. Sturgess, comps., *Register of Admissions to the Honourable Society of the Middle Temple* (1949), 1:350; some letters to Corbin in Richard Corbin Letter Book (1758–1768), Richard Corbin Papers, CW; Council appointment in PRO CO 324/43, 150–151; *JHB, 1773–1776*, 173; *Legislative Journals of Council*, 3:1590; Colonial Papers, folder 50, no. 22, RG 1, LVA; gravestone inscription giving precise age at death printed in *VMHB* 30 (1922): 313.

BRENT TARTER

CORBIN, Hannah Lee (6 February 1728–by 7 October 1782), planter and early advocate of women's rights, was born at Matholic, the Westmoreland County plantation of her parents, Thomas Lee and Hannah Ludwell Lee. Her immediate family was one of the most prominent in Virginia. Her mother's Harrison and Ludwell kinsmen included many wealthy planters and burgesses and several members of the governor's Council, and her father was president of the Council and acting governor when he died in 1750. Her brothers included a member of the Council, Philip Ludwell Lee; two signers of the Declaration of Independence, Francis Lightfoot Lee and Richard Henry Lee; a member of the Convention of 1776, Thomas Ludwell Lee; and two of the first United States diplomats during the American Revolution, Arthur Lee, who also served in the Confederation Congress, and William Lee, who was an alderman and sheriff of London on the eve of the Revolution.

Lee grew up in the family's new Westmoreland County mansion, Stratford Hall, was educated by private tutors alongside her brothers, and read widely in her father's well-stocked library. On an unknown date, but probably about 1747, she married Gawin Corbin, a cousin whose family was almost as prominent as hers; his brother Richard Corbin and nephew Gawin Corbin (1739–1779) both served on the governor's Council, and another nephew, Francis Corbin, was a member of the Convention of 1788. Hannah Corbin and her husband lived at his Peckatone plantation in Westmoreland County, about twenty miles downriver from Stratford Hall. They had one daughter, Martha Corbin, born in 1748. Gawin Corbin died sometime during the winter of 1759–1760. Under the terms of his will, which named his wife one of the executors of his large estate, she was to control and profit from her husband's vast property until their daughter married or reached age twenty-one; but his will also stipulated that Hannah Corbin must reside in Westmoreland and not remarry in order to retain her interest in his estate.

Though presumably displeased by the constraints her husband's will imposed, Corbin flourished in widowhood. Peckatone prospered under her careful management, as she oversaw operations on the plantation and dealt directly with London merchants who bought and marketed her tobacco. Corbin's brothers, several of whom were themselves great planters, respected her business and managerial skills and sometimes solicited her advice.

Corbin found spiritual fulfillment in the Baptist revivals of the 1760s. Virginia authorities, however, sought to suppress the Baptists, who challenged the privileged position of the established Church of England and whose egalitarian views threatened to undermine the social hierarchy. On 29 May 1764 a Westmoreland County grand jury presented Corbin and Richard Lingan Hall for not attending Anglican church services. Hall was a Baptist physician who had attended Gawin Corbin during his final illness, and by 1762 he had fallen in love with Hannah Corbin and was living with her at Peckatone. Both financial and religious considerations discouraged Corbin and Hall from marrying. If Corbin had remarried, she would have lost the property she controlled after her husband's death. Baptist convictions enabled the couple to justify their choice inasmuch as only marriages performed by an Anglican clergyman were legally valid in the colony. It is possible a Baptist minister married them extralegally.

In 1769 Corbin's daughter took possession of her inheritance, including Peckatone, and two years later Corbin and Hall moved to Corbin's Woodberry estate, in Richmond County. They had one son, whom they named Elisha Hall Corbin, and one daughter, whom Hall sometimes referred to as Martha Corbin and Corbin as Martha Hall or as her Baptist daughter.

Religious heterodoxy and Corbin's association with Hall, who died late in the spring or early in the summer of 1774, did not damage her relations with her family, with whom she shared in the patriotic opposition to British policies before the American Revolution. Corbin may have expected the Revolution to improve the status of women. Writing to her brother Richard Henry Lee in March 1778 (a letter that is now lost), she applied the Revolutionary dictum of no taxation without representation to propertied single women and widows, such as herself, who, like American colonists faced with Parliamentary levies, were taxed without their consent because they had no right to vote. Although Lee took seriously his sister's complaint and privately stated that he supported

enfranchising such women, he never said so publicly. Nor, for that matter, did she.

Corbin's outspoken and unconventional life suggests the possibilities and limits of women's independence in eighteenth-century Virginia. Wealth, connections, and ability combined to allow her to live independently as a widow for more than two decades. Financial imperatives and religious conviction, which contemporaries increasingly identified as a hallmark of feminine virtue, won her relationship with Hall grudging acceptance, even if not outright approval. Access to books, to newspapers, and especially to influential men led her to express political opinions and ponder the role and status of women in a revolutionary world. Corbin's legacy, however, was ultimately conservative. She never challenged marriage as an institution. She expected her own daughters to marry and took no steps to create separate estates to preserve their property rights after they married. Unlike some other early Baptists and other Virginia revolutionaries, she never freed her slaves. Her call for suffrage, for which she is chiefly remembered, was more an individual protest against taxation without representation than a broader assertion of women's rights.

Hannah Lee Corbin died, probably in Westmoreland County, still owning sixty-four slaves and more than 1,700 acres of land in Caroline, Fauquier, King George, Richmond, and Westmoreland Counties. The date of her death is not recorded, but it probably occurred not long before her will was proved in the Richmond County Court on 7 October 1782.

Birth date recorded with no middle name in Richard Henry Lee Bible records, VHS; name occasionally recorded by county clerk as Hannah Ludwell Corbin, but never in facsimile signatures (see, for example, Westmoreland Co. Orders [1761–1764], 68a, 95a, 125a); biographies in Ethel Armes, *Stratford Hall: The Great House of the Lees* (1936), 199–217, Elizabeth Dabney Coleman, "Two Lees, Revolutionary Suffragists," *Virginia Cavalcade* 3 (autumn 1953): 18–21, Louise Belote Dawe and Sandra Gioia Treadway, "Hannah Lee Corbin: The Forgotten Lee," *Virginia Cavalcade* 29 (autumn 1979): 70–77, Elizabeth Spencer James Pardoe, "Four Outstanding Women," *Northern Neck of Virginia Historical Magazine* 32 (1982): 3660–3668, and Rees Watkins, "Hannah Lee Corbin Hall—A Baptist," *Virginia Baptist Register* 28 (1989): 1443–1451; correspondence in Peckatone Papers, VHS, and Ethel Armes Collection of Lee Family Papers,

LC; Hening, *Statutes*, 7:458–461; Richard Henry Lee to Hannah Corbin, 17 Mar. 1778, in James Curtis Ballagh, ed., *The Letters of Richard Henry Lee* (1911–1914), 1:392–394; Gawin Corbin's will in Westmoreland Co. Deeds and Wills, 13:265–266; Richard Hall's will in Fauquier Co. Will Book, 1:257–259; Hannah Lee Corbin's will and estate inventories in Richmond Co. Will Book, 7:416–417, 436–439, 8:26–28.

Cynthia A. Kierner

CORBIN, Henry. See **CORBYN, Henry**.

CORBIN, Percy Casino (2 June 1888–6 July 1952), civil rights activist, was born in Athens, Texas, and was the son of Edward Corbin and Priscilla Wright Corbin. He grew up on the family farm and received his early education in public schools in Athens and nearby Corsicana before enrolling in a private institution in El Paso in order to prepare for studying medicine. Corbin attended the medical school at Howard University, in Washington, D.C., for one year and then transferred to the Leonard School of Medicine at Shaw University, in Raleigh, North Carolina. He received an M.D. in 1911.

Corbin opened a medical practice in Salem, Virginia, with a roommate from medical school, but in 1913 he moved to the town of Pulaski. Settling there afforded him the opportunity to serve a rural community in need of medical care and also made good business sense, as there were no other African American doctors in the area. On 31 October 1914 he married Evelyn Carrie Linscom, an El Paso native who had also attended Shaw University. They had one daughter and four sons.

Corbin's patients initially came from the black community, but over time his practice also attracted white clients. His medical skills were on dramatic display in the autumn of 1918 during the influenza pandemic that gripped the town for several weeks and forced the closing of local schools, churches, and businesses. As officials called for additional medical supplies and set up an emergency hospital, Corbin and four other doctors worked around the clock to stem the spread of the disease. Ninety-two townspeople died before the epidemic subsided.

In 1920 Corbin erected a two-story building that housed his office and home until 1936, when he moved into a new residence. By 1921 he had organized the Pulaski Mutual Savings Society and served as its first president. A partner in the Graham, Corbin and Lewis Concrete Block Manufacturing Company, Corbin in 1923 erected the three-story Corbin Building from block the company produced. He moved his office there, rented the first floor to African American businesses, and let the upper floors as apartments.

Corbin was deeply concerned about education, and while president of the Calfee Training School's improvement league he appeared before the Pulaski County school board in May 1936 to request an accredited school for African Americans. The Calfee Training School had long been neglected, and after it burned in November 1938, he launched a campaign to equalize school facilities for black students with those available to white children. Enlisting the help of Chauncey Depew Harmon, principal of the Calfee Training School, and of state representatives from the National Association for the Advancement of Colored People, Corbin petitioned the school board for a new facility and for equal pay for African American teachers. He also appealed to the community, and his letter to the local *Southwest Times* outlining the plight of black children won a sympathetic editorial and generated support from the white public and local civic groups. Despite such public sentiment, Corbin achieved only partial success. The board agreed to fund a new elementary school but decided to transport black high school students to the Christiansburg Industrial Institute in Montgomery County.

After the Calfee Training School burned, Corbin had sent his high school–age son to Washington, D.C., for instruction. When his youngest son, Mahatma N. Corbin, was preparing to enter high school, Corbin decided to send him to the Christiansburg Industrial Institute. After discovering, however, that his son would not be able to use the library or participate in after-school activities because the bus departed for Pulaski immediately after classes ended, Corbin again sought legal assistance from the NAACP. Attorneys Oliver W. Hill, Martin A. Martin, and Spottswood William Robinson (1916–1998) filed suit on behalf of Corbin's son late in December 1947 in the United States District Court in Roanoke, alleging that the school arrangement violated the equal-protection clause of the Fourteenth Amendment. In the case of *Corbin et al.* v. *County School Board of Pulaski County, Virginia, et al.*, Judge Alfred Dickinson Barksdale ruled in the school board's favor on 2 May 1949. On appeal the following November the United States Court of Appeals for the Fourth Circuit held that there were "manifest inequalities" among Pulaski's three white high schools and the Christiansburg facility. It reversed the lower court's decision and instructed it to grant relief to the plaintiffs. Corbin's victory was one of only six successful lawsuits supported by the NAACP in its legal campaign to equalize school facilities before *Brown* v. *Board of Education* (1954).

Active in professional and civic affairs, Corbin joined the Magic City Medical Society, the National Medical Association, the Old Dominion Medical Society, and the Freemasons. He served as president of the Pulaski chapter of the NAACP and was a leader and benefactor of the local African American branch of the Young Men's Christian Association, which was named in his honor. At a time when blacks faced official hostility and a discriminatory poll tax, Corbin regularly exercised his right to vote and encouraged other African Americans to do so. An outspoken reformer, he sometimes adopted views that caused agitation in the black as well as in the white community.

While visiting two of his sons in Detroit, Percy Casino Corbin became ill suddenly and was rushed to a black-owned hospital, where he died on 6 July 1952. His body was returned to Pulaski for burial in Pinehurst Cemetery.

Birth date on World War I Selective Service System Draft Registration Cards (1917–1918), RG 163, NARA, and in Caldwell, *History of the American Negro*, 388–390 (por.); variant birth year of 1887 on gravestone; BVS Marriage Register, Pulaski Co.; family information provided by daughter Evelyn Jacqueline Corbin Pleasants (2003); Corbin letter in *Pulaski Southwest Times*, 15 Nov. 1938, reprinted in *Norfolk Journal and Guide*, 17 Dec. 1938; *Norfolk Journal and Guide* and *Afro-American and Richmond Planet*, both 25 Mar. 1939; *Pulaski Southwest Times*, 2 May, 15 Nov. 1949; *Roanoke Times*, 3 May 1949; Pulaski Co. School Board Minutes (1938–1950), Pulaski Co. Public Schools; *Corbin et al.* v. *County School Board of Pulaski County, Virginia, et al.* (1949), *Federal Reporter*, 2d ser., 177:924–928 (quotation on 927); *Corbin* v. *Pulaski* Case File, U.S. District Court, Western District of Virginia, Roanoke Division, RG 21, NARA;

Conway Howard Smith, *The Land That Is Pulaski County* (1981), 424, 469; Chauncey D. Harmon, "A History of the Origin of the Black Citizens of Pulaski" (typescript dated 1 May 1986), 19, copies in *DVB* Files and at Pulaski Co. Public Library; N. Wayne Tripp, "Chauncey Depew Harmon, Senior: A Case Study in Leadership for Educational Opportunity and Equality in Pulaski, Virginia" (Ed.D. diss., VPI, 1995), 21–22, 34–37, 167, 221–223, 264, 282–288; obituary and accounts of funeral in *Pulaski Southwest Times*, 7, 9, 13 (por.) July 1952, and *Norfolk Journal and Guide*, 26 July 1952.

N. WAYNE TRIPP

CORBIN, Richard (1713 or 1714–20 May 1790), member of the Council, was born in Middlesex County and was the son of Gawin Corbin (1669–1745) and the second of his three wives, Jane Lane Wilson Corbin, who was herself a widow when she married Gawin Corbin. Richard Corbin grew up in Middlesex County and in King and Queen County, where his mother and her family held property. He probably attended the College of William and Mary late in the 1720s. He was appointed to the King and Queen County Court in 1735 but by 1738 was residing on his father's property in Middlesex County, where he also served on the county court. In July 1737 Corbin married Betty Tayloe, daughter of John Tayloe (1687–1747), a member of the governor's Council. Their three daughters and five sons included Gawin Corbin (1739–1779), who sat on the governor's Council at the end of the colonial period, and Francis Corbin, who served in the Convention of 1788.

From his father Corbin acquired and inherited valuable land in Caroline, Essex, King and Queen, Middlesex, and Spotsylvania Counties. He later distributed portions of his property to his sons, but at the end of his life his landholdings still ranked among Virginia's largest. Corbin moved back to King and Queen County in 1745, resumed his position on the county court, and replaced his father on the vestry of Stratton Major Parish. As a capable and prosperous man with excellent family connections, he was soon considered for appointment to the governor's Council. In 1747 Lieutenant Governor Sir William Gooch placed his name at the bottom of a list of potential appointees. The following year Corbin won election to the House of Burgesses from Middlesex County, but his service in the lower house of the General Assembly was brief, because on 19 January 1750 the king appointed him to the Council. He took office in Williamsburg on 7 May 1750.

By the 1750s Corbin was a successful planter who speculated in western land and acted as a collection agent for British mercantile firms. He also had begun to build Laneville, his magnificent residence in King and Queen County. There is no evidence that Corbin ever visited England, but like many other Virginians he sent his sons there to be educated. Clearly his feelings about the mother country were warm and his respect for the British government strong. This attachment was apparent in the 1750s when he supported Lieutenant Governor Robert Dinwiddie's imposition of a fee of one pistole for signing land patents, an action that the leading members of the House of Burgesses and some other Council members strongly opposed.

Corbin opposed a bill to print paper money during the French and Indian War and to make it legal tender, in part because he feared the bill's effect on creditors. The bill passed both in the House of Burgesses and in the Council. On 30 July 1762 Corbin became deputy receiver general of Virginia, responsible for collecting quitrents that were payable to the Crown. In lieu of a salary he annually received 5 percent of the money he collected. This tax was payable in paper currency, which meant that Corbin would lose money if paper currency depreciated in value. His opposition to paper money was not popular in Virginia, and when he warned the Council's agent in London of the House of Burgesses' efforts to hire its own agent, who presumably would provide firmer support for the use of paper currency, he asked that his name not appear. Corbin continued to lobby London officials against paper money and got his wish when Parliament passed the Currency Act of 1764, which effectively prohibited the colonies from issuing paper money and making it legal tender for all private and public transactions.

Corbin emerged as a force to be reckoned with during his first fifteen years on the Council. George Washington turned to him for help when seeking appointment as a lieutenant colonel in the expedition he was planning to lead against the French. Corbin was also close to Dinwiddie and after the lieutenant governor returned to England collected debts that Virginians owed him. Such positions and associations reveal something of Corbin's personality and beliefs. He was a self-confident man of convictions, especially in avoidance of debt; unlike many of his contemporaries, he was never heavily indebted.

Corbin's political influence declined after the mid-1760s. He was unable to get his eldest son appointed to the profitable post of collector of customs for the district of upper James River, and he took an unpopular stand against the colony's opposition to the Stamp Act. When the imperial crisis deepened in the 1770s, Corbin refused to sign the Virginia Association of 1774 unless a majority of the Council did. After the royal governor, John Murray, earl of Dunmore, removed gunpowder from the public magazine in Williamsburg in April 1775, Patrick Henry raised a troop of volunteers and marched toward the capital threatening to retake the powder unless the receiver general compensated the colony for its value. Corbin offered his personal note for the value of the powder, but Henry refused to accept it. Instead, he accepted a note from Thomas Nelson Jr., and Corbin repaid him.

That summer, the king believed that the worsening political condition of the colony might compel Dunmore to return to Great Britain and leave Virginia without a loyal chief executive. On 29 July 1775 George III issued a commission appointing Corbin lieutenant governor. Corbin was the only native Virginian ever commissioned to so high an office in the colony. Dunmore did not depart Virginia for more than a year, however, and he began hostile actions in the Chesapeake Bay and its tributaries. Respected by both Loyalists and Revolutionaries, Corbin was the only man in Virginia who was trusted enough by both sides to act as an emissary in January 1776 when Dunmore and the Virginia Committee of Safety unsuccessfully tried to open negotiations. Corbin then retired to Laneville, where he lived throughout the Revolutionary War, unmolested by either side. His daughter Elizabeth Corbin married Carter Braxton, who signed the Declaration of Independence, but most of the rest of his family remained loyal to the Crown.

Corbin's retreat from public life was complete, and he lived nearly fifteen more years as a wealthy but private man. His wife died on 13 May 1784, and Richard Corbin died at Laneville on 20 May 1790. They were buried at Buckingham, the family's ancestral residence in Middlesex County. In 1941 the surviving family gravestones were moved to Christ Episcopal Church in that county. The author of a remarkably generous obituary of a man who had remained loyal to the king wrote of Corbin that "no man had the true interest of his native state more sincerely at heart, if he differed with the majority of his countrymen about the *means* of promoting it. . . . If he was *too little* of an American, it was, in truth, owing to his being *too much* of a *Virginian*."

Biographies in Elizabeth C. Johnson, "Colonel Richard Corbin of Laneville," *Bulletin of the King and Queen County Historical Society of Virginia* 22 (Jan. 1967), unpaginated, printing text of gravestone inscription with death date at age seventy-six, and Robert Doares, "The Man Who Would Not Be Governor," *Colonial Williamsburg* 22 (winter 2000–2001): 74–78; marriage in *Williamsburg Virginia Gazette*, 29 July 1737; Richard Corbin Papers, CW (including Corbin Letter Book, 1758–1768), VHS, and W&M; other Corbin documents and references in Edmund Jennings Letter Book (1753–1769), VHS, *Executive Journals of Council*, vols. 4–6, *Washington: Colonial Series, Revolutionary Virginia*, esp. vols. 3 and 6, C. G. Chamberlayne, ed., *The Vestry Book of Stratton Major Parish, King and Queen County, 1729–1783* (1931), R. A. Brock, ed., *The Official Records of Robert Dinwiddie . . .* (1883–1884), Louis Knott Koontz, ed., *Robert Dinwiddie: Correspondence Illustrative of His Career in American Colonial Government and Westward Expansion* (1951), George Reese, ed., *The Official Papers of Francis Fauquier, Lieutenant Governor of Virginia, 1758–1768* (1980–1983), and John C. Van Horne and George Reese, eds., *The Letter Book of James Abercromby, Colonial Agent, 1751–1773* (1991); appointments to Council in PRO CO 324/38, 142, as deputy receiver general in *Executive Journals of Council*, 6:229, and as lieutenant governor in PRO CO 324/43, 209–210; Alexander Wilbourne Weddell, ed., *A Memorial Volume of Virginia Historical Portraiture, 1585–1830* (1930), por. facing 199; transcription of will printed in Beverley Fleet, *Virginia Colonial Abstracts*, vol. 4: *King and Queen County. Records Concerning 18th Century Persons* (1939), 63–66; obituary with date of death "in the 77th year of his age" in *Richmond Independent Chronicle and General Advertiser*, 26 May 1790 (quotation).

EMORY G. EVANS

CORBYN, Henry (1628 or 1629–ca. 8 January 1676), member of the Council, was the son of Thomas Corbyn and Winifred Grosvenor Corbyn and was born probably at Hall End, in Polesworth, Warwickshire, England. Contemporaries spelled the family name variously as Corbin, Corbyn, and Corbyne. He signed his surname as Corbyn, but by the end of the seventeenth century Virginia members of the family all used the spelling Corbin. Although tradition states that Corbyn fled England after assisting in the escape of the exiled King Charles II from the battlefield at Worcester in September 1651, documentary proof of such an exploit is lacking. It is more likely that as a young man engaged in commerce, Corbyn was already attracted to opportunities in Virginia. In 1652 he received a bequest from a Virginia colonist, and two years later, while living in London and working as a draper, he acknowledged receipt of his legacy from his father's will.

Corbyn sailed for Virginia early in 1654, but his ship was blown off course and landed in Maryland. There in a deposition dated 23 June 1654 he gave his age as twenty-five and his occupation as merchant. His testimony concerned the tempestuous voyage and the mariners on board the *Charity* who had accused an old woman of witchcraft and executed her at sea. Corbyn probably entered Virginia soon thereafter. The earliest dated evidence of his presence is the bond he executed on 3 January 1657 for his intended marriage to Alice Eltonhead Burnham, the recently widowed mother of four children. During the next fifteen years they had five daughters and three sons. The union tied Corbyn into the complex kinship networks of the colonial political elite; his wife's sisters had married William Brocas, John Carter (ca. 1613–1670), and Ralph Wormeley (d. 1651), all members of the governor's Council, and Sir Henry Chicheley, later a member of the Council and lieutenant governor.

Through purchase and patenting unsettled land, Corbyn acquired several large and valuable properties between the Mattaponi and Rappahannock Rivers, including one that he purchased in 1660 with a proviso that he settle it as soon as the Native Americans who resided there had departed. He acquired plantations known then or later as Corbin Hall, Machotick, and Peckatone, and he resided at Buckingham, one of the finest houses of its time, in the portion of Lancaster County that became Middlesex County about 1669. Well-liked and hospitable, Corbyn along with three associates built a banqueting house in 1670 for entertaining friends and guests at Peckatone. His success and that of several close relatives gave rise to a Virginia phrase, "as rich as Corbin."

In the several counties in which Corbyn transacted business or owned land, his name frequently appeared in the records as an officeholder, as party to land transactions or disputes, as a trustee of property, and as attorney in fact for a third party. On 6 June 1657 he became a justice of the quorum in Lancaster County (that is, one of the members of the county court whose presence was required for the conduct of business), and he may have also sat on the court of Rappahannock County as needed. At least one session of the Lancaster County Court, that of 17 November 1657, met at his house, as did many gatherings of the vestry for Christ Church Parish, on which he also sat. As a landowner and as a justice of the peace Corbyn dealt with local Native Americans several times and in several roles. He presided over cases concerning land disputes, protection of a young man known as Indian Ned from his tribal enemies, and injuries inflicted on Indians in violation of the peace treaty. In 1659 Corbyn won election to represent Lancaster County in the one-week session of the General Assembly that met that spring, when he served on the Committee for Private Causes. A colonel in the militia by April 1668, he was also a deputy escheator and collector of customs for the Rappahannock River district.

On an unrecorded date during or before the spring of 1663, Corbyn became a member of the governor's Council. His first documented responsibility was to take part in negotiations with Maryland to reduce production of tobacco in order to raise its price. The agreement then reached never took effect. Corbyn's tenure on the Council, which continued until his death, is not well documented because the surviving records are incomplete, but he was a trusted adviser to Governor Sir William Berkeley. In October 1669 the governor entered an unusual order, probably to resolve a local controversy,

granting Corbyn authority to issue marriage licenses in Rappahannock County and directing that "noe Clerkes of County Cort. are to meddle in it." Corbyn's service on the Council spanned most of the so-called Long Assembly of 1661–1676; the failed Berkenhead Conspiracy of 1663, in which indentured servants from Gloucester and York Counties planned to march on Jamestown to demand their freedom; the Second and Third Anglo-Dutch Wars, which required large outlays for defense; and the first hints of trouble with Native Americans that led to Bacon's Rebellion in 1676.

When Corbyn wrote his will on 25 July 1675, he stated that although he was in reasonably good health, he was "of short memory." Family tradition holds that Henry Corbyn died at the hands of Indians on 8 January 1676, but there is no known documentary record of the date or circumstance of his death. His brother wrote in April of that year that on the day of the funeral Indians carried off and killed about forty people and that they later attacked the widow's plantation. Corbyn most likely was buried at Buckingham, but if his grave was marked by a stone it had disappeared by the time the family gravestones were moved to the yard at Christ Episcopal Church in Middlesex County. Corbyn's widow married Henry Creyke within a year of her second husband's death, and in April 1681 in Corbyn's memory they donated his silver trencher plate, engraved with his coat of arms, to Christ Church.

Brief biographies and family history in "The Corbin Family," *VMHB* 28 (1920): 281–283 (with undocumented death date of 8 Jan. 1675 Old Style), 372 (abstract of marriage bond from deed records in possession of the earl of Beauchamp), and ibid. 29 (1921): 374–382 (por. facing 374), and *The Madresfield Muniments with an Account of the Family and the Estates* (1929), 55; signatures on letters of the governor and Council to the earl of Arlington, 13 July 1666, and to the Privy Council, July 1673, PRO CO 1/20, pt. 1, fol. 200, and CO 1/30; deposition giving age as twenty-five on 23 June 1654 in William Hand Browne, ed., *Archives of Maryland: Proceedings of the Council of Maryland, 1636–1667* (1885), 306–307; numerous references in Lancaster, Middlesex, and old Rappahannock Co. records (first quotation in old Rappahannock Co. Deed Book, 4:106 [transcription]), and in *Minutes of Council and General Court*; first record as Council member in governor and Council to the earl of Clarendon, 28 Mar. 1663, Egerton MSS 2395, British Library; copy of will, dated 25 July 1675 and proved

8 Mar. 1676, Tayloe Family Papers, VHS (second quotation); another copy printed in *VMHB* 29 (1921): 376–378.

KATHARINE E. HARBURY

COREY, Charles Henry (12 December 1834–5 September 1899), president of Richmond Theological Seminary (later Virginia Union University), was born in New Canaan, New Brunswick, and was the son of Gardner Corey, a farmer, and Elizabeth Humphreys Corey. Raised in the Baptist faith, he attended a seminary in Fredericton. In 1854 Corey matriculated at Acadia College (later Acadia University) in Wolfville, Nova Scotia, where he learned about the English abolitionist movement, a revelation, he stated later, that prepared him for his life's work as an educator of freedpeople. He graduated with a B.A. in 1858 and then enrolled at Newton Theological Institute (later Andover Newton Theological School), near Boston. In 1861 Corey received both a divinity certificate from Newton and an A.M. from Acadia. He was ordained on 18 September of that year and became pastor of First Baptist Church in Seabrook, New Hampshire.

In January 1864 Corey joined the United States Christian Commission, founded in 1861 by the Young Men's Christian Association to minister to soldiers and sailors during the Civil War. As a delegate in Indianola and Brownsville, Texas, and in Port Hudson and Alexandria, Louisiana, he distributed supplies and reading materials and preached in Union camps. Corey returned to New England and the Maritime Provinces of Canada during the summer of 1864 to recover his health. That autumn the commission sent him to Morris Island, South Carolina, where he continued his ministry among the soldiers and also took charge of Wentworth Street Baptist Church, in Charleston, until May 1865. Corey described his experiences in a series of letters that were published in Saint John, New Brunswick, in the *Christian Visitor* under the pseudonym Viator. He returned to Seabrook, where he married Fannie Sanborn on 26 August 1865. They had two sons.

After the war Corey became affiliated with the American Baptist Home Mission Society, which had committed itself to educating and ministering to the new freedpeople in the South. The society sent Corey back to Charleston in September 1865. There he spent two years organizing churches for African Americans, raising money for new buildings, and ordaining ministers throughout South Carolina. In November 1867 Corey moved to Augusta, Georgia, where he took charge of the recently established Augusta Institute (later Morehouse College), which operated under the aegis of the National Theological Institute and University, an organization headquartered in Washington, D.C., and also devoted to providing a Christian education for former slaves. Corey remained at Augusta until July 1868, when he was transferred to Richmond, Virginia, to manage the new seminary there.

In 1867 the National Theological Institute and University had opened a school for black ministerial students in Richmond. Corey's predecessor, Nathaniel Colver, held classes in Lumpkin's Jail, a former holding cell of a slave trader. Corey arrived in Richmond in September 1868 and the following month began teaching day and evening classes for more than 120 students. In May 1869 the American Baptist Home Mission Society took responsibility for the developing theological school, popularly called the Colver Institute in honor of its first superintendent. Corey arranged for the purchase of a former hotel in January 1870, and he and the students spent several months repairing the building for use as their permanent facility.

Corey and his wife taught classes at the school, which in 1876 was incorporated as the Richmond Institute. His duties as president also included developing the curriculum, raising funds, and preaching. Although intended primarily to train young men for the ministry, the institute also offered a general education for students, including women until 1883, at a variety of levels. The rapid growth of Baptist churches organized by African Americans, coupled with the desire to train missionaries for service in Africa, increased the need for a school devoted solely to ministerial education. In 1882, recognizing the institute as a leading center for black Baptists, the American Baptist Home Mission Society determined that Richmond would be the best location for such training, and on 5 February 1886 the Richmond Institute became the Richmond Theological Seminary. Corey continued as president. During a leave of absence in 1890 he visited Egypt, Palestine, and several European countries in an effort to recover from poor health.

In 1896 Richmond Theological Seminary joined with Hartshorn Memorial College, a nearby school for women, to incorporate as Virginia Union University. Still usually known by its former name, the school soon began negotiating to absorb Wayland Seminary, a Baptist institution in the District of Columbia. Corey pursued the merger, which the institutions had accepted by May 1897. The arrangement was formalized in February 1900 with the school's reincorporation as Virginia Union University.

Continued ill health forced Corey to resign late in 1898. He was named president emeritus. During his thirty-year presidency about 1,200 students received their education at the seminary, including more than 530 who prepared for the ministry. Corey attracted donors who provided money for endowed professorships, a scholarship fund, and expansion of the library. He wrote two histories of the seminary, *Historical Sketch of the Richmond Institute* (1876) and *A History of the Richmond Theological Seminary, with Reminiscences of Thirty Years' Work among the Colored People of the South* (1895). In recognition of his work, Corey received honorary doctorates in divinity from Richmond College (later the University of Richmond) and Baylor University in 1881 and from Acadia University in 1892. Toronto Baptist College (later McMaster University) honored him with a courtesy recognition in 1884.

While staying at his summer house in Seabrook, New Hampshire, Charles Henry Corey died of Bright's disease on 5 September 1899. He was buried in Elmwood Cemetery in that town.

Corey, *A History of the Richmond Theological Seminary, with Reminiscences of Thirty Years' Work among the Colored People of the South* (1895), frontispiece por.; birth date on gravestone; biographies in William Cathcart, ed., *The Baptist Encyclopædia* (1881), 279, George Braxton Taylor, *Virginia Baptist Ministers*, 4th ser. (1913), 323–324, and Mary C. Reynolds, *Baptist Missionary Pioneers among Negroes* (1915), 35–38; marriage in Seabrook, N.H., Marriages, Births, and Deaths (1850–1872), 86; Corey correspondence and other materials in Richmond Theological Seminary Records, VUU; *Saint John [New Brunswick] Chris-* *tian Visitor*, 9 Feb., 6, 13 Apr., 11, 25 May, 1 June 1865; State of New Hampshire Death Register, Seabrook; obituaries in *Boston Daily Globe*, 5 Sept. 1899, *Richmond Dispatch*, 6 Sept. 1899, *Exeter News-Letter*, 8 Sept. 1899, *Richmond Planet*, 9 Sept. 1899, and *Boston Watchman*, 14 Sept. 1899; memorials in *Minutes of the Baptist General Association of Virginia* (1899), 70–71, and *Baptist Home Mission Monthly* 22 (Oct . 1900): 279–287.

SUZANNE K. DURHAM

CORNISH, Richard, alias **Richard Williams** (d. after 3 January 1625), principal in a cause célèbre, was master of the merchant ship *Ambrose* in 1624 and the following year was tried, condemned, and hanged for forcibly sodomizing William Couse, a nineteen-year-old member of his crew. Apart from the name of Cornish's brother and the controversial aftermath of the trial, nothing else is known about him. He may have been from Devonshire, England, where families named Cornish and Couse lived in the 1590s.

On 30 November 1624 Couse testified before the governor's Council that on the afternoon of 27 August 1624 "Richard Williams als Cornushe" had forcibly sodomized him aboard the ship, then riding at anchor in the James River, and caused him "payne in the fundement" that left him "sore 3 or 4 dyes." He also reported that Cornish had apologized but later put his hands inside Couse's codpiece "many tymes . . . and plaid and kiste him." The testimony indicated that on one occasion when Cornish called Couse to him but Couse refused to go, Cornish stood him "before the maste and forbad all the shipps Company to eate wth him" and made him "Cooke for all the rest."

On 3 January 1625 Walter Mathew, the boatswain's mate on the *Ambrose*, testified that he had overheard part of a conversation between Cornish and Couse when the two were in the master's locked cabin. Mathew stated that Couse had protested that what Cornish proposed "would be an overthrow to him both in soule and bodye" and that Couse had cited Scripture in opposition to the proposal. When Mathew later questioned Couse about what had taken place, Couse "replied he would keepe that to himself till he cam into England." He later told Mathew only that Cornish "would have Bugard him" but refused to state whether the captain "did the fact."

Perhaps what began as a forced act of sodomy became a consensual relationship, but a ship's master had considerable authority over a cabin boy, and Couse may have had few means of effective resistance. His comment to Mathew about not mentioning what Cornish had done until they returned to England hints that Couse may have intended to lodge a complaint with the English authorities. Perhaps Couse's humiliation in front of the rest of the crew prompted him to leave the ship in Virginia, charge Cornish with forcible sodomy, and take his complaint directly to the governor and Council. The two depositions of Couse and Mathew are all that survive in the Council's fragmentary records that predate Cornish's trial and execution.

Cornish may have been tried summarily before the governor or, more likely, the governor and Council. He was convicted and executed on an unrecorded date, probably not long after Mathew's testimony on 3 January 1625. The few references to the case do not mention a jury. Perhaps Cornish unsuccessfully threw himself on the mercy of the court.

Several mariners and Virginia residents later asserted that Cornish, an excellent mariner, had been unjustly hanged, and they blamed the governor, Sir Francis Wyatt. Criticism of the trial reverberated throughout the maritime community for more than a year. During the winter of 1625–1626, the Council heard testimony from several mariners indicating that aboard the *Swan* in far-off Canadian waters, Edward Nevell, who stated that he had been present at the trial and hanging, had told Jeffry Cornish that his brother had been wrongfully condemned and executed. William Foster informed the Council that Nevell had reported that Richard Cornish "was hangd for a rascally boye wrongfully," and Arthur Aveling testified that Nevell had said that Cornish was executed "through a scurvie boys meanes, & no other came against him."

Jeffrey Cornish swore to kill those responsible for Richard Cornish's death, but he did not avenge his brother. Instead, for Nevell's offense of insulting the governor, the Council ordered that he lose both of his ears, serve the colony for a year, and be incapable of ever becoming a free man in Virginia. Thomas Hatch, a young Vir-ginia servant who also had criticized the governor, was sentenced to be whipped from the fort to the gallows and back, lose one ear, and begin an additional seven-year term of service.

Henry Read McIlwaine published the surviving documents relating to Cornish in the *Minutes of the Council and General Court of Colonial Virginia* in 1924 but erroneously transcribed Couse's age as twenty-nine, rather than nineteen. No historian discussed the case until 1971, when Edmund S. Morgan mentioned it in an article that formed the basis of a chapter in his *American Slavery, American Freedom: The Ordeal of Colonial Virginia* (1975). Focusing on the arbitrary punishments imposed on Wyatt's critics, Morgan analyzed the controversy as evidence of the colony's increasing tendency to reduce servants to the status of chattels, but other scholars have subsequently emphasized the sexual aspects of the case. America's gay community discovered the episode. Jonathan Katz reprinted the documents in modernized form in *Gay American History* (1976), and more recently several World Wide Web sites have highlighted the case. In 1993 the William and Mary Gay and Lesbian Alumni/ae, Inc., created the Richard Cornish Endowment Fund for Gay and Lesbian Resources, which within a decade raised more than $66,000 to purchase materials for the college library. After the Supreme Court of the United States ruled in the summer of 2003 that sodomy between consenting adults was a constitutionally protected right of privacy, one man left a small, informal memorial to Cornish at Jamestown ("In memoriam RICHARD CORNISH, First American Sodomite. Rest in Peace.") and recounted the case in a *New York Times* op-ed piece.

Between 1637 and 1652, at least one woman and four men named Cornish (Mary, Robert, William, and two Johns) immigrated to Virginia, and by 1662 a William Cornish owned land in Northampton County, but no evidence links any of them to Jeffrey or Richard Cornish.

Original depositions and court orders in Thomas Jefferson Papers, ser. 8, vol. 15, LC (quotations from Couse testimony, 30 Nov. 1624; quotations from Mathew testimony, 3 Jan. 1625; quotation from Foster testimony, 12 Dec. 1625; quotation from Aveling testimony, 3 Jan. 1626), printed in *Min-*

utes of Council and General Court, 34, 42, 78, 81, 83, 85, 93; Edmund S. Morgan, "The First American Boom: Virginia 1618 to 1630," *WMQ*, 3d ser., 28 (1971): 194, 198; Morgan, *American Slavery, American Freedom: The Ordeal of Colonial Virginia* (1975), 124–125; Jonathan Katz, ed., *Gay American History: Lesbians and Gay Men in the U.S.A., a Documentary* (1976), 16–19; Richard Godbeer, *Sexual Revolution in Early America* (2002), 123–124, 366–367; John M. Murrin, " 'Things Fearful to Name': Bestiality in Early America," in Angela N. H. Creager and William Chester Jordan, eds., *The Animal/Human Boundary: Historical Perspectives* (2002), 119; *New York Times*, 3 July 2003 (final quotation).
JOHN M. MURRIN

CORNSTALK (d. 10 November 1777), Shawnee leader, whose Indian name was variously rendered in colonial records as Comblade, Coolesqua, Hokoleskwa, Keightughque, Semachquaan, and Tawnamebuck, may have been a son or grandson of the Shawnee leader Paxinosa, a man known to be friendly to the British. During the first half of the eighteenth century Paxinosa's band lived at various locales in present-day Pennsylvania, and it is possible that Cornstalk was born in that colony. Some members of this band moved to the Scioto plains north of the Ohio River during the 1740s, and Paxinosa followed in 1760. Little is known of Cornstalk's life, in part because of a general confusion about the historical antecedents of the Shawnee before the mid-eighteenth century, by which time most Shawnee dwelt on the banks of the Scioto River in what became the state of Ohio.

As the British colonies expanded, both Virginia and Pennsylvania claimed the Ohio country and formed distinctive policies toward its Native American inhabitants. The French also maintained a presence in the area until the end of the Seven Years' War in 1763. There are undocumented reports that Cornstalk led raids into the Virginia frontier on behalf of the French during that war, and he was also said to have led several attacks on settlers in the Greenbrier region during Pontiac's Rebellion of 1763–1764. The earliest documented reference to Cornstalk is in the record of the peace conference in November 1764 at which Henry Bouquet, a British colonel, held him and five other hostages at Fort Pitt to ensure the Indians' cooperation. Cornstalk soon escaped and remained a powerful advocate of peaceful relations between Indians and whites.

The years after that conference witnessed periodic violence and acts of retaliation by both sides. On 25 April 1774 the royal governor of Virginia, John Murray, fourth earl of Dunmore, called out the militia of several western counties to defend the frontier settlements from the Indians. Dunmore's action led to an escalation of violence against friendly Indians, as well. On 30 April a party of whites killed several peaceable Mingoes, including a woman, at Yellow Creek, and infuriated Mingoes set out to avenge the deaths, aided by sympathetic members of other tribes. There is evidence that Cornstalk sought to avert open warfare and preserve the neutrality of the Shawnee. Through emissaries he assured Dunmore that the "foolish young people" who desired war were under control, and he sent word to John Connolly, Dunmore's representative at Fort Pitt (which Connolly called Fort Dunmore), that he would restrain his warriors until he learned the governor's intentions. Cornstalk also directed three men, including his brother Silver Heels, to escort British traders in the Ohio Valley back to the safety of Pittsburgh.

Acting under Dunmore's authority, Connolly sent a party of militia after the departing Shawnee. Silver Heels was shot and wounded. As the Shawnee prepared for war, Dunmore led an army southwest from Pittsburgh to rendezvous with a militia force of about 1,100 men commanded by Colonel Andrew Lewis, marching toward the Ohio River from the east. Just before sunrise on 10 October 1774, two of Lewis's men encountered a combined force of Delaware, Mingoes, Shawnee, Wyandot, and others waiting at the mouth of the Kanawha River near Point Pleasant. One escaped to warn the other Virginians. At sunrise the Indians under Cornstalk's command attacked. Several Virginians identified the loud, clear voice of Cornstalk encouraging his men throughout the battle. After several hours of intense fighting and heavy casualties on both sides, the Indians fell back, using the swampy terrain to cover their retreat.

Having prevented the Virginia armies from launching an invasion of the Scioto, Cornstalk approached Dunmore and asked for peace in order to protect the Shawnee villages. Some of Cornstalk's warriors and other chiefs wanted to continue to fight, to which Cornstalk replied that they might as well kill their women and children before fighting to the death themselves. He agreed to terms with Dunmore later that month in the treaty of Camp Charlotte, through which the Shawnee returned white prisoners and property and ceded hunting rights in Kentucky. Cornstalk was reported to have spoken eloquently at the peace talks and to have insisted that the whites share the blame for inciting the violence. Lewis's son later wrote that his father recalled that Cornstalk was "the most dignified looking man, particularly in council, he ever saw."

Despite persistent bitterness on both sides after what later historians called Dunmore's War, Cornstalk evidently adhered to the treaty and continued to advocate nonviolence. He championed neutrality when the Revolutionary War began, even though other Native American leaders allied themselves with the British in hopes of dislodging American settlements from the western country. Cornstalk took part in conferences with Connolly at Fort Dunmore in July 1775 and with commissioners appointed by the House of Burgesses that autumn. In the spirit of neutrality, he and Red Hawk, a Delaware, approached Fort Randolph at Point Pleasant in October 1777. According to one account, Cornstalk warned the American officers that most Indians were inclined toward the British and that despite his own desire for peace he and his tribe would have to "run with the stream." In an attempt to ensure Shawnee neutrality, Captain Matthew Arbuckle detained Cornstalk and his companions as hostages. On 10 November 1777 while Cornstalk's son Elinipsico (Allanawissica) was visiting the fort, Indians shot and killed a soldier nearby. A vengeful mob quickly formed, and despite Arbuckle's orders, the enraged men stormed Cornstalk's cabin. They shot everyone inside and killed Cornstalk, his son, and two other Indians.

Governor Patrick Henry denounced the murders and offered a reward for apprehension of the killers. In the spring of 1778 James Hall and three other men were separately examined in the Rockbridge County Court, which then had jurisdiction over all that portion of western Virginia, on suspicion of being responsible. No witnesses appeared to testify against any of the men, however, and the court found them not guilty. One week after Hall's acquittal, he took the oath of office as a captain in the county militia.

Cornstalk's known surviving relatives included his sister Nonhelema, also known as the Grenadier Squaw, and a son named Cutemwha, or the Wolf. Cornstalk was buried near Fort Randolph. After builders accidentally unearthed his presumed grave in 1840, the remains were moved to the grounds of the Mason County courthouse, and in 1954 they were moved again to Tu-Endie-Wei State Park on the site of the Battle of Point Pleasant.

Influential early accounts include John Stuart, "Memoir of Indian Wars, and Other Occurrences; By the Late Colonel Stuart, of Greenbrier," ed. Charles A. Stuart, in *Collections of the Virginia Historical and Philosophical Society* 1 (1833): 37–66 (third quotation on 58), in Frederick Webb Hodge, ed., *Handbook of American Indians North of Mexico*, in *Smithsonian Institution Bureau of American Ethnology Bulletin* 30, pt. 1 (1907): 350 (with undocumented birth date of ca. 1720), and Lyman C. Draper, "Sketch of Cornstalk, 1759–1777," *Ohio Archaeological and Historical Quarterly* 21 (1912): 245–262; identified as 1764 hostage in *Minutes of the Provincial Council of Pennsylvania*, Pennsylvania Archives, 1st ser., 9 (1852): 229–232; *Williamsburg Virginia Gazette* (Pinkney), 13 Oct. 1774, supplement (first quotation); *Virginia Historical Register, and Literary Advertiser* 1 (1848): 30–33 (second quotation on 33); most of the essential documents relating to the 1770s and Cornstalk's death, many in Draper MSS, printed in Reuben Gold Thwaites and Louise Phelps Kellogg, eds., *Documentary History of Dunmore's War, 1774* (1905), *The Revolution on the Upper Ohio, 1775–1777* (1908), and *Frontier Defense on the Upper Ohio, 1777–1778* (1912), and others in *Revolutionary Virginia*, vols. 3–4, 7; Cornstalk's mark, 19 July 1775, on MS Treaty of Fort Dunmore, 44, George Chalmers Collection, New York Public Library; death date in Patrick Henry proclamation, 27 Mar. 1778, printed in *Williamsburg Virginia Gazette* (Purdie), 3 Apr. 1778; Rockbridge Co. Order Book (1778–1783), 8–9, 13, 17, 20.

LAURA T. KEENAN

CORPREW, Edenborough G. (d. 16 July 1881), Baptist minister, was born late in the 1820s or in 1830 probably in Norfolk County, where he grew up. His parents, George W. Corprew and Grace Corprew, were slaves. George W. Corprew had learned to read and write, skills that he passed along surreptitiously to his son, and before the Civil War he had contracted to purchase himself, his wife, and their underage children. By that time, E. G. Corprew was owned by another master, had married, and about 1851 had fathered a son. He reportedly suffered the experience of having both his first and second wives sold away from him. Silvia A. Corprew, who is recorded with him in the 1870 census, was most likely his third wife. After her death on an unrecorded date, Corprew married Mary Etta Lane Gordon, a widow, on 22 November 1877. No children are recorded from his third or fourth marriages, but sometime after 1870 he adopted and raised a daughter.

When and how Corprew secured his freedom are not known. Former slaves flocked to Norfolk after Union forces occupied the city on 10 May 1862. Corprew and his father became leaders among the freedpeople there. Norfolk men discussed the need to organize in order to protect their rights when civil government was restored in Virginia, and E. G. Corprew reportedly attended the Colored Men's Conference in Syracuse, New York, in 1864. His father became treasurer of Norfolk's Colored Monitor Union Club, founded on 4 April 1865 to promote unity among the freedmen and to advocate universal suffrage and other rights of citizens.

Simultaneously, African Americans began to take control of their religious institutions, authority previously denied them under Virginia law. Corprew was prominent among the 318 black members of the Court Street Baptist Church, in Portsmouth, who requested a letter of dismissal from the white church in order to found their own congregation. After the letter was granted on 9 March 1865, he served as the first clerk for meetings of the new Zion Baptist Church's deacons. On 28 May a committee consisting of a representative from the church, a Union army chaplain, and representatives from the Court Street Church and from two Norfolk Baptist churches met and, after administering an examination, ordained Corprew to the ministry. Already the congregation's spiritual leader, he became its pastor and continued in that office until his death.

Corprew had no formal education, but church records in his handwriting reportedly display a good hand and adequate spelling. After his ordination, the congregation gave him leave to study theology for a short period at the Rich-

mond Theological School for Freedmen (popularly known as the Richmond Theological Institute or Colver Institute and a predecessor of Virginia Union University), but his continuing education came primarily from books. Contemporaries considered his library the largest owned by any black clergyman in Virginia.

In May 1865 Corprew and other leaders of the Zion Baptist Church formally requested that the Court Street Baptist Church transfer to them a lot on Green Street that the latter church had purchased in 1859 with the intention of building a separate church there for its black members. The white church's trustees readily agreed to the transfer, although complications prevented proper recording of the deed until 1870. In the meantime Corprew's congregation proceeded to erect a frame church on the site, which opened for worship about July 1866. Fire destroyed the building in the winter of 1869–1870, but the congregation built a new brick structure, which was dedicated in July 1876.

On 4 May 1867 fifteen clergy- and laymen met at the Zion Baptist Church to form the Virginia Baptist State Convention. Corprew not only hosted the meeting but also was elected first vice president of the convention. He served as superintendent of the Zion Baptist Sunday School and as president of the Norfolk, Portsmouth, and Berkley Sunday School Union. The Portsmouth city council, under Republican control at the time, elected him clerk of the city market for two years, but he did not play a prominent role in politics as an activist or officeholder.

Corprew acquired quite a bit of property. At the time of his death he owned four lots with houses, along with a vacant lot, all in Portsmouth, in addition to his own house on Effingham Street. He served on the advisory committee of the Norfolk Freedman's Savings and Trust Company bank and also held stock in the Home Savings Bank of Norfolk, of which he was a director.

Edenborough G. Corprew fell ill with consumption (probably tuberculosis) and wrote his will on 28 March 1881. He died at his Portsmouth home on 16 July of that year. His funeral followed two days later from Zion Baptist Church, which could accommodate only a quarter of those who came to mourn. No fewer than nine brother clergymen participated in the funeral services and followed his remains to the cemetery. Corprew, like his father, was one of those obscure yet remarkable men who emerged from slavery to found lasting institutions after emancipation. "His loss to his community," reported the *Washington People's Advocate*, was "well nigh irreparable."

Biography in *Zion Baptist Church: An Authentic History . . .* [1949], 11–12 (por.), with birth ca. 1822 in Norfolk Co.; Census, Norfolk Co., 1870 (age forty on 9 Aug. 1870), 1880 (age fifty on 1 June 1880); Portsmouth Marriage Register (1877), with age as forty-nine on 22 Nov. 1877 and birthplace of Norfolk Co., most likely provided by Corprew; Portsmouth Death Register (age fifty-five on 16 July 1881 and birthplace of North Carolina provided by widow); Portsmouth Hustings Court Will Book, 1:237–238; death and funeral notices in *Norfolk Landmark*, 17 (age "about fifty"), 19 July 1881, *Norfolk Virginian*, 17 (age "about 55"), 19 July 1881, and *Norfolk Public Ledger*, 18 July 1881; obituaries in *Richmond Virginia Star*, 23 July 1881, and *Washington People's Advocate*, 30 July 1881 (quotation).

JOHN T. KNEEBONE

CORSE, Montgomery Dent (14 March 1816–11 February 1895), Confederate army officer, was born in Alexandria and was the son of John Corse and Julia G. Corse. He attended local schools before going to work in his father's banking business. Fascinated from his youth by uniforms and the manual of arms, Corse helped raise a volunteer company during the Mexican War. Elected captain of the 1st Virginia Volunteers on 26 December 1846, he served along the Rio Grande but saw little combat. After months of occupation duty he mustered out in August 1848 and returned home.

News of the California gold discoveries inspired Corse to make his way west. Early in April 1849 he arrived in Sacramento and quickly continued on to the gold fields. He dug and panned for about seventeen months but by August 1850 had produced only modest results. Frustrated, Corse returned to Sacramento, where he lived for the next six years and supported himself by working variously as a deputy marshal, steamboat agent, hotel proprietor, and customs house officer. He also helped organize the Sutter's Rifles militia company in 1852 and became its captain.

Corse decided to return to Alexandria and arrived home in December 1856. He joined his brothers' banking partnership and worked there until the Civil War began. As sectional tensions increased, Corse joined several local militia companies. He became a lieutenant colonel in the 175th Regiment in 1857 and later served as a captain in a Home Guard unit. On 7 January 1861 he was elected captain of the Old Dominion Rifles. This and other Alexandria militia units attached to the 175th Regiment organized as a battalion in February of that year, with Corse as major. The battalion disbanded the following month, and in April the militia units reorganized as the 6th Battalion Virginia Volunteers, again with Major Corse commanding. After Virginia seceded from the Union, he received a state commission as colonel to rank from 17 May 1861. Beginning on 10 June of that year Corse commanded the 17th Regiment Virginia Infantry, formed from the battalion and two other companies. On 1 July the regiment was absorbed into the Provisional Army of the Confederate States.

Corse led his regiment at the First Battle of Manassas (Bull Run) and during the Peninsula campaign fought at Williamsburg and at Seven Pines. In the Seven Days' Battles around Richmond his regiment suffered heavy losses at White Oak Swamp (Frayser's Farm). Corse commanded a brigade at the Second Battle of Manassas (Bull Run) until he received a leg wound. He was wounded again at South Mountain and at Sharpsburg (Antietam), where he was captured but escaped. Having distinguished himself in combat, Corse was promoted to brigadier general on 1 November 1862. Shortly thereafter he took leave to marry Elizabeth Beverley on 22 November in Albemarle County. They had two daughters and two sons.

On 28 November 1862 Corse assumed command of a brigade at Fredericksburg but was not engaged in the battle that took place there two weeks later. His brigade participated in operations at Suffolk in the spring of 1863 and during the Gettysburg campaign guarded the railroad hubs at Richmond and at Gordonsville. In October his brigade joined Major General Samuel Jones's army on detached duty in western Virginia and was assigned to Robert Ransom's division. Early in December, at the conclusion of the Knoxville campaign, that division was attached to General James Longstreet's army and retreated toward Virginia. On 21 January 1864 Corse's brigade was ordered to Petersburg.

By early in February, Corse was in eastern North Carolina. His command participated in operations in the Kinston–New Bern area until 6 May, when the brigade was ordered to rejoin the Army of Northern Virginia. En route his troops fought near Drewry's Bluff on 16 May, and Corse was slightly wounded. His men skirmished at Cold Harbor and then took up positions on the Howlett Line above Petersburg from June 1864 until January 1865. The brigade saw action at Dinwiddie Court House in March and was engaged on 1 April at Five Forks and five days later at Saylers Creek, where Corse was captured. While imprisoned at Fort Warren, in Boston Harbor, Massachusetts, he petitioned for a presidential pardon on 16 June 1865 and was released on 24 July.

After returning to Alexandria late in the summer of 1865, Corse joined with several of his brothers in reviving the family banking business and worked with them until the company dissolved in 1874. He served as a vestryman at Saint Paul's Episcopal Church from 1867 to 1894 and sat on the board of visitors of the Virginia Military Institute from 1876 to 1882. Corse was a charter member of the R. E. Lee Camp, United Confederate Veterans, organized in Alexandria in 1884, and in May 1889 he was a guest of honor when one of his daughters unveiled the city's Confederate monument, to which he had contributed his monthly Mexican War pension.

Corse was visiting the State Capitol in Richmond on 27 April 1870 when the gallery and floor of the Supreme Court of Appeals collapsed. He escaped serious injury, but the disaster killed about sixty people, including the man who had been standing next to him. During the 1880s Corse developed cataracts in both eyes, and despite two operations he lost all sight in one eye and partial sight in the other. His wife died on 31 December 1894. Montgomery Dent Corse died at his Alexandria residence about six weeks later, on 11 February 1895. He was buried in the family plot in the cemetery of Saint Paul's Episcopal Church.

Biographies in Ezra J. Warner, *Generals in Gray: Lives of the Confederate Commanders* (1959), 63–64 (por.), William B. Hurd, "Montgomery Dent Corse," *Alexandria History* 4 (1982): 10–14, and George G. Kundahl, *Alexandria Goes to War: Beyond Robert E. Lee* (2004), 51–75; undated MS biography by son Montgomery Beverley Corse, Eva McCorkle, "Corse Annals" (undated MS), and Montgomery Dent Corse Papers, including letters and military commissions, all in Special Collections, Alexandria Library; Albemarle Co. Marriage License; BVS Marriage Register, Albemarle Co.; Lee A. Wallace, Jr., *17th Virginia Infantry* (1990), 109; Compiled Service Records; *OR*; Presidential Pardons; BVS Death Register, Alexandria City; obituary and funeral notices in *Alexandria Gazette*, 11 (por.), 12, 13 Feb. 1895.

RANDY I. CLEAVER

COSBY, Dabney (11 August 1779–8 July 1862), builder, was the son of Zaccheus Cosby and Susan Dabney Cosby. He was born at Cub Creek in Louisa County and by late in the 1790s had moved to Staunton, where he worked as a brickmaker and bricklayer. Cosby executed a marriage bond on 5 March 1801 and on that date or soon thereafter married Frances Davenport Tapp. They had six daughters, seven sons (two of whom also became builders), and another child who died in infancy.

Few details are known about Cosby's early career in Staunton, but it is clear from testimonials in his behalf that he became a successful and respected local builder. In December 1818 Cosby responded to Thomas Jefferson's advertisement seeking a brickmason to manufacture and lay bricks for the construction of Central College (later the University of Virginia) with a successful proposal to make several hundred thousand bricks each year of the project. Cosby was the principal brickmason for Hotels D and E and eight dormitories on the university's West Range. He hoped he would be considered trustworthy enough to help build the Rotunda and "see it executed in a stile, which for neatness and strength, should equal it in importance, and granduer of design," but there is no evidence that he contributed to its construction.

Cosby's association with the university exposed him to the building practices and adornments of the nineteenth-century Classical Revival, considered by Jefferson an appropriate model for public buildings. Cosby moved to Buckingham County about 1824 and soon contracted with several nearby counties to build new courthouses. Although he likely was not the sole designer of any of the buildings, he ensured that their classical features were correctly employed. As the undertaker, or contractor, Cosby provided and supervised the workmen who also manufactured the bricks and milled the lumber used in the construction. He owned about twenty slaves and regularly rented four others who labored on his projects. Working with the builder Valentine Parrish, Cosby completed the Goochland County courthouse, fronted by a Tuscan-style portico, in 1826. Cosby and another partner, William A. Howard, used the Roman Doric order for the Lunenburg County courthouse, finished in 1827. The following year, working alone, Cosby completed the Sussex County courthouse, which featured a pedimented pavilion and arcaded ground floor. All three buildings were placed on the Virginia Landmarks Register and the National Register of Historic Places during the 1970s.

About 1830 Cosby moved to Prince Edward County, where some of his buildings reflected a stylistic shift to Greek Revival architecture. Between 1829 and 1831 he designed several buildings for Union Theological Seminary, then affiliated with Hampden-Sydney College. He constructed part of Venable Hall and may have contributed to two residence halls, Boston House (later Middlecourt) and North Carolina House (later Penshurst). In October 1830 Cosby and Howard contracted to build the main hall (1832) at Randolph-Macon College, in Boydton. Cosby designed and built residences in Halifax County, including Glennmary (1837–1840), added to the Virginia Landmarks Register in 1978 and to the National Register in 1979. He and his namesake son used Greek Ionic columns to support the portico of the T-shaped Halifax County courthouse (1839), also placed on the state and national registers in 1978 and 1979, respectively. Early in the 1840s Cosby assisted in reconstructing Tabb Street Presbyterian Church, in Petersburg. Fine Flemish bond brickwork and tooled mortar joints characterize many of his buildings.

About 1840 Cosby moved to Raleigh, North Carolina, where he continued his building career and operated a brickyard. He supervised the masonry work on Alexander Jackson Davis's additions to the Old West building at the University of North Carolina, in Chapel Hill. Between 1847 and 1850 he constructed two buildings for the state's school for deaf and blind children in Raleigh, where he also built several houses and a hotel. Dabney Cosby often traveled during his later years but likely resided in Raleigh until his death there on 8 July 1862. The original place of his burial, which was conducted with Masonic rites, is unknown, but sometime after 1869 his remains were moved to Oakwood Cemetery, in Raleigh.

Biographical information, correspondence, transcript of will, and copy of editorial tribute from unidentified Raleigh newspaper in Dabney Cosby Papers, UNC; Cosby correspondence in Thomas Jefferson Papers and in Proctors Papers (quotation in Cosby to Arthur Spicer Brockenbrough, 31 Mar. 1821), both UVA; Dabney Cosby Papers, LVA; Dabney Cosby Account Book (1826–1854), VHS; James Marshall Bullock, "The Enterprising Contractor, Mr. Cosby" (M.A. thesis, UNC, 1982); Thomas W. Dolan, "Origins of the First Campus of Randolph-Macon College: An Architectural Note," *VMHB* 93 (1985): 431, 433; Richard Charles Cote, "The Architectural Workmen of Thomas Jefferson in Virginia" (Ph.D. diss., Boston University, 1986); K. Edward Lay, "Charlottesville's Architectural Legacy," *Magazine of Albemarle County History* 46 (1988): 50–51; Catherine W. Bishir, Charlotte V. Brown, Carl R. Lounsbury, and Ernest H. Wood III, *Architects and Builders in North Carolina: A History of the Practice of Building* (1990), 148 (daguerreotype por. identified as Cosby but more likely his namesake son); obituary in *Raleigh Semi-Weekly Standard*, 12 July 1862.

SUSAN HOLBROOK PERDUE

COTTEN, Joseph Cheshire (15 May 1905–6 February 1994), actor, was born in Petersburg. His parents, Sally Willson Cotten and Joseph Cheshire Cotten, hoped that he would follow an uncle into the banking business, but at Petersburg High School his interests lay in sports and theater. While attending the Hickman School of Speech and Expression, in Washington, D.C., in 1923, Cotten tried to lose his southern accent and supported himself by playing center on a semiprofessional football team. In 1924 he made an unsuccessful attempt to break onto the Broadway stage but spent most of his time in New York working in a paint warehouse. Cotten then tried his luck in Miami, where with a friend he manufactured and sold potato salad, an unlicensed enterprise health inspectors closed down. Cotten sold advertising in the *Miami Herald*, for which he also occasionally wrote reviews. He appeared with the Miami Civic Theatre and at least once glowingly reviewed his own performance for the *Herald*.

In the summer of 1930 Cotten returned to New York and secured an introduction to the celebrated theatrical impresario David Belasco, who hired him as assistant stage manager for *Dancing Partner*. In Belasco's next production, *Tonight or Never* (1930), Cotten was Melvyn Douglas's understudy. The Copley Theatre, in Boston, engaged him for the 1931–1932 season. While in Miami, Cotten had met West Virginia native Lenore Kipp La Mont, a pianist and divorcée with one young daughter. They married in Nashua, New Hampshire, on 18 October 1931 and registered their union in Boston the next month. They had no children.

Over the next few years Cotten appeared occasionally on Broadway, including productions of *Jezebel* (1933) and *The Postman Always Rings Twice* (1936). Under the aegis of the Works Progress Administration's Federal Theatre Project he starred in the farce *Horse Eats Hat* (1936), directed by Orson Welles. Using the stage name Joseph Wooll, he performed a small role in Welles's landmark, racially integrated production of Christopher Marlowe's *Tragical History of Doctor Faustus* (1937). After Welles helped found the Mercury Theater in 1937, Cotten joined that company and played in a minimalist, modern-dress *Julius Caesar* (1937), in *The Shoemakers' Holiday* (1938), and in *Danton's Death* (1938).

In 1939 Cotten created the role of C. K. Dexter Haven opposite Katharine Hepburn in the Broadway production of *The Philadelphia Story*. Although he was passed over in favor of Cary Grant when filming of the movie version began in 1940, he went to Hollywood and with other Mercury Theater veterans was recruited for Welles's masterpiece *Citizen Kane* (1941), in which Cotten played the idealistic drama critic Jedediah Leland. After starring in Alexander Korda's *Lydia* (1941), Cotten appeared in Welles's production of *The Magnificent Ambersons* (1942). Cotten assisted Welles in adapting the screenplay for the World War II spy thriller *Journey into Fear* (1942) and starred in the film.

The two remained close friends until Welles's death in 1985, and Cotten made uncredited appearances as a Venetian senator in Welles's *Othello* (1952) and as an alcoholic coroner in *Touch of Evil* (1958).

In 1942 Cotten became a contract player for David O. Selznick, an independent producer with whom he became fast friends. Selznick lent Cotten to Universal Studios for Alfred Hitchcock's *Shadow of a Doubt* (1943), in which the same honesty that Cotten displayed in his romantic roles rendered him equally believable as Teresa Wright's beloved Uncle Charlie, whom she discovers is a serial killer. He starred with Deanna Durbin in *Hers to Hold* (1943) and with Claudette Colbert in *Since You Went Away* (1944). Cotten played a Scotland Yard detective in *Gaslight* (1944), a traumatized soldier redeemed by parolee Ginger Rogers in *I'll Be Seeing You* (1944), and a soldier who secretly longs for Jennifer Jones in *Love Letters* (1945). He appeared with Jones again in *Duel in the Sun* (1946) and as Loretta Young's employer, political opponent, and love interest in *The Farmer's Daughter* (1947).

National polls of moviegoers in the mid-1940s routinely placed the debonair, courtly Cotten among their favorite romantic screen actors. During World War II he stumped for the American Red Cross's blood bank, and in October 1947 he flew cross-country to Washington, D.C., with about forty other performers to protest the House Un-American Activities Committee's actions related to the motion picture industry.

Cotten's performance as Eben Adams, an artist obsessed with a mysterious girl, in the haunting *Portrait of Jennie* (1948) won the International Prize for Best Actor at the 1949 Venice International Film Festival. Perhaps his finest work came under Carol Reed's direction in *The Third Man* (1949), in which Cotten played Holly Martins, a writer of pulp Westerns searching postwar Vienna for the truth about his best friend, played by Welles.

Compared to his critically acclaimed movies of the 1940s, Cotten's string of films in the 1950s and 1960s was less memorable. He appeared in Alfred Hitchcock's *Under Capricorn* (1949), in King Vidor's *Beyond the Forest* (1949) with Bette

Davis, in Robert Wise's *Two Flags West* (1950), in *September Affair* (1950) with Joan Fontaine, in *The Man with a Cloak* (1951) as the titular Edgar Allan Poe, and in *Untamed Frontier* (1952). He starred in *Niagara* (1953) as an unbalanced newlywed whom Marilyn Monroe plots to kill and in *From the Earth to the Moon* (1958), an awkward adaptation of the Jules Verne novel. Because Cotten played a cowardly Confederate deserter in *The Last Sunset* (1961), he elicited promises from the director and producer not to release the film in Tidewater Virginia so long as his mother lived.

From 1953 to 1954 Cotten returned to Broadway in the original romantic comedy *Sabrina Fair* opposite a fellow Virginian, Margaret Brooke Sullavan, but their roles went to Humphrey Bogart and Audrey Hepburn in the 1954 film version. In 1958 and 1959 he trod the boards in the comedy *Once More, with Feeling* with costars Arlene Francis and Walter Matthau. Cotten made frequent guest appearances on television, including several on the original *Alfred Hitchcock Presents* and as a recurring character on *It Takes a Thief* (1968–1970). He also hosted three television anthology series, *20th Century–Fox Hour* (1955–1956); *On Trial*, later retitled *The Joseph Cotten Show* (1956–1959); and *Hollywood and the Stars* (1963–1964). In the 1960s he pitched Bufferin pain-reliever in television commercials.

Cotten's wife hated traveling, and beginning in the 1940s they were often apart. Both had extramarital affairs. Cotten explained in his memoirs, "I was an actor. A roamer. A lover. I made pictures, I made love, and I made martinis." His wife died of leukemia on 7 January 1960 in Rome while Cotten was there filming *The Angel Wore Red* with Ava Gardner. On 20 October of that year at the Beverly Hills house of David O. Selznick and Jennifer Jones he married the English actress Patricia Medina, whose first marriage to the actor Richard Greene had ended in divorce in 1952. Cotten and Medina had no children. They starred together on tour in several plays, on Broadway in the murder mystery *Calculated Risk* (1962), and in the Japanese science-fiction adventure film *Latitude Zero* (1969).

Cotten's later films of note included the gothic *Hush . . . Hush Sweet Charlotte* (1965), *Petulia* (1968), *Tora! Tora! Tora!* (1970), the campy horror film *The Abominable Dr. Phibes* (1971), and Edward Albee's *Delicate Balance* (1973) with Katharine Hepburn and Paul Scofield. In *Soylent Green* (1973) he had a small but pivotal role as an executive whose murder sets the plot in motion. As his box office appeal declined, Cotten appeared in the requisite ensemble disaster picture (*Airport '77*, as Olivia de Havilland's love interest) and in episodes of the star-hungry television anthologies *Fantasy Island* (1979) and *Love Boat* (1981). Among his last screen appearances were the Mexican film *Guyana, Crime of the Century* (1979; released in the United States in 1980 as *Guyana, Cult of the Damned*) and the big budget Western flop, *Heaven's Gate* (1980). His final movie was an Australian adaptation of James Herbert's thriller, *The Survivor* (1981).

Cotten's smooth, cultured voice remained one of his most distinctive attributes. He narrated the Virginia Civil War Centennial Commission's film *Manassas to Appomattox*, and in 1978 he returned to Petersburg to narrate *The Echoes Still Remain*, a short film for the Siege Museum. He also recorded *She's Called Virginia*, a dramatized compilation of the words of famous Virginians from Captain John Smith to Carter Glass and Richard Evelyn Byrd, produced for the centennial of the Life Insurance Company of Virginia in 1971. Cotten was one of thirty-five Virginians honored by the governor in September 1972 for outstanding national achievement in the arts and humanities. On that occasion he received a pewter Jefferson cup engraved with the words "distinguished Virginian" and joked to the governor that he considered the phrase redundant.

Cotten suffered a stroke in June 1981 and only with great difficulty learned to speak again. In 1987 he published a stylish autobiography, *Vanity Will Get You Somewhere*. After cancer forced the removal of his larynx in 1990, Cotten was able to speak using a prosthesis but remained weak. His acting career over, he expressed himself by sculpting whimsical large-scale modern pieces in metal and wood.

Joseph Cheshire Cotten died of pneumonia in his Los Angeles condominium on 6 February 1994. His cremated ashes were returned to his native Petersburg for private burial in Blandford Cemetery. At Petersburg High School the Joseph Cotten Stage honors his achievements.

Cotten, *Vanity Will Get You Somewhere* (1987), including many pors., quotation on 73, and partial filmography on 219–220; Patricia Medina Cotten, *Laid Back in Hollywood: Remembering* (1998); Massachusetts Department of Public Health, Registry of Vital Records and Statistics, Marriage Certificate (1931); California Certificate of Registry of Marriage, Los Angeles Co. (1960); *Richmond Times-Dispatch*, 29 Sept. 1940; *Washington Post*, 7 Oct. 1944, 28 Nov. 1956, 17 June 1987; *Los Angeles Times*, 3 May, 29 July 1987; *Miami Sun-Sentinel*, 5 July 1987; Charles Slack, "From Petersburg to Tinseltown and Back," *64* 1 (Aug. 2000): 44–48; obituaries in *Los Angeles Times*, *New York Times*, *Petersburg Progress-Index*, *Richmond Times-Dispatch* (with partial filmography), and *Washington Post*, all 7 Feb. 1994; memorial tributes in *Los Angeles Times* and *Richmond Times-Dispatch*, both 8 Feb. 1994.

SARA B. BEARSS

COTTON, Ann (fl. 1650s–1670s), author of a narrative of Bacon's Rebellion, was the wife of John Cotton, of York County. Nothing is known about the date and place of her birth, her maiden name, the date of her marriage or marriages, or whether she had any children. Historians who have identified her husband as a native of the Eastern Shore of Virginia believed that they resided in Hungars Parish, Northampton County, and had a daughter in the spring of 1660 and a son in December 1662, but no documents demonstrate that either of the Cottons had a relationship to any Eastern Shore families. The first reference to Ann Cotton in extant Virginia documents is dated 4 November 1657, when she and her husband witnessed the will of William Evans in York County, where she and her husband evidently lived from sometime before that date until after Bacon's Rebellion of 1676. Her husband was an attorney and for a time owned a plantation on Queen's Creek. It is evident from her narrative of the rebellion that she knew most or all of the important people in the county, including Edmund Cheesman and his wife, both prominent supporters of Nathaniel Bacon (1647–1676).

Unlike many other women in her time and place, Cotton was literate and educated. She corresponded with at least one friend in England, for whom she composed a highly personal narrative of the rebellion. Much of what is known about Cotton must be gleaned from that lost document, which was first published without a note on its provenance on 12 September 1804 in the *Richmond Enquirer*. In that source the letter was signed "An. Cotton. From Q. Creeke" and was addressed "To Mr. C. H. at Yardly in Northamptonshire."

Cotton's narrative, probably based on the longer account that her husband had written sometime after the end of 1676, appeared in a long letter probably addressed to Christopher Harris, whom the Cottons had known in Virginia in the 1650s. As Ann Cotton's letter indicates, Harris had requested information about the rebellion, possibly a copy of her husband's narrative, which for reasons she did not state Harris could not obtain. In order to satisfy Harris's curiosity, she prepared a short version of her husband's narrative and added a good many parenthetical references addressed to Harris to remind him of some of the people to whom she referred. If Harris knew of and requested a copy of John Cotton's narrative, or even if Harris and Ann Cotton had exchanged letters after the conclusion of the rebellion, she could not have composed her narrative before the latter part of 1677.

Like the Cottons, Harris would have known many of the major figures in the rebellion. His wife was a stepdaughter of Nathaniel Bacon (ca. 1620–1692), who resided in York County and was a member of the Council and supporter of the governor against the rebellion that his namesake kinsman led. In her narrative, Cotton referred to the elder Bacon as "your late wives father-in-law." Harris and his wife had sold some land to him in 1661 and apparently departed for England soon afterward. Evidently the Cotton and Harris families had kept in touch, for she referred to previous correspondence: "as hath by a former letter bin hinted to you" and "hinted in my former Letter."

Ann Cotton's narrative style, like the longer work by her husband, is laced with parenthetical remarks, but many of hers are addressed specifically to Harris. A reference to Colonel John Washington is followed by the aside, "(him whom you have somtimes seene at your Howse)." After naming several members of the governor's Council, she reminded her reader that they were "all persons, with whom you have bin formerly acquainted." Naming some of the rebels who were executed in 1676 and 1677, she mentioned "James Wilson (once your servant)" and Henry Page "(one that my Husband bought of Mr. Lee, when he kep store at your howse)."

When Cotton's account was published in 1804, the printer noted that John Cotton had written to his wife from Jamestown on 9 June 1676 recounting one of the dramatic events at the opening of the rebellion. The whereabouts of that document and the original of Ann Cotton's letter are not known. Relying on the 1804 newspaper text, Peter Force reprinted Cotton's letter in 1836 in the first volume of *Tracts and Other Papers, Relating Principally to the Origin, Settlement, and Progress of the Colonies in North America* and there gave it the title by which it is usually known, "An Account of Our Late Troubles in Virginia. Written in 1676, By Mrs. An. Cotton, of Q. Creeke." Because her letter was one of the first personal accounts of Bacon's Rebellion to be published and was included in Force's influential *Tracts*, Cotton became well known as an early American author, even though her life remains largely a mystery. The time and place of Ann Cotton's death and the place of her burial are not recorded.

Jay B. Hubbell, "John and Ann Cotton, of 'Queen's Creek,' Virginia," *American Literature* 10 (1938): 179–201; C. E. Schorer, "'One Cotton, of Acquia Creek, Husband of Ann Cotton,'" ibid. 22 (1950): 342–345; earliest Virginia reference in York Co. Deeds, Wills, Etc., 3: fol. 10; Francis Burton Harrison, "Footnotes Upon Some XVII Century Virginians," *VMHB* 50 (1942): 289–299; Jane Carson, *Bacon's Rebellion, 1676–1976* (1976), 16–20; Cotton's letter printed in *Richmond Enquirer*, 12 Sept. 1804 (all quotations), and Peter Force, ed., *Tracts and Other Papers, Relating Principally to the Origin, Settlement, and Progress of the Colonies in North America, from the Discovery of the Country to the Year 1776* (1836–1846), vol. 1; improbable attribution to Cotton of four-paragraph refutation of supposed Welsh origins of American Indians in *Richmond Enquirer*, 22 Jan. 1805.

VIRGINIA BERNHARD

COTTON, John (d. after 24 October 1683), chronicler of Bacon's Rebellion, has sometimes been identified as the posthumous son of Anne Graves Cotton and William Cotton, the rector of Hungars Parish in Northampton County who died about 1640 or 1641, and as the John Cutten who with his wife Hannah Cutten, of that county, had a daughter in 1660 and a son in 1662, but extant records do not sustain either identification. The clergyman's only known surviving child was a daughter, and it has been impossible to establish any relationship between John Cotton and any members of the several Eastern Shore families whose surnames in the local records were spelled Cotten, Cotton, Cutten, Cutton, Cutting, or Cuttinge. The earliest known reference to John Cotton in Virginia documents is in the will of William Evans, of York County, which John Cotton and Ann Cotton witnessed on 4 November 1657, when a son of the Northampton clergyman would have been no more than sixteen years old. It is more likely that Cotton and his wife were married adults already living in York County by that date.

Nothing is known for certain about Cotton's origins, the date and place of his marriage or marriages, whether he had any children, or other details about his family; but his writings demonstrate that he received a good education and read widely in English and classical literature. York County records between 1657 and 1683 indicate that he lived on Queen's Creek, where for several years he owned a plantation. Although active as an agent and attorney, he did not serve on the county court, and there is no record of his holding a commission in the county militia.

Cotton was in Jamestown during the first week of June 1676 and saw the governor arrest and release Nathaniel Bacon (1647–1676), one of the episodes that set the rebellion in motion. Cotton's long narrative of the rebellion does not note whether he personally witnessed any of the other episodes he described, nor does it disclose what he himself did during that dramatic year. He appears to have had some sympathy with the rebels' initiative in defending the colony against the Indians, but he also sharply criticized Bacon for burning Jamestown. Cotton's name does not appear on any of the surviving documents that Bacon's supporters signed, nor on the official list of those who suffered property losses as a consequence of their adherence to the government of Sir William Berkeley.

The numerous similarities in wording, style, and content between a brief account of the rebellion that Ann Cotton wrote and the much longer one that has been attributed to John Cotton confirm his authorship, and her letter seems to substantiate that his was written first. His narrative was passed down through the Burwell family of Virginia and in 1814 was published for the first time as "The Burwell Papers" in the *Collections of the Massachusetts Historical Society*. Peter Force reprinted that version in the first volume of his *Tracts and Other Papers, Relating Principally to the Origin, Settlement, and Progress of the Colonies in North America* (1836). The 1814 edition being error-filled and modernized in spelling and punctuation, the Massachusetts Historical Society reprinted it in 1866 and at that time gave it the title by which it is usually known, "The History of Bacon's and Ingram's Rebellion." In 1915 Charles McLean Andrews reprinted the 1866 edition in his *Narratives of the Insurrections, 1675–1690.*

There is no sample of Cotton's handwriting by which to identify him as the person who indited the manuscript of his narrative that is at the Virginia Historical Society. That document appears to be in a late seventeenth- or early eighteenth-century handwriting, but the cover is dated 27 July 1764 in another hand. The text begins in mid-sentence on page five (the only numbered page) and ends abruptly in mid-sentence at the foot of the fifty-fifth page. The document is neither signed nor dated, and it contains no hint of the circumstances of the composition of the original. Another manuscript copy in the same library appears to be a transcription made for the printer's use in 1814 when the text was first published.

Cotton's narrative of the rebellion is witty, bombastic, and full of literary allusions, and as a consequence it is frequently quoted (almost always from the early and imperfect printed texts). Written in a florid style, it includes two poems, the first of which, "Bacon's Epitaph," has been lauded as the first notable poem composed in America, but it is not known whether Cotton wrote either or both of the poems. Cotton's original served as the basis for a much shorter account of the rebellion that his wife wrote and that was first published in 1804. That her account of the rebellion concludes with Berkeley's execution of the principal leaders suggests that his did, too, and that John Cotton may have composed his history not long after the execution, early in 1677. Cotton's original or another copy of it was probably the manuscript from which the Maryland poet Ebenezer Cooke derived his "History of Colonel Nathaniel Bacon's Rebellion in Virginia, Done into Hudibrastick Verse, from an Old MS," first published in *The Maryland Muse* in 1731.

There was more than one man named John Cotton in Virginia between the 1650s and 1680s, but only one is known for certain to have lived in York County. The last documented references to him in the records of that county concern a case that he evidently agreed on 24 August 1683 to postpone to the next meeting of the county court. At that meeting, on 24 October, the justices of the peace postponed the case again. John Cotton was presumably still alive on the latter date, but there is no further record of the case, and it may have abated as a consequence of his death a few days, weeks, or months later. His date of death and place of burial remain unknown.

Jay B. Hubbell, "John and Ann Cotton, of 'Queen's Creek,' Virginia," *American Literature* 10 (1938): 179–201; C. E. Schorer, "'One Cotton, of Acquia Creek, Husband of Ann Cotton,'" ibid. 22 (1950): 342–345; Jane Carson, *Bacon's Rebellion, 1676–1976* (1976), 16–20; numerous references in York Co. records, the earliest dated 4 Nov. 1657 (York Co. Deeds, Wills, Etc., 3: fol. 10) and latest dated 24 Aug. and 24 Oct. 1683 (York Co. Deeds, Orders, Wills, Etc., 6:514, 524); Minutes of Council and General Court, 220; Cotton's narrative printed in *Collections of the Massachusetts Historical Society*, 2d ser., 1 (1814): 27–80, in Peter Force, ed., *Tracts and Other Papers, Relating Principally to the Origin, Settlement, and Progress of the Colonies in North America, from the Discovery of the Country to the Year 1776* (1836–1846), vol. 1, in *Proceedings of the Massachusetts Historical Society* 9 (1866): 299–342, and in Charles M. Andrews, ed., *Narratives of the Insurrections, 1675–1690* (1915), 43–98; Lawrence C. Wroth, "The Maryland Muse by Ebenezer Cooke, A Facsimile, with an Introduction," *Proceedings of the American Antiquarian Society*, new ser., 44 (1935): 293–298, 299–308.

VIRGINIA BERNHARD

COUCH, James Henry (3 August 1821–23 or 24 November 1899), member of the Convention of 1861, was the son of Daniel Couch, a farmer, and Sarah Richardson Couch. He was born in Hanover County but grew up in Mason County, where the family moved when he was a child. His father is believed to have died about 1824. Little is known of Couch's education, but he may have attended Ohio University, in Athens. He married Helen Jane Waggener in Mason County on 2 May 1844. During a period of twenty-seven years they had eight sons and three daughters. Couch practiced law in Point Pleasant, where he owned a house and lot and resided until after the Civil War. By 1860 he also owned four parcels containing about 4,000 acres of land in Mason County, and in that year he paid taxes on four slaves.

The county was overwhelmingly pro-Union, as demonstrated by a large public meeting on 29 December 1860 that branded supporters of secession as traitors. On 4 February 1861 the Unionist Couch won election by a reported one thousand votes to represent Mason County in the state convention called to consider the issue of secession. He attended from 13 February through 18 April 1861 but did not speak a single time. Couch voted against secession on 4 April 1861 and again on 17 April, and on the latter date he also voted against the preamble to the Ordinance of Secession that the convention was considering. That is the last time Couch's name appears in the convention journals. He may have gone home or left Richmond, but he evidently returned for the opening of the brief second session in June. Even though there is no indication of his presence in the published convention proceedings, on 1 July 1861 he received a final payment for thirteen days of service. On an unrecorded date before 20 June, Couch resigned.

Couch practiced law in Point Pleasant until about 1870 and then retired to his farm on the banks of the Kanawha River. He refused one or more requests that he campaign for a seat on the West Virginia Supreme Court of Appeals and seemingly did not resume his career at the bar. James Henry Couch died of heart disease at his farm during the night of 23–24 November 1899 and most likely was buried there.

Family history, with birth in Hanover Co. and birth and marriage dates, in Mason County History Book Committee, *History of Mason County, West Virginia* (1987), 80–82 (por.);

biography in W. S. Laidley, *History of Charleston and Kanawha County, West Virginia, and Representative Citizens* (1911), 2:512 (with birth in Hanover Co. and death date of 24 Nov. 1899); Julie Chapin Hesson with Sherman Gene Hesson and Jane J. Russell, eds., *Mason County, West Virginia, Marriages, 1806 to 1915* (1997), 34; Census, Mason Co., 1850, 1860, 1870, 1880; Land and Personal Property Tax Returns, Mason Co., 1860, LVA; *Wheeling Daily Intelligencer*, 8 Feb. 1861; Reese and Gaines, *Proceedings of 1861 Convention*, 3:163, 4:144, 145; *Report of the Committee of Elections upon the Resolution of Mr. Wysor in Regard to Absent Members*, Convention of 1861 Doc. No. 27 (n.d., reported 20 June 1861); Convention of 1861 Pay List, RG 93, LVA; final illness and obituary (giving erroneous birthplace of Harrison Co. and variant marriage date of 20 May 1844 and reporting death during the night of Thursday, 23 Nov. 1899) in *Point Pleasant State Gazette*, 21, 24, 28 Nov. 1899.

BRENT TARTER

COUPER, William (20 September 1853–22 June 1942), sculptor, was born in Norfolk and was the son of John Diedrich Couper, founder of Couper Marble Works, and Euphania Ann Monroe Cowling Couper. His namesake nephew (1884–1964) became a historian and administrator at the Virginia Military Institute. Couper showed an aptitude for carving while still in his teens. He exhibited a cameo of a bacchante in Norfolk in 1872 and the following year displayed several pieces at the city's agricultural fair. Couper then moved to New York and, supported by a scholarship, enrolled in the art school at the Cooper Union for the Advancement of Science and Art. In 1874, bearing letters of introduction from the Richmond sculptor Edward Virginius Valentine and from Virginia governor James Lawson Kemper, he sailed for Germany, where he enrolled in the Royal Academy of Fine Arts and also studied anatomy in Munich.

Couper received a diploma from the academy in 1875 and moved to Florence. The Italian city was internationally popular with sculptors, who were attracted by the famed marble quarries, skilled Italian workmen, and reasonable cost of living. Couper found himself part of a large expatriate community. The turning point in his personal and professional life came when he met the Boston sculptor Thomas Ball, who had settled in Florence with his family in 1869. Couper began studying with Ball late in 1876 and moved into his villa on the Via Dante da Castiglione, where he occupied a room that had been recently vacated by another American pupil, Daniel Chester French. Couper married Ball's only daughter, Eliza Chickering Ball, on 9 May 1878. They had three sons. The two families maintained residences and studios together in Italy and in the United States.

Much of Couper's sculpture consisted of portraits, but he also began to undertake ideal subjects. Some, such as *Evening* (1878) and *Morning* (1882), were marble medallions sold through Tiffany and Company, of New York, which also served as the agent for a number of Couper's ideal busts. Pieces inspired by literature and classical mythology included *Evangeline* (1880), *Psyche* (1882), and *Iphigenia* (1882). Critics praised Couper's later figures of angels, with their detail and fine carving, as some of his most evocative pieces. In 1892 he was named to the committee charged with selecting sculpture by American artists in Italy for exhibition at the World's Columbian Exposition in Chicago the following year.

In 1897 the Couper and Ball families left Florence and settled in Montclair, New Jersey, where Couper built an Italianate villa he named Poggioridente. He opened a studio in New York City and embarked on an active career in public sculpture. Much of his American work continued to comprise medallions, bas reliefs, and portrait busts in marble and bronze, including ones of William McKinley (1903) and John Davison Rockefeller (1910). Some pieces were large in scale, such as the marble statue of *Moses* (1899) Couper executed for the Manhattan Appellate Courthouse in New York. To the Dewey Arch, a temporary monument in New York on which a number of sculptors collaborated, he contributed a relief entitled *Protection of Our Country* (1899), a reduced copy of which was used for the Commodore Richard Dale Monument in Portsmouth, Virginia.

Couper won a bronze medal in 1901 for *A Crown for the Victor* (1896) when it was shown in Buffalo, New York, at the Pan-American Exposition. His portrait statues included a variety of well-known people, most notably the engineer John Augustus Roebling (1906), located in Trenton, New Jersey, and the poet Henry Wadsworth Longfellow (1909), located in Washington, D.C.

Couper also received commissions for six works for the National Military Park in Vicksburg, Mississippi, for which he produced *Peace* (1907) for the Minnesota Monument; busts of Colonel Isham Warren Garrott (1909), Major General Francis Preston Blair (1911), and Brigadier General Isaac F. Quinby (1911); and statues of Rear Admiral Andrew Hull Foote (1911) and Captain Andrew Hickenlooper (1912). For the Sailors' Memorial (1911) at the United States Naval Academy in Annapolis, he executed a large bronze relief depicting a frigate's gun crew in honor of Revolutionary War sailors.

In 1906 Couper designed his most notable work in his native state, a fifteen-foot-tall *Confederate Soldier*, installed atop Norfolk's Confederate Monument, a fifty-foot-tall granite shaft that Couper Marble Works had erected in 1899. Other commissions in Virginia included a bronze tablet to George Dod Armstrong (1900) in Norfolk's First Presbyterian Church and a statue of Captain John Smith (1909) at Jamestown for the Association for the Preservation of Virginia Antiquities. In Richmond are a bust of John Patteson Branch (1903) and large bronze statues of Hunter Holmes McGuire (1904), in Capitol Square, and of Joseph Bryan (1910), in Monroe Park. Recognized for the faithfulness of his portraiture, Couper once stated that a likeness "must be absolute, else the work fails of its first purpose."

Couper retired in 1913 and devoted himself thereafter to painting seascapes and watercolors. He sold his large Montclair house in 1925 and moved to smaller quarters. About two years after the death of his wife on 20 July 1939, he moved to the home of one of his sons in Bozman, Talbot County, Maryland. William Couper died on 22 June 1942 in a hospital in nearby Easton. His cremated remains were interred in the family plot in Elmwood Cemetery in Norfolk, where his *Recording Angel* had been installed in 1906.

NCAB, 9:58; Lorado Taft, *The History of American Sculpture* (1924), 418–424; Greta Elena Couper, *An American Sculptor on the Grand Tour: The Life and Works of William Couper (1853–1942)* (1988), including a checklist of Couper's works and several pors.; Norfolk City Birth Register; Couper family genealogical chart, in William Couper (1884–1964) Papers, VMI, and in Couper Family Papers, VHS; William Couper Biographical File, Norfolk Public Library; correspondence and other documents in William Couper and Couper Family Papers and in Greta Elena Couper Research Material on Thomas Bell and William Couper, all Archives of American Art, Smithsonian Institution, Washington, D.C., in Edward V. Valentine Papers, VRHC, and in Couper Marble Works Records (1848–1942), VHS; *Norfolk Virginian*, 20 Mar. 1872, 1 May 1883; *Norfolk Landmark*, 9 Oct. 1873; *Washington Post*, 13 Dec. 1908 (quotation); obituaries in *New York Times*, 25 June 1942, and *Norfolk Ledger-Dispatch* and *Norfolk Virginian-Pilot*, both 26 June 1942.

BETSY FAHLMAN

COUPER, William (16 November 1884–15 February 1964), college administrator and historian, was born in a section of Norfolk County that in 1902 became part of the city of Norfolk. He was the son of Fannie Bernard Capps Couper and John D. Couper, president of Couper Marble Works, and a nephew of William Couper (1853–1942), a prominent sculptor noted for his portraits and historical works. Couper received his preparatory education at the Norfolk Academy and entered the Virginia Military Institute as a third classman, or sophomore, in 1901. He graduated in 1904 and received a bachelor's degree in civil engineering from the Massachusetts Institute of Technology in 1906.

After completing his studies Couper embarked on a career in civil engineering and construction management. From 1906 to 1917 he worked for the Pennsylvania Railroad Company and was a senior manager of several projects constructing terminals and tunnels in the New York City area. He married Laura Eloise Hirst in Purcellville, Loudoun County, Virginia, on 9 October 1912. They had one son and one daughter.

During World War I, Couper accepted a commission in the United States Army Quartermaster Corps and rose to the rank of lieutenant colonel. He supervised the construction of Camp (later Fort) Jackson in Columbia, South Carolina, and later was officer in charge of matériel and equipment disposal for the construction division. In 1920 Couper resumed his civilian career, and over the next four years he held engineering and management positions with companies in Washington, D.C., and in Texas and was business executive of the Veterans' Bureau (later the Department of Veterans Affairs) station at Perry Point, in Cecil County, Maryland.

Throughout this period Couper maintained close ties to VMI and helped lead the institute's first major fund-raising campaign of the twentieth century. At the request of the school's board of visitors, in 1920 he compiled the first long-range plan charting the future development of VMI. Couper was recruited in 1925 to serve as the Virginia Military Institute's first executive officer. He devoted the next thirty years of his professional life to his alma mater in numerous official and unofficial capacities and shaped virtually all aspects of VMI's growth and development through the mid-1950s. He oversaw a wide range of operations, including finance and budget, construction projects, long-range planning, intercollegiate athletics, personnel, admissions, and student records.

During his tenure Couper supervised extensive improvements to the school's infrastructure, including the construction of a new library, gymnasium, mess hall, and physics and engineering buildings, as well as a major addition to the barracks and the renovation of other structures. Long active in VMI's alumni association, he served as its secretary-treasurer from 1931 to 1933. In 1934 he was elected to a single term as president of the Association of Military Colleges and Schools in the United States. Couper had a strong interest in athletics and served as secretary-treasurer (1934–1945), vice president (1946), and president (1947–1948) of the Southern Conference, the athletic association of which VMI was then a member.

Couper was a noted authority on the history of VMI, Lexington and Rockbridge County, and the Shenandoah Valley. He was also widely regarded as an expert on the life and times of Confederate general Thomas J. "Stonewall" Jackson. In recognition of his work as a historian, VMI appointed him its official historiographer in October 1934. Couper wrote *The VMI New Market Cadets* (1933), which contained biographical sketches of the school's cadets and staff members who had fought in that Civil War battle, and *Claudius Crozet: Soldier-Scholar-Educator-Engineer (1789–1864)* (1936), a biography of the nineteenth-century civil engineer published in the Southern Sketches series. His most important books were *One Hundred Years at VMI* (1939), a four-volume history of the college from its founding in 1839, and the three-volume *History of the Shenandoah Valley* (1952).

Couper was also responsible for the initial organization and preservation of the institute's rich archives, then numbering more than 18,000 items including significant biographical and genealogical records on every former VMI cadet. He helped compile and publish this information in 1927 and 1939 as the *Register of Former Cadets of the Virginia Military Institute*, and subsequent editions relied on Couper's archival foundation.

Couper retired from VMI in December 1954. He remained in Lexington and was active in the Rockbridge Historical Society and other community organizations. After suffering a heart attack, William Couper died at his home on 15 February 1964 and was buried in Elmwood Cemetery, in Norfolk. VMI held a memorial service in his honor and lowered the school's flags to half-staff. Five years after Couper's death the VMI Foundation, Incorporated, presented its first Distinguished Service Award to him.

Biographies in Couper, *History of the Shenandoah Valley* (1952), 3:478–479 (por.), Morton, *Virginia Lives*, 215–216, John L. Couper, "Some Recollections of Colonel William Couper," *Proceedings of the Rockbridge Historical Society* 8 (1970–1974): 161–169, and *Virginia Military Institute Alumni Review* 31 (winter 1954–1955): 6, 13; extensive biographical information, correspondence, research materials, manuscripts, speeches, and photographs in William Couper Papers and administrative papers in various collections, all VMI; diaries, correspondence, notebooks, and genealogical materials in Couper Family Papers, VHS; BVS Marriage Register, Loudoun Co.; Military Service Records; publications include Couper, "War and Work," *Proceedings of the Rockbridge Historical Society* 1 (1939–1941): 26–42, and "Virginia Military Institute: An Educational Pioneer," *Commonwealth* 6 (June 1939): 7–9; *Richmond Times-Dispatch*, 23 Dec. 1954; obituaries in *Lynchburg News*, *Norfolk Virginian-Pilot*, *Richmond Times-Dispatch*, and *Roanoke Times*, all 16 Feb. 1964, and *Lexington News-Gazette*, 19 Feb. 1964.

DIANE B. JACOB

COURTNEY, John (d. 18 December 1824), Baptist minister, was born in the early or mid-1740s in King and Queen County. He was the son of Robert Courtney, but his mother's name is not known. After his father died, Courtney's elder brother apprenticed him to a carpenter. As a young man, he married a woman named Jane, but the date and place of the wedding are not known, nor is his wife's maiden name. Before her death on 19 March 1808, they had two daughters and one son. Sometime before the American Revolution, and probably early in the 1770s, Courtney and one of his brothers were converted as the result of the preaching of several Baptist ministers. By 1775 Courtney had become pastor of Upper College Baptist Church (later Sharon Baptist Church) in King William County. He served as a private in the army during the Revolutionary War and afterward moved to Richmond, where in 1788 he became minister of the eight-year-old Richmond Baptist Church (later First Baptist Church).

Not as well educated as many contemporary clergymen in the capital, Courtney continued to work as a carpenter to support his family while ministering to the growing congregation. He lived simply in a rented house and never owned his own home. About 1798 the members erected their first modest frame building, and in 1802 they built a substantial brick church, later the home of First African Baptist Church of Richmond. The congregation was probably racially integrated from the beginning, as were many other Baptist churches, and Courtney became well known for ministering to the city's African Americans. In 1796 he escorted a black man convicted of theft to the place of execution, where the condemned man, whom Courtney had converted in jail, made an affecting address to a large crowd before being hanged. One of the members of the church early in the nineteenth century was Lott Cary, an enslaved man who with assistance from other church members gained his freedom and in 1821 immigrated to the west coast of Africa, a mission that led to the founding of what became Liberia. Courtney's personal opinions about slavery are not clear. At the time of the Revolution when he became a minister, many Baptists regarded slavery as immoral, but by the early years of the nineteenth century, members of the denomination increasingly accepted slavery as an institution sanctioned by the Bible. Evidence suggests that early in the century Courtney may have owned two or more slaves.

On 7 December 1802, after the House of Delegates had decided by a close vote to appoint a chaplain, the members chose Courtney over two other clergymen, one the popular local Presbyterian, John Durburrow Blair. Courtney's election probably reflected the increased importance of Baptists throughout Virginia, but his lack of education and his ministry among African Americans drew some sharp criticism in the state's newspapers.

The church's congregation had grown to about 1,200 members by 1814 and an even larger number by 1820, when several members, including William Crane, a noted white lay leader, withdrew to form the Second Baptist Church of Richmond. The split stemmed from disagreement about the formation of a Sunday school. Although Courtney accepted the organizing of women in order to support the church's missionary work, he resisted establishing a Sunday school. He compiled *The Christian Pocket Companion, Being a Collection of the Newest and Most Admired Spiritual Songs, Now Made Use of by the United Baptists in Virginia* (1802), yet he was remembered for refusing to use hymnals during services for fear that they distracted the congregation from worship.

Although Courtney continued to visit members of the church during the latter years of his life, he became too feeble to preach regularly. In 1810 a member of the congregation assumed some of his pastoral duties, and for six months in 1821 Andrew Broaddus joined Courtney as assistant pastor. Had it not been for Courtney's poor health and inability to attend, his seniority and service as pastor of one of the state's largest Baptist congregations would have given him a prominent role at the founding of the Baptist General Association of Virginia in 1822. John Courtney died in Richmond on 18 December 1824 and was buried in a private cemetery in the city.

Biography in *Evangelical Inquirer* 1 (1826): 22–25 (with birth year of ca. 1744), reprinted in James B. Taylor, *Virginia Baptist Ministers*, 1st ser. (1859), 96–99, and abstracted in Robert B. Semple and G. W. Beale, *A History of the Rise and Progress of the Baptists in Virginia*, rev. ed. (1894), 472; Blanche Sydnor White, *First Baptist Church, Richmond, 1780–1955* (1955), 11–38, 219–220; Edward C. Carter II et al., eds., *The Virginia Journals of Benjamin Henry Latrobe, 1795–1798* (1977), 1:191–193; *JHD*, 1802–1803 sess., 5–6; *Richmond Virginia Argus*, 8, 15 Dec. 1802; *Richmond Virginia Gazette, and General Advertiser*, 11, 18 Dec. 1802; *Richmond Enquirer*, 22 Mar. 1808; *Richmond Daily Dispatch*, 29 June 1882; obituary in *Richmond Commercial Compiler*, 20 Dec. 1824 (with death "in the eighty-third year of his life").

FRED ANDERSON

COWAN, George Rutledge (22 September 1837–14 October 1904), member of the Convention of 1867–1868, was born in Lebanon, Russell County, and was the son of Mary Gilmore Cowan and George Cowan, a prosperous farmer who served several terms in the House of Delegates and the Senate of Virginia. Little is known of Cowan's early life. He probably attended local schools.

On 2 May 1861 Cowan enlisted as a private in the New Garden Fearnots, later organized as Company I of the 37th Regiment Virginia Infantry. Four of his brothers also served in the unit, one as captain. In June the regiment departed for northwestern Virginia to join Brigadier General Robert Selden Garnett's command. While skirmishing at Laurel Hill, Cowan's company learned of the defeat of Confederate forces at Rich Mountain and joined in the general retreat. By 20 July, his unit had escaped to safety at Monterey. The regiment fought in Robert Edward Lee's failed Cheat Mountain campaign in September. The 37th Regiment was then attached to Thomas J. "Stonewall" Jackson's command, and late in March 1862 Cowan was wounded in the hip in the fighting at Winchester. During the Shenandoah Valley campaign he fought at Kernstown, where one of his brothers was mortally wounded. After receiving a severe wound at Cedar Mountain on 9 August 1862, Cowan was placed on furlough and returned home.

On 1 January 1863 Cowan won election as clerk of Russell County and served in that capacity until 1869. In his application for a special presidential pardon in August 1865, he cited both his work as county clerk and a very brief stint as tax assessor but made no mention of his service in the Confederate army. Cowan married Sarah E. Fuller on 12 June 1866. They had seven daughters and three sons before her death from consumption (probably tuberculosis) on 16 August 1888.

In a referendum held on 22 October 1867 Russell County by a large majority and Buchanan

County by a narrow margin approved holding a convention to draft a new state constitution. Cowan placed second in a field of five candidates in Russell County, and in Buchanan County he easily led a three-candidate field to win an overall majority and the convention seat representing the two counties. Appointed to the Committee on Taxation and Finance and to the Committee on Prisons and the Prevention and Punishment of Crime, he did not speak formally on the floor of the convention that met in Richmond from 3 December 1867 to 17 April 1868. Characterized by the commander of Military District Number One as an *"unreconstructed"* "Original Secessionist," Cowan aligned consistently with Conservatives on key roll-call votes. He did not support John Curtiss Underwood for convention president and voted with a minority who sought an investigation of his conduct in that office. Cowan opposed racial integration of public schools and voted against efforts to disfranchise white Virginians who had supported secession or the Confederacy and also against the so-called test oath that would have prevented all such men from holding office. He did not vote on the adoption of the new constitution but with twenty-eight other Conservatives signed a public address protesting most of its provisions.

During and after the Civil War, Cowan acquired several tracts of land, and when he returned home from the convention he resumed buying and selling various properties. In 1888 he paid taxes on 968 acres that he owned outright, and by 1891 he had added another 105 acres to his holdings. Cowan was still residing in Russell County in July 1893, but by the next year he had sold all but 143 acres and moved west. In April 1894 he was living in Orlando, Logan County, Oklahoma Territory, where he resumed farming. Cowan remained in that county until at least 24 August 1898 and probably until August 1903, when he traveled to Colorado Springs, Colorado, to arrange for the burial of his youngest daughter. By 1904 Cowan had moved to Colorado Springs. He lived with another daughter, a schoolteacher, before moving into his own residence. George Rutledge Cowan died of recurrent skin cancer on 14

October 1904. He was buried beside his youngest daughter in Evergreen Cemetery in Colorado Springs.

Biography in *The Heritage of Russell County, 1786–1986* (1985), 1:28, *1786–1988* (1989), 2:220–221 (with variant death date of 12 Oct. 1904); F. Johnston, comp., *Memorials of Old Virginia Clerks* (1888), 355; BVS Marriage Register, Russell Co.; Russell Co. Deed Book, 28:373, 29:70, 86, 32:457; Russell Co. Law Order Book, 14:454, 15:423, 425, 16:204; Compiled Service Records; Presidential Pardons; Election Records, no. 427, RG 13, LVA; *Journal of 1867–1868 Convention*, 4, 28, 29, 86, 89, 213, 221, 284, 295, 308, 340; Hume, "Membership of Convention of 1867–1868," 461, 479, 480, 481; Lowe, "Virginia's Reconstruction Convention," 359 (quotations); *Richmond Daily Dispatch*, 20 Apr. 1868; Colorado Springs, Colo., Death Register; death notice in *Colorado Springs Gazette*, 15 Oct. 1904.

KEVIN CONLEY RUFFNER

COWAN, Robert Edwin (9 November 1830–14 July 1887), member of the third session of the Convention of 1861, was the son of Arthur Cowan and Elizabeth Cowan (maiden name unknown) and was born probably in Staunton. In 1830 the family was living in Monongalia County and by 1840 had moved to Harrison County. From 1851 to 1852 Cowan studied law at Washington College (later Washington and Lee University) and in the latter year was admitted to the bar in Monongalia County. By 1853 he was representing clients in Preston County, where he was also a commissioner in chancery until compelled to relinquish the position by the demands of his growing practice. On 22 December 1853 Cowan married Susan Louisa Cresap, of Preston County. They had at least four children, two sons and two daughters.

In 1857 Cowan won election to represent Preston County in the House of Delegates, where he was appointed to the Committee on Banks. Reelected in 1859, he sat on the Committee of Schools and Colleges and the Committee on Banks. Late in that session he opposed a bill calling for a state convention to consider the issue of secession because it failed to provide Virginians with an opportunity to review the convention's actions. Cowan voted in favor of a defeated amendment proposing a popular referendum on the question of whether to hold a convention and supported an amendment that allowed voters to decide whether to ratify the convention's decision. To keep his constituents informed of the General Assembly's proceedings, Cowan published letters in the *Kingwood Chronicle*, the local newspaper whose Unionist stance mirrored Preston County's overwhelming opposition to secession.

On 17 April 1861 the convention approved the Ordinance of Secession, and by 27 May Cowan was a major in the 25th Regiment Virginia Infantry (also known as Heck's Regiment) operating against Union forces in the northwestern part of the state. His duties included collecting and transporting arms and supplies and gathering recruits. In June the state convention formally expelled twelve western delegates who opposed secession and had abandoned their seats. The governor ordered special elections to be held at military encampments to fill these vacated positions. On 24 October 1861 at Camp Bartow, in Pocahontas County, Cowan's brother-in-law Charles James Pindall Cresap, Cresap's brother, and two other Preston County men selected Cowan to replace one of the county's convention delegates, and Cresap's brother and the two other men elected Cresap to the remaining seat. Cowan resigned his clerkship in the Auditor's Office of the Post Office Department and took his seat on 20 November 1861. He served only about two weeks in the third and final convention session but added his signature to the Ordinance of Secession.

On 28 January 1862 Cowan was appointed a captain in the regular Confederate service to rank from 18 January of that year and served as an assistant commissary of subsistence in the Commissary Department. His regimental duties permitted him to reside for much of the time in Richmond. Cowan was elected to another term in the House of Delegates that met in four sessions from 2 December 1861 to 31 March 1863, but he did not take his seat until 9 March 1863. His absence no doubt resulted from his military service. Cowan suffered from rheumatism and by October 1862 planned to leave the army, but not until 5 June 1863 did he tender his resignation.

Special elections held at several military encampments and among refugees in Richmond on 28 May 1863 sent Cowan and Cresap to the House of Delegates with sixteen and twelve votes, respectively. Although in June 1863 Preston County became part of the new state of West Virginia, Cowan continued to represent the county in the Virginia legislature in three sessions between 7 September 1863 and 15 March 1865. He served on the Committees for Courts of Justice and on Confederate Relations. When not attending to his legislative obligations Cowan periodically sought various positions with the Confederate Treasury Department and described himself in one 1864 letter of application as a refugee "destitute of the means of Support."

After the Civil War, Cowan went west. He began keeping a daily journal when he left Cincinnati in April 1867. He traveled to Texas, where he practiced law in Dallas, before visiting the Oklahoma Territory. On 12 September he arrived in Independence, Missouri, and recorded his final journal entry. Cowan settled in Jackson County, Missouri, where his father had owned property, and opened a law office in Kansas City. In May 1868 his wife and children joined him. That year he was admitted to the Missouri bar and became a partner in a local law firm. From 1873 until 1880 Cowan served as judge of the Jackson County Special Law and Equity Court. He campaigned on behalf of the Democratic Party and for the 1876 presidential candidate Samuel Jones Tilden.

Cowan was a member of several fraternal and benevolent societies, including the Royal Arch Masons and the Independent Order of Odd Fellows. Rising to prominence in the Knights of Pythias, he won election as Grand Chancellor of Missouri in 1877 and later served as Supreme Representative of the Grand Lodge of Missouri. Early in the 1880s he became Supreme Keeper of Records and Seal and moved to Saint Louis. Hailed as the "Uncrowned King of Pythian Jurisprudence," Robert Edwin Cowan died at his Saint Louis home on 14 July 1887 after surgery to remove a tumor. Following a funeral service at Cook Avenue Southern Methodist Church, ranking officials of the Knights of Pythias led the procession that carried his body to the Bellefontaine Cemetery for interment in a lot furnished by the fraternal order.

Cowardin

Biographies in A. J. D. Stewart, ed., *The History of the Bench and Bar of Missouri* (1898), 353, William D. Kennedy, *Pythian History* (1904), 170–171 (including birth date and variant birthplace of Monongahela Co.), *Kansas City Star*, 5 Nov. 1933 (por.), and "Forgotten Journal Brings Early Day Jurist Alive," *Jackson County [Mo.] Historical Society Journal* (July/Sept. 1983), 6–7 (por.); Robert Edwin Cowan Papers, Jackson County Historical Society Archives, Independence, Mo., including Knights of Pythias memorial resolution, 22 July 1887 (second quotation); Roy L. Lockhart, comp., *Preston County WV (then VA) Records, 1853–1860* (1998), Marriage Register, 1 (with variant birthplace of Marion Co.); Compiled Service Records, including Cowan to Christopher Gustavus Memminger, 9 Apr. 1864 (first quotation); Election Records, Papers of the Convention of 1861, RG 93, LVA; Reese, *Journal and Papers of 1861 Convention*, vol. 1, Journal, 334, 336; Election Records, no. 440, RG 13, LVA; S. T. Wiley, *History of Preston County (West Virginia)* (1882), 121, 123–125, 132, 161, 324, 355; obituaries in *Saint Louis Post-Dispatch*, 14 (including birth date and birthplace of Staunton), 15 July 1887.

DONALD W. GUNTER

COWARDIN, Charles O'Brien (23 October 1851–5 July 1900), newspaper publisher, was born in Richmond and was the son of James Andrew Cowardin, a founder of the *Richmond Daily Dispatch*, and Anna Maria Purcell Cowardin. He spent part of his childhood in Ashland, at his father's farm near Richmond, and at his father's country estate in Greenbrier County but before the end of the Civil War had moved back to Richmond. Growing up in the country gave Cowardin a fondness for rural life that he maintained into adulthood. Having completed his early education in Ashland and Richmond, he received a B.A. from Georgetown College (later Georgetown University), in Washington, D.C., in 1874 and an M.A. from that school in 1885.

Soon after receiving his bachelor's degree Cowardin went to work for his father, first in the editorial section, and then in the business of running the *Richmond Daily Dispatch* (beginning in 1886 the *Richmond Dispatch*). Cowardin, a vice president of the company, took over management of the paper after his father suffered a stroke in October 1879 and purchased his father's interest in the company. On 17 April of that year he married Kate Spotswood Evans, of Richmond. Before she died on 19 February 1886, they had two sons and one daughter. Cowardin married Anna Margaretta Moale, of Baltimore, on 4 October 1888. They had one son.

Cowardin became president of the *Dispatch* on 5 April 1882, several months before his father died. Throughout Cowardin's presidency, the *Dispatch* had by far the largest pressrun and circulation of any daily newspaper in Virginia, and it was one of the few in the state to attempt to publish complete election returns for all of Virginia's congressional and legislative districts. The newspaper consistently supported the state's Democratic Party, which became increasingly a party of white supremacy during the latter years of the nineteenth century.

Late in the summer of 1882 the editors of the *Dispatch* and of its main political rival, the *Richmond Daily Whig*, traded sharp editorials during the height of the competition between the Readjusters, whom the *Whig* supported, and the Funders, whom the *Dispatch* supported. So strong were some of the articles that appeared in the *Dispatch* that the editor of the *Whig*, William Cecil Elam, attributed them to the publisher rather than to the paper's editor and denounced Cowardin as "a liar and a scoundrel." Cowardin replied in language that suggested his willingness to challenge Elam to a duel. Both men were required to post bonds to maintain the peace. It was Cowardin's only known close brush with dueling, a practice that was then dying out among Virginia's highly competitive editors, but it was not Elam's.

During the 1890s the *Dispatch* supported the faction of the Democratic Party that favored the inflationary coinage of silver, an issue that divided the party both nationally and in Virginia. Cowardin never sought public office, but he received from three Democratic governors appointment to the governor's military staff, an honorary recognition that brought with it the title of colonel. From 1894 to 1895 and again in 1898 he was the governor's chief of staff. In 1898 when the state's adjutant general was called into the field on active duty at the time of the war with Spain, Cowardin stepped into the office temporarily for a few days.

During the 1890s Cowardin was a director of the Southern Associated Press. He helped organize the Newspaper Publishers' Association of Richmond in 1892 and served as its first president. A founding member of the Southern

Publishers' Association, Cowardin was its vice president in 1898 and president in 1899. He also sat on the board of the socially prestigious and politically elite Westmoreland Club for several years and was vice president in 1890 and 1891 and president for the two following years. A skilled musician, both as a singer and performer on several instruments, Cowardin contributed to the culture of Richmond as choir director of Saint Peter's Cathedral (later Saint Peter's Catholic Church), as an officer of the city's Mozart Association, and by directing and singing in a number of amateur opera productions. He was also a popular after-dinner speaker. While en route to his country home in Gloucester County in June 1900, he came down with typhoid fever and lingered for three weeks, sometimes improving, sometimes relapsing. Charles O'Brien Cowardin returned to Richmond and died at his home there on 5 July 1900. All four of the city's daily newspapers published long obituaries and editorial tributes. He was buried in Richmond's Hollywood Cemetery.

Biographies in Tyler, *Men of Mark*, 4:73–76 (por. facing 73), and Lacy Yeatts, "Charles O'Brien Cowardin," *Richmond Magazine* 2 (Apr. 1976): 56–57, 60–61; Cowardin family Bible records (1879–1968) and a few letters, VHS; BVS Marriage Register, Richmond City (1879); *Richmond Daily Whig*, 25 Aug., 2 Sept. 1882 (quotation); *Richmond Daily Dispatch*, 26 Aug., 2 Sept. 1882, 6 Oct. 1888; *Washington Post*, 3 Sept. 1882; Virginius Dabney, *Pistols and Pointed Pens: The Dueling Editors of Old Virginia* (1987), 78–82; obituaries in *Richmond Evening Leader* and *Richmond News*, both 5 July 1900, and *Atlanta Constitution*, *New York Times*, *Richmond Dispatch* (por.), *Richmond Times*, and *Washington Post*, all 6 July 1900; editorial tributes in *Richmond Dispatch*, *Richmond Evening Leader*, *Richmond News*, and *Richmond Times*, all 6 July 1900.

MARY E. GLADE

COWARDIN, James Andrew (6 October 1811–21 November 1882), journalist, was born in Bath County and was the son of John Lewis Cowardin and Polly Rhodes Cowardin. At age thirteen he became a printer's apprentice at the *Roanoke Sentinel*, published in Danville. Cowardin moved to Lynchburg about 1827 to become foreman of the *Jeffersonian Republican* (in 1830 retitled the *Jeffersonian*), where he came under the influence of the newspaper's editor, Richard Kenner Crallé, a staunch supporter of John C.

Calhoun's doctrine of states' rights and nullification. Late in 1831 or early in 1832 Crallé moved his paper to Richmond, where Cowardin joined him at the renamed *Jeffersonian and Virginia Times*. After that newspaper ceased publication, Cowardin was chief clerk to Thomas Ritchie, publisher of the Democratic *Richmond Daily Enquirer*, from 1834 until about 1837. By 1 January 1838 he had purchased an interest in the *Richmond Compiler* (after 1844 the *Richmond Times and Compiler*). On 25 July 1838 Cowardin married Anna Maria Purcell, who died of consumption (probably tuberculosis) on 20 October 1878. They had four sons and two daughters.

Cowardin remained co-editor of the *Times and Compiler* until about 1848, when he left journalism temporarily to engage in banking with his brother-in-law. In October 1850 Cowardin helped establish the *Richmond Daily Dispatch* and installed Hugh Rose Pleasants as editor. The appearance of the *Dispatch* heralded the beginning of a new age of newspaper publishing in Virginia. The first daily penny press published south of Baltimore, the *Dispatch* proclaimed itself nonpartisan. Envisioned as the primary source of information on local news and state and national economic developments for Richmond's commercial and industrial elite, the *Dispatch* departed from most contemporary newspapers, which functioned mainly as vitriolic propaganda organs for their respective political parties.

Cowardin's approach to publishing reflected his own political and economic philosophy. Despite the *Dispatch*'s officially nonpartisan editorial line, he was a southern Whig who numbered among the civic boosters advocating the development of industry and commerce in order to gain economic independence in a time of growing sectional tension. In 1853 Richmond voters gave Cowardin the opportunity to promote his views when they elected him to the House of Delegates. He sat on the Committee on Finance and did not seek reelection at the end of his two-year term.

Cowardin devoted his efforts to encouraging industry and commerce in the city and state. He believed that one of the most important prerequisites for Virginia's economic independence was the creation of a skilled, educated class of artisans and mechanics. In 1854 he supported the organization of the Virginia Mechanics' Institute, which established an apprenticeship program and public library, and he served as first vice president on its inaugural board of managers. Believing also, however, in the compatibility of slavery and industrialization, Cowardin contended that it was possible to build an industrial city in the image of New York or Philadelphia with slave labor. His fight against attempts to abolish Sunday labor at the *Dispatch* created tension with white artisans in Richmond, as did his use of several slaves to help produce and distribute his newspaper.

Cowardin reported $12,000 in real estate and $77,000 in personal property to the census enumerator in 1860 and maintained that the *Dispatch* boasted a circulation of 18,000, by far the largest among the city's dailies. Although a Whig and Unionist, he came to support secession after South Carolina withdrew from the Union in December 1860. With the formation of the Confederate States of America early in February 1861, Cowardin believed that Virginia faced the stark choice between becoming an economically marginalized region in a Northern-dominated Union or an economic and industrial powerhouse of the new Southern nation. If Virginia joined the Confederacy, he argued, it "would become the chief merchant and the manufacturer of the South. Her waters would be filled with sails and her rivers be indicated by the ever rising smoke of the fast-moving steam vessels actively conducting her commerce with all nations."

During the Civil War, the *Richmond Daily Dispatch* ardently defended the Confederate cause. Cowardin did not serve in the military; his pen was certainly mightier than any fifty-year-old with a rifle could be. At various times the *Dispatch*'s pages described Abraham Lincoln as a vulgar tycoon and portrayed Union soldiers as thieves and cutthroats. Despite his rhetoric, Cowardin maintained contact with Northern newspaper friends, and on at least one occasion in 1863 he delivered provisions and money to Union prisoners in Richmond on behalf of a Bal-

timore publisher. The *Dispatch* defended the city's Jewish population against common accusations of usury and extortion during the economically harsh war years.

The publication of a daily newspaper in a city short of everything, including paper, ink, and printing presses, became more and more difficult. The *Dispatch* suspended publication beginning on 16 March 1865 because all its employees had been impressed into military service. On 3 April a fire set by the retreating Confederates that destroyed much of the business district also consumed the newspaper's office. Cowardin took the amnesty oath on 1 July and spent most of the remainder of the year farming in Halifax County. The value of his property required that he apply for a presidential pardon, which he received on 13 July 1865.

When the first postwar issue of the *Dispatch* appeared on 9 December 1865, Cowardin plunged headlong back into Virginia politics. Converted into a staunch conservative Democrat, he left his nonpartisan past behind as his paper attacked Radical Reconstruction and lashed out against those who cooperated with federal authorities. In 1869 Cowardin supported the efforts of the so-called Committee of Nine, which met with the president-elect to arrange a compromise by which to end Reconstruction in Virginia. Its terms permitted the state electorate to vote separately on the ratification of the constitution prepared by the Convention of 1867–1868 and on its clauses that would have disfranchised many former Confederates. Cowardin accompanied the group to Washington and sent dispatches about the proceedings to his newspaper's office. His advocacy of the committee's work helped sway voters to ratify the constitution and defeat the disqualification clauses.

Throughout the postwar era Cowardin remained active in civic affairs. In March 1874 he helped found the Virginia Press Association and two years later was elected president for the first of two consecutive terms. In October 1879 he suffered a stroke that left him paralyzed and that effectively ended his editorial career. His son, Charles O'Brien Cowardin, took over the day-to-day management of the *Richmond Daily Dispatch*. James Andrew Cowardin died at his son's home in Richmond on 21 November 1882 and was buried in Hollywood Cemetery.

Biographies in *NCAB*, 2:51–52 (with birth date), and Virginius Dabney, *Pistols and Pointed Pens: The Dueling Editors of Old Virginia* (1987), 61–78 (por.); Richmond City Marriage Bonds (bond dated 24 July 1838); *Richmond Enquirer*, 31 July 1838; *Richmond Daily Dispatch*, 11, 16, 18 Feb. 1852, 15 June, 31 July 1854, 14 Feb. 1861 (quotation), 12–15, 18 Jan. 1869; *Richmond Times-Dispatch*, 15 Oct. 2000; Presidential Pardons; BVS Death Register, Richmond City; obituaries, accounts of funeral, and editorial tributes in *Richmond Daily Dispatch*, 22–24 Nov. 1882, *Richmond Daily Whig*, 22, 23 Nov. 1882, and *Washington Post*, 22 Nov. 1882.

WERNER STEGER

COWGILL, Clinton Harriman (6 September 1890–28 December 1975), architect and educator, was born in Sterling, Kansas, and was the son of Elias Branson Cowgill, editor of the *Kansas Farmer*, and Rena Harriman Cowgill. He attended Washburn College in Topeka during the 1910–1911 academic year and later enrolled at the University of Illinois, where in 1916 he received a B.S. in architecture. From 1916 to 1917 Cowgill (pronounced "Coe'-gill," according to college press releases) taught architecture and architectural engineering at Oklahoma Agricultural and Mechanical College (later Oklahoma State University). For the next three years he worked variously as a draftsman in Topeka and in Kansas City, Missouri, and as an office manager for an Oklahoma City contracting company. On 19 January 1918 Cowgill married Mabel Claire Huey. They had no children. From 1920 to 1928 he was an associate professor of architectural engineering at Iowa State College of Agriculture and Mechanic Arts, where his wife also taught the subject from 1921 to 1925. He received an M.A. in architecture from the University of Illinois in 1925.

In July 1928 Cowgill successfully sought appointment as professor of architectural engineering at Virginia Agricultural and Mechanical College and Polytechnic Institute (later Virginia Polytechnic Institute and State University), where he established and managed the architectural engineering department. His pragmatic, thorough approach toward constructing buildings demanded a close association among architect, engineer, and contractor. Cowgill developed four

areas of study in the program: structural design, mechanical equipment, contracting, and architectural design. Originally much of the coursework was the same for the four divisions, but by 1946 three distinct curricula had developed with markedly different coursework specific to each. Cowgill was instrumental in organizing architectural students into college chapters of the American Institute of Architects. In a joint effort with Pendleton Scott Clark at the University of Virginia, the first student chapters at these institutions were formed in 1940.

Along with his administrative and teaching duties Cowgill served as an advisory architect for VPI and helped plan the physical development of the campus. He assisted University Club officers with the design and construction of the University Clubhouse, completed late in 1929. Cowgill also designed the college's airport hanger, the Dairy Husbandry Building, and several private residences in Blacksburg.

Cowgill held key offices in local and national architectural organizations, civic clubs, and educational committees. From 1934 to 1937 he served as president of the Virginia State Board for the Examination and Certification of Architects, Professional Engineers, and Land Surveyors. From 1940 to 1948 Cowgill sat on the National Architectural Accrediting Board, from 1949 to 1952 as president, and he also was a member of the Board of Review of the National Council of Architectural Registration Boards from 1942 to 1949. Cowgill served as treasurer of the Virginia chapter of the American Institute of Architects in 1938, secretary in 1939, vice president in 1940, and president in 1941. On 22 March 1950 he became a fellow of the AIA, one of the highest honors given by that organization.

In 1947 Cowgill's typed lectures were reproduced by the VPI bookstore as *Notes on Architectural Practice*, which he then expanded with the New York architect Ben John Small and published as *Architectural Practice* (1947). Intended as a guide for architectural schools to use in training students, the text became a reference work for professional architects and others involved in construction projects. It was revised in 1949 and 1959 and translated into Japanese in 1965. Among Cowgill's other publications were *Building for*

Investment (1951) and articles for the *Journal of the American Institute of Architects* on "The Library Building" and "Modern Travel Accommodations."

Cowgill retired from VPI in the summer of 1956 after almost thirty years as head of the department of architecture. During his tenure the architectural engineering program had grown from two faculty members and thirty-four students to thirteen full-time faculty members and more than two hundred students. The curriculum also expanded to include architecture, architectural engineering, and building construction. After his retirement Cowgill worked for the American Institute of Architects in Washington, D.C., as editor of the *Handbook of Architectural Practice* (1958). He stayed on as department head until 1961. After his second retirement Cowgill moved to La Jolla, California, where he resided for the rest of his life.

Based on faculty recommendations, early in 1967 VPI named a new building housing its architectural program Cowgill Hall. Health concerns prevented the honoree from attending the dedication ceremony on 30 April 1970. Clinton Harriman Cowgill died in La Jolla on 28 December 1975. His cremated remains were interred in the Cyprus View Mausoleum, in San Diego.

Birth date (probably provided by Cowgill) in George S. Koyl, ed., *American Architects Directory* (1955), 112; Clinton Harriman Cowgill Papers (including correspondence, contracts, draft MSS, diplomas, professional certificates, newspaper clippings, photographs of buildings designed, and program for dedication of Cowgill Hall, 30 Apr. 1970), and Cowgill biographical file, both VPI; publications include Cowgill, *Comparative Cost Studies of School Buildings*, in *Bulletin of the Virginia Polytechnic Institute, Engineering Experiment Station Series* (1955), *Law Office Layout and Design* (1959), "Modern Travel Accommodations," *Journal of the American Institute of Architects* 33 (Mar. 1960): 73–92, and with George E. Pettengill, "The Library Building," ibid. 31 (May 1959): 55–66 and (June 1959): 103–114; *Richmond Times-Dispatch*, 31 May 1941 (por.); *Christiansburg Montgomery News Messenger*, 12 Apr. 1956; *VPI Techgram*, 15 Apr. 1956; Duncan Lyle Kinnear, *The First 100 Years: A History of Virginia Polytechnic Institute and State University* (1972), 292, 347, 376, 458; obituaries in *San Diego Union*, 1 Jan. 1976, *Roanoke Times*, 6 Jan. 1976, *Blacksburg-Christiansburg News Messenger*, 13 Jan. 1976, and *Virginia Tech Techgram* 53 (Jan. 1976): 1.

KELLEY M. EWING

COWLINGE, Christopher (fl. May 1630), member of the Council, is perhaps the least known of all the men who served in a responsible government office during the early years of the Virginia colony. His name appears only once in the extant records of the period. In an enclosure in a letter that Governor Sir John Harvey sent to the Privy Council on 29 May 1630, reporting his safe arrival in Virginia on an unspecified date earlier that year, Harvey identified Cowlinge among the six men he had appointed to the governor's Council since landing. The date of the appointment and the duration of the service are not known, nor is it certain whether Cowlinge had traveled to Virginia with Harvey or was already in the colony when Harvey arrived.

Available parish and local records of several English counties document christenings and marriages of several men named Christopher Cooling, Cowling, Cowlinge, Colling, Collinge, Collins, and Collyn during the decades preceding Cowlinge's appointment to the Council in Virginia, but none of them has been identified as the man Harvey selected. Land records and other scant surviving Virginia documents from the 1620s and 1630s do not mention him under any recognizable variant spelling of his surname, which suggests that he may have arrived with Harvey and left or died soon thereafter. It is possible that Cowlinge was the Christopher Knollinge, probably a merchant mariner, who gave testimony before a Virginia court in December 1625 about events that had occurred in Canadian waters earlier that year. At least two men named Cowlinge lived in Virginia later in the century, but no records clearly link either of them to him. Unlike most of Cowlinge's colleagues on the Council, his life is virtually unrecorded. However interesting or important his presumably brief residence in Virginia may have been, it is known for certain only from one list, on which his name is spelled Christopher Cowlinge.

Sir John Harvey to Privy Council, 29 May 1630, second enclosure, PRO CO 1/5, fol. 206; *Minutes of Council and General Court*, 78.

BRENT TARTER

COWPER, Ann Pierce Parker (d. 21 March 1849), principal in a divorce suit, was born between 1780 and 1785, probably in Portsmouth or Isle of Wight County. She was the only child of Mary Pierce Bridger Parker and her second husband, Josiah Parker, a wealthy merchant, planter, and Revolutionary War officer. Her maternal uncle Thomas Pierce was a member of the Convention of 1788. While her father served in the House of Representatives from 1789 to 1801, she joined him in Philadelphia and received a superior education. Throughout her life she was esteemed for her learning and character, despite her unfortunate marriage.

On 4 May 1802 at Macclesfield, her father's Isle of Wight County plantation, Ann Parker married William Cowper, a former naval officer whose uncle William Cowper (d. 1784) had served in the Convention of 1776. Her father reportedly did not approve of the match, though as former chair of a House committee charged with investigating naval matters he probably knew of the captain's distinguished career during the recent undeclared naval war with France. William Cowper had been discharged from the navy in 1801 as part of a reduction of the American naval forces and had joined his brothers in a Norfolk mercantile business. Soon after the marriage, the company went bankrupt, and Cowper and her husband moved to Macclesfield. At Parker's insistence, his son-in-law returned to sea but stayed at Macclesfield between voyages. The first two of their four sons were born before 1805, when William Cowper retired from the sea again and opened a store with profits from the New York–West Indies trade.

Until that time the relationship between Cowper and her husband had been satisfactory, but after the store failed she experienced her husband's ferocious temper. She returned to Macclesfield and he begged forgiveness, but her father proposed petitioning the General Assembly for a divorce. Dreading the public exposure, she refused. Then while her husband was at sea in 1810, her father died. In his will, he left her $250, an annuity of £100, six slaves, and the use of Macclesfield for as long as she chose to remain there; the rest of the large estate was set aside for her first son, Josiah Cowper, on condition that he assume the Parker surname.

When Cowper's husband returned to Virginia, he petitioned the General Assembly for the name change in order to gain control of the underage boy's inheritance. Cowper objected. For two nightmarish years she fought her husband in chancery court to gain her annuity and the use of her property and in the legislature to keep her son's surname from being changed before he came of age. She prevailed in both efforts, but at home her husband cursed, beat, whipped, starved, and threatened her repeatedly. In 1811 while Cowper was pregnant for the fourth time, he unsuccessfully tried to force an abortion and then a miscarriage. Court orders and fines failed to restrain him. Finally, believing in 1812 that her husband meant to murder her, Cowper fled with her infant son to the protection of relatives. She left her husband at Macclesfield, where he held on to their other sons and squandered the estate. Meanwhile Parker's executor died, and no one replaced him with authority to manage the estate for her benefit as the will directed.

By 1816 Cowper's husband was an insolvent debtor, and in November of that year she petitioned for a divorce, which the General Assembly granted on 9 January 1817 as a legal separation without permission to remarry. The Isle of Wight County Court then made her executrix of her father's estate and the legal guardian of her children. During the next few years Cowper successfully fought to evict her former husband from Macclesfield and to maintain her guardianship against the prejudices of a patriarchal society that often made it difficult for her to protect her rights and the rights of her sons in court. Meanwhile, she also battled the creditors of her father's estate. William Cowper died within a few years, and in 1823 Josiah Cowper came of age, legally changed his surname to Parker, and received his inheritance. He then deeded Macclesfield and its 500 acres of land to his mother in lieu of all past and future annuities and moved to a nearby plantation that he had also inherited from his grandfather.

The remainder of Cowper's life is not well documented, but she evidently lived at Macclesfield, quietly and without the public scrutiny that the consequences of her unhappy marriage had focused on her family life. Her sons lived nearby or in Portsmouth. At the time of her death her personal property, including seven slaves, was worth more than $3,000. Ann Pierce Parker Cowper died at Macclesfield on 21 March 1849, according to family records, and most likely was buried in the Parker family graveyard there. Her youngest son, Leopold Copeland Parker Cowper, with whom she had fled from Macclesfield in 1812, was executor of her estate and later served as lieutenant governor of Virginia.

Family history in James F. Crocker, "The Parkers of Macclesfield, Isle of Wight County, Va.," *VMHB* 6 (1899): 420–424 (with undocumented death date); R. S. Thomas, *The Old Brick Church, Near Smithfield, Virginia* (1892), 18–19; Census, Isle of Wight Co., 1810 (age between twenty-six and forty-five), 1820 (age between twenty-six and forty-five), 1830 (age between forty and fifty); Josiah Parker's will in Isle of Wight Co. Will Book, 13:89–90; *Norfolk Herald*, 8 May 1802; Legislative Petitions, Isle of Wight Co. (from Ann P. P. Cowper, received 19 Dec. 1811 and 20 Nov. 1816; from William Cowper, received 19 Dec. 1811, 16 Dec. 1812, 6 Dec. 1815, 14 Nov. 1816, and 12 Dec. 1817; and from Josiah Cowper, received 8 Dec. 1823), RG 78, LVA; *Acts of Assembly*, 1816–1817 sess., 175–176; Isle of Wight Co. Order Book (1816–1818), 154–155, 168; Thomas E. Buckley, S.J., *The Great Catastrophe of My Life: Divorce in the Old Dominion* (2002), 155–167; will, estate inventory, and accounts in Isle of Wight Co. Common Law Will Book (1833–1902), 32–33, 37–43, 67–68.

THOMAS E. BUCKLEY, S.J.

COWPER, Leopold Copeland Parker (March 1811–17 July 1875), lieutenant governor of Virginia, was born at Macclesfield, the Isle of Wight County estate of his parents, William Cowper, a former naval officer, and Ann Pierce Parker Cowper. Because of his father's vicious emotional and physical abuse of his mother during her pregnancy, Cowper was born prematurely and remained sickly during his first year. In 1812 his mother, fearing for her life, fled Macclesfield with him and sought asylum with friends and relatives. The General Assembly granted his parents a legal separation early in January 1817, and his mother became his sole legal guardian. Perhaps as a consequence of his parents' violent union, Cowper never married, but later in life he formally adopted the four surviving daughters of his eldest brother and provided for them in his will. He also helped support several nephews, whose educational expenses strained his finances.

Cowper read law and practiced in Portsmouth and surrounding Norfolk County. Nominated on the Whig Party ticket, he narrowly won election in April 1847 to the first of two consecutive one-year terms in the House of Delegates as one of two men representing Norfolk County. During both terms he sat on the minor Committees to Examine the Enrolled Bills and to Examine the Public Armory.

At the beginning of the Civil War, Cowper owned one taxable slave, probably one of two men he had purchased from his mother's estate in 1849. The city of Norfolk fell to Union forces in May 1862, and the surrounding area came under the military control of the Union army and the civilian authority of the loyal Restored government, then meeting in Wheeling. During the summer of 1863 Cowper became a key figure in a clash between local civilian and military authorities that began over provision of relief for destitute families. The Portsmouth common council adopted an ordinance authorizing the mayor to collect rents due on all property owned by persons who refused to take an oath of allegiance to the United States and Restored governments and to use those funds for poor relief and to defray the costs of city government. Brigadier General Henry Morris Naglee, the newly arrived district commander, refused to enforce the law because he believed it infringed on military prerogative, although he did provide for destitute families Cowper identified late in July. In response, the common council passed a resolution on 1 August 1863 refusing to recognize Naglee's authority and appointing Cowper to a three-man committee to call on the Restored governor, President Abraham Lincoln, and the Union secretary of war in order to seek Naglee's removal and also clarification of the respective authorities of the civilian and military officials.

In mid-May 1863 a meeting of Norfolk and Portsmouth Unionists unanimously selected Cowper as candidate for lieutenant governor in the Restored government to replace a Berkeley County nominee who had declined to run. When it learned of the choice, the Unionist convention meeting in Alexandria acquiesced and substituted Cowper on the ticket for its own replacement candidate from Alexandria County. The candidates for governor and attorney general ran unopposed, but Cowper faced opposition from Gilbert S. Miner, whom he easily outpolled in the election on 28 May to win office with 2,361 votes.

Cowper's term was not scheduled to begin until 1 January 1864, but he started using his new title about the time that West Virginia attained statehood on 20 June 1863 and the sitting lieutenant governor, a resident of Mason County, resigned. Governor Francis Harrison Pierpont moved the Restored government to Alexandria effective 26 August 1863 and on 17 November appointed Cowper lieutenant governor so that the Restored Senate of Virginia would have a presiding officer when it opened on 7 December 1863. At the two assembly sessions that convened in Alexandria in that month and in December 1864, Cowper presided over a body that consisted at its full strength of six members, representing the districts of Accomack and Northampton Counties, Alexandria and Fairfax Counties, Elizabeth City County and the city of Hampton, Loudoun County, the city of Norfolk, and Norfolk and Princess Anne Counties. The session of 1863–1864 authorized calling a convention to revise the state constitution.

After the defeat of the Confederacy in April 1865, the Restored government moved to Richmond and assumed administrative responsibility for the entire state. Cowper presided over a five-day extra session of the Senate in June 1865 during which the General Assembly, at Pierpont's urging, restored voting rights to most supporters of the Confederacy, provided they took the amnesty oath or received special pardon from the president. Elections in October 1865 returned three of the six Restored senators, but most of the other thirty state senators who convened for the session of 1865–1866 were former Confederates. Cowper was not present on 4 December 1865 for the opening day of the new Senate and did not oversee the organization of the chamber, although he took his seat the next day. He presided during the two subsequent sessions and made his final appearance on 29 April 1867, when the Senate passed its traditional resolution of thanks for his services during the session.

Cowper's term expired on 1 January 1868, but late in March of that year a general order of the military commander with responsibility for Virginia extended his term until a successor could

be named and qualified. Although the commanding general soon replaced Pierpont with a military governor, he did not name a new lieutenant governor, most likely because the General Assembly never met under Radical Reconstruction and therefore no presiding officer was required. Neither the Radical Republicans nor the coalition of moderates calling themselves True Republicans considered naming Cowper to their respective tickets in 1869. His successor won election in July and qualified on 8 September 1869.

Cowper returned to Portsmouth and continued to practice law. He may have fallen into straitened circumstances; two of his adopted daughters, who lived with him, taught school, and he also took in at least one boarder. Early in the 1870s he unsuccessfully sought compensation from the United States Senate for his valuable library, which he had stored at Smithfield during the Civil War and which Union troops had carried off or destroyed in April 1864. Leopold Copeland Parker Cowper died at his Portsmouth home of dropsy on 17 July 1875. After services at Saint John's Episcopal Church, his body was carried by steamer to Smithfield for burial with Masonic rites in the family cemetery at Macclesfield. His achievements had made so little mark locally that one Norfolk newspaper on successive days misreported Cowper's funeral as that of the nonexistent S. C. Cooper, the late governor.

Birth date in Ann Pierce Parker Cowper, petition for divorce, 20 Nov. 1816, pp. 3–4, Legislative Petitions, Isle of Wight Co., RG 78, LVA; biography in Manarin, *Senate Officers*, 91–92; Census, Norfolk Co., 1860 (age forty-six on 10 Aug. 1860), 1870 (age fifty-six on 28 June 1870); some Cowper letters at Duke and VHS, in Francis Harrison Pierpont Executive Papers, RG 3, LVA, and printed in *Report of Brigadier-General Henry M. Naglee of His Command of the District of Virginia . . .* (1863), 38, and John C. Emmerson Jr., ed., *Some Aspects and Incidents of Military Rule in Portsmouth, Virginia: From the Letter Book of Captain Daniel Messinger, Provost Marshal of Portsmouth, . . . November 9, 1863, to June 27, 1864* (1946); *Norfolk and Portsmouth Herald*, 24 Apr. 1847; *Alexandria Gazette*, 26, 28–30 May, 14 Dec. 1863; *OR*, 1st ser., vol. 29, pt. 2, 54–58; *Report [of] the Committee on Claims [on] . . . the Memorial of L. C. P. Cowper*, 42d Cong., 2d sess., 1872, Senate Rept. 148, serial 1483; Portsmouth Hustings Court Will Book, 1:221–223; BVS Death Register, Portsmouth (variant death date of 19 July 1875 at age sixty-four); death notice in *Richmond Daily*

Dispatch, 19 July 1875 (with death date of 17 July 1875); accounts of funeral in *Norfolk Virginian*, 20, 21 July 1875 (misidentified as former governor S. C. Cooper); memorial resolutions in *Norfolk Landmark*, 20 July 1875 (with death date of 17 July 1875).

SARA B. BEARSS

COWPER, William (d. by 26 October 1784), member of the Convention of 1776, was born probably in Nansemond County sometime between 1730 and 1735. He was the son of John Cowper and his first wife, Elizabeth Cowper, whose maiden name may have been Wills. About 1765 Cowper married Mary Godwin. They had one son and three daughters. Personal and family data are scarce and unreliable for several reasons, among them confusion between Cowper and several near contemporaries of the same name, conflated references to him and his brother and business partner, Wills Cowper, and loss of most of the county, family, and business records. One of Cowper's brothers also married a member of the Godwin family, thus making them and their sons and daughters all related in ways unusually complicated even for Virginians.

Cowper and his brothers ran a commercial and shipping company known before the Revolutionary War by the style Wills Cowper and Company, but details about it are nearly as scarce as details about the family. Evidence suggests that some of the younger brothers may have spent time at sea while Cowper remained in charge in Nansemond County. They may have constructed ships as well. Cowper was elected to the Suffolk Parish vestry on 23 April 1772, was appointed to the county court on 9 December of that year, and was a captain in the militia by the spring of 1775 and a major by June 1776.

A member of the county committee formed late in 1774 or early in 1775, Cowper was one of two militia officers who confronted the rector of Suffolk Parish during a church service in the spring of 1775 and demanded that he vacate the church rather than continue to preach that colonial protestors were traitors. Finding that parishioners had barred the church doors against him, the minister left the county. A vestry committee on which Cowper sat declared the ministry vacant, and the county committee found the rector guilty of opposing the cause of American liberty and ordered him jailed.

On 8 April 1776 Cowper was elected to the fifth Revolutionary Convention, where he sat on the Committee of Privileges and Elections. The convention directed him on 17 June to report on proper places to erect defensive batteries on the Nansemond River. Cowper attended nearly every session of the convention until the last three days and was almost certainly present on 15 May when the convention unanimously voted for independence, on 12 June when it unanimously adopted the Virginia Declaration of Rights, and on 29 June when it unanimously adopted the first constitution of Virginia.

Cowper returned to Williamsburg in October 1776 as a member of the new House of Delegates and was again named to the Committee of Privileges and Elections. He won election to a full one-year term in the spring of 1777 and during the next session served as one of the commissioners to ascertain the losses of Norfolk citizens whose property had been burned on 1 January 1776.

On 15 January 1778 in Chowan County, North Carolina, Cowper married the twice-widowed Christian Gregory Granbery Doeber. They had no children. He resigned from the Suffolk Parish vestry later that year and about that time moved to Portsmouth. Cowper attempted to revive his trading company and after the end of the Revolutionary War began construction of a large new residence. In addition to 1,120 acres of land he owned, in the summer of 1783 he obtained title to 100 acres of escheated land of his former neighbor, friend, and shipping competitor John Goodrich, one of Nansemond County's most obdurate Loyalists, as well as land in Norfolk that had belonged to another Loyalist when the Revolution began. William Cowper wrote his will on 24 January 1784 and died, probably in Portsmouth, before he completed construction of his new house and before 26 October of that year, when an entry in the lost Wills Cowper and Company daybook recorded the first dated payment to his estate.

Albert Wallace Cowper, *The Cowper Family* (1983), 6, 8, 42, 65, 78, 85, citing evidence from records no longer extant, including lost will mentioned in deed dated 13 Feb. 1797;

Joseph B. Dunn, *The History of Nansemond County, Virginia* (ca. 1907), 40–43; *Revolutionary Virginia*, 2:314, 6:349, 355–356, 7:24, 61, 338, 534, 682, 748–749; second marriage in *North Carolina Historical and Genealogical Register* 1 (1900): 244; Virginia State Land Office Grants, H:95–96, 109–110, RG 4, LVA; Land Tax Returns, Nansemond Co., 1783, RG 48, LVA.

BRENT TARTER

COX, Earnest Sevier (24 January 1880–26 April 1966), cofounder of the Anglo-Saxon Clubs of America and writer, was born near Knoxville, in Blount County, Tennessee, and was the son of Ann Maria Earnest Cox Cox and her second husband, Samuel Thompson Cox (who was the brother of her first husband). His father, a farmer and sometime Methodist preacher, died when Cox was about twelve years old. Cox attended private schools in Blount County. After receiving a B.S. in 1899 from Roane College, an unaccredited Tennessee institution, he spent time in Georgia, Louisiana, and Oklahoma. Cox took a business course, considered studying law, and worked as a schoolteacher, loan officer, and reporter. In 1902 he enrolled in the Moody Bible Institute in Chicago, where he trained as a public speaker and street-corner preacher. A year later, he moved to Nashville and continued his theological education at Vanderbilt University. Although Cox soon found his own fundamentalism at odds with the teachings of the faculty, he remained at Vanderbilt for three years and devoted all available time to preaching. He was forced to rethink his career aspirations when a chronically sore throat prevented him from earning steady income as a preacher.

After leaving Vanderbilt in 1906 without a degree, Cox enrolled in the graduate course in sociology at the University of Chicago. As a result of the coursework he had completed at Roane and at Vanderbilt, the University of Chicago determined that he had earned the equivalent of a bachelor's degree. During his three years at Chicago, Cox began to articulate racial views that consumed him for the remainder of his life. He fervently believed in the inferiority of the black race, an assumption held by many other whites at the time, but he also insisted that whites and blacks could not coexist. The only solution, he concluded, was the removal of blacks from white society.

During the summers of 1907, 1908, and 1909 Cox traveled to Norfolk and Pittsburgh giving lectures that accompanied the presentation of cycloramas with biblical and Civil War themes. He left the University of Chicago in 1909, again without a degree. Encouraged by a Chicago professor, he decided to visit Africa in order to compare the living conditions of blacks in Africa and in the United States and also the racial policies of colonial powers in Africa with those developed by authorities in the United States. Setting sail in February 1910, Cox began a five-year trip that enabled him, in subsequent decades, to present himself as an ethnographer and expert in racial matters. Earning money along the way by working in the South African gold and diamond mines, he traveled from Cape Town to Cairo and then to Australia, New Zealand, Hong Kong, Singapore, and the Philippines. After a brief respite in the United States, Cox continued his travels in Central and South America. He returned to the United States in 1915 and began supporting himself by lecturing and writing newspaper articles on his travels.

After spending about six months in Alexandria, Virginia, Cox in 1917 joined the United States Army and earned promotion to captain. A year later his commanding officer in France found him unfit to serve on the front lines because Cox's subordinates refused to take orders from him. Removed to the support lines, Cox nevertheless received an honorable discharge in September 1919. He subsequently entered the reserves and rose to the rank of major in 1920 and lieutenant colonel in 1929.

In January 1920 Cox moved to Richmond, where he began selling real estate. Before long, he fell in with John Powell, a Richmond native and world-renowned composer and pianist who shared Cox's extreme racial views. In September 1922 Cox and Powell founded the Anglo-Saxon Clubs of America. The organization, headquartered in Richmond, eventually encompassed more than two dozen chapters in Virginia and also included several in northern states. Deriving intellectual sanction from the burgeoning eugenics movement, Cox and Powell warned that an increase in miscegenation threatened to destroy white civilization by wiping out all its desirable, racially exclusive traits and characteristics. Cox cited Egypt, South Africa, and other countries that he had visited as evidence that interracial mixing always led to the destruction of the superior race. Consequently, the pair asserted that white Americans must enforce a rigid color line. To that end, Cox and Powell led a vocal band of supporters who in 1924 convinced the General Assembly to pass the Virginia Act to Preserve Racial Integrity, probably the nation's strictest anti-miscegenation statute. Two years later, the legislature, again acting at Cox and Powell's urging, passed the so-called Massenburg Bill, a measure sponsored by Delegate George Alvin Massenburg that mandated the separation of the races in all places of public assemblage.

By the time Cox testified before the General Assembly on behalf of the racial integrity act, he had become a local celebrity with the publication of *White America* (1923). Based entirely on Cox's own travels and observations, *White America* developed the thesis that white civilizations could not survive an influx of nonwhites. Cox concluded that whites were faced with two choices: amalgamate and eventually cease to exist, or separate completely. Although hardly novel at the time in warning of the dangers of interracial mixing, Cox went a step farther than most of his contemporaries and argued that effective separation would occur only when black Americans had been repatriated to Africa. He reiterated *White America*'s central themes in subsequent books, pamphlets, and broadsides, including *The South's Part in Mongrelizing the Nation* (1926), *Lincoln's Negro Policy* (1938), *Three Million Negroes Thank the State of Virginia* (1940), *Teutonic Unity* (1951), *Unending Hate: Supreme Court School Decision a Milestone in the Federal Program to Break the Will of the White South in Its Dedicated Purpose to Remain White* (1955), and *Herman's Brother*, a speech published in *The Monument to Herman: Whom the Romans Called "Arminius"* (1959).

In September 1924 Cox entered into an unlikely alliance with Marcus Garvey, the Jamaican-born black nationalist who founded the Universal Negro Improvement Association.

Garvey's black nationalism stood in stark contrast to Cox's racial views, but Garvey nonetheless shared Cox's belief that the repatriation of blacks to Africa offered the only viable solution to the nation's racial issues. For his part, Garvey had concluded that blacks would never receive a fair chance in the United States and thus must leave. Cox wrote an open letter read at a UNIA meeting and dedicated his booklet *Let My People Go* (1925) to Garvey. The partnership between Cox and Garvey ended in 1927 when federal authorities deported Garvey after his conviction for mail fraud.

Cox then formed an alliance of convenience with the Peace Movement of Ethiopia, a little-known African American group, based in Chicago, that advocated federal assistance for the repatriation of blacks to Africa. In 1936 he prevailed on the General Assembly to recommend that the federal government provide such funds. Cox and the PME soon joined forces with Theodore Gilmore Bilbo, a United States senator and unapologetic racist from Mississippi, who introduced legislation to provide federal funds for repatriation. Bilbo's bill unmistakably bore the influence of *White America*. For nearly a decade Bilbo reintroduced his bill while Cox urged the senator to temper his language in order to ensure the support of both blacks and whites. After Bilbo's death in 1947, Senator William Langer, of North Dakota, repeatedly sponsored similar legislation, and on at least two occasions Cox testified before congressional committees as an expert on the subject. Langer's death in 1959 signaled the end of congressional attempts to introduce such legislation.

In 1958 Cox retired from the real estate business that had provided him a modest income. He published *Black Belt around the World at the High Noon of Colonialism* (1963), an autobiographical account of his early life and travels in the 1910s, and sent copies to every member of Congress and to prominent federal officeholders. In his later years he remained popular in white supremacist circles. Earnest Sevier Cox, who never married, died in a Richmond hospital from complications related to emphysema on 26 April 1966 and was buried in Arlington National Cemetery two days later.

Birth date from gravestone; Cox, *Black Belt around the World at the High Noon of Colonialism* (1963); Cox and John Powell, "Is White America to Become a Negroid Nation?" *Richmond Times-Dispatch Sunday Magazine* (22 July 1923), 2 (por.); Earnest Sevier Cox Papers, including correspondence and draft MSS, Duke; Ethel Wolfskill Hedlin, "Earnest Cox and Colonization: A White Racist's Response to Black Repatriation, 1923–1966" (Ph.D. diss., Duke, 1974); Richard B. Sherman, "The 'Teachings at Hampton Institute': Social Equality, Racial Integrity, and the Virginia Public Assemblage Act of 1926," *VMHB* 95 (1987): 275–300; Sherman, "'The Last Stand': The Fight for Racial Integrity in Virginia in the 1920s," *JSH* 54 (1988): 69–92; J. Douglas Smith, "The Campaign for Racial Purity and the Erosion of Paternalism in Virginia, 1922–1930: 'Nominally White, Biologically Mixed, and Legally Negro,'" *JSH* 68 (2002): 65–106; Smith, *Managing White Supremacy: Race, Politics, and Citizenship in Jim Crow Virginia* (2002), esp. 76–78, 80–85, 101–104; obituaries in *Richmond News Leader* and *Richmond Times-Dispatch* (por.), both 27 Apr. 1966; editorial tribute in *Richmond News Leader*, 30 Apr. 1966.

J. DOUGLAS SMITH

COX, Edwin (20 September 1902–22 February 1977), chemical engineer, was born in Richmond and was the son of Sallie Bland Clarke Cox and Edwin Piper Cox, later Speaker of the House of Delegates. His mother died in April 1906, and his father remarried six years later. Cox graduated from John Marshall High School at the age of fourteen. He received a B.S. in chemical engineering from the Virginia Military Institute in 1920 and five years later successfully applied for an M.S. from that institution based on his professional work. On 19 May 1927 Cox married Virginia Bagby DeMott, a former Latin teacher then working as a research associate for the Southern Woman's Educational Alliance. Active in civic and social organizations, she was president of the Woman's Club of Richmond from 1956 to 1957 and for more than a decade edited the *Bulletin of the King and Queen County Historical Society of Virginia*. They had one son.

Known generally as Pete Cox, he began work in 1920 as a chemist in the fertilizer analytical laboratory of the Virginia-Carolina Chemical Company (after 1926 the Virginia-Carolina Chemical Corporation). In 1925 he was a founding director of Phipps and Bird, Incorporated, a Richmond laboratory supply and chemical company. Early in the 1920s Cox joined Tobacco By-Products and Chemical Corporation, a subsidiary of Virginia-Carolina Chemical co-owned

by the American Tobacco Company, and by 1927 he had responsibility for research and development. That year he became a vice president at Phosphate Products Corporation, another V-C subsidiary, in charge of sales and technical development. When Virginia-Carolina Chemical Corporation established its chemicals division about 1935, Cox became an assistant manager and later manager. During this period he also organized the laboratory and quality-control department at the state's Department of Alcoholic Beverage Control and helped establish the research department of the American Tobacco Company.

Long active in the Virginia National Guard, Cox was promoted to lieutenant colonel of the 91st Infantry Brigade (later the 88th Brigade) on 29 July 1940. Called to active duty shortly after the United States entered World War II, he was promoted to colonel and given command of the 176th (formerly 1st Virginia) Infantry Regiment, stationed in Washington, D.C. In July 1942 Cox was placed in charge of the Mobile Force, Military District of Washington, which included the 176th Infantry and other units responsible for local security. He directed the 176th Infantry as a demonstration regiment at the infantry school in Fort Benning, Georgia, in 1943 and 1944. Reassigned in the latter year to the War Department General Staff, Cox served under the Joint Chiefs of Staff as secretary of a committee on new weapons and as chair of both the joint and combined technical intelligence committees. As a member of the general staff of the Supreme Headquarters Allied Expeditionary Force, he assisted in the initial stages of rebuilding Germany after World War II. For his wartime service he received the Bronze Star and the Legion of Merit.

After returning to the United States in 1946, Cox reorganized the 176th Combat Team, Virginia National Guard. He resigned on 1 December 1948, at which time he became a brigadier general. Cox also returned to the Virginia-Carolina Chemical Corporation and continued as manager of its chemicals division until he was promoted to one of three company vice presidencies in 1949. Poor health caused him to retire in September 1957, but he remained a consultant. After retiring he formed Cox and

Gillespie, a Richmond chemical and engineering consulting firm.

A recognized authority on phosphorus and nicotine compounds and their uses as fertilizers and insecticides, respectively, Cox published many scholarly articles on such topics as nicotine synthesis, defluorination of phosphoric acid, rancidity in wheat flour, and protein precipitation, as well as articles about the chemical industry for nonscientific magazines. He held several patents related to nicotine production, use of nicotine in sheep dip, nicotine alkaloid, nicotine dusts, and rancidity inhibitors.

Cox served as secretary, as vice chair, and for the 1929–1930 term as chair of the Virginia Section of the American Chemical Society, from which he received a distinguished service award in 1951. He was a fellow of the American Association for the Advancement of Science and of the American Institute of Chemists, and by 1926 he had joined the Virginia Academy of Science. The American Institute of Chemists in 1965 awarded Cox the Gold Medal, its highest honor.

Cox chaired the Third District Democratic Committee and was secretary of the State Democratic Central Committee. Interested in local and state history, he sat from 1959 to 1969 on the board of the Virginia State Library (later the Library of Virginia), from 1961 to 1963 as chair. He also was a member of the advisory board of the Association for the Preservation of Virginia Antiquities, a vice president of the Valentine Museum (later the Valentine Richmond History Center), and chair of the King and Queen County Committee in 1957 during the Jamestown 350th Anniversary Festival. Cox served as a governor of the General Society of Colonial Wars, Virginia Society, and of the Jamestowne Society. From 1972 to 1975 he was president of the Virginia Historical Society's executive committee. He received the VMI Foundation's distinguished service award in 1974.

Following his retirement, Cox and his wife moved permanently to Holly Hill, their King and Queen County estate that in 1973 was placed on the Virginia Landmarks Register and on the National Register of Historic Places. He farmed, experimented with soil chemistry and fertiliz-ers, and remained involved in numerous civic and cultural affairs. Edwin Cox died in Richmond of a heart attack on 22 February 1977 at a dinner of the Sons of the Revolution in the State of Virginia. He was buried in Hollywood Cemetery, in Richmond.

Biographies in Morton, *Virginia Lives*, 217–218, and American Institute of Chemists, *Edwin Cox* (1965); Virginia Meade Cox, "Grandfather: A Portrait of General Edwin Cox," *Richmond Quarterly* 3 (spring 1981): 26–29; BVS Marriage Register, Lynchburg; published writings include Cox, "The Chemical Industry of Virginia," *Commonwealth* 1 (June 1934): 12, 17, 20–21, and (Nov. 1934): 14–15, *Chemistry, Culture and the Common Weal—Through the Looking Glass* (1965), and "Gleanings of Fluvanna History . . . ," *Bulletin of the Fluvanna County Historical Society*, nos. 2–3 (Sept. 1966): 1–42; correspondence in several collections, VHS; *Richmond News Leader*, 18 Nov. 1948; *Richmond Times-Dispatch*, 27 Sept. 1957, 23 Apr. 1965; *Virginia Military Institute Alumni Review* 34 (spring 1958): 5; ibid. 51 (winter 1975): 4–5 (pors.); Hall, *Portraits*, 56–57 (por.); obituaries and editorial tributes in *Richmond News Leader*, 23 Feb. 1977, *Richmond Times-Dispatch*, 23, 25 Feb. 1977, and *Virginia Military Institute Alumni Review* 53 (spring 1977): 45–46.

MAURI R. WINEGARDNER

COX, Edwin Piper (2 May 1870–11 March 1938), Speaker of the House of Delegates, was born in Bland County. He was the son of first cousins Henry Winston Cox, a civil engineer, and Martha Hannah Wooldridge Cox and the grandson of James Henry Cox, who represented Chesterfield County in the Conventions of 1850–1851 and 1861. Cox's mother died when he was an infant, and he grew up in his maternal grandparents' home in Richmond. After attending Pantops Academy in Albemarle County and Worsham Academy in Prince Edward County, he graduated from Hampden-Sydney College in 1888 and from the law school at the University of Virginia in 1892.

Cox practiced law in Richmond until the summer of 1924. He married Sallie Bland Clarke, of Richmond, on 12 April 1898. They had one son, Edwin Cox, who became a chemical engineer, and one daughter, Ellen Bland Cox Bruns, who served three terms in the Louisiana legislature during the 1950s. Cox's wife died on 29 April 1906, and on 30 December 1912 he married Rhoda Ethel Freeman, a Rockbridge County native. They had two daughters.

A Democrat, Cox won election to the House of Delegates in 1903 as one of five delegates from the city of Richmond. Reelected six times, he served continuously through 1915 and rapidly rose into the ranks of the leadership. In his first session, in 1904, he served on the Committees on Counties, Cities, and Towns, on General Laws, and on Immigration. From 1906 until 1914 he chaired the influential Committee on General Laws and from 1906 through 1910 was ranking member of the Committee on Immigration. Cox gained a seat on the powerful Committee on Rules in 1908 and two years later became the ranking member. At the latter time he also became a member of the Committee on Militia and Police. In 1912 he began sitting on the Committee on Privileges and Elections.

In January 1914 Cox was elected Speaker of the House of Delegates. The preferred candidate of the Democratic Party leadership, he faced down opposition from at least three other candidates who failed to gain support from a significant number of party members. Cox pursued a modest agenda as Speaker. He urged that committees open their meetings to the public and divided the powerful Committee on Finance, giving it control over revenue bills and creating a separate Committee on Appropriations, to the chair of which he appointed a future Speaker, Richard Lewis Brewer. At the end of his term as Speaker, Cox retired from the General Assembly.

During World War I, Cox chaired one of the two district boards that oversaw the administration of conscription in Virginia. On 7 June 1924, about two years after Cox had moved to Chesterfield County, the governor appointed him to fill the vacant office of judge of the Fourth Judicial Circuit, which comprised the city of Petersburg and the counties of Amelia, Chesterfield, Dinwiddie, Nottoway, and Powhatan. The next session of the assembly elected him on 21 January 1926 to the balance of the eight-year term, and it reelected him to another eight-year term on 18 January 1932. One of the few decisions Cox rendered while on the court that attracted wide attention was his disallowance of a Chesterfield County ordinance in April 1935 that licensed walking and dancing marathons. He ruled that

the ordinance was so vague that it would countenance rather than prohibit fund-raising events that "can only appeal to those who are so depraved as to delight in the physical suffering of humanity."

His family's long residence in Chesterfield County led Cox from time to time to speak or write about local history. In January 1899 he gave an oration at the presentation of a portrait of the Civil War officer John Pelham to the R. E. Lee Camp, No. 1, Confederate Veterans, and in September 1936 he delivered an address on the county's history, which was published later that year as a thirty-six-page pamphlet, *A Brief Outline of Some Salient Facts Relating to the History of Chesterfield County, Virginia*. At least one researcher gathering material on Chesterfield County for the Works Progress Administration's Virginia Historical Inventory interviewed him about local sites and subjects. Edwin Piper Cox died of liver cancer in a Richmond hospital on 11 March 1938 and was buried in the family cemetery at Clover Hill, in Chesterfield County.

Biographies in Bruce, Tyler, and Morton, *History of Virginia*, 5:101–103, in Jamerson, *Speakers and Clerks, 1776–1996*, 121 (por. on 120), and in Ernest P. Gates and Lucille C. Moseley, comps., *The 1917 Courthouse of the Circuit Court of Chesterfield County, Virginia: Its History and Portraits* (1994), 28–29 (por.); BVS Marriage Register, Richmond City (1898, 1912); *Richmond Dispatch*, 17 Jan. 1899; *Richmond Times-Dispatch*, 13, 14 Jan. 1914, 10 Jan. 1916, 8 June 1924, 28 Apr. 1935 (quotation); *JHD*, 1914 sess., 5–6, 1926 sess., 70, 1932 sess., 44; address on Pelham printed in *SHSP* 26 (1898): 291–295; BVS Death Certificate, Richmond City (with birth date provided by son); obituaries in *Richmond News Leader* and *Richmond Times-Dispatch*, both 12 Mar. 1938; editorial tributes in *Richmond Times-Dispatch*, 13 Mar. 1938, and *Richmond News Leader*, 14 Mar. 1938; memorials in *JHD*, 1938 sess., 1059, and *Virginia State Bar Association Proceedings* (1939), 221–224.

BRENT TARTER

COX, Frank Woodard (25 February 1903–16 March 1976), educator, was born in York County and was the son of William B. Cox, a farmer, and Resser V. Carmine Cox. After receiving an A.B. from the College of William and Mary in 1926, he was appointed principal of Newport High School in Giles County. On 28 July 1928 Cox married Evelyn Lizabeth Huffman, a Giles County native then living in Oceana, in Princess Anne County. They had one son and one daughter. In 1929 Cox became principal of Oceana High School.

Cox received an M.A. at the University of Virginia in 1931. Two years later, after some controversy about the candidates, the Princess Anne County school board appointed him superintendent of schools. Taking up his new position during the Great Depression, Cox aggressively sought school funding at the local, state, and federal levels. In 1934 he urged the county's representative in the House of Delegates to oppose legislation reducing the amount of money school boards could borrow from the Literary Fund, which provided revenue for school construction. Three years later Cox lobbied for passage of a failed congressional bill that would have appropriated $1 billion in federal funds for schools nationwide during a five-year period.

World War II and the population growth it helped trigger posed new challenges for Cox. Between 1940 and 1942 Princess Anne County school enrollment rose about 20 percent, and the influx of new students and the demand for manpower and supplies for the war effort limited his ability to maintain an adequate number of school buses and teachers. Cox worked tirelessly to secure funds for school expansion and construction. To combat overcrowded schools in 1947 and 1948, he favored a 2 percent sales tax to provide additional funding for school construction. After Virginia Beach was incorporated as a city in 1952, Cox became school superintendent there as well as retaining direction of the Princess Anne County schools. As the area's growth continued and educational demands expanded in the 1950s and 1960s, he advocated multiple bond referenda. In May 1952 a $2.8 million bond referendum for school construction passed by a vote of 2,467 to 266. In 1963, the year the county merged with the city of Virginia Beach, residents overwhelmingly supported a $7.3 million bond issue for school additions and construction. Cox encouraged approval of an $18.5 million bond referendum in January 1968, with a majority of the money earmarked for new school buildings and additions to existing ones. Voters approved the referendum by a margin of three to one, in spite of a possible tax increase.

As superintendent Cox faced the issues of school segregation and integration. Since at least the mid-1920s African American parents had worked to raise funds and gain permission to open a high school for their children, but the county school board had remained unresponsive. Under Cox's leadership, however, the school board approved a school, and after Cox successfully applied for a grant through the Works Progress Administration, the Princess Anne Training School opened in Euclid in 1938. The county's black leaders continued to press for improved educational facilities, and in 1946 a state survey committee assessed the deplorable conditions facing Princess Anne's black children. Cox subsequently emphasized the need to consolidate the several one-room schools that black students attended and to float a $250,000 bond to finance a black high school. Voters defeated the referendum in December 1947 and again in June 1948, while at the same time they approved bonds earmarked for improving white schools. Following both votes, black parents, with the assistance of the National Association for the Advancement of Colored People, prepared lawsuits in an effort to secure better educational facilities for their children. A third referendum, providing $250,000 for the construction of a new African American elementary school, passed in March 1950 by a vote of 718 to 190. In addition, Cox announced that he would allocate educational funds provided by the state solely to the black schools in the county.

After the Supreme Court of the United States overturned legalized school segregation with its decision in *Brown* v. *Board of Education* (1954), Cox adopted a wait-and-see attitude. He stated that current building projects for separate black schools would continue as though no ruling had been handed down. The Virginia Beach schools did not integrate until 1965, when Cox, like many other Virginia school superintendents, organized a freedom-of-choice plan that placed the responsibility of integrating students in the hands of parents, rather than the school board. After the federal government rejected the plan in 1966, Cox cooperated with federal officials to phase in a more comprehensive integration plan, a process completed by the end of 1969.

In 1966 Cox received the Virginia Beach First Citizen Award for his professional and civic efforts. He promoted both the Boy Scouts of America and the Girl Scouts of the USA and raised funds for the General Hospital of Virginia Beach (later Sentara Virginia Beach General Hospital). Cox served on the board of visitors of the College of William and Mary from 1964 to 1972 and on the board of the Coastal Turnpike Authority from 1964 to 1973. He was board chair of Scott Memorial Methodist Church for a dozen years. The school board named the Princess Anne High School stadium and a high school in his honor in 1955 and 1961, respectively.

Cox retired on 29 February 1968 after thirty-four years as superintendent and with sixteen months left on his contract. During his long tenure he oversaw exponential growth of the school system from 3,053 students, 91 teachers, and school property valued at $446,700 in 1933 to 39,987 students, 1,494 teachers, and property valued at $36.5 million in 1967. Cox played a key role in completing $25 million in school construction, with more than $10 million provided by federal sources. In February 1968 the Virginia Beach Education Association honored him with a testimonial dinner attended by 700 guests, and in March of that year the Virginia Beach city council adopted a resolution thanking him for his many achievements. Frank Woodard Cox died in Virginia Beach on 16 March 1976 and was buried in the city's Rosewood Memorial Park.

Birth date in Social Security application, Social Security Administration, Office of Earnings Operations, Baltimore, Md.; BVS Marriage Register, Princess Anne Co.; Cox correspondence in Harry B. Davis Papers, Virginia Wesleyan College, Norfolk–Virginia Beach; *Norfolk Ledger-Star*, 9 Feb. 1966, 11 Aug. 1967; *Virginia Beach Sun*, 10 Feb. 1966, 29 Feb. (por.), 28 Mar. 1968; *Norfolk Virginian-Pilot*, 9 Oct. 1966, 11 Aug. 1967, 29 Feb. 1968; obituary in *Norfolk Virginian-Pilot*, 17 Mar. 1976.

KELLEY M. EWING

COX, Henry (b. December 1832), member of the House of Delegates, was born in Powhatan County, whether free or enslaved is not certain. The maiden name and surname of his mother, an African American woman named Louisa, are not known, nor is the name of his father. It is likely that Cox was closely related to Joseph Cox, a Powhatan County native a few years younger than he who served in the Convention of 1867–1868. Details about Cox's life are scarce, and researchers have occasionally confused him with Henry Coy, a freeborn black carpenter in the county who was approximately six years older. When Cox married Rachel E. Harris on 23 November 1867, he identified himself as a thirty-five-year-old widower and shoemaker. They had two daughters, and the 1870 census (which listed him as a farmer able to read and write) indicates that in that year he also had a sixteen-year-old son. In 1871 Cox purchased a thirty-seven-acre farm worth $666.

Described later as a plain man well-liked by his fellow citizens, Cox became interested in politics during Reconstruction and beginning in 1870 served concurrent two-year terms as a Powhatan County justice of the peace and constable. In July 1869, in the first election in which African Americans voted for members of the General Assembly, he won one of three seats representing Chesterfield and Powhatan Counties in the House of Delegates. A conservative newspaper characterized all three delegates, two of whom were African Americans, as "*Ultra Radicals.*" Following a redistricting of the assembly, Cox won reelection to two-year terms in 1871, 1873, and 1875 as the sole delegate from Powhatan County. He did not seek a fifth term in 1877.

In his first term Cox was appointed to the lowest-ranking seat on the Committee on Labor and the Poor and was also the lowest-ranking member of the Committee on Militia and Police. He retained his assignment on the latter during his second and third terms, and during his third and fourth he also held a low-ranking seat on the Committee on Officers and Offices at the Capitol. None of the appointments was to an influential committee, and there is no evidence that Cox introduced any significant bills during his eight years in the House of Delegates. The assembly's records and newspaper accounts of its sessions do not indicate whether he spoke during debates. Characterizing his service is difficult because he was sometimes absent or did not vote when present, but at election times newspaper reports usually identified him as a Republican or a Radical.

In April 1870 Cox attended a Richmond convention of African American workingmen that adopted resolutions calling for organizing laborers, accused the state's Democrats of attempting to reduce the number of Republican voters, and advised "colored men to be honest, sober, and industrious." Later that month Cox also attended the state convention of the Republican Party, which called for enforcement of the Fourteenth and Fifteenth Amendments to the Constitution, advocated education at public expense, and endorsed the new state constitution. On 10 January 1872 he and several other African American members of the assembly joined legislators from other states in Washington, D.C., to discuss federal civil rights legislation with the president. Two days later Cox was back at work in Richmond, where he voted with the majority of House members in favor of reducing the per diem and mileage allowance for members of the General Assembly. He was a member of the Resolutions Committee at an 1875 state convention of approximately one hundred African American delegates who met in Richmond to address a lack of jobs and who organized a short-lived Laboring Men's Mechanics' Union Association.

Cox and his wife moved to Washington, D.C., about 1881. Seven years later his property in Powhatan County was sold, possibly for nonpayment of taxes. Cox last appears in public records in 1910, when the Washington city directory listed him as a shoemaker residing at 202 Massachusetts Avenue, N.W., where he had lived for a decade or more. His name does not appear in the census taken in April of that year. The date, place, and circumstances of Henry Cox's death are not known, nor is his place of burial.

Biography in Jackson, *Negro Office-Holders*, 9; Census, Powhatan Co., 1870, 1880, and District of Columbia, 1900 (with birth date of Dec. 1832); BVS Marriage Register, Powhatan Co. (age thirty-five on 23 Nov. 1867); Land Tax Returns, Powhatan Co. (1871–1887), RG 48, LVA; Election Records, nos. 2, 3, 10, RG 13, LVA; *Richmond Daily Dispatch*, 8 July 1869 (first quotation), 12 (second quotation), 22 Apr. 1870, 8 Nov. 1871, 3, 6 Nov. 1875; *Richmond Enquirer*, 20, 21 Aug. 1875; Herbert Aptheker, ed., *A Documentary History of the Negro People in the United States*

(1951–1994), 1:636–637; Richard T. Couture, *Powhatan: A Bicentennial History* (1980), 294, 296.

ERVIN L. JORDAN, JR.

COX, James Henry (10 February 1810–18 February 1877), member of the Convention of 1850–1851 and of the Convention of 1861, was born at Sappony, the Chesterfield County plantation of his parents, Henry Cox and Mary Traylor Cox. He matriculated at Hampden-Sydney College in 1825 and received an A.B. in 1829. For about two years he read law in Chesterfield with his mother's cousin, John Winston Jones, a member of the Convention of 1829–1830 and later Speaker of the United States House of Representatives. On 23 August 1832 Cox married Martha Reid Law in Petersburg. Before her death on 18 August 1872, they had five sons and two daughters, one of whom died as an infant.

Soon after his marriage Cox moved to Florida, where he served as headmaster of a Tallahassee academy. He had returned to Chesterfield County by the autumn of 1834 and settled along Winterpock Creek on a 527-acre tract of land owned by his father. After purchasing the land for one dollar in 1839, Cox named the plantation Clover Hill, enlarged the house, and implemented agricultural innovations. He also operated a boarding school for young men at his home. In January 1840, about three years after the discovery of a coal deposit on his land, Cox helped incorporate the Clover Hill Coal Mining and Iron Manufacturing Company. The following year he sold the land to the company for $30,000 and five hundred shares of stock, although as a condition of the deed he continued to live in the main house.

In addition to his business interests, Cox practiced law. He began an almost uninterrupted lifetime of service in Chesterfield County's local affairs in October 1840, when he was appointed to the county court. He had become presiding justice by 1852. On 13 January 1837 Cox began filling an unexpired term representing Chesterfield County in the House of Delegates. He was added to the Committees of Finance and of Schools and Colleges. The following year Cox won election to the first of five consecutive one-year terms. During his tenure he sat on the Committees of Agriculture and Manufactures, to

Examine the Bonds of Public Officers, of Schools and Colleges, and on Trade and Mechanic Arts. He chaired the Committee to Examine the Penitentiary from 1839 to 1842.

In 1842 Cox won election to the Senate of Virginia to complete the last year of an unexpired term representing Petersburg and the counties of Amelia, Chesterfield, and Powhatan. He wanted to retire from public service in 1843 and again in 1847, but he was convinced to seek reelection both times and was returned to the Senate for another four-year term on each occasion. Cox resigned in 1848, with three years left in his term. He sat at various times on the Committees of Claims, to Examine the Penitentiary, and of Internal Improvement (on which he became the ranking member) and also on a joint committee to examine the library. He chaired a joint committee to examine the treasurer's accounts during three sessions from 1844 to 1847.

Early in the 1850s Cox possessed real estate worth approximately $8,000. He owned about twenty slaves and employed more than seventy bondsmen at the Clover Hill Coal Mining and Iron Manufacturing Company. In August 1850 Cox was one of four delegates elected from a ten-candidate field to represent the district comprising Petersburg and the counties of Chesterfield and Prince George in a constitutional convention that met in Richmond from 14 October 1850 to 1 August 1851. Appointed to the Committee on the Basis of Apportionment of Representation, he spoke often during the proceedings and served as temporary chair of the committee of the whole on 17 June 1851.

A Democrat, Cox believed that the United States Constitution granted the federal government only limited powers. During the convention he argued that the new state constitution should reflect the fundamental principles of government only, rather than include detailed laws that would be too inflexible in an era of rapid change and too broad for localities that differed widely from one another. Although Cox supported establishing a board of public works, educating the poor, and reapportioning judicial districts, he vehemently opposed addressing these issues in the constitution and believed they should instead be left to the legislature and

local officials to manage. He grew frustrated that the convention seemed intent on strengthening the constitution and correspondingly weakening the powers and responsibilities of the General Assembly. Cox did not vote on a key compromise on reapportioning representation in the General Assembly or on the final adoption of the constitution, but on 31 July 1851 he paired in opposition on a vote engrossing the new constitution.

Despite personal business losses during the financial panic of 1857, Cox remained a prosperous and optimistic spokesman for expanding industry. On 3 March 1858 he joined several others in incorporating the Chester Hotel and Mining Company in Chesterfield County. Early in the 1860s Cox owned about fifty slaves, while his Clover Hill Coal Mining and Iron Manufacturing Company employed more than sixty others.

In October 1860 Cox, backed by both Unionist Democrats and the Opposition party, unsuccessfully sought a seat in the Senate of Virginia representing Chesterfield, Cumberland, and Powhatan Counties. During that autumn's presidential campaign he also was an unsuccessful elector for Stephen Arnold Douglas, the regular Democratic Party candidate. As the sectional crisis deepened, Cox remained a Unionist, and on 4 February 1861 he won election by several hundred votes to represent Chesterfield County in a convention called to consider the issue of secession. When the delegates convened in Richmond on 13 February, he was elected temporary chair before the selection of a permanent president. Confident that the convention would conduct an orderly and careful deliberation, Cox declared that the delegates assembled bore the responsibility for the honor and safety of Virginia, as well as the destiny of the nation and its republican institutions. On 5 March he submitted a resolution calling for a conference of border slave-states. Arguing that Virginia should take no action in isolation, especially concerning secession, he maintained that the commonwealth should act in concert with the commercially and politically similar border states.

Cox desired to maintain the Union, but he also continued to believe in a limited federal government. He affirmed the right of sovereign, independent states to secede, even while he condemned South Carolina and other states for doing so. Strongly believing that federal coercion of these states not only was unconstitutional but also would lead to civil war, Cox called for an unequivocal declaration that Virginia would support other Southern states if the federal government used force. In introducing his proposal on a border-state conference he exclaimed, "I love the Union, but as much as I love the Union and venerate the memories of the great men who gave us the Union, rather than live in this Union disgraced, rather than live upon terms of inequality I would tear the Union into fragments and trample it under foot."

Despite his forceful rhetoric and a petition from his Chesterfield constituents endorsing disunion, Cox paired against secession in the vote on 4 April 1861 when the convention defeated a motion to withdraw from the Union. On 17 April, after President Abraham Lincoln called for troops to put down the rebellion, Cox voted with the majority to secede. He signed the Ordinance of Secession and attended two subsequent sessions of the convention in June and November 1861. As presiding justice of the Chesterfield County Court during the Civil War, he attended to such matters as organizing efforts to recruit soldiers and ensuring that rail lines fulfilled military needs.

After the war, Cox took the amnesty oath on 20 June 1865 and received a presidential pardon on 3 July. In the latter month he was reelected to the county court and unanimously named presiding justice at its first meeting in August. Cox announced his candidacy in September 1865 for a seat in the House of Representatives from the fourteen-county Fourth District. He soon withdrew from the race, however, because he could not take the prescribed test oath affirming loyalty to the Union during the Civil War. Removed as a justice of the peace during Radical Reconstruction, he returned to the Chesterfield bench in April 1870 when the General Assembly appointed him the first county judge under the new state constitution. James Henry Cox died at Clover Hill on 18 February 1877, approximately two weeks after suffering what was probably a stroke, and was buried on the

estate. Local newspapers reported that as many as seven hundred people attended his funeral.

Biographies in Harry D. Forsythe (great-grandson), "James Henry Cox of 'Clover Hill,' Chesterfield County, Virginia, 1810–1877" (undated typescript), Chesterfield Historical Society of Virginia (including birth and marriage dates), and Ernest P. Gates and Lucille C. Moseley, comps., *The 1917 Courthouse of the Circuit Court of Chesterfield County, Virginia: Its History and Portraits* (1994), 17–18 (por.); *Petersburg American Constellation*, 4 Oct. 1834; *Petersburg Republican*, 24 Feb. 1843, 17 Nov. 1848; *Richmond Enquirer*, 27 Aug. 1850, 12, 19 Oct. 1860; *Petersburg Daily Index*, 16, 18, 30 Sept. 1865; *Richmond Daily Dispatch*, 6 May 1868; *Petersburg Rural Messenger*, 24 Aug. 1872; *Journal of 1850–1851 Convention*, 58; *Debates and Proceedings of 1850–1851 Convention*, 28, 47, 51–53, 277; *Supplement, 1850–1851 Convention Debates*, nos. 64, 66, 67, 70, 87, 90, 92; Reese and Gaines, *Proceedings of 1861 Convention*, 1:3–4, 380–381 (quotation), 482–485, 2:420–421, 3:164, 4:144; Presidential Pardons; BVS Death Register, Chesterfield Co.; obituaries, tributes, and accounts of funeral in *Petersburg Index and Appeal*, 20, 22 Feb., 16 Mar. 1877, and *Petersburg Daily Post*, *Richmond Daily Whig*, and *Richmond Enquirer*, all 20 Feb. 1877.

JOHN HERBERT ROPER

COX, Joseph (d. 16 April 1880), member of the Convention of 1867–1868, was born in the mid-1830s in Powhatan County. He may have been the son of a free black named Joseph Cox. His mother's name is not known for certain, but she may have been Lizza Smith, a free woman of color who late in 1836 married a Joe Cox in Powhatan County. It is likely that Cox was closely related to Henry Cox, a Powhatan native a few years older than he who served four terms in the House of Delegates beginning in 1869. The details of Cox's early life are not known. By 1850 he had most likely moved to Richmond with his father, who was a laborer in the city. Cox worked for a time in a tobacco factory and for nine years in the rolling mills on Belle Isle and at the Tredegar ironworks. Like many other free blacks in Richmond, he held a variety of odd jobs. Later recollections reported that he had at one time been a bartender, a day laborer, and a huckster. The 1860 census listed Cox as a blacksmith. By June of that year he had married a woman named Eliza, whose maiden name is not known and who worked as a washer. They had at least one daughter.

After the Civil War, Cox took advantage of his relative prosperity and assumed a leadership role in Richmond's African American community. Buoyed by emancipation but hampered by a devastated economy, discriminatory policies, and white hostility, Richmond blacks created a network of secret societies that provided relief aid and offered a platform for addressing grievances. Cox emerged as president of one of the largest such organizations, the Lincoln Union Aid Society. He may also have headed up a mounted militia unit, three of whose members attempted to integrate a Richmond streetcar in April 1867. Cox's leadership within the black community did not escape the notice of federal authorities. After Congress passed the First Reconstruction Act in March 1867, an officer of the Bureau of Refugees, Freedmen, and Abandoned Lands identified Cox as a local leader who could take the ironclad oath and therefore serve in government. In the spring of 1867 he sat on the petit jury called to hear the case against former Confederate president Jefferson Davis on charges of treason.

Cox helped organize the Union Republican Party in Virginia. Despite efforts of more-conservative Unionists to promote a Republican Party that might prove more appealing to native Virginia whites, radical activists, particularly those in Richmond, succeeded in forging an organization that pushed for a decisive break from the past. Aligning himself with the more-radical faction, Cox in April 1867 was a Richmond delegate to the party's state convention, which adopted an egalitarian platform. During that summer he bolstered his position within the party's Richmond organization, perhaps by marginalizing centrist black leaders, such as Fields Cook and John Oliver. He also canvassed outlying rural areas to strengthen the party there. A meeting of Republicans in Richmond's Madison Ward in September 1867 named Cox to a committee created to coordinate party-building with committees from other city wards. He was also elected vice president of the Republican organization in Monroe and Fifth Wards. Grounding his radical policy goals with an inclusive political sensibility, he cooperated with centrists when appropriate and sought the participation of prominent white Unionists.

Cox's hard work was rewarded on 14 October 1867 when a convention of city Republicans nominated him and four other candidates (one black, three white) as delegates to a statewide convention called to write a new constitution for Virginia. Richmond's African American population mobilized and by a margin of 404 votes elected the Radical Republican slate, which also received 48 votes from whites. The defeated Conservative candidates alleged fraud but failed to overturn the results. Meeting from 3 December 1867 to 17 April 1868, the convention developed a constitution that granted universal manhood suffrage, instituted a public school system, reorganized the state's system of local government, and proposed disfranchising Confederate loyalists.

Cox sat on the Committees on the Legislative Department and on County and Corporation Courts and County Organizations, as well as on the Committee on Finance, which had a largely organizational function within the convention. Taking great interest in issues associated with the franchise, Cox introduced four resolutions that supported Radical measures on suffrage. Other than a few procedural statements, however, he was silent on other issues. He consistently supported the Radical majority in every major vote without becoming a lightning rod for the Conservative opposition. On 17 April 1868 Cox joined other Republican delegates in approving the new constitution, which voters ratified without the disfranchising provisions in July 1869.

After the convention Cox chaired local meetings of Republicans and African American groups and also officiated at public celebrations. The power of grassroots activists in the Republican Party was declining, however. As white centrists consolidated control over the party and as Conservatives reasserted their power in Richmond, Cox seems to have refocused most of his efforts on nonpartisan movements devoted to improving the economic and political standing of blacks. In April 1870 he became a vice president of the Richmond chapter of the Colored National Labor Union. Cox numbered among the approximately one hundred African American delegates from across the state who met in Richmond in August 1875 to address the lack of jobs and to advance the interests of Virginia blacks. He received a patronage appointment as janitor of the customs house, a position he held throughout much of the decade. Joseph Cox died of consumption (probably tuberculosis) on 16 April 1880 at the Manchester home of his sister. A reported three thousand people turned out to pay their respects two days later when he was buried at Mount Olivet Cemetery, in the section of Chesterfield County that in 1914 became part of the city of Richmond.

Biographies in *Richmond Daily Dispatch*, 20 Aug. 1875 (age given as forty-two), and Jackson, *Negro Office-Holders*, 9; Census, Henrico Co., 1860 (age twenty-four on 23 June 1860); *Daily Richmond Enquirer*, 10 May 1867; *Richmond Southern Opinion*, 17 Aug., 7 Dec. (caricature por.) 1867; *Richmond Daily Dispatch*, 1, 15, 26 Oct. 1867, 7 May 1869; *Richmond Daily Enquirer and Examiner*, 15 Oct. 1867; *New York Times*, 18 Oct. 1867; *Daily Richmond Whig*, 9 Dec. 1867; *Debates and Proceedings of 1867–1868 Convention*, 30, 60, 198, 381–382, 485, 659; *Journal of 1867–1868 Convention*, 28, 389; Hume, "Membership of Convention of 1867–1868," 481; Lowe, "Virginia's Reconstruction Convention," 347; Peter J. Rachleff, *Black Labor in the South: Richmond, Virginia, 1865–1890* (1984), 41, 46, 50, 51, 59, 62, 68, 99; BVS Death Register, Manchester (death on 10 Apr. 1880 at age forty-three); Mount Olivet Cemetery Interment Records (death at age forty-eight of "Softening of the Brain" and burial on 16 Apr. 1880); obituaries and tributes in *Richmond Daily Whig*, 17 Apr. 1880 (died "yesterday morning"), and *Richmond Daily Dispatch* and *Richmond Southern Intelligencer*, both 19 Apr. 1880.

WILLIAM BLAND WHITLEY

COX, Katherine Hamilton Cabell Claiborne (15 September 1854–25 December 1925), president of the National Society of the Colonial Dames of America, was born in Richmond and was the only daughter of Jane C. Alston Cabell and Henry Coalter Cabell, a Confederate artillery officer, attorney, and civic leader. She attended private schools in Richmond and New York City and on 1 February 1882 became the third wife of Herbert Augustine Claiborne (1819–1902), the sixty-two-year-old president of the Mutual Assurance Society. Before his death on 15 February 1902 they had one daughter, who died in childhood, and two sons, the elder of whom, Herbert Augustine Claiborne (1886–1957), became a noted Richmond contractor and preservationist. On 21 June 1905 she married seventy-three-year-old William Ruffin Cox, a former Confederate brigadier general, member of the House of Representatives from North Carolina, and secretary of the United States Senate. She was his third wife, and they had no children. During her second marriage, she continued to live in Richmond but also spent time in North Carolina before William Ruffin Cox's death on 26 December 1919.

One of the most active clubwomen in Virginia, Cox was a member of many service, patriotic, and preservation societies. For more than thirty years she served as financial secretary of the Memorial Home for Girls, successor of the antebellum Female Humane Association of the City of Richmond. Cox was president of the Woman's Club of Richmond from March 1906 to March 1909 and Virginia vice regent of the Mount Vernon Ladies' Association of the Union from 1921 until her death. The Association for the Preservation of Virginia Antiquities, the National Society of the Colonial Dames of America, and the Society of the Colonial Dames in the State of Virginia (later the National Society of the Colonial Dames of America in the Commonwealth of Virginia) were her principal interests. She was corresponding secretary of the APVA from 1898 to 1900, vice president from 1903 to 1924, and honorary vice president from 1924 until her death. A charter member of the Virginia chapter of the Colonial Dames and president from 1898 until her death, she was also vice president of the national society from 1900 to 1902, when she won election to the first of six consecutive two-year terms as president. Under Cox's leadership, the state and national branches of the Colonial Dames worked closely with the APVA to preserve and memorialize places and events of special importance from the colonial period. Cox participated in the APVA's celebration of the three-hundredth anniversary of the English settlement of Virginia and oversaw the Colonial Dames' project to rebuild the seventeenth-century church at Jamestown, which the APVA owned. Later, when John Marshall's house in Richmond was threatened with destruction, the Colonial Dames protested and saved the building, which the APVA later purchased and preserved.

Under Cox's direction, the Colonial Dames also worked to collect, preserve, and transcribe volumes of Virginia county and church records, and the members sponsored publication of abstracts of many city and county government documents. The Dames erected monuments and memorials around Virginia to commemorate persons, places, and special events in Virginia's history. In 1902 the national society dedicated a monument in Arlington National Cemetery to Spanish-American War servicemen, and two years later the society presented to the cemetery a Book of Patriots listing the names of every American soldier and sailor who had died during the war. The state society unsuccessfully lobbied to move Jean-Antoine Houdon's life-size marble statue of George Washington from the State Capitol to a fireproof building, helped restore the clock in Williamsburg's Bruton Parish Church, and presented a steel case to the Virginia State Library (later the Library of Virginia) to protect the state's most valuable archival records.

After Cox declined renomination as national president in 1914, the Colonial Dames named her honorary president and established the Kate Cabell Cox Scholarship in American History at the University of Virginia, where she had earlier helped set up the Henry Coalter Cabell Scholarship in honor of her father. During World War I she was a member of the Council of National Defense and the Red Cross, and she participated in Richmond's Liberty Loan drives. She was a contributing member of the Virginia War History Commission.

In 1922 Cox published *The Society of the Colonial Dames of America in the State of Virginia, October 1892–October 1922*, a thirty-page history listing the organization's achievements. She completed a fifteen-page pamphlet, *Some Facts Regarding the Houdon Statue of George Washington in the Capitol at Richmond, Virginia*, in 1924 and the following year published a sixty-page booklet, *Historical Sketch of Richmond's Oldest Chartered Charity, Memorial Home for Girls, Formerly Female Humane Association, 1805–1925*. Katherine Hamilton Cabell Claiborne Cox died at her Richmond home on 25 December 1925 from pneumonia contracted during treatment for a malignant growth on her neck. She was buried in the city's Hollywood Cemetery.

Biographies in Brent Witt, "Toilers in the Sun: Richmond's Wonderful World of Women," *Everywoman's Magazine* 1 (Nov. 1917): 59–60, and Margaret Wootten Collier, *Biographies of Representative Women of the South, 1861–1923* (1920–1923), 2:55 (por. on 54); birth date from gravestone in Dorman, *Claiborne of Virginia*, 600 (por. on 601); variant birth date of 15 Sept. 1855 on BVS Death Certificate, Richmond City; BVS Marriage Register, Richmond City (1882, 1905); Claiborne family Bible records (1784–1941), VHS; *Richmond News Leader* and *Richmond Times-Dispatch*, both 21 June 1905; letters and diaries in Claiborne Family Papers and some letters in Ellett–Saint Catherine's Alumnae Association Papers, both VHS; APVA Minutes, vols. 1–4, including memorial on 4:181, VHS; APVA *Yearbook* (1898–1926); Clarinda Huntington Pendleton Lamar, *A History of the National Society of the Colonial Dames of America from 1891 to 1933* (1934), 13, 14, 53, 79, 125–126; obituaries in *Richmond Times-Dispatch*, 26 Dec. 1925, *Washington Post*, 27 Dec. 1925, and *New York Times*, 29 Dec. 1925; obituary and editorial tribute in *Richmond News Leader*, 28 Dec. 1925; memorials in Mount Vernon Ladies' Association of the Union *Annual Report* (1926), 12, 34–35, and *Woman's Club, Richmond, Virginia, Annual Report* (1926), 51.

CASSANDRA BRITT FARRELL

COX, Lucy Ann White (d. 17 December 1891), vivandière, was born in Fredericksburg, probably late in the 1820s, although various official records that collected ages and vital statistics provide birth years ranging from as early as 1826 to as late as 1840. Her parents were Jesse White and Lucinda Snellings White. Her father, publisher of the *Fredericksburg Weekly Advertiser*, employed James A. Cox, a young man about ten years her junior, in his printing business. After the Civil War began, Cox enlisted on 22 April 1861 in Company A of the 30th Regiment Virginia Infantry. According to some later accounts, Lucy White accompanied Cox to the front at the beginning of the war and was present at the First Battle of Manassas (Bull Run) in July 1861, but she probably did not permanently join his regiment in the field as a vivandière, or daughter of the regiment, until after they married in Fredericksburg on 9 January 1862, not long before the regiment left for North Carolina.

The 30th Virginia fought most notably in the 1862 Maryland campaign and at the battles of Fredericksburg (1862) and Petersburg (1864). Because Lucy Cox was not officially detailed to the regiment, it is difficult to determine the exact nature or length of her service, but she seems to have acted as a cook, laundress, nurse, and general helpmate for the men in Company A. She was widely known by the *nom de guerre* Pawnee.

James Cox was hospitalized on several occasions, once in 1864 to have his right thumb amputated after sustaining wounds at Cold Harbor. He deserted briefly late in October 1863 and permanently in February 1865. Lucy Cox likely left the regiment to tend to her husband during his illnesses and accompanied him home in February 1865.

After the war, the Coxes returned to her parents' home in Fredericksburg, where James Cox resumed the printing trade with Jesse White. Very little is known about Lucy Cox's postwar life. The Maury Camp of Confederate Veterans in Fredericksburg unanimously elected her an honorary member, and she and her husband both attended reunions of the 30th Virginia held in the 1880s, at which she was honored for her devotion to the Confederacy.

The Coxes are not known to have had any children. Lucy Ann White Cox died in Fredericksburg on 17 December 1891, after a lingering illness, perhaps dropsy. Her widower died on 28 October 1905. Although Lucy Cox had been buried in the Fredericksburg Confederate Cemetery, her husband was interred in the neighboring City Cemetery.

Cox might have been lost to history had her wartime service not been celebrated after her death. Local camps of Confederate Veterans and Sons of Confederate Veterans marched in her funeral procession to the music of Andrew Benjamin Bowering's brass band. Following the elaborate funeral, Cox's memorialists lavishly praised her willingness to undertake "the perils and hardships of the field and march" in order to minister to her husband and his regiment. They opened a subscription to install a monument over her grave in the Confederate Cemetery. The marker inscription reads, in part, "A sharer of the toils, dangers & privations of the 30th Regt. Va. Infy. C.S.A. 1861–1865, and died beloved and respected by the veterans of that command." An 1894 speech calling for the erection of a monument in Richmond to the women of the Confederacy specifically cited Cox and the effort to raise a monument to her as inspiration for the larger endeavor. The Fredericksburg chapter of the Order of Southern Gray, a Virginia women's Civil War preservation organization, bears her name.

Biographies in S. J. Quinn, *The History of the City of Fredericksburg, Virginia* (1908), 246, Alvin T. Embrey, *History of Fredericksburg, Virginia* (1937), 180, and Robert A. Hodge, comp., *These We Know: Brief Biographical Sketches of 644 of the More than 3500 Confederate Soldiers Buried in Fredericksburg, Virginia* (n.d.), 38; Fredericksburg Marriage Register (age twenty-two on 9 Jan. 1862); husband's Compiled Service Records and other records related to his desertion in Document Files 1385 and 6268, War Department Collection of Confederate Records, RG 109, NARA; Census, Fredericksburg, 1870 (age forty-one on 1 June 1870), 1880 (age forty-four on 2 June 1880); *Fredericksburg Star*, 8 Aug. 1885, 28 Oct. 1905; *SHSP* 22 (1894): 54–55; Robert K. Krick, *30th Virginia Infantry* (1983), esp. 14, 92; Edward D. C. Campbell, Jr., and Kym S. Rice, eds., *A Woman's War: Southern Women, Civil War, and the Confederate Legacy* (1996), 218–219 (por.); Fredericksburg Death Register (death at age sixty-four); obituaries in *Fredericksburg Star*, 19 (died in her sixty-fourth year), 23 Dec. 1891, and *Fredericksburg Free Lance*, 22 Dec. 1891 (first quotation and death in her sixty-fourth year); gravestone inscription (second quotation and death at age sixty-four).

MICHELLE A. KROWL

COX, Richard Henry (24 November 1824–20 June 1886), member of the Convention of 1861, was born in Essex County and was the son of William Cox, a merchant, and Fanny Temple Broaddus Cox. His maternal grandfather, Andrew Broaddus, was an important evangelical Baptist minister during the Second Great Awakening. This religious heritage fundamentally shaped Cox as a community and political figure. In 1844 Cox graduated from the Medical Department of Hampden-Sydney College (later the Medical College of Virginia), in Richmond. That same year on 18 July the young physician married Sarah Ann Elizabeth Saunders in King William County. They had two daughters and two sons, one of the latter of whom did not survive childhood. They lived on the Mattaponi River in King and Queen County, and Cox established a medical practice in nearby King and Queen Court House. Failing health later forced him to move his family to Centreville, where he owned a farm worked by eight slaves in 1850 and six slaves in 1860.

In addition to his medical practice, Cox served as a King and Queen County justice of the peace beginning in June 1852. A Whig, he supported building roads and establishing schools in order to develop well-educated citizens who could engage successfully in business and manufacturing. During the 1850s, as the Whig Party collapsed and the sectional conflict over slavery came to a boiling point, Cox focused his political energies on the defense of slavery without surrendering his Whig agenda of good roads, good schools, and a new economy of industry and trade.

On 4 February 1861 voters of Essex and King and Queen Counties elected Cox, an ardent supporter of secession, to a state convention summoned to decide Virginia's response to the secession crisis. He defeated six other candidates, including Thomas Croxton, later a member of the United States House of Representatives. Cox seldom spoke at the convention, which opened on 13 February, and did not serve on any standing committees. He voted for secession on 4 April, when the measure failed. In response, King and Queen County residents held a public meeting that night to express their displeasure at the results. Strongly opposed to organizing a convention of border slave-states or to seeking concessions from Northern states, those at the meeting insisted that the preservation of slavery required immediate secession. On 10 April, Cox presented to the convention a letter from this public meeting that praised him but roundly criticized the delegates who had voted against secession. On 17 April, following the firing on Fort Sumter and Abraham Lincoln's call for troops to put down the rebellion, Cox joined the majority of delegates who voted to secede from the Union. Later he signed the Ordinance of Secession.

Cox did not attend the second and third sessions of the convention and had resigned his seat by mid-June 1861. On 1 July he became a general surgeon with the rank of major in the medical department of the Confederate States Army. He served as post surgeon at Gloucester Point, where King and Queen County soldiers enlisted in the 26th Regiment Virginia Infantry were stationed. Long hours in the hospital aggravated his diabetes and heart problems, and Cox resigned on 21 August 1862, citing poor health.

During Reconstruction, Cox became a Conservative but maintained his Whig support of schools, roads, and business development. From 1875 to 1879 he served two terms in the House of Delegates representing King and Queen

County. During his first term Cox was named to the Committees on Propositions and Grievances, on Asylums and Prisons, and on Federal Relations and Resolutions. During his second term he sat on the Committees on Militia and Police and on Asylums and Prisons, and he also chaired the Committee on Executive Expenditures. Cox became interested in institutional reform, especially of institutions for the mentally impaired. He served on the board of directors for the Eastern Lunatic Asylum from 1875 to 1881, when Readjuster politicians removed him. In his final years he was a summer physician at the Warm Springs resort in Bath County.

About 1883 he moved to West Point, in King William County. Several days after suffering a stroke that paralyzed one side of his body and rendered him unable to speak, Richard Henry Cox died at his residence there on 20 June 1886. He was buried at Old Church Cemetery, in King and Queen County.

Full name on 1844 diploma, Tompkins-McCaw; variant middle initial E. in *Bulletin of the Medical College of Virginia* 11 (1914): 6; Census, King and Queen Co., 1850, 1860, 1870, and Slave Schedule, King and Queen Co., 1850, 1860; "Brown, Saunders, Etc., Bible Records," *VMHB* 33 (1925): 91; *Richmond Enquirer*, 6 Aug. 1844; *Daily Richmond Enquirer*, 8 Feb. 1861; Convention of 1861 Election Records, 4 Feb. 1861, Acc. 40586, LVA; Reese and Gaines, *Proceedings of 1861 Convention*, 3:163, 444, 4:144; Reese, *Journals and Papers of 1861 Convention*, vol. 1, Journal, 246; Compiled Service Records; *Annual Reports of the Eastern Lunatic Asylum* (1876–1879, 1881); BVS Death Register, King William Co. (variant birthplace of King and Queen Co.); obituary in *Richmond Dispatch*, 22 June 1886, with birth date and birthplace; memorial in Medical Society of Virginia *Transactions* (1886), 390 (variant birthplace of Caroline Co.).

JOHN HERBERT ROPER

CRABTREE, Asa Routh (11 August 1889–15 April 1965), Baptist missionary, was born in Russell County. His parents, George M. Crabtree, a farmer, and Lydia Alice Musick Crabtree, named him for a pioneering Baptist preacher of Lebanon, the county seat. A. R. Crabtree, as he usually gave his name, received a B.A. from Richmond College (later the University of Richmond) in 1914 and then moved to Jarratt, in Greensville County, where he taught at the high school and for one year served as its principal. He matriculated at the Southern Baptist Theological Seminary, in Louisville, Kentucky, but military service during World War I interrupted his studies. Crabtree accepted the pastorate of Mount Paran Baptist Church, in Montebello, Nelson County, and in that county on 12 June 1918 married Mabel R. Henderson, a schoolteacher to whom he had been engaged for about five years. They had two daughters and one son. In 1919 they moved to the Richmond area, where Crabtree served as pastor of Bethlehem Baptist Church, in Dumbarton, Henrico County, while attending Union Theological Seminary in Virginia (later Union Theological Seminary and Presbyterian School of Christian Education). He received a B.D. in 1921.

Crabtree's interest in missions dated from his youth. In college he had been secretary of the Volunteer Mission Band, and the example of a Brazilian classmate prompted him to consider ministry in that country. Soon after graduating from the seminary Crabtree sought appointment to the foreign field. On 8 June 1921 the Foreign Mission Board of the Southern Baptist Convention assigned him and his wife to the mission in South Brazil. The Crabtrees arrived in Rio de Janeiro on 1 September 1921. Appointed dean of the Rio Baptist College and Seminary, he became the head of its Old Testament department in 1922. In that year Crabtree also accepted the pastorate of Tijuca Baptist Church, a small Rio congregation of fewer than fifty members that grew to more than four hundred during his twenty-five-year tenure. During a furlough in the United States, Crabtree completed a Th.D. at the Southern Baptist Theological Seminary in 1928 and returned to Brazil later that year. In 1930 the Foreign Mission Board appointed him treasurer of the South Brazil Mission, an office he held for about a year and a half.

Although the mission grew rapidly, it suffered from a lack of trained ministers, and in 1936 the Rio Theological Seminary (later the South Brazil Baptist Theological Seminary) separated from the college. Crabtree remained at the seminary, where he taught classes in apologetics, church history, Hebrew, and the Old Testament. Named interim president for the 1939–1940 academic year and again in 1945, he served as seminary president from 1946 until

1954. During Crabtree's presidency the school improved its finances, increased student enrollment, and beginning in 1949 rebuilt the campus. At dedication ceremonies in 1953, the board of trustees named the main building Crabtree Hall.

Crabtree also contributed to theological education in Brazil through prolific writing and as an editor at the Baptist publishing house in Rio de Janeiro. He wrote sixteen widely used books in Portuguese, including five biblical commentaries, an introduction to the New Testament, a Hebrew-Portuguese dictionary, and works on homiletics, ministry, theology, Hebrew syntax, biblical archaeology, and the history of Baptists in Brazil. Crabtree published two works in English, *Baptists in Brazil* (1953) and *Stephen Lawton Watson of Brazil: A Good Name* (1954). He also wrote an essay on the Baptist mission in Brazil for the first volume of the *Encyclopedia of Southern Baptists* (1958).

Crabtree served in Brazil for more than thirty years. In 1955 he was a guest professor at the Carver School of Social Missions and Social Work in Louisville, Kentucky (later the Baylor University School of Social Work, in Waco, Texas). From 30 January through 15 October 1959 he and his wife served as fraternal representatives to Portugal charged with assessing the possibility of beginning cooperative work between the Foreign Mission Board and Portuguese Baptists. Based on Crabtree's recommendation, the mission board agreed to send missionaries and financial assistance to Portugal. On 1 September 1959 Crabtree received emeritus missionary status. He spent the following year as a visiting professor at the Rio seminary before returning to the United States.

Crabtree settled in Roanoke, where he worked as a supply minister, taught mission classes, and completed a book in Portuguese on the minor prophets. Asa Routh Crabtree died at a local hospital on 15 April 1965 and was buried at Fairview Cemetery, in Roanoke.

Crabtree, *Baptists in Brazil* (1953), esp. 7–12, 156–159, 193–194; *Encyclopedia of Southern Baptists* (1958–1971), 1:186–189, 3:1667–1668; BVS Birth Register, Russell Co. (includes 1942 notarized correction of name based on family Bible records); Nelson Co. Marriage Register, 2:160; BVS Marriage Register, Nelson Co. (variant marriage date of 17 June 1918); Mabel Henderson Crabtree, "My Life on the Mission Field" (undated typescript), and Minutes of the Foreign Mission Board, Southern Baptist Convention, both International Mission Board Archives and Record Center, Richmond; David Mein, ed., *O Que Deus Tem Feito: Compilação* (1982), 43, 127–131, and bibliography of Portuguese-language publications on 360–361; obituaries in *Roanoke World-News*, 15 Apr. 1965, and *Roanoke Times*, 16 Apr. 1965; memorial in *Journal of the Baptist General Association of Virginia* (1965), 107 (por. facing 107).

H. B. CAVALCANTI

CRABTREE, August Fletcher (29 August 1905–13 October 1994), shipwright of miniatures, was born in Portland, Oregon, and was the son of Fletcher Crabtree and Mollie Gilmore Crabtree. After completing high school, he took college courses for several months, but his talents lay elsewhere. At an early age Crabtree showed an unusual dexterity in carving small objects from wood. He enrolled in a sculpting class, his only formal artistic instruction. In grade school his skill was such that a wood medallion he had carved for a contest was attributed to an adult and rejected. In boyhood Crabtree enjoyed solitary rambles along the Columbia River, where he developed a fascination with sailing vessels. At the local library he lingered over romantic depictions of ships, and at home his father told stories of a great-grandfather who had been a shipbuilder on the River Clyde in Scotland.

When Crabtree was about twelve years old, he went to work in a meat-packing plant to assist his family. After his father died in January 1919, Crabtree found better wages across the river at a shipyard in Vancouver, Washington. A display of ship models caught his eye. Charmed by their size and detail, Crabtree determined to apply the lessons learned in the shipyard to his love of carving and to sculpt miniatures built as nearly as possible like the original ships. In an inspired moment of youthful enthusiasm he envisioned a fleet of models depicting the evolution of water transport.

Crabtree set to work locating original ship plans. In the 1920s implements for carving fine detail were not readily available, and hobbyists created simplified models from blocks of wood using ordinary tools. For his small vessels Crabtree improvised with dental instruments. The work proceeded slowly as he used tiny chisels and a magnifying glass to shape individual parts and painstakingly assemble them. Crabtree experimented with dyes and studied the seasoning process and a wide variety of woods. He settled on one kind for framing, another for planking, and close-grained, dense wood for carving. Crabtree employed the plank-on-frame technique as the best means by which to duplicate original construction. He took odd jobs to reserve time and energy for what he began to call "the Project."

This pleasurable pursuit gave way to obsession as Crabtree began to devote virtually all of his waking hours to his models. A careful researcher, he corresponded with nautical repositories at home and abroad. He married Helen Nelson in Multnomah County, Oregon, on 17 July 1926, but the childless union did not last. Even the joy of carving became eclipsed by the exacting standards and tedious labor to which he had bound himself. In one instance Crabtree spent an estimated 300 hours carving an inch-high ornate ship's lantern. He decorated the relief panels on the bow and stern of a mid-seventeenth-century Venetian galleass with 359 elegantly carved figures. His reward became the finished product, not the process.

At the suggestion of a Los Angeles architect, Crabtree moved to Hollywood early in the 1930s with five completed ships. Metro-Goldwyn-Mayer, Universal, and other motion picture studios hired him to create miniature figures and ships and employed him as a technical adviser. Among the most notable films on which Crabtree worked were *Mutiny on the Bounty* (1935), *Captain Caution* (1940), *That Hamilton Woman* (1941), and *Reap the Wild Wind* (1942). Although his talents were in demand, he frequently refused job offers and chose instead to live modestly and devote time to his models.

In 1938 Crabtree met Winnifred Clark, who was so impressed by his ship models that she became his assistant and learned to paint and gild decorations and to sew sails by hand. They married on 15 January 1942 and moved to Portland. During the Second World War, Crabtree worked as a supervisor at the Kaiser shipyard in Vancouver. They later settled in Long Island, New York, where in 1949 he completed the Project—sixteen models ranging from a primitive raft and an ancient Egyptian galley to an 1840 passenger ship that employed both sail and steam. All the moving parts, including winches, pulleys, hatches, and gun ports, functioned. Later that year Crabtree moved to Florida and built a small private museum near Miami, which proved unsuccessful. In 1955 he traveled to Newport News, Virginia, where officials at the Mariners' Museum examined his handiwork and the next year purchased the models. Experts regard the miniature fleet as an influential work of exceptional beauty and detail, virtually unmatched in conception and construction. It became the jewel of the museum's collection.

Crabtree settled in York County, where he carved ship models and showed visitors his other sculptures, including miniature busts of the United States presidents and of celebrities and historical figures. He gave tours and woodcarving demonstrations at the Mariners' Museum for the next thirty-five years, and he also enjoyed a collection of about forty thousand classical and jazz recordings. On 10 January 1982 Christopher Newport College (later Christopher Newport University) awarded Crabtree an honorary doctorate of humane letters. In 1990 he and his wife moved to West Palm Beach, Florida. When his health failed, they returned to York County, where he entered a nursing home. August Fletcher Crabtree died there on 13 October 1994. His remains were cremated.

Birth date and second marriage date in Vincent P. Scott Jr., "The Story of August Fletcher Crabtree" (typescript dated 22 July 1999 and based on conversations with Crabtree and Winnifred Clark Crabtree), copy in *DVB* Files; Crabtree, *The Crabtree Collection of Miniature Ships* (1969), por. on 4; Mariners' Museum, *The Ship Models of August F. Crabtree* (1981); Multnomah Co., Ore., Marriage Certificate (1926), with variant middle name of Frederick and birth date of 29 Aug. 1904; *Portland Oregonian*, 9 May 1942, 17 May 1999; *Portland Sunday Oregonian*, 22 Jan. 1950; *Norfolk Virginian-Pilot*, 3 Nov. 1968, 4 Feb. 1973, 15 June 1977, 27 Aug. 1981; *Norfolk Ledger-Star*, 8 Jan. 1973, 29 May 1978; *Newport News Times-Herald*, 18 Feb. 1978; *Norfolk Virginian-Pilot and Ledger-Star*, 24 Aug. 1985; *Newport News Daily Press*, 26 Aug. 1990; Oregon Maritime Center and Museum, Portland, owns Crabtree's personal collection of books, ship models, miniature busts, scrapbook, and other materials; obituaries in *Newport News Daily Press*, 15 Oct. 1994, and *Portland Oregonian*, 18 Nov. 1994; editorial tribute in *Norfolk Virginian-Pilot*, 19 Oct. 1994; memorial in Mariners' Museum, *August F. Crabtree, Excellence Forever: A Tribute* (1995), copy in *DVB* Files.

VINCENT P. SCOTT JR.

CRADDOCK, John Wimbish (14 August 1858–6 February 1941), shoe manufacturer, was born in Halifax County. His father, Charles James Fox Craddock, a physician and former member of the House of Delegates, died on 1 January 1866. Craddock studied at a school his mother, Fanny Yancey Easley Craddock, had opened in their home and later attended local public schools. After working on the family farm and in a country store, he moved at age twenty to Lynchburg, where he held several jobs including as a traveling salesman for a shoe distribution company. Craddock moved to Baltimore about 1884 and became a junior partner in a wholesale boot and shoe business. On 7 December 1886 he married Mary Peachy Gilmer in Pittsylvania County. Before her death on 13 January 1909, they had three sons and one daughter.

Craddock returned to Lynchburg and in July 1888 established a wholesale boot and shoe business with his brother and a Halifax County friend. The firm was incorporated as the Craddock-Terry Company on 12 November 1898, with Craddock as president. Successful in selling shoes throughout Virginia and the South, the Craddock-Terry Company built a shoe factory in Lynchburg in 1900 in order to expand into manufacturing. By 1907 the company had enlarged the plant, which made shoes for women and children, and built a second factory to produce men's shoes.

Through building, purchasing, developing, and expanding its factories and distribution centers over the next several decades, Craddock-Terry became the dominant industry in Lynchburg. Although it was not, as some secondary accounts assert, the first shoe factory in the South, in Virginia, or even in Lynchburg, it grew to number among the leading shoe manufacturers and distributors in the country. In 1922, just before Craddock retired from its presidency, the company operated three shoe factories in Lynchburg, four in Missouri, and one in Wisconsin, as well as several associated plants. In that year it also owned wholesale distribution houses in Lynchburg, Saint Louis, and Milwaukee and had a net income of $1.85 million. Craddock-Terry was particularly known for its Long Wear Shoes brand. In 1939 the company made nearly five million pairs of shoes.

Craddock was president of the Lynchburg Board of Trade and of the National Shoe Wholesalers Association. Widely recognized for his local civic and philanthropic work, he served on the Lynchburg school board and on the University of Virginia's board of visitors and also conducted fund-raising campaigns at Randolph-Macon Woman's College and at Sweet Briar College. During World War I he led Liberty and Victory Loan drives in Lynchburg and Campbell County, and in February 1918 he was called to Washington, D.C., for six months' service as chief of the shoe, leather, and rubber goods branch of the Quartermaster Corps. On 13 October 1939 almost 3,500 people attended a commemoration of Lynchburg's founding, at which time Craddock received the Civic Club Council of Lynchburg's First Citizen Award for his contributions to the city.

Craddock retired as president of Craddock-Terry in January 1923 and then took the newly created position of chairman of the board. He remained chair after the company was reorganized as the Craddock-Terry Shoe Corporation in December 1938. Craddock married Eliza Deane Baker, a Lynchburg widow, on 7 February 1911. They had no children. John Wimbish Craddock died on 6 February 1941 at his Lynchburg home and was buried in Spring Hill Cemetery.

Biographies in Tyler, *Men of Mark*, 2:83–86, Bruce, Tyler, and Morton, *History of Virginia*, 5:401–402 (por. facing 401), and Betsy Lawson Willis and Martha Barksdale Craddock, comps., *Sketches and Genealogy of the Bailey-Craddock-Lawson Families of Virginia and North Carolina* (1974), 184–186; BVS Birth Register, Halifax Co.; BVS Marriage Register, Pittsylvania Co. (1886); Lynchburg Marriage Register (1911); family papers in possession of grandson, John W. Craddock (2004); SCC Charter Book, 36:586–589, 190:63–67; *Moody's Manual of Railroads and Corporation Securities* (1922), 1:215–217; *Moody's Manual of Investments, American and Foreign* (1941), 480–481; *New York Times*, 11 July 1917; *Washington Post*, 29 Jan. 1923; *Richmond News Leader*, 9 Oct. 1923; *Lynchburg News*, 11 Oct. 1936; *Lynchburg Daily Advance*, 10, 14 Oct. 1939; *Commonwealth* 6 (Nov. 1939): 19; *Lynchburg News and Advance*, 27 Dec. 2001; obituaries in *Lynchburg Daily Advance*, 6 Feb. 1941 (por.), and *Richmond Times-Dispatch*, 7 Feb. 1941.

GEORGE A. KEGLEY

CRAFORD, William (d. by 15 April 1762), founder of Portsmouth, was the son of George Craford and Abigail Mason Craford. Contemporaries sometimes spelled the family name Crawford, but several extant autograph signatures and many transcriptions of it in Norfolk County records indicate that he consistently used the spelling Craford. The place and date of his birth are not known for certain, but probably he was born in Virginia in the 1680s and was orphaned early in childhood. Craford and his sister were both younger than eighteen when in September 1699 their immigrant grandfather, who owned land in Norfolk and Princess Anne Counties and also in North Carolina, wrote his will and made them his principal heirs.

Little is known about Craford's personal life. There is no evidence that he ever married, but during the 1710s he cared for his paternal grandmother during her second widowhood. In the spring of 1711 he patented 173 acres of land in Nansemond County, and on 31 October 1716 he patented 1,129 acres in Norfolk County across the Elizabeth River from the port of Norfolk, land that had once belonged to William Carver, who had been executed in 1676 for his part in Bacon's Rebellion. Craford was a partner in erecting and operating a mill in Norfolk County, constructed a wharf for the county, and probably planted tobacco and engaged in trade. He recorded at least one deed of sale for an enslaved woman and her children, but it is not certain whether he regularly traded in laborers, either free or enslaved. Craford was almost certainly a member of the county court for several years before the governor appointed him sheriff of the county on 4 May 1725. He had become a colonel of militia by 1742 and was county lieutenant, or commander of the county's militia, in 1748.

First elected to the House of Burgesses representing Norfolk County in 1712, Craford served with one interruption for more than thirty years. He gave up his seat in the summer of 1734 after becoming county sheriff for the second time in a decade but was reelected to the House the following year. His name appears in the journals of the session that met early in 1746, but it is not clear whether he took part in the summer session of that year or the session of the following spring, as he was eligible to do. Craford sat on the Committee of Claims in 1723 and again in 1744 and 1746, and twice he served on the committee that drafted the reply of the House to the governor's message. He did not become a powerful legislative leader during his many years as a burgess, however. One of the last responsibilities that he shouldered as a member of the assembly was as a manager of a £600 fund that the legislature set aside early in 1746 to support British soldiers whose ship had blown into Virginia waters while en route to Cape Breton.

Early in the 1750s Craford hired a surveyor to lay off the land that he had acquired in 1716 into streets and lots. Probably at his request, in the spring of 1752 the General Assembly established the town of Portsmouth there, and in the summer of that year he began selling lots. Craford prepared to erect a market and a new courthouse for the county in Portsmouth, but during his lifetime the courthouse remained in the borough of Norfolk. He was in poor health when he wrote his will on 27 January 1762. He bequeathed part of his property to his sister and portions to members of the Dale and Veale families; he singled out the children of his late housekeeper, Mary Veale, for special favors. William Craford died, probably in Portsmouth, sometime before 15 April 1762, when his will was proved in the Norfolk County Court. The place of his burial is not known.

Parents identified in *Adventurers of Purse and Person*, 2:575–576; grandfather's will in Norfolk Co. Deed Book, vol. 6, pt. 1, fols. 181–182; numerous references in surviving Norfolk Co. Order Books (1742–1752), Norfolk Co. Deed Book, vols. 8–20, Norfolk Co. Miscellaneous Records (1652–1748), including some autographs, and Portsmouth and Norfolk Co. Documents (1636–1759), including some autographs, Portsmouth Public Library; *Executive Journals of Council*, 4:86, 5:393; Land Office Patent Book, 10:30, 299–300, RG 4, LVA; Hening, *Statutes*, 6:265–266; Mildred M. Holladay, "History of Portsmouth," *Portsmouth Star*, 19 Jan. 1936; Marshall W. Butt, *Portsmouth under Four Flags, 1752–1961* (1961), 2–3; Craford's holograph will in Chesapeake Circuit Court; Norfolk Co. Will Book, 1: fols. 79–80; Norfolk Co. Order Book (1759–1763), fol. 168.

BARNABAS W. BAKER
DEAN BURGESS

CRAFT, James Belt (17 April 1859–4 September 1941), Baptist minister, was born in Scott County. His parents, Margaret Stewart Craft and William Craft, a successful farmer, were devout Methodists and named him for a local minister. His father was a steward in the church, and one of Craft's favorite pastimes was playing church and exhorting other youngsters from his make-believe pulpit. His mother died when he was about two years old. Craft attended a subscription school until a free school opened in the county and also helped work the family farm.

When Craft was about twenty years old, he attended a revival meeting. Deeply moved by the experience, he made a public profession of faith. On 16 September 1880 he married Rachel Penola Gillenwater. They lived on a farm that she had inherited and had one daughter and one son, Ryland Glenmore Craft, later a prominent Scott County leader and member of the Convention of 1956. Rachel Craft and her family were Baptists, and at her suggestion Craft, who wanted her to join him in the Methodist Church, began to study the Bible on the subject of baptism. He concluded that the proper way to conduct the rite was by immersion and over his father's objections joined the Cartertown Baptist Church at Rye Cove. Although warned that he would be disinherited, Craft was baptized on 1 January 1883 in the Clinch River. That same day he received a license to preach and three days later delivered his first sermon in a private home. His father having carried out his threat, a painful estrangement ensued that lasted until William Craft reconciled with his son and was baptized by him.

On 25 March 1883 Craft was ordained at the Cartertown Church and soon became a leader in Scott County. In November 1887 he was elected as a Republican to a single term in the House of Delegates, where he sat on the Committees on Agriculture and Mining and on Immigration. He did not seek reelection in 1889, when his brother won the seat campaigning as a Democrat. Craft first attended the Clinch Valley Baptist Association annual conference in 1887. During the next few years he served regularly on the standing committees on foreign missions and state missions, and in 1889 he was chosen moderator of the conference. He continued to work his farm during the week and preached on Saturdays and Sundays at area churches.

For the next two decades Craft was a driving force in Baptist activities in southwestern Virginia. In 1891 the State Mission Board appointed him a missionary for Scott County and assigned him to the Riverview Baptist Church, where he served until 1892. Possessed of an impressive memory, he never wrote out a sermon but sometimes scribbled brief notes that he discarded before preaching. Craft was elected moderator of at least fifteen Clinch Valley Baptist Association annual meetings. He often delivered the annual sermon and frequently represented Clinch Valley at the yearly Southern Baptist conventions. In the mid-1890s Craft was pastor at five churches in Carroll, Scott, and Wise Counties. His wife died on 18 February 1896, and for a time his children lived with her relatives. In 1897 the State Mission Board employed Craft as a missionary in Wise County. He married Susan P. Carter on 14 April of that year and moved his family to Coeburn. They had one daughter.

By 1898 Craft had built a church at Coeburn and secured lots and building funds for a church at Wise Court House. Later that year he helped organize the First Baptist Church of Gate City, which chose him as pastor on 20 November. Craft returned to Scott County soon thereafter to serve his new congregation. In 1903 he was named a state evangelist, one of only four appointed to that time, and resigned his pastorate. For the next six years he traveled southwestern Virginia on horseback over mountain trails to remote settlements, preached in schoolhouses and private homes, and often relied on his flock for lodging.

Craft resigned this post in 1909 to become pastor at Big Stone Gap in Wise County, where by 1910 he and his family were living in a rented house. In his nine years there he paid off the church debt, built a parsonage, constructed a church at nearby Appalachia, and completed a church at East Stone Gap. Craft preached at these locations and at two churches in Lee County. His efforts in building congregations laid the foundation for the Wise County Baptist churches to leave the Clinch Valley Baptist Association in 1927 in order to form their own association. In 1918 Craft returned to his former Gate City congregation in what he called the "Kingdom of Scott." His second wife died on 11 April 1914 while visiting Louisville, Kentucky, and on 27 July 1918 in Loudoun County he married Louise Tyler Ford.

Despite his age, Craft's spiritual leadership and devotion to grassroots ministry remained undiminished. He regularly attended the annual conferences of the Baptist General Association of Virginia and served as vice president in 1912 and 1921. Craft sat almost continuously on the board of trustees for the Baptist orphanage in Salem beginning in 1900. He possessed a keen interest in education and assisted a number of students in attending college. He served on the Baptist General Association's Board of Missions and Education and for many years as a trustee of Virginia Intermont College. Several times in the 1920s and 1930s he was also a trustee of Bluefield College.

Known as the "bishop of Scott" during much of his fifty-nine years as a minister, Craft is reported to have officiated at 2,500 baptisms, more than 5,000 marriages, 10,000 professions of faith, and an untold number of funerals. He is credited with establishing eleven churches and helping to build many more. Although invited to become a pastor elsewhere, Craft declined to leave his beloved highlands. In February 1941 he attended the Baptist General Association for the last time. That summer he became ill and in July underwent surgery in a Baltimore hospital. After two weeks he returned home but was soon hospitalized again. James Belt Craft died at his Gate City home on 4 September 1941 and was buried in Holston View Cemetery, in Scott County.

Birth date in BVS Birth Register, Scott Co.; variant birth date of 16 Apr. 1859 on gravestone; biographies in Robert M. Addington, *History of Scott County, Virginia* (1932), 343–344 (por.), and in Joseph Hathaway Cosby, 1977 typescript continuation of *Virginia Baptist Ministers*, VBHS (both with variant birth date of 16 Apr. 1859); [Louise Tyler Ford Craft], "J. B. Craft, Baptist Bishop of The Kingdom of Scott" (undated typescript, VBHS), 15 (first quotation); BVS Marriage Register, Scott Co. (1880, 1897), Loudoun Co. (1918); *Minutes of the Clinch Valley Baptist Association* (1884–1941); *Minutes of the Baptist General Association of Virginia* (1897–1941); *Religious Herald*, 11 Sept. 1980 (second quotation); obituary in *Norton Coalfield Progress*, 11 Sept. 1941 (with variant birth date of 16 Apr. 1859); memorials in *Reli-*

gious Herald, 25 Sept. 1941, *Minutes of the Clinch Valley Baptist Association* (1942), n.p., and *Virginia Baptist Annual* (1942), 149–152.

DONALD W. GUNTER

CRAFT, James Pressley (14 June 1885–27 March 1975), president of Averett College, was the son of John Franklin Craft and Eleanor Gordon Goss Craft. Born in Hartwell, Georgia, he attended local public schools and received a B.S. from Mercer University in 1906, an M.A. from Harvard University in 1909, and a graduate degree in theology from the Southern Baptist Theological Seminary, in Louisville, Kentucky, in 1912. An accomplished scholar, Craft won a science essay medal and a general excellence medal at Mercer in 1905 and 1906, respectively, and was a Thayer Scholar at Harvard. On 29 June 1910 he married Edith Rickenbacker Galphin, of Toccoa, Georgia. They had one son and one daughter.

While attending graduate school Craft taught at the Hearn Academy, in Floyd County, Georgia, during the 1906–1907 school year and served as principal of the Nuberg School, in Hart County, during the 1909–1910 term. Following his graduation from seminary and his ordination, Craft served as minister for several Georgia Baptist churches from 1912 to 1919. In the latter year he began teaching Bible and social science at Shorter College, in Rome, Georgia. In May 1921 Craft was elected president of Averett College (later Averett University), a Baptist preparatory school and junior college for women in Danville, Virginia.

Craft arrived at Averett following a bitter controversy about the types of dancing allowed at the school that had resulted in the firing of the previous president, Clayton Edward Crosland. Although the students preferred to adopt the modern attitudes of the Roaring Twenties, Craft generally maintained the college's strict adherence to Baptist moral teachings and viewed himself as a father figure to Averett's female scholars. He did, however, expand extracurricular activities such as the Modern Languages Club and intercollegiate athletics; approve visits outside Danville (with parental permission); increase the time available for dating, shopping, and dormitory phone calls; allow attendance at dances held at nearby male colleges; and permit dating in

cars (if chaperoned). During his six-year tenure as president Craft expanded the physical facilities to include a new dormitory, gymnasium, and swimming pool. He also increased enrollment and urged Virginia Baptists to send their daughters to the college. Working to improve Averett's standards, Craft established a science department, hired a full-time librarian, instituted an honor system, and organized a faculty-directed student government. With the financially solvent institution advancing academically, Craft resigned early in May 1927 to become the president of Hardin College, a Baptist institution in Mexico, Missouri.

After serving as president of Hardin College for the 1927–1928 academic term, Craft returned to Georgia and the pulpit. From 1929 to 1936 he was pastor of the South Broad Baptist Church, in Rome. The next year he became principal of Lyerly High School. From about 1948 to his retirement in 1954 he taught at the Rome Center of the University of Georgia, a satellite institution that offered evening classes to working adults. After a long illness James Pressley Craft died at his Rome residence on 27 March 1975. He was buried in East View Cemetery in that city.

Biographies in Bruce, Tyler, and Morton, *History of Virginia*, 6:479, and Robert C. Cook, ed., *Who's Who in American Education*, 7th ed. (1936), 168; Averett College documents in General Education Board Archives, Rockefeller Archive Center, North Tarrytown, N.Y.; *Virginia Baptist Annual* (1921), 76–77; ibid. (1922), 66; ibid. (1923), 67–68; ibid. (1924), 58; ibid. (1925), 61; ibid. (1926), 66–67; *Danville Register*, 8 May 1921, 5, 19 May, 1 June 1927; *Religious Herald*, 12 May, 30 June, 14 July 1921 (por.), 26 May 1927; *Danville Bee*, 4, 18 May 1927; David Wesley Gray, "A History of Averett College" (M.A. thesis, University of Richmond, 1960), 162–163; J. I. Hayes, *A History of Averett College* (1984), 77–82; obituary in *Rome [Ga.] News-Tribune*, 28 Mar. 1975 (por.).

TRUDY MCCARTY
JOHN G. DEAL

CRAFT, Ryland Glenmore (21 May 1889–19 October 1960), business and civic leader, was born in Scott County and was the son of James Belt Craft, a prominent Baptist minister, and his first wife, Rachel Penola Gillenwater Craft. His mother died when he was six years old, and for a time before his father remarried Craft and his sister lived with their mother's family. He attended Fork Union Military Academy and Richmond College (later the University of Richmond). After receiving an LL.B. from Washington and Lee University in 1913, Craft was admitted to the Virginia bar and moved to Gate City. He left the practice of law in order to devote himself fully to automobile sales and wholesale oil and gasoline distribution.

After the United States entered World War I, Craft completed officer training at Fort Myer, in Alexandria County, and was commissioned a first lieutenant. At the end of his service in the infantry, he returned to Gate City and resumed selling automobiles. On 5 June 1920 Craft married Nichatie Cecil Taylor, of Catonsville, Maryland. They had two daughters and one son before her death from a heart attack on 15 July 1932. Craft married Ruth Louise Vines, of Johnson City, Tennessee, on 29 August 1933. They had one son.

With a partner Craft founded the Gate City Motor Company, selling Ford automobiles. Through the years he expanded its operations to include the sale of farm machinery and equipment, auto repair, and a service station. His successful dealership (at the time of his death reportedly one of the oldest Ford dealerships in the country) won a regional Ford sales promotion that sent him and a salesman to San Diego for the California Pacific International Exposition in September 1935. Craft also helped establish another Ford dealership in nearby Kingsport, Tennessee, which he operated for more than twenty years, as well as a wholesale distributorship for Standard Oil merchandise. He served as president of R. G. Craft, Distributor, Inc., and Craft Transport Company and owned a large grazing farm in Scott County.

Craft helped organize the Peoples National Bank, which, through mergers, later became the First National Bank of Gate City. He served as a director, chairman of the board, and, at the time of his death, president of the institution. Craft also was president of the Scott County Tobacco Warehouse, Incorporated, and was instrumental in establishing a tobacco market in Scott County. He was a director of the Holston Valley Community Hospital in Kingsport, president of the

Gate City Rotary Club, commander of the local American Legion post, a Freemason, and a member of the Baptist Board of Missions and Education in Virginia. Despite leaving the formal practice of law, Craft maintained his membership in the Scott County and Virginia bar associations. Keenly aware of the importance of transportation to the development of southwestern Virginia, Craft served at various times as an officer in several road associations. In 1943 he became a state director and Scott County chair of the Virginia War Fund, part of a national program during World War II to assist American and Allied servicemen and destitute civilians in occupied countries. He received public recognition from the governor for his efforts.

As an active member of the Republican Party, Craft also participated in the political life of the region. He represented Scott County in the Democrat-controlled House of Delegates for the 1922–1923 session, when he sat on the Committees on Claims, on Finance, on Militia and Police, and on House Expenses. He introduced bills relating to issuing county bonds for improving roads and bridges and for the regulation of fishing in Scott County. In November 1927 Craft defeated the Democratic incumbent to win a seat in the Senate of Virginia, representing Lee and Scott Counties. During the 1928 and 1930 legislative sessions he served on the Committees for Courts of Justice, on Fish and Game, and to Examine the Treasurer's Office.

Craft was a member of the Scott County Republican Committee and also a delegate to the 1940 Republican National Convention, which nominated Wendell Wilkie for president. In 1943 county Republican leaders convinced Craft to run once again for the House of Delegates. Despite a vigorous campaign from his opponent, and a corresponding inactive canvass by Craft, he defeated the Democratic incumbent by about 400 votes of almost 7,000 cast. Craft was one of only four Republicans in the 140-member General Assembly. During two terms from January 1944 to January 1947, he served on the Committees on Game and Inland Fisheries, on Immigration, on Militia and Police, on Mining and Mineral Resources, and on Roads and Internal Navigation. In the spring of 1945 he introduced bills authorizing Scott and Tazewell county officials to maintain an office to assist returning war veterans and for the Gate City council to erect a veterans' memorial or home.

After the Supreme Court of the United States handed down its 1954 decision in *Brown* v. *Board of Education* declaring segregation in public schools unconstitutional, the General Assembly initiated the calling of a limited constitutional convention in order to amend the Virginia constitution to allow tuition grants to nonsectarian private schools. On 21 February 1956 Craft won election to represent Lee and Scott Counties at the convention, which met in Richmond from 5 through 7 March 1956. He served on the Committee on Rules and seldom spoke during the proceedings. Craft joined the other delegates in unanimously approving an amendment to permit state appropriations for private schools, but he was one of only three delegates to vote against a resolution endorsing the doctrine of interposition, an assertion of a state's right to interpose its sovereignty between its citizens and the federal government.

Ryland Glenmore Craft died in a hospital in Kingsport, Tennessee, on 19 October 1960. He was buried in Holston View Cemetery, in Scott County.

Questionnaire returned to clerk of the House of Delegates, Convention of 1956 Records, RG 79, LVA; biography in E. Griffith Dodson, *The General Assembly of the Commonwealth of Virginia, 1940–1960* (1961), 518–519; BVS Birth Register, Scott Co.; Maryland Department of Health, Report of Marriage (1920); personal and family history information provided by son, James Vines Craft (2004); SCC Charter Book, 220:587, 315:181, 317:359; *Washington Post*, 10 Nov. 1927; *Bristol News Bulletin*, 30 Aug. 1933; *Gate City Herald*, 29 Aug. 1935, 29 Apr., 23, 30 Sept., 4, 18 Nov. 1943; *Journal of the Constitutional Convention of the Commonwealth of Virginia to Revise and Amend Sec. 141 of the Constitution of Virginia* (1956), 17, 70, 89, 101; sound recording, Constitutional Convention Proceedings, 5–7 Mar. 1956, WRVA Radio Collection, Acc. 38210, LVA; obituaries in *Bristol Herald Courier* and *Bristol Virginia-Tennessean*, both 21 Oct. 1960, and *Gate City Herald*, 28 Oct. 1960; memorial in *Virginia State Bar Association Proceedings* (1961), 138–139 (por.).

LAURA BETH SHIELDS

CRAIG, Elijah (ca. 1745–18 May 1808), Baptist minister and distiller, was born in Orange County and was the son of Tolever Craig and Mary Hawkins Craig. He received a rudimentary education and lived an unremarkable life until 1764, when the preaching of David Thomas led him to a religious conversion. The following year Craig attended meetings held by Samuel Harriss, another prominent evangelist, who convinced him to spread the gospel. Along with other new believers Craig began holding worship services almost daily in his tobacco barn. In 1766 he journeyed to North Carolina and persuaded a clergyman, James Read, to return with him to Orange County in order to baptize the converts. Craig soon began preaching but did not abandon farming because he believed ministers should not rely solely on pastoral duties for their livings. An uncompromising Calvinist with a solemn yet powerful presence (a contemporary described him as like "a man who had just come from the dead"), he quickly established himself as a leading Baptist preacher. In 1769 he helped found Blue Run Church in Orange County, became its presiding elder, and later, probably in June 1770, was ordained as a minister.

Like many other nonconformist evangelicals, Craig ran afoul of the law and the established Anglican Church. At least twice he was arrested and imprisoned in Culpeper and Orange Counties. During a month of incarceration in the Culpeper County jail, he was fed only rye bread and water; though weak he preached to passersby through the bars of his cell. His boldness ensured him a wide following among the Baptists, and the Separate Baptist Association delegated him on several occasions to lobby the Virginia General Assembly on behalf of religious dissenters.

Although many traditional accounts list Craig as a member of the so-called Traveling Church, a large group of Baptists who migrated in 1781 from Spotsylvania County to central Kentucky, he did not accompany his two elder brothers, Joseph Craig and Lewis Craig (also Baptist ministers), who led that famed party. He remained in Virginia, but during the next few years he speculated in Kentucky land and may several times have visited the area in which his brothers had settled. Craig participated in a meeting of Baptist preachers in the area in 1785 but may not have permanently moved to what became Scott County, Kentucky, until 1786, the year he sold his Orange County farm. In 1787 he became pastor of the Baptist church at Great Crossing. About five years later the congregation split because some members wished to replace Craig with another minister. Excluded in 1791, Craig later regained his pulpit but left about 1795 to lead nearby churches at McConnel's Run and Silas.

It was not as a religious leader, however, that Craig left his principal mark in the western district of Virginia. Within a few years of his arrival, he had established himself as a prominent entrepreneur and land speculator. Craig acquired approximately one thousand acres of land in Scott County, where he laid out the town of Lebanon, which the General Assembly incorporated as Georgetown in 1790. Historians have credited him with establishing Kentucky's first paper mill, some of the earliest saw- and gristmills, a ropewalk, a fulling mill, and a ferry across the Kentucky River. Among his other enterprises was distilling, and Craig's fame derives largely from his reputation as the Baptist minister who created bourbon whiskey. Though he distilled a significant quantity of whiskey from corn—he paid $140 in federal excise taxes in 1798—there is no evidence that he developed the bourbon formula, nor did he make such an assertion.

In December 1787 Craig announced that the following month he intended to open an academy for boys at Lebanon. The planned curriculum of the boarding school, designed to serve about fifty students, included Greek, Latin, and the sciences. Later Craig organized the board of trustees of Rittenhouse Academy, which the Kentucky legislature incorporated in 1798 and which was a forerunner of Georgetown College. Craig continued to preach almost until his death. He defended his variant of Baptist theology in at least three pamphlets, *A Few Remarks on the Errors That Are Maintained in the Christian Churches of the Present Day* (1801), *Three Letters from Philemon to Onesimus* (1803), and *A Portrait of Jacob Creath* (ca. 1807).

About 1763 Craig married a woman named Frances whose surname may have been Smith. The *Kentucky Gazette*, published in Lexington, reported the death of his wife in April 1802, and

many accounts maintain that he later married Margaret Kay (or Tabb) Gatewood. There is no record of their marriage, however, and she is not mentioned in his will, which he dictated on 13 May 1808. It is likely that Craig and his first wife had four sons and three daughters, but some accounts attribute three of these children to a second wife. Elijah Craig died in Georgetown on 18 May 1808 and probably was buried there. In a brief eulogy, the editor of the *Kentucky Gazette* declared, "If virtue consists in being useful to our fellow citizens, perhaps there were few more virtuous men than Mr. Craig."

Biographies in Robert B. Semple, *A History of the Rise and Progress of the Baptists in Virginia* (1810), 414–417, James B. Taylor, *Virginia Baptist Ministers* (1859), 1:65–67, William Cathcart, ed., *The Baptist Encyclopædia* (1881), 284–285 (with birth ca. 1743), J. H. Spencer, *A History of Kentucky Baptists* (1885), 1:27–28, 87–89, and Morgan Edwards, *Materials Towards a History of the Baptists*, ed. Eve B. Weeks and Mary B. Warren (1984), 2:60 (with undocumented birth date of 15 Nov. 1745); Lewis Collins and Richard H. Collins, *History of Kentucky* (1874), 1:516, 2:183, 194, 700; B. O. Gaines, *The B. O. Gaines History of Scott County* (1905), 2:19; Lewis Peyton Little, *Imprisoned Preachers and Religious Liberty in Virginia* (1938); Gerald Carson, *The Social History of Bourbon: An Unhurried Account of Our Star-Spangled American Drink* (1963), 36–40; John Taylor, *Baptists on the American Frontier: A History of Ten Baptist Churches of Which the Author Has Been Alternately a Member*, ed. Chester Raymond Young (1995), 90 (first quotation); *Lexington Kentucky Gazette*, 19 Jan. 1788; Scott Co., Ky., Will Book, A:410; obituary in *Lexington Kentucky Gazette*, 24 May 1808 (second quotation).

THOMAS H. APPLETON JR.

CRAIG, John (17 August 1709–22 April 1774), Presbyterian minister, was born in Donegore Parish, County Antrim, Ireland. His parents, who have not been identified, may have moved from Scotland to Ireland in the 1690s. Little is known of his early life other than that he did well as a student at an academy, was baptized at age fourteen or fifteen at a Presbyterian meetinghouse, and received an M.A. in 1733 from the University of Edinburgh. Craig declined the small Scottish lairdship of the octogenarian uncle for whom he was named and instead chose to immigrate to America.

Craig arrived in New Castle, Delaware, on 17 August 1734. The following month, after hearing Gilbert Tennent plead for so-called New

Light, or evangelical, ministers to be admitted to the Synod of Philadelphia, Craig affiliated with the so-called Old Light conservatives who opposed the Great Awakening. While teaching school and studying for the ministry, he lived for three years with a Presbyterian clergyman in Lancaster County, Pennsylvania. Craig received a license to preach in August 1738 and for the next two years supplied congregations in Pennsylvania, Maryland, and Virginia. He was ordained on 3 September 1740 for the Triple Forks of Shenandoah congregation in the new county of Augusta.

The first settled Presbyterian minister in Virginia west of the Blue Ridge Mountains, Craig registered as a dissenter in February 1741, as required by law, and for nearly a decade traveled as far south as the later site of Roanoke and west into the Allegheny Mountains to preach, baptize, and organize congregations in frontier settlements. He was for a few years the only Presbyterian minister in the area, and his record of 883 baptisms performed during the 1740s is the earliest surviving document of its kind from the region. Craig's own congregation had two churches, one at Tinkling Spring (later Fishersville) and the other at Augusta Stone (later Fort Defiance). Following clashes with some members of the Tinkling Spring church, he was formally discharged on 4 May 1764, but he remained pastor at the Augusta Stone Church and was regularly appointed to supply other congregations in the region.

In 1743 Craig purchased 335 acres of land in Beverley Manor about four miles northeast of present-day Staunton. On 11 June 1744 he married Isabella Helena Russell, who was also from Ireland. They had five daughters, three sons, and another child who died in infancy. Craig and his wife began housekeeping and farming without servants, but by the time of his death he owned five slaves. In 1763 a young man of mixed-race ancestry successfully sued Craig for his freedom. During the Seven Years' War, when many frontier Presbyterians fled to safer territory, Craig counseled his congregation to remain and defend their homes. Among those who attended Craig's church were William Preston, who had become one of the most prominent men in southwestern

Virginia by the time of the American Revolution, and Selim, an Algerine who after a remarkable captivity in the West was converted from Islam to Christianity under Craig's supervision.

Craig adhered to the Donegal Presbytery, Synod of Philadelphia, during the split of American Presbyterians between the Old Lights and New Lights. He kept his distance from the Hanover Presbytery, which the New Light Synod of New York formed in 1755. After the unification of the Synods of New York and Philadelphia in 1758, however, Craig was ordered to join the reconstituted Presbytery of Hanover. He had reluctantly acquiesced by the following year, when he was chosen moderator. After Craig and other western ministers complained to the synod of the hardships of traveling to Hanover, the synod ordered that meetings of the Hanover Presbytery alternate between eastern and western locations. He served several times as moderator, collected funds for the College of New Jersey (later Princeton University) beginning in 1769, and in 1773 advocated passage of an act of religious toleration in Virginia. John Craig died on 22 April 1774 in Augusta County and was buried in the graveyard at Augusta Stone Church.

Autobiographical "A preacher preaching to himself from a long text of no less than sixty years: On review of past life" (ca. 1769), with birth and marriage dates, and John Craig Papers, both Presbyterian Historical Society, Montreat, N.C.; variant birth and death dates on gravestone erected by son in 1798 ("In memory of the Revd. John Craig, D.D., commencer: of the Presbyterian Ministerial Service, in this place, Ano Domini, 1740, and faithfully discharged his duty in the same. To April the 21st, Ano Domini, 1774, then departed this life with fifteen hours affliction: from the hand of the Great Creator. Aged 63 years and 4 months"); biographies in Foote, *Sketches of Virginia*, 28–33, Alfred Nevin, ed., *Encyclopædia of the Presbyterian Church in the United States of America* (1884), 161 (with variant birth date of 21 Sept. 1710), J. N. Van Devanter, *History of the Augusta Church, from 1737 to 1900* (1900), 12–21, Henry Alexander White, *Southern Presbyterian Leaders* (1911), 32–35, and Lillian Kennerly Craig, *Reverend John Craig, 1709–1774: His Descendants and Allied Families* (1963), 39–61, 63–74 (text of farewell sermon at Tinkling Spring, his only surviving sermon); Howard McKnight Wilson, *The Tinkling Spring, Headwater of Freedom: A Study of the Church and Her People, 1732–1952*, 2d ed. (1974), 64–83, 97–101, 123–134; Record of Baptisms (1740–1749), Augusta Stone Church, Fort Defiance, alphabetized and transcribed in Wilson, *Tinkling Spring*, 470–484; Donegal Presbytery Minutes, Presbyterian Historical Society, Philadelphia; Hanover Presbytery Minutes (including death on 22 Apr. 1774 noted on 13 Oct.

1774, 1:55), UTS; Orange Co. Deed Book, 7:125–128; Augusta Co. Order Book, 7:462, 8:122–123; Robert Doares Jr., "'But for the Saviour, I Could Not Bear It': The Story of Selim the Algerine," *Colonial Williamsburg* 24 (summer 2002): 15–18 (por. silhouette believed to be of Craig on 16); appraisal of estate in Augusta Co. Will Book, 6:505–506.

KATHARINE L. BROWN

CRAIG, Lewis (ca. 1737–by July 1825), Baptist minister, was born in Orange County and was the son of Tolever Craig and Mary Hawkins Craig. One of his younger brothers, Elijah Craig, also became a prominent Baptist minister and distiller in Kentucky. Largely self-taught, Craig lived, by his own account, a life of folly and vanity until he was about thirty, when he experienced a religious conversion through the sermons of Samuel Harriss. Although not yet ordained and also without possessing a license as required by law for dissenting ministers, Craig began preaching in Orange and the neighboring counties. On several occasions he was arrested and held in jail for such offenses as disturbing the peace and conducting unlicensed religious services. In June 1768 authorities seized Craig and several other ministers during a worship service. Offered freedom if they promised not to preach again for a full year, the men refused and were incarcerated in Fredericksburg. A defiant Craig reportedly preached through the grates of his jail cell to large and supportive crowds during his one month of imprisonment.

In November 1770 Craig was ordained and named pastor of the Upper Spotsylvania Baptist Church, which steadily increased in membership. Known more for his practical nature and common sense than as a scholar of the Bible, Craig had a congenial personality and melodious voice that made him effective in the pulpit. He conducted revivals and assisted in forming congregations in at least six Virginia counties. He continued to run afoul of the law and in 1771 was confined to the Caroline County jail for three months.

Like many of his contemporaries, Craig became fascinated with the opportunities said to be awaiting in Kentucky. According to Baptist lore, he once described God's celestial kingdom as a Kentucky of a place. When he informed his congregation of his intention to move west, he was astonished to learn that more than half of them desired to accompany him. In September 1781, as Craig, his brother Joseph Craig (who was also a minister), and their party set out from Spotsylvania County bound for Kentucky, he likened their 600-mile journey to the exodus of Moses and the Israelites to the Promised Land. Perhaps as many as 600 people, 200 of them members of his church, formed what was probably the largest group of pioneers ever to enter the Kentucky District. After three months the members of the so-called Traveling Church arrived at their new home on what became Gilbert's Creek, a tributary of Dick's River (later Dix River), in the portion of Lincoln County that became Garrard County, Kentucky. In the autumn of 1783 Craig and most of his followers moved to South Elkhorn, in Fayette County, approximately five miles from Lexington, where they formed the first congregation of any denomination north of the Kentucky River.

After nine years as pastor of the South Elkhorn Church, Craig chose to leave that congregation in 1792. Although one account speculates that he may have been embarrassed because of land dealings that went sour, he offered no explanation for his decision. Craig purchased a farm near the small community of Minerva, in Mason County, where the following year he organized the Bracken Baptist Church. He served as its pastor until 1807 and remained active in ecclesiastical matters in the region until at least 1812.

Although Craig's name is among the most recognizable in the history of the Baptist Church in Virginia and Kentucky, many aspects of his life remain shrouded in mystery. By 14 November 1766 he had married Elizabeth Sanders, of Spotsylvania County. They may have had as many as five daughters and five sons. When Craig composed his will in June 1821, he listed four living sons. Even the date and manner of his death are uncertain. Lewis Craig died probably late in the spring or early in the summer of 1825; his will was first presented for probate during the July session of the Mason County Court. His grave was unmarked and unheralded until 1930, when local Baptists surrounded the presumed site with an iron picket fence and placed a commemorative stone tablet.

Biographies in Robert B. Semple, *A History of the Rise and Progress of the Baptists in Virginia* (1810), revised by G. W. Beale (1894), esp. 29–30, 32, 472–473 (with death ca. 1824), James B. Taylor, *Virginia Baptist Ministers* (1859), 1:85–91, William Cathcart, ed., *The Baptist Encyclopædia* (1881), 285 (with approximate year of birth), J. H. Spencer, *A History of Kentucky Baptists* (1886), esp. 1:26–32, and Lewis N. Thompson, *Lewis Craig: The Pioneer Baptist Preacher* (1910); marriage date derived from Spotsylvania Co. Deed Book, G:228; some Craig letters in George Stovall Smith Papers, Kentucky Historical Society, Frankfort; John Taylor, *A History of Ten Baptist Churches of Which the Author Has Been Alternately a Member . . .* (1823), 27, 41–55; Lewis Peyton Little, *Imprisoned Preachers and Religious Liberty in Virginia* (1938); George W. Ranck, " 'The Travelling Church': An Account of the Baptist Exodus from Virginia to Kentucky in 1781," *Register of the Kentucky Historical Society* 79 (1981): 240–265; Mason Co., Ky., Will Book, F:291–292; gravesite restoration described in John T. Simpson Jr., letter dated 28 Jan. 1982, in Lewis Craig Biography File, Kentucky Historical Society.

THOMAS H. APPLETON JR.

CRAIG, Robert (1792–25 November 1852), member of the House of Representatives, was born near Christiansburg and was the son of James Craig and Anne Craig (whose maiden name is unknown). After attending local schools, he enrolled in Washington Academy (later Washington and Lee University) for the 1809–1810 academic session. Craig settled into the life of a planter in Montgomery County and occasionally practiced law. He executed a marriage bond in Botetourt County on 18 February 1824 and on that date or soon afterward married Melinda O. Walton. They had no children.

In 1817 Montgomery County voters elected Craig to the House of Delegates, where he served on the Committee of Privileges and Elections. Elected again in 1825 to the first of four consecutive one-year terms, he sat on the Committees for Courts of Justice and of Roads and Internal Navigation from 1825 to 1829 and on the Committee for Schools and Colleges from 1826 to 1829. Craig chaired the Committee to Examine the Office of the Auditor of Public Accounts during his last two terms. Beginning in February 1818 he served five consecutive one-year terms as a director of the first district of the Board of Public Works.

In 1829 Craig defeated Fleming Bowyer Miller by 265 votes of 2,643 cast to win election to the House of Representatives from the Twentieth Congressional District, comprising Alleghany, Botetourt, Giles, Montgomery, and Rockbridge Counties. Two years later Miller withdrew from the congressional campaign in the face of the district's strong support of Craig. When Craig ran for a third time in 1833, Montgomery County had been placed in the redrawn Seventeenth Congressional District, which also encompassed Alleghany, Augusta, Botetourt, Floyd, and Rockbridge Counties. That year he lost a tight race to Samuel McDowell Moore, of Rockbridge County, by fewer than 100 votes of 3,452 cast. In their rematch in 1835 Craig won by a vote of 2,617 to 2,364. In 1837 and 1839 he handily defeated Whig opponents.

Craig entered Congress as a supporter of Andrew Jackson, and like most other followers of Old Hickory he found his way into the Democratic Party. Craig advocated limited federal government and tended to be wary of tariffs and federally funded internal improvements. On occasion, however, he supported specific measures that conflicted with his general principles if his constituents favored those projects or measures. In 1830 Craig joined other members of the House in petitioning the president to use army troops in constructing a tunnel through the Allegheny Mountains in order to connect the eastern and western sections of the country. Although Craig did not serve on any standing committees during his first term, in his second term he was appointed to the Committee on Roads and Canals. From 1835 to 1841 he sat on the Committee on Revolutionary Claims, during his last two terms as chair.

Craig chose not to seek reelection in 1841. He returned to Montgomery County but by 1845 had moved to Green Hill, a 380-acre plantation near Salem worked by about a dozen slaves. He represented Roanoke County in the House of Delegates for two terms beginning in December 1850. During the 1850–1851 session Craig chaired the Committee on Roads and Internal Navigation. In 1851 he helped establish a new county carved from parts of Botetourt, Giles, Monroe, and Roanoke Counties. The General Assembly honored him by naming it Craig County.

Robert Craig, ill and unable to travel to Richmond for the beginning of the 1852–1853 assembly session, died at Green Hill on 25 November 1852 and was buried there. Both the House of Delegates and the Senate of Virginia passed memorial resolutions and voted to wear mourning armbands for thirty days.

Biography, with birth year, in T. V. Moore, *A Funeral Discourse on the Death of Robert Craig, Esq., of Roanoke, Late a Member of the Virginia House of Delegates, Preached by Request of His Family, in the First Presbyterian Church, Richmond, Virginia, January 9, 1853* (1853); Botetourt Co. Marriage Bonds; Craig correspondence in Edmundson Family Papers, John Letcher Papers, and Preston Family Papers, all VHS; *Richmond Enquirer*, 12, 19 Aug. 1831, 30 Apr. 1833, 5 May 1835, 16 May 1837, 31 May 1839; *Register of Debates in Congress*, 21st Cong., 1st sess., 674–678 (separately printed as *Speech of Mr. Craig of Virginia on the Bill to Construct a National Road from Buffalo to New Orleans: Delivered in the House of Representatives of the United States, March 1830* [1830]), 22d Cong., 1st sess., 2298–2300, 2366–2370; Pratt, *General Assembly, 1852* (por.); Roanoke Co. Wills, Inventories, Appraisements, 2:251–252; obituaries and editorial tributes in *Richmond Daily Dispatch*, 1, 2 Dec. 1852, and *Richmond Enquirer*, 3, 7 Dec. 1852; memorial resolutions in *JHD*, 1852–1853 adj. sess., 41 (with death date of 25 Nov. 1852), and *JSV*, 1852–1853 adj. sess., 16–17 (with variant death date of 26 Nov. 1852).

TRENTON E. HIZER

CRAIGHILL, Lloyd Rutherford (3 September 1886–13 March 1971), Episcopal missionary and bishop, was born in Lynchburg and was the son of George Peyton Craighill, a chemist, and Lydia Eliza Langhorne Craighill. The family worshiped at Grace Memorial Episcopal Church, where Craighill's father and uncle served on the vestry. The death of his father in 1905 during Craighill's senior year at Lynchburg High School delayed his matriculation at college. After three years of study, he received a B.A. from Washington and Lee University in 1912 and also earned a Phi Beta Kappa key.

In September 1912 Craighill entered the Protestant Episcopal Theological Seminary in Virginia (popularly known as Virginia Theological Seminary) to study for the ministry. During his final year a visit to the seminary by Edmund Lee, a missionary on leave from Anqing, China, inspired him to volunteer for the mission field. On 12 May 1915 the Board of Missions of the Domestic and Foreign Missionary Society of the Protestant Episcopal Church appointed Craighill a missionary to Anqing. He received a bachelor of divinity degree

on 3 June 1915 and was ordained to the diaconate the following day. He sailed for China on 25 August and arrived in September.

During his first eighteen months Craighill studied Chinese at the missionary language school at the university in Nanjing. He was ordained to the priesthood on 18 June 1916 and assigned first as principal of the Kuling American School, in a mountain resort near Jiujiang, and later as an assistant at Saint James School for Boys, in Wuhu. On 13 June 1918, in a village near Nanjing, he married Marian Wakelee Gardner, a Presbyterian missionary from New Jersey. They had three sons, one of whom died in infancy, and one daughter.

Late in 1918 Craighill arrived at what became his longest assignment, as the missionary in charge of the work at Nanchang, a city of 500,000 on the Yangtze River and the capital of Jiangxi Province. At the time of his arrival the mission comprised a congregation worshiping in a room of a decrepit house and schools meeting in inadequate buildings. In February 1921 the Department of Missions of the Domestic and Foreign Missionary Society authorized Craighill to raise $25,000 for a church and school buildings. His efforts were successful, and on 20 April 1925 the bishop of Anqing consecrated the new Saint Matthew's Church, Saint Matthew's School for Boys, and Langhorne School for Girls. Additions to the work included the founding in 1931 of a leper asylum and in 1934 of the Pure in Heart Church. Craighill and his wife kept Virginia Episcopalians informed of the Nanchang mission's work through speaking engagements during furloughs and articles in church publications, including the Richmond-based *Southern Churchman*.

Craighill's work in Nanchang took place during difficult and dangerous times. During the autumn of 1926 Communist and Nationalist troops fought around the city, and in December he and the secretary for the local Young Men's Christian Association left Nanchang under heavy fire and negotiated a truce with the attacking forces. In the winter of 1926–1927 and again in 1930, additional fighting led to military occupation of mission buildings and the evacuation of foreign-born missionaries. In both instances Craighill returned to Nanchang in the face of famine caused by fighting and flooding to rebuild the nearly destroyed facilities and programs.

Craighill's final evacuation from Nanchang occurred in 1937 following the Japanese invasion of China. While the bishop was on furlough, Craighill was responsible for the district of Anqing, and he arranged for the evacuation of missionaries to Kuling and Shanghai. He himself remained at the diocesan compound at Wuhu, where he continued to oversee the district and assisted refugees fleeing the Japanese army. Craighill and the remaining staff sheltered approximately 5,000 Chinese refugees after the Japanese invaded Wuhu in December 1937. As the battlefront moved farther west, many missionaries returned to their posts in areas occupied by the Japanese. Unable to return to Nanchang, Craighill remained in Wuhu assisting the bishop and acting as diocesan treasurer.

In December 1939 the bishop of Anqing resigned, and the House of Bishops of the Chinese Church nominated Craighill in October 1940 to succeed him. His elevation to the Episcopate culminated a decade of increasing diocesan responsibility. Since 1929 Craighill had served on the bishop's council of advice and had administered the Missionary District of Anqing as commissary during the bishop's furloughs in 1931 and 1937. The House of Deputies of the General Convention ratified his election, and he was consecrated on 30 November 1940. Advances by the Japanese army divided the district into occupied and "free" zones, and Craighill, protected by his United States citizenship, administered the occupied eastern portion. After the United States entered World War II, the Japanese immediately placed him under house arrest and subsequently imprisoned him at a camp near Shanghai. Craighill was repatriated in 1943 and arrived in New York on 1 December. The Virginia Theological Seminary and Washington and Lee University recognized his achievements in China with honorary doctorates of divinity in 1941 and 1943, respectively.

After recovering from malnutrition suffered during his internment, Craighill continued to assist the Missionary District of Anqing from the United States through communicating with his assistant bishop in China. He returned to China as soon as possible after the end of the war and arrived late in December 1945. With the assistant bishop, the remaining indigenous clergy, and returning American missionaries, Craighill conducted visitations and worked to gather the congregations scattered by war. He attempted to rebuild churches and schools and to reestablish them on a self-supporting basis during rampant inflation and the increasing success of Communist forces. Realizing that the antiforeign Communists would soon control China, Craighill concluded that the Episcopal Church would have a greater chance of survival if foreigners departed and left its work in Chinese hands. On 28 September 1949 the House of Bishops accepted his resignation as bishop of Anqing.

Early in 1950 Craighill realized a long-held dream of pastoring a small country parish and accepted a call to the rectorship of Saint James Parish, in Anne Arundel County, Maryland. After he retired in 1956, Craighill and his wife moved to Lexington, Virginia, where they became active members of Robert E. Lee Memorial Church. He occasionally fulfilled requests to supply vacant parishes and to assist bishops with church duties, and in 1965 and 1966 he served as a member of the Department of Missions for the Diocese of Southwestern Virginia. In 1966 he was elected president of the Rockbridge Historical Society but resigned after four months as a result of poor health. Lloyd Rutherford Craighill died in Lexington of a heart attack on 13 March 1971 and was buried in the Stonewall Jackson Memorial Cemetery.

Marian G. Craighill, *The Craighills of China* (1972); Craighill correspondence in National Council/Domestic and Foreign Missionary Society, China Records (1835–1951), Archives of the Episcopal Church, Austin, Texas, and in China Records Project Miscellaneous Personal Papers Collection, RG 8, Yale University Divinity Library; information provided by son Peyton G. Craighill (2004); *New York Times*, 19 June 1918, 20 May 1921, 17 Dec. 1926, 18 Aug. 1935, 16 Oct. 1940; *Southwestern Episcopalian* 19 (Oct. 1939): 4; ibid. 20 (Nov. 1940): 9; obituaries in *Lynchburg News*, 15 Mar. 1971, *Lexington News-Gazette*, 17 Mar. 1971 (por.), and *Southwestern Episcopalian* 71 (May 1971): 1.

JULIA E. RANDLE

CRAIGIE, Walter Williams (7 November 1904–10 February 1989), investment banker and civic leader, was born in Richmond and was the son of Francis John Craigie Jr. and Mary Hooper Williams Craigie. He attended local public schools but was forced to end his formal education at age eleven because of his parents' divorce. Craigie helped support his family by working as an office boy for the Chesapeake and Potomac Telephone Company. His long career in banking began in 1917, when he joined the National State and City Bank of Richmond as a clerk. The next year Craigie became a junior department head at the Federal Reserve Bank of Richmond, a position he held until 1922. For the next five years he managed the Richmond Car Works, a company that built railroad boxcars. By the time he was twenty-one years old, Craigie was supervising more than five hundred workers at the plant. On 19 June 1926 he married Helen Pendleton Walker, a Madison County native. They had two sons and one daughter.

In 1926 Craigie founded the Stock Investment Company, Inc., with himself as president. The company became Walter W. Craigie, Inc., the following year. He continued as president until 1935, when the business foundered during the Great Depression, went into receivership, and lost its charter. By the next year he and his brother Frank Willson Craigie had established F. W. Craigie and Company, specializing in municipal bond investments. A senior partner, Walter Craigie managed the trading department. In 1962 he founded Craigie and Company, Inc., which in 1965 became F. W. Craigie and Company, Inc. He retained the presidency in 1968, when the company became Craigie Incorporated, and in 1972, when a merger with Mason-Hagen, Inc., of which he was board chairman, formed Craigie, Mason-Hagen, Inc. Four years later the company reverted to Craigie Incorporated. Craigie served as chairman of the board until 1980 and then as chair of the executive committee until 1988.

Craigie's business interests were not limited to the banking and investment industry. Credited with saving the Cardwell Machine Company from bankruptcy, he served as treasurer between 1934 and 1950, when he became president and oversaw operations until he was appointed chairman of the board in 1961. Craigie also was president and director of Liberty Lime-

stone Corporation in Buchanan, Botetourt County, from 1972 to 1975, a director of the Richmond Guano Company from 1955 to 1983, and chairman of the board of Drum Financial Corporation in Omaha, Nebraska, from 1975 to 1981. Considered a leading expert in municipal bond finance, Craigie served the Investment Bankers Association of America as vice president and member of its board of governors and at various times chaired its municipal securities committee and its subcommittee on finance and local governments. For more than twenty years he was a financial consultant for Fairfax County.

An influential civic leader, Craigie was president of the Family Service Society of Richmond and the Richmond Area Community Council, a board member of the Richmond Children's Aid Society and the Richmond Urban League, a member of the Young Women's Christian Association Advisory Committee, and a trustee of Richmond Memorial Hospital. In 1948 he served on a mayor's study committee established to recommend minimum standards for Richmond Welfare Department operations and later was a member of the city's Public Welfare Advisory Committee. About this time Craigie successfully intervened on behalf of African American residents whose neighborhood had been targeted for takeover and demolition by developers. He sat on the City of Richmond Tax Study Commission from 1959 to 1961 and the Richmond–Henrico County Merger Study Commission of 1960–1961. He was a member of the Richmond Chamber of Commerce and served as president of both the Richmond Ballet and the Central Richmond Association, which worked to stem downtown decay and loss of businesses.

Among Craigie's great loves were horses and foxhunting. He was a president of the Deep Run Hunt Club, and for thirty-three years beginning in 1939 he wrote a weekly column called "Hoof Prints" for the *Richmond Times-Dispatch*. He served on the vestry of Saint Paul's Episcopal Church and in 1948 was elected president of the Episcopal Churchmen of the Diocese of Virginia. Craigie was national vice chairman of the National Conference of Christians and Jews (later the National Conference for Community and Justice), and in 1958 the Anti-Defamation League of B'nai B'rith named him its Man of the Year. The Richmond First Club presented him with its Good Government Award in 1963.

Deeply interested in education, Craigie was an honorary trustee of Virginia Union University and established trust funds at Woodberry Forest School, in Madison County, and at Randolph-Macon College, in Ashland, where he was a trustee from 1969 to 1987. Randolph-Macon used the fund to create the Walter Williams Craigie Teaching Endowment to support teaching and the research of deserving faculty members. Craigie received the college's honorary alumnus award in 1980 and an honorary doctorate of laws in 1984. He was one of twenty-two Virginians recognized in 1986 by the Virginia Cultural Laureate Society for his work in commerce.

In part as a result of his wife's death on 27 December 1987, Craigie retired from Craigie Incorporated during the summer of 1988. He remained on the board of directors of the company, which in 1997 was acquired by Branch Banking and Trust Corporation in Winston-Salem, North Carolina. Walter Williams Craigie died in a local hospital on 10 February 1989 and was buried in Hollywood Cemetery, in Richmond.

Biographies in Morton, *Virginia Lives*, 221, and *Who Was Who in America with World Notables* (1989), 81; Richmond City Department of Health Birth Ledger; BVS Marriage Register, Madison Co.; SCC Charter Book, 140:52–55, 146:40–42, 358:676–678, 405:209–210, 468:5–9, 553:216–219, 667:755–757; *Richmond News Leader*, 8 Oct. 1953, 7 July 1988; *Richmond Times-Dispatch*, 14 Jan. 1954, 22 Jan. 1958, 27 Nov. 1988 (feature article with por.); *Bulletin of Randolph-Macon College* 52 (Aug. 1980): 2; ibid. 55 (winter 1984): 10; ibid. 55 (fall 1984): 11; obituaries in *Richmond News Leader* and *Richmond Times-Dispatch*, both 11 Feb. 1989, *Washington Post*, 13 Feb. 1989, and *Randolph-Macon College Bulletin* 60 (spring 1989): 42; editorial tribute in *Richmond Times-Dispatch*, 15 Feb. 1989.

CARL M. C. CHILDS

CRAIK, James (1730 or 1731–6 February 1814), physician, was born in Kirkcudbright, Scotland. Some undocumented accounts identify him as the illegitimate son of Robert Craik and a mother whose name is not recorded. Educated as an army surgeon, possibly at the medical college of the University of Edinburgh (although his name does not appear on its roll of graduates), Craik may have spent a short

time in the Caribbean before arriving in Virginia early in the 1750s. The earliest record of his presence in the colony is a grant to him on 16 May 1753 from the Northern Neck Proprietary of a lot in the town of Winchester.

Craik was an officer in George Washington's ill-fated march toward the Forks of the Ohio that resulted in the surrender of Fort Necessity in 1754 and was surgeon of the 1st Virginia Regiment that Washington commanded during much of the ensuing French and Indian War. In 1755 when Edward Braddock's expedition met disaster near the site of Fort Necessity, Craik attended the fatally wounded general. For his service in the war, Craik received warrants for bounty lands in the West, and in 1770 he accompanied Washington on a tour of the Ohio Valley to view the land set aside for the officers and soldiers.

Craik married Mariamne Ewell, of Prince William County, on or about 13 November 1760. They lived in Charles County, Maryland, where he owned a plantation, built a large house, and practiced medicine. They had six sons and three daughters. Craik was a founding member of the Charles County Committee of Correspondence formed on 14 June 1774 to coordinate the county's response with those of other Maryland counties to Parliament's passage of the Coercive, or Intolerable, Acts. In the spring of 1777 he accepted Washington's offered appointment as senior physician of the army hospital in the middle department. After a reorganization of the medical corps, early in October 1780 Craik became the third-ranking medical officer in the Continental army with the title of chief hospital physician and surgeon, and in March 1781 he advanced to second-ranking officer with the title of chief physician and surgeon. The doctor was the first to warn Washington early in 1778 that other officers were criticizing his conduct and perhaps plotting to supersede him. Craik served throughout the Revolutionary War, often at camp with Washington, and in 1781 attended wounded soldiers on the field at Yorktown, where the general charged him to give first attention to the marquis de Lafayette, should the Frenchman be wounded.

For forty years Craik was a frequent visitor at Mount Vernon, often with his wife and children. It is unlikely that any man who was not closely related to Washington had a longer friendship with him than Craik, who also served as the physician for the family and often treated Washington's laborers. In 1785 Washington promised to pay for the education of Craik's son George Washington Craik, who became Washington's private secretary in 1796. As president, Washington also appointed one of Craik's sons-in-law auditor of the Department of the Treasury.

Craik made another trip to the West with Washington in 1784. Sometime after the end of the Revolution he moved back to Virginia and lived in Alexandria. In 1787 Craik introduced Mason Locke Weems to Washington. Neither knew that Weems would later write one of the first and most adulatory book-length biographies of Washington, a book of the sort that Washington had told Craik in 1783 he did not want written during his lifetime. In October 1795 Craik purchased a large house in Alexandria, where he resided for another decade or more, and was a member of the same lodge of Freemasons as Washington. When Washington was called out of retirement in 1798 to command the army in the event of war with France, he named Craik physician general with the rank of lieutenant colonel. The war did not take place, and Craik retired effective 15 June 1800.

Craik had a distinguished career as a military doctor, but it was his relationship with Washington for which he is best known. The general described the doctor as "my compatriot in arms, and old & intimate friend" and bequeathed him a chair and bureau, items that Craik treasured and mentioned proudly when he made special provision in his will for which of his grandchildren would inherit the pieces of furniture "willed me by George Washington Esquire." Craik and his fellow physicians Gustavus Brown and Elisha Cullen Dick attended Washington on his deathbed in December 1799, and Craik and Dick wrote a brief memorandum on their treatment of Washington and on his death. The first detailed published account of Washington's death, it appeared in the *Alexandria Times; and District of Columbia Daily Advertiser* for 21 December 1799 and was reprinted early in the following year as an appendix to the published funeral sermon of Hezekiah N. Woodruff. Craik also

attended Martha Dandridge Custis Washington during her final illness and death in May 1802.

A few years later Craik moved from Alexandria to his Fairfax County plantation, Vaucluse Farm, where he spent the last years of his life. At the time he wrote his will in June 1813, he owned thirty-three slaves, town lots in Washington, D.C., and Alexandria, and land in Kentucky and Maryland as well as in Virginia. James Craik died at Vaucluse Farm on 6 February 1814 and was buried probably in the family cemetery on the plantation, although a memorial stone erected in 1928 in the yard at the Alexandria Presbyterian Church appears to suggest that he was buried there or nearby.

Biographies in Timothy Alden, *A Collection of American Epitaphs and Inscriptions, with Occasional Notes* (1814), 5:91–94, and James Thacher, *American Medical Biography* (1828), 238–239, both derived from *Alexandria Gazette* obituary; other biographies in F. L. Brockett, *The Lodge of Washington: A History of the Alexandria Washington Lodge, No. 22, A. F. and A. M. of Alexandria, Va., 1783–1876* (1876), 112–113 (with birth year of 1730), J. M. Toner, "A Sketch of the Life and Character of Dr. James Craik, of Alexandria, Va.," Medical Society of Virginia *Transactions* (1879), 95–105, James Evelyn Pilcher, *The Surgeon Generals of the Army of the United States of America* (1905), 18–24, and Wyndham B. Blanton, *Medicine in Virginia in the Eighteenth Century* (1931), esp. 301–307 (frontispiece silhouette por.); undocumented marriage date in Hayden, *Virginia Genealogies*, 341; reminiscences by grandson in *VMHB* 46 (1938): 135–137, 143–145; numerous references in *Washington Diaries*; numerous references and letters in *Washington: Colonial Series* (place of birth on 5:453), *Revolutionary War Series*, *Confederation Series*, *Presidential Series*, and *Retirement Series* (first quotation on 4:486); Craik letters in George Washington Papers, LC, Papers of the Continental Congress, RG 360, NARA, Bartholomew Booth Papers, Maryland State Archives, and several collections, VHS; Northern Neck Grants, L:4 (first record in Virginia), RG 4, LVA; Craik and Elisha Cullen Dick, Appendix to Hezekiah N. Woodruff, *Sermon, Occasioned by the Death of Gen. George Washington* (1800), 14–16; Thomas M. Boyd, "Death of a Hero, Death of a Friend: George Washington's Last Hours," *Virginia Cavalcade* 33 (1984): 136–143 (por. on 139); Peter R. Henriques, *The Death of George Washington: He Died as He Lived* (2000); will in Fairfax Co. Will Book, K-1:180–184 (second quotation on 181), and inventory of Vaucluse Farm in Fairfax Co. Will Book, L-1:158; birth year of 1727 and variant death date of 4 Feb. 1814 on 1928 memorial stone at Alexandria Presbyterian Church, supposed to be a replication of a table stone destroyed during the Civil War; obituary in *Alexandria Gazette, Commercial and Political*, 10 Feb. 1814 (died "in the 84th year of his age"); death notice in *Washington Daily National Intelligencer*, 11 Feb. 1814 (died "in the 84th year of his age").

BRENT TARTER

CRALLE, John (d. by 11 January 1813), member of the Convention of 1776, was born in Northumberland County about 1730 or 1731 and was the son of John Cralle and the thrice-widowed Hannah Kenner Hull Harris Cralle Cralle, her third husband having been the younger brother of her fourth husband. Even though his father died in 1758, he was known until the mid-1770s as John Cralle Jr., a convenient way of distinguishing him from his elder half brother and other relatives of the same name, most of whom lived in the same part of Saint Stephen's Parish. Occasional references to members of the family as Crallé or Crawley suggest the pronunciation of the surname. About April 1752 Cralle married Sarah Harding. They had at least two sons and two daughters before her death.

In July 1765 and in November 1768 Cralle was an unsuccessful candidate for the House of Burgesses. He had not yet become a justice of the peace, the principal local office to which young men with political aspirations usually won early appointment, and he did not become a captain in the county militia until 1771. During the winter of 1774–1775 Cralle was elected to the Northumberland County Committee, established to enforce regulations the Continental Congress and the colonial conventions adopted. In April 1776 he won election to the last of the Revolutionary Conventions. Cralle was appointed to the Committee of Privileges and Elections and was almost certainly present on 15 May when the convention unanimously voted for independence and again on 12 June when it unanimously adopted the Virginia Declaration of Rights. He left Williamsburg about 21 June to take command of his militia company, which was charged with keeping an eye on British raiding parties operating in the Chesapeake Bay. Cralle therefore missed the final convention debates and vote on adoption of the first constitution of Virginia and the election of the first governor of the commonwealth.

Cralle returned to Williamsburg in October 1776 as a member of the House of Delegates and resumed his seat on the Committee of Privileges and Elections. It is unclear whether it was he or another man (identified in the House journal as John Crawley) who petitioned the General Assembly in the autumn of 1776 for compensation for property damaged when a British party occupied his house in June and July. The delegates never passed on the merits of the claim. Either defeated or choosing not to seek reelection in 1777, Cralle did not again serve in state government, but he finally became a member of the county court in the summer of that year and sheriff in 1790.

Cralle was a member of the vestry of Saint Stephen's Parish as early as 1778, but within five years he had joined the Baptists. He was an early member and perhaps a founder of Morattico Baptist Church. After executing a bond on 18 February 1793 he married a widow, Mary Leland Haynie. They had no children during their nearly twenty years of marriage. Cralle was described as "very aged & infirm" in June 1811 when he verified a signature on an old will, and on 23 September 1812 he made his mark rather than signing his name on the last document he is known to have executed. The date on which John Cralle died is not recorded. He and his namesake son both died about the same time and without leaving wills. On 11 January 1813 the county court awarded his widow dower rights to her third of his estate. At the time of his death Cralle owned at least thirty-two slaves and more than 400 acres of land, and an estate inventory valued his personal property at more than $10,000.

Family history, with some inaccuracies and conflations, in Hayden, *Virginia Genealogies*, 117–120; signature verifying name in Revolutionary War Receipt Book (Aug.–Oct. 1776), RG 2, LVA; Northumberland Co. Marriage Bonds (1793); Northumberland Co. Order Book (1770–1773), 82; Northumberland Co. Record Book, 19:70–71 (quotation on 70), 277 (last recorded document); Land and Personal Property Tax Returns, Northumberland Co. (1782–1813), both RG 48, LVA; *Revolutionary Virginia*, 2:264, 6:383, 385, 7:24, 61, 232, 577; *Calendar of Virginia State Papers*, 6:621; J. Motley Booker, "The Middle Meeting House: An Early Church of the Baptists in Northumberland County," *Bulletin of the Northumberland County Historical Society* 16 (1979): 6–8; wife's dower rights, estate inventory and sale, division of slaves, and related documents in Northumberland Co. Record Book, 19:325–326, 483–490, 531, 20:60–62, 110–111, and Northumberland Co. Order Book (1811–1815), 141, 192, 310, 314.

BRENT TARTER

CRALLÉ, Richard Kenner (1800–10 June 1864), journalist, was born probably at the Lunenburg County estate of his parents, Richard

Kenner Crallé and Sarah Montfort Jones Crallé. Late in the 1810s and early in the 1820s he attended Hampden-Sydney College and the College of William and Mary, after which he settled in Nottoway County and began to practice law. On 5 February 1829 Crallé married Judith Scott Cabell in Lynchburg. They had two daughters, one of whom died as an infant, before his wife's death on 19 April 1835.

By June 1830 Crallé had moved to Lynchburg, at which time he became editor of the *Jeffersonian Republican*, soon renamed the *Jeffersonian*. His father-in-law and a partner published the newspaper, and its foreman was James Andrew Cowardin, later a founder and publisher of the *Richmond Daily Dispatch*. Crallé's support for the doctrine of states' rights found fertile ground for development, as South Carolina's fight with the federal government over tariffs and centralized power was entering its crucial stages. Supporters of John C. Calhoun hoped to swing Virginia into the isolated movement of South Carolinians, and in 1831 Governor John Floyd and Duff Green, editor of the *United States Telegraph* in Washington, D.C., urged Crallé to move the *Jeffersonian* to Richmond. Assuring Calhoun that Crallé was "the man in the world to suit us," Floyd provided funds for the venture, and Green organized the collection of hundreds of subscriptions for the new paper. By April 1832 Crallé, joined by Cowardin, had moved the *Jeffersonian* to Richmond, where it was published as the *Jeffersonian and Virginia Times*. Renamed the *Richmond Jeffersonian* in 1833, the newspaper survived the Nullification Crisis but ceased publication on 10 December 1833.

In 1835 Calhoun, with whom Crallé had become friends, recommended to Green that Crallé would be a suitable associate to assist Green with the *Telegraph*. Crallé took over as editor of the Washington newspaper in October 1836 and continued its opposition to the Andrew Jackson administration until Green stopped publication in February 1837. That same month Crallé began editing the *Washington Reformer*, a new paper that merged with the *Baltimore Merchant* before going out of business in October 1837. In January 1838 he became editor of the *Washington Chronicle*, which ceased publication the following year.

Crallé's newspapers served as an organ for Calhoun and supported his theories of limiting federal power to protect the interests of the South. After becoming secretary of state, Calhoun appointed Crallé his chief clerk on 10 April 1844. Crallé effectively functioned as Calhoun's assistant and even served as acting secretary when Calhoun was away from Washington. He resigned on 10 March 1845 and returned to Lynchburg. From there he continued to keep Calhoun informed about political opinion in Virginia. Although Crallé never ran for public office, he often consulted with leaders of the state's Democratic Party, attended political meetings, and occasionally delivered speeches.

Crallé began planning to write a biography of Calhoun late in the 1840s, and before the South Carolinian died in March 1850 he requested that his letters and papers be deposited with Crallé. Calhoun's crucial essays on political theory, *A Disquisition on Government* and *A Discourse on the Constitution and Government of the United States*, survive only in the edition Crallé published in 1851. These two essays were republished as the first volume in Crallé's six-volume series entitled *The Works of John C. Calhoun* (1853–1856), which included many of his speeches, public letters, and reports.

In an age in which religious disputes were occasionally very public and bitter, Crallé also became one of the better-known practitioners of Swedenborgianism. Based on the writings of the eighteenth-century Swedish scientist and theologian Emanuel Swedenborg, the doctrines of the Church of the New Jerusalem (also known as the New Church) emphasized reason, free will, and a loving, forgiving God. Crallé's letter to his fellow church member Nathaniel Francis Cabell defending the faith from detractors was published as part of Cabell's *Reply to Rev. Dr. Pond's "Swedenborgianism Reviewed"* (1848).

On 10 May 1843 in Goochland County, Crallé married Elizabeth W. Morris. They had four daughters and three sons. Soon after their marriage he built a large brick house in Lynchburg that became known as Crallé's Folly because of its size and extravagance. Crallé advocated internal improvements for the region. He petitioned the General Assembly in 1830 for improved steamboat navigation on the James River and also worked late in the 1840s to secure a railroad line west from Lynchburg. In 1845 Crallé began acquiring land in Greenbrier County, where he established a summer home for his family and raised livestock. Crallé moved there early in the 1850s. He managed his plantation, worked by about thirty slaves in 1860, and continued to practice law. During the Civil War, Richard Kenner Crallé moved his family to Lunenburg County, where he died on 10 June 1864. He was buried probably in the family cemetery in that county.

Biographies in Frederick W. Moore, ed., "Calhoun as Seen by His Political Friends: Letters of Duff Green, Dixon H. Lewis, Richard K. Crallé During the Period from 1831 to 1848," *Publications of the Southern History Association* 7 (1903): 163–164 (with birth year and death date), Alfred J. Morrison, *College of Hampden Sidney: Dictionary of Biography, 1776–1825* (1921), 208, and Ruth Hairston Early, *Campbell Chronicles and Family Sketches: Embracing the History of Campbell County, Virginia, 1782–1926* (1978), 221–222; Richard K. Crallé Papers at Clemson University, LC, and UVA; Crallé letters in John J. Cabell Papers, Clemson University, and in David Hubbard Papers, Tennessee State Library and Archives, Nashville, and printed in Robert L. Meriwether et al., eds., *Papers of John C. Calhoun* (1959–2003), esp. 11:537 (quotation), 18:188 (appointment as chief clerk); second marriage in Goochland Co. Marriage Register and Morris family Bible records (1736–1968), LVA; *Lynchburg Virginian*, 9 Feb. 1829, 27 Apr. 1835; *Washington United States Telegraph*, 4 Oct. 1836, 21 Feb. 1837; *Richmond Times-Dispatch*, 1 June 1913; Lunenburg Co. Will Book, 14:164–166.

PAUL C. ANDERSON

CRANE, William (6 May 1790–28 September 1866), Baptist lay leader, was born in Newark, New Jersey, and was the son of Rufus Crane and his second wife, Charity Campbell Crane. His parents had few resources except a sense of their families' former prominence in New Jersey history and their evangelical faith. Crane's formal schooling lasted only a few years, but he became an avid reader. His conversion experience in 1807 sharpened his desire for knowledge, and he developed a lifelong interest in Christian missions. Crane learned the shoemaker's trade and in November 1811 joined an elder brother in Richmond, Virginia, to sell a consignment of shoes.

He returned to Newark to marry Lydia Dorsett, of Perth Amboy, New Jersey, on 9 July 1812. They lived in Richmond, where he became a successful merchant. Their four daughters and five sons included William Carey Crane, who became a prominent Baptist minister and president of Baylor University.

Crane and his wife joined the First Baptist Church. He persuaded William Sands to launch the Baptist *Religious Herald* in 1828 and financially supported the paper during its early years when it failed to make a profit. From 1830 until at least 1832 Crane was a trustee of the Virginia Baptist Education Society, which purchased land and organized the Virginia Baptist Seminary (later the University of Richmond). In 1816 he helped organize a Sunday school, which met in a shoe store and later in the First Baptist Church. The opposition of some Baptists to Sunday schools led to a rupture in the church and the founding in 1820 of the Second Baptist Church, of which Crane was a member and which included black as well as white members.

Crane's concern for missionary work began to focus on Africa, and he assisted in organizing the Foreign Missionary Society of Virginia in November 1813. He and Lott Cary, a free black member of the church, founded the Richmond African Baptist Missionary Society in April 1815. Crane has often received credit as the primary founder, but he maintained that the society owed its origins more to Cary than to himself. Crane became the president and corresponding secretary and Cary the recording secretary. One of Crane's brothers was also active in the society, and Crane's wife directed the Richmond Female Missionary Society from 1823 until her death on 26 September 1830.

About 1815 Crane began leading a night school for the African American members of the church. Often he read to the students from current newspapers. One news item about African American Baptists in Sierra Leone inspired seven men and women, meeting in Crane's house, to form themselves into a Baptist church, with Cary as pastor, and to make plans to immigrate to Liberia. A member of the American Society for Colonizing the Free People of Color of the United States (popularly known as the American

Colonization Society) since shortly after its founding in December 1816, Crane hoped that colonization of free blacks in Africa would provide an expanded opportunity for missionary activity and also offer a means to end slavery in the United States through emancipation and emigration. Crane helped found the Richmond and Manchester auxiliary of the colonization society in 1823, served as one of its managers, and worked for ten years to send money and supplies to Liberia and promote the colony's interest among free blacks in Richmond.

More than a decade of work supporting emigration led Crane to conclude that few free black Virginians were interested in Liberia. He and others in sympathy with African Americans were becoming politically isolated in Virginia and losing the support of their church congregations. Crane realized that colonization would not end slavery and was beneficial only in demonstrating that African Americans could govern themselves and perhaps disrupt the continued exportation of slaves from Africa. By 1833, after an indecisive debate about slavery in the Virginia General Assembly, Crane wrote, "I must say, frankly, that I can see no possible ultimate remedy for this evil, but for the white man, in this boasted land of liberty, to lay aside his *pride of color*, and to admit what was never denied till within the last few centuries, that 'God has made of one blood all nations of men,' that 'all men are born free and equal,' and without any regard to complexion, all naturally possess the same inalienable rights." He predicted that unless slavery were abolished, "possibly *nullification*, or some similar ground of fanatical discord, may array North and South, anti-slavery and pro-slavery, in a deadly strife, such as may break up the bonds of our Union in scenes of blood and ultimately thus break off the shackles of the slave."

On 20 July 1831 Crane married Jean Nivin Daniel, a sister of Raleigh Travers Daniel, who later served as Virginia's attorney general, and niece of Peter V. Daniel (1784–1860), later an associate justice of the Supreme Court of the United States. They had four daughters and four sons. Discouraged after his work in Richmond for colonization, and fearing that slavery would divide the country, Crane moved to Baltimore

in 1834 and entered the wholesale leather business and later the manufacture of boots and shoes. In 1845 he joined several other men in incorporating the Chesapeake and Liberia Trading Company in order to trade goods between Baltimore and the west coast of Africa.

Crane continued to help form both white and black Baptist churches. In his first year in Baltimore, he invited Moses Clayton, a free black carpenter and Baptist preacher in Richmond, to become the minister to black Baptists in Baltimore, where Clayton organized the First Baptist Church Colored in 1836. Clayton and Crane assisted Noah Davis, an enslaved preacher in Fredericksburg, in raising money to purchase himself. Once in Baltimore, Davis organized the Second Baptist Church Colored (later called the Saratoga Street African Baptist Church). The new church sponsored a high school for blacks, for which Crane helped finance the construction of a four-story building. He rented the ground floor, the church met on the second floor, the school used the third floor, and the fourth floor contained rooms to be rented to civic groups. The school did not last, the rooms could not be profitably rented, and in the face of increasing hostility to free blacks in Baltimore, Crane was left with an almost empty building. Regular in attending the triennial General Missionary Convention of the Baptist Denomination in the United States of America for Foreign Missions (after 1845 the American Baptist Missionary Union) for more than thirty years, he remained active in both the northern and southern branches of the Baptist Church after the denomination split in 1845, including service as a vice president of the Southern Baptist Convention's Board of Foreign Missions for about a dozen years.

Although Crane opposed slavery and manumitted the few slaves who came under his control from his second wife's family, he did not consider himself a northern-style abolitionist. His religious beliefs made it possible for him to see African Americans as his spiritual equals and black Baptists as his true brothers and sisters. In his pamphlet *Anti-Slavery in Virginia: Extracts from Thos. Jefferson, Gen. Washington and Others Relative to the "Blighting Curse of Slavery"* (1865), based in part on writings completed while he lived in Richmond early in the 1830s, Crane was as severe in his criticism of abolitionists as he was of secessionists. He regarded slavery not as a sin of individuals but as an institution created by unjust public policies. William Crane, one of the purest examples of evangelical conscience yoked to the pragmatism of the small businessman, died at his Baltimore home on 28 September 1866 and was buried in the city's Green Mount Cemetery.

Biographies in James B. Taylor, "William Crane," *Religious Herald*, 4 Apr. 1867, George F. Adams, *A Brief Sketch of the Life and Character of the Late William Crane, of Baltimore* (1868), including birth date on 5, William Cathcart, ed., *The Baptist Encyclopædia* (1881), 1:287–289 (por.), and John S. Moore, "William Crane (1790–1866), Enterprising Baptist Layman," *Virginia Baptist Register* 35 (1996): 1758–1765; marriage dates in *Religious Herald*, 8 Oct. 1830, and *Fredericksburg Virginia Herald*, 23 July 1831; some letters in American Colonization Society Papers, LC; publications include an unsigned biography of Lott Cary in *Richmond Family Visitor*, 15 Oct. 1825, and *Anti-Slavery in Virginia: Extracts from Thos. Jefferson, Gen. Washington and Others Relative to the "Blighting Curse of Slavery." Debates on the "Nat Turner Insurrection," Queries by William Crane, &c.* (1865), quotations on 21, 22; obituaries in *Baltimore Sun*, 1 Oct. 1866 (reprinted in *Daily Richmond Whig*, 2 Oct. 1866), and *Religious Herald*, 4 Oct. 1866; tribute by son in *Religious Herald*, 29 Nov. 1866.

MARIE TYLER-MCGRAW

CRAWFORD, George (2 February 1897–15 August 1955), principal in a criminal case, was born in Jacksonville, Florida. His parents, John Crawford and a woman whose name is not known, may have been natives of Cuba. He received only limited schooling. Crawford joined a sister in Richmond about 1918 and worked at a hospital and as a chauffeur. About 1920 he married a woman named Catherine, surname unknown. In March 1921 Crawford was sentenced to three years' imprisonment for receiving and concealing stolen goods. He escaped on 28 May 1922, but several months later he was arrested and convicted on a new charge of grand larceny, for which he was sentenced to a five-year prison term, with an additional two years for his escape and two years for being a repeat offender. He escaped again in 1925 for one day and received another year on his sentence.

Crawford was working in Loudoun County on the state convict road force when he rescued a guard from an attack by another prisoner. His action won a commutation of one year of his sentence in January 1929, and he was discharged from the penitentiary on 23 November 1930. Richard H. Holt, a Middleburg physician who had treated the injured guard, hired Crawford in March 1931 to work for him as a handyman.

Holt lived in a cottage owned by Agnes Boeing Ilsley, a wealthy forty-year-old widow and horsewoman. Crawford began to work for Ilsley as a chauffeur. Early in September 1931 he departed for Boston with Bertie DeNeal, a married woman employed by Holt as a domestic servant. DeNeal later testified that they returned from Boston on 20 December 1931 but that she left Crawford in Washington, D.C., and did not see him again until 26 December. On Christmas Eve, Ilsley's house was robbed of a gold watch and Christmas packages, and it was later reported that Ilsley suspected Crawford and may have consulted with a detective about securing his arrest.

In the early hours of 13 January 1932 Ilsley and her white maid were bludgeoned to death. Flesh under Ilsley's fingernails appeared to come from an African American. Police found her stolen automobile abandoned near Alexandria. That neither woman had been raped and that apparently nothing had been stolen seemed to rule out standard motivations for the crime. In February 1932 Crawford was indicted in Loudoun County for the murders, but he was nowhere to be found.

One year to the day after the murders, Boston police took Crawford into custody on an unrelated housebreaking charge. John Galleher, commonwealth's attorney of Loudoun County, went to Boston, where Crawford confessed to him that a man named Charlie Johnson, with whom he had fallen in on his way back to Middleburg, had committed the murders. Intending only robbery, Crawford had stood lookout while Johnson killed the women. Afterward they quarreled, and Crawford returned to Boston. Crawford, however, refused to sign the confession.

Early reports stated that Crawford agreed to return to Loudoun without extradition proceedings, but two weeks after his arrest he was fighting extradition with help from the National Association for the Advancement of Colored

People. About seven months earlier Walter White, secretary of the organization, had received an anonymous letter from a white woman who reported rumors in Middleburg that Ilsley's brother, who had discovered the bodies, had murdered the two women. White sent the anonymous letter to the president of the NAACP's Boston branch and suggested he share the information with the governor of Massachusetts, who might then delay extradition while the NAACP investigated the case in Loudoun County. Meanwhile White arranged for Helen Boardman, a white activist, to visit Loudoun County in order to determine whether Crawford could receive a fair trial there. She testified at Crawford's extradition hearing that many white residents were convinced of his guilt, but one white magistrate had hinted to her that there was a cover-up to protect Ilsley's brother.

On 25 January 1933 Crawford deposed for the NAACP's lawyers that he had been in Boston when the murders occurred. The governor of Massachusetts approved Crawford's extradition, but his lawyers filed for a writ of habeas corpus, in part arguing that because Loudoun County juries never included blacks, Crawford would not receive justice there. In April, Judge James Arnold Lowell granted the writ, which blocked the extradition on the grounds that the exclusion of African Americans from jury service in Virginia rendered Crawford's indictment and all subsequent legal action unconstitutional. The United States Circuit Court of Appeals for the First Circuit reversed Lowell's ruling in mid-June. Crawford's Boston defense team appealed that decision to the Supreme Court of the United States, but the high court on 16 October 1933 declined to review the extradition. Walter White announced that Charles Hamilton Houston, vice dean of the law school at Howard University, would head Crawford's defense, with the assistance of three African American lawyers from Washington, Leon A. Ransom, Edward P. Lovett, and James G. Tyson.

Virginia's white leaders feared that the trial might become a cause célèbre, as had the ongoing trials in Alabama of the so-called Scottsboro boys, youths facing death sentences on flimsy charges of rape. Because Houston intended to make jury selection an issue and the judge in Loudoun County was a likely witness, the governor of Virginia named James L. McLemore, of Suffolk, to preside. On 7 November, McLemore overruled Houston's motion to quash Crawford's indictment, filed on the grounds that African Americans had been excluded from the grand jury that handed it down. Crawford then pleaded not guilty to Ilsley's murder.

The trial in the matter of *Commonwealth of Virginia* v. *George Crawford* began in Leesburg on 12 December 1933. The defense waived an opening statement. Bertie DeNeal was among several witnesses who took the stand for the prosecution. Just days before, Houston had interviewed DeNeal at the jail, where she was held as a material witness. She told him that Crawford had been in Middleburg the day before the murders. Houston then told Crawford how she would testify, and Crawford confessed to him that he had been present when Johnson killed the women.

In court the circumstantial evidence continued to mount up as witnesses placed Crawford near Middleburg at the time of the murders. Yet the state's case ultimately rested on Crawford's unsigned Boston confession to being Johnson's accomplice. Unable to prevent the confession's admission into the record, Houston then concentrated on avoiding the death penalty. After Ransom's skilled cross-examination of a pathologist won the admission that the flesh found under Ilsley's nails could not be identified with certainty as Crawford's and might belong to an accomplice, Houston emphasized to the all-white jury that executing Crawford would silence the only witness to Johnson's crime. The jury found Crawford guilty and recommended life in prison in the verdict delivered on 16 December 1933.

The Communist Party, which had undertaken the defense of the Scottsboro boys, declared in the *Daily Worker* that the result proved the ineffectiveness of the NAACP. White fueled the controversy by proclaiming in the January 1934 issue of the *Crisis* that the trial had been a great victory because a guilty man, defended by black attorneys, had escaped the electric chair and, as a consequence of the

NAACP's effort in the extradition hearing, southern states had begun admitting blacks to juries.

Meanwhile, in an interview published in the *Norfolk Journal and Guide* on 10 February 1934, Crawford complained that he had been framed. He declared that he did not know anyone named Charlie Johnson and would not of his own free will plead guilty to murdering Ilsley's maid. Houston was livid. When Crawford appeared before a Leesburg judge on 12 February to answer charges that he had killed the maid, Houston refused to accept the responsibility of entering a guilty plea on behalf of his client and reminded Crawford of his pledge to help locate and identify Johnson. Crawford pleaded guilty to the murder charge and received a second life term.

Disagreement about the Crawford case roiled in the NAACP. In May 1934 W. E. B. Du Bois, the independent-minded editor of the *Crisis*, complained in an editorial that "either we should never have taken the case in the first place, or we should have fought it to the last ditch." The following month Boardman and Martha Gruening, another white NAACP activist, wrote in the *Nation* that Houston's decision not to appeal "shows that he dared not put Virginia justice to any real test." Houston and Ransom responded in July 1934 that they had not appealed Crawford's conviction because their client did not want an appeal, and they believed that at a second trial he would most likely have received a death sentence. They argued that their own investigations in Virginia had revealed evidence that made it impossible to use Crawford's Boston alibi at the trial. Given these constraints, the attorneys considered the case a success because it had prompted Virginia officials to begin including blacks on juries without generating resentment among white residents through an appeal.

Boardman and Gruening, along with other radicals, attempted to communicate with Crawford in prison as they continued to argue that his attorneys had betrayed him. To counter the criticism, Houston received authorization from Crawford to publish an account of the pretrial confession in which Crawford had admitted being present during the murders. Houston's article, "The George Crawford Case: A Statement by the NAACP," appeared in the April and May 1935 issues of the *Crisis* and included photographic reproductions of Crawford's handwritten statement that he shared guilt in the crime and was satisfied with Houston's defense. Crawford, however, clouded the situation by contacting Boardman and Gruening to complain that his attorneys had not defended him adequately. On 1 April 1935 the Supreme Court of the United States overturned the convictions of two of the Scottsboro boys because African Americans had been excluded from sitting on the juries at their trials, the constitutional principle that the NAACP had hoped to establish first by defending Crawford. That summer Boardman and Gruening published a pamphlet repeating their charges, but the Crawford case had finally retreated from the public eye.

Charlie Johnson was never found. Crawford last wrote to Walter White in August 1937 asking for cigarettes. There is no record of a reply. George Crawford's life sentences ended on 15 August 1955 when he died of a stroke at the state penitentiary in Richmond. His body was donated to the state for medical research.

Birth and death dates and birthplace confirmed by BVS; Virginia Penitentiary Prisoner Register (1916–1922), 366–367, Prisoner Registers and Indexes, 11:496–497 (age twenty-four on 4 Apr. 1921 and variant birthplace of Richmond), 12: unnumbered entry for 20 Nov. 1922, and Photographs of Escaped Inmates (including por., physical description, family information, and age twenty-four on 28 May 1922), all Virginia Penitentiary Papers, RG 42, LVA; Papers of the NAACP, Parts 8 and 11 (with variant name of Joseph Crawford, variant birthplace of Augusta, Ga., and age twenty-eight on 25 Jan. 1933 in typescript deposition in Part 8, Series A), LC; murders and trials documented in *Leesburg Loudoun Times-Mirror* (1932–1934), including por., 26 Jan. 1933; Crawford trial file in John Garland Pollard Executive Papers, RG 3, LVA; *Richmond News Leader*, 14 Jan. 1932, 27 Feb. 1935; *Richmond Times-Dispatch*, 15 Jan. 1932; *Washington Post*, 10 Nov. 1933; *Daily Worker*, 18 Dec. 1933; *True Detective Mysteries* 18 (June 1932): 6–13, 87–88; *Nation* (8 Mar. 1933), 258–260; ibid. (27 June 1934), 730–732 (second quotation); ibid. (4 July 1934), 17–19; *Crisis* 41 (Jan. 1934): 15; ibid. (May 1934): 149 (first quotation); ibid. 42 (Apr. 1935): 104–105, 116–117, 125; ibid. (May 1935): 143, 150–151, 156; Helen Boardman and Martha Gruening, *The Crawford Case: A Reply to the "N.A.A.C.P."* (1935); Walter White, *A Man Called White: The Autobiography of Walter White* (1948), 152–156; Genna Rae McNeil, *Groundwork: Charles Hamilton Houston and the Struggle for Civil Rights* (1983), 89–94, 102–104.

JOHN T. KNEEBONE

CRAWFORD, Martha Paxton Moffett (15 January 1891–25 March 1981), Presbyterian lay leader, was born in Kentucky and was the daughter of Alexander Stuart Moffett, a Presbyterian minister, and Carrie Lena Crawford Moffett. The Moffetts had been frustrated in their desire to serve the church as foreign missionaries, but six of their eight children followed that path. Paxton Moffett, as she was known, grew up in Lexington, Missouri, and in Lebanon, Kentucky, where her father held pastorates. She matriculated at Randolph-Macon Woman's College in 1909 and received a B.A. in 1912. From the latter year until 1916 she taught mathematics at Palmer College, a Presbyterian school in De Funiak Springs, Florida.

During the summer of 1914 Moffett accompanied her father to China to visit her brother and three of her sisters, all working in missions there. Moffett entered the mission field in October 1916 and the following month began working at a girls' school in Suzhou, China. On 17 May 1917 she married Francis Randolph Crawford, a physician who had been born in Kernstown, Virginia, and who was then working at the Jiangyin mission. They had no children. The couple transferred to Jiaxing in Zhejiang Province, where he was superintendent of the hospital and she taught English and Bible classes at the training school for nurses, in addition to serving occasionally as the hospital's secretary and treasurer. The Crawfords left China in 1932 as tensions increased between Nationalist and Communist forces. They settled in Farmville, where F. R. Crawford practiced medicine until his death on 3 March 1966.

Crawford continued to serve the Presbyterian Church in the United States as a member of Farmville Presbyterian Church. In 1936 she was elected president of the Woman's Auxiliary of the West Hanover Presbytery. During her tenure as president of the Woman's Auxiliary of the Synod of Virginia from 1938 to 1940, Crawford focused the auxiliary's efforts on evangelism through conferences held across the state. From 1939 until 1941 she served as president and dean of the Synodical Training School at Massanetta Springs, in Rockingham County. She chaired its program committee in 1948 and

1949 and also taught at the weeklong Woman's Auxiliary training school held there in 1943. Beginning in January 1946 Crawford served two one-year terms as a vice president of the Virginia Council of Churches, a new ecumenical group. Active also in the affiliated Virginia Council of Church Women, she became its vice president in 1946. *Presbyterian Outlook* recognized her in January 1947 as one of eleven notable Presbyterians for her contributions to the work of the church.

In 1943 and 1944 Crawford chaired the Board of Women's Work of the Presbyterian Church in the U.S. Also during the mid-1940s she was the only woman member of the Presbyterian Church's committee on evangelism. Reflecting her interest in Christian cooperation, she served from 1946 until 1957 on the board of the United Council of Church Women (later Church Women United). Crawford was elected to a two-year term as the corresponding secretary of the UCCW's reorganized General Department of United Church Women in December 1950. From 1954 to 1957 she served as president of the Virginia Council of United Church Women, which emphasized increasing interdenominational missions around the world and training women for leadership in the church. Although the General Assembly of the Presbyterian Church in the U.S. declared in 1964 that women were eligible for ordination at all levels, Farmville Presbyterian Church resisted electing Crawford as its first woman elder until 1971. Her energy and commitment compelled her pastor to assert that he would not "swap her for any four elders" in the denomination.

In 1936 Crawford helped organize the Farmville chapter of the American Association of University Women and served as its first president. During World War II she was vice chair of the Prince Edward County Red Cross chapter and was the rationing officer for the county's Office of Price Administration in 1943 and 1944, for which she received a certificate of award in 1945. A member of the Woman's Club of Farmville, she also organized and chaired the Prince Edward County Community Chest.

Martha Paxton Moffett Crawford moved to Richmond about 1976 and died at a retirement community there on 25 March 1981. She was buried next to her husband's grave in Mount Hebron Cemetery, in Winchester.

Biographies in P. Frank Price, comp., *Our China Investment: Sixty Years of the Southern Presbyterian Church in China with Biographies, Autobiographies, and Sketches of All Missionaries since the Opening of the Work in 1867* (1927), 111 (with birth and marriage dates), and Morton, *Virginia Lives*, 224–225; correspondence in Francis Randolph Crawford Papers (1890–1941), Presbyterian Historical Society, Montreat, N.C.; *Presbyterian Outlook* (20 Jan. 1947), 5–6 (por. and quotation); *Virginia Council News*, 1 Apr. 1956; obituaries in *Farmville Herald* and *Richmond Times-Dispatch*, both 27 Mar. 1981, and *Presbyterian Outlook* (20 Apr. 1981), 32.

BARBARA C. BATSON

CRAWFORD, Robert Baxter (14 April 1895–5 November 1973), president of the Defenders of State Sovereignty and Individual Liberties, was born in Buffalo Gap, in Augusta County, and was the son of Robert Lee Crawford and Sallie B. McClintic Crawford. He attended Augusta Military Academy before matriculating in 1914 at the Virginia Agricultural and Mechanical College and Polytechnic Institute (later Virginia Polytechnic Institute and State University), from which he received a two-year degree in agronomy. Crawford served as a second lieutenant during World War I and for about a year managed a 12,000-acre farm in Alabama. He returned to Virginia and worked as an agricultural agent in Clarke and Warren Counties. On 26 April 1922 in Martinsburg, West Virginia, Crawford married Regina Lauck Shaffer. They had three daughters and one son.

In 1925 Crawford moved to Farmville to become the agricultural agent for Prince Edward County. Two years later he entered private business and was president of the Kilkare Laundry from then until he retired in 1970. Crawford held leadership positions in several business organizations, including the presidency of a regional laundry owners' association in 1940 and of the state association in 1943. Active in the American Legion, he held office in his home post, at the state level, and as a member of the national executive and legislative committees, and in August 1946 he was elected to a one-year term as department commander of Virginia. Crawford

was a member of the Prince Edward County school board from 1931 to 1946, the last seven of those years as chair, and in 1945 he received a distinguished service certificate as the outstanding school board member in Virginia.

In response to the decision of the Supreme Court of the United States in May 1954 declaring racial segregation in public schools unconstitutional, Crawford and other opponents of desegregation in Virginia's Fourth Congressional District established the Defenders of State Sovereignty and Individual Liberties, of which he became president in October of that year. Effectively mobilizing segregationists throughout the state, the Defenders organized dozens of chapters and had recruited nearly 12,000 members by 1958. Those members included powerful state legislators and two congressmen from south-central Virginia, Watkins Moorman Abbitt and William Munford Tuck, both major figures in the state's dominant Democratic political organization led by United States senator Harry Flood Byrd (1887–1966). In 1955 Crawford also helped found the Federation for Constitutional Government, a short-lived organization seeking to thwart integration across the South, and served on its executive committee.

On 8 June 1955 Crawford unveiled the Defenders' *Plan for Virginia*, a package of proposals intended to block enforcement of the Supreme Court's ruling. The Defenders' plan would have permitted localities to close public schools threatened with desegregation and allowed white students to enroll in segregated private academies subsidized by state tuition grants. The Defenders recommended amending the state's constitution and code to eliminate compulsory school-attendance laws, prohibitions on using state money for private tuition grants, and if necessary even the requirement that Virginia provide a statewide system of free public schools. The plan also included a provision to cut off state funds for and to close schools that desegregated. Second only to Crawford's uncompromising commitment to segregation was his unwavering insistence that the Defenders rely solely on legal and peaceful tactics in resisting desegregation. In that significant respect, the Defenders distinctly differed from pro-segregation groups in other southern states during the turbulent decade following the Supreme Court's ruling.

A limited constitutional convention in March 1956 amended the Virginia constitution to allow tuition grants to nonsectarian private schools. At a special session at the end of the summer of 1956 the General Assembly adopted many of the Defenders' recommendations as the central components of its program of Massive Resistance to the Supreme Court's orders. In the autumn of 1958 Governor James Lindsay Almond Jr. enforced the new laws and closed public schools in Charlottesville, Front Royal, and Norfolk that were under court orders to desegregate. The school closings sparked a reaction among business leaders in several cities, and many middle-class white citizens expressed a willingness to accept some desegregation in order to preserve public education. As public support for Massive Resistance receded, the Defenders proved unable to substitute segregated private education for the closed public schools. After both federal and state courts ruled the school-closing laws unconstitutional on 19 January 1959, the governor, who had been elected in 1957 with enthusiastic backing from the Defenders, announced his retreat from Massive Resistance. In April by a narrow majority the General Assembly adopted a plan of limited desegregation.

Crawford and the Defenders felt betrayed. They unsuccessfully attempted to revive Massive Resistance with a Bill of Rights Crusade, which sponsored a rally on 31 March 1959, and by supporting segregationist candidates in the July 1959 Democratic primary. After that year, the Defenders lost their cohesiveness, and only a few chapters continued to operate into the 1960s. Prince Edward County closed its public schools from 1959 to 1964 to avoid desegregation, but the county chapter of the Defenders became moribund as residents focused on raising money for private schools in the county. The State Corporation Commission revoked the Defenders' charter in 1967. With Massive Resistance defeated and statewide support waning, Crawford had resigned as president of the Defenders by June 1963. He remained secretary-treasurer of the Virginia Education Fund, organized as a fund-raising arm of the Defenders

to support private-school education, at least until 1967 and probably until his death. Robert Baxter Crawford died in Farmville on 5 November 1973 and was buried in the city's Westview Cemetery.

Biography with birth date in *Virginia Journal of Education* 39 (1946): 206 (por.); BVS Birth Register, Augusta Co. (month and year only); some Crawford correspondence in Watkins Moorman Abbitt Congressional Papers, University of Richmond; *Staunton News-Leader*, 10 May 1922; *Richmond Times-Dispatch*, 22 Aug. 1946, 27 Oct. 1954, 9 June 1955; *Richmond News Leader*, 25 May 1959, 14 Jan. 1967; "The Defenders," *Virginia Record* 77 (Aug. 1955): 26–27, 45; Haldore Hanson, "No Surrender in Farmville, Virginia: Townsmen Describe How They Expect to Defy the Supreme Court Segregation Decision," *New Republic* 133 (10 Oct. 1955): 11–15; *A Plan for Virginia, Presented to the People of the Commonwealth* (1955), Defenders of State Sovereignty and Individual Liberties pamphlet (copy in *DVB* Files); Bob Smith, *They Closed Their Schools: Prince Edward County, Virginia, 1951–1964* (1965), 87–107; Robbins L. Gates, *The Making of Massive Resistance: Virginia's Politics of Public School Desegregation, 1954–1956* (1962), 36–37, 158–163; David Pembroke Neff, "The Defenders of State Sovereignty and Individual Liberties, 1954–1967" (M.A. thesis, Old Dominion University, 1992); obituaries in *Richmond News Leader*, 6 Nov. 1973, *Farmville Herald* and *Richmond Times-Dispatch*, both 7 Nov. 1973, and *Washington Post*, 9 Nov. 1973; editorial tribute in *Farmville Herald*, 9 Nov. 1973.

DAVID PEMBROKE NEFF

CRAWFORD, Robert Bruce (5 December 1893–15 August 1993), journalist, was born in Dooley, in Wise County, and was the son of Douglas Bruce Crawford, a builder and machinist, and Nancy Louise Powers Crawford. The family moved to Oklahoma, to Fayette County, West Virginia, and then when he was a teenager to Norton, Virginia. Crawford worked at odd jobs, including repairing coal cars at Dante, in Russell County, and in 1911 attended high school in Norton. In 1912 he entered West Virginia University as a subfreshman, a classification that implies he had yet to meet the institution's entrance requirements for college students, but he left after one term.

Bruce Crawford, as he was known as an adult, began newspaper work in Wise County in 1915 as editor and owner of the *Norton Reporter*, which merged with another newspaper and became the *Norton Reporter and Miner's Enterprise*. From July 1918 to mid-February 1919 he served as a sergeant in an army engineers company that did not go overseas during World War I. After the war Crawford was adjutant of a local American Legion post and chaired Wise County's War History Commission, part of a statewide project that gathered information about wartime military and civilian activities.

In 1919 Crawford began publishing *Crawford's Weekly* in Norton. The newspaper's lively copy quickly drew attention, and in 1924 some of his columns appeared in the compilation *Nuggets: Choice Clippings from Crawford's Weekly*, including a humorous story of a moonshiner in the style of a Horatio Alger tale. Crawford visited Tennessee and West Virginia nosing about for subjects. The regional flavor of his paper helped earn him a reputation as a spokesman for Appalachia. Major newspapers in Chicago, New York, and Washington, D.C., quoted *Crawford's Weekly*. Crawford also wrote freelance articles for such state and national publications as *Commonwealth*, the *Nation*, the *New Republic*, and the *Virginia Quarterly Review*. On 26 December 1922 in Bristol he married Kate Lay, a Coeburn schoolteacher. They are not known to have had any children. In May 1923 he chartered the Crawford Printing Company, Incorporated, with himself as president and his wife as both secretary and treasurer.

At a University of Virginia seminar on economic development in August 1929 Crawford argued for better pay and working conditions in southern industry. He made several trips to Harlan County, Kentucky, in 1931 to write about striking coal miners. The county sheriff, John Henry Blair, viewed as a supporter of the coal companies, disliked the attention so much that he traveled to Norton in order to complain about the newspaper's coverage. On 28 July 1931, during one of Crawford's trips to Harlan County, someone fired eight shots at him and a companion and slightly wounded the editor in his right leg. The shooting received widespread publicity. Crawford was convinced that coal-mine operators were responsible for the attack, but no one was ever charged. Later that year he returned to Kentucky with writers of the National Committee for the Defense of Political Prisoners to gather and publish information about the strike. Others on the trip included Sherwood Anderson, John Dos Passos, and Theodore Dreiser, with whom Crawford corresponded regularly.

In 1934 Crawford ran as an independent candidate for the House of Representatives from the Ninth Congressional District, which comprised the city of Bristol and the twelve counties in southwestern Virginia. Making ample use of his newspaper, he mounted a vigorous campaign. Crawford accused the incumbent, John William Flannagan, a Democrat and supporter of the New Deal, of participating in the theft of more than $800,000 from several banks in the district. He also charged that Flannagan was regularly under the influence of alcohol in public. Crawford's platform, which he published on the front page of his newspaper, included his support of "ownership of the means of production and distribution by the government and ownership of the government itself by the working people." Those words, which closely linked the editor with socialists and communists, certainly did not endear him to coal-mine and railroad operators. Crawford attacked political corruption in southwestern Virginia, including the easily abused absentee voting process. He lost by a large margin, which seemed to bother him very little. In the edition of *Crawford's Weekly* after his defeat, he published a mock advertisement for the sale of twenty-seven black bags of the kind that dishonest Democratic officeholders supposedly used.

In 1935 Crawford sold his newspaper to the publishers of the rival *Coalfield Progress*. He soon afterward visited Birmingham, Alabama, during labor unrest directed at its coal and steel companies. City officials had enacted a law that prohibited people from possessing more than one copy of any radical publication. Testing the law, Crawford and others distributed such periodicals as the *Daily Worker* and *New Republic* in front of the city hall but were not charged in the incident. Crawford maintained he had been shot at in Alabama, as well.

Crawford moved to Bluefield, West Virginia, later in 1935 to edit the *Sunset News*, an afternoon Democratic paper owned by a Republican family. His Democratic friends thought him better suited for working in the Works Progress Administration's Writers' Project in West Virginia, of which he became director late in 1938.

Its major publication was *West Virginia: A Guide to the Mountain State*. Ever the lightning rod, Crawford got into trouble in his new job. The section of the book on labor unrest, among other topics, met strong opposition from the governor, Homer Adams Holt, and delayed publication of the book until 1941, after Holt left office.

Crawford had moved to Charleston, West Virginia, by 1941 and that year became secretary of the West Virginia Publicity Commission. By 1944 he headed the Highway Safety Bureau of the West Virginia State Police, and within three years he had started an advertising company that worked to elect Democratic political candidates. Crawford retired in 1961 and moved to Saint Petersburg, Florida, where he continued to keep up with West Virginia news and correspond with radical friends about current events. His wife died on 28 September 1979. Robert Bruce Crawford died in a local hospital on 15 August 1993 and was buried in Memorial Park Cemetery, in Saint Petersburg.

Birth date and place provided by Crawford in World War I Selective Service System Draft Registration Cards (1917–1918), RG 163, NARA; I. M. Warren, "Present-Day Author: Bruce Crawford" (typescript dated 19 Feb. 1938), WPA Biographies (with variant birthplace of Norton and partial bibliography of publications); Arthur C. Prichard, " 'In West Virginia I Had More Freedom': Bruce Crawford's Story," *Goldenseal* 10 (spring 1984): 34–37 (several pors.); Bruce Crawford Collection, University of Virginia's College at Wise; correspondence in Theodore Dreiser Papers, University of Pennsylvania, and John C. Rogers Papers, UVA; Sullivan Co., Tenn., Marriage Records; *Norton Crawford's Weekly*, 5 Jan. 1923, 2 (quotation), 9 Nov. 1934, 8 Feb. 1935; *Richmond News Leader*, 11, 18 Aug. 1924; *Richmond Times-Dispatch*, 29 July 1931, 13 Oct. 1934, 12 Feb. 1935; *Washington Post*, 19 July 1934, 31 July 1935; *Nation* (18 Sept. 1935), 319–320; Crawford, "Labor Situation in the South" (paper delivered 6 Aug. 1929), in *Proceedings of the 1929 Institute of Public Affairs* (1929), vol. 1; Jerry B. Thomas, " 'The Nearly Perfect State': Governor Homer Adams Holt, the WPA Writers' Project and the Making of *West Virginia: A Guide to the Mountain State*," *West Virginia History* 52 (1993): 91–108; death notice in *St. Petersburg Times*, 17 Aug. 1993 (with death at age ninety-eight).

G. W. POINDEXTER

CRAWFORD, William (d. by 15 April 1762). See **CRAFORD, William**.

CRAWFORD, William (ca. 1722–11 June 1782), Continental army and militia officer, was born probably either in Westmoreland County or in the lower Shenandoah Valley in the part of Orange County that in 1738 became Frederick County. His father's name was almost certainly William Crawford; his mother's name appears in various records as Honor, Honoria, or Onora Crawford. After his father died, his mother married Richard Stephenson, and Crawford grew up on his stepfather's Bullskin Run farm in the part of Frederick County that later became Jefferson County. In 1742 Crawford married Ann Stewart, who died sometime after the birth of their daughter. He married Hannah Vance in 1744. They had one son and two daughters who lived to adulthood. In 1750 George Washington purchased land along Bullskin Run, and most likely Crawford met him at that time.

On 27 December 1755, during the Seven Years' War, Crawford was commissioned an ensign in Christopher Gist's scouts, organized as the 17th Company in the Virginia Regiment, commanded by Colonel George Washington. He took his oath on 6 January 1756 at the Frederick County Court session but was allowed to postpone joining his company until the beginning of March. Initially the regiment protected the settlements along the northern Virginia, Maryland, and south-central Pennsylvania frontier from attacks by the French and their Indian allies. After the regiment was reduced from seventeen to ten companies in May 1757 and its troops redistributed, Crawford began garrison duty on the Augusta County frontier. On 27 July he received a lieutenant's commission and the following year served in Brigadier General John Forbes's expedition against Fort Duquesne. Crawford continued in the service until the British victory in 1763 and returned to active duty during Pontiac's Rebellion. By the close of the war he had achieved the rank of captain.

Like many other veterans who served on the Allegheny frontier, Crawford was drawn to the lands near the Forks of the Ohio, a region claimed by both Virginia and Pennsylvania. By 1766 he had established his family near the Stewart's Crossing settlement on the Youghiogheny River. At first lying within Augusta County, the settlement became part of the District of West Augusta and was later organized as part of Yohogania

County. Crawford surveyed and purchased additional tracts. George Washington secretly enlisted him as a land agent in September 1767 to acquire tracts in the Ohio Valley. After his initial surveys, Crawford conferred with Washington during a six-day visit at Mount Vernon in April 1768. Resuming the periodic surveying trips on Washington's behalf that lasted until 1773, he returned to Mount Vernon on several occasions to discuss strategy and met with Washington when he traveled west. The two men corresponded about western lands until 1781. Beginning in 1771 Crawford conducted extensive surveys for the Virginia government of western lands set aside for the Virginia Regiment.

In July 1770 Crawford was appointed a justice of the peace for Cumberland County, Pennsylvania, and he likely held similar offices when that county was divided into others, including Westmoreland County, in 1773. In the latter year he became official surveyor for the Ohio Company of Virginia. In 1774 Crawford volunteered for service in the campaign of Virginia's royal governor, John Murray, the fourth earl of Dunmore, against the Shawnee Indians. During Dunmore's War, Crawford helped erect Fort Fincastle at what became Wheeling, conducted scouting operations, and led an attack against two Indian villages located above the Ohio River. The presence of the Virginia governor at the Forks exacerbated tensions with Pennsylvania, and in the squabble Crawford sided with Virginia. Appointed a justice of the peace for Augusta County on 6 December 1774, he took the oath of office on 16 May 1775, the same day he was selected for the county's committee formed in response to the deepening crisis with Great Britain.

The fourth Virginia Revolutionary Convention raised troops for service in the Revolutionary War and on 12 January 1776 commissioned Crawford lieutenant colonel of the 5th Virginia Regiment. Beginning on 14 August of that year he served as colonel in the 7th Virginia Regiment. For equipping that unit he received $20,000 in compensation from the Continental Congress. Crawford may have been present with elements of the regiment at the Battles of Trenton and Princeton, but by March 1777 he had relinquished his command because of concerns about Indian attacks at the Forks of the Ohio and his need to settle the estate of his deceased brother. Back in western Pennsylvania, Crawford took command of Continental troops and militiamen in the western department and in the spring of 1778 constructed Fort Crawford northeast of Pittsburgh.

Although much of Crawford's time was taken up with frontier defense, in December 1776 he was named a justice of the peace for Yohogania County. Crawford may also have signed a document prepared at the September 1780 session of the county court petitioning the Continental Congress to create a separate state in the region.

The war in the west intensified as British agents from Fort Detroit provided supplies to Indian allies, principally the Mingo, Shawnee, and Delaware, and urged them to escalate their attacks on American settlements. In response to a series of raids during the winter of 1781–1782, Colonel David Williamson mounted a militia expedition. In March 1782 he launched a surprise attack on Gnadenhutten, a village of about a hundred Delaware, converts to Moravian Christianity. Williamson's men killed nearly all of the inhabitants, many of them old men, women, and children, and destroyed the village. Authorities in Virginia and Pennsylvania denounced the attack, but Ohio Valley Indians stepped up their raids. Crawford was elected to command a retaliatory strike against the Sandusky River Indian villages. His expedition comprised approximately 500 Virginia and Pennsylvania volunteers, among whom were Williamson and other veterans of the Gnadenhutten massacre. Anticipating a perilous campaign, Crawford made out his will on 16 May 1782, before departing. On 4 June his force engaged the Indians, but faced with a reinforced enemy the next day, he ordered a retreat after nightfall. During the withdrawal Crawford became separated from his command and with several other men was captured by Delawares. Nearly all were killed; William Crawford was burned with black powder and coals, beaten, and scalped before his death on 11 June 1782. Two prisoners escaped. Their account of Crawford's gruesome torture and death appeared the next year in a pamphlet entitled *Narratives of a Late*

Expedition Against the Indians with an Account of the Barbarous Execution of Col. Crawford. Reprinted several times, the survivors' tale conferred on Crawford a lasting distinction in the chronicles of border warfare.

Biographies in Draper MSS 3D87–94, with dates and places of birth and death, and James H. Anderson, "Colonel William Crawford," *Ohio Archæological and Historical Publications* 6 (1898): 1–34 (frontispiece por.); C. W. Butterfield, ed., *The Washington-Crawford Letters. Being the Correspondence Between George Washington and William Crawford, from 1767 to 1781, Concerning Western Lands* (1877); Butterfield, *Washington-Irvine Correspondence . . .* (1882); numerous references in *Washington Diaries* and *Washington: Colonial Series, Revolutionary War Series*, and *Confederation Series*; Frederick Co. Order Book, 7:8; *Revolutionary Virginia*, 3:137, 5:392; Francis B. Heitman, ed., *Historical Register of Officers of the Continental Army during the War of the Revolution*, rev. ed. (1914), 177; Hugh Henry Brackenridge, ed., *Narratives of a Late Expedition Against the Indians with an Account of the Barbarous Execution of Col. Crawford; and the Wonderful Escape of Dr. Knight and John Slover from Captivity in 1782* (1783), esp. 9–13; Butterfield, *An Historical Account of the Expedition against Sandusky Under Col. William Crawford in 1782* (1873); Grace U. Emahiser, *From River Clyde to Tymochtee and Col. William Crawford* (1969); transcription of will, Acc. 25781, LVA.

LEONARD J. SADOSKY

CREED, Robert Andy Kyle (20 September 1912–26 November 1982), musician and instrument maker, was born in Round Peak, Surry County, North Carolina, and was the son of Isaac Qualey Stanfield Creed, a farmer, and Arthusa Isabell Lowe Creed. Known as Kyle Creed, he grew up in a large family surrounded by music, especially British and indigenous American ballads, fiddle dance-tunes, and hymns. His father taught him to play the fiddle, and Creed took up the banjo when he was about sixteen. He learned his distinctive way of playing from his uncle John Lowe rather than from Charlie Lowe, who influenced most of the other Round Peak banjo players. While spending a winter in Winchester, Virginia, Creed consolidated his musical style by playing at home with his uncle every night. Creed's melodic, brisk banjo playing followed fiddle melodies note for note; the silences surrounding his notes emphasized their crispness. Late in his life he became an avid fiddler.

By 1930 Creed was farming in Stewarts Creek, Surry County, North Carolina. On 1 July 1932, across the state border in Galax, Virginia, he married Callie Percy Hicks. They had two daughters. During this period Creed belonged to the Round Peak Band, which became renowned for its strong, intricate interaction between Fred Cockerham's fiddle and Creed's banjo. Creed spent the next several decades working around the country as a carpenter and sawmiller, including building Quonset huts in Norfolk during World War II. He settled in the mountains of Virginia early in the 1960s. Creed and his wife ran a country store near Pipers Gap on the Blue Ridge Parkway, not far from Galax. Playing banjo and sometimes fiddle, he reestablished ties with former members of the Round Peak Band and in 1963 formed the Camp Creek Boys, a group that featured Cockerham and Ernest East on fiddles, Verlin Clifton on mandolin, and Paul Sutphin and Ronald Collins on guitars.

For a decade the big-band sound of the Camp Creek Boys gave them the power to compete successfully with bluegrass bands in the days before separate old-time music and bluegrass categories existed. The band and its members won many prizes at the fiddling conventions and bluegrass festivals held in Union Grove, Iredell County, North Carolina, and at the Old Fiddlers Convention in Galax. Enthusiastically received by audiences at national concerts and festivals, Creed and his bandmates gained respect throughout the region and beyond. In 1967 they recorded the *Camp Creek Boys Old-Time String Band* for County Records. The landmark album received national attention and has been credited with reviving interest in the musical traditions of the Blue Ridge Mountains.

Creed was a featured performer at music festivals throughout North Carolina, Virginia, and West Virginia. He appeared at the National Folk Festival and the Smithsonian Institution's Festival of American Folklife and played for albums recorded live in concert at the annual Old Fiddlers Convention. In 1966 he recorded the influential *Clawhammer Banjo* album with Cockerham, George Stoneman, and Wade Ward. Creed's focused and precise clawhammer banjo playing, ringing with harmonics and sometimes referred to as the Round Peak style, influenced a generation of musicians.

In 1972 Creed and Bobby Patterson organized Mountain Records, which during the next decade produced releases for local and international traditional musicians. Creed also recorded several important albums for that label and for Patterson's Heritage Records during the 1970s. With Patterson on guitar, Audine Lineberry on bass, and the renowned fiddler and singer Tommy Jarrell, Creed played banjo on *June Apple* (1972). The album was one of the most significant band recordings from the region and was later reissued as a compact disc with additional cuts. Other recordings with his bandmates and additional performers include *Blue Ridge Style Square Dance Time* (1972), *Virginia Reel* (1973), *Mountain Ballads* (1974), and *Liberty* (1977).

In addition to his accomplished musicianship, Creed also was well-known for his custom-style banjos. After moving to Carroll County, he began making banjos and became one of the finest instrument makers in the Blue Ridge. Fashioning his banjos from local wood (apple for the necks and maple for the pots), Creed combined traditional craftsmanship with more modern details, such as metal parts that he made himself and sometimes engraved pearl nameplates inlaid on the neck. He made fretted and fretless banjos with eleven-inch and twelve-inch pots, with or without tone rings. Most of the fretless banjos had the formica fingerboard so well-suited for sliding and bending notes and for hammering on and pulling off with the left hand. The percussive sound of Creed's instruments and the big bassy sound of the banjo pots proved widely popular with traditional and revival players alike. He filled orders from across the United States as well as Canada, Europe, and Japan.

Creed's banjos were played best in his style—over the fingerboard rather than above the skinhead over the pot—and he configured them with high action that allowed the harmonics to ring easily. Dave Forbes and Mac Traynham were the first builders to embrace Creed's ideas and construction techniques; and Tom Barr, of Galax, completed several banjos that remained unfinished when Creed died. Creed's custom-built instruments continued to influence banjo makers in the twenty-first century. A banjo that he made for Fred Cockerham is in the collection of the Smithsonian Institution's National Museum of American History, in Washington, D.C. Robert Andy Kyle Creed died of cancer in a Galax hospital on 26 November 1982 and was buried in Monta Vista Memory Gardens there.

Full name and birth date in Surry Co., N.C., Delayed Birth Certificate (1953); biography in Marty McGee, *Traditional Musicians of the Central Blue Ridge: Old Time, Early Country, Folk and Bluegrass Label Recording Artists, with Discographies* (2000), 1–3, 53–55 (pors.); BVS Marriage Register, Grayson Co.; field recordings in Archive of Folk Culture, LC, and in Southern Folklife Collection, UNC; Cecelia Conway, *African Banjo Echoes in Appalachia: A Study of Folk Traditions* (1995), 185, 186, 214; Kevin Donleavy, *Strings of Life—Conversations with Old-Time Musicians from Virginia and North Carolina* (2004), 42–44; *Clawhammer Banjo: Volume One*, County Records CO-CD-2716 (2004), recording with brochure notes by Bob Carlin and Charlie Faurot; information provided by Tom Barr (2005); death notice in *Roanoke Times and World-News*, 28 Nov. 1982; obituary in *Galax Gazette*, 1 Dec. 1982.

CECELIA CONWAY

CREIGHTON, Martha Gladys (27 September 1894–19 February 1960), home economist, was born in Rock Hill, South Carolina, and was the daughter of William Samuel Creighton, a farmer, and his second wife, Willie Jane McFadden Creighton. After attending local public schools, she graduated in 1913 from Winthrop College (later Winthrop University), in Rock Hill, with a three-year Normal degree and a teaching certificate. Creighton taught home economics at schools in Prosperity, Newberry County, South Carolina, and Kinston, North Carolina, before entering the Agricultural Extension Service as the first home demonstration agent in Lancaster County, South Carolina. She later served as a home agent in Mecklenburg County, North Carolina, and as the district home demonstration agent for western North Carolina. Creighton received a B.S. and M.A. from Teachers College, Columbia University, in 1930 and 1937, respectively. She pursued further graduate studies at Iowa State College of Agriculture and Mechanic Arts (later Iowa State University). She never married.

After completing her undergraduate studies in 1930, Creighton moved to Richmond, where she joined the staff of the Virginia Department of Education, first as assistant state supervisor

Creighton

of home economics education and in 1934 as state supervisor. Under her direction, the department in 1943 issued a revised curriculum for home economics that tied together the needs of the family with those of the community while addressing topics including childcare, health, housing, and inflation. From 1945 until 1947, when Creighton retired as state supervisor, she helped to develop a home economics curriculum for high schools under Virginia's new twelve-year school system. By the latter year more than 400 public schools in the state offered home economics classes.

Creighton updated Virginia's home economics curriculum as the United States moved from the crises of the Great Depression and World War II into the family-centered lifestyle of the postwar years. During the Depression, she supported policies that allowed the Virginia Department of Education's home economics programs to work cooperatively with the National Youth Administration in providing lunches for impoverished schoolchildren, in teaching girls to use sewing machines for clothing repairs, and in establishing barbershops and showers in schools. Her courses reached out not just to schoolchildren but also to their parents and community residents. In some secondary schools the home economics department worked in conjunction with agricultural programs to train students in the planting of summer and autumn vegetable gardens. By introducing such uncommon varieties as brussels sprouts, cauliflower, celery, and okra, the programs expanded local food supplies. To cope with wartime shortages and postwar inflation, Creighton urged the establishment of classes teaching students to produce and preserve meat, dairy, and agricultural products at home. In the affluent society of the 1950s, Americans worried less about doing without than about creating comfortably relaxed suburban homes to shelter their growing families and to provide safe havens from the accelerating arms race between the United States and the Soviet Union. Embracing a slogan of the Future Homemakers of America, "Better homes for a better nation," Creighton recommended that home economics courses place more emphasis on childcare and home beautification training.

After briefly operating a North Carolina automotive repair business for her dying sister, Creighton in 1949 joined the faculty at Virginia Polytechnic Institute (later Virginia Polytechnic Institute and State University), where she initiated a graduate program to train teachers in home economics education. In December 1952 she was the first Virginian and the second woman elected president of the American Vocational Association. During her one-year term the AVA successfully lobbied to prevent a 25 percent cut in federal funds for vocational education. In 1956 the AVA recognized Creighton's contributions to vocational and home economics education with its Outstanding Service Award. She retired from VPI at the end of September 1959 and became professor emerita.

Martha Gladys Creighton died on 19 February 1960 in a Roanoke hospital and was buried in Laurelwood Cemetery, in Rock Hill, South Carolina. Virginia's home economics teachers honored her by creating a scholarship in her name, and friends solicited funds to establish the Martha Creighton Memorial Library Fund at Virginia Polytechnic Institute for purchasing books on home economics and vocational education.

Biography in Virginia Iota State Organization, Delta Kappa Gamma Society, *Adventures in Teaching: Pioneer Women Educators and Influential Teachers* (1963), 45–47, including por. and variant death date of 20 Feb. 1960 based on newspaper obituaries; published works include Creighton, *A Guide to the Development of the Homemaking Education Program in Virginia Public Schools* (1940), *A Course of Study for Homemaking Education in Virginia Public Schools* (1943), "Education in Family Life," *Virginia Journal of Education* 34 (1941): 310–312, "Homemaking Education in Virginia, 1946–47," ibid. 40 (1946): 182–183, and "Vocational Homemaking Education in Virginia," ibid. 45 (May 1952): 18–19; *Richmond Times-Dispatch*, 6 Dec. 1952 (por.); AVA presidential reports in *American Vocational Journal* 28 (Jan. 1953): 3, and 29 (Jan. 1954): 23–24; *Virginia Vocational Education News* (Feb. 1957), 1, and (Oct. 1959), 1; death date confirmed by BVS; obituaries (all with variant death date of 20 Feb. 1960) in *Roanoke World-News*, 20 Feb. 1960, and *Newport News Daily Press*, *Richmond Times-Dispatch*, and *Roanoke Times*, all 21 Feb. 1960; obituaries (all with death date of 19 Feb. 1960) in *Virginia Journal of Education* 53 (Apr. 1960): 34, *Virginia Vocational Educational News* (Apr. 1960), 1, 3, and *American Vocational Journal* 35 (Apr. 1960): 36.

MARY CARROLL JOHANSEN

CRENSHAW, Fanny Graves (17 January 1890–8 October 1984), educator and athletic director, was born in Richmond and was the daughter of Spottswood Dabney Crenshaw, a Richmond and Louisa County entrepreneur, and Anne Warfield Clay Crenshaw, a woman suffrage activist. She attended Virginia Randolph Ellett's school (later Saint Catherine's School) and in 1908 entered Bryn Mawr College to study economics, history, and politics. An outstanding athlete, she was a member of the varsity field hockey team and also fenced, swam, and played basketball, tennis, and water polo. Captain of the indoor track team for three years, Crenshaw set women's world records in four events during her senior year. She received a B.A. in 1912 and returned to Virginia Randolph Ellett's school, where she taught history and mathematics until 1922. During the summers of 1914 and 1915 she pursued graduate studies in physical education at Columbia University. She did not marry.

In 1914, May Lansfield Keller, dean of the newly established Westhampton College, a women's institution coordinate with Richmond College (later the University of Richmond), hired Crenshaw as the school's first faculty member to teach physical education, which she did three afternoons each week. Because it was not considered suitable for a young, unmarried woman to travel alone on the streetcar out to the college's countryside location, Crenshaw took a younger brother along as her chaperon. Westhampton College had no athletic facilities, and the equipment consisted of a single basketball. From such unpromising beginnings Crenshaw, who became director of physical education in 1921, built a strong program.

In a career that spanned four decades Crenshaw, affectionately called "Fanny G." on campus, developed enthusiastic and winning varsity teams in tennis and track. She coached the varsity basketball team from 1919 to 1955, with undefeated seasons in 1949–1950, 1952–1953, and 1953–1954. She encouraged intramural sports, added archery and other individual sports to the physical education curriculum, and taught her students swimming and life-saving techniques in the Westhampton Lake. Instrumental in establishing physical education as a major in 1933, Crenshaw was also a key figure in promoting the construction of a gymnasium in 1936 to provide adequate accommodations for the school's growing physical education program.

Crenshaw was most noted for her contributions to field hockey, one of the few women's team sports early in the twentieth century. Introduced to the sport at Bryn Mawr by the Englishwoman Constance M. K. Applebee, her coach who had started women's field hockey in the United States, Crenshaw organized a team at Westhampton College in 1915. One of the first varsity field hockey teams in the state, it was scheduled to meet the Sweet Briar College team in December 1919 in one of the earliest women's intercollegiate athletic competitions in Virginia, but a sudden snowstorm forced postponement of the game until the following year. Crenshaw helped organize the United States Field Hockey Association in 1921 and was elected second vice president for the 1922–1923 term. She later served as president of the Virginia Field Hockey Association, as a national judge and umpire for the sport, and in 1954 as a member of the national selection committee for the United States field hockey team.

Crenshaw was not only a gifted athlete but also a skillful, dedicated teacher and mentor whose influence on students extended beyond the playing fields and courts. She advocated equal opportunities for women in collegiate sports, believed that women should be knowledgeable and independent in financial affairs, and in September 1920 was among the first Richmond women to register to vote. Interested in broadening her own knowledge, she traveled extensively, including a six-month trip to Egypt and Europe in 1952.

After retiring in 1955 Crenshaw served as a national judge for the Richmond Board of Women's Basketball Officials and as southeast chair of the United States Field Hockey Association, and she officiated at basketball and hockey games. At age seventy-five she earned a Red Cross award for swimming fifty miles during three-times-a-week stints in the Westhampton College pool, which in 1963 had been named for her. During the 1975–1976 academic year Constance Applebee established a Westhampton scholarship in her honor. A road and a playing field on the University of Richmond campus bear her name. In 1979 Crenshaw was the first woman inducted into the college's Athletic Hall of Fame, and in 1988 the Virginia Sports Hall of Fame inducted her as well.

Phlebitis in Crenshaw's last years and blood poisoning, probably caused by diabetes, necessitated the amputation of one leg and confined her to a wheelchair, and at the end of her life she suffered from senile dementia. Fanny Graves Crenshaw, the last surviving original Westhampton College faculty member, died in a Richmond retirement home on 8 October 1984 and was buried in Hollywood Cemetery.

Autobiographical information, including birth date, on University of Richmond Alumni-ae Data Blank, Mar. 1955, VBHS; Crenshaw faculty files, including clippings, "Historical Sketch of Physical Education at Westhampton College, 1914–1939" (undated typescript probably by Crenshaw), and *Women of Westhampton: A Brief Description of Their Portraits* (1989), VBHS; Woodford B. Hackley, *Faces on the Wall: Brief Sketches of the Men and Women Whose Portraits and Busts Were on the Campus of the University of Richmond in 1955* (1972), 17–18; Claire Millhiser Rosenbaum, *A Gem of a College: The History of Westhampton College, 1914–1989* (1989), 29, 37, 43, 55; Dorothy Wagener, "She Could Outrun Us All: A Tribute to Fanny Crenshaw," *University of Richmond Magazine* 47 (winter/spring 1985): 6–7 (pors.); information provided by Jane Thorpe Stockman and niece Sally Clay Crenshaw Witt (2003); *University of Richmond Collegian*, 1 Dec. 1977; *Richmond News Leader*, 24 Mar. 1988; obituaries in *Richmond News Leader* and *Richmond Times-Dispatch*, both 9 Oct. 1984, and *University of Richmond Collegian*, 11 Oct. 1984 (1954 por. by Marcia Silvette).

ELISABETH E. WRAY

CRENSHAW, John Bacon (2 May 1820–10 May 1889), Quaker leader, was born in Henrico County and was the son of Nathaniel Chapman Crenshaw, a wealthy planter who joined the Society of Friends and freed his slaves, and Deborah Darby Crew Crenshaw. His mother died shortly after his birth, and he was raised in the Quaker faith by a maternal aunt and his father. The family later moved to Shrubbery Hill in Hanover County, where his father became a leader of the local Cedar Creek Monthly Meeting. Crenshaw attended Richmond area schools before matriculating in 1837 at the Haverford School (later Haverford College), a Quaker insti-

tution in Pennsylvania. He studied engineering but after one year returned to Henrico County, where he operated a gristmill for about five years and served as a representative, or clerk, for the Cedar Creek Monthly Meeting.

On 12 September 1844 Crenshaw married Rachel Hoge, of Loudoun County. Of their four sons and four daughters, two sons and three daughters survived childhood. Crenshaw settled in the Goose Creek area of Loudoun County, where he assumed control of a portion of the Hoge family's land. After farming for two years, he returned to live in the Henrico County home where he had been born. Engaging in such business enterprises as farming, running a dairy, and investing in roads that connected Richmond with Hanover and Henrico Counties, Crenshaw had accumulated $28,000 in real estate by 1850. He reported to the census taker in 1860 real estate valued at $45,000 and personal property valued at $16,000. In May 1854 Crenshaw was recommended to lead the Cedar Creek Monthly Meeting. He frequently visited other southern and western meetings and Quaker homes, particularly in North Carolina. His wife died on 20 November 1858, and on 5 June 1860 Crenshaw married Judith Ann Willitts, a Philadelphia native. Of their three daughters and three sons, only two daughters survived childhood.

As the leading Quaker in Richmond, Crenshaw became a pivotal figure during the Civil War. Quakers' abolitionist and pacifist beliefs made them in many respects politically and culturally alien to the new Confederacy. Crenshaw labored to ensure that the rights of religious dissenters received a fair hearing from Confederate military and political authorities. With other leading Quakers, including his father, Crenshaw petitioned the government to respect the denomination's pacifism. Their lobbying succeeded in gaining exemptions for religious dissenters, provided they paid a $500 tax and proved that they had been members of their denominations before October 1862.

The act was unevenly honored, however, so Crenshaw developed cordial relations with War Department officials, particularly Assistant Secretary of War John A. Campbell, and facilitated pleas for relief from religious dissenters throughout Virginia and North Carolina who had been conscripted into Confederate military service. In addition to his efforts on behalf of Quakers, Crenshaw provided aid and comfort to captured Union troops held in Richmond and to wounded Confederate soldiers. His home became temporary headquarters for Confederate officers, and he provided food and a place for convalescence. Beginning in the autumn of 1864 Crenshaw edited and published the *Southern Friend: A Religious, Literary and Agricultural Journal*, a newspaper that provided religious solace and practical advice, including information on exemption laws, for Quakers deprived of northern Society of Friends publications.

After the war Crenshaw expanded his political influence. As symbolized by his leadership of efforts to secure the freedom of Campbell in June 1865, he chose a conciliatory path. Crenshaw embraced the Republican Party but acted with its conservative wing. Even after he placed second in a three-candidate field and lost his bid for an at-large seat representing Hanover and Henrico Counties in the Convention of 1867–1868, he continued to seek middle ground. He worked to provide better opportunities for African Americans while rejecting efforts to negate the political authority of non-Radical whites. Some accounts erroneously name Crenshaw as a member of the Committee of Nine, a group of centrist leaders who proposed accomplishing Virginia's readmission to the Union by holding separate votes on ratification of the new state constitution and on qualification clauses that would have disfranchised most former Confederates. Although not a member of this committee, he assumed a conspicuous role throughout 1869 in convincing Washington politicians to accept the compromise that brought an end to Reconstruction in Virginia. That year Crenshaw supported the nomination of the conservative Republican state ticket led by Gilbert Carlton Walker, whose election victory ousted Radicals from power.

Crenshaw's political alignments afforded him a number of opportunities. Military authorities appointed him engineer of Richmond in 1869, and later that year he won election to the House of Delegates for a two-year term representing Henrico County and the city of Richmond. He served on the Committee on Resolutions. As chair of the Committee on Asylums and Prisons, Crenshaw in March 1870 introduced a resolution and helped secure passage of a bill establishing the Central Lunatic Asylum (later Central State Hospital), in Petersburg, to meet the needs of the state's African Americans.

Crenshaw continued to serve as minister of the Cedar Creek Monthly Meeting (after 1875 the Richmond Monthly Meeting), to which he added many newly converted members, and he also helped found the Friends' Asylum for Colored Orphans, a Richmond orphanage and educational institution incorporated in March 1872 with Crenshaw as a trustee. Balancing his leadership role within the Richmond area's Quaker community with his business activities, he became president of the Richmond and Henrico Railroad, Turnpike, and Graded Road Company in 1871.

Although Crenshaw possessed more than $72,000 in real estate and more than $9,000 in personal property in 1870, financial reversals forced him to sell his Henrico County estate in 1879. He moved his family closer to Richmond, where he became a merchant specializing in agricultural equipment and also developed a plowshare with a slip point. In the last years of his life he campaigned against the death penalty and continued to preach at Quaker meetings. John Bacon Crenshaw died on 10 May 1889 from the effects of a stroke and was buried at Shrubbery Hill, his father's former estate in Hanover County.

Biography by daughter Margaret E. Crenshaw in Society of Friends, *Quaker Biographies: Brief Biographical Sketches Concerning Certain Members of the Religious Society of Friends*, 2d ser., 3 [1926]: 165–208, with birth date on 167, second marriage date on 173, and pors. facing 165 and 173; Loudoun Co. Marriage Record (1844); Society of Friends, Richmond Monthly Meeting Record Books, Acc. 23607, 23608, LVA; correspondence in John Bacon Crenshaw Papers, Guilford College, Greensboro, N.C., and War Department Collection of Confederate Records, RG 109, NARA; diary extracts in Fernando G. Cartland, *Southern Heroes or The Friends in War Time* (1895), 345–362; Edward Needles Wright, *Conscientious Objectors in the Civil War* (1931); Election Records, no. 427, RG 13, LVA; *Richmond Daily Dispatch*, 3, 5 Oct. 1880; obituaries in *Richmond State*, 10 May 1889, and *Richmond Daily Times* and *Richmond Dispatch*, both 11 May 1889.

WILLIAM BLAND WHITLEY

CRENSHAW, Lewis Dabney (26 November 1817–27 December 1875), businessman, was born in Lynchburg and was the son of Spotswood Dabney Crenshaw and Winifred Graves Crenshaw. His father, a carpenter and real estate speculator, suffered a serious financial reversal during the panic of 1819 and relocated the family to Richmond, where he worked to pay off his Lynchburg debts and eventually prospered as a hotel owner and real estate investor. Lewis Crenshaw attended a primary school in Orange County, where his mother's family lived, but he struggled throughout his youth with a stutter. At various times he attended a Philadelphia school that specialized in overcoming speech impediments. His efforts had likely succeeded by the end of the 1830s. In Richmond on 26 November 1840 he married Ann Abigail Bosher. They had six daughters, one of whom died young, and two sons.

Having studied bookkeeping early in the 1830s and worked as his father's assistant, Crenshaw had already immersed himself in the Richmond business world. In the 1840s he, along with his father and brothers, organized a commission merchandising and wholesale grocery company. Taking advantage of trade between Richmond and Lynchburg along the James River and Kanawha Canal, Crenshaw and Company became a profitable enterprise. Richmond was experiencing rapid economic growth and industrialization, and its flour mills emerged as one of the most important aspects of the antebellum boom. By partnering with David Currie, a local shipping agent, the Crenshaws acquired a fleet of clipper ships that carried Richmond flour to ports in South America and California and returned with Brazilian coffee and Peruvian guano. The leaders of the business were Crenshaw and his younger brother William Graves Crenshaw, who later served as a Confederate artillery officer and who after the Civil War formed several profitable industrial enterprises.

In 1853 Lewis Crenshaw left the family company and with a partner built his own flour mill. Crenshaw and Fisher added to Richmond's reputation as a leading producer of flour, but the business was dwarfed by its neighbors, the Gallego and Haxall mills. In 1858 Crenshaw merged his milling operation with the Haxall operation to form Haxall, Crenshaw, and Company. He transformed the Crenshaw and Fisher mill into a textile factory and incorporated it in 1860 as the Crenshaw Woolen Company, with himself as president. In addition to his industrial enterprises, Crenshaw built the Spotswood Hotel, which until it burned in 1870 was one of the city's most prestigious establishments. In 1860 he reported to the census enumerator a fortune of more than half a million dollars.

Crenshaw did not serve the Confederacy in any formal capacity, but his loyalty to the South was never in question. In 1861 he sold the John Brockenbrough house, where he had lived for four years, to the city to serve as the official residence of the Confederate president. Crenshaw advertised his woolen factory as a Southern alternative to Northern manufacturers, and it was a main supplier of cloth for Confederate military purposes until it burned in 1863. His mills contracted with the Confederate Commissary Department to supply flour and breadstuffs. Despite the damage that the war effort inflicted on Richmond's flour industry, Crenshaw retained much of his wealth. The Haxall-Crenshaw mills survived the fire that swept through Richmond's business district in April 1865, and the international nature of the family's business had allowed them to deposit their money in London banks. He received a presidential pardon on 19 June 1865, but he had already successfully negotiated with military authorities in Richmond to allow the resumption of his mills' operations.

Other than a short tenure as a trustee of Hampden-Sydney College, Crenshaw focused on his commercial ventures. Still, his devotion to Richmond's economic well-being often placed him at the center of the city's civic life, particularly after the Civil War. He helped rebuild the devastated business district and was among the businessmen who in 1867 called for the organization of a chamber of commerce. At the chamber's first meeting Crenshaw became one of its directors. Early in the 1870s he served as president of the Richmond Corn and Flour Exchange, which the chamber had instituted to regulate the grain trade in the city. When an economic panic threatened the solvency of Richmond's financial institutions in 1873, Crenshaw presided over a public meeting at the exchange that helped avert a run on the city's banks. The following year his health began to fail. Lewis Dabney Crenshaw died of liver disease at his home on 27 December 1875 and was buried in Hollywood Cemetery.

Crenshaw family Bible records (1757–1927), with birth, marriage, and death dates, Crenshaw Family Papers (1807–1977), and signed presidential pardon, all VHS; Crenshaw Family Genealogical Notes, LVA; *Acts of Assembly*, 1859–1860 sess., 624; *Richmond Enquirer*, 27 Nov. 1840; *Richmond Daily Dispatch*, 20 Jan. 1859, 25 Feb. 1861, 9 Dec. 1865, 10 Oct. 1867, 25 Sept. 1873; Presidential Pardons; BVS Death Register, Richmond City; obituary in *Richmond Daily Dispatch*, 28 Dec. 1875.

WILLIAM BLAND WHITLEY

CRENSHAW, Spottswood Dabney (15 August 1854–5 February 1940), business executive, was born in Richmond and was the son of Fanny Elizabeth H. Graves Crenshaw and William Graves Crenshaw. His father and his uncle Lewis Dabney Crenshaw were prominent Richmond merchants and industrialists. Following his father's appointment late in 1862 as a special agent to procure Confederate supplies, the family moved to England, where Crenshaw attended schools in Rugby and Liverpool. After returning to the United States, he matriculated at Hanover Academy and from 1873 to 1876 studied languages, mathematics, and agricultural and industrial chemistry at the University of Virginia.

Late in the 1870s S. Dabney Crenshaw, as he usually gave his name, moved to Elizabeth, New Jersey, and joined his father and brother in their fertilizer business operating near New York City. He was founding secretary and treasurer of the family's Virginia Chemical Company, incorporated in 1880, and founding secretary of its Atlantic and Virginia Fertilizing Company, chartered in Virginia in January 1881. The importance of sulfuric acid in manufacturing fertilizers prompted the Crenshaws to investigate using pyrites instead of brimstone in the chemical process to create the acid. After his namesake son observed the method in England and tested ore from a Louisa County mine, William G. Crenshaw acquired and organized the Sulphur Mines Company of Virginia in 1882 to supply pyrites for the production of sulfuric acid. S. Dabney Crenshaw was president of the Louisa-based company (after 1900 reorganized as the Sulphur Mining and Railroad Company) from 1898 until 1937. One of the earliest such enterprises in the United States, the family business expanded rapidly and added Atlantic and Virginia Fertilizing Company factories in Baltimore, Henrico County, and New York.

Early in the 1880s Crenshaw returned to Richmond, and by 1891 he had become president of the Atlantic and Virginia Fertilizing Company. In 1895 he joined a group of other industrialists, led by Samuel Tate Morgan and Samuel Winfield Travers, who sought to modernize their factories and combine their output of fertilizers, acids, and related chemical products in order to undercut competitors' prices. The group consolidated eight manufacturing operations in Norfolk, Petersburg, Richmond, and Durham, North Carolina, as the Virginia-Carolina Chemical Company, incorporated in New Jersey on 12 September of that year. Crenshaw served as company secretary until 1912, when he also became a vice president, and remained in both positions until 1926. He was an aggressive organizer. Working to secure a supply of raw materials that would make the company self-sufficient, he acquired sulfur and phosphate mines throughout the Southeast and as far away as Mexico. Crenshaw also encouraged V-C Chemical to expand into the production of cottonseed oil by purchasing the Interstate Cotton Oil Company in 1900 and by acquiring control of the Southern Cotton Oil Company and Wesson Process Company, both in 1901. By 1915 the Virginia-Carolina Chemical Company encompassed 135 plants, had sales offices from New York to Florida, and through its numerous subsidiaries largely controlled the market in the southeastern region. By early in the 1920s it and its main competitor produced one-third of the nation's fertilizer. In 1924 industrywide financial difficulties forced the company into receivership, from which it emerged in 1926 as the Virginia-Carolina Chemical Corporation. From 1920 to 1933 Crenshaw served as president of one of its Richmond subsidiaries, the Phosphate Products Corporation.

Crenshaw sat on the board of directors of the First and Merchants National Bank in Richmond beginning in 1900. A promoter of economic development in Louisa County as well, he organized the Bank of Louisa, of which he was president, in 1898 and in that same year was instrumental in establishing the Louisa Telephone Company, of which he was vice president. Crenshaw held a seat on the Richmond Chamber of Commerce, was a member of the Virginia Historical Society, and from January 1902 to January 1904 served as president of the Commonwealth Club, of Richmond.

On 6 November 1886 in Lexington, Kentucky, Crenshaw married Anne Warfield Clay, daughter of Cassius Marcellus Clay, a prominent abolitionist and former minister to Russia, and granddaughter of Green Clay, a member of the Virginia Convention of 1788. Their two sons and two daughters included Fanny Graves Crenshaw, longtime athletic director at Westhampton College (later part of the University of Richmond). Anne Crenshaw, whose sister Laura Clay helped found the Kentucky Equal Rights Association in 1888, hosted the founding meeting of the Equal Suffrage League of Virginia in November 1909. Spottswood Dabney Crenshaw retired from most of his businesses in 1935 and died in a Staunton hospital on 5 February 1940 following a fall that fractured his hip. He was buried in Hollywood Cemetery, in Richmond.

Biographies in Tyler, *Men of Mark*, 5:75–76 (por.), and Paul Brandon Barringer, James Mercer Garnett, and Rosewell Page, eds., *University of Virginia: Its History, Influence, Equipment and Characteristics* (1904), 2:239–240; birth date in L. T. Christian Funeral Home Records, Acc. 34483, LVA, and *NCAB*, 36:203–204 (por.); variant birth date of 20 Aug. 1854 in BVS Birth Register, Richmond City; Crenshaw Family Papers (1807–1977), VHS; Fayette Co., Ky., Marriage Records, Kentucky Department for Libraries and Archives, Frankfort; Virginia-Carolina Chemical Corporation, *In Partnership with the Soil* (1955); William Kiblinger, "The Crenshaw Sulphur Mines, 1871–1920," *Louisa County Historical Magazine* 20 (spring 1989): 46–48; obituaries in *New York Times*, *Richmond News Leader*, and *Richmond Times-Dispatch*, all 6 Feb. 1940.

GREGORY HARKCOM STONER

CRENSHAW, William Graves (7 July 1824–24 May 1897), Confederate artillery officer and industrialist, was born in Orange County and was the son of Spotswood Dabney Crenshaw and Winifred Graves Crenshaw. His elder brother Lewis Dabney Crenshaw became one of the leading flour-millers in Richmond. On 25 May 1847 Crenshaw married a second cousin, Fanny Elizabeth H. Graves, in Orange County. Her father gave the couple an Orange County estate, later known as Hawfield, which contained about 500 acres and where they spent summers and holidays. Their four daughters and two sons included Spottswood Dabney Crenshaw, a Richmond business executive. In the 1860 census Crenshaw reported his wealth at $100,000 in real estate and $80,000 in personal property, including thirty slaves at Hawfield, which he had enlarged to about 1,700 acres of land valued at more than $50,000.

During the 1840s Crenshaw joined his father and brothers in establishing Crenshaw and Company, a commission merchant and grocer business. By 1860 he was in charge of the company, which had developed into an important flour distribution business that shipped goods to South American ports and returned with Brazilian coffee and Peruvian guano.

In the winter of 1861–1862 Crenshaw joined several other Richmond businessmen in raising a company of light artillery for Confederate service. As the chief organizer and financier of the battery, he paid $50 enlistment bounties and provided gray uniforms made in his family's woolen factories. Consequently the unit took the name Crenshaw's Artillery. On 14 March 1862 Crenshaw was commissioned a captain in the Confederate army, and in mid-April the battery, comprising about 140 men, received four cannons, two howitzers, forty horses, and new Confederate uniforms. Assigned to Major General Ambrose Powell Hill's division, Crenshaw's Artillery fought at Gaines's Mill in June 1862 and at Sharpsburg (Antietam) in September.

Crenshaw's business contacts and mercantile experience led the Confederate government to send him in December 1862 on a mission to England, where he procured military supplies and acquired a fleet of ships, with vessels sometimes bearing the names of his family members, to run the Union blockade into Southern ports. The enterprise operated under the auspices of Crenshaw and Company, with his brother James

R. Crenshaw handling transactions from an office in Charleston, South Carolina. The Crenshaws received a commission on the supplies they shipped from England and also on the cotton that they transported on the return trip. Because he was acting as a commercial agent for the Confederate government and receiving payment for his services, Crenshaw resigned his military commission on 15 April 1863. Crenshaw's Battery, however, retained his name even without him and participated in engagements at Chancellorsville, Gettysburg, the Wilderness, and Cold Harbor.

Crenshaw had moved his family to England by the summer of 1864 and remained there for several years after the end of the Civil War. He returned to Virginia several times to manage personal and professional affairs, however. On 13 July 1865 President Andrew Johnson granted him a pardon, to take effect when Crenshaw took the oath of allegiance, which he did on 19 August.

After his permanent return to the United States late in the 1860s, Crenshaw lived in New York, where he was one of the organizers and charter members of the New York Cotton Exchange. By April 1876 he had moved to Elizabeth, New Jersey, and at that time became a director of the Haxall Crenshaw Company. In August of that year he helped form and became vice president of the Crenshaw Warehouse Company, which leased and purchased warehouses for the storage and inspection of tobacco and other goods. In 1880 Crenshaw incorporated the Virginia Chemical Company for the purpose of manufacturing and selling fertilizers, with himself as president and his son S. Dabney Crenshaw as secretary and treasurer. Several years earlier he had established a company to mine and manufacture fertilizer. This enterprise he incorporated in January 1881 as the Atlantic and Virginia Fertilizing Company with an initial capital stock of $200,000 and with himself as president and his sons as vice president, treasurer, and secretary. Atlantic and Virginia Fertilizing operated factories in Henrico County, Virginia, in Baltimore, Maryland, and on Long Island, New York. In 1895 it merged with several other Virginia and North Carolina businesses to form the Virginia-Carolina Chemical Company, with S. Dabney Crenshaw as secretary.

Crenshaw became interested in the commercial manufacture of sulfuric acid, which was produced in the United States from brimstone but in Europe from pyrites. He acquired land in Louisa County that contained pyrite deposits, mined the ore, and sent it to England to ascertain if sulfuric acid could be profitably produced. In April 1882 Crenshaw helped found and became vice president of the Sulphur Mines Company of Virginia, which mined coal, iron, lead, gold, and pyrites for use in manufacturing. One of the earliest businesses in the country to make sulfuric acid from pyrites, it revolutionized mineral production in the United States. By the mid-1890s the company was reportedly the largest manufacturer of pyrites in the country and also one of the largest producers of sulfuric acid.

Early in the 1880s Crenshaw and his wife moved back to Orange County, from which he continued to run his many businesses. At Hawfield, which he eventually enlarged to more than 3,000 acres of land, he tested his fertilizers and publicized his increased production of wheat. Crenshaw's wife died of pneumonia on 27 October 1896. His health had also been failing, exacerbated by a fall that summer in which he fractured his hip. Despite seeking treatment in Richmond, he began to suffer paralysis. William Graves Crenshaw died at Hawfield on 24 May 1897. Following a funeral at the Emmanuel Episcopal Church in Rapidan, Culpeper County, his body was transported to Richmond and buried in Hollywood Cemetery.

Birth and marriage dates in Crenshaw family Bible records (1757–1927), VHS; Orange Co. Marriage Register; Crenshaw Family Papers (1807–1977), including family history compiled by son William G. Crenshaw Jr., and signed presidential pardon, both VHS; *Richmond Whig and Public Advertiser*, 8 June 1847; *Richmond Daily Dispatch*, 18 Feb. 1862; Compiled Service Records; military correspondence in William Graves Crenshaw Papers, Military Records Collection, LVA; William G. Crenshaw III (grandson), comp., "Captain William G. Crenshaw, C.S.A.: The War Years" (1960), in Crenshaw Family Genealogical Notes, LVA; *OR*, 1st ser., vol. 11, pt. 2, 902–904, 4th ser., 2:244–245, 478–482, 535–543, 587–590, 623–630; Peter S. Carmichael, *The Purcell, Crenshaw and Letcher Artillery* (1990), 58–107, 108 (por.), 113; SCC Charter Book, 3:61–64, 94–97, 471–474,

Crenshaw

4:37–40, 292–295; obituaries in *Richmond State* and *Richmond Times*, both 25 May 1897, *Richmond Dispatch*, 25 (por.), 26 May 1897, and *Washington Post*, 25, 27 May 1897.

JOHN G. DEAL

CRESAP, Charles James Pindall (17 August 1836–21 October 1886), member of the third session of the Convention of 1861, was born in Preston County and was the son of Gustavus Cresap, an attorney, and Ruhama Pindall Cresap. Admitted to the bar in 1857, he practiced law with his father in the town of Kingwood. Incomplete evidence suggests that Cresap owned no slaves, but in the spring of 1861 his sympathies clearly lay with the secessionists. He traveled to Richmond and on 17 May received a commission as a second lieutenant in the Provisional Army of Virginia. Cresap took part in the engagements at Laurel Hill in July, Cheat Mountain in September, and Greenbrier River early in October.

Even though Cresap's commission expired at the beginning of September, he remained in the field and was at Camp Bartow, in Pocahontas County, on 24 October 1861 when a special election was held to replace the western delegates who had been expelled from the secession convention in June. He and the three other Preston County men in camp elected Robert Edwin Cowan, one of the county's veteran legislators (and Cresap's brother-in-law) to one of the seats, and the other three men (one of whom was his younger brother) elected Cresap. Cowan and Cresap took their seats in Richmond on 20 November 1861, about two weeks before the convention's final adjournment, and both signed the Ordinance of Secession that the convention had adopted in April.

While in Richmond, Cresap unsuccessfully lobbied for a commission in the Confederate army, and in the spring of 1862 he enlisted as a private in the 25th Regiment Virginia Infantry. A variety of afflictions confined him to hospitals several times and offered him little chance to distinguish himself. On 28 May 1863 Cresap and Cowan won election to the Virginia House of Delegates with twelve and sixteen votes, respectively, from county soldiers in several military camps and from refugees in Richmond. Cresap resigned from the army during the sum-

mer and practiced law in Randolph County until the General Assembly convened. He served in the sessions that met in September and October 1863 and from December 1863 through 10 March 1864 and was appointed to the Committee of Propositions and Grievances and to the Joint Committee to Examine the Second Auditor's Office. In November 1863 he successfully petitioned the Confederate president for permission to recruit a company of soldiers in his home region, but he was unable to enlist enough men.

Returning to Richmond early in January 1865, a month after the assembly reconvened, Cresap resumed his seat in the House of Delegates. As the desperate military situation provoked debates about using slaves or free African Americans in the Confederate army, he made one last attempt to contribute to the cause. On 15 March 1865 Cresap asked Jefferson Davis for a commission "above the rank of Captain, to Command Colored troops." Neither the president nor the secretary of war left any record of his response to the request.

After the Civil War, Cresap practiced law in Beverly, in Randolph County, West Virginia. On 25 January 1870 he married a widow, Agnes Crawford. They appear to have had no children. A Democrat, he served a single term in the West Virginia House of Delegates from the district comprising Randolph and Tucker Counties in 1881 and did not seek reelection the next year. Charles James Pindall Cresap died at his home in Beverly on 21 October 1886 and was buried in Maplewood Cemetery, in Kingwood, West Virginia.

S. T. Wiley, *History of Preston County (West Virginia)* (1882), 324; J. R. Cole, *A History of Preston County, West Virginia* (1914), 658–659; Joseph Ord Cresap and Bernarr Cresap, comps., *The History of the Cresaps* (1937), 310; Census, Preston Co., 1860, Randolph Co., W.Va., 1870, 1880; James I. Robertson Jr., ed., *Proceedings of the Advisory Council of the State of Virginia, April 21–June 19, 1861* (1977), 93; Election Records, Papers of the Convention of 1861, RG 93, LVA; Reese, *Journals and Papers of 1861 Convention*, vol. 1, Journal, 334, 336; Election Records, no. 440, RG 13, LVA; Compiled Service Records, including Cresap's letters to Jefferson Davis dated 20 Nov. 1863 and 15 Mar. 1865 (quotation); Richard L. Armstrong, *25th Virginia Infantry and 9th Battalion, Virginia Infantry* (1990), 148; Janice Cale Sisler, *In Remembrance: Tombstone Readings of Preston County,*

West Virginia (1995–), 1:76 (variant birth date of 17 Aug. 1835 and incorrect death date of 2 Oct. 1886); obituaries in *Wheeling Register*, 24 Oct. 1886, and *Wheeling Intelligencer*, 27 Oct. 1886 (with birth, marriage, and death dates).

BRENT TARTER

CREWES, James (1622 or 1623–26 January 1677), participant in Bacon's Rebellion, was born in England and was the brother of Edward Crewes and Francis Crewes, residents of London. The place or places of their births and names of their parents are not known. James Crewes consistently signed his name in that fashion, but contemporaries sometimes spelled the surname without the second *e*. While in London on 1 December 1652, Crewes signed a deposition concerning the death of an acquaintance in Virginia the previous year. At that time Crewes described himself as a twenty-nine-year-old merchant. Little else is known about his life in England other than that he was educated; he later owned a Latin Bible, which suggests he knew that language.

The 1652 deposition indicates that Crewes had been in Virginia in 1651, and the appearance of his name on headright lists suggests that in his capacity as a merchant he may have made four or more trips to Virginia. Like many other merchants, he eventually settled in the colony, certainly not later than 1655. He acquired 541 acres of land on Turkey Island in Henrico County. The house that he owned there twenty years later was substantial, with four fireplaces, brick chimneys, and a separate kitchen. As part of his continued commercial interests, Crewes also kept a store, engaged in the fur trade, and dealt with business associates back in England. By 1670 he was a captain of militia.

Charles City County Court records beginning in December 1655 contain references to Crewes acting as a merchant, witness, jury member, trustee, and executor of estates. During the winter of 1655–1656 one of the disputes in which he was involved led to blows and a stabbing that was not fatal. Crewes acquired a few servants, including two or more of African descent, and he obtained permission to keep an Indian servant. He probably married Margaret Llewellin, who witnessed a will as Margaret Crewes on 1 May 1662, but when Crewes wrote his own will in 1676, he had no living wife or children. He bequeathed property to relatives of Giles Carter, but whether he was related to Carter by marriage or otherwise is not certain.

During the winter of 1675–1676, Crewes, William Byrd (ca. 1652–1704), and a few other residents of Henrico County persuaded their near neighbor Nathaniel Bacon (1647–1676) to take the lead in organizing local men to defend the colony against anticipated Indian attacks. In the spring, after Bacon had attacked and defeated some Indians and Governor Sir William Berkeley had rebuked him and removed him from his seat on the Council, Crewes and Bacon won election to the House of Burgesses from Henrico County. On 26 May 1676, a week before the General Assembly met, Crewes told Berkeley that Bacon wished to appeal to the Crown the governor's condemnations of his actions. When the assembly met, Bacon made repeated demands that he be commissioned a general to wage war on the Indians, and the colony then erupted into civil war. Crewes took the side of Bacon against the governor. In Berkeley's colorful phrase, Crewes acted throughout as "Bacons Parasite, and Trumpett that continually went about the Country extollinge all Bacons actions & Justifyinge the Rebellion."

The actions of Crewes are poorly documented, but he took the precaution of writing his will on 23 July. Eleven days later, on 3 August 1676, when Bacon issued one of his proclamations at Middle Plantation, Crewes signed the document. He was probably one of the men who circulated copies for subscription and perhaps carried along his small English-language Bible to administer oaths of allegiance. It is possible that he marched with a company of Bacon's men as far southeast as Lower Norfolk County during the autumn. Crewes may have been one of the last of Bacon's principal followers to be captured. He was almost certainly among the fifteen or sixteen men the captain of the warship *Young Prince* delivered to the governor on 19 January 1677.

Berkeley presided at a court-martial at Green Spring, in James City County, on 24 January 1677 at which Crewes and six other men were tried and convicted of treason and rebellion against the king. The trial record singled out

Crewes as "a most notorious Actor & Assistor in the Rebellion." James Crewes was sentenced to be hanged at Jamestown on the following Friday, 26 January 1677. The place of his burial is not recorded. The property of the condemned men was subject to confiscation, but the king declined to proceed against Crewes's estate. In August 1684 William Randolph purchased a portion of the Turkey Island property, which became the seat of the subsequently influential Randolph family of Virginia.

Deposition, 1 Dec. 1652 (giving age as twenty-nine), in PRO C 24/762, pt. 1, no. 13; numerous references in Charles City Co. records (1655–1664); affidavit, 26 May 1676, in Coventry Papers, 77, no. 90, Longleat House, Wiltshire, Eng.; declaration, 3 Aug. 1676, in PRO CO 1/37, fol. 130–131; log of *Young Prince* in PRO CO 1/37, fol. 186; Berkeley's list of men hanged, in Samuel Wiseman's Book of Record, unpaginated (first quotation), Pepysian Library 2582, Magdalene College, University of Cambridge; Hening, *Statutes*, 2:366–377, 3:569; *Minutes of Council and General Court*, 215, 257, 265, 408, 455 (trial record and second quotation), 528; will and 1681 estate records in Henrico Co. Records (Deeds and Wills, 1677–1692), pt. 1, 139–140, 155, 161, 169, 369–370; estate inventory, May 1677, including description of two Bibles, in PRO CO 5/1371, fols. 225–227.

KATHARINE E. HARBURY

CRINKLEY, Richmond Dillard (20 January 1940–29 January 1989), theatrical producer, was born in Blackstone, in Nottoway County, and was the son of James Epes Crinkley, a commissioner of revenue, and Sarah Beck Crinkley. Educated in the local public schools, he attended the University of Virginia, from which he received a B.A. with honors in 1961, an M.A. in 1962, and a Ph.D. in English in 1966. While a Fulbright Fellow at the University of Oxford, he became friends with William F. Buckley and for three years wrote the pseudonymous Cato column for the *National Review* and the Winston column for the *National Review Bulletin*. In 1967 Crinkley became assistant professor of English at the University of North Carolina and in 1971 published his only book, *Walter Pater, Humanist*. He never married.

In 1969, at the urging of his mentor, the noted scholar and poet Osborne Bennett Hardison, who had just become director of the Folger Shakespeare Library, in Washington, D.C., Crinkley accepted the position of director of programs at the library. He transformed the Folger's 250-seat re-creation of William Shakespeare's Globe Theatre from a museum exhibit into a working stage with a resident acting company, the Folger Theatre Group. In his four years at the Folger, Crinkley's productions displayed, in the words of a *Washington Post* critic, a marriage of "strong literary values to an avant-garde sensibility." His noted productions included a rock-music version of Euripides' *Bacchae* entitled *Dionysus Wants You!*, a racially integrated *Twelfth Night* in which one actor played both Viola and Sebastian, and a *Romeo and Juliet* set as a family feud in a nineteenth-century Italian circus. Crinkley's enthusiasm and innovative artistic directorship at the Folger attracted the attention of Roger L. Stevens, chair of the John F. Kennedy Center for the Performing Arts. In the autumn of 1973 Stevens hired Crinkley as his special assistant. Crinkley brought in more experimental theater and co-produced the Kennedy Center's national bicentennial season, which included successful stagings of *The Royal Family* with Rosemary Harris and Eva Le Gallienne and of *Sweet Bird of Youth* with Irene Worth and Christopher Walken.

In July 1976 Crinkley became executive director of the American National Theater and Academy in New York. As a Broadway producer, Crinkley oversaw the premieres of the revue *Tintypes*, which received a 1981 Tony Award nomination for best musical, and the Peter Nichols drama *Passion*. His production of *The Elephant Man* won the 1979 Tony Award for best play, as well as several prestigious critics' awards. The five years following the triumph of *The Elephant Man*, however, were among the most frustrating of Crinkley's career. "He always stayed charming, and he always stayed hungry," remembered one colleague. Late in 1978 Crinkley succeeded the theatrical legend Joseph Papp as executive director of the struggling Vivian Beaumont Theater, Inc., at the Lincoln Center for the Performing Arts, and in November 1980 he reopened the long-dark theater with ambitious plans. His inaugural season comprised a revival of *The Philadelphia Story*, *Macbeth*, in which the opera conductor Sarah Caldwell debuted as stage director, and *The Floating Light Bulb*, a new play by Woody Allen. The three-play season was a critical failure, with *The Philadelphia Story* and *Macbeth* targeted for especially harsh barbs. Thereafter, the Beaumont remained dark and unoccupied.

Almost from the outset, Crinkley clashed with Martin E. Segal, chair of Lincoln Center's board of directors. Crinkley believed that sight-line and technical problems, present since the Beaumont was built, rendered the theater unfit for both production and viewing. He refused to reopen the Beaumont again unless substantial (and expensive) renovations were completed. The conflict between Crinkley and the Lincoln Center board became increasingly acrimonious. The theater board's early decision in July 1983 to reappoint Crinkley for a two-year term before his contract expired exacerbated tensions, and in August the Lincoln Center board barred the Beaumont from using the title "Lincoln Center Theater Company" and froze the theater's funds. After a packing of the theater board diluted support for Crinkley, he resigned as executive director in October 1984.

Crinkley was the founding president of Cerberus Enterprises, Inc., a theatrical, film, and television production company. In addition to his work in the theater, he produced television programs for ABC and PBS and wrote reviews and opinion pieces for the *New York Times*, the *Washington Post*, and *Shakespeare Quarterly*. He lobbied for funding to combat the AIDS epidemic among the theater community and served on the Kennedy Center board of trustees from 1981 until shortly before his death. Richmond Dillard Crinkley died in a Richmond hospital of multiple myeloma on 29 January 1989 and was buried in Lakeview Cemetery, in Blackstone.

Family information verified by brother James Epes Crinkley Jr. (2002); *Washington Post*, 10 Sept. 1969, 10 Sept. 1973 (por.), 23 July 1976; *Blackstone Courier-Record*, 7 June 1979; *New York Times*, 28 Feb. 1980, 10 Jan., 13, 15, 23 July, 18, 25 Aug., 8 Sept. 1983, 16 Oct. 1984; *New Republic* (10 Oct. 1983), 22–23; obituaries in *New York Times*, *Richmond News Leader*, *Richmond Times-Dispatch* (por.), and *Washington Post*, all 31 Jan. 1989, and *Blackstone Courier-Record*, 2 Feb. 1989; memorial tributes by William F. Buckley in *National Review* (10 Mar. 1989), 17, in *Congressional Record*, 101st Cong., 1st sess., E654 (extended remarks, 6 Mar. 1989), and in *Washington Post*, 12 Feb. 1989 (quotations).

JOHN W. FRICK

CRISMOND, Horace Frazer (15 June 1849–17 January 1903), member of the Convention of 1901–1902, was born in Spotsylvania County and was the son of John B. Crismond, a farmer, and Jane McDaniel Crismond. Educated in private schools in the county, Crismond in March 1868 moved to Fredericksburg, where he worked as a clerk in the firm of J. H. Bradley and Son. By March 1873 he had established Willis and Crismond, a commission merchant business specializing in fertilizer, plows, and other agricultural implements. On 1 March 1875 Crismond married Bettie Kay Coleman in Spotsylvania County. They had four sons and four daughters.

Crismond was at various times a city councilman, member of the chamber of commerce, member of the governing board of Fredericksburg's normal school, and twice a member of committees dispatched to invite President Grover Cleveland to attend the city's annual agricultural fair. Throughout his life Crismond remained focused on mercantile pursuits, and in 1891, citing the press of his business concerns, he declined an appointment as city treasurer, despite that position's annual salary of about $1,000. Because of his commercial interests, which included being the secretary of the Rappahannock, Fredericksburg, and Piedmont Telephone Company, Crismond was a conservative Democrat who supported the pro-business policies of Thomas Staples Martin, a United States senator who controlled the dominant faction of Virginia's Democratic Party. Crismond was both a delegate to state party conventions and a member of the Democratic State Central Committee. In November 1885 voters in Spotsylvania County and Fredericksburg elected him to the House of Delegates for the 1885–1887 assembly. He was appointed to the Committees on Asylums and Prisons, on Banks, Currency, and Commerce, and on Militia and Police. After winning reelection to the House of Delegates for the 1887–1888 assembly, Crismond chaired the Committee on Enrolled Bills and sat on the Committees on Asylums and Prisons, on Counties, Cities, and Towns, and on Finance.

In April 1901 Spotsylvania County Democrats nominated Crismond by acclamation to represent that county and the city of Fredericksburg at a state convention called to revise Virginia's constitution. On 23 May of that year Crismond won election over token opposition. He was appointed to the temporary Committee on Organization to arrange the convention proceedings and to the standing Committee on the Organization and Government of Cities and Towns. Crismond spoke little during the convention and did not propose any resolutions, though he did present two petitions from his constituents relating to the sale of intoxicating liquors. Unlike the Democratic majority, he voted against suffrage restrictions designed to reduce the number of black voters, perhaps because he feared that such measures would disfranchise too many poor white voters as well. Crismond favored submitting the constitution to a popular referendum, but the delegates voted to proclaim the constitution in effect rather than risk public defeat. Despite his opposition to these key provisions, he voted on 6 June 1902 to approve the final version of the constitution.

Horace Frazer Crismond died unexpectedly, possibly of a heart attack, at his home in Fredericksburg on 17 January 1903 and was buried in the Confederate Cemetery in that city. He did not leave a will, but estimates valued his estate and life insurance at $75,000.

Birth date in Pollard Questionnaires; biographical sketches in *Richmond Dispatch*, 21 Apr. 1901, and *Richmond Times*, 12 June 1901; Crismond family genealogical notes, Acc. 33833, LVA; Crismond correspondence in William Emmet Bibb Papers, James Taylor Ellyson Papers, William Atkinson Jones Papers, and William Hodges Mann Papers, all UVA; BVS Marriage Register, Spotsylvania Co.; Election Records, no. 47, RG 13, LVA; *Journal of 1901–1902 Convention*, 24, 50, 174, 180, 486–487, 504, 535; *Convention of 1901–1902 Photographs* (por.); Wythe Holt, *Virginia's Constitutional Convention of 1901–1902* (1990), 122, 134–135; obituaries and accounts of funeral in *Fredericksburg Free Lance*, 22, 24 Jan. 1903, and *Richmond Times*, 18 (por.), 20 Jan. 1903.

JOHN G. DEAL

CRITCHER, John (11 March 1820–27 September 1901), member of the Convention of 1861 and of the House of Representatives, was born in Westmoreland County and was the son of John Critcher, a planter, and Sally Winter Covington Critcher. Educated by tutors and at private schools in Northumberland and Stafford Counties, he studied law, mathematics, modern languages, and natural philosophy at the University of Virginia from 1835 to 1839. On 4 July of the latter year, in the company of George Tucker, professor of moral philosophy at the university and a former congressman, Critcher departed on a grand tour of Europe, with stops in England, France, and Switzerland. He returned home in March 1842 and studied law for almost two years before taking his oath as an attorney on 27 November 1843. He owned about twenty slaves in 1850 and approximately the same number a decade later. Critcher married Elizabeth Kennon Whiting, a Hampton native, on 12 November 1857. Their one son and four daughters included Catharine Carter Critcher, a noted Washington, D.C., landscape and portrait painter who was the only female member of the Taos Society of Artists.

Critcher was elected commonwealth's attorney for Westmoreland County in 1856 and the next year ran unsuccessfully for the First Congressional District seat in the House of Representatives as a Distribution candidate, a combined Whig and American Party ticket that sought the equitable distribution among the states of funds generated by the sale of public lands. In January 1861 he replaced Richard Lee Turberville Beale in the Senate of Virginia representing Lancaster, Northumberland, Richmond, and Westmoreland Counties for the remaining months of the assembly session. He was added to the Committee for Courts of Justice and the joint committee on the library. The following month the Unionist Critcher defeated Willoughby Newton, a former Whig congressman, for election to represent Richmond and Westmoreland Counties in the convention called to consider the issue of secession. At the behest of his constituents, in the early days of the convention he outlined for William Henry Seward in private correspondence the Unionists' conditions for preventing Virginia's secession. Critcher voted against secession when the convention first considered it on 4 April 1861 but joined the majority in approving secession in the second vote on 17 April. After the governor nominated Robert Edward Lee to command Virginia's military forces, Critcher, who represented in both the state senate and the secession convention the county where Lee had been born, escorted Lee to the State Capitol and moved that the convention endorse the nomination. The boast that his own home lay between the birthplaces of Lee and George Washington became a mainstay in Critcher's public addresses for the next forty years. He returned to Richmond in June and November 1861 for the second and third sessions of the convention.

Critcher enlisted in the 9th Virginia Cavalry on 25 May 1861 and rose to sergeant by October. He helped organize the 15th Battalion Virginia Cavalry in the spring of 1862, and he was commissioned a lieutenant colonel on 11 September of that year when the 14th and 15th Cavalry Battalions were combined into the 15th Regiment Virginia Cavalry. In November, Critcher commanded elements of the regiment at Fredericksburg, where they were surprised in a Union cavalry raid but managed to repel their attackers. During the Chancellorsville campaign in 1863 the regiment poorly performed its assignment to protect the Confederate right flank along the Rappahannock River, and Union raiders again surprised some of the unit's horsemen as they slept. On 26 May 1863 Lee exhorted Critcher to do a better job screening the right wing and tracking Union movements. The admonition came too late, however, because Union troops had captured Critcher on 23 May as he slipped back from a visit to Westmoreland County after the death of one of his daughters. Believing he was on the north side of the Rappahannock River to organize irregulars and to monitor troop movements, Union officials kept him in captivity as long as possible, first at the Old Capitol Prison in Washington, D.C., and then on Johnson's Island in Ohio. Critcher returned to the Army of Northern Virginia in the spring of 1864 and at Cold Harbor temporarily commanded Brigadier General Lunsford Lindsay Lomax's brigade. He resigned on 12 June 1864 after being denied command of the regiment.

Critcher returned to Westmoreland County and resumed practicing law. On 15 February 1866 the governor appointed him a judge of the eleven-county Eighth Judicial Circuit. Three years later a congressional resolution that prohibited anyone in Mississippi, Texas, and Vir-

ginia who had taken up arms against the United States from holding public office removed him from the bench.

In November 1870 two Republican candidates split their party's vote, and Critcher, running as a Conservative, handily won election to the House of Representatives from the First Congressional District, comprising the counties of Accomack, Caroline, Elizabeth City, Essex, Gloucester, James City, King and Queen, King George, King William, Lancaster, Mathews, Middlesex, Northampton, Northumberland, Richmond, Warwick, Westmoreland, and York. He sat on the Committee on Coinage, Weights, and Measures. In his single term Critcher supported aids to navigation and the restoration of voting and office holding rights to former Confederate officials and criticized Reconstruction and enforcement of the Fourteenth Amendment. He did not seek reelection in 1872.

Voters returned Critcher to the Senate of Virginia in 1874 for one three-year term representing King George, Lancaster, Northumberland, Richmond, and Westmoreland Counties. He chaired the Committee on Roads and Internal Navigation and sat on the Committees for Courts of Justice and on Federal Relations. In July 1876 Critcher, disappointed in the Democratic Party's national platform, declared himself an independent candidate for Congress, but he may have heeded the excoriations in the Democratic press and dropped out of the race. In the November election he received only six votes, none in his home county. Critcher moved to the District of Columbia in 1879 and to Alexandria in 1884 in pursuit of a more lucrative law practice. A friend and ally of William Mahone, he regularly corresponded with the Readjuster leader and United States senator about political appointments, patronage, and other party issues. Critcher sat on the Committee on Resolutions at the 1881 Readjuster State Convention.

Critcher had a variety of business interests. He was attorney and agent of the Virginia Mining and Manufacturing Company in 1889 and during the 1890s was a partner in a Westmoreland County land syndicate. He appeared several times before the Virginia Supreme Court of Appeals and argued, but lost, two cases before the Supreme Court of the United States. In 1893 Critcher represented Pottawatomie Indians of Indiana and Michigan in a treaty dispute with the federal government for which he received a fee of more than $36,000. In *Corralitos Company* v. *United States and the Apache Indians* (1900), he represented a New York company seeking damages from the federal government for property stolen by Apache Indians in Mexico and brought to the United States. John Critcher died of pulmonary edema on 27 September 1901 at his Alexandria home and was buried in Ivy Hill Cemetery in that city.

James Duncan Gatewood, "Family History" (1911 type-script), VHS, including Aug. 1896 autobiography by Critcher on 29–61, with birth date on 30 and variant marriage date of 10 Nov. 1857 on 38; Thomas William Herringshaw, ed., *Herringshaw's Encyclopedia of American Biography of the Nineteenth Century* (1898), 264; BVS Marriage Register, Elizabeth City Co.; *Fredericksburg News*, 13 Apr., 11 May, 4 June 1857, 24, 31 July, 3, 7 Aug., 4 Sept., 20 Nov. 1876; *Richmond Whig and Advertiser*, 29 Nov. 1870; *Fredericksburg Ledger*, 6 Dec. 1870; Reese and Gaines, *Proceedings of 1861 Convention*, 2:582–583, 3:163, 164, 171, 4:144, 363; Compiled Service Records; *OR*, 2d ser., 5:706; John Fortier, *15th Virginia Cavalry* (1993), 2–5, 9–13, 16–20, 24–26, 30–31, 71, 75–77, 129; political speeches printed as Critcher, *Fellow Citizens of the First District* (1870), *Speech in the Virginia Senate on the Texas and Pacific R.R.* (1876), and *To the Voters of the First District* (1876); *Congressional Globe*, 42d Cong., 1st sess., 175, Appendix, 300–303, 2d sess., 800–801, 1776, 1955, 3d sess., 1151; Critcher correspondence in William Mahone Papers, Duke, and printed in *Washington Post*, 26 Jan. 1895, and *VMHB* 5 (1897): 220–221; *Phineas Pam-To-Pee* v. *United States* and *Pottawatomie Indians of Michigan and Indiana* v. *United States* (1893), *United States Reports*, 148:691–705; *Corralitos Company* v. *United States* (1900), *United States Reports*, 178:280–289; pors. in Barnes Publishing Company Photo Archives, Georgetown University, and Westmoreland Co. Circuit Court; obituaries in *Alexandria Gazette*, 27 Sept. 1901, and *Washington Evening Star* and *Washington Post*, both 28 Sept. 1901; bar association memorial in *Washington Post*, 29 Sept. 1901.

G. W. POINDEXTER

CROCKER, Wiley Horace (26 June 1873–9 July 1943), manager of the Tidewater Fair Association of Suffolk, Virginia, Incorporated, was born in Southampton County and was the son of Sandy Crocker and Jane Doles Crocker. Educated in local schools, he attended Centenary Collegiate Institute (later Centenary College) in Hackettstown, New Jersey, from 1899 to 1900 and also Wyoming Seminary Business College

in Kingston, Pennsylvania, and Howard University in Washington, D.C. On 10 September 1902 Crocker married Virginia E. Lee in Suffolk. They had no children. That year he started an undertaking business and by 1910 had formed W. H. Crocker and Company, which incorporated in 1920 with Crocker as president. He also worked in insurance and real estate enterprises and established a reputation as one of the area's preeminent African American businessmen.

Crocker helped found the Nansemond Development Company, incorporated in 1907 to develop properties for black homeowners and businessmen, and became the company's longtime manager and treasurer. He also helped establish the Nansemond County Farmers' Conference to instruct black farmers in modern agricultural techniques. In 1911 Crocker began a three-year term on the board of the Nansemond Normal and Industrial Institute, Inc. This church-supported facility later closed and reopened in 1914, chartered as the Nansemond Collegiate Institute with a curriculum emphasizing classical education. In 1928 the institute became the first county school accredited by the state Department of Education. Crocker came to the financial aid of the school several times before it closed in 1939.

At the urging of the Hampton Normal and Agricultural Institute faculty, in 1910 Crocker and other local black leaders sponsored a farmers' conference and fair in Suffolk. Such events had become popular among African Americans since the 1895 Cotton States and International Exposition in Atlanta had included an exhibit focused on African American achievements. In Virginia, the 1907 Jamestown Ter-Centennial Exposition had featured a "Negro Building," and in October 1910 the governor attended a Colored State Fair in Richmond. The Suffolk fair, held at the white fairgrounds, ran for two days in November and featured speakers from the United States Department of Agriculture, horse races, and livestock, poultry, and farm-product exhibitions for which local merchants donated prizes. At the 1911 fair the guest speaker was William Henry Lewis, an African American recently appointed United States assistant attorney general. As president of the fair in 1912 and 1913, Crocker worked with Hampton Institute extension agents to teach farmers better ways to cultivate and fertilize crops, breed livestock and poultry, and plant new varieties of seeds. He and other businessmen contributed to the fair, which also received financial support from the white community. Some whites attended, and in 1912 many white businesses made donations and gave employees time off for the event. In 1915 Suffolk's mayor delivered an address at the agricultural fair, and the town council endorsed and appropriated funds for it.

Crocker secured a tract of land that in 1913 became the fair's permanent location. On 14 March 1914 the Tidewater Fair Association of Suffolk, Virginia, Incorporated, was formed with Crocker as treasurer. By the next year he was also officially managing the agricultural fair. Under his direction the Tidewater Fair, or Suffolk Colored Fair as it was also known, grew larger each year. It expanded to five days in 1927 before returning to four days in 1935.

In 1921 Crocker arranged for Maggie Lena Mitchell Walker, president of Saint Luke Penny Savings Bank, to address the crowd on the fair's Woman's Day. By that time the association owned thirty-three acres of improved land and had paid shareholders a dividend each year. The association continued to promote agricultural programs even as it began in 1926 to emphasize an industrial component. Crocker worked to establish a statewide presence. Luring visitors from eastern Virginia and North Carolina, the Tidewater Fair successfully competed with other black fairs held in nearby Newport News and Norfolk and also in Raleigh, North Carolina, and eclipsed Suffolk's white fair both in attendance and influence. Taking advantage of a state extension service designation, Crocker advertised the event as "Endorsed as the Colored State and Premier Fair of the State of Virginia" and as the "Negro State Fair." Each year the official state exhibit traveled from the state fair in Richmond to Suffolk for display at the Tidewater Fair.

Crocker continued to attract prominent speakers, such as the black nationalist Marcus Garvey, who in 1924 addressed the thousands who packed the midway. By 1925 the association's assets had increased from $3,500 at its founding to about $25,000. An estimated 100,000 people had visited the grounds that boasted an administration building, grandstand and bleachers, a large exhibits building, county school and state extension exhibits buildings, stables, and other structures. In 1928 about 25,000 visitors passed through the gates. By then the Tidewater Fair had become one of the largest, most successful black-owned businesses in Virginia, and its economic influence extended to nearby counties, where improved farming methods translated into higher incomes that in turn meant more money for black education in surrounding rural areas.

Crocker guided the fair through the Great Depression and the demographic changes that occurred as rural life increasingly gave way to urban living. By 1940 he was again president and served until his death. He was a vice president of the Negro Organization Society, president of the Virginia State Association of the Improved Benevolent Protective Order of the Elks of the World, and founder of the Suffolk and Nansemond County Civic League. Wiley Horace Crocker died at his home in Suffolk on 9 July 1943. State and city officials, education leaders, and representatives of various professional and fraternal groups attended his funeral. He was buried in Oaklawn Cemetery, in Suffolk.

Birth date in BVS Birth Register, Southampton Co., with variant dates of 10 June 1876 in *Who's Who in Colored America*, 3d ed. (1930/1932), 112, of 10 June 1870 in *Norfolk Journal and Guide*, 17 July 1943, and of June 1877 on BVS Death Certificate, Suffolk City; BVS Marriage Register, Nansemond Co. (age twenty-six on 10 Sept. 1902); SCC Charter Book, 84:89–91; Tidewater Fair Association photographs in Hamblin Studio Collection (1910–1975), Morgan Memorial Library, Suffolk; *Norfolk Virginian-Pilot and the Norfolk Landmark*, 7 Oct. 1912; *Norfolk Journal and Guide*, 24 Sept. 1921, 17 Oct. 1925 (por.); Sarah S. Hughes, "The Suffolk Fair," in Jane H. Kobelski, ed., *Readings in Black and White: Lower Tidewater Virginia* (1982), 34–38; death notice in *Suffolk News-Herald*, 10 July 1943; obituary and editorial tribute in *Norfolk Journal and Guide*, 17 July 1943.

DONALD W. GUNTER

CROCKETT, Walter (d. by 10 December 1816), member of the Convention of 1788, was born in the 1730s. His parents, Joseph Louis Crockett and Jeanne de Vigné Crockett, emigrated from Ireland to Pennsylvania and eventually settled along the Roanoke River in an area of shifting boundaries that became Orange County in 1734, Augusta County in 1738, Botetourt County in 1769, Fincastle County in 1772, and Montgomery County in 1776. Little is known about his youth or education, but by April 1764 Crockett had become a sergeant in the Augusta County militia. Recommended in 1769 for selection to the Augusta County Court, he took his oath as a justice for the new county of Botetourt on 13 March 1770, by which time he had also won promotion to captain of the county militia. Crockett was appointed a member of the court for newly established Fincastle County in December 1772 while continuing to serve as a militia captain. During Dunmore's War in 1774 he led a company across the Ohio River against the Shawnee. Crockett had married Margaret Steele Caldwell, a widow, by September 1771. They had at least one son and two daughters.

On 20 January 1775 Crockett attended the first meeting of the Fincastle County Committee and signed its resolutions, which called for breaking from Great Britain if the rights of the Virginia colonists were not safeguarded. In the spring of 1777 he won election to the House of Delegates representing Montgomery County, which had been created the previous year. Arriving about a month after the assembly session opened, he was added to the Committee of Public Claims. Reelected to a second term, he missed the first session, arrived late for the second session in October 1778, and served again on the same committee.

Crockett's involvement in planning the defense of Montgomery County probably accounts for his lackluster attendance at the General Assembly. He missed the first session of his third term in May 1779, but he had been busy suppressing a Loyalist rebellion that threatened the lead mines in southwestern Virginia. That October the General Assembly passed an act protecting Crockett, William Campbell (1745–1781), and their men from any penalties or lawsuits that might arise from their extralegal actions during that effort. Crockett arrived at the House of Delegates in November 1779 for the session that had begun the previous month but was not added to any committees.

Conflict between Loyalists and Patriots in the western part of the state continued, and in August 1780 Crockett led about 250 militiamen against Loyalists along the New River. On 2 July 1781 he accepted command of one of two Montgomery County militia battalions and received orders to raise men for General Nathanael Greene's campaign in the Carolinas. The next year Crockett served as one of Colonel William Preston's field officers for Montgomery and attempted to raise a company of militia to guard the frontier, but he had difficulty attracting enough recruits. He was also appointed sheriff of the county. Crockett continued to bear responsibility throughout the 1780s for defending the county from attacks by Native Americans and often wrote the governor concerning the dangers that backcountry settlers faced. By February 1789 he had become county lieutenant.

In the spring of 1788 Crockett was one of two Montgomery County delegates elected to a convention called to consider ratification of the proposed constitution of the United States. Present throughout the proceedings, he voted on 25 June in favor of requiring the addition of a bill of rights to the Constitution before ratification, and after that motion failed, he voted with the minority against ratifying the Constitution. Two days later he joined antifederalists in voting to limit the taxing power of Congress.

Crockett represented Montgomery County in the House of Delegates for a final term in 1789, when he served on the Committee of Propositions and Grievances. In that year, the area of the county in which he lived became part of Wythe County, and in 1790 he was named to the new county's court and also became the county clerk. Beginning in 1792 Crockett served as a trustee for the town of Evansham as well as for Wythe Academy. He continued to farm along the New River for the rest of his life. Walter Crockett wrote his will on 9 January 1807 and died on an unrecorded date not long before 10 December 1816, when his will was proved in the Wythe County Court. He was reportedly buried near the Austinville lead mines in Wythe County.

Janie Preston Collup French and Zella Armstrong, *Notable Southern Families: The Crockett Family and Connecting Lines* (1928), 204–205, 256–258 (with birth year about 1732 based on birth order and presumed death year of 1811); David B. Trimble, *Crockett and Graham of Southwest Virginia* (1992), 1, 26 (with birth year about 1737 based on different birth order and death year of 1811); numerous references in Mary B. Kegley and F. B. Kegley, *Early Adventurers on the Western Waters* (1980–1998); Crockett correspondence in Draper MSS 5QQ48, in Preston Family Papers, VHS, and published in "Preston Papers," *Branch Papers* 4 (1915): 306, 310, 319, 324–325, 330–331, 338, 342, "Preston Papers," *VMHB* 26 (1918): 371–372, 377–378, ibid. 27 (1919): 49, 165–166, ibid. 28 (1920): 242–245, 347–348; *Revolutionary Virginia*, 2:255, 4:176, 347, 484, 5:375, 6:130–131, 136, 327, 7:286, 439, 441, 446; *Calendar of Virginia State Papers*, 4:31, 159–160, 295–296, 408, 564, 5:42, 205–206; Hening, *Statutes*, 10:195; Kaminski, *Ratification*, 10:1539, 1541, 1557; will and estate inventory in Wythe Co. Will Book, 2:171, 179–180.

MARIANNE E. JULIENNE

CROMWELL, John Wesley (5 September 1846–14 April 1927), educator and journalist, was born in Portsmouth. His parents, Willis Hodges Cromwell and Elizabeth Carney Cromwell, were both slaves. Yeates's Free School, located in Nansemond County, owned his father but permitted him to live in Portsmouth, where he worked as a carpenter and transported freight aboard his small sloop. In a scenario probably devised by Willis Cromwell, in January 1849 B. W. Dobson purchased Elizabeth Cromwell from Thomas Twine, of Elizabeth City County. Evidently Dobson set her free, because in that same month, most likely with her husband's earnings, she paid $2,950 to Twine for their seven children, ranging in age from almost two and a half years old to twenty-five. In July 1850 she paid $300 for her husband and in June of the next year put her mark on documents that freed him and their children. Once free, the family settled in Philadelphia. John Wesley Cromwell attended grade school there until 1856, when he enrolled at the Institute for Colored Youth, a Quaker school that included instruction in the classical languages, history, and mathematics.

After graduating in 1864 with a cash prize for superiority in Greek and Latin studies, Cromwell took a teaching job in Columbia, Pennsylvania. That school soon closed, however, and from the spring of 1865 until the end of the year he operated a private school in Portsmouth. The Baltimore Association for the Moral and Educational Improvement of the Colored People then employed him, but Cromwell's stay in Maryland was cut short in March 1866, when someone fired a gun at him and unknown persons burned down the church in which he held school. He returned to Portsmouth, where he taught Sunday school at the Emanuel African Methodist Episcopal Church. Believing strongly in the importance of education for African Americans, Cromwell declared that he desired "to assist in the elevation of my *own* down-trodden, unfortunate, illiterate yet not God-forsaken people." In the autumn of 1866 the American Missionary Association hired him as a teacher at Providence Church, in Norfolk County. The school closed in June 1867, and for a time he was an agent for the Society of Friends.

In 1867 Cromwell may have attended the Republican Party's first and second state conventions held in Richmond, although his name does not appear on the official lists of delegates. Later he was an organizer for the Republican Party and for the Philadelphia-based Union League Association. Returning to the classroom, he taught in Wytheville during the winter of 1869–1870, in Richmond the following year, and in Southampton County during the summer of 1871.

Cromwell entered Howard University's law school in the autumn of 1871 and three years later graduated and was admitted to the bar. Having in the meantime passed the civil service examination in 1872 and become a clerk at the Treasury Department, he rose through the ranks to become chief examiner of the money order department. Later he worked in the auditor's office of the post office department until 30 June 1885, when he was dismissed, probably for political reasons, soon after a Democrat became president.

After leaving the Treasury Department, Cromwell practiced law. When he appeared before the Interstate Commerce Commission as counsel for the plaintiff in *William H. Heard* v. *the Georgia Railroad Company* in December 1887, he was likely the first African American attorney to argue a case before that new body. Cromwell resumed his career in education in September 1889 and taught or served as principal at several District of Columbia schools until at least 1919. In 1914 he received an honorary degree from Wilberforce University, in Ohio.

While working for the federal government and studying for his law degree, Cromwell continued strong advocacy of African American education. At a Richmond meeting of the Virginia Educational and Literary Association late in August 1875, he was elected second vice president and delivered a keynote speech before the convention, later published as an *Address on the Difficulties of the Colored Youth, In Obtaining an Education in the Virginias* (1875). Cromwell also chaired the convention's Committee on Organization, which created the Virginia Educational and Historical Association, and was named president of the new organization.

In April 1876 Cromwell published the inaugural issue of the *People's Advocate* in Alexandria. By 1878 he had moved the weekly newspaper to Washington, D.C., where its pages continued to reflect his concerns about racial issues and the importance of studying history and literature. Cromwell remained proprietor and managing editor at least through the spring of 1884, when he wrote a history of area black churches that ran in three installments. In 1880 he was a key figure in founding the National Colored Press Association (after 1894 the National Afro-American Press Association).

A gifted organizer, Cromwell in 1877 helped found the short-lived Negro American Society. In 1881 he helped establish the Bethel Literary and Historical Association, whose meetings attracted Frederick Douglass and other leading black scholars and activists. Cromwell served on its advisory board, sat on the executive committee, and in 1886 and 1887 was elected president. To commemorate its fifteenth anniversary he wrote the *History of the Bethel Literary and Historical Association* (1896). During this period Cromwell was elected an honorary member of the Philosophian Literary Society of Lincoln University. He sat on the board of the Progressive Co-operative Society, was an officer in the Mutual Benefit Association, and represented the District of Columbia at the World's Industrial and Cotton Centennial Exposition, which opened in New Orleans in December 1884.

A staunch supporter of industrial and agricultural education, Cromwell in 1879 was president of the Banneker Industrial Education Association. In May of that year he attended the Nashville meeting of the National Conference of Colored Men of the United States, was elected its secretary, and chaired the Committee on Education and Labor. Cromwell's essay in the *Southern Workman* entitled "The Chance for Skilled Negro Labor in the South" (1897) hailed the new trade school at Hampton Normal and Agricultural Institute (later Hampton University) as a forerunner of educational institutions that would boost black participation in the region's industrial development. He attended the inaugural meeting of the Hampton Negro Conference in 1897 and continued to serve on its various committees until at least 1903. Cromwell initially supported Booker Taliaferro Washington's vision of black education and defended him against critics at a meeting of the Bethel Literary and Historical Association in 1895. Cromwell's support of Washington waned, however, as Cromwell came to believe that African American leaders should subordinate the quest for education and material success to seeking political solutions to racial problems.

Cromwell played a key role in founding the American Negro Academy, and at its organizational meeting on 5 March 1897 he was elected corresponding secretary, an office he held until 1919. As a member of the executive committee between 1898 and 1903, he emerged as a dominant force and became the public face of the ANA. Elected the academy's fourth president in 1919, Cromwell made strong efforts to revitalize the organization. He chose not to seek reelection the following year, probably because of his age. During the absences of his successor, Arthur Alfonso Schomburg, Cromwell conducted association business as a member and occasional chair of the executive committee.

Desiring to promote the work of black scholars, Cromwell in 1910 helped establish the American Negro Monograph Company. The enterprise published four papers during its eleven months in business. His interest in book collecting led to an association with other bibliophiles, including Schomburg, with whom he corresponded frequently between 1912 and 1926. In 1915 the two men helped organize the Negro Book Collectors Exchange, with Cromwell as vice president.

Throughout his career Cromwell wrote on educational and historical subjects, including *The Early Negro Convention Movement* and *The Jim Crow Negro* (both 1904), *The Negro in American History: Men and Women Eminent in the Evolution of the American of African Descent* (1914), *The Challenge of the Disfranchised: A Plea for the Enforcement of the 15th Amendment* (1924), and articles for the *Journal of Negro History* entitled "The Aftermath of Nat Turner's Insurrection" (1920) and "The First Negro Churches in the District of Columbia" (1922), a revised version of his history of black churches.

On 13 November 1873 Cromwell married Lucy A. McGuinn in Washington, D.C. They had five daughters and two sons, one of whom died in infancy. His wife died on 6 April 1887, and on 20 October 1892 he married Annie E. Conn in Cumberland County, Pennsylvania. They had no children. John Wesley Cromwell died at his Washington residence on 14 April 1927 and was buried in Woodlawn Cemetery in the District of Columbia.

Biographies in William J. Simmons, *Men of Mark: Eminent, Progressive and Rising* (1887; repr. 1968), 898–907, with birth date and por. opposite 904, and I. Garland Penn, *The Afro-American Press, and Its Editors* (1891), 154–158; manumission papers, correspondence, deeds (with age two years and four months in Thomas Twine, deed of sale to Betsy Cromwell, Jan. 1849), writings, association materials, and scrapbooks in Cromwell Family Papers, Moorland-Spingarn Research Center, Howard University, Washington, D.C.; teaching reports and correspondence in American Missionary Association Archives, Amistad Research Center, Tulane University, New Orleans, La. (quotation in Cromwell to Samuel Hunt, 17 Sept. 1866); other family papers in possession of granddaughter Adelaide Cromwell, who provided information in several interviews (2005); Supreme Court of the District of Columbia Marriage Record, 6:89 (1873); Cumberland Co., Pa., Marriage License (1892); *New York Anglo-African*, 9 Sept. 1865; *Richmond Daily Dispatch*, 24, 25 Aug. 1875; *Washington People's Advocate*, 17 May 1879; Alfred A. Moss Jr., *The American Negro Academy: Voice of the Talented Tenth* (1981), esp. 23–34, 62–71, 195–221 (por. following 112); death notice in *Washington Evening Star*, 15 Apr. 1927; obituary in *Journal of Negro History* 12 (1927): 563–566.

DONALD W. GUNTER

CRONK, Katharine Killinger Scherer (14 July 1877–12 March 1927), Lutheran lay leader, was born in Marion and was the daughter of Elizabeth Katharine Killinger Scherer and John Jacob Scherer (1830–1919), a prominent Lutheran minister who founded Marion Female College (later Marion College) in Smyth County. She and her siblings, including John Jacob Scherer (1881–1956), a Lutheran minister and president of the Virginia Synod, and Minerva May Scherer, longtime dean of Marion College, grew up on the school's campus. She graduated from Marion Female College in 1893 and on 29 May 1895 married Eli Calvin Cronk, a Lutheran minister. They had one son.

In the years following their marriage Cronk moved with her husband as he served congregations in western Virginia. They lived in Atlanta for five years beginning in 1903 and then settled in Columbia, South Carolina. The family moved to Richmond in 1918 and then to New York City the following year. They returned to Richmond in 1921 when Eli Cronk began a two-year term as the superintendent of the Virginia Synod of the United Lutheran Church in America (later the Evangelical Lutheran Church in America).

As her husband continued his ministry, Cronk established her own career. Although a devoted Lutheran, she circulated in a burgeoning ecumenical community that was reorienting Protestant groups away from denominational competition and toward an emphasis on global Christianization. Cronk began writing books and pamphlets that encouraged women and children to participate in church missions, as she herself had done from a young age. Combining a keen sense of humor with clear prose in such works as *Missionary Methods for Church and Home* (1927), she sought to make missionary work inspiring and attractive. Cronk's *Brave Adventurers* (1925), considered by contemporaries the finest book for teaching children about missions and prayers, gained a wide and appreciative interdenominational audience. With her elder sister Laura Lu Scherer Copenhaver, another prominent Lutheran lay leader, she wrote many pageants, including *The Search for the Light: A Pageant of Man's Quest for God* (1900), *The Striking of America's Hour: A Pageant of Christian Liberty* (1919), and *The Way of Peace: A Pageant* (1924). Cronk also occasionally collaborated with her friend Elsie Singmaster Lewars, with whom she wrote *Under Many Flags* (1921).

In 1905 Cronk founded the monthly periodical *Tidings: Sunday School and Missionary Journal for the United Synod of the Lutheran Church, South*. Three years later she became editor and secretary of literature for the Woman's Missionary Conference of the United Synod of the Evangelical Lutheran Church in the South. Cronk was at various times an associate editor of *Lutheran Woman's Work*, of *Lutheran Boys and Girls*, and of the interdenominational children's magazine *Everyland*. From 1918 until her death she edited the "Best Methods" department of the *Missionary Review of the World*. Cronk served for seven years on the board of directors of the Missionary Review Publishing Company. In addition to her writing and editorial work, she became a noted lecturer and addressed churches and conferences in California, Illinois, Maine, Massachusetts, New York, North Carolina, and Wisconsin. She also taught regularly in Saint Petersburg, Florida, at a school for missions.

Active in organizational work as well, Cronk in 1920 helped establish the Light Brigade, the children's missionary organization of the ULCA, and was its general superintendent until her death. She served as president of the Women's Missionary Society of the Virginia Synod from 1921 to 1922. In the latter year Cronk assisted in the merger of the women's missionary societies of the Virginia, Southwestern Virginia, and Holston Synods to form the Women's Missionary Society of the Lutheran Synod of Virginia. Reflecting on her family's rich heritage of service to the church, she often remarked that she was born not with a silver spoon in her mouth but with Martin Luther's catechism.

In 1923 the family moved to Philadelphia, where Eli Cronk was an associate secretary of the ULCA Laymen's Missionary Movement for Stewardship and later executive secretary of the Lutheran Orient Mission Society. On 12 December 1926 Katharine Killinger Scherer Cronk suffered a stroke as she concluded an address at Saint Mark's Lutheran Church in Williamsport, Pennsylvania. After several months of convalescence she had another stroke and died shortly thereafter in a Montgomery County hospital, near Philadelphia, on 12 March 1927. A funeral service held at Saint John's Lutheran Church in the Melrose Park township of Montgomery included a eulogy by Frederick H. Knubel, president of the ULCA. Cronk's remains were taken to Richmond, where her brother officiated at a second funeral service at First English Lutheran Church. She was buried in Hollywood Cemetery, in Richmond. One memorialist counted Cronk "among the most potent influences of our generation in helping to expand the missionary work of all the churches." For many years beginning in 1935 the United Lutheran Church Women of the United Lutheran Church in America offered in her honor Cronk Memorial Scholarships to assist young women enrolled in Lutheran colleges.

Biographical materials, including birth date on ULCA Record of Deceased Members, correspondence, missionary work pamphlets, and Laura Lu Scherer Copenhaver's memorial booklet *Katharine Scherer Cronk* [1927], in ULCA Biographical Files, Evangelical Lutheran Church in America Archives, Elk Grove Village, Ill.; Cronk correspondence, plays, handbooks, and other writings in Crumley Lutheran Archives, Lutheran Theological Southern Seminary, Columbia, S.C.; Smyth Co. Marriage Register; John William Leonard, ed., *Woman's Who's Who of America, 1914–1915* (1914), 217; C. W. Cassell, W. J. Finck, and Elon O. Henkel, eds., *History of the Lutheran Church in Virginia and East Tennessee* (1930), 72, 143, 327, 329–331, 333–335; William Edward Eisenberg, *The Lutheran Church in Virginia, 1717–1962* (1967), 301, 309 (por.), 311, 313, 314; *Marion News*, 12 May 1921; obituaries in *Philadelphia Inquirer* and *Richmond News Leader*, both 14 Mar. 1927, *Richmond Times-Dispatch*, 16 Mar. 1927, and *Marion Smyth County News*, 24 Mar. 1927; memorials and tributes in *Lutheran Woman's Work* 20 (1927): 226–234 (quotation on 229), 271–275, *Missionary Review of the World* 50 (1927): 244 (por.), 249–250, 294, 534, 537, and *United Lutheran Church in America Convention Minutes* (1928), 298–299.

KELLY GILBERT

CROPPER, John (23 December 1755–15 January 1821), Continental army and militia officer, was born at Bowman's Folly, the Accomack County plantation of his parents, Sebastian Cropper and Sabra Corbin Cropper. His father died in the spring of 1776 and his mother in December of that year, leaving him a modest inheritance. On 15 August 1776 Cropper married Margaret Pettit. They had four daughters. Two of them, both named for his mother, died in infancy. Of the surviving daughters, one married Thomas Monteagle Bayly and was the mother of Thomas Henry Bayly, both of whom served in the House of Representatives; and one married John Wise, a Speaker of the House of Delegates, and was the mother of Henry Alexander Wise, a congressman and governor of Virginia.

John Cropper Jr., as he signed his name for most of his life, is reported to have begun recruiting a company of minutemen in Accomack County in 1775. In April 1776 the company became part of the new 9th Virginia Regiment, created during the winter of 1775–1776 for the defense of the exposed Eastern Shore counties. Cropper was commissioned a captain in the regiment, to date from 5 February 1776. Early the next year he headed north to join the Continental army and received promotion to major of the 7th Virginia Regiment on 4 January 1777. Wounded on 11 September at the Battle of Brandywine, where his unit suffered substantial losses, Cropper was promoted to lieutenant colonel effective 27 October of that year. He endured the winter of 1777–1778 at Valley Forge and saw duty at Monmouth, New Jersey. In October 1778 he received a 190-day leave to return home for the first time in almost two years.

While Cropper was home on leave in mid-February 1779, a Loyalist's privateer raided and plundered his house. Although Cropper rejoined his regiment at the beginning of August 1779, he disliked being apart from his family, became disenchanted with the condition of his unit, and complained of inadequate pay. On 16 August he resigned his commission. The Continental Congress declined to accept his resignation, but he was allowed to leave his regiment.

Cropper returned to Bowman's Folly. That winter he and the local militia tried unsuccessfully to ambush a British row galley, or barge, marauding among the Eastern Shore inlets. In May 1780 Cropper became a member of the county court. Appointed county lieutenant, or commander of the local militia, during the summer of 1781, he presided at the court-martial of a local Anglican clergyman accused of Loyalism and aiding the enemy. Cropper's most famous exploit occurred late in November 1782, when he and twenty-five volunteers joined a Maryland naval force intent on attacking six British row galleys that had been cruising unmolested in the Chesapeake Bay. On 30 November,

Cropper, the Maryland commander, and their men engaged in the futile but heroic battle of the barges in the bay. Cropper sustained several wounds and according to a local legend, repeated many years later in his obituary, was saved from death by one of his former slaves who had run away and was serving on one of the British row galleys. Cropper was briefly a British prisoner but was released after promising the British commander that he would look after and tend wounded members of the British crew.

A portrait painted by Charles Willson Peale, whom Cropper had met during the Revolutionary War, and dated 1792 depicts him as a handsome young man with dark hair and a thickening waist. Although Cropper remained attentive to family matters, his military reputation and lifelong desire for command continued to pull him into public affairs. He lost an election bid to the House of Delegates in 1780 and unsuccessfully contested the polling, but he won election to one-year terms representing Accomack County in 1784, 1785, 1786, 1787, and 1790. Cropper sat on the Committee of Propositions and Grievances during the 1784–1785 and 1785–1786 sessions of the assembly and also on the Committee of Claims in the latter session. In October 1786 and October 1787 he arrived too late to receive assignment to a standing committee. During the 1790 session he served on the Committees of Claims, Privileges and Elections, and Propositions and Grievances.

Cropper's wife died on 3 June 1784 while he was in Richmond attending his first assembly, and two years later when the General Assembly authorized creation of a school on the Eastern Shore, it was almost certainly Cropper who arranged to have it named the Margaret Academy, in honor of his late wife. In June 1803 he became president of the academy's board, which eventually erected a large brick building for the boarding school that opened for its first session in 1807 and operated until the Civil War.

On 18 September 1790 Cropper married Catharine Bayly. They had five daughters (among them a third daughter named for his mother, who also died in infancy) and five sons. After a reorganization of the state's militia, in May 1793 Cropper became lieutenant colonel of the 2d

Regiment. When war with France threatened in 1799, George Washington placed Cropper's name on a list of possible regimental commanders to be submitted to the president. Before offering Cropper the command, Washington asked John Marshall for advice. Knowing that Cropper was a firm Federalist, Marshall pronounced him "a man of fair character correct politics & unquestionable courage" but cautioned against offering him a commission at a lower rank than he had held during the Revolution lest Cropper feel insulted and decline. Flattered by the letter that Washington sent, Cropper on 4 July 1799 advised the general that any appointment the commanding officer and the president made would be accepted; but the war scare soon dissipated, and Cropper did not serve.

Although Cropper temporarily retired from elective politics in 1791, he remained a committed Federalist and detested the administrations of Thomas Jefferson and James Madison. From August 1801 until August 1803 he served as sheriff of Accomack County. In August 1812 Cropper helped draft a protest against the declaration of war that Congress had recently adopted against Great Britain. He was elected the following year to the Senate of Virginia for a four-year term representing Accomack and Northampton Counties. During the session that began in December 1815 Cropper chaired a committee to inspect the state's arms manufactory, but the records of the Senate disclose little else about his legislative influence. In spite of his initial opposition to the War of 1812, he retained command of his militia regiment and worked to protect the Eastern Shore from British raids. After the General Assembly elected a colonel junior to him as the new brigadier general, Cropper resigned his commission in March 1813. The assembly created a new 21st Brigade for the Eastern Shore in January 1815 and elected Cropper its first brigadier general.

In 1815 Cropper built a new, large, three-story frame mansion at Bowman's Folly. He was elected president of the Virginia Society of the Cincinnati in December 1816 and again the following year. A prosperous and respected local leader, he paid taxes on twenty slaves age twelve or older and almost 1,300 acres of land

in 1820. John Cropper died at Bowman's Folly on 15 January 1821 and was buried in the family cemetery there.

Biographies in Barton Haxall Wise, *Memoir of General John Cropper of Accomack County, Virginia*, in *Collections of the Virginia Historical Society*, new ser., 11 (1892): 273–315, and Alton Brooks Parker Barnes, *John Cropper: A Life Fully Lived* (1989); birth and death dates on gravestone; birth and marriage dates in Cropper family Bible records (1755–1900), VHS; John Cropper Papers, VHS; Cropper letters in Papers of the Continental Congress, RG 360, NARA, in *Washington: Retirement Series*, 4:116 (quotation), 125–128, 174, and in Executive Papers of several Virginia governors, RG 3, LVA; Revolutionary War Pension and Bounty-Land Warrant Applications, RG 15, NARA; William H. Gaines Jr., "The Battle of the Barges," *Virginia Cavalcade* 4 (autumn 1954): 33–37 (por. by Charles Willson Peale on 35); election as brigadier general in *JHD*, 1814–1815 sess., 151; will in Accomack Co. Wills (1819–1821), 336–337; obituaries in *Richmond Enquirer*, 30 Jan. 1821, and *Washington Daily National Intelligencer*, 1 Feb. 1821.

JOHN G. KOLP

CROSBY, Alanson (28 March 1879–24 February 1955), journalist, was born in Corry, Pennsylvania, and was the son of Manley Crosby, a lawyer, and Frances Clark Crosby. Even before he completed high school, he began working for a local newspaper at about age thirteen. By 1906 Crosby had become editor of the *Evening Courier* in Titusville, Pennsylvania, and in that year married Julia Yost. They had one son and one daughter, who died young. By 1911 Crosby was not only the editor of the newspaper but also secretary and treasurer of the company that published it.

For reasons not recorded and on a date not known, Crosby moved to Virginia, where on 1 April 1914 he purchased 22.5 acres of land near Belroi, in Gloucester County. He subsequently built a house there. It is likely that Crosby had accepted a job with the *Gloucester News-Reporter*, a weekly paper founded in 1912. The first reference to him in that capacity appeared on 6 July 1916 in the *Mathews Journal*, published in neighboring Mathews County, which announced that Crosby was editing the *News-Reporter* during the editor's vacation.

After the *News-Reporter* went out of business, Crosby purchased its printing press and other equipment for $600 in October 1918, and on the following 9 January he began publishing the weekly *Gloucester Gazette*. One year later he organized the Gazette Printing Company, Inc., which owned and published the newspaper and also undertook job printing. The *Gazette* carried the normal mix of local news and advertising. Crosby's editorials were well written but tediously long, and they rarely touched on local issues. During the 1930s he supported the New Deal and criticized United States senator Harry Flood Byrd (1887–1966) for opposing the administration of Franklin Delano Roosevelt. It is doubtful that the editorials had much local effect, although Crosby later blamed his downfall on rejection of his editorial positions.

The 1920s may have been good years for the *Gazette*, but it and most other businesses began feeling the effects of the Great Depression early in the 1930s. As economic conditions worsened, it became obvious that both the *Gloucester Gazette* and the *Mathews Journal* would have to take strong measures in order to continue operating. By early in 1937 the Bank of Gloucester and the Farmers Bank of Mathews had suggested a merger to save both newspapers and protect the loans that the banks had made to them. In their respective issues on 14 October 1937, the newspapers announced that as of 1 November, Tidewater Newspapers, Inc., would publish the merged *Gloucester-Mathews Gazette-Journal*, with Crosby as editor and Paul Titlow, formerly publisher of the *Journal*, as business manager. The first issue of the new weekly appeared on 11 November 1937.

Crosby and Titlow seem to have gotten along well in their managerial roles. Crosby's trouble began with disagreements with the corporation's other directors, including representatives of the two banks, who had reserved for themselves "control of the policies, both editorial and administrative," of the newspaper. At a board meeting on 14 April 1938, one director suggested "that the editor refrain from writing editorials on controversial political subjects and devote more space to subjects of purely local interest." Crosby replied that if the board insisted on changes in editorial policies, he would resign. Relations between Crosby and other members of the board deteriorated, perhaps as a consequence of continuing differences over editorial

policy and in response to the banks' dissatisfaction with the manner in which Crosby was managing the paper and with the corporation's inability to pay off its loans.

Twice Crosby volunteered to reduce his and Titlow's salaries. At the annual meeting of the board in December 1938 Crosby offered to resign if the company's business did not improve. At a meeting on 6 March 1939 he reported that he could not satisfy the banks' demands on their loans. The board then declared that the conditions of Crosby's earlier promise to resign had been fulfilled, and it accepted his resignation effective immediately. In a front-page valedictory in the *Gazette-Journal* on 6 April 1939, Crosby wrote, "In my editorial policy I have consistently contended for and supported a liberal Democracy, have sought to uphold the right as I saw it, to defend the weak, and to champion the cause of the underprivileged. There is nothing vital in that record that I would change if I could." He concluded, "I still believe in a free, unmuzzled press." The following week the board of Tidewater Newspapers printed a long rebuttal to Crosby's last article and stated that his management and financial failures had produced most of the disagreements between him and the other board members, although it singled out his editorial policy as an abuse of freedom of the press and damaging to business.

Crosby's resignation and his stated reasons for leaving received additional coverage in the state's major newspapers, which took their lead from Crosby and portrayed his troubles as the consequence of conservative business and political leaders trying to silence his liberal editorial voice. They also covered his success in finding sufficient local financial support to begin an opposition newspaper, the *Gloucester Free Press*, which began publication on 10 July 1939. Crosby, both editor and publisher, declared on the front page of the first issue that the newspaper owed "no allegiance to any financial or political group and there are no 'sacred cows' in its pasture. Its editor, and its editor alone, will determine its editorial policy, which is founded on those broad principles of personal freedom and economic justice which, seemingly, are so distasteful to our local oligarchy." The eight-page

Free Press was a financial failure and ceased publication on 7 February 1940. Crosby asserted that local advertisers had been pressured not to purchase space in his paper. In debt and unable to pay his bills, he lost his house in November 1940, when his property at Belroi was sold at public auction.

The following year Crosby moved to Richmond, where he worked for the Virginia Employment Service for about a decade before retiring in 1953. Alanson Crosby died in a Richmond hospital on 24 February 1955 and was buried in that city's Forest Lawn Cemetery.

Lucille B. Jayne, "Life History of a Newspaper Man & Family" (typescript dated 8 May 1939), WPA Biographies; birth date confirmed by BVS; Tidewater Newspapers, Inc., board of directors minutes (first quotation in bylaws adopted 29 Oct. 1937, second quotation in minutes of 14 Apr. 1938), Gloucester, Va.; *Richmond Times-Dispatch*, 30 Mar., 7 Apr., 17 May, 15 July 1939, 11 Feb. 1940; *Gloucester-Mathews Gazette-Journal*, 6 (third quotation), 13 Apr. 1939; *Gloucester Free Press*, 10 July 1939 (fourth quotation); *Washington Post*, 16 July 1939; Virginia Press Association *Bulletin* 21 (Apr. 1939): 2, 5; obituaries in *Richmond News Leader*, 24 Feb. 1955, *Richmond Times-Dispatch* and *Washington Post*, both 25 Feb. 1955, and *Gloucester-Mathews Gazette-Journal*, 3 Mar. 1955.

JOHN WARREN COOKE

CROSBY, John Fletcher Harris (9 September 1868–15 May 1948), creator of the city manager plan, was born on the Augusta County farm of his parents, William Crosby and Sarah Ann Moyers Crosby. He was educated in the local public schools and graduated from Dunsmore Commercial and Business College, in Staunton, in 1886. That same year he became the deputy clerk for Augusta County and held that position until 1891, when he began working as an accountant for a private company. After receiving a license on 28 October 1891, in Washington, D.C., Crosby married Janet Burnett, an Augusta County native. They had two sons. He returned to the deputy clerk's position in 1900.

In June 1906 Crosby was elected to Staunton's common council. The city's population had expanded to more than 10,000 following a recent annexation, thus making it a city of the first class. As such, Staunton was required by the state constitution to have a mayor, a common council, and a board of aldermen. The bicameral government, consisting of eight aldermen and fourteen councilmen, organized itself into fifteen committees to deliver services to city residents. The unwieldy arrangement soon proved disastrous.

Although there was no evidence of corruption in Staunton's municipal government, its operating procedures were ineffective, and contractors regularly entered higher-priced bids for city work than for private businesses. The poor condition of the city's streets brought these practices to a head. Citizens petitioned the council for road paving and maintenance, but the superintendent of streets kept no records of how the appropriated money had been spent. Disbursing nearly $45,000 in four years had resulted in only about one block a year being paved in the business district, while residential streets were ignored. Public concern grew as it became evident that despite an annual income of $160,000 the city was in debt for almost $600,000, a sum that exceeded the debt limit established by the state constitution.

Crosby and other members of the council searched for a solution. As deputy clerk for Augusta County, one of the largest and wealthiest counties in the state, he balanced its $500,000 budget and in effect functioned as its business manager. Comparing city government to a private corporation, he believed that having a single executive officer who reported to the council would be less cumbersome than numerous committees. Employing the motto "increased service, decreased taxes," Crosby called for instituting progressive reforms that would establish responsible, efficient government based on sound business principles.

In October 1906 the *Staunton Daily Leader* urged the council and the board of aldermen to adopt an ordinance creating an office of municipal director to oversee the city's management. The city council voted in February 1907 to establish an executive department, based in part on Crosby's ideas and a proposal by a fellow councilman who recommended that a professional engineer be hired to take charge of the street department. Most of the aldermen did not approve of such a step and instead appointed a joint committee to study the issue further. As the committee's chair, Crosby studied the commission form of city government that employed salaried commissioners to oversee municipal services and reviewed that model's application in Galveston, Texas; Des Moines, Iowa; and Norfolk. The committee issued its report on 13 January 1908 recommending that the council and board jointly appoint a salaried general manager to assume control of Staunton's administrative work, take responsibility for city employees, and make all contracts for labor and supplies. The council passed the ordinance that day, and the board of aldermen followed three days later.

In April, Charles Edward Ashburner was appointed the nation's first city manager, as the position was dubbed by the *Staunton Daily Leader*, and soon improved Staunton's infrastructure with great savings for the city. Similar improvements over the next several decades in other localities that used this system prompted Crosby to observe, "Eliminate politics in local government and you've gone a long way toward efficiency." By the 1960s most of Virginia's municipalities employed the city manager plan, and it had been adopted throughout the country as well.

Reelected to a second four-year term in 1910, Crosby served as president of the council from 1908 to 1912. He did not seek a third term in 1914 but later led a drive to petition the General Assembly for a constitutional amendment to permit smaller city councils, necessary for the success of the city manager plan. In December 1917 Crosby left his position as deputy clerk of Augusta County to become assistant clerk of the foreign relations committee of the United States House of Representatives. He resigned two months later, however, and on 1 February 1918 became the auditor-statistician for the State Department of Education. During his thirty-year tenure he reorganized the auditing department and established a bookkeeping system for tracking federal funds for vocational education.

John Fletcher Harris Crosby died of a heart attack at his home in Richmond on 15 May 1948. He was buried next to his wife, who had died in 1944, in Staunton's Thornrose Cemetery.

Biographical feature article in *Richmond Times-Dispatch*, 16 May 1937 (por. and quotations); BVS Birth Register, Augusta Co.; full name in Christos Christou Jr. and John Anthony Barnhouser Sr., *Prominent Families of Augusta Co. and Rockingham Co., VA* (1999), 113–114; publications include Crosby, "Staunton's General Manager," *Municipal Journal and Engineer* 27 (29 Dec. 1909): 954–956; Superior Court of the District of Columbia Marriage Licenses; *Staunton Spectator*, 4 Nov. 1891; *Staunton Daily Leader*, 16 Oct. 1906; *Staunton Evening Leader*, 3 Nov. 1917, 30 Jan. 1918; William M. E. Rachal, "Staunton Steps Out of the Mud: The World's First City Manager Applied Business Methods to Municipal Government," *Virginia Cavalcade* 1 (spring 1952): 9–11 (por. on 10); William A. Grubert, *The Origin of the City Manager Plan in Staunton, Virginia* (1954); obituaries in *Richmond News Leader*, 15 May 1948, and *Staunton News-Leader* and *Washington Post*, both 16 May 1948.

SUSANNE SIMMONS

CROSLAND, Clayton Edward (25 July 1886–31 March 1972), president of Averett College, was born in Selma, Alabama, and was the son of Edward Davidson Crosland and Marie Antoinette Goodwin Crosland. He grew up in East Lake, outside Birmingham, Alabama, experienced religious conversion in 1896, and received an A.B. in 1907 from Howard College (later Samford University), in Birmingham. After graduation, Crosland worked as the Sunday school secretary of the Baptist State Mission Board of Alabama and from 1908 to 1910 was the educational field secretary of the Southern Baptist Sunday School Board, headquartered in Nashville, Tennessee. In 1910 Crosland became a Rhodes Scholar and received a B.A. in 1913 and an M.A. in 1925 in modern languages from Wadham College, University of Oxford. While in Europe he also attended classes at the Sorbonne and at the Universities of Göttingen, Heidelberg, Marburg, and München. After returning to the United States in 1913, Crosland was president of the Southeast Alabama Agricultural College for one year. During the summer of 1914 he worked as director of assemblies for the George Peabody College for Teachers (later part of Vanderbilt University), in Nashville. On 19 August 1914 Crosland married Ida Holley, of Abbeville, Alabama. They had one daughter and two sons.

Less than a week after his wedding, Crosland became president of Fork Union Military Academy, a college preparatory school supported by the Baptist General Association of Virginia. During his three-year tenure, he spearheaded a successful fund-raising and building campaign that caught the attention of George A. Lea, a Danville tobacconist and treasurer of the board of trustees of Averett College (after 2001 Averett University), in Danville, who recruited Crosland to become president of the women's college in July 1917 and instructor of French, German, Latin, and philosophy. Crosland's wife, an accomplished pianist, taught piano and became lady principal.

Crosland quarreled with the college's board of trustees over finances and student conduct throughout his short administration. Despite drastic fluctuations in student enrollment as a result of World War I and a local influenza panic, the board required Crosland to improve the school's finances. The trustees complained that Crosland failed to regulate the students' social behavior in accordance with Baptist moral teachings. In November 1919 the annual meeting of the Baptist General Association of Virginia approved a resolution prohibiting modern, mixed dance at Baptist schools under its jurisdiction. At the subsequent November meeting, the Baptist Education Board condemned a statement in the Averett catalog that the college's Department of Physical Training taught aesthetic and interpretive dancing. Crosland and Lea assured the education board that they would strike all mention of dancing from their next catalog in accordance with the policy.

Nevertheless, in January 1921 Crosland authorized dancing in the college gymnasium to improve student morale during the quarantine from the flu epidemic. The Averett board of trustees convened to review the incident, and on 11 February a majority of the trustees voted to request Crosland's resignation. After prolonged debate on Crosland's fitness as president, the trustees compromised with Crosland's supporters and resolved to withhold action for thirty days, but at a closed meeting held two days later they resumed deliberating the future of Crosland's presidency and decried the negative publicity surrounding the dancing incident.

In an interview published in local newspapers, Crosland asserted that the contentious issues between him and the board went beyond granting the students permission to dance. The trustees, he maintained, were pressuring him to adopt narrow and sectarian views, such as prohibitions against dancing, smoking, and attending movies, in opposition to his belief that institutions of learning should be liberal and democratic. Although Crosland's supporters offered petitions urging arbitration and settlement, the trustees voted on 11 March 1921 to discharge Crosland, citing only his alleged mismanagement of the institution's finances as the grounds for his dismissal. In the *Danville Register*, Crosland responded to the allegations by addressing each of the charges and accusing Lea of misrepresenting the college's financial circumstances in order to secure him as president. Protesting Crosland's forced resignation, students threatened to withdraw from the school, and alumni petitioned the board of trustees, but none of these measures prompted the board to reverse its decision. Days after Crosland was formally dismissed the Averett College senior class obtained permission from Lea to hold a dance show but were restricted to featuring traditional clog and square dances. On 10 April 1921 about 3,500 members of the Danville community and students from Averett College honored Crosland in a tribute at the Blue Ridge Tabernacle with the presentation of gifts valued at approximately $1,800, including a loving cup, a silver service, and stock in a local textile company.

Crosland returned to Tennessee and in the autumn of 1921 became associate president of the Ward-Belmont School for Young Women (later Belmont University), in Nashville. In 1923 he acquired a controlling financial interest in the Columbia Military Academy, in Columbia, Tennessee, and as president and superintendent, with the rank of colonel, increased the school's enrollment by 40 percent his second year. Crosland then moved to Lake Wales, Florida, where he served as principal—in effect superintendent—of the public school from 1927 to 1934. Seeking more lucrative employment, he entered the insurance business late in 1933 as an underwriter for the Equitable Life Assurance Society. By 1940 he had moved to nearby Lakeland and for several decades continued his successful insurance career. His wife died on 13 February 1970.

Clayton Edward Crosland died on 31 March 1972 in Lakeland, Florida, and was buried in a local cemetery.

Crosland questionnaire in "The Autobiographical Notes of Various Students of the Southern Baptist Theological Seminary" (ca. 1936), Southern Baptist Theological Seminary Archives, Louisville, Ky.; Equitable Life Assurance Society *Equitable Agency Items* (24 July 1939), 15 (por.); *Register of Rhodes Scholars, 1903–1945* (1950), 145; *Who Was Who in America, with World Notables, 1977–1981* (1981), 133; *Danville Register*, 15 July 1917, 12, 13, 15–17, 19–20 Feb., 9, 12, 13 (por.), 15, 30, 31 Mar., 5, 7, 9, 12 Apr. 1921; *Religious Herald* (2 Aug. 1917), 8; *Richmond Times-Dispatch*, 14, 16, 18 Feb., 12, 21 Mar., 11 Apr. 1921; Charles Goodall Snead, *History of Fork Union Military Academy: Recollections and Review* (1926), 75–105, 107 (por.); J. I. Hayes, *A History of Averett College* (1984), 71–77; Janyce Barnwell Ahl, *Crown Jewel of the Highlands: Lake Wales, Florida* (1983), 146–150; death notice in *Tampa Tribune*, 1 Apr. 1972.

TERRY L. STOOPS

CROSS, Hardy (10 February 1885–11 February 1959), civil engineer, was born in Nansemond County and was the son of Thomas Hardy Cross, who served two terms in the House of Delegates, and Eleanor Elizabeth Wright Cross. After attending Norfolk Academy, he received an A.B. and a B.S. from Hampden-Sydney College in 1902 and 1903, respectively. Cross taught English, chemistry, and physics at Norfolk Academy from 1903 to 1906. He received a B.S. in civil engineering from the Massachusetts Institute of Technology in 1908 and three years later completed a Master of Civil Engineering degree at Harvard University.

From 1908 to 1910 Cross worked for the Missouri Pacific Railway Company as an engineer in the bridge department. In 1911 he joined the faculty of Brown University as an assistant professor and taught in the engineering department until 1918. Cross then went to New York and Boston, where for three years he engaged in the general practice of structural engineering, particularly the design of bridges and buildings. On 5 September 1921 in Washington, D.C., he married Edythe Hopwood Fenner Bridgham, who had three children from a previous marriage. They had no children of their own.

From 1921 until 1937 Cross served as a professor of structural engineering at the University of Illinois. During this period his innovative ideas changed methods of structural analysis in construction. Cross became famous as a result of his ten-page paper entitled "Analysis of Continuous Frames by Distributing Fixed-End Moments," published in the American Society of Civil Engineers *Proceedings* (1930). In it, he presented an entirely new method of analyzing complex structural frames used in buildings, bridges, and other structures. After publication of Cross's final version with comments by thirty-eight of his peers in the ASCE's *Transactions* (1932), he was immediately recognized as having solved one of the most difficult problems in structural analysis. In 1933 the ASCE awarded him the Norman Medal for his paper. Also known as the Hardy Cross method, his moment distribution method greatly simplified the many complicated calculations previously required for computing stress in rigid frames, such as those of reinforced concrete. His technique was quickly adopted and had immense practical importance around the world. Although computer programs later replaced Cross's method, it continued to be taught in engineering departments in the twenty-first century.

In 1932 Cross and Newlin Dolbey Morgan published *Continuous Frames of Reinforced Concrete*, which presented an elaboration of the former's theory, analysis, and design of buildings and bridges. In *Analysis of Flow in Networks of Conduits or Conductors* (1936), Cross applied his insights to the design of pipe networks and solved problems of water flow and pressure in municipal water systems. At the beginning of the twenty-first century, computer software for such pipe systems used the Hardy Cross method to make preliminary calculations. Designers of gas pipeline networks also applied the method to their analyses. The translation of his works into many other languages permitted their use worldwide not only in civil engineering but also in other engineering disciplines.

In 1937 Cross began sixteen years as head of the civil engineering department at Yale University. He served on an insurance industry committee that investigated the 1940 collapse of the Tacoma Narrows Bridge into Puget Sound and later published articles on the design of suspension bridges. The Society for the Promotion of

Engineering Education (later the American Society for Engineering Education) honored Cross with its Lamme Medal in 1944 for his rigorous training of future engineers. In 1952 he published *Engineers and Ivory Towers*, a collection of articles, speeches, and graduate lectures in which he emphasized the importance of good engineering to social welfare. Cross wrote numerous other articles and reports, and a collection of his most significant works appeared posthumously in a volume entitled *Arches, Continuous Frames, Columns, and Conduits: Selected Papers* (1963).

Throughout his long career Cross received frequent accolades. Hampden-Sydney awarded him an honorary doctorate of science in 1934, and three years later he received an honorary M.A. from Yale and an honorary doctorate of engineering from Lehigh University. In 1936 the American Concrete Institute awarded Cross its Wason Medal for Most Meritorious Paper. He became a fellow of the American Academy of Arts and Sciences in 1945, and the American Society of Civil Engineers granted him honorary membership in 1947. A few months before his death Cross received the Gold Medal of the British Institution of Structural Engineers. In 1959 the Franklin Institute posthumously awarded him its Frank P. Brown Medal for his contributions to engineering education and the profession.

Cross retired from Yale in 1953 and moved to Virginia Beach. Despite poor health he continued to consult with engineering firms. Hardy Cross died at his Virginia Beach residence on 11 February 1959 and was buried in Ivy Hill Cemetery, in Smithfield. The Norfolk branch of the American Society of Civil Engineers named its Hall of Fame for Cross, and the Virginia section of the ASCE established the Hardy Cross Memorial Award for the best paper presented by an engineering student.

Biographies in *Who's Who in Engineering* (1954), 535 (with birth and marriage dates), and Leonard K. Eaton, *Hardy Cross: American Engineer* (2005), with several pors.; variant birth year of 1884 in BVS Birth Register, Nansemond Co.; marriage license recorded in *Washington Post*, 3 Sept. 1921; Hardy Cross Papers, University of Illinois at Urbana-Champaign; *Engineering News-Record*, 13 July 1944, 20 Nov. 1958; *Civil Engineering* 18 (1948): 37; ibid. 29 (1959): 892; *Norfolk Virginian-Pilot*, 16 June 1995; obituaries in *New York Times*, *Norfolk Ledger-Dispatch and Portsmouth Star*, *Norfolk Virginian-Pilot*, and *Washington Post and Times Herald*, all 12 Feb. 1959, *Engineering News-Record* (19 Feb. 1959), 28, *Civil Engineering* 29 (1959): 193, and *Virginia Engineer* 9 (spring 1959): 31; editorial tribute in *Norfolk Virginian-Pilot*, 13 Feb. 1959.

ZIA RAZZAQ

CROWE, Morrill Martin (17 August 1901–10 June 1994), mayor of Richmond, was born in Saint Louis, Missouri, and was the son of Thomas Crowe, a railroad worker, and Della Meyer Crowe, a schoolteacher. His parents divorced when he was a child. By working in an uncle's drugstore he paid his way through Washington University in Saint Louis, from which he received a degree in chemical engineering in 1923. Crowe held a city job overseeing street paving while he trained to become a registered pharmacist. He then ran a Saint Louis drugstore for several years before moving to New York City as a sales agent for a pharmaceutical manufacturing firm. There on 16 April 1938 he married Kathryne Skarry, later president of the Richmond Council of Women's Organizations and the Inter-Faith Council of Richmond Area Church Women. They had no children but adopted and raised a niece. The following year Crowe moved to Richmond to become promotional director for a pharmaceutical manufacturer, William P. Poythress and Company, where he was a vice president for more than twenty years until he retired in 1966. His work earned him the nickname "Doc" Crowe.

Membership in the Kiwanis Club of Richmond enabled Crowe to become well acquainted with the city's business and industrial leaders. As president in 1953 he inaugurated a popular series of travelogue programs featuring speakers and films to raise money for local projects. An avid traveler, Crowe presented his own travel programs, and between 1958 and 1964 he visited every city in the United States with a population of more than 100,000. His other civic interests included the Richmond chapter of the Virginia Manufacturers Association and the Richmond Community Chest. Early in the 1960s he served as president of the American Cancer Society's Richmond affiliate.

In 1964 Crowe ran for city council on a slate of candidates advanced by Richmond Forward, a new civic organization that promised to improve city services and reduce tensions between the city and its neighboring counties as well as chronic conflict among members of the council. He prepared for his campaign by spending several days in the Richmond Public Library making extensive notes from newspaper reports of city council meetings. The Richmond Forward ticket comprised Crowe, seven other white candidates (most of them successful attorneys or business leaders), and one African American businessman, Benjamin Addison Cephas. Crowe and five other members of the slate, including Cephas, won election on 9 June 1964 and took office on 1 July.

On that first day the council elected Crowe mayor of the city for a two-year term. He and several Richmond Forward incumbents were reelected to the council two years later, and the council elected him to a second two-year term as mayor. Following his third election to the council in 1968, Crowe stepped down as mayor. During his tenure the city manager had responsibility for administration of the city bureaucracy, while the mayor served as presiding officer of the council and as Richmond's principal spokesman, a role for which Crowe was well suited. He spoke out against the governor's proposed sales tax in 1966 because he believed the city would receive less than its fair share, and he denounced a proposed civilian review panel to investigate charges of police misconduct, a measure that the city's African American community supported. Crowe advocated construction of a thirteen-mile express highway system and erection of a downtown coliseum to spur commercial development. He also sought public and private funds for housing, educational, recreational, and employment programs to improve the lives of low-income residents.

Even though Crowe and some of the Richmond Forward candidates won endorsements in 1968 from a local black political organization, they did not end the tensions between the city's white and black populations. Selection of a route for the new downtown expressway and construction of public housing intensified political conflict in the city. Crowe's strong endorsement of law and order in 1968, during a time of vio-

lent demonstrations elsewhere in the United States, may have seemed like support for racial segregation because that phrase was then often used by opponents of the civil rights movement.

No issue during Crowe's council service was more contentious than the city's repeated attempts to annex adjacent suburban areas. A plan for Richmond to acquire part of Henrico County was abandoned soon after he became mayor. Crowe and several other council members then began private negotiations with Chesterfield County that led in 1970 to the annexation of twenty-three square miles of that county and the addition of about 47,000 people, most of them white, to the city's population. Charging that the annexation was driven by desires to add white voters and thus halt a demographic trend that was on the verge of making Richmond a black-majority city, African Americans filed suits in federal court under the Voting Rights Act of 1965. During the protracted litigation, testimony disclosed that several council members had indeed hoped to preserve a white voting majority in the city through annexation. Crowe was not one of the leading negotiators of the transfer, and his opinion on the racial issue is not clear, but in 1968 and 1969 he vigorously supported annexation and defended its significant cultural and financial benefits to the city. As divisive legacies of the annexation and subsequent litigation, the city held no municipal elections between 1970 and 1977, and a state law of 1979 granted immunity from annexation to Richmond's neighboring counties and thus prohibited the city from again expanding its boundaries.

Late in November 1969 Crowe became the Republican nominee for a vacant seat representing the city in the Senate of Virginia. He outpolled two candidates in the four-man race, including the retiring Democratic lieutenant governor Fred Gresham Pollard, but lost the election to Lawrence Douglas Wilder, a Democrat and later the first African American governor of Virginia. Crowe announced after the election that he would not run for city council in June 1970, citing both his desire to keep the partisanship generated by the Senate race from further fracturing Richmond Forward and also the city charter's ban on partisanship in municipal elections.

In the spring of 1969 Crowe became the first executive director of the Greater Richmond Community Foundation, a charitable trust. He and his wife received a brotherhood award in December 1968 from the Richmond chapter of the National Conference of Christians and Jews (later the National Conference for Community and Justice), and in 1974 the Richmond First Club honored him with its Good Government Award. Kathryne Skarry Crowe died on 20 January 1988, and Morrill Martin Crowe died in a Richmond retirement community on 10 June 1994. Both were buried in the city's Mount Calvary Cemetery.

Feature articles in *Richmond News Leader*, 26 June 1964 (with birth date), and *Richmond Times-Dispatch*, 14 Jan. 1968; family history provided by niece Dolores Rogers Metz (2003); municipal politics covered in *Richmond Afro-American*, *Richmond News Leader*, and *Richmond Times-Dispatch*; addresses on city government in *Richmond News Leader*, 7 Mar., 28 June 1968; campaign interviews in *Richmond Afro-American*, 8 June 1968, and *Richmond News Leader*, 28 Nov. 1969; John V. Moeser and Rutledge M. Dennis, *The Politics of Annexation: Oligarchic Power in a Southern City* (1982), 48–56; obituary in *Richmond Times-Dispatch*, 11 June 1994 (por.).

BRENT TARTER

CROWN, John Randolph (12 May 1878–14 November 1940), journalist and civic leader, was born in Clarke County and was the son of Sarah Jane Smith Crown and John Oliver Crown, editor of the weekly *Clarke Courier*, published in Berryville. He studied engineering at the Shenandoah University School in Berryville, but at age seventeen he left to begin an apprenticeship at the *Courier*. When his father died in November 1899 he became editor and publisher of the newspaper.

In 1902 Crown sold the *Courier* and moved to Nebraska, where he became state editor of the *Omaha Bee*. Later he served as news editor of the *Augusta Herald* in Georgia and as city editor of the *Norfolk Virginian-Pilot*. About 1910 Crown began working as an editor in the Washington bureau of the *Baltimore Sun*. During his eight years at that newspaper, contemporary accounts credited him with being the first to report that William Jennings Bryan would support Thomas Woodrow Wilson for president in 1912 and that Wilson would attend the Versailles

peace conference after World War I. On 27 September 1915 in Washington, D.C., Crown married Martha Elizabeth Lipscomb, daughter of a Mississippi cotton planter. They had two sons and one daughter.

Crown left the *Sun* in 1918 to take his recently deceased brother's place as publisher of the *Clarke Courier*. He sold that paper in 1927. Crown became editor of the *Harrisonburg Daily News-Record* in 1923 at the request of its new owner, Harry Flood Byrd (1887–1966), a friend and influential member of the Senate of Virginia who later became governor of Virginia and a United States senator. Also close to United States senator Carter Glass and Republican congressman Campbell Bascom Slemp, Crown was recognized among his peers for extensive connections with congressional and state politicians in Virginia and Maryland. Such contacts enabled him to write many exclusive articles for the *Baltimore Sun*, even after he had begun editing the *Daily News-Record*.

An ardent promoter of community and regional development, Crown served as a director of the Harrisonburg–Rockingham County Chamber of Commerce and as secretary of the Chesapeake and Western Railway. Through his newspaper he supported Shenandoah Valley, Incorporated, a regional chamber of commerce formed at a mass meeting in January 1924 to increase residential population and tourism, expand transportation and agricultural and industrial facilities, publicize the area's natural resources, and promote the formation of a national park. He had become a director of the organization by September of that year.

Crown's greatest civic contribution to the region was his crucial role in establishing Shenandoah National Park. Known as the father of the park movement, he wrote many articles in the *Daily News-Record* extolling the scenic charms of the Blue Ridge Mountains and the economic value of tourism, while also using his political contacts to generate legislative support for the project. In 1933 he edited the *Shenandoah National Park Souvenir Book*, a promotional pamphlet containing a history and official photographs of the park, which was completed two years later.

By 1939 Crown's failing health had rendered him unable to conduct daily business at the *News-Record*. After several days in a coma John Randolph Crown died in his Harrisonburg home on 14 November 1940. He was buried in Woodbine Cemetery the following day. The Harrisonburg–Rockingham County Chamber of Commerce requested that on the day of his funeral all businesses in Harrisonburg close between 4:00 and 4:15 P.M. in tribute.

Birth date in Clarke Co. Birth Register; biographies in Bruce, Tyler, and Morton, *History of Virginia*, 5:460–461, and John W. Wayland, ed., *Men of Mark and Representative Citizens of Harrisonburg and Rockingham County, Virginia* (1943), 96–97 (with variant birth date of 12 May 1879 and por.); *Washington Post*, 28 Sept. 1915; *Harrisonburg Daily News-Record*, 11 Jan. 1924; obituaries in *Richmond News Leader* and *Winchester Evening Star*, both 14 Nov. 1940, and *Harrisonburg Daily News-Record* (with variant birth date of 12 May 1879) and *Richmond Times-Dispatch*, both 15 Nov. 1940.

JOHN F. HORAN JR.

CROXTON, Thomas (15 March 1822–3 July 1903), member of the House of Representatives, was born in Tappahannock and was the son of Richard Croxton, an Essex County justice of the peace, and his first wife, Mary S. Clements Croxton. He was raised by his father and stepmother, Frances G. Ware Croxton. After attending a local academy, Croxton received a law degree from the University of Virginia in 1842. On 5 July 1843 he married Louisiana Gatewood, of Essex County. They had six daughters and four sons, including Richard Clayborne Croxton, who graduated from the United States Military Academy, at West Point, and who during the Spanish-American War commanded the 6th Virginia Regiment of Volunteers, a black militia unit that did not go overseas, in part because of disagreement whether its experienced black officers should be replaced with white commanders.

Croxton practiced law in Essex County. In 1852 he won the first popular election for commonwealth's attorney and was reelected in 1856 and 1860. He owned seven slaves and possibly employed another by 1860, but later that year he tripled his slaveholdings and acquired more than 1,000 acres of land in Essex County when his wife inherited her father's estate. He sought election to represent Essex and King and Queen Counties in the convention called to consider Virginia's response to the secession crisis but lost in a seven-candidate field by a margin of 60 votes among 992 cast.

On 10 June 1861 Croxton enlisted as a corporal in the 9th Virginia Cavalry. In October of that year he became an aide to George Edward Pickett, then a colonel commanding Confederate forces along the Rappahannock River. Croxton accepted a commission as first lieutenant and assistant adjutant general on 10 January 1862 but resigned for unspecified health reasons on 12 May of that year during the Peninsula campaign. By the autumn of 1862 he was again prosecuting cases in the Essex County Court. In December that court appointed Croxton to an ad hoc police force to keep order in the county. His successes as a lawyer gave him a large enough income that after the final Confederate defeat he was required to seek a presidential pardon, granted on 12 April 1866.

After the Civil War, Croxton practiced law, was active in Democratic Party politics, and in 1880 was a presidential elector for Winfield Scott Hancock. In 1884 he defeated Robert Murphy Mayo, another Confederate veteran, for the House of Representatives seat from the First Congressional District, which consisted of thirteen Tidewater counties stretching from the Eastern Shore to Spotsylvania County. Croxton served on the Committees on Elections and on Private Land Claims. He rarely spoke but supported navigational improvements, such as lighthouses, buoys, and dredging projects, for his district. He was renominated without opposition in 1886, but the Republican candidate, Thomas Henry Bayly Browne, unseated him that autumn. A newspaper blamed Croxton's unexpected defeat on Democratic Party disaffection.

In January 1892 Croxton became commonwealth's attorney for Essex County to fill an unexpired term. He held the position for little more than a month before the General Assembly elected him on 23 February 1892 to a six-year term as judge of the Essex County Court. Reelected in 1897, he resigned before 6 February 1901.

Thomas Croxton died on 3 July 1903 in Tappahannock. After a funeral at Saint John's

Episcopal Church in that town, he was buried probably in an unmarked grave in a family cemetery at Poplar Spring, a nearby farm that had once belonged to him.

Birth date in French Biographies; variant birth date of 8 Mar. 1822 in *Biographical Directory of the United States Congress, 1774–1989* (1989), 852; Croxton correspondence in Virginia Political Correspondence (1779–1930), UVA; Croxton-Saunders family Bible records, LVA; South Farnham Parish Register (1825–1870, 1875), 75; Essex Co. Marriage Register; *Richmond Daily Whig*, 11 July 1843; *Warsaw Northern Neck News*, 5 Sept., 24 Oct. 1884, 13 Aug., 5 Nov. 1886, 8 Jan. 1892; *Richmond Times*, 4 Feb. 1900; Compiled Service Records; Presidential Pardons; *Congressional Record*, 49th Cong., 1st sess., 3455–3457; Woman's Club of Essex County, *Old Homes of Essex County* (1940; rev. ed. 1957), 44; death date and place of burial in Saint John's and Saint Paul's Episcopal Churches, South Farnham Parish, Register (1871–1925), 34–35; obituaries in *Richmond Times-Dispatch*, 4 July 1903, and *Warsaw Northern Neck News*, 10 July 1903.

G. W. POINDEXTER

CROZET, Claudius (31 December 1789–29 January 1864), civil engineer, was born Claude Crozet in Villefranche-sur-Saône, France. After his mother, Pierrette Varion Crozet, died, he and two of his siblings moved to Paris about 1800 with their father, François Crozet, a wine merchant. In 1805 Crozet secured admission to the École Polytechnique, where he received a technical education and military training. After graduating in 1807, he entered the artillery school at Metz and two years later was commissioned a second lieutenant in a combat engineers unit. During Napoléon I's invasion of Russia in 1812, Crozet served in an artillery corps and on 22 July won promotion to captain. Taken prisoner in September of that year at the Battle of Borodino, he was released in 1814 and returned to service in the French army.

In April 1816 Crozet resigned his commission. He entered into a marriage contract with Agathe DeCamp on 5 June of that year and married in Paris two days later. Before her death on 14 March 1861, they had two daughters and one son. Soon after his marriage he immigrated to the United States and began using the name Claudius Crozet. He started teaching at the United States Military Academy, at West Point, New York, in the autumn of 1816. Taking his place alongside several other French émigrés on the faculty, Crozet added to the curriculum his expertise in the science of artillery and developed courses in geometry. He published a textbook entitled *A Treatise on Descriptive Geometry: For the Use of the Cadets of the United States Military Academy* (1821). Despite his academic success, Crozet feuded with administrators and in 1821 sought without success a position at the University of Virginia, which had not yet opened. He finally left West Point in 1823 to become principal engineer for the Virginia Board of Public Works, effective on 2 June of that year.

Although the Board of Public Works had existed for seven years, by the time of Crozet's appointment its program of supporting private internal improvement projects had yet to reap many economic benefits for the state. The directors immediately charged their new principal engineer with the tasks of aiding in surveying small-scale projects and examining the feasibility of a statewide route linking the Ohio River and Tidewater Virginia. During the summer of 1825 Crozet undertook a detailed survey of western Virginia, and over the next few years he strongly urged the General Assembly to authorize construction of a transportation system comparable to New York's Erie Canal. At first he recommended extending the existing water route along the James River across the state to the Kanawha River, but he soon began advocating a railroad as the most efficient and cost-effective means of linking the Ohio River with the Chesapeake Bay.

Crozet found, however, that sectional interests rendered members of the General Assembly unsympathetic to a centralized statewide plan of internal improvements. The shortsighted goals of local politicians consistently frustrated the forward-looking engineer, who believed that such improvements would make Virginia the most important state in the country. In 1831 the legislature cut the principal engineer's salary and refused to act on his plans for a state-funded railroad in western Virginia. In response to these difficulties, made worse by the death of his elder daughter the year before, Crozet resigned.

Crozet's expertise in internal improvements and his French background led him to Louisiana, where he became the state engineer in 1832. He found the politics there just as complicated as they had been in Virginia, and in 1834 he resigned in order to accept the presidency of Jefferson College, a preparatory school in Saint James Parish. Two years later Crozet left to become a civil engineer with the city of New Orleans, but after briefly struggling with the city's drainage problems he decided to leave Louisiana altogether. This restlessness was typical of Crozet, whom contemporaries frequently described as irritable, intolerant of anyone who disagreed with him, and unpopular. Despite his difficult personality, on 5 April 1837 the Virginia Board of Public Works rehired him as principal engineer. The General Assembly eliminated the office in March 1843. Five years later on order of the assembly Crozet prepared a lithographic map of internal improvements and an accompanying brief history entitled *Outline of the Improvements in the State of Virginia* (1848).

From 1837 to 1845 Crozet served as the first president of the board of directors of the Virginia Military Institute, which opened in Lexington in 1839. Using his own formal military training he helped install a curriculum patterned after his experiences at the École Polytechnique and at the United States Military Academy. He worked from 1845 to 1849 as principal of the financially plagued Richmond Academy. In 1848 Crozet published *An Arithmetic for Colleges and Schools*, which appeared in two subsequent editions. He also wrote another textbook, *First Lessons in Arithmetic: Being an Introduction to the Complete Treatise for Schools and Colleges* (1857).

In 1849 Crozet embarked on the work that earned him a national reputation as the chief engineer for the Blue Ridge Railroad Company (later part of the Chesapeake and Ohio Railroad Company). On the planned railroad route extending from Charlottesville to Staunton, he tested many of his ideas concerning the construction of railroad tunnels through mountainous terrain. In an era when tunneling through solid mountain rock was considered prohibitively expensive, Crozet proposed four manually drilled single-track tunnels through the Blue Ridge Mountains ranging from 100 to more than 4,200 feet in length at a cost of about $803,000. Construction took eight years. The longest tunnel, located at Rockfish Gap and usually designated the Crozet Tunnel, opened in April 1858. The expense and large-scale coordination required inflamed Crozet's testy personality, which was exacerbated by the death of his son in April 1855.

In 1857 Crozet became the principal assistant engineer in charge of building an aqueduct to secure a fresh water supply for Washington, D.C. His position was eliminated in July 1859, and the next year he became the chief engineer of the Virginia and Kentucky Railroad. Sectional tensions complicated work on this rail line, and construction stopped when Kentucky did not secede from the Union. Claudius Crozet died at his son-in-law's home in Chesterfield County on 29 January 1864. Initially buried in an unmarked grave in Richmond's Shockoe Cemetery, his body was reinterred in 1942 on the grounds of the Virginia Military Institute. The Albemarle County town of Crozet and the VMI mess hall bear his name. The Richmond residence where he lived from 1828 to 1832 was added to the Virginia Landmarks Register and the National Register of Historic Places in 1971 and 1972, respectively.

Baptismal record reproduced in *Bulletin de la Société des Amis de la Bibliothèque de l'Ecole Polytechnique* no. 6 (June 1990): 12; William Couper, *Claudius Crozet: Soldier-Scholar-Educator-Engineer (1789–1864)* (1936), with variant birth name of Benoît Crozet on 6; Ulrich Troubetzkoy, "Colonel Claudius Crozet," *Virginia Cavalcade* 12 (spring 1963): 5–10; Robert F. Hunter and Edwin L. Dooley Jr., *Claudius Crozet: French Engineer in America, 1790–1864* (1989), with variant birth date of 2 Jan. 1790 on 1 and frontispiece por.; Claudius Crozet Papers, VMI (including French military records and marriage contract, all with birth name of Claude Crozet and birth date of 31 Dec. 1789); other official reports, correspondence, maps, and surveys in Board of Visitors Minutes and Superintendent's Records, VMI, in Virginia Military Institute Records (1837–1850), LVA, in Board of Public Works, RG 57, House of Delegates Executive Communications, RG 79, and *Annual Reports of the Board of Public Works*, all LVA, and in various collections at LVA, NARA, United States Military Academy, UVA, VHS, and W&M; Elizabeth Dabney Coleman, "The Story of the Virginia Central Railroad, 1850–1860" (Ph.D. diss., UVA, 1957), 56–92; Daniel L. Schodek, *Landmarks in American Civil Engineering* (1987), 165–168; *Richmond Times-Dispatch*, 14 Aug. 1941, 7 Nov. 1942; will and estate inventory in Richmond City Hustings Will Book, 22:550–552, 571–572; death notices in *Daily Richmond Enquirer*, *Richmond Daily Dispatch*, and *Richmond Whig*, all 4 Feb. 1864.

SEAN PATRICK ADAMS

CRUMP, Beverley Tucker (10 June 1854–30 March 1930), judge of the State Corporation Commission and president of the Special Court of Appeals, was born in Richmond and was the son of William Wood Crump, a prominent attorney, and Mary Susan Tabb Crump. He attended private schools in Richmond and in 1873 graduated first in a class of fifty-one at the Virginia Military Institute. After studying at the Universities of Berlin and Göttingen, Crump enrolled as a law student at the University of Virginia in 1877. He received an LL.B. in June 1878 and that autumn began practicing law in Richmond with his father. Although their practice focused on corporate law, they also represented criminal defendants. In the spring of 1885 the Crumps joined two other regionally prominent lawyers in unsuccessfully defending Thomas Judson Cluverius, of King and Queen County, in a sensational and highly publicized murder trial. Crump practiced law on his own after his father died in February 1897.

On 15 October 1884 Crump married Henrietta Ogle Tayloe. They had one son and three daughters. In 1893 he won election to one of five seats representing the city of Richmond in the House of Delegates. During his one-year term Crump served on the Committees for Courts of Justice, for Banks, Currency, and Commerce, and for Federal Relations and Resolutions. The General Assembly elected him a judge on the Richmond Circuit Court in 1902. Before he could take office, however, the governor named him, along with Henry Fairfax and Henry Carter Stuart (1855–1933), to the new State Corporation Commission. The legislature confirmed the appointment on 19 November 1902.

At their first meeting on 2 March 1903, his fellow commissioners chose Crump, the only attorney, as chair of the SCC. The judges possessed executive, judicial, and legislative powers to charter and regulate corporations in Virginia. No member had regulatory experience, but Crump worked with the nascent national trade and industrial associations, as well as with experts from federal and state governments, to impose consumer-friendly regulations on Virginia railroads. During its first years the SCC set uniform classifications for freight traffic on the state's railroads and prescribed telegraph rates.

Crump was reappointed to a six-year term beginning in February 1904 and remained chair. The next year Senator Thomas Staples Martin, an early opponent of the SCC, attacked Crump for having purchased a $100 share of stock in the Virginia Corporation Company, which drafted charters for applicants to the SCC. Crump, who had been appointed by Martin's rival, Andrew Jackson Montague, argued that his support of the service company facilitated the technical work of the SCC. Montague privately fretted at Crump's indiscretion but publicly defended him as a good citizen who had the state's best interest at heart. Shortly before resigning from the commission effective 1 June 1907, Crump wrote a landmark decision on 27 April that made Virginia one of the first southern states to set maximum rates that railroads could charge passengers.

In November 1911 the governor appointed Crump to fill a vacancy on the Law and Equity Court of the city of Richmond, a post he held until his death. In a 1921 decision holding that workers' compensation insurance did not cover an employee's accident while off the clock, Crump wrote that the lunch hour was not a risk incident of employment, "for the place may have no connection with the employment, and lunch is rather an incident of life generally."

The General Assembly created a Special Court of Appeals in 1924 to aid in clearing the congested docket of the Virginia Supreme Court of Appeals. The judges of the Supreme Court named Crump to the Special Court on 18 June 1924. He was sworn in five days later and immediately elected president by his fellow judges. After having disposed of all its designated cases, the court dissolved on 24 June 1926. Another backlog of cases required the creation of a second Special Court of Appeals, which met from 19 July 1927 until 18 December 1928. Crump again sat on the court as president.

About fifty of Crump's opinions written during the two sessions of the Special Court were collected and printed with the decisions of the

Supreme Court of Appeals. His judicial opinions displayed a straightforward approach to complex legal problems and avoided arcane legal language. In 1928 he refused to order election officials to permit an African American Democrat to vote in a party primary. Crump argued that primary elections were private affairs, not subject to Fourteenth and Fifteenth Amendment constitutional protections, and thus Democratic Party officials could determine who would be allowed to vote.

When the Richmond Bar Association unanimously endorsed him to fill a vacancy on the state's highest court in February 1925, the seventy-year-old Crump declined consideration because he did not want to change the character of his daily life and work. In 1928 the president of the Supreme Court of Appeals named him to the Judicial Council of Virginia, a body established by the General Assembly to survey the conditions of the state's courts and recommend improvements in their rules and practices. He traveled to Florida in March 1930 in hopes that the mild climate would improve his failing health. Beverley Tucker Crump died in a Saint Petersburg hotel early in the morning of 30 March 1930. The president and judges of the Supreme Court of Appeals were honorary pallbearers at his funeral two days later at Saint Paul's Episcopal Church, in Richmond, on whose vestry he had served for many years. He was buried in Hollywood Cemetery.

Biographies in Tyler, *Men of Mark*, 1:281–282 (por. facing 281), and Henry C. Riely, "Beverley Tucker Crump," *Virginia State Bar Association Proceedings* (1930), 207–221 (por. facing 207); birth and death dates in Tabb family Bible records (1824–1930) and marriage date in Tayloe family Bible records (1687–1969), both LVA; BVS Marriage Register, Richmond City; Crump Family Papers, VHS; *Washington Post*, 19 Nov. 1902, 13 Apr. 1907; *Richmond News Leader*, 31 May 1907, 24 June 1924, 14 Feb. 1925, 19 July 1927; *Richmond Times-Dispatch*, 1 June 1907, 20 Dec. 1922, 14 Feb. 1925, 31 Mar. 1928; *JSV*, 1902 sess., 68–69, 74, 1904 sess., 29, 41; *JHD*, 1908 sess., 135, 137, 1912 sess., 46, 62; Case No. 99 (27 Apr. 1907), *Fifth Annual Report of the State Corporation Commission of Virginia for the Year Ending December 31, 1907* (1908), 71–102; Supreme Court of Appeals Order Book, 39:330, RG 100, LVA; Special Court of Appeals Order Book, 4:1, 133, 135, 218, RG 107, LVA; *Virginia Law Register*, new ser., 7 (1922): 827–835 (quotation on 829); George Harrison Gilliam, "Making Virginia Progressive: Courts and Parties, Railroads and Regulators, 1890–1910," *VMHB* 107 (1999): 189–222; obituaries and tributes in *Richmond Times-Dispatch*, 30, 31 Mar., 24 June 1930, 11 Mar. 1931, and *Richmond News Leader*, 31 Mar. 1930, 5 Nov. 1931; Richmond Bar Association memorial published as *Beverley Tucker Crump: In Memoriam* (1930).
GEORGE HARRISON GILLIAM

CRUMP, Frank Thomas (6 January 1867–26 September 1951), Baptist lay leader, was born in Augusta, Georgia, and was the son of George R. Crump and Regina Pocahontas Gunn Crump, natives of Richmond and Henrico County, Virginia, respectively. He was educated in Richmond public schools and early in the 1880s joined the lumber business of his maternal relatives as a clerk and bookkeeper. By 1892 he had established F. T. Crump and Company, which manufactured boxes. On 12 December 1895 Crump married Nannie Moore Ellyson, daughter of James Taylor Ellyson, later lieutenant governor of Virginia. They had one son. Crump's father-in-law chaired the State Democratic Committee at the turn of the century, and Crump assisted him with managing several campaigns. He was also an active member of Second Baptist Church, where he served as superintendent of the Sunday school for thirty years between 1897 and 1931.

His business acumen and zeal for Baptist causes drew the notice of church leaders. When the treasurer of the Baptist General Association of Virginia resigned in November 1919, Crump was appointed in his stead. On 1 January 1920 he began his duties, which also included serving as treasurer of the Woman's Missionary Union, an auxiliary of the General Association. He was formally elected to the position at the association's annual meeting in November 1920.

Crump took office during a period of innovation and challenge. In 1919 the Southern Baptist Convention launched a campaign to raise $75 million over five years to fund its missions and other benevolent and educational institutions. Agreeing to participate, the General Association elected to raise $7 million. Before this effort by the SBC, Baptist missions had been funded through special appeals by agency officials who traveled from church to church raising money, and although persuasive speakers and emotional causes thrived, many others did not. When the 75 Million Campaign, which centralized fund-raising efforts, concluded in 1924, Crump had managed the more than $6 million given by Virginia Baptists, which was disbursed around the state and throughout the South.

In 1925 the Southern Baptist Convention, convinced of the need for more business-oriented approaches, adopted a Cooperative Program as its method of denominational funding, in which church gifts were sent to treasurers of the state conventions who then distributed them on a local and national level according to an approved formula. Crump became a tireless champion of the cooperative system as an efficient and equitable way to finance the work of the church. Through the weekly page allotted to him in the *Religious Herald* he exhorted readers to increase their giving and especially to tithe consistently each week. During the next twenty-five years an estimated $30 million passed through Crump's office on the way to support a network of Baptist institutions in Virginia and around the world.

During the Great Depression many of the state's churches and missions suffered financially. Crump proposed that the General Association set aside a portion of the state's share of funds from the Cooperative Program to liquidate their debts. The plan succeeded, and after the debts were paid Crump established a reserve fund of more than $100,000 for future financial emergencies.

Following the incumbent's death, in June 1936 Crump was appointed acting executive secretary of the Virginia Baptist Board of Missions and Education. On 28 January 1937 he was unanimously elected the board's executive secretary, with responsibility for overseeing the work of all the board's departments, including pastoral aid, mission and Sunday schools, training programs, and prison ministries. Crump remained in that office until February 1944, when he declined to be a candidate for reelection. Throughout his long career with the Baptist General Association of Virginia, Crump also served on the Laymen's Missionary Movement Committee from 1917 to 1920, as the corresponding secretary for the Education Board from 1919 to 1935, as a member of the State Mission Board at various times

between 1920 and 1946, and as treasurer of the Baptist Extension Board after 1943.

In April 1949 Crump broke his leg after falling on the steps of the Baptist Building in Richmond. He continued to work from home during his seven-month recuperation but retired effective 31 December 1949, having served thirty years as treasurer, the longest tenure to that date. Frank Thomas Crump died of arteriosclerosis at his Richmond home on 26 September 1951 and was buried in Hollywood Cemetery.

Biography in *Encyclopedia of Southern Baptists* (1958–1971), 1:338; BVS Marriage Register, Richmond City; *Richmond Dispatch*, 13 Dec. 1895; *Religious Herald*, 1 Jan. 1920, 11 Feb. 1937, 24 Feb., 16 Mar. 1944, 5 Jan. 1950; *Richmond News Leader*, 28 Jan. 1937, 4 Jan. 1950; writings include Crump, "Our Virginia Baptist Program," in James Edgar Dillard, *We Southern Baptists, 1937–8* (ca. 1938), 55–62; obituaries in *Richmond News Leader*, 26 Sept. 1951, and *Richmond Times-Dispatch*, 27 Sept. 1951; editorial tributes and memorials in *Religious Herald*, 4, 11 Oct. 1951, Baptist General Association of Virginia *Journal* (1951), 5–6 (por. facing 5), 219–221, and Woman's Missionary Union of Virginia *Report* (1952), n.p.

MICHAEL J. CLINGENPEEL

CRUMP, George William (26 September 1786–1 October 1848), member of the House of Representatives, was born in Powhatan County and was the son of Goodrich Crump, who early in 1779 had married Judith Howlett. He enrolled at Washington Academy (later Washington and Lee University) in 1800 but was suspended in 1803 for outlandish high jinks, which included running naked through the streets of Lexington. Crump matriculated at the College of New Jersey (later Princeton University) in November 1803 and graduated in 1805, after which he studied medicine at the University of Pennsylvania from 1806 to 1808. Although he did not complete a degree at the latter institution, contemporaries routinely referred to him as Doctor Crump.

Crump settled in Cumberland County, where he executed a marriage bond in April 1813 and soon afterward married Ann P. Macon. Before her death on an unrecorded date before 1820 they had one son, who became a midshipman and died at sea before his twentieth birthday. From 1817 to 1822 Crump served consecutive one-year terms representing Cumberland County in the House of Delegates. During all five terms he sat on the Committee of Schools and Colleges. Crump also served on the Committee on Claims in 1817, on the Committee of Finance from 1818 to 1821 (in the latter year as chair), on the Committee of Propositions and Grievances from 1818 to 1820 (as chair in 1819 and 1820), and on the Committee of Privileges and Elections in 1821. Elected again in 1825, he was ranking member of the Committee of Finance.

Crump resigned his seat in the House of Delegates on 31 January 1826 following his election on 21 January to the House of Representatives to fill the seat of John Randolph of Roanoke, who had been elected to the United States Senate the previous month. An ardent supporter of Randolph and the states' rights school of Virginia politics, Crump aligned himself with the Jacksonian Democrats while representing the Fifth Congressional District, consisting of Buckingham, Charlotte, Cumberland, and Prince Edward Counties. He did not serve on any standing committees during his single term, but he was appointed to select committees for examining the Patent Office and for adjusting certain customs duties and excise taxes. Crump introduced one resolution for augmenting postal routes in Virginia and occasionally presented petitions from constituents, but otherwise he seldom spoke during congressional proceedings. His record showed staunch support for fiscal retrenchment. He voted against most federal spending projects that came before the House and unflinchingly opposed appropriations for internal improvements. The sole area in which Crump seemed willing to loosen the federal purse strings involved relief for Revolutionary War veterans; his support in this regard probably influenced his later appointment to the Pension Office.

Crump did not campaign for Congress in 1827 because Randolph returned to claim his former seat. Instead, that year he was elected to the House of Delegates, again representing Cumberland County. Although not appointed to any standing committees, Crump was ranking member of a select committee to examine the Bank of Virginia and the Farmers' Bank of Virginia. At a meeting in January 1828 supporting Andrew Jackson's presidential candidacy, he spoke in

favor of endorsing John C. Calhoun for vice president, but he later became estranged from the states' rights vanguard. In March 1831 Jackson appointed Crump consul for the island of Saint-Barthélemy, but Crump apparently declined the position and that summer mounted an unsuccessful campaign to return to the House of Representatives.

During the 1820s Crump found himself in straitened circumstances. Failure to pay off a $2,500 banknote forced the sale at public auction in 1828 of a 342-acre parcel in Powhatan County in which he held life interest through his deceased wife. Crump became a temporary clerk in the Pension Office in 1832, and the following year the president named him its chief clerk. Crump's performance evidently pleased the next four presidential administrations, because he continued as chief clerk until his death.

During the last several months of his life a severe illness left George William Crump gravely incapacitated. He wrote his will on 15 August 1848 and that autumn returned to Virginia to stay with relatives in Powhatan County, where he died on 1 October 1848. His place of burial is unknown.

French Biographies (with erroneous death year of 1850); Crump correspondence in Tazewell Family Papers, LVA, and Nash Family Papers and Robert Lee Traylor Papers, both VHS; Cumberland Co. Marriage Bonds (bond undated but endorsed Apr. 1813); Powhatan Co. Deed Book, 10:214–216, 12:446–447; *Richmond Enquirer*, 30 Dec. 1825, 24–28 Jan. 1826, 20 Jan. 1827, 15 Mar., 15 July, 16 Aug. 1831; *JHD*, 1825–1826 sess., 145; *Journal of the House of Representatives*, 19th Cong., 1st sess., 220, 239, 2d sess., 160, 182; William Cabell Bruce, *John Randolph of Roanoke, 1773–1833* (1922), 1:541–542, 2:2–5, 758; Powhatan Co. Will Book, 13:349–350; obituary in *Washington Daily Union*, 8 Oct. 1848 (died at age "62 years and 5 days"), reprinted in part in *Daily Richmond Enquirer* and *Washington Daily National Intelligencer*, both 9 Oct. 1848.

ERIC TSCHESCHLOK

CRUMP, Josiah (ca. 1838–15 February 1890), member of the Richmond city council, was born in Richmond and was the son of Johanna Crump (whose maiden name is unknown) and Josiah Crump, who was later said to have been the only African American in Richmond who ran a hotel for white customers. Whether Crump was born free or enslaved is unclear, and records pertaining to his early life are scarce. By 1860 he was free, residing in Richmond with his mother and stepfather, James Robinson, and working with the latter as a teamster. After Robinson's death, Crump ran wagons and hauled freight until 1871, by which time he was working as a clerk in the Richmond post office. The city's postmaster, Elizabeth Van Lew, was a leader of the city's Republican Party, and Crump's appointment likely indicates that he had begun taking part in Republican Party politics. He purchased his first property in Richmond in October 1872 and thereafter owned one or two lots and houses in the city.

In 1870 and 1875 Crump attended conventions organized to advance the interests of African American laboring men in Richmond. In May 1876 he won election to Richmond's bicameral city council. He represented Jackson Ward on the board of aldermen from 1876 to 1884 and again from 1888 to 1890. Crump sat on committees that were important to his constituents, such as the committees for the first and second markets, as well as the committees on the police and on streets, to which African American members usually were appointed. He also served on the committee on ordinances, a rarity for a black alderman, and on relatively less-prestigious committees including those on public grounds and buildings and on claims and salaries.

Crump and other African American community leaders succeeded in many ways in protecting or improving the lives of their constituents in spite of opposition from a white Democratic majority that was usually united. Even during the growing racial hostility of the 1880s and 1890s, Crump and his colleagues established a night school for adults, provided fuel for poor residents, made improvements to streets and installed better lighting, and ended the practice of grave-robbing by which medical schools obtained African American cadavers for dissecting laboratories. Such achievements were not matched until the post–World War II generation of civil rights pioneers.

Crump served as a member of the Republican State Committee in 1880. A loyal supporter of Ulysses S. Grant, he was one of 306 delegates at that year's Republican National Convention who tried to nominate Grant for a third term as president. Like many other politically active African Americans, Crump supported the Read-

justers, who proposed to refinance and reduce the principal and interest rate on Virginia's large antebellum public debt. At the 1881 Republican State Convention, he was elected temporary chair of the faction that successfully pushed for a coalition with the Readjusters.

In 1882 the governor appointed Crump to a two-year term on the board of the Central Lunatic Asylum, in Petersburg, the state's first black mental hospital. Crump was the board's president pro tempore, a member of the executive committee, and briefly acting president when the presiding officer resigned in January 1883. Throughout the 1880s Crump offered advice on local politics and patronage policy to William Mahone, the Readjuster leader who joined the Republican Party while a member of the United States Senate from 1881 to 1887.

Crump may have lived with his mother until he married Fernella Meriweather, a member of a prominent middle-class African American family, on 19 December 1883. They had two daughters and one son. Sometime after his marriage Crump joined Saint Philip's Episcopal Church. He lost his job as a postal clerk after a Democrat won the presidential election in 1884, and late in the 1880s he operated a grocery near his home. A member of Davis Fountain 106, Grand Fountain United Order of True Reformers, he was also a captain in the Attucks Guard, one of the city's black militia companies.

Josiah Crump died of pyaemia at his Richmond home on 15 February 1890. He had won respect in both the black and white communities in the increasingly segregated city. Richmond's aldermen passed resolutions of mourning that praised their former colleague as "one of the most active and zealous members of the Board who by his courteous and kind bearing won the esteem and good will of his fellow members, . . . who was always faithful and conscientious in the discharge of his duties to his constituents, and who was ever watchful of the interests of the city." Many aldermen and common council members joined a crowd estimated at five or six thousand in paying their respects and riding in the procession to the funeral service at the Third Street African Methodist Episcopal Church. (His own church had been too small for the throngs of people expected to attend.) Crump was buried in Union Mechanics Cemetery.

Biographies in *Richmond Daily Dispatch*, 20 Aug. 1875 (age thirty-seven), Jackson, *Negro Office-Holders*, 27 (por.), 57 (birth year of 1838 probably provided by daughter), 84, 85, and Eric Foner, ed., *Freedom's Lawmakers: A Directory of Black Officeholders during Reconstruction* (1993), 54–55; Census, Richmond City, 1860 (free and age twenty-three on 14 Aug. 1860), 1880 (listed as Joseph Crump, age forty on 2 June 1880); BVS Marriage Register, Richmond City (age forty-five on 19 Dec. 1883); *Richmond Daily Whig*, 20 Dec. 1883; some Crump letters in William Mahone Papers, Duke; Michael B. Chesson, "Richmond's Black Councilmen, 1871–96," in Howard N. Rabinowitz, ed., *Southern Black Leaders of the Reconstruction Era* (1982), 191–222; BVS Death Register, Richmond City (age fifty-three on 15 Feb. 1890); obituaries and accounts of funeral in *Richmond Dispatch*, 16 (died in his fifty-second year), 18 Feb. 1890, *Richmond Times*, 16 Feb. 1890, and *Richmond Planet*, 22 Feb. 1890 (died in his fifty-third year; quotation).

MICHAEL B. CHESSON

CRUMP, Pleasants Roper "Snowball" (1 September 1905–1 August 1995), tap dancer, was born in Richmond and was the son of Rosa Smith Crump and her first husband, Robert Crump. While he was a boy, his father died, and his mother, who worked as a domestic servant, married William Gordon in 1914. Crump dropped out of Armstrong High School to help support his family. While a student, he observed the young men who danced on the street corners at Second and Clay Streets in Jackson Ward, the lively entertainment center of Richmond's African American community. A self-taught tap dancer, Crump performed as the Dancing Busboy in local black nightclubs. He offered tap-dancing lessons at community centers and became a successful entertainer in the city's white clubs. By 1926 he had obtained engagements as far away as New York, where he performed in Schenectady as the Van Curler Kid. On 7 April 1929, in Richmond, he married Fannie Bell Snow, a native of Lynchburg. They had two daughters and one son.

Crump later recalled that he had received the nickname Snowball in 1930, while performing at the Richmond Hotel's rooftop garden. Several prominent businessmen complimented him and said that his tap dancing reminded them of the Richmond-born and inter-nationally famous dancer Bill "Bojangles" Robinson. Having previously given Robinson the nickname "Snowbird," they christened Crump "Snowball." Encouraged by Richmond's mayor, Crump went to New York City early in the 1930s to study with Robinson. He impressed Robinson with his abilities, and they danced together at prominent New York hotels and nightclubs. In 1938 Crump performed at the Hotel New Yorker and at the Belmont Plaza, and in August of that year he won first place on the *Major Bowes Amateur Hour*. As a result he joined Bowes's *Rodeo Rhythm Revue*, a vaudeville road show that toured the nation. Crump later asserted that he was the first black entertainer to tour with the troupe.

The diminutive Crump (he stood five feet, three inches tall) was known for his debonair stage costume composed of a tuxedo, top hat, and white gloves and cane, along with a white carnation boutonnière in his lapel and a cigar in his hand. Skilled at clog, buck and wing, and fancy tap styles, he displayed a distinctive flashing, energetic, and bold dancing. At the crowd-pleasing climax of Crump's act, he lay flat on his back and tap-danced on the seat of an overturned chair.

About 1940 Crump returned to Richmond to raise his family, but he continued to dance. During World War II he toured with United Service Organization troupes and stage shows for military camps. Crump's travels took him throughout the United States and also to other countries, including appearances in Havana, Mexico City, and London. Like his mentor Robinson, he danced with Shirley Temple. Crump was among the first African Americans to appear on such early television programs as *The Bob Hope Show*, *The Ed Sullivan Show*, and *What's My Line?* In Richmond he appeared on at least one radio broadcast of WRVA's *Old Dominion Barn Dance*.

Crump worked as a clerk for the Internal Revenue Service until he retired in 1960. In the years that followed he had several part-time jobs, but his passion for tap dancing kept him performing well into his eighties. Delighting Richmond-area audiences, Crump appeared at countless public and private events. He entertained at local festivals, schools, hospitals, civic centers, charity events, and before governors at the State Capitol. For more than forty years he danced to "Tea for Two" and "Sweet Georgia Brown" on top of the dugout at Richmond's minor-league baseball fields, including the inaugural game at the Diamond in 1985. When asked what kept him dancing, Crump answered, "I don't want to sit down and dry out. If you keep on moving, you keep on moving."

Known as the unofficial mayor of Southside Richmond, Crump was highly regarded for his extensive community work at churches, schools, and nursing homes and also for tutoring aspiring tap dancers. In 1991 the Retired Senior Volunteer Program of the United Way presented him with an award for 5,000 hours of service at the South Richmond Senior Center. His wife died on 1 June 1985. Pleasants Roper "Snowball" Crump died on 1 August 1995 at his home in Richmond. His remains were cremated.

Birth and death dates confirmed by BVS; feature articles in *Richmond Times-Dispatch*, 1 May 1972, 28 Dec. 1979 (pors.), and *Richmond News Leader*, 1 Sept. 1987; BVS Marriage Register, Richmond City; *Norfolk Journal and Guide*, 8 Jan. 1927; *Richmond Planet*, 6 Oct. 1934 (por.); *Chicago Defender*, 4 June 1938; *Afro-American and Richmond Planet*, 20 Aug. 1938; *Richmond News Leader*, 23 Aug. 1938, 16 Apr. 1985 (quotation); *Richmond Style Weekly*, 21 July 1987; obituaries in *Richmond Times-Dispatch*, 3 Aug. 1995 (with variant death date of 2 Aug. 1995), and *Richmond Free Press*, 3–5 Aug. 1995; tribute in *Richmond Free Press*, 10–12 Aug. 1995.

KATHRYN H. FULLER-SEELEY

CRUMP, William Wood (25 November 1819–27 February 1897), attorney, was born in Richmond and was the son of Sterling Jamieson Crump and Elizabeth Wood Crump. He attended the College of William and Mary from 1835 to 1840 and received a law degree in the latter year. Crump maintained a close association with the college for the rest of his life and with his former law professor, the prominent states' rights theorist Nathaniel Beverley Tucker, until Tucker's death in 1851. In an 1843 address Crump extolled the college's historic role in Virginia and lamented that the perceived decline in Virginia's status was in part a consequence of the neglect and concomitant decline of the college. On 1 January 1846 he married Mary Susan Tabb, of

Gloucester County, who died on 7 April 1891. Their three daughters and three sons included Beverley Tucker Crump, who became a judge of the State Corporation Commission and president of the Special Court of Appeals.

Crump began practicing law in Richmond in 1840 and soon gained professional success as a persuasive advocate and notable trial tactician who was effective with juries and adept in examining witnesses. In September 1851, to fill a vacancy caused by resignation, the governor appointed him judge of the circuit court for Henrico County and the city of Richmond, one of the state's busiest jurisdictions. Crump was not a candidate for election under the new Virginia constitution, which made the office of circuit court judge elective. He stepped down from the bench at the completion of the term on 1 July 1852.

Judge Crump, as he was thereafter known, also had a long career of political involvement. He delivered addresses on some of the central political issues of his time. A member of Richmond's common council for a single term from 1845 to 1846, he chaired a study committee in the former year that called for the council to recommend that the General Assembly incorporate a company for the purpose of converting the city from oil lamps to gas lighting. In national politics, as befit a student and admirer of Tucker, Crump supported John C. Calhoun and the annexation of Texas. He was a close friend of John Moncure Daniel, editor of the Democratic *Richmond Examiner*, and kept him apprised of local and state politics while Daniel served as American minister to the Kingdom of Sardinia. During the presidential campaign of 1856, Crump warned the southern states against "the relentless pursuit of us by northern fanaticism."

In March 1864 Crump became assistant secretary of the treasury in the Confederate government. Later that year he successfully argued that a proposal made to the Confederate Congress to draft the department's clerks who were younger than age forty for the defense of Richmond would severely disrupt the treasury's work. In his application for a pardon after the Civil War, Crump described his wartime office as "Assistant to the Secretary of the Treasury of the late Confederate States," a position he characterized as "purely subordinate and ministerial." He received a presidential pardon on 26 June 1865. Crump was later one of twenty men who posted $5,000 each for the release of Jefferson Davis while the former Confederate president awaited trial for treason.

In 1866 Crump won a special election to fill one of Richmond's vacant seats in the House of Delegates. He chaired the Committee on Finance and served on the Committees for Courts of Justice and of Resolutions. An early supporter of the Conservative Party, Crump vigorously opposed adoption of the new state constitution drafted by the Convention of 1867–1868 because he believed that it jeopardized the traditional antebellum political, racial, and social order. In 1875 he was elected to a two-year term in the House of Delegates. During the session of 1875–1876 he again chaired the Committee on Finance but did not return for the assembly's second session.

Crump was perhaps best remembered in Richmond as defense counsel for James Jeter Phillips, who stood trial in that city during the winter of 1867–1868 for the murder of his wife, and for Thomas Judson Cluverius, who in 1885 was convicted of the murder of his pregnant cousin. Crump excelled as a courtroom advocate, and his arguments and cross-examination of witnesses in those and other trials earned him a long-lasting reputation as one of the stars of the Richmond bar.

Crump served on the board of visitors of the College of William and Mary in 1853 and again from 1859 to 1890. He was elected the college's rector in 1883 and president of the board in 1888. Crump received credit for helping the college survive its long period of financial difficulty after the Civil War. He opposed an 1873 effort to align the college more closely with the Episcopal Diocese of Virginia.

William Wood Crump died at his home in Richmond on 27 February 1897. Following a funeral at Saint Paul's Episcopal Church, he was buried in the city's Shockoe Cemetery.

Biographies in Tyler, *Men of Mark*, 5:77–80, George L. Christian, "Reminiscences of Some of the Dead of the Bench and Bar of Richmond," *Virginia Law Register* 14 (1909): 669–670, and Valentine Museum, *Richmond Portraits in an Exhibition of Makers of Richmond, 1737–1860* (1949), 52–53 (por.); William Wood Crump Papers, Huntington; Crump Family Papers and John Moncure Daniel Papers, both VHS; published speeches include *An Address Delivered before the Society of Alumni of William & Mary College, Upon the 5th of July 1843, by Wm. W. Crump* (1843), *Speech of Judge Wm. W. Crump Delivered before the Democratic Association of the City of Richmond on the 12th of September 1856* [1856] (first quotation on 12), *Daily Richmond Whig*, 11 May 1868, and *Speech of Judge W. W. Crump before the Senate Committee on Roads and Internal Navigation . . . Delivered February 13, 1873* (1873); *Daily Richmond Enquirer* and *Richmond Daily Whig*, both 15 Jan. 1846; Presidential Pardons (second and third quotations); obituaries and accounts of funeral in *Richmond Dispatch* and *Richmond Times*, both 28 Feb., 2 Mar. 1897; "Memorial of Judge W. W. Crump by the Bar Association of Richmond, Va.," *Virginia Law Register* 2 (1897): 915–917.

STEVEN L. DALLE MURA

CRUTCHFIELD, Andrew Fletcher (13 March 1824–24 July 1889), journalist, was born in Richmond and was the son of Ralph Crutchfield, a merchant, and Mary Ann Williams Crutchfield. He attended a local academy and became a printer's apprentice at the *Richmond Christian Advocate*, a Methodist newspaper. Crutchfield worked as a printer in Richmond while also contributing local news items to area newspapers and serving occasionally as a correspondent for Virginia and for various out-of-state papers. On 3 March 1847 he married Sarah Louisa Davies, a native of England then residing in Richmond. Of their eight children, four sons and one daughter lived to adulthood.

In April 1852 Crutchfield became general manager of the *Petersburg Daily Express*, a new penny newspaper. He and two partners bought the paper a month later and operated as A. F. Crutchfield and Company. As editor, Crutchfield adopted an emphasis on news. The *Daily Express* became popular throughout Southside Virginia and northern and central North Carolina, for which Petersburg was a trade center. Although Crutchfield published a politically neutral newspaper, during the sectional crises of the 1850s he defended the South against attacks on its social institutions, moral standards, and commercial interests. As an owner of three slaves in 1860, he firmly believed that abolitionists violated the United States Constitution and the property rights of slaveholders. After John Brown's raid on Harpers Ferry in October 1859, Crutchfield likened abolitionism to "Satanic doctrines" and accused abolitionist newspapers such as the *Liberator* of having "done more to disgrace and distract the country than all the external enemies which could be banded against it could do."

Crutchfield opposed the election of Abraham Lincoln in 1860 and strongly supported the infant Confederacy. From the first clash of arms, the *Daily Express* featured war news with a decidedly Southern slant. Paper shortages caused the editor to shrink its four-page format to a front-and-back sheet by 1864, and the newspaper may have ceased daily issues during the siege of Petersburg. Crutchfield did not give up, however. As residents prepared for a winter under siege in 1864, he appealed for men to join the Confederate ranks to help fend off Ulysses S. Grant's imminent occupation of Petersburg.

After the Confederate army withdrew from the city, Union soldiers seized the *Daily Express* printing presses early in April 1865 and used them to publish several editions of *Grant's Petersburg Progress*. Crutchfield resumed publishing the *Daily Express* later in the month and tried to continue issuing an informative newspaper in a ruined city. Among the items he regularly included was a guide to the Union officers who governed Petersburg. Despite his earlier feelings about Lincoln, in the edition of 17 May 1865 he decried the assassination of the president as a crime unrivaled in American history. Crutchfield held a more moderate view of Reconstruction than many of his contemporaries, who criticized him for being too pro-northern. He had sold the *Daily Express* by September 1866 and had returned to Richmond by August 1868, at which time he established a short-lived weekly journal entitled the *Richmond Literary Pastime*.

About 1869 Crutchfield moved to Baltimore, where for several years he worked at the *Baltimore Daily Sun* and the *Baltimore Sunday Telegram*. In June 1872 he and a partner founded the *Baltimorean*, a weekly journal devoted to political, literary, scientific, and social news. Printed on large paper, most issues featured a biographical profile of a prominent national figure along with an engraved portrait. In mid-July 1889 remittent fevers caused by kidney disease forced him from his editing duties at the *Balti-

morean. Andrew Fletcher Crutchfield died at his Baltimore home on 24 July 1889 and three days later was buried in the city's Loudon Park National Cemetery.

Birth date in *The Biographical Cyclopedia of Representative Men of Maryland and District of Columbia* (1879), 603; Edward A. Wyatt, ed., *Preliminary Checklist for Petersburg, 1786–1876* (1949), 268–271; Richmond City Marriage Bonds; Petersburg Hustings Court Deed Book, 19:311, 29:339–340; *Richmond Enquirer*, 5 Mar. 1847; *Petersburg Daily Express*, 24 Apr. 1858, 13, 19 (quotations) Oct. 1859, 9 Oct. 1860, 5 Mar., 23 Dec. 1861, 6 Oct. 1864, 17 May 1865; *Richmond Literary Pastime*, 8 Aug. 1868; *Baltimorean*, 8 June 1872; Crutchfield letter in Baldwin Family Papers, VHS; Baltimore Health Department Death Certificate; obituaries and editorial tributes in *Baltimore Sun*, *Petersburg Daily Index-Appeal*, and *Richmond Dispatch*, all 25 July 1889; newspaper obituary clipping with por., probably from *Baltimorean*, in Mary Lecock Keen Armistead Scrapbook (1887–1890), Acc. 13766, LVA.

G. W. POINDEXTER

CRUTCHFIELD, John Jeter (20 September 1844–21 November 1920), Richmond police court judge, was born in Richmond and was the son of Ann Marie Clark Crutchfield and George K. Crutchfield, a prosperous painter who later served on the common council and represented the city in the House of Delegates from 1877 to 1879. He was privately educated, and in mid-August 1861, at age sixteen, he enlisted in Confederate service as a private in Company G of the 4th Virginia Cavalry. He received a furlough during the summer of 1863 because of an injury to his horse and spent several stretches in 1862, 1863, and 1864 on medical leave for scabies and rheumatism. On 13 October 1868 Crutchfield married Rose Alice Brown, also of Richmond. They had three sons and three daughters.

Crutchfield served five terms as a justice of the peace for the city of Richmond from 1870 until 1880. Occasionally he presided over the police court when the sitting judge was ill. He also worked as a grocer, and during the 1880s he was a clerk in a railroad office. On 2 July 1888 the board of aldermen and the common council jointly elected Crutchfield judge of Richmond's police court. Meeting six days a week, his court had jurisdiction over all violations of city ordinances as well as initial hearings for state criminal cases. Beginning in April 1912 Crutchfield also presided over the city's new juvenile court. He heard hundreds of cases until a separate Juvenile and Domestic Relations Court was established in 1916.

Crutchfield won respect for serving the city long and well, but it was his demeanor, especially his humor, that soon made his court into one of Richmond's most popular tourist attractions. Many newspapers likened his courtroom to a theatrical production—"The Justice's Big Matinee" read one headline. "Justice John," as he was generally known, imposed stiff penalties that looked to contemporary observers to be prejudicial, precipitous, and frequently hilarious. When more than one luckless culprit admitted that he came from North Carolina, a state Crutchfield despised, the judge peremptorily responded: "That's what I thought. Thirty days!"

Many arraigned before Crutchfield were African Americans or immigrants, and although he could be prejudiced, the *Richmond Planet*, a weekly black newspaper, occasionally praised him for being kindhearted and respectful despite his brusque manner. In truth, much of his bluster was show. He aimed barbs not just at defendants, black and white, but at least as often at lawyers, whose book-learning he held in contempt. Crutchfield's severe sentences were easily misunderstood. He regularly imposed the highest possible penalties to awaken a healthy reverence of the law but later reduced them to more proportional dimensions. Although such erratic and outspoken behavior by a judge later in the twentieth century might have brought lawsuits and censure, during Crutchfield's tenure his manner was singled out for praise.

Crutchfield's reputation for wit and an understanding of human nature spread far beyond Virginia. By the time of his death he had become a symbol of old-time justice: swift judgment mixed with mercy, meted out with gruff and knowing good humor. In the course of his thirty-two years on the bench, Crutchfield's fame became such that his courtroom matinees advanced the careers of several Richmond reporters, including the future literary icon James Branch Cabell. Some Richmonders credited Crutchfield as the inspiration for Walter C. Kelly's vaudeville character, "The Virginia Judge," although Kelly himself stated that his model was John Dudley George Brown, judge of the Newport News police court. The *Richmond News Leader* countered that Crutchfield was in still more rarified company: "Well it was that no vaudeville performe[r] attempted to imitate Justice John! He was inimitable. There was none like him. There never will be."

Crutchfield was a Freemason and late in life joined the Baptist Church. Despite periods of asthma and heart disease, he continued to preside over the police court until just weeks before his death. John Jeter Crutchfield died of a heart attack on 21 November 1920 in the Richmond home of one of his daughters. He was buried in Hollywood Cemetery next to his wife, who had died the previous year.

Biographies in *Illustrated Richmond Police and Fire Department Directory* (1896), 40 (por. on 41), and John H. Gwathmey, *Justice John: Tales from the Courtroom of the Virginia Judge* (1934), second quotation on 141; Richmond City Marriage Register; correspondence, clippings, and other materials in John Jeter Crutchfield Scrapbooks, VHS; Compiled Service Records; *Richmond Daily Dispatch*, 17 Oct. 1868, 3 July 1888, 16 Feb. 1892 (first quotation); *Richmond Planet*, 9 July 1892, 28 Jan. 1893, 6 Feb. 1915; *Washington Post*, 30 Aug., 6 Sept. 1931; *Richmond Afro-American*, 18 Aug. 1945; John A. Cutchins, *Memories of Old Richmond (1881–1944)* (1973), esp. 146–147; BVS Death Certificate, Richmond City; obituaries in *Atlanta Constitution* and *Washington Post*, both 22 Nov. 1920; obituaries and editorial tributes in *Richmond News Leader* (third quotation and por.) and *Richmond Times-Dispatch*, both 22 Nov. 1920; editorial tribute in *Richmond Planet*, 27 Nov. 1920.

MICHAEL AYERS TROTTI

CRUTCHFIELD, Oscar Minor (16 January 1800–15 May 1861), Speaker of the House of Delegates, was born at Spring Forest, the Spotsylvania County estate of his parents, Elizabeth Lewis Minor Crutchfield and Stapleton Crutchfield (d. 1818). His father, who commanded a militia battalion in action at Hampton during the War of 1812, represented Spotsylvania County in the House of Delegates from 1808 to 1811 and was a member again at the time of his death. His mother sponsored a school and took in boarding students for a time after his father's death, but Crutchfield's education is undocumented. From 1822 until 1825 he was deputy sheriff of Spotsylvania County. Named to the committee to arrange the marquis de Lafayette's November

1824 visit to Fredericksburg, Crutchfield sold tickets to the celebratory ball and organized local guard units for the ceremonies. In other expressions of the civic religion of the American Revolution, Crutchfield was assistant marshal at the unveiling of a monument to Mary Ball Washington in 1833, a manager of George Washington's birthday ball in 1839, and a member of a committee pressing Congress in 1857 to erect a monument in Fredericksburg to the Revolutionary War general Hugh Mercer.

During 1825 and 1826 Crutchfield toured Europe, including England, France, Italy, and Switzerland, and while in the Netherlands he inspected dikes and windmills with the civil engineer Moncure Robinson. Commissioned a justice of the Spotsylvania County Court on 15 August 1825 before leaving for Europe, Crutchfield qualified on 2 March 1829 and served until his death, after 28 June 1852 as presiding judge. On 24 October 1833 he married his cousin Susan Elizabeth M. Gatewood, of Essex County, who died in December 1853. Their one daughter and seven sons included Stapleton Crutchfield (1835–1865), a Confederate artillery officer killed at Saylers Creek in the last days of the Civil War.

In 1834 Crutchfield won election to the first of nine consecutive one-year terms in the House of Delegates representing Spotsylvania County. From 1834 through 1839 he served on the Committee on the Militia Laws, where he employed expertise gained as a brigade inspector with the rank of major. From 1835 through 1841 and again for the 1842–1843 term Crutchfield sat on the Committee of Roads and Internal Navigation and was chair for the two sessions that met between 1839 and 1841. He chaired the Committee to Examine the Public Armory in 1839, the Committee to Examine the Banks for the 1840–1841 term, and the Committee of Claims during the 1842–1843 session.

While sitting in the House, Crutchfield was Grand Master of the Grand Lodge of Virginia from 14 December 1841 through 12 December 1843, even though he had never presided over his local Masonic lodge, service usually considered a prerequisite for holding the statewide office. From 7 February 1843 through 10 December 1844 he served as Spotsylvania County sher-

iff. Crutchfield practiced law occasionally but devoted most of his efforts to farming a 1,167.5-acre Mat River plantation called Green Branch. He owned twenty-two taxable slaves in 1845, twenty-five in 1850, and thirty-two at the time of his death eleven years later.

Although Crutchfield had been a Whig since at least 1840, as that party disintegrated he moved gradually into the Democratic ranks. In August 1850 he finished ninth in an eleven-candidate field for the five seats representing Caroline, Hanover, King William, and Spotsylvania Counties in a convention called to revise Virginia's constitution. Spotsylvania voters returned him to the House of Delegates for the 1850–1851 session, and he won reelection for the succeeding five terms. He received assignment to no major standing committees during the 1850–1851 session. On 12 January 1852 Crutchfield overwhelmed token opposition from Fleming Bowyer Miller to win election as Speaker of the House of Delegates with a vote of 138 to 2, a measure of support commonplace for the nonpartisan office in the decades preceding the Civil War. During escalating sectional tensions, both on the national stage and within the state, Crutchfield was noted for his courtesy, evenhandedness, and impartiality in presiding over the House. He remained the unanimous choice as Speaker during the three sessions that met between 1853 and 1858, and with a vote of 126 to 1 he defeated James Lawson Kemper for reelection to the Speakership in December 1859.

Crutchfield's position as Speaker made him an attractive candidate for other offices. Knowing that he had shifted parties once before, the American (or Know Nothing) Party approached him through the Whig press in 1855 about accepting its nomination for governor against Henry Alexander Wise, even though Crutchfield had chaired the Democratic State Convention that selected the maverick Wise as its gubernatorial candidate. Three years later Crutchfield was mentioned both in his home district and in southwestern Virginia as a possible candidate for lieutenant governor on the Democratic ticket with John Letcher.

Crutchfield presided over the House during the special session that on 19 January 1861 approved the calling of a state convention to consider Virginia's response to the secession crisis. Citing poor health and financial obligations to several estates for which he served as trustee, he announced his intention to retire from the House after completing his term. Following Virginia's secession in April, however, he reversed his decision and offered himself for reelection as a non-party candidate who favored "merging all former party affiliations in one universal party for the achiev[e]ment and maintenance of Southern Liberty, Southern Rights, and a *Southern Union forever* separated from a *Northern Union*." Eight days before the election, after a hard day of supervising his plantation operations, Oscar Minor Crutchfield died suddenly of apoplexy at Green Branch on 15 May 1861. He was buried on the estate.

Jamerson, *Speakers and Clerks, 1776–1996*, 77; S. J. Quinn, *Historical Sketch of Fredericksburg Lodge, No. 4, A.F.&A.M.* (1890), 65; French Biographies; birth date in Sue K. Gordon, "Spring Forest" (typescript dated 12 July 1937), 2, in Works Progress Administration, Virginia Historical Inventory, LVA, citing family Bible records; Crutchfield family Bible records (typescript), VHS; Essex Co. Marriage Bonds (dated 14 Oct. 1833); *Fredericksburg Virginia Herald*, 4 Sept., 20 Nov. 1824, 4 May, 2 Nov. 1833, 1 Feb., 30 Apr. 1855, 6 Nov. 1858; *Fredericksburg Political Arena*, 1 Nov. 1833, 25 Jan. 1839, 8 May, 28 July 1840; *Richmond Enquirer*, 27 Aug., 3, 13 Sept. 1850; *Richmond Whig and Public Advertiser*, 30 Jan. 1855; *Fredericksburg Weekly Advertiser and Chronicle of the Times*, 14 Nov. 1857; *Fredericksburg News*, 3 May 1861 (quotation); Pratt, *General Assembly, 1852* (por.); estate accounts, inventories, and sales in Spotsylvania Co. Will Book, W:539–546, 670–673, 684–685; obituaries in *Fredericksburg News*, 17 May 1861, and *Richmond Enquirer*, 21 (reprinting in part unidentified issue of *Fredericksburg Democratic Recorder*), 24 May 1861.

SARA B. BEARSS

CRUTCHFIELD, Stapleton (21 June 1835–6 April 1865), Confederate artillery officer, was born on the Spotsylvania County plantation of his parents, Oscar Minor Crutchfield, Speaker of the House of Delegates from 1852 to 1861, and Susan Elizabeth M. Gatewood Crutchfield. He matriculated at the Virginia Military Institute in 1851 but was sent home after only a few months for disciplinary reasons. He returned to the institute the next year and graduated first in his class in 1855. For the next six years Crutchfield served on the VMI faculty, first as an assis-

tant and after 1858 as a full professor of mathematics, one highly regarded by his students. While living in Lexington, Crutchfield was confirmed in the Episcopal Church and joined the Franklin Society and Library Company of Lexington, a lending library and debating club.

When the Civil War began in the spring of 1861, Crutchfield remained in Lexington and served for about three months as temporary superintendent of VMI. In this capacity he supervised the shipment to Richmond of 10,000 muskets from the state arsenal located at the school and served as a drillmaster for new units raised in the region. On 1 May 1861 Crutchfield was commissioned a major in Confederate service. Assigned on 7 July to the 9th Regiment Virginia Volunteers, he reported for duty at Craney Island later that month. On 1 October, Crutchfield became a major in the 58th Regiment Virginia Infantry, but illness prevented his participation in the autumn campaign in western Virginia. Elected lieutenant colonel in the 58th Regiment early in 1862, he was dropped from the roster when the regiment reorganized on 1 May. Two days later he was elected colonel of the 16th Regiment Virginia Infantry but for health reasons declined to serve.

On 17 May 1862 his friend and former VMI colleague Thomas J. "Stonewall" Jackson secured for him a commission as colonel and appointed Crutchfield his chief of artillery. Crutchfield saw his first action in Jackson's Shenandoah Valley campaign when, on the morning of 8 June 1862, Union cavalry surprised Jackson and his staff at Port Republic. Captured while attempting to leave the village, Crutchfield escaped during a Confederate counterattack and rejoined Jackson's army. That summer he participated in the Seven Days' Battles around Richmond, Cedar Mountain, Second Manassas (Bull Run), and the capture of Harpers Ferry during the Maryland campaign. In November 1862 Jackson's command became the 2d Corps of the Army of Northern Virginia, and Crutchfield directed its artillery. At Fredericksburg he commanded the guns on the southern part of the battlefield.

In mid-April 1863 Jackson recommended Crutchfield for promotion to brigadier general, but the request was passed over and Crutchfield remained a colonel. At Chancellorsville he was severely wounded by a shell fragment that shattered a bone in his right leg below the knee. Crutchfield left the battlefield in the same ambulance that carried the mortally wounded Jackson. The leg wound removed Crutchfield from active service for the remainder of 1863. In the autumn of that year the VMI board of visitors elected Crutchfield to fill Jackson's former chair as professor of natural philosophy. He declined the offer of a permanent position but taught on a temporary basis while he recuperated.

On 16 March 1864, having sufficiently recovered, Crutchfield was assigned to duty in the Confederate Bureau of Ordnance and Hydrography as inspector of seacoast batteries. He petitioned for field service and on 18 January 1865 returned to active duty with the Army of Northern Virginia as commander of a heavy-artillery brigade stationed at Chaffin's Bluff in the Richmond defenses. During the Appomattox campaign, Crutchfield's brigade was attached to George Washington Custis Lee's division. On 6 April 1865 at Saylers Creek, Stapleton Crutchfield was leading a charge when an artillery shell decapitated him. His body was left on the field by the retreating Confederate forces and probably was buried there by local citizens.

Biographies in Charles D. Walker, *Memorial, Virginia Military Institute: Biographical Sketches of the Graduates and Élèves of the Virginia Military Institute Who Fell during the War between the States* (1875), 143–159, Stewart Sifakis, *Who Was Who in the Civil War* (1988), 156, and Richard M. McMurry, *Virginia Military Institute Alumni in the Civil War: In Bello Praesidium* (1999), 114; variant birth date of 21 June 1836 in Crutchfield family Bible records (typescript), VHS; Stapleton Crutchfield alumnus file (including birth date of 21 June 1835 and Oct. 1973 genealogy), correspondence, and oil por. in Confederate uniform, VMI Archives; MS of Crutchfield's 1855 Fourth of July address, VHS; Compiled Service Records; *Daily Richmond Examiner*, 12 May 1863; *Orders and Circulars Issued by the Army of the Potomac and the Army and Department of Northern Virginia, C.S.A, 1861–1865* (1974 microfilm); *Special Orders of the Adjutant and Inspector General's Office, Confederate States* (n.d.), 4:158; numerous references in *OR*, including death reported in 1st ser., vol. 46, pt. 1, 1297.

GRAHAM T. DOZIER

CULLEN, John (1 February 1797–25 December 1849), medical educator, was born in Dublin, Ireland. The names of his parents are not known,

but one of them was closely related to Patrick Curtis, the learned rector of the Irish College in Salamanca, Spain, and later archbishop of Armagh, Ireland, who worked for Catholic emancipation. Cullen may have attended Trinity College, in Dublin. About 1814 he traveled to Paris, where he studied anatomy and surgery. He returned to Ireland in the summer of 1815 but soon sailed to New York, where he found work as a chemist. In 1816 Cullen matriculated at the medical school of the University of Pennsylvania and received an M.D. in April 1819. Afterward he spent about a year as the resident physician in a Philadelphia almshouse.

Early in the 1820s Cullen traveled to Virginia, reportedly to confer with Thomas Jefferson about a position at the new University of Virginia. He gave a series of lectures on chemistry in Petersburg but became ill while passing through Richmond. Persuaded by his new friends to remain there, he had begun practicing medicine in the city by 1822. Cullen executed a marriage bond on 28 February 1828 and on that date or soon thereafter married Charlotte Eliza Howard. Their two daughters and two sons included John Syng Dorsey Cullen, who became a surgeon and later dean of the Medical College of Virginia.

Cullen's library eventually numbered more than one hundred volumes related to medicine. He was not known as a particularly innovative physician, and he rarely published in medical journals. Noted for his devotion to his profession, Cullen relied on such typical prescriptions as calomel, mercury, and opium, and he was a strong proponent of bleeding his patients. He enjoyed a successful practice, and by the 1830s he had started acquiring several lots in Richmond. He built a three-story brick house and office as well as several rental properties.

On 9 July 1832 the Richmond common council selected Cullen to serve on the city's board of health. In October 1837 he and several other physicians petitioned Hampden-Sydney College, located in Prince Edward County, to establish a department of medicine in Richmond. The group argued that the capital city's excellent location would attract those Virginians and other southerners who were going north for their medical education. On 1 December 1837 the college board voted to create a medical school in Richmond, which in 1854 became the Medical College of Virginia. One of the first four appointed professors, Cullen held the chair of theory and practice of medicine for the next decade. A tall man who enjoyed stylish dress, he was considered an excellent orator, and students later recalled that he kept his listeners hanging onto every word of his lectures.

At an 1846 meeting in New York, Cullen and other delegates discussed establishing the American Medical Association. He served on a committee that at the organizational meeting of the AMA the following year presented a resolution declaring that those physicians who taught medicine should not also be responsible for licensing doctors. The committee called for creating one board in each state that would confer medical licenses rather than relying on the usual combination of medical colleges and local medical societies.

By August 1848 Cullen had become too ill to continue teaching, and on 11 April 1849 he resigned from the medical school. He sought treatment in Philadelphia during the summer and autumn of that year without success. John Cullen died at his Richmond home on 25 December 1849 and was buried in the city's Hollywood Cemetery. The faculty of the Hampden-Sydney medical department published a tribute noting that he was "among the foremost in energy, liberality and zeal in founding our cherished institution."

Birth date on gravestone; biographies in T. Pollard, "Sketch of the Life of Dr. John Cullen," *Atlantic Journal of Medicine* 1 (1883): 191–199, Wyndham B. Blanton, "John Cullen," *Virginia Medical Monthly* 54 (1927): 356–358 (pors.), and "John Cullen: First Professor of Theory and Practice of Medicine, 1797–1849," *Medicovan* 15 (Mar. 1962): 8; Blanton, *Medicine in Virginia in the Nineteenth Century* (1938), 40, 43–44, 102, 238; Cullen alumnus record, University of Pennsylvania, Philadelphia; some Cullen accounts, VHS; Richmond City Marriage Bonds; Hampden-Sydney Medical Department Faculty Minutes (1847–1854), Tompkins-McCaw; will and estate inventory in Richmond City Hustings Wills, Inventories, and Accounts, 12:487–497; death notice in *Richmond Whig and Public Advertiser*, 28 Dec. 1849; obituary and medical department tribute in *Richmond Enquirer*, 28 Dec. 1849, 8 Jan. 1850 (quotation).

MARIANNE E. JULIENNE

CULLEN, John Syng Dorsey (29 July 1832–22 March 1893), physician and medical educator, was born in Richmond and was the son of Charlotte Eliza Howard Cullen and John Cullen, a distinguished physician and founding faculty member of Hampden-Sydney College's Richmond medical department (beginning in 1854 the Medical College of Virginia). Named for his father's favorite medical school professor, J. S. Dorsey Cullen, as he was known, studied mathematics and ancient and modern languages at the University of Virginia during the 1850–1851 academic year. In 1853 he received an M.D. from the medical school that his father had helped establish. Cullen continued his studies in Philadelphia, where he attended private lectures on chest diseases and received training at Saint Joseph's Hospital and at the Blockley township hospital (later Philadelphia General Hospital). About 1855 he returned to Richmond and joined the practice of Charles Bell Gibson, a prominent surgeon. On 27 November 1856 Cullen married Jennie Maben, also of Richmond. They had four daughters and one son.

On 21 April 1861, just days after Virginia had voted to secede from the Union, Cullen enlisted in the 1st Regiment Virginia Infantry. He was appointed surgeon on 3 May. Announced as medical director of James Longstreet's division in October 1861, Cullen had become medical director of Longstreet's First Corps by the next year. He served with him at Antietam (Sharpsburg), Fredericksburg, and Gettysburg, and in Tennessee. During the Peninsula campaign from May to July 1862, Cullen supervised the treatment of Confederate wounded and also was ordered to superintend the removal of sick and wounded Union soldiers. In February 1863 Longstreet assumed command of the Department of Virginia and North Carolina and appointed Cullen as its medical director.

At the Battle of the Wilderness on 6 May 1864, a stray Confederate rifle shot seriously wounded Longstreet. The bullet lifted him from the saddle as it passed through his throat. Cullen stanched the hemorrhaging before Longstreet was taken to a nearby hospital tent and then took charge of the general's care after he was moved to Lynchburg. Longstreet's wounds healed, although he never recovered the use of his right arm and could only whisper when he spoke. In 1864 Cullen was recommended for promotion to lieutenant colonel. He remained with Longstreet until the surrender at Appomattox Court House and was paroled on 9 April 1865.

Cullen returned to Richmond and resumed his surgical practice. He gained a reputation as one of several brilliant Virginians responsible for advances in surgery. In 1869 Cullen became professor of diseases of women and children at the Medical College of Virginia and made infirmities in children a focus of study. He was surgeon to the Richmond City Almshouse and city hospitals from at least 1870 through 1885, and he also served on the staff of the College Infirmary (later the Retreat for the Sick and still later Retreat Hospital). In 1872 Cullen directed Richmond's preparations for a smallpox epidemic that had swept through several northern cities. He was a charter fellow of the Medical Society of Virginia, organized in 1870, and also president of the Richmond Academy of Medicine in 1889. After helping to establish the *Virginia Clinical Record* in 1871, Cullen edited the journal and contributed many case reports, primarily related to patients at the almshouse, before the *Record* ceased publication in 1874.

Beginning with the 1881–1882 academic session, Cullen replaced Hunter Holmes McGuire as professor of surgery at the Medical College of Virginia, and in May 1886 he became dean of the faculty. In 1888 the editors of the *Journal of the American Medical Association* charged that the Medical College of Virginia was producing incompetent physicians and denounced the faculty for supporting students' efforts to win exemption from examination by the Virginia State Board of Medical Examiners. As dean, Cullen defended the college in a letter to the editor dismissing the accusations as misrepresentations put forth by enemies of the school. In a scathing reply the editors accused Cullen of being offensive and ungrammatical and of misunderstanding the charges against his institution.

After a protracted illness, during which he continued to practice medicine and to fill his two academic posts, John Syng Dorsey Cullen died at his Richmond home on 22 March 1893. At his funeral two days later the sixteen honorary pallbearers included former fellow officers in the Army of Northern Virginia. He was buried in Hollywood Cemetery.

Biographies in William B. Atkinson, ed., *The Physicians and Surgeons of the United States* (1878), 315–316 (including birth date), Howard A. Kelly, *A Cyclopedia of American Medical Biography* (1912), 1:213 (including partial bibliography of published writings), and "The First 125 Years, 1838–1963," Medical College of Virginia *Bulletin* 61 (1963): 38 (por.); a few Cullen letters in Carrington Family Papers and Johnston Family Papers, VHS; BVS Marriage Register, Richmond City; Compiled Service Records; *OR*, 1st ser., 18:896, vol. 51, pt. 2, 357, 2d ser., 4:176; *Journal of the American Medical Association* 11 (1888): 345–347, 527–528, 848–849, 861–863; Wyndham B. Blanton, *Medicine in Virginia in the Nineteenth Century* (1933), esp. 43, 59, 61, 120, 121, 158, 263; Robert M. Steckler and Jon D. Blachley, "The Cervical Wound of General James Longstreet," *Archives of Otolaryngology—Head and Neck Surgery* 126 (2000): 353–359; BVS Death Register, Richmond City; obituary in *Richmond Dispatch*, 23 Mar. 1893; memorials in Medical Society of Virginia *Transactions* (1893), 220, and *Virginia Medical Monthly* 20 (Apr. 1893): 103–104.

RICHARD B. DAVIS

CULPEPER, Thomas, second baron Culpeper of Thoresway (bap. 21 March 1635–27 January 1689), governor of Virginia and proprietor of the Northern Neck, was the son of Sir John Culpeper (after 1644 first baron Culpeper of Thoresway) and his second wife, Judith Culpeper Culpeper. He was born at Greenway Court, his father's English estate in Hollingbourne Parish in Kent, where he was christened on 21 March 1635. His family included several prominent investors in the Virginia Company of London and other men who sought large grants of land in North America. One of his second cousins, the widowed Frances Culpeper Stephens, married Sir William Berkeley and was a major influence in Virginia politics in the 1670s and 1680s.

Culpeper's father was master of rolls under King Charles I and accompanied the royal family into exile at the end of the English Civil Wars. His loyalty to the Crown was well rewarded. On 18 September 1649 Charles II granted John Culpeper and six other close associates ownership of the Northern Neck, the land between the Potomac and Rappahannock Rivers in Virginia. Even though Parliament condemned and sold the Culpeper estates in 1651, the exiled king offered to restore to the family what it had lost. Culpeper lived with his father in the Netherlands during most of the royal exile, and at The Hague on 3 August 1659 he married Margaretta van Hesse, a wealthy Dutch heiress. They had one daughter. In later years his wife resided in Kent at Leeds Castle, which Culpeper purchased with her money, and he lived openly on the Isle of Wight and in London with his mistress, Susanna Willis. They had two daughters.

Culpeper's father died a few months after the Restoration in 1660, but Charles II did not fulfill his promise to restore the Culpeper estates, which the elder Culpeper had valued at £12,000. Succeeding his father as baron, Culpeper enjoyed royal patronage for much of his life. In July 1661 the king appointed him captain of and in mid-1664 governor of the Isle of Wight, a post he filled competently until 1668. In 1671 Culpeper won appointment to the Council for Foreign Plantations, a select committee of the royal council, and he became vice president when it was reorganized in September 1672. From then until the council was dissolved in December 1674 he received an annual salary of £600.

Culpeper's interest in Virginia dated from that experience. He and the secretary of state, Henry Bennet, earl of Arlington, obtained from the king on 25 February 1673 a grant allowing them for thirty-one years to receive escheats and quitrents collected in Virginia, as well as the power to grant all land not already granted by the governor. In 1681 Culpeper bought out Arlington's interest in their joint grant and also secured five-sixths ownership of the Northern Neck Proprietary (the remaining one-sixth belonged to his cousin, Alexander Culpeper). Those transactions caused considerable consternation among the colonists, who perceived a threat to their land titles and a loss of independence for the General Assembly. In May 1684, after much lobbying by the colonists, Culpeper surrendered to the Crown his interest in the Arlington grant for an annual pension of £600 for twenty and a half years.

Culpeper's ambitions included more than just proprietary interests. On 8 July 1675 the king granted him a patent for the office of governor of Virginia to succeed Sir William Berke-ley whenever he died, resigned, or was recalled. Culpeper held the governorship from Berkeley's death on 9 July 1677 until August 1683 but seemed more interested in collecting his salary and perquisites than in governing and living in the colony. For more than two years Herbert Jeffreys and, following his death, Sir Henry Chicheley administered the government as lieutenant governors. Not until late in 1679 did Culpeper yield to increasingly blunt prodding from the Crown and sail to Virginia.

Culpeper arrived in the colony on 3 May 1680 with royal instructions that sought clearly to define the subordinate status of the colony and the General Assembly within the Restoration empire. Culpeper's orders restricted his power to convene the assembly, which had usually met annually. The king also commanded the governor to secure passage of a law authorizing regular taxes on the export of tobacco, on persons transported to the colony, and on every ship that docked there, with the revenue thus raised going to support the salaries and other expenses of the provincial government. Despite the protests of the colonists, Culpeper persuaded the assembly to enact the taxes, which diminished the assembly's ability to influence the governor by reducing or enlarging his income. Culpeper also secured passage of an act to establish towns and tobacco inspection warehouses in every county and a general act of indemnity that ended the continuing litigation that followed Bacon's Rebellion.

Culpeper's instructions required him to curtail the capacity of the burgesses to initiate legislation and thus placed the shaping of legislation in the hands of the governor and Council. The instructions also required the governor to terminate the assembly's jurisdiction as the court of highest appeal in the colony and threw final jurisdiction of Virginia disputes to the Privy Council in England. Culpeper failed to press the first of those instructions, and he implemented the second indirectly by neglecting to appoint Council members to meet with the burgesses' Committee for Private Causes. With pending appeals hanging in limbo, it was left to Culpeper's successor, Francis Howard, baron Howard of Effingham, to settle the issue forthrightly.

Having accomplished the king's agenda to his own satisfaction, Culpeper departed for New England on 11 August 1680, a mere three months after arriving, and then returned to England. He left the colony in economic crisis, suffering from abundant harvests of tobacco and declining prices. Some prominent Virginians began pleading for a mandatory cessation of tobacco planting, and during the winter of 1681–1682 many other Virginians petitioned for a meeting of the assembly to pass the necessary laws. Lieutenant Governor Sir Henry Chicheley called an assembly for April 1682, but having received orders not to summon the assembly until later in the year he dismissed the disappointed burgesses. Denied legislative relief, some of the colonists took matters into their own hands in May and began cutting tobacco plants in Gloucester, Middlesex, and New Kent Counties. While Chicheley acted decisively to suppress the riots and prevent them from spreading, the reports from Virginia understandably alarmed the Crown. On 17 June 1682 the king ordered Culpeper to return to Virginia.

Culpeper obeyed his instructions reluctantly and without haste. He sailed from England early in October and reached the colony in December 1682. His arrival coincided with a rise in tobacco prices, which largely pacified the planters. Culpeper denounced the tobacco cutters and by way of example executed two of them, although he offered pardons to all who took an oath of allegiance. With order restored, he left the colony soon after 29 May 1683 to report in person to the king. His departure violated an express order that colonial governors not leave their posts without royal permission, and the king deprived Culpeper of his office on 16 August 1683.

Culpeper submitted several petitions seeking repayment for various expenses he had incurred as governor. He continued to speculate in colonial lands and in 1685 purchased land in the Narragansett territory, an acquisition confirmed by the Crown in April 1688. In July 1688 he petitioned for a renewal of his Northern Neck grant, which James II approved in September. Despite that favor from the king, Culpeper was one of about thirty members of the House of Lords who met in December of that year to set up a provisional government after the king fled London, and he favored inviting William of Orange to assume the English throne.

Thomas Culpeper, second baron Culpeper of Thoresway, died in London on 27 January 1689. The place of his burial is not recorded. Culpeper's widow and daughter, Katherine Culpeper, and son-in-law, Thomas Fairfax, fifth baron Fairfax of Cameron, spent a decade in court and in Parliament attempting with but partial success to regain control of property that Culpeper had alienated to his mistress and her daughters. Culpeper had settled the Northern Neck Proprietary on his legitimate daughter, and it descended to the Fairfax family following her death in 1719.

Fairfax Harrison, *Proprietors of the Northern Neck: Chapters of Culpeper Genealogy* (1926), 62–88, with date of baptism from Hollingbourne Parish register and frontispiece por.; David A. H. Cleggett, *History of Leeds Castle and Its Families* (1992), 86–96, 212–213; Cleggett, "Leeds Castle and its Families," *Northern Neck of Virginia Historical Magazine* 44 (1994): 5098–5101, with marriage date from marriage settlement in Maastricht, Netherlands, notary archives 1256; Culpeper letters in PRO CO 1/44, CO 1/47, CO 5/1356, SP 29/428, and Wykeham-Martin Papers, Kent County Archives Service, Maidstone, Kent, Eng.; instructions in PRO CO 5/1355, 326–356; records of administration in *Executive Journals of Council*, vol. 1, and *JHB, 1659/60–1693*; Warren M. Billings, John E. Selby, and Thad W. Tate, *Colonial Virginia: A History* (1986), 103–110; Billings, *A Little Parliament: The Virginia General Assembly in the Seventeenth Century* (2004), 54–57, 79–81, 120, 160–161, 178–179; judgment of disputed will in Prerogative Court of Canterbury, Dyke 401; death "on or about" 27 Jan. 1689 and inventory of household effects in PRO C 9/282/87.

KEVIN R. HARDWICK

CUMMING, Hugh Smith (17 August 1869–20 December 1948), surgeon general of the United States Public Health Service, was born in Hampton. The son of Samuel Cumming, a Scots immigrant, and Diana Whiting Smith Cumming, he attended Hampton Academy and a preparatory school in Baltimore. Cumming received an M.D. from the University of Virginia in 1893. While an intern at Saint Luke's Hospital, in Richmond, he continued his medical training at the University College of Medicine (later the Medical College of Virginia) and received a second M.D. in 1894.

On 11 May 1894 Cumming was appointed assistant surgeon in the Marine-Hospital Service of the United States (after 1912 the United States Public Health Service) and assigned to hospital duty on Staten Island. Between 1896 and 1900 he served at quarantine stations at Norfolk, Philadelphia, New York, and Blackbeard Island, off the Georgia coast. Cumming was promoted to passed assistant surgeon in January 1900 and the following year was transferred to San Francisco to manage the Angel Island Quarantine Station. For several years beginning in 1906 he worked in the office of the United States consul general in Yokohama, Japan. While there he focused on issues of immigration and quarantinable diseases. This international approach to protecting the health of Americans became an important component of his career.

After returning to the United States, Cumming served as quarantine officer at the Hampton Roads Station. On 15 March 1911 he was promoted to surgeon. Assigned to the Hygienic Laboratory, in Washington, D.C., from 1913 to 1917, Cumming investigated the health risks from consuming shellfish harvested in sewage-polluted tidal waters from Virginia to New York. After the United States entered World War I in 1917, he joined other Health Service officers in requesting military assignment and later served as a sanitary adviser to the navy. At the war's end Cumming led efforts to improve the sanitation of ports and military camps in Europe and to prevent disease among homeward-bound American troops. He also represented the Public Health Service at several international conferences on sanitation in 1918 and 1919, served as United States delegate to the Office Internationale d'Hygiène Publique, and led an inter-allied medical commission that studied typhus fever in Poland.

On 27 January 1920 President Woodrow Wilson nominated Cumming to be the fifth surgeon general of the Public Health Service. Recalled to Washington, D.C., he received the official appointment on 3 March. During Cumming's sixteen-year tenure the Public Health Service expanded dramatically. The service provided medical care for the nation's veterans immediately after World War I, but once the Veterans' Bureau assumed that task in 1922, the PHS focused on research and intervention in health

promotion. Cumming supervised the replacement of state-run quarantine stations with a system of federally directed stations and the establishment of a national hospital for lepers. In 1929 the PHS created a Narcotics Division (later the National Institute of Mental Health) and in 1935 opened the nation's first hospital to study and treat drug addiction.

Under Cumming's direction the PHS continued to expand its research into a wide variety of public health issues, and in 1930 the Hygienic Laboratory became the National Institute of Health (later the National Institutes of Health). The PHS's regular commissioned corps increased in number and added dentists, pharmacists, and sanitary engineers to its ranks. As part of its efforts to control venereal disease, the Health Service, under Cumming's direction, began an experiment at Tuskegee, Alabama, in which syphilis in a test group of African American males was left untreated.

Cumming expanded the role of the United States in the field of international health, despite the nation's decision not to join the League of Nations. Through his continued affiliation with the Office Internationale d'Hygiène Publique, he was able to formalize what was at first an advisory and consultative role in the League's Health Section. Cumming promoted international sanitation treaties, and the Hygienic Laboratory became a center for international health research. He directed the International Sanitary Bureau (later the Pan American Health Organization) from 1920 until 1947, when he became director emeritus. The PHS continued its interest in preventing disease transmission via immigration, and Cumming's experience in international health was critical in establishing a system to screen immigrants for infectious diseases before they embarked for American shores. He also emphasized the dangers of air travel in quickly spreading contagious diseases from other countries to the United States.

Always optimistic about the ability of medical science to improve human health, Cumming viewed his work as a crusade in which "the stethoscope and test tube have replaced the sword and spear; vaccines the shield." Although he was expansive about the government's proper role in international health and in studying and preventing disease, he opposed compulsory health insurance and federal grants for state health programs. Citing his many years of service and failing health, he resigned as surgeon general on 31 January 1936.

Cumming received decorations from nearly a dozen nations and became an honorary fellow of the American College of Surgeons, the American College of Physicians, and the Royal Society of Medicine in London. Honorary degrees he received included doctorates of science from the Medical College of Virginia (1927) and from the University of Pennsylvania (1930) and an LL.D. from Yale University (1933). In 1935 the National Academy of Sciences awarded him its public welfare medal for his work on yellow fever epidemics. Cumming served as president of the American Public Health Association, the Association of Military Surgeons of the United States, the National Board of Medical Examiners, and the Southern Medical Association. Although he was a prominent member of the American Medical Association, he twice narrowly lost bids to become its president. He was a member of the Medical Society of Virginia for fifty-two years.

On 26 October 1896, in James City County, Cumming married Lucy Almira Booth, who became a partner in his efforts and served on the Board of Public Welfare in the District of Columbia. They had one son and two daughters, one of whom died as an infant. Hugh Smith Cumming suffered a stroke in November 1947 and died of a heart attack at his residence in Washington, D.C., on 20 December 1948. He was buried in the cemetery of Saint John's Episcopal Church, in Hampton.

Biography in Bruce, Tyler, and Morton, *History of Virginia*, 4:416–417; BVS Birth Register, Elizabeth City Co.; BVS Marriage Register, James City Co.; Hugh S. Cumming Papers and Cumming materials in several other collections, National Library of Medicine, Bethesda, Md.; unpublished memoirs in Cumming Family Papers, UVA; publications include Cumming, *Safe Ice* (1914), *Investigation of the Pollution and Sanitary Conditions of the Potomac Watershed . . .* (1916), *Investigation of the Pollution of Tidal Waters of Maryland and Virginia with Special Reference to Shellfish-bearing Areas* (1916), *Investigation of the Pollution of Certain Tidal Waters of New Jersey, New York, and Delaware . . .* (1917), and with Arthur M. Stimson, "The Outlook of Public Health

Work," in *Biology in Human Affairs*, ed. Edward M. East (1931), 240–271; *Washington Post*, 28 Jan. 1920, 8 Jan. 1928, 27–29 Jan. 1936; *Richmond Times-Dispatch*, 29 May, 1 June 1927 (quotation), 27 Jan. 1936; *New York Times*, 10 June 1928, 27 Jan. 1936; Ralph Chester Williams, *The United States Public Health Service, 1798–1950* (1951), esp. 482–484 (por. facing 484); Bess Furman, *A Profile of the United States Public Health Service, 1798–1948* (1973), esp. 329–390 (por. on 336); obituaries in *New York Times*, *Richmond Times-Dispatch*, and *Washington Post*, all 21 Dec. 1948, *Journal of the American Medical Association* 139 (1949): 46, and *Virginia Medical Monthly* 76 (1949): 104; editorial tribute in *Richmond Times-Dispatch*, 23 Dec. 1948.

CHRISTIAN S. WARREN

CUMMINGS, Charles (ca. 1733–25 March 1812), Presbyterian minister, is believed to have been born in County Donegal, Ireland, and to have been the son of John Cummings and Sarah Polk Cummings. He immigrated to the British colonies as a young man and in Lancaster County on 13 February 1766 married Millicent Carter. Of their at least seven sons and five daughters, three sons and two daughters died as children. In preparation for the ministry, Cummings learned Greek and Latin. On 7 November 1765 he delivered a trial sermon and was rigorously examined by the Hanover Presbytery in the ancient languages, geography, philosophy, and his religious experiences. The presbytery licensed him to preach on 18 April 1766 and ordained him on 14 May 1767.

In October 1766 Cummings accepted a call to become the minister of Brown's Meeting House in Augusta County. While serving that church he also itinerated among other congregations in western Virginia in order to serve the rapidly increasing number of Presbyterians in that part of the colony. On 2 June 1773 he accepted a call from two congregations, Ebbing Spring and Sinking Spring, in the Holston River region of southwestern Virginia, where he had preached on a recent tour. Cummings was probably the first clergyman of any denomination to reside in that area. Those were dangerous years in western Virginia, even apart from the emerging imperial crisis, as violent conflicts between colonists and Native Americans erupted throughout the backcountry. Cummings reportedly carried a rifle with him wherever he went, including to church services. A member of his congregation later recalled that in 1776, after Cummings had moved his family to the safety of a fort, he was traveling with his slave and several neighbors when Indians attacked and killed a member of the party. Cummings and his slave held off the attackers until help arrived.

Early in 1775 leading residents of Fincastle County elected Cummings to a committee to enforce the regulations adopted by the Virginia Revolutionary Conventions and the First Continental Congress. The following year he was the first of about 230 men who signed a petition asking that the huge county be divided for the convenience of the residents. As a result, later in 1776 the General Assembly created Kentucky, Montgomery, and Washington Counties. Cummings lived in the part of Fincastle County that then became Washington County, and for many years he was a prominent citizen and community leader as well as Presbyterian minister. He took part as a chaplain in at least one expedition against the Cherokee. As one of the few Presbyterian ministers who served in the field during the American Revolution, he saw some of the most brutal violence of the war, as racial hostility, competition for land, and the struggle for independence intersected on the frontier. After the Revolution, like many other residents of that part of Virginia, Cummings was eager to see the region become a separate state. In 1784 and 1785 he chaired a group that unsuccessfully attempted to persuade Congress to create a new state of Franklin west of the Blue Ridge Mountains.

The Sinking Spring congregation split early in the 1780s after Cummings introduced a new set of church hymns. During the controversy he requested that the presbytery dismiss him, and on 23 May 1782 he received permission to preach in Kentucky. He returned to the Sinking Spring and Knobs congregations in May 1784. Cummings served as moderator of the Hanover Presbytery at meetings in August 1783 and September 1784. He petitioned for the division of Hanover Presbytery in 1785 and the creation of Abingdon Presbytery, which included churches throughout western Virginia and North Carolina and eastern Tennessee. From 1788 to 1803 the new presbytery came under the authority of the Synod of the Carolinas, rather than the Virginia Synod.

Cummings's wife died about the end of the eighteenth century, and early in the nineteenth century he built a large brick manse near Abingdon to replace the log house he had erected and in which he had lived since the 1770s. Charles Cummings retired from the ministry about 1796 and died, probably at his home in Washington County, on 25 March 1812. He was buried near Abingdon in the cemetery of Sinking Spring Presbyterian Church.

Biographies by David Campbell based on personal and family papers in Sprague, *American Pulpit*, 3:285–288 (with marriage date and estimated age eighty at death in Mar. 1812), by Hugh Blair Grigsby in *Washington and Lee University Historical Papers* 2 (1890): 38–40 (with birth year about 1743 but age eighty at death), Lewis Preston Summers, *History of Southwest Virginia, 1746–1786, Washington County, 1777–1870* (1903), 747, Henry Alexander White, *Southern Presbyterian Leaders* (1911), 100–102, and Douglas Summers Brown, "Charles Cummings: The Fighting Parson of Southwest Virginia," *Virginia Cavalcade* 28 (1979): 138–143 (with photograph of later memorial gravestone with year of death "in the 80th year of his age"); undocumented family history with parents' names in Joseph Lyon Miller, *The Descendants of Capt. Thomas Carter of "Barford," Lancaster County, Virginia . . .* (1912), 87–90; copy of call to Sinking Spring, 5 Jan. 1773, in Draper MSS 9DD75; Hanover Presbytery Minutes, esp. 1:82–84, 95, 101, 2:47, 117, 154, 168, UTS; "Memorial of the Freemen," docketed 17 Jan. 1785, Patrick Henry Executive Papers, RG 3, LVA; Victoria Alice Gilliam, "The Old Manse" (typescript dated 26 May 1937), in Works Progress Administration, Virginia Historic Inventory, LVA; Mattie Rountree Stephenson, comp., *Historical Sketch of Sinking Spring Presbyterian Church at Abingdon, Virginia: 1773–1948* (1948), 8–14 (with date of death from presbytery minutes); Washington Co. Will Book, 4:280–281.

MONICA NAJAR

CUMMINGS, Helen Norris (15 February 1865–4 June 1949), woman's club leader, was born in Philadelphia, Pennsylvania, and was the only child of Norris Stanley Cummings, a shipping merchant, and Emma Ricketts Cummings. She received her education in Philadelphia and moved to Alexandria with her parents about 1894. She never married.

Inspired by a club to which she had belonged in Philadelphia, Cummings founded a woman's club in Alexandria in April 1894. The members of the Current Events Club met weekly to present reports on world news, but over time the club's interests expanded to include art, literature, music, and science. The group changed its name to the Cameron Club in 1896 and in the following decade began working closely with other community leaders to undertake civic improvements in Alexandria. Cummings served as president of the club from its inception through the mid-1940s, when her health began to fail.

In May 1907 Cummings and another member represented the Cameron Club in Lynchburg at the organizational meeting of the Virginia Federation of Women's Clubs. The Cameron Club was a charter member of the state federation, and Cummings became an enthusiastic leader in VFWC activities. She served as the first chair of its literature committee and in 1909 was elected a vice president. In May 1915 Cummings began a two-year term as president of the federation. From 1922 to 1923 she edited its short-lived magazine, *Club Life in the Old Dominion*, and at the same time chaired the department of press and publicity.

Cummings's most significant role in the Virginia Federation of Women's Clubs was her involvement with the department of American citizenship, which she chaired for a decade beginning in 1925. From 1935 until 1938 she chaired the federation's division of Americanization and afterward served as an adviser. During this period many Americans feared that communists were infiltrating the United States, and through her articles in *Virginia Club Woman* and in speeches around the state Cummings emphasized the need for vigilance against the dangers of communism and atheism, particularly among the nation's youth. She also produced a number of half-hour radio programs on patriotism and other national issues. At the same time Cummings joined the National Patriotic Council, which called for a strong national defense against the threat posed by the Soviet Union. She chaired its membership committee in 1930 and served on its executive committee two years later. Cummings's work also reflected the national movement to restrict the number of immigrants coming to the United States from Eastern Europe and from Central and South America, and on several occasions she introduced resolutions at VFWC meetings urging Congress to continue limiting such immigration. Cummings served as the official representative in Washington, D.C., for the Mass-

achusetts Public Interests League, a fiercely xenophobic and anticommunist group that favored restrictions on immigration. After adoption of the Nineteenth Amendment she exhorted women to learn about political issues and vote. The Virginia Federation of Women's Clubs honored her many years of leadership with a medal awarded at its state convention in 1940.

Cummings represented Virginia in the General Federation of Women's Clubs, the national organization for women's associations. She served as the Virginia Federation's director on the GFWC's national board for four years, helped revise the GFWC's constitution, and chaired the membership committee. From 1920 to 1922 she sat on the committee that selected Washington, D.C., as the national headquarters of the GFWC. Cummings was also president of the Council of the Original Thirteen States. In spite of poor health, in 1941 she attended the GFWC convention in order to support Virginia's candidate for the office of second vice president.

Cummings helped found Alexandria's Civic Improvement League and raised funds for both the Alexandria Children's Home and the Alexandria Playground Association. During World War I she assisted the city's Liberty Loan campaign and chaired the Women's Federated Council on Employment in Alexandria. After the war she chaired the local committee for the Virginia War History Commission (later known as the World War I History Commission). In 1932 Cummings joined the Alexandria Association, Inc., an organization founded to preserve the city's architecture and history and also to promote residential, riverfront, and social development. She served as president of the local chapter of the National Society of the Colonial Dames of America. A longtime member of Christ Episcopal Church, she wrote a history of the church originally published in the *Southern Churchman*, anthologized in *Colonial Churches: A Series of Sketches of Churches in the Original Colony of Virginia* (1907), and published as a separate pamphlet under the title *Christ Church, Alexandria, Virginia* (1915).

Known for her hospitality, Cummings often hosted Cameron Club meetings and entertained members of the state and national Federation of

Women's Clubs at her home on Cameron Street. Contemporaries described her as elegant, as distinguished, and as a forceful speaker. Helen Norris Cummings died on 4 June 1949 at an Alexandria hospital and was buried in Woodlands Cemetery, in Philadelphia.

Biography in Henry Brantly Handy, ed., *The Social Recorder of Virginia* (1928), 42; Cummings family Bible (with birth date), correspondence, and diaries in Helen Norris Cummings Papers, Alexandria Library; some biographical documents and other materials in Virginia Federation of Women's Clubs Records (1907–1958), LVA; Cameron Club Papers and Virginia Federation of Women's Clubs Papers, both Alexandria Library; reports and articles by Cummings in *Virginia Club Woman* (1928–1938); Mrs. Norwood Lee Beville, *Brief History of the Virginia Federation of Women's Clubs* (1951), 8; Etta Belle Walker Northington, *A History of the Virginia Federation of Women's Clubs, 1907–1957* (1958), esp. 50–52, 183–184 (por. facing 256); obituary in *Alexandria Gazette*, 6 June 1949; editorial tribute in *Virginia Club Woman* 22 (Oct. 1949): 12.

KATHLEEN FEENEY CHAPPELL

CUNNINGHAM, Edward (9 August 1771–14 March 1836), manufacturer, was born in Maghera Parish, County Down, Ireland, and was the son of Richard Cunningham and Elizabeth Hoope Cunningham. According to family tradition, he and an elder brother may have immigrated to Virginia as early as 1784 to establish a mercantile firm. He had certainly arrived in the state by 3 May 1790, when he took a citizenship oath in Petersburg. Settling in Cartersville, Cumberland County, Cunningham worked with his brother in the mercantile firm of John Cunningham and Company. He married a Richmond widow, Ariana Gunn McCartney, on 18 August 1796. Three of their four sons and one of their two daughters lived to adulthood.

After the American Revolution the economy of Richmond shifted from tobacco shipment to new commercial and manufacturing enterprises. Although Cunningham continued to live in Cumberland County, he became one of several Europeans who established prominent businesses in Richmond during the early years of the republic. He entered the expanding flour-milling business in the city in 1799 when he and his brother joined Joseph Gallego in leasing a mill on the James River canal. Cunningham had moved to Richmond by 1812, at which time he began milling flour with Thomas Rutherfoord. After one year Cunningham continued the operation on his own. During the War of 1812 he served for ten days in March 1813 as a private in the 19th Regiment, Virginia militia. That year he purchased a lot in Richmond and two years later built a house designed by the eminent architect Robert Mills.

Cunningham's flour business thrived until the mid-1820s, when he began increasingly to shift his mills to processing cotton and tobacco. In 1829 he sold part of his property and mills to his son Richard Hoope Cunningham and a partner. In December 1831 Cunningham leased Richmond Mills, his remaining property along the canal, to a group of businessmen that included the prominent flour manufacturer Peter Joseph Chevallié. Cunningham joined his sons and several others in January 1832 in incorporating the Richmond Manufacturing Company, a manufactory of cotton, iron, and wool. After his death in 1836 the Richmond Mills passed to his two other surviving sons, Edward Cunningham and John Atkinson Cunningham, and his son-in-law Francis Browne Deane. The following year they incorporated the Tredegar Iron Company, which merged with the Virginia Foundry Company in 1838 to establish what later became Tredegar Iron Works.

Cunningham served as a director of the Bank of Virginia and of the Mutual Assurance Society, against Fire on Buildings, of the State of Virginia. He also was a member of the Richmond common council from December 1820 to July 1821 and a vestryman of Saint James Northam Parish, in Goochland County. In 1825 Cunningham sold his house in Richmond and moved to Howard's Neck, a parcel of land along the James River in Goochland County that he had purchased in 1807. There he built a Federal-style residence, perhaps also designed by Robert Mills, which later was listed on the Virginia Landmarks Register and on the National Register of Historic Places. Edward Cunningham died at his Goochland County residence on 14 March 1836 and was buried in the family cemetery at Howard's Neck.

Biography in Valentine Museum, *Richmond Portraits in an Exhibition of Makers of Richmond, 1737–1860* (1949), 54–55 (por.); Cunningham family genealogical materials (including birth, marriage, and death dates), correspondence, and business papers, all Richard E. Cunningham Papers, VHS; other Cunningham correspondence in Ambler Family Papers and John Randolph Papers, both VHS; *Richmond and Manchester Advertiser*, 3 Sept. 1796; Henrico Co. Deed Book, 5:693–695; Richmond City Hustings Court Deed Book, 7:370–371, 23:107–109, 27:540–547; Mutual Assurance Society Declarations, nos. 1694–1698, 2267 (all 1815), 3460, 4442–4445 (all 1822), 6928–6930 (all 1829), LVA; Tredegar Iron Works Records (1836–1957), esp. volume entitled Copies of Deeds, Agreements, etc., Involving the Company (ca. 1812–1925), 14–15, LVA; Thomas S. Berry, "The Rise of Flour Milling in Richmond," *VMHB* 78 (1970): 387–408; will in Goochland Co. Deed Book, 30:517–518; obituary in *Richmond Whig and Public Advertiser*, 18 Mar. 1836.

MARIANNE BUROFF SHELDON

CUNNINGHAM, John Atkinson (24 June 1846–9 October 1897), president of the State Female Normal School (later Longwood University), was born in Richmond. He was the son of Mary Morris Johnston Dillon Cunningham and her second husband, the physician John Atkinson Cunningham, and the grandson of the Richmond flour and tobacco manufacturer Edward Cunningham. Educated at home by a French governess because of his delicate health and later at New London Academy in Bedford County, Cunningham enlisted on 5 June 1864 in Captain Willis Jefferson Dance's Company (Powhatan Artillery), in which he served until the end of the Civil War.

After studying ancient languages and mathematics at the University of Virginia from 1865 through 1868, Cunningham moved to New Castle, Kentucky, where he taught at a military academy founded by the former Confederate general Edmund Kirby Smith. After a fire destroyed the school in 1870, Smith became chancellor of the University of Nashville (later George Peabody College for Teachers and still later a part of Vanderbilt University), and Cunningham joined the faculty in the Latin chair. On 14 June 1875 he married Florence M. Boyd, of Nashville. They had one son. Cunningham moved back to Richmond, where his wife died on 9 November 1876. For a time he worked as a druggist but then returned to teaching. In 1877 he became principal of the Madison School, a large public school in Richmond. Cunningham married Martha (or Mattie) Macon Eggle-

ston, of Cumberland County, on 3 April 1884. They had two daughters and one son.

On 20 July 1887 Cunningham was elected superintendent of the State Female Normal School, in Farmville, three years after it became Virginia's first public college to prepare white women to teach in the state's public schools. When he arrived, the school had just instituted a new curriculum consisting of two years of academic education and one year of professional training at the college's practice school. Cunningham oversaw the construction of several modern brick buildings and in 1891 the installation of incandescent electric lighting. He nearly doubled the size of the faculty, to fourteen, by hiring teachers educated at such institutions as the Harvard Annex (later Radcliffe College), the George Peabody College for Teachers, the University of Virginia, and Vassar College. Enrollment grew from about 90 in 1887 to 250 in 1897, and the annual number of graduates rose from 14 to 40. By all accounts Cunningham was a popular teacher of psychology and didactics, an able administrator, and a strong believer in both moral and physical education in addition to rigorous academic training. He exchanged the title of superintendent for president in 1893. Neighboring Hampden-Sydney College awarded him an honorary LL.D. in 1896.

Early in his eleventh year at the State Female Normal School, John Atkinson Cunningham died of meningitis at his Farmville home on 9 October 1897. He was buried next to the grave of his first wife in Hollywood Cemetery, in Richmond. A student dormitory at Longwood University bears his name.

"A Brief Biographical Sketch of Dr. John Atkinson Cunningham" and "Dr. Cunningham's Administration" (undated typescripts), Longwood University Archives, including birth date, also on gravestone; biographies in Charles Edward Burrell, *A History of Prince Edward County, Virginia* (1922), 316–317, Rosemary Sprague, *Longwood College: A History* (1989), 64–77 (por. on 67), and Richard L. Nicholas and Joseph Servis, *Powhatan, Salem and Courtney Henrico Artillery* (1997), 203; Compiled Service Records; Davidson Co., Tenn., Marriage Bonds and Licenses (1875), Metropolitan Government Archives of Nashville and Davidson County; BVS Marriage Register, Culpeper Co. (1884); State Female Normal School at Farmville, Virginia, *Catalogues* (1887–1898); obituaries in *Richmond Dispatch*, *Richmond State*, and *Richmond Times*, all 10 Oct. 1897, *Lynchburg*

News, 12 Oct. 1897, *Farmville Herald*, 15 Oct. 1897 (variant birth date of 24 June 1845), and *Virginia School Journal* 6 (1897): 219–220 (variant birth year of 1845); memorials and faculty and student resolutions in *Normal Record* 2 (Nov. 1897): 1, 4–16 (variant birth year of 1845).

BRENT TARTER

CUNNINGHAM, William Edmund (18 February 1803–3 September 1855), journalist, was the son of James B. Cunningham, a prosperous commission merchant, and Penelope Gregory Cunningham. He was born in Norfolk and baptized on 11 December 1803 at Christ Protestant Episcopal Church in that city. He studied at the new University of Virginia during its first two sessions in 1825 and 1826. The Norfolk personal property tax lists record that in 1826 Cunningham owned one slave, and five years later he owned a town lot. He read law and by early in the 1830s had become a partner in the commission merchants Watson and Cunningham. There is no evidence that he married.

Early in April 1833 Cunningham was appointed an alderman, and later that month he won a close election to represent Norfolk in the House of Delegates for a one-year term. Reelected five times, he served until 1839. From 1833 to 1837 he sat on the Committee of Schools and Colleges and on a joint committee to examine the Bank of Virginia and Farmers' Bank of Virginia. He was ranking member on both committees in the 1836–1837 session. During the 1838 assembly Cunningham served on the Committee on Roads and Internal Navigation. The following year he was reappointed to the Committee of Schools and Colleges and also sat on a joint committee to examine the public library.

In the autumn of 1840 Cunningham purchased from Hugh Blair Grigsby, a historian and member of the Convention of 1829–1830, the *American Beacon, and Norfolk and Portsmouth Daily Advertiser*, established in 1815. Publishing the paper with two others as William E. Cunningham and Company, he took editorial control on 1 October 1840. Cunningham's introductory editorial announced that the newspaper would focus on commerce and be dedicated to Norfolk's commercial interests. He also emphasized that although his affiliation with the Whig Party was well known, the newspaper would be politically neutral. Decrying what he perceived as neglect of mercantile interests in the state, Cunningham promoted direct trade between Virginia and foreign ports and sought to end dependence on northern cities for the importation and exportation of goods. He supported the United States Navy's interests in the region, internal improvements, agriculture and industry, and public education.

Cunningham owned four slaves, three of whom worked in the *American Beacon* office. On 20 November 1847 the newspaper's printing office burned. Temporarily the *American Beacon*, with a curtailed number of pages, had to be printed on the press of the *Virginia Temperance Advocate*. Quickly recovering, Cunningham had resumed publishing his full newspaper on new printing presses by 8 December. The fire spurred changes in ownership. Cunningham's partners left the business, and he operated the newspaper single-handedly for several weeks until early in January 1848, when he announced his partnership with Richard Gatewood Jr., a young journalist who became the junior editor and proprietor.

Cunningham assumed sole editorship in November 1851, although Gatewood remained as a business partner. With this change came a profound alteration in the character of the newspaper. Cunningham believed that Virginia had entered a new era following the recent adoption and approval of a new state constitution that implemented a number of reforms he favored, including universal white male suffrage, increased western representation in the House of Delegates, and popular election of most local and state officers. On 4 November he shortened his newspaper's title to the *American Beacon*, eliminated the focus on commerce, and transformed the paper into a partisan organ of the Whig Party. He directly commented on politics. He affirmed his support of the Union but called on the federal government and the northern states to adhere strictly to the United States Constitution. He blamed sectional discord on northern states' legislation that had encroached on southern property rights.

After the Whig Party disintegrated, the *American Beacon* supported the American Party, or Know Nothings. The newspaper adopted the anti-Catholic and strongly anti-immigration stances of the larger party. Cunningham participated in local American Party rallies and associations, and in 1854 and 1855 the party controlled Norfolk's municipal offices.

In June 1855 a devastating yellow fever epidemic struck Norfolk. By the time it had subsided late in October, more than two thousand residents had perished. Cunningham, Gatewood, and most of the *American Beacon* staff contracted yellow fever late in August. Gatewood died about a week later. William Edmund Cunningham died on 3 September 1855, probably at the City Hotel, where he lived and which had been turned into a temporary hospital. He was most likely buried in an unmarked grave in the Cunningham family plot in Cedar Grove Cemetery. The *American Beacon*, the longest-running daily newspaper in Norfolk's history to that time, did not survive the deaths of Cunningham and his partner.

Full name and birth date in Norfolk City Birth Register and in baptismal record printed in George Holbert Tucker, comp., *Abstracts from Norfolk City Marriage Bonds (1797–1850) and Other Genealogical Data* (1934), 209; several Cunningham letters in Hugh Blair Grigsby Papers and Tompkins Family Papers, both VHS; *American Beacon, and Norfolk and Portsmouth Daily Advertiser*, 2 Apr. 1833, 1, 12 Oct. 1840, 2 Dec. 1847, 1 Jan. 1848; *Norfolk and Portsmouth Herald*, 23 Nov. 1847; *American Beacon*, 4 Nov. 1851, 27 Apr. 1855; Norfolk Death Register; death notices in *Richmond Daily Dispatch*, 5, 6 Sept. 1855, *Richmond Enquirer*, 6, 11 Sept. 1855, and *Richmond Whig and Public Advertiser*, 7 Sept. 1855.

JOHN G. DEAL

CURLE, William Roscow Wilson (d. by 7 February 1782), member of the Convention of 1776 and judge of the Virginia Court of Appeals, was the son of Wilson Curle and Priscilla Meade Curle. He was born probably in Elizabeth City County, but the date is not known. The destruction of most of the county's records leaves much about his personal life undocumented. Curle married Euphan Wallace, who was probably the mother of his only known son. She died early in 1774, and in August or September 1776 he married a widow, Sarah Lyon. They are not known to have had any children before her death on an unrecorded date. Curle and his third wife, Mary Kello, had at least one daughter.

Curle eventually owned more than 730 acres of land in Elizabeth City County, but early in his career he practiced law in Norfolk. At the end of March 1766 he joined the Norfolk Sons of Liberty to protest the Stamp Act, and on 24 June 1772 he was elected to the borough's common council. In December 1773 Curle and several other Norfolk attorneys announced that as a consequence of the difficulty they were having collecting fees from clients, they would accept only payments in advance from all but the local merchants. Curle seems to have possessed a volatile temperament. Having once waited half an hour for a play to begin in Norfolk's theater, he threw a bottle at one of the performers and set off a riot that led to the destruction of the stage and scenery.

After moving back to Elizabeth City County in 1774, Curle was elected a member and chair of the Elizabeth City County–Hampton Town Joint Committee on 22 November of that year. The committee vigorously enforced the regulations that the Continental Congress and the Virginia Revolutionary Conventions had adopted. He took part in selecting officers for the minutemen recruited in the counties near Hampton during the autumn of 1775. Early in December of that year Curle took charge of a cache of intercepted letters from Loyalists and merchants. On one of the letters he entered a fiercely patriotic annotation, *"False as hell."* He branded the writers as "base, vile, secret and malicious Enemys" of American liberty and complained to the Committee of Safety in Williamsburg that "if Scotchmen continue in our Land thus free; Virginians must be Slaves."

In the aftermath of the fire that destroyed much of Norfolk on 1 January 1776, Curle lost property valued at more than £600. As an owner of a city lot, he was eligible to vote on 22 May 1776 when the few Norfolk residents who had not been burned out elected a replacement for Joseph Hutchings, who had represented the borough in the first three Revolutionary Conventions but who had been captured in a skirmish at Kemp's Landing the previous November. The voters elected Curle, who took his seat in the fifth and final Revolutionary Convention five days later. He was appointed to the Committees of Privileges and Elections and of Propositions and Grievances. Curle also served on the committee that presented drafts of the Virginia Declaration of Rights and the first constitution of the commonwealth and was almost certainly present when the convention unanimously adopted the Declaration of Rights on 12 June and the constitution on 29 June.

Curle represented Norfolk in the House of Delegates in the autumn of 1776 and sat on the Committees for Courts of Justice, of Privileges and Elections, of Propositions and Grievances, and of Religion. Reelected in the spring of 1777, he served in the session of the General Assembly that met in May of that year as a member of the Committees for Courts of Justice, of Privileges and Elections, of Propositions and Grievances, for Religion, and of Trade, an impressive list of committee assignments for a man who had never been elected to the House of Burgesses. Curle arrived late to the autumn session and was added to the committees for establishing the state's courts and to the Committee for Courts of Justice. After winning election to a third term in 1778, he again sat on the Committees for Courts of Justice, of Propositions and Grievances, and of Trade. He won a final term in the spring of 1779, served on the same committees as in the previous year, and rejoined the Committee of Privileges and Elections.

On 17 June 1779 the General Assembly elected Curle one of the three judges of the state's Court of Admiralty. Surviving records of the court do not indicate how often it met or how busy its docket was. As a member of that court Curle became ex officio a member of the Virginia Court of Appeals, and he took his seat on its first day of business, 30 August 1779. As a judge of the Court of Appeals during the formative period of the commonwealth's first appellate court, he initially shouldered light responsibilities.

Curle remained active in the defense of his region throughout the Revolutionary War, but it is not clear whether his successful petition to the governor and Council of State in November 1777 asking permission to manumit a male slave for meritorious service was in connection with the war effort. Curle was by then or soon became county lieutenant, or commander of the Elizabeth City County militia. When British officers

were scouring the county in 1780 in search of supplies, one of them included Curle's name on his list of "very bad men. in other words Damned Rebels." On 7 March 1781, after a British raiding party entered the county, Curle called out and commanded the militia to repulse them, but his small force was outnumbered, and he was captured. Curle remained a prisoner of war for about a month and became gravely ill before being exchanged. The experience may have led to his death. William Roscow Wilson Curle died on an unrecorded date late in 1781 or early in 1782. The place of his burial is not known. On 7 February 1782 the governor and Council appointed a new member of the Court of Admiralty "in the room of William R. W. Curle deceased."

Imperfectly documented family history in *WMQ*, 1st ser., 9 (1900): 126, 130; *Williamsburg Virginia Gazette* (Purdie and Dixon), 30 Dec. 1773; *Williamsburg Virginia Gazette* (Purdie), 6 Sept. 1776; *Richmond Virginia Gazette* (Dixon and Nicolson), 10 Mar. 1781; *Norfolk and Portsmouth Herald and General Advertiser*, 19 June 1839; numerous references and several letters in *Revolutionary Virginia*, vols. 1–7 (first quotation on 4:433, second and third quotations on 5:45); appointment to court in *JHD*, May 1779 sess., 54; Court of Appeals Order Book, 1:1, RG 100, LVA; *Journals of Council of State*, 2:28; Cornwallis Papers, PRO CO 30/11/3, no. 12, fol. 18 (fourth quotation); *Jefferson Papers*, 5:95–96, 293–294, 324, 330–331 (printing a Curle letter in New-York Historical Society, New York, N.Y.), 352, 365, 366–367, 383–385, 428; fragmentary estate accounts in Elizabeth City Co. Order Book (1784–1788), 59, 283, 373, 548; death without date reported in *Journals of Council of State*, 3:41 (final quotation).

THOMAS M. COSTA

CURRIE, Ellyson (d. by 28 August 1829), member-elect of the Convention of 1829–1830, was the son of David Currie, an Anglican minister who for almost fifty years served at Christ Church in Lancaster County, and his second wife, Elizabeth Armistead Currie. On 15 September 1803 he married Ann Gilliam in Petersburg. They had at least one son and one daughter. After her death on an unrecorded date, Currie on 14 December 1812 married Elizabeth F. Jones, daughter of the Northumberland County physician Walter Jones, who was a member of the Convention of 1788 and served five terms in the House of Representatives. No children are recorded from the second marriage, and after

Currie's death his widow became the fourth wife of the Lancaster County planter and merchant Rawleigh William Downman.

Two years after receiving an A.B. from the College of William and Mary in 1797, Currie qualified as an attorney in Lancaster and Northumberland Counties. He practiced law in both counties until his death and on occasion served as their commonwealth's attorney. Currie represented Lancaster County in the House of Delegates during four terms from 1801 to 1805. He sat on the Committees of Propositions and Grievances, of Privileges and Elections, and for Courts of Justice. From 1806 to 1810 Currie represented the counties of Lancaster, Northumberland, and Richmond in the Senate of Virginia, where he was appointed to the Committee of Privileges and Elections during the 1806–1807 assembly and served as its chair from 1808 to 1810. Currie returned to the House of Delegates for the 1812–1813 session and served on the Committee for Courts of Justice and the Committee of Finance.

On 12 April 1813 Currie accepted an interim appointment by the governor and Council of State to a vacant seat on the General Court. His tenure on the bench was brief. On 25 May of that year the General Assembly elected William Alexander Gibbons Dade, of Prince William County, to the office. The next year Currie served as quartermaster for the 92d Regiment, Virginia militia. He was a presidential elector for William Harris Crawford in 1824 and Andrew Jackson in 1828.

In May 1829, along with Dade and two other men, Currie won election in a nine-candidate field to represent the counties of King George, Lancaster, Northumberland, Prince William, Richmond, Stafford, and Westmoreland at a convention summoned to revise the Virginia constitution. At the convention, which met in Richmond from 5 October 1829 through 15 January 1830, eastern delegates successfully thwarted the reform efforts of their western counterparts to extend the suffrage and gain more-proportionate representation in the General Assembly. Neither Dade nor Currie attended the convention, however. Dade resigned just as the convention began and died later that month.

Ellyson Currie had died by 28 August 1829, when a Lancaster County constituent informed the governor of the necessity of calling a special election to fill Currie's vacant convention seat. In three-day polling beginning on 28 September the district voters sent Augustine Neale to the convention in Currie's stead. At the time of his death Currie owned about 1,200 acres of land in Lancaster County and more than 460 acres in Northumberland County, as well as more than thirty slaves. He was buried probably at Verville, the Currie family estate in Lancaster County.

Biography in Edward Chase Earle Jr. and Mildred Towles Wooding, "Verville: Once Called 'Gordonsville,'" *Northern Neck of Virginia Historical Magazine* 7 (1957): 610–614; Petersburg Hustings Court Marriage Register (1784–1865); Virginia Genealogical Society, *Virginia Marriages in Rev. John Cameron's Register and Bath Parish Register* (1963), 8; Stratton Nottingham, *The Marriage License Bonds of Northumberland County, Virginia, from 1783–1850* (1929), 25; Personal Property Tax Returns, Lancaster Co., RG 48, LVA; Land Tax Returns, Lancaster Co., Northumberland Co., RG 48, LVA; Council of State Journal (1812–1813), 159, 169, and (1828–1829), 155, RG 75, LVA; Executive Letter Book (29 July 1812–1 Dec. 1813), 224, RG 3, LVA; Currie to governor, 12 Apr. 1813, 18 Apr. 1814, in *Calendar of Virginia State Papers*, 10:226, 322–323; *Fredericksburg Virginia Herald*, 13 Oct. 1824, 11 Oct. 1828, 9 Sept., 3 Oct. 1829; *Richmond Enquirer*, 29 May, 2 June 1829; *Proceedings and Debates of 1829–1830 Convention*, 5; Records of Convention of 1829–1830, RG 91, LVA; Lancaster Co. Will Book, 28:294–295; Lancaster Co. Estate Book, 30:530–533; Lancaster Co. Order Book, 27a:117; death reported in Addison Hall to governor, 28 Aug. 1829, William Branch Giles Executive Papers, RG 3, LVA.

JOHN G. DEAL

CURRIE, Leonard James (28 July 1913–23 April 1996), architect and educator, was born in Stavely, Alberta, Canada. His parents, Andrew Currie and Florence McIntyre Currie, nurtured in him a love for the arts and history that he cultivated throughout his life. In 1932 he became a naturalized citizen of the United States. Currie graduated with a bachelor's degree in architecture in 1936 from the University of Minnesota. There he met Virginia Herz, whom he married on 8 February 1937. They had two daughters and one son.

Currie continued his education at Harvard University, where he received a master's degree in architecture in 1938. He benefited from the teaching of Walter Gropius, founder of the

Bauhaus school in Germany, which promoted the synthesis of the visual arts and the adaptation of science and technology into architectural design. Gropius hired Currie to work for his firm in Cambridge, Massachusetts. Gropius and his partner, Marcel Breuer, made a lasting impression on Currie, who later recalled that through Breuer's encouragement, "I became convinced that I could redesign the world."

In 1940 Currie won the prestigious Arthur W. Wheelwright Fellowship from Harvard University, which allowed him to travel to Honduras and work with the Carnegie Institution of Washington in pioneering archaeological research at the ancient Mayan city of Copán. He remained as an architectural consultant for more than a year, and his work became part of the reference documentation for all subsequent studies of the archaeological site.

In 1941 and 1942 Currie worked on a Pan American Airways project to construct airport buildings in Central America. He served as an officer in the United States Army in the European theater during World War II and later retired as a lieutenant colonel in the Army Reserve. The year 1946 marked a turning point for Currie. After having worked in Denver for about a year as an assistant campus planner for the University of Colorado, he received an invitation from Gropius to join the faculty at Harvard as an assistant professor of architecture. At the same time Currie joined Gropius in The Architects Collaborative (TAC), a new Cambridge firm that garnered international acclaim as one of the leaders of the Modern movement. Working as a designer and draftsman for TAC, Currie collaborated on several important projects, including the celebrated Six Moon Hill planned residential community near Boston. He left in 1951 to head a study of housing in Costa Rica for the Department of State's Technical Cooperation Administration.

In 1951 Currie and his family moved to Bogotá, Colombia, where he spent five years as the organizer and director of the Inter-American Housing Center, a project of the Organization of American States dedicated to improving housing and community development in impoverished sections of Latin American cities. In several

of the public housing projects initiated under his direction, he found that Gropius's lessons in prefabrication, standardization, and rationalization served him well. Currie later regarded his contributions to alleviating the housing problems of the poor in Latin America as his most worthwhile work.

In 1956 Currie became head of the department of architecture at Virginia Polytechnic Institute (later Virginia Polytechnic Institute and State University), in Blacksburg. There, drawing inspiration from the influential modernist curriculum of Gropius at Harvard, he laid the groundwork for the eventual establishment of the College of Architecture and Urban Studies. Currie worked to change the four-year architecture program into a five-year professional program. He pushed for the department's transformation into a separate school and urged the construction of an architecture building.

While teaching at Virginia Tech, Currie founded the architectural firm of Atkins, Currie, and Payne, for which he produced some of his best designs. Most notable was his own residence in Blacksburg, dubbed Pagoda House. Completed in 1961, the building received a First Honor Award in the Homes for Better Living Competition of the American Institute of Architects (1963) and the Test of Time Award from the Virginia Society of the AIA (1982). In 1994 Pagoda House was listed on both the Virginia Landmarks Register and the National Register of Historic Places. In his design, Currie found a personal expression of Modernism that departed from the machine aesthetic favored by Gropius and Breuer and that in its use of natural materials and a spreading hipped roof was more reminiscent of the organic architecture of Frank Lloyd Wright.

In 1962 Currie accepted an invitation to become the founding dean of the College of Fine and Applied Arts (later the College of Architecture and the Arts) at the University of Illinois's undergraduate division in Chicago (after 1982 the University of Illinois at Chicago). During his nineteen years as dean and professor he continued to accumulate an impressive record of professional achievements. As an independent practitioner he restored a nineteenth-century house as his own residence—a project that served as a catalyst for numerous rehabilitation, restoration, and adaptive reuse projects in the Near West Side neighborhood of Chicago. In 1982 the University of Illinois honored him with its Distinguished Service Award.

Continuing his international activity, Currie was an architectural consultant for two universities in Managua, Nicaragua, and one in Patras, Greece. In 1972 and 1973 he traveled to Malaysia on a senior Fulbright Fellowship and served as acting dean for the School of Housing, Building, and Planning at the Universiti Sains Malaysia, in Penang. Currie, joining other distinguished architects from around the world, represented the United States in 1977 as a co-signer of the Charter of Machu Picchu, a document that assessed the state of architecture and urbanism and identified the most pressing challenges confronting the design professions.

After he retired from the University of Illinois in 1981, Currie and his wife returned to Blacksburg, where he established Leonard J. Currie and Associates. He devoted himself to general practice with a special emphasis on solar and alternative energy projects. Currie believed that "in order to conserve energy and raw materials, the human race must come to realize that we simply cannot afford to keep throwing away our buildings." He constructed a new house for himself using innovative strategies for energy efficiency and incorporating recycled components and fragments of demolished structures. His rehabilitation and restoration of Preston Place, a former hotel in Blacksburg, received an award for historic commercial building rehabilitation from the New River Valley Preservation League. Currie also won national acclaim in 1987 for operating a free clinic that provided architectural services to low-income residents in the region.

Currie received numerous honors during his career. The Colombian government awarded him a medal of merit in 1956. He became a fellow of the American Institute of Architects in 1969 and was also a fellow of the International Institute of Arts and Letters. In 1993 the Virginia Society of the American Institute of Architects recognized Currie's distinguished body of accomplishments throughout his fifty-five-year career

by conferring on him its highest honor, the William C. Noland Medal. Reflecting his many interests and commitment to community service, Currie sat on many boards, including Virginia's advisory committee for school construction from 1956 to 1962 and the advisory board for *Architecture in Virginia*, published by the Virginia Museum of Fine Arts, in 1968.

After returning to Blacksburg, Currie maintained a close relationship with Virginia Tech, where he frequently lectured and participated in design reviews. With his wife, he established two endowments to promote excellence in architectural education: the Michelle Currie Memorial Scholarship for an incoming undergraduate student and the Leonard and Virginia Currie Faculty Professional Development Award. For his achievements and outstanding service to the College of Architecture and Urban Studies, Leonard James Currie received a special Lifetime Contributions Award shortly before he died of a heart attack in Blacksburg on 23 April 1996. He was buried in Westview Cemetery.

Biographies in John F. Gane, ed., *American Architects Directory*, 3d ed. (1970), 195, Clara B. Cox, "Educator Leaves His Mark World-Wide, His Generosity Closer to Home," *Virginia Tech Magazine* 9 (winter 1987): 24–26 (first quotation on 26 and several pors.), and *Inform* 5 (special issue, 1994): 34–35 (second quotation), 58; correspondence and other materials in Leonard and Virginia Currie Collection, University of Illinois, Chicago; some Currie letters in Marcel Breuer Papers, Archives of American Art, Smithsonian Institution, Washington, D.C.; publications include Currie, *Housing in Costa Rica* (1951), "Changing Roles in Architectural Education," *AIA Journal* 41 (May 1964): 26–31, *Planning of Central American Campuses* (1964), and *Designing Environments for the Aging: Policies and Strategies* (1977); *Washington Post*, 6 Dec. 1958; *Chicago Tribune*, 7 July 1963 (por.); *Virginia Record* 107 (May/June 1985): 27–30; *Architectural Record* 175 (Mar. 1987): 9; *Roanoke Times*, 12 Nov. 1993; *Richmond Times-Dispatch*, 14 Nov. 1993; *Christiansburg, Blacksburg, and Radford News*, 17 Nov. 1993; obituaries in *Roanoke Times*, 24 Apr. 1996, *Chicago Sun-Times* and *Chicago Tribune*, both 25 Apr. 1996, *Richmond Times-Dispatch*, 26 Apr. 1996, *Washington Post*, 28 Apr. 1996, and *Virginia Tech Spectrum*, 9 May 1996.
HUMBERTO RODRÍGUEZ-CAMILLONI

CURRY, Elinor Wise (28 September 1903–25 October 1995), Presbyterian lay leader, was the daughter of Carrie Wise Curry and Lucien Ralston Curry, a bookkeeper and later a realtor. Soon after her birth in Harrodsburg, Kentucky, the family moved to Richmond, Virginia. Curry attended the Collegiate School for Girls and the General Assembly's Training School for Lay Workers, Inc. (after 1959 the Presbyterian School of Christian Education, Inc., and after 1997 Union Theological Seminary and Presbyterian School of Christian Education), a Presbyterian institution that trained women for a vocation of church work. After graduating in 1925, she spent nine months operating synod Bible schools in Mississippi. She never married.

Curry returned to Richmond and accepted a position as director of Christian education at Ginter Park Presbyterian Church. Exposure to the plight of African Americans at home and in Mississippi prompted a life of activism and powerful concern. By the 1930s she was working to combat racial discrimination and volunteering at the 17th Street Mission, a ministry in Richmond's East End that students at the Union Theological Seminary in Virginia had organized in 1911 to help local African Americans. Curry encouraged members of her church to become involved with the mission. Many of them, along with students from Union Theological Seminary and the Training School, experienced their first interracial contacts and developed friendships as a result of her efforts.

In 1945 Curry resigned from the Ginter Park Church over differences with some members who opposed her mission work. For the next year she was an assistant dietician in the dining room at Saint Philip Hospital, a facility for African Americans at the Medical College of Virginia, while she continued volunteering at the 17th Street Mission. She sponsored a weekly fellowship supper, taught classes, conducted a reading room, arranged entertainment, and provided support for the mission's clients. Curry's work there led *Presbyterian Outlook* to recognize her in January 1946 as one of ten notable Presbyterians. The Hanover Presbytery, the church's governing assembly for central Virginia, hired Curry in 1947 to take charge of the mission. As a result of her efforts to organize an official church, in 1952 the 17th Street Mission became Eastminster Presbyterian Church. Curry served as Eastminster's director of Christian education and at the time of her retirement in 1969 was director of church

and community services. In 1963, a year after the General Assembly of the Presbyterian Church in the U.S. voted to allow women to serve in a variety of church offices, Curry became the first woman elected elder in the Hanover Presbytery (later Presbytery of the James). In 1972 she was elected the presbytery's first woman moderator.

In retirement Curry became a member of All Souls Presbyterian Church, which she helped organize, and was a part-time coordinator for the Volunteers-in-Education program in the Richmond public schools. Believing strongly that the church should capitalize on the abilities and experience of its older parishioners, she served in 1975 on a committee at the Presbyterian School of Christian Education charged with developing a curriculum specializing in ministry to the elderly. At various times Curry sat on the board of directors of the Capital Area Agency on Aging, the Richmond Community Senior Center, the Richmond Urban League, and the Young Women's Christian Association. She also served on the Model City Committee for the East End, the advisory committee for Upward Bound, and the advisory council for the Richmond Community Action Program. From 1977 to 1979 she chaired the Hanover Presbytery's division of Mission to Society.

In 1970 the president of the United States honored Curry with a certificate of commendation for exceptional service to others in her efforts to improve race relations. Five years later the Presbyterian School of Christian Education presented her with an award for faithful service. Elinor Wise Curry died in a Richmond-area retirement community on 25 October 1995. She donated her body to science, but her name is inscribed on her parents' grave marker in Union Cemetery, in Leesburg. The Union Theological Seminary and Presbyterian School of Christian Education annually recognizes congregations for effective work in their communities with the Elinor Curry Award for Outreach and Social Concern.

Birth date in Social Security application, Social Security Administration, Office of Earnings Operations, Baltimore, Md.; *Presbyterian Outlook* (14 Jan. 1946), 6–7 (with cover por.); *Presbyterian Survey* 59 (Jan. 1969): 13–15 (several pors.); *Richmond News Leader*, 3 Nov. 1972, 29 July 1978; *Richmond Times-Dispatch*, 17 May 1975; Church Educators of Hanover Presbytery, *The Ministry of Church Education* (video recording), including Curry interview conducted by Jeff Kellam, 21 Feb. 1983, UTS; information provided by sister, Margaret Curry Worsham (2003); Robert P. Davis et al., *Virginia Presbyterians in American Life: Hanover Presbytery (1755–1980)* (1982), 203, 236–237, 260; obituaries in *Richmond Times-Dispatch*, 29 Oct. 1995, and *Presbyterian Outlook* (20 Nov. 1995), 24.

JANET B. SCHWARZ

CURRY, Jabez Lamar Monroe (5 June 1825–12 February 1903), educational reformer, was born in Lincoln County, Georgia, and was the son of William Curry, a merchant and member of the state legislature, and his first wife, Susan Winn Curry. As a young man he changed his middle name from Lafayette to Lamar. His mother died in 1827, and two years later his father married a widow with one son. Curry was educated in the local schools and for one year at Willington Academy, a school in Abbeville County, South Carolina, established by the noted educator Moses Waddel. In 1838 Curry's family moved to Talladega County, Alabama.

The following year Curry entered Franklin College (later the University of Georgia), where he excelled in debating and was elected orator during his junior and senior years. He graduated in 1843 and later that year entered the law school of Harvard University, where he studied with Simon Greenleaf and Joseph Story, the latter an associate justice of the Supreme Court of the United States. Curry's classmates included Rutherford B. Hayes, and while in Massachusetts he heard speeches by the radical abolitionist William Lloyd Garrison, the common-school reformer Horace Mann, and the Unitarian minister Theodore Parker. After receiving a law degree in 1845, Curry continued his legal studies in Alabama. He served briefly as a private in a Texas company during the war with Mexico, but he returned home to attend to an ill compatriot before he saw any action. In 1846 Curry was admitted to the Talladega County bar and during the next few years settled into the life of a southern gentleman. He practiced law and operated a plantation, worked at the time of the Civil War by about fifty slaves.

Curry married Ann Alexander Bowie on 4 March 1847. Of their four children, one son and one daughter survived childhood. Dissatisfied with farming and the law and fired by sectional controversies, Curry entered politics as a member of the states' rights wing of the Alabama Democratic Party. Elected to represent Talladega County in the Alabama House of Representatives for biennial terms in 1847, 1853, and 1855, he favored aid to railroads and advocated the establishment of state-supported common schools. Curry was a presidential elector for James Buchanan in 1856 and won election the following year from Alabama's Seventh Congressional District to the United States House of Representatives. He quickly developed a reputation for oratory and as an able defender of southern interests. During his two terms Curry delivered several addresses that asserted slavery's central importance to the national, and not just the southern, economy, blasted northern Republicans for their attempts to bar the spread of slavery, and predicted that abolition would result in a decline of character and productivity among southern blacks.

After the election of Abraham Lincoln intensified the sectional crisis, Alabama named Curry its commissioner to Maryland to urge that state's governor and legislature to side with other slaveholding states. When Alabama seceded from the Union in January 1861, Curry resigned from the United States Congress and was elected a deputy to the Provisional Confederate Congress, which met in Montgomery, Alabama. He won election to the First Confederate Congress, which assembled in Richmond in February 1862. Curry became Speaker pro tempore of the House of Representatives in 1863 and in that capacity has been credited with authorship of the *Address of Congress to the People of the Confederate States*, in which the Confederate Congress reviewed the causes of the Civil War, its goals in the struggle, and the North's stubborn refusal to negotiate a peace. In August 1863 Curry lost his bid for reelection, and later that year he failed in his attempt to be elected to the Confederate States Senate. After his term in Congress ended he prosecuted home-front disloyalty as a habeas corpus commissioner. He served as special aide to General Joseph Eggleston Johnston and to Major General Joseph Wheeler and finished the war as a lieutenant colonel commanding the 5th

Alabama Cavalry. Curry was paroled in Alabama on 13 May 1865. Almost simultaneously with the defeat of the Confederacy, his wife died on 8 April 1865.

Immediately after the Civil War, the Baptist Church provided the venue for most of Curry's professional activities. He had joined the denomination in 1847 and been active in local Alabama Baptist associations. Curry was elected president of the Alabama State Baptist Convention in 1865 and also became president of Howard College (later Samford University), a Baptist-affiliated institution in Marion, Alabama. Ordained a Baptist minister in January 1866, he regularly preached in various pulpits and was twice reelected president of the state convention.

On 25 June 1867 Curry married Mary Wortham Thomas, daughter of a prosperous Richmond merchant. They had no children. The next year he left Howard College to join the faculty of Richmond College (later the University of Richmond), where he taught English, moral philosophy, and constitutional and international law. Curry was a popular professor and remained a dynamic Baptist leader and Sunday school organizer, both locally and nationally. He served as president of the Baptist General Association of Virginia for five years during the 1870s, as president of the National Baptist Sunday School Convention, and as president of the Foreign Mission Board from 1871 to 1872 and again from 1874 to 1885.

Although not particularly active in Virginia politics, Curry sided with the Funders in their struggle with the Readjusters in the debate about public finance and repayment of the state debt late in the 1870s. Disenchanted after Readjusters swept to power in 1879, Curry continued to look for opportunities for public service and in October 1885 accepted an appointment by President Grover Cleveland as American minister to Spain. Curry served in Madrid until 5 July 1888, and in May 1902 President Theodore Roosevelt named him the American special envoy for ceremonies marking King Alfonso XIII's coming of age as the Spanish monarch.

Curry's most notable accomplishments were in the field of public education. In 1881 he resigned from the Richmond College faculty to become general agent of the Peabody Education Fund (named for its founder, the Massachusetts financier and philanthropist George Peabody), which sought to stimulate the expansion of common schools in the South largely through improving the training of teachers and establishing state-funded normal schools. In November 1890 Curry accepted an offer from the John F. Slater Fund for the Education of Freedmen to chair its education committee. In effect the fund's general agent, he assumed his new duties the following year.

Established in 1882, the Slater Fund was then the most important southern philanthropy dedicated to African American education. Under Curry's leadership the fund focused its resources on a small number of institutions that emphasized industrial schooling, a blend of manual training and moral improvement that in the last decades of the nineteenth century achieved popularity at such institutions as Hampton Normal and Agricultural Institute (later Hampton University) and Tuskegee Normal and Industrial Institute (later Tuskegee University). Throughout the 1890s he often visited southern schools supported by the Peabody and Slater Funds and made numerous public addresses about educational improvement.

As efforts at school improvement expanded across the South, Curry developed contacts with other incipient reformers throughout the region. Eventually, a full-scale crusade emerged in 1898 with the first of several Conferences for Education in the South, held at Capon Springs in Hampshire County, West Virginia. Although not present at the conference's first meeting, Curry was chosen vice president. The following year he was elected president and delivered a keynote address proposing a transformation of southern white public education. Curry believed that education of African Americans was important but declared that a greater need existed for improvements in schools for white students. As he stated, "The white people are to be the leaders, to take the initiative, to have the directive control in all matters pertaining to civilization and the highest interests of our beloved land."

When the conference met in Winston-Salem, North Carolina, in April 1901, Curry served on the Committee on Platform and Resolutions, which outlined the establishment of what became the Southern Education Board, a coordinating council of educational reformers that represented southern whites and northern philanthropists. He subsequently helped to establish the General Education Board, which, with the support of John D. Rockefeller, soon became the best-financed and most-professionally managed northern philanthropy involved in southern social policy.

By 1900 Curry had become the nation's best-known advocate of southern education. He had participated early in the 1880s in the unsuccessful campaign for congressional passage of a bill to provide money to states with high rates of illiteracy. His credentials among white southerners were unassailable, and he worked effectively with post-Reconstruction Redeemer regimes. At the same time, though he did not favor integrated or equal schools for white and black children, he supported basic justice for African Americans. Curry vigorously opposed efforts to fund racially segregated public schools based on the actual tax contributions of the members of each race, a breakdown that would have drastically reduced tax support for black schools. His main weapon in the educational campaign remained his oratory, which he used with great effectiveness. In the decades after the Civil War he addressed all of the state legislatures of the South, some of them multiple times.

As Curry's speaking ability became legendary, he also wrote prolifically. Along with numerous addresses that appeared in pamphlet form or as articles in educational journals, he published widely on government and history topics. His most significant works include *Constitutional Government in Spain* (1889), *William Ewart Gladstone* (1891), *The Southern States of the American Union Considered in Their Relations to the Constitution of the United States and to the Resulting Union* (1894), and *Civil History of the Government of the Confederate States with Some Personal Reminiscences* (1901).

During the time Curry lived in Richmond, he served as an officer of the Virginia Historical Society and as a visitor of the Medical College of Virginia. After he resigned from the faculty of Richmond College he became a member of

its governing board and served until his death. In 1902 the College of William and Mary chapter elected him a member of Phi Beta Kappa.

By the mid-1890s Jabez Lamar Monroe Curry had moved to Washington, D.C. After a long struggle with Bright's disease, he died on 12 February 1903 at the home of his brother-in-law near Asheville, North Carolina. Following a funeral in the chapel of Richmond College, he was buried in the city's Hollywood Cemetery. A native of Georgia and longtime resident of Virginia, Curry is one of two citizens of Alabama whose statues stand in the National Statuary Hall Collection in the United States Capitol. The school of education at the University of Virginia is named in his honor.

Biographies include Edwin Anderson Alderman and Armistead Churchill Gordon, *J. L. M. Curry: A Biography* (1911), with frontispiece por., Jessie Pearl Rice, *J. L. M. Curry: Southerner, Statesman and Educator* (1949), Woodford B. Hackley, *Faces on the Wall: Brief Sketches of the Men and Women Whose Portraits and Busts Were on the Campus of the University of Richmond in 1955* (1955), 21–23 (por. facing 62), and W. Hamilton Bryson, ed., *Legal Education in Virginia, 1779–1979: A Biographical Approach* (1982), 161–170, including bibliography of Curry's writings; principal collections of letters include J. L. M. Curry Family Papers, Alabama Department of Archives and History, Montgomery, J. L. M. Curry Papers, LC, and J. L. M. Curry Collection, VBHS; BVS Marriage Register, Richmond City (1867); *Congressional Globe*, 35th and 36th Cong.; *OR*, 1st ser., vol. 49, pt. 1, 1038, vol. 52, pt. 2, 648, 4th ser., 1:30, 38–42, 46–47; *Richmond Daily Dispatch*, 30 Jan. 1878; Curry, "Education in the Southern States," *Proceedings of the Second Capon Springs Conference for Christian Education in the South* (1899), 25–32 (quotation on 28); obituaries and tributes in *New York Times*, *Richmond News Leader*, and *Richmond Times-Dispatch*, all 13 Feb. 1903, *Washington Post*, 13, 15, 16 Feb. 1903, and *Minutes of the Baptist General Association of Virginia* (1903), 98–101.

WILLIAM A. LINK

CURTIS, Florence Rising (30 September 1873–6 October 1944), librarian and educator, was born in Ogdensburg, New York, and was the daughter of Emeline Clark Curtis and Newton Martin Curtis, a Union brigadier general during the Civil War, a farmer and Treasury Department agent in the 1870s, and a Republican member of the House of Representatives for three terms beginning in 1891. She attended the Ogdensburg Free Academy and then in 1891 entered Wells College, in Aurora, New York, but left in 1894 to attend the New York State Library School, in Albany. While enrolled in the latter school Curtis began working in February 1895 as a cataloger at the Children's Neighborhood Library, in Troy, New York, and from November 1895 to June 1896 as an assistant librarian at the Diocesan Lending Library at the Cathedral of All Saints, also in Albany. She completed her degree requirements in 1896 but did not receive her diploma until 1898. For the next dozen years she was a librarian at various public libraries in Pennsylvania, New Jersey, and New York, including a stint from 1899 until October 1906 at the State Normal and Training School Library in Potsdam, New York.

Curtis's career path then led her toward training librarians. From 1908 until 1920 she taught at the Library School of the University of Illinois, in Urbana, and also was an instructor at the Indiana Public Library Commission's Summer School for Librarians. Curtis received both a B.A. from the University of Illinois and a B.L.S. from the New York State Library School in 1911. Six years later the University of Minnesota granted her an M.A. and in 1918 published her research calling for the establishment of libraries in such institutions as asylums, juvenile halls, prisons, and sanatoriums. Curtis served from 1915 to 1921 as the first secretary of the Association of American Library Schools. From 1920 to 1922 she taught English at government schools in China and the Philippines. After returning to the United States, she became the assistant director of the Drexel Institute Library School in Philadelphia, Pennsylvania, in 1922 before being hired in 1925 as the first and only director of the Hampton Institute Library School.

In the segregated South, states only grudgingly funded public and school libraries for African Americans. Improvements in libraries at black schools came from $1 million in aid donated by several northern educational foundations. An American Library Association study early in the 1920s found that 72 percent of southerners lived in areas without libraries and that, except in a few of the larger cities, the African American population in the South completely lacked access to libraries. Determined to develop more libraries for African Americans, the

Carnegie Corporation, on advice from the American Library Association, the General Education Board, and the Julius Rosenwald Fund, in 1925 granted Hampton Normal and Agricultural Institute (later Hampton University) funds to found the Hampton Institute Library School. Accredited by the American Library Association, Hampton was the first school for African Americans to offer a bachelor's degree in library science. The Carnegie Corporation selected Hampton both because it already possessed a library of 55,000 books and two trained professional librarians, and because Hampton's administrators were white. Influenced by the American Library Association and the Carnegie Corporation, the school selected Curtis as director based on her "broad experience and the tolerance which comes with it."

The school opened in the autumn of 1925 with four pupils, all black female librarians from the South, two of whom received diplomas the following year. Initially students needed only a high school diploma and one year of college to enter the library school, but by 1934 Hampton accepted only students who had completed four years at the collegiate level. Curtis, who both directed and taught at the school, modeled a curriculum focusing as much on practical problem-solving as on theoretical studies. She encouraged students to institute programs at the libraries for which they worked and to draw up lists of books, including children's materials, suitable for their patrons' needs and interests. A grant of $16,000 from the Rosenwald Fund enabled Curtis to visit black colleges to examine their library needs and to encourage them to develop modern library facilities. Based on her visits, Curtis prepared, and the Rosenwald Fund published, a list of recommended college library books.

In March 1927 at Hampton, Curtis convened a conference of librarians and educators to design a program for creating and encouraging libraries in African American schools. The conference recommended launching model schools in each southern state and at teacher-training institutes at black colleges in order to train librarians and teachers to use books in education. By December 1927 five colleges had established book funds and agreed to meet the conditions for setting up model programs: hiring a trained librarian; providing modern book-stacks, shelves, and reading room space; and allowing Curtis to approve their lists of books to purchase. These institutions became the first of forty-three colleges that received Rosenwald Fund grants for library development within the first five years. As the fund added new colleges, Curtis visited each to assess its needs, plan adequate library facilities and budgets, and select graduates to take Hampton's library course. As a result, Curtis noted, more black colleges and schools received accreditation from the Association of Colleges and Secondary Schools of the Southern States.

Curtis served as vice president of the Virginia Library Association in 1932 and as president in 1933. She decided that she could give the greatest service to segregated southern libraries by helping to develop extension service programs for black high schools and colleges, and in 1929 she first indicated to the General Education Board her desire to leave Hampton. In the mid-1930s, as Curtis approached retirement age, the Carnegie Corporation reevaluated its commitment to the library school. Carnegie had contributed more than 80 percent of the school's funding between 1925 and 1936, but Hampton had provided only about 9 percent. The corporation concluded that qualified applicants would be more interested in attending a library school located at an academically stronger institution. Over Hampton's objections, the corporation endorsed a plan to move the school to Atlanta University (later Clark Atlanta University). The Hampton Institute Library School closed on 29 May 1939. During the fourteen years the school had been in existence, it had graduated 183 librarians, the largest number of whom took positions at four-year colleges.

Florence Rising Curtis, who never married, returned to Ogdensburg after her retirement and died of a cerebral hemorrhage on 6 October 1944, while visiting her sister in Richmond, Indiana. She was buried in the Ogdensburg (later Odgensburgh) Cemetery.

Birth and death dates from Indiana State Board of Health BVS Death Certificate, Wayne Co.; biographies in *New York State Library School Register, 1887–1929*, James I. Wyer Memorial Edition (1959), 23, Bohdan S. Wynar, ed., *Dictionary of American Library Biography* (1978), 108–109, and Arthur Clinton Gunn, "Early Training for Black Librarians in the U.S.: A History of the Hampton Institute Library School and the Establishment of the Atlanta University School of Library Service" (Ph.D. diss., University of Pittsburgh, 1986), 74–79 (quotation from Sarah C. N. Bogle to W. S. Learned, 24 July 1925, on 75, por. on 78); Curtis materials in American Library Association Archives at University of Illinois, Urbana-Champaign, and in Hampton University Archives; publications include Curtis, *The Collection of Social Survey Material* (1915), *The Libraries of the American State and National Institutions for Defectives, Dependents, and Delinquents* (1918), "The Contribution of the Library School to Negro Education," *Library Journal* 51 (1926): 1086–1088, and "Librarianship as a Field for Negroes," *Journal of Negro Education* 4 (Jan. 1935): 94–98; S. L. Smith, "The Passing of the Hampton Institute Library School," *Journal of Negro Education* 9 (Jan. 1940): 51–58; Lucy B. Campbell, *Black Librarians in Virginia: The Story of the Hampton Institute Library School, 1925–1939* (1976), 1–27; obituaries and funeral announcements in *Ogdensburg Journal*, 6, 7 Oct. 1944, and *Ogdensburg Advance*, 8 Oct. 1944; memorial in *Library Journal* 69 (1944): 1060.

MARY CARROLL JOHANSEN

CURTIS, Natalie Josef (1 March 1889–6 June 1968), hospital superintendent, was born in Petersburg and was the daughter of Patrick Henry Curtis, an Irish immigrant, and Mollie M. Bannan Curtis. About 1895 the family moved to Richmond, where her father worked as a traveling salesman. Inspired by her mother's charity work, Curtis in 1910 entered the nursing school at the Philadelphia Orthopedic Hospital and Infirmary for Nervous Diseases. She graduated in 1913 and received specialized training at other Philadelphia-area institutions, including the Episcopal and obstetrical hospitals. While in school she became lifelong friends with a fellow nursing student, Hazel Hill, of Columbus, Ohio.

After returning to Richmond, Curtis enrolled in a new public health course that the state health commissioner had instituted. She convinced Hill to join her, and after the six-week class Curtis took a position with the Richmond Department of Public Health and Hill was assigned to a milk station. By 1919 Curtis had become the assistant superintendent at Tucker Sanatorium, a private psychiatric facility. Her leadership qualities and dedication to her profession attracted the attention of the state inspector of nurses' training schools, who encouraged Curtis to apply for the position of superintendent of Sheltering Arms Hospital.

Sheltering Arms Free Hospital had been founded in Richmond in 1889 as a private facility offering free medical services. By early in the 1920s it was suffering from a rapid turnover in administration and had recently failed to meet state standards for nurses' training. Offered the job in April 1922, Curtis arrived at her new post to find the institution in complete disarray, with too few qualified nurses, too little essential equipment, and a foundering nursing program. Realizing she needed help, Curtis prevailed on Hill to join her staff in October and to take on much of the responsibility for training the nurses. Together, during their tenure the two women taught more than three hundred nurses. Curtis begged, borrowed, and bartered for much-needed educational and operating room equipment. She even placed a donation box in the operating room and charged doctors a quarter every time they used profanity. Through her hard work, determination, and never-ending supply of resourcefulness and inspiration, the hospital began to prosper. Once the physical state of the hospital was restored and the nurses' training program placed back on course, Curtis turned her efforts toward obtaining accreditation for the hospital, which she achieved in 1926.

Under the able leadership of Curtis, Sheltering Arms continued to expand and improve. A twelve-room house donated in 1929 became a nurses' residence, and a new wing added in 1941 increased capacity to 103 patients. Donations decreased during the Great Depression, but the hospital was still able to provide hot meals for neighborhood children and added many unemployed nurses to the staff. Sheltering Arms discontinued its training school for nurses in 1934, but a nursing shortage during World War II led to the establishment of its school for practical nurses in 1944. Curtis, a Catholic, received an apostolic benediction from Pope Pius XII in 1951 for her tireless efforts on behalf of the poor and the sick through her work at the hospital. Curtis retired as superintendent on 31 December 1954. She and Hill traveled for a short time, and after returning to Richmond they lived together and volunteered at the Medical College of Virginia hospital, where in 1956 they received recognition as Volunteers of the Year.

Although she never married, Curtis became the foster mother of a boy who arrived at Sheltering Arms in 1923 as a three-month-old baby. His mother was dying and his father was unable to raise him alone, so Curtis took responsibility for his care. Natalie Josef Curtis died in Richmond on 6 June 1968 and was buried in Saint Joseph's Catholic Church Cemetery, in Petersburg.

BVS Birth Register, Petersburg; biographical information in Sheltering Arms Rehabilitation Hospital Records (1889–1989), VHS; family information provided by foster son Thomas J. Curtis (2002); *Richmond Times-Dispatch*, 16 June 1935; *Richmond News Leader*, 18 Apr. 1951, 25 Oct. 1954; *Richmond Catholic Virginian*, 20, 27 Apr. 1951; Eda Carter Williams, *Sheltering Arms Hospital, Richmond, Virginia, 1889–1949* (1949); Nita Ligon Morse and Eda Carter Williams, *The History of Sheltering Arms Hospital: The First 75 Years, 1889–1964* (1964), 12–13; Anne Rutherford Lower, *Sheltering Arms Hospital: A Centennial History (1889–1989)* (1989), 88–98 (several pors.); obituaries in *Richmond News Leader* and *Richmond Times-Dispatch*, both 7 June 1968.

L. EILEEN PARRIS

CURTISS, Gaston G. (September 1819–15 November 1872), member of the Convention of 1867–1868, was born possibly in the village of Constantia in Oswego County, New York. His early life and education are undocumented. His mother's name is not known, but his father was Hastings Curtiss, who about 1820 moved his family to the nearby village of Central Square, where he built a hotel. In 1824 he served a term in the state legislature, and the next year a newly incorporated Oswego County town was named Hastings in his honor. By 1845 Gaston Curtiss had married Floretta Anna Allen and had at least one son, but four years later he was in debt and forced to sell his real and personal property in order to pay his creditors. In 1850 he was living in Hastings, where he was a merchant and a town supervisor. By 1860 he and his family had moved to the port city of Oswego.

Curtiss arrived in Virginia about 1861 but does not appear in the Bedford County records until 29 December 1865, when he purchased 344 acres of land near the town of Liberty (later Bedford) and took up farming. He also became active in the Republican Party. On 22 October 1867 Bedford County voters approved the calling of a convention to write a new state constitution and elected Curtiss and David Staley, both Radical

Republicans, as delegates to the convention. An election return published in a local newspaper indicates that all but a handful of white Virginians shunned Curtiss, while he received overwhelming support from the freedmen voting for the first time.

The radical faction of the Republican Party dominated the convention, which met in Richmond from 3 December 1867 to 17 April 1868. Curtiss chaired a thirteen-member committee that organized the business of the convention by identifying the numbers and duties of the standing committees. He also chaired the Committee on the Executive Department of Government, was ranking member of the Committee on Limitations and Guaranties, and at the end of the convention was added to the Committee of Revision and Adjustment. He participated in the convention's day-to-day business, sat on various ad hoc committees, and spoke often but not at great length on the convention floor. Curtiss aligned with the Radicals on key roll calls and voted with the convention majority on 6 and 24 March 1868 in support, respectively, of a disabling clause and of a test-oath provision that extended, beyond the requirements of the Congressional Reconstruction Acts, the disfranchisement of many white Virginians who had championed the Confederacy. On 17 April, Curtiss voted for the new constitution, which included among its reforms universal manhood suffrage, the establishment of a public school system, and more elective local offices. On 6 July 1869 voters ratified the constitution but rejected the two disfranchising clauses.

On 20 January 1869 Curtiss chaired a Republican mass meeting at Liberty, and his son, Allen H. Curtiss, was installed as secretary. The two served on a committee charged with recommending to the state's military commander candidates for county offices. Allen Curtiss was nominated for county clerk and on 25 January appeared before the Bedford County Court with a letter signed by the military commander, but the next day the court declared him "whol[l]y incompetent" and petitioned for his removal. Later he was appointed clerk of the Third District Court of Appeals, but evidently he did not serve. The military commander also appointed

Gaston Curtiss to the Bedford County Court. Curtiss took his seat on 22 March but two days later relinquished it to become assistant revenue assessor.

In March 1869 a Republican convention in Richmond appointed Curtiss to the party's State Central Committee, and on 8 June of that year Radical Republicans meeting in Lynchburg nominated him as their candidate for the ten-county Fifth District seat in the House of Representatives. The *Petersburg Index* excoriated the choice and opined that "Curtiss is a very bad man—one of the worst of the whole carpet-bag tribe." The *Lynchburg Daily Virginian* expressed similar contempt and in the weeks leading up to the election published a rumor that Curtiss had fled forgery charges in New York. Described as the "loathsome leader of the flock of carpetbag buzzards," he was also accused of furnishing his home with stolen goods. During the statewide campaign, centrist Conservatives forged an alliance with moderate Republicans that weakened the radical faction of the Republican Party. Curtiss lost the election to Robert Ridgway, whose victory was but one of many for the triumphant Republican and Conservative coalition.

Gaston G. Curtiss returned to farming and died of consumption at his Liberty home on 15 November 1872. In a terse death notice the local press observed, "Probably no man has ever died in any community less regretted than the deceased." His remains were returned to Central Square, New York, and interred in Hillside Cemetery there. His wife and son were later buried beside him.

Birth date derived from BVS Death Register, Bedford Co. (recording age at death as fifty-three years, one month, and twenty-two days); variant birth year of 1820 on gravestone; John C. Churchill, ed., *Landmarks of Oswego County, New York* (1895), 222, 553, 555–556; Oswego Co., N.Y., Deed Liber, 33:466–467, 51:440–443; Bedford Co. Deed Book, 43:71–73; Bedford Co. Order Book, 35:586, 591 (first quotation), 618, 632–633; *Journal of 1867–1868 Convention*, 28, 380; *Debates and Proceedings of 1867–1868 Convention*, 745; Hume, "Membership of Convention of 1867–1868," 481; Lowe, "Virginia's Reconstruction Convention," 348 (Curtiss misidentified by John McAllister Schofield as a former New York state legislator); *Lynchburg Daily Virginian*, 24 Oct. 1867, 14, 19 (third quotation), 30 June 1869; *Bedford Sentinel*, 22 Jan. 1869; *Petersburg Index*, 11 June 1869 (second quotation); *Daily Richmond Whig*, 11

Mar. 1869; *General Orders and Circulars, Headquarters First Military District, 1869* (1870), "Returns of Election of July 6, 1869," 7; estate inventory in Bedford Co. Will Book, 22:420–422; estate division in Bedford Co. Deed Book, 46:424–425; death notice in *Lynchburg Daily Virginian*, 20 Nov. 1872 (fourth quotation).

DONALD W. GUNTER

CUSHING, Jonathan Peter (12 March 1793–25 April 1835), president of Hampden-Sydney College, was born in Rochester, New Hampshire, and was the son of Peter Cushing, a merchant, and Hannah Hanson Cushing. In 1806, two years after being orphaned, he bound himself to his uncle, a saddler. Determined to further his meager education, Cushing redeemed his apprenticeship in 1811 and matriculated at Phillips Exeter Academy, from which he graduated four years later. Despite academic deficiencies he entered Dartmouth College and received a B.A. in August 1817. Chronic lung trouble prompted Cushing, who had intended to qualify for the bar, to leave immediately for Charleston, South Carolina. On the way, he visited John Holt Rice, founding pastor of First Presbyterian Church in Richmond and also a trustee and former teacher at Hampden-Sydney College, in Prince Edward County. Through Rice he met a fellow Dartmouth alumnus who had been engaged to teach at Hampden-Sydney but who had fallen ill. With Rice's encouragement, Cushing signed on as a substitute for the autumn 1817 term.

From the outset Cushing favorably impressed the leaders of the college, especially its president Moses Hoge (1752–1820). Hoge persuaded him to continue teaching at the school, where he became the star of the four-person faculty. The board of trustees readily acquiesced to Cushing's request for new chemistry equipment, and he quickly instituted modern instruction in science. In 1819 he became the school's first professor of chemistry and natural philosophy.

After Hoge died in 1820, Cushing was named acting president, and in September 1821 he was elected president of Hampden-Sydney College while retaining his teaching position. He was the first president who was not also a Presbyterian minister. Cushing's wide-ranging operational innovations began at once and

included issuing in 1821 one of the first college catalogs in America, expanding the faculty, securing more authority for professors, improving salaries, increasing enrollment (with provisions for graduate work), and improving student morale and discipline. He also broadened and strengthened the curriculum, a program of study that was not extensively modified until the 1880s.

In 1820 Cushing proposed erecting a single edifice to replace the inadequate campus buildings constructed between 1775 and 1803. He contributed $500 to the building campaign, an amount matched by fewer than ten other donors. The massive structure, which ultimately cost $45,000, went up in sections over thirteen years. Named Cushing Hall early in the twentieth century, the new structure was the college's primary building until the 1890s and continued to be used as a dormitory in the twenty-first century. The resulting criticism over the construction costs and schedule was probably the chief factor in Cushing's resignation in 1831 to accept an offer to become professor of chemistry and natural philosophy at the College of William and Mary. After reconsideration he agreed to remain at Hampden-Sydney, and the board reelected him president on 25 April 1832.

In 1823 Cushing assisted John Holt Rice in relocating the theological school that had been operating at the college since 1812 to its own permanent buildings on the south end of the campus. Revitalized, it became Union Theological Seminary in 1827 and in 1898 moved to Richmond, where it later became Union Theological Seminary and Presbyterian School of Christian Education.

The effect of Cushing's imposing stature was softened by his kindliness, modesty, patience, courtesy, and fair-mindedness. Students respected him highly as both teacher and disciplinarian. He gave liberally to purchase laboratory equipment and, mindful of his own difficulty in getting an education, quietly supported needy students, including his nephew George Washington Dame, who later became a prominent Episcopal minister and educator. Cushing had come to the school entirely by accident, but his almost eighteen-year tenure as a teacher and president was the longest before the Civil War.

His remarkable combination of vision and practical sense in reviving Hampden-Sydney placed him at the forefront of its presidents.

Cushing's lively interest in all levels of public and private education, cultural advancement, and preservation of history was manifested in his founding of the Literary and Philosophical Society at Hampden-Sydney College in 1824 and also in 1831 of the Institute of Education of Hampden-Sydney College (forerunner of the Educational Association of Virginia, established in 1863). He helped organize the Virginia Historical and Philosophical Society in 1831. At its founding Cushing was elected second vice president. In February 1833 he gave the society's first annual address, in which he called for its acquisition and preservation of manuscripts, papers, and books related to Virginia history.

On 30 July 1827 Cushing executed a marriage bond in Cumberland County and on that day or soon afterward married Lucy Jane Page, daughter of a Hampden-Sydney trustee. They had three daughters, one of whom died in infancy. Cushing began the school year in November 1834 in unusually good health and spirits but soon fell ill. His condition deteriorated dramatically and forced him to resign from Hampden-Sydney College late in March 1835. Hoping to find relief in the West Indies, he and his wife traveled as far as Raleigh, North Carolina, in a torturous three-week carriage trip. Jonathan Peter Cushing died there in a hotel on 25 April 1835. He was buried in Raleigh's City Cemetery, where the trustees of the college later erected a monument. His remains were reinterred in College Presbyterian Church Cemetery at Hampden-Sydney on 25 April 1954.

Biographies in *Southern Literary Messenger* 2 (1836): 163–166, George W. Dame (nephew), "Sketch of the Life and Character of Jonathan P. Cushing, M.A.," *American Quarterly Register* 11 (1838): 113–128, *NCAB*, 2:23–24, and Joseph D. Eggleston, "Jonathan Peter Cushing," *VMHB* 39 (1931), 289–291 (silhouette por. facing 289); Cumberland Co. Marriage Bonds; Cushing, *Collections of the Virginia Historical and Philosophical Society, To Which is Prefixed An Address, Spoken Before the Society at an Adjourned Anniversary Meeting . . . on Monday, Feb. 4th, 1833* (1833); Alfred J. Morrison, *The College of Hampden-Sidney: Calendar of Board Minutes, 1776–1876* (1912), 71–108; Morrison, ed., *Six Addresses on the State of Letters and Science in Virginia . . .* (1917), 31–34, 51–53 (frontispiece por.); Herbert Clarence Bradshaw, *History of Hampden-Sydney College*, vol. 1: *From the Beginnings to the Year 1856* (1976); John Luster Brinkley, *On This Hill: A Narrative History of Hampden-Sydney College, 1774–1994* (1994); obituaries in *Richmond Enquirer*, 8 May 1835, and *Richmond Whig and Public Advertiser*, 19 May 1835.

JOHN LUSTER BRINKLEY

CUSSONS, John (1838–4 January 1912), defender of the Lost Cause and entrepreneur, was born in Horncastle, Lincolnshire, England, and was the son of John Cussons and Elizabeth Jackson Cussons. Educated in Doncaster, he immigrated to the United States in 1855 and traveled west. For a time Cussons worked at the *Detroit Free Press*. He lived for several years on the northern plains frontier, where his six-foot-three-inch, 240-pound frame led the Lakotah Sioux to confer on him the name Wau-zee-hos-ka (tall pine tree). In later years he proudly defended Indian culture and harshly condemned white stereotypes of, and attacks on, the Sioux.

About 1859 Cussons moved to Selma, Alabama, where he worked at a local newspaper. He was a member of the governor's guard that in the spring of 1861 became part of the 4th Regiment Alabama Infantry. As a Confederate private, Cussons exploited the skills he had acquired among the Sioux and served as a scout and sharpshooter during the First Battle of Manassas (Bull Run) and other campaigns in Virginia during 1862 and 1863. By August 1862 he had joined Colonel Evander M. Law's staff as an aide-de-camp and was promoted to first lieutenant. He may have attained the rank of captain by the war's end. In April 1863, while participating in the Suffolk campaign, Cussons fought a duel with another officer who had accused Cussons of maligning a North Carolina regiment. Cussons was not injured, but he slightly wounded his opponent. On 2 July 1863 Cussons was captured at Gettysburg. After being held in a series of prisons for eight months, he was paroled on 16 March 1864 and later served in the western theater.

On 19 May 1864 Captain Cussons, as he was known for the rest of his life, married Susan Ann Sheppard Allen, a wealthy widow almost twenty years his senior who lived north of Richmond in Henrico County. They had no children.

After the Civil War he settled at his wife's estate, Glen Allen, where late in the 1860s he established a prosperous printing business employing as many as fifty men and women at a time. Cussons, May, and Sheppard specialized in such items as druggists' labels, postcards, and thermometer cards. Beginning in 1881 Cussons received several patents for two popular inventions, a cardboard dial calendar and a flap-pad desk calendar, which he used as a means of advertising by securing a tablet to a heavy card and pasting an ad at the top. In 1897 he incorporated Cussons, May, and Company, which continued to operate for many years after his death.

A devoted member of Virginia's Grand Camp Confederate Veterans, Cussons served as grand commander for the 1896–1897 term. He also sat on the organization's influential history committee, which criticized the history textbooks used in the state's public schools as antisouthern and successfully pressured the superintendent of public instruction to adopt works that defended the justice of the Confederate cause. In *A Glance at Current American History* (1897), republished as *United States "History" as the Yankee Makes and Takes It* (1900), Cussons accused northern writers of distorting the history of the nation. He reprinted that essay as well as several of his lectures in *A Glance at Current History* (1899), in which he expressed his outrage that Virginia students "are taught to believe that their fathers were traitors" and urged southerners to "relate the annals of our own war to our own children in our own way."

In 1897 Cussons became embroiled in a controversy in which the chair of the history committee was accused of taking bribes from a publisher to retain unacceptable textbooks. He testified against James New Stubbs before an investigating committee of the Grand Camp and subsequently engaged in a heated exchange of letters in the Richmond newspapers with Stubbs's lawyer. Both men were arrested and required to post bonds of $1,000 in January 1898 as a guarantee that they would preserve the peace.

Cussons spent many years developing his property at Glen Allen, 253 acres of which he purchased from the estate of his wife's first husband in 1874. During the next two decades he acquired a total of almost 1,000 acres of land and built a grand hotel of his own design. Known as Forest Lodge, it could boast of more than one hundred rooms, a ballroom, an auditorium, and hand-painted murals. The grounds included a deer park, artificial lakes for boating and fishing, and rose gardens patrolled by peacocks. In 1902 Cussons incorporated the Forest Lodge Association, with himself as president, to operate the establishment as a summer and winter resort. He hoped that Forest Lodge would become a regular stop along the adjacent Richmond, Fredericksburg, and Potomac Railroad line, but despite the attractive accommodations, proximity to Richmond, and his extensive promotional efforts, the resort never attracted the patronage commanded by better-known spas.

Cussons poured his energy into developing the rest of Glen Allen. He laid out roads and lots, but his dream of a village never materialized. As a member of the Tuckahoe Farmers' Club, he joined in urging the General Assembly in the 1890s to pay for new roads in the county. Cussons's later years were marked by disputes with his neighbors, many of whom resented his autocratic manner. He accused them of numerous incidents of vandalism, including the slaughter of his beloved fawns. In retaliation Cussons advertised his Glen Allen property for sale as a "New Afro-American Development," and Richmond newspapers carried headlined accounts of the quarrels. Although he offered his property for sale throughout much of the first decade of the twentieth century, he never sold Forest Lodge. John Cussons died of pneumonia at Forest Lodge on 4 January 1912 and was buried in Richmond's Hollywood Cemetery.

Birth year in England and Wales Civil Registration Index and on gravestone; undocumented birth date of 6 Apr. 1838 in Robert E. L. Krick, *Staff Officers in Gray: A Biographical Register of the Staff Officers in the Army of Northern Virginia* (2003), 107–108; biographies in Tyler, *Men of Mark*, 3:104–108, James R. Short, "The Strange Lodge of Wauzee-hos-ka: A Tale of Honor Upheld and a Dream That Died," *Virginia Cavalcade* 5 (winter 1955): 30–33 (pors.), and Henry L. Nelson, "A Dream Not Realized: The Story of Captain Cussons and 'Forest Lodge,'" *Henrico County Historical Society Magazine* 10 (fall 1986): 3–20; correspondence and other materials in United Confederate Veterans, Virginia Division, Records (1890–1903), LVA, and in Cussons, May, and Company Records, John Cussons Papers, Kate Mason

Rowland Papers, and Virginia Bryce Scrapbook (third quotation in advertising broadside, n.d.), all VHS; other publications include Cussons, *A Glance at Current History* (1899), with first quotation on 78–79 and second quotation on 81, *The Passage of Thoroughfare Gap and the . . . Assembling of Lee's Army . . . for the Second Battle of Manassas* (1906), *Jack Sterry, the Jessie Scout* (1907), and *Comments on "Irregular Warfare"* (n.d.); Compiled Service Records; *Richmond Daily Dispatch*, 24 May 1864; *Richmond Dispatch*, 11 Mar. 1893, 20 Oct., 9–11 Dec. 1897; *Richmond Times*, 19 Dec. 1897, 2 Jan. 1898, 12 May 1901; *Washington Post*, 19 Jan. 1898, 27 Apr. 1901; *Richmond News Leader*, 10 Jan. 1911; *Richmond Times-Dispatch*, 5 Dec. 1920, 3 Jan. 1932; Fred Arthur Bailey, "Free Speech and the Lost Cause in the Old Dominion," *VMHB* 103 (1995): 237–266; obituaries in *Richmond News Leader*, 5 Jan. 1912, and *New York Times* and *Richmond Times-Dispatch*, both 6 Jan. 1912; memorial in Grand Camp Confederate Veterans, Department of Virginia, *Proceedings* (1912), 8–9.

CARY HOLLADAY

CUSTALOW, George F. "Thunder Cloud"

(17 January 1865–18 March 1949), Mattaponi chief, was the son of Norman C. Custalow and Adeline Custalow (whose maiden name is unknown). He was born in King William County, probably on the reservation that had been set aside for the Mattaponi by an act of the General Assembly in March 1658. Although largely self-taught, he may have attended the Pamunkey school with other Mattaponi children for several months after it began in 1877. In the city of Richmond, on 23 May 1889, he married Emma L. "Water Lily" King, who had grown up in Hanover County. They lived on the Mattaponi reservation, where they reared six daughters and at least four sons, including Otha Thomas "Blue Wing" Custalow, also called Hos-Ki-No-Wa-Na-Ah, and Daniel Webster "Little Eagle" Custalow, who each later served as Mattaponi chief.

A farmer and fisherman by trade, Custalow was best known to Virginia sportsmen as a fishing guide. On 24 March 1914 he was elected chief of the Mattaponi, an office he held until his death. The Mattaponi had been officially recognized as a separate tribe only since 1894, and there was a mistaken belief at the time that they were a branch of the Pamunkey. Custalow played a central role in delineating the Mattaponi as a separate tribe in the Powhatan nation. He worked to forge this identity by instituting reforms, including establishing a separate Mattaponi school. Custalow met with the governor late in 1914 to discuss opening a public free school for Mattaponi children, who had been attending school on the Pamunkey reservation ten miles away. A Mattaponi school opened for the 1916–1917 school year and operated directly under state supervision, as did the Pamunkey school. A decrease in the number of Pamunkey children on the reservation caused the two schools to be consolidated into the Mattaponi Indian School in 1950.

About 1916 the tribe established a shad hatchery on the Mattaponi River to increase jobs available on the reservation. Custalow framed the Mattaponi tribal laws and asserted that violations of law on the reservation were subject to his council's authority, rather than that of King William County officials. Beginning in 1917 he engaged in an ongoing dispute with the Chesapeake Paper and Pulp Company, whose employees trespassed on the reservation grounds and stacked cordwood on the wharf to await removal along the Mattaponi River.

As the county, state, and federal tax systems were refined and codified early in the twentieth century, Virginia's Indian tribes again came under scrutiny. In June 1917 the Virginia attorney general ruled that the Mattaponi and Pamunkey who lived and worked on their reservations were legal wards of the state and thus exempt from state and local taxation. In 1919, however, the county attempted to tax Custalow for operating a store on the Mattaponi reservation. He successfully sued the county, and the circuit court reiterated the decision specifically for the Mattaponi tribe. In 1924 King William County tried once more to tax the reservation store, and Custalow once again had to appeal to the attorney general, who broadened his earlier decision by determining that neither reservation property nor reservation businesses could be taxed.

After the United States entered World War I, both Mattaponi and Pamunkey were drafted into military service. To prove their separate status, several Pamunkey brought suit against the King William County draft board. They maintained that because they were noncitizens and wards of the state—status that had been legally determined earlier that year—their draft notices were invalid. In December 1917 Virginia's attorney general rendered a decision that the Pamunkey on the reservation were indeed wards of the state and could not be drafted into the armed forces. The Mattaponi decided to test the specificity of the ruling, and in 1918 the new state attorney general, the Provost Marshal General's Office, and the United States Bureau of Indian Affairs examined the ruling's application to the Mattaponi and determined that Pamunkey and Mattaponi men living on their respective reservations were exempted from compulsory military service. Once they had proved the principle, members of the two tribes enlisted voluntarily.

Custalow also viewed religious reform as important in fostering Mattaponi autonomy. In the first half of the nineteenth century, some members of the tribe had joined a white church in King William County. In 1865 the Pamunkey and Mattaponi organized a new Baptist church on the Pamunkey reservation, but the ten miles separating the two reservations caused attendance to decline among the Mattaponi. Wanting to encourage his tribe to participate more fully in the Christian life, Custalow began leading a Sunday school on the Mattaponi reservation in 1922. Ten years later the members formally organized as the Mattaponi Indian Baptist Church. The congregation completed its church building in 1935, with the chief's son, Harvey Nathaniel Custalow, as its first pastor.

Custalow recognized the need for a distinct Mattaponi public image. Each autumn he ensured that the Mattaponi presented their tribute to Virginia's governor alongside, but separate from, the Pamunkey tribe. In 1931 Custalow used the weeklong sesquicentennial celebration of the British surrender at Yorktown as an opportunity to gain publicity. He saw to it that the Mattaponi performed war and ceremonial dances and demonstrated their work in the commemoration's Indian exhibitions. He also delivered a speech in which he explained the pivotal role of Virginia's Indians in the American Revolution.

Mattaponi tribal identity, like that for all other Native Americans in the state, was challenged in March 1924 with the passage of the Virginia Act to Preserve Racial Integrity. That statute, promoted by Walter Ashby Plecker, state registrar of vital statistics, classified all Virginians in rigid categories of white and colored and consequently subjected those defined as nonwhite to discriminatory racial segregation laws. The following year Custalow spoke out forcefully against the measure. Rather than lose their distinct designation as Indians and be categorized with African Americans, he asserted, the Mattaponi "would prefer to be banished to the wilds of the forest, there to let the wild fowls of the air and the wild animals of the field devour our bodies and leave our bones to bleach white in the sunlight of the Great Spirit." Along with George Major Cook, chief of the Pamunkey, and other Indian leaders, Custalow successfully campaigned to quash more-restrictive legislation in 1926 and 1928, but in 1930 the General Assembly adopted an amendment that specified that any ascertainable African ancestry officially classified a person as colored.

As Custalow grew older, he maintained his reform efforts. He called for electrification and rural mail delivery for the reservation and requested paved state roads to aid an incipient tourist trade. Custalow's wife died on 30 April 1936. Early in the 1940s he began sharing his duties with his son O. T. Custalow, who became assistant chief. George F. "Thunder Cloud" Custalow died on the Mattaponi reservation on 18 March 1949. His funeral, conducted at the Mattaponi Indian Baptist Church, included both Christian elements and Indian chants and prayers. The casket, draped with an Indian blanket, was escorted to the grave in the church's cemetery by the other Powhatan chiefs.

Birth date and variant death date of 19 Mar. 1949 on gravestone; variant birth date of Jan. 1867 in Census, King William Co., 1900; BVS Marriage Register, Hanover Co. (age twenty-two on 23 May 1889); *Richmond News Leader*, 13 July 1925 (quotation); *Richmond Times-Dispatch*, 4 Feb. 1928, 16, 18 Oct. 1931, 3 Jan. 1938 (por.); *Annual Report of the Attorney General to the Governor of Virginia for the Year 1917* (1918), 160–164; *Annual Report of the Attorney General . . . for 1918* (1919), 86; *Annual Report of the Attorney General . . . from October 1, 1923, to June 30, 1925* (1925), 224; Mrs. Fred Pfaus, *Our Indian Neighbors* [1949], 5, 16–18, copy of Dover Baptist Association pamphlet at LVA; Arthur L. Singleton, "Powhatan's Heirs in Modern Times: A Study of Virginia's Reservation Indians since the 1890s" (M.A. thesis, George Washington University, 1965), 16; obituaries in *Richmond News Leader* and *Richmond Times-Dispatch*, both 19 Mar. 1949; accounts of funeral in *Richmond Times-Dispatch*, 20 Mar. 1949, and *Richmond News Leader*, 23, 24 Mar. 1949.

PATRICIA FERGUSON WATKINSON

CUSTALOW, Otha Thomas "Blue Wing," also known as Hos-Ki-No-Wa-Na-Ah, Hos-Ki-No-Wana-H, or Hos-Ki-Wa-Naah (17 March 1898–18 October 1969), Mattaponi chief, was the son of George F. "Thunder Cloud" Custalow and Emma L. "Water Lily" King Custalow and was born on the reservation in King William County that had been set aside for the Mattaponi by an act of the General Assembly in March 1658. He probably attended school on the neighboring Pamunkey reservation and for much of his life was identified on census returns and in other official records as a freshwater fisherman. For about fifteen years, probably beginning in the 1920s, he toured the country as a professional wrestler, and for a time he was also a traveling salesman.

On 23 June 1918 Custalow married Marie Jane Miles, or Min-Ne-Ha-Ha, also a Mattaponi. They had seven sons and six daughters before her death on 6 January 1943. The Virginia Act to Preserve Racial Integrity, passed in 1924, classified as colored all Virginians not demonstrably 100 percent "white," thereby subjecting them to discriminatory racial segregation laws. Walter Ashby Plecker, the registrar of vital statistics, entered a memorandum on the state's copy of the marriage record to alter Custalow's identification as a Mattaponi: "Custalow-Miles—These are colored people descendants of free negroes. See Racial files for Kg Wm Co." The latter part of the memorandum referred to records and other unofficial materials Plecker had accumulated that convinced him that there were no Native Americans in Virginia who were not also descendants of African Americans. Custalow may never have learned of the alteration of his marriage record, but he certainly knew about Plecker's campaign to reclassify Virginia's Native Americans as African Americans.

Custalow became assistant chief of the Mattaponi early in the 1940s and acting chief on the death of his father in 1949. Soon thereafter he was elected chief. At his father's funeral in March 1949, after the conclusion of the Christian por-

tion of the service, Custalow offered a Mattaponi prayer that was reported to be the first such ceremony in a century and a half. Although sometimes criticized for wearing headdresses and other clothing not always clearly authentic to Powhatan traditions, and even suspected of having made up the funeral prayer, Custalow was a skillful showman and persisted during his quarter century as chief in exploiting every opportunity to publicize the Mattaponi and cultivate a public perception of Virginia's Native Americans as a distinct people with an honorable history. He and other leaders of the Mattaponi and chiefs of the Pamunkey annually presented the governor with gifts of wild fish and game in a ceremony that usually attracted press attention and offered him opportunities for gaining publicity. Achievements of Virginia tribes during the period, which were early years of heightened Native American consciousness and little intertribal cooperation, included federal recognition of the right to vote in 1948, state adoption of a more-expansive definition of Indians in 1954, and an exemption in 1957 from having to purchase county automobile license plates.

By 1954 Custalow had married Elizabeth Newton Scheneman, a widow with two sons and aunt of the performer Wayne Newton. They had one son. In 1960 he was ordained and later became pastor of the Mattaponi Indian Baptist Church, of which his brother Harvey Nathaniel Custalow had been minister. Custalow and his wives had Mattaponi names, and they gave their children a combination of English and tribal names. One son was called Sitting Bull and another Thundercloud.

Custalow founded the Mattaponi museum on the reservation. Separately and together with his daughter Gertrude Minnie Ha-Ha Custalow he presented programs to educate people about the history and culture of the Mattaponi. Custalow's serious educational objectives were occasionally undermined by his showmanship, as when he exhibited at the museum what he identified without any authenticating provenance as the very club with which Powhatan intended to pound out the brains of Captain John Smith.

Custalow's son-in-law Curtis Lee "War Horse" Custalow (husband of Gertrude Minnie

Ha-Ha Custalow) succeeded him as chief, and Custalow's younger brother Daniel Webster "Little Eagle" Custalow in turn succeeded Curtis Custalow. The two chiefs carried on the work that he had advanced and forged new alliances with other tribes in Virginia and with others elsewhere as Native American organizations became increasingly active and national in outlook.

Otha Thomas "Blue Wing" Custalow died of a heart attack in a Richmond hospital on 18 October 1969. After funeral services at the Mattaponi Indian Baptist Church, he was buried in the church cemetery. In settling his estate (which had an estimated value of $150,000), the family and the local judge, bolstered by an official opinion of the state attorney general, carefully distinguished between Custalow's property that was subject to taxation and his property that, because he was a resident of the reservation, was exempt under terms of the 1658 act of the assembly.

Birth date confirmed by BVS; variant birth date of Mar. 1897 in Census, King William Co., 1900; family information provided by daughter Gertrude Minnie Ha-Ha Custalow and widow Elizabeth Newton Custalow (both 2004); BVS Marriage Register, King William Co. (1918), with memorandum (quotation); feature articles and editorials in *Richmond Times-Dispatch*, 24 May 1940, 14 Dec. 1954, 23 Jan. 1960, 11 May 1964, 25 May 1969, *Richmond News Leader*, 24 Mar. 1949, *Norfolk Virginian-Pilot*, 5 Mar. 1962, and *West Point Tidewater Review*, 14 May 1964; Indian School Files, ser. 1, Department of Education, RG 27, LVA; *Opinions of the Attorney General* (1970), 277–278; Helen C. Rountree, *Pocahontas's People: The Powhatan Indians of Virginia through Four Centuries* (1990), esp. 239–240, 261; obituaries in *Richmond News Leader*, 18 Oct. 1969 (por.), *Newport News Daily Press* and *Richmond Times-Dispatch*, both 19 Oct. 1969, and *Washington Post* and *West Point Tidewater Review*, both 23 Oct. 1969; memorials in *Richmond Times-Dispatch*, 26 Oct. 1969, and *Virginia Baptist Annual* (1969), 136.

BRENT TARTER

CUSTIS, Daniel Parke (15 October 1711–8 July 1757), planter, was born in York County on the Queen's Creek plantation of his parents, John Custis (1678–1749), who became a member of the governor's Council in 1727, and Frances Parke Custis. His uncle William Byrd (1674–1744), also a member of the Council, and Lieutenant Governor Alexander Spotswood stood as his godfathers. A member of one of the colony's wealthiest landed families, Custis was the child of an unhappy marriage. His parents were both hot-tempered and eccentric. Sometime after the death of his mother from smallpox in March 1715 but before 1717, Custis's father moved into a brick townhouse on Francis Street in Williamsburg and indulged his interest in horticulture by planting a notable garden with many new and experimental plants. Custis grew up in the capital and may have attended the grammar school and College of William and Mary.

His father's unhappy marriage, stingy attitude toward dowries and marriage settlements, and preoccupation with social status made it difficult for Custis and his elder sister to marry. Custis courted a woman named Betty (most likely a member of the Lightfoot or Tayloe families) in 1731 and 1732 and later his cousin Anne Byrd, daughter of William Byrd (1674–1744), but his father's demands prevented him from marrying the latter, as well as perhaps other eligible young women. His father was also reluctant to turn over control of any of his plantations to Custis until 1735, when he deeded Custis 275 acres of land in New Kent County on the Pamunkey River, where he may already have been living. As he entered his mid-twenties, Custis maintained a bachelor establishment there at White House plantation with almost one hundred slaves. He came into his own as a vestryman of Saint Peter's Parish, an officer of the county militia, and a successful planter.

In 1748 Custis began courting Martha Dandridge, daughter of a local planter and county clerk. She was the niece of William Dandridge, a naval officer and member of the governor's Council who had died four years earlier, and the elder sister of Bartholomew Dandridge, who served in the Convention of 1776, on the Council of State, and on the Virginia Court of Appeals. She was then seventeen years old, twenty years Custis's junior. Custis's father objected strenuously to the Dandridge family's inability to provide a substantial dowry and to what he perceived as her inferior social status. Eventually the young woman persuaded Custis's father to relent and give permission for them to marry. Late in 1749, not long after he had signed a will in favor of his son, Custis's father died. Custis then inherited nearly 18,000 acres of prime farmland, houses in Williamsburg and Jamestown, about two hundred additional slaves, and English treasury notes and cash worth several thousand pounds. He married Martha Dandridge on 15 May 1750 at Chestnut Grove, her New Kent County residence.

At White House and in Williamsburg, Custis and his wife enjoyed the life of a wealthy and elite Virginia planter family. They had four children, all given the middle name Parke in order to preserve their eligibility to inherit as descendants of his great-grandfather, Daniel Parke, a member of the Council who had died in 1679. Custis's first son and first daughter died early in childhood. His younger son, John Parke Custis, lived to adulthood and became heir to the Custis wealth and its entangled lawsuits; his second daughter, Martha Parke Custis, died at age seventeen after an epileptic seizure.

As one of the richest men in the colony, Custis could have taken a leading role in public affairs but never chose to do so. He and his second son became ill on 4 July 1757. His son survived, but Daniel Parke Custis died at White House on 8 July 1757. The medicines prescribed for treating his illness suggest that he died of some sort of virulent throat infection, such as scarlet fever, a streptococcal infection, diphtheria, or quinsy. He was buried beside his mother and children in the family burial ground at the Queen's Creek plantation in York County. Custis died without a will. His widow inherited the property that was her dower right and managed the large estate for the benefit of their children. Martha Dandridge Custis was one of the wealthiest young widows in Virginia when on 6 January 1759 she married George Washington, who then took over as manager of the Custis property for the benefit of the children and gained additional wealth and social stature as a consequence of the marriage. Although Daniel Parke Custis was a successful planter, his principal claim to fame is as the first husband of Martha Dandridge Custis Washington and his indirect contribution to George Washington's rise to greatness.

Biographies in E. G. Swem, ed., *Brothers of the Spade: Correspondence of Peter Collinson, of London, and of John Custis, of Williamsburg, Virginia, 1734–1746* (1957), 117–121, and Lynch, *Custis Chronicles: Virginia Generations*, 102–116; birth and marriage dates in Custis family Bible records (1710–1859), VHS; Custis Family Papers, including library catalog, estate accounts, and letters, and Lee Family Papers, including Custis's Memorandum Book (1749–1757), with death date in widow's draft gravestone inscription, both VHS; Jo Zuppan, "Father to Son: Letters from John Custis IV to Daniel Parke Custis," *VMHB* 98 (1990): 81–100 (por. by John Wollaston on 91); Joseph E. Fields, ed., *"Worthy Partner": The Papers of Martha Washington* (1994), 3–9; Patricia Brady, *Martha Washington: An American Life* (2005), 27–51.

PATRICIA BRADY

CUSTIS, Edmund (d. after 18 October 1797), member of the Convention of 1788, was born probably early in the 1740s on the Northampton County estate of his parents, Edmund Custis and Katherine Sparrow Custis. Still a minor at the time of his father's death in 1748, Custis inherited four slaves and a 300-acre plantation. By the mid-1760s he had vacated his pew in the local church, sold his Northampton County property, and moved to neighboring Accomack County. Custis's activities during the next decade remain uncertain, but by 1779 he had begun to acquire land in Accomack, including property near Onancock, which became his home base. On an unrecorded date between 1 December 1779 and 29 February 1780 Custis married Elizabeth Drummond. It is not known whether they had any children. During the next decade he and his wife bought and sold a number of properties in the county, including town lots in Onancock.

Although Custis appears to have supported the patriot cause during the Revolutionary War, he often exhibited strong pro-British sentiments, as did a significant minority on the Eastern Shore. In 1781 he joined several other men in requesting that the governor reduce or remit the sentence of a local minister convicted of aiding the enemy. The next year the governor and the Council of State initiated an investigation into Custis's wartime dealings with British merchants, but prominent local politicians came to his defense and the issue was eventually dropped. Custis continued to advance in local politics, and in April 1785 he became a vestryman of Saint George's Parish. On 1 April 1787 he outpolled three other candidates to win one of two seats representing the county in the House of Delegates. He was not appointed to any standing committees. While in the General Assembly he supported legislation authorizing payment of debts to British subjects and their American partners and insisted that glebe lands remain in the hands of the new Episcopal Church.

On 25 March 1788 Custis was elected one of two Accomack County delegates to the convention called to consider the proposed constitution of the United States. Despite a dire warning from "An American" published in several newspapers in May and June that the Eastern Shore would be set adrift if Virginia did not ratify the Constitution, Custis joined other antifederalists in voting to require prior amendments to the Constitution and after that effort failed voted against ratification on 25 June. Two days later he voted to restrict the federal taxing power. His fellow delegate from Accomack, George Parker, voted exactly the opposite on the three key issues.

Reelected to the House of Delegates in 1788 and 1789, Custis served on the Committees of Claims and of Propositions and Grievances during both terms. He generally voted with the majority on key legislation. In December 1788 Custis mounted an unsuccessful attempt to gain a seat on the Council of State. He placed last among three candidates and lost his reelection bid to the House of Delegates on 27 April 1790.

Custis acquired more than one thousand acres in Accomack County and owned more than a dozen slaves during the 1780s, but in the 1790s he often found himself in court facing his creditors. By the spring of 1797 he had moved to Baltimore, probably to escape his debts. Edmund Custis last appeared as a defendant in the Accomack County courthouse on 18 October 1797 and afterward disappeared from the county records. The date and place of his death are unknown. He may have been the Edmund Custis, of the city of Baltimore, who late in 1805 petitioned the Maryland House of Delegates to declare him insolvent.

Biographical information in Ralph T. Whitelaw, *Virginia's Eastern Shore: A History of Northampton and Accomack Counties* (1951), 1:141, 2:921–922, 926–927, 936–937, 1015, 1173, 1260; some correspondence and election materials in John Cropper Papers, VHS; numerous mentions in Accomack Co. deed, district court, and order books (1779–1797);

Calendar of Virginia State Papers, 2:344–345, 509–510, 3:161; Kaminski, *Ratification*, 9:564, 10:1538, 1540, 1557; last appearance in Accomack Co. District Court Order Book (1797–1805), 21–22; *Votes and Proceedings of the House of Delegates of the State of Maryland*, 1805–1806 sess., 63.

JOHN G. KOLP

CUSTIS, Eleanor "Nelly" Parke (31 March 1779–15 July 1852), preserver of George Washington's legacy, was born at Mount Airy, her maternal grandfather's estate in Prince George's County, Maryland. She was the daughter of Eleanor Calvert Custis and John Parke Custis, a planter and member of the House of Delegates who died in November 1781. Two years later she and her younger brother, George Washington Parke Custis, were informally adopted by their grandmother Martha Dandridge Custis Washington and stepgrandfather George Washington when the latter returned to Mount Vernon, in Fairfax County, at the close of the American Revolution. Her two elder sisters, Elizabeth Parke Custis (later Law) and Martha Parke Custis (later Peter), remained with their mother and stepfather, David Stuart, a physician and member of the Convention of 1788.

Nelly Custis was educated at Mount Vernon by tutors, including Washington's personal secretary Tobias Lear, as well as by music and dancing masters. After Washington's inauguration as president of the United States, Martha Washington and the Custis children joined him in May 1789 in New York City, the nation's temporary capital. Custis attended private schools and studied music with the composer and performer Alexander Reinagle and art with William Dunlap. When the capital moved to Philadelphia in 1790, she continued her studies there.

As she grew to be a beautiful young woman and a talented musician, dancer, and artist, Custis helped entertain guests at the presidential mansion and accompanied her adoptive parents to social events. After Washington retired in March 1797, she continued in that role at Mount Vernon. A flood of uninvited visitors came to see the retired hero at his estate, and Custis was invaluable in helping her grandmother entertain guests while allowing George Washington time for his own projects. She was introduced to society at balls in Alexandria and Georgetown. Late in 1797 Washington's nephew Lawrence Lewis, a widower, joined the family at Mount Vernon as a deputy host and occasional secretary. He and Custis married on Washington's birthday, 22 February, in 1799.

The couple remained at Mount Vernon, where their first three children were born. Of their four sons and four daughters, only one son and two daughters lived to adulthood. George Washington died on 14 December 1799 and bequeathed the Lewises about 2,000 acres of the Mount Vernon plantation, as well as a gristmill and whiskey distillery. They continued to live with Martha Washington while beginning to build a house on their property, but after her death on 22 May 1802, the Lewis family was obliged to move because the Mount Vernon mansion and home farm had been left to Washington's nephew, Bushrod Washington.

The central block of their house was not yet inhabitable, so in 1802 the Lewises moved into one of the small dependencies. Completed in 1805, their new home was named Woodlawn, probably for the estate in one of Martha Washington's and Nelly Custis's favorite novels, *The Children of the Abbey*. Designed by William Thornton, architect of the United States Capitol and a friend of George Washington, Woodlawn was an elegant red-brick Georgian manor house flanked by one-and-a-half-story dependencies connected by hyphens. There Lewis managed her extensive household and lavishly entertained numerous guests.

As agricultural land in eastern Virginia became less productive and Alexandria declined as a port, profitable farming at Woodlawn became impossible for the Lewises. Their surviving son moved to Audley plantation, in Clarke County, which became the family's major source of income. Their two daughters married men who settled in Louisiana, and beginning in the mid-1830s the couple divided their time between Louisiana and Virginia. Lawrence Lewis died on 20 November 1839, following a daughter's death two months earlier. Nelly Custis Lewis went to live permanently at Audley. A noted needle-woman and artist, she completed numerous needlepoint and embroidered keepsakes for her relatives and friends.

Throughout her life, Lewis regarded herself as the keeper of George Washington's legacy. She shared memories and mementos, entertained and corresponded with those seeking information, and verified or debunked new accounts. Her husband had been one of Washington's executors and was instrumental in having a grand tomb erected at Mount Vernon, completed in 1835. At the time of Lewis's death, she had little fortune to leave but her remaining Mount Vernon artifacts, which she distributed among her grandchildren. Woodlawn was sold in 1846, and after numerous vicissitudes, in 1951 the house and a portion of the grounds became the first property of the National Trust for Historic Preservation.

Nelly Custis was the delight of George and Martha Washington's lives and the most accurate purveyor of information about them. During her long life, stretching from the American Revolution until the crucial decade leading up to the Civil War, she was a living point of connection with the most important of the founding fathers. Eleanor Parke Custis Lewis suffered partial paralysis during the last two years of her life. She died at Audley on 15 July 1852 and was buried at Mount Vernon in an enclosure adjoining George Washington's tomb. In 1915 Lunt Silversmiths designed a Nellie Custis silver pattern, and her name also appears in various guises on the landscape of Northern Virginia, including Nelly Custis Park, in Arlington County, and the Nelly Custis Chapter of the National Society Daughters of the American Revolution, in Fort Belvoir, Fairfax County.

Biographies in David L. Ribblett, *Nelly Custis: Child of Mount Vernon* (1993), and Lynch, *Custis Chronicles: Virginia Generations*, 204–222; birth date in Custis family Bible records (1710–1859), VHS; some correspondence in Custis-Lee-Mason Family Papers, LVA; primary collection of correspondence in Eleanor Parke Custis Lewis Papers, Mount Vernon Library and Archives, published in Patricia Brady, ed., *George Washington's Beautiful Nelly: The Letters of Eleanor Parke Custis Lewis to Elizabeth Bordley Gibson, 1794–1851* (1991), with several pors.; Patricia Brady Schmit, ed., *Nelly Custis Lewis's Housekeeping Book* (1982); numerous mentions in *Washington: Confederation Series, Presidential Series*, and *Retirement Series*, and in *Washington Diaries*, vols. 4–6, esp. 6:335 (marriage date); Clarke Co. Will Book, C:63–64; obituary in *Alexandria Gazette*, 22 July 1852.

PATRICIA BRADY

CUSTIS, Elizabeth Parke (21 August 1776–31 December 1831), social leader, was born at Mount Airy, the home of her maternal grandparents, in Prince George's County, Maryland, and was the daughter of Eleanor Calvert Custis and John Parke Custis, a planter and after 1778 a member of the House of Delegates. An intelligent, lively child, she suffered a series of losses and disappointments early in life, beginning with the death of her father in November 1781. Her younger sister, Eleanor "Nelly" Parke Custis, and her brother, George Washington Parke Custis, went to live at Mount Vernon, in Fairfax County, with their paternal grandmother, Martha Dandridge Custis Washington, and her second husband, George Washington, while Custis and another sister remained with their mother. In November 1783 her mother married David Stuart, an Alexandria physician and later a member of the Convention of 1788. Her mother's frequent pregnancies deprived Eliza Custis of the attention she craved. George Washington's election to the presidency and the Stuarts' subsequent move to Hope Park, a country estate in Fairfax County, further isolated her from the grandparents she loved and the stimulation of Georgetown and Alexandria society. Custis later complained that because she was a girl her education had been limited to less rigorous topics than she would have preferred. She was fond of music and horses, and a relative later commented that "in her tastes and pastimes she is more man than woman and regrets that she can't wear pants."

Later in Washington's presidency Custis visited her paternal grandparents (who called her Betsy) in Philadelphia for long stays. Her eccentricities worried her grandmother, and her stepgrandfather sent her a long letter on the subject of marriage shortly after her eighteenth birthday. It is among the most personally revealing letters that the usually reticent Washington ever composed and suggests that he, too, was concerned. It was probably during a visit with the Washingtons in 1795 that Custis met Thomas Law, an Englishman twenty years her senior. His family was prominent in church, legal, and political circles, and he had made a fortune with the East India Company before immigrating to the United States in 1794 with at least one of his three half-Indian sons and becoming a developer in the new national capital. Custis and Law married at Hope Park on 21 March 1796. They had one daughter.

The Laws, among the earliest residents of Washington, D.C., enjoyed a lavish lifestyle. They took an active part in society in Washington and Georgetown, entertained many dignitaries, and numbered members of both emerging political parties among their friends. Following his extended business trip to England, however, the couple separated in the summer of 1804. Rumors about the breakup were widespread, but his correspondence from the period cast no blame on her, and family members believed that the couple's thorny personalities were equally at fault. A legal settlement at the time of the separation allowed her $1,500 per year, but her husband received legal custody of their daughter.

Law spent the first year after the separation at Riversdale, the Maryland home of an uncle, and subsequently purchased a small country property outside Alexandria, which she called Mount Washington. She lived there until 1809, when, disenchanted with isolated life in the country, she sold the property (later the site of the Protestant Episcopal Theological Seminary in Virginia). In unfinished memoirs written in an 1808 letter to a friend, she revealed a bitter, self-absorbed personality, with a penchant for melodrama and ancestor-worship. After her husband obtained a divorce in Vermont on 15 January 1811, she began calling herself Mrs. Custis. She had a series of unsuccessful romances, and at least one engagement, with French diplomats and military officers. Despite her divorce, Custis continued to move in powerful social circles and remained friends with Dolley Payne Todd Madison.

In her final years, Custis lived a peripatetic existence, traveling between friends and relatives. Her daughter died in 1821, and estrangement from her son-in-law limited contact with her three grandchildren. Like her younger brother and sisters, Custis saw herself as one of the stewards of the Washington legacy. She had family memorabilia in her care and often made gifts of items that had belonged to her grandmother and stepgrandfather. Custis took care to identify, for the benefit of her grandchildren, the objects that she still retained. Elizabeth Parke Custis died in the home of a Richmond friend on 31 December 1831 and was buried six days later in the family vault at Mount Vernon.

Biography in Lynch, *Custis Chronicles: Virginia Generations*, 158–188 (with variant, undocumented marriage date of 20 Mar. 1796 on 165 and texts of divorce documents on 174, 175); birth date in Custis family Bible records (1710–1859), VHS (given name spelled Elisabeth); autobiographical fragment in William D. Hoyt Jr., ed., "Self-Portrait: Eliza Custis, 1808," *VMHB* 53 (1945): 89–100; some possessions and papers at Mount Vernon Library and Archives; correspondence in Thomas Law Family Papers and in David Bailie Warden Papers (including original letter of 20 Apr. 1808 containing her autobiographical fragment), both Maryland Historical Society, Baltimore; George Washington to Custis, 14 Sept. 1794, Pierpont Morgan Library, New York; numerous references in Joseph E. Fields, ed., *"Worthy Partner": The Papers of Martha Washington* (1994), Patricia Brady, ed., *George Washington's Beautiful Nelly: The Letters of Eleanor Parke Custis Lewis to Elizabeth Bordley Gibson, 1794–1851* (1991), with marriage date on 26, and Margaret Law Callcott, ed., *Mistress of Riversdale: The Plantation Letters of Rosalie Stier Calvert, 1795–1821* (1991), with quotation in Calvert to Isabelle van Havre, 18 Feb. 1805, on 111; Robert G. Stewart, *Robert Edge Pine: A British Portrait Painter in America, 1784–1788* (1979), 51 (por.); Mount Vernon Ladies' Association of the Union *Annual Report* (1992), 26 (por.); brief obituaries in *Richmond Enquirer*, 3 Jan. 1832 (noting death "on Saturday night, ten minutes before 12 o'clock"), *Washington Daily National Intelligencer*, 7 Jan. 1832, and *Alexandria Phenix Gazette*, 9 Jan. 1832.

MARY V. THOMPSON

CUSTIS, George Washington Parke (30 April 1781–10 October 1857), writer and orator, was born at Mount Airy, his maternal grandfather's estate in Prince George's County, Maryland. His elder sisters included Elizabeth Parke Custis Law and Eleanor "Nelly" Parke Custis Lewis, both of whom shared his devotion to preserving the legacy of George Washington. Their father, John Parke Custis, a planter and member of the House of Delegates, died on 5 November 1781, and on 20 November 1783 their mother, Eleanor Calvert Custis, married David Stuart, a physician and later a member of the Convention of 1788, and began a second family. Custis and his sister Nelly Custis grew up in the household of their paternal grandmother, Martha Dandridge Custis Washington, and her second husband, George Washington, but Stuart, as Custis's stepfather, remained his official guardian.

Custis was expelled from the College of New Jersey (later Princeton University) in September 1797 for repeated misbehavior and left Saint John's College, in Annapolis, in July 1798 without completing his studies. Commissioned on 10 January 1799 a cornet in the army called up to meet the threat of war with France and promoted to second lieutenant on 3 March of that year, he served with a troop of Alexandria light dragoons and was discharged on 15 June 1800 with the brevet rank of major. In April 1802 Custis stood for election to the House of Delegates from Fairfax County as an old-line Federalist, opposing any further erosion of property qualifications for voting. He outpolled his stepfather but placed third among four candidates vying for the two seats.

Less than a month after the election Martha Washington died. After an unsuccessful attempt to purchase Mount Vernon from George Washington's nephew and heir, Custis moved to an 1,100-acre Alexandria County estate inherited from his father that he first called Mount Washington but soon renamed Arlington, for an ancestral property on the Eastern Shore. The estate lay in the area that Virginia had ceded to the federal government to become part of the District of Columbia and that Congress retroceded after a referendum in 1846. Custis owned two other large plantations totaling approximately 9,000 acres of land, Romancock in King William County and White House in New Kent County, which provided the foodstuffs and revenues to support him on his park estate at Arlington. He also inherited property in Northampton County, including Smith Island, and through marriage acquired land in Richmond, Stafford, and Westmoreland Counties. Custis believed slavery was an economic detriment to southern agriculture and blamed the institution for his financial problems. He supported the efforts of the American Society for Colonizing the Free People of Color of the United States (popularly known as the American Colonization Society), but his opposition to the institution in theory did not lead him to manumit more than a handful of his slaves, nor did it prevent him from putting slaves on the auction block as punishment or when he became strapped for money.

On 7 July 1804 in the city of Alexandria, Custis married Mary Lee Fitzhugh, daughter of William Fitzhugh (1741–1809), a member of the Convention of 1776 and of the Continental Congress, and sister of William Henry Fitzhugh, a member of the Convention of 1829–1830. A prominent Episcopal lay leader and supporter of manumission and colonization, she died on 23 April 1853. Of their four daughters, only Mary Anna Randolph Custis, who married Robert Edward Lee, survived infancy. With a Custis family slave, Airy Carter, Custis had a daughter, Maria Carter, whom he educated and informally freed and to whom he gave about seventeen acres of the Arlington estate. She married and became the matriarch of a distinguished family that included her sons John B. Syphax, a member of the House of Delegates, and William Syphax, a prominent educator in Washington, D.C.

Deeply concerned about American dependency on foreign manufactures, Custis promoted commercial independence through agricultural reform and the improvement of domestic varieties of livestock. He described his vision in *An Address to the People of the United States, on the Importance of Encouraging Agriculture and Domestic Manufactures* (1808). Custis developed two breeds of sheep, the long-wooled Arlington Improved and the fine-wooled Smith's Island, also noted for the flavor of its mutton. Annual sheep shearings he held at Arlington from 1805 through 1812 evolved into full-scale agricultural fairs offering premiums for the best blankets, stockings, and yarn and to the family relying the least on imported material. Held on 30 April, the date Washington had taken the oath of office as first president and therefore regularly celebrated by Federalists, the event became highly partisan. Custis closed each fair with an oration advocating the Federalist program, decrying the dangers of universal manhood suffrage, or warning of the threat to American liberty posed by Napoléon I.

During the War of 1812 Custis, an animated, gifted orator, became a speaker much in demand. On 1 September 1812 he delivered the funeral oration for James M. Lingan, a Revolutionary War veteran murdered by a Jeffersonian mob in Baltimore after helping to reopen and defend a Federalist newspaper office. Custis's stirring address, a tribute to the freedom of the press, was printed in Federalist pamphlets under various titles and circulated throughout the country. The following 5 June he addressed a Georgetown audience celebrating the failure of Napoléon's campaign in Russia. Custis helped man a battery at the Battle of Bladensburg on 24 August 1814 and after the rout of the American army stopped at the White House to make sure that Dolley Payne Todd Madison moved Gilbert Stuart's portrait of Washington to safety.

During the marquis de Lafayette's triumphal tour of the United States in 1825, Custis began recording Lafayette's reminiscences of Washington, the Revolutionary War, and his own life and published them in sixteen parts in Alexandria's *Phenix Gazette* as "Conversations of La Fayette." The enthusiastic public response led Custis to begin setting down his own recollections of growing up at Mount Vernon. For the next three decades he wrote occasional essays on various aspects of Washington's life and the Revolution. These recollections often ran in the Alexandria or Washington newspapers on such anniversaries as Washington's Birthday or the Fourth of July or at times of national crisis, such as the sectional clash preceding the Compromise of 1850, in order to rekindle the fires of reconciliation and patriotism by reminding Americans of the achievements and sacrifices of Washington. Important for the details they contain about Washington in private life, Custis's recollections are also significant because in many cases they were the first appearance in print of certain stories. An 1826 essay on Mary Ball Washington, for example, was the first detailed piece ever printed about Washington's mother, and it remained the chief source for all nineteenth-century historians examining Washington's childhood. In "His Portrait," another 1826 essay, Custis wrote that Washington had once thrown a piece of slate the size and shape of a dollar coin across the Rappahannock River. Custis never consummated plans to publish his essays in a single volume, but his daughter and the editor and illustrator Benson John Lossing collected many of the newspaper articles and family letters after his death and published them as

Recollections and Private Memoirs of Washington in several editions in 1859, 1860, and 1861.

At about the same time he embarked on the recollections, Custis began writing historical plays. Texts of only three of his ten plays survive. The lyrics of four songs from another appeared in contemporary newspapers. The plots of the others must be reconstructed from advertisements, playbills, reviews, and enigmatic comments in correspondence. All but one of his ten plays revolve around episodes in America's past and fit securely in the National Drama genre. *Indian Prophecy; or Visions of Glory*, premiered in Philadelphia on 4 July 1827 and was published with a variant subtitle the next year. A prosy, static drama with little action, the story of a meeting in 1770 between George Washington and an Indian chief who recounts an incident from the Seven Years' War and predicts military glory for Washington during the American Revolution nevertheless attracted such nationally prominent actors as Edwin Forrest and Joseph Jefferson Jr. and was revived at theaters across the country for the next dozen years. *The Rail Road* (1828), an operetta set in Baltimore and billed in the District of Columbia in 1829 as *The Rail Road and Canal*, had received at least 100 performances by December 1833. The operetta *The Eighth of January, or, Hurra for the Boys of the West!* celebrated Andrew Jackson's victory at the Battle of New Orleans and premiered in New York City sometime before 1830. Custis wrote *The Pawnee Chief; or, Hero of the Prairie* about 1830, but it was not performed until 1832.

Pocahontas; or, The Settlers of Virginia (1830), dedicated to John Marshall, was Custis's most popular and durable work. Modern drama anthologies occasionally reprint it as the best surviving example of the historical genre. *North Point, or, Baltimore Defended* (1833) included a spectacular reenactment of the British bombardment of Fort McHenry during the War of 1812 and featured as a major character an African American veteran of the Revolutionary War. Custis planned a three-act *Tecumseh, or The Last of the Braves* (1833) for production in New York with Edwin Forrest in the title role but may never have completed it. *The Launch of the Columbia, or, America's Blue Jackets Forever* (1836) was a musical farce celebrating a frigate's launch in Washington. Custis wrote *Montgomerie, or, The Orphan of a Wreck* in 1830, but this unsuccessful melodramatic pastiche of *Hamlet* and Sir Walter Scott received its only recorded performances in 1836. In the latter year he completed *Monongahela, or, Washington on the First Great Field of His Fame*, which he sent to Edward Everett in 1839 in a failed effort to have the work mounted in Boston.

Custis used both his plays and his recollections of Washington to arouse patriotic feelings. As sectional tensions intensified, he sought to remind northerners and southerners of their common heritage by calling to mind the days of the Revolution when the separate colonies had come together and thrown off the British yoke. Only by recovering the legacy of Washington and the Revolution could the declension be halted. As part of his memorializing and preservation efforts, Custis placed a marker at Washington's birthplace in 1815 and enthusiastically supported an abortive congressional resolution in 1832 to disinter the president and his wife from Mount Vernon and to rebury them under the dome of the United States Capitol. He made his own Washington Treasury, as he called his collection of Washington items, available for public viewing and distributed Washington relics in order to inspire public figures to follow in Washington's footsteps. Henry Clay, for example, received a fragment of Washington's coffin, which he brandished on the floor of the United States Senate when he introduced his compromise resolutions in 1850. By his own reckoning, Custis averaged one letter a week from people seeking information on Washington or asking for Washington autographs. He usually obliged autograph-seekers, and after he had given the last available signature to Queen Victoria, he began cutting up the account books in which Washington had recorded his management of the Custis estate. By distributing relics of Washington, Custis hoped to preserve the legacy of the Revolution and save the increasingly fragile Union.

Custis also contributed to the visual record of Washington. A number of artists went to Arlington to copy or engrave the Custis and Washington family portraits. Other painters, including Emmanuel Leutze, corresponded with Custis about which life portrait best represented the first president. In his last years, Custis devoted increasing attention to painting charmingly naive scenes from the American Revolution as described to him by Washington. He occasionally exhibited his monumental canvases at the United States Capitol, and several were reproduced in *Harper's New Monthly Magazine* in 1853. The days of the Revolution became his life. In 1848 he wrote, "The old Orator you know boasts of having *two Religions*, (most people have but one & many none) while I have the Religion of Christianity & the Religion of the Revolution."

For four decades Custis regularly gave speeches, often supporting the national independence movements of Greece, Poland, and South America. The cause of Irish independence he held particularly dear. A favored orator and sometime president of the Friends of Civil and Religious Liberty, Custis counted Saint Patrick's Day with Washington's Birthday and the Fourth of July as the three "holydays" he celebrated. George Washington Parke Custis, who enjoyed playing the role of the Child of Mount Vernon and the Last Survivor of the Family of Washington, died of influenza at Arlington on 10 October 1857 and was buried there. His will ordered the emancipation of his 196 slaves within five years of his death.

Biography by daughter in Custis, *Recollections and Private Memoirs of Washington, by His Adopted Son* (New York, 1860), 9–72 (frontispiece por.); birth and marriage dates in Custis family Bible records (1710–1859), VHS; Custis correspondence in Boston Public Library, Harvard University, Historical Society of Pennsylvania, Huntington, LC, Maryland Historical Society (including first quotation in Custis to John Spear Smith, 24 Oct. 1848, MS 1814), Mount Vernon Library and Archives, New York Public Library, VHS, and W&M; orations and writings include *Letter from George W. P. Custis, Addressed to the Speaker, Enclosing Sundry Resolutions Agreed to by the Inhabitants of Alexandria County Relative to the Recession of the Jurisdiction of That Part of the Territory of Columbia Which Was Ceded to the United States by the State of Virginia . . .* (1804), *An Address Occasioned by the Death of General Lingan, Who Was Murdered by the Mob at Baltimore . . .* (1812), *Oration by Mr. Custis, of Arlington; with an Account of the Funeral Solemnities in Honor of the Lamented Gen. James M. Lingan* (1812), *The Celebration of the Russian Victories, in Georgetown, District of Columbia; on the 5th of June, 1813* (1813), *Oration by Mr. Custis, of Arlington, Delivered before the Washington Society of Alexandria, on the Anniversary of the 22d February, 1820* (1820), and *Oration Delivered by the Hon. Henry S. Foote, on the Fourth of July, 1850, . . . and the Address of G. W. P. Custis, Esq.* (1850); Arlington Co. (formerly Alexandria Co.) Marriage Bonds (dated 6 July 1804); *Alexandria Advertiser and Commercial Intelligencer*, 29 Apr., 3 May 1802; *Washington Daily National Intelligencer*, 10 Apr. 1839 (second quotation); Benson J. Lossing, "Arlington House, the Seat of G. W. P. Custis, Esq.," *Harper's New Monthly Magazine* 7 (1853): 433–454; Murray H. Nelligan, "American Nationalism on the Stage: The Plays of George Washington Parke Custis (1781–1857)," *VMHB* 58 (1950): 299–324; Nelligan, "Old Arlington: The Story of the Lee Mansion National Memorial" (Ph.D. diss., Columbia University, 1954); David G. Lowe, "A Son's Tribute," *American Heritage* 17 (Feb. 1966): 16–21, 85–87; Sara B. Bearss, "The Federalist Career of George Washington Parke Custis," *Northern Virginia Heritage* 8 (Feb. 1986): 15–20; Bearss, "The Farmer of Arlington: George W. P. Custis and the Arlington Sheep Shearings," *Virginia Cavalcade* 38 (1989): 124–133 (pors.); will, inventories, and estate accounts in Alexandria City Will Book, 7:267–269 (will), 278–279, 369–371 (White House, Romancock, and Arlington inventories), 485–493, 8:92–97; obituaries, memorial tributes, and funeral accounts in *Alexandria Gazette*, 12–15 Oct. 1857, *Washington Daily National Intelligencer*, 12–14 Oct. 1857, *Washington Evening Star*, 14 Oct. 1857 (with incorrect birth date of 13 Apr. 1781), and *New-York Times*, 15 Oct. 1857.

SARA B. BEARSS

CUSTIS, John (ca. 1629–29 January 1696), member of the Council and founder of the Custis family in Virginia, may have been born in Rotterdam, in the Netherlands. He was the son of Johanna Wittingham Custis and Henry Custis, a native of Gloucestershire, England, who operated a Rotterdam victualling house, or tavern, that served as the hub of the city's English expatriate community. Custis's father was a member of an extended family engaged in international commerce, and it is possible that as a young man Custis worked in one of the family's commercial houses. About 1649 or 1650 he moved to the Eastern Shore of Virginia, where his sister Ann Custis Yeardley lived with her husband Argall Yeardley, son of Governor Sir George Yeardley and a prominent planter and member of the governor's Council. Several other members of the Custis family also lived on the Eastern Shore of Virginia and Maryland, including another John Custis, probably an uncle or cousin, who has sometimes been misidentified as the father of the immigrant founder of the Custis family of Virginia.

With his family's trading connections and his brother-in-law's help, Custis grew wealthy through trade, land speculation, and tobacco planting. He had accumulated more than a thousand acres of land by 1664 and an additional ten thousand acres during the next quarter century. The Custis workforce of servants and slaves grew into one of the largest on the Eastern Shore. His commercial activities centered on New Amsterdam, a logical trading destination for a man with his background. He assembled cargoes of tobacco for shipment to the Dutch colony and acted as the Virginia agent for merchants from New Netherland and Rotterdam, as well as New England. Custis's facility in the Dutch language enhanced his value as an intermediary in international commerce. When Peter Stuyvesant, the governor of New Netherland, corresponded with the governor and Council of Virginia on an important admiralty matter in 1663, Virginia officials relied on Custis to translate the documents.

Sometime before 15 January 1652 Custis married a widow, Elizabeth Robinson Eyer (or Eyre). Before she died two or three years later they had one son, John Custis (ca. 1654–1714), who also served on the governor's Council. About 1656 Custis married the thrice-widowed Alicia Travellor Burdett Walker (whose maiden name is unknown), and about 1679 he married the twice-widowed Tabitha Scarburgh Smart Browne, a daughter of Edmund Scarburgh (d. 1671), one of the Eastern Shore's leading planters and a former Speaker of the House of Burgesses. Custis and his second and third wives had no children who grew to adulthood. Early in the 1670s he built a three-story brick mansion on the south bank of Old Plantation Creek, in southwestern Northampton County. He named the house Arlington, probably after the Custis family's ancestral village in Gloucestershire. With a foundation measuring 54 feet by 43 ½ feet, the imposing double-pile structure was perhaps the finest mansion erected in the seventeenth-century Chesapeake, rivaled only by Governor Sir William Berkeley's Green Spring, near Jamestown. Early in the nineteenth century, the name of the mansion inspired Custis's descendant George Washington Parke Custis, who gave the same name to his estate outside Washington, D.C.

Custis's lordly surroundings and imperious manner, which involved him in several disputes with his neighbors, earned him the sobriquet King Custis. As his wealth grew, so did his political power. During the 1650s, before he became a legal denizen of the colony, he held such offices as surveyor and appraiser of estates. Although nominated for sheriff in 1655, Custis did not receive the appointment because of his foreign birth. The assembly removed that obstacle to political advancement in 1658 by passing a law naturalizing him and his brother William Custis. In 1659 Custis became county sheriff, and the following year the governor appointed him to the Northampton County Court. Except for another term as sheriff in 1665 and 1666, he remained a justice of the peace until 1677.

Custis became a captain in the county militia in 1664, was commissioned a colonel in 1673, and ended his career in 1692 as commander in chief of all forces on the Eastern Shore. During Bacon's Rebellion in 1676, he was a major general in Governor Sir William Berkeley's army. After the governor fled Jamestown and took refuge on the Eastern Shore, he made his temporary headquarters at Arlington. Custis's loyalty to the government won plaudits from two of the commissioners the king sent to investigate the rebellion. Sir John Berry praised Custis's courage and generous offer to lend the Crown £1,000 sterling to provision the king's ships, and Francis Moryson once addressed him as "Honest Jack."

Custis probably won election to the House of Burgesses in the spring of 1676 when the rebellion broke out, but the sparse surviving records of the assembly session that met in June of that year do not include his name. He was present at the next session, which met at Green Spring in February 1677, after the conclusion of the rebellion. On an unrecorded date before 5 July of that year the lieutenant governor appointed Custis to the Council. As a councillor he often sat as an additional member of the Accomack and Northampton County Courts. Rumors that Custis was dead or dying resulted in the Privy Council omitting his name from the list of Council members when Francis Howard, baron Howard of Effingham, was appointed governor in October 1683. Custis petitioned the Crown for reinstatement in 1685 and continued to serve until "Extreame violent Sicknesses," "Extreame fitts," and "the faileing of his Memory and hearing" forced him to retire on 15 April 1692.

Custis achieved dynastic as well as financial and political success. He established a family that remained prominent in Virginia for two centuries. When he prepared his will in 1691, he provided handsomely for his grandson John Custis (1678–1749), who later became the third man of that name to serve on the governor's Council. John Custis died, almost certainly at Arlington in Northampton County, on 29 January 1696 and was buried near his mansion.

Biography in Lynch, *Custis Chronicles: Migration*, 157–181, including mother's will from Dutch records on 218–222; depositions recording age as about thirty on 29 Jan. 1659 (Northampton Co. Order Book [1657–1664], fol. 43) and forty-three on 30 Dec. 1671 (Northampton Co. Order Book, 9: fol. 120); date of death at age sixty-six on eighteenth-century gravestone; Nicholas M. Luccketti, Edward A. Chappell, and Beverly A. Straube, *Archaeology at Arlington: Excavations at the Ancestral Custis Plantation, Northampton County, Virginia* (1999); act of denization in *JHB, 1619–1658/59*, 112, and Hening, *Statutes*, 1:499; earliest service on Council in log of HMS *Bristol*, PRO Adm 51/134 (entries for 5, 6 July 1677), and Northampton Co. Order Book, Wills, Etc., 10:173; numerous references in *Minutes of Council and General Court*, *Executive Journals of Council*, vol. 1, and Billings, *Effingham Papers*; Sir John Berry and Francis Moryson to John Custis, n.d. [ca. spring 1677], PRO CO 5/1371, fols. 29–30 (first quotation on 30), and their commendation of Custis on 181; petition and re-appointment to Council in PRO CO 1/57, fols. 265–266, PRO CO 5/1356, 322–324, and PRO CO 391/5, 140–141; Custis to Sir Francis Nicholson, 15 Apr. 1692, PRO CO 5/1306, fol. 413 (all other quotations); will in Northampton Co. Orders and Wills, 13:355–360.

JOHN RUSTON PAGAN

CUSTIS, John (ca. 1654–26 January 1714), member of the Council, was the son of John Custis (ca. 1629–1696) and the first of his three wives, Elizabeth Robinson Eyer (or Eyre) Custis. He was born in Northampton County, and although information about his early years is limited, he apparently received a good education and developed the sense of noblesse oblige expected of the son of a socially prominent family. By mid-1678 Custis had married Margaret Michael. They had two daughters and seven sons. The eldest son, also named John Custis

(1678–1749), later served on the governor's Council. Custis's wife died after the birth of their second daughter, whom he named Sorrowful Margaret Custis. By 1691 he had married Sarah Littleton Michael, the widow of his first wife's eldest brother. They had no children.

Sometimes referred to as John Custis, of Wilsonia (his Northampton County plantation), he was one of the principal planters and wealthiest men on the Eastern Shore, where he owned thousands of acres of land and a large number of enslaved laborers. His public career began on 29 July 1675 when his father, then the coroner of Northampton County, made him deputy coroner. Custis replaced his father as a justice of the peace in the summer of 1677 when his father was elevated to the governor's Council. He served as sheriff of the county in 1682, 1684, and 1688. In the summer of 1691 Custis became a member of the new Hungars Parish vestry and insisted on ordering the first and finest pew when the new church was erected. He also advanced from captain to colonel in the county militia. Evidence suggests that he often appeared in court in the role of an attorney, employing his considerable ability and self-confidence in the interest of his clients.

In 1684 Custis was elected to represent Northampton County in the House of Burgesses, but he was disqualified after being chosen sheriff of the county. In the election held to fill the open seat in the House, voters again selected Custis. Records for the 1685 sessions are not extant, but he was returned again in 1686. During the assembly session that met in the autumn of that year he emerged as a respected member of the House and was appointed ranking member of the Committee of Propositions and Grievances. After several years out of the assembly, Custis was returned in the spring of 1693, resumed his influential seat on the Committee for Propositions and Grievances, and joined the Committee for Elections and Privileges. After less than a month, illness forced him to return home, and during the brief session of the assembly held that autumn he chaired the Committee for Elections and Privileges before leaving early because of illness in his family. Elected again in 1695, Custis missed the assembly session that met in the spring of the following year but in the autumn of 1696 once again became chair of the Committee for Elections and Privileges and retained his high-ranking seat on Propositions and Grievances. He missed the session of October 1697 and most of the brief session in October of the following year, but during the long session that began in April 1699 he was once again one of the most active members and kept his two prized committee seats. He also chaired the committee of burgesses that reported to the governor and Council on the choice of Middle Plantation for the new capital of the colony.

On the recommendation of Governor Francis Nicholson, the king appointed Custis to the governor's Council on 26 December 1699. Custis took his seat on 9 July 1700 and attended the Council for the last recorded time on 30 April 1713. His tenure spanned two politically contentious periods, the final years of Nicholson's second administration and the first years of the administration of Lieutenant Governor Alexander Spotswood, as well as the initial construction of the capitol and governor's mansion at Middle Plantation, which became Williamsburg.

Custis wrote his will in December 1708. He provided for his wife and children as well as friends and relatives and in the process itemized many valuable items of silver, almost 7,000 acres of land, and more than thirty slaves and half a dozen Indians whose legal status is not clear. On 12 May 1705 the Council had distributed several Nanzatico children to responsible planters in order to protect them from presumed dangers from other Indians, with an order that they be held as servants until the age of twenty-four and then freed. Unless Custis changed the name of the one infant girl assigned to him, he did not mention her in his will. Declining health and gout forced Custis to remain at home and miss some meetings of the Council. In a letter to his namesake son in June 1713 he mentioned crippled hands, which might have been the consequence of gout or arthritis. John Custis died in Northampton County on 26 January 1714 and was buried on his plantation at Wilsonia Neck.

Biography in Lynch, *Custis Chronicles: Migration*, 183–197; depositions recording age as about twenty-seven on 29 Dec.

1681 (Northampton Co. Order Book, 11:206), about twenty-eight on 11 Feb. 1683 (ibid., 11:273), about forty on 28 Nov. 1694 (ibid., 11:306), and about forty-seven on 28 Nov. 1701 (Northampton Co. Orders, Wills, Etc., 14:84); father's will in Northampton Co. Orders and Wills, 13:355–360; appointment to Council in PRO CO 324/27, 102; one letter, New-York Historical Society; numerous references in *Executive Journals of Council*, vols. 2 and 3, and *Legislative Journals of Council*, 295–542; will in Northampton Co. Wills, Deeds, Etc. (1711–1718), 58–64; widow's will and estate inventory in Northampton Co. Wills, Etc., 15:81–84, 85–87, 127; date of death (in sixtieth year) on gravestone, transcribed in "Wilsonia Farm Graveyard" (undated typescript), 2, in Works Progress Administration, Virginia Historical Inventory, LVA.

KATHARINE E. HARBURY

CUSTIS, John (August 1678–after 14 November 1749), member of the Council, was born in Northampton County, at the Hungars Creek plantation of his parents, John Custis (ca. 1654–1714), later a member of the governor's Council, and his first wife, Margaret Michael Custis. A bequest of £100 from his grandfather John Custis (ca. 1629–1696), also a member of the governor's Council, helped support his education in England, where for almost seven years he studied the intricacies of the tobacco trade with the London consignment merchant Micajah Perry. Indirect evidence in a commonplace book Custis compiled suggests that he also had some formal schooling in England. He returned to Virginia probably about 1699 but certainly by 25 April 1701, when he was named a justice of the peace for Northampton County.

From his paternal grandfather Custis inherited thirteen slaves, Smith Island in the Chesapeake Bay, and Arlington, a fine three-story brick mansion on 550 acres of land in Northampton County. He acquired additional property in that county and in 1704 paid quitrents on 3,250 acres there. Custis represented Northampton County in the House of Burgesses for the sessions that met from October through November 1705 and from April through June 1706.

On 4 May 1706 in York County, Custis married Frances Parke, the elder legitimate daughter and heiress of Daniel Parke (d. 1710), a former member of the governor's Council then serving as governor of the Leeward Islands. Parke did not pay the promised marriage settlement of £4,000, but he placed the management of his Virginia properties in Custis's hands and awarded him one-fifth of the net proceeds of the plantation profits. Parke's murder in 1710 plunged Custis into the morass of an estate dispute that lasted three generations. Parke had bequeathed his properties in England and Virginia to Frances Custis and his properties in the Leeward Islands to an illegitimate daughter there. In order to pay Parke's considerable debts and desired legacies, Custis and his wife secured passage of legislative acts in 1712 to break the entail and allow them to sell portions of the estate. William Byrd (1674–1744), who had married Frances Custis's younger legitimate sister, agreed to accept the land and slaves designated to be sold in exchange for assuming Parke's English debts and the legacies charged to the Virginia estate. In the 1720s the Antiguan heirs sought to force Custis to pay Parke's debts in the Leeward Islands. Custis prophetically warned his adversary, "I would go to Law the whole Course of my Life; spend the last penny I have in the world rather than I will pay one farthing of your unjust and unreasonable demand. . . . I must confess you may give me some trouble; and put me to some Charge; but depend upon it; where you put me to one penny worth you will put your self to a pound." The transatlantic suits and countersuits, appeals and counterappeals, consumed Custis's time and patience for the rest of his life and dragged on until the American Revolution rendered the dispute moot.

Custis and his wife had two daughters and two sons and divided their time between Arlington and a former Parke family plantation on Queen's Creek in York County. Their marriage was a stormy one between two strong-willed people who were not well-suited for each other. In June 1714 they drew up but never formally executed articles of agreement in which Custis promised to provide a plentiful maintenance for his wife and children and not to interfere with her running of their household if she forbore calling him vile names or using ill language. After Frances Custis died of smallpox on 13 March 1715, their surviving daughter grew up under the care of her maternal grandaunt. Custis's surviving son, Daniel Parke Custis, became a successful planter but did not marry until he was almost forty.

Later in life, Custis had an affair with Ann Moody, the wife of a tavern owner, to whom he provided many gifts that his son later tried to recover and also a £20 annuity. With his slave Alice, Custis had a son christened John (but called Jack) whom he freed in February 1748. At that time Custis deeded him 250 acres of land on Queen's Creek in York County and the boy's mother, all her other children, and four male slaves about ten years old of his own choosing. Custis had a portrait painted of his son, posted a bond that required his heirs to provide John with £20, fine clothing, and provisions each year until he reached age twenty-one, and in his will instructed Daniel Parke Custis to build John a house furnished with Russian leather chairs, two black walnut tables, and three feather beds.

By 1717 Custis had moved to Williamsburg. (Later writers often refer to him as John Custis, of Williamsburg, to distinguish him from his grandfather, father, and other relatives of the same name.) He enjoyed reading, delighted in prints and fine paintings, and at his house on Francis Street created a magnificent garden that eventually encompassed almost four acres and featured topiary, classical statues, and formal gravel walkways. Two portraits depict Custis with cut tulips and holding a small book entitled *Of the Tulip*. He may have written an essay, no longer extant, on that topic for circulation among his friends. Custis avidly collected, imported, traded, and cultivated plant specimens, especially flowers, trees, and shrubs. He knew Mark Catesby during the English naturalist's sojourn in Williamsburg (and owned a copy of his *Natural History of Carolina, Florida and the Bahama Islands*), welcomed John Bartram when the Pennsylvania botanist traveled to Virginia, and enjoyed a friendly correspondence for more than a dozen years with Peter Collinson, a Quaker horticulturist and member of the Royal Society of London for Improving Natural Knowledge.

Custis was able to indulge his love of gardening and fine art because he was a canny tobacco planter. After his father died in 1714, Custis inherited additional property in Accomack County, and by that date he owned more than 15,000 acres of land, principally in Northampton,

King William, New Kent, and York Counties. At the time of his death he owned approximately 200 slaves. His experience in a London mercantile house gave him a keen understanding of the transatlantic economy. Rather than confine his trade to one merchant, Custis varied the merchants and ports he did business with in order to secure better prices for his tobacco. He carefully measured the bolts of cloth and medicines he received from London, Bristol, and Glasgow, complained sharply when the goods he had ordered failed to meet his expectations, and threatened when cheated to take his business elsewhere. As a wealthy planter who was not in debt to the British merchants, Custis was able to parley his relationship with his various overseas merchants into political lobbying at critical times.

Custis represented the College of William and Mary in the House of Burgesses that met in three sessions in 1718. Although initially he was close enough to Alexander Spotswood to persuade the new lieutenant governor to stand as godfather to his son, Custis's connection by marriage to the powerful Byrd and Ludwell families eventually placed him in opposition to Spotswood. Political differences became personal in 1717 after Spotswood created a vista for the governor's palace by cutting down valuable timber on Custis's property. For a time Custis ceased speaking to Spotswood, and in 1721 he supported Commissary James Blair's trip to England to secure the removal of the lieutenant governor. In 1725 Spotswood's replacement, Hugh Drysdale, recommended Custis for appointment to the governor's Council, and after extensive lobbying by one of Custis's London commission merchants, the king acquiesced on 2 June 1727. Custis took his seat on 11 September of that year. As a member of the Council, he opposed the Tobacco Inspection Act of 1730 and two years later warned his consignment merchants that by pressing for a "cruell and unjust" act to help them more easily recover debts in the colonies they had "so incensd the Country; that you will force them as soon as convenient to have nothing to do with you."

Beginning late in the 1710s Custis suffered long bouts of ill health, including blinding headaches, sensitivity to light, and crippling pain in his joints that occasionally confined him to his house for months at a time. By 1742 he may have contracted yaws from some diseased slaves he had purchased and tried to treat. Although Custis diligently attended Council meetings for almost twenty years, he appeared only sporadically after April 1747 and sat for last time on 14 April 1749. The lieutenant governor planned to depart for England in August of that year, and during his absence Custis, as senior member of the Council, would have become president, or acting governor. On 25 August 1749 Custis declared his incapacity to serve, and the next day the lieutenant governor suspended him from the Council. John Custis wrote his will on 14 November 1749 and died on an unrecorded date not long thereafter, probably within a few days. His death was known in London as early as March 1750. His will was proved in the James City County Court on 9 April 1750 and in the Prerogative Court of Canterbury on 19 November 1753. In his will Custis required that "my Real Dead Body and not a Sham Coffin" be buried next to his grandfather's grave at Arlington. Custis set aside £100 for a handsome tomb of the finest white marble and directed his son, on pain of being cut off with only one shilling, to place on it the infamous wording that he had "Yet lived but Seven years which was the Space of time he kept a Batchelors House at Arlington on the Eastern Shoar of Virginia. This Inscription put on this Stone by his own positive Orders."

Jo Zuppan, "John Custis of Williamsburg, 1678–1749," *VMHB* 90 (1982): 177–197 (por. attributed to Charles Bridges on 192); Lynch, *Custis Chronicles: Virginia Generations*, 19–101; Custis family Bible records (1710–1859), VHS; Custis correspondence and other MSS at Chicago Historical Society, LC, LVA, Mount Vernon Library and Archives, New-York Historical Society, Rosenbach Museum and Library, Philadelphia, Pa., and VHS and printed in E. G. Swem, ed., *Brothers of the Spade: Correspondence of Peter Collinson, of London, and of John Custis, of Williamsburg, Virginia, 1734–1746* (1957), *Byrd Correspondence*, Zuppan, ed., "Father to Son: Letters from John Custis IV to Daniel Parke Custis," *VMHB* 98 (1990): 81–100, and Zuppan, ed., *The Letterbook of John Custis IV of Williamsburg, 1717–1742* (2005), with first quotation in Custis to Thomas Dunbar, 15 Jan. 1725, 68, second and third quotations in Custis to Lionel Lyde, 1732, 122, and birth date in Custis to Peter Collinson, [2 May] 1742, 228; *VMHB* 4 (1896): 64–66; York Co. Deed Book, 5:236–239; British Library, Add. MSS 36217, fols. 161–171 (including marriage date); PRO CO

5/1319, fols. 235–237; PRO CO 5/1320, fols. 121–122; PRO CO 324/35, fols. 336–337; *Executive Journals of Council*, 4:147, 5:141, 299–300; Mary A. Stephenson, "Custis Square Historical Report, Block 4 Lot 1–8" (1959), Colonial Williamsburg Foundation Library Report, ser. 1070; Ivor Noël Hume, "Custis Square: The Williamsburg Home and Garden of a Very Curious Gentleman," *Colonial Williamsburg* 16 (summer 1994): 12–26 (cover por.); will in Prerogative Court of Canterbury, Searle 287 (all other quotations).

SARA B. BEARSS

CUSTIS, John Parke (27 November 1754–5 November 1781), planter, was born probably at White House, the New Kent County plantation of his parents, Daniel Parke Custis and Martha Dandridge Custis. After the death of his father in 1757, he inherited more than 17,880 acres of land in the counties of Hanover, King William, New Kent, Northampton, and York; town lots in Jamestown and Williamsburg; two islands, Mockhorn and Smith, in the Chesapeake Bay; personal property and slaves worth £30,000; and liquid assets of £10,000. A convoluted estate battle, dating from 1723, with relatives in the Leeward Islands led his mother to seek assistance from John Robinson (1705–1766), who agreed to represent Custis and his surviving sister in the transatlantic lawsuit but was unwilling to take on management of all their property. On 6 January 1759 Custis's mother married George Washington and moved with her children to Mount Vernon, in Fairfax County. In April of that year Washington acquired limited rights to administer his stepchildren's estates and on 21 October 1761, after posting a £20,000 bond, became their guardian.

Privately tutored at Mount Vernon in classical Latin and New Testament Greek until the end of 1767, Custis (usually called Jack or Jacky) began studying in June 1768 at Jonathan Boucher's Caroline County boarding school and continued with the Anglican minister after he moved to Annapolis. Critical of Custis's early interest in the opposite sex, Boucher once exclaimed that he had never had a pupil "so exceedingly indolent, or so surprizingly voluptuous" and concluded that perhaps "Nature had intended Him for some Asiatic Prince." The schoolmaster hoped that escorting Custis on a grand tour of Europe in 1772 would improve his student's mind. Instead, Custis entered King's

College (later Columbia University) late in May 1773, but partly because of the death of his sister after an epileptic seizure the following month, he left the school in September.

On 3 February 1774, after overcoming initial resistance from the Washingtons because of his youth, Custis married Eleanor Calvert at Mount Airy, her father's estate in Prince George's County, Maryland. They had six daughters, including the social leaders Elizabeth Parke Custis Law and Eleanor "Nelly" Parke Custis Lewis, and one son, the writer and orator George Washington Parke Custis. Until late in 1778 Custis and his family divided their time among White House, Mount Vernon, and Mount Airy. Two years after his death, his widow married David Stuart, a physician and later a member of the Convention of 1788, and had at least seven more children.

Not long after his marriage Custis began to consolidate his landholdings. In 1778 he disposed of his 1,980-acre Mount Pleasant estate in King and Queen County and began selling off land in Hanover and New Kent Counties, as well as his family's town lots in Jamestown and Williamsburg. Desiring to own property in northern Fairfax County (after 1801 Alexandria County), he acquired two adjoining estates a few miles above Alexandria. One, an 1,100-acre tract his son later named Arlington, he purchased outright for £12,100. The other, a 904-acre tract called Abingdon, he mortgaged at £12 per acre with compound interest, the entire sum payable at the end of twenty-four years, an injudicious arrangement that would require him to produce £48,000 in 1802. In December 1778 Custis moved his family to Abingdon and during the summer of 1781 attempted to renegotiate the land transaction on more favorable terms. Eleven years after Custis's death, David Stuart, as guardian of Custis's minor son, reconveyed Abingdon to its former owner after paying £2,400 in rent for the time the estate had remained in Custis hands.

Custis was a conservative revolutionary and during the early days of the American Revolution criticized several Maryland counties for allowing anyone who bore arms to vote. His dissatisfaction with Virginia's ineffective conduct of the war eventually moved him to stand for election to the House of Delegates in 1778. Declaring himself "a true Friend to the Independency of America" who had "laid aside every Thought of returning to our former Masters," he was simultaneously a candidate in both Fairfax and New Kent Counties. Custis was elected to represent Fairfax County but arrived late at the session that began on 4 May 1778 and was added to the Committees of Propositions and Grievances and of Religion. He was sometimes lax in attendance, and when the House reconvened in October, it ordered the sergeant at arms to take him and other absent members into custody. Custis won reelection to the assemblies of 1779 and 1780–1781 but missed assignments to important committees because of his habitual late arrival, usually the result of the press of personal business or his wife's pregnancies.

As the only male in his family and as his mother's only surviving child, Custis faced determined opposition from his mother and stepfather and did not join the Continental army at the beginning of the Revolution. The danger to his native state and the direct threat to his property along the Pamunkey River later spurred him to action. In September 1781 as the French and American armies moved to Yorktown, Custis persuaded his stepfather to allow him to serve as a civilian aide-de-camp. Custis put his affairs in order, but shortly before he was to leave for camp he became ill with one of the occasional fevers that were a regular part of life in the Tidewater. Finally, at the end of the month, he left for Yorktown. As he rode through the countryside, he made enquiries about a number of his slaves who had absconded but was unable to locate any. Custis served with his stepfather during the siege of Yorktown but in the fetid environment of smallpox and camp fever fell ill again. John Parke Custis was taken to Eltham, the New Kent County plantation of his uncle Burwell Bassett (1734–1793), and died there on 5 November 1781. Two days later he was interred near Williamsburg in the Custis family burial ground at Queen's Creek plantation, in York County. His grave marker, if he had one, was no longer standing by 1895, when the local camp of Confederate Veterans removed the surviving Custis stones to Bruton Parish Church in Williamsburg.

Biographies in E. G. Swem, *Brothers of the Spade: Correspondence of Peter Collinson, of London, and of John Custis, of Williamsburg, Virginia, 1734–1746* (1957), 121–123, Lynch, *Custis Chronicles: Virginia Generations*, 128–157, and Frank E. Grizzard Jr., *George Washington: A Biographical Companion* (2002), 67–70; birth date in Eleanor Parke Custis Lewis to Elizabeth Bordley Gibson, 27 Nov. 1820, in Patricia Brady, ed., *George Washington's Beautiful Nelly: The Letters of Eleanor Parke Custis Lewis to Elizabeth Bordley Gibson, 1794–1851* (1991), 93; Custis letters at CW, LVA, Louisiana State University, Mount Vernon Library and Archives, and VHS, printed in part in *Washington Papers: Colonial Series* (including first quotation in Jonathan Boucher to George Washington, 18 Dec. 1770, 8:414), *Washington Papers: Revolutionary War Series* (second quotation in Custis to Washington, 26 Mar. 1778, 14:316), Billy J. Harbin, ed., "Letters from John Parke Custis to George and Martha Washington, 1778–1781," *WMQ*, 3d ser., 43 (1986): 267–293, and Joseph E. Fields, ed., *"Worthy Partner": The Papers of Martha Washington* (1994); marriage in *Washington Diaries*, 3:231 (por. on 3:109), and *Williamsburg Virginia Gazette* (Purdie and Dixon) and *Williamsburg Virginia Gazette* (Rind), both 17 Feb. 1774; children identified in Custis family Bible records (1710–1859), VHS, and Elizabeth Parke Custis Law to David Bailie Warden, 20 Apr. 1808, David Bailie Warden Papers, Maryland Historical Society, Baltimore, printed in *VMHB* 53 (1945): 93; nineteenth-century circumstantial evidence, laid out in Henry Wiencek, *An Imperfect God: George Washington, His Slaves, and the Creation of America* (2003), 284–290, has suggested to several historians that Custis may also have had a son with Ann Dandridge, a mixed-race slave; William S. Simpson Jr., "A Comparison of the Libraries of Seven Colonial Virginians, 1754–1789," *Journal of Library History* 9 (1974): 54–65; burial recorded in Jonathan Trumbull Diary, 7 Nov. 1781, Munn Collection, Fordham University Library; estate inventories in Fairfax Co. Will Book, D-1:274–288, E-1:11–18; death notice, with incorrect place of death, in *Philadelphia Pennsylvania Gazette, and Weekly Advertiser*, 28 Nov. 1781.

SARA B. BEARSS

CUSTIS, Mary Lee Fitzhugh (22 April 1788–23 April 1853), Episcopal lay leader, was born probably at Chatham, the Stafford County estate of her parents, Ann Randolph Fitzhugh and William Fitzhugh (1741–1809), a member of the Convention of 1776 and of the Continental Congress. In the 1790s her father advertised Chatham for sale and moved the family to northern Virginia, where he owned Ravensworth, a Fairfax County plantation, and also a house in Alexandria. On 7 July 1804 in the city of Alexandria, Fitzhugh married George Washington Parke Custis, an orator and writer devoted to preserving the legacy of George Washington. They lived nearby at Arlington, an 1,100-acre plantation in

Alexandria County, an area the Commonwealth of Virginia had ceded to the federal government to become part of the District of Columbia and which Congress retroceded after a referendum in 1846. She and her husband had four daughters, of whom one was stillborn and two died in infancy; the surviving child, Mary Anna Randolph Custis, married Robert Edward Lee. Custis's husband also had a daughter, Maria Carter (later Syphax), with one of the Custis family slaves.

Molly Custis inherited £2,000 and several slaves when her father died in 1809. She considered her religious faith "the one thing needful" and devoted her life to causes affiliated with the Episcopal Church. She was a member of Christ Church, in Alexandria, which had organized a Sunday school by May 1820 and by the end of the decade had established both a missionary association and a benevolent society. In 1824 women belonging to several churches in Alexandria and Georgetown joined together in founding a ladies' auxiliary to the Society for the Education of Pious Young Men for the Ministry of the Protestant Episcopal Church, an organization Custis supported with annual gifts of $10 for much of the decade. The society provided funds for students as well as salaries for professors at the Protestant Episcopal Theological Seminary in Virginia (known as the Virginia Theological Seminary). Custis also raised money for the American Society for Colonizing the Free People of Color of the United States (popularly known as the American Colonization Society) by selling flowers grown in her gardens at Arlington.

Custis was a member of a family network in northern Virginia that revived the state's Episcopal Church early in the nineteenth century. She was a spiritual influence on the children of her cousin Mary Fitzhugh Grymes Meade, among them Ann Randolph Meade Page, Susan Meade, and William Meade, who served as the bishop of Virginia from 1841 until his death in 1862. During the 1820s and 1830s these evangelical Episcopalians promoted Sunday schools for both white and black children, missionary work, and the gradual emancipation of slaves and colonization. Custis was a strong influence on her younger brother, William Henry Fitzhugh,

a member of the Convention of 1829–1830. In September 1829 they jointly sold a male slave to a local apothecary for $1 so that the purchaser could free him. Custis's brother was a vice president for Virginia of the American Colonization Society and in his will provided unconditionally for emancipating his slaves after 1850 and offering them incentives to immigrate to Liberia. Although Custis and her husband supported colonization, only Custis and her daughter took an active role in educating slaves. Because Bible literacy was central to spiritual improvement, the slaves at Arlington learned to read and write under the women's tutelage. Custis held family prayers twice daily and taught a Sunday school for black children in the sewing room in her home. Many of the Arlington slaves had joined the Baptist Church by the 1850s.

Custis did not write a will, but she left a sealed letter to her daughter directing the distribution of her prized possessions, including clothing to certain favored female slaves. Her daughter also recorded that Molly Custis's greatest desire was that all the family's slaves would be manumitted and enabled to immigrate to Africa. One family, William C. Burke, Rosebella Burke, and their four children, departed for Liberia on 9 November 1853. The will of Custis's husband, who died in October 1857, specified that all his slaves be freed once the legacies from his estate were paid but no later than five years after his death. Mary Lee Fitzhugh Custis died at Arlington on 23 April 1853 and was buried near the mansion. Three weeks later the minister at Christ Church published an unusually long obituary in the local newspaper. In addition to conventional comments on Custis's character and devotion to her family and the church, he wrote, "In the death of Mrs. Custis, the *community* has sustained no ordinary loss. . . . Her life was one of great practical usefulness, for she was deeply interested 'in every good work.'"

Birth date, marriage date, and children's birth dates recorded in Custis's handwriting in copy of *Annual Visitor: or, Almanac for the Year of our Lord, 1802*, Annfield Collection, Clarke County Historical Association, Berryville; Arlington Co. (formerly Alexandria Co.) Marriage Bonds (dated 6 July 1804); children's variant birth dates in Custis family Bible records (1710–1859), VHS; some letters and related documents in Arlington House Archives, George Washington

Memorial Parkway, in Annfield Collection, Clarke County Historical Association, in Lydia Huntley Sigourney Papers, Connecticut Historical Society, Hartford, in William Meade Papers, General Theological Seminary, New York, in Custis-Lee-Mason Papers, LVA, and in other collections at UVA and VHS; Alexandria City Deed Book, S-2:387–388; charitable work documented in *African Repository, and Colonial Journal, Episcopal Recorder*, and *Washington Theological Repertory and Churchman's Guide*; Deborah L. Sisum, "'A Most Favorable and Striking Resemblance': The Virginia Portraits of Cephas Thompson (1775–1856)," *Journal of Early Southern Decorative Arts* 23 (summer 1997): 20–21 (por.); bequests in lieu of will in Custis to Mary Anna Randolph Custis Lee, 19 Aug. 1848, George Bolling Lee Papers, VHS; death notice in *Alexandria Gazette*, 26 Apr. 1853; tributes in *Alexandria Gazette*, 16 May 1853 (quotations), and *Washington Daily National Intelligencer*, 27 May 1853, and by Lydia Huntley Sigourney in *Southern Literary Messenger* 20 (Feb. 1854): 120.

TATIANA VAN RIEMSDIJK

CUSTIS, William Henry Bagwell (28 December 1814–7 October 1889), member of the Convention of 1861 and member-elect of the House of Representatives, was born in Accomack County and was the only surviving son of Henry Bagwell Custis, a slaveholding planter, and Elizabeth Fletcher Custis. After the death of his father in 1817, Custis inherited 575 acres of his father's 975-acre seaside plantation. Custis's mother remarried in September 1819 and began a new family. His relations with his stepfather, William Robinson Custis, were strained. The stepfather died in the autumn of 1839 and by his will denied his stepchildren any inheritance from his estate and forbade his children to entangle themselves financially with their half siblings. Custis disobeyed and the next year gave bond for the marriage of his half sister and ward. He himself posted a marriage bond on 19 September 1840 and on that date or soon thereafter married Emeline V. S. Conquest. Of their five sons and four daughters, only two daughters, who never married, survived Custis.

In 1834 Custis received an A.B. from Indiana College (later Indiana University) in Bloomington, and three years later the college, following a practice in force until 1876, automatically awarded him an A.M. without further academic study. Accounted an eloquent, persuasive speaker, Custis, a Democrat, represented Accomack County in the House of Delegates for the 1842–1843 session. He sat on the Committees on the Militia

Laws and on Trade and Mechanic Arts. Reelected to the 1843–1844 assembly, he served on a committee to examine the clerk's office and again on the Committee on Trade and Mechanic Arts. Accomack voters returned Custis to the House for the 1845–1846 term. He chaired a committee to examine executive expenditures and also served on the Committee to Examine the Public Library. In August 1850 he campaigned for one of the two seats representing Accomack and Northampton Counties in a convention called to revise the state constitution but finished third in the four-candidate poll.

During the next decade Custis devoted himself to farming. The number of his slaves more than doubled, from nineteen in 1850 to forty-eight on the eve of the Civil War. In 1861 Custis represented Accomack County at the convention called to consider Virginia's response to the secession crisis. In his only speech, he decried secession as a declaration of war and viewed remaining in the Union as the best protection for the Eastern Shore's slaves and property. Even if no other delegate would vote against secession, he vowed to "stand here solitary and alone and do it." As good as his word, Custis opposed secession on 4 April when it failed and again on 17 April when it passed. Despite an earlier protest that he would rather cut off his arm than sign the Ordinance of Secession, he affixed his name to the document and attended the two subsequent adjourned sessions of the convention. He took no other recorded part in the Civil War, and his Unionist sympathies led him to visit Wheeling at least once during the conflict.

In August 1865 Custis entered a tight five-man race for election to represent the twenty-county First Congressional District, embracing the Eastern Shore, the Northern Neck, and most of the Tidewater. Campaigning on his eligibility because he could take the prescribed test oath affirming that he had not borne arms against the United States or otherwise supported the Southern cause, Custis narrowly defeated his opponents despite missing campaign opportunities at several district court days and neglecting to run the requisite election announcements in the regional newspapers. Along with all the other members of the Thirty-ninth Congress elected from the former Confederate states, he was denied his seat when Radical Republicans in the House of Representatives instructed the clerk to omit those states in the organizational roll call of members-elect.

In March 1869 the commander of the First Military District named Custis clerk of the Accomack County Court to fill a vacancy caused by the removal of the incumbent under a federal law that required replacement of all Virginia, Mississippi, and Texas officials who had any recorded Confederate activity. Custis continued in office through June 1887 and from 1869 until 1875 simultaneously served as clerk of the circuit court. About 1872 he moved from his home estate at Ravenswood to a 3.75-acre parcel he acquired at the county seat. After several weeks of declining health, William Henry Bagwell Custis died at Accomac Court House on 7 October 1889 and was buried in the family cemetery at Ravenswood, in Accomack County.

Birth and death dates in Custis family Bible records (1722–1889), VHS; Ralph T. Whitelaw, *Virginia's Eastern Shore: A History of Northampton and Accomack Counties* (1951), 2:881–882, 1021–1022; father's and stepfather's wills in Accomack Co. Will Book (1817–1818), 218–221, and (1828–1846), 315–323, respectively; Accomack Co. Marriage Licenses and Bonds; *Richmond Whig and Public Advertiser*, 27, 30 Aug. 1850; *Richmond Enquirer*, 27 Aug., 6 Sept. 1850; Reese and Gaines, *Proceedings of 1861 Convention*, 3:163, 4:135–137 (quotation on 136), 144; congressional election reported in *Fredericksburg Ledger*, 19 Sept., 17, 20 Oct. 1865; Alan B. Bromberg, "The Virginia Congressional Elections of 1865: A Test of Southern Loyalty," *VMHB* 84 (1976): 80–81, 85–86, 92, 97; Accomack Co. Official Bonds (1859–1870), 475–476; Accomack Co. Will Book (1882–1901), 168–169; obituaries in *Richmond Dispatch*, 8 Oct. 1889, and *Accomac Court House Peninsula Enterprise*, 12 Oct. 1889.

SARA B. BEARSS

CUTCHIN, Joel Holleman (2 February 1846–20 September 1917), mayor of Roanoke, was born in Nansemond County and was the son of John A. Cutchin, a farmer, and his second wife, Treacy Holland Cutchin. Little is known about his early years or education. On 2 January 1864 Cutchin enlisted as a private in the 32d Regiment Virginia Infantry. He was promoted to corporal and served through the end of the Civil War. Paroled at Appomattox Court House on 9 April 1865, Cutchin returned home, where he

married Mary Frances Norfleet on 15 February 1866. They had four daughters. For the next decade he assisted his father in managing the family farm.

By 1880 Cutchin had moved his family to Norfolk, where he founded the Norfolk Peanut Company about 1885. The business proved unsuccessful, and before the end of the decade he had settled in the rapidly expanding railroad city of Roanoke, where he hoped to capitalize on the real estate boom that was inflating land prices in southwestern Virginia. The market collapsed, however, and although he was nearing fifty, Cutchin entered the law school at Richmond College (later the University of Richmond). He received a B.L. in June 1894 and established a Roanoke practice specializing in commercial law. In 1898 Cutchin won election to the city council, took his seat in July, and served on the Committee of Ordinances. The following July he was elected president of the council. After winning the Democratic primary in April 1902, Cutchin won the first of four general elections as mayor.

During a decade as mayor Cutchin embraced progressive goals that sought to bring order, reform, and efficiency to municipal government. He studied books on urban planning, attended conferences on the subject throughout the country, and in 1906 was elected president of the League of Virginia Municipalities. Involved in nearly every aspect of local governance, he expanded the police force and convinced the council to issue revolvers and batons to officers. Cutchin advocated such health measures as citywide garbage collection, smallpox vaccinations for schoolchildren, and the hiring of a city food and milk inspector, a health officer, and a city electrician. A believer in the City Beautiful ideal, he worked to pave muddy streets, replace wooden sidewalks, and build parks and protect green spaces. Cutchin's combative personality often placed him at odds with the council, but many of his proposals succeeded, including a $400,000 bond issue in December 1905 to finance improvements of the city's fire department, sewers, and streets. Four years later he encouraged the council to provide funds supporting the good roads movement. Cutchin urged women to become more active in city affairs, particularly civic improvement. After the founding of the Woman's Civic Betterment Club of Roanoke in 1906, he was its staunchest ally in efforts to improve sanitation and schools.

Two riots brought Roanoke national publicity while Cutchin was mayor. At the end of January 1904 Alice Shields and her young daughter were brutally attacked. They identified a black man as the assailant. Despite condemnation of the attack and donations of reward money by some African Americans, area blacks were targets of intimidation and violence during the two weeks before the suspect's capture. Some lost their jobs, others were threatened, and a black man living in nearby Salem was tied to a post and whipped. Cutchin denounced the mob violence as "unmanly and cowardly" but declined to protect a black pastor rumored to have wrongly accused Shields's husband of being her assailant. Forced to abandon his home, the pastor later filed an unsuccessful lawsuit against Cutchin. Determined to prevent a lynching and the rioting and racial unrest that had previously marred the city's reputation, Cutchin acquiesced in the governor's order calling up 800 militiamen to protect the prisoner during his trial in Roanoke the next month.

Roanoke made headlines again in 1907 when a minor dispute at one of the city's Greek-owned restaurants escalated into a fistfight. An unruly crowd of whites resisted police orders to disperse. Summoned by Cutchin, the fire company turned its hoses on the mob that, undeterred, began ransacking other Greek restaurants. Order was restored by morning, but news of the riot reached the secretary of state and Greek officials in New York. Cutchin, who was among those who suffered minor injuries, and other city leaders persuaded a reluctant city council to provide reimbursement for some of the property damage and destruction.

Cutchin's opposition to prohibition and Sunday closing laws created conflict with many Roanokers, but his attitude toward prostitution proved his undoing. Unable to persuade the council to build a detention facility for women and believing it useless to force prostitutes to leave town, he resisted calls for raids of the red-light district and making public the names of the women and their clients. On 29 March 1911 Cutchin was charged with malfeasance and misfeasance in office and neglect of official duty for allowing houses of ill-repute and gambling dens to flourish. Also accused of consorting with prostitutes, he denounced the charges as politically motivated. One of the city's well-known madams testified to a friendship with Cutchin and insisted that her gifts to him were payment for his legal services, not protection. Cutchin maintained his innocence but was convicted of all charges on 1 June 1911. The Virginia Supreme Court of Appeals upheld the decision on 28 March 1912, and Cutchin was immediately removed from office.

Undaunted by his conviction, Cutchin ran for mayor in the Democratic primary in May 1912 but was defeated. He retained a measure of his popularity and in April 1916 lost his final attempt to become the Democratic candidate for mayor by only 377 votes of 2,699 cast. In November 1913 he won election as a trial justice for the city and in the Democratic primary on 7 August 1917 was nominated for reelection by a large majority. Joel Holleman Cutchin died of apoplexy at his Roanoke home on 20 September 1917 and was interred in Evergreen Burial Park there. The local newspapers memorialized him as a "veritable landmark of Roanoke" and lauded his efficiency, honesty, and civic-minded leadership.

Biographies in WPA Biographies and Brenda McDaniel, "Impeached!" *Roanoker* 7 (Oct. 1980): 62–67 (several pors.); publications include Cutchin, "Municipal Government under the Virginia Constitution," *Fourth Annual Convention of the League of Virginia Municipalities* (1909), 39–45; BVS Marriage Register, Nansemond Co.; Compiled Service Records; *Roanoke Times*, 23 May 1902, 9 Feb. 1904 (first quotation), 30 Nov. 1905, 22, 25, 30 Sept., 4 Oct. 1906, 14, 16–19 July 1907, 30–31 Mar., 16 May, 2 June 1911, 29 Mar. 1912, 14 Mar. 2004; Raymond P. Barnes, *A History of Roanoke* (1968); Paul R. Dotson, "'Magic City': Class, Community, and Reform in Roanoke, Virginia, 1882–1912" (Ph.D. diss., Louisiana State University, 2003), 327–330, 343–345, 347–349, 354–356, 367–371; BVS Death Certificate, Roanoke City; obituaries in *Roanoke World-News*, 20 Sept. 1917, and *Roanoke Times*, 21 Sept. 1917; editorial tributes in *Roanoke Times* (second quotation) and *Roanoke World-News*, both 21 Sept. 1917.

ANN FIELD ALEXANDER

CUTSHAW, Wilfred Emory (25 January 1838–19 December 1907), civil engineer, was born in Harpers Ferry and was the son of George W. Cutshaw, a merchant tailor, and Martha J. Moxley Cutshaw. He was educated at home and at a local academy. After graduating from the Virginia Military Institute in 1858, Cutshaw became an instructor of mathematics and artillery tactics at John Baytop Cary's Hampton Male and Female Academy, often referred to as the Hampton Military Academy.

After resigning his teaching position in the spring of 1861, Cutshaw secured a commission as second lieutenant in the Confederate provisional army. He served as an engineer under Thomas J. "Stonewall" Jackson until March 1862, when Cutshaw received permission to organize an artillery company, of which he was elected captain. During an assault on Winchester in May of that year, he was wounded in the left knee and captured soon after the battle. Federal officers paroled Cutshaw in August 1862 on condition that he remain within Union lines in Frederick or Jefferson Counties. In April 1863 he was imprisoned at Fort McHenry and exchanged the following month. Deemed unfit for duty in June, Cutshaw returned to VMI, where he served as acting commandant of cadets until the end of August. He was assigned to the Army of Northern Virginia as an artillery inspector and promoted to major on 27 February 1864. Cutshaw had taken command of an artillery battalion with the Second Corps of the Army of Northern Virginia by 19 March 1864. He led the battalion in the Battle of Spotsylvania Court House, where it suffered heavy losses on 12 May defending the salient known as the Mule Shoe. Cutshaw received a wound in the right arm but remained in command when his unit accompanied the Second Corps to the Shenandoah Valley. The battalion fought in the trenches around Petersburg early in 1865. After receiving promotion to lieutenant colonel in the last month of the war, Cutshaw was wounded on 6 April at the Battle of Saylers Creek and lost his right leg above the knee. Captured again, he was paroled in June 1865.

By 1866 Cutshaw had become assistant professor of mathematics and assistant commandant of cadets at the Virginia Military Institute. He left Lexington in January 1868 to work at the Dover Coal and Iron Company in Henrico County, but by the next year he had returned to VMI as an assistant professor of physics and later of civil and military engineering. He took charge of the engineering department during the 1872–1873 academic year.

On 23 June 1873 Cutshaw became engineer for the city of Richmond. Despite the bleak economic climate of the 1870s, he urged that the developing city adopt a comprehensive approach to planning and begin implementing systematic improvements. One of his first acts was the assessment and demolition in 1874 of Richmond's city hall (1814–1816), designed by the noted architect Robert Mills. Cutshaw's dispassionate judgment of the structure's vulnerabilities marked the first occasion of many when he played a decisive role in determining the architectural landscape of the city.

Cutshaw often viewed improvements to the Richmond cityscape with the pragmatism of a civil engineer, but his personal tastes drove the city's architectural program. A majority of the armories, markets, and schools constructed during Cutshaw's thirty-four years as city engineer were in the Italianate style, seen in such diverse municipal buildings as Steamer Company No. 5, a combination fire station and police precinct house, and in his designs for the Marshall Street Market (1875), the Clay Ward Market (1891), West End School (later Stonewall Jackson School, 1887), and Randolph Street School (1896). His career coincided with the height of armory construction in the United States. The distinctive castellated armories built under Cutshaw's direction included those for the First Virginia Regiment (1882), the First Regiment Cavalry Virginia Volunteers (1895), the First Virginia Volunteers Battalion (1895), and the Richmond Howitzers Battalion (1895).

Cutshaw saw public parks as essential elements of a modern city. Under his direction, the city acquired more than 300 acres of land on its western edge to provide space and facilities for a new pumping station and reservoir. He designed this multiple-use area (which became known as New Reservoir Park and later as William Byrd Park) to accommodate a tree nursery from which the streets of Richmond were landscaped.

Cutshaw's 1904 report *Trees of the City* emphasized the importance of planting tree species appropriate for their locations. Believing that public spaces for recreation, especially for children, were of great importance, he designed several other city parks and expanded existing ones.

Cutshaw established goals of permanent, rational, and comprehensive design for his concept of municipal improvement. In 1875 he used the improvement of the Union Hill section of Richmond as a demonstration. Cutshaw's plan began with the installation of main sewers, followed by grading streets for drainage; laying branch sewer, gas, and water lines; installing sidewalks, gutters, and stone curbs; and finally paving roads. Cutshaw maintained that these were basic principles of modern city design and construction and that the example of Union Hill could be applied consistently to the entire city.

In 1883 Cutshaw's intervention led the city council to award the design for a new city hall to Elijah E. Myers. Cutshaw became supervising engineer for the building, and despite considerable cost overruns, his reputation was undiminished. Although the Confederate Soldiers and Sailors Monument on Richmond's Libby Hill was not a municipal project, Cutshaw's influence came to the fore in 1888 when he was named to the design committee, which proposed a monument based on Pompey's Pillar, near Alexandria, Egypt. Cutshaw was the engineer in charge of constructing the column surmounted by a statue of a Confederate soldier, which was completed in 1894.

On 21 December 1876 Cutshaw married Emma S. Thornton Norfleet, a widow. She died of cholera thirteen days later. He married Margaret Watkins Morton on 21 January 1890. They had no children before her death on 15 December of that year. Continuing his work as city engineer through his final illness, Wilfred Emory Cutshaw died of kidney disease at the Richmond home of his niece on 19 December 1907. He was buried in the city's Hollywood Cemetery. In 1908 a small triangular park bordered by Stuart and Park Avenues and Meadow Street was renamed Cutshaw Place, and by 1923 Cutshaw Avenue bore his name.

Biographies in Henry and Spofford, *Eminent Men*, 432–433, and Selden Richardson, "'Architect of the City': Wilfred Emory Cutshaw (1838–1907) and Municipal Architecture in Richmond" (M.A. thesis, VCU, 1996); BVS Marriage Register, Richmond City (1876, 1890); Compiled Service Records; Richmond City Council Records (1873–1874), 129; Architectural Drawings and Plats, Office of City Engineer, Richmond, LVA; obituaries and editorial tributes in *Richmond News Leader* and *Richmond Times-Dispatch* (por.), both 20 Dec. 1907; obituary in *Confederate Veteran* 16 (1908): 83–84.

SELDEN RICHARDSON

D

DABBS, Isaac (d. after 27 April 1910), member of the House of Delegates, was born into slavery, probably late in the 1840s, on the Charlotte County plantation of John Garnett. George Dabbs and Frankie Dabbs were his parents, but nothing else is known about his childhood, nor is it certain when or under what circumstances he became free. In Charlotte County on 29 December 1869 Dabbs married Sarah Ann Brown. Before her death on an unrecorded date after 17 December 1884, they had at least two sons.

In the census taken in August 1870 Dabbs was described as a twenty-one-year-old farm laborer who could neither read nor write. It is unclear how he first became involved in post–Civil War politics, but in October 1875 Radical Republicans in Charlotte County selected him as the party's candidate for the House of Delegates in what the *Charlotte Gazette* described as a "somewhat excited and stormy discussion." In the election the following month he received 1,283 votes, while the incumbent and a third candidate tallied 630 and 261 ballots, respectively. As a member of the assembly that met in two sessions from December 1875 through March 1876 and then from December 1876 until April 1877, Dabbs served on the Committee on Labor and the Poor. He spoke little, but in January 1877 he introduced a bill to amend a sheep protection law in Charlotte, Clarke, and Frederick Counties. Later that month, the resolution was dismissed.

At a meeting in October 1877 the county's Radical Republicans, by one vote, rejected Dabbs in favor of another candidate to seek the House of Delegates seat. He continued to speak at county meetings, however, and to support party candidates. Dabbs aligned himself with the Readjuster faction of the Republican Party, which supported a partial repudiation of the state's antebellum public debt. In November 1882 he dictated a letter to United States senator William Mahone affirming his loyalty and service to the Readjusters, while requesting an appointment as a railway postal clerk for a young man in Charlotte County.

Dabbs canvassed Charlotte County in the weeks leading up to the November 1883 election. He stumped in nearly every precinct for the Readjuster candidate for the House of Delegates. Dabbs dictated another letter to Mahone in October informing him that the canvass was going well and predicting that party turnout at the polls would be substantial. Dabbs emphasized that he would continue his work until the election but informed Mahone that the candidate did not have the resources to pay him. He explained that his family required his support and they would suffer while he canvassed unless he could be paid from the campaign fund.

A civic leader in the black community, Dabbs served on the committee of arrangements in April 1896 for a gathering of African Americans discussing issues of citizenship as well as mental, moral, religious, and financial advancement. On 30 March 1898 he married twenty-one-year-old Sarah Catherine Howell in Charlotte County. No children are recorded from the marriage. Although he received little, if any, formal education, Dabbs may have learned to read and write by 1900, as reported by the census enumerator. By 1910 he and his wife had moved to Baltimore, where he worked as a brickyard laborer. Isaac Dabbs died on an unknown date after the census enumeration of his ward on 27 April 1910.

Biography in Jackson, *Negro Office-Holders*, 9 (with birth year of 1846); correspondence in William Mahone Papers, Duke; Charlotte Co. Marriage Register (1869, with age twenty-one on 29 Dec. 1869, and 1898, with age forty-three on 30 Mar. 1898); Census, Charlotte Co., 1870 (age twenty-one on 26 Aug. 1870), 1880 (age twenty-eight on 23 June 1880), 1900 (birth date of Mar. 1855); Election Records, no. 10, RG 13, LVA; *JHD*, 1876–1877 sess., 92, 107, 150; Charlotte Co. Deed Book, 38:314, 40:335, 41:266 (Dabbs signing with his mark); *Charlotte Gazette*, 23 Oct. (quotation), 13 Nov. 1875, 8 Jan. 1876, 25 Oct. 1877, 7 Apr. 1887, 9 Apr. 1896, 7 Apr. 1898; last appearance in Census, Baltimore City, Md., 1910 (age forty-eight on 27 Apr. 1910).

JOHN G. DEAL

DABNEY, John (ca. 1824–7 June 1900), caterer, was born into slavery in Hanover County and was the son of Eliza, or Elizabeth, Dabney, a cook and maid, and London Dabney, a carriage driver who lived on a neighboring farm. Cora Williamson DeJarnette owned Dabney and his mother and later hired him out to a relative, William Williamson, who had him trained as a jockey. A success on the racecourses of central Virginia, Dabney earned lasting fame from his bartending, catering, and cooking. After he grew too big to compete as a jockey, he worked as a waiter at Hanover Junction (later Doswell), as a head waiter in Gordonsville, and then as a bartender at a Richmond hotel that Williamson managed. Williamson arranged for various chefs to instruct Dabney in preparing special dishes. His signature culinary items at the Richmond hotels where he worked were mint juleps, terrapin stew, and canvasback. On several occasions Richmond residents presented Dabney with large trophy cups in recognition of his champion juleps, and in October 1860 he served one to the Prince of Wales (later Edward VII), who was then visiting the United States.

By 1856 Dabney had married Elizabeth Foster, who was also enslaved. Virginia law did not recognize slave marriages, and the union produced no documentary record. With earnings from his bartending, Dabney enlisted the aid of sympathetic white men in purchasing his wife from her owner, who intended to sell her out of Richmond. He arranged for her to be freed, probably late in the 1850s and certainly before mid-1864, and it is possible that he also arranged for his mother's freedom. Dabney and his wife had five sons and four daughters. Two sons and two daughters died young. Their surviving daughters became Richmond schoolteachers; one son, John Milton Dabney (originally Milton Williamson Dabney), played baseball professionally before becoming a postal worker; and another son, Wendell Phillips Dabney, became a musician, writer, and founding editor of two Cincinnati newspapers, the *Ohio Enterprise* and the *Union*.

By the beginning of the Civil War, Dabney had paid DeJarnette part of the sum they had agreed on for him to purchase his freedom, but before he completed the payments the war and slavery had ended. Nevertheless, he later gave her the balance he owed. Praised for his honesty in fulfilling the obligation, Dabney reportedly could thereafter secure credit at any bank in Richmond. The episode, publicized in the summer of 1868, later inspired Thomas Nelson Page's poem "Little Jack" (which the author dedicated to Dabney) and continued to appear in the reminiscences of Richmond residents well into the twentieth century.

Dabney kept bar in several fashionable Richmond hotels before, during, and immediately after the Civil War. His wife acquired a valuable city lot in 1864, she being unmarried in the eyes of the law and therefore able to own real estate. It is possible that Dabney provided money from his earnings to white friends who purchased the property and transferred it to her. After the war he and his wife bought and sold several pieces of real estate. Dabney always made his mark on the deed rather than signing his name. In November 1866 they purchased a large house near First African Baptist Church, of which they were or became members, and lived there the remainder of their lives. Early in the 1870s Dabney opened a restaurant; but before doing so, he carefully deeded all his real estate and restaurant equipment to his wife in trust so that their property, then worth about $4,000, would not be at risk if his new business failed. It succeeded. As Dabney's fame spread beyond Richmond, his services were often in demand during the summer season at many of the finest western Virginia resorts, and the prominent people who tasted his specialties at those hotels secured his services at their homes or local establishments.

Dabney was a dignified, portly man with what his son described as a reddish-brown complexion. Bald from early manhood, he wore a wig with long, curling black hair. He dressed well as a businessman and won the trust and even measured respect of many white people, not only for his cooking and integrity but also for his courtesy, good humor, and politeness. On the other hand, he was hot-tempered and sometimes violent, and he kept a gun handy in the house or at the bar. Dabney knew where he stood in his relationship with his white customers. As his son

Wendell Phillips Dabney wrote, his "reputation and business standing rendered him almost immune to segregation, ostracism or racial prejudice." The son quoted Dabney as remarking that "white folks are awfully wicked" and that "if you do everything white folks want you to do, you will go either to the penitentiary or the gallows." He cautioned his son "never to let a white man know how much you really do know about anything except hard work." While outwardly conforming to the expectations of white society, Dabney inwardly experienced the "two-ness" that sociologist W. E. B. Du Bois described in *The Souls of Black Folk* (1903): such a man as Dabney was "an American, a Negro; two souls, two thoughts, two unreconciled strivings; two warring ideals in one dark body, whose dogged strength alone keeps it from being torn asunder."

Dabney may have retired from managing his restaurant and catering business early in the 1890s, but he continued to work until the week of his death. John Dabney died at his Richmond home on 7 June 1900. All four of the city's daily newspapers reported his death, but none indicated in which of Richmond's African American cemeteries he was buried.

Census, Henrico Co., 1880 (age fifty-six on 16 June 1880); *Richmond Southern Opinion*, 20 June 1868; feature articles derived wholly or in part from interviews with sons in *Richmond News Leader*, 15 Apr. 1938 (por.), *Richmond Planet*, 28 May 1938, and *Norfolk Journal and Guide*, 21 Dec. 1957 (reprinting article from *Newark [N.J.] Sunday News*); biographical and family information in typescript autobiography of son Wendell Phillips Dabney, Cincinnati Historical Society, Cincinnati, Ohio (first quotation on 17, second on 46, third on 50, fourth on 67); deed of trust, 29 Oct. 1869, in Richmond City Hustings Court Deed Book, 89A:372–374; "Little Jack," *Century Illustrated Monthly Magazine* 33 (1887): 800; *Washington Post*, 13 Aug. 1893; W. E. Burghardt Du Bois, *The Souls of Black Folk: Essays and Sketches* (1903), 3 (fifth quotation); obituaries in *Richmond Dispatch*, *Richmond Evening Leader*, *Richmond News*, and *Richmond Times* (age at death about seventy-five), all 8 June 1900.
PHILIP J. SCHWARZ

DABNEY, Richard Heath (29 March 1860–16 May 1947), historian, was born in Memphis, Tennessee, and was the son of two native Virginians, Ellen Maria Heath Dabney, who died of complications from his birth, and Virginius Dabney (1835–1894), an educator and popular writer. While his father served in the Civil War, he lived in Richmond with his maternal grandmother, Elizabeth Ann Macon Heath, and was cared for part of the time by Lucy Parke Chamberlayne, who in 1863 married the writer George William Bagby and later became a noted Richmond civic leader. Heath Dabney, as he was known, rejoined his father and new stepmother in 1867. At boys' schools operated by his father in Loudoun County and later in Princeton, New Jersey, and New York City, he showed promise in subjects ranging from Latin and French to history and geography.

Dabney enrolled in the University of Virginia in 1878 and received an M.A. in history in 1881. The years in Charlottesville made an indelible impression on him. Dabney found there his vocation of history, his eventual home-place and employer, and a close and influential friend, Woodrow Wilson. After graduating, Dabney taught for a year at his father's New York Latin School and then began advanced studies in history in Europe. He attended lectures at the universities of Munich and Berlin before choosing to pursue his doctorate at the University of Heidelberg, which did not require completion of a dissertation. Dabney was fascinated by the oratorical passion of Berlin's Heinrich von Treitschke, but that historian's insistence on German ethnic superiority and justification of German military expansion repelled him. Dabney's scholarly interests increasingly focused on France, and throughout his life he urged American opposition to Germany.

Dabney received a Ph.D. in 1885 after a rigorous oral examination. Returning to the United States, he temporarily settled in New York while looking for a university teaching job. At Washington and Lee University in March 1886 he delivered lectures that formed the basis of his only book-length scholarly work, *Causes of the French Revolution* (1888). In 1886 Dabney accepted an offer, which Woodrow Wilson had declined, to join the history faculty at Indiana University. Dabney improved the history curriculum, but he was often blunt and caustic. He was openly disdainful of Hoosiers, and his years there were full of controversy. The local annoyances faded into insignificance after Dabney published a short article entitled "Indiana 'Floaters'" in the *Nation* on 22 November 1888 in which he described election abuses, especially vote-buying, as standard Republican Party practice in Indiana. In response, Republican newspapers throughout the state insulted Dabney's origins, character, and motivations. He was soon relieved to secure appointment as adjunct professor of history at the University of Virginia beginning on 1 October 1889.

While still living in Bloomington, Indiana, Dabney married Mary Amanda Bentley in Richmond on 19 June 1888. She died on the following 18 May after giving birth to a daughter who died two months later. Eager to escape the private grief and public turmoil of the preceding year, Dabney threw himself into the life of the University of Virginia. He taught all the courses in American, ancient, medieval, and modern European history. Even after gaining full faculty status and acquiring colleagues, he taught all the history classes at the university for thirty-four years and also all of the courses in economics for nine of those years. Once he began teaching economics, he reoriented the curriculum away from the broad economic approach favored by his predecessor toward a focus on current events that allowed him to preach the virtues of the gold standard. Dabney served also as the first dean of graduate studies from 1904 to 1923. Among the first doctorates in history that the university granted during his tenure were to three historians who made major contributions to Virginia studies: John Walter Wayland (1907), Thomas Jefferson Wertenbaker (1910), and Richard Lee Morton (1918).

Dabney publicly advocated some administrative changes at the university, such as organizing students and alumni by the year of their graduation in order to facilitate fund-raising, and opposed others, among them the admission of women to the undergraduate program. By speaking at numerous public events he continued to try to shape broader political debates. Dabney published a long article in the *Richmond Times* of 6 October 1901 encouraging the state constitutional convention then sitting to minimize African American suffrage and to free white taxpayers from the obligation of supporting the education of black children. He was later an outspoken critic of Prohibition.

In spite of the favorable reception of *Causes of the French Revolution* and of a revised edition in 1906, Dabney's scholarly output was limited. He wrote *John Randolph: A Character Sketch* (1898) for a series on the American character and also a number of short works, some of them first delivered as speeches or published as letters to newspapers, but he never again completed a major work of original research. Dabney remained too active as a teacher, faculty leader, and broadly interested citizen to devote the necessary time to extended study and writing. He abandoned a history of Reconstruction he had agreed to write for a series under the auspices of the Johns Hopkins University and during the 1920s made little progress on a planned one-volume biography of Robert Edward Lee.

On 27 November 1899 Dabney married Lily Heth Davis, of Albemarle County. They left Charlottesville for a few days' honeymoon, the only time, according to family tradition, that Dabney missed a class during his forty-nine years of teaching at the university. They had two daughters and one son, Virginius Dabney (1901–1995), who became a journalist and writer. Richard Heath Dabney retired in 1938 and died in Charlottesville on 16 May 1947. He was buried in the University of Virginia Cemetery.

Biographies in *NCAB*, 13:348–349, *University of Virginia Alumni News* 45 (Nov. 1956): 6–7, 19, Virginius Dabney, "Richard Heath Dabney: A Memoir," *Magazine of Albemarle County History* 33/34 (1975/1976): 53–140 (several pors.), and Howard F. McMains, "Richard Heath Dabney: A Virginian in Indiana, 1886–1889," *Indiana Magazine of History* 82 (1986): 334–357; BVS Marriage Register, Richmond City (1888), Albemarle Co. (1899); Dabney Family Papers, UVA; Dabney letters in several other collections, UVA, and in Arthur S. Link et al., eds., *The Papers of Woodrow Wilson* (1966–1994); obituaries in *Charlottesville Daily Progress*, 16 May 1947, and *Richmond Times-Dispatch*, 17 May 1947; editorial tributes in *Richmond News Leader*, 17 May 1947, and *Norfolk Ledger-Dispatch*, 19 May 1947; memorials in *JSH* 13 (1947): 424, and by Thomas Jefferson Wertenbaker in *University of Virginia Alumni News* 35 (June 1947): 5, 7.

JOHN C. WILLIS

DABNEY, Robert Lewis (5 March 1820–3 January 1898), Presbyterian minister, was born in Louisa County and was the son of Elizabeth Randolph Price Dabney and Charles Dabney, a member of the county court and an elder in the local

Presbyterian church. At age seven he began his education in a small log school near his home. He learned Latin from an elder brother and later began to study Greek. In June 1836, following several months of tutoring in mathematics, Dabney entered Hampden-Sydney College as a sophomore. He left after September 1837, returned home to assist his widowed mother, and found time to teach two terms at a local school. In the autumn of 1839 he matriculated at the University of Virginia and in 1842 received an M.A.

For the next two years Dabney helped his mother manage the family plantation, taught school, and began his long and productive career as an author by writing articles for Richmond newspapers. Having joined the Presbyterian Church in 1837, he enrolled in November 1844 at the Union Theological Seminary, then affiliated with Hampden-Sydney College. After graduating in June 1846, Dabney returned to Louisa County and preached at Providence Presbyterian Church. On 16 July 1847 he was ordained and installed as minister of Tinkling Spring Presbyterian Church, in Augusta County. Dabney married Margaretta Lavinia Morrison in Rockbridge County on 28 March 1848. Of their six sons, three died as children.

The Union Theological Seminary (later Union Theological Seminary and Presbyterian School of Christian Education) awarded Dabney a D.D. in 1852, and in August of the following year he joined the faculty as professor of church history and church government. In 1859 he took over the duties of the chair of theology and began teaching systematic theology with a rigorous emphasis on Calvinist orthodoxy. The following year he declined offers of a prestigious pulpit in New York and a position on the faculty of Princeton Theological Seminary.

Initially opposed to secession, Dabney sided with his state after Virginia joined the Confederacy in the spring of 1861. In May of that year he began four months of service as chaplain to the 18th Regiment Virginia Infantry before returning to his duties at the seminary. Thomas J. "Stonewall" Jackson often heard Dabney preach during those months and asked Dabney to serve as his adjutant, or chief of staff, a position for which he had neither experience nor skill.

Although Dabney preferred resuming the role of chaplain, Jackson was persuasive, and Dabney was commissioned a major, to rank from 22 April 1862. Illness forced him to resign on 15 August, but his respect for Jackson never wavered. When Jackson's widow later asked Dabney to write a biography of the general, Dabney threw himself into the effort. His *Life and Campaigns of Lieut.-Gen. Thomas J. Jackson (Stonewall Jackson)*, which highlighted the subject's fervent piety, appeared in a two-volume edition published in London between 1864 and 1866 and a one-volume edition published in New York in 1866.

As soon as his health allowed, Dabney resumed teaching at the Union Theological Seminary. He had been a reluctant secessionist but steadfastly defended the Confederate cause until the day of his death. Terribly embittered by the defeat of the South and by the end of slavery, Dabney was decidedly undemocratic in his politics and racist to the core. He defended an idealized version of the Old South as the apex of Christian civilization. He spoke and wrote against allowing freedpeople to vote and denounced free public education for blacks and whites. Dabney was as opposed to new theories in science as he was to new ideas about politics, education, and a whole range of so-called progressive concepts, and his Calvinism grew more inflexible as his social and political views calcified. He employed his formidable learning to defend a variety of reactionary causes. From Dabney's pen flowed a series of publications, mounting a rearguard defense of older ways as suggested by the titles: *A Defence of Virginia, [and Through Her, of the South] in Recent and Pending Contests Against the Sectional Party* (1867), *Ecclesiastical Relation of Negroes* (1868), *A Caution Against Anti-Christian Science* (1871), *The Sensualistic Philosophy of the Nineteenth Century, Considered* (1875), and *The Practical Philosophy* (1897).

Dabney emerged as one of the most influential leaders of the southern Presbyterian Church. In 1863 he chaired a committee that brought about the merger of New School and Old School factions in the South to create the Presbyterian Church in the U.S. While serving as moderator of the denominational general assembly in 1870, Dabney helped scuttle efforts to promote fraternal relations between southern and northern Presbyterians, and he vehemently opposed any efforts toward reunification. His essays and sermons appeared frequently in Presbyterian periodicals or in pamphlet form. The publication of his theological texts, *Sacred Rhetoric* (1870) and *Syllabus and Notes of the Course of Systematic and Polemic Theology* (1871), both of which went through several editions, ensured that his influence over southern Presbyterian divinity students was unmatched.

Dabney's unhappiness with the postwar situation led him to consider leaving the United States, and in 1883 health problems convinced him to leave Virginia and accept the professorship of moral philosophy at the new University of Texas, in Austin. He liked the climate and at first was optimistic about the prospects for Christian society in Texas, where he helped to found the Austin School of Theology. But modernity soon intruded there, too, and an exasperated Dabney grew ever more embittered. In 1894 the university asked for his resignation, and the following year he and his wife moved to the home of a son in Victoria, Texas.

Though a spirited lecturer and prolific writer, Dabney suffered from ill heath for much of his life, and toward the end his afflictions were multiplied by blindness. He nevertheless saw through to publication *Discussions* (1890–1897), a four-volume collection of his writings. Robert Lewis Dabney died in Victoria, Texas, on 3 January 1898. At his request he was buried at the Union Theological Seminary in Virginia Cemetery, at Hampden-Sydney College.

Biographies in Thomas Cary Johnson, *The Life and Letters of Robert Lewis Dabney* (1903), with birth and marriage dates and frontispiece por., Henry Alexander White, *Southern Presbyterian Leaders* (1911), 382–393, and Sean Michael Lucas, *Robert Lewis Dabney: A Southern Presbyterian Life* (2005); selected bibliography of writings in Frank Bell Lewis, "Robert Lewis Dabney: Southern Presbyterian Apologist" (Ph.D. diss., Duke, 1946), 237–246; principal collections of MSS include Dabney-Jackson Collection, LVA, Charles William Dabney Papers, UNC, Robert Lewis Dabney Papers, Presbyterian Historical Society, Montreat, N.C., Robert Lewis Dabney Papers (including sermon and lecture notes), UTS, Dabney Family Papers, UVA, and Dabney Family Papers, VHS; Rockbridge Co. Marriage Bonds; variant marriage date of 29 Mar. 1848 in Rockbridge Co. Ministers Returns; Compiled Service Records; Charles Reagan Wilson, "Robert Lewis Dabney: Religion and the Southern Holocaust," *VMHB* 89 (1981): 79–89; obituaries in *Richmond Dispatch*, 5 Jan. 1898, *Richmond Times*, 9 Jan. 1898, and *Louisville Christian Observer*, 12 Jan. 1898; *In Memoriam Robert Lewis Dabney, Born, March 5th, 1820; Died, January 3rd, 1898* (1899).

JOHN B. BOLES

DABNEY, Virginius (8 February 1901–28 December 1995), journalist, writer, and recipient of the Pulitzer Prize, was born at the University of Virginia. His father, Richard Heath Dabney, a history professor, was the son of Virginius Dabney (1835–1894), an author of romantic tales about Virginia; and his mother, Lily Heth Davis Dabney, a Charlottesville *grande dame*, was a descendant of Martha Jefferson Carr, Thomas Jefferson's sister. Tutored at home until he was thirteen, Dabney attended Episcopal High School of Virginia, in Alexandria, from 1914 to 1917. He received a B.A. from the University of Virginia in 1920 and an M.A. the following year. His impressive academic record earned him a Phi Beta Kappa key, and he was also a star tennis player, a game that he played passionately until age eighty-six.

Dabney taught French at Episcopal High School for a year and in 1922 moved to Richmond, where he became a reporter for the *Richmond News Leader*. The publisher, John Stewart Bryan, was a longtime family friend and invited him to live at Laburnum, the Bryan family home. On 10 October 1923 Dabney married Douglas Harrison Chelf, of Richmond, who died on 29 January 1994. They had two daughters and one son. Dabney began contributing articles to the *Baltimore Evening Sun* in 1925, which he considered a turning point in his career. Like many other young journalists of the time, he admired the iconoclastic critic H. L. Mencken. Some of Dabney's older colleagues worried about Mencken's influence, but Dabney soon developed his own prose style, less exaggerated and more complimentary than Mencken's.

By June 1928 Dabney had contributed articles to some of the nation's leading magazines, and the *Richmond Times-Dispatch* wooed him away from the *News Leader* with an offer to become its chief political reporter. The following year, he also became the Upper South correspondent for the *New York Times*. Dabney's complex relationship with Harry Flood Byrd (1887–1966) began during these years. His first article for the *Sun* predicted that if Byrd were elected governor, the state's political machine would continue public policies that Dabney considered detrimental, but a few months after Byrd took office, Dabney began praising the reforms that the governor introduced.

Religious fundamentalists, prohibitionists, and machine politicians were Dabney's favorite targets early in his career. He saw them coalescing in Virginia under the leadership of James Cannon, a Methodist bishop, ardent advocate of Prohibition, and one of the men behind the anti-Catholic campaign against Alfred E. Smith, the 1928 Democratic presidential candidate. During the summer and autumn of 1929 Dabney took leave from the *Times-Dispatch* in order to complete a book about Cannon. The manuscript was scathing and hastily written, and he could not find a publisher. Not until 1949, after Cannon's death, did Dabney publish a revised version with the title *Dry Messiah: The Life of Bishop Cannon*.

In the 1930s Dabney's writings expanded into new areas as he began urging liberal reforms in industrial regulation and civil rights. His increasing stature as a spokesman for southern liberals was confirmed in 1932 when he published *Liberalism in the South*. Twice disappointed when other men were appointed editor of the *Richmond Times-Dispatch*, Dabney applied for and accepted an Oberlaender Trust grant to study in several European countries in 1934. While he was in Germany, he received an offer to become chief editorial writer for the *Times-Dispatch*, and finally, two years later, he was named editor.

In 1935 Dabney helped found the Southern Policy Committee, a group that studied such issues as tenant farming, industrial conditions, and racial injustice. He also agreed to work with the Southern Conference for Human Welfare, but growing suspicious that Communists were playing an influential role, he withdrew his support before the first conference in 1938. By the end of the decade, Dabney's liberal credentials were well established. He had supported the protection of civil liberties for striking workers and Communists, proposed that African Americans serve on Virginia juries, advocated a federal antilynching law, fought for abolition of the poll tax, and criticized Byrd, who had been appointed to a vacant seat in the United States Senate in 1933, for his opposition to New Deal relief and reform measures. Washington and Lee University's Lee School of Journalism and the Virginia Press Association honored Dabney with the Lee Editorial Award for his editorials supporting the county manager form of government in Henrico County in 1937, and three years later the University of Richmond awarded him an honorary doctorate, lauding him as one who "fearlessly champions justice and brotherhood" and as a "tireless contender for freedom of thought and expression."

In 1940 Dabney lectured on the New South for a semester at Princeton University. His next book, *Below the Potomac* (1942), exposed many problems of the region, but the volume's tone was positive and emphasized the progress that was being made. By then Dabney was questioning whether a federal antilynching law was any longer necessary, and he cautioned that litigation by the National Association for the Advancement of Colored People that sought to break down legal racial segregation could make race relations in the South worse. During World War II he also became concerned about national security and less concerned with the civil liberties of laborers. The real test of Dabney's status as a liberal, however, came in the area of race relations. As the pressure for desegregation mounted, he held to the separate-but-equal policy and feared that it would take generations for accumulated racial prejudices to fade away. In January 1943 he drew heated responses when he shared those sentiments in an *Atlantic Monthly* article.

At the same time, Dabney began working with others to keep southern control over the movement to improve conditions for African Americans. He wrote favorably about the Durham Manifesto, an outline of specific reforms issued by southern black leaders in December 1942, and he participated in the 1943 Atlanta and Richmond conferences on the substance of the manifesto. The Southern Regional Council grew out of those meetings, with Dabney as an original member of its board. As a further sign of good faith, he looked for areas where he thought desegregation might be brought about peacefully. In November 1943 Dabney wrote editorials in the *Richmond Times-Dispatch* urging the integration of streetcars and buses. The following year he received honorary doctorates from Lynchburg College and the College of William and Mary, but public transportation remained segregated in Virginia.

As criticism of the South mounted, Dabney became more defensive about the region. "Is the South That Bad?" was the title of an article he published in the *Saturday Review of Literature* on 13 April 1946. Privately, he began to wonder whether he still qualified as a liberal under the changing conditions that prevailed after World War II. He opposed the 1947 report of the President's Committee on Civil Rights, which called for a strong federal program to eliminate segregation, but he was dismayed that he had been forced to choose sides.

When Dabney received the Pulitzer Prize in 1948 for his editorial writing of the previous year, his national prestige seemed secure, but there were signs of trouble. His editor at the *New York Times* had complained about the local themes of his columns, and in April 1947, after one of his columns was rejected, Dabney severed the relationship. He was bothered, too, by what he perceived as a rift between himself and Byrd. In 1946 a Dabney editorial praised but did not endorse Byrd's opponent in the Democratic Party primary, and even though Dabney ultimately endorsed Byrd, the senator stopped responding to Dabney's letters. The breach widened in 1948 after Dabney lambasted the Byrd-dominated General Assembly for attempting to keep Harry S. Truman's name off the presidential ballot in Virginia. Byrd's allies in the House of Delegates retaliated by voting to have Richmond Newspapers, Inc., owner of the *Richmond Times-Dispatch*, investigated. Dabney fired back with an editorial in which he declared, "The *Times-Dispatch* will not be intimidated." He won a Sigma Delta Chi award for that editorial.

More threatening to Dabney's security was his deteriorating relationship with John Dana Wise, vice president and general manager of Richmond Newspapers. In 1943 they had a bitter argument about a syndicated column that the *Times-Dispatch* carried, and Dabney, without naming names, took his case to the public in a 1945 *Saturday Review of Literature* article critical of publishers who dictated editorial policy. Wise later required that Dabney justify his outside activities that took time from his newspaper work.

Dabney was accustomed to coaxing his readers into moderately liberal positions with conservative arguments or flattery, but he never strayed far from the dominant conservative opinion at home. In 1949, estranged from Byrd and from his publisher, he grew wary and made no endorsement in the Democratic Party gubernatorial primary, even though he had worked on the Southern Policy Committee with Byrd's sometime adversary, Francis Pickens Miller, who was one of the unsuccessful candidates. Dabney subsequently moved closer to Byrd with a 1951 laudatory magazine article, and in 1952 he withdrew from the Southern Regional Council after it adopted a policy calling for an end to segregation in the South. The *Richmond Times-Dispatch* took the unprecedented step of supporting a Republican for president in 1952. Dabney's editorial in favor of Dwight David Eisenhower won him a second Sigma Delta Chi award. That year he also gave a strong endorsement to Byrd when Miller challenged him for the senatorial nomination.

In the spring of 1954 Dabney received an invitation to lecture at the annual Fulbright Conference on American Studies at the University of Cambridge. On 17 May 1954, two months before he left for England, the Supreme Court of the United States ruled that racial segregation in public schools was unconstitutional. Dabney urged calm and predicted that the decision would take a long time to implement. He helped establish and was the first chair of the Southern Education Reporting Service, which sought to ensure access to accurate, objective information about how southern communities were adjusting to the Court's decision. In a *Saturday Evening Post* article explaining how an illustrious Virginian, John Marshall, had made the

Supreme Court the final interpreter of the Constitution, he indirectly told his readers that the 1954 Court order must be obeyed.

Early in 1956 it became clear that Byrd's political organization had something else in mind. In January voters approved a constitutional convention to authorize tuition grants as part of what appeared to be a local-option plan, but in February the Speaker of the House of Delegates headed a large group that introduced a resolution committing the state's schools to remain segregated during the next year. Dabney accused the organization of a breach of faith in abandoning the local-option plan. The following week Byrd issued a public statement calling for coordinated, massive resistance to enforcement of the Court's orders. James Jackson Kilpatrick, editor of the *Richmond News Leader*, supported Massive Resistance, and Dabney's publishers fell in line with Byrd. Dabney acquiesced.

Dabney's professional colleagues elected him president of the American Society of Newspaper Editors in 1957, but his decision to accept Massive Resistance undermined his reputation. In September 1958, when the governor closed schools in several Virginia communities rather than allow them to integrate, *Life* magazine asked Dabney to explain the state's position. He presented the commonwealth's case in an article published on 22 September and entitled "Virginia's 'Peaceable, Honorable Stand.'" Both the federal courts and the Virginia Supreme Court of Appeals declared the Massive Resistance laws unconstitutional, however, and after the school closings, some influential Virginia politicians abandoned Massive Resistance. Dabney had once been one of the best-known liberals in the South, but when he retired as editor of the *Richmond Times-Dispatch* in January 1969, the *New York Times* reported that, among liberals, he had come to be considered an apologist for Massive Resistance.

In April 1968 Dabney agreed to serve as rector of the new Virginia Commonwealth University, formed by the merger of the Medical College of Virginia and Richmond Professional Institute. His association with Byrd and Massive Resistance produced protests from the Students for Afro-American Philosophy at the university in

April 1969, but he had the support of the university's board. Nevertheless, he resigned at the end of July in order to work on a history of Virginia. He remained on the university's governing board for many years.

In retirement Dabney devoted more time to his interest in history. For more than thirty years he sat on the executive committee of the Virginia Historical Society and from 1969 to 1972 served as its president. Assisted by a Guggenheim Fellowship, he published a large one-volume history, *Virginia: The New Dominion* (1971). Both it and *Richmond: The Story of a City* (1976) remained in print for many years. Dabney told his own story in *Across the Years: Memories of a Virginian* (1978). *The Jefferson Scandals: A Rebuttal* (1981) attempted to refute assertions that Thomas Jefferson had children with the enslaved Sally Hemings. Dabney wrote institutional histories of the two universities he knew best, *Mr. Jefferson's University: A History* (1981) and *Virginia Commonwealth University: A Sesquicentennial History* (1987). He drew on his own reporting for *The Last Review: The Confederate Reunion, Richmond, 1932* (1984), an event he had covered for the *Richmond Times-Dispatch*, and he also wrote *Pistols and Pointed Pens: The Dueling Editors of Old Virginia* (1987). A collection of his previously published articles, *Virginius Dabney's Virginia: Writings about the Old Dominion* (1986), contained an introductory essay about Dabney by the internationally recognized writer and Richmond native Tom Wolfe.

Virginius Dabney died in his sleep at his Richmond home on 28 December 1995 and was buried in the city's Hollywood Cemetery.

Dabney, *Across the Years: Memories of a Virginian* (1978), including several pors.; Dabney, "Reflections," *VMHB* 93 (1985): 279–290; Marie Morris Nitschke, "Virginius Dabney of Virginia: Portrait of a Southern Journalist in the Twentieth Century" (Ph.D. diss., Emory University, 1987); BVS Marriage Register, Richmond City; Virginius Dabney Papers, UVA; Morton Sosna, *In Search of the Silent South: Southern Liberals and the Race Issue* (1977), esp. 121–139; John T. Kneebone, *Southern Liberal Journalists and the Issue of Race, 1920–1944* (1985); Earle Dunford, *Richmond Times-Dispatch: The Story of a Newspaper* (1995); Alex Leidholdt, "Virginius Dabney and Lenoir Chambers: Two Southern Liberal Newspaper Editors Face Virginia's Massive Resistance to Public School Integration," *American Journalism* 15 (fall

1998): 35–68; *Richmond Times-Dispatch*, 20 Apr. 1940 (first quotation), 15 Mar. 1948 (second quotation); obituaries in *New York Times, Richmond Times-Dispatch*, and *Norfolk Virginian-Pilot*, all 29 Dec. 1995, and in *Washington Post*, 30 Dec. 1995.

MARIE MORRIS NITSCHKE

DABNEY, Walter Davis (13 May 1853–12 March 1899), attorney and educator, was born at Dunlora, the Albemarle County home of his parents, Susan Fitzhugh Gordon Greene Dabney and her second husband, William S. Dabney, an attorney and prominent farmer. His elder brother William Cecil Dabney became a distinguished physician and professor of medicine at the University of Virginia. Dabney attended private schools. After studying civil engineering for one year at the University of Virginia beginning in 1871, he left to teach at Hanover Academy. He returned to the university in 1874, studied law, and received a B.L. in 1875. Dabney married Mary B. Douglass in Albemarle County on 23 September 1878. They had four sons and three daughters before her death on 2 October 1896.

Establishing himself as an attorney in Charlottesville, Dabney quickly developed an excellent reputation for his clear and thorough, yet concise, work. His 1879 article in the *Virginia Law Journal* entitled "The Virginia Married Woman's Act" discussed provisions of the 1877 state law concerning married women's property. In 1886 he published an article in the same journal on a related subject, "Post-Nuptial Settlements: *Perry* v. *Ruby*."

In 1885 Dabney won election to the first of three terms in the House of Delegates representing Albemarle County. He served on the Committees on Finance, on Officers and Offices at the Capitol, and on Executive Expenditures. During his second term Dabney retained his seat on the Committee on Officers and Offices at the Capitol, became chair of the Committee on Roads and Internal Navigation, and was ranking member of the Committee on Counties, Cities, and Towns and of the Committee on Federal Relations and Resolutions. In his third and final term, which began in 1889, he continued to sit on the Committees on Federal Relations and Resolutions and on Roads and Internal Nav-

igation and also chaired the important Committee on Finance.

In 1887 Dabney chaired a three-member legislative commission established to consider removing James River dams owned by the Richmond and Alleghany Railroad Company, without violating the railroad's charter obligations. His experiences as chair of the Committee on Roads and Internal Navigation led him to write *The Public Regulation of Railways* (1889), published in G. P. Putnam's Sons' Questions of the Day series. This work won Dabney national renown and brought him to the attention of the members of the Interstate Commerce Commission, which in 1891 hired him as its solicitor. He became indispensable in trying cases before district and circuit courts across the country. A particularly compelling argument before an Illinois court in 1892 impressed federal judge Walter Quintin Gresham, who after he became secretary of state the following year appointed Dabney as solicitor of the Department of State.

In 1892 Dabney published "The Basis of the Demand for Public Regulation of Industries" in the *Annals of the American Academy of Political and Social Science*, and in July 1894 he presented a paper before the Virginia State Bar Association entitled "The Legal Evolution and Status of American Paper Money," at the time considered one of the best essays on the subject. He accepted appointment in September 1895 as professor of law at the University of Virginia, where he replaced the longtime, celebrated incumbent, John Barbee Minor, who had died. The month after Dabney arrived, the Rotunda burned, and he served on a faculty committee raising funds for its restoration. Dabney's clear elucidation of his subject and personal warmth won the esteem of his students, while his intellect and modesty impressed his colleagues. He taught, among other courses, the law of pleading and practice in civil cases; law of contracts, torts, bailments, and carriers; and law of evidence. In 1897 Dabney published a textbook, *Outlines of Federal Jurisdiction and Law Procedure, Prepared as a Basis of Lectures to Law Students at the University of Virginia*. He was working on a book on equity practice in the federal courts when he became ill with tuberculosis during the 1897–1898 academic year. He suspended teaching and traveled south to recover his health. About ten days after returning to Charlottesville, Walter Davis Dabney died at his home on 12 March 1899. He was buried in the University of Virginia Cemetery.

Biographies in Glass and Glass, *Virginia Democracy*, 37–38, and W. Hamilton Bryson, *Legal Education in Virginia, 1779–1979: A Biographical Approach* (1982), 171–173 (por.); BVS Birth Register, Albemarle Co.; BVS Marriage Register, Albemarle Co.; several Dabney letters in various collections, UVA, and in Basil Brown Gordon Papers, VHS; publications include Dabney, "The Virginia Married Woman's Act," *Virginia Law Journal* 3 (1879): 193–204, "Post-Nuptial Settlements: *Perry* v. *Ruby*," ibid. 10 (1886): 265–267, "The Basis of the Demand for Public Regulation of Industries," *Annals of the American Academy of Political and Social Science* 2 (1892): 433–449, and "The Legal Evolution and Status of American Paper Money," *Virginia State Bar Association Proceedings* (1894), 181–217; *Washington Post*, 28 Sept. 1891, 14 Sept. 1895; death notice in *Virginia School Journal* 8 (1899): 120; obituaries in *Charlottesville Daily Progress*, 13 Mar. 1899, and *Richmond Dispatch* and *Washington Post*, both 14 Mar. 1899; memorial in *Virginia State Bar Association Proceedings* (1899), 89–93.

KATHARINE E. HARBURY

DABNEY, William Cecil (4 July 1849–20 August 1894), physician, was born at Dunlora, the Albemarle County home of his parents, Susan Fitzhugh Gordon Greene Dabney and her second husband, William S. Dabney, an attorney and well-to-do farmer. His younger brother Walter Davis Dabney became a noted attorney and law professor. After receiving his early education from home tutors, Dabney in 1866 matriculated at the University of Virginia, where he studied anatomy, chemistry, medicine, physiology, and surgery. He received an M.D. in 1868 and then served for a year as resident physician at a Baltimore hospital before returning to Virginia to practice medicine in Big Lick (later the city of Roanoke). Dabney soon moved to Charlottesville, where he married Jane Bell Minor, of Albemarle County, on 16 March 1869. They had five daughters, three sons, and one other child who died young.

As a result of poor health, Dabney temporarily closed his medical practice in 1872 and took up farming in Albemarle County. He did not abandon medicine, however, and in 1873 he became a fellow of the Medical Society of Virginia. That same year Harvard College awarded him the Boylston Prize for an essay on *The Value of Chemistry to the Medical Practitioner* (1873). Dabney resumed his practice in Charlottesville in 1874, but four years later he suffered a physical breakdown, possibly the early stages of tuberculosis. On the advice of a colleague he took a voyage to Japan. Dabney returned to the United States in December 1878 and resided in San Diego, California, for a number of months. By 1880 he was again practicing medicine in Charlottesville.

Concerned about unqualified physicians practicing in the state, the Medical Society of Virginia appointed Dabney chair of a committee in 1881 to petition the General Assembly for the creation of a board of medical examiners. Dabney's efforts proved successful, and on 31 January 1884 the legislature passed an act establishing the Medical Examining Board of Virginia. At its first meeting on 15 November 1884 the board unanimously elected Dabney as its president. During his tenure of almost two years the board licensed dozens of physicians and denied some applicants their certifications; when two who failed the examination began to practice anyway, the board secured convictions against them.

Dabney resigned as president in August 1886 following his appointment as professor of medicine, obstetrics, and medical jurisprudence in the University of Virginia's medical department, where he modernized the curriculum. Emphasizing the importance of good observation skills and clinical instruction, he established a class to train students in using a microscope and instituted a free clinic at the university where they could gain experience in examining patients. Dabney published a 300-page *Abstract of a Course of Lectures on the Practice of Medicine* (1891). Two years later he presented a paper at the Pan-American Medical Congress on "The Aims and Methods of Medical Education," in which he urged medical schools to raise their graduation standards in order to improve the caliber of new physicians.

Dabney continued to practice medicine while teaching at the university. Early in June 1888 he identified the first recorded North American cases of pleurodynia, commonly known as "the devil's grip" because patients suffered excruciating, paroxysmal pain on the left side of the chest. Dabney recorded his observations of twenty-nine Charlottesville-area cases in an "Account of an Epidemic Resembling Dengue" in the *American Journal of the Medical Sciences* the following November. His name became associated with the disease, and after a 1923 outbreak of more than three thousand cases the State Board of Health began calling pleurodynia "Dabney's Grip," a term used during later epidemics in the state. Beginning in 1889 Dabney served as the resident physician at White Sulphur Springs, in West Virginia, and his article on "The Physiological Action and Therapeutic Uses of the Water of the Greenbrier White Sulphur Springs, West Virginia," appeared in *Gaillard's Medical Journal* in April 1890.

A prolific writer, Dabney contributed numerous treatises and articles to a variety of journals, including the *American Journal of the Medical Sciences*, *Medical News*, and the Medical Society of Virginia's *Transactions*. His interest embraced a wide range of topics, such as diphtheria, liver disease, lung infections, typhoid fever, and the importance of medical education and regulation. Dabney contributed an entry on "Maternal Impressions" to the first volume of John M. Keating's *Cyclopedia of the Diseases of Children* (1889). In addition, he translated and abstracted more than one hundred medical articles from French and German publications for the *Virginia Medical Monthly*. A member of the American Medical Association and the Association of American Physicians, Dabney presented papers at their annual meetings, and in 1887 he represented the state's medical society at the ninth International Medical Congress, in Washington, D.C.

While preparing articles for a medical encyclopedia and organizing a paper for presentation to the New York Medical Association, William Cecil Dabney contracted typhoid fever and died from related complications at his home in Charlottesville on 20 August 1894. He was buried in the University of Virginia Cemetery.

Biographies in Henry and Spofford, *Eminent Men*, 433–434 (with birth date probably provided by Dabney), Howard A. Kelly and Walter L. Burrage, *Dictionary of American Medical Biography* (1928), 285–286, and Byrd S. Leavell, "Distinguished Virginia Professor: Dr. William Cecil Dabney," *Virginia Medical* 106 (1979): 799–803 (por. on 798); Albemarle Co. Marriage Licenses; major publications include Dabney, "State Regulation of the Practise of Medicine," *Physician's Magazine* 1 (1885): 115–122, "The Topical Uses of Ergot," *American Journal of the Medical Sciences* 78 (1879): 101–105, "The Treatment of Empyema," ibid. 84 (1882): 403–427, "Account of an Epidemic Resembling Dengue, Which Occurred in and around Charlottesville and the University of Virginia, in June 1888," ibid. 96 (1888): 488–494, "A Contribution to the Study of Hepatic Abscess," ibid. 104 (1892): 125–151, "An Outbreak of Typhoid Fever Presenting Unusual Features," *Medical News* 63 (1893): 630–632, and "The Aims and Methods of Medical Education," ibid. 63 (1893): 729–731; *Report of the State Board of Health and the State Health Commissioner for [1921–1923]* (1924), 5; F. J. Spencer, "The Devil and William Dabney: An Epidemiological Postscript," *Journal of the American Medical Association* 195 (21 Feb. 1966): 645–648; obituary in *Richmond Times*, 11 Sept. 1894; memorials in *Virginia Medical Monthly* 21 (1894): 574–575, Medical Society of Virginia *Transactions* (1894), 195–197, and *VMHB* 2 (1895): 332–333.

AMANDA MORRELL

DADE, Francis. See **SMITH, John** (d. 1663).

DADE, Francis Langhorne (22 February 1792–28 December 1835), army officer, was born most likely in King George County and was the son of Townshend Dade and Elizabeth Dade Dade. Little is known about his early life or education. On 29 March 1813 he received a commission as a third lieutenant in the 12th United States Infantry, which saw service during the War of 1812. Promoted to second lieutenant on 31 January 1814, he was transferred to the 4th Infantry the following year. Dade made first lieutenant on 4 September 1816 and on 24 February 1818 was promoted to captain. He served principally at posts in Alabama, Louisiana, North Carolina, and Virginia.

While stationed at Fort San Carlos de Barrancas, near Pensacola, Florida, beginning in August 1818, Dade participated in operations against the Indians, cleared roads, and built forts. In July 1825 he reported to Fort Brooke, on Tampa Bay. When an appeal for reinforcements came from the Indian agent a hundred miles to the north, near where Fort King and the city of Ocala were later built, Dade set out with two infantry companies on an arduous five-day march along an Indian trail and arrived in a show of force designed to thwart any outbreak of hostilities by the Seminoles. The next year he arrested and disarmed tribe members involved in subsequent disturbances at the agency. William Pope Duval, the territorial governor of Florida and a native Virginian, commended Dade for his vigilance and credited him with restoring order to the area.

After serving recruiting duty in Albany, New York, Dade returned to Pensacola in March 1827. There on 6 December he married Amanda Malvina Middleton, then about sixteen years old. They set up housekeeping in Pensacola and had a daughter. Dade was brevetted major on 24 February 1828. During the next few years he was posted successively to New Orleans, Albany, and Baltimore, and by November 1833 he was again on duty in Florida, at Key West.

In December 1835 Dade received orders to proceed to Fort Brooke as part of an expedition assembling to reinforce Fort King. Later that month he and other officers learned that about 250 Seminole warriors had gathered in the north. Although some officers were intimidated by the news and reluctant to aid the fort, Dade believed that the number was exaggerated and urged action. Volunteering to lead the expedition and hoping to duplicate his feat of a decade earlier, Dade set out on 23 December with seven other officers and about a hundred men from artillery and infantry units. Slowed by an oxen-drawn cannon, the two companies moved cautiously along the twenty-foot-wide road through hostile territory. On the morning of 28 December 1835 an estimated 180 Seminoles led by Chief Micanopy ambushed the columns near the present-day city of Bushnell. Shot in the chest, Francis Langhorne Dade was killed in the first volley. After several hours of fighting the Seminoles withdrew. The survivors scraped together makeshift breastworks as the Indians prepared to renew the attack. When the fighting subsided, everyone in the expedition had been killed except for three soldiers who escaped. The dead lay unburied until 20 February 1836, when an American force reached the battlefield and interred the remains of enlisted men and officers in separate mass graves. In August 1842 the remains were moved to a military burying ground (later Saint Augustine National Cemetery) in Saint Augustine.

Known as the Dade Massacre, the battle precipitated the Second Seminole War, which lasted seven years. One year after the fight a new fort constructed on the south bank of the Withlacoochee River was named for Dade. The settlement that grew up in the shadow of the fort came to be known as the Fort Dade Community and, in the 1880s, Dade City. In Alabama a small town took the name of Dadeville, while Florida and Georgia each established counties named for Dade. Although he was not a graduate of the United States Military Academy, the school erected a monument in his honor in 1845. Each year since its founding in 1977 the Dade Battlefield Society, Inc., has reenacted the surprise attack at the Dade Battlefield Historic State Park.

Tyler's Quarterly 17 (1935): 55 (with birth date and parents' names), 58–59; *NCAB*, 12:196–197 (with incorrect names of parents); Francis B. Heitman, *Historical Register and Dictionary of the United States Army* (1903): 1:350; *Washington Daily National Intelligencer*, 4 Jan. 1828; Frank Laumer, *Massacre!* (1968) and *Dade's Last Command* (1995); William P. Duval to Secretary of War James Barbour, 29 Jan. 1827, Letters Received by the Office of Indian Affairs (1824–1881), Florida Superintendency (1824–1853), RG 75, NARA; accounts of battle and Dade's death in *Washington Daily National Intelligencer*, 25–27 Jan. 1836, and *Richmond Enquirer*, 26, 28, 30 Jan. 1836.

FRANK LAUMER

DADE, William Alexander Gibbons (1782 or 1783–15 October 1829), member-elect of the Convention of 1829–1830, was born probably in Stafford County and was the son of Langhorne Dade and Sarah Ashton Dade. Little is known about his education, but he studied law and by 1805 had begun practicing in Prince William County. In June 1805 Dade was appointed commonwealth's attorney for the district court that met in the county, and he held that position until becoming a judge eight years later. He acquired more than 1,000 acres of land in Prince William County, where his more than forty slaves raised wheat and other crops and tended cattle, sheep, hogs, and horses. By May 1809 Dade had married Elizabeth Westwood James. They had one daughter and three sons.

In 1807 Prince William County voters elected Dade to the House of Delegates. During his single one-year term he sat on the Committees on Claims, for Courts of Justice, and on Propositions and Grievances. In 1812 and 1813 Dade represented Fairfax and Prince William Counties in the Senate of Virginia but resigned his seat after the General Assembly elected him a judge of the General Court on 25 May 1813. On the bench he heard criminal appeals and cases involving fiscal matters. By virtue of his service on the General Court, Dade was also judge of the Third Circuit Court and presided over civil and criminal trials in Fairfax, King George, Lancaster, Northumberland, Prince William, Richmond, Stafford, and Westmoreland Counties. He remained a judge until his death sixteen years later. In 1828 he was a candidate for presidential elector for John Quincy Adams.

Valuing education, Dade served as a trustee for the new Dumfries academy in 1806 and in 1822 established a classical school for his own children and others in the vicinity. He also acquired a library of more than 400 volumes, primarily on legal topics. In 1818 the General Assembly appointed Dade to a commission authorized to determine a location for the new University of Virginia. He attended the meeting held at Rockfish Gap beginning on 1 August of that year and joined the majority who voted to place the school in Charlottesville. Dade was among the six commissioners at the meeting, including Thomas Jefferson and James Madison (1751–1836), chosen to compose a report on a plan for the school's organization and curriculum. In June 1825 Jefferson, having been turned down by several other men, offered Dade the position of law professor at the new university. He declined on the grounds that it would require too many "personal sacrifices" at a stage in his career when he was "tolerably well established."

In May 1829 Dade received the most votes of the four men elected to represent the counties of King George, Lancaster, Northumberland, Prince William, Richmond, Stafford, and Westmoreland in a convention called to revise the state constitution. On 5 October 1829, the day the convention opened, Dade, citing poor health, wrote to resign his seat. Five days later his letter was read and accepted by the convention, and on 12 October the district's remaining delegates

chose Alexander F. Rose as his replacement. Had Dade attended the convention, he likely would have voted with the other Tidewater delegates to limit the reforms sought by westerners, who called for extension of the suffrage and a more-equitable apportionment in the General Assembly. William Alexander Gibbons Dade did not survive to see the state's new constitution. He died on 15 October 1829 at his Clover Hill estate in Prince William County and was buried in the family plot at Effingham plantation, in that county.

French Biographies (with birth year of 1782); full name in Prince William Co. District Court Order Book (1804–1807), 165, 274; genealogical notes compiled by Dade printed as "Some Dade History" in Sigismunda Mary Frances Chapman, *A History of Chapman and Alexander Families* (1946), 175–178; variant birth year of 1785 in Susan Rogers Morton, "Effingham" (typescript dated 31 Aug. 1937), 4, in Works Progress Administration, Virginia Historical Inventory, LVA; election as judge in *JHD*, 1813–1814 sess., 38; *JHD*, 1818–1819 sess., 9–10; *Fredericksburg Virginia Herald*, 9 Feb. 1822, 11 Oct. 1828; Thomas Jefferson to Dade, 21 June 1825, and Dade to Jefferson, 30 June, 28 July (quotations) 1825, Thomas Jefferson Papers, LC; *Richmond Enquirer*, 29 May, 2 June 1829; *Proceedings and Debates of 1829–1830 Convention*, 23; estate inventory in Prince William Co. Will Book, N:279–283; obituaries in *Alexandria Phenix Gazette*, 20 Oct. 1829, *Fredericksburg Virginia Herald*, 21 Oct. 1829 (reporting death "in the 47th year of his age"), and *Richmond Enquirer* and *Richmond Whig*, both 22 Oct. 1829.

MARIANNE E. JULIENNE

DAILEY, Daphne Lowell (2 October 1912–3 October 1995), journalist, was born in Madison County, Arkansas, and was the daughter of Ozzie L. Dailey and Ada Jane Mullins Dailey. She graduated from high school in Fayetteville and in 1932 received a bachelor's degree in journalism from the University of Arkansas. Dailey pursued graduate studies in English and history at that institution until 1934. While a student she worked at the university newspaper and later as a reporter for the *Fayetteville Daily Democrat*. From 1934 to 1936 Dailey taught journalism at a high school and junior college in Fort Smith, Arkansas, where she met Clara Margaret Payne, with whom she later formed a business partnership.

In July 1936, after Payne secured a divorce, she and Dailey moved to Caroline County, Virginia, and purchased the weekly Bowling Green newspaper, the *Caroline Progress*. Dailey edited the paper, Payne was business manager, and the latter's son Howard Allen Payne served as publisher. They also purchased Tappahannock's weekly, the *Rappahannock Times*, but sold it in 1938. In November 1936 Dailey and Clara Payne bought the *Quantico Sentry* (later the *Quantico Marine Sentry*), the newspaper circulated at Marine Corps bases throughout the world, and published it until July 1944.

As editor of the *Caroline Progress*, Dailey began to make her mark locally with editorials that encouraged and initiated change within the county. In 1940 Washington and Lee University's Lee School of Journalism and the Virginia Press Association honored her with the Lee Editorial Award for distinguished writing and service to the community. Throughout the previous year Dailey had run a sometimes controversial series of editorials that called for the county to establish a public health unit, a goal accomplished in 1941. Dailey strongly opposed the United States Army's plan to locate a new training facility in Caroline County, in part because the proposed 110,000-acre camp would displace hundreds of residents and encompass about a third of the county's territory, including most of its best farmland. Once Camp A. P. Hill had been established in June 1941, however, *Caroline Progress* editorials encouraged readers to accept the army's decision and provided free advertising to farmers selling their land.

Throughout her years at the *Progress*, Dailey continued to make outstanding contributions to journalism. Her editorials commented on a variety of issues, ranging from federal programs, national elections, and international collaboration by the United States to such local concerns as support for the Red Cross, the War Fund, and the construction of a cannery. Other editorials chided local officers and boards for their inability to plan appropriately for Caroline County's future. In 1943 the Virginia Press Association presented Dailey with an award for outstanding editorial leadership in weekly newspapers. The following year the organization recognized her persistent community involvement and her emphasis on providing the best in local news with its Distinguished Service Award. Dailey chaired the VPA's Legislative Committee from 1943 to 1944. She became a vice president in July 1944 and was unanimously elected the first female president of the press association in July 1945. During her one-year term the association instituted a program of inviting foreign journalists to work temporarily with Virginia newspapers and to report on life in America.

Dailey and Payne sold the *Caroline Progress* in the autumn of 1947. Two years later Dailey began working for the Bank of Virginia as the director of advertising and public relations. In 1962 the bank named her a vice president. Maintaining residences in Richmond and Bowling Green, Dailey was active in the community affairs of both localities. She volunteered with the Caroline County American Red Cross and served on the board of directors for the Richmond chapter. During World War II, Dailey chaired the Caroline County Junior Red Cross and the public information committee of the Caroline County War Fund. She served as the first female president of the Richmond Public Relations Association during the 1952–1953 term. In 1968 the governor appointed Dailey to the Advisory Committee on Emergency Medical Services. She wrote two histories, *The First Seventy Years, 1902–1972: A History of Union Bank and Trust Company* (1972) and *Queen Caroline* (1981).

Dailey never married and had no children. In 1985 she returned to her native state. On 3 October 1995 Daphne Lowell Dailey died in Springdale, Arkansas. She was buried at Fairview Memorial Gardens, in Fayetteville.

Biographical information in *Richmond Times-Dispatch*, 20 July 1941 (several pors.); Daphne Dailey Papers, University of Arkansas, Fayetteville; other publications include Dailey, "The Bank of Virginia," *Virginia and the Virginia County* 6 (July 1952): 18–19; *Quantico Sentry*, 24 Nov. 1936; *Richmond News Leader*, 26 Jan. 1940, 29 Jan. 1945; *Richmond Times-Dispatch*, 28 Jan. 1945, 18 Sept. 1962; *Commonwealth* 7 (Feb. 1940): 18; ibid. 12 (July 1945): 17; Virginia Press Association *Bulletin* 25 (Feb. 1943): 6; ibid. 27 (Feb. 1945): 1, 12; ibid. 27 (July 1945): 1, 8; ibid. 28 (Feb. 1946): 12, 21; ibid. 28 (Sept. 1946): 6, 10–11; ibid. 29 (Oct. 1947): 7; obituaries in *Bowling Green Caroline Progress* and *Fayetteville Northwest Arkansas Times*, both 11 Oct. 1995.

CASSANDRA BRITT FARRELL

DALE, Sir Thomas (d. 9 August 1619), deputy governor of Virginia and member of the Council, may have been a member of the Dale family of Surrey County, England, or of an Anglo-Dutch family. No known documents record the date and place of his birth, the names of his parents, or any details about his education. He wrote equally well in English and Dutch, was probably fluent in French, knew at least some Latin, and was a deeply committed Protestant. Dale stated late in 1617 that he had begun his lifelong career in the military as a common soldier in the service of the States General of the Netherlands about thirty years earlier, at which time England and the Netherlands were at war with Spain. By 1594 he was a captain in the English army. Dale may have volunteered without a commission to fight against the Spanish, as young gentlemen seldom served in the ranks, and men from the laboring and yeoman classes seldom became officers. He may also have made a socially and financially advantageous first marriage about which nothing is now known.

In 1598 and 1599 Dale commanded an English company in Ireland under Robert Devereux, second earl of Essex, and was briefly detained two years later after the earl was charged with treason. Dale was personally known to Henry IV, the king of France, on whose recommendation the States General appointed him captain of a Dutch infantry company in August 1603. England's James I knighted him on 19 June 1606. Dale was evidently close to King James's young son and heir, Prince Henry, who early in 1611 requested that the States General grant Dale a three-year leave of absence without pay to serve in Virginia. Dale married Elizabeth Throckmorton before he departed for Virginia in the spring of 1611; they are not known to have had any children.

The Virginia Company of London, in which Dale owned shares, appointed him the colony's marshal, or the army officer in charge of discipline and order. The company also designated him deputy, or acting, governor in the event that both the governor, Thomas West, baron De La Warr, and the lieutenant governor, Sir Thomas Gates, were absent from Virginia. Dale and about 300 well-armed soldiers reached the colony in May 1611. He immediately issued orders to erect palisades at the James River settlements to secure them from attack. With De La Warr and Gates both out of the colony, Dale was acting governor until Gates returned in August 1611. Dale was a member of the governor's Council after March 1612 and was acting governor again from March 1614 to April 1616.

On 22 June 1611 Dale issued military regulations under which his soldiers were to act while in Virginia. They supplemented civil orders that De La Warr and Gates had promulgated in 1610 at the company's direction. In 1612 the combined orders were printed in London with the title *For The Colony in Virginea Britannia. Lawes Divine, Morall and Martiall, &c.* The civil orders prescribed severe corporal punishment or death for many infractions, as did Dale's military code. Although sharply criticized for governing Virginia by brutal martial law, Dale did not hesitate to impose the severe penalties specified by the codes, including forced labor, capital punishment, and condemning a man who stole food to be tied to a tree and left to starve to death as a warning to others. The civilian and military regulations, harsh as they were, were not notably more severe than the orders that other English officers imposed in Ireland and elsewhere, and by the standards of the time the soldiers and many of the residents of Virginia were not all entitled to the protections of the common law.

Dale's imposition of discipline and his directions for organizing necessary work converted the fractious, inefficient colony into a reasonably well-run military and commercial outpost. As soon as he arrived, Dale ordered men to sow grain and tend the large stock of cattle and swine that the company had sent to Virginia. In June 1611 he attacked and defeated the Nansemond Indians and burned their towns. Later in the summer he marched against Indians farther up the James River and established a settlement on a bluff that he called the City of Henrico, or Henricus, in honor of his patron Prince Henry. In December, Dale attacked the Appamattuck towns in that vicinity and later founded on their land the settlement known as Bermuda Hundred. After Samuel Argall, later deputy governor of Virginia, captured Pocahontas early in 1613, Dale held her as a guarantee of peace with her father, Powhatan. Dale and Alexander Whitaker, the minister at Jamestown and Henricus, directed her conversion to Christianity, and in 1614 Dale assented to her marriage to John Rolfe.

The first professional military man in Virginia to command a large and properly equipped force, Dale succeeded where previous commanders had failed and earned commendations from company officers, the king, and some of the surviving colonists. His campaigns against the Indians were the concluding actions in the First Anglo-Powhatan War and allowed the colonists to live in comparative peace for nearly a decade. Dale fended off a Spanish incursion into Virginia and reportedly threatened to hang some French Jesuits who, en route to New France, were driven into Virginia during a storm. His stern enforcement of discipline and careful husbandry of the colony's livestock and other resources helped make Virginia largely self-sufficient within five years and marked the end of the repeated failings that had plagued the colony's founding. Dale sent samples of iron to England, established a fishing settlement and saltworks on the Eastern Shore at a site called Dale's Gift, and acquired property near Henricus.

When his three-year leave of absence expired in 1614, Dale was more than ready to leave Virginia and resume command of his Dutch company, but he stayed on, and the king himself requested that the States General extend his leave of absence. Dale finally left Virginia with John Rolfe and Pocahontas in the spring of 1616, having had primary responsibility for the colony's military affairs and a major role in its governance for more than half of its nine-year history. He returned to England with a cargo showing what the colony could produce: pitch, potash, sassafras, sturgeon (and caviar), and tobacco, among other commodities. The cargo and the condition of the colony presented vivid contrasts to Virginia's desperate straits at the time that the company had recruited Dale to take charge of its defenses. Safely home in England, he boasted that he had "returned from the hardest taske that ever I undertooke & by the blessing of god have wth poor means left the Collonye in great prosperitye & peace contrarye to many men's expectation."

Late in 1617 Dale petitioned the States General for full pay for the whole time of his absence,

which with the assistance of the English ambassador he received. Rather than resume his career in the Netherlands, he took command of another large-scale and important enterprise, an English force that the East India Company sent to the Indian Ocean to counter the commercial influence of the Dutch East India Company. Dale wrote a short will on 20 February 1618 leaving to his wife his estates in England and Virginia, which his widow still owned at the time of her death in 1640. En route to India, Dale almost drowned in an accident at Penguin Island, off the coast of modern-day Namibia. In December 1618 he engaged Dutch forces in heavy fighting off the coast of Java, where he occupied Dutch trading posts. The following summer Sir Thomas Dale sailed to Machilipatnam, or Masulipatam, on the east coast of India, where he became ill and died on 9 August 1619. He was buried there in a tomb erected for the purpose.

Biographies in Massachusetts Historical Society *Collections*, 4th ser., 9 (1871): 52–59, and Alexander Brown, *The Genesis of the United States* (1890), 2:869–874, as corrected by Darrett B. Rutman, "The Historian and the Marshal: A Note on the Background of Sir Thomas Dale," *VMHB* 68 (1960): 284–294, and David Dewey Scarboro Jr., "Sir Thomas Dale: A Study of the Marshal and Deputy-Governor of Virginia" (M.A. thesis, Emory University, 1963); J. Frederick Fausz, "An 'Abundance of Blood Shed on Both Sides': England's First Indian War, 1609–1614," *VMHB* 98 (1990): 3–56; Vaughn Baker, "The Elusive Marshall of Virginia: Sir Thomas Dale, Third Governor of Virginia, Research Manuscript" (2003), with undocumented marriage date of 19 Feb. 1611 on 59 and n. 58, VHS; photocopies of documents from National Archives of the Netherlands, The Hague, at VHS, and those and others abstracted and printed in translation in E. B. O'Callaghan, ed., *Documents Relative to the Colonial History of the State of New-York* (1856), 1:1–3, 9–10, 17–21; documents concerning Dale and some letters from various collections printed or abstracted in Kingsbury, *Virginia Company*, Ralph Hamor, *A True Discourse of the Present Estate of Virginia* (1615), and Sainsbury, *Calendar of State Papers, Colonial Series: East Indies, China and Japan, 1617–1621*, and *Colonial Series: America and West Indies, 1675–1676, also Addenda, 1574–1674*; Dale to Sir Ralph Winwood, 3 June 1616, PRO CO 1/1, fols. 113–114 (quotation); contrasting discussions of Dale's laws in Walter F. Prince, "The First Criminal Code of Virginia," *Annual Report of the American Historical Association for the Year 1899* (1900), 1:309–363, *For The Colony in Virginea Britannia: Lawes Divine, Morall and Martiall, Etc., Compiled by William Strachey*, ed. David H. Flaherty (1969), xi–xxxvii, and David Thomas Konig, "'Dale's Laws' and the Non–Common Law Origins of Criminal Justice in Virginia," in Eric H. Monkkonen, ed., *Crime and Justice in American History* (1991),

Dale

1:368–389; William H. Gaines Jr., "The Discipline of Sir Thomas Dale," *Virginia Cavalcade* 3 (spring 1954): 14 (por.); will in Prerogative Court of Canterbury, Dale 1; death date in narrative of Martin Pring in Samuel Purchas, *Purchas His Pilgrimes* (1625; repr. 1905–1907), 5:21.

BRENT TARTER

DALGLEISH, John (bap. 27 February 1726–September 1771), physician, was the son of Robert Dalgleish, a clergyman, and Susanna Symmer Dalgleish. He was born in Linlithgow, Linlithgowshire (later West Lothian), Scotland, and was baptized there on 27 February 1726. While still young he and two of his brothers immigrated to Gloucester County, Virginia, probably with their maternal uncle, a physician named John Symmer. The fear of contagious diseases that Dalgleish witnessed during his boyhood led him to study medicine, most likely informally under the tutelage of his uncle, as did his elder brother Alexander Dalgleish, who lived in Gloucester County until his death in September 1770. Neither man married or had children, so they left scant records of their lives in the colony. Their younger brother Robert Dalgleish, who probably had no surviving children either, was a Gloucester County merchant who died in March 1770.

By the mid-1750s Dalgleish was practicing medicine in Chesterfield County and studying contagious diseases. He recorded how different classes of people, both free and enslaved, contracted and reacted to infectious diseases, and he also noted how diseases spread among horses and dogs. He deduced that the most contagious afflictions were imported: fatal intestinal complaints arrived from Africa aboard slave-trading ships; jail fever entered Virginia aboard vessels transporting convicts to the colonies from England and Ireland; yellow fever arrived on ships that traded with the West Indies; and smallpox reached Virginia from many parts of the world. Dalgleish read the scientific literature but also experimented with unconventional treatments and was one of the few physicians then in the colony known to have inoculated against smallpox. He carefully observed the effects of inoculation administered at different stages of the disease and with material obtained from poxes at different states of maturity. Beginning about

1758 Dalgleish inoculated fifty or sixty people. Only one of them died, a much higher rate of survival than among people who contracted the disease naturally.

Dalgleish moved to Norfolk early in the 1760s and practiced with Archibald Campbell, but Campbell gradually relinquished medicine for commerce and left Dalgleish as one of the port's few physicians and perhaps manager of an apothecary shop. In June 1768, in spite of opposition from many local citizens, Dalgleish inoculated some of Campbell's family members and the families of several other prominent merchants, among them James Parker and Cornelius Calvert, the mayor of Norfolk. Even though the persons inoculated were sequestered about three miles from town, a mob attacked the residences of Calvert, Campbell, and Parker. Outraged opponents denounced Dalgleish for trying to start an epidemic in order to increase his business. An attempt to prosecute Dalgleish failed in the General Court at the April 1769 session because inoculation was not a crime, but the incident provoked a hot debate between the governor and some members of the Council about the potential dangers and benefits of inoculation. A separate trial resulted in the conviction of several leaders of the 1768 riot.

In May 1769 Calvert asked Dalgleish to inoculate an employee who had been exposed to smallpox, action that led to a second riot. Afterward the doctor was jailed, and he and Parker were formally charged in June with disturbing the peace. A writ of habeas corpus removed the case from the jurisdiction of the Norfolk County Court to the General Court, where it languished while Parker repeatedly attempted without success to have it transferred to London.

The two riots and the trial pitted native Virginians against Scottish merchants but also divided Norfolk families, such as Mayor Calvert's, whose brothers were among the most virulent opponents of inoculation. Dalgleish published more than half a dozen long letters in the Williamsburg newspapers to explain and defend his medical practice, and his critics and defenders also published their own versions of events. This public discussion inflamed passions of both advocates and opponents of inoculation. In the spring of 1769 angry Norfolk County residents petitioned the General Assembly demanding a law to prohibit inoculation, and other petitioners asked for strict regulation of the practice. The following year the assembly forbade inoculation except of persons who might have been exposed to smallpox and even then only authorized the procedure with the consent of the local magistrates.

The case of the *King* v. *John Dalgleish* was still pending when John Dalgleish died in Norfolk late in September 1771, possibly of yellow fever. It is not known where he was buried.

Baptismal date in Linlithgow Parish Register, 3:248, New Register House, Edinburgh, Scot.; identity of father and death in Sept. 1771 confirmed in Norfolk Co. Deed Book, 26: fols. 242–244; biographical details in Dalgleish's letters in *Williamsburg Virginia Gazette* (Purdie and Dixon), 14 Apr., 20 Oct., 17 Nov. 1768, 20 Apr. 1769, 8 Nov. 1770, and *Williamsburg Virginia Gazette* (Rind), 24 Nov. 1768, 2 Nov. 1769, 15 Mar. 1770; Norfolk Co. Order Book (1768–1771), fol. 99; riots described in *Williamsburg Virginia Gazette* (Rind), 25 Aug. 1768 (supplement), *Williamsburg Virginia Gazette* (Purdie and Dixon), 8 Sept. 1768 (supplement), 9 Jan. 1772, and letters of Margaret Parker to James Steuart, 21 Aug. 1768, and James Parker to Charles Steuart, May 1769–June 1773, Charles Steuart Papers, National Library of Scotland, Edinburgh, Scot.; Patrick Henderson, "Smallpox and Patriotism: The Norfolk Riots, 1768–1769," *VMHB* 73 (1965): 413–424; death notice without date in *Williamsburg Virginia Gazette* (Purdie and Dixon), 3 Oct. 1771.

BRENT TARTER

DALTON, Grady William (19 June 1908–5 March 1986), civic leader, was born in Stuart and was the son of Lilla Shockley Dalton and Booker Dalton, a longtime commissioner of revenue who represented Patrick County in the House of Delegates for one term. Dalton grew up on a farm and attended the local high school before moving to Bluefield, West Virginia, where he worked in a coal company commissary and a clothing shop. In 1930 he traveled to Chicago, where on 19 June he married Freya Louise Howell, whom he had met in Patrick County. They had one son. Dalton took a job with the Commercial Bank of Bluefield in 1934. He completed coursework offered by the American Institute of Banking, held at nearby Bluefield College in Virginia, and earned promotion to assistant cashier. In 1940 Dalton moved to Richlands to become cashier at the Richlands National Bank. For about ten years he occasionally taught at the American Institute of Banking.

Although warned that the town could not support a second newspaper, Dalton founded the *Richlands Press*, incorporated on 24 August 1944 with himself as president. The first issue appeared on 25 January 1945. His weekly column, "Around the Hills and Down the Cricks," ran for at least six years. Mixing light topics and folksy humor, the column also addressed such concerns as enforcement of game and fishing laws and pollution of the Clinch River. Dalton opposed what he regarded as an elitist group of leading citizens who exerted undue social and political influence over community affairs.

On a slow news-day in June 1947 Dalton lightheartedly agreed to demonstrate the veracity of the journalistic adage that, although a dog biting a man is not news, a man biting a dog is. Newspapers across the country and overseas carried an Associated Press photograph of the banker using his teeth to lift a small dog. Dalton resigned as president of the *Richlands Press* in 1966 and sold it to Southwest Virginia Newspapers, Inc. He sat on the board of directors, which merged the *Press* with the *Richlands News Progress* to form the *Richlands News-Press*.

In January 1945 the aeronautic division of the State Corporation Commission identified Richlands as a suitable site for an airfield. Fascinated by flight and recognizing the benefits of having a local airport, Dalton arranged for the purchase of a tract of land and with a former navy flight instructor formed Clinch Valley Airways. In February the SCC authorized the company to build and operate a commercial airport, and by June the facility had opened for business. Expecting individual flying to become popular, the company sponsored a series of articles on flight instruction that appeared in the *Richlands Press* beginning in September. Over the next seven years more than 350 students, many of them World War II veterans, attended the airport's flight school. Dalton himself learned to fly and purchased the first of several airplanes. He organized the Richlands Squadron Civil Air Patrol in 1945 and was commanding officer for the next twelve years.

In 1946 Dalton acquired full ownership of Clinch Valley Airways. He became president when the company incorporated in 1950, but mounting financial considerations compelled him to sell the facility two years later. Dalton's activities earned him appointment in 1950 to a vacated seat on the state Advisory Committee on Aviation. He served until 1952 and again from 1954 until 1962, for part of that time as chair. The Virginia Department of Aviation awarded him a certificate of recognition in 1983 for distinguished service in promoting aviation, and in November 1985 he was inducted into the Virginia Aviation Hall of Fame.

A Democrat, Dalton in 1957 won election to Tazewell County's seat in the House of Delegates. Unopposed in the next four elections, he scored narrow victories over opponents in 1967 and 1969. During fourteen years in office Dalton served on the Committees on Education and on Mining and Mineral Resources and chaired the latter for three sessions. He also sat at various times on the Committees on Appropriations, on Health, Welfare, and Institutions, on Manufactures and Mechanic Arts, and on Public Institutions. During legislative sessions Dalton wrote weekly reports for the Richlands newspaper. On 9 January 1962 he was elected secretary of the Democratic caucus. He was appointed to two-year terms on the advisory board on the state budget in 1965, 1967, and 1969.

Dalton sponsored bills that increased limits on coal-truck tonnage and in 1962 was instrumental in creating Richlands Municipal Airport. Committed to education, he chaired the Clinch Valley College advisory board for two terms, served on the executive committee of the Rural Affairs Study Commission, and sponsored a bill that located Southwest Virginia Community College in Richlands. Dalton supported Massive Resistance policies during the emergency legislative sessions in 1959 and also introduced a bill allowing teachers who wished to avoid working in integrated public schools to cancel their contracts. When the General Assembly met in 1969 to rewrite Virginia's constitution, Dalton drafted an amendment, modeled on the right-to-bear-arms provision in the United States Constitution, that was incorporated in the new state constitution.

In 1971 Dalton's district was redrawn to encompass three counties with two delegate seats. After he failed to win his party's endorsement at the district nominating convention, he ran as an independent. Dalton carried Tazewell County but fared poorly in Buchanan and Russell Counties and was not reelected. His political career over, he continued his banking and real estate pursuits. In May 1985 Dalton retired as president and chairman of the board of Richlands National Bank.

A keen sportsman, Dalton also kept bees, enjoyed firing muzzle-loading rifles, and collected vintage cars and firearms. He moved a reassembled Methodist log church and a Civil War cannon onto his property, and he was proud of a reputed family connection to the notorious Dalton Gang. He was president and lieutenant governor of the Richlands Kiwanis, director of the Richlands Area Industrial Development Corporation, a state counselor for the Junior Order United American Mechanics, and president of the local chamber of commerce. Grady William Dalton suffered from colon cancer and died of cardiopulmonary arrest on 5 March 1986 at the University of Virginia Medical Center in Charlottesville. He was buried in Stuart Cemetery, in Patrick County.

Birth date, family papers, and other information provided by son Richard Dalton and granddaughter Anne Dalton Boothe (both 2004); biographical file, Virginia Aviation Museum, Richmond; E. Griffith Dodson, *The General Assembly of the Commonwealth of Virginia, 1940–1960* (1961), 519–520; Cook Co., Ill., Marriage License; SCC Charter Book, 205:337–338, 234:46–47; *Richlands Press*, 19 June 1947 (por.), 26 Feb., 11 Mar., 6 May 1948, 22 Jan. 1959, 31 Oct. 1963 (por.); *Newport News Daily Press*, 2 June 1957; *Clinch Valley News*, 8 Nov. 1957; *Richlands News-Press*, 9 Nov. 1967, 5 Nov. 1969, 21 Oct. 1970, 15 Sept., 3 Nov. 1971; *Richmond Times-Dispatch*, 18 Nov. 1985; obituaries in *Richmond Times-Dispatch* and *Roanoke Times and World-News*, both 6 Mar. 1986, and *Clinch Valley News*, 12 Mar. 1986 (por.).

DONALD W. GUNTER

DALTON, John Nichols (11 July 1931–30 July 1986), governor of Virginia, was born John Clay Nichols, in Emporia. His parents, Jessie Snow Turner Nichols and her first husband, Luther Clay Nichols, a baker, divorced when he was young. He divided his time between his mother's house in Bedford (she later married J. Clyde Key, of that city) and the childless family of his mother's sister, Mary Lou Turner Dalton, and her husband, Theodore Roosevelt Dalton, of Radford. His aunt and uncle adopted him and changed his name to John Nichols Dalton. He graduated from Radford High School and attended the College of William and Mary, where he was president of the student body in his senior year and a member of the Reserve Officer Training Corps. Dalton completed his senior-year studies and first-year law coursework simultaneously. He graduated with an A.B. in 1953 and entered the University of Virginia as a second-year law student but in 1954 began two years of active duty in an army field artillery command. On 18 February 1956 Dalton married Edwina Jeanette Panzer in Jeffersonville, Indiana. They had two daughters and two sons.

Dalton completed his legal education, received a B.L. from the University of Virginia in 1957, and joined his adoptive father's Radford law firm. In addition to Ted Dalton, who was a leader of the Republican Party of Virginia, a member of the Senate of Virginia, and later a United States district court judge, the other partners were Richard Harding Poff, then a congressman and later a judge of the Supreme Court of Virginia, and James Clinton Turk, who also became a United States district court judge. Dalton practiced law in Radford, acquired several large tracts of land in the area, and took part in civic affairs. Following his uncle into Republican Party politics, he worked in campaigns and served in many responsible capacities. He was president of the Young Republican Federation in Virginia in 1959 and 1960 and a member of the Republican Party's central committee from 1959 to 1972.

In 1965 Dalton won election to the first of three consecutive two-year terms in the House of Delegates representing Radford and Montgomery County. One of a small minority of House Republicans, who until that time had seldom been named to influential standing committees, he was appointed to low-ranking seats on the Committee on Labor and the relatively inconsequential Committees on Manufactures and Mechanic Arts and on Retrenchment and

Economy. In his second term Dalton also served on the more-important Committee for Courts of Justice and in his third on the Committee on Appropriations and the Committee on Mining and Mineral Resources. Perhaps the most important debates in which he took part were in the special session of 1969 when the General Assembly acted as a constitutional convention and rewrote the state constitution. Dalton proposed a failed amendment that a judicial selection commission recommend persons to the governor for appointment to the state bench and that voters approve or reject the judge after he or she had served for a specified time. He also unsuccessfully tried to include a provision mandating that local governing bodies select school boards. Although Dalton questioned some aspects of the new constitution, he voted on 17 February 1970 to submit it to the voters, who ratified it in a referendum.

Following a reapportionment of the assembly in 1971, voters in Radford and the counties of Carroll, Floyd, Montgomery, and Wythe elected Dalton to the House of Delegates. He retained his seats on the same committees he had served on during his third term. In 1972 Dalton won a special election to fill a vacant seat in the Senate of Virginia representing the counties of Carroll, Floyd, Grayson, and Montgomery and the cities of Galax and Radford. He sat on the Committees on Commerce and Labor, for Courts of Justice, and on Local Government. During his single session in the Senate, Dalton was chief patron of a bill to issue revenue bonds supporting higher education.

In 1973 the Republican State Convention nominated Dalton for lieutenant governor and selected former Democratic governor Mills Edwin Godwin Jr. as the Republican gubernatorial candidate. In the general election Dalton defeated the Democratic nominee, James Harry Michael, later a United States district court judge, and independent candidate Flora S. Crater after a campaign in which most of the attention was focused on Godwin's contest with Lieutenant Governor Henry Evans Howell Jr. Dalton attempted to raise the profile of the lieutenant governor's office, which he believed should be a full-time position.

Dalton easily won the party's nomination for governor in 1977. In his race against Howell, this time the Democratic candidate, Dalton mounted a fiscally conservative, small government, pro-business campaign. He and his supporters attacked Howell as a dangerous liberal closely allied with organized labor. In a campaign characterized by deep differences of opinion between the two candidates and personal attacks by both parties, Dalton cancelled scheduled public debates with Howell. Dalton, overwhelmingly successful in traditionally Republican western districts and in the state's growing suburbs, won the election on 8 November 1977 with almost 56 percent of the vote.

As governor of Virginia from 14 January 1978 to 16 January 1982, Dalton worked productively with the General Assembly, in which conservative Democrats still held the majority. He emphasized economical management of the state bureaucracy and reduced the rate of growth in the number of state employees. Dalton settled a legal dispute, which Godwin had insisted on pursuing, with the federal government over desegregation of higher education in Virginia. In spite of the fiscal conservatism that was one of his trademarks, in 1980 Dalton proposed an increase of four cents per gallon in the state gasoline tax in order to provide money for highway construction (the assembly agreed to an increase of two cents). He also supported creating a law school at George Mason University and a new school of veterinary medicine at Virginia Polytechnic Institute and State University. Dalton made several trips overseas to improve trade between Virginia and foreign countries. When coal miners went on strike in southwestern Virginia and some violence resulted, he placed the National Guard on alert and sent in state troopers, actions that union officials denounced as anti-union strikebreaking. In October 1979 Dalton began a year-long term as chair of the Southern Governors' Association.

In December 1981 Dalton vetoed a redistricting bill that preserved the tradition of not having legislative districts bisect county or city boundaries. Legislators then for the first time had to redistrict the assembly entirely with single-member districts. As an unanticipated long-term consequence of that redistricting, Republican candidates found it easier to win election in single-member districts than they had in the large multimember districts that Democrats had traditionally dominated. During the ensuing years Republican membership increased in both houses of the General Assembly.

Virginia Democrats and some veteran journalists regarded Dalton's administration as more intensely partisan than those of his immediate predecessors, both Republicans. He occasionally had a testy relationship with the press and attempted to keep the Capitol press corps at a distance from his office. Dalton drew sharp public criticism on several occasions, for awarding a political ally and consultant a large state contract, for choosing expensive and showy modes of transportation for his administration while reining in the travel budgets of other state employees, and for purging political correspondence from the official office files even after it had been deposited in the state archives.

Prohibited by the state constitution from seeking reelection in 1981, Dalton joined the Richmond law firm of McGuire Woods and Battle and lived in suburban Henrico County after leaving the governor's mansion. Although he did not smoke, Dalton learned in 1983 that he had lung cancer, which was treated with surgery. Evidently enjoying the practice of corporate law and service on the boards of several major Virginia corporations, he declined to consider campaigning for governor again in 1985. The following year, the cancer returned, and John Nichols Dalton died in a Richmond hospital on 30 July 1986. After funeral services in Richmond and in Radford, he was interred in Sunrise Burial Park, in Radford. His widow (who later married John Burwell Phillips) won election to the Senate of Virginia from Henrico County in 1987 and was the unsuccessful Republican Party nominee for lieutenant governor in 1989.

Biographies in Richard Lobb, "63rd Governor of the Commonwealth of Virginia—John Nichols Dalton," *Virginia Record* 100 (Jan. 1978): 13–22, 87–88, and Manarin, *Senate Officers*, 178–181 (por.); family information provided by widow, Edwina Jeanette Panzer Dalton Phillips (2005); *Proceedings and Debates of the Virginia House of Delegates Pertaining to Amendment of the Constitution, Extra Session 1969, Regular Session 1970* (1970), esp. 125–130, 282, 782;

feature article in *Washington Post*, 29 May 1977; Ted Dalton Papers, W&M; John Nichols Dalton Executive Papers, RG 3, LVA; excerpts of retrospective conference held in Charlottesville, 20–21 July 2000, in *Richmond Times-Dispatch*, 23 July 2000, John H. Chichester, "The Legacy of Governor Dalton," *Virginia News Letter* 76 (Aug. 2000), and *No Higher Honor: John N. Dalton, Governor of Virginia, 1978–1982*, video recording (Commonwealth Public Broadcasting, 2001); obituaries in *Radford News Journal, Richmond News Leader, Richmond Times-Dispatch, Roanoke Times and World-News*, and *Washington Post*, all 31 July 1986; editorial tributes in *Roanoke Times and World-News* and *Richmond Times-Dispatch*, both 31 July 1986, and *Radford News Journal* and *Washington Post*, both 1 Aug. 1986.

BRENT TARTER

DALTON, Theodore Roosevelt (3 July 1901–30 October 1989), Republican Party leader and United States district court judge, was born in Carroll County and was the son of Currell Dalton, a merchant and farmer, and Lodoska V. Martin Dalton. At age sixteen Ted Dalton, as he was always known, began taking high school courses at the College of William and Mary. He attended the University of Virginia for one year and then returned to William and Mary, where he received an A.B. in 1924 and a B.L. in 1926. Dalton joined a small law firm in Radford. His later law partners included James Clinton Turk, who became a United States district court judge. On 4 January 1932 Dalton married Mary Lou Turner. They had no children but adopted her sister's son, John Clay Nichols. At the time of the adoption they changed his name to John Nichols Dalton. He joined Dalton's law firm and from 1978 to 1982 served as governor of Virginia.

Dalton was commonwealth's attorney for the city of Radford from 1929 to 1937. Appointed in 1941 to a Virginia Advisory Legislative Council subcommittee that studied the poll tax, he signed the subcommittee's report calling for abolition of the tax as a prerequisite for voting. After a close but unsuccessful Republican candidacy for the House of Delegates in 1939, Dalton was elected to fill a vacancy in the Senate of Virginia in February 1944. His victory was an extraordinary achievement. Running as a write-in candidate in a predominantly Democratic district (Radford and the counties of Franklin, Montgomery, and Roanoke), Dalton launched an intense weeklong campaign against four opponents and won a narrow victory. When

he took office a few days later, he was one of only two Republicans in the forty-member Senate. During his years in the Democratically controlled chamber, Dalton received low-ranking seats on the Committees on Agriculture, Mining, and Manufacturing, for Courts of Justice, and on Public Institutions and Education and occasionally on other, less-influential committees. In 1947 he faced a difficult reelection campaign against a formidable opponent and a united Democratic Party, but he was a popular man and a tireless campaigner and eked out another narrow victory. After Dalton won reelection by larger margins in 1951 and 1955, he gained a reputation as the most electable Republican in the state. He was never able to persuade the Senate's Democratic leaders to name Republicans to their share of influential committees.

As the most successful young Republican in Virginia at mid-century, Dalton sought to change the political status quo and make Virginia into a vigorous two-party state in every election at every level of government. In a guest column entitled "The Virginia GOP Feels Hamstrung" in the *Washington Post* on 3 September 1950, he described the obstacles the Virginia Republican Party faced. Its political organization was inefficient, its most talented members refused to run for office, and a defeatist attitude permeated the ranks. Republicans also faced a residue of Civil War–era prejudices that Democrats exploited. Democrats controlled the redistricting process, placed restrictions on registration and voting, and monopolized the appointive power. A key element in every Dalton campaign was electoral reform.

Dalton mounted unsuccessful candidacies for state Republican Party chair in 1944 and national committeeman in 1948. He won a seat on the national committee in 1952 after carefully navigating between the groups in the state party backing Dwight David Eisenhower and Robert Alphonso Taft for the presidential nomination. Dalton endorsed Eisenhower only after the Virginia delegation to the Republican National Convention, a majority of whom supported Taft, had elected him to the national committee.

Although Dalton preferred to wait until 1957, he was under intense pressure to run for governor in 1953 and in that year mounted the most serious Republican challenge to Democratic control of state government in three-quarters of a century. His progressive views contrasted with those of the dominant conservative Democratic faction headed by his friend, United States senator Harry Flood Byrd (1887–1966). Dalton's "Program of Progress" summarized his commitment to move Virginia forward and create a statewide two-party system. His proposals included abolition of the poll tax, reform of the absentee-voters law, limits on campaign spending, lowering the voting age to eighteen, popular election of school boards, nonpartisan selection of judges, removal of judges' appointive powers, increased spending on education and state hospitals, and establishment of a community college system.

Dalton's campaign energized his supporters and appealed to many independents and anti-organization Democrats. Tall, slim, and silver-haired, he commanded attention and was an effective, inspiring speaker on the campaign trail. His opponent, Thomas Bahnson Stanley, a congressman and former Speaker of the House of Delegates, was a Byrd organization stalwart. His campaign speeches were dull, and his reluctance to take positions on issues contrasted starkly and unfavorably with Dalton's forthrightness. Even though no Republican candidate for governor in the twentieth century had ever received more than 37 percent of the vote, knowledgeable observers were predicting late in September that Dalton might win. The following month brought events that jeopardized his chances for victory, however. The indictment of the Democratic campaign manager on an income tax charge in mid-October shocked Democratic loyalists into action; and on 19 October, Dalton announced support for a $100 million bond issue for highway construction. He endorsed revenue bonds to be redeemed by gas tax revenues, but even that modest deviation from the pay-as-you-go political orthodoxy that had reigned in Virginia since the 1920s was enough to cause Byrd to increase his campaign activity dramatically in Stanley's behalf. Dalton lost the election but received an unprecedented 44 percent of the vote.

Six months after the election, the Supreme Court of the United States ruled that mandatory racial segregation in public schools was unconstitutional. Like almost every other elected official in Virginia, Dalton supported segregation, but he was a moderate and a realist who believed that some desegregation was inevitable and that the public schools must remain open. During the next two years he denounced the Massive Resistance policies that Byrd, Stanley, and their legislative allies enacted to thwart desegregation. Dalton ridiculed the General Assembly's interposition resolution and described tuition grants as futile and impracticable. He also opposed holding a constitutional convention to legalize using state funds to pay tuition at private, nonsectarian, all-white schools.

Dalton was the Republican candidate for governor again in 1957 when Massive Resistance was at the height of its popularity among white Virginia voters. His Democratic opponent was Attorney General James Lindsay Almond Jr., a fiery orator and supporter of Massive Resistance. Democrats charged that Dalton favored integration and associated him in the public mind with such national Republicans as Chief Justice Earl Warren, who had written the desegregation decision, and Attorney General Herbert Brownell, who supported the Civil Rights Act of 1957. The crushing blow to Dalton's candidacy was Eisenhower's decision to send federal troops to enforce desegregation of a high school in Little Rock, Arkansas. Dalton called for the troops' withdrawal, but he refused to criticize the president. Events in Little Rock recalled Reconstruction to the minds of many white Virginians and made the Democrats' task even easier. On election day Almond won a landslide victory, and Dalton received only 36 percent of the vote.

Fourteen months later federal and state courts both invalidated the Massive Resistance laws. Vindicated by events, Dalton joined a legislative majority in April 1959 in enacting a plan that permitted limited school desegregation, essentially what he had advocated unsuccessfully in 1957.

On 21 July 1959 Eisenhower nominated Dalton to be judge of the United States District Court for the Western District of Virginia. Personally friendly with the state's two Democratic senators, Dalton experienced no difficulty winning confirmation by the Senate in August. He served as chief judge of the court from 1960 to 1971 and again from 1972 until 1973. He retired with senior status on 12 October 1976. Dalton handled a wide variety of federal cases, including suits involving the desegregation of public facilities, religious instruction in public schools, the rights of organized labor, student protests at state universities during the Vietnam War, tax fraud, voting rights, and in 1970 a Roanoke city school desegregation case that had been in litigation for ten years as a consequence of the state's Massive Resistance policies. In that case, Dalton approved a plan to integrate the public school system.

Dalton's most enduring significance for Virginia was to inspire younger men to join the Republican Party and run for office. His law partner Richard Harding Poff won election to Congress in 1952, and in 1970 Abner Linwood Holton Jr., who had worked in Dalton's campaigns, became Virginia's first Republican governor of the twentieth century. In January 1978 Dalton administered the oath of office to his adopted son as the third consecutive Republican governor of Virginia. Dalton's wife died on 28 September 1988. Theodore Roosevelt Dalton died of a respiratory illness at a Radford hospital on 30 October 1989. Both were interred in Sunrise Burial Park in that city. Dalton Hall, a student services building at Radford University, is named jointly for Dalton and his adopted son. The university also offers a Judge Ted Dalton Memorial Scholarship.

Biography with birth date in Morton, *Virginia Lives*, 241; Ted Dalton Papers, W&M, and correspondence in several collections at UVA and VHS; Dalton concession speeches, Nov. 1953 and Nov. 1957, and interview, 1957, sound recordings, WRVA Radio Collection, Acc. 38210, LVA; BVS Marriage Register, Radford; J. Harvie Wilkinson III, *Harry Byrd and the Changing Face of Virginia Politics, 1945–1966* (1968); James W. Ely Jr., *The Crisis of Conservative Virginia: The Byrd Organization and the Politics of Massive Resistance* (1976); George Leonard Vogt, "The Development of Virginia's Republican Party" (Ph.D. diss., UVA, 1978); Frank B. Atkinson, *The Dynamic Dominion: Realignment and the Rise of Virginia's Republican Party since 1945* (1992); "Program of Progress" in *Richmond Times-Dispatch*, 13 Aug. 1953; feature articles in *Richmond News Leader*, 9 Oct. 1953, and *Richmond Times-Dispatch*, 22 Oct. 1953; obituaries (all with pors.) in *Radford News Journal*, *Richmond News Leader*, *Richmond Times-Dispatch*, and *Roanoke Times and World-News*, all 31 Oct. 1989, *Washington Post*, 1 Nov. 1989, and *New York Times*, 2 Nov. 1989.

JAMES R. SWEENEY

DALY, John Joseph (31 August 1905–5 November 1964), journalist and Catholic lay leader, was born in Naugatuck, Connecticut, and was the son of Patrick H. Daly, an Irish immigrant and grocer, and Mary Brennan Daly. He attended the Catholic University of America, in Washington, D.C., where he edited the college newspaper and received a B.A. in 1927.

After garnering some experience as a sports writer for the *Washington Post*, Daly returned to Connecticut and worked as a reporter and editor at the *Naugatuck Daily News*. In January 1938 he became state editor for the nearby *Waterbury Republican* and in October of the next year became its city editor. The morning *Republican* and its sister publication, the afternoon *Waterbury American*, received a Pulitzer Prize for meritorious public service in 1940 for a campaign against graft in municipal government. Starting in 1945 Daly also read the evening newscasts six days a week for a local radio station.

In 1946 Bishop Peter Leo Ireton of the Catholic Diocese of Richmond hired Daly as editor and general manager of the *Richmond Catholic Virginian*. Despite its name, the diocese encompassed part of West Virginia and most of Virginia, including the fast-growing areas in Northern Virginia and the Tidewater. Under Daly's editorship the monthly magazine became a weekly newspaper in November 1946. The publication reported diocesan, national, and international news of religious events and services, the activities of clergy- and laymen, and Catholic education. The *Catholic Virginian* defended the faith from detractors, and Daly's editorials regularly castigated Communist regimes for repressing Catholics. In 1958 Daly was one of sixty American business, civic, and religious leaders who traveled to West Germany and Portugal to tour the facilities of Radio Free Europe. During the 1950s he also provided commentaries for a Richmond radio station.

In 1947 black and white Catholics at a Richmond convention of the Holy Name Union dined, deliberated, and worshiped together. A priest advocating integration before a General Assembly committee said they did so knowing they violated state law. Daly reported the statement on the front page of the *Catholic Virginian*, as he did Ireton's May 1954 announcement that Catholic schools would desegregate. Ten days later the Supreme Court of the United States overturned legal school segregation in *Brown* v. *Board of Education*. In his editorial supporting the decision, Daly described the separation of the races as "a moral and religious problem," rather than a political one. The *Catholic Virginian* remained silent on Massive Resistance until many of the movement's supporters lost Democratic primary elections in 1959. Daly uncharacteristically appended his initials to his editorial celebrating their defeat. The publication and its editor often won honors from the national Catholic Press Association, including a first prize for general excellence in editorial content in 1960.

Daly was active in Catholic circles and in the Richmond community. For many years he sat on the board of the Diocesan Bureau of Catholic Charities and from 1954 to 1956 was its president. He was elected vice president of the National Council of Catholic Charities in 1955. Daly served two one-year terms as president of the Catholic Press Association in 1958 and 1959. He was a member of the board of the Virginia chapter of the National Conference of Christians and Jews (later the National Conference for Community and Justice) and sat for four years on its National Commission on Religious Organizations.

Daly received numerous honors throughout his career. In 1950 the Virginia department of Catholic War Veterans recognized his leadership in journalism and in the community by selecting him as the state's Catholic Layman of the Year. Four years later Pope Pius XII named Daly a Knight of Saint Gregory the Great, among the highest honors for Catholic laymen, for his numerous civic activities in behalf of the church. Spring Hill College in Mobile, Alabama, awarded him an honorary doctorate of letters in 1957. The National Conference of Christians and Jews honored him in 1963 with its brotherhood award.

Daly married Helen Fisk, of New Haven, Connecticut, on 30 June 1930. They had three sons. John Joseph Daly died of a stroke in his Richmond home as he prepared for work on 5 November 1964. More than thirty priests attended his funeral four days later at Richmond's Cathedral of the Sacred Heart. He was buried in the city's Mount Calvary Cemetery.

Biographical information in clipping file of *Waterbury Republican-American* Archives, copies in *DVB* Files; some correspondence concerning Daly in Catholic Diocese of Richmond Archives; other published writings include "They Were Here Well Before Jamestown," *Commonwealth* 17 (Oct. 1950): 15–16; *Richmond Times-Dispatch*, 16 Apr. 1950, 24 May 1958, 11, 12 Dec. 1963; *Richmond Catholic Virginian*, 21 May 1954 (quotation); Gerald P. Fogarty, S.J., *Commonwealth Catholicism: A History of the Catholic Church in Virginia* (2001), 405, 468, 484; obituaries and tributes in *Richmond News Leader*, 5 Nov. 1964 (por.), *Richmond Times-Dispatch*, 6, 7 Nov. 1964, *Washington Post*, 6 Nov. 1964, and *Richmond Catholic Virginian*, 13, 20 Nov. 1964.

G. W. POINDEXTER

DAME, George Washington (27 July 1812–24 December 1895), Episcopal minister and educator, was born in Rochester, New Hampshire, and was the son of Jabez Dame, a merchant, and Elizabeth Hanson Cushing Dame. In 1823 he moved to Prince Edward County, Virginia, to live with his maternal uncle, Jonathan Peter Cushing, president of Hampden-Sydney College. Dame received an A.B. from Hampden-Sydney in 1829 and began studying medicine at the University of Pennsylvania the following year. After his uncle became ill, Dame returned to Hampden-Sydney and received an A.M. in 1832. He joined the school's faculty as a tutor the next year. In 1834 he was appointed chair of geology and mineralogy and a professor of natural philosophy and chemistry. On 22 July 1835 Dame married Mary Maria Page. They had nine children, of whom two daughters and four sons lived to adulthood. Among his grandchildren were George MacLaren Brydon, who also became an Episcopal minister and historian of the church, and Mary Evelyn Brydon, a physician and public health officer.

After contracting tuberculosis, Dame resigned from Hampden-Sydney in 1836. He stayed with his wife's family in Cumberland County while recovering, but health problems continued to plague him for the rest of his life. In May 1836 Dame joined the Episcopal Church and soon became convinced that it was his duty to enter the ministry despite his concerns about his health, speaking abilities, and finances. He prepared for the ministry at night while operating a school for girls in Lynchburg in 1838 and in Prince Edward County in 1839. Ordained a deacon on 15 January 1840, Dame took charge of the church at Prince Edward Court House (later Worsham). He was ordained a priest on 10 August 1841.

In September 1840 Dame accepted an invitation to become principal of the Danville Female Academy. He successfully managed the school for many years and was able both to pay off his accumulated debts and to provide free schooling for impoverished students. When Dame arrived in Danville, he agreed also to serve as rector of Camden Parish, which at that time included the counties of Franklin, Henry, Patrick, and Pittsylvania. The parish reportedly had only eight Episcopalians, and he worked tirelessly to build the church in and around Danville. Dame traveled more than a hundred miles each month to hold services in Competition (later Chatham), Martinsville, and Rocky Mount. During his nearly fifty-five-year tenure he established ten churches throughout the region with more than five hundred members. Having raised the funds for its construction, he held the first service at the Church of the Epiphany, in Danville, in 1844.

During the Civil War, Dame ministered to wounded Confederate soldiers and Union prisoners. He received a commission as chaplain of the general hospital in Danville on 9 June 1864 (to date from 14 April of that year). After the collapse of the Confederacy, he took the oath of allegiance on 12 May 1865. The following year Dame closed the Danville Female Academy. He remained committed to education, however, and in 1870 was appointed the first school superintendent for Pittsylvania County, with responsibility for examining and licensing teachers, supervising school boards, and monitoring the management of each school in his district. During his first year Dame noted the enthusiasm of

county residents for the new system of public schools and logged 1,000 miles visiting Pittsylvania schools. Believing that a strong system of public education was vital to the country's future success, he consistently urged greater funding for teachers' salaries and construction of adequate school buildings. Dame remained county superintendent until August 1879, when he became superintendent for the schools in the city of Danville. He was reappointed in 1883 but had resigned by April 1884.

Dame became a Freemason in 1833 and in January 1842 was elected Worshipful Master of Danville's Roman Eagle Lodge, a position he held until 1869 and resumed for one year in 1876. He was a district deputy grand master for more than twenty years and also the grand chaplain for the Grand Lodge of Virginia from 1863 to 1895. Not long before his death Dame completed a *Historical Sketch of Roman Eagle Lodge* (1895). He was a member of the local lodge of the Independent Order of Odd Fellows for almost fifty years and served as Most Worthy Grand Master of the state lodge for the 1867–1868 term. He also supported the temperance movement.

Hampden-Sydney College awarded Dame an honorary D.D. in 1891. On 20 April 1894 he retired as rector of Camden Parish and the Church of the Epiphany. George Washington Dame died at his Danville home on 24 December 1895. He was buried in the city's Green Hill Cemetery next to his wife, who had died three months earlier.

Typescript autobiographies, 1892 (with birth and marriage dates) and 1895, in Materials Concerning the Reverend George Washington Dame, VHS; autobiography in Marshall W. Fishwick, ed., *George Washington Dame (1812–1895): Missionary to Southwestern Virginia* (1961); biographies in Edward Pollock, *Illustrated Sketch Book of Danville, Virginia: Its Manufactures and Commerce* (1885), 119, and A. J. Morrison, *College of Hampden Sidney: Dictionary of Biography, 1776–1825* (1921), 281–282; Cumberland Co. Marriage Bonds; Compiled Service Records; George Washington Dame Papers and Dame Family Papers, VHS; writings include Dame, "Flute Melodies," Acc. 20613, LVA, "Sketch of the Life and Character of Jonathan P. Cushing, M.A.," *American Quarterly Register* 11 (1838): 113–128, *Proceedings of the Grand Lodge of Virginia, Independent Order of Odd Fellows* (1868), 318–328, "Supt. Dame on the Danville Schools," *Educational Journal of Virginia* 10 (1879): 428–430, and *Historical Sketch of Roman Eagle Lodge* (1895), with frontispiece por.; *Church of the Epiphany,*

Dame

Danville, Virginia: Centennial, 1840–1940 (1940), 6–22; obituaries in *Richmond Dispatch, Richmond Times,* and *Washington Post,* all 25 Dec. 1895.

JEFFREY W. MCCLURKEN

DANDRIDGE, Bartholomew (25 or 26 December 1737–18 April 1785), member of the Convention of 1776, member of the Council of State, and judge of the Virginia Court of Appeals, was born in New Kent County and was the son of John Dandridge and Frances Jones Dandridge. His father and his father's brother, William Dandridge, a naval officer who served on the governor's Council, emigrated from England by the mid-1710s and were merchants in Hampton before marrying into prominent Virginia planter families. One of Dandridge's sisters, Martha, married Daniel Parke Custis and George Washington, and another, Anna Maria, married Burwell Bassett (1734–1793), a member of the Convention of 1788.

As a young man Dandridge embarked on a successful legal career and became wealthy through his inheritance, professional income, and marriages. His first marriage to a cousin, Elizabeth Macon, early in the 1760s was short-lived. She died in 1764 soon after the birth of a daughter. Not long afterward Dandridge married Mary Burbidge, who inherited a New Kent County estate called Pamocra. They resided there and had four sons and three daughters. Their large household included several live-in wards, slaves, and after 1768 both of their mothers.

Dandridge won election to the House of Burgesses in January 1772 and again in July 1774. He sat on the Committee of Privileges and Elections at each assembly session he attended and on the Committee of Propositions and Grievances at all sessions except that of March 1773. In 1774 he joined the Committee for Courts of Justice. Dandridge's rising status is indicated by his membership on a select committee in June 1775 that sparred with the royal governor after he removed the colony's gunpowder from the public magazine in Williamsburg.

Dandridge represented New Kent County in all five of the Revolutionary Conventions that met between the summer of 1774 and the summer of 1776. On 17 August 1775 he came within one vote of being elected to the Committee of

Safety that in effect governed Virginia for the next ten months. One of the more active members of the last two Revolutionary Conventions, Dandridge was frequently appointed to select committees to investigate charges of election irregularities, and when the Convention of 1776 finally named a standing Committee of Privileges and Elections, he was a member. In May 1776 Dandridge introduced a resolution declaring that because actions of the king and Parliament had endangered American liberties, "the Union that has hitherto subsisted between Great Britain and the American Colonies is hereby totally dissolved, and that the Inhabitants of America are discharged from any Allegiance to the Crown of Great Britain." His draft resolution and two others of similar import formed the basis for the convention's unanimous instruction, adopted on 15 May, that the Virginia delegates in the Continental Congress move that the colonies be declared independent. Dandridge was a member of the large and distinguished committee that prepared the Virginia Declaration of Rights and the first constitution of Virginia, both of which the convention unanimously adopted.

On 29 June 1776 the convention elected Dandridge to the Council of State. It is possible that he took the oath of office and began serving on 6 July 1776, the day that Patrick Henry became governor, but the surviving records of the Council do not begin until 12 July, by which time Dandridge was seated. As the governor's advisory board, the Council oversaw many details of putting the government under the new constitution into operation and raising and supplying forces to serve in the Revolutionary War. Dandridge attended Council meetings regularly, with occasional short breaks to take care of personal and family business, through 8 January 1778. Twelve days later the Speaker of the House of Delegates laid Dandridge's letter of resignation before the General Assembly.

Elected to the House of Delegates the following April, Dandridge once again served on the Committee of Privileges and Elections, was ranking member of the Committees for Courts of Justice and of Propositions and Grievances, and chaired the Committee of Trade. On 29 May

1778 the General Assembly elected him to the General Court, which had jurisdiction in cases involving common and criminal law. The following year the assembly created a new Court of Appeals, composed of the judges of the General Court, the Court of Admiralty, and the High Court of Chancery, all ex officio. Although the Court of Appeals met for the first time in the spring of 1779, Dandridge did not take his seat until 29 March 1780. One of the most interesting cases presented to the Court of Appeals during his tenure was *Commonwealth* v. *Caton et al.*, heard in November 1782 under a statute that may have violated the state constitution. Some of the judges stated that the court had the power to declare the law invalid because it conflicted with the constitution, but Dandridge cautiously declined to express an opinion whether the court possessed the power of judicial review.

With his appointment to the bench at age forty, Dandridge reached the height of his public career as well as his greatest prosperity. In addition to his New Kent County plantation, he had purchased 4,000 acres of land in North Carolina and 8,000 acres in Fayette County. Engaged also in the management of Custis family land that his sister inherited and as executor of the estate of his nephew, John Parke Custis, Dandridge was a busy man with large-scale responsibilities. On 18 April 1785 Bartholomew Dandridge died of unknown causes, probably at Pamocra in New Kent County, where he was buried.

Biographies in (4 Call), *Virginia Reports*, 8:xix–xx, and *Journals of Council of State*, 5:383; birth at "12 O'Clock A.M." on 25 Dec. 1737 and death date in Dandridge family Bible records (1728–1798), Mount Vernon Library and Archives, with copies at LVA and VHS; birth date of 26 Dec. 1737 and christening date of 13 Mar. 1738 in C. G. Chamberlayne, ed., *The Vestry Book and Register of St. Peter's Parish: New Kent and James City Counties, Virginia, 1684–1786* (1937), 536; family history in Wilson Miles Cary, "The Dandridges of Virginia," *WMQ*, 1st ser., 5 (1896): 30–39, and Lyon G. Tyler, "The Dandridge Family," ibid. 6 (1898): 250–251; Dandridge letters and documents in George Washington Papers, LC, in several collections, LVA, in Custis Family Papers and other collections, VHS, and in Dandridge Papers, W&M; numerous references in Joseph E. Fields, ed., *"Worthy Partner": The Papers of Martha Washington* (1994), in *Revolutionary Virginia* (quotation on 7:145, election to Council on 7:655), and *Journals of Council of State*, vols. 1–3; *JHD*, 1777–1778 sess., 129 (resignation from Council); *JHD*, May–June 1778 sess., 38 (election to General Court); *Commonwealth v. Caton et al.* (1782) (4 Call), *Virginia Reports*, 8:5–21; David John Mays, ed., *The Letters and Papers of Edmund Pendleton, 1734–1803* (1967), 2:426; death notice, without date, in *Richmond Virginia Gazette, or the American Advertiser*, 23 Apr. 1785.

THOMAS J. LITTLE

DANDRIDGE, Raymond Emmett (30 August 1913–12 February 1994), baseball player, was born in Richmond and was the son of Archer Dandridge and Alberta Thompson Dandridge. He grew up in the city's Church Hill neighborhood, where he attended the local elementary school. At about age ten Dandridge moved to Buffalo, New York, to live with his mother. There he attended integrated schools before dropping out in the ninth grade. He played baseball, basketball, and football while attending vocational school part-time.

By age eighteen Dandridge had returned to Richmond and was playing semiprofessional baseball for local African American teams, the Paramount All Stars, the Richmond Grays, the Violets, and the Albemarle All-Stars. In 1933 the Detroit Stars of the Negro National League played an exhibition game against the Paramounts in Richmond, and the Stars' manager, Candy Jim Taylor, signed Dandridge to play outfield. Taylor transformed Dandridge from a long-ball to a contact hitter by training him to adjust to each pitch and to drive the ball to different parts of the field. Dandridge hit .218 before the Stars disbanded later that year, but he soon developed into a feared "bad-ball" hitter. He appeared in one game with the Nashville Elite Giants before returning to Richmond.

In 1934 the manager of the Newark Dodgers signed Dandridge and moved him to third base. Although league statistics are incomplete and box scores imprecise, extant records show that he developed into a superb hitter. Dandridge batted .408 and in the next season, when his nine triples led the league, hit .340. He also went four for eleven while facing white major-league competition in exhibition games played in October 1935. After the Dodgers merged with the Brooklyn Eagles to form the Newark Eagles, Dandridge's average fell to .287 in 1936 but rebounded to well above .300 the next two seasons. In 1937 he led his team to the league's

World Series, in which he batted six for sixteen. Dandridge also excelled with the glove and as a member of the Eagles' so-called Million-Dollar Infield was known for his quickness and his ability to time his throws to first base so that the runner would be narrowly thrown out. Named by Cum Posey, owner of the Homestead Grays, to his annual All American team as the best third baseman in the Negro Leagues from 1936 to 1938, Dandridge was regarded as one of the finest fielding third basemen in professional baseball.

Known as "Dandy" to his teammates and as "Squatty" or "Hooks" to his opponents, the five-foot-six-inch, bow-legged infielder left the Eagles after the 1938 season when he was offered substantially more money to play for a team in Venezuela. By this time he had married Florence Alberta Cooper, with whom he had two sons and one daughter. Leaving most of his advance money with his wife, Dandridge went to Caracas, where he played for two seasons and led his team to the league championship in 1939. During the winter of 1937–1938 he had also begun playing winter baseball in Cuba, where for more than twelve seasons he batted about .282.

In 1940 Dandridge joined the Mexican League, for which the millionaire Jorge Pasquel recruited players from the Negro Leagues in the United States by paying significantly higher salaries. The right-hander played shortstop for most of the next nine seasons and compiled a career average of .347 with the Vera Cruz and Mexico City clubs. In 1941 Dandridge was a member of the pennant-winning Vera Cruz team. One of the most popular players in Mexico, he earned as much as $10,000 in a season. Dandridge returned to the Newark Eagles briefly in 1942 and played the entire 1944 season, during which he batted .370 and led the league in hits, runs, and total bases. In 1947 the owner of Major League Baseball's Cleveland Indians offered him a contract, but the higher pay and more congenial atmosphere south of the border persuaded him to remain with his Mexico City team, where he had taken over as manager while continuing to play shortstop.

In 1949 Dandridge left Mexico to manage and play second base for the New York Cubans. He led them to first place in June before signing with the New York Giants, two years after Jackie Robinson had broken the color barrier in Major League Baseball. Sent to the club's triple-A franchise in the American Association, Dandridge batted .362 for the Minneapolis Millers and was voted runner-up for the league's rookie of the year. In 1950 he hit .311, led the Millers to the American Association championship, and was voted the league's most valuable player. During four seasons with the club he sparkled in the field and at the plate, compiled a .318 batting average, and mentored young African American players, most notably Willie Mays.

Despite these accomplishments, Dandridge was deprived of a chance to play in the majors. Passing him over for younger talent, the Giants refused to trade him to another major league franchise and opted to keep the Millers' star attraction and most popular player in Minneapolis. An informal quota system limiting the number of African Americans on each team may also have been a factor. In 1953 Dandridge's contract was sold to the Sacramento Solons in the Pacific Coast League, which then sent him to the Oakland Acorns. He sat out a year with an injury before signing with the Bismarck Barons of the Manitoba-Dakota (Man-Dak) Baseball League. Playing third base and batting about .360, he led the league in hits. The Barons won the regular season pennant but lost in the playoffs.

Dandridge returned to Newark, where he had bought a house about 1940 and lived during the off-season. He retired from baseball, tended bar, and managed a liquor store while occasionally scouting for the New York (later San Francisco) Giants. His wife died in 1961, and Dandridge married Heneritta Newmones Shepherd in 1966. He worked for the Newark recreation department for about eight years and was honored by the city council in 1980 for his service to children as a supervisor of public works. In 1985 Newark named a baseball field in the city's Westside Park for Dandridge, who moved to Palm Bay, Florida, about that time.

Dandridge benefited from an awakening interest in the Negro Leagues during the 1970s and 1980s and was recognized as one of the great third basemen in all of baseball's history. The Committee on Baseball Veterans elected him to the National Baseball Hall of Fame in 1987, and he returned to Minneapolis to throw out the ceremonial first pitch before the second game of the 1987 World Series between the Minnesota Twins and the Saint Louis Cardinals. Two years later he was inducted into the Mexican Baseball Hall of Fame. Raymond Emmett Dandridge died of prostate cancer on 12 February 1994 in Palm Bay, Florida, and was buried in Fountainhead Memorial Park there. He was posthumously inducted into the Greater Buffalo Sports Hall of Fame in 1994 and into the Virginia Sports Hall of Fame in 1999.

Birth date in Richmond City Department of Public Health Birth Records Index and in Social Security application, Social Security Administration, Office of Earnings Operations, Baltimore, Md.; biographies in John B. Holway, "Dandy at Third: Ray Dandridge," *National Pastime* 1 (fall 1982): 7–11, James A. Riley, *Dandy, Day, and the Devil* (1987), 1–53 (with variant birth date of 31 Aug. 1913 on 21 and several pors.), and Holway, *Blackball Stars: Negro Leagues Pioneers* (1988), 353–374; player file in National Baseball Hall of Fame, Cooperstown, N.Y.; career statistics in Holway, *The Complete Book of Baseball's Negro Leagues: The Other Half of Baseball History* (2001), Pedro Treto Cisneros, *The Mexican League: Comprehensive Player Statistics, 1937–2001* (2002), 122, and Jorge S. Figueredo, *Who's Who in Cuban Baseball, 1878–1961* (2003), 376; *Our World* 2 (July 1947): 25–29 (several pors.); *Chicago Defender*, 9 July 1949; *Newark Star-Ledger*, 4 Mar., 23 July 1987; *New York Times*, 4 Mar., 10 May, 27 July 1987; *Richmond News Leader*, 4 Mar. 1987; *Richmond Times-Dispatch*, 4, 5, 10 Mar., 26, 27 July, 19 Oct. 1987; obituaries in *Richmond Times-Dispatch*, 13 Feb. 1994, *Newark Star-Ledger* and *New York Times*, both 14 Feb. 1994, and *Richmond Free Press*, 17–19 Feb. 1994.

TRENTON E. HIZER
MARIANNE E. JULIENNE

DANDRIDGE, William (29 December 1689–28 August 1744), member of the Council, was the son of John Dandridge, a London member of the company of painters and stainers, and his second wife, Ann Dandridge (whose maiden name is not known). Several of his siblings were born in their father's native Oxfordshire, but Dandridge's birthplace is uncertain. Commissioned a lieutenant in the Royal Navy on 20 October 1709, he left active duty within a few years and sometime before 1715 sailed to Virginia, probably in company with his brother, John Dandridge, later the father of Martha Dandridge Custis Washington. Dandridge lived at Hampton, where he owned a wharf and a ship and was a merchant. In 1715 Lieutenant Governor Alexander Spotswood commissioned him to carry soldiers in his sloop *William* from Hanover County to Charleston, South Carolina. Dandridge may have accompanied Spotswood on his expedition to the Shenandoah Valley the following year. The members of that party later received commemorative golden horseshoes.

By late in July 1715 Dandridge had married a young widow, Euphan Wallace Roscow. They had one son before her death on 22 April 1717. Two years later Dandridge moved to Elsing Green, a large King William County estate that he acquired when he married Unity West on 17 or 18 March 1719. One of their four daughters and one of their two sons married children of Alexander Spotswood.

On 1 June 1727 George I appointed Dandridge to the governor's Council. Dandridge took his seat on 11 September, at which time the news of the king's death and the accession of George II were officially proclaimed in Williamsburg. On the following 14 December the lieutenant governor appointed Dandridge one of the commissioners to survey the boundary between Virginia and North Carolina. With William Byrd (1674–1744) and Richard Fitzwilliam, he accompanied both surveying parties that were in the field from 27 February to 9 April and from 17 September to 22 November 1728. In Byrd's private manuscript account of the surveying expeditions, usually designated the *Secret History of the Dividing Line* and not published until the twentieth century, he assigned type names to all of the main characters of his fanciful narrative. He called Fitzwilliam "Firebrand" and Dandridge "Meanwell." Byrd's *Secret History* offers the best information available about Dandridge's personality. Much of the dramatic tension in the story comes from the conflict between the irascible Fitzwilliam and the prudent, even-tempered Dandridge. From the pages of Byrd's narrative, Dandridge emerges as a good-natured gentleman, a keen conversationalist, and a spirited companion. In a letter of introduction to the bishop of London, James Blair, another member of the Council, confirmed Byrd's evaluation of Dandridge and called him "a very honest Gentleman."

In August 1734 Dandridge obtained a one-year leave of absence from the Council in order to return to England, where he intended to resume his naval career. He was commissioned a lieutenant and extended his leave of absence from Virginia for two more years, but he eventually found a way to return home while remaining in the navy. Dandridge became commander of a ship assigned to patrol the coast of Virginia and the colonies to its south. Though he had been absent from Virginia for more than three years, he very much wanted to continue serving on the Council once he returned, and he successfully requested permission from the absentee royal governor, William Anne Keppel, second earl of Albemarle, to do so.

Promoted to commander on 11 April 1738 and given charge of the twelve-gun sloop *Wolf*, Dandridge also received from the second duke of Montagu that same month a handsome, inscribed sword that a descendant presented to the Virginia Historical Society in 1969. Although Dandridge had difficulty fitting out the ship and completing his crew, he sailed in the *Wolf* from Portsmouth, England, before the end of June. Traveling by way of Madeira, he encountered stormy weather that battered the ship and left less-seasoned crew members seasick. Serious illness struck others, who died or had to be put ashore. Dandridge reached Virginia on 29 September 1738. The following week the *Virginia Gazette* reported his arrival and announced his mission: "to protect the valuable Trade of this Country, against any Insults that may be attempted upon it." During the following two years he spent much time aboard the *Wolf* cruising the Virginia and Carolina coasts.

Dandridge was promoted to captain in November 1741 and took command of the forty-four-gun *Southsea Castle*, which he sailed from England to Virginia. He arrived early in 1742, in time to take part in the British attack on Saint Augustine and the siege of Cartegena during the War of the Austrian Succession. After being ordered back to England the next year, he attended the Council for the last recorded time on 4 August 1743. William Dandridge was given command of the forty-gun *Mary Galley* the following July, but he died little more than a month later, at Greenwich, England, on 28 August 1744.

Family history in W. S. Bristowe, "News of Martha Washington," *Genealogists' Magazine* 15 (1968): 610 (with undocumented birth date), Wilson Miles Cary, "The Dandridges of Virginia," *WMQ*, 1st ser., 5 (1896): 30–33, and Mary Selden Kennedy, *Seldens of Virginia and Allied Families* (1911), 2:13–17; naval career and letters in PRO Adm 1/1695, 2/55, 2/57, 2/478, 3/46, 7/569, 52/490; PRO Adm 2/474, fols. 533–534; appointment to Council in PRO CO 324/35, fol. 336, and *Executive Journals of Council*, 4:146–147; leaves of absence from Council in PRO CO 5/1337, fols. 166–167, and William Dandridge to earl of Albemarle, 6 Mar. 1737, British Library, Add. MSS 32691; boundary commissioners' reports in PRO CO 5/1321, fols. 52–57, and CO 5/1322, fols. 38–50; *William Byrd's Histories of the Dividing Line betwixt Virginia and North Carolina*, ed. William K. Boyd (1929), esp. 95, 99, 175; some Dandridge documents in Colonial Papers, RG 1, LVA; James Blair to bishop of London, 11 Aug. 1734, Fulham Palace Papers, Lambeth Palace Library, Eng. (first quotation); *Williamsburg Virginia Gazette*, 6 Oct. 1738 (second quotation); *Gentleman's Magazine* 11 (Nov. 1741): 609; ibid. 14 (July 1744): 395 (appointment to command *Mary Galley*); ibid. 14 (Aug. 1744): 452 (appointment of successor "in room of Capt. *Dandridge*, decd."); "A Fine Sword to Capt. Dandridge," Virginia Historical Society *An Occasional Bulletin* 18 (Apr. 1969): 11–13; Hall, *Portraits*, 66–67 (por.); extract from lost will in Hening, *Statutes*, 6:322, 428–430; undocumented death date in Culpepper-Dandridge-Spotswood-Rolfe family genealogical notes, Acc. 37554, LVA.

KEVIN J. HAYES

DANIEL, John Hannah (1 March 1896–20 March 1972), businessman and member of the House of Delegates, was born in Charlotte County and was the son of Edward Flournoy Daniel, a banker and county treasurer, and Virginia Hannah Daniel. Educated in local public schools, the industrious Daniel (universally called Jack) earned money during the summer of 1913 by raising tobacco and building a sidewalk in Charlotte Court House. That autumn he managed a dairy farm in Orange County, New York. Daniel moved to Charleston, South Carolina, early in 1915. There he apprenticed at the American Agricultural Chemical Company and by 1917 had become supervisor of its chemical plants in Alexandria, Virginia, and in Atlanta and Baltimore.

On 12 October 1920 Daniel married Eloise Burney, in Rome, Georgia. They had one daughter. The following year he began managing his father-in-law's department store in Rome. About 1928 he founded the John H. Daniel Company, which produced men's custom-made clothing sold through direct mail. After several years Daniel moved the business office to Knoxville,

Tennessee, where his factories were. He sold the company in 1970, but it continued to operate under his name in the twenty-first century.

Daniel returned to Charlotte County about 1941 and established a successful cattle ranch on more than 1,300 acres of land. With his son-in-law and two others, in 1947 he founded Virginia Crafts, Incorporated, a carpet-manufacturing company, in Keysville. Daniel remained president until he sold the business in 1969, by which time it had expanded from six employees and a 10,000-square-foot factory to more than 300 workers in a plant of 160,000 square feet.

In 1943 voters in Charlotte and Prince Edward Counties elected Daniel to the House of Delegates. Reelected twelve times, he represented those localities, as well as Cumberland County in his last two terms, until 1969. Emerging as an influential delegate, he chaired the Committee on Manufactures and Mechanic Arts from 1950 to 1956, the Committee on Roads and Internal Navigation from 1958 to 1964, and the important Committee on Appropriations in 1966 and 1968. He also sat at various times on the Committees on Agriculture, on Asylums and Prisons, on Public Institutions, on Retrenchment and Economy, on Rules, and on Schools and Colleges.

Allied with the conservative Democratic Party organization of Harry Flood Byrd (1887–1966), Daniel served on the Virginia State Central Democratic Committee from 1948 to 1968 and also chaired the Charlotte County Democratic Committee from 1948 to 1962. Concurrently he sat on many legislative and governor's commissions relating to the budget, highways, police, public education, state agencies, and the livestock industry. From 1944 to 1967 Daniel chaired the State Soil Conservation Committee (after 1964 the Virginia Soil and Water Conservation Commission), which in 1961 received the National Soil and Water Conservation Merit Award. He served from 1947 to 1957 on the Advisory Council on the Virginia Economy, a forty-five-member body responsible for encouraging expansion of agriculture, commerce, and industry. Daniel was also a member from 1953 to 1969 of the Virginia Advisory Legislative Council, a General Assembly panel that met between sessions to examine a variety of issues

and to recommend legislation. As chair of the VALC from 1958 to 1960, he oversaw studies presented to the 1960 General Assembly on proposals relating to peaceful uses of atomic energy, forest management, health insurance, industrial development, and teacher salaries and on laws concerning child labor, eminent domain, drunk driving, and workers' compensation.

During the 1950 assembly session, Daniel and several other delegates joined Armistead Lloyd Boothe in proposing an unsuccessful bill that would have ended segregation on public transportation and established a commission on race relations. In March 1958 Daniel introduced an amendment to the state constitution requiring the legislature to consider land area, in addition to population figures, when reapportioning seats in the General Assembly. Urban legislators defeated the resolution, which would have allowed the rural counties to maintain their majority in the face of population growth in the cities. In August 1968 the governor appointed Daniel to a bipartisan, ten-member committee organized to secure passage of $81 million in bonds to finance construction at colleges and mental health facilities. Approved by the voters in November, it was the first bond issue since state adoption of pay-as-you-go policies during the 1920s. Reginald Hoffman Pettus, a former Charlotte County commonwealth's attorney, challenged Daniel for his seat in the House of Delegates in 1969. Despite his long tenure and influence in the assembly, Daniel lost the Democratic Party primary on 15 July by 674 votes of about 7,000 cast.

Daniel sat on the board of the Patrick Henry Memorial Foundation for more than two decades and was a trustee of the Virginia Museum of Fine Arts from 1961 to 1970. Widely acknowledged as a leader in protecting the state's natural resources, he was recognized as Virginia Conservationist of the Year in 1959 by the Soil Conservation Society of America (later the Soil and Water Conservation Society), and in 1965 the Virginia and the National Wildlife Federations and the Sears Roebuck Foundation honored him with the Legislative Conservation Award. The local Ruritan Club named him Charlotte County's outstanding citizen in 1964.

A longtime advocate of higher education, Daniel sat on the Southern Regional Education Board from 1958 to 1962 and served on the board of visitors of the College of William and Mary during the 1969–1970 academic term. In December 1968 he donated land in Keysville for a branch campus of Southside Virginia Community College. Classes at the John H. Daniel Campus of SVCC began in September 1971. John Hannah Daniel died at a Richmond hospital on 20 March 1972 and was buried in the cemetery of Village Presbyterian Church, in Charlotte Court House.

Biography in *NCAB*, 57:113–114 (por. facing 113); birth date in General Assembly of Virginia, *Manual of the Senate and House of Delegates*, 1968 sess., 250; *Washington Post*, 28 July 1947, 7 Feb. 1950, 6 Mar. 1958, 20 May 1960, 10 Aug., 4 Dec. 1967, 14 Aug. 1968, 17 July 1969; *Richmond Times-Dispatch*, 5, 6 Mar. 1958; *Charlotte Gazette*, 10, 17, 24 July 1969, 23 Sept. 1971; SCC Charter Book, 216:207–209, 487:410–416; obituaries in *Richmond News Leader*, 21 Mar. 1972, *Richmond Times-Dispatch* and *Washington Post*, both 22 Mar. 1972, and *Charlotte Gazette*, 23 Mar. 1972.

JOHN G. DEAL

DANIEL, John Moncure (24 October 1825–30 March 1865), journalist and member of the Council of State, was born in Stafford County and was the son of John Moncure Daniel, a physician, and his first wife, Eliza Mitchell Daniel. He was educated by his father and attended school in Richmond, where he lived with his granduncle Peter V. Daniel (1784–1860), a member of the Council of State and associate justice of the Supreme Court of the United States. Early in the 1840s he read law in Fredericksburg in the office of John Tayloe Lomax.

Penniless after the death of his father, Daniel moved to Richmond in 1845 and worked initially as librarian of the Patrick Henry Society, a gentleman's literary club. Late in 1846 he became coeditor of the monthly *Southern Planter*, and from December 1847 to June 1849 he was sole editor. By early in 1848 he was also working at the *Richmond Examiner*, a recently established newspaper that supported the Democratic Party. Daniel soon became the paper's chief editor. In December 1848 he purchased a part interest in the paper and later bought out his partner. He

also contributed articles to the *Southern Literary Messenger*, including one on Edgar Allan Poe—who once challenged him to a duel—that helped establish the poet's reputation.

As a young man, Daniel may have opposed slavery, but influenced by his granduncle the judge and by the writings of Louis Agassiz and Thomas Carlyle, he later adopted a strongly proslavery position. Early in the 1850s Daniel's paper warned readers that northern opposition to slavery imperiled the Union, and he advised southerners to counter the threat by presenting a united front in national politics. Daniel believed that secession was a legitimate course of action but warned that it would lead to civil war and should be employed only as a last resort. His editorials, often abrasive and sarcastic, fiercely attacked the Whig Party's local majority in Richmond as well as the party's national leaders, including Zachary Taylor and Millard Fillmore. Daniel's writing led to a duel in January 1852 with Edward W. Johnston, editor of the *Richmond Whig*; neither was wounded.

On 10 January 1850 the Democratic majority in the General Assembly elected Daniel to the Council of State in place of his uncle Raleigh Travers Daniel, then a Whig and later attorney general of Virginia. Daniel served on the governor's advisory panel from 29 April 1851 until 15 January 1852, when under the terms of a new state constitution it ceased to exist. Prominent in the Young America wing of the Democratic Party, he was a delegate to the 1852 Democratic National Convention.

In July 1853 President Franklin Pierce appointed Daniel chargé d'affaires at Turin, capital of the Kingdom of Sardinia, after another Virginian had declined the posting. Soon after arriving, Daniel wrote to a Richmond friend that the women there were uglier than in the United States, the noblemen he dealt with had empty heads, and the whole country stank of garlic. The letter leaked to the press, and for a time it appeared that Daniel would have to resign, but neither the president nor the secretary of state thought his resignation necessary. Daniel was promoted to minister resident at Turin in 1854 and remained at his post throughout the administrations of Franklin Pierce and, with support from John Buchanan Floyd, a former Virginia governor who became secretary of war in 1857, of James Buchanan. Two secretaries of state commended Daniel for his reporting on the reunification of Italy. During Daniel's absence in 1854 a New York jury found him guilty of libel in a case stemming from an 1851 review in the *Examiner*. He was forced to sell his personal library to pay the damages. Daniel never married, but while in Turin he was close to Marie de Solms, a relative of Napoléon I who later married a prime minister of Italy.

In February 1861 Daniel returned to Richmond, resumed control of the *Examiner*, and, believing Southern unity to be paramount, became perhaps the most influential proponent of Virginia's secession. After the Civil War began, in May 1861 he called for the Confederate capital to be moved to Richmond and for Jefferson Davis to become dictator of the new nation. Daniel received a commission as a major in the autumn of 1861 and served briefly on the staff of Floyd, who was then a brigadier general in the Confederate army.

Daniel found grave defects in the manner that Davis conducted the war, which he thought should be waged more aggressively. As he had been in the forefront in the campaign for secession in 1861, Daniel was soon in the vanguard among Davis's sharpest critics. Although the *Examiner* expressed optimism that the South would win the war, it commented frankly on Southern defeats, which Daniel attributed to Davis's appointment of incompetent generals. In February 1864 the paper charged the president with nepotism after the government awarded a contract to the president's brother-in-law for construction of a large distillery.

Daniel returned to the field as a staff officer under Major General Ambrose Powell Hill and in June 1862 was wounded in the right arm at the Battle of Gaines's Mill. In August 1864 he received a leg wound in a duel with Edward C. Elmore, the Confederate treasurer, who had challenged him after the *Examiner* reported that a treasury official was gambling with government funds. Physically slight and often in poor health, Daniel suffered symptoms of tuberculosis for several years and perhaps contracted mercury

poisoning from the medicine called blue mass. After battling pneumonia for several months, John Moncure Daniel died of acute tuberculosis in Richmond on 30 March 1865. The *Richmond Examiner* died with him, and four days later the capital of the Confederacy fell to the United States Army. Daniel's body was buried in Richmond's Hollywood Cemetery.

Biographies include memoir by Frederick S. Daniel (brother) in *The Richmond Examiner during the War; or, The Writings of John M. Daniel, With a Memoir of His Life* (1868), 218–232 (with birth date), George William Bagby, *John M. Daniel's Latch-Key: A Memoir of the Late Editor of the Richmond Examiner* (1868), Robert W. Hughes, "John Moncure Daniel: His Times and Career," *Baltimorean*, 10 Jan. 1885, and Peter Bridges, *Pen of Fire: John Moncure Daniel* (2002), with por. on 52; family history with variant death date of 29 Mar. 1865 in Hayden, *Virginia Genealogies*, 315–317; Daniel letters in Daniel Family Papers, Huntington, John Moncure Daniel Papers, UVA and VHS, various collections at W&M, and Turin Legation Letter Books, RG 84, NARA; election to Council in *JHD*, 1850–1851 sess., 73; Council of State Journal (1850–1852), 15, RG 75, LVA; Compiled Service Records; will and estate inventory in Richmond City Hustings Court Wills, 23:520–521, 662–664; obituaries in *Richmond Daily Dispatch*, 31 Mar. 1865, *Richmond Whig*, 31 Mar., 1 Apr. 1865, and *New-York Times*, 7 Apr. 1865.

PETER BRIDGES

DANIEL, John Warwick (5 September 1842–29 June 1910), member of the House of Representatives, of the United States Senate, and of the Convention of 1901–1902, was born in Lynchburg. Through his father, William Daniel, a judge of the Virginia Supreme Court of Appeals, he was connected to many of the leading families in the state. His mother, Sarah Ann Warwick Daniel, was the daughter of a wealthy Lynchburg tobacco merchant. After she died in August 1845, Daniel was raised in the Lynchburg household of his maternal grandparents. He attended local primary schools and from 1855 to 1859 Lynchburg College. He then matriculated at a preparatory academy that operated for one year in Albemarle County and the following year in Nelson County.

After Virginia seceded from the Union in April 1861, Daniel enlisted in a Lynchburg cavalry troop, but early in May he secured a commission as a second lieutenant in the 27th Regiment Virginia Infantry. He was wounded at the First Battle of Manassas (Bull Run) and after convalescing gained a commission as a second lieutenant in the 11th Regiment Virginia Infantry. On 11 July 1862 Daniel was promoted to first lieutenant and adjutant (to rank from 17 June of that year), and on 24 March 1863 he was named assistant adjutant general for Major General Jubal Anderson Early and promoted to major (to rank from 30 April). At the Battle of the Wilderness in May 1864 a minié ball shattered Daniel's femur. The injury required him to use a crutch for the rest of his life and later earned him the nickname "The Lame Lion of Lynchburg."

After the Civil War, Daniel studied law at the University of Virginia for one year and then joined his father's practice in Lynchburg. When not busy with cases, he continued his legal studies and indulged his passion for oratory by memorializing the Confederate war effort and speaking out against Reconstruction. In 1868 Daniel published one of his lectures as *The Character of Stonewall Jackson*, followed the next year by a compilation entitled *The Law and Practice of Attachment, under the Code of Virginia*. On 24 November 1869 he married Julia Elizabeth Murrell, also of Lynchburg. They had two daughters and three sons, the youngest of whom died in a horseback-riding accident in 1894.

Daniel's political career began with his election as a Conservative to the House of Delegates in July 1869. As one of three men representing Campbell County from 1869 to 1871, he served on the Committee for Courts of Justice and chaired the Committee on the Library. Although Daniel did not seek reelection in 1871, he may already have set his sights on higher office. He unsuccessfully sought nomination to the Sixth Congressional District seat in the House of Representatives in 1872 and 1874 and canvassed the state in behalf of Conservative candidates during the 1873 campaign. Most of his time during this period, however, was devoted to the law. Through intensive study of the legal codes governing financial transactions Daniel made his most important contribution to the profession, *A Treatise on the Law of Negotiable Instruments* (1876). Reprinted several times, the two-volume work became the standard text on the subject throughout the United States and gained a substantial reading in other English-speaking courts.

Virginia's massive public debt emerged as the principal fault line of state politics. In 1871 the General Assembly passed the Funding Act, which committed the state to assume the full burden of its antebellum debt. The issue split the Conservative Party into two factions. Opponents of the act, later known as Readjusters, favored a debt adjustment that would leave Virginia in a better position to maintain government services, particularly the new public education system, while defenders of the act, called Funders, argued that the state's honor and future ability to attract capital depended on paying its creditors in full. Although Daniel had voted against the Funding Act, he emerged as one of the most prominent Funder spokesmen.

In 1875 Campbell County voters elected Daniel to the Senate of Virginia, where his growing reputation was reflected in assignments to important committees. He chaired the Committee of Privileges and Elections in 1875 and 1876 and the Committee for Courts of Justice from 1877 to 1880. He was an at-large elector for Samuel J. Tilden, the unsuccessful Democratic presidential candidate in 1876. In a spirited contest for the Conservative gubernatorial nomination in 1877, Daniel became the principal Funder candidate opposing the leading Readjuster, William Mahone. Eventually Mahone withdrew his candidacy and threw his support behind a third candidate whose stance on the debt was less clear.

Despite the loss, Daniel's popularity was growing, and he continued to help lead the Funder faction in the state senate. Although not opposed in principle to a new debt settlement, he vehemently fought any plan that did not make debt payment the state's top budgetary priority. In making his case during one debate, Daniel argued that it "were better to burn the schools," the key focus of the Readjuster camp, "than sustain them on money taken by force" from the state's creditors. Although not intended as an attack on the public schools, Daniel's clumsy rhetoric provided fodder for Readjuster assertions that Funders opposed not only a debt adjustment but public education as well. The publicity that the incident aroused and the philosophy that it reflected—that the property rights of bondholders superseded all other interests—helped spur the Readjusters to sweeping victories in the 1879 elections, although Daniel himself easily won reelection.

Daniel stepped onto the national stage for the first time in 1880 when, as a delegate to the Democratic National Convention, he gave a celebrated nominating speech in behalf of Winfield Scott Hancock. He praised Hancock as a candidate who offered the best hope for reconciliation between North and South, a theme that often appeared in his rhetoric. The following year Daniel secured the Conservative Party nomination for governor. Despite an energetic campaign, he lost by almost 12,000 votes, of more than 211,000 cast, to William Evelyn Cameron, the candidate of a coalition of Readjusters and Republicans.

Daniel's defeat did not significantly diminish his reputation. Having resigned from the state senate during the campaign, he retreated from politics in order to focus again on his law practice. He cemented his status as a leading tribune of Confederate remembrance and was chosen as the keynote speaker at the unveiling of Edward Virginius Valentine's recumbent statue of Robert Edward Lee for the chapel at Washington and Lee University. Daniel's oration, delivered on 28 June 1883 and reprinted in newspapers throughout the country, strengthened Lee's image as the embodiment of all that was noble, even sacred, about the South and the cause for which it had fought. Daniel also used the speech to assert Virginia's central place in the nation, a theme that he elaborated on in an address during ceremonies dedicating the Washington Monument in the nation's capital on 21 February 1885.

Pride in Virginia and in the efforts of its white people during the Civil War emerged as primary vehicles in the resurgence of the Conservatives. Reorganized as the Democratic Party in 1883, they regarded the state debt controversy as settled and placed race and the presumed cronyism of their opponents at the heart of the 1883 campaign. Although not running for office, Daniel campaigned vigorously and in a celebrated speech, which linked the Readjuster-Republican coalition with Reconstruction-era hostility toward former Confederates, summarized the reasons

for supporting his party: "I am a Democrat because I am a white man and a Virginian."

One of the first acts of the victorious Democrats in the General Assembly was a reapportionment of the state's ten congressional districts. Daniel was removed from the same district as the popular John Randolph Tucker, and when Republicans challenged the plan, Daniel successfully defended it before the Supreme Court of Appeals. In November 1884 Daniel easily won election to the House of Representatives from the Sixth District, which comprised Lynchburg and the counties of Bedford, Botetourt, Campbell, Charlotte, Halifax, Montgomery, and Roanoke. Already well-known at the national level, he received prestigious assignments to the Committees on Foreign Affairs and on Labor. Daniel's tenure in the House was short-lived, however; in December 1885 the General Assembly elected him to succeed Mahone in the United States Senate.

Reelected four times, Daniel remained a senator until his death. As a Democrat in an era when Republicans dominated Congress, he wielded little power. His committee assignments tended to be relatively inconsequential, although during a brief period when Democrats held the majority he chaired the Committee on the Revision of the Laws of the United States and gained a spot on the influential Committee on Foreign Relations. In later years Daniel was the ranking Democratic member of the Committee on Finance. He introduced no major legislation but often represented the minority position on such issues as the tariff and other fiscal policy. His courtly manners, oratorical prowess, and somewhat iconoclastic positions made him a beloved fixture in the Senate, and his popularity in Virginia remained unparalleled.

Although an adherent to states' rights Virginia conservatism and aligned with a nascent party organization that had isolated political power in the hands of a few business-oriented brokers, Daniel often took positions that appealed to the mass of voters. He supported an education bill that would have secured federal funding for schools in the South. Most important, Daniel became a leading advocate of a more-inflationary monetary policy. Although opposed to the free circulation of greenbacks and other more-radical measures, he believed that a significant portion of the nation's currency should be based on silver, in addition to gold. In perhaps his most important congressional speech, Daniel argued against repeal of the Sherman Silver Purchase Act, which gold advocates had blamed for the economic panic of 1893. He excoriated the deflationary constraints that had governed the nation's economic policy since British creditors had gained influence after the Civil War.

Daniel's silver stance placed him at the center of the revolt within the national Democratic Party against the hard-money policy of Grover Cleveland's administration. At the 1896 Democratic National Convention, Daniel's election as keynote speaker and temporary chair signaled the triumph of the pro-silver faction and paved the way for the nomination of William Jennings Bryan. Daniel remained a significant force at every subsequent national convention during his lifetime. Although his commitment to silver cooled during the next four years, he acceded to Bryan's nomination at the 1900 convention. As he had in 1896, Daniel squelched efforts to nominate him for vice president. By the 1904 convention he had come to view silver as an impracticable policy, and he helped lead the conservative counterrevolt against Bryan. Named chair of the platform committee, Daniel supervised the removal of a pro-silver plank and mandated silence on more-radical proposals, such as a federal income tax and stringent regulation of trusts.

Daniel's deepening conservatism likewise affected Virginia's political structure. Although staking out independent positions on some issues, he largely cooperated with the Democratic organization led by Thomas Staples Martin, his Senate colleague, including helping to delay the party's adoption of primary elections and opposing party mavericks who challenged the organization. The two senators disagreed about calling a convention to revise the state constitution, which Daniel advocated as early as 1895. Momentum for the convention became too strong even for Martin to withstand, and after voters approved calling it in the spring of 1900, Daniel ran unopposed to represent Campbell County in the convention, which met in Richmond from 12 June 1901 until 26 June 1902.

As chair of the Committee on the Elective Franchise, Daniel was expected to exercise a controlling influence over the key question facing the convention, the disfranchisement of African Americans. On the committee he led the minority faction, which proposed slightly less-onerous suffrage restrictions than did the majority plan. The convention could not decide between the plans, and Daniel was widely viewed as having failed to provide the leadership necessary to break the deadlock. Exhausted and ill, he retreated to Lynchburg and had to be dissuaded from resigning. Daniel returned in March 1902 and served as a chief floor advocate for Carter Glass's amended plan, which the convention eventually adopted. Daniel's address before the convention deprecated the loss of suffrage that many white voters would face but declared it proof that "the Anglo-Saxon . . . will accept tyranny rather than . . . surrender to the inevitable consequences of a putrid electorate." Although he maintained his opposition to proclaiming the constitution in force, rather than submitting it to the electorate for approval in a referendum, he crafted the compromise scheme that made proclamation virtually inevitable. Daniel sat on the Committee on Final Revision, and on 6 June 1902 he voted to approve and place in effect the new constitution.

Daniel spent his last years as elder statesman of the Democratic Party. He remained responsive to reform-minded Virginia voters and acceded to stronger regulatory powers over interstate commerce and a federal eight-hour work law. More-radical proposals drew his sharp rebukes, however, and in 1908 many conservative Democrats considered him a promising alternative to Bryan as a presidential nominee. Despite Daniel's precarious health, he easily won election to the Senate for the fifth time in January 1910. He had suffered a stroke in October 1909 while in Philadelphia, and a second stroke, suffered the following March while he was resting in Florida, paralyzed his left side. Never fully recovering, John Warwick Daniel died in a Lynchburg sanitarium of a cerebral hemorrhage on 29 June 1910 and was buried in Spring Hill

Cemetery in that city. His family declined the governor's offer of a state funeral at the Capitol in Richmond. Lynchburg citizens honored Daniel with a bronze statue, unveiled on 26 May 1915 with the inscription, "Foremost and best beloved Virginian of his time."

Biographies in Sylvia D. Vecellio, "John Warwick Daniel, Lame Lion of Lynchburg: Youth, Soldier, and Rising Politician, 1842–1885" (M.A. thesis, UVA, 1950), and Richard B. Doss, "John Warwick Daniel: A Study in the Virginia Democracy" (Ph.D. diss., UVA, 1955); birth date in Daniel family Bible records, UVA; BVS Marriage Register, Lynchburg; John W. Daniel Papers at Duke, LVA, Lynchburg Public Library, and UVA; Civil War diary and memoir, VHS; published works include Daniel, "The Work of the Constitutional Convention," *Virginia State Bar Association Proceedings* (1902), 257–294, and Edward M. Daniel (son), ed., *Speeches and Orations of John Warwick Daniel* (1911), with frontispiece por.; Compiled Service Records; *Congressional Record*, 49th–61st Cong.; *Richmond Daily Dispatch*, 24 Sept. 1879 (first quotation), 26 Oct. 1883 (second quotation); *Journal of 1901–1902 Convention*, 49–50, 535; *Proceedings and Debates of 1901–1902 Convention*, 1:9–12, 43–47, 418–419, 517–522, 2:2943–2957 (third quotation on 2956), 3100–3104; obituaries in *Lynchburg News, New York Times, Richmond News Leader*, and *Washington Post*, all 30 June 1910, and *Harper's Weekly* 54 (9 July 1910): 21; memorials in *Virginia State Bar Association Proceedings* (1910), 73–80, *Congressional Record*, 61st Cong., 3d sess., 2953–2968, Lynchburg Daniel Monument Committee, *Proceedings Connected with the Unveiling of the Statue of Senator John Warwick Daniel* (1915), and *Lynchburg News*, 27 May 1915 (with statue inscription).

WILLIAM BLAND WHITLEY

DANIEL, Peter V. (24 April 1784–31 May 1860), member of the Council of State, United States district court judge, and associate justice of the Supreme Court of the United States, was born at Crow's Nest, a family estate near the mouth of Potomac Creek in Stafford County. He was the son of Travers Daniel, a prominent planter, and Frances Moncure Daniel. He almost always signed his name with a middle initial, and although relatives and namesakes used the spelling Vivian, there are indications, including a surviving calling card, that he himself may have preferred Vyvian. Among the many family members whom Daniel influenced later in life were two grandnephews, the reformer and writer Moncure Daniel Conway and the journalist and diplomat John Moncure Daniel.

Educated by private tutors, Daniel briefly attended the College of New Jersey (later Princeton University), where he joined the Cliosophic Society, many of whose members went on to distinction in politics and law. From 1805 to 1807 he studied law in Richmond with Edmund Randolph, a former governor and attorney general of the United States. On 21 April 1810 Daniel married Randolph's daughter, Lucy Nelson Randolph. They had two daughters and one son, Peter Vivian Daniel (1818–1889), who became president of the Richmond, Fredericksburg, and Potomac Railroad Company. A nephew, Raleigh Travers Daniel, also lived with him, studied law under his direction, and became a member of the Council of State during the 1840s and attorney general of Virginia after the Civil War.

Daniel qualified to practice law in Stafford County on 11 May 1807 and began practicing in Falmouth. In November 1808 he fought a duel with John Seddon, possibly over political differences. Daniel was unhurt in the exchange of pistol shots at a site in Maryland, but he mortally wounded Seddon. That same year Daniel won election to the first of two consecutive one-year terms representing Stafford County in the House of Delegates. He served on the Committees for Courts of Justice and of Privileges and Elections during his first term and on the Committees for Courts of Justice and of Finance during his second. From the start, Daniel was more successful in politics than in law. He became a champion of agrarianism, states' rights, and strict construction of the Constitution, principles associated with the Virginia and Kentucky Resolutions of 1798.

On 7 January 1812 the General Assembly elected Daniel to the Council of State. He took office two days later and served without interruption until 31 March 1835, when his term under the new state constitution concluded. He was elected president of the Council in 1818, and thereafter when the governor was absent he presided as lieutenant, or acting, governor. One of the longest-serving members of the Council of State, Daniel lived in Richmond and became an influential member of the so-called Richmond Junto, which adhered to old Republican principles of states' rights and a very limited role for the federal government. Almost one-third of the members of the assembly voted for him for governor in January 1830. When Whigs enjoyed a slim majority in the General Assembly in January 1835, they refused to reelect Daniel to the Council, but after Democrats regained control of the legislature in the next election, they elected him on the following 16 December to fill a new vacancy.

Daniel supported the presidential candidacies of William Harris Crawford in 1824, Andrew Jackson in 1828 and 1832, and Martin Van Buren in 1836. For Daniel's party loyalty, more than for his legal acumen, in 1833 Jackson offered to appoint him attorney general, but Daniel declined. On 6 April 1836 Jackson nominated him judge of the United States District Court for the Eastern District of Virginia, an appointment confirmed by the Senate on 19 April. Daniel presided over the court for five relatively undemanding years until 27 February 1841, when Van Buren nominated him to the Supreme Court of the United States to succeed Philip Pendleton Barbour, a Virginian who had died in office. Facing strong opposition, Daniel's Democratic supporters in the Senate outmaneuvered the Whigs. Late at night on 2 March, two days before Van Buren's term as president ended and with only a few Whig senators present, they rammed through his confirmation by a vote of twenty-two to five.

Daniel was appointed to the Supreme Court's fifth circuit during the 1841 term and joined the Court at its next session, which began in January 1842. He ascended the bench with confidence that he would bring true constitutional principles to the Supreme Court, which in his view had long since permitted the encroachment of national power on state authority. Daniel took a particularly restrictive view of Congress's power to regulate commerce. He sharply dissented in the *Passenger Cases* (1849), in which the majority of justices invalidated state efforts to regulate and tax immigrants as violating the Constitution's commerce clause. Fearing the majority's interpretation of that clause, as well as his colleagues' strict reliance on the language of treaties guaranteeing the rights of British subjects in American ports, Daniel bluntly warned of the implications of allowing the commerce clause to override the authority of the southern

states: "if it should suit the commercial speculations of British subjects to land within the territory of any of the States cargoes of negroes from Jamaica, Hayti, or Africa, it would be difficult, according to the broad interpretation of the commercial privileges conferred by those stipulations, to designate any legitimate power in the States to prevent this invasion of their domestic security." Such concerns demonstrated the way in which Daniel identified southern interests with state and local autonomy.

Daniel's views, which some observers and historians interpreted as narrow provincialism, were also evident in his attempts to restrict the reach of the federal courts. In *Propeller Genesee Chief et al.* v. *Fitzhugh et al.* (1852), when the rest of the justices voted to expand federal admiralty jurisdiction to include navigable inland waterways, Daniel dissented and based his opinion on the traditional common-law rule that admiralty law was confined to the high seas and tidal waters. Moreover, in a series of cases regarding corporations, he wrote that corporations lacked the right to sue or be sued in federal courts. Thus, for Daniel, national power in any form posed a threat to state and local interests. His unswerving devotion to these principles prompted him to dissent at a higher rate than any of his colleagues—nearly a third of all of his written opinions were dissents.

Daniel spoke for the majority of the Court in *West River Bridge Company* v. *Dix et al.* (1848), a major constitutional case involving eminent domain, the power of a state to take private property, with compensation, for the sake of the public good. A 1795 Vermont charter had authorized a company to maintain a toll bridge for a hundred years, but the state later decided to turn the bridge into a free public highway and compensated its owners. The owners contended that the state's action violated the Constitution's contract clause. Daniel's opinion sustained the state's actions on the ground that no difference existed between incorporated and unincorporated property when it came to eminent domain. His hostility to corporations (even though at the time of his death he owned stock in several railroad companies) and his belief in state sovereignty lay behind his opinion. Although the majority did not share Daniel's extreme views on these subjects, they agreed on the need for states to have extensive power of eminent domain in order to promote economic development.

Known for his dry wit and acerbic tongue, Daniel clung tenaciously throughout his life to his political principles. Remaining a staunch proponent of traditional agrarianism and strict construction of the Constitution, he was the most conservative Supreme Court justice of the mid-nineteenth century. Not surprisingly, Daniel was a strong supporter of slavery, which he viewed as the foundation of southern society. A slave owner himself, he believed that state control over slavery was the only way to preserve the region's way of life. In *Prigg* v. *The Commonwealth of Pennsylvania* (1842), Daniel concurred in upholding the Fugitive Slave Law of 1793 and invalidating Pennsylvania's personal liberty law. Daniel wrote a separate opinion denying the national government's exclusive power over the return of fugitives and highlighting the role of individual states and slave owners in the process.

Over time, Daniel became more strident in his support of slavery and more sectional in his constitutional positions. A visit to New England in 1847 confirmed his worst opinions of the region, for he detested its bustling mercantilism and uncouth incivility. By 1857, when Daniel wrote a separate opinion in *Dred Scott* v. *Sandford* (1857), he was the most pro-southern and proslavery of all the justices. Like most of his colleagues, he denied that African Americans, enslaved or free, could be citizens, and he held that Congress lacked the power to legislate on slavery in the territories. But unlike his fellow justices, Daniel even maintained that the Northwest Ordinance of 1787, which had banned slavery north of the Ohio River, was unconstitutional. That position made Daniel's opinion even more extreme than the infamous proslavery opinion of Chief Justice Roger Brooke Taney.

Daniel was not wealthy, but he furnished his Richmond residence well, kept a fine wine cellar, and accumulated a library of nearly 600 volumes in addition to the very large law library that he owned, which alone was appraised after his death at $853. The last years of Daniel's life were difficult ones. His wife died on 14 November 1847. Daniel married Elizabeth Harris, of Philadelphia, on 20 October 1853. They had one daughter and one son. In their Washington residence on 4 January 1857 she accidentally set her clothing on fire with a candle and died of the burns, leaving Daniel bitter and lonely for the remainder of his life. Peter V. Daniel died in Richmond on 31 May 1860 and was buried in Hollywood Cemetery in that city.

Birth date on gravestone; biographies in Lawrence Burnette Jr., "Peter V. Daniel: Agrarian Justice," *VMHB* 62 (1954): 289–305, John P. Frank, *Justice Daniel Dissenting: A Biography of Peter V. Daniel, 1784–1860* (1964), with frontispiece por., and Frank Otto Gatell, "Peter V. Daniel," in Leon Friedman and Fred L. Israel, eds., *The Justices of the United States Supreme Court, 1789–1969: Their Lives and Major Opinions* (1969), 1:795–805; marriages in Henrico Co. Marriage Bonds, *Richmond Enquirer*, 24 Apr. 1810, and *Daily Richmond Enquirer*, 24 Oct. 1853; principal collections of Daniel letters in Daniel Family Papers, Huntington, Daniel Family Papers, Acc. 23652, LVA, Gooch Family Papers and Peter V. Daniel Papers (with calling card of Peter Vyvian Daniel), both UVA, and Daniel Family Papers (including Daniel's memoir of first wife, 5 Dec. 1847) and Gooch Family Papers, both VHS; *Passenger Cases* (1849) (7 Howard), *United States Reports*, 48:283–573 (quotation on 508); will and estate inventory in Richmond City Circuit Court Will Book, 1:594–600, 608–620; obituaries (both with middle name Vyvian and birth in 1785) in *Richmond Daily Whig*, 1 June 1860, and *Richmond Enquirer*, 5 June 1860; obituary in *Richmond Daily Dispatch*, 1 June 1860; memorials in *Richmond Enquirer*, 5 June 1860, and (24 Howard), *United States Reports*, 65:iii–vii.

TIMOTHY S. HUEBNER

DANIEL, Peter Vivian (17 April 1818–2 April 1889), railroad executive, was born in Henrico County at the country farm of his parents, Peter V. Daniel (1784–1860), then a member of the Council of State and later an associate justice of the Supreme Court of the United States, and his first wife, Lucy Nelson Randolph Daniel. His maternal grandfather was Edmund Randolph, a former governor and attorney general of the United States. While Daniel was growing up, his cousin Raleigh Travers Daniel, who became a member of the Council of State and attorney general of Virginia, lived in the Daniel household and studied law with Daniel's father.

Peter V. Daniel Jr., as he always identified himself even after the death of his father, was privately educated until age eighteen, when he decided to become a civil engineer. He worked for several years for his kinsman Moncure Robinson during the construction of the Louisa Railroad Company line and the initial surveying and construction of the Richmond and Petersburg Railroad Company line. Daniel then studied law under his father's direction and qualified to practice on 10 March 1843. While practicing in Richmond he took part in civic affairs. At a conference on education in August 1845 he offered resolutions requesting that the General Assembly establish a statewide system of public schools. In December 1854 he was the founding president of the Richmond Young Men's Christian Association. The following year Daniel wrote a preface to and reprinted *A Vindication of Edmund Randolph*, which his grandfather had published in 1795 after being dismissed from the president's cabinet. On 1 December 1846 in Philadelphia, Daniel married Mary Robertson. They had one son and one daughter. After his father died in 1860, Daniel became the guardian of his two orphaned half siblings.

On 31 May 1853 Daniel was elected president of the Richmond and Petersburg Railroad Company. He oversaw the refinancing of its debt and replaced old track with new, heavy-duty rails. He rebuilt a spur to Port Walthall, on the James River, which for a time was the terminus of connecting steamboat service that carried passengers to and from Norfolk. The Richmond and Petersburg Railroad leased the twenty-one-mile Clover Hill Railroad that transported coal from the fields of western Chesterfield County to the main line north of Petersburg.

Daniel was elected president of the allied Richmond, Fredericksburg, and Potomac Railroad Company on 18 June 1860 to succeed Edwin Robinson, a brother of Moncure Robinson. The RF&P operated seventy-five miles of track from Richmond to a wharf at Aquia Creek in Stafford County. Passengers to and from Washington, D.C., traveled between that city and the railroad terminus on steamboats of the railroad's Potomac Steamboat Company. On 19 April 1861, two days after Virginia seceded from the Union, the federal government seized four of the steamboats and ended connecting service between Aquia Creek and Washington.

Throughout the Civil War, Daniel strove to keep the railroad running. Raids on its track and bridges required constant repair and rebuilding, and Daniel and executives of other railroads had to combat proposals to employ old iron rails for other purposes, such as construction of naval vessels. Daniel estimated in the spring of 1863 that Virginia's railroads needed more than 4,000 tons of iron rails each month to keep operating. The RF&P and four other Virginia railroads jointly sent an agent to England to procure supplies. Daniel cooperated with the Confederate government and army to keep troops and supplies moving while lobbying Confederate congressmen and bureaucrats in opposition to proposals that the Confederacy's railroads be operated under government or military authority. In 1863 he cut salaries and dismissed laborers as a result of reduced traffic on the truncated line, but he also argued that railroad employees should be exempt from conscription. RF&P men formed Company G of the 19th Regiment Virginia militia under the command of Captain Samuel Ruth, superintendent of the railroad. Unknown to Daniel or to the Confederate government, Ruth was a secret agent of the United States and was able throughout the war to slow the movement of trains at vital times.

Because Daniel possessed more than $20,000 in personal property at the end of the Civil War, he applied for and on 3 July 1865 received a presidential pardon. Ruth asserted that Daniel had been an early advocate of secession, but Daniel maintained that he operated the railroad as a commercial enterprise and had kept known Unionists on the job during the war. After the war, the RF&P borrowed $100,000 at 8 percent interest to finance reconstruction of the railroad and hired Edmund Trowbridge Dana Myers, a former major in the Confederate army, to direct the work. The railroad resumed service between Richmond and Aquia Creek in September 1865. Daniel reported at the annual stockholders meeting in 1866 that with the collapse of the Confederacy the company and its stockholders had lost $700,000, including a large award in Confederate securities that the RF&P had received in 1863 after successfully suing the Orange and Alexandria Railroad for operating a competing mail service in violation of the RF&P's

charter. In the spring of 1866 the RF&P joined the Richmond and Petersburg Railroad in a venture to build and operate a 1.25-mile connection between the two lines in Richmond.

At the RF&P's annual meetings in November 1867 and 1868, Daniel reported that the company's income remained low, an occurrence he attributed to a general business depression. He also successfully fended off what he believed was an attempt by officers of the recently chartered Alexandria and Fredericksburg Railroad Company to acquire a controlling interest in the RF&P. Early in 1871 Daniel also became president of the Potomac Railroad Company, which constructed a short connecting line between Quantico Creek and the RF&P's northern terminus that enabled passenger trains beginning in May 1872 to run directly from Richmond to Alexandria. The RF&P then discontinued its steamboat service at Aquia Creek.

Daniel declined reelection to another term as president of the RF&P in December 1871 but remained president of the Potomac Railroad until 1880. He served as general counsel of the RF&P for several years after he left its presidency and then returned to the private practice of law for about two years before poor health forced him to retire. Peter Vivian Daniel died of the effects of paralysis, possibly after suffering a stroke, at his Richmond home on 2 April 1889. He was buried in the city's Hollywood Cemetery.

Family history, with birth date of 17 Apr. 1818, in Hayden, *Virginia Genealogies*, 317; French Biographies, with birth date of 17 Apr. 1818; variant birth date of 17 Mar. 1818 on gravestone; collections of Daniel Family Papers at Huntington, LVA (including law license), and VHS; personal correspondence in Gooch Family Papers and Daniel H. London Papers, both VHS; *Richmond Daily Whig*, 7 (misdated 6) Dec. 1846; annual reports of Richmond and Petersburg Railroad Company (1853–1860) and of Richmond, Fredericksburg, and Potomac Railroad Company (1860–1871), Records of the Board of Public Works, RG 57, LVA; Richmond, Fredericksburg, and Potomac Railroad Company Papers, including por., Acc. 36460, LVA; Daniel Letter Book (1860–1871), in Richmond, Fredericksburg, and Potomac Railroad Company Records, VHS; numerous reports and references in *OR*; Presidential Pardons; BVS Death Register, Richmond City, with age at death as seventy-one years, eleven months, and fifteen days; Hollywood Cemetery Burial Register, 2:235; obituaries in *Richmond State*, 2 Apr. 1889, and *Richmond Daily Times* and *Richmond Dispatch*, both 3 Apr. 1889.

MARTIN STAKES LANE

DANIEL, Raleigh Travers (15 October 1805–16 August 1877), member of the Council of State and attorney general of Virginia, was born in Falmouth, Stafford County, and was the son of John Moncure Daniel, an army surgeon, and the second of his three wives, Margaret Stone Daniel. His sister married William Crane, a prominent Baptist lay leader in Richmond and Baltimore. After the death of his father in 1813, Daniel lived with and was educated in the Richmond home of his uncle and guardian, Peter V. Daniel (1784–1860), a member of the Council of State and later an associate justice of the Supreme Court of the United States. R. T. Daniel studied law with his uncle and on 21 November 1826 received his law license. He married Elizabeth Susan Tabb Riddle, a Gloucester County widow, on 7 November 1831. They had at least four daughters and three sons. She died on 13 June 1874.

Daniel served for a time in the 1830s and 1840s as commonwealth's attorney for Henrico County. Although he earned a reputation as an able attorney, politics consumed much of his time. A Whig well-known locally, he won election to the House of Delegates from the city of Richmond in 1841 and was reelected each of the succeeding three years. Daniel served on the Committees on Banks and for Courts of Justice all four years and chaired the Committee on Banks during the 1844–1845 session. He sat on the Committee on Roads and Internal Navigation during his first term and on the committee on the library during his second. Daniel was a candidate for presidential elector when Henry Clay ran in 1844. On 30 January of the following year, the slim Whig majority in the General Assembly elected Daniel to the Council of State by a two-vote margin to replace John Rutherfoord, a veteran Democratic member.

Daniel took his seat on the governor's advisory Council for a three-year term on 1 April 1845 and narrowly won reelection three years later, when a few Democrats voted for him. Service on the Council was not arduous, and the three members often rotated duty so that only one member attended. On several occasions when the governor was absent from Richmond, Daniel presided as lieutenant governor, as his uncle and guardian had done many times during the 1820s and 1830s. On 10 December 1850, with partisan feelings running high in the assembly, the Democratic majority replaced Daniel with his nephew, John Moncure Daniel (1825–1865), then editor of the *Richmond Examiner*. Even though Daniel's term did not expire until the end of March 1851, he attended the Council for the last time on 26 December 1850.

In August 1850 Daniel campaigned in a fourteen-candidate field for one of six seats representing Richmond and the counties of Charles City, Henrico, and New Kent in a convention called to revise the state constitution. An opponent of all the proposed democratic reforms, he lost badly. In the presidential election of 1860 he supported John Bell, a former Whig and candidate of the Constitutional Union Party. Although Daniel initially opposed secession, he warmly embraced the Confederate cause after the spring of 1861 and in November of that year was a presidential elector for Jefferson Davis. Lacking a record of distinction in the militia and being too old for military service, Daniel did not fight in the Civil War but served instead as commonwealth's attorney of Richmond.

Daniel gained statewide prominence in the altered political environment after the war. In April 1867 he made a patronizing address before a Richmond meeting of African Americans who were soon to vote for the first time in which he suggested that they follow the advice of the state's established political leaders. That tactic failed to dissuade freedmen from supporting radical reformers for seats in the Convention of 1867–1868. To promote white supremacy and mobilize opposition to Republicans and radicals, Daniel took part in December 1867 in founding the Conservative Party, of which he was state chair until 1873. He severely criticized the convention's draft constitution, which provided for universal manhood suffrage while disfranchising many Confederate veterans. During the stalemate that followed the convention's proposal, Daniel initially opposed but later joined conservatives' successful campaign to convince President Ulysses S. Grant to allow separate referenda on the constitution and on the sections pertaining to Confederate disfranchisement. As expected, the voters ratified the constitution and defeated the disqualification clauses.

In 1870 Daniel was a candidate for congressman at-large from Virginia, a seat that members of the Convention of 1867–1868 created, perhaps on the erroneous assumption that the state was entitled to nine members in the House of Representatives rather than the eight from the existing districts. In July 1870 the House refused to seat Joseph Eggleston Segar, who had been elected to the at-large seat in 1869. After Daniel was elected without serious opposition in November 1870, Virginia members of Congress submitted his credentials to the House of Representatives, but the Committee on Elections made no report on his eligibility, and he did not attempt to take his seat.

After winning election to the House of Delegates for a two-year term in 1871, Daniel became chair of the important Committee on Finance. In August 1873 the Conservative Party nominated him for attorney general of Virginia. A supporter of the controversial Funding Act of 1871 but running on a ticket that included an opponent of that measure, Daniel did not campaign in areas where the act was unpopular. He ran strongest in the regions of Virginia with the fewest African Americans and the weakest Republican Party organizations. On 6 November 1873 Daniel defeated the Republican candidate, David Fultz, by a margin of more than 27,000 votes of about 207,000 cast.

Daniel's four-year term as attorney general began on 1 January 1874. He represented the state in federal court, defended the state's interests in the state courts, and rendered opinions when requested to do so by Virginia public officials needing legal guidance in the conduct of their duties. He opposed allowing inmates in the state penitentiary time off for good behavior as permitted by prison rules unless the governor specifically ordered a reduction of the sentence as an act of clemency. Daniel resisted enforcement of federal laws prohibiting Virginians from obstructing African American attempts to vote because he argued the measures violated the state's right to control elections. He did not, however, recommend enforcement of state or local laws against those obstructive tactics. Daniel also represented Virginia before an arbitration commission that settled a boundary dispute with Maryland. The arbitrators ruled against Virginia's claim to the Potomac River and drew the line across the Chesapeake Bay farther south than Daniel believed was justified.

Raleigh Travers Daniel died of a bowel hemorrhage at his home in Richmond on 16 August 1877, a few days after securing nomination for a second term as attorney general. He was buried in Hollywood Cemetery.

Biographies in *Richmond Enquirer*, 8 Aug. 1873 (with birth date), in Conservative Party campaign pamphlet, *Speech of Hon. R. M. T. Hunter, Delivered at Richmond, Aug. 22, 1873* . . . (1873), 19–20, and in George L. Christian, "Reminiscences of Some of the Dead of the Bench and Bar of Richmond," *Virginia Law Register* 14 (1909): 19–20; variant birth date of 7 Oct. 1805 in *Richmond Enquirer*, 17 Aug. 1877; incomplete family history in Hayden, *Virginia Genealogies*, 308, 313–314; Daniel Family Papers, VHS; some Daniel letters in Robert Anderson Papers, Huntington, in James Lawson Kemper Executive Papers, RG 3, LVA, in other collections at LVA and VHS, and printed in John Y. Simon et al., eds., *The Papers of Ulysses S. Grant* (1967–), 19:166, 167, 171; Council of State Journal, esp. (1845–1846), 2, and (1850–1851), 134, RG 75, LVA; *Richmond Enquirer*, 11 Nov. 1831; *Richmond Daily Whig*, 31 Jan., 3 Feb. 1845, 16 Apr. 1867; *Daily Richmond Enquirer*, 13 Mar. 1848, 13 Dec. 1850; *Richmond Daily Enquirer and Examiner*, 2, 17 Feb. 1869; Election Records, no. 1 (1873), RG 13, LVA; *Annual Reports of the Attorney General of the State of Virginia* (1874–1877); Hummel and Smith, *Portraits and Statuary*, 31 (pors.); obituaries, accounts of funeral, and tributes in *Richmond Daily Dispatch*, *Richmond Daily Whig*, and *Richmond Enquirer*, all 17, 18 Aug. 1877; memorial in *Virginia Law Journal* 1 (1877): 510.

BRENT TARTER

DANIEL, Robert Prentiss (2 November 1902–5 January 1968), president of Virginia State College, was born on the school's campus at Ettrick, near Petersburg. He was the son of Carrie Tabitha Green Daniel and Charles James Daniel, who was the institution's secretary from 1888 to 1916. Daniel attended the school's preparatory department until his father's death in 1916, when the family moved to Richmond. He graduated in 1920 from Wayland Academy, the high school division of Virginia Union University, where he worked as an assistant instructor of mathematics while completing his bachelor's degree. After graduating from Virginia Union in 1924, Daniel

became a mathematics instructor at Wayland. The following year he taught English at Virginia Union and in 1926 was named an assistant professor of education and acting head of that department. On 11 September 1929 Daniel married Blanche Ardelle Taylor, a Virginia Union graduate with master's degrees from Columbia University and the Union Theological Seminary, in New York. The childless couple raised two nephews.

Daniel received an M.A. in education from Columbia University in 1928 and became permanent department chair, full professor, and director of Virginia Union's Extension Division. In the last role, he supervised the formation of the Norfolk Unit of Virginia Union University (later Norfolk State University). After completing a dissertation published as *A Psychological Study of Delinquent and Non-Delinquent Negro Boys* (1932), Daniel received a Ph.D. in educational psychology from Columbia in 1932 and began teaching both education and psychology courses. When Virginia Union organized academic departments into divisions in 1934, he became director of the Division of Education, Psychology, Philosophy, and Religious Education. During the summers of 1935 and 1936 Daniel was a visiting graduate professor of education at Hampton Institute (later Hampton University), and in the 1940s he engaged in postdoctoral study at the Union Theological Seminary, in New York.

In 1936 the board of trustees of Shaw University in Raleigh, North Carolina, selected Daniel as its fifth president, and only its second black president. Under his leadership during the next fourteen years all campus buildings were renovated, enrollment doubled, and donations totaled more than $1 million. In December 1949 Daniel was elected the fifth president of Virginia State College (later Virginia State University). Taking office the following February, he steered the school through an era of major social upheaval, including the integration of the student body and faculty following the *Brown* v. *Board of Education* decision in 1954 and nonviolent student protests against segregated facilities in the neighboring community. Daniel launched an extensive building campaign, doubled the number of faculty members with doctoral degrees, and established the Division of Field Services to coordinate off-campus community services. The Norfolk Division, which he had helped establish while at Virginia Union and which had become part of Virginia State College in 1944, continued to flourish.

Daniel's articles on race, psychology, and education appeared in the *Journal of Educational Psychology*, the *Journal of Educational Sociology*, and the *Journal of Negro Education*. He advocated an increase in scholarly standards and training in fields not traditionally open to African Americans in order to prepare students for civic leadership in the black community's struggle for equal rights. Daniel held high office in many professional organizations. He served as president of the Virginia State Teachers Association (1934–1936), of the North Carolina Negro College Conference (1938–1939), of the Association of Colleges and Secondary Schools for Negroes (1953–1954), and of the Council of Presidents of Institutions of the Central Intercollegiate Athletic Association (1960–1962). Daniel was secretary of the board of directors of the United Negro College Fund, Incorporated (1946–1949), and the first black president of the Association of Northern Baptist Educational Institutions (1948–1949). He served as director of training for African American scouts in the Richmond area and in 1939 was appointed to the Interracial Work Committee of the National Council of the Boy Scouts of America.

Daniel received a National Urban League Certificate for Distinguished Service in Education in 1948 and honorary degrees from Virginia Union University and Morris Brown College, in Atlanta, Georgia, in 1949. He was the only African American whom President Harry S. Truman named to the new eleven-member Advisory Board on International Development in 1950. Reappointed by President Dwight David Eisenhower, Daniel served until the board disbanded in 1957. He chaired a team that evaluated the federal technical assistance program in Liberia in 1954. The following year Daniel joined the Virginia delegation to the White House Conference on Education, and in 1960 he was a resource leader at the White House Conference on Children and Youth. From 1963 to 1964 he served as a trustee of the Prince Edward Free School Association, which organized free schooling in Prince Edward County after the county closed its public schools to prevent desegregation.

Daniel's wife died on 13 December 1965. In Roanoke Rapids, North Carolina, in December 1966 he married a widow, Marie Plummer Orsot. They had no children. Daniel suffered a heart attack in July 1967 and announced in October that he would retire the following June. Robert Prentiss Daniel died at his home after a second heart attack on 5 January 1968 and was buried in Blandford Cemetery, in Petersburg.

Biographies in *Current Biography* 13 (1952): 14–16, and *NCAB*, vol. K (1967): 53–56 (por. facing 53), with birth date provided by Daniel; family information in Luther Porter Jackson, "The Daniel Family of Virginia," *Negro History Bulletin* 11 (1947): 51–58 (por. on 54); biographical sketch, personal and professional correspondence, and other documents in Robert Prentiss Daniel Papers, Virginia State University; publications include Daniel, "Basic Considerations for Valid Interpretations of Experimental Studies Pertaining to Racial Differences," *Journal of Educational Psychology* 23 (1932): 15–27, "Personality Differences Between Delinquent and Non-Delinquent Negro Boys," *Journal of Negro Education* 1 (1932): 381–387, "Negro-White Differences in Non-Intellectual Traits, and in Special Abilities," ibid. 3 (1934): 411–423, "One Consideration of Redirection of Emphasis of the Negro College," ibid. 5 (1936): 479–483, "The Impact of the War upon the Church-Related College and University," ibid. 11 (1942): 359–364, "Relationship of the Negro Public College and the Negro Private and Church-Related College," ibid. 29 (1960): 388–393, and with Walter G. Daniel, "The Curriculum of the Negro College," *Journal of Educational Sociology* 19 (1946): 496–502; BVS Marriage Register, Richmond City (1929); *Richmond News Leader*, 11 June 1936, 15 Dec. 1949, 14, 17 Oct., 30 Nov. 1950; *Norfolk Journal and Guide*, 19 Oct. 1946; *New York Times*, 15 Oct. 1950; *Richmond Times-Dispatch*, 30 Nov. 1950, 18 Oct. 1959; *Richmond Afro-American*, 10 Dec. 1966; *Washington Post*, 8 Oct. 1967; *Commonwealth* 17 (Dec. 1950): 48–49; obituaries in *Richmond News Leader*, 5, 6 Jan. 1968, *Richmond Times-Dispatch* and *Washington Post*, both 6 Jan. 1968, and *New York Times*, 9 Jan. 1968; editorial tribute in *Richmond Times-Dispatch*, 11 Jan. 1968.

KARA MILES TURNER

DANIEL, Wilbur Clarence "Dan" (12 May 1914–23 January 1988), member of the House of Representatives, was born in Pittsylvania County and was the son of Reuben Earl Daniel, a sharecropper, and his second wife, Georgia Lee Grant Daniel. He attended Mecklenburg County public schools until age fifteen, when he went to work as a store clerk to help support his family. In 1933 Daniel (called Clarence until adulthood, when he acquired the nickname Dan) joined the Civilian Conservation Corps in Spotsylvania County. He married Daisy Rivers Greene Fines on 2 June 1934 in Hyattsville, Maryland. The childless couple separated three years later. By 1939 Daniel had discovered that Fines's divorce from her first husband had not been made final at the time she married Daniel. He sued for a declaration of annulment, which the Stafford County circuit court granted on 16 September 1939.

In July 1934 Daniel began working as a shipping clerk for a clothing-manufacturing company in Fredericksburg. He also played semiprofessional baseball, and by 1937 a major-league team was scouting him. In that year he fractured his shoulder after falling from a bus and at a hospital received ether twice. The procedure may have weakened his lungs, and Daniel developed tuberculosis. He was treated at the Blue Ridge Sanatorium in Charlottesville from the autumn of 1937 until April 1939 and at a Danville sanatorium from then until July 1939. While hospitalized he met Ruby Gordon McGregor. They married in Chatham on 30 September 1939 and had one son.

Daniel moved to Danville, where he worked first as a cloth handler and then as a junior foreman at the Riverside and Dan River Cotton Mills. During World War II he enlisted in the navy but received a medical discharge because of a collapsed lung, the result of his treatment for tuberculosis. After four years of adult evening classes, Daniel graduated from high school first in his class in 1948. He won steady promotion at Dan River Mills, from supervisor of hourly employees, to employment manager, and finally in 1957 to assistant to the chairman of the board.

Daniel joined the local chapter of the American Legion in 1944. He served as state commander for the 1951–1952 term and four years later was the first Virginian to be named national commander. Throughout his Legion service Daniel championed the conservative themes of the 1950s: limited government, self-reliance, nationalism and a strong national defense, and above all anticommunism. With three million members the American Legion was a formidable

pressure group, and Daniel was able to lobby nationally for veterans' rights and benefits.

In Virginia politics Daniel comfortably aligned with the Democratic Party organization controlled by United States senator Harry Flood Byrd (1887–1966). Daniel opposed integration of the public schools, supported Massive Resistance, and publicly called for a congressional investigation of the National Association for the Advancement of Colored People. He also served on Virginia's Commission on Constitutional Government, which developed philosophical attacks on the civil rights movement and theoretical justification for states' rights and nullification.

Daniel represented Danville in the House of Delegates for nine years beginning with the assembly session of 1960. His committee assignments included Education, Finance, General Laws, Militia and Police (which he chaired during the 1968 session), Privileges and Elections, and Public Property, as well as the Commission of Veterans' Affairs and the Virginia State Crime Commission. A Byrd loyalist, Daniel supported retaining the poll tax, helped gerrymander legislative and congressional districts to protect organization stalwarts, and often joined his colleagues in thwarting Governor James Lindsay Almond Jr.'s legislative proposals after the governor deserted Byrd on Massive Resistance. Although Daniel attended the Democratic National Conventions in 1960 and 1964, he followed Byrd's lead in remaining silent on the party tickets and, by implication, in supporting the respective Republican presidential candidates.

During the first administration of Mills Edwin Godwin Jr., Daniel shifted from conservatism to conservative moderation by endorsing a state sales tax, an increase in teachers' salaries, a statewide system of community colleges (which he helped construct as a member of the House Committee on Education), and a 2 percent automobile titling tax earmarked for improvements in transportation. In foreign affairs he remained strongly conservative; in 1966 he publicly denounced opponents of the Vietnam War as cowards unworthy of their country.

In 1966 Daniel managed the successful statewide senatorial campaign of Harry Flood Byrd Jr. (b. 1914). The following year he leaked to the press his intention to seek the Democratic nomination for governor in 1969. Unfavorable reaction in the press forced him retreat to the more attractive option of running for the House of Representatives. In 1968 Democrats in the Fifth Congressional District (comprising the cities of Danville, Galax, Martinsville, and South Boston and eleven counties in the southern part of Virginia along the North Carolina border) unanimously chose Daniel. Garnering 70,681 votes in the November election, he soundly defeated the Republican candidate, Weldon W. Tuck, who received 34,608 votes, and an independent candidate, Ruth LaCountess Harvey Wood Charity, a prominent Danville attorney and civil rights activist, who tallied 24,196 votes.

Reelected to the House of Representatives nine times, Daniel did not disappoint his conservative constituency. During nineteen years in Congress, he often received 100 percent ratings from the conservative Americans for Constitutional Action. He served on the Armed Services Committee in each of his terms and chaired its Readiness subcommittee during the 100th Congress (1987–1988). Daniel was also appointed to the Committee on the District of Columbia during the 94th and 95th Congresses (1975–1976, 1977–1978). He sat on the Permanent Select Committee on Intelligence during the 99th and 100th Congresses (1985–1986, 1987–1988) and during the latter was named to its Program and Budget Authorization subcommittee. Daniel worked tirelessly to strengthen national defense. He called for massive military operations to defeat the communists in Vietnam but ultimately acquiesced in American withdrawal. Daniel opposed détente and prodded the military into creating forces adept at antiterrorism and brushfire wars.

During the Watergate investigation Daniel supported Richard Milhous Nixon until the release of audiotapes finally demonstrated the president's complicity in obstructing justice. Daniel was one of thirty-four friendly legislators invited to the White House on the evening of the president's resignation. During Ronald Reagan's administration Daniel became a leader of the Boll Weevils, a group of conservative Sunbelt Democrats who supported supply-side econom-

ics and increases in defense spending. He helped write the Omnibus Anti-Drug Act of 1986, which provided money for interdiction, enforcement, rehabilitation, and education.

On 19 January 1988 Daniel announced that because of heart disease he would not seek reelection. Four days later, while visiting his son in Charlottesville, he was admitted to the University of Virginia Medical Center after suffering chest pains. Wilbur Clarence "Dan" Daniel died of an aortic dissection later that afternoon, on 23 January 1988. He was interred in Highland Burial Park, in Danville. In 1990 Averett College (after 2001 Averett University), of which Daniel had been a trustee, established a professorship bearing his name. Three years later Danville leaders named a 170-acre recreational facility Dan Daniel Memorial Park.

Jack Irby Hayes Jr., *Dan Daniel and the Persistence of Conservatism in Virginia* (1997), with pors.; congressional papers, personal correspondence, memorabilia, and photographs in Dan Daniel Collection, Averett University; Daniel correspondence in Harry Flood Byrd (1887–1966) Papers, UVA; State Board of Elections, Abstracts of Votes, Acc. 33132, RG 14, LVA; *Danville Bee*, 3 Oct. 1939; *Richmond Times-Dispatch*, 9 Sept. 1956, 26 Jan. 1966, 6 Nov. 1968, 26 July 1982; *Danville Register*, 6 Nov. 1968; *Washington Post*, 30 Dec. 1985, 20 Jan. 1988; *Richmond News Leader*, 17 May 1989; obituaries, accounts of funeral, and editorial tributes in *Richmond Times-Dispatch*, 24 Jan. 1988, *Danville Register*, 24–27 Jan. 1988, *Richmond News Leader* and *Washington Post*, both 25 Jan. 1988, and *Danville Bee*, 25–27 Jan. 1988.

JACK IRBY HAYES JR.

DANIEL, William (26 November 1806–28 March 1873), judge of the Virginia Supreme Court of Appeals, was the son of William Daniel, a Cumberland County attorney, and his first wife, Margaret Baldwin Daniel. He was born most likely in his mother's hometown of Winchester and was related to many influential Virginians. His sister Martha Daniel married Wood Bouldin (1811–1876), a member of the Supreme Court of Appeals after the Civil War, and his sister Elvira Augusta Daniel married a noted civil engineer, Charles Ellet, and became the mother of Mary Virginia Ellet Cabell, one of the founding officers of the National Society Daughters of the American Revolution. In 1813 Daniel's father became a judge of the General Court. The family moved from Cumberland County to Lynchburg about 1819, and they later lived at Point of Honor, a residence then just outside the city in an area that became known as Daniel's Hill.

William Daniel Jr., as he continued to sign his name even after the death of his father in November 1839, graduated from Hampden-Sydney College in 1826. He attended three academic sessions at the University of Virginia from February 1827 through July 1829 and during the final session studied law. He numbered among the first generation of Virginia attorneys educated in law schools rather than by reading law as apprentices. The experience fostered in Daniel and his contemporaries a sense of professionalism and began to mark the end of the planter-lawyer image that had characterized preceding generations of Virginia's legal culture. Daniel maintained a thriving law practice in Lynchburg and soon became one of the celebrities of the bar. On 8 December 1841 he married Sarah Ann Warwick, also of Lynchburg. Before her death on 8 August 1845, they had one daughter and one son, John Warwick Daniel, a Democratic Party leader who served in the House of Representatives and the United States Senate.

In August 1831 Daniel won election to the House of Delegates from Campbell County. He was twenty-four years old when elected and therefore not old enough to take office, but he met the minimum age requirement by the time the assembly convened in December. Daniel served on the standing Committees for Courts of Justice and of Finance and on a joint committee to examine the records of the Bank of Virginia and the Farmers' Bank of Virginia. He made his legislative debut during one of the General Assembly's most important debates, on the future of slavery in Virginia. Although he had probably not yet acquired any slaves, at that time his father paid taxes on about thirty age twelve or older. On 14 January 1832 Daniel spoke in opposition to a proposal for emancipation *post nati*, which would have freed children born to enslaved mothers and thus slowly extinguished the institution of slavery as older slaves died. Daniel's proslavery argument was premised on his strong commitment to the sanctity of the private property rights of slave owners.

Daniel was not reelected in 1832, but he returned to the House of Delegates for the 1835–1836 and 1838 sessions. During the first term he was ranking member of the Committee of Privileges and Elections and chaired the Committee to Examine the Second Auditor's Office; during the second he was a member of the Committee for Courts of Justice. Daniel, a Democrat and defender of states' rights doctrines, in 1845 delivered a long eulogy in Lynchburg after the death of Andrew Jackson.

On 15 December 1846 the General Assembly elected Daniel to a vacant seat on the Virginia Supreme Court of Appeals. One of the unsuccessful candidates was Richard Cassius Lee Moncure, who won election to the court in 1851. Daniel's maternal uncle, Briscoe Gerard Baldwin, sat on the court until 1852, and Daniel joined the family of another court member on 6 June 1850 when he married Elizabeth Hannah Cabell, a celebrated beauty and daughter of William H. Cabell, who was also a former governor. They lived at Rivermont, Daniel's house on Daniel's Hill. They had no children.

Daniel took his seat on the bench during the January 1847 term and wrote his first of more than one hundred majority opinions for the court in the combined cases *Sheppards* v. *Turpin* and *Sheppards* v. *Stubbs*. These cases dealt with questions of equity jurisprudence and property rights, realms of law in which Daniel excelled and that provided the subject matter for many of his subsequent opinions. His opinions were generally long essays that often recounted the legal history of the statute or precept in question and reflected a strong grasp of the procedural and conceptual technicalities characteristic of Virginia's laws.

The Constitution of 1851 altered the method of appointing judges by establishing five judicial districts, each of which popularly elected one justice to the Supreme Court of Appeals. Daniel's section comprised the city of Lynchburg and twelve counties to its south and east, including Campbell, Charlotte, and Pittsylvania. As a testament to his standing in the community, four hundred Lynchburg residents endorsed his candidacy in an open letter published in a local newspaper days before the election. On 27 May 1852 he defeated James Murray Whittle, a member of the Convention of 1850–1851, and John Robertson, a former member of the House of Representatives.

Daniel delivered his most notable opinion on 9 April 1861 in *Baker* v. *Wise, Governor*, which upheld a Virginia law that required state inspectors to verify that ships owned by residents of another state departing Virginia for northern ports carried no escaping slaves. Daniel, who reported forty-one slaves and $200,000 in real estate in the 1860 census, ruled that the statute was a valid exercise of the police powers reserved to the states and not an infringement of Congress's power to regulate interstate and foreign commerce.

The court sat through the Civil War and last met on 8 February 1865. The judges intended to sit again in April but did not as a result of the evacuation of Richmond. In February 1866 the General Assembly, which under the constitution adopted by the Restored government had again taken responsibility for electing judges, did not return Daniel to his seat on the bench.

Because the value of his property exceeded $20,000 after the Civil War, Daniel was required to apply for a presidential pardon, which he received on 14 July 1865. He resumed practicing law in Lynchburg with his son and son-in-law. William Daniel died of apoplexy while attending a session of court in the Nelson County courthouse on 28 March 1873. He was buried in the Old City Cemetery (also known as the Old Methodist Cemetery) in Lynchburg, where his memorial stone bears the inscription, "Be just and fear not."

Biographies in *Virginia Law Register* 7 (1901): 1–14 (frontispiece por. and quotation on 14), A. J. Morrison, *College of Hampden Sidney: Dictionary of Biography, 1776–1825* (1921), 272–273, and Lucy Harrison Miller Baber and Evelyn Lee Moore, *Behind the Old Brick Wall: A Cemetery Story* (1968), 43–44; birth date in Daniel family Bible records (1717–1935), UVA (name recorded as William Allen Daniel jr., with middle name struck out); Lynchburg City Marriage Register (1841); Richmond City Marriage Bonds (dated 6 June 1850); Richmond City Consents, Certificates, Ministers' Returns, and Marriage Licenses (1850); correspondence in Daniel Family Papers, LVA, William Daniel Jr. Papers, UVA, and Bouldin Family Papers and Brown Family Papers, both VHS; *Lynchburg Virginian*, 9 Feb. 1832 (legislative address), 13 Dec. 1841, 24 July 1845 (oration on Jackson), 24 May, 3 June 1852; *Richmond Enquirer*, 18 Dec. 1841, 25 May 1852; *Richmond Whig and Public Advertiser*, 11 June 1850; first election to court in *JHD*, 1846–1847 sess., 36–37; *Sheppards* v. *Turpin* and *Sheppards* v. *Stubbs* (1847) (3 Grattan), *Virginia Reports*, 44:357–386 (Daniel's opinion on 366–386); *Baker* v. *Wise, Governor* (1861) (16 Grattan), *Virginia Reports*, 57:139–229 (Daniel's opinion on 190–229); Presidential Pardons; obituaries in *Lynchburg Tri-Weekly News* and *Richmond Daily Dispatch* (erroneously reporting death occurred at Amherst Court House), both 31 Mar. 1873.

CHRISTOPHER M. CURTIS

DANIELS, Edward Dwight (19 January 1828–19 April 1916), agricultural reformer, was born in Cambridge, Massachusetts. When he was about eight years old, his father, Nathaniel Daniels, died. His widowed mother, Nancy Hay Daniels, moved the family to Orleans County in western New York. Daniels attended Oberlin Collegiate Institute from 1843 until poor health caused him to leave the Ohio school in 1846. He then joined a government survey and helped build railroads before moving to Ripon, Wisconsin, in 1848 to live in a cooperative agricultural community.

Daniels studied geology informally with several prominent northeastern professors, including Louis Agassiz, and then returned to Wisconsin, where he was appointed the first state geologist in 1853. Removed by the governor the following year, Daniels in effect regained the position in 1857 when he became one of the state's commissioners of geology. An abolitionist by 1856, he led the State Kansas Aid Society of Wisconsin. Under its auspices Daniels helped mount two colonizing expeditions to Kansas to counter with free labor, free schools, and free men the influx of slave-owning settlers. He married Ione Gove on 1 March 1859, most likely in Waukesha County, Wisconsin. Of their one son and three daughters, one died as an infant.

Shortly after the Civil War began, Daniels was commissioned a colonel and authorized to organize the 1st Wisconsin Cavalry, which he had readied for combat by March 1862. His military career was short and undistinguished. Assigned to guard Cape Girardeau, Missouri, in April 1862, Daniels violated his orders and led incursions into northeastern Arkansas, a maneuver that left his post vulnerable to a Confederate raid. He resigned his commission on 5 February 1863 as a result of continued poor health.

During the Civil War, Daniels investigated the possibility of manufacturing iron in Chicago. He invested in a patent for a new type of furnace and in the Illinois Valley Coal Company in La Salle, Illinois. He tried to settle a labor dispute by the novel method of offering his employees the opportunity to participate in a cooperative arrangement. After Daniels suffered a severe case of pneumonia during the winter of 1867–1868, his doctor suggested he move to the South. Daniels sold his interest in the company, as well as other midwestern assets, and purchased Gunston Hall, the one-time Fairfax County residence of the Revolutionary-era statesman George Mason (1725–1792). On 6 February 1868 Daniels paid $20,000 for the house and approximately 1,000 acres of land. Between that year and mid-1891, he attempted to transform Gunston Hall plantation into a varied economic enterprise infused with the free-labor principles typical of the New England and New York of his youth and the Wisconsin of his young manhood. Concentrating on the production of fruits and vegetables, Daniels hired African American laborers and trained them in scientific farming techniques with the intention that they would embrace northern ideals of thrift, independence, and upward mobility and eventually acquire their own land. In spite of the difficulties in turning a profit in capital-starved postwar Virginia, he paid his workers relatively high wages, and several were able to purchase their own land.

As part of his goal of creating a community of independent farmers and artisans, Daniels was a founding director of the Co-operative Industrial Association of Fairfax County (later the Industrial Home Company), incorporated in 1876 as a cooperative, self-sufficient community. He also tried to establish a suburban settlement called Sunnyside near Gunston Hall. After he improved the estate's wharf, he became a founding director and member of the executive committee of the Upper Potomac Steamboat Company.

Daniels extended his ambitions for reform into politics. In 1871 he purchased a Richmond newspaper, the *Evening State Journal*, which he edited and published in support of the Republi-

can Party for three years before selling it. Also in 1871 Daniels and Westel Willoughby, a New York native who had served on the Virginia Supreme Court of Appeals for a few months in 1869 and 1870, were the unsuccessful Republican candidates for the two seats in the Senate of Virginia representing the city of Alexandria and the counties of Alexandria, Fairfax, Loudoun, and Prince William. Daniels attended the Republican National Convention in 1872 as an at-large delegate. That year he ran for the House of Representatives in the Eighth Congressional District (comprising the counties of Alexandria, Clarke, Culpeper, Fairfax, Fauquier, Frederick, Loudoun, Madison, Orange, Rappahannock, and Warren and the cities of Alexandria and Winchester) but lost by about 2,500 votes of more than 19,200 cast.

Daniels addressed the Republican State Convention on the currency issue in 1876 and blamed the country's economic problems on moneyed elites. Late in the 1870s he joined the Greenback movement, perhaps as a consequence of his increasing indebtedness and the unprofitability of Gunston Hall. In 1880 and 1881 Daniels served on the party's executive committee. He also supported the emerging Readjusters, a biracial political coalition in Virginia that hoped to improve the state's economy and schools and reduce the burden of paying off the antebellum public debt. In December 1881 Daniels testified in behalf of Charles Julius Guiteau at his trial for assassinating President James Abram Garfield.

Gunston Hall's financial problems made it difficult for Daniels to implement his educational philosophy and to train freedpeople and poor whites in agriculture and as artisans. He helped found a primary school for black children that survived into the 1920s, but two other efforts failed as a result of his inability to obtain adequate funding. In 1882 Daniels incorporated and served as general agent for the Society to Promote Industrial Education, to which he promised one hundred acres for establishing the George Mason Industrial University of the Potomac. The land never changed hands, however, because the school did not raise the money that Daniels had stipulated. He printed and circulated a "Plan for Industrial Schools" and in 1890 was a founding manager of the Mount Vernon Children's Industrial Home Society, which also failed for a lack of money.

By the 1880s Gunston Hall teetered on the edge of financial ruin. Daniels spent about a year in Saint Paul, Minnesota, where in 1883 he volunteered his efforts to help the Saint Paul Academy of Natural Sciences recover from a devastating fire. In 1885 and 1886 he edited a labor newspaper, *Our Country*, in New York City. His wife, tired of frequent moves, constant traveling, debt, and suspected adultery, left Daniels in 1886 and lived her final years with her adult children in Nebraska and Iowa. She died in September 1899.

On 18 June 1891 Daniels sold Gunston Hall but retained a small plot of land for himself. He spent much time in the West visiting his children, lecturing, and writing for an agricultural journal published in Omaha, Nebraska. In letters to the editors of various newspapers Daniels continued to decry the lack of a national fiscal system, advocated civil service reform, and encouraged the development of rural, largely self-sufficient communities. On 5 March 1901, in Omaha, he married Julia E. Rennie, a schoolteacher. They had no children. Edward Dwight Daniels died at his farm near Gunston Hall on 19 April 1916 of heart and liver failure and was buried in Arlington National Cemetery.

Full name, birth date, and other information provided by Daniels on 20 Aug. 1908, Alumni and Development Records, Oberlin College Archives; James Harrison Daniels Jr., comp., *The Daniels-Daniells Family*, vol. 2: *A Genealogical History of the Descendants of William Daniell . . .* (1959), 366–374 (with variant birth year of 1826 on 366 and por. on 367); Jerald E. Podair, "The Limits of Free Labor in the Post–Civil War South: Edward Daniels and the Gunston Hall Experiment," paper delivered in Apr. 2002 at Southern Labor Studies Conference, Florida International University, Miami (copy in *DVB* Files); Edward Daniels Papers, Wisconsin Historical Society, Madison; other Daniels correspondence in Topolobampo Collection, California State University, Fresno, in William Mahone Papers, Duke, and at Gunston Hall Library, Lorton; Ione Gove Daniels Papers, Gunston Hall Library, Lorton; *OR*, 1st ser., 13:16, 64–68; Fairfax Co. Deed Book, I-4:286–287, K-5:638–639; Election Records, nos. 4, 5, RG 13, LVA; letters to the editor in *Washington Post*, 5 Sept. 1886, 16 Mar. 1903, 8 Feb. 1904, 6 Feb., 8 Apr. 1905, and in *Fairfax Herald*, 4 Jan. 1907, 17 July 1908, 1 Nov. 1912; P. J. Staudenraus, ed., "Immigrants or Invaders? A Document," *Kansas Historical Quarterly* 24 (1958): 394–398; David H. Overy Jr., *Wisconsin Carpetbaggers in Dixie* (1961), 39–45; Lawrence N. Powell, *New Masters: Northern Planters during the Civil War and Reconstruction* (1980), 30; BVS Death Certificate, Fairfax Co. (with variant birthplace of Boston, Mass., provided by widow); obituaries in *Alexandria Gazette*, 29 Apr. 1916, and *Ripon [Wis.] Weekly Press*, 11 May 1916.

JERALD E. PODAIR

Library of Congress Cataloging-in-Publication Data

Dictionary of Virginia biography / editors, John T. Kneebone . . . [et al.].
             p. cm.
      Includes bibliographical references and index.
      Contents: v. 1. Aaroe–Blanchfield. v. 2. Bland–Cannon. v. 3. Caperton–Daniels.
      ISBN 0-88490-189-0 (v. 1)
      ISBN 0-88490-199-8 (v. 2)
      ISBN 0-88490-206-4 (v. 3)
      1. Virginia—Biography—Dictionaries.   I. Kneebone, John T.
      F225.D54 1998   98-39746
      920.0755—dc21   CIP

Jacket illustrations, from left beginning on back flap:

Maybelle Addington Carter, Alvin Pleasant Delaney Carter, and Sara Elizabeth Dougherty Carter (Carter Family Memorial Music Center, Inc., Hiltons, Virginia)

George Major Cook (Library of Virginia, from Mrs. Fred Pfaus, *Our Indian Neighbors* [1949])

Mary Lee Fitzhugh Custis (portrait by Cephas Thompson. Oil on canvas, 69.2 cm x 56.8 cm. Object No. 76.21.1. Virginia Museum of Fine Arts, Richmond. Gift of Mrs. A. Smith Bowman. © Virginia Museum of Fine Arts)

Robert "King" Carter (Shirley Plantation in Charles City, Virginia)

John Wesley Cromwell (Library of Virginia, from D. W. Culp, ed., *Twentieth Century Negro Literature; or, A Cyclopedia of Thought on the Vital Topics Relating to the American Negro by One Hundred of America's Greatest Negroes* [1902])

Sir Thomas Dale (detail of portrait by unknown British artist, ca. 1615. Oil on canvas, 204.7 cm x 115.7 cm. Object No. 52.8. Virginia Museum of Fine Arts, Richmond. The Adolph D. and Wilkins C. Williams Fund. Photo: Ron Jennings. © Virginia Museum of Fine Arts)

Jean Esther Outland Chrysler (portrait by Christopher Clark, 1949. Oil on canvas, 43 x 34 inches. Accession 63.58.6. Chrysler Museum of Art, Norfolk, Virginia. Gift of Jean Outland Chrysler in tribute to her parents, Mr. and Mrs. Grover Cleveland Outland.)

Langdon Taylor Christian (Library of Virginia, from Lyon Gardiner Tyler, ed., *Men of Mark in Virginia* [1906–1909], vol. 2)

George Rogers Clark (portrait attributed to Matthew Harris Jouett, after John Wesley Jarvis. Library of Virginia)

Edna Meade Colson (Library of Virginia, from *Virginia Education Bulletin* 33 [Oct. 1953])

Dictionary of Virginia Biography, Volume 3: *Caperton–Daniels* was designed by Sara Daniels Bowersox of the Library of Virginia. Page layout was produced by Betty Saxman of the Virginia Department of General Services, Office of Graphic Communications, using Macintosh PowerPC G4 and QuarkXpress 6.5. Text was composed in Times Roman and Italic. Printed on acid-free, Glatfelter Writers Offset Natural, 50-lb. text, by Sheridan Books, Inc., in Ann Arbor, Michigan.